# Essentials of Business Communication

## 10e

**MARY ELLEN GUFFEY**
Professor Emerita of Business
Los Angeles Pierce College

**DANA LOEWY**
Business Communication Program
California State University, Fullerton

CENGAGE Learning

Australia • Brazil • Japan • Korea • Mexico • Singapore • Spain • United Kingdom • United States

**CENGAGE Learning**

**Essentials of Business Communication, Tenth edition**

**Mary Ellen Guffey**
**Dana Loewy**

Vice President, General Manager: Erin Joyner
Product Director: Michael Schenk
Product Manager: Michele Rhoades
Sr. Content Developer: Mary Emmons
Product Assistant: Brian Pierce
Marketing Manager: Jeff Tousignant
Content Project Manager: Jana Lewis
Media Developer: John Rich and Deepak Kumar
Marketing Coordinator: Christopher Walz
Manufacturing Planner: Ron Montogomery
Marketing Communications Manager: Sarah Greber
Production Service: Cenveo
Sr. Art Director: Stacy Shirley
Internal Designer: KeDesign, Mason, OH
Cover Designer: KeDesign, Mason, OH
Cover Image: denphumi/iStock/Thinkstock
Intellectual Property
   Analyst: Diane Garrity
   Project Manager: Sarah Shainwald

© 2016, 2013 Cengage Learning

WCN: 01-100-101

ALL RIGHTS RESERVED. No part of this work covered by the copyright herein may be reproduced, transmitted, stored, or used in any form or by any means graphic, electronic, or mechanical, including but not limited to photocopying, recording, scanning, digitizing, taping, Web distribution, information networks, or information storage and retrieval systems, except as permitted under Section 107 or 108 of the 1976 United States Copyright Act, without the prior written permission of the publisher.

---

For product information and technology assistance, contact us at
**Cengage Learning Customer & Sales Support, 1-800-354-9706**

For permission to use material from this text or product, submit all requests online at **www.cengage.com/permissions**
Further permissions questions can be emailed to
**permissionrequest@cengage.com**

---

Library of Congress Control Number: 2014947986
ISBN: 978-1-285-85891-3
Student Edition ISBN: 978-1-285-85889-0

**Cengage Learning**
20 Channel Center Street
Boston, MA 02210
USA

Cengage Learning is a leading provider of customized learning solutions with office locations around the globe, including Singapore, the United Kingdom, Australia, Mexico, Brazil, and Japan. Locate your local office at **www.cengage.com/global**

Cengage Learning products are represented in Canada by Nelson Education, Ltd.

To learn more about Cengage Learning Solutions, visit **www.cengage.com**

Purchase any of our products at your local college store or at our preferred online store **www.cengagebrain.com**

Printed in the United States of America
Print Number: 03    Print Year: 2017

# Essentials of Business Communication

**10E**

**Dr. Mary Ellen Guffey**
Emerita Professor of Business
Los Angeles Pierce College
m.e.guffey@cox.net

**Dr. Dana Loewy**
Business Communication Program
California State University, Fullerton
dloewy@fullerton.edu

**Dear Business Communication Student:**

The **Tenth Edition** of *Essentials of Business Communication* brings you a four-in-one learning package including (a) an authoritative textbook, (b) a convenient workbook, (c) a self-teaching grammar/mechanics handbook, and (d) a comprehensive student website at www.cengagebrain.com.

In preparing this Tenth Anniversary edition, your authors examined every topic and added new coverage to prepare you for success in today's thoroughly networked and hyper-connected digital-age workplace. Here are a few of the major features:

- **Workplace relevance.** This edition continues to stress the practical and immediate importance of this course to your career success.
- **Communication technologies.** You'll find integrated coverage of cutting-edge digital technologies and mobile devices, emphasizing best practices for e-mail, texting, instant messaging, blogging, wikis, and social media.
- **Job search and interviewing coverage.** The Tenth Edition covers the latest trends and tips in preparing résumés and successful employment interviewing.
- **Premier website at www.cengagebrain.com.** All students with new books have access to chapter review quizzes, PowerPoint slides, flashcards, and a wide assortment of learning resources.
- **Grammar and writing improvement exercises.** One of the best ways to improve your writing skills is to revise poorly written messages. This edition provides many new grammar/mechanics and writing assignments to help you hone your skills.
- **Writing plans.** Clear, step-by-step writing plans structure the writing process so that you can get started quickly and stay focused on the writing experience.

The many examples and model documents in *Essentials of Business Communication,* 10e, including winning résumés and cover letters, have made this book a favorite to keep as an on-the-job reference.

We wish you well in your studies!
Cordially,

*Mary Ellen Guffey & Dana Loewy*

Dana Loewy and Mary Ellen Guffey

Photographer: Barbara D'Allessandro

ESSENTIALS OF BUSINESS COMMUNICATION, 10E

# Digital Resources with Guffey/Loewy

Mastering workplace communication is now easier than ever. Access numerous, robust study resources that complement your textbook at **cengagebrain.com**, and improve your business communication grade.

ESSENTIALS OF BUSINESS COMMUNICATION, 10E

ESSENTIALS OF BUSINESS COMMUNICATION, 10E

# Access these resources to improve your grade:

### CHAPTER REVIEW QUIZZES

Quizzing capabilities allow you to brush up on important chapter concepts throughout the course or just prior to exams. Each quiz question includes feedback that further improves your understanding of important topics.

### POWERPOINT REVIEWS

PowerPoint slides review important concepts from each chapter and help you comprehend and retain these concepts as you prepare for exams or internalize your learning.

### DOWNLOADABLE DOCUMENTS

Avoid having to do the extra work rekeying documents by downloading them from the premium website. Or use these documents for additional practice, beyond instructor requirements.

### PERSONAL LANGUAGE TRAINER

Personal Language Trainer is a comprehensive learning resource that ensures mastery of the grammar/mechanics required in the business communication course. Take a diagnostic quiz to assess your current knowledge base. Complete warmup activities and exercises to brush up on problem areas. Then test your knowledge with a comprehensive test that helps you track your progress.

### FLASHCARDS

Improve your vocabulary and understanding of business communication terminology by using these interactive, online study aids.

### WRITING RESOURCES

This handy resource includes references to links and online writing resources to help you more easily complete writing assignments. Specifically, access Online Writing Labs, MLA and APA formats, and other valuable writing resources.

# 5 REASONS to buy your textbooks and course materials at CENGAGEbrain.com

**1. SAVINGS:**
Prices up to 65% off, daily coupons, and free shipping on orders over $25

**2. CHOICE:**
Multiple format options including textbook, eBook and eChapter rentals

**3. CONVENIENCE:**
Anytime, anywhere access of eBooks or eChapters via mobile devices

**4. SERVICE:**
Free eBook access while your text ships, and instant access to online homework products

**5. STUDY TOOLS:**
Free study tools* for your text, plus writing, research, career and job search resources
*availability varies

Find your course materials and start saving at:
**www.cengagebrain.com**

# Brief Contents

## Unit 1 — Business Communication in the Digital Age 1
1. Communicating in the Digital-Age Workplace 2

## Unit 2 — The Business Writing Process in the Digital Age 35
2. Planning Business Messages 36
3. Organizing and Drafting Business Messages 63
4. Revising Business Messages 90

## Unit 3 — Workplace Communication 119
5. Short Workplace Messages and Digital Media 120
6. Positive Messages 156
7. Negative Messages 192
8. Persuasive Messages 226

## Unit 4 — Business Reports 263
9. Informal Reports 264
10. Proposals and Formal Reports 299

## Unit 5 — Professionalism, Teamwork, Meetings, and Speaking Skills 351
11. Professionalism at Work: Business Etiquette, Ethics, Teamwork, and Meetings 352
12. Business Presentations 389

## Unit 6 — Employment Communication 425
13. The Job Search and Résumés in the Digital Age 426
14. Interviewing and Following Up 474

## Appendixes
A. Correction Symbols and Proofreading Marks A-1
B. Document Format Guide A-4
C. Documentation Formats A-13

## End Matter
Grammar/Mechanics Handbook GM-1
Key to Grammar/Mechanics Checkups K-1
Index I-1

# Contents

## UNIT 1 Business Communication in the Digital Age

### 1 Communicating in the Digital-Age Workplace 2

1-1 Mastering the Tools for Success in the Twenty-First-Century Workplace 2
1-2 Developing Listening Skills 10
1-3 Learning Nonverbal Communication Skills 11
1-4 Recognizing How Culture Affects Communication 14
1-5 Building Intercultural Workplace Skills 18

Summary of Learning Objectives 22
Chapter Review 23
Critical Thinking 24
Activities and Cases 24
Grammar/Mechanics Checkup—1 29
Editing Challenge—1 30
Communication Workshop 31
Endnotes 32
Acknowledgments 33

## UNIT 2 The Business Writing Process in the Digital Age

### 2 Planning Business Messages 36

2-1 Understanding the Communication Process 36
2-2 Using the 3-x-3 Writing Process as a Guide 38
2-3 Analyzing and Anticipating the Audience 41
2-4 Using Expert Writing Techniques to Adapt to Your Audience 44
2-5 Developing Additional Expert Writing Techniques 47

Summary of Learning Objectives 52
Chapter Review 53
Critical Thinking 54
Writing Improvement Exercises 54
Radical Rewrites 58
Activities 59
Grammar/Mechanics Checkup—2 59
Editing Challenge—2 60
Communication Workshop 61
Endnotes 62
Acknowledgments 62

### 3 Organizing and Drafting Business Messages 63

3-1 Drafting Workplace Messages 63
3-2 Organizing Information to Show Relationships 66
3-3 Composing the First Draft With Effective Sentences 69
3-4 Developing Business Writing Techniques 71
3-5 Drafting Well-Organized, Effective Paragraphs 75

Summary of Learning Objectives 76
Chapter Review 77
Critical Thinking 79
Writing Improvement Exercises 79
Radical Rewrites 85
Grammar/Mechanics Checkup—3 86
Editing Challenge—3 87
Communication Workshop 88
Endnotes 89
Acknowledgments 89

## 4 Revising Business Messages 90

4-1 Taking Time to Revise: Applying Phase 3 of the Writing Process   90
4-2 Making Your Message Clear   95
4-3 Enhancing Readability Through Document Design   98
4-4 Proofreading to Catch Errors   103
4-5 Evaluating the Effectiveness of Your Message   105

Summary of Learning Objectives   105

Chapter Review   106
Critical Thinking   107
Writing Improvement Exercises   108
Radical Rewrites   114
Grammar/Mechanics Checkup—4   115
Editing Challenge—4   116
Communication Workshop   117
Endnotes   118
Acknowledgments   118

# UNIT 3 Workplace Communication

## 5 Short Workplace Messages and Digital Media 120

5-1 Preparing Digital-Age E-Mail Messages and Memos   120
5-2 Workplace Messaging and Texting   127
5-3 Making Podcasts and Wikis Work for Business   130
5-4 Blogging for Business   132
5-5 Web 2.0: Social Networking   136

Summary of Learning Objectives   139
Chapter Review   140

Critical Thinking   141
Writing Improvement Exercises   142
Radical Rewrites   144
Activities and Cases   146
Grammar/Mechanics Checkup—5   150
Editing Challenge—5   152
Communication Workshop   153
Endnotes   154
Acknowledgments   155

## 6 Positive Messages 156

6-1 Routine Messages: E-Mails, Memos, and Letters   156
6-2 Typical Request, Response, and Instruction Messages   158
6-3 Direct Claims and Complaints   164
6-4 Adjustment Messages   168
6-5 Goodwill Messages   171

Summary of Learning Objectives   175
Chapter Review   176

Critical Thinking   177
Writing Improvement Exercises   177
Radical Rewrites   179
Activities and Cases   182
Grammar/Mechanics Checkup—6   188
Editing Challenge—6   189
Communication Workshop   190
Endnotes   191
Acknowledgments   191

# 7 Negative Messages 192

7-1 Communicating Negative News Effectively  192
7-2 Analyzing Negative News Strategies  194
7-3 Composing Effective Negative Messages  197
7-4 Refusing Typical Requests and Claims  202
7-5 Managing Bad News Within Organizations  206

Summary of Learning Objectives  211
Chapter Review  212
Critical Thinking  213
Writing Improvement Exercises  213
Radical Rewrites  215
Activities and Cases  217
Grammar/Mechanics Checkup—7  222
Editing Challenge—7  223
Communication Workshop  224
Endnotes  225
Acknowledgments  225

# 8 Persuasive Messages 226

8-1 Understanding Persuasion in the Digital Age  226
8-2 Planning and Writing Persuasive Requests  228
8-3 Writing Effective Persuasive Claims and Complaints  229
8-4 Crafting Persuasive Messages in Digital-Age Organizations  232
8-5 Creating Effective Sales Messages in Print and Online  233

Summary of Learning Objectives  243
Chapter Review  244
Critical Thinking  246
Writing Improvement Exercises  246
Radical Rewrites  247
Activities and Cases  250
Grammar/Mechanics Checkup—8  258
Editing Challenge—8  259
Communication Workshop  260
Endnotes  261
Acknowledgments  262

# UNIT 4  Business Reports

## 9 Informal Reports 264

9-1 Reporting in the Digital Age  264
9-2 Report Formats and Heading Levels  268
9-3 Defining the Purpose and Gathering Data  273
9-4 Writing Short Informational Reports  275
9-5 Preparing Short Analytical Reports  279

Summary of Learning Objectives  288
Chapter Review  289
Critical Thinking  290
Activities and Cases  290
Grammar/Mechanics Checkup—9  294
Editing Challenge—9  296
Communication Workshop  297
Endnotes  298
Acknowledgments  298

## 10 Proposals and Formal Reports 299

10-1 Preparing Business Proposals 299
10-2 Writing and Editing Formal Business Reports 305
10-3 Conducting Primary and Secondary Research 308
10-4 Documenting and Citing Sources in Business Reports 316
10-5 Incorporating Meaningful Visual Aids and Graphics 318
10-6 Understanding Report Components 325

Summary of Learning Objectives 339
Chapter Review 340
Critical Thinking 341
Activities and Cases 342
Grammar/Mechanics Checkup—10 347
Editing Challenge—10 348
Communication Workshop 349
Endnotes 350
Acknowledgments 350

# UNIT 5 Professionalism, Teamwork, Meetings, and Speaking Skills

## 11 Professionalism at Work: Business Etiquette, Ethics, Teamwork, and Meetings 352

11-1 Developing Professionalism and Business Etiquette Skills at the Office and Online 352
11-2 Communicating Face-to-Face on the Job 355
11-3 Following Professional Telephone and Voice Mail Etiquette 361
11-4 Adding Value to Professional Teams 364
11-5 Planning and Participating in Face-to-Face and Virtual Meetings 368

Summary of Learning Objectives 376

Chapter Review 377
Critical Thinking 378
Activities and Cases 378
Grammar/Mechanics Checkup—11 383
Editing Challenge—11 385
Communication Workshop 386
Endnotes 386
Acknowledgments 388

## 12 Business Presentations 389

12-1 Preparing Effective Business Presentations 389
12-2 Organizing Content for Impact and Audience Rapport 392
12-3 Understanding Contemporary Visual Aids 398
12-4 Preparing Engaging Multimedia Presentations 400
12-5 Polishing Your Delivery and Following Up 406

Summary of Learning Objectives 411

Chapter Review 412
Critical Thinking 413
Activities and Cases 414
Grammar/Mechanics Checkup—12 420
Editing Challenge—12 421
Communication Workshop 422
Endnotes 423
Acknowledgments 423

Purestock/Thinkstock

Contents xiii

# UNIT 6 Employment Communication

## 13 The Job Search and Résumés in the Digital Age 426

- 13-1 Job Searching in the Digital Age 426
- 13-2 Developing a Job-Search Strategy Focused on the Open Job Market 429
- 13-3 Pursuing the Hidden Job Market With Networking 431
- 13-4 Creating a Customized Résumé 435
- 13-5 Optimizing Your Job Search With Today's Digital Tools 448
- 13-6 Creating Customized Cover Messages 454

Summary of Learning Objectives 462
Chapter Review 463
Critical Thinking 464
Radical Rewrites 465
Activities and Cases 467
Grammar/Mechanics Checkup—13 469
Editing Challenge—13 471
Communication Workshop 472
Endnotes 472
Acknowledgments 473

## 14 Interviewing and Following Up 474

- 14-1 Purposes and Types of Employment Interviews 474
- 14-2 Before the Interview 476
- 14-3 During the Interview 482
- 14-4 After the Interview 491
- 14-5 Preparing Additional Employment Documents 494

Summary of Learning Objectives 498

Chapter Review 499
Critical Thinking 501
Activities and Cases 501
Grammar/Mechanics Checkup—14 507
Editing Challenge—14 508
Communication Workshop 509
Endnotes 510
Acknowledgments 511

## Appendixes

Appendix A Correction Symbols and Proofreading Marks A-1

Appendix B Document Format Guide A-4
Appendix C Documentation Formats A-13

**Grammar/Mechanics Handbook GM-1**
Key to Grammar/Mechanics Checkups K-1
Index I-1

# Appreciation for Support

No successful textbook reaches a No. 1 position without a great deal of help. We are exceedingly grateful to the reviewers and other experts who contributed their pedagogic and academic expertise in shaping *Essentials of Business Communication*.

We extend sincere thanks to many professionals at Cengage Learning, including Jack W. Calhoun, Senior Vice President; Erin Joyner, Vice President, General Manager; Michael Schenk, Product Director, Business, Management & Marketing; Michele Rhoades, Senior Product Manager; Kristen Hurd, Senior Brand Manager; John Rich, Senior Media Developer; Jeff Tousignant, Marketing Manager; Shirley Stacy, Senior Art Director; and Jana Lewis, Content Project Manager. We are also grateful to Crystal Bullen, DPS Associates, and Malvine Litten, LEAP Publishing Services, who ensured premier quality and excellent accuracy throughout the publishing process.

Our very special thanks go to Mary Emmons, Senior Content Developer, whose wise counsel, exceptional management skills, friendship, and unfailingly upbeat outlook have kept us sane and on track as she shepherded many editions of our books to market leadership.

Our heartfelt appreciation goes to the following for their expertise in creating superior instructor and student support materials: Jane Flesher, Chippewa Valley Technical College; Janet Mizrahi, University of California, Santa Barbara; Joyce Staples, Bellevue College; and Christina Turner, Des Moines Area Community College.

*Mary Ellen Guffey*
*Dana Loewy*

## Grateful Thanks to the Following

Faridah Awang
*Eastern Kentucky University*

Joyce M. Barnes
*Texas A & M University - Corpus Christi*

Patricia Beagle
*Bryant & Stratton Business Institute*

Nancy C. Bell
*Wayne Community College*

Ray D. Bernardi
*Morehead State University*

Karen Bounds
*Boise State University*

Daniel Brown
*University of South Florida*

Cheryl S. Byrne
*Washtenaw Community College*

Jean Bush-Bacelis
*Eastern Michigan University*

Mary Y. Bowers
*Northern Arizona University*

Therese Butler
*Long Beach City College*

Derrick Cameron
*Vance-Granville Community College*

Brennan Carr
*Long Beach City College*

Steven V. Cates
*Averett University*

Irene Z. Church
*Muskegon Community College*

Lise H. Diez-Arguelles
*Florida State University*

Dee Anne Dill
*Dekalb Technical Institute*

Dawn Dittman
*Dakota State University*

Elizabeth Donnelly-Johnson
*Muskegon Community College*

Jeanette Dostourian
*Cypress College*

Nancy J. Dubino
*Greenfield Community College*

Donna N. Dunn
*Beaufort County Community College*

Cecile Earle
*Heald College*

Valerie Evans
*Cuesta College*

Bartlett J. Finney
*Park University*

Pat Fountain
*Coastal Carolina Community College*

Marlene Friederich
*New Mexico State University – Carlsbad*

Christine Foster
*Grand Rapids Community College*

JoAnn Foth
*Milwaukee Area Technical College*

Gail Garton
*Ozarks Technical Community College*

Nanette Clinch Gilson
*San Jose State University*

Robert Goldberg
*Prince George's Community College*

Margaret E. Gorman
*Cayuga Community College*

Judith Graham
*Holyoke Community College*

Lauren Gregory
*South Plains College*

Bruce E. Guttman
*Katharine Gibbs School, Melville, New York*

Susan E. Hall
*University of West Georgia*

April Halliday
*Georgia Piedmont Technical College*

Tracey M. Harrison
*Mississippi College*

Debra Hawhee
*University of Illinois*

L. P. Helstrom
*Rochester Community College*

Jack Hensen
*Morehead State University*

Rovena L. Hillsman
*California State University, Sacramento*

Karen A. Holtkamp
*Xavier University*

Michael Hricik
*Westmoreland County Community College*

Jodi Hoyt
*Southeast Technical Institute*

Sandie Idziak
*University of Texas, Arlington*

Karin Jacobson
*University of Montana*

Bonnie Jeffers
*Mt. San Antonio College*

Edna Jellesed
*Lane Community College*

Jane Johansen
*University of Southern Indiana*

Pamela R. Johnson
*California State University, Chico*

Edwina Jordan
*Illinois Central College*

Sheryl E. C. Joshua
*University of North Carolina, Greensboro*

Diana K. Kanoy
*Central Florida Community College*

Ron Kapper
*College of DuPage*

Jan Kehm
*Spartanburg Community College*

Karen Kendrick
*Nashville State Community College*

Lydia Keuser
*San Jose City College*

Linda Kissler
*Westmoreland County Community College*

Deborah Kitchin
*City College of San Francisco*

Frances Kranz
*Oakland University*

Keith Kroll
*Kalamazoo Valley Community College*

Rose Marie Kuceyeski
*Owens Community College*

Richard B. Larsen
*Francis Marion University*

Mary E. Leslie
*Grossmont College*

Ruth E. Levy
*Westchester Community College*

Gary R. Lewis
*Southwest Florida College*

Maryann Egan Longhi
*Dutchess Community College*

Nedra Lowe
*Marshall University*

Elaine Lux
*Nyack College*

Margarita Maestas-Flores
*Evergreen Valley College*

Jane Mangrum
*Miami-Dade Community College*

Maria Manninen
*Delta College*

Tim March
*Kaskaskia College*

Paula Marchese
*State University of New York College at Brockport*

Tish Matuszek
*Troy University Montgomery*

Kenneth R. Mayer
*Cleveland State University*

Victoria McCrady
*University of Texas at Dallas*

Karen McFarland
*Salt Lake Community College*

Pat McGee
*Southeast Technical Institute*

Bonnie Miller
*Los Medanos College*

Mary C. Miller
*Ashland University*

Willie Minor
*Phoenix College*

Nancy Moody
*Sinclair Community College*

Suman Mudunuri
*Long Beach City College*

Nancy Mulder
*Grand Rapids Junior College*

Paul W. Murphey
*Southwest Wisconsin Technical College*

Nan Nelson
*University of Arkansas Phillips Community College*

Lisa Nieman
*Indiana Wesleyan University*

Jackie Ohlson
*University of Alaska – Anchorage*

Richard D. Parker
*Western Kentucky University*

Martha Payne
*Grayson County College*

Catherine Peck
*Chippewa Valley Technical College*

Carol Pemberton
*Normandale Community College*

Carl Perrin
*Casco Bay College*

Jan Peterson
*Anoka-Hennepin Technical College*

Susan Peterson
*Scottsdale Community College*

Kay D. Powell
*Abraham Baldwin College*

Jeanette Purdy
*Mercer County College*

Carolyn A. Quantrille
*Spokane Falls Community College*

Susan Randles
*Vatterott College*

Diana Reep
*University of Akron*

Ruth D. Richardson
*University of North Alabama*

Carlita Robertson
*Northern Oklahoma College*

Vilera Rood
*Concordia College*

Rich Rudolph
*Drexel University*

Rachel Rutledge
*Carteret Community College*

Joanne Salas
*Olympic College*

Rose Ann Scala
*Data Institute School of Business*

Joseph Schaffner
*SUNY College of Technology, Alfred*

Susan C. Schanne
*Eastern Michigan University*

James Calvert Scott
*Utah State University*

Laurie Shapero
*Miami-Dade Community College*

Lance Shaw
*Blake Business School*

Cinda Skelton
*Central Texas College*

Estelle Slootmaker
*Aquinas College*

Margaret Smallwood
*The University of Texas at Dallas*

Clara Smith
*North Seattle Community College*

Nicholas Spina
*Central Connecticut State University*

Marilyn St. Clair
*Weatherford College*

Judy Sunayama
*Los Medanos College*

Dana H. Swensen
*Utah State University*

James A. Swindling
*Eastfield College*

David A. Tajerstein
*SYRIT College*

Marilyn Theissman
*Rochester Community College*

Zorica Wacker
*Bellevue College*

Lois A. Wagner
*Southwest Wisconsin Technical College*

Linda Weavil
*Elan College*

William Wells
*Lima Technical College*

Gerard Weykamp
*Grand Rapids Community College*

Beverly Wickersham
*Central Texas College*

Leopold Wilkins
*Anson Community College*

Anna Williams
*College of Central Florida, Ocala*

Charlotte Williams
*Jones County Junior College*

Donald Williams
*Feather River College*

Janice Willis
*Bellevue College*

Janice Willis
*College of San Mateo*

Almeda Wilmarth
*State University of New York – Delhi*

Barbara Young
*Skyline College*

Appreciation for Support

# About the Authors

## Dr. Mary Ellen Guffey

A dedicated professional, Mary Ellen Guffey has taught business communication and business English topics for over thirty-five years. She received a bachelor's degree, *summa cum laude*, from Bowling Green State University; a master's degree from the University of Illinois, and a doctorate in business and economic education from the University of California, Los Angeles (UCLA). She has taught at the University of Illinois, Santa Monica College, and Los Angeles Pierce College.

Now recognized as the world's leading business communication textbook author, Dr. Guffey corresponds with instructors around the globe who are using her books. She is the founding author of the award-winning *Business Communication: Process and Product,* the leading business communication textbook in this country. She also wrote *Business English,* which serves more students than any other book in its field; *Essentials of College English*; and *Essentials of Business Communication,* the leading text/workbook in its market. Dr. Guffey is active professionally, serving on the review boards of the *Business and Professional Communication Quarterly* and the *Journal of Business Communication*, publications of the Association for Business Communication. She participates in national meetings, sponsors business communication awards, and is committed to promoting excellence in business communication pedagogy and the development of student writing skills.

## Dr. Dana Loewy

Dana Loewy has been teaching business communication at California State University, Fullerton for the past eighteen years. She enjoys introducing undergraduates to business writing and honing the skills of graduate students in managerial communication. Most recently, she has also taught various German classes. Dr. Loewy is a regular guest lecturer at Fachhochschule Nürtingen, Germany. Having earned a PhD from the University of Southern California in English with a focus on translation, she is a well-published freelance translator, interpreter, brand-name consultant, and textbook author. Dr. Loewy has collaborated with Dr. Guffey on recent editions of *Business Communication: Process & Product* as well as on *Essentials of Business Communication*.

Fluent in several languages, among them German and Czech, her two native languages, Dr. Loewy has authored critical articles in many areas of interest—literary criticism, translation, business communication, and business ethics. Before teaming up with Dr. Guffey, Dr. Loewy published various poetry and prose translations, most notably *The Early Poetry* of Jaroslav Seifert and *On the Waves of TSF*. Active in the Association for Business Communication, Dr. Loewy focuses on creating effective teaching/learning materials for undergraduate and graduate business communication students.

# Business Communication in the Digital Age

## UNIT 1

**CHAPTER 1**
Communicating in the Digital-Age Workplace

# CHAPTER 1

# Communicating in the Digital-Age Workplace

**OBJECTIVES**
After studying this chapter, you should be able to

**1-1** Describe how solid communication skills will improve your career prospects and help you succeed in today's challenging digital-age workplace.

**1-2** Confront barriers to effective listening, and start building your listening skills.

**1-3** Explain the importance of nonverbal communication and of improving your nonverbal communication skills.

**1-4** Explain five common dimensions of culture, and understand how culture affects communication and the use of social media and communication technology.

**1-5** Discuss strategies that help communicators overcome negative cultural attitudes and prevent miscommunication in today's diverse networked workplace.

## 1-1 Mastering the Tools for Success in the Twenty-First-Century Workplace

You may wonder what kind of workplace you will enter when you graduate and which skills you will need to be successful in it. Expect a fast-moving, competitive, and information-driven digital environment. Communication technology provides unmatched mobility and connects individuals anytime and anywhere in the world. Today's communicators interact using mobile electronic devices and access information stored on remote servers, "in the cloud." This mobility and instant access explain why increasing numbers of workers must be available practically around the clock and must respond quickly.

This first chapter presents an overview of communication in business today. It addresses the contemporary workplace, listening skills, nonverbal communication, the cultural dimensions of communication, and intercultural job skills. The remainder of the book is devoted to developing specific writing and speaking skills.

### 1-1a Solid Communication Skills: Your Pass to Success

Your ability to communicate is a powerful career sifter.[1] Strong communication skills will make you marketable even in a tough economic climate. When jobs are few and competition is fierce, superior communication skills will give you an edge over other job applicants. Recruiters rank communication high on their wish lists.[2]

In a Fortune poll, 1,000 executives cited writing, critical-thinking, and problem-solving skills along with self-motivation and team skills as their top choices in new-hires. Effective writing skills can be a stepping-stone to great job opportunities; poorly developed writing skills, on the other hand, will derail a career.

Perhaps you are already working or will soon apply for your first job. How do your skills measure up? The good news is that you can learn effective communication. This textbook and this course can immediately improve your communication skills. Because the skills you are learning will make a huge difference in your ability to find a job and to be promoted, this will be one of the most important courses you will ever take.

## 1-1b The Digital Revolution: Why Writing Skills Matter More Than Ever

People in today's workforce communicate more, not less, since information technology and the Internet have transformed the world of work. Thanks to technology, messages travel instantly to distant locations, reaching potentially huge audiences with a minimum of expense and effort. Work team members collaborate even when they are physically apart. Moreover, social media are playing an increasingly prominent role in business. In such a hyperconnected world, writing matters more than ever. Digital media require more written communication, and workers' skills are always on display.[3]

As a result, employers seek employees with a broader range of skills and higher levels of knowledge in their field than in the past.[4] Unfortunately, a great number of workers can't deliver.[5] A survey of American corporations revealed that two thirds of salaried employees have some writing responsibility. About one third of them, however, do not meet the writing requirements for their positions.[6] "Businesses are crying out—they need to have people who write better," said Gaston Caperton, business executive and former College Board president.[7]

Not surprisingly, many job listings mention the need for excellent oral and written communication skills. In a poll of recruiters, oral and written communication skills were by a large margin the top skill set sought.[8] Among the top choices in two other surveys were teamwork, critical-thinking, analytical-reasoning, and oral and written communication skills.[9] In addition, as you will learn in later chapters, recruiters will closely examine your social media presence to learn about your communication skills and professionalism. Naturally, they will not hire candidates who write poorly or post inappropriate content online.[10]

**Techies Write Too.** Even in technical fields such as accounting and information technology, you will need strong communication skills. A poll of 1,400 chief financial officers sponsored by Accountemps revealed that 75 percent said that verbal, written, and interpersonal skills are more important today than they were in the past.[11] Technical experts must be able to communicate with others and explain their work clearly, says an IBM systems specialist.[12] A survey of Web professionals showed that those with writing and copyediting skills were far less likely to have their jobs sent offshore.[13] Another survey conducted by the Society for Information Management revealed that network professionals ranked written and oral communication skills among the top five most desired skills for new-hires.[14]

**Businesses Generate a Wide Range of Messages.** Be prepared to use a variety of media. In addition to occasional traditional letters and memos, expect to communicate with the public and within the company by e-mail,* instant messaging and

---

## OFFICE INSIDER

"Communicating clearly and effectively has NEVER been more important than it is today. Whether it's fair or not, life-changing critical judgments about you are being made based solely on your writing ability."
—Victor Urbach, management consultant

**LEARNING OBJECTIVE 1**
Describe how solid communication skills will improve your career prospects and help you succeed in today's challenging digital-age workplace.

**Note: Small superscript numbers in the text announce information sources. Full citations begin on page N-1 near the end of the book. This edition uses a modified American Psychological Association (APA) reference format.**

---

*The usage standard in this book is *Merriam-Webster's Collegiate Dictionary,* Eleventh Edition. Words such as *e-mail* and *Web* are in a state of flux, and a single standard has yet to establish itself. *Merriam-Webster's* continues to show conventional usage patterns.

texting, company blogs, collaboration software such as wikis, and social media sites such as Facebook, Twitter, Pinterest, Instagram, and YouTube. You will learn more about workplace communication technology in Chapter 5.

**Writing Is in Your Future.** Regardless of career choice, you will probably be sending many digital messages, such as the e-mail shown in Figure 1.1. In fact, e-mail is "today's version of the business letter or interoffice memo."[15] Because electronic mail and other digital media have become important channels of communication in today's workplace, all digital business messages must be clear, concise, and professional. Notice that the message in Figure 1.1 is more businesslike and more professional than the quick e-mail or text you might send socially. Learning to write professional digital messages will be an important part of this course.

## Figure 1.1 Businesslike, Professional E-Mail Message

*Because e-mails have all but replaced business letters and interoffice memos in most workplaces, they must be written carefully, provide complete information, and sound businesslike and professional. Notice that this message is more formal in tone than e-mail messages you might send to friends.*

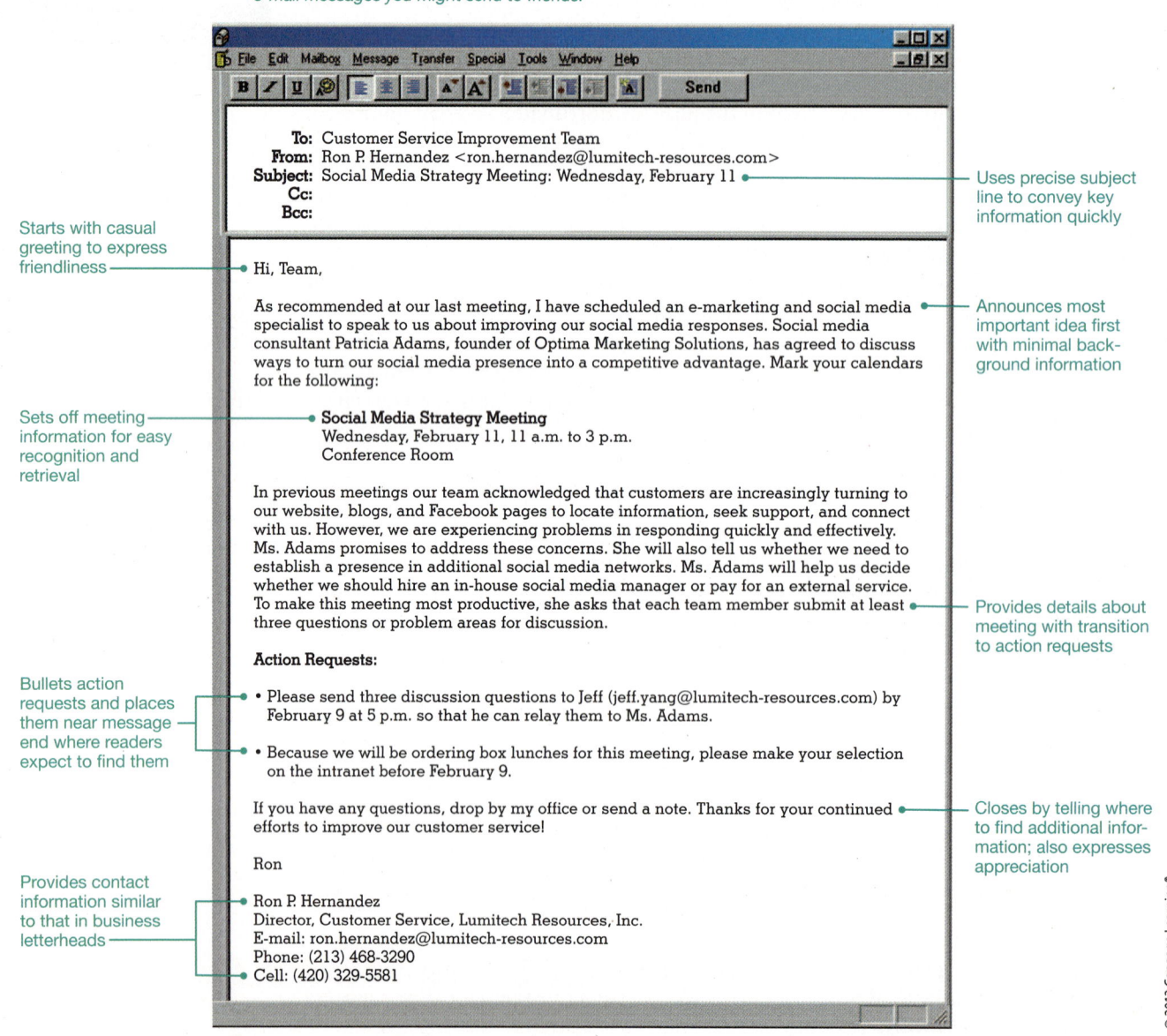

**To:** Customer Service Improvement Team
**From:** Ron P. Hernandez <ron.hernandez@lumitech-resources.com>
**Subject:** Social Media Strategy Meeting: Wednesday, February 11
**Cc:**
**Bcc:**

Hi, Team,

As recommended at our last meeting, I have scheduled an e-marketing and social media specialist to speak to us about improving our social media responses. Social media consultant Patricia Adams, founder of Optima Marketing Solutions, has agreed to discuss ways to turn our social media presence into a competitive advantage. Mark your calendars for the following:

**Social Media Strategy Meeting**
Wednesday, February 11, 11 a.m. to 3 p.m.
Conference Room

In previous meetings our team acknowledged that customers are increasingly turning to our website, blogs, and Facebook pages to locate information, seek support, and connect with us. However, we are experiencing problems in responding quickly and effectively. Ms. Adams promises to address these concerns. She will also tell us whether we need to establish a presence in additional social media networks. Ms. Adams will help us decide whether we should hire an in-house social media manager or pay for an external service. To make this meeting most productive, she asks that each team member submit at least three questions or problem areas for discussion.

**Action Requests:**

- Please send three discussion questions to Jeff (jeff.yang@lumitech-resources.com) by February 9 at 5 p.m. so that he can relay them to Ms. Adams.
- Because we will be ordering box lunches for this meeting, please make your selection on the intranet before February 9.

If you have any questions, drop by my office or send a note. Thanks for your continued efforts to improve our customer service!

Ron

Ron P. Hernandez
Director, Customer Service, Lumitech Resources, Inc.
E-mail: ron.hernandez@lumitech-resources.com
Phone: (213) 468-3290
Cell: (420) 329-5581

*Annotations:*
- Starts with casual greeting to express friendliness
- Sets off meeting information for easy recognition and retrieval
- Bullets action requests and places them near message end where readers expect to find them
- Provides contact information similar to that in business letterheads
- Uses precise subject line to convey key information quickly
- Announces most important idea first with minimal background information
- Provides details about meeting with transition to action requests
- Closes by telling where to find additional information; also expresses appreciation

## 1-1c What Employers Want: Professionalism

Your future employer will expect you to show professionalism and possess what are often referred to as "soft skills" in addition to your technical knowledge. Soft skills are essential career attributes that include the ability to communicate, work well with others, solve problems, make ethical decisions, and appreciate diversity.[16] Sometimes called employability skills or key competencies, these soft skills are desirable in all business sectors and job positions.[17]

Not every job seeker is aware of the employer's expectations. Some new-hires have no idea that excessive absenteeism or tardiness is grounds for termination. Others are surprised to learn that they are expected to devote their full attention to their duties when on the job. One young man wanted to read novels when things got slow.[18] Some recent graduates had unrealistic expectations about their salaries and working hours.[19] Moreover, despite well-publicized warnings, some people continue to post racy photos and otherwise questionable content online, thus sabotaging their careers.[20]

Projecting and maintaining a professional image can make a real difference in helping you obtain the job of your dreams. Once you get that job, you are more likely to be taken seriously and promoted if you look and sound professional. Don't send the wrong message with unwitting and unprofessional behavior. Figure 1.2 reviews areas you will want to check to be sure you are projecting professionalism. You will learn more about soft skills and professionalism in Chapter 11.

## 1-1d How Your Education Drives Your Income

As college tuition rises steeply and student debt mounts, you may wonder whether going to college is worthwhile. Yet the effort and money you invest in earning your college degree will most likely pay off. College graduates earn more, suffer less unemployment, and can choose from a wider variety of career options than workers without a college education. Moreover, college graduates have access to the highest-paying and fastest-growing careers, many of which require a degree.[21] As Figure 1.3 on page 7 shows, graduates with bachelor's degrees earn nearly three times as much as high school dropouts and are almost three times less likely to be unemployed.[22]

Writing is one aspect of education that is particularly well rewarded. One corporate president explained that many people climbing the corporate ladder are good. When he faced a hard choice between candidates, he used writing ability as the deciding factor. He said that sometimes writing is the only skill that separates a candidate from the competition. A survey of employers confirms that soft skills such as communication ability can tip the scales in favor of one job applicant over another.[23] Your ticket to winning in a tight job market and launching a successful career is good communication skills.

## 1-1e Meeting the Challenges of the Information Age Workplace

Today's digital workplace is changing profoundly and rapidly. As a businessperson and as a business communicator, you will be affected by many trends, including new communication tools such as social media, the "anytime, anywhere" office, and team-based projects. Other trends are flattened management hierarchies, global competition, and a renewed emphasis on ethics. The following overview reveals how communication skills are closely tied to your success in a constantly evolving networked workplace.

- **Rapidly changing communication technologies.** New communication technology is dramatically affecting the way workers interact. In our always-connected world, businesses exchange information by e-mail, instant

### OFFICE INSIDER

*"The ability to write well is unquestionably a skill necessary for 21st-century success in college and the workplace. . . . Strong writing skills are essential."*

—Gaston Caperton, former president, College Board

## Figure 1.2 Projecting Professionalism When You Communicate

| Unprofessional | | Professional |
|---|---|---|
| *Uptalk*, a singsong speech pattern, making sentences sound like questions; *like* used as a filler; *go* for *said*; slang; poor grammar and profanity. | **Speech habits** | Recognizing that your credibility can be seriously damaged by sounding uneducated, crude, or adolescent. |
| Messages with incomplete sentences, misspelled words, exclamation points, IM slang, and mindless chatter; sloppy messages signal that you don't care, don't know, or aren't smart enough to know what is correct. | **E-mail** | Messages with subjects, verbs, and punctuation marks. Employers dislike IM abbreviations. They value conciseness and correct spelling, even in brief e-mail messages and texts. |
| E-mail addresses such as *hotbabe@outlook.com*, *supasnugglykitty@yahoo.com*, or *buffedguy@gmail.com*. | **Internet** | E-mail addresses should include a name or a positive, businesslike expression; they should not sound cute or like a chat room nickname. |
| An outgoing message with strident background music, weird sounds, or a joke message. | **Voice mail** | An outgoing message that states your name or phone number and provides instructions for leaving a message. |
| Soap operas, thunderous music, or a TV football game playing noisily in the background when you answer the phone. | **Telephone presence** | A quiet background when you answer the telephone, especially if you are expecting a prospective employer's call. |
| Using electronics during business meetings for unrelated purposes or during conversations with fellow employees; raising your voice (cell yell); forcing others to overhear your calls. | **Cell phones, tablets** | Turning off phone and message notification, both audible and vibrate, during meetings; using your smart devices only for meeting-related purposes. |
| Sending and receiving text messages during meetings, allowing texting to interrupt face-to-face conversations, or texting when driving. | **Texting** | Sending appropriate business text messages only when necessary (perhaps when a cell phone call would disturb others). |

messaging, text messaging, smartphones, fax, voice mail, powerful laptop computers, and tablets. Satellite communications, wireless networking, teleconferencing, and videoconferencing help workers conduct meetings with associates around the world. Social media sites such as Facebook, Twitter, Pinterest, and YouTube as well as blogs, wikis, forums, and peer-to-peer tools help businesspeople collect information, serve customers, and sell products and services. Figure 1.4 on pages 8 and 9 illustrates many new technologies you will encounter in today's workplace.

- **"Anytime, anywhere" and nonterritorial offices.** High-speed and wireless Internet access has freed millions of workers from nine-to-five jobs in brick-and-mortar offices. Flexible working arrangements allow them to work at home or on the road. Meet the "work shifter," a telecommuter or teleworker who largely remains outside the territorial office. The "anytime, anywhere" office requires only a mobile electronic device and a wireless connection.[24]

Figure **1.3** The Education Bonus: Higher Income, Lower Unemployment

| Education | Median Weekly Earnings | Unemployment Rate |
|---|---|---|
| High school dropout | $ 471 | 12.4% |
| High school diploma | 652 | 8.3% |
| Some college, no degree | 727 | 7.7% |
| Associate's degree | 785 | 6.2% |
| Bachelor's degree or higher | 1,367 | 4.5% |

*Source:* U.S. Bureau of Labor Statistics. (2013, February 5). Labor force statistics from the current population survey; and U.S. Bureau of Labor Statistics (2013, May 22). Employment Projections: Earnings and unemployment rates by educational attainment.

Teleworkers now represent almost 20 percent of the U.S. working adult population.[25] To save on office real estate, some industries provide "nonterritorial" workspaces, or "hot desks." The first to arrive gets the best desk and the corner window.[26] At the same time, 24/7 availability has blurred the line between work and leisure, so that some workers are always "on duty."

- **Self-directed work groups and virtual teams.** Teamwork has become a reality in business. Many companies have created cross-functional teams to empower employees and boost their involvement in decision making. You can expect to collaborate with a team in gathering information, finding and sharing solutions, implementing decisions, and managing conflict. You may even become part of a virtual team whose members are in remote locations. Increasingly, organizations are also forming ad hoc teams to solve particular problems. Such project-based teams disband once they have accomplished their objectives.[27] Moreover, parts of our future economy may rely on "free agents" who will be hired on a project basis, a far cry from today's full-time and relatively steady jobs.

- **Flattened management hierarchies.** To better compete and to reduce expenses, businesses have for years been trimming layers of management. This means that as a frontline employee, you will have fewer managers. You will be making decisions and communicating them to customers, to fellow employees, and to executives.

- **Heightened global competition.** Because many American companies continue to move beyond domestic markets, you may be interacting with people from many cultures. To be a successful business communicator, you will need to learn about other cultures. You will also need to develop intercultural skills including sensitivity, flexibility, patience, and tolerance.

- **Renewed emphasis on ethics.** Ethics is once again a hot topic in business. On the heels of the banking crisis and the collapse of the real estate market, a calamitous recession followed, caused largely, some say, by greed and ethical lapses. With the passage of the Sarbanes-Oxley Act, the U.S. government now requires greater accountability. As a result, businesses are eager to regain public trust by building ethical environments. Many have written ethical mission statements, installed hotlines, and appointed compliance officers to ensure strict adherence to their high standards and the law.

These trends mean that your communication skills will constantly be on display. Those who can write clear and concise messages contribute to efficient operations and can expect to be rewarded.

---

**OFFICE INSIDER**

*"Rare is the new college hire who lacks skills involving Facebook, texting or any other form of electronic communication. But face to face, many of these same people have difficulty reading interpersonal signals and communicating, especially in the increasingly multigenerational workplace. Most of the gaps I see are on the social, soft skills side."*

—Cindy Warkentin, CIO, Maryland Automobile Insurance Fund

Figure 1.4 Communication and Collaborative Technologies

# Communication Technologies
## Reshaping the World of Work

Becoming familiar with modern communication technology can help you be successful on the job. Today's digital workplace is changing dramatically as a result of innovative software; social media networks; superfast broadband and wireless access; and numerous technologies that allow workers to share information, work from remote locations, and be more productive in or away from the office. With today's tools you can exchange ideas, solve problems, develop products, forecast performance, and complete team projects any time of the day or night anywhere in the world.

### Cloud Computing and Web 2.0
Increasingly, applications and data are stored in remote locations online, "in the cloud." *Cloud computing* means that businesses and individuals no longer need to maintain costly hardware and software in-house; instead, they can pay for digital storage space and software applications offered by providers online. Photo- and video-sharing sites such as Picasa and Flickr keep your photos "in the cloud." Similarly, Dropbox, a popular file-synchronization service, and online backup provider Carbonite allow users to edit and sync files online independent of the device used to access them. Websites and Web applications have moved from "read only" to "read–write," thus enabling users to participate, collaborate, and network in unprecedented ways.

### Telephony: VoIP
Savvy businesses are switching from traditional phone service to voice over Internet protocol (VoIP). This technology allows callers to communicate using a broadband Internet connection, thus eliminating long-distance and local telephone charges. Higher-end VoIP systems now support unified voice mail, e-mail, click-to-call capabilities, and softphones (phones using computer networking). Free or low-cost Internet telephony sites, such as the popular Skype, are also increasingly used by businesses, although their sound and image quality is often uneven.

### Voice Recognition
Computers equipped with voice recognition software enable users to dictate up to 160 words a minute with accurate transcription. Voice recognition is particularly helpful to disabled workers and to professionals with heavy dictation loads, such as physicians and attorneys. Users can create documents, enter data, compose and send e-mails, browse the Web, and control their desktops—all by voice. Smart devices can also execute tasks as directed through voice command apps.

### Voice Conferencing
Telephone "bridges" join two or more callers from any location to share the same call. *Voice conferencing* (also called *audioconferencing, teleconferencing,* or just plain *conference calling*) enables people to collaborate by telephone. Communicators at both ends use enhanced speakerphones to talk and be heard simultaneously.

### Open Offices
The widespread use of laptop computers, tablets, and other smart devices; wireless technology; and VoIP have led to more fluid, flexible, and open workspaces. Smaller computers and flat-screen monitors enable designers to save space with boomerang-shaped workstations and cockpit-style work surfaces rather than space-hogging corner work areas. Smaller breakout areas for impromptu meetings are taking over some cubicle space, and digital databases are replacing file cabinets. Mobile technology allows workers to be fully connected and productive on the go.

8     Chapter 1: Communicating in the Digital-Age Workplace

## Smart Mobile Devices and Digital Convergence

A new generation of lightweight, handheld devices provide phone, e-mail, Web browsing, and calendar options anywhere there is a cellular or Wi-Fi network. Tablets and smartphones such as Android devices, iPhones, and iPads now allow workers to tap into corporate databases and intranets from remote locations. They can check customers' files, complete orders, and send out receipts without returning to the office. Increasingly, businesses are issuing smartphones to their workforces, abandoning landlines completely. At the same time, the need for separate electronic gadgets is waning as digital smart devices are becoming multifunctional and highly capable. With streaming video on the Web, connectivity between TVs and computers, and networked mobile devices, technology is converging, consolidating into increasingly powerful devices. Many smart devices today are fully capable of replacing digital point-and-shoot still photography and video cameras. Mobile smart devices are also competing with TVs and computers for primacy.

## Videoconferencing

Videoconferencing allows participants to meet in special conference rooms equipped with cameras and television screens. Individuals or groups see each other and interact in real time, although they may be far apart. Faster computers, rapid Internet connections, and better cameras now enable 2 to 200 participants to sit at their own computers or mobile devices and share applications, spreadsheets, presentations, and photos. The technology extends from the popular Internet applications Skype and FaceTime to sophisticated videoconferencing software that delivers HD-quality audio, video, and content sharing.

## Electronic Presentations

Business presentations in PowerPoint, Keynote, SlideRocket, or Prezi can be projected from a laptop or tablet or posted online. Sophisticated presentations may include animation, sound effects, digital photos, video clips, or hyperlinks to Internet sites. In some industries, electronic slides ("decks") are replacing or supplementing traditional hard-copy reports.

## Presence Technology

Presence technology makes it possible to locate and identify a computing device as soon as users connect to the network. This technology is an integral part of communication devices including smartphones, laptop computers, tablets, and GPS devices. Collaboration is possible wherever and whenever users are online.

## Web Conferencing

With services such as GoToMeeting, WebEx, and Microsoft LiveMeeting, all you need is a computer or a smart device and an Internet connection to hold a meeting (*webinar*) with customers or colleagues in real time. Although the functions are constantly evolving, Web conferencing currently incorporates screen sharing, chats, slide presentations, text messaging, and application sharing.

## Social Media

Never before in history have so many people been connected in online communities called social networks. Broadly speaking, the term *social media* describes technology that enables participants to connect and participate in social networks online. For example, tech-savvy companies and individuals send *tweets*, short messages of up to 140 characters, to other users to issue up-to-date news about their products, to link to their blogs and websites, or to announce events and promotions. The microblogging service Twitter also allows businesses to track what is being said about them and their products. Similarly, businesses use social networks such as Facebook, YouTube, and Instagram to interact with customers and to build their brands. Companies may also prospect for talent using social media networks.

## Collaboration With Blogs, Podcasts, and Wikis

Businesses use *blogs* to keep customers and employees informed and to receive feedback. Company news can be posted, updated, and categorized for easy cross-referencing. An audio or video file streamed online or downloaded to a digital music player is called a *podcast*. A *wiki* is a website that allows multiple users to collaboratively create and edit pages. Information can get lost in e-mails, but wikis provide an easy way to communicate and keep track of what has been said.

Chapter 1: Communicating in the Digital-Age Workplace

## OFFICE INSIDER

*Did you know?*

- *It is estimated that more than 50 percent of our work time is spent listening.*
- *Immediately following a 10-minute presentation, average people retain about half of what they hear and only one quarter after 48 hours.*
- *Sixty percent of all management problems are related to listening.*
- *We misinterpret, misunderstand, or change 70 to 90 percent of what we hear.*

—Valarie Washington, CEO, Think 6 Results

**LEARNING OBJECTIVE 2**

Confront barriers to effective listening, and start building your listening skills.

## 1-2 Developing Listening Skills

In an age that thrives on information and communication technology, listening is an important skill. However, by all accounts most of us are not very good listeners. Do you ever pretend to be listening when you are not? Do you know how to look attentive in class when your mind wanders far away? How about "tuning out" people when their ideas are boring or complex? Do you find it hard to focus on ideas when a speaker's clothing or mannerisms are unusual?

You probably answered *yes* to one or more of these questions because many of us have poor listening habits. In fact, some researchers suggest that we listen at only 25 to 50 percent efficiency. Such poor listening habits are costly in business and affect professional relationships. Messages must be rewritten, shipments reshipped, appointments rescheduled, contracts renegotiated, and directions restated.

To develop better listening skills, we must first recognize barriers that prevent effective listening. Then we need to focus on specific techniques for improving listening skills.

### 1-2a Overcoming Barriers to Effective Listening

As you have seen, bad habits and distractions can interfere with effective listening. Have any of the following barriers and distractions prevented you from hearing what has been said?

- **Physical barriers.** You cannot listen if you cannot hear what is being said. Physical impediments include hearing disabilities, poor acoustics, and noisy surroundings. It is also difficult to listen if you are ill, tired, or uncomfortable.

- **Psychological barriers.** Everyone brings to the communication process a unique set of cultural, ethical, and personal values. Each of us has an idea of what is right and what is important. If other ideas run counter to our preconceived thoughts, we tend to "tune out" speakers and thus fail to receive their messages.

- **Language problems.** Unfamiliar words can destroy the communication process because they lack meaning for the receiver. In addition, emotion-laden, or "charged," words can adversely affect listening. If the mention of words such as *bankruptcy* or *real estate meltdown* has an intense emotional impact, a listener may be unable to focus on the words that follow.

- **Nonverbal distractions.** Many of us find it hard to listen if a speaker is different from what we view as normal. Unusual clothing or speech mannerisms, body twitches, or a radical hairstyle can cause enough distraction to prevent us from hearing what the speaker has to say.

- **Thought speed.** Because we can process thoughts at least three times faster than speakers can say them, we can become bored and allow our minds to wander.

- **Faking attention.** Most of us have learned to look as if we are listening even when we are not. Such behavior was perhaps necessary as part of our socialization. Faked attention, however, seriously threatens effective listening because it encourages the mind to engage in flights of unchecked fancy. Those who fake attention often find it hard to concentrate even when they want to.

- **Grandstanding.** Would you rather talk or listen? Naturally, most of us would rather talk. Because our own experiences and thoughts are most important to us, we grab the limelight in conversations. We sometimes fail to listen carefully because we are just waiting politely for the next pause so that we can have our turn to speak.

### 1-2b Building Powerful Listening Skills

You can reverse the harmful effects of poor habits by making a conscious effort to become an active listener. This means becoming involved. You can't sit back and hear whatever a lazy mind happens to receive. The following keys will help you become an active and effective listener:

- **Stop talking.** The first step to becoming a good listener is to stop talking. Let others explain their views. Learn to concentrate on what the speaker is saying, not on what your next comment will be.
- **Control your surroundings.** Whenever possible, remove competing sounds. Close windows or doors, turn off TVs and smartphones, and move away from loud people, noisy appliances, or engines. Choose a quiet time and place for listening.
- **Establish a receptive mind-set.** Expect to learn something by listening. Strive for a positive and receptive frame of mind. If the message is complex, think of it as mental gymnastics. It is hard work but good exercise to stretch and expand the limits of your mind.
- **Keep an open mind.** We all sift through and filter information based on our own biases and values. For improved listening, discipline yourself to listen objectively. Be fair to the speaker. Hear what is really being said, not what you want to hear.
- **Listen for main points.** Heighten your concentration and satisfaction by looking for the speaker's central themes. Congratulate yourself when you find them!
- **Capitalize on lag time.** Make use of the quickness of your mind by reviewing the speaker's points. Anticipate what is coming next. Evaluate evidence the speaker has presented. Don't allow yourself to daydream. Try to guess what the speaker's next point will be.
- **Listen between the lines.** Focus both on what is spoken and what is unspoken. Listen for feelings as well as for facts.
- **Judge ideas, not appearances.** Concentrate on the content of the message, not on its delivery. Avoid being distracted by the speaker's looks, voice, or mannerisms.
- **Hold your fire.** Force yourself to listen to the speaker's entire argument or message before responding. Such restraint may enable you to understand the speaker's reasons and logic before you jump to false conclusions.
- **Take selective notes.** In some situations thoughtful notetaking may be necessary to record important facts that must be recalled later. Select only the most important points so that the notetaking process does not interfere with your concentration on the speaker's total message.
- **Provide feedback.** Let the speaker know that you are listening. Nod your head and maintain eye contact. Ask relevant questions at appropriate times. Getting involved improves the communication process for both the speaker and the listener.

### OFFICE INSIDER

*"Listening is hard work. Unlike hearing, it demands total concentration. It is an active search for meaning, while hearing is passive."*

—Alfonso Bucero, consultant and author

## 1-3 Learning Nonverbal Communication Skills

**LEARNING OBJECTIVE 3**
Explain the importance of nonverbal communication and of improving your nonverbal communication skills.

Understanding messages often involves more than merely listening to spoken words. Nonverbal cues, in fact, can speak louder than words. These cues include eye contact, facial expression, body movements, time, space, territory, and appearance. All of these nonverbal cues affect how a message is interpreted, or decoded, by the receiver.

**What Is Nonverbal Communication?** Nonverbal communication includes all unwritten and unspoken messages, whether intended or not. These silent signals have a strong effect on receivers. However, understanding them is not simple. Does a downward glance indicate modesty? Fatigue? Does a constant stare reflect

Chapter 1: Communicating in the Digital-Age Workplace

coldness? Dullness? Aggression? Do crossed arms mean defensiveness, withdrawal, or just that the person is shivering?

**What If Words and Nonverbal Cues Clash?** Messages are even harder to decipher when the verbal and nonverbal cues do not agree. What will you think if Scott says he is not angry, but he slams the door when he leaves? What if Alicia assures the hostess that the meal is excellent, but she eats very little? The nonverbal messages in these situations speak more loudly than the words. In fact, researchers believe that the bulk of any message we receive is nonverbal.

Successful communicators recognize the power of nonverbal messages. Cues broadcast by body language might be helpful in understanding the feelings and attitudes of senders. It is unwise, however, to attach specific meanings to gestures or actions because behavior and its interpretations strongly depend on context and on one's cultural background, as you will see.

### 1-3a Your Body Sends Silent Messages

Psychologist and philosopher Paul Watzlawick claimed that we cannot not communicate.[28] In other words, it's impossible to not communicate. This means that every behavior is sending a message even if we don't use words. The eyes, face, and body convey meaning without a single syllable being spoken.

**Eye Contact.** The eyes have been called the windows to the soul. Even if they don't reveal the soul, the eyes are often the best predictor of a speaker's true feelings. Most of us cannot look another person straight in the eyes and lie. As a result, in North American culture we tend to believe people who look directly at us. Sustained eye contact suggests trust and admiration; brief eye contact signals fear or stress. Good eye contact enables the message sender to see whether a receiver is paying attention, showing respect, responding favorably, or feeling distress. From the receiver's viewpoint, good eye contact, in North American culture, reveals the speaker's sincerity, confidence, and truthfulness.

**Facial Expression.** The expression on a person's face can be almost as revealing of emotion as the eyes. Experts estimate that the human face can display over 250,000 expressions.[29] To hide their feelings, some people can control these expressions and maintain "poker faces." Most of us, however, display our emotions openly. Raising or lowering the eyebrows, squinting the eyes, swallowing nervously, clenching the jaw, smiling broadly—these voluntary and involuntary facial expressions can add to or entirely replace verbal messages.

**Posture and Gestures.** A person's posture can convey anything from high status and self-confidence to shyness and submissiveness. Leaning toward a speaker suggests attentiveness and interest; pulling away or shrinking back denotes fear, distrust, anxiety, or disgust. Similarly, gestures can communicate entire thoughts via simple movements. However, the meanings of some of these movements differ in other cultures. Unless you know local customs, they can get you into trouble. In the United States and Canada, for example, forming the thumb and forefinger in a circle means everything is OK. But in parts of South America, the OK sign is obscene.

What does your own body language say about you? To take stock of the kinds of messages being sent by your body, ask a classmate to critique your use of eye contact, facial expression, and body movements. Another way to analyze your nonverbal style is to record yourself making a presentation. Then study your performance. This way you can make sure your nonverbal cues send the same message as your words.

### 1-3b Time, Space, and Territory Send Silent Messages

In addition to nonverbal messages transmitted by your body, three external elements convey information in the communication process: time, space, and territory.

**Time.** How we structure and use time tells observers about our personalities and attitudes. For example, when Warren Buffett, industrialist, investor, and philanthropist, gives a visitor a prolonged interview, he signals his respect for, interest in, and approval of the visitor or the topic to be discussed.

**Space.** How we order the space around us tells something about ourselves and our objectives. Whether the space is a bedroom, a dorm room, or an office, people reveal themselves in the design and grouping of their furniture. Generally, the more formal the arrangement, the more formal and closed the communication style. An executive who seats visitors in a row of chairs across from his desk sends a message of aloofness and a desire for separation. A team leader who arranges chairs informally in a circle rather than in straight rows conveys her desire for a more open exchange of ideas.

**Territory.** Each of us has a certain area that we feel is our own territory, whether it is a specific spot or just the space around us. Your father may have a favorite chair in which he is most comfortable, a cook might not tolerate intruders in the kitchen, and veteran employees may feel that certain work areas and tools belong to them. We all maintain zones of privacy in which we feel comfortable. Figure 1.5 categorizes the four zones of social interaction among Americans, as formulated by anthropologist Edward T. Hall.[30] Notice that North Americans are a bit standoffish; only intimate friends and family may stand closer than about 1.5 feet. If someone violates that territory, North Americans feel uncomfortable and may step back to reestablish their space.

## 1-3c Appearance Sends Silent Messages

Much like the personal appearance of an individual, the physical appearance of a business document transmits immediate and important nonverbal messages. Ideally, these messages should be pleasing to the eye.

**Eye Appeal of Business Documents.** The way an e-mail, letter, memo, or report looks can have either a positive or a negative effect on the receiver. Sloppy e-mails send a nonverbal message that you are in a terrific hurry or that you do not care about the receiver. Envelopes—through their postage, stationery, and printing—can suggest that they are routine, important, or junk mail. Letters and reports can look neat, professional, well organized, and attractive—or just the opposite. In succeeding chapters you will learn how to create business documents that send positive nonverbal messages through their appearance, format, organization, readability, and correctness.

**Personal Appearance.** The way you look—your clothing, grooming, and posture—telegraphs an instant nonverbal message about you. Based on what they see, viewers make quick judgments about your status, credibility, personality, and potential. If you want to be considered professional, think about how you present yourself. One

Figure 1.5 Four Space Zones for Social Interaction

Intimate Zone
(1 to 1½ feet)

Personal Zone
(1½ to 4 feet)

Social Zone
(4 to 12 feet)

Public Zone
(12 or more feet)

## Workplace in Focus

One of the latest fads is body art in the form of tattoos and piercings. Once seen primarily on bikers, prisoners, and sailors, inked images increasingly adorn the bodies of Americans today. The Food and Drug Administration estimates that as many as 45 million Americans have at least one tattoo. A Pew Research study found the highest incidence of tattoos in eighteen- to twenty-nine-year-olds (38 percent). Think twice, however, before displaying "tats" and piercings at work. *Conspicuous body art may make you feel distinctive and slightly daring, but how might it affect your career?*

marketing manager said, "I'm young and pretty. It's hard enough to be taken seriously, and if I show up in jeans and a teeshirt, I don't stand a chance."[31] As a businessperson, you will want to think about what your appearance says about you. Although the rules of business attire have loosened up, some workers show poor judgment. You will learn more about professional attire and behavior in later chapters.

### 1-3d Building Strong Nonverbal Skills

Nonverbal communication can outweigh words in the way it influences how others perceive us. You can harness the power of silent messages by reviewing the following tips for improving nonverbal communication skills:

- **Establish and maintain eye contact.** Remember that in North America appropriate eye contact signals interest, attentiveness, strength, and credibility.
- **Use posture to show interest.** Encourage interaction by leaning forward, sitting or standing erect, and looking alert.
- **Reduce or eliminate physical barriers.** Move out from behind a desk or lectern; arrange meeting chairs in a circle.
- **Improve your decoding skills.** Watch facial expressions and body language to understand the complete verbal and nonverbal messages being communicated.
- **Probe for more information.** When you perceive nonverbal cues that contradict verbal meanings, politely seek additional cues (*I'm not sure I understand, Please tell me more about . . .*, or *Do you mean that . . .*).
- **Interpret nonverbal meanings in context.** Make nonverbal assessments only when you understand a situation or a culture.
- **Associate with people from diverse cultures.** Learn about other cultures to widen your knowledge and tolerance of intercultural nonverbal messages.
- **Appreciate the power of appearance.** Keep in mind that the appearance of your business documents, your business space, and yourself sends immediate positive or negative messages to receivers.
- **Observe yourself on video.** Ensure that your verbal and nonverbal messages are in sync by recording and evaluating yourself making a presentation.
- **Enlist friends and family.** Ask friends and family to monitor your conscious and unconscious body movements and gestures to help you become an effective communicator.

**LEARNING OBJECTIVE 4**
Explain five common dimensions of culture, and understand how culture affects communication and the use of social media and communication technology.

## 1-4 Recognizing How Culture Affects Communication

Global business, new communication technologies, the Internet, and social media span the world, shrinking distances. However, cultural differences still exist and can cause significant misunderstandings. Comprehending the verbal and nonverbal meanings of a message is difficult even when communicators are from the same culture. When they come from different cultures, special sensitivity and skills are necessary.

**What Is Culture?** For our purposes, *culture* may be defined as "the complex system of values, traits, morals, and customs shared by a society, region, or country." Culture is a powerful operating force that molds the way we think, behave, and communicate. The objective of this section is to broaden your view of culture and open your mind to new attitudes so you can avoid frustration when cultural adjustment is necessary. Despite globalization, growing diversity, and widespread social networking, we need to make adjustments and adopt new attitudes.

So that you will better understand your culture and how it contrasts with other cultures, we will describe five key dimensions of culture: context, individualism, time orientation, power distance, and communication style. The section closes with a look at the interaction between culture and social media.

### 1-4a Context

Context is probably the most important cultural dimension and also the most difficult to define. In a model developed by cultural anthropologist Edward T. Hall, context refers to the stimuli, environment, or ambience surrounding an event. Hall arranged cultures on a continuum, shown in Figure 1.6, from low to high in relation to context. This figure also summarizes key comparisons for today's business communicators.

Figure **1.6** Comparing Low- and High-Context Cultures

*Culture has a powerful effect on business communicators. The following observations point out selected differences. However, these are simplifications and practices within a given culture vary considerably. Moreover, as globalization expands, low- and high-context cultures are experiencing change and differences may be less pronounced.*

**Lower Context**: Swiss, German, Northern European, American, Australian, Central European

**Higher Context**: South American, African, South European, Arabian, Asian

- Tend to prefer direct verbal interaction
- Tend to understand meaning at only one sociocultural level.
- Are generally less proficient in reading nonverbal cues
- Value individualism
- Rely more on logic
- Say *no* directly
- Communicate in highly structured, detailed messages with literal meanings
- Give authority to written information

- Tend to prefer indirect verbal interaction
- Tend to understand meanings embedded at many sociocultural levels
- Are generally more proficient in reading nonverbal cues
- Value group membership
- Rely more on context and feeling
- Talk around point, avoid saying *no*
- Communicate in sometimes simple, sometimes ambiguous messages
- Understand visual messages readily

Chapter 1: Communicating in the Digital-Age Workplace

Communicators in low-context cultures (such as those in North America, Scandinavia, and Germany) depend little on the context of a situation to convey their meaning. They assume that messages must be explicit, and listeners rely exclusively on the written or spoken word. Low-context cultures tend to be logical, analytical, and action oriented. Business communicators stress clearly articulated messages that they consider to be objective, professional, and efficient. Words are taken literally.

Communicators in high-context cultures (such as those in China, Japan, and Arab countries) assume that the listener does not need much background information.[32] Communicators in high-context cultures are more likely to be intuitive and contemplative. They may not take words literally. Instead, the meaning of a message may be implied from the social or physical setting, the relationship of the communicators, or nonverbal cues. For example, a Japanese communicator might say *yes* when he really means *no*. From the context of the situation, his Japanese conversation partner would conclude whether *yes* really meant *yes* or whether it meant *no*. The context, tone, time taken to answer, facial expression, and body cues would convey the meaning of *yes*.[33] Communication cues are transmitted by posture, voice inflection, gestures, and facial expression.

### 1-4b Individualism

An attitude of independence and freedom from control characterizes individualism. Members of low-context cultures, particularly North Americans, tend to value individualism. They believe that initiative and self-assertion result in personal achievement. They believe in individual action and personal responsibility, and they desire much freedom in their personal lives.

Members of high-context cultures are more collectivist. They emphasize membership in organizations, groups, and teams; they encourage acceptance of group values, duties, and decisions. They typically resist independence because it fosters competition and confrontation instead of consensus. In group-oriented cultures such as those in many Asian societies, for example, self-assertion and individual decision making are discouraged. "The nail that sticks up gets pounded down" is a common Japanese saying.[34] Business decisions are often made by all who have competence in the matter under discussion. Similarly, in China managers also focus on the group rather than on the individual, preferring a consultative management style over an autocratic style.[35]

Many cultures, of course, are quite complex and cannot be characterized as totally individualistic or group oriented. For example, European Americans are generally quite individualistic, whereas African-Americans are less so, and Latinos are closer to the group-centered dimension.[36]

### 1-4c Time Orientation

North Americans consider time a precious commodity. They correlate time with productivity, efficiency, and money. Keeping people waiting for business appointments is considered a waste of time and also rude.

In other cultures time may be perceived as an unlimited resource to be enjoyed. A North American businessperson, for example, was kept waiting two hours past a scheduled appointment time in South America. She wasn't offended, though, because she was familiar with South Americans' more relaxed concept of time.

The perception of time and how it is used are culturally learned. In some cultures time is perceived analytically. People account for every minute of the day. In other cultures, time is holistic and viewed in larger chunks. People in Western cultures tend to be more analytical, scheduling appointments at 15- to 30-minute intervals. Those in Eastern cultures tend to be more holistic, planning fewer but longer meetings. People in one culture may look at time as formal and task oriented. In another culture, time is seen as an opportunity to develop interpersonal relationships.

## 1-4d Power Distance

One important element of culture is power distance, a concept first introduced by influential social psychologist Geert Hofstede. The Power Distance Index measures how people in different societies cope with inequality; in other words, how they relate to more powerful individuals. In high power distance countries, subordinates expect formal hierarchies and embrace relatively authoritarian, paternalistic power relationships. In low power distance cultures, however, subordinates consider themselves as equals of their supervisors. They confidently voice opinions and participate in decision making. Relationships between high-powered individuals and people with little power tend to be more democratic, egalitarian, and informal in these cultures.

As you probably guessed, in Western cultures people are more relaxed about social status and the appearance of power.[37] Deference is not generally paid to individuals merely because of their wealth, position, seniority, or age. In many Asian cultures, however, these characteristics are important and must be respected. Walmart, facing many hurdles in breaking into the Japanese market, admits having had difficulty training local employees to speak up to their bosses. In the Japanese culture, lower-level employees do not question management. Deference and respect are paid to those in authority and power. Recognizing this cultural pattern, Marriott Hotel managers learned to avoid placing a lower-level Japanese employee on a floor above a higher-level executive from the same company.

## 1-4e Communication Style

People in low- and high-context cultures tend to communicate differently with words. To Americans and Germans, words are very important, especially in contracts and negotiations. People in high-context cultures, on the other hand, place more emphasis on the surrounding context than on the words describing a negotiation. A Greek may see a contract as a formal statement announcing the intention to build a business for the future. The Japanese may treat contracts as statements of intention, and they assume changes will be made as projects develop. Mexicans may treat contracts as artistic exercises of what might be accomplished in an ideal world. They do not necessarily expect contracts to apply consistently in the real world. An Arab may be insulted by merely mentioning a contract; a person's word is more binding.[38]

In communication style North Americans value straightforwardness, are suspicious of evasiveness, and distrust people who might have a "hidden agenda" or who "play their cards too close to the chest."[39] North Americans also tend to be uncomfortable with silence and impatient with delays. Some Asian businesspeople have learned that the longer they drag out negotiations, the more concessions impatient North Americans are likely to make.

## 1-4f Intercultural Communication, Social Media, and Communication Technology

Much has been made of the connectedness that social media and communication technology provide today. With minimal resources, communicators can reach out to larger and more varied audiences than ever before. Social media offer the potential for intercultural engagement. They may overcome cultural differences or reinforce them, depending on their users.

**Social Networking: Bridging Cultural Divides?** What we make of the potential for intercultural connectedness online is as much up to us as it would be at a dinner party where we don't know any of the other guests. "Digital media is an amplifier.

It tends to make extroverts more extroverted and introverts more introverted," says Clay Shirky, social media expert at New York University.[40] At the same time, the online environment may deepen feelings of isolation; it can make interpersonal contact more difficult because all contact is mediated electronically.[41]

In real life, as online, we instinctively tend to gravitate toward people who seem similar to us, believes Gaurav Mishra, a social media strategist from India: "[H]uman beings have a strong tendency to prefer the familiar, so we pay attention to people with a shared context and treat the rich Twitter public stream as background noise."[42] Twitter and other social media can boost intercultural communication; however, we must be willing to reach out across the boundaries that separate us. Yet, the public around the world is witnessing firsthand, real-time accounts of political unrest and natural and human-caused disasters on social media—often long before traditional media reporters arrive on the scene.

**Whether social media networks will allow business communicators to engage across cultures and bridge intercultural differences will depend on the users' attitudes and openness.**

**Social Networking: Erasing Cultural Differences?** Despite the equalizing influence of globalization, regional and cultural differences persist, as those who design media for markets in other countries know. Asian users may prefer muted pastel colors and anime-style graphics that North Americans would find unusual. Conversely, Korean and Japanese employees may balk at being compelled to post photos of themselves on company intranet pages. They opt for avatars or pictures of pets instead, possibly as an expression of personal modesty or expectations of privacy, whereas North Americans believe photos promote cohesion and make them seem accessible.[43]

It remains to be seen whether social networking will slowly erase many of the cultural differences present today or whether distinct national, even local, networks will emerge.[44]

**LEARNING OBJECTIVE 5**
Discuss strategies that help communicators overcome negative cultural attitudes and prevent miscommunication in today's diverse networked workplace.

## 1-5 Building Intercultural Workplace Skills

Being aware of your own culture and how it contrasts with others is a first step in learning intercultural skills. Another important step involves recognizing barriers to intercultural accommodation and striving to overcome them. The digital age economy needs workers who can thrive on diverse teams and interact effectively with customers and clients at home and abroad. This section addresses how to overcome barriers to productive intercultural communication, develop strong intercultural skills, and capitalize on workplace diversity.

### 1-5a Curbing Ethnocentrism and Stereotyping

The process of understanding and interacting successfully with people from other cultures is often hampered by two barriers: ethnocentrism and stereotyping. These barriers, however, can be overcome by developing tolerance, a powerful and effective aid to communication.

**Ethnocentrism.** The belief in the superiority of one's own culture is known as *ethnocentrism*. This natural attitude is found in all cultures. Ethnocentrism causes us to judge others by our own values. If you were raised in North America, values such as punctuality and directness described previously probably seem "right" to you, and you may wonder why the rest of the world doesn't function in the same sensible fashion. A North American businessperson in an Arab or Asian country might be upset at time spent over coffee or other social rituals before any "real" business is transacted. In these cultures, however, personal relationships must be established and nurtured before earnest talks may proceed.

**Stereotypes.** Our perceptions of other cultures sometimes cause us to form stereotypes about groups of people. A *stereotype* is an oversimplified perception of a behavioral pattern or characteristic applied to entire groups. For example, the Swiss are hardworking, efficient, and neat; Germans are formal, reserved, and blunt; Americans are loud, friendly, and impatient; Canadians are polite, trusting, and tolerant; Asians are gracious, humble, and inscrutable. These attitudes may or may not accurately describe cultural norms. When applied to individual business communicators, however, such stereotypes may create misconceptions and misunderstandings. Look beneath surface stereotypes and labels to discover individual personal qualities.

**Tolerance.** As global markets expand and as our society becomes increasingly multiethnic, tolerance is critical. *Tolerance* here means learning about beliefs and practices different from our own and appreciating them. It means being open-minded and receptive to new experiences. One of the best ways to develop tolerance is to practice *empathy*, defined as trying to see the world through another's eyes. It means being less judgmental and more eager to seek common ground.

For example, BMW Group and the United Nations Alliance of Civilizations jointly award projects around the world that promote international understanding and the overcoming of religious and cultural boundaries. A pair of recent finalists, a Palestinian school principal and an Israeli school principal, joined forces to counter the political turmoil in Jerusalem with their peace-building project billed "an ark of tolerance and understanding."[45] Students of both schools collaborate on environmental protection activities and study each other's languages. Getting along well with others is always a good policy, but doubly so in the workplace. Some job descriptions now include statements such as *Must be able to interact with ethnically diverse personnel*.

The suggestions in the following section can help you prevent miscommunication in oral and written transactions across cultures.

## 1-5b Successful Oral Communication With Intercultural Audiences

When you have a conversation with someone from another culture, you can reduce misunderstandings by following these tips:

- **Use simple English.** Speak in short sentences (under 20 words) with familiar, short words. Eliminate puns, sport and military references, slang, and jargon (special business terms). Be especially alert to idiomatic expressions that can't be translated, such as *burn the midnight oil* and *throw a curve ball*.
- **Speak slowly and enunciate clearly.** Avoid fast speech, but don't raise your voice. Overpunctuate with pauses and full stops. Always write numbers for all to see.
- **Encourage accurate feedback.** Ask probing questions, and encourage the listener to paraphrase what you say. Don't assume that a *yes*, a nod, or a smile indicates comprehension or assent.
- **Check frequently for comprehension.** Avoid waiting until you finish a long explanation to request feedback. Instead, make one point at a time, pausing to check for comprehension. Don't proceed to B until A has been grasped.
- **Observe eye messages.** Be alert to a glazed expression or wandering eyes. These tell you the listener is lost.
- **Accept blame.** If a misunderstanding results, graciously accept the responsibility for not making your meaning clear.

## OFFICE INSIDER

"Not everyone can travel, but since we live and work in a global economy, we should expect undergraduate programs to prepare students with a fundamental understanding of the cultural differences, historical perspectives and common business practices employed by all the major countries within it."

—Craig Cuyar, CIO, Cushman & Wakefield Inc.

- **Listen without interrupting.** Curb your desire to finish sentences or to fill out ideas for the speaker. Keep in mind that North Americans abroad are often accused of listening too little and talking too much.
- **Smile when appropriate.** The smile is often considered the single most understood and most useful form of communication. In some cultures, however, excessive smiling may seem insincere.[46]
- **Follow up in writing.** After conversations or oral negotiations, confirm the results and agreements with written messages—if necessary, in the local language.

## 1-5c Successful Written Communication With Intercultural Audiences

When you write to someone from a different culture, you can improve your chances of being understood by following these suggestions:

- **Consider local styles and conventions.** Learn how documents are formatted and how letters are addressed and developed in the intended reader's country. Decide whether to use your organization's preferred format or adjust to local styles. Observe titles and rank. Be polite.
- **Hire a translator.** Engage a professional translator if (a) your document is important, (b) your document will be distributed to many readers, or (c) you must be persuasive.
- **Use short sentences and short paragraphs.** Sentences with fewer than 20 words and paragraphs with fewer than 8 lines are most readable.
- **Avoid ambiguous wording.** Include relative pronouns (*that, which, who*) for clarity in introducing clauses. Stay away from contractions (especially ones such as *Here's the problem*). Avoid idioms (*once in a blue moon*), slang (*my presentation really bombed*), acronyms (*ASAP* for *as soon as possible*), abbreviations (*DBA* for *doing business as*), jargon (*ROI, bottom line*), and sports references (*play ball, slam dunk*). Use action-specific verbs (*buy a printer* rather than *get a printer*).
- **Cite numbers carefully.** In international trade learn and use the metric system. In citing numbers, use figures (*15*) instead of spelling them out (*fifteen*). Always convert dollar figures into local currency. Spell out the month when writing dates. In North America, for example, *March 5, 2015*, might be written as *3/5/15*, whereas in Europe the same date might appear as *5.3.15*.

## 1-5d Globalization and Workplace Diversity

While North American companies are expanding global operations and adapting to a variety of emerging markets, the domestic workforce is also becoming more diverse. This diversity has many dimensions—race, ethnicity, age, religion, gender, national origin, physical ability, sexual orientation, and other qualities.

No longer, say the experts, will the workplace be predominantly male or Anglo oriented. By 2020 many groups now considered minorities (African-Americans, Hispanics, Asians, Native Americans) are projected to become 36 percent of the U.S. population. Between 2040 and 2050, these same groups will reach the "majority–minority crossover," the point at which they will represent the majority of the U.S. population.[47] Women will comprise nearly 50 percent of the workforce, and the number of workers aged fifty-five and older will grow to 20 percent.[48]

What do all these changes mean for you? Simply put, your job may require you to interact with colleagues and customers from around the world. You will need to cooperate with individuals and teams. What's more, your coworkers may differ from you in race, ethnicity, gender, age, and other ways.

### 1-5e Benefits of a Diverse Workforce

As society and the workforce become more diverse, successful communication among the various identity groups brings distinct advantages. Customers want to deal with companies that respect their values. They are more likely to say, "If you are a company whose ads do not include me, or whose workforce does not include me, I will not buy from you."

A diverse staff is better able to respond to the increasingly diverse customer base in local and world markets. "We find that more and more of our clients are demanding that our partners and staff—involved in securing new business as well as delivering the work—reflect diversity within their organizations," said Toni Riccardi. She represents PricewaterhouseCoopers, the world's largest accounting firm.[49] Theo Fletcher, a vice president at IBM, agrees: "It is important that we have a supply base that looks like our employee base and that looks like the market we are trying to attract."[50]

In addition, organizations that set aside time and resources to cultivate and capitalize on diversity will suffer fewer discrimination lawsuits, fewer union clashes, and less government regulatory action. Most important, though, is the growing realization among organizations that diversity is a critical bottom-line business strategy to improve employee relationships and to increase productivity. Developing a diverse staff that can work together cooperatively is one of the biggest challenges facing business organizations today.

### 1-5f Tips for Communicating With Diverse Audiences on the Job

Harmony and acceptance do not happen automatically when people who are dissimilar work together. This means that companies must commit to diversity. Harnessed effectively, diversity can enhance productivity and propel a company to success. Mismanaged, it can become a drain on a company's time and resources. How companies deal with diversity will make all the difference in how they compete in a networked global environment. The following suggestions can help you find ways to improve communication and interaction:

- **Seek training.** If your organization is experiencing diversity problems, it may benefit from sensitivity training. Spend time reading and learning about workforce diversity and how it can benefit organizations. Look upon diversity as an opportunity, not a threat. Intercultural communication, team building, and conflict resolution are skills that can be learned in diversity training programs.

- **Understand the value of differences.** Diversity makes an organization innovative and creative. Sameness fosters an absence of critical thinking called *groupthink*. Case studies, for example, of the *Challenger* shuttle disaster suggest that groupthink prevented alternatives from being considered. Even smart people working collectively can make dumb decisions if they do not see different perspectives.[51] Diversity in problem-solving groups encourages independent and creative thinking.

- **Learn about your cultural self.** Begin to think of yourself as a product of your culture, and understand that your culture is just one among many. Try to stand outside and look at yourself. Do you see any reflex reactions and automatic thought patterns that are a result of your upbringing? These may be invisible to you until challenged by people who are different from you. Be sure to keep what works and yet be ready to adapt as your environment changes.

- **Make fewer assumptions.** Be careful of seemingly insignificant, innocent workplace assumptions. For example, don't assume that everyone wants to observe the holidays with a Christmas party and a decorated tree. Celebrating only Christian holidays in December and January excludes those who honor Hanukkah, Kwanzaa, and the Lunar New Year. Moreover, in workplace discussions don't assume anything about others' sexual orientation or attitude toward marriage. For invitations, avoid phrases such as *managers and their*

---

**OFFICE INSIDER**

*"I need to find the best set of skills to do the assignment rather than someone who looks like me, acts like me, or went to the same school or fits into the old mold."*

—Ken Henderson, managing director of IMCOR, a national executive search firm

*wives. Spouses* or *partners* is more inclusive. Valuing diversity means making fewer assumptions that everyone is like you or wants to be like you.

- **Build on similarities.** Look for areas in which you and others not like you can agree or at least share opinions. Be prepared to consider issues from many perspectives, all of which may be valid. Accept that there is room for various points of view to coexist peacefully. Although you can always find differences, it is much harder to find similarities. Look for common ground in shared experiences, mutual goals, and similar values.[52] Concentrate on your objective even when you may disagree on how to reach it.

## SUMMARY OF LEARNING OBJECTIVES

**1-1** Describe how solid communication skills will improve your career prospects and help you succeed in today's challenging digital-age workplace.
- Employers hire and promote job candidates who have excellent communication skills; writing skills make or break careers.
- Because workers interact more than ever using communication technology, even technical fields require communication skills.
- New-hires and other employees must project a professional image and possess soft skills.
- Job challenges in the information age include changing communication technologies, mobile 24/7 offices, flatter management, an emphasis on teams, and global competition.

**1-2** Confront barriers to effective listening, and start building your listening skills.
- Most of us are poor listeners; we can learn active listening by removing physical and psychological barriers, overlooking language problems, and eliminating distractions.
- A fast processing speed allows us to let our minds wander; we fake attention and prefer to talk than to listen.
- Poor listening can be overcome as long as we stop talking, focus fully on others, control distractions, keep an open mind, and listen for the speaker's main ideas.
- Capitalizing on lag time, listening between the lines, judging ideas instead of appearances, taking good notes, and providing feedback are other methods for building listening skills.

**1-3** Explain the importance of nonverbal communication and of improving your nonverbal communication skills.
- Be aware of nonverbal cues such as eye contact, facial expression, and posture that send silent, highly believable messages.
- Understand that how you use time, space, and territory is interpreted by the receiver, who also "reads" the eye appeal of your business documents and your personal appearance.
- Build solid nonverbal skills by keeping eye contact, maintaining good posture, reducing physical barriers, improving your decoding skills, and probing for more information.
- Interpret nonverbal meanings in context, learn about other cultures, and understand the impact of appearance—of documents, your office space, and yourself.

**1-4** Explain five common dimensions of culture, and understand how culture affects communication and the use of social media and communication technology.
- Culture is a complex system of values, traits, and customs shared by a society; culture molds the way we think, behave, and communicate both offline and online.
- Culture can be described using key dimensions such as context, individualism, time orientation, power distance, and communication style.
- Today's communicators need to be aware of low- and high-context cultures, individualistic versus collectivist societies, differing attitudes toward time, clashing perceptions of power, and varying reliance on the written word.
- Whether social media and technology can bridge cultural divides and erase differences will depend on the users as much as it would among strangers who meet at a dinner party.

**1-5** Discuss strategies that help communicators overcome negative cultural attitudes and prevent miscommunication in today's diverse networked workplace.
- Beware of ethnocentrism and stereotyping; instead, embrace tolerance and keep an open mind.
- When communicating orally, use simple English, speak slowly, check for comprehension, observe eye messages, accept blame, don't interrupt, smile, and follow up in writing.

- When writing, consider local styles, hire a translator, use short sentences, avoid ambiguous wording, and cite numbers carefully.
- As the domestic workforce becomes more diverse, appreciate diversity as a critical business strategy.
- To communicate well with diverse audiences, seek training, understand the value of diversity, learn about your own culture, make fewer assumptions, and look for similarities.

## CHAPTER REVIEW

1. Based on what you have learned in this chapter, describe the kind of work environment you can expect to enter when you graduate. (Obj. 1)

2. Why are writing skills more important in today's workplace than ever before? (Obj. 1)

3. List six trends in the information-age workplace that affect business communicators. Be prepared to discuss how they might affect you in your future career. (Obj. 1)

4. List bad habits and distractions that can act as barriers to effective listening. (Obj. 2)

5. List 11 techniques for improving your listening skills. Be prepared to discuss each. (Obj. 2)

6. What is nonverbal communication, and are nonverbal cues easy to read? (Obj. 3)

7. How do we send messages to others without speaking? (Obj. 3)

8. What is culture, and what are five key dimensions that can be used to describe it? (Obj. 4)

9. Can social media connect cultures and bridge cultural divides? (Obj. 4)

10. List seven or more suggestions for enhancing comprehension when you are talking with nonnative speakers of English. Be prepared to discuss each. (Obj. 5)

## CRITICAL THINKING

11. Do you consider your daily texting, Facebook updates, blog entries, e-mails, and other informal writing to be "real writing"? How might such writing differ from the writing done in business? (Obj. 1)

12. Why do executives and managers spend more time listening than do workers? (Obj. 2)

13. What arguments could you give for or against the idea that body language is a science with principles that can be interpreted accurately by specialists? (Obj. 3)

14. Consider potential culture clashes in typical business situations. Imagine that businesspeople from a high-context culture, say, Japan or China, meet their counterparts from a low-context culture, the United States, for the first time to negotiate and sign a manufacturing contract. What could go wrong? How about conflicting perceptions of time? (Obj. 4)

15. A stereotype is an oversimplified perception of a behavioral pattern or characteristic applied to entire groups. For example, the Germans are formal, reserved, and blunt; Americans are loud, friendly, and impatient; Asians are gracious, humble, and inscrutable. In what way are such stereotypes harmless or harmful? (Obj. 5)

## ACTIVITIES AND CASES

### 1.1 Test Your Communication Skills (Obj. 1)
Web

This course can help you dramatically improve your business communication skills. How much do you need to improve? This assessment exercise enables you to evaluate your skills with specific standards in four critical communication skill areas: writing, reading, speaking, and listening. How well you communicate will be an important factor in your future career—particularly if you are promoted into management, as many college graduates are.

**YOUR TASK.** Either here or at **www.cengagebrain.com**, select a number from 1 (indicating low ability) to 5 (indicating high ability) that best reflects your perception of yourself. Be honest in rating yourself. Think about how others would rate you. When you finish, see a rating of your skills. Complete this assessment online to see your results automatically!

| | Low | | | | High |
|---|---|---|---|---|---|

**Writing Skills**

1. Possess basic spelling, grammar, and punctuation skills — 1 2 3 4 5
2. Am familiar with proper e-mail, memo, letter, and report formats for business documents — 1 2 3 4 5
3. Can analyze a writing problem and quickly outline a plan for solving the problem — 1 2 3 4 5
4. Am able to organize data coherently and logically — 1 2 3 4 5
5. Can evaluate a document to determine its probable success — 1 2 3 4 5

**Reading Skills**

1. Am familiar with specialized vocabulary in my field as well as general vocabulary — 1 2 3 4 5
2. Can concentrate despite distractions — 1 2 3 4 5
3. Am willing to look up definitions whenever necessary — 1 2 3 4 5
4. Am able to move from recreational to serious reading — 1 2 3 4 5
5. Can read and comprehend college-level material — 1 2 3 4 5

**Speaking Skills**

1. Feel at ease in speaking with friends — 1 2 3 4 5
2. Feel at ease in speaking before groups of people — 1 2 3 4 5
3. Can adapt my presentation to the audience — 1 2 3 4 5
4. Am confident in pronouncing and using words correctly — 1 2 3 4 5
5. Sense that I have credibility when I make a presentation — 1 2 3 4 5

**Listening Skills**

1. Spend at least half the time listening during conversations — 1 2 3 4 5
2. Am able to concentrate on a speaker's words despite distractions — 1 2 3 4 5
3. Can summarize a speaker's ideas and anticipate what's coming during pauses — 1 2 3 4 5
4. Provide proper feedback such as nodding, paraphrasing, and asking questions — 1 2 3 4 5
5. Listen with the expectation of gaining new ideas and information — 1 2 3 4 5

Total your score in each section. How do you rate?

- 22-25  Excellent! You have indicated that you have exceptional communication skills.
- 18-21  Your score is above average, but you could improve your skills.
- 14-17  Your score suggests that you have much room for improvement.
- 5-13   You need serious study, practice, and follow-up reinforcement.

Where are you strongest and weakest? Are you satisfied with your present skills? The first step to improvement is recognition of a need. The second step is making a commitment to improve. The third step is following through, and this course will help you do that.

## 1.2 Pump Up Your Language Muscles (Obj. 1)

**Web**

You can enlist the aid of your authors to help you pump up your basic language muscles. As your personal trainers, Drs. Guffey and Loewy provide a three-step workout plan and hundreds of interactive questions to help you brush up on your grammar and mechanics skills. You receive immediate feedback in the warm-up sessions, and when you finish a complete workout, you can take a short test to assess what you learned. These workouts are completely self-taught, which means that you can review them at your own pace and repeat them as often as you need. *Your Personal Language Trainer* is available at your premium website, **www.cengagebrain.com**. In addition to pumping up your basic language muscles, you can also use *Spell Right!* and *Speak Right!* to improve your spelling and pronunciation skills.

Chapter 1: Communicating in the Digital-Age Workplace

**YOUR TASK.** Begin using *Your Personal Language Trainer* to brush up on your basic grammar and mechanics skills by completing one to three workouts per week, or as many as your instructor advises. Be prepared to submit a printout of your "fitness" (completion) certificate when you finish a workout module. If your instructor directs, complete the spelling exercises in *Spell Right!* and submit a certificate of completion for the spelling final exam.

## 1.3 Introduce Yourself (Obj. 1)
`Communication Technology` `E-mail`

Your instructor wants to know more about you, your motivation for taking this course, your career goals, and your writing skills.

**YOUR TASK.** Send an e-mail or write a memo of introduction to your instructor. See Chapter 5 for formats and tips on preparing e-mails. In your message include the following:

a. Your reasons for taking this class
b. Your career goals (both short term and long term)
c. A brief description of your employment, if any, and your favorite activities
d. An evaluation and discussion of your current communication skills, including your strengths and weaknesses

For online classes, write a message of introduction about yourself with the preceding information. Post your message (memo or letter) to your discussion board. Read and comment on the posts of other students. Think about how people in virtual teams must learn about each other through online messages.

Alternatively, your instructors may assign this task as a concise individual voice mail message to establish your telephone etiquette and speaking skills.

## 1.4 Small-Group Presentation: Introduce Each Other (Objs. 1, 2)
`Team`

Many business organizations today use teams to accomplish their goals. To help you develop speaking, listening, and teamwork skills, your instructor may assign team projects. One of the first jobs in any team is selecting members and becoming acquainted.

**YOUR TASK.** Your instructor will divide your class into small groups or teams. At your instructor's direction, either (a) interview another group member and introduce that person to the group or (b) introduce yourself to the group. Think of this as an informal interview for a team assignment or for a job. You will want to make notes from which to speak. Your introduction should include information such as the following:

a. Where did you grow up?
b. What work and extracurricular activities have you engaged in?
c. What are your interests and talents? What are you good at doing?
d. What have you achieved?
e. How familiar are you with various computer technologies?
f. What are your professional and personal goals? Where do you expect to be five years from now?

To develop listening skills, practice the listening techniques discussed in this chapter and take notes when other students are presenting. In addition to mentioning details about each speaker, be prepared to discuss three important facts about each speaker.

## 1.5 Rating Your Listening Skills (Obj. 2)
`Web`

You can learn whether your listening skills are excellent or deficient by completing a brief quiz.

**YOUR TASK.** Take *Dr. Guffey's Listening Quiz* at **www.cengagebrain.com**. What two listening behaviors do you think you need to work on the most?

## 1.6 Remembering a Time When Someone Didn't Listen to You (Obj. 2)
`Communication Technology` `E-mail` `Team`

Think of a time when you felt that someone didn't listen to you—for example, on the job, at home, at the doctor's office, or at a store where you shop. Your instructor will split the class into pairs of speakers and listeners. The speakers will share their stories. The listeners must try to recognize two things: (a) what the poor listener in the story did that demonstrated nonlistening and (b) what impact this had on the speaker's feelings. The speakers and listeners then reverse roles. After this second round, the class compares notes to debrief. All ideas are collected to identify patterns of nonlistening behavior and its negative impact on the speakers.

**YOUR TASK.** In pairs or individually, identify behavior that would reverse what happened in the stories told in class. Based on your insights, write an e-mail or memo that describes several principles of good listening illustrated with brief examples. You could end by concisely telling of an encounter that shows ideal active listening.

## 1.7 Listening: An In-Person or Virtual Social Media Interview (Obj. 2)
*Communication Technology* | *Social Media* | *Team* | *E-mail*

How much and to whom do businesspeople listen?

**YOUR TASK.** Interview a businessperson about his or her workplace listening. Connect with a worker in your circle of friends, family, and acquaintances; in your campus network; at a prior or current job; or via LinkedIn or Facebook. Come up with questions to ask about listening, such as the following: (a) How much active listening do you practice daily? (b) To whom do you listen on the job? (c) How do you know that others are listening or not listening to you? (d) Can you share anecdotes of poor listening that led to negative outcomes? (e) Do you have tips for better listening?

## 1.8 Listening and Nonverbal Cues: Skills Required in Various Careers (Objs. 2, 3)
*Team*

Do the listening skills and behaviors of individuals differ depending on their careers?

**YOUR TASK.** Your instructor will divide you into teams and give each team a role to discuss, such as business executive, teacher, physician, police officer, attorney, accountant, administrative assistant, mentor, or team leader. Create a list of verbal and nonverbal cues that a member of this profession would display to indicate that he or she is listening.

## 1.9 Body Language (Obj. 3)

Can body language be accurately interpreted?

**YOUR TASK.** What attitudes do the following body movements suggest to you? Do these movements always mean the same thing? What part does context play in your interpretations?

a. Whistling, wringing hands
b. Bowed posture, twiddling thumbs
c. Steepled hands, sprawling sitting position
d. Rubbing hand through hair
e. Open hands, unbuttoned coat
f. Wringing hands, tugging ears

## 1.10 Nonverbal Communication: Universal Sign for *I Goofed* (Obj. 3)
*Team*

To promote tranquility on the highways and reduce road rage, motorists submitted the following suggestions. They were sent to a newspaper columnist who asked for a universal nonverbal signal admitting that a driver had "goofed."[53]

**YOUR TASK.** In small groups consider the pros and cons of each of the following gestures intended as an apology when a driver makes a mistake. Why would some fail?

a. Lower your head slightly and bonk yourself on the forehead with the side of your closed fist. The message is clear: *I'm stupid. I shouldn't have done that.*
b. Make a temple with your hands, as if you were praying.
c. Move the index finger of your right hand back and forth across your neck—as if you were cutting your throat.
d. Flash the well-known peace sign. Hold up the index and middle fingers of one hand, making a V, as in victory.
e. Place the flat of your hands against your cheeks, as children do when they have made a mistake.
f. Clasp your hand over your mouth, raise your brows, and shrug your shoulders.
g. Use your knuckles to knock on the side of your head. Translation: *Oops! Engage brain.*
h. Place your right hand high on your chest and pat a few times, like a basketball player who drops a pass or a football player who makes a bad throw. This says, *I'll take the blame.*
i. Place your right fist over the middle of your chest and move it in a circular motion. This is universal sign language for *I'm sorry.*
j. Open your window and tap the top of your car roof with your hand.
k. Smile and raise both arms, palms outward, which is a universal gesture for surrender or forgiveness.
l. Use the military salute, which is simple and shows respect.
m. Flash your biggest smile, point at yourself with your right thumb, and move your head from left to right, as if to say, *I can't believe I did that.*

## 1.11 Nonverbal Communication: Signals Sent by Casual Attire (Obj. 3)
**Communication Technology | E-mail | Team | Web**

Although many employers allow casual attire, not all employers and customers are happy with the results. To learn more about the implementation, acceptance, and effects of casual-dress programs, select one of the following activities, all of which involve some form of interviewing.

**YOUR TASK.**
a. In teams, gather information from human resources directors to determine which companies allow casual or dress-down days, how often, and under what specific conditions. The information may be collected by personal interviews, e-mail, telephone, instant messaging, or on the Web.
b. In teams, conduct inquiring-reporter interviews. Ask individuals in the community how they react to casual dress in the workplace. Develop a set of standard interview questions.
c. In teams, visit local businesses on both casual days and traditional business dress days. Compare and contrast the effects of business dress standards on such factors as the projected image of the company, the nature of the interactions with customers and with fellow employees, the morale of employees, and the productivity of employees. What generalizations can you draw from your findings?

## 1.12 Nonverbal Communication Around the World (Objs. 3, 4)
**Intercultural | Web**

Gestures play an important role when people communicate. Because culture shapes the meaning of gestures, miscommunication and misunderstanding can easily result in international situations.

**YOUR TASK.** Use the Web to research the meanings of selected gestures. Make a list of ten gestures (other than those discussed in the text) that have different meanings in different countries. Consider the fingertip kiss, nose thumb, eyelid pull, nose tap, head shake, and other gestures. How are the meanings different in other countries?

## 1.13 Making Sense of Idioms (Obj. 4)
**Intercultural**

Many languages have idiomatic expressions that do not always make sense to outsiders.

**YOUR TASK.** Explain in simple English what the following idiomatic expressions mean. Assume that you are explaining them to non-native speakers of English.

a. have an axe to grind
b. under wraps
c. come out of left field
d. hell on wheels
e. drop the ball
f. get your act together
g. stay the course
h. in the limelight
i. low on the totem pole

## 1.14 Examining Cultural Stereotypes (Objs. 4, 5)
**Intercultural | Team | Web**

Generalizations are necessary as we acquire and categorize new knowledge. As long as we remain open to new experiences, we won't be stymied by rigid, stereotypical perceptions of other cultures. Almost all of us are at some point in our lives subject to stereotyping by others, whether we are immigrants, minorities, women, members of certain professions, or Americans abroad. Generally speaking, negative stereotypes sting. However, even positive stereotypes can offend or embarrass because they fail to acknowledge the differences among individuals.

**YOUR TASK.** Think about a nation or culture about which you have only a hazy idea. Jot down a few key traits that come to mind. For example, you may not know much about the Netherlands and the Dutch people. You may think of gouda cheese, wooden clogs, Heineken beer, tulips, and windmills. Anything else? Then consider a culture with which you are very familiar, whether it is yours or that of a country you visited or studied. For each culture, in one column, write down a few stereotypical perceptions that are positive. Then, in another column, record negative stereotypes you associate with that culture. Share your notes with your team or the whole class, as your instructor may direct. How do you respond to others' descriptions of your culture? Which stereotypes irk you and why? For a quick fact check and overview at the end of this exercise, google the *CIA World Factbook* or *BBC News Country Profiles*.

## 1.15 Examining Diversity in Job Interviews (Objs. 4, 5)

Today's workforce benefits from diversity, and most businesses have embraced explicit nondiscrimination policies. The federal government and many state governments have passed legislation that makes it illegal to discriminate based on race, color, creed, ethnicity, national origin, disability, sex, age, and other factors such as sexual orientation and gender identity. Some public institutions have the most far-reaching nondiscrimination policies on their books—for example, the Massachusetts Institute of Technology (MIT): "The Institute does not discriminate against individuals on the basis of race, color, sex, sexual orientation, gender identity, religion, disability, age, genetic information, veteran status, ancestry, or national or ethnic origin."[54]

**YOUR TASK.** Consider how such differences could affect the communication, for instance, between an interviewer and a job candidate. If negatively, how could the differences and barriers be overcome? Role-play or discuss a potential job interview conversation between the following individuals. After a while summarize your findings, either orally or in writing:
a. A female top executive is interviewing a prospective future assistant, who is male.
b. A candidate with a strong but not disruptive foreign accent is being interviewed by a native-born human resources manager.
c. A manager dressed in a conventional business suit is interviewing a person wearing a turban.
d. A person over fifty is being interviewed by a hiring manager in his early thirties.
e. A recruiter who can walk is interviewing a job seeker who uses a wheelchair.

# GRAMMAR/MECHANICS CHECKUP—1

These checkups are designed to improve your control of grammar and mechanics, which includes punctuation, spelling, capitalization, and number use. The checkups systematically review all sections of the Grammar/Mechanics Handbook. Answers are provided near the end of the book. You will find a set of alternate Bonus Grammar/Mechanics Checkups with immediate feedback at your premium website (www.cengagebrain.com). These Bonus G/M Checkups use different exercises but parallel the items in the textbook. Use the Bonus G/M Checkups to reinforce your learning.

## Nouns

Review Sections 1.02–1.06 in the Grammar/Mechanics Handbook. Then study each of the following statements. Underscore any inappropriate form, and write a correction in the space provided. Also record the appropriate G/M section and letter to illustrate the principle involved. If a sentence is correct, write C. When you finish, compare your responses with those provided. If your answers differ, study carefully the principles shown in parentheses.

sexes _____ (1.05b) **EXAMPLE** The tennis match turned out to be a battle of the sex's.

1. American marketing efforts are increasing in all Pacific Rim countrys.
2. None of the CEO's used their smartphones during the meeting.
3. We were surprised that the companies' two highly paid attornies disagreed on the best defense.
4. That restaurant is open on Sunday's but not on Monday's.
5. Many turkies had to be destroyed after the virus outbreak.
6. Only the Bushes and the Alvarez's brought their entire families.
7. Congress established the Small Business Administration in the 1950's.
8. President Lincoln had four brother-in-laws serving in the Confederate Army.
9. I have never seen so many klutz's on one dance floor.
10. Congress conducted several inquirys regarding new taxes.
11. The instructor was surprised to have three Anthonies in one class.
12. All the mountains and valleys were visible on Google Earth.
13. The IRS required copies of all documents showing the company's assets and liabilitys.
14. My tablet monitor makes it difficult to distinguish between *i*'s and *l*'s.
15. The four sisters-in-law joined many other woman in fighting for human rights.

# EDITING CHALLENGE—1

To fine-tune your grammar and mechanics skills, in every chapter you will be editing a message. These are the skills that employers frequently find lacking in employees. It's during the revising process that you will put these skills to work. That's why we provide a completed message with errors in proofreading, grammar, spelling, punctuation, capitalization, word use, and number form. Your job is to find and correct all errors. This first Editing Challenge focuses on nouns but other writing faults also need revision.

You can complete this exercise (a) by correcting errors in your textbook or on a photocopy using proofreading marks from Appendix A or (b) by downloading the exercise from your premium website at **www.cengagebrain.com** and correcting at your computer. Your instructor may show you a possible solution.

---

**To:** Amanda Stapleton <a.stapleton@dobbsmfg.com>
**From:** Kevin Williams <k.williams@dobbsmfg.com>
**Subject:** Tip for Working From Home
**Cc:**
**Bcc:**

---

Hi, Amanda,

Because you will be working from home during the next 6 months, we have some tips on how to do it efficiently while stay in touch with the office.

- **Set boundarys for your work.** Establish a starting and ending time, and when its quitting time, wrap every thing up and shut down.
- **Check your e-mail regularly.** Such as 3 times a day. Answer all message promply, and send copys of relevant messages to the appropriate office staff.
- **Transmit all work order to Andrea.** She will analyze each weeks activitys and update all sales assignments and inventorys.
- **Provide a end of week report.** Send a summary of your weeks work to me indicating the major accounts you serviced.

If your not a big e-mail user get acquainted with it right away and don't be afraid to use it. Please shoot e-mails to any staff member. When you need clarification on a project or if you just want to keep us updated.

We will continue to hold once a week staff meeting on Friday's at 10 a.m. in the morning. Do you think it would be possible for you to attend 1 or 2 of these meeting. The next one is Friday, May 5th.

I know you will enjoy working at home Amanda. Following these basic guideline should help you complete your work, and provide the office with adequate contact with you.

Kevin Williams
[Full contact information]

# COMMUNICATION WORKSHOP

## TECHNOLOGY

### Scouring Job Boards to Explore Career Prospects in Your Field

Most job seekers today start with the Internet, whether searching job boards or, increasingly, social media networks. This communication workshop will help you use the big job boards to study openings in your field. Looking for jobs or internships online has distinct advantages. For a few job hunters, the Internet delivers with leads to bigger salaries, wider opportunities, and faster hiring. The Internet, however, can devour huge chunks of time and produce slim results.

Internet job searches seem to work best for professionals looking for similar work in their current fields and for those who are totally flexible about location. However, Internet job boards are an excellent place for any job seeker to learn what is available, what qualifications are necessary, and what salaries are being offered. To be sure, with tens of thousands of job boards and employment websites deluging the Internet, it's hard to know where to start.

**CAREER APPLICATION.** Assume that you are about to finish your degree or certification program and you are now looking for a job. At the direction of your instructor, conduct a survey of online job advertisements in your field. What's available? How much is the salary? What are the requirements?

**YOUR TASK**

- **Visit Monster**, one of the most popular job boards.
- **Study the opening page.** Ignore the clutter and banner ads or pop-ups. Close any pop-up boxes.
- **Select keyword, category, city, and state.** Decide whether you want to search by a job title (such as *nurse, accountant, project manager*) or a category (such as *Accounting/Finance, Administrative/Clerical, Advertising/Marketing*). Enter your keyword job title or select a category—or do both. Enter a city, state, or region. Click **Search**.
- **Study the job listings.** Click the links to read more about the job openings.
- **Refine your search techniques.** For many helpful hints on precise searching, click **Search tips** or **Advanced Search**. Browsing this information may take a few minutes, but it is well worth the effort to learn how to refine your search.
- **Select the best ads.** In your career and geographical area, select the three best ads and print them. If you cannot print, make notes on what you find.
- **Visit another site.** Try CollegeRecruiter, which claims to be the leading internship and entry-level job site for students and recent graduates, or CareerBuilder, which says it is the largest online career site with more than 1.6 million jobs and 24 million unique visitors every month. Become familiar with the site's search tools, and look for jobs in your field. Select and print three ads.
- **Analyze the skills required.** How often do the ads you printed mention communication, teamwork, computer skills, or professionalism? What tasks do the ads mention? What is the salary range identified in these ads for the positions they feature? Your instructor may ask you to submit your findings and/or report to the class.

---

Communication Workshops (such as the one on this page) provide insight into special business communication topics and skills not discussed in the chapters. Topics include ethics, technology, career skills, and collaboration. Each workshop includes a career application to extend your learning and help you develop skills relevant to the workshop topic.

# ENDNOTES

[1] O'Rourke, J. (2012). *Managerial communication*. 5th ed. Upper Saddle River, NJ: Prentice Hall.

[2] The MetLife Survey of the American Teacher: Preparing students for college and careers. (2011, May). Retrieved from http://www.metlife.com/assets/cao/contributions/foundation/americanteacher/MetLife_Teacher_Survey_2010.pdf

[3] Canavor, N. (2012). *Business writing in the digital age*. Los Angeles: Sage, pp. 1-3; National Writing Project with DeVoss, D. N., Eidman-Aadahl, E., & Hicks, T. (2010). *Because digital writing matters*. San Francisco: Jossey-Bass, pp. 1–5.

[4] The Association of American Colleges and Universities/Hart Research Associates. (2009, November). Raising the bar: Employers' views on college learning in the wake of the economic downturn, pp. 5–6. Retrieved from http://www.aacu.org/leap/documents/2009_EmployerSurvey.pdf

[5] Appleman, J. E. (2009, October). Don't let poor writing skills stifle company growth. *T + D*, *63*(10), 10. Retrieved from http://search.ebscohost.com; Timm, J. A. (2005, December). Preparing students for the next employment revolution. *Business Education Forum*, *60*(2), 55–59. Retrieved from http://search.ebscohost.com; Messmer, M. (2001, January). Enhancing your writing skills. *Strategic Finance*, p. 8. See also Staples, B. (2005, May 15). The fine art of getting it down on paper, fast. *The New York Times*, p. WK13(L).

[6] Do communication students have the "write stuff"?: Practitioners evaluate writing skills of entry-level workers. (2008). *Journal of Promotion Management*, *14*(3/4), 294. Retrieved from http://search.ebscohost.com; The National Commission on Writing. (2005, July). Writing: A powerful message from state government. CollegeBoard. Retrieved from http://www.collegeboard.com/prod_downloads/writingcom/powerful-message-from-state.pdf; The National Commission on Writing. (2004, September 14). Writing skills necessary for employment, says big business. [Press release]. Retrieved from http://www.writingcommission.org/pr/writing_for_employ.html

[7] Survey shows workers shud write better. (2004, September 14). Associated Press. Retrieved from MSNBC at http://www.msnbc.msn.com/id/6000685

[8] Employers rank top 5 candidate skills. (2010, January 20). [Weblog post]. Retrieved from http://blog.resumebear.com/2010/01/20/employers-rank-top-5-candidate-skills; Moody, J., Stewart, B., & Bolt-Lee, C. (2002, March). Showcasing the skilled business graduate: Expanding the tool kit. *Business Communication Quarterly*, *65*(1), 23.

[9] American Management Association. (2010). AMA 2010 critical skills survey: Executives say the 21st century requires more skilled workers. Retrieved from http://www.p21.org/documents/Critical%20Skills%20Survey%20Executive%20Summary.pdf; Vance, E. (2007, February 2). College graduates lack key skills, report says. *The Chronicle of Higher Education*, p. A30.

[10] Wong, V. (2013, June 27). Hey job applicants, time to stop the social-media sabotage. *Bloomberg Businessweek*. Retrieved from www.businessweek.com/articles/2013-06-27/for-job-applicants-social-media-sabotage-is-still-getting-worse#r=read

[11] Musbach, T. (2009, November 11). Secret weapon in the job hunt today: Personality. FastCompany.com. [Weblog post]. Retrieved from http://www.fastcompany.com/user/tom-musbach; Gallagher, K. P., Kaiser, K. M., Simon, J., Beath, C. M., & Goles, J. (2009, June). The requisite variety of skills for IT professionals. *Communications of the Association for Computing Machinery*, *53*(6), 147. doi: 10.1145/1743546.1743584

[12] English, A. (2012, October). What makes a great techie? *IBM Systems Magazine*. Retrieved from http://www.ibmsystemsmag.com/aix/trends/whatsnew/great_techie

[13] Willmer, D. (2009, April 21). Leveraging soft skills in a competitive IT job market. Computerworld.com. Retrieved from http://www.computerworld.com; Morisy, M. (2008, February 28). Networking pros can avoid outsourcing with soft skills. Global Knowledge. Retrieved from http://www.globalknowledge.com/training/generic.asp?pageid=2119&country=United+States; Stranger, J. (2007, July). How to make yourself offshore-proof. *Certification Magazine*, *9*(7), 34–40. Retrieved from http://search.ebscohost.com

[14] Marsan, C. D. (2007, December 31). Job skills that matter: Where you can leave a mark. *Network World*, *24*(50), 38–40. Retrieved from http://search.ebscohost.com

[15] Robinson, T. M. (2008, January 26). Quoted in Same office, different planets. *The New York Times*, p. B5.

[16] Mitchell, G. A., Skinner, L. B., & White, B. J. (2010) Essential soft skills for success in the twenty-first-century workforce as perceived by business educators. *The Delta Pi Epsilon Journal*, *52*(1). Retrieved from http://www.faqs.org/periodicals/201001/2036768821.html

[17] McEwen, B. C. (2010). Cross-cultural and international career exploration and employability skills. *National Business Education Association Yearbook 2010: Cross-Cultural and International Business Education*, *48*, 142.

[18] King, J. (2009, September 21). Crossing the skills gap. *Computerworld*, p. 30. Retrieved from http://search.ebscohost.com; Professional demeanor and personal management. (2004, January). *Keying In*, National Business Education Association Newsletter, p. 1.

[19] King, J. (2009, September 21). Crossing the skills gap. *Computerworld*, p. 30. Retrieved from http://search.ebscohost.com

[20] Wong, V. (2013, June 27). Hey job applicants, time to stop the social-media sabotage. *Bloomberg Businessweek*. Retrieved from www.businessweek.com/articles/2013-06-27/for-job-applicants-social-media-sabotage-is-still-getting-worse#r=read

[21] Rampell, C. (2013, February 19). College premium: Better pay, better prospects. Economix Blogs, New York Times. Retrieved from http://economix.blogs.nytimes.com/2013/02/19/college-premium-better-pay-better-prospects/?_r=0; Crosby, O., & Moncarz, R. (2006, Fall). The 2004-14 job outlook for college graduates. *Occupational Outlook Quarterly*, *50*(3), 43. Retrieved from http://www.bls.gov/opub/ooq/2006/fall/art03.htm

[22] Shah, N. (2013, April 2). College grads earn nearly three times more than high school dropouts. WSJ Blogs. Retrieved from http://blogs.wsj.com/economics/2013/04/02/college-grads-earn-nearly-three-times-more-than-high-school-dropouts

[23] Employers rank top 5 candidate skills. (2010, January 20). Retrieved from http://blog.resumebear.com/2010/01/20/employers-rank-top-5-candidate-skills

[24] Holland, K. (2008, September 28). The anywhere, anytime office. *The New York Times*, p. 14 BU Y.

[25] Telework 2011: A WorldatWork special report, p. 3. Retrieved from www.worldatwork.org/waw/adimLink?id=53034

[26] Silverman, R. E., & Sidel, R. (2012, April 17). Warming up to the officeless office. *The Wall Street Journal*. Retrieved from http://online.wsj.com/article/SB10001424052702304818404577349783161465976.html; Holland, K. (2008, September 28). The anywhere, anytime office. *The New York Times*, p. 14 BU Y.

[27] Edmondson, A. C. (2012, April). Teamwork on the fly. *Harvard Business Review*. Retrieved from http://hbr.org/2012/04/teamwork-on-the-fly/ar/1

[28] Watzlawick, P., Beavin-Bavelas, J., & Jackson, D. (1967). Some tentative axioms of communication. In: *Pragmatics of human communication: A study of interactional patterns, pathologies and paradoxes*. New York: W. W. Norton.

[29] Birdwhistell, R. (1970). *Kinesics and context*. Philadelphia: University of Pennsylvania Press.

[30] Hall, E. T. (1966). *The hidden dimension*. Garden City, NY: Doubleday, pp. 107-122.

[31] Wilkie, H. (2003, Fall). Professional presence. *The Canadian Manager*, *28*(3), 14–19. Retrieved from http://search.ebscohost.com

[32] Davis, T., Ward, D. A., & Woodland, D. (2010). Cross-cultural and international business communication—verbal. *National Business Education Association Yearbook: Cross-Cultural and International Business Education*, p. 3; Hall, E. T., & Hall, M. R. (1990). *Understanding cultural differences*. Yarmouth, ME: Intercultural Press, pp. 183–184.

[33] Chaney, L. H., & Martin, J. S. (2011). *Intercultural business communication* (5th ed.). Upper Saddle River, NJ: Prentice Hall, p. 93.

[34] Beamer, L., & Varner, I. (2008). *Intercultural communication in the global workplace*. Boston: McGraw-Hill Irwin, p. 129.

[35] Sheer, V. C., & Chen, L. (2003, January). Successful Sino-Western business negotiation: Participants' accounts of national and professional cultures. *The Journal of Business Communication*, *40*(1), 62; see also Luk, L., Patel, M., & White, K. (1990, December). Personal attributes of American and Chinese business associates. *The Bulletin of the Association for Business Communication*, 67.

[36] Gallois, C., & Callan, V. (1997). *Communication and culture*. New York: Wiley, p. 24.

[37] Ibid., p. 29.

[38] Copeland, L. & Griggs, L. (1985). *Going international*. New York: Penguin, p. 94. See also Beamer, L., & Varner, I. (2008). *Intercultural communication in the global workplace*. Boston: McGraw-Hill Irwin, p. 340.

[39] Copeland, L. & Griggs, L. (1991). *Going international*. New York: Penguin, p. 12.

[40] Klass, P. (2012, January 9). Seeing social media more as portal than as pitfall. *The New York Times*. Retrieved from http://www.nytimes.com/2012/01/10/health/views/seeing-social-media-as-adolescent-portal-more-than-pitfall.html

[41] Aragon, S. R. (2003, Winter). Creating social presence in online environments. *New Directions for Adult and Continuing Education, 100*, 59.

[42] Carter, J. F. (2010, October 14). Why Twitter influences cross-cultural engagement. Mashable Social Media. Retrieved from http://mashable.com/2010/10/14/twitter-cross-cultural

[43] McGrath, C. (2009, August 5). Five lessons learned about cross-cultural social networking. ThoughtFarmer. Retrieved from http://www.thoughtfarmer.com/blog/2009/08/05/5-lessons-cross-cultural-social-networking/#comments

[44] Kunz, B. (2012, April 19). Facebook, Google must adapt as users embrace "unsocial" networks. *Bloomberg Businessweek*. Retrieved from http://www.businessweek.com; Jackson, E. (2012, June 5). Will Facebook exist in five years? [Video]. *Bloomberg Businessweek*. Retrieved from http://www.businessweek.com/videos/2012-06-05/will-facebook-exist-in-five-years

[45] BMW Group. (2010, November 18). The intercultural innovation award. Retrieved from http://www.bmwgroup.com/e/0_0_www_bmwgroup_com/verantwortung/gesellschaft/lifeaward/ausschreibung2010/_pdf/profils_finalists_engl.pdf

[46] Martin, J. S., & Chaney, L. H. (2006). *Global business etiquette*. Westport, CT: Praeger, p. 36.

[47] Ortman, J. M., & Guarneri, C. E. (2009). United States population projections: 2000–2050, p. 4. Retrieved from http://www.census.gov/population/projections; see also 2000 U.S. Census figures, as reported by Little, J. S., & Triest, R. K. (2001). Proceedings from the Federal Reserve Bank of Boston Conference Series. The impact of demographic change on U.S. labor markets. Seismic shifts: The economic impact of demographic change. Retrieved from http://www.bos.frb.org/economic/conf/conf46/conf46a.pdf

[48] Ten Tips for the awkward age of computing. (n.d.). *Microsoft accessibility, technology for everyone*. Retrieved from http://www.microsoft.com/enable/aging/tips.aspx

[49] Hansen, F. (2003, April). Tracing the value of diversity programs. *Workforce*, p. 31.

[50] Carbone, J. (2005, August 11). IBM says diverse suppliers are good for business. *Purchasing*, p. 27. Retrieved from http://search.ebscohost.com

[51] Schoemaker, P. J. H., & Day, G. S. (2009, Winter). Why we miss the signs. *MIT Sloan Management Review, 50*(2), 43; Schwartz, J., & Wald, M. L. (2003, March 9). Smart people working collectively can be dumber than the sum of their brains. Appeared originally in *The New York Times*. Retrieved from http://www.mindfully.org/Reform/2003/Smart-People-Dumber9mar03.htm

[52] White, M. D. (2002). *A short course in international marketing blunders*. Novato, CA: World Trade Press, p. 46.

[53] What's the universal hand sign for "I goofed"? (1996, December 16). *Santa Barbara News-Press*, p. D2.

[54] MIT Reference Publications Office. (2009, December). Nondiscrimination policy. Retrieved from http://web.mit.edu/referencepubs/nondiscrimination

## ACKNOWLEDGMENTS

**p. 3** Office Insider based on Canavor, N. (2012). *Business writing in the digital age*. Los Angeles: Sage, p. 4.

**p. 5** Office Insider based on The College Board. (2008, April 24). Teens say electronic writing is different from their real writing. [Press release]. Retrieved from http://press.collegeboard.org/releases/2008/teens-say-electronic-writing-different-their-real-writing

**p. 7** Office Insider based on King, J. (2009, September 21). Crossing the skills gap. *Computerworld*, p. 30. Retrieved from http://search.ebscohost.com

**p. 10** Office Insider is based on Washington, V. (n.d.). The high cost of poor listening. EzineArticles.com. Retrieved from http://ezinearticles.com/?The-High-Cost-of-Poor-Listening&id=163192

**p. 11** Office Insider based on Bucero, A. (2006, July). Listen and learn. *PM Network*. Retrieved from http://search.ebscohost.com

**p. 14** Workplace in Focus based on Schepp, D. (2010, July 26). People@work: How to job hunt with tattoos. *Daily Finance*. Retrieved from http://www.dailyfinance.com/2010/07/26/tattoos-job-hunt-interviews-career

**p. 19** Office Insider based on King, J. (2009, September 21). Crossing the skills gap. *Computerworld*, p. 32. Retrieved from http://search.ebscohost.com

**p. 21** Office Insider based on Papiernik, R. L. (1995, October 30). Diversity demands new understanding. *Nation's Restaurant News, 29*(43), 54. Retrieved from http://www.nrn.com

**p. 26** Activity 1.6 is based on Gough, V. (2010, July 12). Trainers' tips: Active listening exercises. Retrieved from http://www.trainingzone.co.uk/topic/trainers-tips-active-listening-exercises/143120

# The Business Writing Process in the Digital Age

## UNIT 2

**Chapter 2**
Planning Business Messages

**Chapter 3**
Organizing and Drafting Business Messages

**Chapter 4**
Revising Business Messages

# CHAPTER 2

# Planning Business Messages

**OBJECTIVES**
After studying this chapter, you should be able to

**2-1**
Discuss the five steps in the communication process.

**2-2**
Recognize the goals of business writing, summarize the 3-x-3 writing process, and explain how it guides a writer.

**2-3**
Analyze the purpose of a message, anticipate its audience, and select the best communication channel.

**2-4**
Employ adaptive writing techniques such as incorporating audience benefits, developing the "you" view, and using conversational but professional language.

**2-5**
Develop additional expert writing techniques including the use of a positive and courteous tone, bias-free language, plain language, and precise words.

## 2-1 Understanding the Communication Process

The digital revolution has profoundly changed the way we live our lives, do business, and communicate. People are sending more and more messages, and they are using exciting new media as the world becomes increasingly interconnected. However, even as we have become accustomed to e-mail, instant messaging, Facebook, Twitter, and other social media, the nature of communication remains unchanged. No matter how we create or send our messages, the basic communication process consists of the same five steps. It starts with an idea that must be transmitted.

In its simplest form, *communication* may be defined as "the transmission of information and meaning from a sender to a receiver." The crucial element in this definition is *meaning*. The process is successful only when the receiver understands an idea as the sender intended it. How does an idea travel from one person to another? It involves a sensitive process, shown in Figure 2.1. This process can be easily sidetracked resulting in miscommunication. It is successful when both the sender and the receiver understand the process and how to make it work. In our discussion we will be most concerned with professional communication in the workplace so that you can be successful as a business communicator in your career.

### 2-1a Sender Has Idea

The communication process begins when the sender has an idea. The form of the idea may be influenced by complex factors surrounding the sender. These factors

36     Chapter 2: Planning Business Messages

may include mood, frame of reference, background, culture, and physical makeup, as well as the context of the situation and many other factors. Senders shape their ideas based on their own experiences and assumptions.

**LEARNING OBJECTIVE 1**
Discuss the five steps in the communication process.

## 2-1b Sender Encodes Idea

The next step in the communication process involves *encoding*. This means converting the idea into words or gestures that will convey meaning. A major problem in communicating any message verbally is that words have different meanings for different people. Recognizing how easy it is to be misunderstood, skilled communicators choose familiar, concrete words. In choosing proper words and symbols, senders must be alert to the receiver's communication skills, attitudes, background, experiences, and culture. Including a smiley face in an e-mail announcement to stockholders may turn them off.

## 2-1c Sender Selects Channel and Transmits Message

The medium over which the message travels is the *channel*. Messages may be delivered by computer, wireless network, smartphone, letter, memorandum, report, announcement, image, spoken word, fax, Web page, or some other channel. Today's messages are increasingly carried over digital networks with much opportunity for distraction and breakdown. Receivers may be overloaded with incoming messages

### Figure 2.1 The Communication Process

**The Communication Process**

1. Sender has idea
2. Sender encodes message
3. Sender selects channel, transmits message
4. Receiver decodes message
5. Feedback returns to sender

**To communicate effectively:**

**Sender should**
- Clarify idea
- Decide on purpose of message
- Analyze idea and how it can best be presented
- Anticipate effect on receiver

**Sender should**
- Consider receiver's background, communication skills, experience, culture, context
- Choose concrete words and appropriate symbols
- Encourage feedback

**Sender should**
- Consider importance of message, feedback required, interactivity
- Choose a channel that the receiver prefers
- Think of ways to reduce channel noise and distractions
- Be aware of competing messages

**Receiver should**
- Avoid prejudging message
- Strive to understand both verbal and nonverbal cues
- Ignore distractions
- Create receptive environment
- Expect to learn

**Receiver should**
- Craft clear and complete response that reveals comprehension of message meaning
- Begin the cycle again when the receiver becomes the sender with the same concerns

Chapter 2: Planning Business Messages

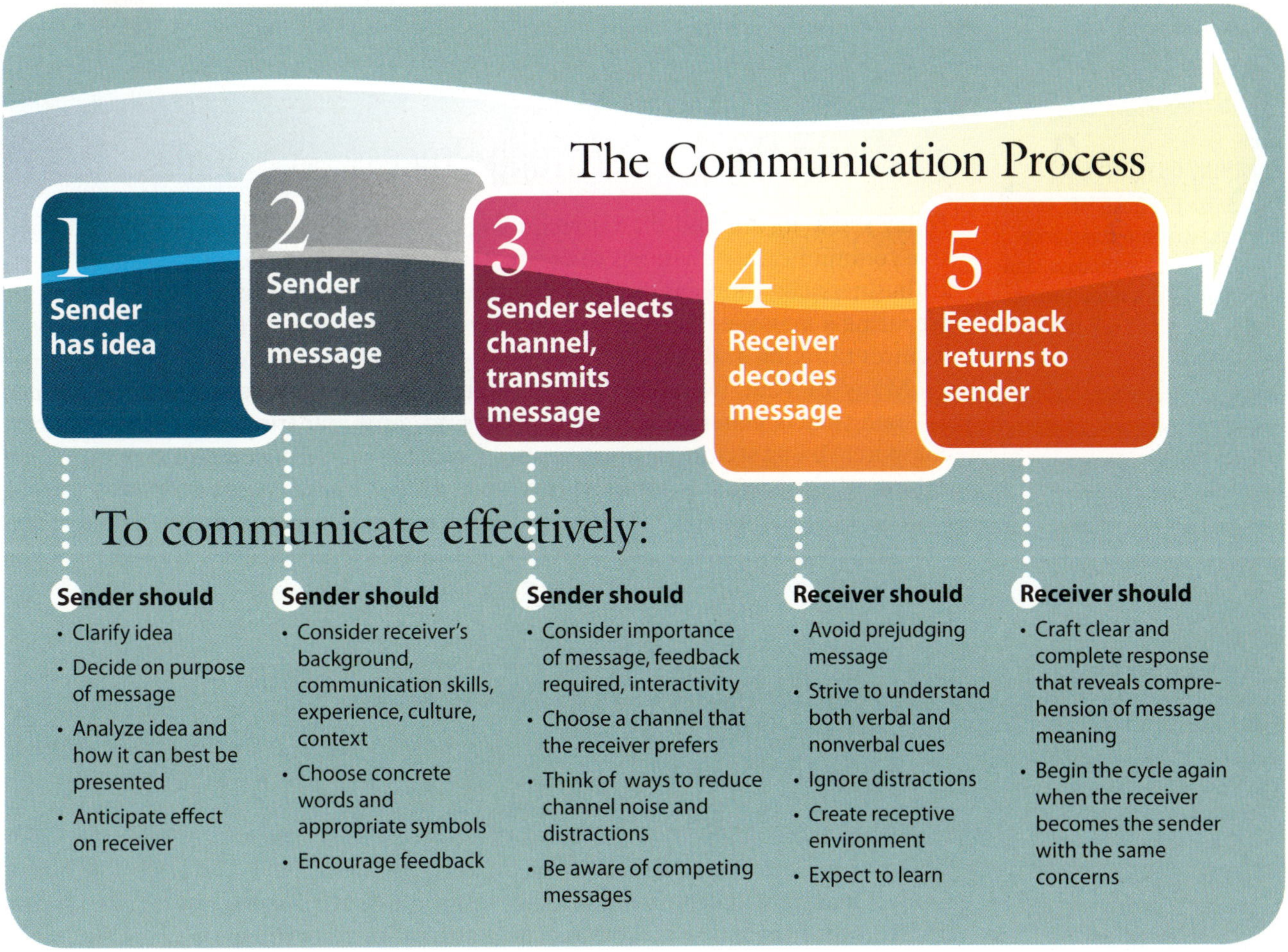

or unable to receive messages clearly on their devices. Only well-crafted messages may be accepted, understood, and acted on. Anything that interrupts the transmission of a message in the communication process is called *noise*. Channel noise may range from a weak Internet signal to sloppy formatting and typos in e-mail messages. Noise may even include the annoyance a receiver feels when the sender chooses an improper channel for transmission or when the receiver is overloaded with messages and information.

### 2-1d Receiver Decodes Message

The individual to whom the message is intended is the *receiver*. Translating the message from its symbol form into meaning involves *decoding*. Only when the receiver understands the meaning intended by the sender—that is, successfully decodes the message—does communication take place. Such success is often difficult to achieve because of a number of barriers that block the process.

### 2-1e Feedback Returns to Sender

The verbal and nonverbal responses of the receiver create *feedback*, a vital part of the communication process. Feedback helps the sender know that the message was received and understood. Senders can encourage feedback by asking questions such as *Am I making myself clear?* and *Is there anything you don't understand?* Senders can further improve feedback by timing the delivery appropriately and by providing only as much information as the receiver can handle. Receivers improve the communication process by providing clear and complete feedback. In the business world, one of the best ways to advance understanding is to paraphrase the sender's message with comments such as *Let me try to explain that in my own words*.

## LEARNING OBJECTIVE 2

Recognize the goals of business writing, summarize the 3-x-3 writing process, and explain how it guides a writer.

## 2-2 Using the 3-x-3 Writing Process as a Guide

Today's new media and digital technologies enable you to choose from innumerable communication channels to create, transmit, and respond to messages. Nearly all business communication, however, revolves around writing. Whether you are preparing a message that will be delivered digitally, orally, or in print, that message requires thinking and writing.

Many of your messages will be digital. A *digital message* may be defined as "one that is generated, stored, processed, and transmitted electronically by computers using strings of positive and nonpositive binary code (0s and 1s)." That definition encompasses many forms, including e-mail, Facebook posts, tweets, and other messages. For our purposes, we will focus primarily on messages exchanged on the job. Because writing is central to all business communication, this chapter presents a systematic plan for preparing business messages in the digital age.

### 2-2a Defining Your Business Writing Goals

One thing you should immediately recognize about business writing is that it differs from other writing you have done. In preparing high school or college compositions and term papers, you probably focused on discussing your feelings or displaying your knowledge. Your instructors wanted to see your thought processes, and they wanted assurance that you had internalized the subject matter. You may have had to meet a minimum word count. Business writing is definitely not like that! It also differs from personal texts you may exchange with your friends and family. These

Chapter 2: Planning Business Messages

messages enable you to stay connected and express your feelings. In the workplace, however, you will want your writing to be:

- **Purposeful.** You will be writing to solve problems and convey information. You will have a definite strategy to fulfill in each message.
- **Economical.** You will try to present ideas clearly but concisely. Length is not rewarded.
- **Audience oriented.** You will concentrate on looking at a problem from the perspective of the audience instead of seeing it from your own.

These distinctions actually ease your task. You won't be searching your imagination for creative topic ideas. You won't be stretching your ideas to make them appear longer. Writing consultants and businesspeople complain that many college graduates entering industry have a conscious—or perhaps unconscious—perception that quantity enhances quality. Wrong! Get over the notion that longer is better. Whether you are presenting your message in an e-mail message, in a business report, or at a wiki site, conciseness and clarity are what count in business.

The ability to prepare purposeful, concise, and audience-centered messages does not come naturally. Very few people, especially beginners, can sit down and compose an effective e-mail message, letter, or report without training. However, following a systematic process, studying model messages, and practicing the craft can make nearly anyone a successful business writer or speaker.

## 2-2b Introducing the 3-x-3 Writing Process

Regardless of what you are writing, the process will be easier if you follow a systematic plan. The 3-x-3 writing process breaks the entire task into three phases: *prewriting*, *drafting*, and *revising*, as shown in Figure 2.2.

To illustrate the writing process, let's say that you own a popular local McDonald's franchise. At rush times, you face a problem. Customers complain about the chaotic multiple waiting lines to approach the service counter. You once saw two customers nearly get into a fistfight over cutting into a line. What's more, customers often are so intent on looking for ways to improve their positions in line that they fail to examine the menu. Then they are undecided when their turn arrives. You want to convince other franchise owners that a single-line (serpentine) system would work better. You could telephone the other owners. However, you want to present a serious argument with good points that they will remember and be willing to act on when they gather for their next district meeting. You decide to send a persuasive e-mail that you hope will win their support.

**Prewriting.** The first phase of the writing process prepares you to write. It involves *analyzing* the audience and your purpose for writing. The audience for your message will be other franchise owners, some highly educated and others not. Your purpose in writing is to convince them that a change in policy would improve customer service. You think that a single-line system, such as that used in banks, would reduce chaos and make customers happier because they would not have to worry about where they are in line.

Prewriting also involves *anticipating* how your audience will react to your message. You are sure that some of the other owners will agree with you, but others might fear that customers seeing a long single line might go elsewhere. In *adapting* your message to the audience, you try to think of the right words and the right tone that will win approval.

**Drafting.** The second phase involves researching, organizing, and then drafting the message. In *researching* information for this message, you would probably investigate other kinds of businesses that use single lines for customers. You might check your competitors. What are Wendy's and Burger King doing? You might do some calling to see whether other franchise owners are concerned about chaotic

---

### OFFICE INSIDER

*"Writing in the* Harvard Business Review, *David Silverman blasts "an educational system that rewards length over clarity." Students learn to overwrite, he says, in hopes that at least some of their sentences "hit the mark." Once on the job, they continue to act as if they were paid by the word, a perception that must be unlearned."*

—David Silverman, businessman, entrepreneur, and blogger

Figure 2.2 The 3-x-3 Writing Process

### 1 Prewriting

**Analyze**
- What is your purpose?
- What do you want the receiver to do or believe?
- What channel should you choose: face-to-face conversation, group meeting, e-mail, memo, letter, report, blog, wiki, tweet, etc.

**Anticipate**
- Profile the audience.
- What does the receiver already know?
- Will the receiver's response be neutral, positive, or negative? How will this affect your organizational strategy?

**Adapt**
- What techniques can you use to adapt your message to its audience?
- How can you promote feedback?
- Strive to use positive, conversational, and courteous language.

### 2 Drafting

**Research**
- Gather data to provide facts.
- Search company files, previous correspondence, and the Internet.
- What do you need to know to write this message?
- How much does the audience already know?

**Organize**
- Organize direct messages with the big idea first, followed by an explanation in the body and an action request in the closing.
- For persuasive or negative messages, use an indirect, problem-solving strategy.

**Draft**
- Prepare a first draft, usually quickly.
- Focus on short, clear sentences using the active voice.
- Build paragraph coherence by repeating key ideas, using pronouns, and incorporating appropriate transitional expressions.

### 3 Revising

**Edit**
- Edit your message to be sure it is clear, concise, conversational, readable.
- Revise to eliminate wordy fillers, long lead-ins, redundancies, and trite business phrases.
- Develop parallelism.
- Consider using headings and numbered and bulleted lists for quick reading.

**Proofread**
- Take the time to read every message carefully.
- Look for errors in spelling, grammar, punctuation, names, and numbers.
- Check to be sure the format is consistent.

**Evaluate**
- Will this message achieve your purpose?
- Does the tone sound pleasant and friendly rather than curt?
- Have you thought enough about the audience to be sure this message is appealing?
- Did you encourage feedback?

---

lines. Before writing to the entire group, you might brainstorm with a few owners to see what ideas they have for solving the problem.

Once you have collected enough information, you would focus on *organizing* your message. Should you start out by offering your solution? Or should you work up to it slowly, describing the problem, presenting your evidence, and then ending with the solution? The final step in the second phase of the writing process is actually *drafting* the letter. At this point many writers write quickly, realizing that they will polish their ideas when they revise.

**Revising.** The third phase of the process involves editing, proofreading, and evaluating your message. After writing the first draft, you will spend considerable time *editing* the message for clarity, conciseness, tone, and readability. Could parts of it be rearranged to make your point more effectively? This is the time when you look for ways to improve the organization and tone of your message. Next, you will spend time *proofreading* carefully to ensure correct spelling, grammar, punctuation, and format. The final phase involves *evaluating* your message to decide whether it accomplishes your goal.

#### 2-2c Pacing the Writing Process

The time you spend on each phase of the writing process varies depending on the complexity of the problem, the purpose, the audience, and your schedule. On

Figure 2.3 Scheduling the Writing Process

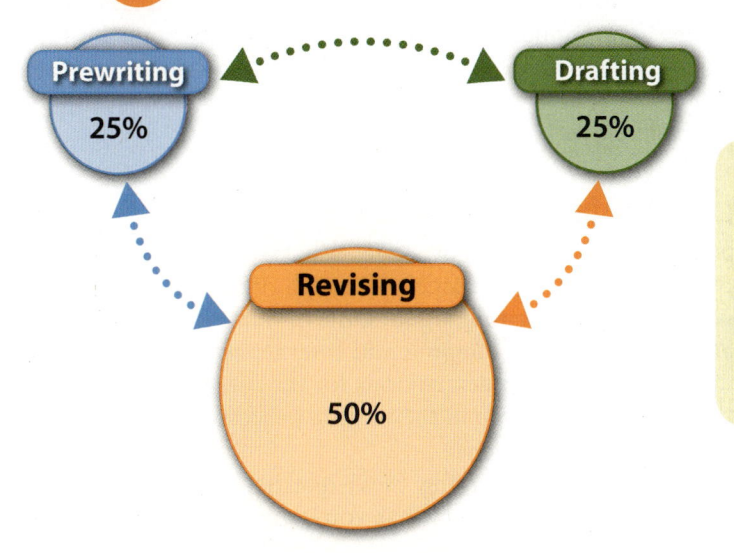

Prewriting 25%
Drafting 25%
Revising 50%

Although the writing process looks like a linear set of steps, it actually is recursive, enabling writers to revise their work continually as they progress. However, careful planning can avoid wasted time and frustration caused by rethinking and reorganizing during drafting.

average, you should expect to spend about 25 percent of your time prewriting, 25 percent drafting, and 50 percent revising, as shown in Figure 2.3.

These are rough guides, yet you can see that good writers spend most of their time on the final phase of revising and proofreading. Much depends, of course, on your project, its importance, and your familiarity with it. What is critical to remember, though, is that revising is a major component of the writing process even if the message is short.

It may appear that you perform one step and progress to the next, always following the same order. Most business writing, however, is not that rigid. Although writers perform the tasks described, the steps may be rearranged, abbreviated, or repeated. Some writers revise every sentence and paragraph as they go. Many find that new ideas occur after they have begun to write, causing them to back up, alter the organization, and rethink their plan. Beginning business writers often follow the writing process closely. With experience, though, they will become like other good writers and presenters who alter, compress, and rearrange the steps as needed.

## 2-3 Analyzing and Anticipating the Audience

**LEARNING OBJECTIVE 3**
Analyze the purpose of a message, anticipate its audience, and select the best communication channel.

Surprisingly, many people begin writing and discover only as they approach the end of a message what they are trying to accomplish. If you analyze your purpose before you begin, you can avoid backtracking and starting over. The remainder of this chapter covers the first phase of the writing process: analyzing the purpose for writing, anticipating how the audience will react, and adapting the message to the audience.

### 2-3a Determining Your Purpose

As you begin to compose a workplace message, ask yourself two important questions: (a) Why am I sending this message? and (b) What do I hope to achieve? Your responses will determine how you organize and present your information.

Your message may have primary and secondary purposes. For college work your primary purpose may be merely to complete the assignment; secondary purposes might be to make yourself look good and to earn an excellent grade. The primary purposes for sending business messages are typically to inform and to persuade. A

Chapter 2: Planning Business Messages

secondary purpose is to promote goodwill. You and your organization want to look good in the eyes of your audience.

Many business messages do nothing more than *inform*. They explain procedures, announce meetings, answer questions, and transmit findings. Some business messages, however, are meant to *persuade*. These messages sell products, convince managers, motivate employees, and win over customers. Persuasive and informative messages are developed differently.

### 2-3b Anticipating and Profiling the Audience

A good writer anticipates the audience for a message: What is the reader or listener like? How will that person react to the message? Although one can't always know exactly who the receiver is, it is possible to imagine some of that person's characteristics. A copywriter at Lands' End, the shopping and Internet retailer, pictures his sister-in-law whenever he writes product descriptions for the catalog.

Profiling your audience is a pivotal step in the writing process. The questions in Figure 2.4 will help you profile your audience.

How much time you devote to answering these questions depends on your message and its context. An analytical report that you compose for management or an oral presentation that you deliver to a big group would, of course, demand considerable audience anticipation. An e-mail message to a coworker or a message to a familiar supplier might require only a few moments of planning.

Preparing a blog on an important topic to be posted to a company website would require you to think about the people in local, national, and international audiences who might read that message. Similarly, posting brief messages at social media sites such as Facebook, Twitter, and Tumblr should make you think about who will read the messages. How much of your day and life do you want to share? Will customers and business partners be reading your posts?

No matter how short your message, though, spend some time thinking about the audience so that you can tailor your words to your readers. Remember that they will be thinking, *What's in it for me (WIIFM)?* One of the most important writing tips you can take away from this book is recognizing that every message you write should begin with the notion that your audience is thinking *WIIFM?*

Figure 2.4 Asking the Right Questions to Profile Your Audience

**Primary Audience**
- Who is my primary reader or listener?
- What are my personal and professional relationships with this person?
- What position does this person hold in the organization?
- How much does this person know about the subject?
- What do I know about this person's education, beliefs, culture, and attitudes?
- Should I expect a neutral, positive, or negative response to my message?

**Secondary Audience**
- Who might see or hear this message in addition to the primary audience?
- How do these people differ from the primary audience?
- Do I need to include more background information?
- How must I reshape my message to make it understandable and acceptable to others to whom it might be forwarded?

## 2-3c Making Choices Based on the Audience Profile

Profiling your audience helps you make decisions about shaping the message. You will discover what language is appropriate, whether you are free to use specialized technical terms, whether you should explain the background, and so on. Profiling the audience helps you decide whether your tone should be formal or informal and whether the receiver is likely to feel neutral, positive, or negative about your message.

Another advantage of profiling your audience is considering the possibility of a secondary audience. For example, let's say you start to write an e-mail message to your supervisor, Sheila, describing a problem you are having. Halfway through the message you realize that Sheila will probably forward this message to her boss, the vice president. Sheila will not want to summarize what you said; instead she will take the easy route and merely forward your e-mail. When you realize that the vice president will probably see this message, you decide to back up and use a more formal tone. You remove your inquiry about Sheila's family, you reduce your complaints, and you tone down your language about why things went wrong. Instead, you provide more background information, and you are more specific in explaining issues with which the vice president is unfamiliar. Analyzing the task and anticipating the audience help you adapt your message so it is effective for both primary and secondary receivers.

## 2-3d Selecting the Best Channel

After identifying the purpose of your message, you'll want to select the most appropriate communication channel. In this digital age, the number of channels continues to expand, as shown in Figure 2.5. Whether to send an e-mail message, schedule a

### Figure 2.5 Comparing Rich and Lean Communication Channels

**Ten Levels of Richness in Today's Workplace Communication Channels—Richest to Leanest**

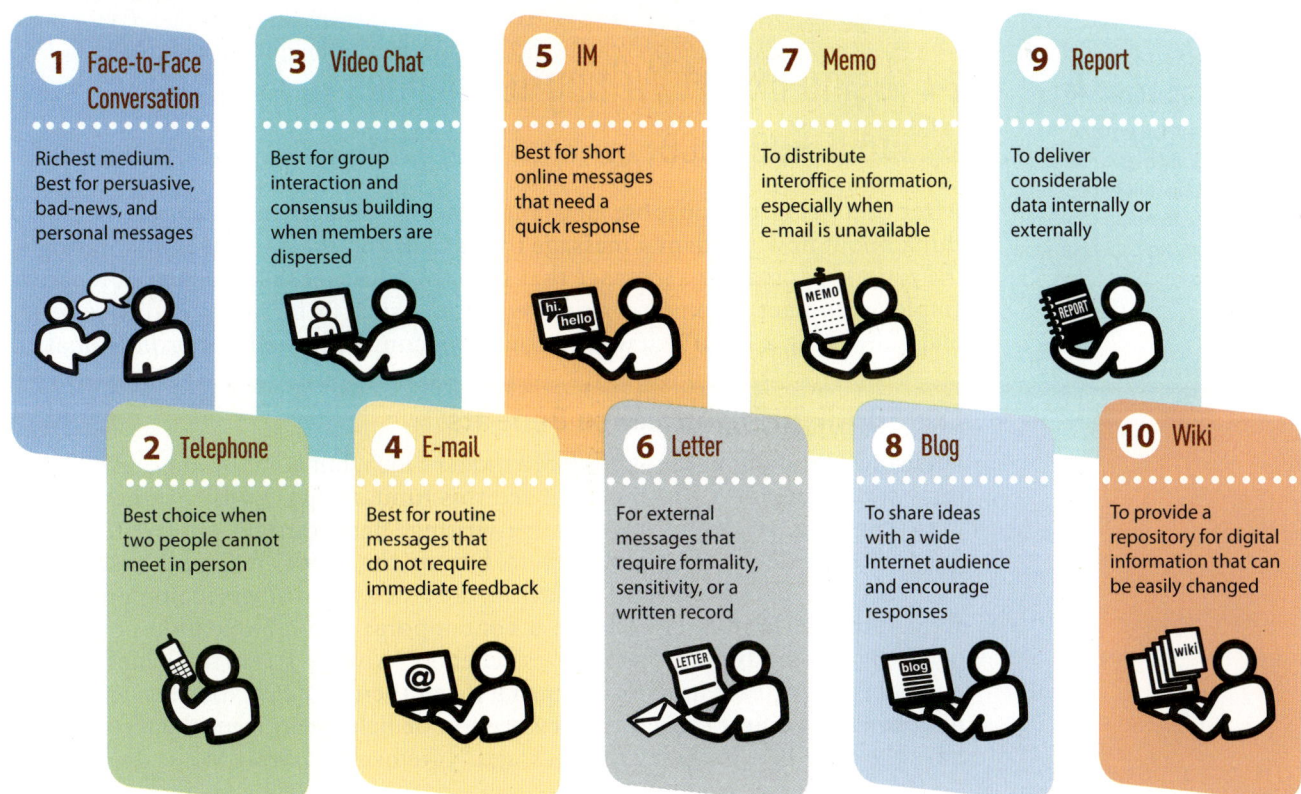

**1 Face-to-Face Conversation** — Richest medium. Best for persuasive, bad-news, and personal messages

**3 Video Chat** — Best for group interaction and consensus building when members are dispersed

**5 IM** — Best for short online messages that need a quick response

**7 Memo** — To distribute interoffice information, especially when e-mail is unavailable

**9 Report** — To deliver considerable data internally or externally

**2 Telephone** — Best choice when two people cannot meet in person

**4 E-mail** — Best for routine messages that do not require immediate feedback

**6 Letter** — For external messages that require formality, sensitivity, or a written record

**8 Blog** — To share ideas with a wide Internet audience and encourage responses

**10 Wiki** — To provide a repository for digital information that can be easily changed

Chapter 2: Planning Business Messages

video conference, or have a face-to-face conversation or group meeting depends on some of the following factors:

- Importance of the message
- Amount and speed of feedback and interactivity required
- Necessity of a permanent record
- Cost of the channel
- Degree of formality desired
- Confidentiality and sensitivity of the message
- Receiver's preference and level of technical expertise

In addition to these practical issues, you will also consider how *rich* the channel is. The *richness* of a channel involves the extent to which it recreates or represents all the information available in the original message. A richer medium, such as a face-to-face conversation, permits more interactivity and feedback. A leaner medium, such as a letter or an e-mail, presents a flat, one-dimensional message. Richer media enable the sender to provide more verbal and visual cues, as well as allow the sender to tailor the message to the audience.

Choosing the wrong medium can result in the message being less effective or even misunderstood. If, for example, marketing manager Connor must motivate the sales force to increase sales in the fourth quarter, he is unlikely to achieve his goal if he merely posts an announcement on the office bulletin board, writes a memo, or sends an e-mail. He could be more persuasive with a richer channel such as individual face-to-face conversations or a group meeting to stimulate sales. For sales reps on the road, a richer medium would be a videoconference. Keep in mind the following tips for choosing a communication channel:

- Use the richest media available.
- Employ richer media for more persuasive or personal communications.

**LEARNING OBJECTIVE 4**
Employ adaptive writing techniques such as incorporating audience benefits, developing the "you" view, and using conversational but professional language.

## 2-4 Using Expert Writing Techniques to Adapt to Your Audience

After analyzing the purpose and anticipating the audience, writers begin to think about how to adapt a message to the task and the audience. Adaptation is the process of creating a message that suits the audience. Skilled communicators employ a number of expert writing techniques such as featuring audience benefits, cultivating a "you" view, and sounding conversational but professional.

### 2-4a Spotlighting Audience Benefits

Focusing on the audience sounds like a modern idea, but actually one of America's early statesmen and authors recognized this fundamental writing principle over 200 years ago. In describing effective writing, Ben Franklin observed, "To be good, it ought to have a tendency to benefit the reader."[1] These wise words have become a fundamental guideline for today's business communicators. Expanding on Franklin's counsel, a contemporary communication consultant gives this solid advice to his business clients: "Always stress the benefit to the audience of whatever it is you are trying to get them to do. If you can show them how you are going to save them frustration or help them meet their goals, you have the makings of a powerful message."[2] Remember, WIIFM!

Adapting your message to the receiver's needs means putting yourself in that person's shoes. It's called *empathy*. Empathic senders think about how a receiver will decode a message. They try to give something to the receiver, solve the receiver's problems, save the receiver's money, or just understand the feelings and position of that person. Which version of each of the following messages is more appealing to the audience?

| DON'T SENDER FOCUS | DO ✓ AUDIENCE FOCUS |
|---|---|
| ✗ All employees are instructed herewith to fill out the enclosed questionnaire so that we can allocate our training funds to employees. | ✓ By filling out the enclosed questionnaire, you can be one of the first employees to sign up for our training funds. |
| ✗ Our warranty becomes effective only when we receive an owner's registration. | ✓ Your warranty begins working for you as soon as you return your owner's registration. |

## 2-4b Developing the "You" View

In concentrating on audience benefits, skilled communicators naturally develop the "you" view. They emphasize second-person pronouns (*you, your*) instead of first-person pronouns (*I/we, us, our*). Whether your goal is to inform, persuade, or promote goodwill, the catchiest words you can use are *you* and *your*. Compare the following examples.

| DON'T "I/WE" VIEW | DO ✓ "YOU" VIEW |
|---|---|
| ✗ We are requiring all employees to respond to the attached survey about health benefits. | ✓ Because your ideas count, please complete the attached survey about health benefits. |
| ✗ I need your account number before I can do anything. | ✓ Please give me your account number so that I can locate your records and help you solve this problem. |

Although you want to focus on the reader or listener, don't overuse or misuse the second-person pronoun *you*. Readers and listeners appreciate genuine interest; on the other hand, they resent obvious attempts at manipulation. The authors of some sales messages, for example, are guilty of overkill when they include *you* dozens of times in a direct-mail promotion. What's more, the word can sometimes create the wrong impression. Consider this statement: *You cannot return merchandise until you receive written approval*. The word *you* appears twice, but the reader may feel singled out for criticism. In the following version, the message is less personal and more positive: *Customers may return merchandise with written approval*.

Another difficulty in emphasizing the "you" view and de-emphasizing *we/I* is that it may result in overuse of the passive voice. For example, to avoid writing *We will give you* (active voice), you might write *You will be given* (passive voice). The active voice in writing is generally preferred because it identifies who is doing the acting. You will learn more about active and passive voice in Chapter 3.

> ## OFFICE INSIDER
>
> "When it comes to writing engaging content, 'you' is the most powerful word in the English language, because people are ultimately interested in fulfilling their own needs."
>
> —Brian Clark, founder of a top marketing blog called Copyblogger

## Workplace in Focus

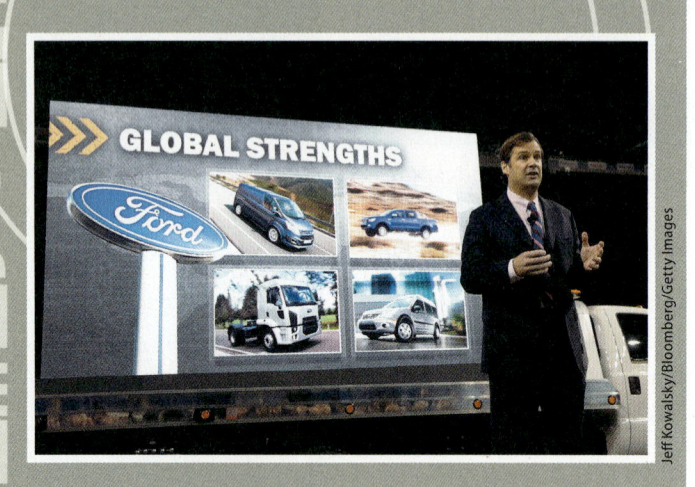

While addressing a panel at the 2014 Consumer Electronics Show, Ford marketing chief Jim Farley stirred controversy in comments meant to showcase the automaker's advanced GPS features. Instead of selling consumers on the benefits of in-dash computers, Farley confirmed their worst suspicions: "We know everyone who breaks the law, and we know when you're doing it," he said. "We have GPS in your car, so we know what you're doing." The remark startled listeners and violated nearly every rule of audience-focused communication. Ford quickly denounced the comments. How might automakers adopt the "you" view to emphasize the benefits of in-dash navigation services to customers?[4]

In recognizing the value of the "you" view, however, you don't have to sterilize your writing and totally avoid any first-person pronouns or words that show your feelings. You can convey sincerity, warmth, and enthusiasm by the words you choose. Don't be afraid of phrases such as *I'm happy* or *We're delighted*, if you truly are. When speaking face-to-face, you can show sincerity and warmth with nonverbal cues such as a smile and a pleasant voice tone. In letters, e-mail messages, memos, and other digital messages, however, only expressive words and phrases can show your feelings. These phrases suggest hidden messages that say, *You are important, I hear you*, and *I'm honestly trying to please you.*

### 2-4c Sounding Conversational but Professional

Most business messages replace conversation. That's why they are most effective when they convey an informal, conversational tone instead of a formal, pretentious tone. Just how informal you can be depends greatly on the workplace. At Google, casual seems to be preferred. In a short message to users describing changes in its privacy policies, Google recently wrote, "we believe this stuff matters."[3] In more traditional organizations, that message probably would have been more formal. The dilemma for you, then, is knowing how casual to be in your writing. We suggest that you strive to be conversational but professional, especially until you learn what your organization prefers.

E-mail, instant messaging, chat, Twitter, and other short messaging channels enable you and your coworkers to have spontaneous conversations. Don't, however, let your messages become sloppy, unprofessional, or even dangerous. You will learn more about the dangers of e-mail and other digital channels later. At this point, though, we focus on the tone of the language.

To project a professional image, you want to sound educated and mature. Overuse of expressions such as *totally awesome, you know*, and *like*, as well as a reliance on unnecessary abbreviations (*BTW* for *by the way*), make a businessperson sound like a teenager. Professional messages do not include texting-style abbreviations, slang, sentence fragments, and chitchat. We urge you to strive for a warm, conversational tone that avoids low-level diction. Levels of diction, as shown in Figure 2.6, range from unprofessional to formal.

Your goal is to convey a warm, friendly tone that sounds professional. Although some writers are too casual, others are overly formal. To impress readers and listeners, they use big words, long sentences, legal terminology, and third-person constructions. Stay away from expressions such as *the undersigned, the writer*, and *the affected party*. You will sound friendlier with familiar pronouns such as *I, we*, and *you*. The following examples illustrate a professional yet conversational tone:

| DON'T — UNPROFESSIONAL | DO — PROFESSIONAL |
|---|---|
| ✗ Hey, boss, Gr8 news! Firewall now installed!! BTW, check with me b4 announcing it. | ✓ Mr. Smith, our new firewall software is now installed. Please check with me before announcing it. |
| ✗ Look, dude, this report is totally bogus. And the figures don't look kosher. Show me some real stats. Got sources? | ✓ Because the figures in this report seem inaccurate, please submit the source statistics. |

| DON'T — OVERLY FORMAL | DO — CONVERSATIONAL |
|---|---|
| ✗ All employees are herewith instructed to return the appropriately designated contracts to the undersigned. | ✓ Please return your contracts to me. |
| ✗ Pertaining to your order, we must verify the sizes that your organization requires prior to consignment of your order to our shipper. | ✓ We will send your order as soon as we confirm the sizes you need. |

**Figure 2.6** Levels of Diction

| Unprofessional (Low-level diction) | Conversational (Middle-level diction) | Formal (High-level diction) |
|---|---|---|
| badmouth | criticize | denigrate |
| guts | nerve | courage |
| pecking order | line of command | dominance hierarchy |
| ticked off | upset | provoked |
| rat on | inform | betray |
| rip off | steal | expropriate |
| If we just hang in there, we'll snag the contract. | If we don't get discouraged, we'll win the contract. | If the principals persevere, they will secure the contract. |

## 2-5 Developing Additional Expert Writing Techniques

**LEARNING OBJECTIVE 5**
Develop additional expert writing techniques including the use of a positive and courteous tone, bias-free language, plain language, and precise words.

As you continue to improve your writing skills, you can use additional expert techniques that improve the clarity, tone, and effectiveness of a message. These skillful techniques include using a positive and courteous tone, bias-free language, simple expression, and precise words. Take a look at Figure 2.7 to see how a writer can improve an e-mail message by applying numerous expert writing techniques.

### 2-5a Being Positive Rather Than Negative

One of the best ways to improve the tone of a message is to use positive rather than negative language. Positive language generally conveys more information than negative language does. Moreover, positive messages are uplifting and pleasant to read. Positive wording tells what *is* and what *can be done* rather than what *isn't* and what *can't be done*. For example, *Your order cannot be shipped by January 10*

Chapter 2: Planning Business Messages

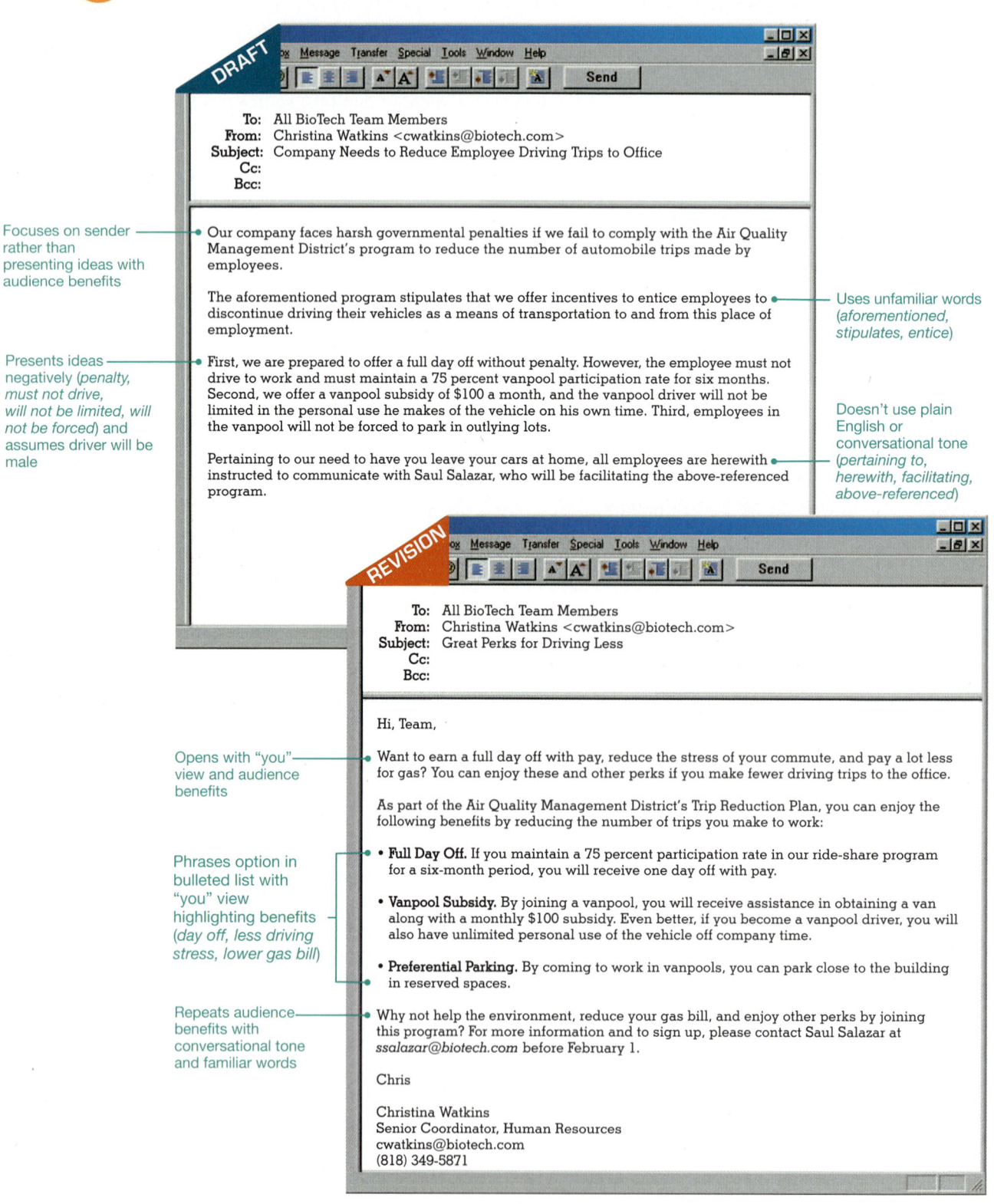

## Figure 2.7 Applying Expert Writing Techniques to Improve an E-Mail Message

**DRAFT**

To: All BioTech Team Members
From: Christina Watkins <cwatkins@biotech.com>
Subject: Company Needs to Reduce Employee Driving Trips to Office
Cc:
Bcc:

Our company faces harsh governmental penalties if we fail to comply with the Air Quality Management District's program to reduce the number of automobile trips made by employees.

The aforementioned program stipulates that we offer incentives to entice employees to discontinue driving their vehicles as a means of transportation to and from this place of employment.

First, we are prepared to offer a full day off without penalty. However, the employee must not drive to work and must maintain a 75 percent vanpool participation rate for six months. Second, we offer a vanpool subsidy of $100 a month, and the vanpool driver will not be limited in the personal use he makes of the vehicle on his own time. Third, employees in the vanpool will not be forced to park in outlying lots.

Pertaining to our need to have you leave your cars at home, all employees are herewith instructed to communicate with Saul Salazar, who will be facilitating the above-referenced program.

*Annotations:*
- Focuses on sender rather than presenting ideas with audience benefits
- Presents ideas negatively (*penalty, must not drive, will not be limited, will not be forced*) and assumes driver will be male
- Uses unfamiliar words (*aforementioned, stipulates, entice*)
- Doesn't use plain English or conversational tone (*pertaining to, herewith, facilitating, above-referenced*)

**REVISION**

To: All BioTech Team Members
From: Christina Watkins <cwatkins@biotech.com>
Subject: Great Perks for Driving Less
Cc:
Bcc:

Hi, Team,

Want to earn a full day off with pay, reduce the stress of your commute, and pay a lot less for gas? You can enjoy these and other perks if you make fewer driving trips to the office.

As part of the Air Quality Management District's Trip Reduction Plan, you can enjoy the following benefits by reducing the number of trips you make to work:

- **Full Day Off.** If you maintain a 75 percent participation rate in our ride-share program for a six-month period, you will receive one day off with pay.
- **Vanpool Subsidy.** By joining a vanpool, you will receive assistance in obtaining a van along with a monthly $100 subsidy. Even better, if you become a vanpool driver, you will also have unlimited personal use of the vehicle off company time.
- **Preferential Parking.** By coming to work in vanpools, you can park close to the building in reserved spaces.

Why not help the environment, reduce your gas bill, and enjoy other perks by joining this program? For more information and to sign up, please contact Saul Salazar at ssalazar@biotech.com before February 1.

Chris

Christina Watkins
Senior Coordinator, Human Resources
cwatkins@biotech.com
(818) 349-5871

*Annotations:*
- Opens with "you" view and audience benefits
- Phrases option in bulleted list with "you" view highlighting benefits (*day off, less driving stress, lower gas bill*)
- Repeats audience benefits with conversational tone and familiar words

© 2013 Cengage Learning®

---

is not nearly as informative as *Your order will be shipped January 15.* An office supply store adjacent to an ice cream parlor in Portland, Maine, posted a sign on its door that reads: *Please enjoy your ice cream before you enjoy our store.* That sounds much more positive and inviting than *No food allowed!*[5]

Using positive language also involves avoiding negative words that create ill will. Some words appear to blame or accuse your audience. For example, opening a letter to a customer with *You claim that* suggests that you don't believe the customer. Other loaded words that can get you in trouble are *complaint, criticism, defective, failed, mistake,* and *neglected.* Also avoid phrases such as *you apparently are unaware of* or *you did not provide* or *you misunderstood* or *you don't understand.* Often you may be unaware of the effect of these words. Notice in the following examples how you can revise the negative tone to create a more positive impression.

| DON'T NEGATIVE | DO POSITIVE |
|---|---|
| ✗ This plan definitely cannot succeed if we don't obtain management approval. | ✓ This plan definitely can succeed if we obtain management approval. |
| ✗ You failed to include your credit card number, so we can't mail your order. | ✓ We look forward to completing your order as soon as we receive your credit card number. |
| ✗ Your letter of May 2 claims that you returned a defective headset. | ✓ Your May 2 letter describes a headset you returned. |
| ✗ Employees cannot park in Lot H until April 1. | ✓ Employees may park in Lot H starting April 1. |

## OFFICE INSIDER

"Negative tone can hurt your company in many ways. It can lose customers, it can generate lawsuits and, if inflammatory rhetoric is found in a discoverable e-mail or log notes, a few words might cost your company a whopping settlement and punitive damages in a bad-faith lawsuit."

—Gary Blake, *National Underwriter Life & Health-Financial Services*

## 2-5b Expressing Courtesy

Maintaining a courteous tone involves not just guarding against rudeness but also avoiding words that sound demanding or preachy. Expressions such as *you should, you must,* and *you have to* cause people to instinctively react with *Oh, yeah?* One remedy is to turn these demands into rhetorical questions that begin with *Will you please....* Giving reasons for a request also softens the tone.

Even when you feel justified in displaying anger, remember that losing your temper or being sarcastic will seldom accomplish your goals as a business communicator: to inform, to persuade, and to create goodwill. When you are irritated, frustrated, or infuriated, keep cool and try to defuse the situation. In dealing with customers in telephone conversations, use polite phrases such as these: *I would be happy to assist you with that, Thank you for being so patient,* and *It was a pleasure speaking with you.*

| DON'T LESS COURTEOUS | DO MORE COURTEOUS AND HELPFUL |
|---|---|
| ✗ Can't you people get anything right? This is the second time I've written! | ✓ Please credit my account for $340. My latest statement shows that the error noted in my letter of May 15 has not yet been corrected. |
| ✗ Stewart, you must complete all performance reviews by Friday. | ✓ Stewart, will you please complete all performance reviews by Friday. |
| ✗ Am I the only one who can read the operating manual? | ✓ Let's review the operating manual together so that you can get your documents to print correctly next time. |

Chapter 2: Planning Business Messages

### 2-5c Employing Bias-Free Language

In adapting a message to its audience, be sure your language is sensitive and bias-free. Few writers set out to be offensive. Sometimes, though, we all say things that we never thought could be hurtful. The real problem is that we don't think about the words that stereotype groups of people, such as *the boys in the mail room* or *the girls in the front office*. Be cautious about expressions that might be biased in terms of gender, race, ethnicity, age, and disability.

Generally, you can avoid gender-biased language by choosing alternate language for words involving *man* or *woman*, by using plural nouns and pronouns, or by changing to a gender-free word (*person* or *representative*). Avoid the *his or her* option whenever possible. It's wordy and conspicuous. With a little effort, you can usually find a construction that is graceful, grammatical, and unself-conscious.

Specify age only if it is relevant, and avoid expressions that are demeaning or subjective (such as *spry old codger*). To avoid disability bias, do not refer to an individual's disability unless it is relevant. When necessary, use terms that do not stigmatize people with disabilities. The following examples give you a quick look at a few problem expressions and possible replacements. The real key to bias-free communication, though, lies in your awareness and commitment. Be on the lookout to be sure that your messages do not exclude, stereotype, or offend people.

| DON'T — GENDER BIASED | DO ✓ BIAS FREE |
|---|---|
| ✗ female doctor, woman attorney, cleaning woman | ✓ doctor, attorney, cleaner |
| ✗ waiter/waitress, authoress, stewardess | ✓ server, author, flight attendant |
| ✗ mankind, man-hour, man-made | ✓ humanity, working hours, artificial |
| ✗ office girls | ✓ office workers |
| ✗ the doctor . . . he | ✓ doctors . . . they |
| ✗ the teacher . . . she | ✓ teachers . . . they |
| ✗ executives and their wives | ✓ executives and their spouses |
| ✗ foreman, flagman, workman, craftsman | ✓ lead worker, flagger, worker, artisan |
| ✗ businessman, salesman | ✓ businessperson, sales representative |
| ✗ Each employee had his picture taken. | ✓ Each employee had a picture taken. All employees had their pictures taken. Each employee had his or her picture taken. |

| DON'T — RACIALLY OR ETHNICALLY BIASED | DO ✓ BIAS FREE |
|---|---|
| ✗ An Indian accountant was hired. | ✓ An accountant was hired. |
| ✗ James Lee, an African-American, applied. | ✓ James Lee applied. |

| DON'T — AGE BIASED | DO ✓ BIAS FREE |
|---|---|
| ✗ The law applied to old people. | ✓ The law applied to people over sixty-five. |
| ✗ Sally Kay, 55, was transferred. | ✓ Sally Kay was transferred. |
| ✗ a sprightly old gentleman | ✓ a man |
| ✗ a little old lady | ✓ a woman |

| DON'T DISABILITY BIASED | DO ✓ BIAS FREE |
|---|---|
| ✗ afflicted with arthritis, crippled by arthritis | ✓ has arthritis |
| ✗ confined to a wheelchair | ✓ uses a wheelchair |

## 2-5d Preferring Plain Language and Familiar Words

In adapting your message to your audience, use plain language and familiar words that you think audience members will recognize. Don't, however, avoid a big word that conveys your idea efficiently and is appropriate for the audience. Your goal is to shun pompous and pretentious language. Instead, use GO words. If you mean *begin*, don't say *commence* or *initiate*. If you mean *pay*, don't write *compensate*. By substituting everyday, familiar words for unfamiliar ones, as shown here, you help your audience comprehend your ideas quickly.

| DON'T UNFAMILIAR | DO ✓ FAMILIAR |
|---|---|
| ✗ commensurate | ✓ equal |
| ✗ interrogate | ✓ question |
| ✗ materialize | ✓ appear |
| ✗ obfuscate | ✓ confuse |
| ✗ remuneration | ✓ pay, salary |
| ✗ terminate | ✓ end |

At the same time, be selective in your use of jargon. *Jargon* describes technical or specialized terms within a field. These terms enable insiders to communicate complex ideas briefly, but to outsiders they mean nothing. Human resources professionals, for example, know precisely what's meant by *cafeteria plan* (a benefits option program), but most of us would be thinking about lunch. Geologists refer to *plate tectonics*, and physicians discuss *metastatic carcinomas*. These terms mean little to most of us. Use specialized language only when the audience will understand it. In addition, don't forget to consider secondary audiences: Will those potential receivers understand any technical terms used?

## 2-5e Using Precise, Vigorous Words

Strong verbs and concrete nouns give receivers more information and keep them interested. Don't overlook the thesaurus (also available online or on your computer) for expanding your word choices and vocabulary. Whenever possible, use precise, specific words, as shown here:

| DON'T IMPRECISE, DULL | DO ✓ MORE PRECISE |
|---|---|
| ✗ a change in profits | ✓ a 25 percent hike in profits<br>a 10 percent plunge in profits |
| ✗ to say | ✓ to promise, confess, understand<br>to allege, assert, assume, judge |
| ✗ to think about | ✓ to identify, diagnose, analyze<br>to probe, examine, inspect |

### OFFICE INSIDER

*"Simple changes can have profound results.... Plain talk isn't only rewriting. It's rethinking your approach and really personalizing your message to the audience and to the reader."*

—Janet Shimabukuro, manager, Taxpayers Services, Department of Revenue, Washington State

Chapter 2: Planning Business Messages

# SUMMARY OF LEARNING OBJECTIVES

**2-1 Discuss the five steps in the communication process.**
- A sender encodes (selects) words or symbols to express an idea in a message.
- The message travels over a channel (such as an e-mail, website, tweet, letter, or smartphone call).
- "Noise" (loud sounds, misspelled words, or other distractions) may interfere with the transmission.
- The receiver decodes (interprets) the message and may respond with feedback.

**2-2 Recognize the goals of business writing, summarize the 3-x-3 writing process, and explain how it guides a writer.**
- Business writing should be purposeful, economical, and audience oriented.
- The 3-x-3 writing process helps writers create efficient and effective messages.
- Phase 1 (prewriting): analyze the message, anticipate the audience, and consider how to adapt the message to the audience.
- Phase 2 (drafting): research the topic, organize the material, and draft the message.
- Phrase 3 (revising): edit, proofread, and evaluate the message.

**2-3 Analyze the purpose of a message, anticipate its audience, and select the best communication channel.**
- Before composing, decide what you hope to achieve.
- Select the appropriate channel to inform, persuade, or convey goodwill.
- After identifying the purpose, visualize both the primary and secondary audiences.
- Remember that receivers will usually be thinking, *What's in it for me (WIIFM)?*
- Select the best channel by considering (a) the importance of the message, (b) the amount and speed of feedback required, (c) the necessity of a permanent record, (d) the cost of the channel, (e) the degree of formality desired, (f) the confidentiality and sensitivity of the message, and (g) the receiver's preference and level of technical expertise.

**2-4 Employ adaptive writing techniques such as incorporating audience benefits, developing the "you" view, and using conversational but professional language.**
- Look for ways to shape the message from the receiver's, not the sender's, view.
- Apply the "you" view without attempting to manipulate.
- Use conversational but professional language.

**2-5 Develop additional expert writing techniques including the use of a positive and courteous tone, bias-free language, plain language, and precise words.**
- Use positive language that tells what can be done rather than what can't be done (*The project will be successful with your support* rather than *The project won't be successful without your support*).
- Be courteous rather than rude, preachy, or demanding.
- Provide reasons for a request to soften the tone of a message.
- Avoid biased language that excludes, stereotypes, or offends people (*lady lawyer, spry old gentleman, confined to a wheelchair*).
- Strive for plain language (*equal* instead of *commensurate*), familiar terms (*end* instead of *terminate*), and precise words (*analyze* instead of *think about*).

# CHAPTER REVIEW

1. Define *communication*. When is it successful? (Obj. 1)

2. List the five steps in the communication process. (Obj. 1)

3. In what ways is business writing different from school essays and private messages? (Obj. 2)

4. Describe the components in each stage of the 3-x-3 writing process. Approximately how much time is spent on each stage? (Obj. 2)

5. What does *WIIFM* mean? Why is it important to business writers? (Obj. 3)

6. What seven factors should writers consider in selecting an appropriate channel to deliver a message? (Obj. 3)

7. What is the "you" view? When can the use of the pronoun *you* backfire? (Obj. 4)

8. How can a business writer sound conversational but also be professional? (Obj. 4)

9. Why is positive wording more effective in business messages than negative wording? (Obj. 5)

10. What are three ways to avoid biased language? Give an original example of each. (Obj. 5)

## CRITICAL THINKING

11. Has digital transmission changed the nature of communication? (Obj. 1)
12. Why do you think employers prefer messages that are not written like high school and college essays? (Obj. 2)
13. Why should business writers strive to use short, familiar, simple words? Does this "dumb down" business messages? (Obj. 5)
14. A wise observer once said that bad writing makes smart people look dumb. Do you agree or disagree, and why? (Objs. 1–5)
15. In a letter to the editor, a teacher criticized an article in *USA Today* on autism because it used the term *autistic child* rather than *child with autism*. She championed *people-first* terminology, which avoids defining individuals by their ability or disability.[6] For example, instead of identifying someone as a *disabled person*, one would say, *she has a disability*. What does *people-first language* mean? Can language change perceptions? (Obj. 5)

## WRITING IMPROVEMENT EXERCISES

### Audience Benefits and the "You" View (Obj. 4)

**YOUR TASK.** Revise the following sentences to emphasize the perspective of the audience and the "you" view.

16. We have prepared the enclosed form that may be used by victims to report identity theft to creditors.

17. To help us process your order with our new database software, we need you to go to our website and fill out the customer information required.

18. We are now offering RapidAssist, a software program we have developed to provide immediate technical support through our website to your employees and customers.

19. We find it necessary to restrict parking in the new company lot to those employee vehicles with "A" permits.

20. To avoid suffering the kinds of customer monetary losses experienced in the past, our credit union now prohibits the cashing of double-endorsed checks presented by our customers.

21. Our warranty goes into effect only when we have received the product's registration card from the purchaser.

22. Unfortunately, you will not be able to use our computer and telephone systems on Thursday afternoon because of upgrades to both systems.

23. As part of our company effort to be friendly to the environment, we are asking all employees to reduce paper consumption by communicating by e-mail and avoiding printing.

## Conversational but Professional (Obj. 4)

**YOUR TASK.** Revise the following to make the tone conversational yet professional.

24. Per your recent e-mail, the undersigned takes pride in informing you that we are pleased to be able to participate in the Toys for Tots drive.

25. Pursuant to your message of the 15th, please be advised that your shipment was sent August 14.

26. Yo, Jeff! Look, dude, I need you to sweet talk Ramona so we can drop this budget thingy in her lap.

27. BTW, Danika was totally ticked off when the manager accused her of ripping off office supplies. She may split.

28. He didn't have the guts to badmouth her 2 her face.

29. The undersigned respectfully reminds affected individuals that employees desirous of changing their health plans must do so before November 1.

## Positive and Courteous Expression (Obj. 5)

**YOUR TASK.** Revise the following statements to make them more positive.

30. Employees are not allowed to use instant messaging until a company policy is established.

31. We must withhold authorizing payment of your consultant's fees because our CPA claims that your work is incomplete.

32. Plans for the new health center cannot move forward without full community support.

33. This is the last time I'm writing to try to get you to record my October 3 payment of $359.50 to my account! Anyone who can read can see from the attached documents that I've tried to explain this to you before.

34. Although you apparently failed to read the operator's manual, we are sending you a replacement blade for your food processor. Next time read page 18 carefully so that you will know how to attach this blade.

35. Everyone in this department must begin using new passwords as of midnight, June 15. Because of flagrant password misuse, we find it necessary to impose this new rule so that we can protect your personal information and company records.

## Bias-Free Language (Obj. 5)

**YOUR TASK.** Revise the following sentences to reduce gender, racial, ethnic, age, and disability bias.

36. Every employee must wear his photo identification on the job.

37. The conference will offer special excursions for the wives of executives.

38. Does each salesman have his own smartphone loaded with his special sales information?

39. A little old lady returned this item.

40. Serving on the panel are a lady veterinarian, an Indian CPA, two businessmen, and a female doctor.

41. Each nurse is responsible for her patient's medications.

## Plain Language and Familiar Words (Obj. 5)

**YOUR TASK.** Revise the following sentences to use plain language and familiar words.

42. The salary we are offering is commensurate with remuneration for other managers.

43. To expedite ratification of this agreement, we urge you to vote in the affirmative.

44. In a dialogue with the manager, I learned that you plan to terminate our contract.

45. Did your car's braking problem materialize subsequent to our recall effort?

46. Pursuant to your invitation, we will interrogate our agent.

## Precise, Vigorous Words (Obj. 5)

**YOUR TASK.** From the choices in parentheses, select the most precise, vigorous words.

47. Government economists (say, hypothesize, predict) that employment will (stabilize, stay the same, even out) next year.

48. The growing number of (people, consumers, buyers) with (devices, gadgets, smartphones) provides an (idea, indicator, picture) of economic growth.

49. Although international trade can (get, offer, generate) new profits and (affect, lower) costs, it also introduces a (different, higher, new) level of risk and complexity.

50. The World Bank sees international trade as a (good, fine, vital) tool for (decreasing, changing, addressing) poverty.

# RADICAL REWRITES

In most chapters you will find Radical Rewrite cases, poorly written messages that invite you to apply the writing techniques you have been learning. Rewriting is an excellent way to help you build writing skills. It enables you to focus on revising and not on supplying a context or generating imaginary facts. Your instructor's feedback regarding your strengths and challenges will speed your growth as a business communicator.

**Note:** Radical Rewrites are provided at **www.cengagebrain.com** for you to download and revise. Your instructor may show a suggested solution.

## 2.1 Radical Rewrite: Watch Your Tone! (Objs. 4, 5)

The following demanding message to be sent by the vice president to all employees suffers from many writing faults, requiring a radical rewrite.

**YOUR TASK.** Analyze the message and list at least five writing faults. Pay special attention to its tone. Your instructor may ask you to revise the message so that it reflects some of the expert writing techniques you learned in this chapter. How can you make this message more courteous, positive, and precise? In addition, think about using familiar words and developing the "you" view.

**To:** All Staff
**From:** Sybil Montrose <smontrose@syracuse.com>
**Subject:** Problematic Online Use by Employees
**Cc:**
**Bcc:**
**Attached:** E-Mail and Internet Policy

Once again I have the decidedly unpleasant task of reminding all employees that you may NOT utilize company computers or the Internet other than for work-related business and essential personal messages. Effective immediately a new policy must be implemented.

Our guys in IT tell me that our bandwidth is now seriously compromised by some of you boys and girls who are using company computers for Facebooking, blogging, shopping, chatting, gaming, and downloading streaming video. Yes, we have given you the right to use e-mail responsibly for essential personal messages. That does **not**, however, include checking your Facebook or other social accounts during work hours or downloading shows or sharing music.

We distributed an e-mail policy a little while ago. We have now found it necessary to amplify and extrapolate that policy to include use of the Internet. If our company fails to control its e-mail and Internet use, you will continue to suffer slow downloads and virus intrusions. You may also lose the right to use e-mail altogether. In the past every employee has had the right to send a personal e-mail occasionally, but he must use that right carefully. We don't want to prohibit the personal use of e-mail entirely. Don't make me do this!

You will be expected to study the attached E-Mail and Internet policy and return the signed form with your agreement to adhere to this policy. You must return this form by March 1. No exceptions!

List at least five specific writing faults and include examples.

# ACTIVITIES

## 2.2 Channel Selection: Various Business Scenarios (Obj. 3)

**YOUR TASK.** Using Figure 2.5 on page 43, suggest the best communication channels for the following messages. Assume that all channels shown are available, ranging from face-to-face conversations to instant messages, blogs, and wikis. Be prepared to justify your choices based on the richness of each channel.

a. As part of a task force to investigate cell phone marketing, you need to establish a central location where each team member can see general information about the task as well as add comments for others to see. Task force members are located throughout the country.
b. You're sitting on the couch in the evening watching TV when you suddenly remember that you were supposed to send Jeremy some information about a shared project. Should you text him right away before you forget?
c. As an event planner, you have been engaged to research sites for a celebrity golf tournament. What is the best channel for conveying your findings to your boss or planning committee?
d. You want to persuade your manager to change your work schedule.
e. As a sales manager, you want to know which of your sales reps in the field are available immediately for a quick teleconference meeting.
f. You need to know whether Amanda in Reprographics can produce a rush job for you in two days.
g. Your firm must respond to a notice from the Internal Revenue Service announcing that the company owes a penalty because it underreported its income in the previous fiscal year.

# GRAMMAR/MECHANICS CHECKUP—2

## Pronouns

Review Sections 1.07–1.09 in the Grammar/Mechanics Handbook. Then study each of the following statements. In the space provided, write the word that completes the statement correctly and the number of the G/M principle illustrated. When you finish, compare your responses with those provided near the end of the book. If your responses differ, study carefully the principles in parentheses.

_its_        1.09d     **EXAMPLE** The Employee Development Committee will make (its, their) recommendation soon.

1. The manager said that Elena would call. Was it (she, her) who left the message?
2. Every member of the men's soccer team must have (his, their) medical exam completed by Monday.
3. Even instant messages sent between the CEO and (he, him) were revealed in the court case.
4. (Who, Whom) have you hired to create cutting-edge ads for us?
5. It looks as if (yours, your's) is the only report that cites electronic sources correctly.
6. Mark asked Catherine and (I, me, myself) to help him complete his research.
7. My friend and (I, me, myself) were interviewed for the same job.
8. To park the car, turn (it's, its) wheels to the left.
9. Give the budget figures to (whoever, whomever) asked for them.
10. Everyone except the interviewer and (I, me, myself) noticed the alarm.
11. No one knows that case better than (he, him, himself).
12. A proposed budget was sent to (we, us) owners before the vote.
13. One of the female travelers left (their, her) smartphone on the seat.
14. Neither the glamour nor the excitement of the Vegas job had lost (its, it's, their) appeal.
15. If neither Cory nor I receive confirmation of our itinerary, (him and me, him and I, he and I) cannot make the trip.

Chapter 2: Planning Business Messages

59

# EDITING CHALLENGE—2

To fine-tune your grammar and mechanics skills, in every chapter you will be editing a message. This e-mail message is a short report about beverage sweeteners from a researcher to his boss. However, the message suffers from proofreading, spelling, grammar, punctuation, and other writing faults that require correction. Study the guidelines in the Grammar/Mechanics Handbook. as well as the lists of Confusing Words and Frequently Misspelled Words at the end of the book to sharpen your skills.

**YOUR TASK.** Edit the following message (a) by correcting errors in your textbook or on a photocopy using proofreading marks from Appendix A or (b) by downloading the message from **www.cengagebrain.com** and correcting at your computer. Your instructor may show you a possible solution.

---

**To:** Vicky Miranda <v.miranda@dino.com>
**From:** Aliriza Kasra <a.kasra@dino.com>
**Subject:** Sending Information on Beverage Sweeteners
**Cc:**
**Bcc:**

---

Vicky,

Per your request, herewith is a short report of the investigation you assigned to Oliver Orenstein and I pertaining to sweeteners. As you probaly already know, Coca-Cola co. and PepsiCo inc. market many drinks using sweeteners that are new to the market. Totally awesome!

Coca-Cola brought out Sprite Green, a reduced calorie soft drink that contains Truvia. Which it considers a natural sweetener because it is derived from an herb. The initial launch focused on locations and events oriented to teenagers and young adults. According to inside information obtained by Ollie and I, this product was tested on the shelfs of grocerys, mass merchants, and conveience stores in 5 citys in Florida.

PepsiCo has it's own version of the herbal sweetener, however it was developed in collaboration with Green earth sweetener co. Its called Pure Via. The first products that contained the sweetener were 3 flavors of zero-calorie SoBe Lifewater. It may also be used in a orange-juice drink with half the calorys and sugar of orange juice. Another new sweetener is Nectresse, marketed by Splenda. It comes from the monk fruit. Which has been cultivated for centurys, and only recently rediscovered as a source of natural sweetness.

BTW, approval by the Food and drug administration did not materialize automatically for these new sweeteners. FDA approval was an issue because studys conducted in the early 1990s suggested that their was possible adverse health effects from the use of stevia-based products. However the herb has been aproved for use in 12 countrys.

Both companys eventually received FDA approval and there products are all ready on the market. We cannot submit our full report until October 15.

Al

Aliriza Kasra
a.kasra@dino.com
Research and Development
Office: (927) 443-9920
Cell: (927) 442-2310

Chapter 2: Planning Business Messages

## COMMUNICATION WORKSHOP

### CAREER SKILLS

## Get Ready for Critical Thinking, Problem Solving, and Decision Making!

Gone are the days when management expected workers to check their brains at the door and do only as told. Today, you will be expected to use your brain and think critically. You will be solving problems and making decisions. Much of this book is devoted to helping you solve problems and communicate those decisions to management, fellow workers, clients, the government, and the public. Faced with a problem or an issue, most of us do a lot of worrying before identifying the issues or making a decision. You can convert all that worrying to directed thinking by channeling it into the following procedure:

- **Identify and clarify the problem.** Your first task is to recognize that a problem exists. Some problems are big and unmistakable, such as failure of an air-freight delivery service to get packages to customers on time. Other problems may be continuing annoyances, such as regularly running out of toner for an office copy machine. The first step in reaching a solution is pinpointing the problem.
- **Gather information.** Learn more about the problem situation. Look for possible causes and solutions. This step may mean checking files, calling suppliers, or brainstorming with fellow workers. For example, the air-freight delivery service would investigate the tracking systems of the commercial airlines carrying its packages to determine what is going wrong.
- **Evaluate the evidence.** Where did the information come from? Does it represent various points of view? What biases could be expected from each source? How accurate is the information gathered? Is it fact or opinion? For example, it is a fact that packages are missing; it is an opinion that they are merely lost and will turn up eventually.
- **Consider alternatives and implications.** Draw conclusions from the gathered evidence and pose solutions. Then weigh the advantages and disadvantages of each alternative. What are the costs, benefits, and consequences? What are the obstacles, and how can they be handled? Most important, what solution best serves your goals and those of your organization? Here is where your creativity is especially important.
- **Choose the best alternative and test it.** Select an alternative, and try it out to see if it meets your expectations. If it does, put your decision it into action. If it doesn't, rethink your alternatives. The freight company decided to give its unhappy customers free delivery service to make up for the lost packages and downtime. Be sure to continue monitoring and adjusting the solution to ensure its effectiveness over time.

**CAREER APPLICATION.** Let's return to the McDonald's problem (discussed on page 39) in which customers and some franchise owners are unhappy with the multiple lines for service. Customers don't seem to know where to stand to be the next served. Tempers flare when aggressive customers cut in line, and other customers spend so much time protecting their places in line that they are not ready to order. As a franchise owner, you want to solve this problem. Any new procedures, however, must be approved by a majority of McDonald's owners in your district. You know that McDonald's management feels that the multi-line system accommodates higher volumes of customers more quickly than a single-line system does. In addition, customers are turned off when they see a long line.

**YOUR TASK**

- Individually or with a team, use the critical-thinking steps outlined here. Begin by clarifying the problem.
- Where could you gather information? Would it be wise to see what your competitors are doing? How do banks handle customer lines? Airlines?
- Evaluate your findings and consider alternatives. What are the pros and cons of each alternative?
- With your team, choose the best alternative. Present your recommendation to your class and give your reasons for choosing it.

## ENDNOTES

[1] Arnold, V. (1986, August). Benjamin Franklin on writing well. *Personnel Journal*, p. 17.
[2] Bacon, M. (1988, April). Quoted in Business writing: One-on-one speaks best to the masses. *Training*, p. 95.
[3] Google (personal communication with Mary Ellen Guffey, January 30, 2012).
[4] Photo essay based on Henkel, K. and Shepardson, D. (2014, January 9). Ford exec apologizes for saying company tracks customers with GPS. *The Detroit News*. Retrieved from http://www.detroitnews.com/article/20140109/AUTO0102/301090127
[5] Be positive. (2009, March). *Communication Briefings*, p. 5. Adapted from Brandi, J. Winning at customer retention at http://www.customercarecoach.com
[6] Link, S. (2012, May 2). Use "person first" language. [Letter to editor]. *USA Today*, p. 6A.

## ACKNOWLEDGMENTS

**p. 39** Office Insider based on Silverman, D. (2009, February 10). Why is business writing so bad? *Harvard Business Review*. Retrieved from http://blogs.hbr.org/silverman/2009/02/why-is-business-writing-so-bad.html

**p. 45** Office Insider based on Clark, B. (n.d.). The two most important words in blogging. Copyblogger. Retrieved from http://www.copyblogger.com/the-two-most-important-words-in-blogging

**p. 46** Workplace in Focus based on Henkel, K. and Shepardson, D. (2014, January 9). Ford exec apologizes for saying company tracks customers with GPS. *The Detroit News*. Retrieved from http://www.detroitnews.com/article/20140109/AUTO0102/301090127

**p. 49** Office Insider based on Blake, G. (2002, November 4). Insurers need to upgrade their employees' writing skills. *National Underwriter Life & Health-Financial Services Edition*, *106*(44), 35.

**p. 53**. Office Insider based on Shimabukuro, J. (2006, December 11). Quoted in Wash. state sees results from 'plain talk' initiative. *USA Today*, p. 18A.

# Organizing and Drafting Business Messages

## CHAPTER 3

## 3-1 Drafting Workplace Messages

Who me? Write on the job? Not a chance! With today's advances in technology, lots of people believe they will never be required to write on the job. The truth is, however, that business, technical, and professional people in this digital age are exchanging more messages than ever before. The more quickly you can put your ideas down and the more clearly you can explain what needs to be said, the more successful and happy you will be in your career.

Being able to write clearly is also critical to promotions. That's why we devote three chapters to teaching you a tried-and-true writing process, summarized in Figure 3.1 This process guides you through the steps necessary to write rapidly but, more important, clearly. Instead of struggling with a writing assignment and not knowing where to begin or what to say, you can use this effective process both in school and on the job.

Chapter 2 focused on the prewriting stage of the writing process. You studied the importance of using a conversational tone, positive language, plain and courteous expression, and familiar words. This chapter addresses the second stage of the process, which involves gathering information, organizing it into outlines, and drafting messages.

### OBJECTIVES
After studying this chapter, you should be able to

**3-1**
Apply Phase 2 of the 3-x-3 writing process, which begins with formal and informal research to collect background information.

**3-2**
Organize information into strategic relationships.

**3-3**
Compose the first draft of a message using a variety of sentence types while avoiding sentence fragments, run-on sentences, and comma splices.

**3-4**
Improve your writing by emphasizing important ideas, employing the active and passive voice effectively, using parallelism, and preventing dangling and misplaced modifiers.

**3-5**
Draft well-organized paragraphs that incorporate (a) topic sentences, (b) support sentences, and (c) transitional expressions to build coherence.

## OFFICE INSIDER

*"With the fast pace of today's electronic communications, one might think that the value of fundamental writing skills has diminished in the workplace. Actually the need to write clearly and quickly has never been more important than in today's highly competitive, technology-driven global economy."*

—Joseph M. Tucci, president and chief executive officer of EMC Corporation

**LEARNING OBJECTIVE 1**

Apply Phase 2 of the 3-x-3 writing process, which begins with formal and informal research to collect background information.

### 3-1a Getting Started Requires Researching Background Information

No smart businessperson would begin drafting a message before gathering background information. We call this process research, a rather formal-sounding term. For our purposes, however, *research* simply means "collecting information about a certain topic." This is an important step in the writing process because that information helps the writer shape the message. Discovering significant information after a message is half completed often means having to start over and reorganize. To avoid frustration and inaccurate messages, writers collect information that answers several questions:

- What does the receiver need to know about this topic?
- What is the receiver to do?
- How is the receiver to do it?
- When must the receiver do it?
- What will happen if the receiver doesn't do it?

Whenever your communication problem requires more information than you have in your head or at your fingertips, you must conduct research. This research may be informal or formal.

### 3-1b Informal Research Methods

Many routine tasks—such as drafting e-mails, memos, letters, informational reports, and oral presentations—require information that you can collect informally. Where can you find information before starting a project? The following techniques are useful in informal research:

- **Search your company's files.** If you are responding to an inquiry or drafting a routine message, you often can find background information such as previous correspondence in your own files or those of the company. You might consult the company wiki or other digital and manual files. You might also consult colleagues.
- **Talk with the boss.** Get information from the individual making the assignment. What does that person know about the topic? What slant should you take? What other sources would that person suggest?
- **Interview the target audience.** Consider talking with individuals at whom the message is aimed. They can provide clarifying information that tells

Figure **3.1** The 3-x-3 Writing Process

**1 Prewriting**

**Analyze:** Decide on the message purpose. What do you want the receiver to do or believe?

**Anticipate:** What does the audience already know? How will it receive this message?

**Adapt:** Think about techniques to present this message most effectively. Consider how to elicit feedback.

**2 Drafting**

**Research:** Gather background data by searching files and the Internet.

**Organize:** Arrange direct messages with the big idea first. For persuasive or negative messages, use an indirect, problem-solving strategy.

**Draft:** Prepare the first draft, using active-voice sentences, coherent paragraphs, and appropriate transitional expressions.

**3 Revising**

**Edit:** Eliminate wordy fillers, long lead-ins, redundancies, and trite business phrases. Strive for parallelism, clarity, conciseness, and readability.

**Proofread:** Check carefully for errors in spelling, grammar, punctuation, and format.

**Evaluate:** Will this message achieve your purpose? Is the tone pleasant? Did you encourage feedback?

you what they want to know and how you should shape your remarks. Suggestions for conducting more formal interviews are presented in Chapter 10.

- **Conduct an informal survey.** Gather unscientific but helpful information through questionnaires, telephone surveys, or online surveys. In preparing a report predicting the success of a proposed company fitness center, for example, circulate a questionnaire asking for employee reactions.
- **Brainstorm for ideas.** Alone or with others, discuss ideas for the writing task at hand, and record at least a dozen ideas without judging them. Small groups are especially fruitful in brainstorming because people spin ideas off one another.

## 3-1c Formal Research Methods

Long reports and complex business problems generally require formal research methods. Let's say you are part of the management team for an international retailer such as Forever 21 and you have been asked to help launch a new store in Canada. Or, let's assume you must write a term paper for a college class. Both tasks require more data than you have in your head or at your fingertips. To conduct formal research, consider the following research options:

- **Access electronic sources.** College and public libraries provide digital retrieval services that permit access to a wide array of books, journals, magazines, newspapers, and other online literature. In this information age, you also could conduct an online Google search turning up thousands of hits, which can be overwhelming. Expect to be deluged with torrents of information, presenting a troubling paradox: research seems to be far more difficult to conduct in the digital age than in previous times.[2] With so much data drowning today's researchers, they struggle to sort through it all, trying to decide what is current, relevant, and credible. Help is on the way, however! You'll learn more about researching and using electronic sources effectively in Chapter 10.
- **Search manually.** Valuable background and supplementary information is available through manual searching of resources in public and college libraries. These traditional paper-based sources include books and newspaper, magazine, and journal articles. Other sources are encyclopedias, reference books, handbooks, dictionaries, directories, and almanacs.
- **Investigate primary sources.** To develop firsthand, primary information for a project, go directly to the source. In helping to launch a new Forever 21 outlet in Canada, you might travel to possible sites and check them out. If you need information about how many shoppers pass by a location or visit a shopping

## Workplace in Focus

At Jump Associates, a San Francisco growth strategy firm, brainstorming may devolve into a kind of competitive-idea tennis match. One "Jumpster" starts with the first idea, and the next Jumpster says, "Yes, and?" which leads to another "Yes, and?" bouncing around its Black Box idea room. Once a storytelling method, this technique became an effective collaboration procedure and a core element of scrum, a daily standing meeting where the same "yes, and" principle is applied in improv games that prepare the company for its unique approach to brainstorming. For its megaclient Target, Jump helped create a product called "Kitchen in a Box," which became a phenomenal success. How does the "Yes, and" concept improve brainstorming?[1]

Chapter 3: Organizing and Drafting Business Messages

center, you might conduct a traffic count. If you need information about consumers, you could search blogs, Twitter, wikis, and Facebook fan pages. To learn more about specific shoppers, you could use questionnaires, interviews, or focus groups. Formal research often includes scientific sampling methods that enable investigators to make accurate judgments and valid predictions.

- **Conduct scientific experiments**. Another source of primary data is experimentation. Instead of merely asking for the target audience's opinion, scientific researchers present choices with controlled variables. Assume, for example, that the management team at Forever 21 wants to know at what price and under what circumstances consumers would purchase jeans from Forever 21 instead of from Abercrombie & Fitch. Instead of jeans, let's say that management wants to study the time of year and type of weather conditions that motivate consumers to begin purchasing sweaters, jackets, and cold-weather gear. The results of such experimentation would provide valuable data for managerial decision making. Because formal research techniques are particularly necessary for reports, you will study resources and techniques more extensively in Unit 4.

**LEARNING OBJECTIVE 2**
Organize information into strategic relationships.

## 3-2 Organizing Information to Show Relationships

Once you have collected data, you must find some way to organize it. Organizing includes two processes: grouping and strategizing. Well-organized messages group similar items together; ideas follow a sequence that helps the reader understand relationships and accept the writer's views. Unorganized messages proceed free-form, jumping from one thought to another. Such messages fail to emphasize important points. Puzzled readers can't see how the pieces fit together, and they become frustrated and irritated. Many communication experts regard poor organization as the greatest failing of business writers. Two simple techniques can help you organize data: the scratch list and the outline.

Some writers make a quick scratch list of the topics they wish to cover in a message. They then compose the message on a computer directly from the scratch list. Most writers, though, need to organize their ideas—especially if the project is complex—into a hierarchy such as an outline. The beauty of preparing an outline is that it gives you a chance to organize your thinking before you get bogged down in word choice and sentence structure. Figure 3.2 shows an outline format.

**Direct Strategy for Receptive Audiences.** After preparing a scratch list or an outline, think about how the audience will respond to your ideas. When you expect the reader to be pleased, mildly interested, or, at worst, neutral—use the direct strategy. That is, put your main point—the purpose of your message—in the first or second sentence. Dianna Booher, renowned writing consultant, pointed out that typical readers begin any message by thinking, "So what am I supposed to do with this information?" In business writing you have to say, "Reader, here is my point!"[3] As quickly as possible, tell why you are writing. Compare the direct and indirect strategies in the following e-mail openings. Notice how long it takes to get to the main idea in the indirect opening.

| DON'T — INDIRECT OPENING | DO — DIRECT OPENING |
|---|---|
| ✗ Our company has been concerned with attracting better-qualified prospective job candidates. For this reason, the Management Council has been gathering information about an internship program for college students. After considerable investigation, we have voted to begin a pilot program starting next fall. | ✓ The Management Council has voted to begin a college internship pilot program next fall. |

66    Chapter 3: Organizing and Drafting Business Messages

Figure 3.2  Format for an Outline

Title: Major Idea or Purpose

I. First major component
   A. First subpoint
      1. Detail, illustration, evidence
      2. Detail, illustration, evidence
      3. Detail, illustration, evidence
   B. Second subpoint
      1.
      2.

II. Second major component
   A. First subpoint
      1.
      2.
   B. Second subpoint
      1.
      2.
      3.

**Tips for Making Outlines**
- Define the main topic in the title.
- Divide the main topic into major components or classifications (preferably three to five).
- Break the components into subpoints.
- Don't put a single item under a major component; if you have only one subpoint, integrate it with the main item above it or reorganize.
- Strive to make each component exclusive (no overlapping).
- Use details, illustrations, and evidence to support subpoints.

Explanations and details follow the direct opening. What's important is getting to the main idea quickly. This direct method, also called *frontloading*, has at least three advantages:

- **Saves the reader's time**. Many of today's businesspeople can devote only a few moments to each message. Messages that take too long to get to the point may lose their readers along the way.
- **Sets a proper frame of mind**. Learning the purpose up front helps the reader put the subsequent details and explanations in perspective. Without a clear opening, the reader may be thinking, "Why am I being told this?"
- **Reduces frustration**. Readers forced to struggle through excessive verbiage before reaching the main idea can become frustrated and begin to resent the writer. Poorly organized messages create a negative impression of the writer.

Typical business messages that follow the direct strategy include routine requests and responses, orders and acknowledgments, nonsensitive memos, e-mails, informational reports, and informational oral presentations. All these tasks have one element in common: none has a sensitive subject that will upset the reader. It should be noted, however, that some business communicators prefer to use the direct strategy for nearly all messages.

**Indirect Strategy for Unreceptive Audiences.** When you expect the audience to be uninterested, unwilling, displeased, or perhaps even hostile, the indirect strategy is more appropriate. In this strategy you reveal the main idea only after you have offered an explanation and evidence. This approach works well with three kinds of messages: (a) bad news, (b) ideas that require persuasion, and (c) sensitive news, especially when being transmitted to superiors. The indirect strategy has these benefits:

- **Respects the feelings of the audience**. Bad news is always painful, but the trauma can be lessened by preparing the receiver for it.
- **Facilitates a fair hearing**. Messages that may upset the reader are more likely to be read when the main idea is delayed. Beginning immediately with a piece of

## Workplace in Focus

When Hurricane Sandy slammed the East Coast of the United States, the superstorm flooded thousands of homes and left citizens displaced, especially in New Jersey and New York. In the weeks that followed, devastated homeowners contacted insurance companies for help rebuilding their lives—only to discover that standard homeowner policies do not cover flood losses. Sympathetic claims adjusters struggled to break the bad news, and heartbroken policyholders expressed anger and disbelief as their claims were denied. "It's traumatic to lose your house and everything you own," said one survivor. "On top of this, you find out your insurance is not helping you." How should claims administrators organize messages when denying claims to disaster victims?[4]

bad news or a persuasive request, for example, may cause the receiver to stop reading or listening.

- **Minimizes a negative reaction**. A reader's overall reaction to a negative message is generally improved if the news is delivered gently.

Typical business messages that could be developed indirectly include e-mails, memos, and letters that refuse requests, deny claims, and disapprove credit. Persuasive requests, sales letters, sensitive messages, and some reports and oral presentations may also benefit from the indirect strategy. You will learn more about using the indirect strategy in Chapters 7 and 8.

In summary, business messages may be organized directly (with the main idea first) or indirectly. How you expect the audience to respond determines which strategy to use, as illustrated in Figure 3.3. Although these two strategies cover many communication problems, they should be considered neither universal nor inviolate. Every business transaction is distinct. Some messages are mixed: part good news, part bad; part goodwill, part persuasion. In upcoming chapters you will practice applying the direct and indirect strategies in typical situations. Then, you will have the skills and confidence to evaluate communication problems and vary these strategies depending on the goals you wish to achieve.

**Figure 3.3  Audience Response Determines Direct or Indirect Strategy**

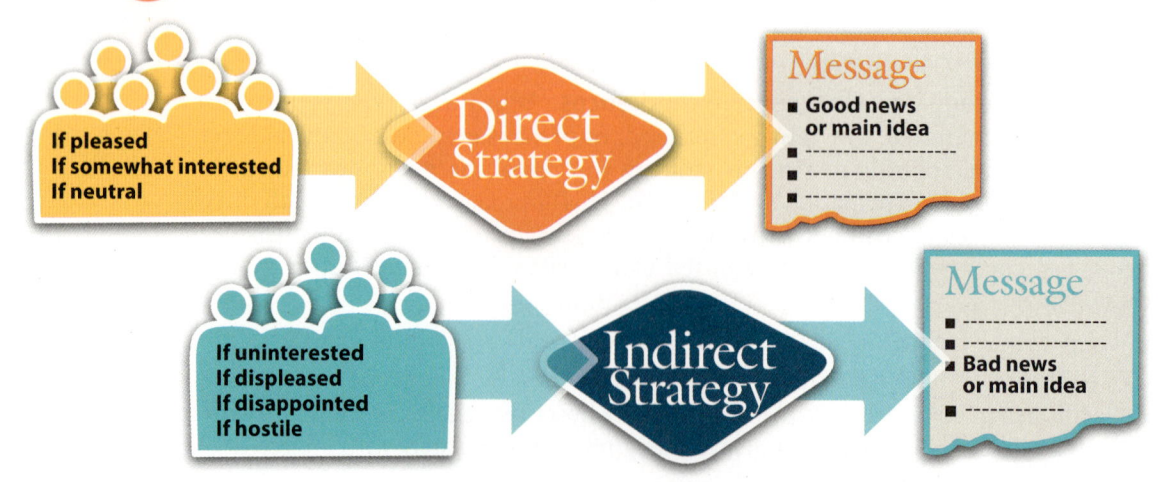

If pleased / If somewhat interested / If neutral → **Direct Strategy** → Message: Good news or main idea

If uninterested / If displeased / If disappointed / If hostile → **Indirect Strategy** → Message: Bad news or main idea

# 3-3 Composing the First Draft With Effective Sentences

**LEARNING OBJECTIVE 3**
Compose the first draft of a message using a variety of sentence types while avoiding sentence fragments, run-on sentences, and comma splices.

Once you have researched your topic, organized the data, and selected a strategy, you're ready to begin drafting. Many writers have trouble getting started, especially if they haven't completed the preparatory work. Organizing your ideas and working from an outline are very helpful in overcoming writer's block. Composition is also easier if you have a quiet environment in which to concentrate, if you set aside time to concentrate, and if you limit interruptions.

As you begin writing, think about what style fits you best. Some experts suggest that you write quickly (*freewriting*). Get your thoughts down now and refine them in later versions. As you take up each idea, imagine that you are talking to the reader. Don't let yourself get bogged down. If you can't think of the right word, insert a substitute or type *find perfect word later*. Freewriting works well for some writers, but others prefer to move more slowly and think through their ideas more deliberately. Whether you are a speedy or a deliberate writer, keep in mind that you are writing the first draft. You will have time later to revise and polish your sentences.

## 3-3a Achieving Variety With Four Sentence Types

Messages that repeat the same sentence pattern soon become boring. To avoid monotony and to add spark to your writing, use a variety of sentence types. You have four sentence types from which to choose: simple, compound, complex, and compound-complex.

### Simple Sentence

Contains one complete thought (an independent clause) with a subject and predicate verb:

The *entrepreneur* *saw* an opportunity.

### Compound Sentence

Contains two complete but related thoughts. May be joined by (a) a conjunction such as *and*, *but*, or *or*; (b) a semicolon; or (c) a conjunctive adverb such as *however*, *consequently*, and *therefore*:

The *entrepreneur* *saw* an opportunity, and *she* *responded* immediately.
The *entrepreneur* *saw* an opportunity; *she* *responded* immediately.
The *entrepreneur* *saw* an opportunity; consequently, *she* *responded* immediately.

### Complex Sentence

Contains an independent clause (a complete thought) and a dependent clause (a thought that cannot stand by itself). Dependent clauses are often introduced by words such as *although*, *since*, *because*, *when*, and *if*. When dependent clauses precede independent clauses, they always are followed by a comma:

When the *entrepreneur* *saw* the opportunity, *she* *responded* immediately.

### Compound-Complex Sentence

Contains at least two independent clauses and one dependent clause:

When the *entrepreneur* *saw* the opportunity, *she* *responded* immediately; however, she *needed* capital.

Chapter 3: Organizing and Drafting Business Messages

## OFFICE INSIDER

*"If you think an apostrophe was one of the 12 disciples of Jesus, you will never work for me. If you think a semicolon is a regular colon with an identity crisis, I will not hire you. If you scatter commas into a sentence with all the discrimination of a shotgun, you might make it to the foyer before we politely escort you from the building."*

—Kyle Wiens, CEO, iFixit, the largest online repair community

### 3-3b Avoiding Three Common Sentence Faults

As you craft your sentences, beware of three common traps: fragments, run-on (fused) sentences, and comma-splice sentences. If any of these faults appears in a business message, the writer immediately loses credibility.

One of the most serious errors a writer can make is punctuating a fragment as if it were a complete sentence. A *fragment* is usually a broken-off part of a complex sentence. Fragments often can be identified by the words that introduce them—words such as *although, as, because, even, except, for example, if, instead of, since, such as, that, which*, and *when*. These words introduce dependent clauses, as italicized in the following fragment examples. They should not be punctuated as sentences. Make sure such clauses always connect to independent clauses, as shown in the revisions.

| DON'T FRAGMENT | DO ✓ REVISION |
|---|---|
| ✗ *Because most transactions require a permanent record.* Good writing skills are critical. | ✓ Because most transactions require a permanent record, good writing skills are critical. |
| ✗ The recruiter requested a writing sample. *Even though the candidate seemed to communicate well.* | ✓ The recruiter requested a writing sample even though the candidate seemed to communicate well. |

A second serious writing fault is the **run-on (fused) sentence**. A sentence with two independent clauses must be joined by a coordinating conjunction (*and, or, nor, but*) or by a semicolon (;) or separated into two sentences. Without a conjunction or a semicolon, a run-on sentence results.

| DON'T RUN-ON SENTENCE | DO ✓ REVISION |
|---|---|
| ✗ Many job seekers prepare traditional résumés some also use websites as electronic portfolios. | ✓ Many job seekers prepare traditional résumés. Some also use websites as electronic portfolios. |
| ✗ One candidate sent an e-mail résumé another sent a link to her Web portfolio. | ✓ One candidate sent an e-mail résumé; another sent a link to her Web portfolio. |

A third sentence fault is a **comma splice**. It results when a writer joins (splices together) two independent clauses with a comma. Independent clauses may be joined with a coordinating conjunction (*and, or, nor, but*) or a conjunctive adverb (*however, consequently, therefore*, and others). Notice that clauses joined by a coordinating conjunctions require only a comma. Clauses joined by a conjunctive adverb require a semicolon and a comma. To rectify a comma splice, try one of the possible revisions shown here:

| DON'T COMMA SPLICE | DO ✓ REVISIONS |
|---|---|
| ✗ Some employees prefer their desktop computers, others prefer their tablets. | ✓ Some employees prefer their desktop computers, but others prefer their tablets. |
| | ✓ Some employees prefer their desktop computers; however, others prefer their tablets. |
| | ✓ Some employees prefer their desktop computers; others prefer their tablets. |

### 3-3c Favoring Short Sentences

Because your goal is to communicate clearly, you should strive for sentences that average 20 words. Some sentences will be shorter; some will be longer. The American Press Institute reports that reader comprehension drops off markedly as sentences become longer.[5] Therefore, in crafting your sentences, think about the relationship between sentence length and comprehension.

| Sentence Length | Comprehension Rate |
|---|---|
| 8 words | 100% |
| 15 words | 90% |
| 19 words | 80% |
| 28 words | 50% |

Instead of stringing together clauses with *and*, *but*, and *however*, break some of those complex sentences into separate segments. Business readers want to grasp ideas immediately. They can do that best when thoughts are separated into short sentences. On the other hand, too many monotonous short sentences will sound "grammar schoolish" and may bore or even annoy the reader. Strive for a balance between longer sentences and shorter ones. Your grammar-checker and spell-checker can show you readability statistics that flag long sentences and give you an average sentence length.

## 3-4 Developing Business Writing Techniques

Business writers can significantly improve their messages by working on a few writing techniques. In this section we focus on emphasizing and de-emphasizing ideas and using active and passive voice strategically.

### 3-4a Developing Emphasis

When you are talking with someone, you can emphasize your main ideas by saying them loudly or by repeating them slowly. You could even pound the table if you want to show real emphasis! Another way you could signal the relative importance of an idea is by raising your eyebrows or by shaking your head or whispering in a low voice. But when you write, you must rely on other means to tell your readers which ideas are more important than others. Emphasis in writing can be achieved primarily in two ways: mechanically and stylistically.

**Achieving Emphasis Through Mechanics.** To emphasize an idea in print, a writer may use any of the following devices:

| | |
|---|---|
| Underlining | Underlining draws the eye to a word. |
| Italics and boldface | Using *italics* or **boldface** conveys special meaning. |
| Font changes | Selecting a large, small, or different font draws interest. |
| All caps | Printing words in ALL CAPS is like shouting them. |
| Dashes | Dashes—used sparingly—can be effective. |
| Tabulation | Listing items vertically makes them stand out: <br> 1. First item <br> 2. Second item <br> 3. Third item |

---

### OFFICE INSIDER

On the topic of comma splices, one well-known writing coach says, "Why do intelligent people make the error? I think people worry that they will come across too informally or too plainly if they use [two] short sentences. They believe using 4-to-6-word sentences, especially two of them in a row, can't be professional. But two short, crisp, clear sentences in a row are professional and punchy."

—Lynn Gaertner Johnson, business writing trainer, coach, blogger

### LEARNING OBJECTIVE 4

Improve your writing by emphasizing important ideas, employing the active and passive voice effectively, using parallelism, and preventing dangling and misplaced modifiers.

Other means of achieving mechanical emphasis include the arrangement of space, color, lines, boxes, columns, titles, headings, and subheadings. Today's software and color printers provide a wonderful array of capabilities for setting off ideas. More tips on achieving emphasis are coming in Chapter 4, in which we cover document design.

**Achieving Emphasis Through Style.** Although mechanical devices are occasionally appropriate, more often a writer achieves emphasis stylistically. That is, the writer chooses words carefully and constructs sentences skillfully to emphasize main ideas and de-emphasize minor or negative ideas. Here are four suggestions for emphasizing ideas stylistically:

**Use vivid, not general, words.** Vivid words are emphatic because the reader can picture ideas clearly.

| DON'T — GENERAL | DO — VIVID |
|---|---|
| ✗ The way we seek jobs has changed. | ✓ The Internet has dramatically changed how job hunters search for positions. |
| ✗ Someone will contact you as soon as possible. | ✓ Ms. Rivera will telephone you before 5 p.m. tomorrow, May 3. |

**Label the main idea.** If an idea is significant, tell the reader.

| DON'T — UNLABELED | DO — LABELED |
|---|---|
| ✗ Consider looking for a job online, but also focus on networking. | ✓ Consider looking for a job online; but, *most important*, focus on networking. |
| ✗ We shop here because of the customer service and low prices. | ✓ We like the customer service, but the *primary reason* for shopping here is the low prices. |

**Place the important idea first or last.** Ideas have less competition from surrounding words when they appear first or last in a sentence. Observe how the concept of *productivity* can be emphasized by its position in the sentence:

| DON'T — MAIN IDEA LOST | DO — MAIN IDEA EMPHASIZED |
|---|---|
| ✗ Profit-sharing plans are more effective in increasing *productivity* when they are linked to individual performance rather than to group performance. | ✓ *Productivity* is more likely to be increased when profit-sharing plans are linked to individual performance rather than to group performance. |

**Give the important idea the spotlight.** Don't dilute the effect of the main idea by making it share the stage with other words and clauses. Instead, put it in a simple sentence or in an independent clause.

| DON'T — MAIN IDEA LOST | DO — MAIN IDEA CLEAR |
|---|---|
| ✗ Although you are the first trainee we have hired for this program, we had many candidates and expect to expand the program in the future. (The main idea is lost in a dependent clause.) | ✓ You are the first trainee we have hired for this program. (Simple sentence) |

**De-emphasizing When Necessary.** To de-emphasize an idea, such as bad news, try one of the following stylistic devices:

**Use general words.**

| DON'T — EMPHASIZES HARSH STATEMENT | DO — DE-EMPHASIZES HARSH STATEMENT |
|---|---|
| ✗ Our records indicate that you were recently fired. | ✓ Our records indicate that your employment status has recently changed. |

**Place the bad news in a dependent clause connected to an independent clause that contains something positive.** In sentences with dependent clauses, the main emphasis is always on the independent clause.

| DON'T — EMPHASIZES BAD NEWS | DO — DE-EMPHASIZES BAD NEWS |
|---|---|
| ✗ We cannot issue you credit at this time, but we have a special plan that will allow you to fill your immediate needs on a cash basis. | ✓ Although credit cannot be issued at this time, you can fill your immediate needs on a cash basis with our special plan. |

## 3-4b Using the Active and Passive Voice Effectively

In active-voice sentences, the subject, the actor, performs the action. In passive-voice sentences, the subject receives the action. Active-voice sentences are more direct because they reveal the performer immediately. They are easier to understand and usually shorter. Most business writing should be in the active voice. However, passive voice is useful to (a) emphasize an action rather than a person, (b) de-emphasize negative news, and (c) conceal the doer of an action.

**Active Voice**

Actor → Action
Justin must submit a tax return.
Actor → Action
Officials reviewed all tax returns.
Actor → Action
We cannot make cash refunds.
Actor → Action
Our CPA made a big error in the budget.

**Passive Voice**

Receiver ← Action
The tax return was submitted [by Justin].
Receiver ← Action
All tax returns were reviewed [by officials].
Receiver ← Action
Cash refunds cannot be made.
Receiver ← Action
A big error was made in the budget.

## 3-4c Developing Parallelism

*Parallelism* is a skillful writing technique that creates balanced writing. Sentences written so that their parts are balanced, or parallel, are easy to read and understand.

Chapter 3: Organizing and Drafting Business Messages

To achieve parallel construction, use similar structures to express similar ideas. For example, the words *computing, coding, recording,* and *storing* are parallel because the words all end in *-ing*. To express the list as *computing, coding, recording,* and *storage* is disturbing because the last item is not what the reader expects. Try to match nouns with nouns, verbs with verbs, and clauses with clauses. Avoid mixing active-voice verbs with passive-voice verbs. Your goal is to keep the wording balanced in expressing similar ideas.

| DON'T — LACKS PARALLELISM | DO ✓ — ILLUSTRATES PARALLELISM |
|---|---|
| ✗ The policy affected all vendors, suppliers, and *those involved with consulting.* | ✓ The policy affected all vendors, suppliers, and *consultants.* (Matches nouns.) |
| ✗ Our primary goals are to increase productivity, reduce costs, and *the improvement of product quality.* | ✓ Our primary goals are to increase productivity, reduce costs, and *improve product quality.* (Matches verbs.) |
| ✗ We are scheduled to meet in Atlanta on January 5, *we are meeting in Montreal on the 15th of March,* and in Chicago on June 3. | ✓ We are scheduled to meet in Atlanta on January 5, *in Montreal on March 15,* and in Chicago on June 3. (Matches phrases.) |
| ✗ Shelby audits all accounts lettered A through L; accounts lettered M through Z are audited by Andrew. | ✓ Shelby audits all accounts lettered A through L; Andrew audits accounts lettered M through Z. (Matches clauses.) |
| ✗ Our Super Bowl ads have three objectives:<br>1. We want to increase product use.<br>2. Introduce complementary products.<br>3. Our corporate image will be enhanced. | ✓ Our Super Bowl ads have three objectives:<br>1. Increase product use<br>2. Introduce complementary products<br>3. Enhance our corporate image<br>(Matches verbs in listed items.) |

### 3-4d Escaping Dangling and Misplaced Modifiers

For clarity, modifiers must be close to the words they describe or limit. A modifier dangles when the word or phrase it describes is missing from its sentence—for example, *After working overtime, the report was finally finished.* This sentence says that the report was working overtime. Revised, the sentence contains a logical subject: *After working overtime, we finally finished the report.*

A modifier is misplaced when the word or phrase it describes is not close enough to be clear—for example, *Firefighters rescued a dog from a burning car that had a broken leg.* Obviously, the car did not have a broken leg. The solution is to position the modifier closer to the word(s) it describes or limits: *Firefighters rescued a dog with a broken leg from a burning car.*

Introductory verbal phrases are particularly dangerous; be sure to follow them immediately with the words they logically describe or modify. Try this trick for detecting and remedying many dangling modifiers. Ask the question *Who?* or *What?* after any introductory phrase. The words immediately following should tell the reader who or what is performing the action. Try the *Who?* test on the first three danglers here:

---

**OFFICE INSIDER**

*Good writers don't let their modifiers dangle in public. "Always suspect an -ing word of dangling if it's near the front of a sentence; consider it guilty until proved innocent."*

—Patricia T. O'Conner, author, *Woe Is I: The Grammarphobe's Guide to Better English in Plain English*

Chapter 3: Organizing and Drafting Business Messages

| DON'T — DANGLING OR MISPLACED MODIFIER | DO ✓ — CLEAR MODIFICATION |
|---|---|
| ✗ Skilled at graphic design, the contract went to DesignOne. | ✓ Skilled at graphic design, DesignOne won the contract. |
| ✗ Working together as a team, the project was finally completed. | ✓ Working together as a team, we finally completed the project. |
| ✗ To meet the deadline, your Excel figures must be sent by May 1. | ✓ To meet the deadline, you must send your Excel figures by May 1. |
| ✗ The recruiter interviewed candidates who had excellent computer skills in the morning. | ✓ In the morning the recruiter interviewed candidates with excellent computer skills. |
| ✗ As an important customer to us, we invite you to our spring open house. | ✓ As you are an important customer to us, we invite you to our spring open house. *OR*:<br>✓ As an important customer to us, you are invited to our spring open house. |

## 3-5 Drafting Well-Organized, Effective Paragraphs

**LEARNING OBJECTIVE 5**
Draft well-organized paragraphs that incorporate (a) topic sentences, (b) support sentences, and (c) transitional expressions to build coherence.

Good business writers develop well-organized paragraphs by focusing on a single main idea. The sentences in their paragraphs cohere, or stick together, by using transitional expressions.

### 3-5a Crafting Topic Sentences

A paragraph is unified when it develops a single main idea. That idea is usually expressed in a topic sentence, which may appear at the beginning, in the middle, or at the end of the paragraph. Business writers generally place the topic sentence first in the paragraph. It tells readers what to expect and helps them understand the paragraph's central thought immediately.

### 3-5b Developing Support Sentences

Support sentences illustrate, explain, or strengthen the topic sentence. One of the hardest things for beginning writers to remember is that all support sentences in the paragraph must relate to the topic sentence. Any other topics should be treated separately. Support sentences provide specific details, explanations, and evidence. The following example starts with a topic sentence about flexible work scheduling and is followed by three support sentences that explain how flexible scheduling could work. Transitional expressions are italicized:

> **Topic sentence:** Flexible work scheduling could immediately increase productivity and enhance employee satisfaction in our organization.
>
> **Support sentences:** Managers would maintain their regular hours. For many other employees, *however*, flexible scheduling provides extra time to manage family responsibilities. Feeling less stress, employees are able to focus their attention better at work; *therefore*, they become more relaxed and more productive.

### 3-5c Building Paragraph Coherence

Paragraphs are coherent when ideas are linked—that is, when one idea leads logically to the next. Well-written paragraphs take the reader through a number of

Figure 3.4 Transitional Expressions to Build Coherence

| To Add or Strengthen | To Show Time or Order | To Clarify | To Show Cause and Effect | To Contradict | To Contrast |
|---|---|---|---|---|---|
| additionally | after | for example | accordingly | actually | as opposed to |
| accordingly | before | for instance | as a result | but | at the same time |
| again | earlier | I mean | consequently | however | by contrast |
| also | finally | in other words | for this reason | in fact | conversely |
| beside | first | put another way | hence | instead | on the contrary |
| indeed | meanwhile | that is | so | rather | on the other hand |
| likewise | next | this means | therefore | still | previously |
| moreover | now | thus | thus | yet | similarly |

steps. When the author skips from Step 1 to Step 3 and forgets Step 2, the reader is lost. Several techniques allow the reader to follow the writer's ideas:

- **Repeat a key idea by using the same expression or a similar one:** *Employees treat guests as VIPs. These VIPs are never told what they can or cannot do.*
- **Use pronouns to refer to previous nouns:** *All new employees receive a two-week orientation. They learn that every staffer has a vital role.*
- **Show connections with transitional expressions:** *Hospitality is our business; consequently, training is critical.* (Use transitions such as *consequently, however, as a result*, and *meanwhile*. For a complete list, see Figure 3.4.)

### 3-5d Controlling Paragraph Length

Although no rule regulates the length of paragraphs, business writers recognize the value of short paragraphs. Paragraphs with eight or fewer printed lines look inviting and readable. Long, solid chunks of print appear formidable. If a topic can't be covered in eight or fewer printed lines (not sentences), consider breaking it into smaller segments.

## SUMMARY OF LEARNING OBJECTIVES

**3-1** Apply Phase 2 of the 3-x-3 writing process, which begins with formal and informal research to collect background information.
- Apply the second phase of the writing process (prewriting) by researching, organizing, and drafting.
- Collect information by answering questions about what the receiver needs to know and what the receiver is to do.
- Conduct informal research for routine tasks by looking in the company's digital and other files, talking with the boss, interviewing the target audience, organizing informal surveys, and brainstorming for ideas
- Conduct formal research for long reports and complex problems by searching electronically or manually, investigating primary sources, and organizing scientific experiments.

**3-2** Organize information into strategic relationships.
- For simple messages, make a quick scratch list of topics; for more complex messages, create an outline.
- To prepare an outline, divide the main topic into three to five major components.

- Break the components into subpoints consisting of details, illustrations, and evidence.
- Organize the information using the **direct strategy** (with the main idea first) when audiences will be pleased, mildly interested, or neutral.
- Organize information using the **indirect strategy** (with explanations preceding the main idea) for audiences that will be unwilling, displeased, or hostile.

**3-3** Compose the first draft of a message using a variety of sentence types while avoiding sentence fragments, run-on sentences, and comma splices.
- Decide whether to compose quickly (*freewriting*) or to write more deliberately—but remember that you are writing a first draft.
- Employ a variety of sentence types including simple (one independent clause), complex (one independent and one dependent clause), compound (two independent clauses), and compound-complex (two independent clauses and one dependent clause).
- Avoid fragments (broken-off parts of sentences), run-on sentences (two clauses fused improperly), and comma splices (two clauses joined improperly with a comma).
- Remember that sentences are most effective when they are short (20 or fewer words).

**3-4** Improve your writing by emphasizing important ideas, employing the active and passive voice effectively, using parallelism, and preventing dangling and misplaced modifiers.
- Emphasize an idea mechanically by using underlining, italics, boldface, font changes, all caps, dashes, tabulation, and other devices.
- Emphasize an idea stylistically by using vivid words, labeling it, making it the sentence subject, placing it first or last, and removing competing ideas.
- For most business writing, use the active voice by making the subject the doer of the action (*the company hired the student*).
- Use the passive voice (*the student was hired*) to de-emphasize negative news, to emphasize an action rather than the doer, or to conceal the doer of an action.
- Employ parallelism for balanced construction (*jogging, hiking, and biking* rather than *jogging, hiking, and to bike*).
- Avoid dangling modifiers (*sitting at my computer, the words would not come*) and misplaced modifiers (*I have the report you wrote in my office*).

**3-5** Draft well-organized paragraphs that incorporate (a) topic sentences, (b) support sentences, and (c) transitional expressions to build coherence.
- Build well-organized, unified paragraphs by focusing on a single idea.
- Always include a topic sentence that states the main idea of the paragraph.
- Develop support sentences to illustrate, explain, or strengthen the topic sentence.
- Build coherence by repeating a key idea, using pronouns to refer to previous nouns, and showing connections with transitional expressions (*however, therefore, consequently*).
- Control paragraph length by striving for eight or fewer lines.

# CHAPTER REVIEW

1. What is *research*, and how do informal and formal research methods differ? (Obj. 1)

2. Before drafting a message, what questions should writers ask as they collect information? (Obj. 1)

3. Why do writers need to outline complex projects before beginning? (Obj. 2)

4. What business messages are better organized directly, and which are better organized indirectly? (Obj. 2)

5. What are the four sentence types? Provide an original example of each. (Obj. 3)

6. What is the relationship between sentence length and comprehension? (Obj. 3)

7. How is a sentence fragment different from a comma splice? (Obj. 3)

8. What is the difference between active-voice and passive-voice sentences? Give an original example of each. When should business writers use each? (Obj. 4)

9. How are topic sentences different from support sentences? (Obj. 5)

10. Name three techniques for building paragraph coherence. (Obj. 5)

# CRITICAL THINKING

11. What trends in business and developments in technology are forcing workers to write more than ever before? (Obj. 1)

12. Molly, a twenty-three-year-old college graduate with a 3.5 GPA, was hired as an administrative assistant. She was a fast learner on all the software, but her supervisor had to help her with punctuation. On the ninth day of her job, she resigned, saying: "I just don't think this job is a good fit. Commas, semicolons, spelling, typos—those kinds of things just aren't all that important to me. They just don't matter."[6] For what kind of job is Molly qualified? (Objs. 1–5)

13. Why is audience analysis so important in the selection of the direct or indirect organization strategy for a business message? (Obj. 2)

14. How are speakers different from writers in the way they emphasize ideas? (Obj. 4)

15. Now that you have studied the active and passive voice, what do you think when someone in government or business says, "Mistakes were made"? Is it unethical to use the passive voice to avoid specifics?

# WRITING IMPROVEMENT EXERCISES

## Sentence Type (Obj. 3)

For each of the following sentences, select the letter that identifies its type:

   a. Simple sentence   c. Complex
   b. Compound sentence   d. Compound-complex

_____   16. Many companies are now doing business in international circles.

_____   17. If you travel abroad on business, you may bring gifts for business partners.

_____   18. In Latin America a knife is not a proper gift; it signifies cutting off a relationship.

_____   19. When Arabs, Middle Easterners, and Latin Americans talk, they often stand close to each other.

_____   20. Unless they are old friends, Europeans do not address each other by first names; consequently, businesspeople should not expect to do so.

_____   21. In the Philippines men wear a long embroidered shirt called a *barong*, and women wear a dress called a *terno*.

## Sentence Faults (Obj. 3)

In each of the following sentences, identify the sentence fault (fragment, run-on, comma splice). Then revise it to remedy the fault.

22. Because 90 percent of all business transactions involve written messages. Good writing skills are critical.

23. Darcy agreed to change her password. Even though she thought her old one was just fine.

24. Major soft-drink companies considered a new pricing strategy, they tested vending machines that raise prices in hot weather.

Chapter 3: Organizing and Drafting Business Messages

25. Thirsty consumers may think that variable pricing is unfair they may also refuse to use the machine.

26. About half of Pizza Hut's 7,600 outlets make deliveries, the others concentrate on walk-in customers.

27. McDonald's sold its chain of Chipotle Mexican Grill restaurants the chain's share price doubled on the next day of trading.

## Emphasis (Obj. 4)

For each of the following sentences, circle (a) or (b). Be prepared to justify your choice.

28. Which is more emphatic?
    a. Our dress code is fine.
    b. Our dress code reflects common sense and good taste.

29. Which is more emphatic?
    a. A budget increase would certainly improve hiring.
    b. A budget increase of $70,000 would enable us to hire two new people.

30. Which is more emphatic?
    a. The committee was powerless to act.
    b. The committee was unable to take action.

31. Which de-emphasizes the refusal?
    a. Although our resources are committed to other projects this year, we hope to be able to contribute to your worthy cause next year.
    b. We can't contribute to your charity this year.

32. Which sentence places more emphasis on the date?
    a. The deadline is November 30 for health benefit changes.
    b. November 30 is the deadline for health benefit changes.

33. Which is *less* emphatic?
    a. One division's profits decreased last quarter.
    b. Profits in beauty care products dropped 15 percent last quarter.

34. Which sentence *de-emphasizes* the credit refusal?
    a. We are unable to grant you credit at this time, but we welcome your cash business and encourage you to reapply in the future.
    b. Although credit cannot be granted at this time, we welcome your cash business and encourage you to reapply in the future.

35. Which sentence gives more emphasis to *leadership*?
    a. Jason has many admirable qualities, but most important is his leadership skill.
    b. Jason has many admirable qualities, including leadership skill, good judgment, and patience.

36. Which is more emphatic?
    a. We notified three departments: (1) Marketing, (2) Accounting, and (3) Distribution.
    b. We notified three departments:
       1. Marketing
       2. Accounting
       3. Distribution

## Active Voice (Obj. 4)

Business writing is more forceful when it uses active-voice verbs. Revise the following sentences so that verbs are in the active voice. Put the emphasis on the doer of the action.

**Passive:** Antivirus software was installed by Craig on his computer.
**Active:** Craig installed antivirus software on his computer.

37. Employees were given their checks at 4 p.m. every Friday by the manager.

38. New spices and cooking techniques were tried by McDonald's to improve its hamburgers.

39. Our new company logo was designed by my boss.

40. The managers with the most productive departments were commended by the CEO.

## Passive Voice (Obj. 4)

Revise the following sentences so that they are in the passive voice.

41. The auditor discovered a computational error in the company's tax figures.

42. We discovered the error too late to correct the balance sheet.

43. Stacy did not submit the accounting statement on time.

44. The Federal Trade Commission targeted deceptive diet advertisements by weight-loss marketers.

## Parallelism (Obj. 4)

Revise the following sentences so that their parts are balanced.

45. (**Hint:** Match adjectives.) To be hired, an applicant must be reliable, creative, and show enthusiasm.

46. (**Hint:** Match active voice.) If you have decided to cancel our service, please cut your credit card in half and the pieces should be returned to us.

Chapter 3: Organizing and Drafting Business Messages

47. (**Hint:** Match verbs.) Guidelines for improving security at food facilities include inspecting incoming and outgoing vehicles, restriction of access to laboratories, preventing workers from bringing personal items into food-handling areas, and inspection of packaging for signs of tampering.

48. (**Hint:** Match adjective-noun expressions.) The committee will continue to monitor merchandise design, product quality, and check the feedback of customers.

49. (**Hint:** Match verb clauses.) To use the fax copier, insert your meter, the paper trays must be loaded, indicate the number of copies needed, and your original sheet should be inserted through the feeder.

50. (**Hint:** Match *ing* verbs.) Sending an e-mail establishes a more permanent record than to make a telephone call.

## Dangling and Misplaced Modifiers (Obj. 4)

Revise the following sentences to avoid dangling and misplaced modifiers.

51. After leaving the midtown meeting, Angela's car would not start.

52. Walking up the driveway, the Hummer parked in the garage was immediately spotted by the detectives.

53. To complete the project on time, a new deadline was established by the team.

54. Acting as manager, several new employees were hired by Mr. Lopez.

55. Michelle Mitchell presented a talk about workplace drug problems in our boardroom.

## Organizing Paragraph Sentences (Obj. 5)

In a memo to the college president, the athletic director argues for a new stadium scoreboard. One paragraph will describe the old scoreboard and why it needs to be replaced. Study the following list of ideas for that paragraph.

1. *The old scoreboard is a tired warhorse that was originally constructed in the 1970s.*
2. *It is now hard to find replacement parts when something breaks.*
3. *The old scoreboard is not energy efficient.*
4. *Coca-Cola has offered to buy a new sports scoreboard in return for exclusive rights to sell soda pop on campus.*
5. *The old scoreboard should be replaced for many reasons.*
6. *It shows only scores for football games.*
7. *When we have soccer games or track meets, we are without a functioning scoreboard.*

_____ 56. Which sentence should be the topic sentence?

_____ 57. Which sentence(s) should be developed in a separate paragraph?

_____ 58. Which sentences should become support sentences?

## Building Coherent Paragraphs (Obj. 5)

59. Use the information from the preceding sentences to write a coherent paragraph about replacing the sports scoreboard. Strive to use three devices to build coherence: (a) repetition of key words, (b) pronouns that clearly refer to previous nouns, and (c) transitional expressions.

60. Revise the following paragraph. Add a topic sentence and improve the organization. Correct problems with pronouns, parallelism, wordiness, and misplaced or dangling modifiers. Add transitional expressions if appropriate.

    *You may be interested in applying for a new position within the company. The Human Resources Department has a number of jobs available immediately. The positions are at a high level. Current employees may apply immediately for open positions in production, for some in marketing, and jobs in administrative support are also available. To make application, these positions require immediate action. Come to the Human Resources Department. We have a list showing the open positions, what the qualifications are, and job descriptions are shown. Many of the jobs are now open. That's why we are sending this now. To be hired, an interview must be scheduled within the next two weeks.*

61. Revise the following paragraph. Add a topic sentence and improve the organization. Correct problems with pronouns, parallelism, wordiness, and misplaced or dangling modifiers.

    *As you probably already know, this company (Lasertronics) will be installing new computer software shortly. There will be a demonstration April 18, which is a Tuesday. You are invited. We felt this was necessary because this new software is so different from our previous software. It will be from 9 to 12 a.m. in the morning. This will show employees how the software programs work. They will learn about the operating system, and this should be helpful to nearly everyone. There will be information about the new word processing program, which should be helpful to administrative assistants and product managers. For all you people who work with payroll, there will be information about the new database program. We can't show everything the software will do at this one demo, but for these three areas there will be some help at the Tuesday demo. Presenting the software, the demo will feature Paula Roddy. She is the representative from Quantum Software.*

62. From the following information, develop a coherent paragraph with a topic and support sentences. Strive for conciseness and coherence.
    - Car dealers and lenders offer a variety of loan terms.
    - To get the best deal, shop around when buying a new or used car.
    - You have two payment options: you may pay in full or finance over time.
    - You should compare offers and be willing to negotiate the best deal.
    - If you are a first-time buyer—or if your credit isn't great—be cautious about special financing offers.
    - Buying a new or used car can be challenging.
    - Financing increases the total cost of the car because you are also paying for the cost of credit.
    - If you agree to financing that carries a high interest rate, you may be taking a big risk. If you decide to sell the car before the loan expires, the amount you get from the sale may be far less than the amount you need to pay off the loan.
    - If money is tight, you might consider paying cash for a less expensive car than you originally had in mind.

# RADICAL REWRITES

**Note:** Radical Rewrites are provided at **www.cengagebrain.com** for you to download and revise. Your instructor may provide a suggested solution.

## 3.1 Radical Rewrite: Seattle Health Club Offers Ailing E-Mail Message (Objs. 2–5)

In Seattle the 24-Hour Gym promises to strengthen bodies. However, its weak e-mail to its clients needs a radical rewrite to improve its effectiveness.

**YOUR TASK.** The following e-mail suffers from numerous writing faults such as dangling modifiers, overuse of the passive voice, and fragments. Notice that small superscript numbers identify each sentence or group of words. Individually or in a group, analyze this message and list the faulty sentences or groups of words. Be sure your group agrees on its analysis. Your instructor may ask you to revise the message to remedy its faults.

**To:** Tyler.Long <tlong@cox.org>
**From:** Janice Rivera <jrivera@24hourgym.com>
**Subject:** Expanding Your Workouts at 24-Hour Gym
**Cc:**
**Bcc:**

Dear Mr. Long,

[1]24-Hour Gym here in Seattle was probably selected by you because it is one of the top-rated gyms in the Northwest. [2]Our principal goal has always been making your workouts productive. [3]To continue to provide you with the best equipment and programs, your feedback is needed.

[4]An outstanding program with quality equipment and excellent trainers has been provided by 24-Hour Gym. [5]However, more individual attention could be given by us to our customers if our peak usage time could be extended. [6]You have probably noticed that attendance at the gym increases from 4 p.m. to 8 p.m. [7]We wish it were possible to accommodate all our customers on their favorite equipment during those hours. [8]Although we can't stretch an hour. [9]We would like to make better use of the time between 8 p.m. and 11 p.m. [10]If more members came later, the gym would have less crush from 4 p.m. to 8 p.m.

[11]To encourage you to stay later, security cameras for our parking area are being considered by my partner and me. [12]Cameras for some inside facilities may also be added. [13]This matter has been given considerable thought. [14]Although 24-Hour Gym has never had an incident that endangered a member.

[15]Please fill in the attached interactive questionnaire. [16]Which will give us instant feedback about scheduling your workouts. [17]By completing this questionnaire, your workouts and training sessions can be better planned so that you can enjoy exactly the equipment and trainers you prefer.

Cordially,

**What three sentences have dangling modifiers?**
**What eight sentences exhibit passive voice?**
**Which three groups of words represent fragments?**

Chapter 3: Organizing and Drafting Business Messages

85

# GRAMMAR/MECHANICS CHECKUP—3

## Verbs

Review Sections 1.10–1.15 in the Grammar Review section of the Grammar/Mechanics Handbook. Then study each of the following statements. Underline any verbs that are used incorrectly. In the space provided, write the correct form (or *C* if correct) and the number of the G/M principle illustrated. When you finish, compare your responses with those provided near the end of the book. If your responses differ, study carefully the principles in parentheses.

has     (1.10c)    **EXAMPLE** Every one of the top-ranking executives <u>have</u> been insured.

_____ 1. Are you convinced that Google's database of customers' messages and private information are secure?

_____ 2. Google's data team have been carefully studying how to shield users from unwarranted government intrusion.

_____ 3. Wells-Fargo, along with most other large national banks, offer a variety of savings plans.

_____ 4. In the next building is the administrative staff and our marketing people.

_____ 5. The city council have unanimously approved the parking fee hike.

_____ 6. If you was in my position, you might agree with my decision.

_____ 7. Everyone except the temporary workers employed during the past year has become eligible for health benefits.

_____ 8. All employees should have went to the emergency procedures demonstration.

_____ 9. The reports have laid on his desk for 11 days and are now overdue.

_____ 10. Either of the flight times are fine with me.

_____ 11. Some of the jury members believes that the prosecution's evidence is not relevant.

In the space provided, write the letter of the sentence that illustrates consistency in subject, voice, tense, and mood.

_____ 12. a. By carefully following the instructions, much time can be saved.
             b. By carefully following the instructions, you can save much time.

_____ 13. a. All employees must fill out application forms; only then will you be insured.
             b. All employees must fill out application forms; only then will they be insured.

_____ 14. a. First, advertise the position; then, evaluate applications.
             b. First, advertise the position; then, applications must be evaluated.

_____ 15. a. Our manager was a computer whiz who was always ready to help.
             b. Our manager was a computer whiz who is always ready to help.

# EDITING CHALLENGE—3

To fine-tune your grammar and mechanics skills, in every chapter you will be editing a message. This message is from a financial planner answering an inquiry about eBay profits. However, the message suffers from proofreading, spelling, grammar, punctuation, wordiness, and other writing faults that require correction. Study the guidelines in the Grammar/Mechanics Handbook.

**YOUR TASK.** Edit the following message (a) by correcting errors in your textbook or on a photocopy using proofreading marks from Appendix A or (b) by downloading the message from **www.cengagebrain.com** and correcting at your computer. Your instructor may show you a possible solution.

---

**ANDALUZ FINANCIAL PLANNING**
CERTIFIED FINANCIAL PLANNERS
2230 GIBSON BOULEVARD SE
ALBUQUERQUE, NM 87108
505.256.1002
marcy.martinez@andaluz.com


September 12, 2016

Ms. Stephanie Jimenez
2509 Blake Road NW
Albuquerque, NM 87110

Dear Stephany:

I just wanted to let you know that, as your Financial Planner, I'm happy to respond to your request for more information and clarification on the Tax status of eBay profits.

As you in all probability are all ready aware of, you can use eBay to clean out your closets or eBay can be used to run a small business. Your smart to enquire about your tax liability. Although there is no clear line that separates fun from profit or a hobby from a business. One thing is certin, the IRS taxes all income.

There are a number of factors that help determine whether or not your hobby should or should not be considered a business. To use eBay safely, the following questions should be considered:

1. Do you run the operation in a businesslike manner? Do you keep records, is your profit and loss tracked, and how about keeping a seperate checking account?

2. Do you devote alot of time and effort to eBay? If you spend eighteen hours a day selling on eBay the IRS would tend to think your in a business.

3. Some people depend on the income from their eBay activitys for their livelihood.

Are you selling items for more then they cost you? If you spend five dollars for a Garage Sale vase and sell it for fifty dollars the IRS would probably consider this a business transaction.

All profits is taxable. Even for eBay sellers who are just playing around. If you wish to discuss this farther please call me at 256-1002.

Sincerely,

*Marcy Martinez*

Marcy Martinez
Certified Financial Planner

---

Chapter 3: Organizing and Drafting Business Messages

# COMMUNICATION WORKSHOP

## SOCIAL MEDIA

### Guidelines for Safe Social Networking

More and more people are becoming accustomed to communicating and sharing information, both business and personal, on Facebook, Twitter, Instagram, Tumblr, and other social media sites. As the popularity of these social networks grows, so do the risks. Savvy business communicators can protect themselves by employing smart practices such as the following:

- **Establish boundaries.** Don't share information, images, and media online that you would not be comfortable sharing openly in the office.
- **Be cautious in clicking links.** Treat links on social media sites with the same caution you use with e-mail messages. Cyber criminals are eager for you to "like" them or open their links.
- **Remember that Big Data is watching you.** Whether you are making business contacts or visiting fun sites, you are leaving a digital trail.
- **Distrust privacy settings.** Even privacy settings don't guarantee complete protection from prying eyes. Facebook has repeatedly come under fire for changing privacy settings and opening unwitting users' profiles for the world to see.
- **Beware of oversharing.** If your employer visits your Facebook page and notices a flurry of activity while you should be working, you might land on the hot seat. If you report that you're sick and then your Facebook location shows you posting from the local movie theater, this could reveal that you're playing hooky.
- **Doubt suspicious messages.** Even if a strange message looks as if it's from a friend, remember that hackers may have broken into that person's account. Use an alternate method to reach your friend to find out.
- **Rein in your friends.** One of your 500 Facebook friends may tag you in an inappropriate photograph. Tags make pictures searchable, so that an embarrassing college incident may resurface years later. Always ask before tagging someone.
- **Expect the unexpected.** Recruiters now routinely check applicants' online presence. Some employers have gone so far as to demand that candidates disclose their Facebook login information. Facebook and lawmakers have criticized the practice.
- **Beware of "friending."** Don't reject friend requests from some coworkers while accepting them from others. Snubbed workers may harbor ill feelings. Don't friend your boss unless he or she friends you first. Send friend requests only once.

**CAREER APPLICATION.** Office workers and businesspeople are using more and more technology to complete their work. Best practices and netiquette rules are still evolving. We've presented nine tips here for smart use of social media.

**YOUR TASK.** In teams discuss the tips presented here. From your own experience, add more suggestions that can make social media users safer. What risky behavior have you experienced or learned about? What violations of netiquette have you seen? Prepare a list of additional helpful tips. Show them using the format shown here, with each statement a command. Submit your list to your instructor and discuss it in class.

# ENDNOTES

[1] Photo essay based on Segal, D. (2010, December 16). In pursuit of the perfect brainstorm. *The New York Times*. Retrieved from http://www.nytimes.com

[2] Head, A., & Eisenberg, M. (2009, February 4). What today's college students say about conducting research in the digital age. Project Information Literacy Progress Report, University of Washington. Retrieved from http://www.educause.edu/library/resources/what-today%E2%80%99s-college-students-say-about-conducting-research-digital-age

[3] Rindegard, J. (1999, November 22). Use clear writing to show you mean business. *InfoWorld*, p. 78.

[4] Photo essay based on Beeson, E. (2013, January 20). Hurricane Sandy to spawn storm of insurance lawsuits. *The Star-Ledger*. Retrieved from http://www.nj.com/business/index.ssf/2013/01/hurricane_sandy_to_spawn_storm.html

[5] Goddard, R. W. (1989, April). Communication: Use language effectively. *Personnel Journal*, 32.

[6] Booher, D. (2007). *The voice of authority*. New York: McGraw-Hill, p. 93.

# ACKNOWLEDGMENTS

**p. 64** Office Insider based on Tucci, J. M. (2004, September 1). Quoted in the National Writing Project, Writing: A ticket to work . . . or a ticket out. Retrieved from http://www.nwp.org/cs/public/print/resource/2154

**p. 70** Office Insider based on Wiens, K. (2012, July 20). I won't hire people who use poor grammar. Here's why. *Harvard Business Review* blog. Retrieved from http://blogs.hbr.org/cs/2012/07/i_wont_hire_people_who_use_poo.html

**p. 71** Office Insider based on Johnson, L. G. (2011, January 12). Avoid this simple "comma splice" error. Retrieved from http://www.businesswritingblog.com/business_writing/2011/01/avoid-this-simple-comma-splice-error.html

**p. 74** Office Insider based on O'Conner, P. (1996). *Woe is I*. New York: Putnam, p. 161.

**p. 88** Communication Workshop based on the following: Horn, L. (2013, June 14). What Emily Post can't teach us about 'netiquette.' Retrieved from http://gizmodo.com/what-emily-post-cant-teach-us-about-netiquette-513423651; Palmer, M. (2012, February 6). The netiquette of working life. Retrieved from http://www.ft.com/intl/cms/s/0/94239bbe-4dae-11e1-b96c-00144feabdc0.html#axzz2ccxWuyPJ; Zwilling, M. (2013, August 17). 7 steps to productive business use of social media. Retrieved from http://www.forbes.com/sites/martinzwilling/2013/08/17/7-steps-to-productive-business-use-of-social-media; Naish, J. (2009, August 11). Is multi-tasking bad for the brain? Experts reveal hidden perils of juggling too many jobs. Retrieved from http://www.dailymail.co.uk/health/article-1205669/Is-multi-tasking-bad-brain-Experts-reveal-hidden-perils-juggling-jobs.html

# CHAPTER 4

# Revising Business Messages

## OBJECTIVES
After studying this chapter, you should be able to

**4-1** Complete business messages by revising for conciseness, which includes eliminating flabby expressions, long lead-ins, *there is/are* and *it is/was* fillers, redundancies, and empty words, as well as condensing for microblogging.

**4-2** Improve clarity in business messages by keeping the ideas simple, dumping trite business phrases, dropping clichés, avoiding slang and buzzwords, rescuing buried verbs, controlling exuberance, and choosing precise words.

**4-3** Enhance readability by understanding document design including the use of white space, margins, typefaces, fonts, numbered and bulleted lists, and headings.

**4-4** Recognize proofreading problem areas, and apply effective techniques to catch mistakes in both routine and complex documents.

**4-5** Evaluate a message to judge its effectiveness.

## 4-1 Taking Time to Revise: Applying Phase 3 of the Writing Process

In this digital age of e-mailing, texting, and tweeting, the idea of stopping to revise a message seems almost alien to productivity. What? Stop to proofread? Crazy idea! No time! However, sending quick but sloppy business messages not only fails to enhance productivity but also often produces the opposite result. Those rushed messages can be confusing and frustrating. They often set into motion a maddening series of back-and-forth queries and responses seeking clarification. To avoid messages that waste time, create confusion, and reduce your credibility, take time to slow down and revise—even for short messages.

The final phase of the 3-x-3 writing process focuses on editing, proofreading, and evaluating. Editing means improving the content and sentence structure of your message. Proofreading involves correcting its grammar, spelling, punctuation, format, and mechanics. Evaluating is the process of analyzing whether your message achieves its purpose.

Rarely is the first or even second version of a message satisfactory. Only amateurs expect writing perfection on the first try. The revision stage is your chance to make sure your message says what you mean and makes you look good. Many professional writers compose the first draft quickly without worrying about language, precision, or correctness. Then they revise and polish extensively. Other writers, however, prefer to revise as they go—particularly for shorter business documents.

Whether you revise immediately or after a break, you will want to examine your message critically. You should be especially concerned with ways to improve its conciseness, clarity, and readability.

## 4-1a Tightening Your Message by Revising for Conciseness

In business, time is indeed money. Translated into writing, this means that concise messages save reading time and, thus, money. In addition, messages that are written directly and efficiently are easier to read and comprehend. In the revision process, look for shorter ways to say what you mean. Examine every sentence that you write. Could the thought be conveyed in fewer words? Your writing will be more concise if you eliminate flabby expressions, drop unnecessary introductory words, get rid of redundancies, and purge empty words.

**Eliminating Flabby Expressions.** As you revise, focus on eliminating flabby expressions. This takes conscious effort. As one expert copyeditor observed, "Trim sentences, like trim bodies, usually require far more effort than flabby ones."[1] Turning out slim sentences and lean messages means that you will strive to "trim the fat." For example, notice the flabbiness in this sentence: *Due to the fact that sales are booming, profits are strong.* It could be said more concisely: *Because sales are booming, profits are strong.* Many flabby expressions can be shortened to one concise word as shown here and illustrated in Figure 4.1. Notice in this figure how you can revise digital documents with strikethrough formatting and color. If you are revising print documents, use proofreading marks.

| FLABBY | CONCISE |
| --- | --- |
| as a general rule | generally |
| at a later date | later |
| at this point in time | now, presently |
| despite the fact that | although |
| due to the fact that, inasmuch as, in view of the fact that | because |
| feel free to | please |
| for the period of, for the purpose of | for |
| in addition to the above | also |
| in all probability | probably |
| in the event that | if |
| in the near future | soon |
| in very few cases | seldom, rarely |
| until such time as | until |

**Limiting Long Lead-Ins.** Another way to create concise sentences is to delete unnecessary introductory words. Consider this sentence: *I am sending you this e-mail to announce that a new manager has been hired.* A more concise and more direct sentence deletes the long lead-in: *A new manager has been hired.* The meat of the sentence often follows the long lead-in.

Chapter 4: Revising Business Messages

## OFFICE INSIDER

*"Regardless of what you may have been taught in school, writing more doesn't necessarily equate to writing better—especially in a business environment, where time is precious. Don't bury your important points under unnecessary verbiage."*

—Edwin Powell, business writing expert and senior editor, *Office Solutions* magazine

**LEARNING OBJECTIVE 1**

Complete business messages by revising for conciseness, which includes eliminating flabby expressions, long lead-ins, *there is/are* and *it is/was* fillers, redundancies, and empty words, as well as condensing for microblogging.

## Figure 4.1 Revising Digital and Print Documents

**Revising Digital Documents Using Strikethrough and Color**

~~This is a short note to let you know that, as~~ As you requested, I ~~made an investigation of~~ investigated several of our competitors' websites. Attached ~~hereto~~ is a summary of my findings. ~~of my investigation.~~ I was ~~really~~ most interested in ~~making a comparison of the employment of strategies for~~ comparing marketing strategies as well as ~~the use of~~ navigational graphics ~~used~~ to guide visitors through the sites. ~~In view of the fact that~~ Because we will be revising our own website ~~in the near future~~ soon, I was ~~extremely~~ intrigued by the organization, ~~kind of~~ marketing tactics, and navigation at each ~~and every~~ site I visited.

> When revising digital documents, you can use simple word processing tools such as strikethrough and color. In this example, strikethroughs in red identify passages to be deleted. The strikethrough function is located on the Font tab. We used blue to show inserted words, but you may choose any color you prefer.

**Revising Printed Documents Using Proofreading Symbols**

When revising printed documents, use standard symbols to manually show your revisions.

~~This is a short note to let you know that,~~ as you requested, I ~~made an~~ investig*ed* ~~ation of~~ several of our competitors' websites. Attached ~~hereto~~ is a summary of my findings. ~~of my investigation.~~ I was ~~really~~ most interested in ~~making a comparison of the employment of~~ *comparing* strategies ~~for marketing~~ *marketing* as well as ~~the use of~~ navigational graphics ~~used~~ to guide visitors through the sites. ~~In view of the fact that~~ *Because* we will be revising our own website ~~in the near future~~ *soon*, I was ~~extremely~~ intrigued by the organization, ~~kind of~~ marketing tactics, and navigation at ~~each and~~ every site I visited.

**Popular Proofreading Symbols**

| Symbol | Meaning |
|---|---|
| Delete | ⌒ |
| Capitalize | ≡ |
| Insert | ∧ |
| Insert comma | ∧, |
| Insert period | ⊙ |
| Start paragraph | ¶ |

---

| DON'T WORDY | DO ✓ CONCISE |
|---|---|
| ✗ We are sending this announcement to let everyone know that we expect to change Internet service providers within six weeks. | ✓ We expect to change Internet service providers within six weeks. |
| ✗ This is to inform you that you may find lower airfares at our website. | ✓ You may find lower airfares at our website. |
| ✗ I am writing this letter because Professor Brian Wilson suggested that your organization was hiring trainees. | ✓ Professor Brian Wilson suggested that your organization was hiring trainees. |

**Dropping Unnecessary *There is/are* and *It is/was* Fillers.** In many sentences the expressions *there is/are* and *it is/was* function as unnecessary fillers. In addition to taking up space, these fillers delay getting to the point of the sentence. Eliminate them by recasting the sentence. Many—but not all—sentences can be revised so that fillers are unnecessary.

92  Chapter 4: Revising Business Messages

| DON'T WORDY | DO ✓ CONCISE |
|---|---|
| ✗ *There are* more women than men enrolled in college today. | ✓ More women than men are enrolled in college today. |
| ✗ *There* is an aggregator that collects and organizes blogs. | ✓ An aggregator collects and organizes blogs. |
| ✗ *It was* a Facebook post that revealed the news. | ✓ A Facebook post revealed the news. |

**Rejecting Redundancies.** Expressions that repeat meaning or include unnecessary words are redundant. Saying *unexpected surprise* is like saying *surprise surprise* because *unexpected* carries the same meaning as *surprise*. Excessive adjectives, adverbs, and phrases often create redundancies and wordiness. Redundancies do not add emphasis, as some people think. Instead, they identify a writer as inexperienced. As you revise, look for redundant expressions such as the following:

| DON'T REDUNDANT | DO ✓ CONCISE |
|---|---|
| ✗ absolutely essential | ✓ essential |
| ✗ adequate enough | ✓ adequate |
| ✗ basic fundamentals | ✓ fundamentals *or* basics |
| ✗ big in size | ✓ big |
| ✗ combined together | ✓ combined |
| ✗ exactly identical | ✓ identical |
| ✗ each and every | ✓ each *or* every |
| ✗ necessary prerequisite | ✓ prerequisite |
| ✗ new beginning | ✓ beginning |
| ✗ refer back | ✓ refer |
| ✗ repeat again | ✓ repeat |
| ✗ true facts | ✓ facts |

**Purging Empty Words.** Familiar phrases roll off the tongue easily, but many contain expendable parts. Be alert to these empty words and phrases: *case, degree, the fact that, factor, instance, nature,* and *quality*. Notice how much better the following sentences sound when we remove all the empty words:

~~In the case of~~ Facebook~~, it~~ increased users but lost share value.

Because of ~~the degree of~~ support from upper management, the plan worked.

We are aware ~~of the fact~~ that sales of new products soar when pushed by social networking.

Except for ~~the instance of~~ Toyota, Japanese imports sagged.

She chose a career in a field that was analytical ~~in nature~~. [OR: She chose a career in an analytical field.]

Student writing in that class is excellent ~~in quality~~.

---

### OFFICE INSIDER

*"Clutter is the disease of American writing. We are a society strangling in unnecessary words, circular constructions, pompous frills, and meaningless jargon."*

—William Zinsser, esteemed writer, editor, literary critic, teacher, and author of the classic *On Writing Well*

Chapter 4: Revising Business Messages
93

Also avoid saying the obvious. In the following examples, notice how many unnecessary words we can omit through revision:

> ~~When it arrived,~~ I cashed your check immediately. (Announcing the check's arrival is unnecessary. That fact is assumed in its cashing.)
>
> As consumers learn more about ingredients ~~and as they become more knowledgeable~~, they are demanding fresher foods. (Avoid repeating information.)

Look carefully at clauses beginning with *that*, *which*, and *who*. They can often be shortened without loss of clarity. Search for phrases such as *it appears that*. These phrases often can be reduced to a single adjective or adverb such as *apparently*.

> Changing the name of a ∧*successful* company ~~that is successful~~ is always risky.
>
> All employees ~~who are among those~~ completing the course will be reimbursed.
>
> Our ∧*final* proposal, ~~which was~~ slightly altered ~~in its final form~~, was approved.
>
> We plan to schedule ∧*weekly* meetings ~~on a weekly basis~~.

## 4-1b Writing Concisely for Microblogging and Posting on Social Media Networks

Concise expression is especially important in microblogging. As its name suggests, *microblogging* consists of short messages exchanged on social media networks such as Twitter, Facebook, and Tumblr. Many businesses are eagerly joining these microblogging networks to hear what's being said about them and their products. When they hear complaints, they can respond immediately and often solve customer problems. Companies are also using microblogging to make announcements, promote goodwill, and sell their products.

Microblogging may be public or private. Twitter and similar social networks are predominantly public channels with messages broadcast externally to the world. Twitter limits each post ("tweet") to 140 characters, including spaces, punctuation, and links. Recognizing the usefulness of microblogging but desiring more confidentiality and security, some companies prefer to keep their messaging internal. IBM, for example, employs Blue Twit, a tool that enables IBMers to share real-time news and get help from colleagues without going outside the organization. BlueTwit extends the length of messages to 400 characters.

Regardless of the microblogging network, conciseness is critical. Your messages must be short—without straying too far from conventional spelling, grammar, and punctuation. Sound difficult? It is, but it can be done, as shown in the following 140-character examples of workplace tweets:

**Sample Response to Customer Complaint**
*@complainer Our manual can be confusing about that problem. Call me at 800-123-4567 or see http://bit.ly/xx for easy fix. Thanks, Henry*[2]

**Zappos CEO Announces Meeting**
*Livestreaming the Zappos Family quarterly all hands meeting 1-5 PM Pacific today! Tune in: http://on.fb.me/allhandslive*[3]

**Southwest Airlines Explains**
*Southwest Airlines responds to loss of pressurization event on flight from PHX to SMF [with a link to a Southwest statement about the event]*[4]

**Starbucks Thanks Customers**
*Throughout April, you contributed 231,000+ hours of community service in 34 countries across five continents. Thank You! #monthofservice*[5]

Chapter 4: Revising Business Messages

When microblogging, (a) include only main ideas, (b) choose descriptive but short words, (c) personalize your message if possible, and (d) be prepared to write several versions striving for conciseness, clarity, and, yes, even correctness. It's like playing a game: can you get your message across in only 140 characters?

## 4-2 Making Your Message Clear

A major revision task involves assessing the clarity of your message. A clear message is one that is immediately understood. Employees, customers, and investors increasingly want to be addressed in a clear and genuine way. Fuzzy, long-winded, and unclear writing prevents comprehension. Readers understand better when information is presented clearly and concisely, as a Dartmouth study about drug facts illustrates in Figure 4.2. Three techniques can improve the clarity of your writing: applying the KISS formula (Keep It Short and Simple), dumping trite business phrases, and avoiding clichés and slang.

### 4-2a Keep It Short and Simple

To achieve clarity, resist the urge to show off or be fancy. Remember that your goal is not to impress a reader. As a business writer, your goal is to *express*, not *impress*. One way to achieve clear writing is to apply the familiar KISS formula. Use active-voice sentences that avoid indirect, pompous language.

| DON'T — WORDY AND UNCLEAR | DO — IMPROVED |
|---|---|
| ✗ Employees have not been made sufficiently aware of the potentially adverse consequences regarding the use of these perilous chemicals. | ✓ Warn your employees about these dangerous chemicals. |
| ✗ In regard to the matter of obtaining optimal results, it is essential that employees be given the implements that are necessary for jobs to be completed satisfactorily. | ✓ To get the best results, give employees the tools they need to do the job. |

Figure **4.2** Conciseness Aids Clarity in Understanding Drug Facts

**72%** — People who correctly quantified a heart drug's benefits after reading concise fact box.

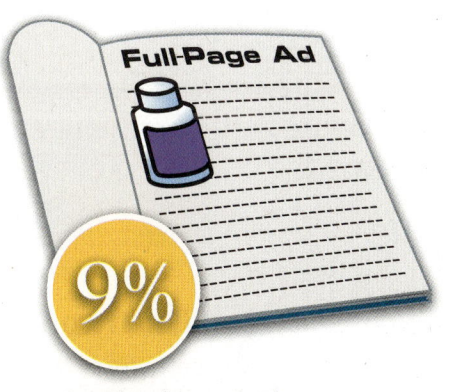

**9%** — People who correctly quantified a heart drug's benefits after reading the company's long ad.

---

### OFFICE INSIDER

"Good writing is brevity, and brevity is marketing. Want to lose me as a customer, forever, guaranteed? Have a grammar error on any form of outward communication."

—Peter Shankman, founder of Geek Factory, blogger, angel investor, author

### LEARNING OBJECTIVE 2

Improve clarity in business messages by keeping the ideas simple, dumping trite business phrases, dropping clichés, avoiding slang and buzzwords, rescuing buried verbs, controlling exuberance, and choosing precise words.

---

Consumers understand drug effects better when the information is presented concisely and clearly. A Dartmouth University study revealed that concise fact boxes were superior to the tiny-type, full-page DTC (direct-to-consumer) advertisements that drug manufacturers usually publish.

Chapter 4: Revising Business Messages

## OFFICE INSIDER

"I took a two-day class in business writing that taught me how to write direct sentences and to avoid extra words. Simplicity makes ideas powerful. Want examples? Read anything by Steve Jobs or Warren Buffet."

—Scott Adams, Dilbert cartoonist

### 4-2b Dumping Trite Business Phrases

To sound "businesslike," some business writers repeat the same stale expressions that others have used over the years. Your writing will sound fresher and more vigorous if you eliminate these trite phrases or find more original ways to convey the idea.

| DON'T — TRITE PHRASE | DO ✓ — IMPROVED |
| --- | --- |
| ✗ as per your request | ✓ as you request |
| ✗ pursuant to your request | ✓ at your request |
| ✗ enclosed please find | ✓ enclosed is |
| ✗ every effort will be made | ✓ we'll try |
| ✗ in accordance with your wishes | ✓ as you wish |
| ✗ in receipt of | ✓ have received |
| ✗ please do not hesitate to | ✓ please |
| ✗ respond forthwith | ✓ respond immediately |
| ✗ thank you in advance | ✓ thank you |
| ✗ under separate cover | ✓ separately |
| ✗ with reference to | ✓ about |

### 4-2c Dropping Clichés

Clichés are expressions that have become exhausted by overuse. Many cannot be explained, especially to those who are new to our culture. Clichés lack not only freshness but also clarity. Instead of repeating clichés such as the following, try to find another way to say what you mean.

| | |
| --- | --- |
| below the belt | last but not least |
| better than new | make a bundle |
| beyond a shadow of a doubt | pass with flying colors |
| easier said than done | quick as a flash |
| exception to the rule | shoot from the hip |
| fill the bill | step up to the plate |
| first and foremost | think outside the box |
| good to go | true to form |

### 4-2d Avoiding Slang and Buzzwords

Slang is composed of informal words with arbitrary and extravagantly changed meanings. Slang words quickly go out of fashion because they are no longer appealing when everyone begins to understand them. If you want to sound professional, avoid expressions such as *snarky, lousy, blowing the budget, bombed, getting burned*, and other slangy expressions.

Chapter 4: Revising Business Messages

Buzzwords are technical expressions that have become fashionable and often are meant to impress rather than express. Business buzzwords include empty terms such as *optimize, incentivize, innovative, leveraging, right-size,* and *paradigm shift*. Countless businesses today use vague rhetoric in the form of phrases such as *cost effective, positioned to perform, solutions-oriented,* and *value-added services with end-to-end fulfillment*.

Consider the following statement of a government official who had been asked why his department was dropping a proposal to lease offshore oil lands: *The Administration has an awful lot of other things in the pipeline, and this has more wiggle room so they just moved it down the totem pole*. He added, however, that the proposal might be offered again since *there is no pulling back because of hot-potato factors*. What exactly does this mean?

## 4-2e Rescuing Buried Verbs

Buried verbs are those that are needlessly converted to wordy noun expressions. Verbs such as *acquire, establish,* and *develop* are made into nouns such as *acquisition, establishment,* and *development*. Such nouns often end in *-tion, -ment,* and *-ance*. Sometimes called *zombie nouns* because they cannibalize and suck the life out of active verbs,[6] these nouns increase sentence length, slow the reader, and muddy the thought. Notice how you can make your writing cleaner and more forceful by avoiding buried verbs and zombie nouns:

| DON'T BURIED VERBS | DO UNBURIED VERBS |
|---|---|
| ✗ conduct a discussion of | ✓ discuss |
| ✗ create a reduction in | ✓ reduce |
| ✗ engage in the preparation of | ✓ prepare |
| ✗ give consideration to | ✓ consider |
| ✗ make an assumption of | ✓ assume |
| ✗ make a discovery of | ✓ discover |
| ✗ perform an analysis of | ✓ analyze |
| ✗ reach a conclusion that | ✓ conclude |
| ✗ take action on | ✓ act |

## 4-2f Controlling Exuberance

Occasionally, we show our exuberance with words such as *very, definitely, quite, completely, extremely, really, actually,* and *totally*. These intensifiers can emphasize and strengthen your meaning. Overuse, however, makes your writing sound unbusinesslike. Control your enthusiasm and guard against excessive use.

| DON'T EXCESSIVE EXUBERANCE | DO BUSINESSLIKE |
|---|---|
| ✗ The manufacturer was *extremely* upset to learn that its smartphones were *definitely* being counterfeited. | ✓ The manufacturer was upset to learn that its smartphones were being counterfeited. |
| ✗ We *totally* agree that we *actually* did not give his proposal a *very* fair trial. | ✓ We agree that we did not give his proposal a fair trial. |

## OFFICE INSIDER

"If you could taste words, most corporate websites, brochures, and sales materials would remind you of stale, soggy rice cakes: nearly calorie free, devoid of nutrition, and completely unsatisfying. . . . Unfortunately, years of language dilution by lawyers, marketers, executives, and HR departments have turned the powerful, descriptive sentence into an empty vessel optimized for buzzwords, jargon, and vapid expressions."

—Jason Fried, software developer and cofounder of the company 37signals

## Workplace in Focus

Ever heard of Internet content that is "snackable"? Do you prefer Web sites that deliver an "immersive experience"? Have you seen the latest pet photos that have "gone viral" because of their "clickability"? Do you know what any of this means? You do if you work in the world of digital marketing, according to technology blog Mashable, which included these words in a list of the most overused buzzwords in the digital media profession. While people use buzzwords to sound smart or trendy, such words are inappropriate in most—but not all—business settings. In what situations should communicators avoid using buzzwords and slang?[7]

©iStockphoto.com/RapidEye

### 4-2g Choosing Clear, Precise Words

As you revise, make sure your words are precise so that the audience knows exactly what you mean. Clear writing creates meaningful images in the mind of the reader. Such writing is sparked by specific verbs, concrete nouns, and vivid adjectives. Foggy messages are marked by sloppy references that may require additional inquiries to clarify their meaning.

| DON'T — LESS PRECISE | DO ✓ — MORE PRECISE |
|---|---|
| ✗ She requested that everyone help out. | ✓ Our manager begged each team member to volunteer. |
| ✗ They will consider the problem soon. | ✓ Our steering committee will consider the recruitment problem on May 15. |
| ✗ We received many responses. | ✓ The Sales Division received 28 job applications. |
| ✗ Someone called about the meeting. | ✓ Russell Vitello called about the June 12 sales meeting |

**LEARNING OBJECTIVE 3**
Enhance readability by understanding document design including the use of white space, margins, typefaces, fonts, numbered and bulleted lists, and headings.

## 4-3 Enhancing Readability Through Document Design

Well-designed documents improve your messages in two important ways. First, they enhance readability and comprehension. Second, they make readers think you are a well-organized and intelligent person. In the revision process, you have a chance to adjust formatting and make other changes so that readers grasp your main points quickly. Significant design techniques to improve readability include the appropriate use of white space, margins, typefaces, fonts, numbered and bulleted lists, and headings for visual impact.

### 4-3a Employing White Space

Empty space on a page is called *white space*. A page crammed full of text or graphics appears busy, cluttered, and unreadable. To increase white space, use headings, bulleted or numbered lists, and effective margins. Remember that short sentences (20 or fewer words) and short paragraphs (eight or fewer printed lines) improve readability and comprehension. As you revise, think about shortening long sentences. Consider breaking up long paragraphs into shorter chunks.

### 4-3b Understanding Margins and Text Alignment

Margins determine the white space on the left, right, top, and bottom of a block of type. They define the reading area and provide important visual relief. Business letters and memos usually have side margins of 1 to 1.5 inches.

Your word processing program probably offers four forms of margin alignment: (a) lines align only at the left, (b) lines align only at the right, (c) lines align at both left and right (*justified*), and (d) lines are centered. Nearly all text in Western cultures is aligned at the left and reads from left to right. The right margin may be either *justified* or *ragged right*. The text in books, magazines, and other long works is often justified on the left and right for a formal appearance.

Justified text, however, may require more attention to word spacing and hyphenation to avoid awkward empty spaces or "rivers" of spaces running through a document. When right margins are *ragged*—that is, without alignment or justification—they provide more white space and improve readability. Therefore, you are best served by using left-justified text and ragged-right margins without justification. Centered text is appropriate for headings and short invitations but not for complete messages.

### 4-3c Choosing Appropriate Typefaces

Business writers today may choose from a number of typefaces on their word processors. A typeface defines the shape of text characters. A wide range of typefaces, as shown in Figure 4.3, is available for various purposes. Some are decorative and useful for special purposes. For most business messages, however, you should choose from *serif* or *sans serif* categories.

Figure 4.3 Typefaces With Different Personalities for Different Purposes

| All-Purpose Sans Serif | Traditional Serif | Happy, Creative Script/Funny | Assertive, Bold Modern Display | Plain Monospaced |
|---|---|---|---|---|
| Arial | Century | Brush Script | Britannic Bold | Courier |
| Calibri | Garamond | Comic Sans | Broadway | Letter Gothic |
| Helvetica | Georgia | Gigi | Elephant | Monaco |
| Tahoma | Goudy | Jokerman | Impact | Prestige Elite |
| Univers | Palatino | Lucinda | Bauhaus 93 | |
| Verdana | Times New Roman | Kristen | SHOWCARD | |

**Serif** typefaces have small features at the ends of strokes. The most common serif typeface is Times New Roman. Other popular serif typefaces are Century, Georgia, and Palatino. Serif typefaces suggest tradition, maturity, and formality. They are frequently used for body text in business messages and longer documents. Because books, newspapers, and magazines favor serif typefaces, readers are familiar with them.

**Sans serif** typefaces include Arial, Calibri, Gothic, Tahoma, Helvetica, and Univers. These clean characters are widely used for headings, signs, and material that does not require continuous reading. Web designers often prefer sans serif typefaces for simple, pure pages. For longer documents, however, sans serif typefaces may seem colder and less appealing than familiar serif typefaces.

For less formal messages or special decorative effects, you might choose one of the "happy" fonts such as Comic Sans or a bold typeface such as Impact. You can simulate handwriting with a script typeface. Despite the wonderful possibilities available on your word processor, don't get carried away with fancy typefaces. All-purpose sans serif and traditional serif typefaces are most appropriate for your business messages. Generally, use no more than two typefaces within one document.

### 4-3d Capitalizing on Type Fonts and Sizes

*Font* refers to a specific style within a typeface family. Here are examples of font styles in the Verdana font family:

| | |
|---|---|
| CAPITALIZATION | underline |
| SMALL CAPS | Outline |
| **boldface** | Shadow |
| *italics* | Emboss |

Font styles are a mechanical means of adding emphasis to your words. ALL CAPS, SMALL CAPS, and **bold** are useful for headings, subheadings, and single words or short phrases in the text. ALL CAPS, HOWEVER, SHOULD **NEVER** BE USED FOR LONG STRETCHES OF TEXT BECAUSE ALL THE LETTERS ARE THE SAME HEIGHT. This makes it difficult for readers to differentiate words. In addition, excessive use of all caps feels like shouting and irritates readers.

**Boldface**, *italics*, and underlining are effective for calling attention to important points and terms. Be cautious, however, when using fancy or an excessive number of font styles. Don't use them if they will confuse, annoy, or delay readers.

As you revise, think about type size. Readers are generally most comfortable with 10- to 12-point type for body text. Smaller type enables you to fit more words into a space. Tiny type, however, makes text look dense and unappealing. Slightly larger type makes material more readable. Overly large type (14 points or more) looks amateurish and out of place for body text in business messages. Larger type, however, is appropriate for headings.

### 4-3e Numbering and Bulleting Lists for Quick Comprehension

One of the best ways to ensure rapid comprehension of ideas is through the use of numbered or bulleted lists. Lists provide high "skim value." This means that readers can browse quickly and grasp main ideas. By breaking up complex information into smaller chunks, lists improve readability, understanding, and retention. They also force the writer to organize ideas and write efficiently.

When revising, look for ideas that could be converted to lists, and follow these techniques to make your lists look professional:

- **Numbered lists:** Use for items that represent a sequence or reflect a numbering system.
- **Bulleted lists:** Use to highlight items that don't necessarily show a chronology.
- **Capitalization:** Capitalize the initial word of each line.
- **Punctuation:** Add end punctuation only if the listed items are complete sentences.
- **Parallelism:** Make all the lines consistent; for example, start each with a verb.

In the following examples, notice that the list on the left presents a sequence of steps with numbers. The bulleted list does not show a sequence of ideas; therefore, bullets are appropriate. Also notice the parallelism in each example. In the numbered list, each item begins with a verb. In the bulleted list, each item follows an adjective/noun sequence. Business readers appreciate lists because they focus attention. Be careful, however, not to use so many that your messages look like grocery lists.

### Numbered List

Our recruiters follow these steps when hiring applicants:

1. Examine the application.
2. Interview the applicant.
3. Check the applicant's references.

### Bulleted List

To attract upscale customers, we feature the following:

- Quality fashions
- Personalized service
- Generous return policy

## OFFICE INSIDER

*An advocate for plain English, Arthur Levitt champions readability in investor documents. He advocates using the active voice, familiar words, and graphic techniques such as boldface, headings, and lists. However, he has been only partially successful, he complains, because such efforts "get tugged into the ditch by the irresistible pull of legal jargon" with documents "buried in an avalanche of impenetrable verbiage."*

—Arthur Levitt, former chair, U.S. Securities and Exchange Commission

### 4-3f Adding Headings for Visual Impact

Headings are an effective tool for highlighting information and improving readability. They encourage the writer to group similar material together. Headings help the reader separate major ideas from details. They enable a busy reader to skim familiar or less important information. They also provide a quick preview or review. Headings appear most often in reports, which you will study in greater detail in Chapters 9 and 10. However, headings can also improve readability in e-mails, memos, and letters. In the following example, notice how *category headings* highlight the listings:

Our company focuses on the following areas in the employment process:

- **Attracting applicants.** We advertise for qualified applicants, and we also encourage current employees to recommend good people.
- **Interviewing applicants.** Our specialized interviews include simulated customer encounters as well as scrutiny by supervisors.
- **Checking references.** We investigate every applicant thoroughly. We contact former employers and all listed references.

In Figure 4.4 the writer converts a dense, unappealing e-mail message into an easier-to-read version by applying professional document design. Notice that the all-caps font shown earlier makes its meaning difficult to decipher. Justified margins and lack of white space further reduce readability. In the revised version, the writer changed the all-caps font to upper- and lowercase and also used ragged-right margins to enhance visual appeal. One of the best document design techniques in this message is the use of headings and bullets to help the reader see

Chapter 4: Revising Business Messages

# Figure 4.4 Document Design Improves Readability

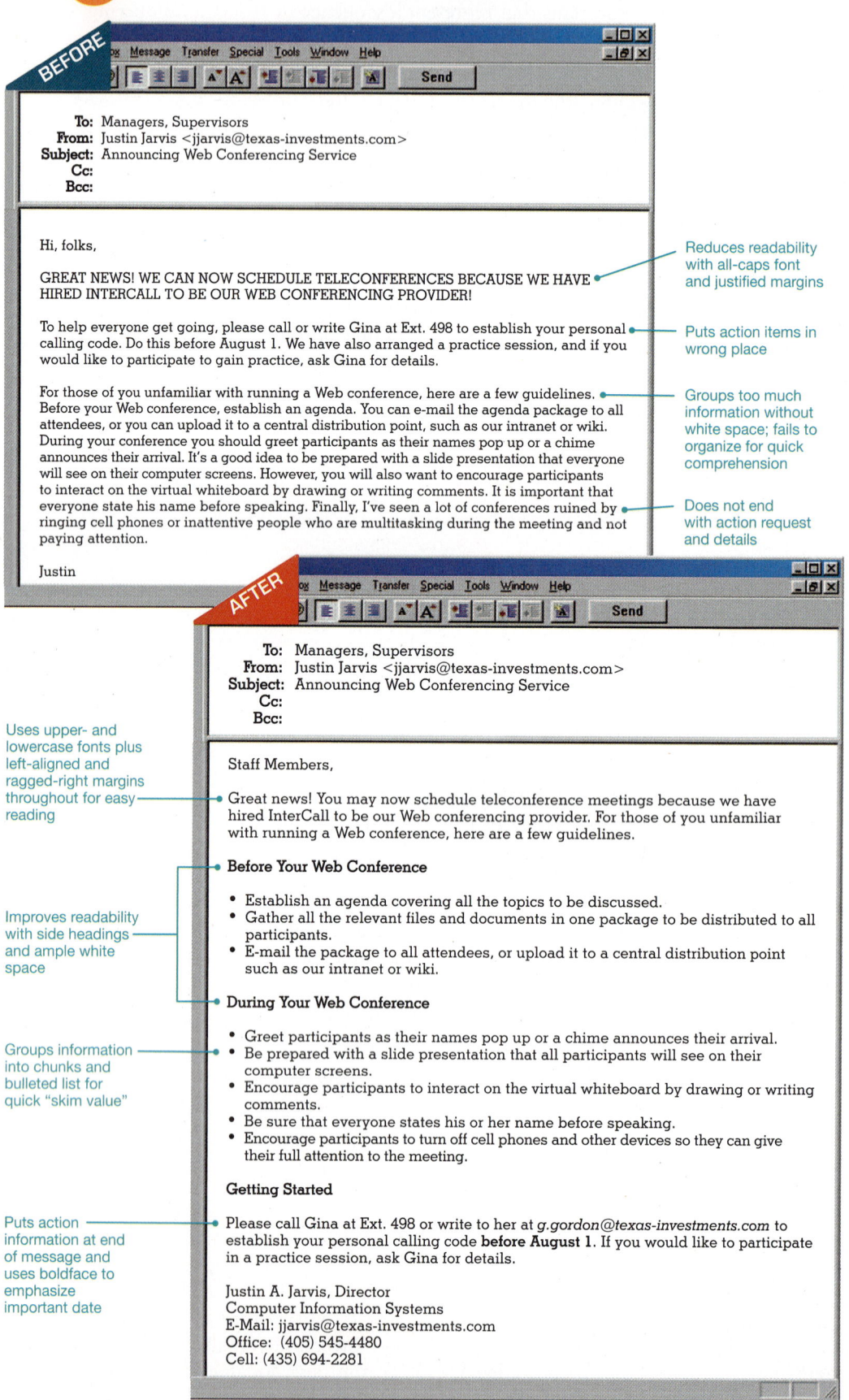

## BEFORE

**To:** Managers, Supervisors
**From:** Justin Jarvis <jjarvis@texas-investments.com>
**Subject:** Announcing Web Conferencing Service
**Cc:**
**Bcc:**

Hi, folks,

GREAT NEWS! WE CAN NOW SCHEDULE TELECONFERENCES BECAUSE WE HAVE HIRED INTERCALL TO BE OUR WEB CONFERENCING PROVIDER!

To help everyone get going, please call or write Gina at Ext. 498 to establish your personal calling code. Do this before August 1. We have also arranged a practice session, and if you would like to participate to gain practice, ask Gina for details.

For those of you unfamiliar with running a Web conference, here are a few guidelines. Before your Web conference, establish an agenda. You can e-mail the agenda package to all attendees, or you can upload it to a central distribution point, such as our intranet or wiki. During your conference you should greet participants as their names pop up or a chime announces their arrival. It's a good idea to be prepared with a slide presentation that everyone will see on their computer screens. However, you will also want to encourage participants to interact on the virtual whiteboard by drawing or writing comments. It is important that everyone state his name before speaking. Finally, I've seen a lot of conferences ruined by ringing cell phones or inattentive people who are multitasking during the meeting and not paying attention.

Justin

- Reduces readability with all-caps font and justified margins
- Puts action items in wrong place
- Groups too much information without white space; fails to organize for quick comprehension
- Does not end with action request and details

## AFTER

**To:** Managers, Supervisors
**From:** Justin Jarvis <jjarvis@texas-investments.com>
**Subject:** Announcing Web Conferencing Service
**Cc:**
**Bcc:**

Staff Members,

Great news! You may now schedule teleconference meetings because we have hired InterCall to be our Web conferencing provider. For those of you unfamiliar with running a Web conference, here are a few guidelines.

**Before Your Web Conference**

- Establish an agenda covering all the topics to be discussed.
- Gather all the relevant files and documents in one package to be distributed to all participants.
- E-mail the package to all attendees, or upload it to a central distribution point such as our intranet or wiki.

**During Your Web Conference**

- Greet participants as their names pop up or a chime announces their arrival.
- Be prepared with a slide presentation that all participants will see on their computer screens.
- Encourage participants to interact on the virtual whiteboard by drawing or writing comments.
- Be sure that everyone states his or her name before speaking.
- Encourage participants to turn off cell phones and other devices so they can give their full attention to the meeting.

**Getting Started**

Please call Gina at Ext. 498 or write to her at *g.gordon@texas-investments.com* to establish your personal calling code **before August 1**. If you would like to participate in a practice session, ask Gina for details.

Justin A. Jarvis, Director
Computer Information Systems
E-Mail: jjarvis@texas-investments.com
Office: (405) 545-4480
Cell: (435) 694-2281

- Uses upper- and lowercase fonts plus left-aligned and ragged-right margins throughout for easy reading
- Improves readability with side headings and ample white space
- Groups information into chunks and bulleted list for quick "skim value"
- Puts action information at end of message and uses boldface to emphasize important date

© 2016 Cengage Learning®

Chapter 4: Revising Business Messages

chunks of information in similar groups. All of these improvements are made in the revision process. You can make any message more readable by applying the document design techniques presented here.

## 4-4 Proofreading to Catch Errors

**LEARNING OBJECTIVE 4**
Recognize proofreading problem areas, and apply effective techniques to catch mistakes in both routine and complex documents.

Alas, none of us is perfect, and even the best writers sometimes make mistakes. The problem, however, is not making the mistakes; the real problem is not finding and correcting them. Documents with errors affect your credibility and the success of your organization, as illustrated in Figure 4.5.

Once the message is in its final form, it's time to proofread. Don't proofread earlier because you may waste time checking items that eventually will be changed or omitted. Important messages—such as those you send to management or to customers or turn in to instructors for grades—deserve careful revision and proofreading. When you finish a first draft, plan for a cooling-off period. Put the document aside and return to it after a break, preferably after 24 hours or longer. Proofreading is especially difficult because most of us read what we thought we wrote. That's why it's important to look for specific problem areas.

Figure 4.5 Why Proofread?

**WHY PROOFREAD? IN BUSINESS, ACCURACY MATTERS**

A survey of business professionals revealed the following:

- **100%** said that writing errors influenced their opinions about a business.
- **57%** will stop considering a company if its print brochure has one writing error.
- **77%** have eliminated a prospective company from consideration in part because of writing errors.
- **75%** thought misspelled words were inexcusable.
- **30%** of Web visitors will leave if a website contains writing errors.

© Goodluz/Shutterstock.com; © 2016 Cengage Learning®

### 4-4a What to Watch for in Proofreading

Careful proofreaders check for problems in the following areas:

- **Spelling.** Now is the time to consult the dictionary. Is *recommend* spelled with one or two *c*'s? Do you mean *affect* or *effect*? Use your computer spell-checker, but don't rely on it totally.
- **Grammar.** Locate sentence subjects; do their verbs agree with them? Do pronouns agree with their antecedents? Review the principles in the Grammar/Mechanics Handbook if necessary. Use your computer's grammar-checker, but be suspicious. It's not always correct.
- **Punctuation.** Make sure that introductory clauses are followed by commas. In compound sentences put commas before coordinating conjunctions *(and, or, but, nor)*. Double-check your use of semicolons and colons.
- **Names and numbers.** Compare all names and numbers with their sources because inaccuracies are not always visible. Especially verify the spelling of the names of individuals receiving the message. Most of us immediately dislike someone who misspells our name.
- **Format.** Be sure that your document looks balanced on the page. Compare its parts and format with those of standard documents shown in Appendix B. If you indent paragraphs, be certain that all are indented and that their spacing is consistent.

### 4-4b How to Proofread Routine Documents

Most routine documents require a light proofreading. If you read on screen, use the down arrow to reveal one line at a time. This focuses your attention at the bottom of the screen. A safer proofreading method, however, is reading from a printed copy. Regardless of which method you use, look for typos and misspellings. Search for easily confused words, such as *to* for *too* and *then* for *than*. Read for missing words and inconsistencies. For handwritten or printed messages, use standard proofreading marks, shown briefly in Figure 4.6 or completely in Appendix A. For digital documents and collaborative projects, use the simple word processing tools also shown in Figure 4.1 or use the **Comment** and **Track Changes** functions discussed in the Communication Workshop at the end of this chapter.

### 4-4c How to Proofread Complex Documents

Long, complex, or important documents demand careful proofreading. Apply the previous suggestions but also add the following techniques:

- Print a copy, preferably double-spaced, and set it aside for at least a day. You will be more alert after a breather.
- Allow adequate time to proofread carefully. A common excuse for sloppy proofreading is lack of time.
- Be prepared to find errors. One student confessed, "I can find other people's errors, but I can't seem to locate my own." Psychologically, we don't expect to find errors, and we don't want to find them. You can overcome this obstacle by anticipating errors and congratulating, not criticizing, yourself each time you find one.
- Read the message at least twice—once for word meanings and once for grammar and mechanics. For very long documents (book chapters and long articles or reports), read a third time to verify consistency in formatting.
- Reduce your reading speed. Concentrate on individual words rather than ideas.

### Figure 4.6 Most Common Proofreading Marks

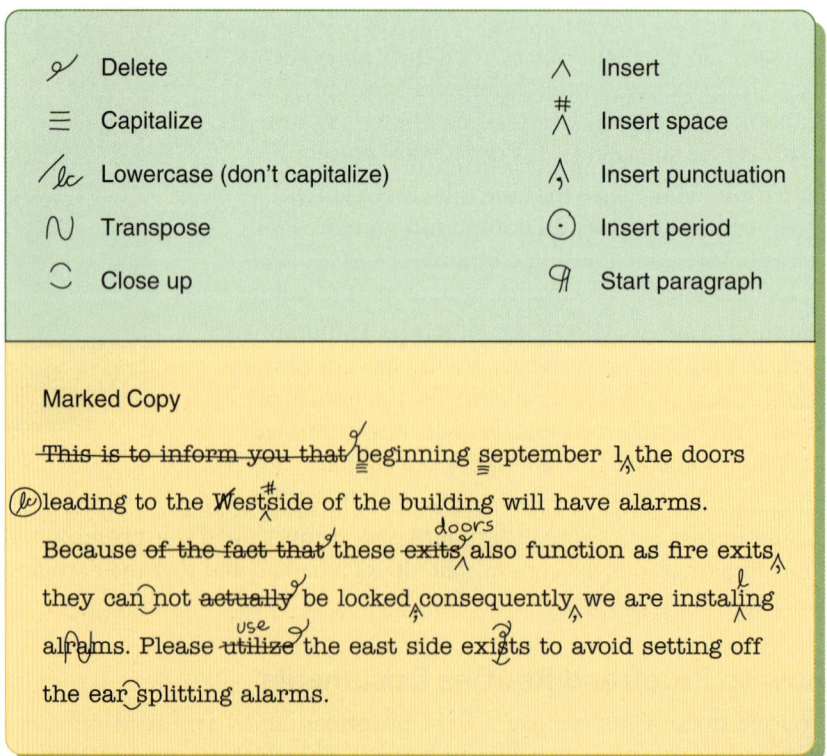

| Symbol | Meaning | Symbol | Meaning |
|---|---|---|---|
| ℓ | Delete | ∧ | Insert |
| ≡ | Capitalize | # | Insert space |
| /lc | Lowercase (don't capitalize) | ∧ | Insert punctuation |
| ∩ | Transpose | ⊙ | Insert period |
| ◡ | Close up | ¶ | Start paragraph |

**Marked Copy**

This is to inform you that beginning september 1, the doors leading to the West side of the building will have alarms. Because of the fact that these exits also function as fire exits, they cannot actually be locked, consequently, we are installing alarms. Please utilize the east side exits to avoid setting off the ear splitting alarms.

- For documents that must be perfect, enlist a proofreading buddy. Have someone read the message aloud, spelling names and difficult words, noting capitalization, and reading punctuation.
- Use the standard proofreading marks shown in Appendix A to indicate changes.

Many of us struggle with proofreading our own writing because we are seeing the same information over and over. We tend to see what we expect to see as our eyes race over the words without looking at each one carefully. We tend to know what is coming next and glide over it. To change the appearance of what you are reading, you might print it on a different colored paper or change the font. If you are proofing on screen, enlarge the page view or change the background color of the screen.

## 4-5 Evaluating the Effectiveness of Your Message

**LEARNING OBJECTIVE 5**
Evaluate a message to judge its effectiveness.

As you apply finishing touches, take a moment to evaluate your writing. Remember that everything you write, whether for yourself or someone else, takes the place of a personal appearance. If you were meeting in person, you would be certain to dress appropriately and professionally. The same standard applies to your writing. Evaluate what you have written to be sure that it attracts the reader's attention. Is it polished and clear enough to convince the reader that you are worth listening to? How successful will this message be? Does it say what you want it to? Will it achieve its purpose? How will you know whether it succeeds?

The best way to judge the success of your communication is through feedback. For this reason you should encourage the receiver to respond to your message. This feedback will tell you how to modify future efforts to improve your communication technique.

Your instructor will also be evaluating some of your writing. Although any criticism is painful, try not to be defensive. Look on these comments as valuable advice tailored to your specific writing weaknesses—and strengths. Many businesses today spend thousands of dollars bringing in communication consultants to improve employee writing skills. You are getting the same training in this course. Take advantage of this chance—one of the few you may have—to improve your skills. The best way to improve your skills, of course, is through instruction, practice, and evaluation.

In this class you have all three elements: instruction in the writing process, practice materials, and someone to guide you and evaluate your efforts. Those three elements are the reasons this book and this course may be the most valuable in your entire curriculum. Because it's almost impossible to improve your communication skills alone, take advantage of this opportunity.

# SUMMARY OF LEARNING OBJECTIVES

**4-1** Complete business messages by revising for conciseness, which includes eliminating flabby expressions, long lead-ins, *there is/are* and *it is/was* fillers, redundancies, and empty words, as well as condensing for microblogging.
- Revise for conciseness by eliminating flabby expressions (*as a general rule, at a later date, at this point in time*).
- Exclude opening fillers (*there is, there are*), redundancies (*basic essentials*), and empty words (*in the case of, the fact that*).
- In microblogging messages, include only main ideas, choose descriptive but short words, personalize your message if possible, and be prepared to write several versions striving for conciseness, clarity, and correctness.

Chapter 4: Revising Business Messages

**4-2 Improve clarity in business messages by keeping the ideas simple, dumping trite business phrases, dropping clichés, avoiding slang and buzzwords, rescuing buried verbs, controlling exuberance, and choosing precise words.**

- To be sure your messages are clear, apply the KISS formula: Keep It Short and Simple.
- Avoid foggy, indirect, and pompous language.
- Do not include trite business phrases (*as per your request, enclosed please find, pursuant to your request*), clichés (*better than new, beyond a shadow of a doubt, easier said than done*), slang (*snarky, lousy, bombed*), and buzzwords (*optimize, paradigm shift, incentivize*).
- Avoid burying nouns (*to conduct an investigation* rather than *to investigate*, *to perform an analysis* rather than *to analyze*).
- Don't overuse intensifiers that show exuberance (*totally, actually, very, definitely*) but sound unbusinesslike.
- Choose precise words (*the report was well-organized* rather than *the report was great*).

**4-3 Enhance readability by understanding document design including the use of white space, margins, typefaces, fonts, numbered and bulleted lists, and headings.**

- Enhance readability and comprehension by using ample white space, appropriate side margins, and ragged-right (not justified) margins.
- Use serif typefaces (fonts with small features at the ends of strokes, such as Times New Roman, Century, and Palatino) for body text; use sans serif typefaces (clean fonts without small features, such as Arial, Helvetica, and Tahoma) for headings and signs.
- Choose appropriate font styles and sizes for business messages.
- Provide high "skim value" with numbered and bulleted lists.
- Include headings to add visual impact and aid readability in business messages as well as in reports.

**4-4 Recognize proofreading problem areas, and apply effective techniques to catch mistakes in both routine and complex documents.**

- In proofreading be especially alert to spelling, grammar, punctuation, names, numbers, and document format.
- Proofread routine documents immediately after completion by reading line by line on the computer screen or, better yet, from a printed draft.
- Proofread more complex documents after a breather.
- Allow adequate time, reduce your reading speed, and read the document at least three times—for word meanings, for grammar and mechanics, and for formatting.

**4-5 Evaluate a message to judge its effectiveness.**

- Encourage feedback from the receiver so that you can determine whether your communication achieved its goal.
- Welcome any advice from your instructor on how to improve your writing skills.

# CHAPTER REVIEW

1. What's involved in the revision process? Is revision still necessary in a digital age when workplace messages fly back and forth in split seconds? (Obj. 1)

2. What's wrong with a message that begins, *I am writing this announcement to let everyone know that* . . . ? (Obj. 1)

3. What is microblogging, and why is conciseness especially important in microblogging messages and social media posts? (Obj. 1)

4. What's wrong with familiar business phrases such as *as per your request* and *enclosed please find*? (Obj. 2)

5. Why should writers avoid expressions such as *first and foremost* and *think outside the box*? (Obj. 2)

6. What are buried verbs and zombie nouns? Give an original example of each. Why should they be avoided? (Obj. 2)

7. How do bulleted and numbered lists improve readability? (Obj. 3)

8. In proofreading, why is it difficult for writers to find their own errors? How could they overcome this barrier? (Obj. 4)

9. What are five items to check in proofreading? Be ready to discuss methods you find useful in spotting these errors. (Obj. 4)

10. How can you overcome defensiveness when your writing is criticized constructively? (Obj. 5)

# CRITICAL THINKING

11. In this digital age of rapid communication, how can you justify the time it takes to stop and revise a message? (Objs. 1–5)

12. Assume you have started a new job in which you respond to customers by using boilerplate (previously constructed) paragraphs. Some of them contain clichés such as *pursuant to your request* and *in accordance with your wishes*. Other paragraphs are wordy and violate the principle of using concise and clear writing that you have learned. What should you do? (Obj. 2)

13. Because business writing should have high "skim value," why not write everything in bulleted lists? (Obj. 3)

14. Conciseness is valued in business. However, can messages be too short? (Obj. 1)

15. What advice would you give in this ethical dilemma? Brittani is serving as interim editor of the company newsletter. She receives an article written by the company president describing, in abstract and pompous language, the company's goals for the coming year. Brittani thinks the article will need considerable revising to make it readable. Attached to the president's article are complimentary comments by two of the company vice presidents. What action should Brittani take?

# WRITING IMPROVEMENT EXERCISES

## Flabby Expressions (Obj. 1)

**YOUR TASK.** Revise the following sentences to eliminate flabby expressions.

16. We are sending a revised proposal at this point in time due to the fact that building costs have jumped at a considerable rate.

17. In the normal course of events, we would seek additional funding; however, in view of the fact that rates have increased, we cannot.

18. In very few cases has it been advisable for us to borrow money for a period of 90 or fewer days.

19. Inasmuch as our Web advertising income is increasing in a gradual manner, we might seek a loan in the amount of $50,000.

20. Despite the fact that we have had no response to our bid, we are still available in the event that you wish to proceed with your building project.

## Long Lead-Ins (Obj. 1)

**YOUR TASK.** Revise the following to eliminate long lead-ins.

21. This is an announcement to tell you that all computer passwords must be changed every six months for security purposes.

22. We are sending this memo to notify everyone that anyone who wants to apply for telecommuting may submit an application immediately.

23. I am writing this letter to inform you that your new account executive is Edward Ho.

24. This is to warn you that cyber criminals use sophisticated tools to decipher passwords rapidly.

25. This message is to let you know that social media services can position your company at the forefront of online marketing opportunities.

## *There is/are* and *It is/was* Fillers (Obj. 1)

**YOUR TASK.** Revise the following to avoid unnecessary *there is/are* and *it is/was* fillers.

26. There is a password-checker that is now available that can automatically evaluate the strength of your password.

27. It is careless or uninformed individuals who are the most vulnerable to computer hackers.

28. There are computers in Internet cafes, at conferences, and in airport lounges that should be considered unsafe for any personal use.

29. A computer specialist told us that there are keystroke-logging devices that gather information typed on a computer, including passwords.

30. If there are any questions that you have about computer safety, please call us.

## Redundancies (Obj. 1)

**YOUR TASK.** Revise the following to avoid redundancies.

31. Because his laptop was small in size, he could carry it everywhere.

32. A basic fundamental of computer safety is to avoid storing your password on a file in your computer because criminals will look there first.

33. The manager repeated again his warning that we must use strong passwords.

34. Although the two files seem exactly identical, we should proofread each and every page.

35. The computer specialist combined together a PowerPoint presentation and a handout.

## Empty Words (Obj. 1)

**YOUR TASK.** Revise the following to eliminate empty words.

36. Are you aware of the fact that social media can drive brand awareness and customer loyalty?

37. Except for the instance of MySpace, social networking sites are booming.

38. If you seek to build an online community that will support your customers, social media services can help.

39. With such a degree of active participation in Facebook and Twitter, it's easy to understand why businesses are flocking to social media sites.

40. We plan to schedule online meetings on a monthly basis.

## Condensing for Microblogging (Obj. 1)

**YOUR TASK.** Read the following real Twitter messages and write a 140-character microblog reply to each. Be selective in what you include. Your instructor may show you the actual responses that the company wrote.

41. @HTWilson94 asks whether grocer Whole Foods stocks Whole Trade–certified flowers all year long.[8] Prepare a response (140 or fewer characters) based on the following information: Yes, at Whole Foods stores we do indeed offer Whole Trade–certified flowers the entire year. We strongly advocate and support the Whole Trade movement, which strives to promote quality, premium price to the producer, better wages and working conditions, and the environment. However, we can't tell you exactly which certified flowers will be available at our stores and when. You would have to check with your local store for its specific selection.

42. @AmyJean64 sent Bank of America a tweet saying she was frustrated with a real estate short sale. "Have a contract on a house and cannot get them to return calls to finalize."[9] Prepare a response based on the following information: You work for Bank of America, and you would very much like to help her, but you can't without certain information. You need her to send you the property address along with her name and phone number so that you can call to see how you can help. She should probably DM (direct message) you with this crucial information.

43. @VickiK wrote to JetBlue: "I have booked a flt in July, CA-VT. Wondering about flying my wedding dress w/me. Is there a safe place to hang it on the plane?"[10] Prepare a response based on the following information: We congratulate you on your coming wedding! We bet your wedding dress is beautiful. We don't have special closets on our planes and certainly nothing big enough for a wedding dress. But here's a suggestion: Have you considered having it shipped ahead of time? All the best wishes on your upcoming happy event!

44. **@ChrisC sent a message to Southwest Airlines saying, "This is extremely frustrating, how is it possible for your website to be down the entire day?"**[11] Prepare a response based on the following information: Southwest is very, very sorry! It's extremely frustrating to us also. We realize that you are accustomed to using this site to book flights. Our IT people tell us that the website functionality is getting better. We are not sure exactly what that means in terms of availability, but we are very hopeful that customers will be able to book their flights soon.

45. **@JamesR. sent a message to the delivery service UPS complaining, "Holy XXX. It's after 6 pm and UPS still hasn't delivered my pkg yet."** Prepare a response based on the following information: UPS makes every effort to deliver all packages promptly. For packages destined for offices, we must deliver by 3 p.m. However, for packages going to residences, our goal is to deliver by 7 p.m. But we can't always make it, so our drivers can sometimes run later. We're sorry about the wait.

46. **@calinelb sent a message to H&R Block: "YOU SUCK! I've been waiting for my return more than 3.5 months."**[12] Prepare a response based on the following: We are sorry that you feel that way. We certainly can't understand the reason for this long delay. We would like to look into the matter, but before we can respond, we need you to send a DM (direct message) to our customer service desk at @HRBlockAnswers. We will definitely check on this and get back to you.

## Trite Business Phrases (Obj. 2)

**YOUR TASK.** Revise the following sentences to eliminate trite business phrases.

47. Pursuant to your request, I will submit your repair request immediately.

48. Enclosed please find the list of customers to be used in our promotion.

49. As per your request, we are sending the contract under separate cover.

50. Every effort will be made to proceed in accordance with your wishes.

51. If we may help in any way, please do not hesitate to call.

## Clichés, Slang, Buzzwords, and Wordiness (Obj. 2)

**YOUR TASK.** Revise the following sentences to avoid confusing clichés, slang, buzzwords, and wordiness.

52. Our manager insists that we must think outside the box in promoting our new kitchen tool.

53. Although we got burned in the last contract, you can be sure we will stand our ground this time.

54. Beyond the shadow of a doubt, our lousy competitor will make another snarky claim that is below the belt.

55. If you refer back to our five-year plan, you will see that there are provisions for preventing blowing the budget.

56. BTW, have you heard the latest buzz about hackers ripping off customer info from Best Buy?

## Buried Verbs (Obj. 2)

**YOUR TASK.** Revise the following sentences to recover buried verbs.

57. After making an investigation, the fire department reached the conclusion that the blaze was set intentionally.

58. Our committee made a promise to give consideration to your proposal at its next meeting.

59. When used properly, zero-based budgeting can bring about a reduction in overall costs.

60. Did our department put in an application for increased budget support?

61. The budget committee has not taken action on any projects yet.

62. Homeowners must make a determination of the total value of their furnishings.

## Lists, Bullets, and Headings (Obj. 3)

**YOUR TASK.** Revise the following poorly written sentences and paragraphs. Use lists, bullets, and category headings, if appropriate. Improve parallel construction and reduce wordiness.

63. **Three Best Twitter Practices**. There are three simple ways you can build an online following, drive your reputation, and develop customers' trust by using these uncomplicated and simple Twitter practices. First off, share some of your photos and information about your business from behind the scenes. Sharing is so important! Next, listen. That is, you should regularly monitor the comments about your company, what's being said about your brand, and any chatter about your products. And, of course, you should respond. In real time it is necessary to respond to statements that are compliments and just general feedback.

64. Revise the following by incorporating a numbered list.

    Computer passwords are a way of life at this point in time. In the creation of a strong password, you should remember a few things. First, you should come up with an eight-word phrase that is easy to remember, such as this: *my goal is a degree in 4 years*. Then take each of those words and the first letter should be selected, such as this: *mgiadi4y*. The last step for creating a really strong password is to exchange—that is, swap out—some of those letters for characters and capital letters: *Mgia$in4Y*.

65. Revise the following paragraph by incorporating a bulleted list with category headings. Eliminate all the wordiness.

    In response to your inquiry with questions about how credit scores are made, this is to let you know that there are four important factors that make up your credit score. Because you say you are interested in improving your score so that it reaches the highest level, you will be interested in this. One of the most important items lenders consider before approving anyone for a loan is your payment history. It is important that you have a long history of making payments on time. Almost as important is the amount of available credit that you have. If you are close to maxing out your accounts, you are a higher risk and will have a lower score. How long you have had accounts is also important. Accounts that have been open for ten years will help your credit score. Finally, if you are opening lots of new accounts, you can lower your credit score.

Chapter 4: Revising Business Messages

# RADICAL REWRITES

**Note:** Radical Rewrites are provided at **www.cengagebrain.com** for you to download and revise. Your instructor may show a suggested solution.

## 4.1 Radical Rewrite: Information E-Mail—Wretched Invitation (Objs. 1–5)

The following wordy, inefficient, and disorganized message invites department managers to three interviewing sessions to select student interns. However, to be effective, this message desperately needs a radical rewrite.

**YOUR TASK.** Study the message and list at least five weaknesses. Then revise to avoid excessive wordiness and repetition. Also think about how to develop an upbeat tone and improve readability. Can you reduce this sloppy 15-sentence message to 6 efficient sentences plus a list—and still convey all the necessary information?

**To:** List - Department Managers
**From:** Aaron Alexander <aalexander@vasco.com>
**Subject:** Upcoming Interviews
**Cc:**
**Bcc:**

For some time our management team has been thinking about hiring several interns. We decided to offer compensation to the interns in our internship program because in two fields (computer science and information systems) interns are usually paid, which is the norm. However, you may be disappointed to learn that we can offer only three internships.

In working with our nearby state university, we have narrowed the field to six excellent candidates. These six candidates will be interviewed. This is to inform you that you are invited to attend three interviewing sessions for these student candidates. Your presence is required at these sessions to help us avoid making poor selections.

Mark your calendars for the following three times. The first meeting is May 3 in the conference room. The second meeting is May 5 in Office 22 (the conference room was scheduled). On May 9 we can finish up in the conference room. All of the meetings will start at 2 p.m. In view of the fact that your projects need fresh ideas and talented new team members, I should not have to urge you to attend and be well prepared.

Please examine all the candidates' résumés and send me your ranking lists.

Aaron Alexander

[Full contact information]

List at least five weaknesses.

# GRAMMAR/MECHANICS CHECKUP—4

## Adjectives and Adverbs

Review Sections 1.16 and 1.17 of the Grammar/Mechanics Handbook. Then study each of the following statements. Underscore any inappropriate forms. In the space provided, write the correct form (or C if correct) and the number of the G/M principle illustrated. You may need to consult your dictionary for current practice regarding some compound adjectives. When you finish, compare your responses with those provided at the end of the book. If your answers differ, carefully study the principles in parentheses.

cost-effective               (1.17e)     **EXAMPLE**   We need a <u>cost effective</u> solution for this continuing problem.

_____ 1. The newly opened restaurant offered many tried and true menu items.

_____ 2. Amazingly, most of the ten year old equipment is still working.

_____ 3. Although purchased ten years ago, the equipment still looked brightly.

_____ 4. Global messages today are exchanged so quick that international business moves more rapidly than ever.

_____ 5. The president's veto of the tax plan couldn't have sent a more clearer message.

_____ 6. You may submit only work related expenses to be reimbursed.

_____ 7. Amanda and Max said that they're planning to open there own business next year.

_____ 8. Haven't you ever made a spur of the moment decision?

_____ 9. Not all decisions that are made on the spur of the moment turn out badly.

_____ 10. The committee offered a well thought out plan to revamp online registration.

_____ 11. You must complete a change of address form when you move.

_____ 12. Each decision will be made on a case by case basis.

_____ 13. I could be more efficient if my printer were more nearer my computer.

_____ 14. If you reject his offer to help, Kurt will feel badly.

_____ 15. The truck's engine is running smooth after its tune-up.

Chapter 4: Revising Business Messages

# EDITING CHALLENGE—4

This message transmits a suggestion from an employee to her boss. However, the message suffers from proofreading, wordiness, spelling, punctuation, and other writing faults that require correction.

**YOUR TASK.** Edit the following message (a) by correcting errors in your textbook or on a photocopy using proofreading marks from Appendix A or (b) by downloading the message from the premium website at **www.cengagebrain.com** and correcting at your computer. Your instructor may show you a possible solution.

**To:** Daniel R. Kesling <daniel.kesling@federalsavings.com>
**From:** Misty McKenney<misty.mckenney@federalsavings.com>
**Subject:** My Idea
**Cc:**
**Bcc:**

Mr. Kesling,

Due to the fact that you recently asked for ideas on how to improve customer relations I am submitting my idea. This message is to let you know that I think we can improve customer satisfaction easy by making a change in our counters.

Last June glass barriers were installed at our branch. There are tellers on one side and customers on the other. The barriers, however, do have air vents to be able to allow we tellers to carry on communication with our customers. Management thought that these bullet proof barriers would prevent and stop thiefs from jumping over the counter.

I observed that there were customers who were surprised by these large glass partitions. Communication through them is really extremely difficult and hard. Both the customer and the teller have to raise there voices to be heard. Its even more of a inconvenence when you are dealing with an elderly person or someone who happens to be from another country. Beyond a shadow of a doubt, these new barriers make customers feel that they are being treated impersonal.

I made an effort to research the matter of these barriers and made the discovery that we are the only bank in town with them. There are many other banks that are trying casual kiosks and open counters to make customers feel more at home.

Although it may be easier said than done, I suggest that we actually give serious consideration to the removal of these barriers as a beginning and initial step toward improving customer relations.

Misty McKenney
E-mail: misty.mckenney@federalsavings.com
Support Services
(316) 448-3910

# COMMUNICATION WORKSHOP

## TECHNOLOGY

### Revising and Editing Documents in MS Word

Collaborative writing and editing projects are challenging. Fortunately, Microsoft Word offers many useful tools to help team members edit and share documents electronically. Three simple but useful editing tools are **text highlight color, font color**, and **strikethrough**, which you learned about earlier in this chapter. These tools enable reviewers to point out editing changes. Complex projects, however, may require more advanced editing tools such as **Track Changes** and Insert **Comments**, as illustrated in Figure 4.7.

**TRACK CHANGES.** To suggest specific editing changes to other team members, **Track Changes** is handy. When this command is in effect, all changes to a document are recorded in a different color, with one color for each reviewer. New text is underlined, and a vertical line appears in the margin to show where changes were made. Text that has been deleted is crossed out. Suggested revisions offered by different team members are identified and dated. The original writer may accept or reject these changes. In Word 2007, 2010, and 2013, you will find **Track Changes** on the **Review** menu.

**INSERT COMMENTS.** By using **Insert Comments**, you can point out problematic passages or errors, ask or answer questions, and share ideas without changing or adding text. When more than one person adds comments, the comments appear in different colors and are identified by the individual writers' names and date/time stamps.

**CAREER APPLICATION.** On the job, you will likely be working with others on projects that require written documents. During employment interviews, employers may ask whether you have participated in team projects using collaborative software. To be able to answer that question favorably, take advantage of this opportunity to work on a collaborative document using some of the features described here.

**YOUR TASK.** Divide into two-person teams to edit the Editing Challenge document. One partner downloads the file from www.cengagebrain.com or retypes it from the textbook. That partner makes all necessary changes using font color, strikethrough, and the **Comment** feature and then saves the file with a file name such as *PartnerName-Editing4*. The first partner then sends an e-mail to the second partner with the attached file and asks the partner to make further edits. The receiving partner prints a copy of the sending partner's file before editing the message further using font color, strikethrough, and the **Comment** feature. The second partner approves or rejects the first partner's edits and then submits the edited copy along with a copy of the message with both partners' edits. Be sure to name each file distinctly. Your instructor will decide whether to require hard copies or e-mail copies.

Figure 4.7 Track Changes and Comment Features Aid Revision Process

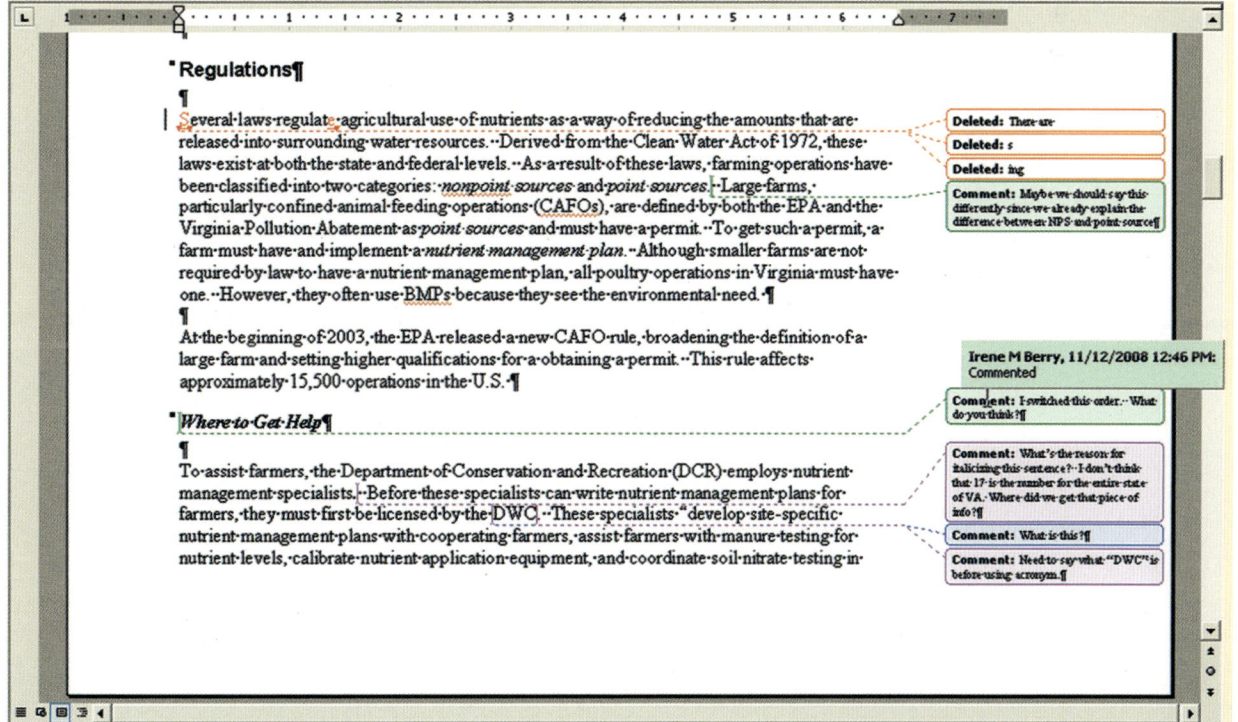

Chapter 4: Revising Business Messages

# ENDNOTES

[1] Cook, C. (1985). *Line by line*. Boston: Houghton Mifflin, p. 17.
[2] Glassman, N. (2010, November 29). 6 tips for brands on responding to customer complaints on Twitter. Retrieved from http://socialtimes.com/responding-customer-complaints-twitter_b29179
[3] Hsieh, T. (2011, May 11). Twitter. Retrieved from http://twitter.com/#!/zappos
[4] Holmes, E. (2011, December 9). Tweeting without fear. Wall Street Journal Online. Retrieved from http://online.wsj.com/article/SB10001424052970204319004577086140865075800.html
[5] Starbucks. (2012, May 30). Retrieved from http://twitter.com/#!/Starbucks
[6] Sword, H. (2012, July 25). Zombie nouns. Retrieved from http://www.3quarksdaily.com/3quarksdaily/2012/07/zombie-nouns.html
[7] Photo essay based on Al-Greene, B. (2013, May 23). 30 overused buzzwords in digital marketing. Mashable. Retrieved from http://mashable.com/2013/05/23/buzzword-infographic/
[8] Based on Van Grove, J. (2009, January 21). 40 of the best twitter brands and the people behind them. Retrieved from http://mashable.com/2009/01/21/best-twitter-brands
[9] Based on Bank of America Twitter Help. (2012, June 3). @AmyJo 63Owen. Twitter. Retrieved from https://twitter.com/#!/BofA_Help
[10] Based on JetBlue Twitter Help. (2012, June 4). VictoriaKlim @vikiybubbles. Twitter. Retrieved from https://twitter.com/#!/JetBlue
[11] Based on Southwest Airlines Twitter. (2012, May 15). Chris Cichon@cichonship. Twitter. Retrieved from https://twitter.com/#!/SouthwestAir
[12] Based on H&R Block. (2012, June 4). Carlos Noriega@calinelbarbaro. Twitter. Retrieved from https://twitter.com/#!/hrblock

# ACKNOWLEDGMENTS

**p. 91** Office Insider based on Powell, E. (2003, November/December). Ten tips for better business writing. *Office Solutions*, 20(6), 36.

**p. 93** Office Insider based on Zinsser, W. (2006). *On writing well* (7th ed.). New York: HarperCollins.

**p. 95** Office Insider based on Shankman, P. (2011, May 20). I will never hire a "social media expert," and neither should you. Retrieved from http://shankman.com/i-will-never-hire-a-social-media-expert-and-neither-should-you

**p. 96** Office Insider based on Adams, S. (2011, April 9-10). How to get a real education. *The Wall Street Journal*, pp. C1–C2.

**p. 97** Office Insider based on Fried, J. (2010, May 1). Why is business writing so awful? *Inc.* magazine. Retrieved from http://www.inc.com/magazine/20100501/why-is-business-writing-so-awful.html

**p. 101** Office Insider based on Levitt, A. (2011, April 2). A word to Wall Street: 'Plain English,' please. Retrieved from Wall Street Journal Online at http://online.wsj.com/article/SB10001424052748704471904576231002037599510.html

# Workplace Communication

## UNIT 3

**Chapter 5**
Short Workplace Messages and Digital Media

**Chapter 6**
Positive Messages

**Chapter 7**
Negative Messages

**Chapter 8**
Persuasive Messages

# CHAPTER 5

# Short Workplace Messages and Digital Media

## OBJECTIVES

After studying this chapter, you should be able to

**5-1** Understand the professional standards for the usage, structure, and format of e-mails and interoffice memos in the digital-era workplace.

**5-2** Explain workplace instant messaging and texting as well as their liabilities and best practices.

**5-3** Identify professional applications of podcasts and wikis.

**5-4** Describe how businesses use blogs to connect with internal and external audiences, and list best practices for professional blogging.

**5-5** Address business uses of social media networks, and assess their advantages as well as risks.

## 5-1 Preparing Digital-Age E-Mail Messages and Memos

The world of communication is rapidly changing in this digital age. The Web has evolved from mere storage of passively consumed information to Web 2.0—a dynamic, hyperconnected environment. Users are empowered, active participants who create content, review products, and edit and share information. They are increasingly adopting mobile electronic devices. Messages are shorter and more frequent, and response time is much speedier. Social media networks such as Facebook, Twitter, and Pinterest have transformed communication from one-on-one conversations to one-to-many transmissions. Social media have also revolutionized the way we keep in touch with friends and family.

In many businesses, desktop computers are being replaced by ever-smaller laptops, netbooks, smartphones, and tablets. These and other mobile devices access data and applications stored in the *cloud*, in remote networks, not individual computers.

Doubtless you are already connecting digitally with your friends and family. However, chances are that you need to understand how businesses transmit information electronically and how they use communication technologies. This chapter explores short forms of workplace communication, beginning with e-mail, which everyone loves to hate, and memos, which are disappearing but still necessary in many organizations. Moving on to newer media, you will learn about workplace functions of instant messaging, text messaging, podcasts, wikis, corporate blogs, and social networking sites. Understanding these workplace technologies and best procedures can save you time, reduce blunders, and help you excel as a professional.

### 5-1a  E-Mail: Love It or Hate It—But It's Not Going Away

Critics say that e-mail is outdated, inefficient, and slowly dying. They complain that it takes too much time, increases stress, and leaves a dangerous "paper" trail. However, e-mail in the workplace is here to stay. Despite the substantial attention that social media receive in the news, most business messages are still sent by e-mail.[1] In the next three to five years, we may see more business messages being sent by social media platforms, predicts Dr. Monica Seeley, author of *Brilliant Email*. "But email will remain a bedrock of businesses for some time to come," she maintains.[2] Typical businesspeople spend at least two hours a day—perhaps much more—writing and replying to e-mail.

E-mail has replaced paper memos for many messages inside organizations and some letters to external audiences. In addition to accessing e-mail in the office, increasing numbers of businesspeople check their e-mail on mobile devices. Because you can expect to use e-mail extensively to communicate at work, it's smart to learn how to do it expertly. You may have to adjust the writing practices you currently use for texting and Facebook, but turning out professional e-mails is an easily attainable goal.

### 5-1b  Why People Complain About E-Mail

Although e-mail is recognized as the mainstay of business communication, it's not always done well. In a recent study of 1,800 global knowledge workers, 40 percent confessed that "they had received e-mails that made no sense whatsoever."[3] A *Wall Street Journal* article reported that many business schools were ramping up their writing programs or hiring writing coaches because of complaints about their graduates' skills.[4] Adding to the complaints, Chris Carlson, recruiting officer at the consulting firm of Booz Allen Hamilton Inc., said that new MBA graduates exchange more than 200 e-mails a day, and some read like text messages. "They're not [even] in complete sentences," he said.[5]

**E-Mail Overload.** In addition to the complaints about confusing and poorly written e-mails, many people are overwhelmed with too many messages. Currently, the average worker receives 11,680 e-mails per year.[6] Some of those messages are unnecessary, such as those that merely confirm receipt of a message or ones that express thanks. The use of "Reply All" adds to the inbox, irritating those who have to plow through dozens of messages that barely relate to them. Others blame e-mail for eliminating the distinction between work life and home life. They feel an urgency to be available 24/7 and respond immediately.

**E-Mail—Everlasting Evidence.** Still other e-mail senders fail to recognize how dangerous e-mail can be. After deletion, e-mail files still leave trails on servers within and outside organizations. Messages are also backed up on other servers, making them traceable and recoverable by forensic experts. Long-forgotten messages may turn up in court cases as damaging evidence. Even writers with nothing to hide should be concerned about what may come back to haunt them. Your best bet is to put nothing in an e-mail message that you wouldn't post on your office door. Also, be sure that you know your organization's e-mail policy before sending personal messages. Estimates suggest that as many as a quarter of bosses have fired an employee for an e-mail violation.[7]

Despite its dark side, e-mail has many advantages and remains a prime communication channel. Therefore, it's to your advantage to learn when and how to use it efficiently and safely.

---

## OFFICE INSIDER

*"E-mail is not dead, it's just evolving. It's becoming a searchable archive, a manager's accountability source, a document courier. . . . Three-quarters of all e-mail is junk, and we're wasting lots of time dealing with less important messages. But it remains the mule of the information age—stubborn and strong."*

—Barry Gill, enterprise consultant and product marketing manager with Mimecast

**LEARNING OBJECTIVE 1**

Understand the professional standards for the usage, structure, and format of e-mails and interoffice memos in the digital-era workplace.

Chapter 5: Short Workplace Messages and Digital Media

## OFFICE INSIDER

*"E-mail is the digital equivalent of DNA evidence, the smoking gun. E-mail has become the place where everybody loves to look."*

—Irwin Schwartz, president of the National Association of Criminal Defense Lawyers

### 5-1c Knowing When E-Mail Is Appropriate

E-mail is appropriate for short, informal messages that request information and respond to inquiries. It is especially effective for messages to multiple receivers and messages that must be archived (saved). An e-mail is also appropriate as a cover document when sending longer attachments.

E-mail, however, is not a substitute for face-to-face conversations or telephone calls. These channels are much more successful if your goal is to convey enthusiasm or warmth, explain a complex situation, present a persuasive argument, or smooth over disagreements. One expert gives this wise advice: "Sometimes it's better to get off the computer and make a phone call. If e-mails are getting too complicated, if the tone is degenerating, if they're just not getting the job done, call or walk over to that colleague."[8] Managers and employees echo this advice, as revealed in recent research. They were adamant about using face-to-face contact, rather than e-mail, for critical work situations such as human resources annual reviews, discipline, and promotions.[9]

### 5-1d Drafting Professional E-Mails

Professional e-mails are quite different from messages you may send to friends. Instead of casual words tossed off in haste, professional e-mails are well-considered messages that usually carry nonsensitive information unlikely to upset readers. Therefore, these messages should be organized directly with the main idea first. The following writing plan will help you create information messages quickly.

---

**WRITING PLAN FOR INFORMATIONAL E-MAILS**

- **Subject line:** Summarize the main idea in condensed form.
- **Opening:** Reveal the main idea immediately but in expanded form.
- **Body:** Explain and justify the main idea using headings, bulleted lists, and other high-skim techniques when appropriate.
- **Closing:** Include (a) action information, dates, or deadlines; (b) a summary of the message; or (c) a closing thought.

---

**Craft a Compelling Subject Line.** The most important part of an e-mail is its subject line. Avoid meaningless statements such as *Help*, *Important*, or *Meeting*. Summarize the purpose of the message clearly and make the receiver want to open the message. Try to include a verb (*Need You to Attend Las Vegas Trade Show*). Remember that in some instances the subject line can be the entire message (*Meeting Changed from May 3 to May 10*). Also be sure to adjust the subject line if the topic changes after repeated replies. Subject lines should appear as a combination of uppercase and lowercase letters—never in all lowercase letters.

**Include a Greeting.** To help receivers see the beginning of a message and to help them recognize whether they are the primary or secondary receiver, include

| DON'T — POOR SUBJECT LINES | DO — IMPROVED SUBJECT LINES |
|---|---|
| ✗ Trade Show | ✓ Need You to Showcase Two Items at Our Next Trade Show |
| ✗ Staff Meeting | ✓ Staff Meeting Rescheduled for May 12 |
| ✗ Important! | ✓ Please Respond to Job Satisfaction Survey |
| ✗ Parking Permits | ✓ New Employee Parking Permits Available From HR |

## Workplace in Focus

From government e-mails that exposed the National Security Agency surveillance program, to affair-related e-mails that ended the career of former CIA chief David Petraeus, leaked e-mails cause headaches for individuals and organizations. In one recent incident, a leader of the Delta Gamma sorority at the University of Maryland sent an 880-word e-mail to sorority members about proper decorum for the Greek Week match-up with the guys of Sigma Nu. After opening with a warning, the e-mail blasted the girls' social graces using no less than 55 expletives, 150 all-caps "shouts," and multiple threats. The message closed with one final profanity-laden insult. The leader resigned after the e-mail went viral online. How can communicators avoid sending embarrassing or legally actionable e-mails?[10]

---

a greeting. The greeting sets the tone for the message and reflects your audience analysis. For friends and colleagues, try friendly greetings (*Hi, Julie; Thanks, Julie; Good morning, Julie;* or *Greetings, Julie*). For more formal messages and those to outsiders, include an honorific and last name (*Dear Ms. Stevens*).

**Organize the Body for Readability and Tone.** After drafting an e-mail, ask yourself how you can make your message more readable. Did you start directly? Did you group similar topics together? Could some information be presented with bulleted or numbered lists? Could you add headings—especially if the message is more than a few paragraphs? Do you see any phrases or sentences that could be condensed? Get rid of wordiness, but don't sacrifice clarity. If a longer sentence is necessary for comprehension, then keep it. To convey the best tone, read the message aloud. If it sounds curt, it probably is.

**Close Effectively.** At the end of your message, include an action statement with due dates and requests. Although complimentary closes are unnecessary, you might include a friendly closing such as *Many thanks* or *Warm regards*. Do include your name because messages without names become confusing when forwarded or when they are part of a long string of responses.

For most messages, include full contact information in a signature block, which can be inserted automatically. Figure 5.1 illustrates a typical e-mail with proper formatting.

### 5-1e Controlling Your Inbox

Business communicators love to complain about e-mail, and some young people even deny its existence. In the business world, however, e-mail writing IS business writing.[11] Instead of letting your inbox consume your time and crimp your productivity, you can control it by observing a few time management strategies.

The most important strategy is checking your e-mail at set times, such as first thing in the morning and again after lunch or at 4 p.m. To avoid being distracted, be sure to turn off your audio and visual alerts. No fair peeking! If mornings are your best working times, check your e-mail later in the day. Let your boss and colleagues

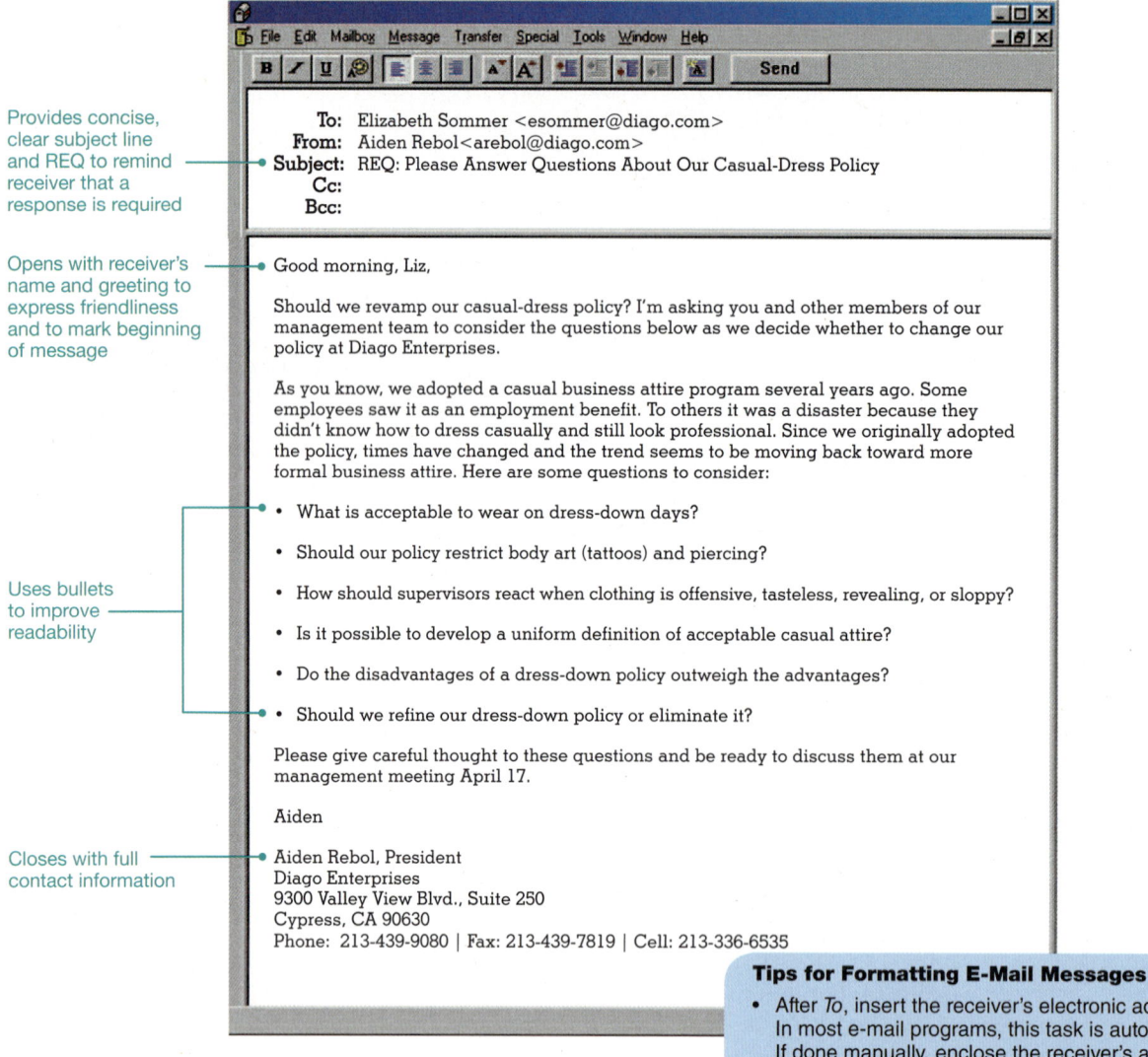

Figure 5.1 Formatting an E-Mail Message That Makes a Request

| | |
|---|---|
| To: | Elizabeth Sommer <esommer@diago.com> |
| From: | Aiden Rebol <arebol@diago.com> |
| Subject: | REQ: Please Answer Questions About Our Casual-Dress Policy |
| Cc: | |
| Bcc: | |

*Provides concise, clear subject line and REQ to remind receiver that a response is required*

Good morning, Liz,

*Opens with receiver's name and greeting to express friendliness and to mark beginning of message*

Should we revamp our casual-dress policy? I'm asking you and other members of our management team to consider the questions below as we decide whether to change our policy at Diago Enterprises.

As you know, we adopted a casual business attire program several years ago. Some employees saw it as an employment benefit. To others it was a disaster because they didn't know how to dress casually and still look professional. Since we originally adopted the policy, times have changed and the trend seems to be moving back toward more formal business attire. Here are some questions to consider:

- What is acceptable to wear on dress-down days?
- Should our policy restrict body art (tattoos) and piercing?
- How should supervisors react when clothing is offensive, tasteless, revealing, or sloppy?
- Is it possible to develop a uniform definition of acceptable casual attire?
- Do the disadvantages of a dress-down policy outweigh the advantages?
- Should we refine our dress-down policy or eliminate it?

*Uses bullets to improve readability*

Please give careful thought to these questions and be ready to discuss them at our management meeting April 17.

Aiden

*Closes with full contact information*

Aiden Rebol, President
Diago Enterprises
9300 Valley View Blvd., Suite 250
Cypress, CA 90630
Phone: 213-439-9080 | Fax: 213-439-7819 | Cell: 213-336-6535

**Tips for Formatting E-Mail Messages**

- After *To*, insert the receiver's electronic address. In most e-mail programs, this task is automated. If done manually, enclose the receiver's address in angle brackets.
- After *From*, type your name and electronic address, if your program does not insert it automatically.
- After *Subject*, present a clear description of the message.
- Insert the addresses of anyone receiving courtesy or blind copies.
- Include a salutation (*Liz; Hi, Liz*) or honorific and last name (*Dear Ms. Sommer*), especially in messages to outsiders.
- Double-space (skip one line) between paragraphs.
- Do not type in all caps or in all lowercase letters.
- Include full contact information in the signature block.

know about your schedule for responding. Another excellent time-saver is the two-minute rule. If you can read and respond to a message within two minutes, then take care of it immediately. For messages that require more time, add them to your to-do list or schedule them on your calendar. To be polite, send a quick note telling the sender when you plan to respond.

124  Chapter 5: Short Workplace Messages and Digital Media

## 5-1f Replying Efficiently With Down-Editing

When answering e-mail, a neat skill to develop is *down-editing*. This involves inserting your responses to parts of the incoming message. After a courteous opening, your reply message will include only the parts of the incoming message to which you are responding. Delete the sender's message headers, signature, and all unnecessary parts. Your responses can be identified with your initials, if more than one person will be seeing the response. Another efficient trick is to use a different color for your down-edits. It takes a little practice to develop this skill, but the down-edited reply reduces confusion, saves writing and reading time, and makes you look super savvy.

Figure 5.2 shows a number of additional best practices for managing your e-mail.

## 5-1g Writing Interoffice Memos

In addition to e-mail, you should be familiar with another workplace document type, the interoffice memorandum. Although e-mail has largely replaced memos, you may still be called on to use the memo format in specific instances. Memos are necessary for important internal messages that (a) are too long for e-mail, (b) require a permanent record, (c) demand formality, or (d) inform employees who may not have access to e-mail. Within organizations, memos deliver changes in procedures, official instructions, and reports.

The memo format is particularly necessary for complex, lengthy internal messages. Prepared as memos, long messages are then delivered as attachments to e-mail cover messages. Memos seem to function better as permanent records than e-mail messages because the latter may be difficult to locate and may contain a trail of confusing replies. E-mails also may change the origination date whenever the file is accessed, thus making it impossible to know the original date of the message.

When preparing e-mail attachments, be sure that they carry sufficient identifying information. Because the cover e-mail message may become separated from the attachment, the attachment must be fully identified. Preparing the e-mail attachment as a memo provides a handy format that identifies the date, sender, receiver, and subject.

> **OFFICE INSIDER**
>
> "E-mail is today's version of a business letter or interoffice memo. Think accordingly. Make it look professional."
>
> —Tennille Robinson, editor, *Black Enterprise*

### Figure 5.2 Best Practices for Better E-Mail

**Getting Started**
- Don't write if another channel—such as IM, social media, or a phone call—might work better.
- Send only content you would want published.
- Write compelling subject lines, possibly with names and dates: *Jake: Can You Present at January 10 Staff Meeting?*

**Replying**
- Scan all e-mails, especially those from the same person. Answer within 24 hours or say when you will.
- Change the subject line if the topic changes. Check the threaded messages below yours.
- Practice down-editing; include only the parts from the incoming e-mail to which you are responding.
- Start with the main idea.
- Use headings and lists.

**Observing Etiquette**
- Obtain approval before forwarding.
- Soften the tone by including a friendly opening and closing.
- Resist humor and sarcasm. Absent facial expression and tone of voice, humor can be misunderstood.
- Avoid writing in all caps, which is like SHOUTING.

**Closing Effectively**
- End with due dates, next steps to be taken, or a friendly remark.
- Add your full contact information including social media addresses.
- Edit your text for readability. Proofread for typos or unwanted auto-corrections.
- Double-check before hitting **Send.**

Chapter 5: Short Workplace Messages and Digital Media

**Comparing Memos and E-Mails.** Memos have much in common with e-mails. Both usually carry nonsensitive information that may be organized directly with the main idea first. Both have guide words calling for a subject line, a dateline, and the identification of the sender and receiver. To enhance readability, both should be organized with headings, bulleted lists, and enumerated items whenever possible.

## Figure 5.3 Formatting a Memo That Responds to a Request

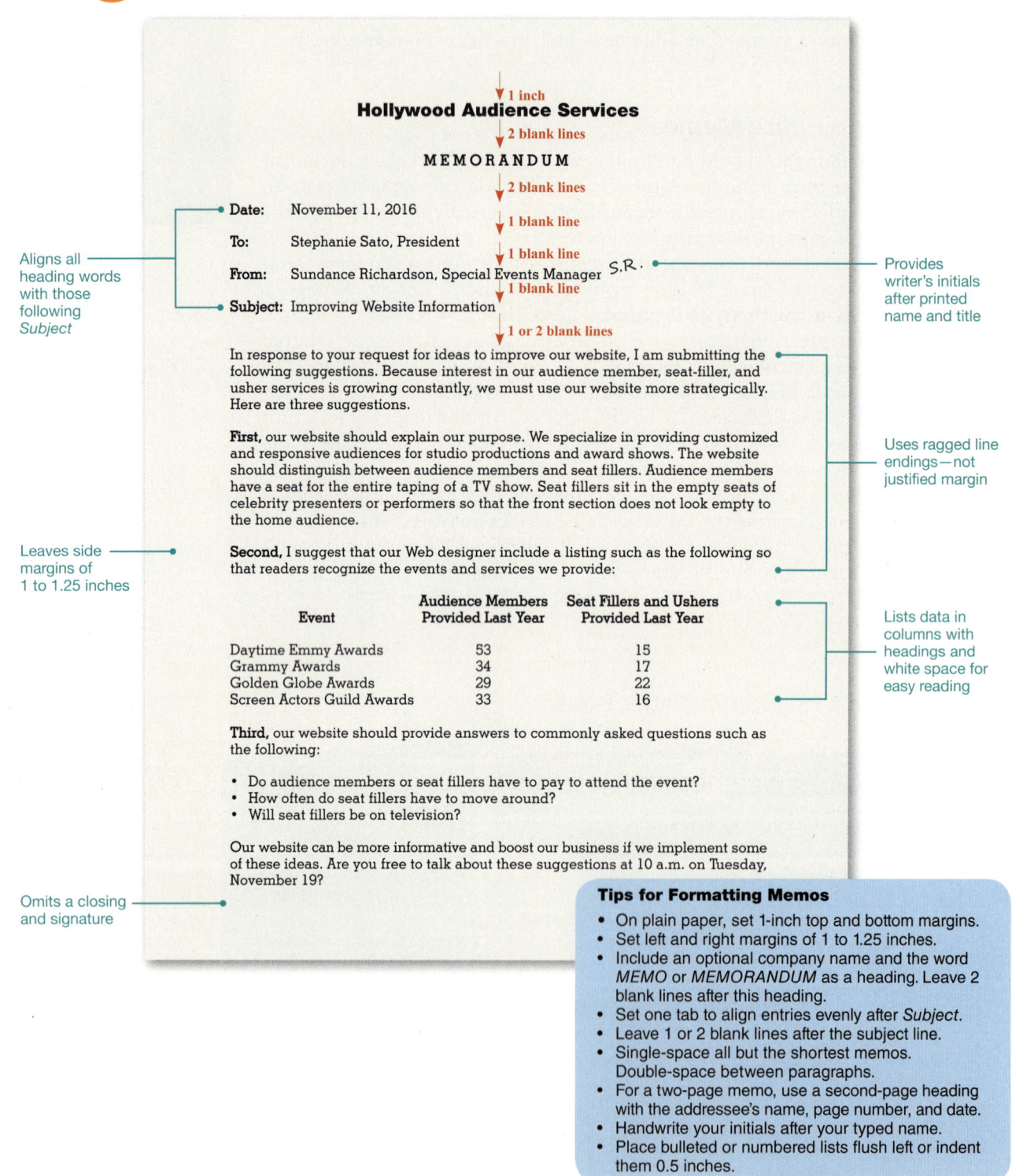

---

**Hollywood Audience Services**

↓ 1 inch
↓ 2 blank lines

**MEMORANDUM**

↓ 2 blank lines

**Date:** November 11, 2016

↓ 1 blank line

**To:** Stephanie Sato, President

↓ 1 blank line

**From:** Sundance Richardson, Special Events Manager  S.R.

↓ 1 blank line

**Subject:** Improving Website Information

↓ 1 or 2 blank lines

In response to your request for ideas to improve our website, I am submitting the following suggestions. Because interest in our audience member, seat-filler, and usher services is growing constantly, we must use our website more strategically. Here are three suggestions.

**First,** our website should explain our purpose. We specialize in providing customized and responsive audiences for studio productions and award shows. The website should distinguish between audience members and seat fillers. Audience members have a seat for the entire taping of a TV show. Seat fillers sit in the empty seats of celebrity presenters or performers so that the front section does not look empty to the home audience.

**Second,** I suggest that our Web designer include a listing such as the following so that readers recognize the events and services we provide:

| Event | Audience Members Provided Last Year | Seat Fillers and Ushers Provided Last Year |
|---|---|---|
| Daytime Emmy Awards | 53 | 15 |
| Grammy Awards | 34 | 17 |
| Golden Globe Awards | 29 | 22 |
| Screen Actors Guild Awards | 33 | 16 |

**Third,** our website should provide answers to commonly asked questions such as the following:

- Do audience members or seat fillers have to pay to attend the event?
- How often do seat fillers have to move around?
- Will seat fillers be on television?

Our website can be more informative and boost our business if we implement some of these ideas. Are you free to talk about these suggestions at 10 a.m. on Tuesday, November 19?

---

Annotations:
- Aligns all heading words with those following *Subject*
- Provides writer's initials after printed name and title
- Uses ragged line endings—not justified margin
- Leaves side margins of 1 to 1.25 inches
- Lists data in columns with headings and white space for easy reading
- Omits a closing and signature

**Tips for Formatting Memos**

- On plain paper, set 1-inch top and bottom margins.
- Set left and right margins of 1 to 1.25 inches.
- Include an optional company name and the word *MEMO* or *MEMORANDUM* as a heading. Leave 2 blank lines after this heading.
- Set one tab to align entries evenly after *Subject*.
- Leave 1 or 2 blank lines after the subject line.
- Single-space all but the shortest memos. Double-space between paragraphs.
- For a two-page memo, use a second-page heading with the addressee's name, page number, and date.
- Handwrite your initials after your typed name.
- Place bulleted or numbered lists flush left or indent them 0.5 inches.

**Similarities.** E-mails and memos both generally close with (a) action information, dates, or deadlines; (b) a summary of the message; or (c) a closing thought. An effective memo or e-mail closing might be, *Please submit your written report to me by June 15 so that we can review your data before our July planning session*. In more detailed messages, a summary of main points may be an appropriate closing. If no action request is made and a closing summary is unnecessary, you might end with a simple concluding thought *(I'm glad to answer your questions* or *This sounds like a useful project).*

**Differences.** You need not close messages to coworkers with goodwill statements such as those found in letters to customers or clients. However, some closing thought is often necessary to avoid sounding abrupt. Closings can show gratitude or encourage feedback with remarks such as *I sincerely appreciate your help* or *What are your ideas on this proposal?* Other closings look forward to what's next, such as *How would you like to proceed?* Avoid closing with overused expressions such as *Please let me know if I may be of further assistance*. This ending sounds mechanical and insincere.

In Figure 5.3, notice how memos are formatted and how they can be created to improve readability with lists and white space.

## 5-2 Workplace Messaging and Texting

Instant messaging (IM) and text messaging have become powerful communication tools, not only among teens and twentysomethings. IM enables two or more individuals to use the Internet or an intranet (an internal corporate communication platform) to "chat" in real time by exchanging brief text-based messages. One such intranet chat window is captured in Figure 5.4.

Companies large and small now provide live online chats with customer service representatives, in addition to the usual contact options, such as telephone and e-mail. The free IM apps most popular among mobile device users are Skype, Facebook Messenger, WhatsApp, and Hangouts.

Text messaging, or texting, is another popular means for exchanging brief messages in real time. Usually delivered by or to a smartphone, texting requires a

**LEARNING OBJECTIVE 2**
Explain workplace instant messaging and texting as well as their liabilities and best practices.

Figure **5.4** Instant Messaging for Brief, Fast Communication

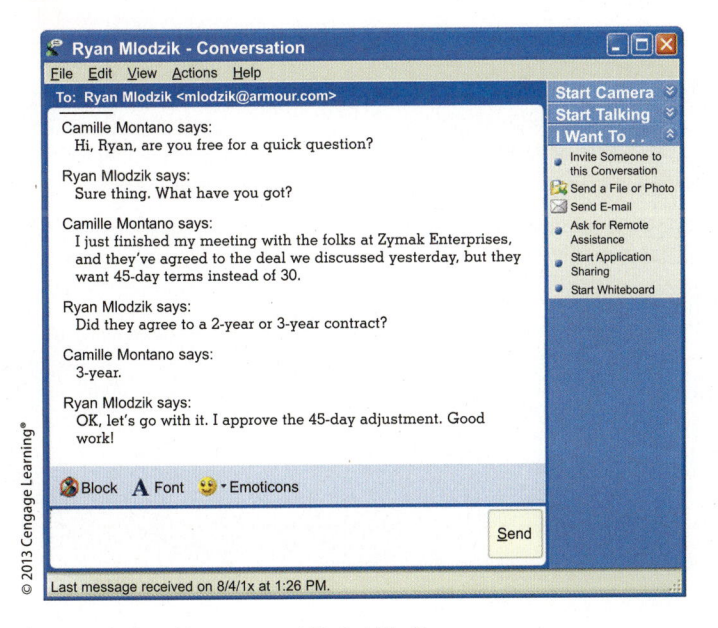

> Brief instant messages or texts can provide quick answers to coworkers who need responses immediately. For security reasons, most large companies use proprietary communication systems behind firewalls. These enterprise-grade communication platforms—for example, Adobe's Unicom—combine functions such as IM, e-mail, voicemail, phone directory, videochat, and presence technology.

Chapter 5: Short Workplace Messages and Digital Media

## OFFICE INSIDER

"[B]ear in mind that messaging sessions can be stored, then copied and pasted elsewhere. . . . The term 'confidential' is somewhat rubbery these days, so . . . think before you hit that enter key."

—Michael Bloch, Taming the Beast, e-commerce development and Web marketing consultant

short message service (SMS) supplied by a cell phone service provider or a voice over Internet protocol (VoIP) service. Some of the most common apps for unlimited mobile text messaging are Facebook Messenger, WhatsApp, LINE, KakaoTalk, and WeChat.

Texting usually requires a smartphone, and users pay for the service, often choosing a flat rate for a certain number of text or media messages per month. VoIP providers such as Skype and Jaxtr also offer texting. For a small fee, subscribers can send text messages to SMS-enabled cell phones in the United States and IM messages both domestically and internationally.

### 5-2a Impact of Instant Messaging and Texting

Text messaging and IM are convenient alternatives to the telephone and are replacing e-mail for short internal communication. French IT giant Atos switched its in-house communication entirely from e-mail to a Facebook-style interface and instant messaging.[12] More than 2.7 billion IM accounts worldwide[13] attest to IM's popularity. Sixty-four percent of business professionals use IM.[14]

**Benefits of IM and Texting.** The major attraction of instant messaging is real-time communication with colleagues anywhere in the world—so long as a cell phone signal or a Wi-Fi connection is available. Because IM allows people to share information immediately and make decisions quickly, its impact on business communication has been dramatic. Group online chat capabilities in enterprise-grade IM applications allow coworkers on far-flung project teams to communicate instantly. Many people consider instant messaging and texting productivity boosters because they enable users to get answers quickly and allow multitasking.[15]

**Low cost, speed, and unobtrusiveness.** Both IM and texting can be low-cost substitutes for voice calls, delivering messages between private mobile phone users quietly and discreetly. Organizations around the world provide news alerts, financial information, and promotions to customers via text. Credit card accounts can be set up to notify account holders by text or e-mail of approaching payment deadlines. Verizon Wireless sends automated texts helping customers track their data usage. The Centers for Disease Control started an SMS text messaging program that now has 15,000 participants receiving regular health alerts and tips on their mobile phones.[16] A few of these text alerts are shown in Figure 5.5.

Figure 5.5 Centers for Disease Control Text Alerts

Responding to the H1N1 flu virus threat, the Centers for Disease Control (CDC) launched a concerted Web 2.0 campaign employing several social networking channels, its website, and texting.

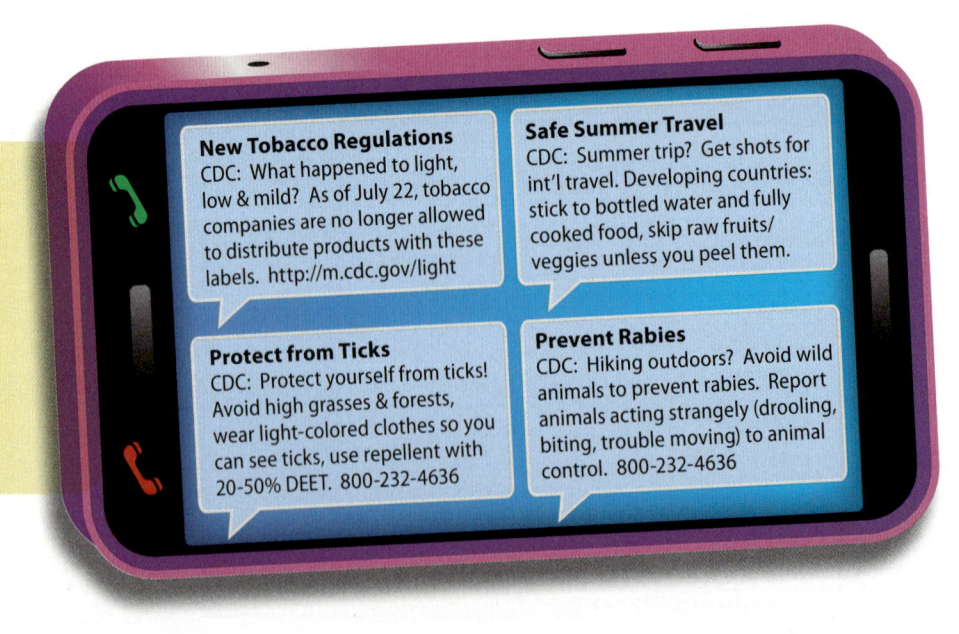

**New Tobacco Regulations**
CDC: What happened to light, low & mild? As of July 22, tobacco companies are no longer allowed to distribute products with these labels. http://m.cdc.gov/light

**Safe Summer Travel**
CDC: Summer trip? Get shots for int'l travel. Developing countries: stick to bottled water and fully cooked food, skip raw fruits/veggies unless you peel them.

**Protect from Ticks**
CDC: Protect yourself from ticks! Avoid high grasses & forests, wear light-colored clothes so you can see ticks, use repellent with 20-50% DEET. 800-232-4636

**Prevent Rabies**
CDC: Hiking outdoors? Avoid wild animals to prevent rabies. Report animals acting strangely (drooling, biting, trouble moving) to animal control. 800-232-4636

**Immediacy and efficiency.** The immediacy of instant and text messaging has created many fans. A user knows right away whether a message was delivered. Messaging avoids phone tag and eliminates the downtime associated with personal telephone conversations. Another benefit includes *presence functionality*. Coworkers can locate each other online, thus avoiding wild goose chases hunting someone who is out of the office.

**Risks of IM and Texting.** Despite their popularity among workers, some organizations forbid employees to use instant and text messaging for a number of reasons. Employers consider instant messaging yet another distraction in addition to the telephone, e-mail, and the Web. Some organizations also fear that employees using free consumer-grade instant messaging systems will reveal privileged information and company records. One UK study found that 72 percent of businesses have banned IM, although 74 percent of the respondents believed that IM could boost collaboration in their organizations. IT directors worried about security risks posed by free consumer IM services, with loss of sensitive business data a primary concern.[17]

**Liability burden.** A worker's improper use of mobile devices while on company business can expose the organization to staggering legal liability. A jury awarded $18 million to a victim struck by a transportation company's big rig whose driver had been checking text messages. Another case resulted in a $21 million verdict to a woman injured by a trucker who had used a cell phone while driving a company truck.[18] Over a third of Americans admit to having texted while driving. In one year alone, 1.3 million crashes, or 23 percent of all collisions, involved cell phones.[19]

**Security and compliance.** Companies also worry about *phishing* (fraudulent schemes), viruses, *malware* (malicious software programs), and *spim* (IM spam). Like e-mail, instant and text messages as well as all other electronic records are subject to discovery (disclosure); that is, they can become evidence in lawsuits. Wall Street regulatory agencies NASD, SEC, and NYSE require that IM exchanged between brokers and clients be retained for three years, much like e-mail and printed documents.[20] Businesses must track and store messaging conversations to comply with legal requirements. Finally, IM and texting have been implicated in inappropriate uses such as bullying and the notorious *sexting*.

## 5-2b How to Use Instant Messaging and Texting on the Job

In today's workplace instant messaging and texting can definitely save time and simplify communication with coworkers and customers. However, before using IM or text messaging on the job, be sure you have permission. Do not download and use software without checking with your supervisor. If your organization does allow IM or texting, you can use it efficiently and professionally by following these best practices:

- Follow company policies: netiquette rules, code of conduct, ethics guidelines, as well as harassment and discrimination policies.[21]
- Don't disclose sensitive financial, company, customer, employee, or executive data.
- Don't forward or link to inappropriate photos, videos, and art.
- Don't text or IM while driving a car; pull over if you must read or send a message.
- Separate business contacts from family and friends.
- Avoid unnecessary chitchat and know when to say goodbye.
- Keep your presence status up-to-date, and make yourself unavailable when you need to meet a deadline.
- Use good grammar and correct spelling; shun jargon, slang, and abbreviations, which can be confusing and appear unprofessional.

## Figure 5.6 Texting Etiquette

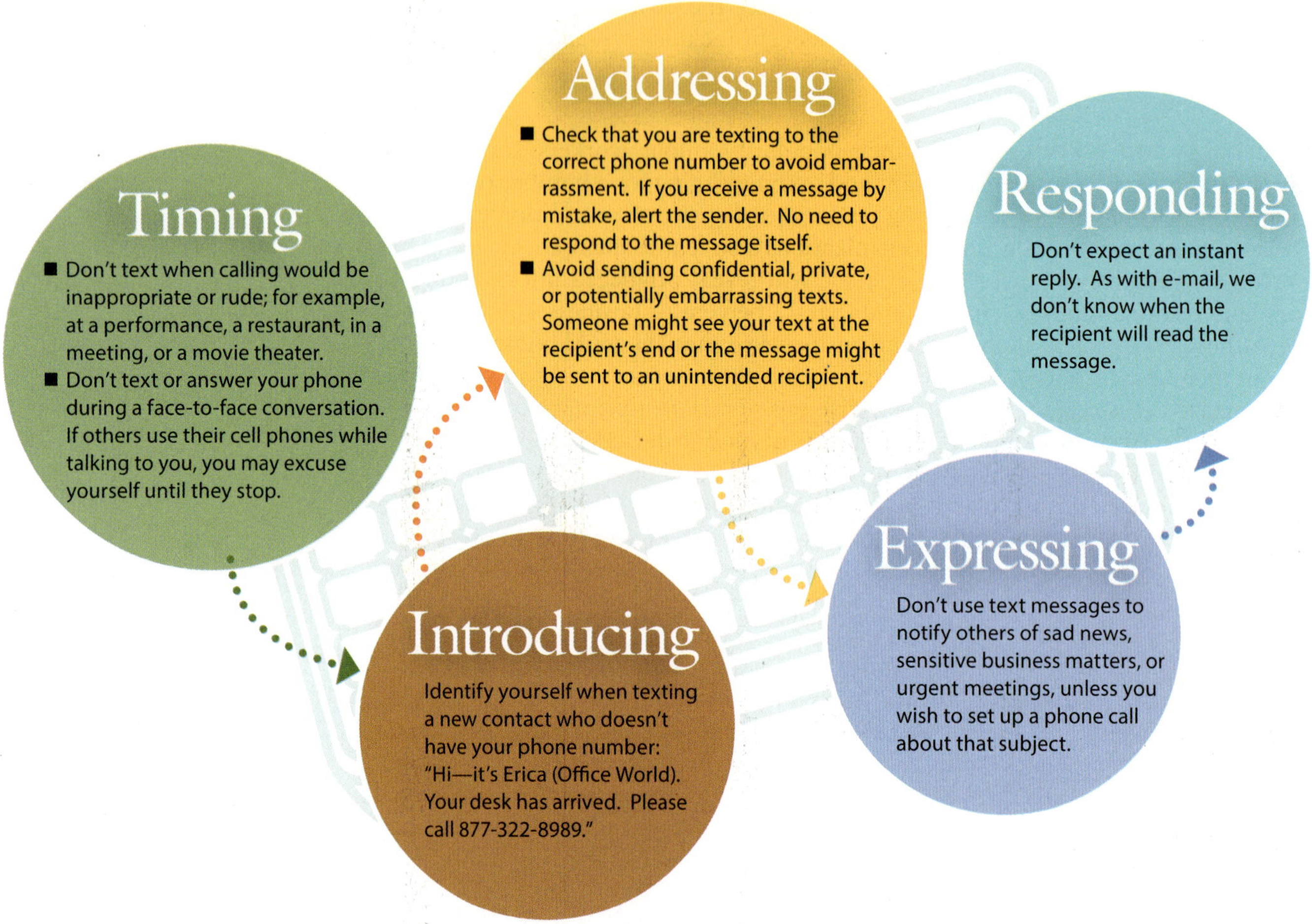

**Timing**
- Don't text when calling would be inappropriate or rude; for example, at a performance, a restaurant, in a meeting, or a movie theater.
- Don't text or answer your phone during a face-to-face conversation. If others use their cell phones while talking to you, you may excuse yourself until they stop.

**Addressing**
- Check that you are texting to the correct phone number to avoid embarrassment. If you receive a message by mistake, alert the sender. No need to respond to the message itself.
- Avoid sending confidential, private, or potentially embarrassing texts. Someone might see your text at the recipient's end or the message might be sent to an unintended recipient.

**Responding**
Don't expect an instant reply. As with e-mail, we don't know when the recipient will read the message.

**Introducing**
Identify yourself when texting a new contact who doesn't have your phone number: "Hi—it's Erica (Office World). Your desk has arrived. Please call 877-322-8989."

**Expressing**
Don't use text messages to notify others of sad news, sensitive business matters, or urgent meetings, unless you wish to set up a phone call about that subject.

### 5-2c Text Messaging and Business Etiquette

Texting is quick and unobtrusive, and for routine messages it is often the best alternative to a phone call or e-mail. Given the popularity of text messaging, etiquette experts are taking note.[22] Figure 5.6 summarizes the suggestions they offer for the considerate and professional use of texting.

**LEARNING OBJECTIVE 3**
Identify professional applications of podcasts and wikis.

## 5-3 Making Podcasts and Wikis Work for Business

In the digital age, individuals wield enormous influence because they can potentially reach huge audiences. Far from being passive consumers, today's Internet users have the power to create Web content; interact with businesses and each other; review products, self-publish, or blog; contribute to *wikis*; or tag and share images and other files. Businesses often rightly fear the wrath of disgruntled employees and customers, or they curry favor with influential plugged-in opinion leaders, the so-called *influencers*. Like social media networks, communication technologies such as podcasts and wikis are part of the new user-centered virtual environment called *Web 2.0*.

This section addresses prudent business uses of podcasts and wikis because you are likely to encounter these and other electronic communication tools on the job.

## 5-3a Business Podcasts or Webcasts

Perhaps because podcasts are more elaborate to produce and require quality hardware, their use is lagging behind that of other digital media. However, they have their place among Web 2.0 business communication strategies. Although the terms *podcast* and *podcasting* have caught on, they are somewhat misleading. The words *broadcasting* and *iPod* combined to create the word *podcast*; however, audio and video files can be played on any number of devices, not just Apple's. *Webcasting* for audio and *vcasting* for video content would be more accurate terms. Podcasts can extend from short clips of a few minutes to 30-minute or longer digital files. Most are recorded, but some are live. They can be streamed on a website or downloaded as media files.

**How Organizations Use Podcasts.** Podcasting has found its place among various user groups online. Major news organizations and media outlets podcast radio shows (e.g., National Public Radio) and TV shows, from ABC to Fox. You may have heard of TED Talks, the subject of Figure 5.7. These thought-provoking podcasts on any imaginable topic in technology, entertainment, and design (TED) are delivered by an intriguing mix of entrepreneurs, scientists, and other opinion leaders. Podcasts are also common in education. You can access instructors' lectures, interviews, and other media files. Apple's iTunes U is perhaps the best-known example of free educational podcasts from prestigious universities.

**Delivering and Accessing Podcasts.** Businesses have embraced podcasting for sending audio and video messages that do not require a live presence yet offer a friendly human face. Because they can broadcast repetitive information that does not require interaction, podcasts can replace costlier live teleconferences. Podcasts are featured on media websites and company portals or shared on blogs and social networking sites, often with links to YouTube and Vimeo.

For example, The Corcoran Group's channel on YouTube features professionally produced videos of luxurious properties in New York. Buyers can enjoy virtual walking tours of available properties at their leisure. IBM's acclaimed massive employee training effort is largely facilitated by podcasts and other media. HR policies can also be presented in the form of podcasts for unlimited viewing on demand.

To browse and learn from popular favorites, search on the Podcast Awards website for podcasts in various categories, including business, science, and technology.

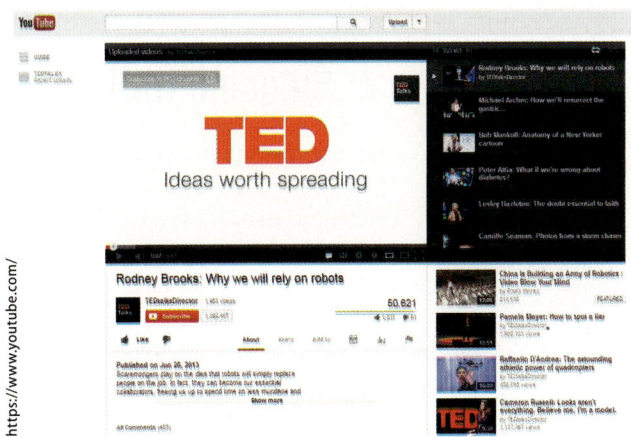

Figure 5.7 TED Talks Media Podcasts

### Figure 5.8 Four Main Uses for Business Wiki

**The global wiki**

For companies with a global reach, a wiki is an ideal tool for information sharing between headquarters and satellite offices. Far-flung team members can easily edit their work and provide input to the home office and each other.

**The wiki knowledge base**

Teams or departments use wikis to collect and disseminate information to large audiences creating a database for knowledge management. For example, human resources managers may update employee policies, make announcements, and convey information about benefits.

**Wikis for meetings**

Wikis can facilitate feedback from employees before and after meetings and serve as repositories of meeting minutes. In fact, wikis may replace some meetings, yet still keep a project on track.

**Wikis for project management**

Wikis offer a highly interactive environment for project information with easy access and user input. All participants have the same information, templates, and documentation readily available.

## 5-3b Collaborating With Wikis

Wikis are another important feature of the interactive, participatory Web 2.0 environment. A wiki is a Web-based tool that employs easy-to-use collaborative software to allow multiple users collectively to create, access, and modify documents. Think Wikipedia, the well-known online encyclopedia. You will find wikis in numerous subject categories on the Internet. Wiki editors may be given varying access privileges and control over the cloud-based material.

**Advantages of Wikis.** Two major advantages of wikis come to mind. First, wikis capitalize on *crowdsourcing*, which can be defined as the practice of tapping into the combined knowledge of an online community to solve problems and complete assignments. Second, working on the same content jointly eliminates the infamous problem of version confusion. Most wikis store all changes and intermediate versions of files, so that users can return to a previous stage if necessary. A survey found that benefits of corporate wikis include enhancing the reputation of expert contributors, making work flow more easily, and improving an organization's processes.[23]

**How Businesses Use Wikis.** Enterprises using wikis usually store their internal data on an intranet, a private network. An enterprise-level wiki serves as an easy-to-navigate, efficient central repository of company information, complete with hyperlinks and keywords pointing to related subjects and media. IBM, for example, uses wikis to publish documentation for its WebSphere and Lotus products and to interact with the community of adopters. The four main uses of wikis in business, shown in Figure 5.8,[24] range from providing a shared internal knowledge base to storing templates for business documents.

Popular simple-to-use wiki hosting services, called *wiki farms*, are PBworks (Project Hub), Wikispaces, and Wikia. Some are noncommercial and offer free hosting. Consider starting a wiki for your next classroom project requiring teamwork. Alternatively, explore Google Docs and Google Sites, a page of which is shown in Figure 5.9.

**LEARNING OBJECTIVE 4**
Describe how businesses use blogs to connect with internal and external audiences, and list best practices for professional blogging.

## 5-4 Blogging for Business

The biggest advantage of business blogs is that they potentially reach a far-flung, vast audience. A blog is a website with journal entries on any imaginable topic usually written by one person, although most corporate blogs feature multiple contributors. Typically, readers leave comments. Businesses use blogs to keep customers, employees, and the public at large informed and to interact with them.

Marketing firms and their clients are looking closely at blogs because blogs can invite spontaneous consumer feedback faster and more cheaply than such staples

Figure 5.9 Creating a Wiki With Google Sites and Google Docs

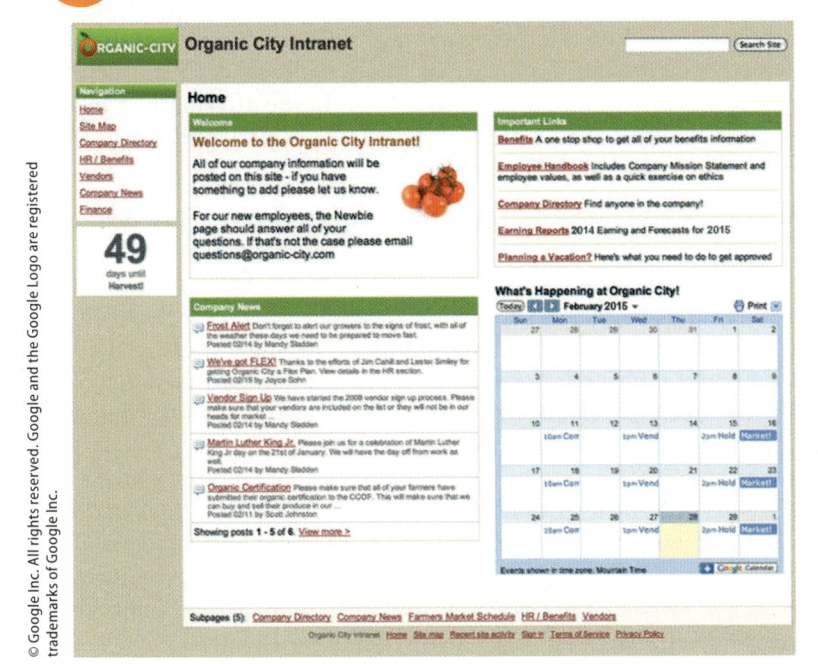

This screenshot shows a template available for customization in Google Sites, a free, user-friendly wiki and website creator. Google Sites and the document editing and revision tool Google Docs allow users to create, edit, share, and manage documents online in real time. Unlike in typical wikis, here multiple editors can modify files simultaneously.

of consumer research as focus groups and surveys. Employees and executives at companies such as Walmart, Exxon, Dell, and Xerox maintain blogs. They use blogs to communicate externally with the public but also internally with employees. Currently, 171 (34 percent) of Fortune 500 companies are blogging, and researchers note a rise in the number of corporations with active blogs.[25] However, a whopping 68 percent of Fortune 500 CEOs have no social presence at all, and of those who do, only a few blog.[26]

In this section you will learn how businesses use blogs and find guidance on professional blogging practices.

### 5-4a How Companies Blog

Like other Web 2.0 phenomena, corporate blogs help create virtual communities, build brands, and develop relationships. In other words, blogs are part of a social media strategy to create *engagement*, resulting in customers' goodwill and brand loyalty. Companies use blogs for public relations, customer relations, crisis communication, market research, viral marketing, internal communication, and recruiting.

**Public Relations, Customer Relations, and Crisis Communication.** One of the prominent uses of blogs is to provide up-to-date company information to the media and the public. Blogs can be written by rank-and-file employees or by top managers. Consider these examples: Executive chairman Bill Marriott is an avid and astute blogger. His Marriott on the Move blog feels personal and honest. Just one of several General Electric blogs, Edison's Desk addresses industry insiders and the interested public. Under the heading Best Buy Unboxed, the electronics retailer operates five niche blogs targeting various constituencies and actively soliciting customer input.

Social media experts believe that brands should embrace negative blog posts and turn them into opportunities to reach out to the customer and strengthen the

## OFFICE INSIDER

"I make [blogging] work because it's a great way to communicate with our customers and stakeholders. . . . When your family's name is on the building or you are the person clearly identified with the company, everything you say or do affects the business, good or bad. In this fascinating information age, you have to be transparent."

—J. W. "Bill" Marriott, Jr., executive chairman, Marriott International, Inc.

relationship.[27] Whether businesses choose to respond angrily or surprise and delight customers, "the world is watching."[28]

An organization's blog is a natural forum for late-breaking news, especially when disaster strikes. Although a blog cannot replace other communication channels in an emergency, it should be part of the overall effort to soothe the public's emotional reaction with a human voice of reason. In the aftermath of hugely devastating Hurricane Sandy, various blogs chronicled recovery and rebuilding efforts, offering vital information to the public.[29]

**Market Research and Viral Marketing.** Because most blogs invite feedback, they can be invaluable sources of opinion and bright ideas from customers as well as industry experts. Starbucks is a Fortune 500 company that understands blogging and crowdsourcing in particular. My Starbucks Idea blog, depicted in Figure 5.10, is a public forum for the sharing of product ideas. Members vote and comment on the suggestions and eliminate poor ideas. Many companies now have appointed employees who scrutinize the blogosphere for buzz and positive and negative postings about their organizations and products.

The term *viral marketing* refers to the rapid spread of messages online, much like infectious diseases that pass from person to person. Marketers realize the potential of getting the word out about their products and services in the blogosphere, where their messages are often picked up by well-connected bloggers, the so-called *influencers*, who boast large audiences. Viral messages must be authentic and elicit an emotional response, but for that very reason they are difficult to orchestrate. Online denizens resent being co-opted by companies using overt hard-sell tactics.

**Online Communities.** Company blogs can attract a devoted community of participants who want to keep informed about company events, product updates, and other news. In turn, those enthusiasts can contribute new ideas. Few companies enjoy the brand awareness and customer loyalty of Coca-Cola. With its blog

Figure 5.10 Starbucks Blog Specializes in Crowdsourcing

### Ideas so far

Search Ideas

**PRODUCT IDEAS**

| | |
|---|---|
| 32,318 | Coffee & Espresso Drinks |
| 3,281 | Frappuccino® Beverages |
| 9,478 | Tea & Other Drinks |
| 14,799 | Food |
| 7,728 | Merchandise & Music |
| 15,806 | Starbucks Card |
| 2,621 | New Technology |
| 10,411 | Other Product Ideas |

**EXPERIENCE IDEAS**

| | |
|---|---|
| 7,761 | Ordering, Payment, & Pick-Up |
| 13,932 | Atmosphere & Locations |
| 10,738 | Other Experience Ideas |

**INVOLVEMENT IDEAS**

SHARE. VOTE. DISCUSS. SEE.

Share your ideas, tell us what you think of other people's ideas and join the discussion.

my STARBUCKS IDEA

**Most Recent Ideas**

| | |
|---|---|
| 2 Hour(s) Ago | More options for decaf coffee |
| 3 Hour(s) Ago | Upgrade to chip card readers for your debit machines please. |
| 6 Hour(s) Ago | Bring Soy and other non-dairy milk alternative back for free! |

© 2012 Starbucks Corporation. All rights reserved.

Chapter 5: Short Workplace Messages and Digital Media

Coca-Cola Conversations, the soft drink maker shares its rich past ("Life without Coca-Cola") and thus deepens Coke fans' loyalty. Coke's marketing is subtle; the blog is designed to provide a unique experience to fans.

**Internal Communication and Recruiting.** Blogs can be used to keep virtual teams on track and share updates on the road. Members in remote locations can stay in touch by smartphone and other devices, exchanging text, images, sound, and video clips. In many companies, blogs have replaced hard-copy publications in offering late-breaking news or tidbits of interest to employees. Blogs can create a sense of community and stimulate employee participation. Furthermore, blogs mirror the company culture and present a priceless opportunity for job candidates to size up a potential employer and the people working there.

## 5-4b Blog Best Practices: Seven Tips for Master Bloggers

Much advice is freely accessible on the Web, but this section offers guidelines culled from experienced bloggers and communication experts that will lead you to successful blog writing. As with any public writing, your posts will be scrutinized; therefore, you want to make the best impression.

**Craft a Catchy but Concise Title.** The headline is what draws online readers to even open your post. Some will be intriguing questions or promises. Online writers often use numbers to structure their posts. Here are some examples: *Six Apps You Don't Want to Miss; 5 Tips to Keep Spear Phishers Out of Your Inbox; Create Powerful Imagery in Your Writing; How Financially Sexy is Your Household?; The False Choice of Mediocrity.*

**Ace the Opening Paragraph.** The lead must deliver on the promise of the headline.

Identify a need and propose to solve the problem. Ask a relevant question. Say something startling. Tell an anecdote or use an analogy to connect with the reader. The author of "How Many Lives Does a Brand Have?" opened with this:

> *It's said that cats have nine lives, but how many lives does a brand have? The answer, it seems, is definitely more than one. Recently, in Shanghai, a friend took me to one of the city's most sophisticated luxury malls. . . .*[30]

**Provide Details in the Body.** Mind the *So what?* and *What's in it for me?* questions. Use vivid examples, quotations and testimonials, or statistics. Structure the body with numbers, bullets, and subheadings. Use expressive action verbs (*buy* for *get*; *own* for *have*; *travel* or *jet* for *go*). Use conversational language to sound warm and authentic. Use contractions (*can't* for *cannot*; *doesn't* for *does not*; *isn't* for *is not*).

**Consider Visuals.** Add visual interest with relevant images and diagrams. Keep paragraphs short and use plenty of white space around them. Aim to make the look simple and easy to scan.

**Include Calls to Action.** Call on readers in the title to do something or provide a take-away and gentle nudge at the end. Chris Brogan, writing in his blog Become a Dream Feeder, had this to say: "So, how will you make your blog into a dream feeder? Or do you do that already? What dreams do your readers have?"[31] Ask open-ended questions or tell the reader what to do: *So, be sure to ask about 360-degree security tactics that aim to stop inbound attacks, but also to block outbound data theft attempts.*

**Edit and Proofread.** Follow the revision tips in Chapter 4 of this book. Cut any unneeded words, sentences, and irrelevant ideas. Fix awkward, wordy, and repetitious sentences. Edit and proofread as if your life depended on it. Your reputation might. The best blogs are error free.

## OFFICE INSIDER

*"In the past the local dry cleaner could mumble whatever he wanted behind the register, but online the repercussions can be so much greater. Anything can go viral."*

—Shama Kabani, author of "The Zen of Social Media Marketing"

**LEARNING OBJECTIVE 5**

Address business uses of social media networks, and assess their advantages as well as risks.

**Respond to Posts Respectfully.** Build a positive image online by posting compelling comments on other bloggers' posts. Politely and promptly reply to comments on your site. This reply to Guy Kawasaki's infographic makes a positive observation about the post and adds a valuable thought albeit with a glaring spelling error and missing commas:

*Great graphic portrayal of the human connection. Three other areas might include 1) use people's first name (something pretty basic but often forgotten) 2) listen before you talk (a great one for bosses when meeting with employees) and 3) don't be afraid to pay complements [sic] when they are warranted.*[32]

Don't ramble. If you disagree with a post, do so respectfully. Remember, your comments may remain online practically forever and could come back to haunt you long after posting.

## 5-5 Web 2.0: Social Networking

Popular social networking sites such as Facebook and Twitter are used by businesses for similar reasons and in much the same way as podcasts, blogs, and wikis. Social networking sites enable businesses to connect with customers and employees, share company news, and exchange ideas. Social online communities for professional audiences (e.g., LinkedIn), discussed in Chapter 13, help recruiters find talent and encounter potential employees before hiring them.

### 5-5a Tapping Into Social Networks

Business interest in social networking sites is not surprising if we consider that 93 percent of millennials, also called Generation Y, go online several times a day. They are most likely to access the Internet wirelessly with mobile phones, laptops, and tablets.[33] Young adults lead in instant messaging, blog reading, listening to music, playing online games, and participating in virtual worlds. However, older age groups are gaining on them and even pulling ahead in some categories; for example, in Facebook growth.

As for Twitter, the heaviest users are people in the eighteen-to-twenty-four age bracket (31 percent), followed by twenty-five- to thirty-four-year-olds (17 percent).[34] Predictably, businesses are trying to adapt and tap the vast potential of social networking. About 70 percent of the Fortune 500 companies are now on Facebook, and 77 percent have corporate Twitter accounts.[35] Excluding celebrities and news media, Facebook (the corporation) leads in the number of Twitter followers with 10.9 million, with Google coming in second (6.7 million), and Samsung Mobile US in third place (4.6 million), followed by Starbucks (4.2 million).[36]

### 5-5b How Businesses Use Social Networks

Companies harness the power of very public online communities to boost their brand image or to provide a forum for collaboration. However, the social Web has also spawned internal networking sites safely located behind corporate firewalls. For example, with almost 600,000 likes, Wells Fargo is a popular company on Facebook with about 50,000 Twitter followers, a comparatively modest number. However, the bank's private social network, Teamworks, connects 280,000 team members worldwide.[37] Insurer MetLife runs MetConnect, an internal networking tool. Similarly, a digital ad agency by the name of Possible turned to its own social network to share a new brand identity with its 20 offices from Cincinnati to Guangzhou, China.[38]

**Adopting the Facebook Model.** Many businesses have found that the Facebook model can be adapted to internal networks, many of which run on Yammer, Salesforce Chatter, or Jive—the most prominent enterprise social networking platforms. For one thing, staff members already intuitively understand how a corporate social network operates because they are familiar with Facebook. Red Robin's corporate social network, by allowing discussions and providing videos, helped cut the introduction of a new burger line from months to days.[39]

**Connecting Far-Flung Workers.** Because social networks are about connections, they also enable companies to match up dispersed employees and their skills as needed, especially when managers in different divisions don't know each other. SUPERVALU supermarket chains built a Yammer-based network connecting 11,000 executives and store managers, eliminating the need for expensive travel. More than 1,000 groups emerged that provided creative solutions to specific problems.[40]

**Crowdsourcing Customers.** Social networks and blogs also help companies invite customer input at the product design stage. On its IdeaStorm site, Dell has solicited over 17,000 new product ideas and suggested improvements, including backlit keyboards that are ideal for working on airplanes.[41] Samuel Adams enlisted social media guru Guy Kawasaki to invite fans and followers of the Boston brewery to vote on the ideal properties of a new beer recipe.[42] As Figure 5.11 shows, large companies have established successful social media presences.

Figure 5.11 Big Companies Rule on Facebook

Facebook has reached 1.15 billion users. For comparison, LinkedIn has 238 million members. Twitter claims more than 200 million active users, and Google Plus has 343 million active users. Facebook allows registered users to create individual home pages as well as group pages based on their interests. Large corporations seem to thrive on Facebook. The top three companies with the most fans after Facebook itself are Coca-Cola (71.6 million), Disney (45 million), and Starbucks (35.2 million).

Chapter 5: Short Workplace Messages and Digital Media

### 5-5c Potential Risks of Social Networks for Businesses

Online social networks hold great promise for businesses while also presenting some risk. Most managers want plugged-in employees with strong tech skills. They like to imagine their workers as brand ambassadors. They fantasize about their products becoming overnight sensations thanks to viral marketing. However, they also fret about incurring productivity losses, compromising trade secrets, attracting the wrath of huge Internet audiences, and facing embarrassment over inappropriate and damaging employee posts.[43] Moreover, network administrators fear security breaches from the unauthorized private use of work-issued devices.[44]

Businesses take different approaches to the "dark side" of social networking. Some, such as Zappos.com, take a hands-off approach and encourage employee

Figure 5.12 Using Media Professionally: Dos and Don'ts

| DON'T — AVOID QUESTIONABLE CONTENT, PERSONAL DOCUMENTS, AND FILE SHARING | DO ✓ — KNOW WORKPLACE POLICIES AND AVOID PRIVATE USE OF MEDIA AT WORK |
|---|---|
| ✗ **Don't spread rumors, gossip, and negative defamatory comments.** Because all digital information is subject to discovery in court, avoid unprofessional content and conduct, including complaints about your employer, customers, and employees. | ✓ **Learn your company's rules.** Some companies require workers to sign that they have read and understand Internet and digital media use policies. Being informed is your best protection. |
| ✗ **Don't download and share cartoons, video clips, photos, and art.** Businesses are liable for any recorded digital content regardless of the medium used. | ✓ **Avoid sending personal e-mail, instant messages, or texts from work.** Even if your company allows personal use during lunch or after hours, keep it to a minimum. Better yet, wait to use your own electronic devices away from work. |
| ✗ **Don't open unfamiliar attachments.** Attachments with executable files or video files may carry viruses, spyware, or other malware (malicious programs). | ✓ **Separate work and personal data.** Keep information that could embarrass you or expose you to legal liability on your personal storage devices, on hard drives, or in the cloud, never on your office computer. |
| ✗ **Don't download free software and utilities to company machines.** Employees can unwittingly introduce viruses, phishing schemes, and other cyber "bugs." | ✓ **Be careful when blogging, tweeting, or posting on social networking sites.** Unhappy about not receiving a tip, a Beverly Hills waiter lost his job for tweeting disparaging remarks about an actress. Forgetting that his boss was his Facebook "friend," a British employee was fired after posting, "OMG, I HATE MY JOB!" and calling his supervisor names. |
| ✗ **Don't store your music and photos on a company machine (or server) and don't watch streaming videos.** Capturing precious company bandwidth for personal use is a sure way to be shown the door. | ✓ **Keep sensitive information private.** Use privacy settings, but don't trust the "private" areas on Facebook, Twitter, Flickr, and other social networks. |
| ✗ **Don't share files, and avoid file-sharing services.** Clarify whether you may use Google Docs and other services that offer optional file sharing. Stay away from distributors or pirated files such as LimeWire. | ✓ **Avoid pornography, sexually explicit jokes, or inappropriate screen savers.** Anything that might "poison" the work environment is a harassment risk and, therefore, prohibited. |

online activity. Others, such as IBM, have drafted detailed policies to cover all forms of self-expression online. According to one survey, 50 percent of businesses block Web access to social networking sites; 61 percent, to gaming sites; and 40 percent, to entertainment sites.[45] However, some experts believe that organizations should embrace positive word-of-mouth testimonials from employees about their jobs, not quash them with rigid policies.[46]

### 5-5d Using Social Networking Sites and Keeping Your Job

Most professionals agree that, as with any public online activity, users of social networking sites would do well to exercise caution. Privacy online is a myth, and sensitive information should not be shared lightly, least of all risqué photographs. Furthermore, refusing *friend requests* or *unfriending* individuals could jeopardize professional relationships.

The advice to think twice before posting online applies to most communication channels used on the job. Many users leave their pages open and risk trouble with their employers by assuming that online comments are hidden.[47] Even privacy settings, however, do not guarantee complete protection from prying eyes.

Among the many risks in the cyber world are inappropriate photographs and tagging. Tags make pictures searchable so that an embarrassing college incident may resurface years later. The dos and don'ts in Figure 5.12 sum up best practices for all digital media.

> **OFFICE INSIDER**
>
> "Security risks rise in businesses because many employees adopt 'my way' work lifestyles in which their devices, work and online behavior mix with their personal lives virtually anywhere—in the office, at home and everywhere in between."
>
> —Cisco Annual Security Report

## SUMMARY OF LEARNING OBJECTIVES

**5-1** Understand the professional standards for the usage, structure, and format of e-mails and interoffice memos in the digital-era workplace.
- Although sometimes annoying, e-mail will likely remain a mainstream communication channel.
- E-mail is especially effective for informal messages to multiple receivers and as a cover document for attachments.
- Business e-mails feature a compelling subject line, include a greeting, are organized for readability, and close effectively.
- Memos are still used for internal messages that are too long for e-mail, require a lasting record, demand formality, or inform workers who don't have e-mail.
- Like e-mails, memos carry nonsensitive information and include a subject line, a dateline, and the names of senders and receivers.

**5-2** Explain workplace instant messaging and texting as well as their liabilities and best practices.
- Individuals use the Internet or corporate intranets to exchange brief text-based messages, which requires a cellular connection or a VoIP service.
- The benefits of messaging are low cost, speed, unobtrusiveness, immediacy, and efficiency.
- The risks of messaging include legal liability, security breaches, and compliance issues.
- Best practices for messaging include minding policies, protecting sensitive data, pulling over to message, separating personal and work contacts, and using correct language.

**5-3** Identify professional applications of podcasts and wikis.
- Whether as short clips or longer digital files, business podcasts offer a friendly human face and can replace costlier live teleconferences.
- A wiki is a Web-based collaborative software tool that allows multiple users to create, access, and modify documents.
- Wikis can help online groups solve problems and complete assignments while preventing version confusion.

Chapter 5: Short Workplace Messages and Digital Media

**5-4** Describe how businesses use blogs to connect with internal and external audiences, and list best practices for professional blogging.
- External or internal corporate blogs help create virtual communities, build brands, and develop relationships.
- Companies use blogs for public relations, customer relations, crisis communication, market research, viral marketing, building online communities, internal communication, and recruiting.
- Best practices include crafting a catchy title and intriguing opening, providing details in the body, using visuals, calling for action, editing carefully, and commenting respectfully.

**5-5** Address business uses of social media networks, and assess their advantages as well as risks.
- Social networking sites enable businesses to connect with customers and employees, share news, exchange ideas, and boost their brand images.
- In addition to Facebook, Twitter, and other very public social media, many businesses also run private social networks behind corporate firewalls.
- The risks of social media use in business include productivity losses, leaked trade secrets, angry Internet audiences, security breaches, and damaging employee posts.
- Savvy users should keep privacy settings up-to-date, avoid risqué images, handle friend requests tactfully, and beware of tagging.

# CHAPTER REVIEW

1. Why do some businesspeople criticize e-mail? (Obj. 1)

2. When is e-mail appropriate? (Obj. 1)

3. Describe the writing plan for informational e-mail messages. (Obj. 1)

4. What are the risks of instant messaging and texting? (Obj. 2)

5. List five best practices for using IM and texting that you consider most important. (Obj. 2)

6. How do organizations use and deliver podcasts? (Obj. 3)

7. Explain what a wiki is and list its advantages. (Obj. 3)

8. How do companies use blogs? (Obj. 4)

9. What seven tips would you give to a beginning blogger? (Obj. 4)

10. Name potential risks of social networks for businesses. (Obj. 5)

## CRITICAL THINKING

11. Many people are concerned that privacy is increasingly rare in our hyperconnected world as our online presence leaves a lasting footprint.[49] Do you fear that disclosing personal matters online will hamper your job search? (Objs. 1–5)

12. Experts have argued that social media fool us into thinking that we are connected when in reality they do not help us develop true friendships.[50] Do you agree that technology diminishes personal relationships rather than bringing us closer together? (Objs. 1–5)

13. Are common abbreviations such as *lol* and *imho* and all-lowercase writing acceptable in texting or instant messaging for business? (Obj. 2)

14. Traditional mainstream media act as so-called *gatekeepers* that decide what kind of content gets published. However, social media networks have changed the game. Now anyone with an Internet connection can potentially publish anything and reach vast audiences. What are the benefits and dangers of this unprecedented access?

15. Some marketers employ machines to inflate the number of likes and fans online.[51] So-called Facebook bot networks (*botnets*) operate large numbers of fake accounts around the world. A rental agency based in Washington, D.C., went from two fans to almost 15,000 within a few days. How do you feel about companies and their brands pretending they have actual traffic on their sites and buying *likes*?

# WRITING IMPROVEMENT EXERCISES

## Message Openers and Subject Lines (Obj. 1)

**YOUR TASK.** Compare the following sets of message openers. Circle the letter of the opener that illustrates a direct opening. Write an appropriate subject line for each opening paragraph.

16. An e-mail requesting information about creating online surveys:

    a. Our company needs to conduct occasional consumer surveys regarding new products. We used to invest in focus groups, but now we would like to try online research, about which we have heard good things. We hope this will save much time and money. We need information on how to do it, and your program called MySurvey might be just what we need. We are especially interested in how incentives such as reward points might work.
    b. Please send information about your program MySurvey so that our company can learn about online surveys.

    **Subject line:**

17. An e-mail announcing a low-cost day-care program:

    a. Employees interested in enrolling their children in our new low-cost day-care program are invited to attend an HR orientation on January 18.
    b. For several years we have studied the possibility of offering a day-care option for those employees who are parents. Until recently, our management team was unable to agree on the exact parameters of this benefit, but now some of you will be able to take advantage of this option.

    **Subject line:**

18. A memo announcing an upcoming employee satisfaction survey:

    a. We have noticed recently increased turnover among our marketing staff. We are concerned about this troubling development and would like to study its causes. We have hired an outside consulting firm to gauge the satisfaction level and attitudes of our marketing staff in confidential qualitative interviews. You may be asked to participate in this important survey in which you can recommend strategies to avoid the situation.
    b. You may be asked to participate in qualitative interviews to explore the satisfaction level among our marketing staff and recommend strategies to stem the tide of recent departures.

    **Subject line:**

19. A memo announcing a new policy:

    a. It has come to our attention that some staff members write blogs, sometimes publicly addressing sensitive company information. Although we respect the desire of employees to express themselves and would like to continue allowing the practice, we have decided to adopt a new policy providing binding rules to ensure the company's and the bloggers' safety.
    b. The following new policy for blog authors will help staff members create posts that maintain the integrity of the company's sensitive information and keep writers safe.

    **Subject line:**

## Bulleted and Numbered Lists (Obj. 1)

E-mails and memos frequently contain numbered (for items in a sequence) or bulleted lists. Study how the following wordy paragraph was revised into a more readable format with a list:

**BEFORE REVISION:**

Our office could implement better environmental practices such as improving energy efficiency and reducing our carbon footprint. Here are three simple things we can do to make our daily work practices greener. For one thing, we can power down. At night we should turn off monitors, not just log off our computers. In addition, we could "Light Right." This means installing energy-efficient lighting throughout the office. A final suggestion has to do with recycling. We could be recycling instantly if we placed small recycling bins at all workstations and common use areas.

**AFTER REVISION:**

Our office could use energy more efficiently and reduce our carbon footprint in three simple ways:
- **Power down:** Turn off monitors rather than just logging off our computers.
- **Light right:** Install energy-efficient lighting throughout the office.
- **Recycle instantly:** Place small recycling bins at all workstations and common use areas to encourage recycling.

**YOUR TASK.** Revise the following wordy, unorganized paragraphs. Include an introductory statement followed by a bulleted or numbered list. Look for ways to eliminate unnecessary wording.

20. If you are a job candidate interviewing for a job, you should follow a few guidelines that most people consider basic. You will be more successful if you do these things. One of the first things to do is get ready. Before the interview, successful candidates research the target company. That is, they find out about it. If you really want to be successful, you will prepare success stories. Wise candidates also clean up any digital dirt that may be floating around the Internet. Those are a few of the things to do before the interview. During the interview, the best candidates try to sound enthusiastic. They answer questions clearly but with short, concise responses. They also are prepared to ask their own questions. After the interview, when you can relax a bit, you should remember to send a thank-you note to the interviewer. Another thing to do after the interview is contact references. One last thing to do, if you don't hear from the interviewer within five days, is follow up with an inquiry.

21. Winning the lottery can bring a colossal chunk of income. What would you do if you had won the lottery and come home with mega millions? Smart winners can save their sanity and their cash, as well as live well for years into the future if they take precautionary steps. Step No. 1 is staying anonymous. Don't broadcast your good news because long-lost friends and relatives become vultures, all seeking handouts. A second step involves seeking out a tax pro immediately. You may think you have a huge chunk of money to spend, but the government will be taking a hefty hunk. You need a tax expert to help minimize the tax burden. Experts also warn against making immediate and major changes in your lifestyle within six months after winning. Examples: quitting your job, buying yachts, or purchasing European castles.

# RADICAL REWRITES

**Note:** Radical Rewrites are provided at **www.cengagebrain.com** for you to download and revise. Your instructor may show a suggested solution.

## 5.1 Radical Rewrite: Informational E-mail—Lining Up "Lunch and Learn" Talks (Obj. 1)

The following e-mail message from Kennedy Freed asks his assistant Camille Chavez to perform a task. However, she will struggle with that task because the message is so poorly written. It badly needs a radical rewrite.

**YOUR TASK.** Study the message in light of what you have learned about how e-mail messages should be organized. What is Camille to do? Should this message have an end date? List at least five weaknesses of this message. Revise it if your instructor directs.

       To:  Camille Chavez <c.chavez@firstfederal.com>
     From:  Kennedy Freed <k.freed@firstfederal.com>
  Subject:  Luncheon Talks
       Cc:
      Bcc:

You've probably seen us working hard to get good speakers to speak at our "Lunch and Learn" sessions. Well, we've finally lined up speakers for September and October. It took a little twisting of arms, but we do have some really good speakers lined up. We're scheduling the talks from 12 to 1, but the speakers should plan to speak for only about 30 minutes and leave 10 to 20 minutes for questions and answer.

I need you to send messages to these speakers to confirm. If any of them has questions or needs to change his date, just have them call my cell at 213.348.4421. We will need to get this done as soon as possible since the listing will be released in early September. The speakers include Alaina Adams, who agreed to speak at our first fall session on Tuesday, September 24. Her topic is "How to Talk So People Will Listen." Another interesting speaker is Caitlyn Cervantes. Her topic is "Ten Top Tips for Eating Healthy." Caitlyn's date is Tuesday, October 22. Another speaker who just agreed is Brandon Tabaldo, and his topic is "Staying Safe, Private, and Secure on Social Networks." We were able to schedule Mr. Tabaldo for Tuesday, October 15.

Oh yes, here are the e-mail addresses: alina.adams@circe.com, btabaldo@intercoastal.com, and caitlyn.cervantes@rio.com. Thank you, Camille!

Kennedy Freed

1. List at least five weaknesses of this message.




2. Outline a writing plan (not the actual message) for this information e-mail.

   **Subject line:**

   **Opening:**

   **Body:**

   **Closing:**

## 5.2 Radical Rewrite: Informational E-mail—Web Conferencing Made Simple (Obj. 1)

Jeremy Harper, a blogger and Web conferencing expert, responds to a request from Christina Cruz, who wants advice for an article she is writing. His advice is good, but his message is poorly organized, contains grammar and other errors, and is hard to read.

**YOUR TASK.** Analyze the following message and note specific weaknesses with examples. Then revise if your instructor advises. Remember that you can download these documents at **www.cengagebrain.com**.

To: Christina Cruz <ccruz @sagepublications.com>
From: Jeremy Harper <jeremy.harper@pcs.com>
Subject: Replying to Your Request
Cc:
Bcc:

Dear Christina Cruz:

Hey, thanks for asking me to make a contribution to the article you are preparing and working up for *Networking Voices*. Appreciate this opportunity! Although you asked me to keep it brief, I could give you an extensive, comprehensive list of dos and don'ts for Web conferencing. If you want this, let me know.

As an alternative to in-person meetings, Web conferencing is increasingly popular. Here's five tips for your article. First and foremost, plan ahead. All participants should be notified of things like the date, time, and duration. It's your job to send log-ins, passwords, and printed documents by e-mail. My next advise is about identifying yourself. Don't assume that attendees will automatically recognize your voice. The first few times you speak, its good to state your name.

Another tip has to do with muting (turning off) your phone. Believe me, there's nothing worse than barking dogs, side conversations. And worst of all is the sound of toilets flushing during a conference. Ick!

You should play with your microphone and speakers until you sound good. And of course, don't shuffle papers. Don't eat. Don't move things while your speaking.

My final tip involves using a lobby slide to open. This is a slide that tells the meeting details. Such as the start time, audio information, and the agenda. This lobby slide should go up about 10 to 15 minutes before the meeting begins.

Hope this helps!

Jeremy Harper

[Full contact information]

1. List at least five weaknesses with examples.

## 5.3 Radical Rewrite: Informational Memo—Lost in the Cloud (Obj. 1)

In the following memo, product manager Alexandra Amato reports to CEO Mason Razipour the high points of a workshop he asked her to attend. Alexandra's jumbled memo offers solid information but is poorly written.

**YOUR TASK.** Analyze the message and list at least five weaknesses. Revise if directed.

Date:     July 10, 2016
To:       Mason Razipour, CEO
From:     Alexandra Amato, Product Manager
Subject:  Cloud Computing

Some time ago you signed me up to attend The Promise of Cloud Computing workshop. I did attend it on July 8. Herewith is a short report, as you requested. If you prefer, I could give a presentation about what I learned at the next management council meeting. Is that meeting coming up in August?

Okay, here's my report. I know you asked that it be brief, so will do! Lisa Moritz, the workshop leader told the group that the big problem today is that in this anytime/anywhere workplace employees are working with tons of devices from various locations. With employees scattered around, software and file storage must be accessible anywhere, anytime. It can't be on one type of device, and it can no longer be stuck in one place to be accessed with incompatible devices. Lisa told us that there are three main ways that cloud computing can improve the workplace. No. 1. Cloud computing makes it possible to access nearly all types of applications or software. A vast number of cloud-based services (e-mail, online storage, online file transfer) can be made available to lots of users—without the problem of compatibility. Another big benefit is the promise of making employees more efficient. How? Free access to unlimited ways to provide on-the-spot solutions eliminates searching and downtime. Cloud computing is also a way to improve communications. It completely transforms the way work is performed. Lisa didn't tell us exactly how this was accomplished, but she said that cloud computing makes for a happier, mentally healthy atmosphere all around.

This is just a bare-bones summary of what I learned. If you want to hear more, please do not hesitate to call.

1. List at least five weaknesses with examples.

# ACTIVITIES AND CASES

## 5.4 Instant Messaging Mess at Auto Dealership (Obj. 2)
**Communication Technology · Social Media · Web**

Read the following log of a live IM chat between a customer service representative and a visitor to an Orlando car dealership's website.

**YOUR TASK.** In class discuss how Mark could have made this interaction with a customer more effective. Is his IM chat with Mr. Kim professional, polite, and respectful? If your instructor directs, rewrite Mark's responses to Mr. Kim's queries.

*Dealer rep:* Hey, I'm Mark. How's it goin? Welcome to Fields BMW South Orlando!
*Customer:* ??
*Dealer rep:* Im supposed to provid live assistance. What can I do you for?
*Customer:* I want buy car.
*Dealer rep:* May I have your name fist?
*Customer:* Young Jae Kim

*Dealer rep:* Whoa! Is that a dude's name? Okay. What kind? New inventory or preowned?
*Customer:* BMW. 2016 model. for family, for business.
*Dealer rep:* New, then, huh? Where are you from?
*Customer:* What car you have?
*Dealer rep:* We got some that will knock your socks off.
*Customer:* I want green car, no high gasoline burn.
*Dealer rep:* My man, if you can't afford the gas on these puppies, you shouldn't buy a Beemer, you know what I mean? Or ya want green color?
*Customer:* ?
*Dealer rep:* Okeydoke, we got a full lineup. Which series, 3, 5, 6, or 7? Or an X3 or X5? A Z4 convertible?
*Customer:* BMW i ActiveE?
*Dealer rep:* Nope. Is that the electric car? Oh I dont recommend those. We got two regular 550i, one for $70,895 and one for 75,020
*Customer:* Eurepean delivery?
*Dealer rep:* Oh, I know zip about that. Let me find someone who does. Can I have your phone number and e-mail?
*Customer:* i prefer not get a phone call yet . . . yjkim@t-tech.net is email
*Dealer rep:* Awsome. Well shoot you an email pronto! Bye.

## 5.5 E-Mail Simulation: Writeaway Hotels (Obj. 1)
**Communication Technology** **E-mail**

At **www.cengagebrain.com**, you can build your e-mail skills in our Writeaway Hotels simulation. You will be reading, writing, and responding to messages in an exciting game that helps you make appropriate decisions about whether to respond to e-mail messages and how to write clear, concise messages under pressure. The game can be played in a computer lab, in a classroom, or even on your own computer and on your own time.

**YOUR TASK.** Check out the Writeaway Hotels simulation at www.cengagebrain.com. If your instructor directs, follow the instructions to participate.

## 5.6 Informational E-Mail: What Exactly Is Business Attire? (Obj. 1)
**E-mail** **Team**

Casual dress in professional offices has been coming under attack. Your boss, Elizabeth Sommer, received the e-mail shown in Figure 5.1. She thinks it would be a good assignment for her group of management trainees to help her respond to that message. She asks your team to research answers to the first five questions in President Aiden Rebol's message. She doesn't expect you to answer the final question, but any information you can supply to the first questions would help her shape a response.

Diago Enterprises, LLC, is a public CPA firm with a staff of 90 CPAs, bookkeepers, managers, and support personnel. Located in Cypress, California, the plush offices on Valley View Boulevard overlook Oak Knoll Park. The firm performs general accounting and audit services as well as tax planning and preparation. Accountants visit clients in the field and also entertain them in the downtown office.

**YOUR TASK.** Decide whether the entire team will research each question in Figure 5.1 or whether individual team members will be assigned certain questions. Collect information, discuss it, and reach consensus on what you will report to Ms. Sommer. As a team write a concise one-page response. Your goal is to inform, not persuade. Remember that you represent management, not students or employees.

## 5.7 How Professional Are Your Instant Messaging Skills? (Obj. 2)
**Communication Technology** **Web** **Team**

Your instructor will direct this role-playing group activity. Using instant messaging, you will simulate one of several typical business scenarios—for example, responding to a product inquiry, training a new-hire, troubleshooting with a customer, or making an appointment. For each scenario, two or more students will chat professionally with only a minimal script to practice on-the-spot yet courteous professional interaction by IM. Your instructor will determine which software you will need and provide brief instructions to prepare you for your role in this exercise.

If you don't have instant messaging software on your computer or smart device yet, download the application first—for example, AOL's Instant Messenger, Yahoo Messenger, Microsoft's Windows Live Messenger, FaceTime, or Skype. Yahoo Messenger allows you to IM your friends on Yahoo Messenger but also on Windows Live Messenger.

You control who sees you online; if you don't wish to be interrupted, you can use stealth settings. All IM software enables users to share photos and large media files. You can make voice calls and use webcam videos as well. These advanced features turn IM software into a simple conferencing tool and video phone. You can connect with users who have the same software all around the world. Unlike landline and cell phone calls, peer-to-peer voice calls are free. Most IM clients also offer mobile applications for your smartphone or tablet, so that you can IM or call other users while you are away from a computer.

**YOUR TASK.** Log on to the IM or chat program your instructor chooses. Follow your instructor's directions closely as you role-play the business situation you were assigned with your partner or team. The scenario will involve two or more people who will communicate by instant messaging in real time.

## 5.8 Checking Out a Podcast (Obj. 3)
`Communication Technology`  `Web`  `E-mail`  `Social Media`

Browsing the podcasts at iTunes, you stumble across the Quick and Dirty Tips series, specifically Money Girl, who dispenses financial advice. You discover that you can sign up for the free podcasts, which cover a variety of business topics. You can also visit the website Quick and Dirty Tips or interact with Laura D. Adams on her Money Girl page. Alternatively, you examine the advice conveyed via podcast, the Web, Facebook, and Twitter by clever Grammar Girl Mignon Fogarty.

**YOUR TASK.** Pick a Money Girl podcast that interests you. Listen to it or obtain a transcript on the website and study it for its structure. Is it direct or indirect? Informative or persuasive? How is it presented? What style does the speaker use? At your instructor's request, write an e-mail that discusses the podcast you analyzed. Alternatively, if your instructor allows, you could also send a very concise summary of the podcast by text message from your cell phone or tweet (140 characters or fewer) to your instructor.

## 5.9 Creating a Simple Business Podcast (Obj. 3)
`Communication Technology`  `Social Media`  `Web`

Do you want to try your hand at producing a podcast? Businesses rely on a host of social media and communication technologies when reaching out to the public or internally to their workers. As you have seen, some companies produce such short audio or video clips on focused, poignant subjects. The following process describes how to create a simple podcast:

**Select software.** In addition to offline software (e.g., Audacity), newer podcast creation software such as Hipcast, Yodio, and Podbean work in the cloud. They allow recordings within a Web browser or from a smartphone.

**Obtain hardware.** For high sound quality, you may need a sophisticated microphone and other equipment. The recording room must be properly shielded against noise, echo, and other interference. Many universities and some libraries provide recording booths.

**Organize the message.** Make sure your broadcast has a beginning, middle, and end. Build in some redundancy. Previews, summaries, and transitions are important to help your audience follow the message.

**Choose an extemporaneous or scripted delivery.** Extemporaneous delivery means that you prepare, but you use only brief notes. It usually sounds more spontaneous and natural than reading from a script, but it can also lead to redundancy, repetition, and flubbed lines.

**Prepare and practice.** Practice before recording. Editing audio or video is difficult and time-consuming. Try to get your recording right, so that you won't have to edit much.

**Publish your message.** Once you post the MP3 podcast to your course website or blog, you can introduce it and request feedback from your audience.

**YOUR TASK.** Create a short podcast about a business-related subject you care about. Producing a simple podcast does not require sophisticated equipment. With free or inexpensive recording, editing, and publishing software such as Audacity or Podbean, you can inform customers, mix your own music, or host interviews. Any digital recorder can be used to create a no-frills podcast if the material is scripted and well rehearsed.

## 5.10 Blogging: Learning From the Best (Obj. 4)
`Communication Technology`  `E-mail`  `Social Media`  `Web`

Visit the blogs of Seth Godin, Chris Brogan, Guy Kawasaki, Bill Marriott, and other acclaimed bloggers. See what tricks of the trade you can adopt and make work for you.

**YOUR TASK.** You may be asked to write a blog entry detailing your analysis of the professional blogs you have examined. Apply the same best practices for professional business blogs outlined in this chapter. Remember to offer a catchy title on a popular topic that will attract browsers or, in this case, your peers in class and your instructor. Share helpful advice in easy-to-read numbered items and, if applicable, provide links to other relevant articles. To motivate readers to respond, ask questions at the end of your blog entry.

## 5.11 Composing a Personal Blog Entry (Obj. 4)
`Communication Technology` `Social Media` `Web`

Review the guidelines for professional blogging in this chapter. Find a recent social media–related study or survey, and target an audience of business professionals who may wish to know more about social networking. Search for studies conducted by respected organizations and businesses such as Pew Internet, Robert Half International, Burson-Marsteller, ePolicy Institute, and U.S. government agencies, as applicable. As you plan and outline your post, follow the advice provided in this chapter. Although the goal is usually to offer advice, you could also weigh in with your opinion regarding a controversy. For example, do you agree with companies that forbid employees to use company computers for social networking? Do you agree that millennials are losing social skills because of excessive online connectivity?

**YOUR TASK.** Compose a one-page blog entry in MS Word and submit it in hard copy. Alternatively, post it to the discussion board on the class course management platform, or e-mail it to your instructor, as appropriate. Because you will be using outside sources, be careful to paraphrase correctly. Visit Chapter 10 to review how to put ideas into your own words with integrity.

## 5.12 Reviewing Corporate Blogs (Obj. 4)
`Communication Technology` `E-mail` `Social Media` `Web`

Here is your opportunity to view and evaluate a corporate blog. As we have seen, about 34 percent of the primary Fortune 500 companies, or 171, are blogging, and researchers note an increase in corporations with active blogs. The companies and their CEOs who do blog can impart valuable lessons.

**YOUR TASK.** Within your favorite browser, search for *CEO blogs, index of corporate blogs, index of CEO blogs*, and similar keywords. You will likely end up at Chief Executive.net, on SlideShare, and at other sites that may list the top 10 or so most popular corporate blogs, perhaps even one penned by a CEO. Select a corporate or CEO blog you find interesting, browse the posts, and read some of the content. Furthermore, note how many of the points the blog makes match the guidelines in this book. If your instructor directs, write a brief informational memo or e-mail summarizing your observations about the business blog, its style, the subjects covered, and so forth.

## 5.13 Monitoring Twitter Chatter and Facebook Posts (Obj. 5)
`Social Media` `Web`

Many large companies monitor Twitter chatter and Facebook posts. They have discovered social media to be a tool for averting public relations disasters. Domino's Pizza deftly responded with a coordinated social media campaign to counter the fallout from a damaging prank. Two employees had posted a disgusting YouTube video showing them engaging in several health code violations.[52] Despite initial damage, the company was able to regain its customers' trust and even enlisted their help via social networking to improve the taste of its pizzas.

Comcast, Coca-Cola, PepsiCo, and others are quick to apologize to irate customers and to correct problems that they discover via Twitter or other social media networking sites. Southwest Airlines employs a six-member "emerging-media team." The former head of social media at Coca-Cola, Adam Brown, now at computer maker Dell, says: "We're getting to a point if you're not responding, you're not being seen as an authentic type of brand."[53]

**YOUR TASK.** You are one of three social media interns working for Adam Brown at Dell. Your job is to comb through tweets and Facebook posts to find those that are both positive about and critical of your company and to inform your boss about any that could potentially end up hurting Dell's image. Deciding which post could cause trouble is difficult, given that even with tracking software, you may need to scan hundreds of posts every day. You know that if many users "retweet," or redistribute the news, the problem may get out of hand. Create a Twitter account and search for posts about Dell or any other company your instructor may assign. Make a list of three positive and three negative tweets. Recommend or draft responses to them. If you identify a trend, make a note of it and report it either in class or in writing as directed by your instructor.

## 5.14 The Dark Side: Hooked on Social Media? (Obj. 5)
`Communication Technology` `Social Media` `Web`

Could you give up your electronic toys for 24 hours without withdrawal symptoms? Would you be able to survive a full day unplugged from all media? A class of 200 students at the University of Maryland, College Park, went media free for 24 hours and then blogged about the experience.[54] Some sounded like addicts going cold turkey: *In withdrawal. Frantically craving. Very anxious. Extremely antsy. Miserable. Jittery. Crazy.* One student lamented: *I clearly am addicted and the dependency is sickening.* In the absence of technology that anchors them to friends and family, students felt bored and isolated. One wrote: *I felt quite alone and secluded from my life. Although I go to a school with thousands of students, the fact that I was not able to communicate with anyone via technology was almost unbearable.*

Chapter 5: Short Workplace Messages and Digital Media

The study reveals a paradigm shift in human interaction. A completely digital generation is viscerally wedded to electronic toys, so much so that technology has become an indispensable part of young people's lives.

Electronically abstinent students stated that they spent more time on course work, took better notes, and were more focused. As a result, they said they learned more and became more productive. They also reported that they spent more time with loved ones and friends face-to-face. Life slowed down and the day seemed much longer to some.

**YOUR TASK.** Discuss in class, in a chat, or in an online post the following questions: Have you ever unplugged? What was that experience like? Could you give up your cell phone, iPod, TV, car radio, online magazines and newspapers, and computer (no texting, no Facebook or IM) for a day or longer? What would you do instead? Is there any harm in not being able to unplug?

## 5.15 Creating Fair Digital Media Policies (Obj. 5)

Communication Technology · E-mail · Social Media · Team

As advances in computer technology continue to change the way we work and play, Internet use on and off the job has become a danger zone for employees and employers. Misuse costs employers millions of dollars in lost productivity and litigation, and it can cost employees their jobs. A survey by the American Management Association revealed that 26 percent of employers fired workers for e-mail misuse. In addition, 2 percent terminated employees for using instant messaging, and another 2 percent for posting offensive blog content from a company machine or, yes, the employee's own computer.[55] Companies struggle with fair Internet use policies knowing that over half of their employees with Web access shop online from the office.[56]

**YOUR TASK.** Your boss is aware of these numbers and is weighing whether to prohibit all personal use of the Internet at work, including IM, texting, visiting shopping websites, viewing YouTube videos, and viewing and posting to Facebook. How would you justify keeping Internet access open? Alone or as a group, brainstorm arguments for allowing unlimited or partial access to the Web. Also, consider arguments for limiting or disallowing access. If asked, develop your ideas into an e-mail, discussion board post, or blog entry that could sway your boss.

# GRAMMAR/MECHANICS CHECKUP—5

## Prepositions and Conjunctions

Review Sections 1.18 and 1.19 in the Grammar Review section of the Grammar/Mechanics Handbook. Then study each of the following statements. Write *a* or *b* to indicate the sentence in which the idea is expressed more effectively. Also record the number of the G/M principle illustrated. When you finish, compare your responses with those provided. If your answers differ, study carefully the principles shown in parentheses.

b_____ (1.18a)   **EXAMPLE**   a. When did you graduate high school?
                                       b. When did you graduate from high school?

_____ 1. a. Your iPad was more expensive than mine.
                 b. Your iPad was more expensive then mine.

_____ 2. a. Don't you hate when your inbox is filled with spam?
                 b. Don't you hate it when your inbox is filled with spam?

_____ 3. a. If the company called you, than it must be looking at your résumé.
                 b. If the company called you, then it must be looking at your résumé.

_____ 4. a. Ethnocentrism is when you believe your culture is best.
                 b. Ethnocentrism involves the belief that your culture is best.

_____ 5. a. Business messages should be clear, correct, and written with conciseness.
                 b. Business messages should be clear, correct, and concise.

_____ 6. a. What type of computer monitor do you prefer?
                 b. What type computer monitor do you prefer?

_____ 7. a. Do you know where the meeting is at?
                 b. Do you know where the meeting is?

Chapter 5: Short Workplace Messages and Digital Media

_____ 8. a. Did you send an application to the headquarters in Los Angeles or to the branch in San Diego?
b. Did you apply to the Los Angeles headquarters or the San Diego branch?

_____ 9. a. Shelby hopes to graduate college next year.
b. Shelby hopes to graduate from college next year.

_____ 10. a. She had a great interest, as well as a profound respect for, historical homes.
b. She had a great interest in, as well as a profound respect for, historical homes.

_____ 11. a. Volunteers should wear long pants, bring gloves, and sunscreen should be applied.
b. Volunteers should wear long pants, bring gloves, and apply sunscreen.

_____ 12. a. His PowerPoint presentation was short, as we hoped it would be.
b. His PowerPoint presentation was short, like we hoped it would be.

_____ 13. a. An ethics code is where a set of rules spells out appropriate behavior standards.
b. An ethics code is a set of rules spelling out appropriate behavior standards.

_____ 14. a. Please keep the paper near the printer.
b. Please keep the paper near to the printer.

_____ 15. a. A behavioral interview question is when the recruiter says, "Tell me about a time. . . ."
b. A behavioral interview question is one in which the recruiter says, "Tell me about a time. . . ."

Chapter 5: Short Workplace Messages and Digital Media

# EDITING CHALLENGE—5

To fine-tune your grammar and mechanics skills, in every chapter you will be editing a message. This message explains a task being assigned to Antonella Doolittle by her boss Jared Kim. However, the message suffers from proofreading, spelling, grammar, punctuation, wordiness, and other writing faults that require correction. Study the guidelines in the Grammar/Mechanics Handbook as well as the lists of Confusing Words and Frequently Misspelled Words to sharpen your skills.

**YOUR TASK.** Edit the following message (a) by correcting errors in your textbook or on a photocopy using proofreading marks from Appendix A or (b) by downloading the message from the premium website at **www.cengagebrain.com** and correcting at your computer. Your instructor may show you a possible solution.

**To:** Antonella Doolittle <antonella.doolittle@circa.com>
**From:** Jared Kim <jared.kim@circa.com>
**Subject:** Big Job for You
**Cc:**
**Bcc:**

Antonella,

Due to the fact that you have done excellent work on various projects here at Circa the vice president and the undersigned has picked you to work on a special project conducting research for next years annual report. In all likelihood, you should plan to visit each and every department head personal to collect department information individually from them.

Staff members of the Corporate Communications division which oversee the production of the annual report is of the opinion that you should concentrate on the following items:
- specific accomplishments—not just activitys—for the past year
- You should also find out about goals of each department for the coming year
- in each department get names of interesting employees who have made a contribution to the department or ones who have contributed to the community.
- Be sure to ask about special events featuring outstanding employees and corporate officers.

Because of the fact that this is an assignment that is big in size, Mary Mansfield has been given the assignment of offering assistance to you. We made the decision that it was better to assign an assistant rather then have you be overwhelmed with this task.

Oh, one more thing. As you do your interviewing, try to collect digital photos that are in color and that illustrate employees and special events.

Inasmuch as the annual report must be completed by August first you must submit this material to Julie Armstrong or I by June 5th. We are greatful for your expertise and have confidence that you will do a terrific job.

Warm regards,
Jared

Jared Kim, Director
Corporate Communications
Circa Industries, Inc.
jared.kim@circa.com
Cell: 288-430-9018

# COMMUNICATION WORKSHOP

## TECHNOLOGY

## Should Employers Curb Social Media, E-Mail, and Other Internet Use?

Most employees today work with computers and have Internet access. They also carry smartphones and tablets to work. Should they be able to use their own devices or work computers for social media posting, online shopping, private messages, and personal work, as well as to listen to music and play games?

### But It's Harmless

Office workers have discovered that it is far easier to shop online than to race to malls and wait in line. To justify her Web shopping at work, one employee, a recent graduate, said, "Instead of standing at the water cooler gossiping, I shop online." She went on to say, "I'm not sapping company resources by doing this."[57]

IM users say that what they are doing is similar to making personal phone calls. So long as they don't abuse the practice, they see no harm. One marketing director justified his occasional game playing and online shopping by explaining that his employer benefits because he is more productive when he takes minibreaks. "When I need a break, I pull up a Web page and just browse," he says. "Ten minutes later, I'm all refreshed, and I can go back to business-plan writing."[58]

### Companies Cracking Down

Employers, however, see it differently. One survey reported that more than one fourth of employers have fired workers for misusing e-mail, and nearly one third have fired employees for misusing the Internet.[59] UPS discovered an employee running a personal business from his office computer. Lockheed Martin fired an employee who disabled its entire company network for six hours because of an e-mail heralding a holiday event that the worker sent to 60,000 employees. Companies not only worry about lost productivity, but they fear litigation, security breaches, and other electronic disasters from accidental or intentional misuse of computer systems.

### What's Reasonable?

Some companies (e.g., Volkswagen and Porsche) impose a zero tolerance policy, prohibiting any personal use of company equipment. Ameritech Corporation tells employees that computers and other company equipment are to be used only for business purposes. Companies such as Boeing, however, have issued guidelines allowing some personal use of e-mail and the Internet. The company strictly prohibits chain letters, obscenity, and political and religious solicitation.

**CAREER APPLICATION.** As an administrative assistant at Lone Star Technologies in Austin, Texas, you have just received an e-mail from your boss asking for your opinion. Many employees have been accessing social media sites, shopping online, and using instant messaging. One person received four personal packages from UPS in one morning. Although reluctant to do so, management is considering installing monitoring software that not only tracks Internet use but also blocks social media, messaging, porn, hate, and game sites.

**YOUR TASK**

- In teams or as a class, discuss the problem of workplace abuse of social media, e-mail, instant messaging, online shopping, and other Internet browsing. Should full personal use be allowed?
- Are computers and their Internet access similar to other equipment such as telephones?
- Should employees be allowed to access the Internet for personal use as long as they limit it to their own smart electronic devices?
- Should management be allowed to monitor all Internet use?
- Should employees be warned if Internet activities including e-mail are to be monitored?
- What reasons can you give to support an Internet crackdown by management?
- What reasons can you give to oppose a crackdown?

Decide whether you support or oppose the crackdown. Explain your views in an e-mail or a memo to your boss, James McKnight, at *jmcknight@lone-star-tech.com*.

Chapter 5: Short Workplace Messages and Digital Media

# ENDNOTES

1. Foster, D. (2010, November 10). How to write better emails. WebWorkerDaily. Retrieved from http://gigaom.com/collaboration/how-to-write-better-emails

2. Seeley, M. quoted in Palmer, M. (2011, December 19). The end of email? *Financial Times* (ft.com/management). Retrieved from http://www.ft.com/intl/cms/s/0/5207b5d6-21cf-11e1-8b93-00144feabdc0.html#axzz1u7265yfu

3. Plantronics. (2010). How we work: Communication trends of business professionals. Retrieved from http://www.plantronics.com/media/howwework/brochure-role-of-voice.pdf

4. Middleton, D. (2011, March 3). Students struggle for words. *The Wall Street Journal*, Executive edition. Retrieved from http://online.wsj.com/article/SB10001424052748703409904576174651780110970.html

5. Ibid.

6. Gill, B. (2013, June). Vision statement: E-mail: Not dead, evolving. *Harvard Business Review*. Retrieved from http://hbr.org/2013/06/e-mail-not-dead-evolving

7. Tugend, A. (2012, April 21). What to think about before you hit 'Send.' *The New York Times*, p. B5.

8. Orrell, L. quoted in Tugend, A. (2012, April 21). What to think about before you hit 'Send.' *The New York Times*, p. B5.

9. Kupritz, V. W., & Cowell, E. (2011, January). Productive management communication: Online and face-to-face. *Journal of Business Communication*, 48(1), 70–71.

10. Photo essay based on Jacobs, P. (2013, December 9). 10 private and embarrassing emails that went viral on college campuses. Business Insider. Retrieved from http://www.businessinsider.com/10-embarrassing-emails-that-went-viral-on-college-campuses-2013-12; Weaver, C. (2013, April 8). The most deranged sorority girl email you will ever read. Gawker. Retrieved from http://gawker.com/5994974/the-most-deranged-sorority-girl-email-you-will-ever-read

11. Terk, N. (2012, January 18). E-mail education: Global headaches and universal best practices. Retrieved from http://www.newswiretoday.com/news/104276

12. Allen, P. (2011, November 30). One of the biggest information technology companies in the world to abolish e-mails. Mail Online. Retrieved from http://www.dailymail.co.uk/news/article-2067520/One-biggest-IT-companies-world-abolish-emails.html

13. Radicati, S. (2012, November 15). Statistics anyone? Retrieved from http://www.radicati.com/?p=8417

14. Plantronics. (2010). How we work: Communication trends of business professionals. Retrieved from http://www.plantronics.com/media/howwework/brochure-role-of-voice.pdf

15. Pazos, P., Chung, J. M., & Micari, M. (2013). Instant messaging as a task-support tool in information technology organizations. *Journal of Business Communication*, 50(1), 78.

16. Marketing News Staff. (2010, March 15). Digital dozen. AMA.org. Retrieved from http://www.marketingpower.com/resourceLibrary/Publications/MarketingNews/2010/3_15_10/Digital%20Dozen.pdf

17. Skinner. C. A. (2008, July 16). UK businesses ban IM over security concerns. CIO. Retrieved from http://www.cio.com/article/437910/UK_Businesses_Ban_IM_over_Security_Concerns

18. Flynn, N. (2012, May 23). Social media rules: Policies & best practices to effectively manage your presence, posts & potential risks. The ePolicy Institute. Retrieved from http://www.ohioscpa.com/docs/conference-outlines/8_social-media-rules.pdf?sfvrsn=4

19. Marino, K. (2012, June 22). DWI: Driving while intexticated—infographic. OnlineSchools.com. Retrieved from http://www.onlineschools.com/in-focus/driving-while-intexticated

20. Flynn, N., & Kahn, R. (2004). E-mail rules: A business guide to managing policies, security, and legal issues for e-mail and digital communication. Columbus, OH: ePolicy Institute, pp. 153–154.

21. Flynn, N. (2012, May 23). Social media rules: Policies & best practices to effectively manage your presence, posts & potential risks. The ePolicy Institute. Retrieved from http://www.ohioscpa.com/docs/conference-outlines/8_social-media-rules.pdf?sfvrsn=4

22. Based on The Emily Post Institute. (n.d.) Text messaging: I love text messaging. Retrieved from http://www.emilypost.com/home-and-family-life/133/391-text-messaging

23. Majchrzak, A., Wagner, C., & Yates, D. (2006). Corporate wiki users: Results of a survey. CiteSeer. Retrieved from http://citeseerx.ist.psu.edu/viewdoc/summary?doi=10.1.1.97.407

24. The five main uses of wikis based on Nations, D. (2009). The business wiki: Wiki in the workplace. About.com: Web Trends. Retrieved from http://webtrends.about.com/od/wiki/a/business-wiki.htm

25. Barnes, N. G., Lescaut, A. M., & Wright, S. (2013). 2013 Fortune 500 are bullish on social media: Big companies get excited about Google+, Instagram, Foursquare and Pinterest. Center for Marketing Research, Charlton College of Business, University of Massachusetts Dartmouth. Retrieved from http://www.umassd.edu/cmr/socialmediaresearch/2013fortune500

26. DOMO & CEO.com. (2013). 2013 Social CEO report: Are America's top CEOs getting more social? Retrieved from http://www.ceo.com/social-ceo-report-2013/#ceoid=rtdb869; Duren, M. (2013, February 12). 9 CEO blogs to watch. Socialmedia Today. Retrieved from http://socialmediatoday.com/martyduren/1235491/nine-ceo-blogs-watch-2013

27. Westergaard, N. (2013, August 18). Social media: Don't fear negative content. *The Gazette*. Retrieved from http://thegazette.com/2013/08/18/social-media-dont-fear-negative-content

28. Devaney, T., & Stein, T. (2012, December 19). How to turn your online critics into fans. *Forbes*. Retrieved from http://www.forbes.com/sites/capitalonespark/2012/12/19/how-to-turn-your-online-critics-into-fans

29. Live blog: Hurricane Sandy targets East Coast. (2012, October 29). *The Wall Street Journal*. Retrieved from http://blogs.wsj.com/dispatch/2012/10/29/live-blog-hurricane-sandy-targets-east-coast; Hurricane Sandy: Covering the storm. (2012, November 6). *The New York Times*. Retrieved from http://www.nytimes.com/interactive/2012/10/28/nyregion/hurricane-sandy.html?_r=0; Izeman, M. (2013, January 25). 10 essential blogs on Hurricane Sandy recovery. Switchboard: Natural Resources Defense Council Staff Blog. Retrieved from http://switchboard.nrdc.org/blogs/mizeman/10_essential_blogs_on_hurrican.html

30. Lindstrom, M. (2012, July 3). How many lives does a brand have? Fast Company. Retrieved from http://www.fastcompany.com/1841927/buyology-martin-lindstrom-lives-of-brands-china-marketing

31. Brogan, C. (2012, July 13). Become a dream feeder. Retrieved from http://www.chrisbrogan.com/dreamfeeder

32. Cairns, B. (2012, January 24). Blog comment. Retrieved from http://blog.guykawasaki.com/2011/06/how-to-increase-your-likability.html#axzz20dk8CnTk

33. Millennials: A portrait of Generation Next. (2010, February 24). Pew Research Center. Retrieved from http://www.pewresearch.org/millennials; How digital behavior differs among Millennials, Gen Xers and Boomers. (2013, March 21). eMarketer. Retrieved from http://www.emarketer.com/Articles/Print.aspx?R=1009748

34. Smith, A., & Brenner, J. (2012, May 31). Twitter use 2012. Pew Internet & American Life Project. Retrieved from http://pewinternet.org/files/old-media//Files/Reports/2012/PIP_Twitter_Use_2012.pdf

35. Barnes, N. G., Lescaut, A. M., & Wright, S. (2013). 2013 Fortune 500 are bullish on social media: Big companies get excited about Google+, Instagram, Foursquare and Pinterest. Center for Marketing Research, Charlton College of Business, University of Massachusetts Dartmouth. Retrieved from http://www.umassd.edu/cmr/socialmediaresearch/2013fortune500

36. Twitter statistics. (2013). Socialbakers.com. Retrieved from http://www.socialbakers.com/twitter

37. Kass, K. (2012). The road to social at Wells Fargo. Simply-communicate.com. Retrieved from http://www.simply-communicate.com/case-studies/chatter/road-social-wells-fargo

38. Parekh, R. (2012, September 17). Internal affairs: Social media at the office. *Ad Age*. Retrieved from http://adage.com/article/digital/internal-affairs-social-media-office/237207

39. Mullaney, T. (2012, May 16). Social media is reinventing how business is done. *USA Today*. Retrieved from http://www.usatoday.com/money/economy/story/2012-05-14/social-media-economy-companies/55029088/1

40. Ibid.

41. Ibid.

42. Kiefarber, D. (2012, January 20). Sam Adams crowdsourcing its next beer: You choose the color, clarity, malt, hops and yeast. *Adweek*. Retrieved from http://www.adweek.com/adfreak/sam-adams-crowdsourcing-its-next-beer-137619

43. Conlin, M., & MacMillan, D. (2009, June 1). Managing the tweets. *BusinessWeek*, p. 20.

44. 2013 Cisco annual security report, pp. 23-25. Retrieved from https://www.cisco.com/web/offer/gist_ty2_asset/Cisco_2013_ASR.pdf

45. Flynn, N. (2012, May 23). Social media rules: Policies & best practices to effectively manage your presence, posts & potential risks. The ePolicy

Institute. Retrieved from http://www.ohioscpa.com/docs/conference-outlines/8_social-media-rules.pdf?sfvrsn=4
[46] Ibid.
[47] Ibid.
[48] Ibid.
[49] Weeks, L. (2011, April 27). Privacy 2.0: The Garbo economy. NPR.org. Retrieved from http://www.npr.org/2011/04/27/135623137/privacy-2-0-the-garbo-economy
[50] Turkle. S. (2011). *Alone together: Why we expect more from technology and less from each other*. New York: Basic Books, p. 1.
[51] Tynan, D. (2012, May 25). How companies buy Facebook friends, likes, and buzz. ITWorld.com. Retrieved from http://www.techhive.com/article/256240/how_companies_buy_facebook_friends_likes_and_buzz.html
[52] Thomas, A., & Applegate, J. (2010). *Pay attention!: How to listen, respond, and profit from customer feedback*. Hoboken, NJ: John Wiley & Sons, pp. 1–2.
[53] Needleman, S. E. (2009, August 4). For companies, a tweet in time can avert PR mess. *The Wall Street Journal*. Retrieved from http://online.wsj.com
[54] Moeller, S. D. (2010). 24 hours: Unplugged. Retrieved from http://withoutmedia.wordpress.com; The Associated Press. (2009, September 6). Center tries to treat Web addicts. *The New York Times*. Retrieved from http://www.nytimes.com
[55] Searcey, D. (2009, November 24). Some courts raise bar on reading employee email. *The Wall Street Journal*, p. A31. Retrieved from http://online.wsj.com/article/SB125859862658454923.html; and Na, G. (2006, October 17). Employee e-mail use: Big brother may be watching. Mondaq Business Briefing. Retrieved https://global.factiva.com
[56] Klein, K. E. (2009, December 1). Putting a fair Internet use policy in place. BusinessWeek.com. Retrieved from http://www.businessweek.com/smallbiz/content/dec2009/sb2009121_245449.htm
[57] Irvine, M. (2009, July 12). Young workers push employers for wider Web access. *USA Today*. Retrieved from http://www.usatoday.com/tech/webguide/internetlife/2009-07-13-blocked-internet_N.htm; DeLisser, E. (1999, September 27). One-click commerce: What people do now to goof off at work. *The Wall Street Journal*. Retrieved from http://www.kenmaier.com/wsj19990927.htm
[58] Cheng, J. (2009, April 2). Study: Surfing the Internet at work boosts productivity. Ars Technica. Retrieved from http://arstechnica.com/web/news/2009/04/study-surfing-the-internet-at-work-boosts-productivity.ars; DeLisser, E. (1999, September 27). One-click commerce: What people do now to goof off at work. *The Wall Street Journal*. Retrieved from http://www.kenmaier.com/wsj19990927.htm
[59] Ford, J. (2009, November 9). Think twice about shopping online from work. Marketwatch.com. Retrieved from http://www.marketwatch.com/story/think-twice-about-shopping-online-from-work-2009-11-29; The 2007 electronic monitoring and surveillance survey. (2008, February 29). GPS Daily. Retrieved from http://www.gpsdaily.com

# ACKNOWLEDGMENTS

**p. 121** Office Insider based on Gill, B. (2013, June). Vision statement: E-mail: Not dead, evolving. *Harvard Business Review*. Retrieved from http://hbr.org/2013/06/e-mail-not-dead-evolving

**p. 122** Office Insider based on E-mail becoming crime's new smoking gun. (2002, August 15). USA Today.com. Retrieved from http://www.usatoday.com/tech/news/2002-08-15-email-evidence_x.htm

**p. 125** Office Insider based on Brown, P. (2008, January 26). Same office, different planets. *The New York Times*, p. B5. Retrieved from http://proquest.umi.com

**p. 128** Office Insider based on Bloch, M. (n.d.). Instant messaging and live chat etiquette tips. Taming the Beast. Retrieved from http://www.tamingthebeast.net/articles6/messaging-chat-etiquette.htm

**p. 134** Office Insider based on Marriott, Jr., J. W. (2012, January 1). Marriott on the move: About my blog. Retrieved from http://www.blogs.marriott.com/marriott-on-the-move//about-marriott-blog.html

**p. 136** Office Insider based on Devaney, T., & Stein, T. (2012). 9 things businesses shouldn't do on social media. Forbes. Retrieved from http://www.forbes.com/sites/capitalonespark/2012/12/20/9-things-businesses-shouldnt-do-on-social-media

**p. 139** Office Insider based on Cisco annual security report: Threats step out of the shadows. (2013). Cisco: The Network. [Press release]. Retrieved from http://newsroom.cisco.com/release/1133334

# CHAPTER 6

# Positive Messages

## OBJECTIVES
After studying this chapter, you should be able to

**6-1** Understand the channels through which typical positive messages travel in the digital era—e-mails, memos, and business letters, and explain how business letters should be formatted.

**6-2** Compose direct messages that make requests, respond to inquiries online and offline, and deliver step-by-step instructions.

**6-3** Prepare messages that make direct claims and voice complaints, including those posted online.

**6-4** Create adjustment messages that salvage customers' trust and promote further business.

**6-5** Write special messages that convey kindness and goodwill.

## 6-1 Routine Messages: E-Mails, Memos, and Letters

Most workplace messages are positive or neutral and, therefore, direct. Positive messages are routine; they help workers conduct everyday business. Such routine messages include simple requests for information or action, replies to customers, and explanations to coworkers. Other types of routine messages are instructions, direct claims, and complaints.

E-mails, memos, and letters are the channels most frequently used. In addition, businesses today must listen and respond to customers on social networks and in the blogosphere. At the same time, in some industries, memos continue to be an important channel of communication within organizations, and letters are a vital paper-based external channel.

Chapter 5 discussed e-mails as well as memos and focused on their format and safe, professional use. This chapter will familiarize you with the direct writing plans for positive messages whether electronic or paper based. First, though, you will learn when to respond by letter and how to format a business letter.

### 6-1a Understanding Business Letters

Despite the advent of electronic communication technologies such as e-mail, in certain situations letters are still the preferred channel of communication for delivering messages *outside* an organization. Such letters go to suppliers, government agencies, other businesses, and, most important, customers.

You may think that everybody is online, but more than a fifth of the U.S. population is still unplugged. Just as they are eager to connect with a majority of consumers online, businesses continue to give letters to customers a high priority. After all, letters, too, encourage product feedback, project a favorable image of the organization, and promote future business.

Whether you send a business letter will depend on the situation and the preference of your organization. Business letters are necessary when the situation (a) demands a permanent record; (b) requires confidentiality; (c) calls for formality and sensitivity; and (d) favors a persuasive, well-considered presentation.

**Providing a Permanent Record.** Many business transactions require a permanent record. For example, when a company enters into an agreement with another company, business letters introduce the agreement and record decisions and points of understanding. Routine letters are used to deliver contracts, explain terms, exchange ideas, negotiate agreements, answer vendor questions, and maintain customer relations.

**Safeguarding Confidentiality.** Business letters are confidential. They are less likely than electronic media to be intercepted, misdirected, forwarded, retrieved, or otherwise inspected by unintended recipients. Today's business communicators know how dangerous it is to entrust confidential and sensitive information to digital channels.

**Conveying Formality and Sensitivity.** Business letters presented on company stationery communicate formality and importance not possible with e-mail. They look important. Letters carry a nonverbal message that the writer considered the message to be significant and values the recipient.

**Delivering Persuasive, Well-Considered Messages.** Business letters represent deliberate, thoughtful communication. Letters can persuade people to change their actions, adopt new beliefs, make donations, contribute their time, and try new products. Direct-mail letters remain a powerful tool to promote services and products, boost online and retail traffic, and enhance customer relations. You will learn more about writing persuasive and sales messages in Chapter 8.

### 6-1b Formatting Business Letters

A letter's appearance and format reflect the writer's carefulness and experience. A short letter bunched at the top of a sheet of paper, for example, looks as though it were prepared in a hurry or by an amateur.

For your letters to make a good impression, you need to select an appropriate format. The block style shown in Figure 6.1 is a popular format. In this style the parts of a letter—dateline, inside address, optional subject line, body, and so on—are set flush left on the page. The letter is arranged on the page so that it is framed by white space. Most letters have margins of 1 to 1.5 inches.

In preparing business letters, use ragged-right margins; that is, don't allow your computer to justify the right margin and make all lines end evenly. Unjustified margins improve readability, say experts, by providing visual stops and by making it easier to tell where the next line begins. Although book publishers use justified right margins, as you see on this page, your letters should be ragged right. Study Figure 6.1 for more tips on making your letters look professional. If you have questions about letter formats, see Appendix B.

---

### OFFICE INSIDER

*"The old-fashioned personal business letter—written on pristine, high-quality paper, sealed in an envelope, and delivered by post or by hand—remains the single most impressive written ambassador for your company. A letter has a dignity that cannot be equaled by electronic mail or faxed correspondence."*

—Emily Post Institute, "Effective Business Letters"

**LEARNING OBJECTIVE 1**

Understand the channels through which typical positive messages travel in the digital era—e-mails, memos, and business letters, and explain how business letters should be formatted.

## Figure 6.1 Formatting a Direct Request Letter—Block Style

**Letterhead**

**Paradigm Communication Solutions**

1909 Avenue of the Stars, Seventh Floor
Los Angeles, CA 90067
Phone: (310) 391-8901 Fax: (310) 391-7893 Web: www.pcs.com

**Dateline** — September 8, 2016

**Inside address** —
Ms. Bridget Rosales, Manager
Meeting and Events Department
The Venetian Resort Hotel Casino
3355 Las Vegas Boulevard South
Las Vegas, NV 89109

**Salutation** — Dear Ms. Rosales:

**Subject line (optional)** — Subject: Need Information on Group Scheduling for March 20–March 26

**Body** —
Can The Venetian Resort Hotel Casino provide meeting rooms and accommodations for about 250 PCS sales representatives from March 20 through March 24?

Your hotel received strong recommendations because of its excellent resort and conference facilities. Our spring sales conference is scheduled for next March, and I am collecting information for our planning committee. Will you please answer these additional questions regarding The Venetian:

- Does the hotel have (a) a banquet room that can seat 250 plus (b) four smaller meeting rooms each to accommodate a maximum of 75?
- What computer facilities are available for electronic presentations?
- What is the nearest airport, and do you provide transportation to and from it?
- Do you have special room rates for groups at this time of the year?

Answers to these questions and any other information you can provide will help us decide which conference facility to choose. Your response before September 18 would be most appreciated since our planning committee meets September 25.

**Complimentary close** — Sincerely yours,

*Richard M. Mahar*

**Author's name and identification** —
Richard M. Mahar, Associate
Corporate Travel Department

**Reference initials** — RMM:gdr

---

**Tips for Formatting Letters**
- Start the date 2 inches from the top or 1 blank line below the letterhead, whichever position is lower.
- For block style, begin all lines at the left margin.
- Leave side margins of 1 to 1.5 inches depending on the length of the letter and font size.
- Single-space the body and double-space between paragraphs.
- Use left, not right, justification.
- Place the title of the receiver wherever it best balances the inside address.
- Place the title of the author wherever it best balances the closing lines.

---

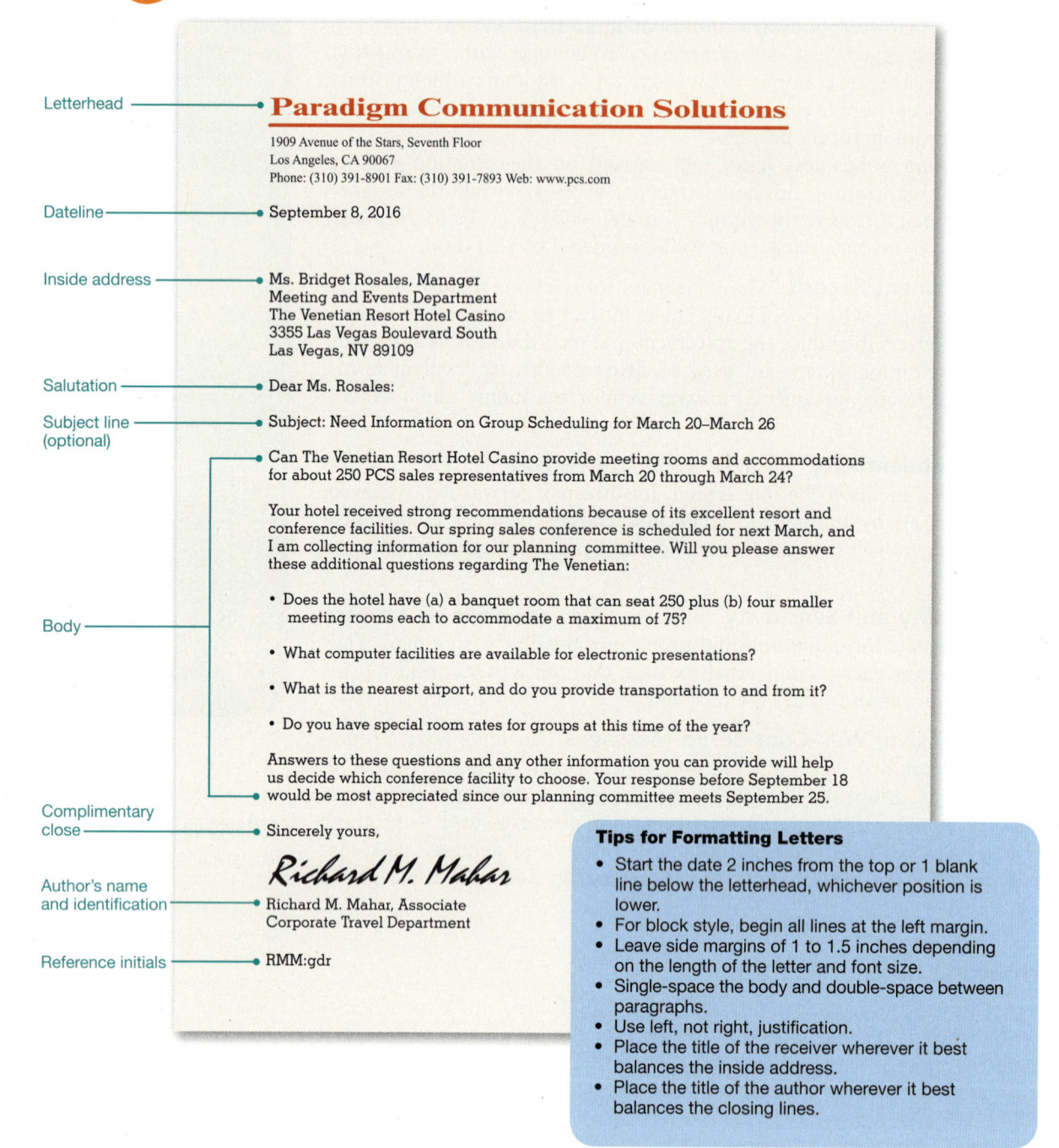

**LEARNING OBJECTIVE 2**

Compose direct messages that make requests, respond to inquiries online and offline, and deliver step-by-step instructions.

## 6-2 Typical Request, Response, and Instruction Messages

In the workplace routine positive messages take the form of e-mails, memos, and letters. Brief positive messages are also delivered by instant messaging, texting, and social media. When you need information from a team member in another office, you might send an e-mail or use IM. If you must explain a new procedure for ordering supplies and rank-and-file workers do not have company e-mail, you would write a memo. When you respond to a customer letter asking about your products, you would prepare a letter. These kinds of routine messages follow a similar pattern:

> **WRITING PLAN FOR DIRECT REQUEST AND RESPONSE MESSAGES**
> - **Opening:** Ask the most important question first or express a polite command.
> - **Body:** Explain the request logically and courteously. Ask other questions if necessary.
> - **Closing:** Request a specific action with an end date, if appropriate, and express appreciation.

### 6-2a Creating Request Messages

When you write a message that requests information or action and you think your request will be received positively, *frontload* your message, which means immediately tell the reader what you want. Readers tend to look at the opening and closing first. As a writer, then, you should capitalize on this tendency by putting the most significant statement first. The first sentence of a direct request is usually a question or a polite command.

**Big Idea First.** A letter inquiring about hotel accommodations, shown in Figure 6.1, begins immediately with the most important idea: Can the hotel provide meeting rooms and accommodations for 250 people? If several questions must be asked, you have two choices. You can ask the most important question first, as shown in Figure 6.1. An alternate opening begins with a summary statement, such as *Please answer the following questions about providing meeting rooms and accommodations for 250 people from March 20 through March 24*. Such a letter might travel by postal mail, or it could be attached to an e-mail.

**Providing Details.** The body of a message that requests information or action provides necessary details. Remember that the quality of the information obtained from a request depends on the clarity of the inquiry. If you analyze your needs, organize your ideas, and frame your request logically, you are likely to receive a meaningful answer that doesn't require a follow-up message. Whenever possible, focus on benefits to the reader (*To ensure that you receive the exact sweater you want, send us your color choice*). To improve readability, itemize the appropriate information in bulleted or numbered lists. Notice that the questions in Figure 6.1 are bulleted, and they are parallel. That is, they use the same balanced construction.

**Closing With Appreciation and a Call for Action.** In the closing tell the reader courteously what is to be done. If a date is important, set an end date to take action and explain why. You can save the reader time by spelling out the action to be taken. Avoid overused endings such as *Thank you for your cooperation* (trite), *Thank you in advance for . . .* (trite and presumptuous), and *If you have any questions, do not hesitate to call me* (suggests that you didn't make yourself clear).

Showing appreciation is always appropriate, but try to do so in a fresh and efficient manner. For example, you could hook your thanks to the end date (*Thanks for returning the questionnaire before May 5, when we will begin tabulation*). You might tie your appreciation to a reader benefit (*We are grateful for the information you will provide because it will help us serve you better*). You could briefly describe how the information will help you (*I appreciate this information that will enable me to . . .*). When possible, make it easy for the reader to comply with your request (*Note your answers on this sheet and return it in the postage-paid envelope*).

### 6-2b Responding to Requests

Many business messages comply with requests for information or action. A customer seeks product information. A supplier asks to arrange a meeting. An employee inquires about a procedure, or a manager requests your input on a marketing campaign. In complying with such requests, apply the same direct pattern you used in making requests:

> **WRITING PLAN FOR E-MAIL, MEMO, AND LETTER REPLIES**
> - **Subject line:** Summarize the main information from your reply. (A subject line is optional in letters.)
> - **Opening:** Start directly by responding to the request with a summary statement.
> - **Body:** Provide additional information and details in a readable format.
> - **Closing:** Add a concluding remark, summary, or offer of further assistance.

A customer reply e-mail that starts with an effective subject line, as shown in Figure 6.2, helps the reader recognize the topic immediately. The subject line refers in abbreviated form to previous correspondence and/or summarizes a message *(Subject: Your July 12 Inquiry About DataQuirk Software)*.

**Figure 6.2 Customer Response E-Mail**

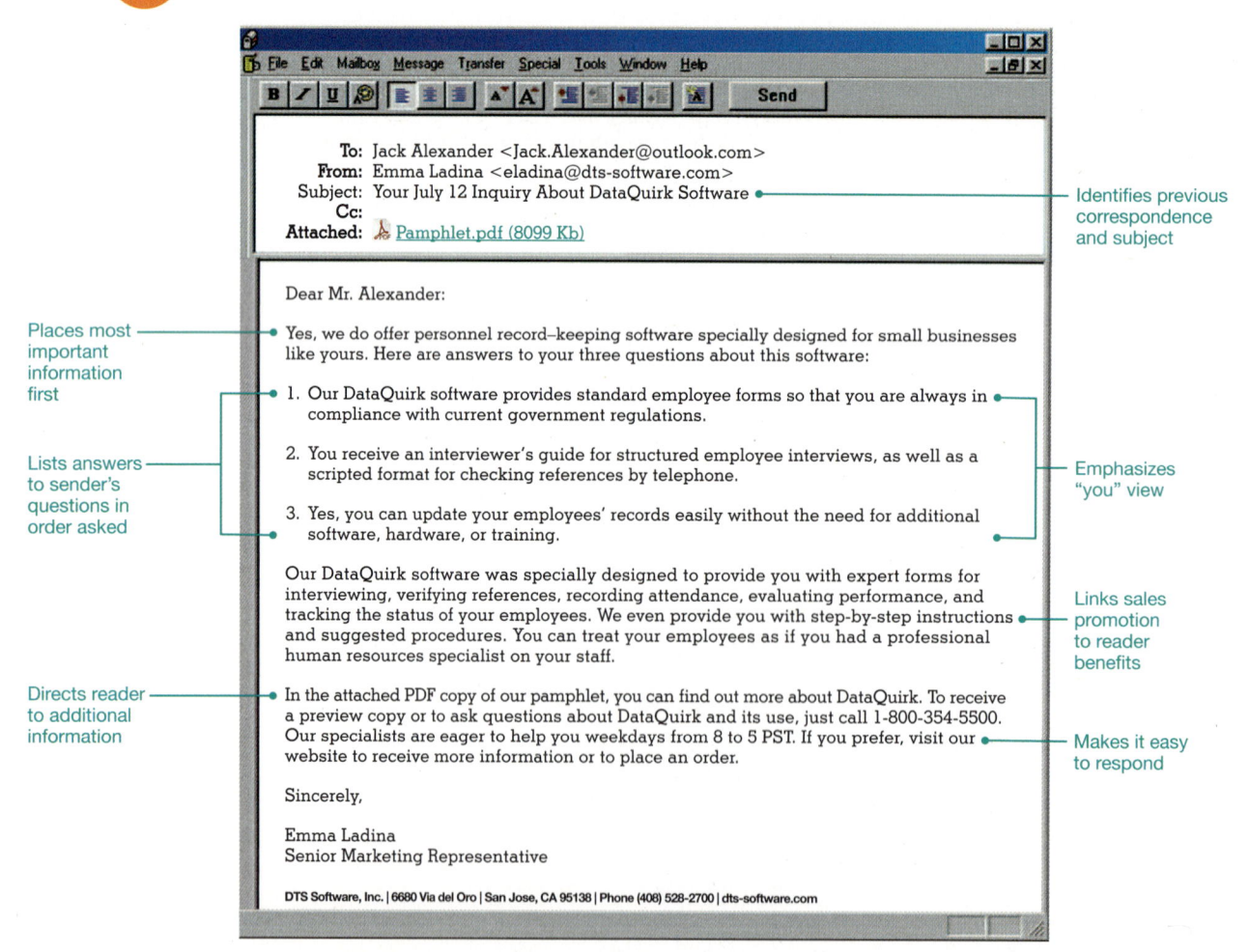

```
To:       Jack Alexander <Jack.Alexander@outlook.com>
From:     Emma Ladina <eladina@dts-software.com>
Subject:  Your July 12 Inquiry About DataQuirk Software
Cc:
Attached: Pamphlet.pdf (8099 Kb)
```

*Identifies previous correspondence and subject*

Dear Mr. Alexander:

Yes, we do offer personnel record–keeping software specially designed for small businesses like yours. Here are answers to your three questions about this software:

1. Our DataQuirk software provides standard employee forms so that you are always in compliance with current government regulations.
2. You receive an interviewer's guide for structured employee interviews, as well as a scripted format for checking references by telephone.
3. Yes, you can update your employees' records easily without the need for additional software, hardware, or training.

Our DataQuirk software was specially designed to provide you with expert forms for interviewing, verifying references, recording attendance, evaluating performance, and tracking the status of your employees. We even provide you with step-by-step instructions and suggested procedures. You can treat your employees as if you had a professional human resources specialist on your staff.

In the attached PDF copy of our pamphlet, you can find out more about DataQuirk. To receive a preview copy or to ask questions about DataQuirk and its use, just call 1-800-354-5500. Our specialists are eager to help you weekdays from 8 to 5 PST. If you prefer, visit our website to receive more information or to place an order.

Sincerely,

Emma Ladina
Senior Marketing Representative

DTS Software, Inc. | 6680 Via del Oro | San Jose, CA 95138 | Phone (408) 528-2700 | dts-software.com

- Places most important information first
- Lists answers to sender's questions in order asked
- Directs reader to additional information
- Emphasizes "you" view
- Links sales promotion to reader benefits
- Makes it easy to respond

In the first sentence of a direct reply, deliver the information the reader wants. Avoid wordy, drawn-out openings (*I am responding to your e-mail of December 1, in which you request information about . . .*). More forceful and more efficient is an opener that answers the inquiry directly (*Here is the information you wanted about . . .*). When agreeing to a request for action, announce the good news promptly (*Yes, I will be happy to speak to your business communication class about . . .*).

Supply additional relevant information in the body of your response. Because any document written for your company is considered a legally binding contract, check facts and figures carefully. If a policy or procedure needs authorization, seek approval from a supervisor or executive before sending the message.

When answering several questions or providing considerable data, arrange the information logically and make it readable by using graphic devices such as lists, tables, headings, boldface, or italics. When customers or prospects inquire about products or services, try to promote your organization. Provide helpful information that satisfies the inquiry, but consider introducing another product as well. Be sure to present the promotional material with the "you" view and reader benefits (*You can use our standardized tests to free you from time-consuming employment screening*).

In concluding a response message, be cordial. Refer to the information provided (*The attached list summarizes our recommendations. We wish you all the best in redesigning your app.*). If further action is required, help the reader with specifics (*The Small Business Administration publishes a number of helpful booklets. Its Web address is . . .*). To prevent abruptness, include a pleasant closing remark that shows your willingness to help. Tailor your remarks to fit this e-mail and this reader. Avoid signing off with clichés (*If I may be of further assistance, don't hesitate to . . .*). In your e-mail provide your contact information to enable the reader to follow up.

## 6-2c Responding to Customer Comments Online

We live in an age when vocal individuals can start a firestorm of criticism online or become powerful brand ambassadors who champion certain products. Therefore, businesses must listen to social media comments about themselves and, if necessary, respond. You may ask, How do companies know when and how to respond? This invaluable knowledge constitutes an evolving field and, some would say, a minefield, littered with disastrous missteps and missed opportunities.

However, social media marketing experts are developing guidelines to provide organizations with tools for strategic decision making in various situations. Businesses can't control the conversation without disabling fans' comments on their Facebook walls or blogs, but they can respond in a way that benefits customers, prevents the problem from snowballing, and shines a positive light on their organizations.

**Embracing Customer Comments.** Customer reviews online are opportunities for savvy businesses to improve their products or services and may serve as a free and efficient *crowdsourced* quality-control system. Retailers such as

Figure **6.3** Responding to Customers Online

As businesses increasingly interact with their customers and the public online, they are developing "rules of engagement" and best practices.

**Be positive.**
- Respond in a friendly, upbeat, yet professional tone.
- Correct mistakes politely.
- Do not argue, insult, or blame others.

**Be transparent.**
- State your name and position with the business.
- Personalize and humanize your business.

**Be honest.**
- Own up to problems and mistakes.
- Inform customers when and how you will improve the situation.

**Be timely.**
- Respond in less than 24 hours.

**Be helpful.**
- Point users to valuable information on your website or other approved websites.
- Follow up with users when new information is available.

## OFFICE INSIDER

*"People unable to express themselves clearly in writing limit their opportunities for professional, salaried employment."*

—Bob Kerrey, chair of the National Commission on Writing

---

Walmart, Amazon, and L.L. Bean use powerful software to sift through billions of social media posts and product reviews. The data offer real-time feedback that may help clear up supply chain bottlenecks, expose product flaws, and improve operating instructions.[1] For example, angry reviews on its website alerted Walmart to a problem with a prepaid wireless Internet stick the retailer was selling and prompted a remedy within two days.

**Guidelines for Responding to Online Posts.** Social media experts say that not every comment on the Web merits a response. They recommend responding to posts only when you can add value—for example, by correcting false information or providing customer service. Additional guidelines for professional responses to customer comments are summarized in Figure 6.3.

### 6-2d Preparing Instruction Messages

Like requests and responses, instruction messages follow a straightforward, direct approach. You may be asked to write instructions about how to access cloud-based information, order supplies, file a grievance, or evaluate employees. Instructions must use plain English and be especially clear. Instructions are different from policies and official procedures, which establish rules of conduct to be followed within an organization. With instructions, business writers should be most concerned with creating messages that clearly explain how to complete a task.

**Dividing Instructions Into Steps.** Before writing instructions for a process, be sure you understand the process completely. Create logical steps in the correct order. Practice completing the procedure yourself first. This writing plan will get you started:

---

### WRITING PLAN FOR INSTRUCTION MESSAGES

- **Subject line:** Summarize the content of the message.
- **Opening:** Expand the subject line by stating the main idea concisely in a full sentence.
- **Body:** Present the instructions in steps in the order in which they are to be carried out. Arrange the items vertically with numbers. Begin each step with an action verb using the imperative (command) mood.
- **Closing:** Request a specific action, summarize the message, or present a closing thought. If appropriate, include a deadline and a reason.

---

The most effective way to list directions is to use command language, which is called the *imperative mood*. Think recipes, owner manuals, and assembly instructions. The imperative mood differs from the *indicative mood* in that it requests an action, whereas the indicative mood describes a statement as shown here:

| INDICATIVE MOOD | IMPERATIVE (COMMAND) MOOD |
|---|---|
| The contract should be sent immediately. | Send the contract immediately. |
| The first step involves installing the app. | Install the app first. |
| A survey of employees is necessary to learn what options they prefer. | Survey employees to learn the options they prefer. |

If you are asked to prepare a list of instructions that is not part of a message, include a title, such as *How to Access Cloud-Based Information*. Include an opening paragraph explaining why the instructions are needed.

Chapter 6: Positive Messages

**Revising a Message Delivering Instructions.** Figure 6.4 shows the first draft of an interoffice memo written by Neil DeLuca. His memo was meant to announce a new method for employees to follow in advertising open positions. However, the tone was negative, the explanation of the problem rambled, and the new method was unclear. Notice, too, that Neil's first draft told readers what they *shouldn't* do (*Do not submit*

## Figure 6.4 Memo Delivering Instructions

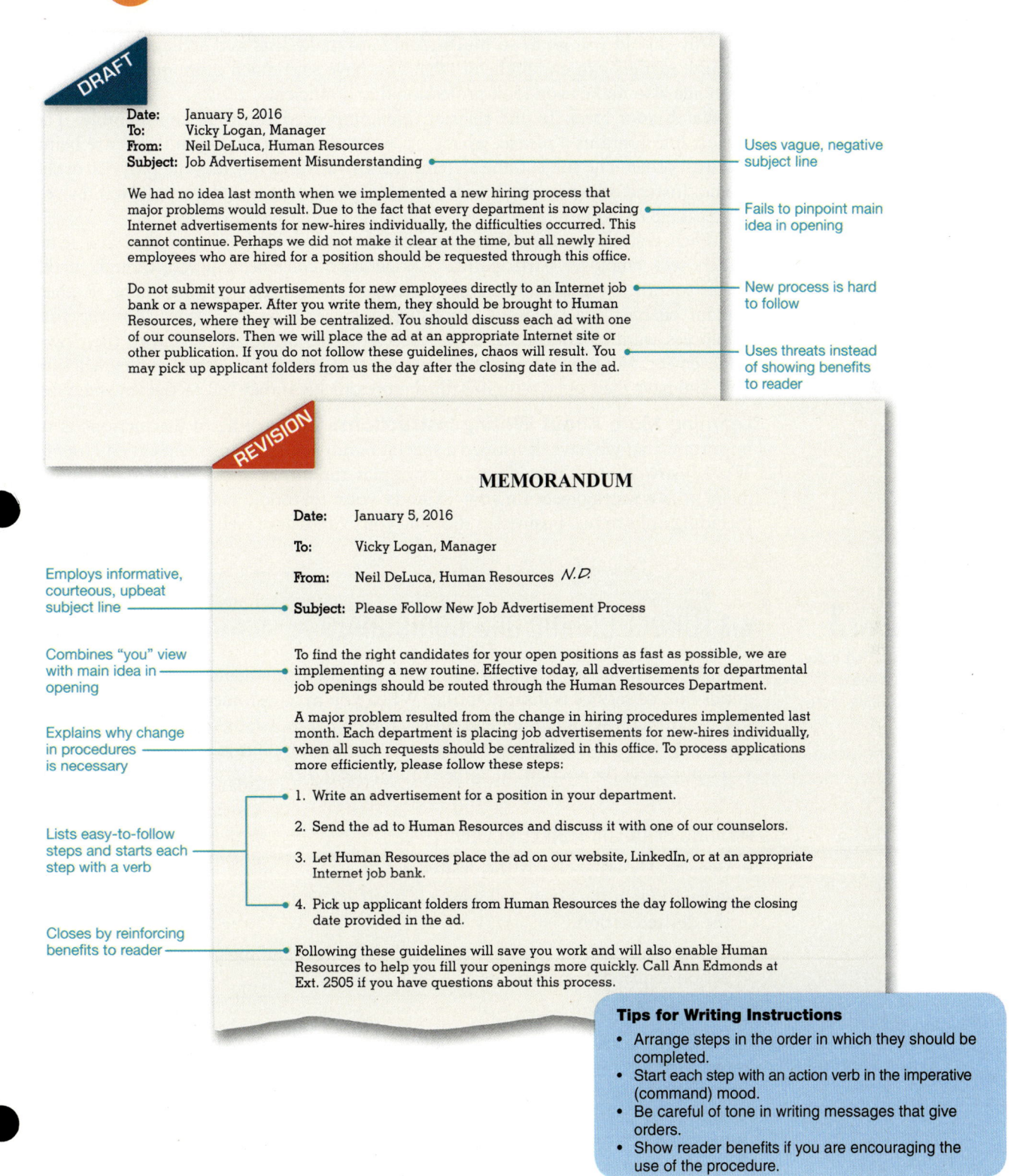

**DRAFT**

Date: January 5, 2016
To: Vicky Logan, Manager
From: Neil DeLuca, Human Resources
Subject: Job Advertisement Misunderstanding —— *Uses vague, negative subject line*

We had no idea last month when we implemented a new hiring process that major problems would result. Due to the fact that every department is now placing Internet advertisements for new-hires individually, the difficulties occurred. This cannot continue. Perhaps we did not make it clear at the time, but all newly hired employees who are hired for a position should be requested through this office. —— *Fails to pinpoint main idea in opening*

Do not submit your advertisements for new employees directly to an Internet job bank or a newspaper. After you write them, they should be brought to Human Resources, where they will be centralized. You should discuss each ad with one of our counselors. Then we will place the ad at an appropriate Internet site or other publication. If you do not follow these guidelines, chaos will result. You may pick up applicant folders from us the day after the closing date in the ad. —— *New process is hard to follow* / *Uses threats instead of showing benefits to reader*

**REVISION**

### MEMORANDUM

Date: January 5, 2016
To: Vicky Logan, Manager
From: Neil DeLuca, Human Resources *N.D.*
Subject: Please Follow New Job Advertisement Process

*Employs informative, courteous, upbeat subject line*

To find the right candidates for your open positions as fast as possible, we are implementing a new routine. Effective today, all advertisements for departmental job openings should be routed through the Human Resources Department.

*Combines "you" view with main idea in opening*

A major problem resulted from the change in hiring procedures implemented last month. Each department is placing job advertisements for new-hires individually, when all such requests should be centralized in this office. To process applications more efficiently, please follow these steps:

*Explains why change in procedures is necessary*

1. Write an advertisement for a position in your department.
2. Send the ad to Human Resources and discuss it with one of our counselors.
3. Let Human Resources place the ad on our website, LinkedIn, or at an appropriate Internet job bank.
4. Pick up applicant folders from Human Resources the day following the closing date provided in the ad.

*Lists easy-to-follow steps and starts each step with a verb*

Following these guidelines will save you work and will also enable Human Resources to help you fill your openings more quickly. Call Ann Edmonds at Ext. 2505 if you have questions about this process.

*Closes by reinforcing benefits to reader*

### Tips for Writing Instructions
- Arrange steps in the order in which they should be completed.
- Start each step with an action verb in the imperative (command) mood.
- Be careful of tone in writing messages that give orders.
- Show reader benefits if you are encouraging the use of the procedure.

*advertisements for new employees directly to an Internet job bank or a newspaper).* It is more helpful to tell readers what they *should* do. Finally, Neil's first memo closed with a threat instead of showing readers how this new practice will help them.

**Provide clear explanations.** Neil realized that his original explanation of the new procedure was vague and unclear. To clarify the instructions, he itemized and numbered the steps. Each step begins with an action verb in the imperative (command) mood (*Write, Bring, Let,* and *Pick up*). It is sometimes difficult to force all the steps in a list into this kind of command language. Neil struggled, but by trying different wording, he finally found verbs that worked.

Why should you go to so much trouble to make lists and achieve parallelism? Because readers can comprehend what you have said much more quickly. Parallel language also makes you look professional and efficient.

**Watch your tone.** In the revision Neil improved the tone considerably. The subject line contains a *please*, which is always pleasant to see even if you are being given an order. The subject line also includes a verb and specifies the purpose of the memo. Instead of expressing his ideas with negative words and threats, Neil revised his message to explain objectively and concisely what went wrong.

When delivering instructions, be careful of tone. Today's managers and team leaders seek employee participation. Cooperation can't be achieved, though, if the writer sounds like a dictator. Avoid making accusations and fixing blame. Rather, explain changes, give reasons, and suggest benefits to the reader. Assume that employees want to contribute to the success of the organization and to their own achievement. Notice in the Figure 6.4 revision that Neil tells readers that they will save time and have their open positions filled more quickly if they follow the new method.

**Learning More About Writing Instructions.** The writing of instructions is so important that we have developed a special bonus online supplement called *How to Write Instructions*. It provides more examples and information. This online supplement at www.cengagebrain.com extends your textbook with in-depth material including links to real businesses showing you examples of well-written instructions.

## 6-3 Direct Claims and Complaints

**LEARNING OBJECTIVE 3**
Prepare messages that make direct claims and voice complaints, including those posted online.

Things can and do go wrong in business—promised shipments are late, warrantied goods fail, or service is disappointing. When you as a customer must write to identify or correct a wrong, the message is called a *claim*. Claims that require persuasion are presented in Chapter 8. However, when your claim is straightforward and you can expect the receiver to agree readily, use a direct approach:

### WRITING PLAN FOR A DIRECT CLAIM

- **Opening:** Describe clearly the desired action.
- **Body:** Explain the claim, tell why it is justified, and provide details describing the desired action.
- **Closing:** End pleasantly with a goodwill statement, and include an end date and action request, if appropriate.

Increasingly, consumers resort to telephone calls, they e-mail their claims, or—as we have seen—they vent their peeves in online posts. However, even in the digital age, claims written as letters command more attention than telephone calls or e-mails. Letters also more convincingly establish a record of what happened. For fast delivery, a letter can be faxed or attached to an e-mail. Regardless of the channel, however, straightforward claims are direct.

### 6-3a Opening a Claim With a Clear Statement

When consumers have a legitimate claim or complaint, they can expect a positive response from a company. Smart businesses want to hear from their customers. They know that retaining a customer is far less costly than recruiting a new customer.

Open a claim with a clear statement of the problem or with the action you want the receiver to take. You might expect a replacement, a refund, a new order, credit to your account, correction of a billing error, free repairs, or cancellation of an order. When the remedy is obvious, state it immediately (*Please correct an erroneous double charge of $59 to my credit card for LapLink migration software. I accidentally clicked the Submit button twice*).

When the remedy is less obvious, you might ask for a change in policy or procedure or simply for an explanation (*Because three of our employees with confirmed reservations were refused rooms September 16 in your hotel, please clarify your policy regarding reservations and late arrivals*).

### 6-3b Explaining and Justifying a Claim

In the body of a claim message, explain the problem and justify your request. Provide all relevant details so that the problem can be corrected without further correspondence. Avoid becoming angry or trying to fix blame. Bear in mind that the person reading your message is seldom the one responsible for the problem. Instead, state the facts logically, objectively, and unemotionally; let the reader decide on the causes.

When sending a letter by postal mail, enclose copies of all pertinent documents such as invoices, sales slips, catalog descriptions, and repair records. Of course, those receipts and other documents can also be scanned and attached to an e-mail. When using paper mail, do *not* send your originals, which could be lost.

When service is involved, cite the names of individuals you spoke to and the dates of calls. Assume that a company honestly wants to satisfy its customers—because most do. When an alternative remedy exists, spell it out (*If you offer store credit only, please apply the $59 to your TurboSpeed software and a LapLink USB cable that I would like to buy too*).

### 6-3c Concluding a Claim With an Action Request

End a claim message with a courteous statement that promotes goodwill and summarizes your action request. If appropriate, include an end date (*I hope you understand that mistakes in ordering online sometimes occur. Because I have enjoyed your prompt service in the past, I hope that you will be able to issue a refund or store credit by May 2*).

Finally, in making claims, act promptly. Delaying claims makes them appear less important. Delayed claims are also more difficult to verify. By taking the time to put your claim in writing, you indicate your seriousness. A written claim starts a record of the problem, should later action be necessary. Save a copy of your message, whether paper or electronic.

### 6-3d Putting It All Together and Revising

When Duncan Rabe received a statement showing a charge for a three-year service warranty that he did not purchase, he was furious. He called the store but failed to get satisfaction. He decided against voicing his complaint online because he wished for a quick resolution and doubted that the small business would notice his social media post. He chose to write an e-mail to the customer service address featured prominently on the Good Vibes website.

You can see the first draft of Duncan's direct claim letter in Figure 6.5. This draft gave him a chance to vent his anger, but it accomplished little else. The

Figure 6.5 Direct Claim E-Mail

**DRAFT**

To: Sandra Bourne <sbourne@goodvibes.com>
From: Duncan K. Rabe <dkrabe@outlook.com>
Subject: Bad Vibes! — *Uses meaningless subject line*
Cc:
Bcc:

Dear Good Vibes:

You call yourselves Good Vibes, but all I'm getting from your service is bad vibes! I'm furious that you have your salespeople slip in unwanted service warranties to boost your sales. — *Sounds angry; jumps to conclusions*

When I bought my Panatronic DVR from Good Vibes, Inc., in August, I specifically told the salesperson that I did NOT want a three-year service warranty. But there it is on my Visa statement this month! You people have obviously billed me for a service I did not authorize. I refuse to pay this charge. — *Forgets that mistakes happen*

How can you hope to stay in business with such fraudulent practices? I was expecting to return this month and look at HDTVs, but you can be sure I'll find an honest dealer this time. — *Fails to suggest solution*

Angrily,

---

**REVISION**

To: Sandra Bourne <sbourne@goodvibes.com>
From: Duncan K. Rabe <dkrabe@outlook.com>
Subject: Requesting Refund for Erroneous Charge — *Provides informative subject line summarizing purpose*
Cc:
Attached: salesinvoice.pdf (2405 Kb)

Dear Ms. Bourne:

*States simply and clearly what to do* — Please credit my Visa account, ending in No. 9421, to correct an erroneous charge of $299. — *Explains objectively what went wrong*

*Doesn't blame or accuse* — On August 1, I purchased a Panatronic DVR from Good Vibes, Inc. Although the salesperson discussed a three-year extended warranty with me, I decided against purchasing that service for $299. However, when my credit card statement arrived this month, I noticed an extra $299 charge from Good Vibes, Inc. I suspect that this charge represents the warranty I declined. Enclosed is a scanned copy of my sales invoice along with my Visa statement showing the charge. — *Uses friendly tone* / *Documents facts*

*Summarizes request and courteously suggests continued business once problem is resolved* — Please authorize a credit immediately and e-mail me a confirmation of the transaction. I'm enjoying all the features of my Panatronic DVR and would like to be shopping at Good Vibes for an HDTV shortly.

Sincerely,
Duncan Rabe

Duncan K. Rabe | dkrabe@outlook.com | 2003 53rd Street | West Palm Beach, FL 33407 | 561.385.2241

---

**Tips for Submitting Claims**
- Begin with a compliment, point of agreement, statement of the problem, brief review of action you have taken to resolve the problem, or clear statement of the action you want taken.
- Prove that your claim is valid; explain why the receiver is responsible.
- Enclose document copies supporting your claim.
- Appeal to the receiver's fairness, ethics, legal responsibilities, or desire for return business.
- Avoid sounding angry, emotional, or irrational.
- Close by restating what you want done and looking forward to future business.

tone was belligerent; the writer assumed that the company intentionally mischarged him. Furthermore, he failed to tell the reader how to remedy the problem. The revision, also shown in Figure 6.5, tempered the tone, described the problem objectively, and provided facts and figures. Most important, it specified exactly what Duncan anted to be done.

### 6-3e Posting Complaints and Reviews Online

Social media experts advise that consumers exhaust all other options for complaints with the company before venting online.[2] Just as you probably wouldn't complain to the Better Business Bureau without giving a business at least one chance to respond, you shouldn't just let off steam online. Most businesses want to please their customers. A well-considered message, whether a letter or an e-mail, allows you to tell the full story and is more likely to be heard. Letting loose in ill-conceived online comments exposes you to risk.

**Angry Posts Are Out of Control.** Social media posts have a way of ending up in the wrong hands, making vicious complainers seem irrational. As always, consider whether people you respect and prospective employers would approve. Even anonymous posts can be traced back to the writer. Moreover, nasty "cyber chest-pounding" might not be taken seriously, and your remarks could be deleted.[3]

**Public Criticism Can Cost You.** Businesses and professionals can take individuals to court for negative comments online. A chiropractor in San Francisco sued a patient for criticizing his billing process on Yelp. The case was settled out of court. Also, libelous statements disguised as opinion (*In my view attorney Jack Miller is stealing $4,000 from his clients*) can get you in trouble.[4]

**You Have a Responsibility; Use It Wisely.** Shoppers read online comments on sites such as Yelp, TripAdvisor, Angie's List, and Amazon. In a Consumer Reports study of more than 4,000 online subscribers, 40 percent stated that they read user reviews when researching a product.[5] Even if posting does not achieve your objective, your well-written complaint or review may help others.

The tips in Figure 6.6, gleaned from Consumer Reports, will allow you to exercise your right to free speech while staying safe when critiquing a product or service online.

Figure **6.6** Writing Online Reviews and Complaints

**Establish your credibility.**
- Zero in on your objective and make your comment as concise as possible.
- Focus only on the facts and be able to support them.

**Check posting rules.**
- Understand what's allowed by reading the terms and conditions on the site.
- Keep your complaint clean, polite, and to the point.

**Provide balanced reviews.**
- To be fair, offset criticism with positives to show that you are a legitimate consumer.
- Suggest improvements even in glowing reviews; all-out gushing is suspicious and not helpful.

**Consider the Web's permanence.**
- Know that your review may be posted indefinitely, even if you change your mind and modify a post later.

**Embrace transparency.**
- Be open; even anonymous comments can be tracked down. Privacy policies do not protect writers from subpoenas.

**Accept offers to help.**
- Reply if a business offers to help or discuss the problem; update your original post as necessary.

**Refuse payment for favorable critiques.**
- Never accept payment to change your opinion or your account of the facts.
- Comply with requests for a review if you are a satisfied customer.

Chapter 6: Positive Messages

## OFFICE INSIDER

"No matter what the laws are in your state, consider the potential repercussions before you post critical or embarrassing comments.... The worst thing is reacting out of anger without taking the time to think about how this is going to be read by other people on the Internet."

—Mark Goldowitz, founder and president of the board of directors of the Public Participation Project

**LEARNING OBJECTIVE 4**

Create adjustment messages that salvage customers' trust and promote further business.

## 6-4 Adjustment Messages

When a company receives a claim and decides to respond favorably, the message is called an *adjustment*. Most businesses make adjustments promptly: they replace merchandise, refund money, extend discounts, send coupons, and repair goods. In fact, social media have shortened the response time drastically to mere hours, not days.

Businesses grant adjustments to legitimate claims for two reasons. First, contract and tort law protects consumers for recovery of damages. If, for example, you find an insect in a package of frozen peas, the food processor of that package is bound by contractual law to replace it. If you suffer injury, the processor may be liable for damages. Second, most organizations genuinely want to satisfy their customers and retain their business.

In responding to customer claims, you must first decide whether to grant the claim. Unless the claim is obviously fraudulent or excessive, you will probably grant it. When you say *yes*, your adjustment message will be good news to the reader. Deliver that good news by using the direct strategy. When your response is *no*, the indirect pattern might be more appropriate. Chapter 7 discusses the indirect pattern for conveying negative news. You have three goals in adjustment messages:

- Rectifying the wrong, if one exists
- Regaining the confidence of the customer
- Promoting further business

A positive adjustment message follows the direct strategy described in the following writing plan:

### WRITING PLAN FOR ADJUSTMENT MESSAGES

- **Subject line (optional):** Identify the previous correspondence and refer to the main topic.
- **Opening:** Grant the request or announce the adjustment immediately.
- **Body:** Provide details about how you are complying with the request. Try to regain the customer's confidence. Apologize, if appropriate, but don't admit negligence.
- **Closing:** End positively with a forward-looking thought; express confidence about future business relations. Include a sales promotion, if appropriate. Avoid referring to unpleasantness.

### 6-4a Revealing Good News Up Front

Don't dwell on what went wrong; present the good news immediately. When Kimberly Lu responded to the claim of customer Optima Ventures about a missing shipment, her first draft, shown at the top of Figure 6.7, was angry. No wonder. Optima Ventures apparently had provided the wrong shipping address, and the goods were returned. Once Kimberly and her company decided to send a second shipment, however, she had to give up the anger. Her goal was to regain the goodwill and the business of the customer.

If you decide to comply with a customer's claim, let the receiver know immediately. Don't begin your message with a negative statement (*We are very sorry that you are having trouble with your dishwasher*). This approach reminds the reader of the problem and may rekindle the unhappy feelings experienced when the claim

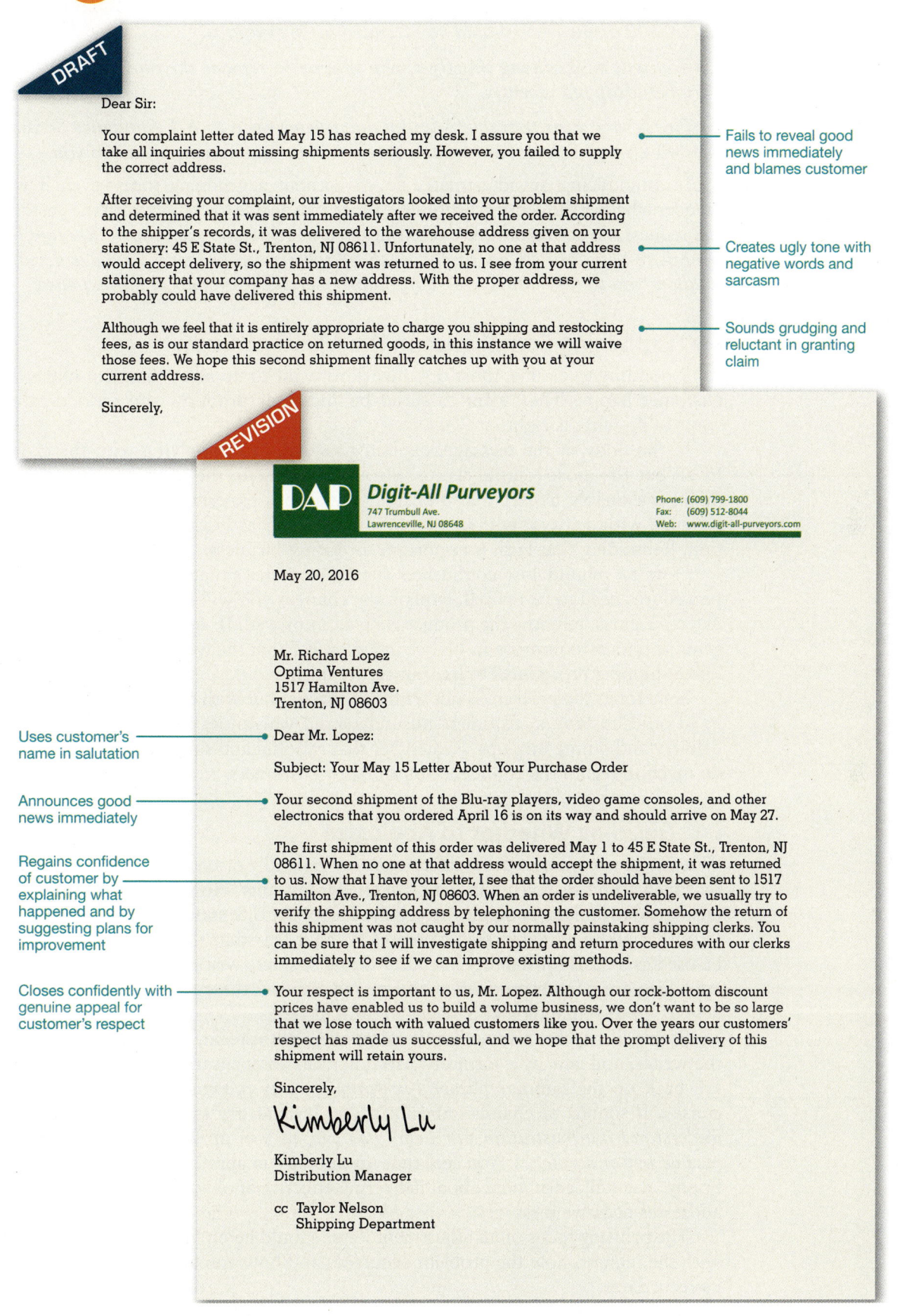

Figure 6.7 Customer Adjustment Letter

**DRAFT**

Dear Sir:

Your complaint letter dated May 15 has reached my desk. I assure you that we take all inquiries about missing shipments seriously. However, you failed to supply the correct address.

- Fails to reveal good news immediately and blames customer

After receiving your complaint, our investigators looked into your problem shipment and determined that it was sent immediately after we received the order. According to the shipper's records, it was delivered to the warehouse address given on your stationery: 45 E State St., Trenton, NJ 08611. Unfortunately, no one at that address would accept delivery, so the shipment was returned to us. I see from your current stationery that your company has a new address. With the proper address, we probably could have delivered this shipment.

- Creates ugly tone with negative words and sarcasm

Although we feel that it is entirely appropriate to charge you shipping and restocking fees, as is our standard practice on returned goods, in this instance we will waive those fees. We hope this second shipment finally catches up with you at your current address.

- Sounds grudging and reluctant in granting claim

Sincerely,

**REVISION**

**DAP  Digit-All Purveyors**
747 Trumbull Ave.
Lawrenceville, NJ 08648

Phone: (609) 799-1800
Fax: (609) 512-8044
Web: www.digit-all-purveyors.com

May 20, 2016

Mr. Richard Lopez
Optima Ventures
1517 Hamilton Ave.
Trenton, NJ 08603

- Uses customer's name in salutation

Dear Mr. Lopez:

Subject: Your May 15 Letter About Your Purchase Order

- Announces good news immediately

Your second shipment of the Blu-ray players, video game consoles, and other electronics that you ordered April 16 is on its way and should arrive on May 27.

- Regains confidence of customer by explaining what happened and by suggesting plans for improvement

The first shipment of this order was delivered May 1 to 45 E State St., Trenton, NJ 08611. When no one at that address would accept the shipment, it was returned to us. Now that I have your letter, I see that the order should have been sent to 1517 Hamilton Ave., Trenton, NJ 08603. When an order is undeliverable, we usually try to verify the shipping address by telephoning the customer. Somehow the return of this shipment was not caught by our normally painstaking shipping clerks. You can be sure that I will investigate shipping and return procedures with our clerks immediately to see if we can improve existing methods.

- Closes confidently with genuine appeal for customer's respect

Your respect is important to us, Mr. Lopez. Although our rock-bottom discount prices have enabled us to build a volume business, we don't want to be so large that we lose touch with valued customers like you. Over the years our customers' respect has made us successful, and we hope that the prompt delivery of this shipment will retain yours.

Sincerely,

*Kimberly Lu*

Kimberly Lu
Distribution Manager

cc  Taylor Nelson
    Shipping Department

was written. Instead, focus on the good news. The following openings for various messages illustrate how to *frontload* the good news:

*You're right! We agree that the warranty on your American Standard Model UC600 dishwasher should be extended for six months.*

*You will be receiving shortly a new iPhone to replace the one that shattered when dropped recently.*

*Please take your portable Admiral microwave oven to A-1 Appliance Service, 200 Orange Street, Pasadena, where it will be repaired at no cost to you.*

In announcing an adjustment, do so without a grudging tone—even if you wonder whether the claim is legitimate. Once you decide to comply with the customer's request, do so happily. Avoid halfhearted or reluctant responses (*Although the American Standard dishwasher works well when used properly, we have decided to allow you to take yours to A-1 Appliance Service for repair at our expense*).

### 6-4b Explaining Compliance in the Message Body

In responding to claims, most organizations want to do more than just make the customer happy. They want to stand behind their products and services; they want to do what is right.

In the body of the message, explain how you are complying with the claim. In all but the most routine claims, also seek to regain the customer's trust. You might reasonably expect that a customer who has experienced difficulty with a product, with delivery, with billing, or with service has lost faith in your organization. Rebuilding that faith is important for future business.

How to rebuild lost confidence depends on the situation and the claim. If procedures need to be revised, explain the changes you will make. If a product has defective parts, tell how the product is being improved. If service is faulty, describe genuine efforts to improve it. Notice in Figure 6.7 that the writer promises to investigate shipping procedures to prevent future mishaps.

Sometimes the problem is not with the product but with the way consumers use it. In other instances customers misunderstand warranties or inadvertently cause delivery and billing mix-ups. Remember that rational and sincere explanations will do much to regain the confidence of unhappy customers.

### 6-4c Deciding Whether to Apologize

Whether to apologize is debatable. Attorneys generally discourage apologies fearing that they admit responsibility and can trigger lawsuits. However, both judges and juries tend to look on apologies favorably. Thirty-six U.S. states have passed *apology laws* that allow an expression of regret without fear that those statements would be used as a basis for liability in court.[6] Some business writing experts caution that apologies are counterproductive and merely remind the customer of unpleasantness. If, however, apologizing seems natural, do so.

People like to hear apologies. It raises their self-esteem, shows the humility of the writer, and acts as a form of "psychological compensation."[7] Don't, however, fall back on the familiar phrase *I'm sorry for any inconvenience we may have caused*. It sounds mechanical and insincere. Instead, try something like this: *We understand the frustration our delay has caused you* or *We're sorry you didn't receive better service*. If you feel that an apology is appropriate, do it early and briefly. You will learn more about delivering effective apologies in Chapter 7, which addresses negative messages.

The primary focus of an adjustment letter should be on how you are complying with the request, how the problem occurred, and how you are working to prevent its recurrence.

### 6-4d Using Sensitive Language

The language of adjustment letters must be particularly sensitive, because customers are already upset. Here are some don'ts:

- Don't use negative words or phrases *(trouble, regret, misunderstanding, fault, error, inconvenience, you claim)*.
- Don't blame customers—even when they may be at fault.
- Don't blame individuals or departments within your organization; it's unprofessional.
- Don't make unrealistic promises; you can't guarantee that the situation will never recur.

To regain the confidence of your reader, consider including resale information. Describe a product's features and any special applications that might appeal to the reader. Promote a new product if it seems appropriate.

### 6-4e Showing Confidence in the Closing

End positively by expressing confidence that the problem has been resolved and that continued business relations will result. You might mention the product in a favorable light, suggest a new product, express your appreciation for the customer's business, or anticipate future business. It is often appropriate to refer to the desire to be of service and to satisfy customers. Notice how the following closings illustrate a positive, confident tone.

> *Thanks for writing. Your satisfaction is important to us. We hope that this refund check convinces you that service to our customers is our No. 1 priority. Our goals are to earn your confidence and continue to merit that confidence with quality products and excellent service.*

> *You were most helpful in informing us of this situation and permitting us to correct it. We appreciate your thoughtfulness in writing to us.*

> *Your Asus Netbook will come in handy whether you are connecting with friends, surfing the Net, listening to music, watching movies, or playing games. For a little more, you can add an HDTV tuner and built-in GPS. Take a look at our website for big savings on essential technology.*

Although the direct pattern works for many requests and replies, it obviously won't work for every situation. With more practice and experience, you will be able to alter the pattern and adapt your skills to other communication problems.

## 6-5 Goodwill Messages

**LEARNING OBJECTIVE 5**
Write special messages that convey kindness and goodwill.

Finding the right words to express feelings is often more difficult than writing routine business documents. That is probably why writers tend to procrastinate when it comes to sending goodwill messages expressing thanks, recognition, and sympathy. Sending a ready-made card or picking up the telephone may seem easier. Remember, though, that the personal sentiments of the sender are more expressive and more meaningful to readers than are printed cards or oral messages. Taking the time to write lends more importance to well-wishing. Personal notes also allow the recipient to reread, savor, and treasure them.

Goodwill notes should always be dispatched promptly. These messages are easier to write while the situation is fresh in your mind. They also mean more to the recipient. A prompt thank-you note carries the hidden message that you care and that the reader is important to you. Instead of learning writing plans for each goodwill message—whether thanks, congratulations, praise, or sympathy—we

## OFFICE INSIDER

*"Saying 'Thank You' is an important concept in our business. When people are sincerely appreciated for their efforts, they tend to be more effective and do a better job."*

—Nowell C. Wisch, editor of *Wearables Business* and veteran of the promotional products industry

recommend that you concentrate on the five Ss. Goodwill messages should have the following characteristics:

- **Selfless.** Focus the message solely on the receiver, not the sender. When praising others, avoid such comments as *I remember when I. . . .*
- **Specific.** Personalize the message by mentioning specific incidents or characteristics of the receiver. Telling a colleague *Great speech* is much less effective than *Great story about McDonald's marketing in Moscow*. Take care to verify names and other facts.
- **Sincere.** Let your words show genuine feelings. Rehearse in your mind how you would express the message to the receiver orally. Then transform that conversational language to your written message. Avoid pretentious, formal, or flowery language *(With the utmost pleasure, I extend felicitations on the occasion of your firm's twentieth anniversary)*.
- **Spontaneous**. Keep the message fresh and enthusiastic. Avoid canned phrases *(Congratulations on your promotion, Good luck in the future)*. Strive for directness and naturalness, not creative brilliance.
- **Short.** Although goodwill messages can be as long as needed, try to accomplish your purpose in only a few sentences. Remembering an individual is most important. Such caring does not require documentation or wordiness. Individuals and business organizations often use special note cards or stationery for brief messages.

### 6-5a Saying Thank You

When someone has done you a favor or when an action merits praise, you need to extend thanks or show appreciation. Letters of appreciation may be written to customers for their orders, to hosts for their hospitality, to individuals for kindnesses performed, to employees for a job well done, and especially to customers who complain. After all, whether in social media posts, by e-mail, or on paper, complaints are actually providing you with free consulting reports from the field. Complainers who feel that their complaints were heard often become the greatest promoters of an organization.[8]

Because the receiver will be pleased to hear from you, you can open directly. The letter in Figure 6.8 thanks a speaker who addressed a group of marketing professionals. Although such thank-you notes can be short, this one is a little longer because the writer wants to lend importance to the receiver's efforts. Notice that every sentence relates to the receiver and offers enthusiastic praise. By using the receiver's name along with contractions and positive words, the writer makes the letter sound warm and conversational.

Written notes that show appreciation and express thanks are significant to their receivers. In expressing thanks, you generally write a short note on special notepaper or heavy card stock. The following messages provide models for expressing thanks for a gift, for a favor, for hospitality, and for employee contributions.

**Expressing Thanks for a Gift.** When expressing thanks, tell what the gift means to you. Use sincere, simple statements.

> *Thanks, Laura, to you and the other members of the department for honoring me with the elegant Waterford crystal vase at the party celebrating my twentieth anniversary with the company. The height and shape of the vase are perfect to hold roses and other bouquets from my garden. Each time I fill it, I will remember your thoughtfulness in choosing this lovely gift for me.*

**Sending Thanks for a Favor.** In showing appreciation for a favor, explain the importance of the gesture to you.

> *I sincerely appreciate your filling in for me last week when I was too ill to attend the planning committee meeting for the spring exhibition. Without your participation, much of my preparatory work would have been lost. Knowing that competent*

Figure 6.8 Thank-You Letter for a Favor

**National eMarketing Association**
645 5th Avenue, Suite 1203
New York, NY 10022
www.nea.com

February 26, 2016

Mr. Paul Rizzoli
Marketing Manager
Fisher-Price Brands
636 Girard Avenue
East Aurora, NY 14052

Dear Paul:

Thank you for providing the Manhattan chapter of the NeA with one of the best presentations our group has ever heard. — *Tells purpose and delivers praise*

Your description of the battle Fisher-Price Brands waged to begin marketing products in Japan was a genuine eye-opener for many of us. Nine years of preparation establishing connections and securing permissions seems an eternity, but obviously such persistence and patience pay off. We now understand better the need to learn local customs and nurture relationships when dealing in Japan or other Asian countries. — *Personalizes the message by using specifics rather than generalities*

In addition to your good advice, we particularly enjoyed your sense of humor and jokes—as you must have recognized from the uproarious laughter. What a great routine you do on faulty translations! — *Spotlights the reader's talents*

We're grateful, Paul, for the entertaining and instructive evening you provided our marketing professionals. — *Concludes with compliments and thanks*

Cordially,

*Roberta B Wilson*

Roberta B. Wilson
Program Chair, NeA

RBW: mef

---

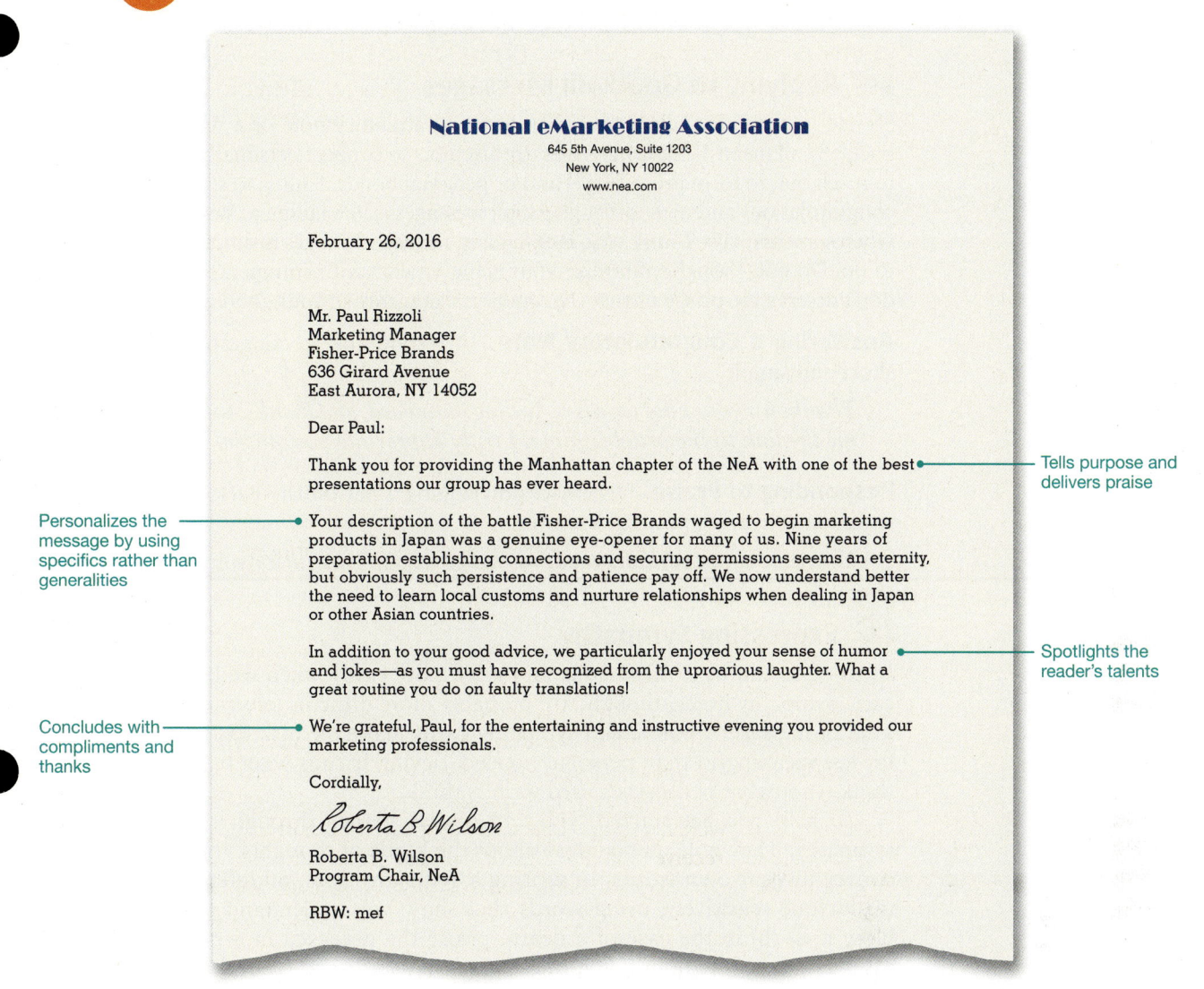

and generous individuals like you are part of our team, Mark, is a great comfort. Moreover, counting you as a friend is my very good fortune. I'm grateful to you.

**Extending Thanks for Hospitality.** When you have been a guest, send a note that compliments the fine food, charming surroundings, warm hospitality, excellent host, and good company.

*Jeffrey and I want you to know how much we enjoyed the dinner party for our department that you hosted Saturday evening. Your charming home and warm hospitality, along with the lovely dinner and sinfully delicious chocolate dessert, combined to create a truly memorable evening. Most of all, though, we appreciate your kindness in cultivating togetherness in our department. Thanks, Barbara, for being such a special person.*

**Recognizing Employees for Their Contributions.** A letter that recognizes specific employee contributions makes the person feel appreciated even if it is not accompanied by a bonus check.

*Jerry, I am truly impressed by how competently you shepherded your team through the complex Horizon project. Thanks to your leadership, team members stayed on target and met their objectives. Your adept meeting facilitation, use of an agenda, and quick turnaround of meeting minutes kept the project on track. However, most of all I appreciate the long hours you put in to hammer out the final report.*

### 6-5b Replying to Goodwill Messages

Should you respond when you receive a congratulatory note or a written pat on the back? By all means! These messages are attempts to connect personally; they are efforts to reach out, to form professional and/or personal bonds. Failing to respond to notes of congratulations and most other goodwill messages is like failing to say *You're welcome* when someone says *Thank you*. Responding to such messages is simply the polite thing to do. Do not, though, minimize your achievements with comments that suggest you don't deserve the praise or that the sender is exaggerating your good qualities.

**Answering a Congratulatory Note.** In responding to congratulations, keep it short and simple.

*Thanks for your kind words regarding my award, and thanks, too, for forwarding me the link to the article online. I truly appreciate your warm wishes.*

**Responding to Praise.** When acknowledging a pat-on-the-back note, use simple words in conveying your appreciation.

*Your note about my work made me feel good. I'm grateful for your thoughtfulness.*

### 6-5c Expressing Sympathy

Most of us can bear misfortune and grief more easily when we know that others care. Sympathy notes, though, are probably more difficult to write than any other kind of message. Commercial sympathy cards make the task easier—but they are far less meaningful than personal notes. Grieving friends want to know what you think—not what Hallmark's card writers think.

To help you get started, you can always glance through cards expressing sympathy. They will supply ideas about the kinds of thoughts you might wish to convey in your own words. In writing a sympathy note, (a) refer to the death or misfortune sensitively, using words that show you understand what a crushing blow it is; (b) in the case of a death, praise the deceased in a personal way; (c) offer assistance without going into excessive detail; and (d) end on a reassuring, forward-looking note. Sympathy messages may be typed, although handwriting seems more personal. In either case, use quality paper stock or personal stationery.

**Sending Condolences.** Mention the loss tactfully, recognize good qualities of the deceased, assure the receiver of your concern, offer assistance, and conclude on a reassuring note.

*We are deeply saddened, Gayle, to learn of the death of your husband. Warren's kind nature and friendly spirit endeared him to all who knew him. He will be missed. Although words seem empty in expressing our grief, we want you to know that your friends at QuadCom extend their profound sympathy to you. If we may help you or lighten your load in any way, you have but to call.*

*We know that the treasured memories of your many happy years together, along with the support of your family and many friends, will provide strength and comfort in the months ahead.*

### 6-5d Is E-Mail Appropriate for Goodwill Messages?

In expressing thanks or responding to goodwill messages, handwritten notes are most impressive. However, if you frequently communicate with the receiver by e-mail and if you are sure your note will not get lost, then sending an e-mail goodwill message is acceptable, according to the Emily Post Institute.[9] To express sympathy immediately after learning of a death or accident, you might precede a phone call or a written condolence message with an e-mail. E-mail is a fast and nonintrusive way to show your feelings. However, advises the Emily Post Institute, immediately follow with a handwritten note. Remember that e-mail messages are quickly gone and forgotten. Handwritten or printed messages remain and can be savored. Your thoughtfulness is more lasting if you take the time to prepare a handwritten or printed message on notepaper or personal stationery.

## SUMMARY OF LEARNING OBJECTIVES

**6-1** Understand the channels through which typical positive messages travel in the digital era—e-mails, memos, and business letters, and explain how business letters should be formatted.
- Most workplace messages are positive or neutral; therefore, adopt the direct strategy. Positive messages are routine; they help workers conduct everyday business.
- Write a letter when the situation (a) demands a permanent record, (b) requires confidentiality, (c) calls for formality, and (d) favors a well-considered presentation.
- Format your letters carefully. Select the block style, leave enough white space, and set margins of 1 to 1.5 inches. Don't justify the right margin.

**6-2** Compose direct messages that make requests, respond to inquiries online and offline, and deliver step-by-step instructions.
- In requests, frontload key information because readers look at the opening and closing first. Provide details in the body, and close with appreciation and a call for action.
- When complying with requests, be direct. Sum up the main idea in the subject line; open directly; provide details in the body; and end with a brief conclusion, a summary, or an offer of help.
- Expect to listen to social media comments about your business; if necessary, respond to benefit customers, prevent escalation, and present your organization in a positive light.
- Be direct and divide instructions into steps in the correct order, arrange items vertically with numbers, and begin each step with an action verb in the imperative mood.

**6-3** Prepare messages that make direct claims and voice complaints, including those posted online.
- Open a claim by describing the desired action; explain and justify your claim. Conclude pleasantly with a goodwill statement, a date, and an action request, if appropriate.
- In making claims, act promptly. Delaying claims makes them appear less important and makes them difficult to verify.
- When posting complaints online, keep in mind that you can't prevent angry posts and that public criticism could cost you; use the power inherent in commenting publicly responsibly.

**6-4** Create adjustment messages that salvage customers' trust and promote further business.
- Favorable responses to claims are called adjustments. In adjustment messages announce the good news up front, explain how you are complying with the request in the message body, and end positively.
- Understand that the three goals in adjustment messages are rectifying wrongs, regaining the confidence of the customer, and promoting further business.
- When appropriate, apologize early and briefly. Don't use negative language, don't blame customers or coworkers, and don't make unrealistic promises.
- Show confidence in the closing; end positively by expressing confidence that the problem has been resolved and that continued business relations will result.

**6-5** Write special messages that convey kindness and goodwill.
- Write goodwill messages to express thanks, recognition, and sympathy; dispatch goodwill notes promptly to show that the reader is important to you.
- Make your goodwill messages selfless, specific, sincere, spontaneous, and short.
- Answer congratulatory notes and respond to praise in simple words that convey your appreciation.
- When expressing condolences, mention the loss tactfully, recognize good qualities of the deceased, assure the receiver of your concern, offer assistance, and end on a reassuring note.
- Sending an e-mail goodwill message is acceptable; however, follow up with a handwritten note.

Chapter 6: Positive Messages

# CHAPTER REVIEW

1. What are routine messages, and why is the direct strategy useful for them? (Obj. 1)

2. When are letters still the preferred channel of communication despite the advent of e-mail, social networking, and other electronic communication technologies? (Obj. 1)

3. Why should businesses welcome customer comments online? (Obj. 2)

4. How should instructions be written? Give an example. (Obj. 2)

5. What is a claim? When should it be straightforward? (Obj. 3)

6. Why should a direct claim be made by letter rather than by e-mail or a telephone call? (Obj. 3)

7. What is an adjustment message? (Obj. 4)

8. What are a writer's three goals in composing an adjustment message? (Obj. 4)

9. What are five characteristics goodwill messages should have? (Obj. 5)

10. What are five groups of people to whom business communicators might write letters of appreciation? (Obj. 5)

## CRITICAL THINKING

11. What are the advantages of mailing a letter as opposed to sending an e-mail, making a phone call, or writing an online post? (Objs. 1, 2)
12. Why is it smart to keep your cool when making a claim, and how should you go about it? (Obj. 3)
13. Is it true that the "squeaky wheel gets the most grease," meaning that the customer complaining the loudest and most aggressively will get noticed and receive the greatest concessions? (Obj. 3)
14. Why is it important to regain the trust of a customer in an adjustment message? How can it be done? (Obj. 4)
15. Is it fair for creditors to continue reporting late payments after the payments have been made? What do you think about experts' suggestion that people with credit blemishes write a sincere "goodwill" letter to creditors asking for compassion and requesting that the records of their late payments be erased? (Obj. 5)

## WRITING IMPROVEMENT EXERCISES

### Improving Subject Lines and Opening Paragraphs in Positive Messages (Objs. 1, 2)

**YOUR TASK.** Study the following paragraphs. Then write an appropriate subject line and opening sentence for each one.

16. My name is Rachel Rivera, and I am looking for a new computing device, and frankly I don't know what is right for me or my small business. I am highly mobile and work from many places. You were recommended as a computing guru who gives great advice. I need a portable yet secure device. I like a big screen and the ability to connect to many peripherals at once. I guess what I am saying is that I need your advice on what computer is right for me—a tablet, notebook, laptop, or desktop PC. What do you think?

17. Our organization, Newborns in Need, has heard that charity golf tournaments can raise a lot of money. However, we know nothing about how to plan such an event. Your recent blog about planning an event was terrific. But we have additional questions, such as how to attract celebrities and whether it would be an amateur event or could local celebrities participate. Another big question has to do with pricing. Can you help us estimate what costs are involved and what expenses we should expect? As you can see, we have many questions, such as what is a "shotgun start" format? We would commission you to help us if you are available.

18. Because the economy seems to be improving, First Federal Bank has been investigating the possibility of initiating an internship program within our Financial Services Department. I have been appointed as the point person to conduct research regarding our proposed program. We are fully aware of the benefits of a strong internship program, and our management team is eager to take advantage of some of these benefits. We would be deeply appreciative if you would be so kind as to help us out with answers to a number of specific questions.

19. Your letter of November 2 has been referred to my desk. Pursuant to your inquiry, I have researched your question in regard to the colors of our European-style patio umbrella. This unique umbrella is one of our most popular items. Its 10-foot canopy protects you when the sun is directly overhead, but it also swivels and tilts to virtually any angle for continuous sun protection all day long. It comes in two colors: cream and forest green.

Chapter 6: Positive Messages

20. I am pleased to receive your inquiry of March 2 regarding the possibility of my acting as a speaker at the final semester meeting of your business management club on June 1. The topic of networking and résumés in the digital age interests me and is one on which I think I could impart helpful information to your members. Therefore, I am responding in the affirmative to your kind invitation.

21. Your complaint message about our XR-310 Amplifier Tubes that were broken in transit to you has been directed to me for response. Thank you for telling us immediately about this mishap with your Order No. 2190. We also thank you for your thoughtfulness in noting the damage carefully on the express receipt. That information is very helpful. We are sending a replacement shipment of your entire order of XR-310 Amplifier Tubes by prepaid express and expect that it will arrive by February 20 to replace your stock.

## Writing Instructions (Obj. 2)

**YOUR TASK.** Revise the following wordy, dense paragraphs into a set of concise instructions. Include a short introductory statement.

22. More and more amateurs are making YouTube videos, but if you have never done it before, here are some important tips. First, of course, you will need some kind of video recording device such as a smartphone, webcam, or camcorder. Another thing you will have to do is make a decision on whether or not to make a video blog, comedy skit, how-to video, or a video that is about travel. Because nothing is perfect the first time, you should record several takes, which you can stitch together later. Next you must transfer the video files to your computer. Finally, be sure to use computer editing software to delete, improve, or change anything in your footage.

23. As a visitor and customer to our catalog website, you can place an order by following certain steps. Let me explain those steps. One of the first things you will want to do is look over everything and find the items you want from our catalog. Then your shopping cart is important. You will add items to your shopping cart. When you are finished adding things to your shopping cart, the next step is to proceed to checkout. But wait! Have you created a new account? After creating a new account, we next need to know what shipping address to ship your items to. We will also need to have you choose a shipping method. Then you will be expected to provide payment information. Finally, you are nearly done! Payment information must be provided, and then you are ready to review your order and submit it.

24. Obtaining credit and keeping good credit can be difficult, especially for young people. Here are five suggestions that will help you obtain credit and maintain a good credit score. One thing I like to suggest first is getting a gas store card. These cards are easier to get than regular credit cards. What's great about them is that you can establish a credit history by making small payments in full and on time. To maintain good credit, you should always pay your bills on time. Delinquencies are terrible. They create the biggest negative effect on a credit score. If you already have credit cards, your balance should be paid down. If you can't afford to do that, you might take a loan from a family member or friend. If you have unused credit card accounts, don't close them. I know it sounds as if you should, but actually, canceling a card can lower your score. Don't do it! Finally, never max out your credit cards. A good rule of thumb to follow is keeping your balance below 30 percent of your credit limit.

# RADICAL REWRITES

**Note:** Radical Rewrites are provided at **www.cengagebrain.com** for you to download and revise. Your instructor may provide a suggested solution.

## 6.1 Radical Rewrite: Direct Request—Patient Privacy Breach at Medical Office (Obj. 2)
**E-mail**

The following serious message requests information, but its poor organization and other writing faults prevent it from accomplishing its goal.

**YOUR TASK.** Analyze this message and list at least five writing weaknesses. If your instructor directs, revise the message using the suggestions you learned in this and previous chapters.

**To:** w.e.vance@securityspecialists.com
**From:** dr.jeremy.chen@valleyinternists.com
**Subject:** Inquiry
**Cc:**
**Bcc:**

Dear Sir:

I am a physician in a small medical practice, and I am worried about protecting patients' medical information. Your website (SecuritySpecialists.com) looks quite promising but I found it overwhelming. I could not find answers to my specific questions, so I am writing this message to ask them. Could you call me within the next two days? I'm usually in surgery until 4 p.m. most days and try to leave at 6 p.m.

First, as I mentioned heretofore, my practice is small. Do you have experience in working with small medical practices? We may already have experienced a security breach. When you investigate, if you find out that privacy laws have been broken, do you report them to government agencies immediately?

We're really extremely interested in how you investigate an incident that may have taken place. If you discover a privacy breach, do you help your client make notification to his patients who are affected? Additionally, are you discreet about it?

I look forward to hearing from you.

Jeremy Chen, M.D.

List at least five weaknesses of this message.

## 6.2 Radical Rewrite: Direct Response—Sending Answers to Data Breach Questions (Obj. 2)
**E-mail**

The following message responds to the inquiry in **Radical Rewrite 6.1**. Dr. Chen asks for information about dealing with a data breach at his medical firm. Mr. Vance, from Security Specialists, wants to respond briefly and answer more fully in a telephone conversation with Dr. Chen. However, the following direct response is disorganized and needs a radical rewrite to be effective in achieving its goal. Study the following poorly written message, list its weaknesses, and revise it if your instructor directs.

Chapter 6: Positive Messages

**To:** dr.jeremy.chen@valleyinternists.com
**From:** w.e.vance@securityspecialists.com
**Subject:** Data Breaches
**Cc:**
**Bcc:**

Dear Dr. Chen:

We have received your inquiry, which has been directed to me for response. I can assure you that our company can do what you want in the way of cyber security, data breach response, and incident analysis solutions. We are specialists. You asked some specific questions, such as having experience with smaller medical establishments. I can assure you that, yes, we certainly do have such experience. Even with limited resources, smaller companies will benefit from basic security awareness training in a manner related to how to properly handle, store, and the processing of patient health information.

In regard to any incident that may have already occurred, we are experienced at investigating incidents, we analyze clues, and we can quickly and defensively uncover critical information. In regard to notifying patients of any breach, we assure you that we can give discreet breach notification that is prompt and we also customize it for your business. However, I must warn you in advance that if we become aware of any wrongdoing, we must notify any applicable government or law enforcement agencies because we are obligated to do so. But I can assure you that such notification is hardly ever necessary. We can discuss your concerns more extensively by telephone. Thank you for your interest in Security Specialists.

Warren E. Vance

[Full contact information]

List at least five weaknesses of this message.

## 6.3 Radical Rewrite: Instruction Memo—New Procedure for Submitting Travel Expenses (Obj. 2)

The following instruction memo is negative and unpolished and lacks the "you" view. It needs a radical rewrite to transform it into an efficient, effective memo. List its weaknesses, and then rewrite it with a bulleted list and more emphasis on benefits to the reader.

**Date:** Current date
**To:** Staff Members
**From:** Marcy Needham, Accounting
**Subject:** Travel Expense Claims

This is to inform you that here in Accounting we cannot process your travel expense claims unless you use the revised Travel Expense Claim form. This form is available on the company intranet.

If you have questions about what can be properly reimbursed, look at the revised Travel Expense Policy. This, too, is available on the company intranet. In fact, everyone should read the policy so that they don't make mistakes about what is reimbursable. You should note that the mileage reimbursement amount has been changed. On personal vehicles it's now 56.5 cents per mile.

Claims for reimbursement will not be approved unless they are submitted within 45 days of the transaction date. This is important to remember. Don't wait too long to submit your claim. You are also reminded that you must secure the signature of your manager for any expense in excess of $200. We are here to serve!

List at least five weaknesses of this message.

## 6.4 Radical Rewrite: Direct Claim—Car Rental Horror Story (Obj. 3)

The writer of the following letter is too angry to compose a logical and rational claim. Her message is more suited to venting than to achieving the goal of receiving a refund.

**YOUR TASK.** Analyze this message, list at least five weaknesses, and revise it if your instructor directs.

---

Current date

Mr. Joseph A. Morgan
Regional General Manager
ProCar Rentals
4510 Cyprus Street
Denver, CO 80246

Dear Regional General Manager Joseph Morgen:

I have a horror story of gargantuan proportions to relate to you so that you know how incompetent the amateurish bozos are that work for you! You should fire the whole Colorado Springs Airport branch. I'm tired of lousy service and of being charged an arm and a leg for extras that end up not functioning properly. Calling your company is useless because no one answers the phone or returns calls!

In view of the fact that my colleague and I were forced to wait for an hour for a car at Colorado Springs Airport on August 15, your local branch people gave us a free navigation device. That would have been really nice in the event that the thing had actually worked, which it didn't. We advised the counter person that the GPS was broken, but it took another half hour to receive a new one and to finally start our business trip.

Imagine our surprise when the "free" GPS showed up on our bill apparently costing a whopping $180, plus tax! What came next would qualify as some dark Kafkaesque nightmare. I spent hours over the next three weeks talking to various employees of your questionable organization who swore that only "the manager" could help me, but this mysterious person was never available to talk. At this point in time, I called your Denver Airport location again and refused to get off the phone until I spoke to "the manager," and, lo and behold, he promised to credit the cost of the GPS to our corporate account. Was my nightmare over? No!

When we checked the status of the refund on our credit card statement, we noticed that he had forgotten to refund about $60 in taxes and surcharges that had also been assessed. So much for a full refund!

Inasmuch as my company is a new customer and inasmuch as we had hoped to use your agency for our future car rentals because of your competitive rates, I trust that you will give this matter your prompt attention.

Your very upset customer,

---

List at least five weaknesses of this message.

# ACTIVITIES AND CASES

## 6.5 Short Responses to Online Comments (Objs. 1–5)
**Social Media**

**YOUR TASK.** Explain the positive and negative attributes of the following online posts.[10] Examine the consumer posts and the companies' responses to them. Do both follow the guidelines in this chapter?

**a.**

**Heather Jones** really really poor customer service by you guys. i am now looking into a new auto insurance provider. . . .
Yesterday at 8:57 am • Like • Comment

25 people like this.

**GEICO** Hi Heather, is there something we can assist with? Please send us your contact info at facebook@geico.com if you would like follow up communication.
22 hours ago • Like • Flag

Write a comment...

**b.**

**Maria Daley** You should extend your 15% off since I tried to order things off the website and it crashed. Then I tried calling the 1 800 number and it is constantly busy. Very disappointed that I can not place my order!
Monday at 11:09 pm • Like • Comment

5 people like this.

**Box and Barrel** Hi Maria. Thanks for bringing this to our attention. We hope that you were able to place your order but if not, please call us at 800.975.9969 – we'd like to help!
Tuesday at 8:55 am • Like • Flag

**Maria Daley** Thank you! I called the customer service department and they were able to help me. I might also add they were very nice.
Tuesday at 11:14 am • Like • Flag

Write a comment...

**c.**

**JD Lopez** when is the LG BANTER coming out?
11 hours ago • Like • Comment

**Sky Horizon Wireless** Hi JD – Please continue visiting our page for the latest news on device launches. Stay tuned !
about an hour ago • Like • Flag

Write a comment...

**d.**

**Dee Innes** Is there any hope that Turbotax could be written for Ubuntu Linux? It would be really great. I know I would appreciate it because I am moving away from windows and I am sure other Ubuntu users would like it too!
October 28 at 11:57 pm • Like • Comment

**Turbo Tax** Hi Dee,

Thanks for sharing your idea. I hope you'll join our inner Circle (it's where we gather new ideas from customers and get customer feedback on our Turbo Tax product). Please join us!

http://intuit.metrix.com/intuitCGT_community/sug...
See more
October 29 at 11:48 am • Like • Flag

**Jack Meghan** Dee... It's not likely we will write a version for Linux. Today we already write for Windows, Mac and the internet. That's a lot of versions. With more and more customers using the Online version of TurboTax, I'd suggest this as your way of using TurboTax.

Thanks for your feedback.
Jack Meghan
VP, TurboTax
November 4 at 6:52 pm • Like • Flag

Write a comment...

## 6.6 Direct Request: Social Media Pro Wanted (Obj. 2)
**E-mail**  **Social Media**

Social media jobs are in great demand. Petco, supplier of pet supplies and services, recently hired Natalie Malaszenko as its director of social media and commerce. Her assignment was to devise the company's social media strategy. She created fan pages on Facebook, opened several Twitter accounts, and wrote a company blog. Other organizations have hired social media officers, including Sears, Panasonic, Citigroup, AT&T, Fiji Water, GoDaddy, and Harrah's Entertainment.

As the director of corporate communication for Home & Yard, a large home supply store, you were asked to look into hiring a social media specialist. You know that other companies have both profited from and been hurt by fast-moving viral news. Social media experts, companies hope, can monitor cyberspace and be ready to respond to both negative and positive messages.

Many issues worry you. For one thing, you are not sure about a reasonable salary for a social media expert. You don't know where to place that person within your hierarchy. Would the media expert operate out of corporate communications, marketing, or customer service? Another thing that disturbs you is how to judge a candidate. What background should you require? How will you know the best candidate? Also, should Home & Yard pay a full-time salary for doing what most people consider to be fun?[11]

**YOUR TASK.** Compose an e-mail inquiry to Robert Mainka, a social media consultant recommended by your CEO, Jack Blum. Explain your situation and list specific questions. Mr. Mainka is a consultant who charges for his information and advice. Make your questions clear and concise. You want answers in writing, so that you can share the information with the CEO.

## 6.7 Direct Request: Paws for Philanthropy and Community Relations (Obj. 2)

As an assistant in the Community Involvement Program of your corporation, you have been given an unusual task. Your boss wants to expand the company's philanthropic and community relations mission and especially employee volunteerism. She heard about Northwestern Guide Dogs, a program in which volunteers raise puppies for 14 to 18 months for guide dog training. She thinks this would be an excellent outreach program for the company's employees. They could give back to the community in their role as puppy raisers. To pursue the idea, she asks you to request information about the program and ask questions about whether a company could sponsor a program encouraging employees to act as volunteers. She hasn't thought it through very carefully and relies on you to raise logical questions, especially about who pays for the costs of raising puppies.

**YOUR TASK.** Write a direct request letter to Helen Adams, Northwestern Guide Dogs, 512 Maynard Alley South, Seattle, WA 98104. Include an end date and a reason.

## 6.8 Direct Request: Planning a Plush Winter Retreat (Obj. 2)

`E-mail` `Web`

Reaves Media Group of Dallas, Texas, has had an excellent year, and the CEO, Henry Reaves, would like to reward "the troops" for their hard work with a rustic yet plush winter retreat. The CEO wants to host a four-day conference/retreat/vacation for his 55 marketing and media professionals with their spouses or significant others at some spectacular winter resort. Ideally, the location would delight any taste, with activities ranging from dining and relaxing in style to downhill and cross-country skiing, snowboarding, snowmobile tours, and other winter sports.

One of the choices is Jackson Hole, Wyoming, a famous ski resort town with steep slopes and dramatic mountain views. As you investigate the options in Jackson Hole, you are captivated by the Four Seasons Resort, a five-star facility with an outdoor pool, a spa tub, ski in/ski out access, and an amply equipped gym and fitness room. Other amenities include an on-site spa with massage and treatment rooms, a sauna, and facial and body treatments. Bathrooms feature separate bathtubs and showers, double sinks, and bathrobes. For business travelers, the hotel offers complimentary wired high-speed Internet access, complimentary wireless Internet access, and multiline phones as well as the use of two desktop computers.

The website of the Four Seasons Jackson Hole is not very explicit on the subject of business and event facilities, so you decide to jot down a few key questions. You estimate that your company will require about 50 rooms. You will also need two conference rooms (to accommodate 25 participants or more) for one and a half days. You want to know about room rates, conference facilities, A/V equipment in the conference rooms, Internet access, and entertainment options for families. You have two periods that would be possible: December 15–19 or January 12–16. You realize that both are peak times, but you wonder whether you can get a discounted group rate. You are interested in entertainment in Jackson Hole, and in tours to the nearby national parks. Jackson Hole airport is 4.5 miles away, and you would like to know whether the hotel operates a shuttle. Also, one evening the CEO will want to host a banquet for about 85 people. Mr. Reaves wants a report from you by September 15.

**YOUR TASK.** Write a well-organized direct request letter or e-mail to Laura O'Malley, Sales Manager, Four Seasons Resort, 7680 Granite Loop Road, Teton Village, WY 83025.

## 6.9 Direct Response: Harbor Sail & Canvas Receives a Poor Customer Rating on Yelp (Obj. 2)

`Social Media`

As you may know, Yelp is a social network for consumer reviews and local searches with approximately 108 million monthly unique visitors and 42 million local reviews.[12] Many users rely on what they hope to be real reviews by real people, as the company claims. They wish to make more informed buying decisions based on Yelp reviews. Dan Wilcox, owner of Harbor Sail & Canvas in Long Beach, California, is not yet on Facebook, but he pays attention to Yelp reviews. Currently, he has six reviews, all five stars. Imagine his surprise when he recently received only one star from Jenna K.:

> Harbor Sail & Canvas does good work, but it seems to have become a casualty of its own success. The company is unresponsive when you call and e-mail. I will take my business elsewhere because after 3 weeks, I still haven't heard about that estimate for my marine canvas. I had left a voice mail message and sent an e-mail. No response. I called again and was received as if my request were outlandish when I expressed the hope of getting a quote that same week. Since then, silence. Not cool. And I am a repeat customer. . . . People, fortunately there are other businesses out there!

Dan sighs because he is shorthanded. His administrative assistant has been sick and inquiries have gone unanswered; communication has been poor. Business is booming and Dan does not have enough qualified installers; as a result, weeks elapse before his small crew can do the work. Dan searches his files and finds Jenna's job completed four years ago. Harbor had made a dodger, sail cover, and other smaller canvas items for Jenna's 30-foot Catalina sailboat.

Chapter 6: Positive Messages

**YOUR TASK.** Consider Dan's options. Should he respond to the one negative review? What could be the consequences of ignoring it? If you believe that Dan should respond, discuss first how. He has the disgruntled customer's e-mail, phone number, and street address. He could post a reply on Yelp to provide a commentary to the bad review. If your instructor directs, plan a strategy for Dan and respond to the customer in the way you believe is best for Dan and his business.

## 6.10 Direct Response: Telling Job Applicants How to Make a Résumé Scannable (Obj. 2)
**Team** **Web**

As part of a team of interns at the outdoor e-tailer Campmor.com, you have been asked to write a form letter to send to job applicants who inquire about your résumé-scanning techniques. The following poorly written response to an inquiry was pulled from the file.

Dear Ms. Fratelli:

Your letter of April 11 has been referred to me for a response. We are pleased to learn that you are considering employment here at Campmor, and we look forward to receiving your résumé, should you decide to send same to us.

You ask if we scan incoming résumés. Yes, we certainly do. Actually, we use SmartTrack, an automated résumé-tracking system. We sometimes receive as many as 300 résumés a day, and SmartTrack helps us sort, screen, filter, and separate the résumés. It also processes them, helps us organize them, and keeps a record of all of these résumés. Some of the résumés, however, cannot be scanned, so we have to return those—if we have time.

The reasons that résumés won't scan may surprise you. Some applicants send photocopies or faxed copies, and these can cause misreading, so don't do it. The best plan is to send an original copy. Some people use colored paper. Big mistake! White paper (8 1/2 × 11-inch) printed on one side is the best bet. Another big problem is unusual type fonts, such as script or fancy gothic or antique fonts. They don't seem to realize that scanners do best with plain, readable fonts such as Helvetica or Arial in a 10- to 14-point size.

Other problems occur when applicants use graphics, shading, italics, underlining, horizontal and vertical lines, parentheses, and brackets. Scanners like plain, unadorned résumés. Oh yes, staples can cause misreading. And folding of a résumé can also cause the scanners to foul up. To be safe, don't staple or fold, and be sure to use wide margins and a quality printer.

When a hiring manager within Campmor decides to look for an appropriate candidate, he is told to submit keywords to describe the candidate he has in mind for his opening. We tell him (or sometimes her) to zero in on nouns and phrases that best describe what they want. Thus, my advice to you is to try to include those words that highlight your technical and professional areas of expertise.

If you do decide to submit your résumé to us, be sure you don't make any of the mistakes described herein that would cause the scanner to misread it.

Sincerely,

**YOUR TASK.** As a team, discuss how this letter could be improved. Decide what information is necessary to send to potential job applicants. Search the Web for additional information that might be helpful. Then, submit an improved version to your instructor. Although the form letter should be written so that it can be sent to anyone who inquires, address this one to Chiara Fratelli, 1019 University Drive, Boise, ID 83725.

## 6.11 Direct Response: Describing Your Major (Obj. 1)

A friend in a distant city is considering moving to your area for more education and training in your field. Your friend has asked you for information about your program of study.

**YOUR TASK.** Write a letter describing a program in your field (or any field you wish to describe). What courses must be taken? Toward what degree, certificate, or employment position does this program lead? Why did you choose it? Would you recommend this program to your friend? How long does it take? Add any information you feel would be helpful.

## 6.12 Instruction Message: Bewildering Skimmer Warning (Obj. 2)
**E-mail**

The following actual message was sent to bewildered faculty and staff members of a large institution. The message warns of the use of "skimmers." Criminals attach these small imaging devices to ATM machines and gas pumps to steal credit card information.

**YOUR TASK.** Revise the following poorly written message with a proper set of instructions including an introduction, body, and conclusion.

| | |
|---|---|
| To: | Faculty and Staff Members |
| From: | Michael Love <mlove@valleyviewpd.gov> |
| Subject: | ATM Safety |

Chapter 6: Positive Messages

Forgot to mention these prevention measures

1. Try to use ATMs that you are familiar with
2. Push pull the card slot and if it comes off, call 911. Skimmers are usually held on by double stick tape.
3. When punching in your PIN, cover the numbers you are punching in with you opposite hand or a sheet of paper
4. Gas pumps are also susceptible to skimming but usually the skimmer is inside so you cannot tell if a skimmer is present, so try to use a pump that is closest and in direct view of the attendance or go in and pay
5. Check your statement ASAP

Thank you for reading.

Detective Michael Love
Valley View Police Department

## 6.13 Instruction Message: Emergency Procedures Urgently Needed (Obj. 2)
*E-mail*

In talking with your boss, Patricia Carter, one day, you learned that she was concerned about fires in and safe evacuation from your office building. She thinks that the two of you can prepare a set of procedures in a conversation, and she begins talking with you.

She notes that if an employee sees a fire, that person should pull the alarm and call the fire department. The number of that department is 9-911. If the fire is small, the employee can attempt to extinguish it with a fire extinguisher. At this point, you ask your boss if the person who discovered the fire should also notify a supervisor, and your boss agrees. The supervisor is probably the one who should size up the situation and decide whether the building should be evacuated. You then begin to think about the evacuation process. What to do? Ms. Carter says that all doors should be closed and employees should secure their workstations. You ask what exactly that means, and she says employees should turn off their computers and put away important documents, but perhaps that information is unnecessary. Just stick to the main points, she says.

If employees are evacuating, they should go to the nearest exit in an orderly manner. In addition, it's very important that everyone remain calm. You ask about people with disabilities. "Sure," she says, "we should assist all visitors and persons with disabilities." Then Ms. Carter remembers that employees have been told about predetermined gathering places, and says that they should go there and wait for more instructions from floor monitors. It's also important that employees not reenter the building until given the all-clear. When they are outside, they should stay out of the way of fire department personnel and equipment.

**YOUR TASK.** Draft an e-mail or memo to employees from Patricia Carter, CEO. Provide brief background data and explain the main idea. List clear fire instructions. Provide your name and office phone number if receivers want more information.

## 6.14 Instruction Message: Copying Pictures and Text From PDFs Is a Snap (Obj. 2)

As a tech-savvy intern, you know that it's easy to copy text and images from PDF documents with a feature called **Snapshot Tool**. Your boss, Esther Garcia, has so much confidence in you that she asks you to draft a memo detailing the steps for copying images and text passages from portable document format (PDF) files.

You start by viewing the **Edit** pull-down menu in an open PDF document. Depending on the Adobe Acrobat or Reader version, a feature called **Take a Snapshot** emerges. This feature is represented by a camera icon. To copy content, you need to select the part of the PDF document that you want to capture by holding down the left mouse button and dragging the mouse across the document. The cursor will change its shape once the feature is activated. You can expand and reduce the selected area. This highlighted area will be copied to a clipboard. When you click the right mouse button, a menu appears that allows you to select **Paste Options**. You click the desired option once you have chosen a location where you want to insert the copied passage or image. The image that you copied to the clipboard can be pasted into a blank Microsoft Office document, whether Word, Excel, or PowerPoint. You can also take a picture of an entire page.

**YOUR TASK.** Prepare a memo addressed to Production Department staff members for the signature of Esther Garcia. Follow the steps described here and arrange all necessary instructions in a logical sequence. You may need to add steps omitted here or add explanations. Remember, too, that your audience may not be as computer literate as you are, so ensure that the steps are clear and easy to follow.

## 6.15 Direct Claim: But It Doesn't Work! (Obj. 3)
*E-mail*

After you receive an unexpected bonus, you decide to indulge and buy a new HDTV. You conduct research to compare prices and decide on a Panasonic 42-inch Plasma HDTV Model TC-P42X1.

You find a great deal at Digital Depot for $599.95 plus tax. Although the closest store is a 45-minute drive, the price is so good you decide it's worth the trip. You sell your old TV to make room for the Panasonic and spend several hours installing the new set.

Chapter 6: Positive Messages

It works perfectly, but the next day when you turn it on, nothing happens. You check everything, but no matter what you do, you can't get a picture. You're irritated! You are without a TV and have wasted hours hooking up the Panasonic. Assuming it's just a faulty set, you pack up the TV and drive back to Digital Depot. You have no trouble returning the item and come home with a second Panasonic.

Again you install the TV, and again you enjoy your new purchase. But the next day, you have no picture for a second time. Now you are fuming! Not looking forward to your third trip to Digital Depot, you repack the Panasonic and return it. The customer service representative tries to offer you another Panasonic, but you decline. You point out all the trouble you have been through and say you would prefer a more reliable TV from a different manufacturer that is the same size and in the same price range as the Panasonic. Digital Depot carries a Samsung (Model PN42B450B1D) that fits your criteria, but at $729, it is more than you had budgeted. You feel that after all the problems you have endured, Digital Depot should sell you the Samsung at the same price as the Panasonic. However, when you call to discuss the matter, you are told to submit a written request.

**YOUR TASK.** Write a direct claim e-mail to Dennis Alvarez, Manager at Digital Depot, in Houston, Texas, asking him to sell you the TV for less than the advertised price.

## 6.16 Direct Claim: Iron Gate Repair (Obj. 3)

You work for JPM, Johnson Property Management, in Portland, Oregon. Your employer specializes in commercial real estate. Just yesterday one of your business tenants in the trendy NW 23rd neighborhood complained about problems with an iron gate you had installed by Chung Iron Works just six months earlier, on August 20. Apparently, the two doors of the gate have settled and don't match in height. The gate gets stuck. It takes much force to open, close, and lock the gate. The iron gate was painted, and in some spots rust is bleeding onto the previously pristine white paint. The tenant at 921 NW 23rd Avenue, Portland, OR 97210, a petite shop owner, has complained to you about struggling with the gate at least twice a day when opening and closing her store.

You realize that you will have to contact the installer, Chung Iron Works, and request that the company inspect the gate and remedy the problem. Only six months have passed, and you recall that the warranty for the gate was for one year. To have a formal record of the claim and because Chung Iron Works does not use e-mail, you decide to write a claim letter.

**YOUR TASK.** Address your letter to Jin Ree at Chung Iron Works, 2255 NW Yeon Avenue in Portland, OR 97210. To jog his memory, you will enclose a copy of the company's proposal/invoice. Your business address is 1960 NE Irving Street, Portland, OR 97209, phone (503) 335-5443. Create professional-looking corporate stationery.

## 6.17 Direct Claim: Righting a Wrong (Obj. 3)

Have you ever bought a product that didn't work as promised? Have you been disappointed in service at a bank, restaurant, department store, or discount house, or from an online merchant? Have you had ideas about how a company or organization could improve its image, service, or product? Remember that smart companies want to know what their customers think, especially if a product could be improved.

**YOUR TASK.** Select a product or service that has disappointed you. Write a claim letter requesting a refund, replacement, explanation, or whatever seems reasonable. For claims about food products, be sure to include bar code identification from the package, if possible. Your instructor may ask you to actually mail this letter. When you receive a response, share it with your class.

## 6.18 Adjustment: Shipping Art Can Be a Stretch (Obj. 4)
*E-mail*

Your company, For Art's Sake, sells paintings online. It specializes in workplace art for offices, executive suites, conference rooms, and common areas. Your art consultants preselect paintings, making sure that the finished product is framed and delivered in perfect shape. You are proud that For Art's Sake can offer fine works of original art at affordable prices.

Recently, you received an e-mail from Southeast Equity Bank claiming that a large oil painting that your company sent had arrived in damaged condition. The e-mail said, "This painting sags, and we can't possibly hang it in our executive offices." You were surprised because the customer had signed for delivery and not mentioned any damage. The e-mail demands a replacement. You find it difficult to believe that the painting is damaged because you are so careful about shipping. You give explicit instructions to shippers that large paintings must be shipped standing up, not lying down. You also make sure that every painting is wrapped in two layers of convoluted foam and one layer of Perf-Pack foam, which should be sufficient to withstand any bumps and scrapes that negligent handlers may cause. Nevertheless, you decide to review your packing requirements with your shippers.

It's against your company policy to give refunds or replace paintings that the receiver found acceptable when delivered. However, you could offer Southeast Equity Bank the opportunity to take the painting to a local framing shop for restretching at your expense. The company could send the restretching bill to For Art's Sake at 18 East 79th Street, New York, NY 10075.

**YOUR TASK.** Compose an e-mail adjustment message that regains the customer's confidence. Send it to Gregory Karipidis at gkaripidis@southeastequitybank.com.

186     Chapter 6: Positive Messages

## 6.19 Adjustment: GPS Rental Nightmare (Obj. 4)

As assistant to Joseph A. Morgan, Regional General Manager at ProCar Rentals, you read a shockingly irate complaint letter from a corporate customer (See **Radical Rewrite 6.4**) addressed to your boss. April Schmitz-Fidalgo, Sales Manager for KPC Construction, Inc., in Tucson, Arizona, has angrily detailed her tribulations with your company's Colorado Springs Airport branch.

Apparently, she and a colleague suffered long delays in obtaining their rental car. To compensate for the late car delivery, the customers received complimentary use of a navigation device, a $180 value plus taxes and surcharges that add up to another $60. However, at the end of their rental period, their bill reflected the full cost of the GPS. After multiple phone calls to the Colorado Springs Airport branch as well as to ProCar Rentals corporate offices, Ms. Schmitz-Fidalgo apparently was finally able to have the $180 credited to KPC's business account. However, soon she realized that the $60 levy had not been credited.

Mr. Morgan asks you to investigate what went so terribly wrong at the Colorado Springs Airport location. You learn that the branch is an independent franchisee, which may explain such a laxness in customer service that is unacceptable under corporate rules. In addition, you find out that the branch manager, Jeffrey Blackson, was traveling on company business during Ms. Schmitz-Fidalgo's rental period and then left town to attend two management training seminars. Mr. Morgan is concerned that ProCar might lose this disappointed customer and decides to offer discount vouchers for KPC's next three rentals at 20 percent off each, valid at any U.S. branch.

**YOUR TASK.** Write a polite adjustment letter to April Schmitz-Fidalgo, KPC Construction, Inc., 5900 East Speedway Blvd., Tucson, AZ 85711 to secure the customer's goodwill and future business.

## 6.20 Richard Branson Sends a Goodwill Message to the People of Ghana (Obj. 5)
*E-mail  Social Media*

Virgin Group President, Richard Branson, wrote a sympathy letter to the people of Ghana after the country's president died. Branson had been a guest of President John Atta Mills on the occasion of Virgin's launch of flights to Ghana's capital.

*It was with much regret and surprise that I learned about the passing of President John Evans Atta Mills of Ghana. I had the singular pleasure to spend some time with him at the Osu Castle when I visited Ghana on 24th May 2010. We were launching new flights to Accra and the warmth and hospitality which the President showed towards me and our entire delegation brought confidence and assurance that we were in good hands.*

*President Mills has served the country and the people of Ghana with a calm, peaceful hand and as a member of the Elders Organisation brought together by Nelson Mandela in 2007 I wish to state that I identify in President Mills many of our goals as I note him to be an elder statesman of Ghana, a follower of peace and an advocate for human rights and dignity.*

*I further laud the smooth transition of power to his immediate successor President John Dramani Mahama as I convey my thoughts to the family, the new Government and the people of Ghana at this difficult time.*[13]

—Sir Richard Branson, the President of Virgin Group

**YOUR TASK.** In a concise social media post or an e-mail, examine the features in this goodwill message and evaluate whether it conforms to the guidelines discussed in this chapter.

## 6.21 Thanks for a Favor: Expressing Appreciation for Business Etiquette Training (Obj. 5)
*Team  Web*

Your business communication class was fortunate to have the etiquette and protocol expert Pamela Eyring speak to you. A sought-after TV commentator and media personality, she runs The Protocol School of Washington, a training center for etiquette consultants and protocol officers. Ms. Eyring emphasized the importance of soft skills. She talked about outclassing the competition and dining like a diplomat. She addressed topics such as business entertaining, invitations, introductions, greetings, seating arrangements, toasting, eye contact, remembering names, and conversation skills. In the table manners segment, among other topics, she discussed dining dos and don'ts, host and guest duties, seating and napkin placement, place settings and silverware savvy, eating various foods gracefully, and tipping. With characteristic poise but also humor, Ms. Eyring used utensils, plates, and napkins to demonstrate correct table manners.

The class was thrilled to receive hands-on training from a nationally known business etiquette expert who was able to lessen their fears of making fools of themselves during business meals or at business mixers.

**YOUR TASK.** Individually or in groups, draft a thank-you letter to Pamela Eyring, director of The Protocol School of Washington, P.O. Box 676, Columbia, SC 29202. Check out the company's website http://www.psow.edu, or find The Protocol School of Washington on Facebook, where you can follow Ms. Eyring's frequent media appearances, interviews, and etiquette advice.

## 6.22 Responding to Good Wishes: Saying Thank You (Obj. 5)

**YOUR TASK.** Write a short note thanking a friend who sent you good wishes when you recently completed your degree.

Chapter 6: Positive Messages

# GRAMMAR/MECHANICS CHECKUP—6

## Commas 1

Review the Grammar Review section of the Grammar/Mechanics Handbook Sections 2.01–2.04. Then study each of the following statements and insert necessary commas. In the space provided, write the number of commas that you add; write *0* if no commas are needed. Also record the number of the G/M principle illustrated. When you finish, compare your responses with those shown at the end of the book. If your answers differ, study carefully the principles shown in parentheses.

<u>2</u> (2.01) **EXAMPLE** Sometimes we are so engrossed in our jobs, our families, or relationships that we forget about ourselves.

1. We think on the other hand that camera phones are not a good idea in offices.
2. We are certain Mr. Nosrati that your UPS delivery will arrive before 11 a.m.
3. Our software helps your employees be more creative collaborative and productive in team projects.
4. The spring leadership conference will take place April 3 at the South Beach Marriott Hotel beginning at 2 p.m.
5. Needless to say we were depressed at the stock market drop.
6. Amazon closed distribution centers in McDonough Georgia and Grand Forks North Dakota to save money.
7. By the way the best things in life aren't things.
8. The last council meeting that was recorded in the minutes was held on March 23 2010 in Phoenix.
9. Mr. Maslow Mrs. Kim and Ms. Garcia were all promoted.
10. The shipment addressed to Galaxy Industries 6920 Fondren Road Houston TX 77074 arrived two weeks late.
11. The manager feels nevertheless that the support of all employees is critical.
12. Successful teams encourage open communication resolve conflict fairly and promote interaction among members.
13. Our team works hard to retain your business Mr. Sherman.
14. President Carson however thinks that all staff members need training.
15. Rachel moved from Hartford Connecticut to Portland Oregon because she was offered a better job.

# EDITING CHALLENGE—6

To fine-tune your grammar and mechanics skills, in every chapter you will be editing a message. This claim message suffers from rudeness and wordiness, as well as from proofreading, spelling, grammar, punctuation, and other writing faults that require correction. Study the guidelines in the Grammar/Mechanics Handbook as well as the lists of Confusing Words and Frequently Misspelled Words to sharpen your skills.

**YOUR TASK.** Edit the following message (a) by correcting errors in your textbook or on a photocopy using proofreading marks from Appendix A or (b) by downloading the message from **www.cengagebrain.com** and correcting at your computer. Your instructor may show you a possible solution.

---

May 25, 2016

SENT BY CERTIFIED MAIL

Mr. Irwin Nelson
Landmark Contractors
657 Wisconsin Avenue
Milwaukee, WI 53203

Dear Mr. Nelsen:

This is to inform you that we are very unhappy with your shoddy work! Please redo the work or pay for the repair of tile installation in the remodeling of a shower at our health club facility at 4493 First Street here in Milwaukee.

In a contract signed on April 28 you and me agreed that the remodel would involve tile work, for which my company paid $3,220 when the work was completed on May 5th. Just 2 weeks' later, on May 19th, we made the discovery that there was some tile in the south portion of the shower that had sank almost as much as half a inch. This caused the shower floor to be really extremely uneven and water pooled in the downhill corner and would not flow into the drain. Such pooling of water could eventually led to mold and mildew. Which would be not healthy for customers at our fitness facility.

In our telephone conversation that we had on May 21, you argued at various times that the problem was all a matter in my imagination, that it was a problem that was our fault, and that it was to miner to worry about. As a result of this messy problem, I have commissioned 3 bids to repair the work, these bids range from the amount of $4,500 to the amount of $5,530 as shown on the inclosed estimates.

We entered into a god faith contract with you and I expected a remodeling job that was first-class. I'm feeling confident that you will want to please your customers' and not force them to file in small claims court. Please contact me before June fifth, to arrange either (a) to re-pay my company the amount to repair the tile or (b) to discuss a plan to retile the job yourself.

Sincerely,

MILWAUKEE FITNESS

*Deborah Olson*

Deborah Olson, Owner

Enclosures

Chapter 6: Positive Messages

# COMMUNICATION WORKSHOP

## ETHICS

### Choosing Tools for Doing the Right Thing

In composing messages or engaging in other activities on the job, business communicators can't help being torn by conflicting loyalties. Do we tell the truth and risk our jobs? Do we show loyalty to friends even if it means bending the rules? Should we be tactful or totally honest? Is it our duty to make a profit or be socially responsible?

Acting ethically means doing the right thing *given the circumstances*. Each set of circumstances requires analyzing issues, evaluating choices, and acting responsibly. Resolving ethical issues is never easy, but the task can be made less difficult if you know how to identify key issues. The following questions may be helpful.

- **Is the action legal?** No matter who asks you to do it or how important you feel the result will be, avoid anything that is prohibited by law. Bribing a buyer to secure a large order is illegal, even if you suspect that others in your field do it and you know that without the kickback you will lose the sale.
- **Would you do it if you were on the opposite side?** Looking at both sides of an issue helps you gain perspective. By weighing both sides of an issue, you can arrive at a more equitable solution.
- **Can you rule out a better alternative?** Would the alternative be more ethical? Under the circumstances, is the alternative feasible?
- **Would a trusted advisor agree?** Suppose you feel ethically bound to report accurate information to a client—even though your boss has ordered you not to do so. Talking about your dilemma with a coworker or with a colleague in your field might give you helpful insights and lead to possible alternatives.
- **Would your family, friends, employer, or coworkers approve?** If the thought of revealing your action publicly produces cold sweats, your choice is probably not a wise one. Losing the faith of your friends or the confidence of your customers is not worth whatever short-term gains you might realize.

**CAREER APPLICATION.** One of the biggest accounting firms uses an ethical awareness survey that includes some of the following situations. You may face similar situations with ethical issues on the job or in employment testing.

**YOUR TASK.** In teams or individually, decide whether each of the following ethical issues is (a) very important, (b) moderately important, or (c) unimportant. Then decide whether you (a) strongly approve of, (b) are undecided about, or (c) strongly disapprove of the action taken.[14] Apply the ethical tools presented here to determine whether the course of action is ethical. What alternatives might you suggest?

- **Recruiting.** You are a recruiter for your company. Although you know company morale is low, the turnover rate is high, and the work environment in many departments is deplorable, you tell job candidates that it is "a great place to work."
- **Training program.** Your company is offering an exciting training program in Hawaii. Although you haven't told anyone, you plan to get another job shortly. You decide to participate in the program anyway because you have never been to Hawaii. One of the program requirements is that participants must have "long-term career potential" with the firm.
- **Thievery.** As a supervisor, you suspect that one of your employees is stealing. You check with a company attorney and find that a lie detector test cannot be legally used. Then you decide to scrutinize the employee's records. Finally, you find an inconsistency in the employee's records. You decide to fire the employee, although this inconsistency would not normally have been discovered.
- **Downsizing.** As part of the management team of a company that makes potato chips, you face the rising prices of potatoes. Rather than increase the cost of your chips, you decide to decrease slightly the size of the bag. Consumers are less likely to notice a smaller bag than a higher price.

# ENDNOTES

[1] Cited in New ways to complain: Airing your gripes can get you satisfaction—or trouble. (2011, August). Consumer Reports.org. Retrieved from http://www.consumerreports.org/cro/money/consumer-protection/new-ways-to-complain/overview/index.htm

[2] Pilon, M. (2009, August 5). How to complain about a company. *The Wall Street Journal*. Retrieved from http://blogs.wsj.com/wallet/2009/08/05/how-to-complain-about-a-company; Torabi, F. (2011, July 28). Bad customer service? 3 smarter ways to complain. CBS News. Retrieved from http://www.cbsnews.com/8301-505144_162-41542345/bad-customer-service-3-smarter-ways-to-complain

[3] New ways to complain: Airing your gripes can get you satisfaction—or trouble. (2011, August). Consumer Reports.org. Retrieved from http://www.consumerreports.org/cro/money/consumer-protection/new-ways-to-complain/overview/index.htm

[4] Ibid.

[5] Ibid.

[6] Ho, B., & Liu, E. (2010, October). Does sorry work? The impact of apology laws on medical malpractice. Social Science Research Network. Retrieved from http://dx.doi.org/10.2139/ssrn.1744225. Quinley, K. (2008, May). Apology programs. *Claims*, pp. 14–16. Retrieved from http://search.ebscohost.com. See also Runnels, M. (2009, Winter). Apologies all around: Advocating federal protection for the full apology in civil cases. *San Diego Law Review*, 46(1), 137–160. Retrieved from http://search.ebscohost.com

[7] Davidow, M. (2003, February). Organizational responses to customer complaints: What works and what doesn't. *Journal of Service Research*, 5(3), 225. Retrieved from http://search.ebscohost.com; Blackburn-Brockman, E., & Belanger, K. (1993, June). You-attitude and positive emphasis: Testing received wisdom in business communication. *The Bulletin of the Association for Business Communication*, 1–5; Mascolini, M. (1994, June). Another look at teaching the external negative message. *The Bulletin of the Association for Business Communication*, p. 46.

[8] Liao, H. (2007, March). Do it right this time: The role of employee service recovery performance in customer-perceived justice and customer loyalty after service failures. *Journal of Applied Psychology*, 92(2), 475. Retrieved from http://search.ebscohost.com; Gilbert, P. (1996, December). Two words that can help a business thrive. *The Wall Street Journal*, p. A12.

[9] Emily Post Institute. (2008). Conveying sympathy Q & A. Retrieved from http://www3.1800flowers.com/Post-Etiquette-Conveying-Sympathy

[10] Based on Buddy Media. (2010). How do I respond to that? The definitive guide to Facebook publishing & moderation. Retrieved from http://honestagency.com/wp-content/uploads/2011/01/Definitive-Guide-Buddy-Media-White-Paper.pdf

[11] Partially based on Gillette, F. (2010, July 19–25). Twitter, twitter, little stars. *Bloomberg Businessweek*, pp. 64–67.

[12] 10 things you should know about Yelp. (2012, July). Retrieved from http://www.yelp.com/about

[13] Sir Richard Branson send [sic] goodwill message to Ghanaians. (2012, July 26). Retrieved from http://www.ameyawdebrah.com/sir-richard-branson-send-goodwill-message-to-ghanaians

[14] Adapted from Conaway, R. N., & Fernandez, T. L. (2000, March). Ethical preferences among business leaders: Implications for business schools. *Business Communication Quarterly*, 23–38.

# ACKNOWLEDGMENTS

p. 157 Office Insider based on Emily Post Institute. [n.d.]. Effective business letters. Retrieved from http://www.emilypost.com/on-the-job/clients-customers-vendors-or-contractors/784-effective-business-letters

p. 162 Office Insider based on National Commission on Writing. (2004, September 14). Writing skills necessary for employment, says big business. [Press release]. Retrieved from http://www.host-collegeboard.com/advocacy/writing

p. 168 Office Insider based on New ways to complain: Airing your gripes can get you satisfaction—or trouble. (2011, August). Consumer Reports.org. Retrieved from http://www.consumerreports.org/cro/money/consumer-protection/new-ways-to-complain/overview/index.htm

p. 172 Office Insider based on Wisch, N. C. (2005, April). Hey . . . Thank you! *Wearables Business*, p. 39. Retrieved from http://search.ebscohost.com

# CHAPTER 7

# Negative Messages

## OBJECTIVES
After studying this chapter, you should be able to

**7-1** Understand the goals of business communicators in conveying negative news.

**7-2** Compare the strategies and ethics of the direct and indirect plans in communicating negative news.

**7-3** Explain the components of effective negative messages, including opening with a buffer, apologizing, showing empathy, presenting the reasons, cushioning the bad news, and closing pleasantly.

**7-4** Apply effective techniques in refusing typical requests or claims, as well as handling customer bad news in print and online.

**7-5** Describe and apply effective techniques for delivering negative news within organizations.

## 7-1 Communicating Negative News Effectively

Bad things happen in all businesses. Goods are not delivered, products fail to perform as expected, service is poor, billing gets fouled up, and customers are misunderstood. You may have to write messages declining proposals, explaining service outages, describing data breaches, refusing requests for donations, turning down invitations, or responding to unhappy customers. You might have to apologize for mistakes in orders or pricing, the rudeness of employees, overlooked appointments, defective products, or jumbled instructions. As a company representative, you may have to respond to complaints posted for the world to see on Twitter, Facebook, or complaint websites.

The truth is that everyone occasionally must deliver negative news in business. Because bad news disappoints, irritates, and sometimes angers the receiver, such messages must be written carefully. The bad feelings associated with disappointing news can generally be reduced if the receiver (a) knows the reasons for the rejection, (b) feels that the news was revealed sensitively, and (c) believes that the matter was treated seriously and fairly.

In this chapter you will learn when to use the direct strategy and when to use the indirect strategy to deliver negative news. You will study the goals of business communicators in working with unfavorable news and learn techniques for achieving those goals.

## 7-1a How to Achieve Your Goals in Communicating Negative News

Delivering bad news is not the happiest communication task you may have, but it can be gratifying if you do it effectively. As a business communicator working with bad news, you will have many goals. Here's how to achieve them:

- **Explain clearly and completely.** Your goal is to make your readers understand and, in the best case, accept the bad news. Recipients should not have to call or write to clarify your message.
- **Project a professional image.** Even when irate customers sound threatening and overstate their claims, you should strive to stay calm, use polite language, and respond with clear explanations of why a negative message was necessary.
- **Convey empathy and sensitivity.** Try to use language that respects the receiver but also attempts to reduce bad feelings. When appropriate, accept blame and apologize; however, strive to do so without creating legal liability for your organization or yourself.
- **Be fair.** When you can show that the decision was fair, impartial, and rational, receivers are far more likely to accept the negative news.
- **Maintain friendly relations.** A final goal is to demonstrate your desire to continue pleasant relations and to regain the confidence of the reader.

These goals are ambitious, and, frankly, you may not be successful in achieving them all. However, many communicators have found the strategies and techniques you are about to learn helpful in conveying disappointing news sensitively and safely. With experience, you will be able to vary these strategies and adapt them to your organization's specific communication tasks.

## OFFICE INSIDER

"*Delivering difficult messages is part of day-to-day life in all social groups, whether the organization is a family, a nation, or a business.*"

—John J. Engels, president of Leadership Coaching Inc. in Rochester, New York

**LEARNING OBJECTIVE 1**
Understand the goals of business communicators in conveying negative news.

## Workplace in Focus

During a recent holiday season, hackers breached Target's computer system and stole the credit card data of an estimated 110 million customers—one of the largest cyber-security heists ever in retail. In a letter to customers, Target CEO Gregg Steinhafel opened with news of the event and got straight to the point: "I am writing to make you aware that your name, mailing address, phone number or e-mail address may have been taken during the intrusion." Steinhafel offered a sincere apology and gave important tips on how to protect against Internet and phone scams. Most important, the CEO offered customers one year of free credit monitoring and identity theft insurance. How would you rate Target's response to this event?[1]

Chapter 7: Negative Messages

**LEARNING OBJECTIVE 2**

Compare the strategies and ethics of the direct and indirect plans in communicating negative news.

## 7-2 Analyzing Negative News Strategies

Unfavorable news in business doesn't always fall into neat categories. To successfully convey bad news, writers must carefully consider the audience, purpose, and context. As a business writer in training, you have at your disposal two basic strategies for delivering negative news: direct and indirect, as compared in Figure 7.1.

Whether to use the direct or indirect strategy depends largely on the situation, the reaction you expect from the audience, and your goals. Which approach is best suited for your particular message? One of the first steps you will take before delivering negative news is analyzing how your receiver will react to this news. In earlier chapters we discussed applying the direct strategy to positive messages. In this chapter we expand on that advice and offer additional considerations to help you decide which strategy to use.

**When to Use the Direct Strategy.** The direct strategy saves time and is preferred by some who consider it to be more professional and even more ethical than the indirect strategy. The direct strategy may be more effective in situations such as the following:

- **When the bad news is not damaging.** If the bad news is insignificant (such as a small increase in cost) and doesn't personally affect the receiver, then the direct strategy makes sense.
- **When the receiver may overlook the bad news.** Changes in service, new policy requirements, legal announcements—these critical messages may require boldness to ensure attention.
- **When the organization or receiver prefers directness.** Some companies and individuals expect all internal messages and announcements—even bad news—to be straightforward and presented without frills.

Figure 7.1 Comparing the Direct and Indirect Strategies for Negative Messages

**Direct Strategy**

If Bad News
- Is not damaging
- May be overlooked
- Is preferred by recipient
- Requires firmness

Bad News
Reasons
Pleasant Close

**Indirect Strategy**

If Bad News
- Is personally upsetting
- May provoke hostile reaction
- Could threaten customer relationship
- Is unexpected

Buffer
Reasons
Bad News
Pleasant Close

- **When firmness is necessary.** Messages that must demonstrate determination and strength should not use delaying techniques. For example, the last in a series of collection letters that seek payment on an overdue account may require a direct opener.

Security breach messages provide a good example of how to employ the direct strategy in delivering bad news. Notice in Figure 7.2 that the writer, Steven Ellis, is fairly direct in announcing that consumer identity information was lost at Conectix Federal Credit Union.

Although he does not blurt out "your information has been compromised," the writer does announce a potential identity theft problem in the first sentence. He then explains that a hacker attack has compromised roughly a quarter of customer accounts. In the second paragraph he recommends that credit union customer Michael Arnush take specific corrective action to protect his identity and offers helpful contact information. The tone is respectful and serious. The credit union's

Figure 7.2 Announcing Bad News Directly: Security Breach Letter

---

**CONECTIX FEDERAL CREDIT UNION**
5234 PARK AVENUE, FAIRFIELD, CT 06825
www.conectix.com   203.448.2101

September 5, 2016

Mr. Michael Arnush
15 Vanderbilt Avenue
Newton, MA 02459

Dear Mr. Arnush:

*[Uses modified direct strategy because urgent action is needed to prevent identity theft]*

We are contacting you about a potential problem involving identity theft. On August 30, names, encrypted social security numbers, birth dates, and e-mail addresses of fewer than 25 percent of accounts were compromised in an apparent hacker attack on our website. Outside data security experts are working tirelessly to identify the causes of the breach as well as prevent future intrusions into our system. Immediately upon detecting the attack, we notified the local police authorities as well as the FBI. We also alerted the three major credit-reporting agencies.

We recommend that you place a fraud alert on your credit file. A fraud alert tells creditors to contact you before they open any new accounts or change your existing accounts. Please call any one of the three major credit bureaus. As soon as one credit bureau confirms your fraud alert, the others are notified to place fraud alerts. All three credit reports will be sent to you, free of charge.

| Equifax | Experian | TransUnion |
|---|---|---|
| 800-685-1111 | 888-397-3742 | 800-680-7289 |

*[Suggests recommended steps and provides helpful information about credit-reporting agencies]*

*[Gives reasons for the recommended action, provides contact information, and offers additional pointers]*

Even if you do not find any suspicious activity on your initial credit reports, the Federal Trade Commission (FTC) recommends that you check your credit reports periodically. Victim information sometimes is held for use or shared among a group of thieves at different times. Checking your credit reports periodically can help you spot problems and address them quickly.

If you find suspicious activity on your credit reports or have reason to believe your information is being misused, call 518-584-5500 and file a police report. Get a copy of the report; many creditors want the information it contains to absolve you of the fraudulent debts. You also should file a complaint with the FTC at www.ftc.gov/idtheft or at 1-877-ID-THEFT (877-438-4338).

Please visit our website at www.conectix.com/databreach for updates on the investigation, or call our privacy hotline at 800-358-4422. Affected customers will receive free credit-monitoring services for one year.

*[Ends by providing more helpful information, company phone number, and offer of one-year free credit monitoring]*

Sincerely,

*Steven Ellis*

Steven Ellis
Customer Service

Chapter 7: Negative Messages

letter is modeled on an FTC template that was praised for achieving a balance between a direct and indirect opening.[2]

**When to Use the Indirect Strategy.** The indirect strategy does not reveal the bad news immediately. This strategy, at least theoretically, enables you to keep the reader's attention until you have been able to explain the reasons for the bad news. Some writing experts suggest that the indirect strategy "ill suits today's skeptical, impatient, even cynical audience."[3] To be sure, in social media, bluntness seems to dominate public debate. Directness is equated with honesty; hedging, with deceit. Regardless, many communicators prefer to use the indirect strategy to soften negative news. Whereas good news can be revealed quickly, bad news may be easier to accept when broken gradually. Here are typical instances in which the indirect strategy works well:

- **When the bad news is personally upsetting.** If the negative news involves the receiver personally, such as a layoff notice, the indirect strategy makes sense. Telling an employee that he or she no longer has a job is probably best done in person and by starting indirectly and giving reasons first. When a company has made a mistake that inconveniences or disadvantages a customer, the indirect strategy also makes sense.
- **When the bad news will provoke a hostile reaction.** When your message will irritate or infuriate the recipient, the indirect method may be best. It begins with a buffer and reasons, thus encouraging the reader to finish reading or hearing the message. A blunt announcement may make the receiver stop reading.
- **When the bad news threatens the customer relationship.** If the negative message may damage a customer relationship, the indirect strategy may help salvage the customer bond. Beginning slowly and presenting reasons that explain what happened can be more helpful than directly announcing bad news or failing to adequately explain the reasons.
- **When the bad news is unexpected.** Readers who are totally surprised by bad news tend to have a more negative reaction than those who expected it. If a company suddenly closes an office or a plant and employees had no inkling of the closure, that bad news would be better received if it were revealed cautiously with reasons first.

The indirect approach does not guarantee that recipients will be pleased, because, after all, bad news is just that—bad. However, many communicators prefer to use it. To apply the indirect strategy effectively, you may use four parts, as shown in Figure 7.3.

### 7-2a Keeping the Indirect Strategy Ethical

You may worry that the indirect organizational strategy is unethical or manipulative because the writer deliberately delays the main idea. Now, consider the alternative. Breaking bad news bluntly can cause pain and hard feelings. By delaying bad news, you soften the blow somewhat, as well as ensure that your reasoning will be

**Figure 7.3** Four-Part Indirect Strategy for Bad News

| Buffer | Reasons | Bad News | Closing |
|---|---|---|---|
| Open with a neutral but meaningful statement that does not mention the bad news. | Explain the causes of the bad news before disclosing it. | Reveal the bad news without emphasizing it. Provide an alternative or compromise, if possible. | End with a personalized, forward-looking, pleasant statement. Avoid referring to the bad news. |

read while the receiver is still receptive. One expert communicator recognized the significance of the indirect strategy when she said, "People must believe the reasons why before they will listen to the details of what and when."[4] Your goal is to be a compassionate, yet effective communicator.

The key to ethical communication lies in the motives of the sender. Unethical communicators *intend to deceive*. Although the indirect strategy is a technique for announcing bad news, it should not be used to avoid or misrepresent the truth. For example, unscrupulous marketers advertise on trusted websites of national news organizations and falsely claim endorsements by Oprah Winfrey and Dr. Oz. Unsuspecting consumers end up paying hundreds of dollars, the Better Business Bureau reports.[5] As you will see in Chapter 8, misleading, deceptive, and unethical claims are never acceptable. In fact, many are simply illegal.

## 7-3 Composing Effective Negative Messages

**LEARNING OBJECTIVE 3**
Explain the components of effective negative messages, including opening with a buffer, apologizing, showing empathy, presenting the reasons, cushioning the bad news, and closing pleasantly.

Although you can't expect to make the receiver happy when delivering negative news, you can reduce resentment by structuring your message sensitively. Most negative messages contain some or all of these parts: buffer, reasons, bad news, and closing. Figure 7.4 presents these four components of the indirect strategy in greater detail.

### 7-3a Opening Indirect Messages With a Buffer

A buffer is a device to reduce shock or pain. To buffer the pain of bad news, begin with a neutral but meaningful statement that encourages the reader to continue reading. The buffer should be relevant and concise and provide a natural transition to the explanation that follows. The situation, of course, will help determine what you should put in the buffer. This section provides some possibilities for opening bad-news messages. Avoid trite buffers such as *Thank you for your e-mail*.

Not all business communication authors agree that buffers actually increase the effectiveness of negative messages. However, many cultures appreciate softening bad news. Following are various buffer possibilities.

**Best News.** Start with the part of the message that represents the best news. For example, a message to workers announced new health plan rules limiting prescriptions to a 34-day supply and increasing co-payments. With home delivery, however, employees could save up to $24 on each prescription. To emphasize the good news, you might write, *You can now achieve significant savings and avoid trips to the drugstore by having your prescription drugs delivered to your home.*

Figure **7.4** Delivering Bad News Sensitively

| Buffer | Reasons | Bad News | Closing |
|---|---|---|---|
| • Best news<br>• Compliment<br>• Appreciation<br>• Agreement<br>• Facts<br>• Understanding<br>• Apology | • Cautious explanation<br>• Reader or other benefits<br>• Company policy explanation<br>• Positive words<br>• Evidence that matter was considered fairly and seriously | • Embedded placement<br>• Passive voice<br>• Implied refusal<br>• Compromise<br>• Alternative | • Forward look<br>• Information about alternative<br>• Good wishes<br>• Freebies<br>• Resale<br>• Sales promotion |

Chapter 7: Negative Messages

## Office Insider

*"These days, apologizing is a leadership skill. We see our decision makers dodging and weaving instead of accepting responsibility, and that disappoints us. We don't expect them to be perfect. Just willing to learn. In the long run apology leads to better outcomes and more durable relationships."*

—John Kador, blogger and author of *Effective Apology*

**Compliment.** Praise the receiver's accomplishments, organization, or efforts, but do so with honesty and sincerity. For instance, in a letter declining an invitation to speak, you could write, *HarvestPlenty has my sincere admiration for using crowdsourcing technology to enable gardeners to donate their excess crops to local food pantries. I am honored that you asked me to speak Friday, November 6.*

**Appreciation.** Convey thanks for doing business, for sending something, for showing confidence in your organization, for expressing feelings, or simply for providing feedback. Suppose you had to draft a letter that refuses employment. You could say, *I appreciated learning about the hospitality management program at Cornell and about your qualifications in our interview last Friday.*

**Agreement.** Make a relevant statement with which both you and the receiver can agree. A letter that rejects a loan application might read, *We both realize how much the slow economic recovery in the past five years has affected customers' purchasing power.*

**Facts.** Provide objective information that introduces the bad news. For example, in a memo announcing cutbacks in the hours of the employee cafeteria, you might say, *During the past five years the number of employees eating breakfast in our cafeteria has dropped from 32 percent to 12 percent.*

**Understanding.** Show that you care about the reader. Notice how in this e-mail to customers announcing a product defect, the writer expresses concern: *We know that you expect superior performance from all the products you purchase from OfficeCity. That's why we are writing personally about the Omega printer cartridges you recently ordered.*

### 7-3b Apologizing

Apologies to customers are important if you or your company erred. They cost nothing, and they go a long way in soothing hard feelings. You learned about making apologies in adjustment letters in Chapter 6. We expand that discussion here because apologies are often part of negative-news messages.

Why apologize? Because sincere apologies work. Peter Post, great-grandson of famed etiquette expert Emily Post and director of the Emily Post Institute, said that Americans love apologies. They will forgive almost anything if presented with a sincere apology.[6] An *apology* is defined as an "admission of blameworthiness and regret for an undesirable event."[7] The following pointers can help you apologize effectively in business messages:

- **Apologize promptly and sincerely.** Credibility suffers when a public figure delays an apology and responds only after causing an outrage. Also, people dislike apologies that sound hollow (*We regret that you were inconvenienced* or *We are sorry that you are disturbed*). Focusing on your regret does not convey sincerity; explaining what you will do to prevent recurrence of the problem does.
- **Accept responsibility.** One CEO was criticized for the following weak apology after angrily and publicly firing an employee: "It was an emotional response at the start of a difficult discussion dealing with many people's careers and livelihoods. . . . [I] apologized for the way the matter was handled at the meeting." Communication experts faulted this apology because it did not acknowledge responsibility or show remorse.[8]
- **Use good judgment.** Before admitting blame, it might be wise to consult a superior or the company legal counsel to avoid litigation.

Consider these poor and improved apologies:

> **Poor apology:** *We regret that you are unhappy with the price of frozen yogurt purchased at one of our self-serve scoop shops.*

**Improved apology:** *We are genuinely sorry that you were disappointed in the price of frozen yogurt recently purchased at one of our self-serve scoop shops. Your opinion is important to us, and we appreciate your giving us the opportunity to look into the problem you describe.*

**Poor apology:** *We are sorry that mistakes were made in filling your order.*

**Improved apology:** *You are right to be concerned. We sincerely apologize for the mistakes we made in filling your order. To prevent recurrence of this problem, we are changing our tracking. . . .*

## 7-3c Showing Empathy

One of the hardest things to do in apologies is to convey sympathy and empathy. As discussed in Chapter 2, *empathy* is the ability to understand and enter into the feelings of another. When ice storms trapped JetBlue Airways passengers on hot planes for hours, CEO Neeleman wrote a letter of apology that sounded as if it came from his heart. He said, "Dear JetBlue Customers: We are sorry and embarrassed. But most of all, we are deeply sorry." Later in his letter he said, "Words cannot express how truly sorry we are for the anxiety, frustration, and inconvenience that you, your family, friends, and colleagues experienced."[9] Neeleman put himself into the shoes of his customers and tried to experience their pain.

You can express empathy in many ways, as illustrated in the following:

- In writing to an unhappy customer: *We did not intentionally delay the shipment, and we sincerely regret the disappointment and frustration you must have suffered.*
- In laying off employees: *It is with great regret that we must take this step. Rest assured that I will be more than happy to write letters of recommendation for anyone who asks.*
- In responding to a complaint: *I am deeply saddened that our service failure disrupted your sale, and we will do everything in our power to respond to any future outages promptly.*
- In showing genuine feelings: *You have every right to be disappointed. I am truly sorry that. . . .*

## 7-3d Presenting the Reasons

Providing an explanation reduces feelings of ill will and improves the chances that readers will accept the bad news. Without sound reasons for denying a request, refusing a claim, or revealing other bad news, a message will fail, no matter how cleverly it is organized or written. For example, if you must deny a customer's request, you probably have good reasons. As part of your planning before writing, think through those reasons so that you can present them strategically in your message. In the indirect strategy, the reasons appear before the bad news. In the direct strategy, the reasons appear immediately after the bad news.

**Explaining Clearly.** If the reasons are not confidential and if they will not create legal liability, you can be specific: *Growers supplied us with a limited number of patio roses, and our demand this year was twice that of last year.* In responding to a billing error, explain what happened: *After you informed us of an error on your January bill, we realized the mistake was ours. Until our new automated system is fully online, we are still subject to human error. Rest assured that you will see a credit on your next bill.* In refusing a speaking engagement, tell why the date is impossible: *On January 15 we have a board of directors meeting that I must attend.* However, in an effort to be the "good guy," don't make dangerous or unrealistic promises: *Although we can't contribute now, we expect increased revenues next year and promise a generous gift then.*

---

### OFFICE INSIDER

*"Business is all about building relationships and the best way to build relationships is to be kind and to show interest in and compassion for the people you work and interact with. Ultimately, that's how you build trust, which is the single most important factor in business and in life."*

—Paul Spiegelman, co-founder and CEO of The Beryl Companies and author of *Why Is Everyone Smiling?*

**Citing Reader or Other Benefits if Plausible.** Readers are more open to bad news if in some way, even indirectly, it may help them. In refusing a customer's request for free hemming of skirts and slacks, Lands' End wrote: "We tested our ability to hem skirts a few months ago. This process proved to be very time-consuming. We have decided not to offer this service because the additional cost would have increased the selling price of our skirts substantially, and we did not want to impose that cost on all our customers."[10] Readers also accept bad news more readily if they recognize that someone or something else benefits, such as other workers or the environment: *Although we would like to consider your application, we prefer to fill managerial positions from within*. Avoid trying to show reader benefits, though, if they appear insincere: *To improve our service to you, we are increasing our brokerage fees*.

**Explaining Company Policy.** Readers resent blanket policy statements prohibiting something: *Company policy prevents us from making cash refunds* or *Company policy requires us to promote from within*. Instead of hiding behind company policy, gently explain why the policy makes sense: *We prefer to promote from within because it rewards the loyalty of our employees. In addition, we have found that people familiar with our organization make the quickest contribution to our team effort*. By offering explanations, you demonstrate that you care about readers and are treating them as important individuals.

**Choosing Positive Words.** Because the words you use can affect a reader's response, choose carefully. Remember that the objective of the indirect strategy is holding the reader's attention until you have had a chance to explain the reasons justifying the bad news. To keep the reader in a receptive mood, avoid expressions with punitive, demoralizing, or otherwise negative connotations. Stay away from such words as *cannot, claim, denied, error, failure, fault, impossible, mistaken, misunderstand, never, regret, rejected, unable, unwilling, unfortunately*, and *violate*.

**Showing Fairness and Serious Intent.** In explaining reasons, show the reader that you take the matter seriously, have investigated carefully, and are making an unbiased decision. Receivers are more accepting of disappointing news when they feel that their requests have been heard and that they have been treated fairly. In canceling funding for a program, board members provided this explanation: *As you know, the publication of* Urban Artist *was funded by a renewable annual grant from the National Endowment for the Arts. Recent cutbacks in federally sponsored city arts programs have left us with few funds. Because our grant has been discontinued, we have no alternative but to cease publication of* Urban Artist. *The board has searched long and hard for some other viable funding, but every avenue of recourse has been closed before us. Accordingly, June's issue will be our last.*

### 7-3e Cushioning the Bad News

Although you can't prevent the disappointment that bad news brings, you can reduce the pain somewhat by breaking the news sensitively. Be especially considerate when the reader will suffer personally from the bad news. A number of thoughtful techniques can cushion the blow.

**Positioning the Bad News Strategically.** Instead of spotlighting it, sandwich the bad news between other sentences, perhaps among your reasons. Don't let the refusal begin or end a paragraph; the reader's eye will linger on these high-visibility spots. Another technique that reduces shock is putting a painful idea in a subordinate clause: *Although another candidate was hired, we appreciate your interest in our organization and wish you every success in your job search*. Subordinate clauses often begin with words such as *although, as, because, if*, and *since*.

**Using the Passive Voice.** Passive-voice verbs enable you to depersonalize an action. Whereas the active voice focuses attention on a person *(We don't give cash refunds)*, the passive voice highlights the action *(Cash refunds are not given because. . .)*. Use the passive voice for the bad news. In some instances you can combine passive-voice verbs and a subordinate clause: *Although franchise scoop shop owners cannot be required to lower their frozen yogurt prices, we are happy to pass along your comments for their consideration.*

**Highlighting the Positive.** As you learned earlier, messages are far more effective when you describe what you can do instead of what you can't do. Rather than *We will no longer allow credit card purchases*, try a more positive appeal: *We are now selling gasoline at discount cash prices.*

**Implying the Refusal.** It is sometimes possible to avoid a direct refusal. Often, your reasons and explanations leave no doubt that a request has been denied. Explicit refusals may be unnecessary and at times cruel. In this refusal to contribute to a charity, for example, the writer never actually says *no*: *Because we will soon be moving into new offices in Glendale, all our funds are earmarked for relocation costs. We hope that next year we will be able to support your worthwhile charity.* The danger of an implied refusal, of course, is that it is so subtle that the reader misses it. Be certain that you make the bad news clear, thus preventing the need for further correspondence.

**Suggesting a Compromise or an Alternative.** A refusal is not so depressing—for the sender or the receiver—if a suitable compromise, substitute, or alternative is available. In denying permission to a group of students to visit a historical private residence, for instance, this writer softens the bad news by proposing an alternative: *Although private tours of the grounds are not given, we do open the house and its gardens for one charitable event in the fall.* You can further reduce the impact of the bad news by refusing to dwell on it. Present it briefly (or imply it), and move on to your closing.

### 7-3f Closing Pleasantly

After explaining the bad news sensitively, close the message with a pleasant statement that promotes goodwill. The closing should be personalized and may include an alternative follow-up, freebies, good wishes, a forward look, resale information, or a sales promotion. *Resale* refers to mentioning a product or service favorably to reinforce the customer's choice. For example, *you chose our best-selling model.*

**Alternative Follow-Up.** If an alternative exists, you might end your letter with follow-up advice. For example, in a letter rejecting a customer's demand for replacement of landscaping plants, you might say: *I will be happy to give you a free inspection and consultation. Please call 301-746-8112 to arrange a date for my visit.* In a message to a prospective home buyer: *Although the lot you saw last week is now sold, we do have two lots with excellent views that are available at a slightly higher price.* In reacting to an Internet misprint: *Please note that our website contained an unfortunate misprint offering $850-per-night Bora Bora bungalows at $85. Although we cannot honor that rate, we are offering a special half-price rate of $425 to those who responded.*

**Freebies.** When customers complain—primarily about food products or small consumer items—companies often send coupons, samples, or gifts to restore confidence and promote future business. In response to a customer's complaint about a frozen dinner, you could write: *Your loyalty and your concern about our frozen entrées are genuinely appreciated. Because we want you to continue enjoying our healthy and convenient dinners, we are enclosing a coupon that you can take to your local market to select your next Green Valley entrée.*

**Good Wishes.** A letter rejecting a job candidate might read: *We appreciate your interest in our company, and we extend to you our best wishes in your search to find the perfect match between your skills and job requirements.*

**Forward Look.** Anticipate future relations or business. A letter that refuses a contract proposal might read: *Thanks for your bid. We look forward to*

## OFFICE INSIDER

*"The most pressing need of angry customers is to be heard. Listen to them without interrupting. Then show you understand their situation by finding common points of frustration."*

—Jonathan Rick, director, Levick Strategic Communications

**LEARNING OBJECTIVE 4**

Apply effective techniques in refusing typical requests or claims, as well as handling customer bad news in print and online.

working with your talented staff when future projects demand your special expertise.

**Resale or Sales Promotion.** When the bad news is not devastating or personal, references to resale information or promotion may be appropriate: *The computer workstations you ordered are unusually popular because of their stain-, heat-, and scratch-resistant finishes. To help you locate hard-to-find accessories for these workstations, we invite you to visit our website where our online catalog provides a huge selection of surge suppressors, multiple outlet strips, security devices, and PC tool kits.*

Avoid endings that sound canned, insincere, inappropriate, or self-serving. Don't invite further correspondence *(If you have any questions, do not hesitate. . .)*, and don't refer to the bad news. To review these suggestions for delivering bad news sensitively, take another look at Figure 7.4, Delivering Bad News Sensitively.

## 7-4 Refusing Typical Requests and Claims

When you must refuse typical requests, first think about how the receiver will react to your refusal and decide whether to use the direct or the indirect strategy. You may receive requests for favors or contributions. You may have to say no to customer claims or invitations to give presentations. You may also deal with disappointment and anger. If you have any doubt, use the indirect strategy and the following writing plan:

### WRITING PLAN FOR REFUSING TYPICAL REQUESTS AND CLAIMS

- **Buffer:** Start with a neutral statement on which both reader and writer can agree, such as a compliment, appreciation, a quick review of the facts, or an apology. Try to include a key idea or word that acts as a transition to the reasons.
- **Reasons:** Present valid reasons for the refusal, avoiding words that create a negative tone.
- **Bad news:** De-emphasize the bad news, use the passive voice, accentuate the positive, or imply a refusal. Suggest a compromise, alternative, or substitute, if possible. The alternative may be part of the bad-news section or part of the closing.
- **Closing:** Renew good feelings with a positive statement. Avoid referring to the bad news. Include resale or sales promotion material, if appropriate. Look forward to continued business.

### 7-4a Rejecting Requests for Favors, Money, Information, and Action

Requests for favors, money, information, and action may come from charities, friends, or business partners. Many are from people representing worthy causes, and you may wish you could comply. However, resources are usually limited. In a letter from Heartland Management Associates, shown in Figure 7.5, the company must refuse a request for a donation to a charity.

Following the indirect strategy, the letter begins with a buffer acknowledging the request. It also praises the good works of the charity and uses those words as a transition to the second paragraph. In the second paragraph, the writer explains why the company cannot donate. Notice that the writer reveals the refusal without actually stating it *(Because of internal restructuring and the economic downturn, we are forced to take a much harder look at funding requests that we receive this year).* This gentle refusal makes it unnecessary to be blunter in stating the denial.

In some donation refusal letters, the reasons may not be fully explained: *Although we can't provide financial support at this time, we all unanimously agree*

Figure 7.5 Refusing Donation Request

**Heartland Management Associates**
212 South Central Avenue
St. Louis, MO 631250
www.heartlandmanagement.com

February 12, 2016

Ms. Denise Moore
Guide Dog Center
2903 Market Street
St. Louis, MO 63103

Dear Ms. Moore:

Here at Heartland Management Associates, we are pleased that over the years we were able to partner with the Guide Dog Center and assist in its admirable program that provides guide and service dogs to blind or visually impaired individuals. We appreciate your recent letter describing the exceptionally worthwhile VetDogs program that offers trained animals to America's returning heroes in need of service dogs.

Supporting the good work and worthy projects of your organization and others, although unrelated to our business, is a luxury we have enjoyed in the past. Because of internal restructuring and the economic downturn, we are forced to take a much harder look at funding requests that we receive this year. We feel that we must focus our charitable contributions on areas that relate more directly to our business.

We are hopeful that the worst of the economic slump is now behind us and that in the future we will be able to again partner with the Guide Dog Center to help defray the costs of breeding, training, and placing guide and service dogs. You provide an admirable service, and Heartland salutes you.

Cordially,

HEARTLAND MANAGEMENT ASSOCIATES

*Nelson M. Felton*

Nelson M. Felton

*Annotations:*
- Opens with praise and compliments
- Transitions with repetition of key ideas (*good work and worthy projects*)
- Closes graciously with praise and a forward look
- Doesn't say *yes* or *no*
- Explains cutback in gifts, thus revealing refusal without actually stating it

---

that the Make-A-Wish Foundation contributes a valuable service to sick children. The emphasis is on the foundation's good deeds rather than on an explanation for the refusal. Businesses that are required to write frequent refusals might prepare a form letter, changing a few variables as needed.

## 7-4b Dealing With Disappointed Customers in Print

Businesses must occasionally respond to disappointed customers. Whenever possible, these problems should be dealt with immediately and personally. Most business professionals strive to control the damage and resolve such problems in the following manner:[11]

- Call or e-mail the individual immediately.
- Describe the problem and apologize.

## Office Insider

"As soon as you realize there is a problem, let your client know by phone or, if possible, in person. It's better to let them hear bad news from you than to discover it on their own because it establishes your candor."

—Kevin Kearns, VP of sales for Huthwaite, a sales force consulting company in Sterling, Virginia

- Explain why the problem occurred, what they are doing to resolve it, and how they will prevent it from happening again.
- Promote goodwill by following up with a print message that documents the phone call.

Written messages are important (a) to communicate when personal contact is impossible, (b) to establish a record of the incident, (c) to formally confirm follow-up procedures, and (d) to promote good relations.

A bad-news follow-up letter is shown in Figure 7.6. Consultant Manuela Lucas Santiago found herself in the embarrassing position of explaining why she had given out the name of her client to a salesperson. The client, Premier Resources International, had hired her firm, Azad Consulting Associates, to help find an appropriate service for outsourcing its payroll functions. Without realizing it, Manuela had mentioned to a potential vendor (QuickPay Services, Inc.) that her client was considering hiring an outside service to handle its payroll. An overeager salesperson from QuickPay Services immediately called on Premier, thus angering the client.

Manuela Lucas Santiago first called her client to explain and apologize. She was careful to control her voice and rate of speaking. She also followed up with the letter shown in Figure 7.6. The letter not only confirms the telephone conversation but also adds the right touch of formality. It sends the nonverbal message that the writer takes the matter seriously and that it is important enough to warrant a hard-copy letter.

Many consumer problems are handled with letters, either written by consumers as complaints or by companies in response. However, e-mail and social networks are also firmly established as channels for delivering complaints and negative messages.

### 7-4c Responding to Negative Posts and Reviews Online

Today's impatient, hyperconnected consumers eagerly embrace the idea of delivering their complaints to social networking sites rather than calling customer service departments. Why rely on word of mouth or send a letter to a company about poor

## Workplace in Focus

What do underwear and hummus have in common? Nothing. But that didn't stop underwear giant Hanes Brands Inc. (HBI) from requesting that food-dip maker Hanes Hummus change its name, destroy its products, and withdraw its trademark application due to possible name infringement. In letters exchanged between the firms, the underwear maker claimed that Hanes Hummus is "essentially identical and confusingly similar" to its own trademark. In its reply, the mashed-chickpeas maker wrote, "No rational person familiar with Hanes Hummus could possibly allege any confusion between Hanes Hummus and HBI's mark or product." The writer added, cheekily, "I was not aware that HBI's t-shirts were edible, made with chickpeas, lemon or garlic." The name "Hanes" is the nickname of the hummus maker Yohannes Petros. What tips should businesses follow when refusing requests?[12]

Chapter 7: Negative Messages

## Figure 7.6 Bad-News Follow-Up Message

### AZAD CONSULTING ASSOCIATES
4350 Speedway Blvd.  
Tucson, AZ 85712  
Voice: (520) 259-0971  
Web: www.azadassociates.com

May 7, 2016

Mr. Carl Bahadur  
Director, Administrative Operations  
Premier Resources International  
538 North Pima Road, Suite 1210  
Phoenix, AZ 85001

Dear Mr. Bahadur:

You have every right to expect complete confidentiality in your transactions with an independent consultant. As I explained in yesterday's telephone call, I am very distressed that you were called by a salesperson from QuickPay Services, Inc. This should not have happened, and I apologize to you again for inadvertently mentioning your company's name in a conversation with a potential vendor, QuickPay Services, Inc.

All clients of Azad Consulting are assured that their dealings with our firm are held in the strictest confidence. Because your company's payroll needs are so individual and because you have so many contract workers, I was forced to explain how your employees differed from those of other companies. Revealing your company name was my error, and I take full responsibility for the lapse. I can assure you that it will not happen again. I have informed QuickPay Services that it had no authorization to call you directly, and its actions have forced me to reconsider using its services for my future clients.

A number of other payroll services offer outstanding programs. I'm sure we can find the perfect partner to enable you to outsource your payroll responsibilities, thus allowing your company to focus its financial and human resources on its core business. I look forward to our next appointment when you may choose from a number of excellent payroll outsourcing firms.

Sincerely,

*Manuela Lucas Santiago*  
Manuela Lucas Santiago  
Partner

- **Opens with** agreement and apology
- **Takes responsibility and promises to prevent recurrence**
- **Closes with forward look**
- **Explains what caused the problem and how it was resolved**

**Tips for Resolving Problems and Following Up**
- Whenever possible, call or see the individual involved.
- Describe the problem and apologize.
- Explain why the problem occurred.
- Take responsibility, if appropriate.
- Explain what you are doing to resolve it.
- Explain what you are doing to prevent recurrence.
- Follow up with a message that documents the personal contact.
- Look forward to positive future relations.

---

service or a defective product when you can jump online and shout your grievance to the entire world? Today's consumers are quick to voice their displeasure with negative posts and reviews via Twitter, Facebook, Angie's List, Yelp, and other sites.

How can organizations respond to negative posts and reviews online? Experts suggest the following pointers:

- **Verify the situation.** Investigate to learn what happened. If the complaint is legitimate and your organization fouled up, it's best to fess up. Admit the problem and try to remedy it.
- **Respond quickly and constructively.** Offer to follow up offline; send your contact information. Be polite and helpful.
- **Consider freebies.** Suggest a refund or a discount on future services. Dissatisfied customers often write a second more positive review if they have received a refund.

Chapter 7: Negative Messages

## OFFICE INSIDER

*"Any declarative sentence starting with 'you' when talking to a customer is best avoided—it comes across as shaking your finger at the customer, and no one wants to feel like we're talking to our mother! Better choices are 'We can' or 'Let's do this together' or 'What I could suggest is.'"*

—Kristin Robertson, KR Consulting, Inc.

- **Learn how to improve.** Look upon online comments as opportunities for growth and improvement. See complaining customers as real-time focus groups that can provide valuable insights.
- **Accept the inevitable.** Recognize that nearly every business will experience some negativity, especially on today's readily accessible social media sites. Do what you can to respond constructively, and then move on.

For advice on answering online comments, see p. 167 in Chapter 6.

### 7-4d Denying Claims

Publisher Malcolm Forbes once observed, "To be agreeable while disagreeing—that's an art."[13] Customers occasionally want something they are not entitled to or something you can't grant. Because these customers are often unhappy with a product or service, they are emotionally involved. Messages that say *no* to emotionally involved receivers will probably be your most challenging communication task.

Fortunately, the reasons-before-refusal plan helps you be empathic and artful in breaking bad news. Obviously, in denial messages you will need to adopt the proper tone. Don't blame customers, even if they are at fault. Avoid *you* statements that sound preachy *(You would have known that cash refunds are impossible if you had read your user agreement)*. Use neutral, objective language to explain why the claim must be refused. Consider offering resale information to rebuild the customer's confidence in your products or organization.

In Figure 7.7 the writer denies the customer's request to be reimbursed for the difference between the price the customer paid for speakers and the price he saw advertised locally (which would have resulted in a cash refund of $100). Although the catalog service does match any advertised lower price, the price-matching policy applies *only* to exact models. This claim must be rejected because the advertisement the customer submitted showed a different, older speaker model.

The e-mail to Stephen Dominique opens with a buffer that agrees with a statement in the customer's e-mail. It repeats the key idea of product confidence as a transition to the second paragraph. Next comes an explanation of the price-matching policy. The writer does not assume that the customer is trying to pull a fast one. Nor does he suggest that the customer is a dummy who didn't read the price-matching policy. The safest path is a neutral explanation of the policy along with precise distinctions between the customer's speakers and the older ones. The writer also gets a chance to resell the customer's speakers and demonstrate what a quality product they are. By the end of the third paragraph, it is evident to the reader that his claim is unjustified.

**LEARNING OBJECTIVE 5**
Describe and apply effective techniques for delivering negative news within organizations.

## 7-5 Managing Bad News Within Organizations

Generally, bad news is better received when reasons are given first. Whether you use a direct or an indirect strategy in delivering that news depends primarily on the anticipated reaction of the audience. A tactful tone and a reasons-first approach help preserve friendly relations with customers. These techniques are also useful when delivering bad news within organizations. Interpersonal bad news might involve telling the boss that something went wrong or confronting an employee about poor performance. Organizational bad news might involve declining profits, lost contracts, harmful lawsuits, public relations controversies, and policy changes. Within organizations, you may find yourself giving bad news in person or in writing.

Figure 7.7 E-Mail Denying a Claim

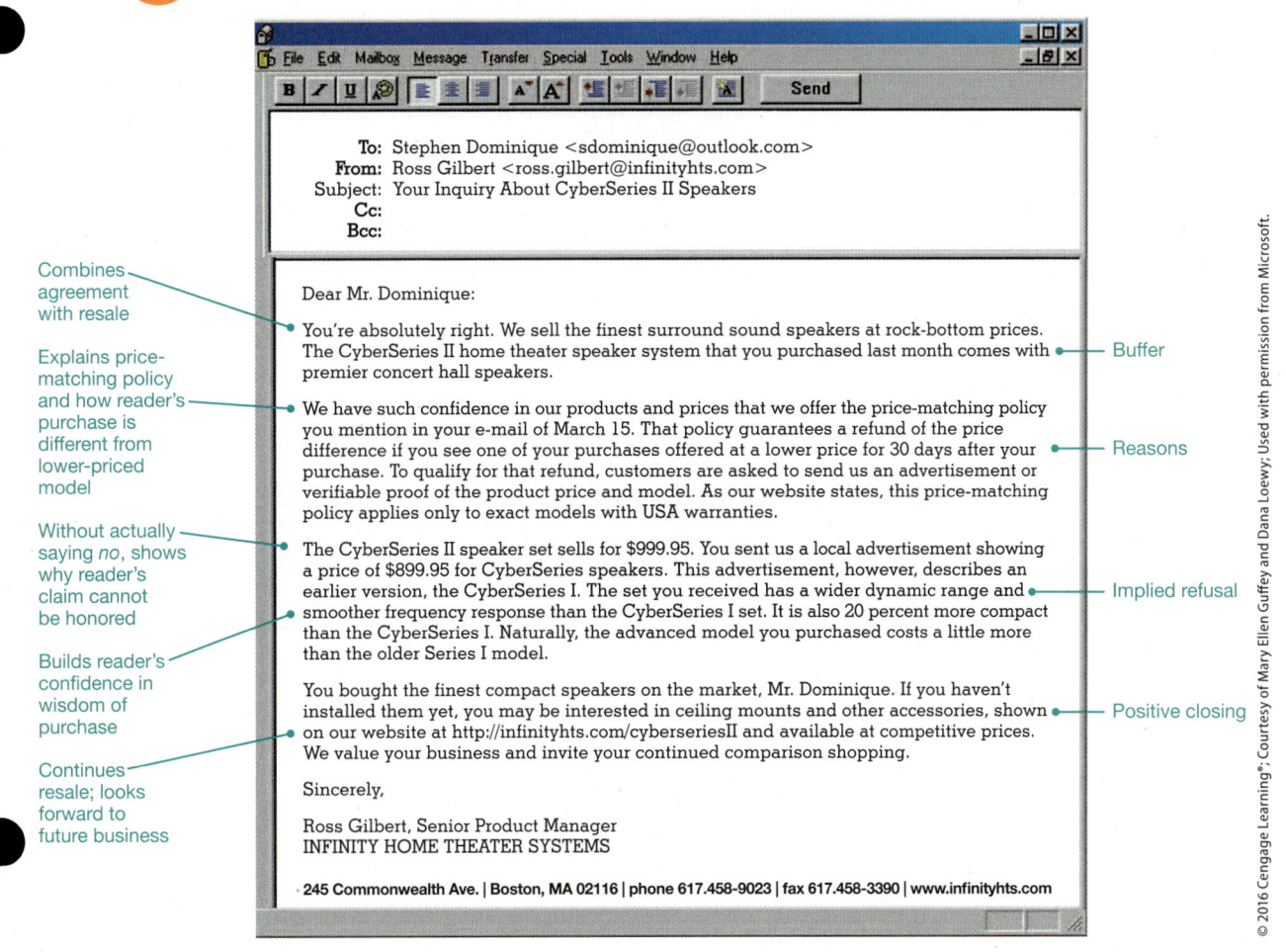

```
To:      Stephen Dominique <sdominique@outlook.com>
From:    Ross Gilbert <ross.gilbert@infinityhts.com>
Subject: Your Inquiry About CyberSeries II Speakers
Cc:
Bcc:
```

Dear Mr. Dominique:

You're absolutely right. We sell the finest surround sound speakers at rock-bottom prices. The CyberSeries II home theater speaker system that you purchased last month comes with premier concert hall speakers. — Buffer

We have such confidence in our products and prices that we offer the price-matching policy you mention in your e-mail of March 15. That policy guarantees a refund of the price difference if you see one of your purchases offered at a lower price for 30 days after your purchase. To qualify for that refund, customers are asked to send us an advertisement or verifiable proof of the product price and model. As our website states, this price-matching policy applies only to exact models with USA warranties. — Reasons

The CyberSeries II speaker set sells for $999.95. You sent us a local advertisement showing a price of $899.95 for CyberSeries speakers. This advertisement, however, describes an earlier version, the CyberSeries I. The set you received has a wider dynamic range and smoother frequency response than the CyberSeries I set. It is also 20 percent more compact than the CyberSeries I. Naturally, the advanced model you purchased costs a little more than the older Series I model. — Implied refusal

You bought the finest compact speakers on the market, Mr. Dominique. If you haven't installed them yet, you may be interested in ceiling mounts and other accessories, shown on our website at http://infinityhts.com/cyberseriesII and available at competitive prices. We value your business and invite your continued comparison shopping. — Positive closing

Sincerely,

Ross Gilbert, Senior Product Manager
INFINITY HOME THEATER SYSTEMS

245 Commonwealth Ave. | Boston, MA 02116 | phone 617.458-9023 | fax 617.458-3390 | www.infinityhts.com

*Annotations:*
- Combines agreement with resale
- Explains price-matching policy and how reader's purchase is different from lower-priced model
- Without actually saying *no*, shows why reader's claim cannot be honored
- Builds reader's confidence in wisdom of purchase
- Continues resale; looks forward to future business

© 2016 Cengage Learning®; Courtesy of Mary Ellen Guffey and Dana Loewy; Used with permission from Microsoft.

## 7-5a Delivering Bad News in Person

When you have the unhappy responsibility of delivering bad news, decide whether the negative information is newsworthy. For example, trivial, noncriminal mistakes or one-time bad behaviors are best left alone. However, fraudulent travel claims, consistent hostile behavior, or failing projects must be reported.[14] For example, you might have to tell the boss that the team's computer crashed and important files have not been backed up. As a team leader or supervisor, you might be required to confront an underperforming employee. If you know that the news will upset the receiver, the reasons-first strategy is most effective. When the bad news involves one person or a small group nearby, you should generally deliver that news in person. Here are pointers on how to do so tactfully, professionally, and safely:[15]

- **Gather all the information.** Cool down and have all the facts before marching in on the boss or confronting someone. Remember that every story has two sides.
- **Prepare and rehearse.** Outline what you plan to say so that you are confident, coherent, and dispassionate.
- **Explain: past, present, future.** If you are telling the boss about a problem such as the computer crash, explain what caused the crash, the current situation, and how and when you plan to fix it.
- **Consider taking a partner.** If you fear a "shoot the messenger" reaction, especially from your boss, bring a colleague with you. Each person should have a

Chapter 7: Negative Messages

consistent and credible part in the presentation. If possible, take advantage of your organization's internal resources. To lend credibility to your view, call on auditors, inspectors, or human resources experts.

- **Think about timing.** Don't deliver bad news when someone is already stressed or grumpy. Experts also advise against giving bad news on Friday afternoon when people have the weekend to dwell on it.
- **Be patient with the reaction.** Give the receiver time to vent, think, recover, and act wisely.

### 7-5b Refusing Workplace Requests

Occasionally, managers must refuse requests from employees. In Figure 7.8 you see the first draft and revision of a message responding to a request from a key specialist, Luke Carson. He wants permission to attend a conference. However, his timing is

Figure 7.8 Refusing an Internal Request

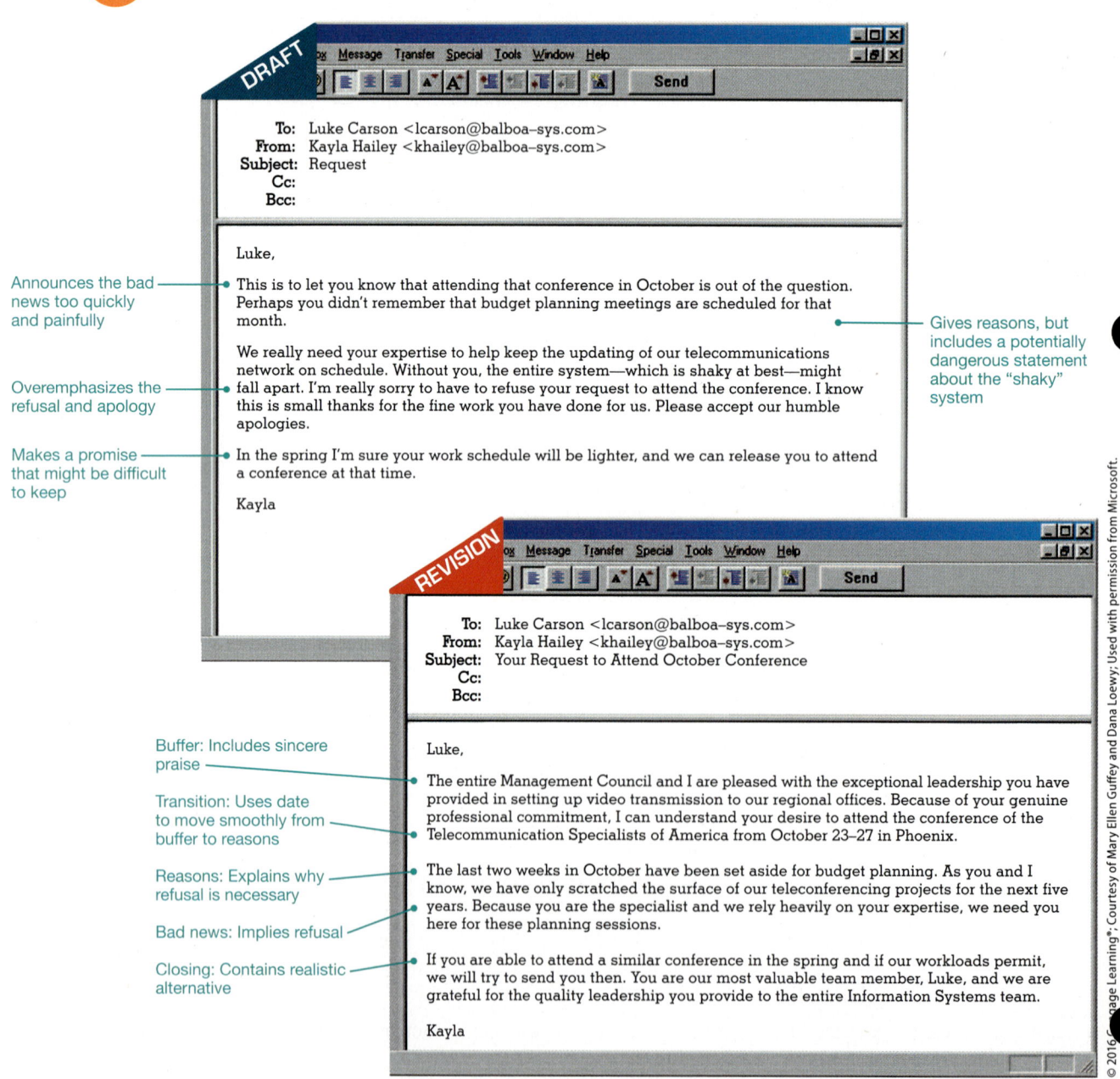

**DRAFT**

To: Luke Carson <lcarson@balboa-sys.com>
From: Kayla Hailey <khailey@balboa-sys.com>
Subject: Request
Cc:
Bcc:

Luke,

- Announces the bad news too quickly and painfully → This is to let you know that attending that conference in October is out of the question. Perhaps you didn't remember that budget planning meetings are scheduled for that month.

- Overemphasizes the refusal and apology → We really need your expertise to help keep the updating of our telecommunications network on schedule. Without you, the entire system—which is shaky at best—might fall apart. I'm really sorry to have to refuse your request to attend the conference. I know this is small thanks for the fine work you have done for us. Please accept our humble apologies. ← Gives reasons, but includes a potentially dangerous statement about the "shaky" system

- Makes a promise that might be difficult to keep → In the spring I'm sure your work schedule will be lighter, and we can release you to attend a conference at that time.

Kayla

**REVISION**

To: Luke Carson <lcarson@balboa-sys.com>
From: Kayla Hailey <khailey@balboa-sys.com>
Subject: Your Request to Attend October Conference
Cc:
Bcc:

Luke,

- Buffer: Includes sincere praise → The entire Management Council and I are pleased with the exceptional leadership you have provided in setting up video transmission to our regional offices. Because of your genuine professional commitment, I can understand your desire to attend the conference of the Telecommunication Specialists of America from October 23–27 in Phoenix.

- Transition: Uses date to move smoothly from buffer to reasons
- Reasons: Explains why refusal is necessary
- Bad news: Implies refusal → The last two weeks in October have been set aside for budget planning. As you and I know, we have only scratched the surface of our teleconferencing projects for the next five years. Because you are the specialist and we rely heavily on your expertise, we need you here for these planning sessions.

- Closing: Contains realistic alternative → If you are able to attend a similar conference in the spring and if our workloads permit, we will try to send you then. You are our most valuable team member, Luke, and we are grateful for the quality leadership you provide to the entire Information Systems team.

Kayla

© 2016 Cengage Learning®; Courtesy of Mary Ellen Guffey and Dana Loewy; Used with permission from Microsoft.

208  Chapter 7: Negative Messages

bad; he must be present at budget planning meetings scheduled for the same two weeks. Normally, this matter would be discussed in person. However, Luke has been traveling among branch offices, and he just hasn't been in the office recently.

The vice president's first inclination was to dash off a quick e-mail, as shown in the Figure 7.8 draft, and "tell it like it is." However, the vice president realized that her first draft was going to hurt and that it had possible danger areas. Moreover, the message missed a chance to give Luke positive feedback. Notice that the revision carefully employs a buffer, gives a rational explanation, and closes positively with an alternative and gratitude.

### 7-5c  Announcing Bad News to Employees and the Public

In an age of social media, damaging information can rarely be contained for long. Executives can almost count on it to be leaked. Corporate officers who fail to communicate effectively and proactively may end up on the defensive and face an uphill battle trying to limit the damage. Many of the techniques used to communicate bad news in person are useful when organizations face a crisis or must deliver negative news to their workers and other groups.

**Keeping Communication Open and Honest.** Smart organizations in crisis prefer to communicate the news openly to employees and other stakeholders. A crisis might involve serious performance problems, a major relocation, massive layoffs, a management shakeup, or public controversy. Instead of letting rumors distort the truth, managers ought to explain the organization's side of the story honestly and promptly.

> **OFFICE INSIDER**
>
> "E-mail and blogging have become such a part of our DNA that people take for granted that it's an OK way to communicate. But actually it's depersonalizing. It chops us off from who we thought we were."
>
> —Ruth Luban, employment counselor and author of *Are You a Corporate Refugee? A Survival Guide for Downsized, Disillusioned, and Displaced Workers.*

> **WRITING PLAN FOR ANNOUNCING NEGATIVE NEWS TO EMPLOYEES**
>
> - **Buffer:** Start with a neutral or positive statement that transitions to the reasons for the bad news. Consider opening with the best news, a compliment, appreciation, agreement, or solid facts. Show understanding.
> - **Reasons:** Explain the logic behind the bad news. Provide a rational explanation using positive words and displaying empathy. If possible, mention reader benefits.
> - **Bad news:** Position the bad news so that it does not stand out. Be positive, but don't sugarcoat the bad news. Use objective language.
> - **Closing:** Provide information about an alternative, if one exists. If appropriate, describe what will happen next. Look forward positively.

**Choosing the Best Communication Channel.** Morale can be destroyed when employees learn of major events affecting their jobs through the grapevine or from news accounts—rather than from management. When bad news must be delivered to individual employees, management may want to deliver the news personally. With large groups, however, this is generally impossible. Instead, organizations deliver bad news through multiple channels, ranging from hard-copy memos to digital media. Such electronic messages can take the form of intranet posts, e-mails, videos, webcasts, internal as well as external blogs, and voice mail.

**Draft of Intranet Post.** The draft of the intranet blog post shown in Figure 7.9 announces a substantial increase in the cost of employee health care benefits. However, the message suffers from many problems. It announces jolting news bluntly in the first sentence. Worse, it offers little or no explanation for the steep increase in costs. It also sounds insincere (*We did everything possible. . .*) and arbitrary. In a final miscue, the writer fails to give credit to the company for absorbing previous health cost increases.

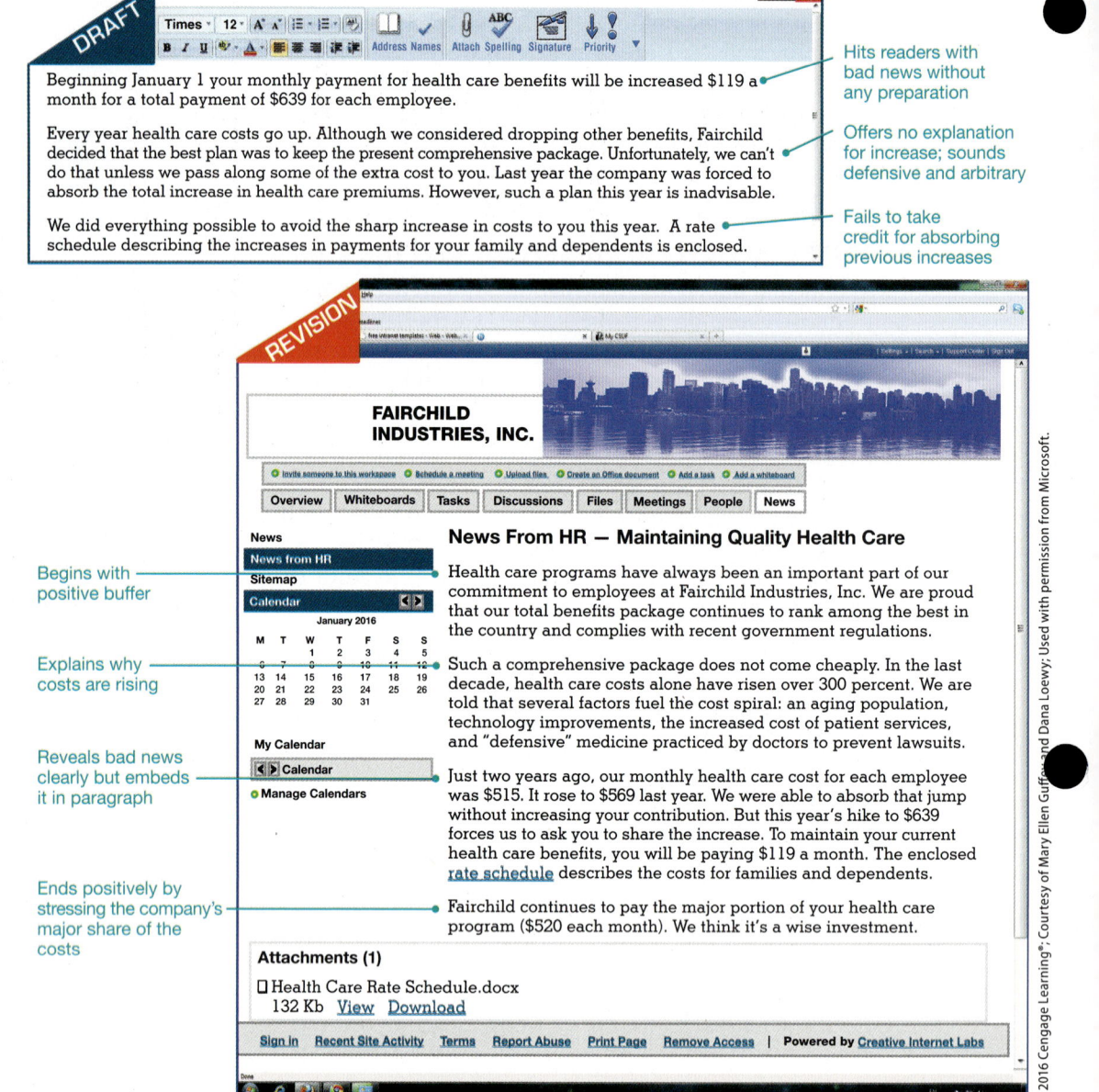

## Figure 7.9 Announcing Bad News to Employees

**DRAFT**

Beginning January 1 your monthly payment for health care benefits will be increased $119 a month for a total payment of $639 for each employee.

Every year health care costs go up. Although we considered dropping other benefits, Fairchild decided that the best plan was to keep the present comprehensive package. Unfortunately, we can't do that unless we pass along some of the extra cost to you. Last year the company was forced to absorb the total increase in health care premiums. However, such a plan this year is inadvisable.

We did everything possible to avoid the sharp increase in costs to you this year. A rate schedule describing the increases in payments for your family and dependents is enclosed.

- Hits readers with bad news without any preparation
- Offers no explanation for increase; sounds defensive and arbitrary
- Fails to take credit for absorbing previous increases

**REVISION**

**FAIRCHILD INDUSTRIES, INC.**

### News From HR — Maintaining Quality Health Care

Health care programs have always been an important part of our commitment to employees at Fairchild Industries, Inc. We are proud that our total benefits package continues to rank among the best in the country and complies with recent government regulations.

Such a comprehensive package does not come cheaply. In the last decade, health care costs alone have risen over 300 percent. We are told that several factors fuel the cost spiral: an aging population, technology improvements, the increased cost of patient services, and "defensive" medicine practiced by doctors to prevent lawsuits.

Just two years ago, our monthly health care cost for each employee was $515. It rose to $569 last year. We were able to absorb that jump without increasing your contribution. But this year's hike to $639 forces us to ask you to share the increase. To maintain your current health care benefits, you will be paying $119 a month. The enclosed rate schedule describes the costs for families and dependents.

Fairchild continues to pay the major portion of your health care program ($520 each month). We think it's a wise investment.

- Begins with positive buffer
- Explains why costs are rising
- Reveals bad news clearly but embeds it in paragraph
- Ends positively by stressing the company's major share of the costs

**Revision of Intranet Post.** The revision of this bad-news message uses the indirect strategy and improves the tone considerably. Notice that it opens with a relevant, upbeat buffer regarding health care—but says nothing about increasing costs. For a smooth transition, the second paragraph begins with a key idea from the opening (*comprehensive package*). The reasons section discusses rising costs with explanations and figures. The bad news (*you will be paying $119 a month*) is clearly presented but embedded within the paragraph. Throughout, the writer strives to show the fairness of the company's position. The ending, which does not refer to the bad news, emphasizes how much the company is paying and what a wise investment it is.

The entire message demonstrates a kinder, gentler approach than that shown in the first draft. Of prime importance in breaking bad news to employees is providing clear, convincing reasons that explain the decision. Parallel to this internal blog post, the message was also sent by e-mail. In smaller companies in which some workers do not have company e-mail, a hard-copy memo would be posted prominently on bulletin boards and in the lunchroom.

# SUMMARY OF LEARNING OBJECTIVES

**7-1 Understand the goals of business communicators in conveying negative news.**
- Explain clearly and completely while projecting a professional image.
- Convey empathy, sensitivity, and fairness.
- Maintain friendly relations, especially with customers.

**7-2 Compare the strategies and ethics of the direct and indirect plans in communicating negative news.**
- Use the direct strategy, with the bad news first, when the news is not damaging, when the receiver may overlook it, when the organization or receiver prefers directness, or when firmness is necessary.
- Use the indirect strategy, with a buffer and explanation preceding the bad news, when the bad news is personally upsetting, when it may provoke a hostile reaction, when it threatens the customer relationship, and when the news is unexpected.
- To avoid being unethical, never use the indirect method to deceive or manipulate the truth.

**7-3 Explain the components of effective negative messages, including opening with a buffer, apologizing, showing empathy, presenting the reasons, cushioning the bad news, and closing pleasantly.**
- To soften bad news, start with a buffer such as the best news, a compliment, appreciation, agreement, facts, understanding, or an apology.
- If you apologize, do it promptly and sincerely. Accept responsibility but don't admit blame without consulting a superior or company counsel. Strive to project empathy.
- In presenting the reasons for the bad news, explain clearly, cite reader or other benefits if plausible, explain company policy if necessary, choose positive words, and strive to show fairness and serious intent.
- In breaking the bad news, position it and word it strategically by (a) sandwiching it between other sentences, (b) presenting it in a subordinating clause, (c) using passive-voice verbs to depersonalize an action, (d) highlighting whatever is positive, (e) implying the refusal instead of stating it directly, and (f) suggesting a compromise or an alternative.
- To close pleasantly, you could (a) suggest a means of following through on an alternative, (b) offer freebies, (c) extend good wishes, (d) anticipate future business, or (e) offer resale information or a sales promotion.

**7-4 Apply effective techniques in refusing typical requests or claims, as well as handling customer bad news in print and online.**
- In rejecting requests for favors, money, information, and action, follow the bad-news strategy: (a) begin with a buffer, (b) present valid reasons, (c) explain the bad news and possibly an alternative, and (d) close with good feelings and a positive statement.
- To deal with disappointed customers in print, (a) call or e-mail the individual immediately; (b) describe the problem and apologize; (c) explain why the problem occurred, what you are doing to resolve it, and how you will prevent it from happening again; and (d) promote goodwill with a follow-up message.
- To handle negative posts and reviews online, (a) verify the situation, (b) respond quickly and constructively, (c) consider giving freebies such as refunds or discounts, (d) learn to improve by considering people who made negative comments as real-time focus groups, and (e) be prepared to accept the inevitable and move on.
- To deny claims, (a) use the reasons-before-refusal plan, (b) don't blame customers (even if they are at fault), (c) use neutral objective language to explain why the claim must be refused, and (d) consider offering resale information to rebuild the customer's confidence in your products or organization.

**7-5 Describe and apply effective techniques for delivering negative news within organizations.**
- To deliver workplace bad news in person, (a) gather all the information; (b) prepare and rehearse; (c) explain the past, present, and future; (d) consider taking a partner; (e) choose the best time to deliver the news; and (f) be patient with the reaction.
- In announcing bad news to employees and to the public, strive to keep the communication open and honest, choose the best communication channel, and consider applying the indirect strategy.
- Be positive, but don't sugarcoat the bad news; use objective language.

# CHAPTER REVIEW

1. When denying a claim from an irate customer who is threatening and overstates the claim, how can you remain professional and fair? (Obj. 1)

2. What is the primary difference between the direct and the indirect strategies? (Obj. 2)

3. When would you be more inclined to use the direct strategy in delivering bad news? (Obj. 2)

4. What is a buffer? Name five or more techniques to buffer the opening of a bad-news message. (Obj. 3)

5. Why should you apologize to customers if you or your company erred? What is the best way to do it? (Obj. 3)

6. In delivering bad news, name five techniques that can be used to cushion that news. (Obj. 3)

7. What is a process used by many business professionals in resolving problems with disappointed customers in print? (Obj. 4)

8. How can negative online comments be turned into positive growth for an organization? (Obj. 4)

9. How can a subordinate tactfully, professionally, and safely deliver upsetting news personally to a superior? (Obj. 5)

10. What are some channels that large organizations may use to deliver bad news to employees? (Obj. 5)

# CRITICAL THINKING

11. Robert Bies, professor of management at Georgetown University, believes that an important ethical guideline in dealing with bad news is never to shock the recipient: "Bad news should never come as a surprise. Failure to warn senior leadership of impending bad news, such as poor sales or a loss of a major client, is a cardinal sin. So is failure to warn subordinates about mistakes in their performance and provide an opportunity for them to make corrections and improve."[16] Discuss the motivation of people who keep quiet and struggle with dispensing bad news. (Objs. 1–3)

12. Suppose you made an honest mistake that could prove expensive for your employer or internship provider. Would you blurt out the bad news immediately or consider strategies to soften the blow somewhat? (Objs. 1–3)

13. Why is the passive voice acceptable, even desirable, in bad-news messages when it's considered poor, impersonal writing in most other situations? (Objs. 1–3)

14. Consider times when you have been aware that others were using the indirect strategy in writing or speaking to you. How did you react? (Obj. 2)

15. Living in Pittsburgh, Lauren Bossers worked virtually by e-mail and phone for a supply chain management software company in Dallas. She was laid off by phone, too. Bossers' manager had given her one day's notice; however, the news was still "shocking," and she responded with just *yes* or *no* to the HR officer who called: "I wasn't rude, but I didn't think it was my job to make them feel better," Bossers said. Software developer Jeff Langr was fired during a teleconference on Skype. What might be some advantages and disadvantages to receiving bad news remotely, if any? Why might it be a good idea to rein in one's frustration and anger? (Obj. 5)

# WRITING IMPROVEMENT EXERCISES

## Passive-Voice Verbs (Obj. 3)

Passive-voice verbs may be preferable in breaking bad news because they enable you to emphasize actions rather than personalities. Compare these two refusals:

**Active voice**: I cannot authorize you to take two weeks of vacation in August.
**Passive voice:** Two weeks of vacation in August cannot be authorized.

**YOUR TASK.** Revise the following sentences to present the bad news with passive-voice verbs.

16. We cannot offer free shipping for orders under $100.

17. This hospital has a strict policy of not admitting patients until we have verified their insurance coverage.

18. Because our liability insurance no longer covers visitors, we are postponing indefinitely requests for company tours.

19. Your car rental insurance coverage does not cover large SUVs.

20. Company policy prevents us from offering health and dental benefits until employees have been on the job for 12 months.

Chapter 7: Negative Messages

## Subordinating Bad News (Obj. 3)

**YOUR TASK.** Revise the following sentences to position the bad news in a subordinate clause. (**Hint:** Consider beginning the clause with *Although*.) Use passive-voice verbs for the bad news.

21. A shipping strike makes it impossible for us to ship your complete order at this point in time. However, we are able to send two corner workstations now, and you should receive them within five days.

22. We were forced to stop taking orders for flowers the week before Mother's Day. To make up for this disappointment, we apologize and ask you to try again with free shipping for the next week.

23. We now offer all of our catalog choices at our website, which is always current. We are sorry to report that we no longer mail print catalogs. Our sustainability goals made it impossible for us to continue doing that.

24. We appreciate your interest in our organization, but we are unable to extend an employment offer to you at this time.

25. The shipment of your last order was late for a reason. We had some really large orders that had to be filled ahead of yours and tied up our facilities. After that tie-up, we realized we had to improve our shipping process. Your next order will arrive within a week. That's a promise.

## Implying Bad News (Obj. 3)

**YOUR TASK.** Revise the following statements to *imply* the bad news. If possible, use passive-voice verbs and subordinate clauses to further de-emphasize the bad news.

**Direct refusal:** We cannot send you a price list, nor can we sell our lawn mowers directly to customers. We sell only through authorized dealers, and your dealer is HomeCo.
**Implied refusal:** Our lawn mowers are sold only through authorized dealers, and your dealer is HomeCo.

26. Unfortunately, we find it impossible to contribute to your excellent and worthwhile fund-raising campaign this year. At present all the funds of our organization are needed to lease equipment and offices for our new branch in Hartford. We hope to be able to support this commendable endeavor in the future.

27. We cannot ship our fresh fruit baskets c.o.d. Your order was not accompanied by payment, so we are not shipping it. We have it ready, though, and will rush it to its destination as soon as you call us with your credit card number.

28. Because of the holiday period, all our billboard space was used this month. Therefore, we are sorry to say that we could not give your charitable group free display space. However, next month, after the holidays, we hope to display your message as we promised.

# RADICAL REWRITES

**Note:** Radical Rewrites are provided at **www.cengagebrain.com** for you to download and revise. Your instructor may provide a suggested solution.

## 7.1 Radical Rewrite: Request Refusal—Bitter Taste of the Beach (Objs. 1–4)

The following blunt refusal from a restaurant owner rejects a previously agreed-to favor. To avoid endangering a friendship and losing community goodwill, this writer needs to draft a radical rewrite.

**YOUR TASK.** List at least five weaknesses and suggest ways to improve this message. If your instructor directs, revise.

Current date

Ms. Diane Hinchcliffe
Taste of the Beach
310 Ocean Avenue, Suite 304
Carmel-by-the-Sea, CA 93521

Dear Ms. Hinchcliffe:

Unfortunately, we cannot participate in this summer's Taste of the Beach event. This may be particularly disappointing to you because, merely as a friendly gesture, I had earlier agreed to provide a selection of tasty hors d'oeuvres from my restaurant, The Zodiac. I'm sorry to let you down like this. We have participated in the past, but we just can't do it this year because our sad kitchen facilities require major and extensive remodeling.

I heard that this year's Taste of the Beach is really going to be a blast with new and old food, wine, music, and artistic offerings. How did you get so many prized vintners and all those well-known chefs, artists, and music groups to participate and perform?

This is probably quite disappointing to you (and to me) because the event supports Big Brothers Big Sisters of America. I know that BBBSA is simply the very best as a youth mentoring organization.

Let me repeat—I'm sorry we can't participate. Don't bother to beg me. But for your silent raffle we can offer you a coupon for a dinner for two. Of course, this could not be used until October when our renovations are completed.

Sincerely,

List at least five weaknesses.

## 7.2 Radical Rewrite: Bad News to Customers—Hackers Hijack E-Mail Addresses (Objs. 1–4)

The following poorly written e-mail tells customers that their e-mail addresses have been hacked. However, the message is clumsy and fails to include essential information in revealing security breaches to customers.

**YOUR TASK.** Analyze the message and list at least seven weaknesses. If your instructor directs, revise it using the suggestions you learned in this chapter about security breach messages.

Chapter 7: Negative Messages

**To:** Kara Khalial [kkhalial@coastal.net]
**From:** Justin Small [jsmall@princetonpayment.org]
**Subject:** Customer Security Incident at Princeton Payment Systems
**Cc:**
**Bcc:**

Companies and individuals across the country are experiencing more and more security breaches. This is just to let you know that you are receiving this e-mail because of a recent unfortunate security breach at Princeton Payment Systems. Rest assured, however, that as a customer of Princeton, your privacy was never at risk. We promise to guard your privacy around the clock.

Hackers last week were able to maliciously exploit a new function that we were trying to use to make the customer log-in process faster for you and our other customers. The hackers were ingenious and malicious, going to extreme lengths to gain access to some customer addresses at Princeton. You should now beware of scams that may result from your address being used in phishing scams. To learn more, go to http://www.fdic.gov/consumers/consumer/alerts/phishing.html.

To provide even more information about this incident, the U.S. postal service will bring you a letter with more information. Taking your privacy very seriously, e-mail addresses are heavily protected here at Princeton. Within hours of the hacker break-in, the log-in mechanism was disabled and a new procedure was established. The user is now required to enter their e-mail address and their password before they can log in successfully. E-mail addresses were the only information the hackers got. Other information such as account information and other personal information were never risked.

We appreciate you being a Princeton customer.

Sincerely,

List at least seven weaknesses.

## 7.3 Radical Rewrite: Claim Denial—Warranty Does Not Mean a New Device (Objs. 1–4)

Following is a letter to a customer who demanded a brand-new replacement smartphone under her wireless phone protection plan.

**YOUR TASK.** Analyze the message. List at least five weaknesses. If your instructor directs, revise the message.

Current date

Ms. Haley Tranquillo
501 Westhampton Way
Richmond, VA 23173

Dear Ms. Tranquillo:

This letter is being sent to you to inform you that warranty repairs or replacements are not available for damage caused by operator fault. The dot inside your smartphone indicates in bright red that the device suffered prolonged exposure to liquid. The phone also shows signs of heavy external abuse—quite rightly excluded from coverage under your protection plan.

Your phone retailer, Westhampton Wireless, at 422 Pleasant Valley Road, forwarded your device to us. Our service technician made an inspection. That's when he discovered that your Droid had not been treated with proper caution and care. He said he had never seen such a gunky phone interior, and that without a doubt the gadget was subjected to blunt force on top of that! You are lucky that the touch screen did not crack or break and that you didn't lose all your data irretrievably since you apparently didn't bother to arrange for a backup. Today's smartphones are sophisticated high-tech devices. They must be handled with utmost respect. You wouldn't believe how many users accidentally drop their phones into the toilet.

The Peace of Mind Plan that you have purchased gets rave reviews from users. They love the protection their expensive equipment enjoys at a low monthly cost of $5.99. However, this plan plus the manufacturer's warranty on your Droid covers only this one thing: manufacturing defects. Your warranty has expired by now, but it wouldn't cover neglect and abuse anyway. Your Peace of Mind Plan is in effect but only covers you for theft, loss, and malfunction. It explicitly excludes liquid and physical damage. In any case, there is always a deductible of $89. We can't replace the Droid at no charge, as you request. But we could sell you a remanufactured model, at a cost of $49 plus tax. Your other option is to purchase a new device at full retail cost. Furthermore, since you have a two-year contract, you will be eligible for an upgrade as you are nearing month 20. You could go to www.alphawireless.com to browse new calling plans and see current smartphones and perhaps order a product or service online.

Let us know what you want to do. We pride ourselves on our unparalleled customer service.

Sincerely,

List at least five weaknesses.

# ACTIVITIES AND CASES

### 7.4 Request Refusal: Advocating for Abused Children (Objs. 1–4)

As a vice president of a financial services company, you serve many clients and they sometimes ask your company to contribute to their favorite charities. You recently received a letter from Paulina Ramirez asking for a substantial contribution to the National Court Appointed Special Advocates (CASA) Association. On visits to your office, she has told you about its programs to recruit, train, and support volunteers in their work with abused children. She herself is active in your town as a CASA volunteer, helping neglected children find safe, permanent homes. She told you that children with CASA volunteers are more likely to be adopted and are less likely to reenter the child welfare system.

You have a soft spot in your heart for children and especially for those who are mistreated. You sincerely want to support CASA and its good work. However, times are tough, and you can't be as generous as you have been in the past. Ms. Ramirez wrote a special letter to you asking you to become a Key contributor, with a pledge of $1,000.

**YOUR TASK.** Write a refusal letter that maintains good relations with your client. Address it to Ms. Paulina Ramirez, 4382 Congress Avenue, Austin, TX 78701.

### 7.5 Request Refusal: Pink Dragons Sink Application (Objs. 1–4)
E-mail  Web

Adobe Systems Incorporated prides itself on its commitment to employees who receive generous benefits and enjoy a supportive corporate culture. This core value may have contributed to the company's ranking among the top 50 of *Fortune* magazine's 100 Best Companies to Work For. The software giant is also known for its community involvement and corporate social responsibility efforts. This is why, like most large companies, Adobe receives many requests for sponsorships of charity events and community projects. True to its innovative spirit, the software company has streamlined the application process by providing an online sponsorship request form at its website.

You work in Corporate Affairs/Community Relations at Adobe and periodically help decide which nonprofits will obtain support. Just yesterday you received an e-mail from the Pink Dragons of San Diego, a dragon boat racing team of breast cancer survivors. The ancient Chinese sport has spread around the globe with competitions held not only in Asia but also in many Western countries. Dragon boat racing has gained popularity in North America among breast cancer patients who bond with fellow survivors, engage in healthy competition, and exercise regularly on the water. Synchronicity and technique are more important than brute strength, which is the main reason even recreational paddlers enjoy this fast-growing water sport.

The newly formed survivor team would like Adobe to sponsor a dragon boat festival in San Diego in less than a month, an event potentially drawing at least 20 survivor teams that would compete against each other. Your company is already funding several cancer charities and has a policy of sponsoring many causes. Naturally, no corporate giving program has infinite funds, nor can it green-light every request. Adobe steers clear of religious, political, and "pornographic" events. The team judging the sponsorship entries wants to ensure that each proposal reaches audiences affiliated with Adobe. Most important, applicants must submit their requests at least six weeks before the event.

**YOUR TASK.** As a junior staff member in Corporate Affairs/Community Relations, write an e-mail to Pink Dragon captain Josephine Rosa (jrosa@pinkdragons.org) refusing her initial request and explaining the Adobe sponsorship philosophy and submission rules.

## 7.6 Request Refusal: No Favors for Jamba Juice (Objs. 1–4)

In an aggressive expansion effort, Jamba Juice became a good customer of your software company. You have enjoyed the business it brought, and you are also quite fond of its products—especially Banana Berry and Mega Mango smoothies. Jamba Inc. is in the midst of expanding its menu with the goal of becoming the Starbucks of the smoothie. "Just as Starbucks defined the category of coffee, Jamba has the opportunity to define the category of the healthy snack," said market analyst Brian Moore. One goal of Jamba is to boost the frequency of customer visits by offering some products that are more filling. Then it could attract hungry customers as well as thirsty ones. It has been experimenting with adding grains such as oatmeal and nuts such as almonds so that a smoothie packs more substance and could substitute for a meal.

You receive a letter from Joe Wong, your business friend and contact at Jamba Juice. He asks you to do him and Jamba Juice a favor. He wants to set up a juice-tasting bar in your company cafeteria to test his new experimental drinks. All the drinks would be free, of course, but employees would have to fill out forms to evaluate each recipe. The details could be worked out later.

You definitely support healthy snacks, but you think this idea is terrible. First of all, your company doesn't even have a cafeteria. It has a small lunchroom, and employees bring their own food. Second, you would be embarrassed to ask your boss to do this favor for Jamba Juice, despite the business it has brought your company.

**YOUR TASK.** Write a letter that retains good customer relations with Jamba Juice but refuses this request. What reasons can you give, and what alternatives are available? Address your message to Joe Wong, Vice President, Product Development, Jamba Inc., 450 Golden Gate Avenue, San Francisco, CA 94102.[17]

## 7.7 Request Refusal: Loud Music Bothers Tenant Neighbor (Objs. 1–4)

**Web**

As the owner of Two Buckhead Plaza, you must respond to the request of Manuel Quinones, one of the tenants in your three-story office building. Mr. Quinones, a CPA, demands that you immediately evict a neighboring tenant who plays loud music throughout the day, interfering with Mr. Quinones' conversations with clients and with his concentration. The noisy tenant, Scott Eslan, seems to operate an entertainment booking agency and spends long hours in his office. You know you can't evict Mr. Eslan because, as a legal commercial tenant, he is entitled to conduct his business. However, you might consider adding soundproofing, an expense that you would prefer to share with Mr. Eslan and Mr. Quinones. You might also discuss limiting the time of day that Mr. Eslan could make noise.

**YOUR TASK.** Before responding to Mr. Quinones, you decide to find out more about commercial tenancy. Use the Web to search the keywords *commercial eviction*. Then develop a course of action. In a letter to Mr. Quinones, deny his request but retain his goodwill. Tell him how you plan to resolve the problem. Write to Manuel Quinones, CPA, Suite 300, Two Buckhead Plaza, 3050 Peachtree Rd., NW, Atlanta, GA 30305. Your instructor may also ask you to write an appropriate message to Mr. Scott Eslan, Suite 330.

## 7.8 Claim Denial: Lost in Flight (Objs. 1–4)

National Airlines had an unhappy customer. Genna Frymoyer-Morris flew from Washington, DC, to Los Angeles. The flight stopped briefly at Denver International Airport, where she got off the plane for half an hour. When she returned to her seat, her $500 prescription reading glasses were gone. She asked the flight attendant where the glasses were, and the attendant said they probably were thrown away since the cleaning crew had come in with big bags and tossed everything in them. Ms. Frymoyer-Morris tried to locate the glasses through the airline's lost-and-found service, but she failed.

Then she wrote a strong letter to the airline demanding reimbursement for the loss. She felt that it was obvious that she was returning to her seat. The airline, however, knows that an overwhelming number of passengers arriving at hubs switch planes for

Chapter 7: Negative Messages

their connecting flights. The airline does not know who is returning. What's more, flight attendants usually announce that the plane is continuing to another city and that passengers who are returning should take their belongings. Cabin cleaning crews speed through planes removing newspapers, magazines, leftover foods, and trash. Airlines feel no responsibility for personal items left in cabins.

**YOUR TASK.** As a staff member of the customer relations department of National Airlines, deny the customer's claim but retain her goodwill using techniques learned in this chapter. The airline never refunds cash, but it might consider travel vouchers for the value of the glasses. Remember that apologies cost nothing. Write a claim denial to Ms. Genna Frymoyer-Morris, 1805 Panorama Drive, Bakersfield, CA 93305.

### 7.9 Claim Denial: Going Ape After Botched Gorilla Party (Objs. 1–4)

E-mail  Web

BuyCostumes, the world's largest online costume and accessories retailer, is proud of its extensive stock of costumes, its liberal return policy, and its many satisfied customers. However, one day an e-mail arrived with a request that went beyond the company's ability to deliver. The customer said that he had ordered the Gorilla Blinky Eye With Chest costume. This popular gorilla costume comes with a unique gorilla mask, attractive suit with rubber chest, foot covers, and hands. The customer complained that the gorilla costume did not arrive until two days after his Halloween party. He planned an elaborate party with a gorilla theme, and he was extremely unhappy that he did not have his costume. He asks BuyCostumes to reimburse $300 that he spent on theme-related decorations, which he says were useless when he failed to receive his costume.

As a customer service representative, you checked his order and found that it was not received until five days before Halloween, the busiest time of the year for your company. It's so busy that your staff grows from 60 core employees to over 300 during this season. His order was filled the next day, but standard shipping requires three to six business days for delivery. The customer did not order express or premium delivery; his shipping option was marked "Standard."

You showed the e-mail to the owner, Mr. Schwartz, who said that this request was ludicrous. However, he wanted to retain the customer's goodwill. Obviously, BuyCostumes was not going to shell out $300 for late delivery of a costume. Mr. Schwartz suggested that the company would allow the customer to return the costume (in its original packaging). In addition, BuyCostumes would send a digital coupon for $20 off the next costume purchase. You can check its return policy at buycostumes.com.

**YOUR TASK.** Mr. Schwartz asks you to write an e-mail that retains the goodwill of this customer. Address your e-mail to Paul Littleton <plittleton@outlook.com>.

### 7.10 Claim Denial: Raising a Stink About a Charge for Smoking in the Room (Objs. 1–4)

Recently, the Metropol Grand Hotel embarked on a two-year plan to provide enhanced value and improved product quality to its guests. It always strives to exceed guest expectations. As part of this effort, Metropol Grand Hotel has been refurbishing many rooms with updated finishes. The new carpet, paint, upholstery, and draperies, however, absorb the heavy odor of cigarette smoke. To protect the hotel's investment, Metropol Grand Hotel enforces a strict nonsmoking policy for its nonsmoking rooms.

Metropol Grand Hotel makes sure that guests know about its policy regarding smoking in nonsmoking rooms. It posts a notice in each nonsmoking room, and it gives guests a handout from the manager detailing its policy and the consequences for smoking in nonsmoking rooms. The handout clearly says, "Should a guest opt to disregard our nonsmoking policy, we will process a fee of $150 to the guest's account." For those guests who prefer to smoke, a smoking accommodation can be provided.

On May 10 Trevor H. Taylor was a guest in the hotel. He stayed in a room clearly marked "Nonsmoking." After he left, the room cleaners reported that the room smelled of smoke. According to hotel policy, a charge of $150 was processed to Mr. Taylor's credit card. Mr. Taylor has written to demand that the $150 charge be removed. He doesn't deny that he smoked in the room. He just believes that he should not have to pay.

**YOUR TASK.** As hotel manager, deny Mr. Taylor's claim. You would certainly like to see Mr. Taylor return as a Metropol Grand Hotel guest, but you cannot budge on your smoking policy. Address your response to Mr. Trevor H. Taylor, 580 Lottie Street, Bellingham, WA 98225.

### 7.11 Customer Bad News: Putting the Brakes on Bakery Deliveries (Objs. 1–4)

As the owner of La Boulangerie Bakery in Baton Rouge, Louisiana, you have a devoted clientele savoring your delicacies. Your salty caramel cupcakes offer an irresistible salty-sweet flavor combination using fleur de sel crystals hand harvested from the pristine seas off Brittany, France. These salt granules complement the sweet buttery caramel that flavors both the cake and frosting. Although your cupcakes are a trendy hit, you also feature delicious cakes, squares, cookies, croissants, and breads. Your bakery has a medium-sized storefront; however, most of your business comes from supplying local restaurants and coffee shops with your tantalizing treats. You own two trucks that make deliveries to customers throughout the Baton Rouge metropolitan area.

Chapter 7: Negative Messages

Although La Boulangerie is financially successful, rising costs have severely undercut your profits over the past few months. You know that you are not the only business owner dealing with rising prices. Many of your suppliers have raised their prices over the past year. Specifically, the higher prices of wheat and sugar have resulted in a drastic increase in your production costs. Previously, you did not charge for deliveries made to your wholesale clients. However, you now feel that you have no choice but to add a delivery charge for each order to cover your increased costs and the rising price of gas.

**YOUR TASK.** As the owner of La Boulangerie Bakery, write a letter to your wholesale clients in which you announce a $20 charge per delivery. Try to think of a special offer to soften the blow. Address the first letter to Mr. Emil Broussard, Café Broussard, 2013 West Lee Drive, Baton Rouge, LA 70820.

### 7.12 Customer Bad News: Blunder in Scheduling Fairytale Cottage Wedding (Objs. 1–4)

As the wedding planner at Sea Island Resort in Georgia, you just discovered a terrible mistake. Two weddings have been scheduled for the same Saturday in June. How could this happen? You keep meticulous records, but six months ago, you were away for two weeks. Another employee filled in for you. She apparently didn't understand the scheduling system and lined up two weddings for the Cloister Chapel on June 14. The month of June, of course, is the busiest month of the year. Weddings in the popular fairytale cottage Cloister Chapel are usually booked for two years in advance, and it can handle only one wedding a day.

It's now January, and Kellie Singer, one of the brides-to-be called to check on her arrangements. That's when you discovered the mistake. However, you didn't reveal the blunder to Kellie on the telephone. From experience, you know how emotional brides can be when their plans go awry. Now you must decide what to do. Your manager has given you complete authority in scheduling weddings, and you know he would back nearly any decision you make to rectify the mistake. Unfortunately, all of your Sea Island wedding venues are booked for June Saturdays. However, you do have some midweek openings for the Cloister Chapel in early June. If one of the brides could change to midweek, you might offer one free night in a sumptuous bridal suite to smooth ruffled feathers.

Sea Island offers dreamlike settings for unforgettable wedding celebrations. Brides, grooms, and their guests can enjoy five-star resort services, five miles of private coastline, glittering ballrooms, custom banquets, and alluringly wooded and landscaped strolling areas.

**YOUR TASK.** Decide what course of action to take. The two brides-to-be are Kellie Singer, 3201 Peachtree Lane, Cumming, GA 30016, and Julie Brehm, 240 Lakeview Avenue, Atlanta, GA 30305. In a memo to your instructor, explain your response strategy. If you plan a phone call, outline what you plan to say. If your instructor requests, write a letter and copy your instructor.

### 7.13 Customer Bad News: Which Elliptical for Commercial Gym? (Objs. 1–4)

**E-mail**

You are delighted to receive a large order from Rudy Cardenas at 24-Hour Fitness gym. This order includes two Olympic Benches (at $349 each), three Stamina Power Towers (at $249 each), three sets of Premier Dumbbells (at $105 each), and two Titanic 20 Ellipticals (at $1,099 each).

You could ship immediately except for one problem. The Titanic 20 Elliptical, as rated by *Consumer Reports*, is intended for home use, not for gym or club use. More and more fitness lovers are purchasing ellipticals because they have better track records than treadmills and stair climbers for aerobic exercise. The Titanic 20 is definitely effective for personal use. However, this is not the model you would recommend for club use. The Titanic 90 is larger, sturdier, and safer for commercial gyms. It also has extras such as a built-in cooling fan, water bottle holder, and speakers that allow users to hook up to any MP3 player (iPod, etc.) for easy listening. You believe that Mr. Cardenas should order the Titanic 90 Elliptical. It's solidly built, comes with a chest-strap heart-rate monitor, has 20 resistance levels, and features a lifetime warranty on its frame. For gym use, the Titanic 90 is clearly better. The bad news is that it is considerably more expensive at $3,100 per machine.

You get no response when you try to telephone Mr. Cardenas to discuss the problem. Should you ship what you can, or hold the entire order until you learn whether he wants the Titanic 20 or the Titanic 90 Elliptical? Another option is to substitute the Titanic 90 and send only one of them. Another possibility is sending one of the home models and one of the gym models.

**YOUR TASK.** Decide what to do and then send an e-mail to Rudy Cardenas (rcardenas@24hourfitness.com).

### 7.14 Employee Bad News: Rising Tuition? You're on Your Own (Objs. 1–5)

Sabrina Sparks, a hardworking bank teller, has sent an e-mail request asking that the company create a program to reimburse the tuition and book expenses for employees taking college courses. Although some companies have such a program, First Federal Bank has not felt that it could indulge in such an expensive employee perk. Moreover, the CEO is not convinced that companies see any direct benefit from such programs. Employees improve their educational credentials and skills, but what is to keep them from moving that education and those skill sets to other employers? First Federal has over 200 employees. If even a fraction of them started classes, the company could see a huge bill for the cost of tuition and books.

Because the bank is facing stiff competition and its profits are sinking, the expense of such a program makes it out of the question. In addition, it would involve administration—applications, monitoring, and record keeping. It is just too much of a hassle. When employees were hard to hire and retain, companies had to offer employment perks. With a soft economy, however, such inducements are unnecessary.

**YOUR TASK.** As director of Human Resources, send an individual response to Sabrina Sparks. The answer is a definite *no*, but you want to soften the blow and retain the loyalty of this conscientious employee.

## 7.15 Employee Bad News: Only Employees Can Play (Objs. 1–5)

E-mail

As director of Human Resources at Portland Paper Company, you received an unusual request. Several employees asked that their spouses or friends be allowed to participate on Portland intramural sports teams. Although the teams play only once a week during the season, these employees claim that they can't afford more time away from friends and family. Over 100 employees currently participate on the eight coed volleyball, softball, and tennis teams, which are open to company employees only. The teams were designed to improve employee friendships and to give employees a regular occasion to have fun together.

If nonemployees were to participate, you fear that employee interaction would be limited. Although some team members might have fun if spouses or friends were included, you are not so sure all employees would enjoy it. You are not interested in turning intramural sports into "date night." Furthermore, the company would have to create additional teams if many nonemployees joined, and you don't want the administrative or equipment costs of more teams. Adding teams also would require changes to team rosters and game schedules. This could create a problem for some employees. You do understand the need for social time with friends and families, but guests are welcome as spectators at all intramural games. Also, the company already sponsors a family holiday party and an annual company picnic.

**YOUR TASK.** Write an e-mail or hard-copy memo to the staff denying the request of several employees to include nonemployees on Portland's intramural sports teams.

## 7.16 Employee Bad News: Nixing Facebook at Work (Objs. 1–5)

E-mail

Your boss at MarketingMatters, a hip midsized public relations agency, is concerned that the youngest employee generation may be oversharing on Facebook. Two supervisors have complained that they spotted inappropriate photos on Facebook posted by a small group of millennials on the company payroll. This group of twentysomethings is close-knit. Its members maintain friendships outside the office and in cyberspace. They are smart and plugged in, but they seem to have trouble recognizing boundaries of age and authority. They party every weekend, which is code for a lot of drinking, marijuana use, and even salacious escapades—all of which the young workers generously document with smartphone cameras on the spot and occasionally in real time. Sometimes they share snarky comments about their workplace, such as "Rough day at work" or "Talked to the most idiotic client ever!" On top of that, the young people think nothing of friending their colleagues and supervisors. Their "friends" rank in the hundreds; some in the group have exceeded 1,000 friends on Facebook.

MarketingMatters has embraced cutting-edge technology because the management believes that information sharing and collaboration tools can lead to networking opportunities and, if used correctly, to increased productivity. The company maintains a permissive stance toward Internet use, but concern is growing that the young people are headed for trouble. The abuses continue despite the company's comprehensive Internet and social media use policy, which was widely disseminated. Probably the biggest risk MarketingMatters fears is the leaking of confidential information on social networking sites. The managers also complain that the millennials spend too much time on Facebook during office hours. Your boss is becoming impatient. After several meetings, the management decides to disallow Facebook use during work hours and to caution all employees against dangerous breaches of company policy and social media netiquette.

**YOUR TASK.** Draft an e-mail for the signature of your boss, Darcy M. Diamond, Director, Human Resources. Your message should remind all employees about the existing social networking policy and tactfully yet clearly announce the end of Facebook use at the office. The prohibition is effective immediately. Your message should also warn about the pitfalls of oversharing online.

# GRAMMAR/MECHANICS CHECKUP—7

## Commas 2

Review the Grammar/Mechanics Handbook Sections 2.05–2.09. Then study each of the following statements and insert necessary commas. In the space provided, write the number of commas you added; write *0* if no commas were needed. Also record the number of the G/M principle(s) illustrated. When you finish, compare your responses with those provided at the end of the book. If your answers differ, study carefully the principles shown in parentheses.

**1** _____ (2.06a) **EXAMPLE** When U.S. organizations engage in overseas business, they must train their staffs accordingly.

_____ 1. If you are based in New York City and working with a sales office in Australia you will be dealing with a 16-hour time difference.

_____ 2. One international support person works with time zones around the world and she keeps several clocks set to different zones.

_____ 3. Dealing with the unfamiliar is less challenging if you are patient and if you are able to avoid becoming irritated at misunderstandings.

_____ 4. Lourdes Luna who was recently transferred to the parent company in France quickly became fluent in French.

_____ 5. The imaginative promising software company opened its offices April 22 in Paris.

_____ 6. Any sales associate who earns at least 1,000 recognition points this year will be honored with a bonus vacation trip to Tahiti.

_____ 7. James Manning the marketing manager for Chevron's Global Power Generation frequently engages in videoconferences that span time zones.

_____ 8. In a period of less than six weeks Mr. Manning made several trips to the West Coast and to Asia.

_____ 9. When you are working with foreign clients for whom English is a second language you may have to speak slowly and repeat yourself.

_____ 10. To be most successful you must read between the lines and learn to pick up on different cultural vibes.

## Review of Commas 1 and 2

_____ 11. Lourdes' new job involved setting up meetings arranging travel plans and communicating with people who did not speak her language.

_____ 12. After she was hired she was told to report for work on Monday June 2 in Paris.

_____ 13. In the fall we expect to open a new branch in Sunnyvale which is an area of considerable growth.

_____ 14. As we discussed on the telephone the ceremony is scheduled for Thursday March 4 at 3 p.m.

_____ 15. Lourdes had to ask a foreign executive with a thick accent to repeat himself several times and she was uncomfortable in this situation.

# EDITING CHALLENGE—7

To fine-tune your grammar and mechanics skills, in every chapter you will be editing a message. This price-increase message suffers from lapses in proofreading, spelling, grammar, punctuation, and other writing problems that require correction. Study the guidelines in the Grammar/Mechanics Handbook as well as the lists of Confusing Words and Frequently Misspelled Words to sharpen your skills.

**YOUR TASK.** Edit the following message (a) by correcting errors in your textbook or on a photocopy using proofreading marks from Appendix A or (b) by downloading the message from the premium website at www.cengagebrain.com and correcting at your computer. Your instructor may show you a possible solution.

---

**ConnexCable**   The Nation's Largest Cable TV Producer

November 14, 2016

Mrs. Conchetta Stacko
467 East Lavacca
Beaumont, TX 77704

Dear Mr. Stacko:

As the nations leading producer of cable entertainment ConnexCable have been working continuous to bring you the highest-quality programming and cable features. Because many next generation technology features are available at this point in time we are investing in them to make sure of the fact that you have more programming choices and improvments in customer service.

Some of the recent improvements include a main dashboard layed out in a tile format. This will give you direct access to recorded and bookmarked shows as well as access to Facebook, Pandora and additional online media. Other improvements include voice commands on your remote control so that you can search with verbal commands for shows, movies, and Web videos based on title, topic, or actors. Our new system is four times faster then the current model and uses less energy then other cable boxs.

However these improvements, when combined with the rising costs of doing business and escalating programming charges has increased our operating budget. Although we are forced to make price adjustments in selected packages many adjustments are small and the cost of some programs in actuality really declines.

If you receive the Basic Cable package you wont see a price increase. Depending on where you live that package will remain at the price of $23 to $28 per month. If you receive the Digital Economy package you will see a rate decline, depending on you're package this decline will range from eight cents to ten dollars per month.

A complete schedule showing rate adjustments are enclosed. Although the cost of some packages are increasing you are receiving the best in voice, video and data transmission. Its a exceptional entertainment value and we are planning even more innovations for future programming. We appreciate you loyalty and we promise to continue to bring you the best in service and entertainment.

Sincerely,

*Colson Bryant*

Colson Bryant, President

Enclosure

# COMMUNICATION WORKSHOP

## INTERCULTURAL SKILLS

### Presenting Bad News in Other Cultures

To minimize disappointment, Americans generally prefer to present negative messages indirectly. Other cultures may treat bad news differently, as illustrated in the following:

- In Germany business communicators occasionally use buffers but tend to present bad news directly.
- British writers tend to be straightforward with bad news, seeing no reason to soften its announcement.
- In Latin countries the question is not how to organize negative messages but whether to present them at all. It is considered disrespectful and impolite to report bad news to superiors. Therefore, reluctant employees may fail to report accurately any negative situations to their bosses.
- In Thailand the negativism represented by a refusal is completely alien; the word *no* does not exist. In many cultures negative news is offered with such subtlety or in such a positive light that it may be overlooked or misunderstood by literal-minded Americans.
- In many Asian and some Latin cultures, one must look beyond an individual's actual words to understand what is really being communicated. One must consider the communication style, the culture, and especially the context. Consider the following phrases and their possible meanings:

**CAREER APPLICATION.** Interview fellow students or work colleagues who are from other cultures. Collect information by asking the following questions:

- How is negative news handled in your culture?
- How would typical business communicators refuse a request for a business favor (such as a contribution to a charity)?
- How would typical business communicators refuse a customer's claim?
- How would an individual be turned down for a job?

**YOUR TASK.** Report the findings of your interviews in class discussion or in a memo report. In addition, collect samples of foreign business letters. You might ask foreign students, your campus admissions office, or local export/import companies whether they would be willing to share business letters from other countries. Compare letter styles, formats, tone, and writing strategies. How do these elements differ from those in typical North American business letters?

| Phrase | Possible Meaning |
| --- | --- |
| I agree. | I agree with 15 percent of what you say. |
| We might be able to... | Not a chance! |
| We will consider... | *We* will consider, but the real decision maker will not. |
| That is a little too much... | That is outrageous! |
| Yes. | Yes, I'm listening. OR: Yes, you have a good point. OR: Yes, I understand, but I don't necessarily agree. |

Chapter 7: Negative Messages

# ENDNOTES

[1] Photo essay based on Hamilton, W. and Lopez, R. (2014, January 10). Target says data breach is far larger than first estimated. *Los Angeles Times*. Retrieved from http://www.latimes.com/business/la-fi-target-breach-20140111,0,987578.story; Steinhafel, G. (2014, January 13). Important message from Target to our guests. Target corporate site. Retrieved from https://corporate.target.com/_media/TargetCorp/global/PDF/GreggEmailToGuests-1-13-14.pdf

[2] Veltsos, J. (2012). An analysis of data breach notifications as negative news. *Business Communication Quarterly, 75*(2), 198. doi: 10.1177/1080569912443081

[3] Canavor, N. (2012). *Business writing in the digital age*. Thousand Oaks, CA: Sage, p. 62.

[4] O'Neal, S. (2003, November). Quoted in Need to deliver bad news? How & why to tell it like it is. *HR Focus*, p. 3. Retrieved from http://search.ebscohost.com

[5] Council of Better Business Bureaus. (2010, January 5). BBB lists top 10 scams and rip-offs of 2009. Retrieved from http://www.buffalo.bbb.org

[6] The "magic words." (2013). Emily Post Etipedia. Retrieved from http://www.emilypost.com/everyday-manners/important-manners-for-every-day/865-the-qmagic-wordsq; Brodkin, J. (2007, March 19). Corporate apologies don't mean much. *Networkworld, 24*(11), 8. PDF file retrieved from http://search.ebscohost.com

[7] Schweitzer, M. E. (2006, December). Wise negotiators know when to say "I'm sorry." *Negotiation*, 4. Retrieved from http://search.ebscohost.com

[8] Grossman, D. (2013, August 21). Hit or miss'ive: AOL CEO Tim Armstrong's apology to employees is pathetic. Retrieved from http://www.yourthoughtpartner.com/blog/bid/69882/AOL-CEO-Tim-Armstrong-s-Apology-to-Employees-is-Pathetic; see also Post, P. (2013, August 15). AOL CEO's impulsive action leads to public apology. Job Doc. Retrieved from http://www.boston.com/jobs/news/jobdoc/2013/08/how_not_to_fire_a_employee.html

[9] Neeleman, D. (2007). An apology from David Neeleman. Retrieved from http://jetblue-happyjetting.blogspot.com/2009/12/apology-from-david-neeleman.html

[10] Letters to Lands' End. (1991, February). 1991 Lands' End catalog. Dodgeville, WI: Lands' End, p. 100.

[11] Zimmerman, E. (2012, April 7). Accentuating the positive to angry customers. *The New York Times*. Retrieved from http://www.nytimes.com; Mowatt, J. (2002, February). Breaking bad news to customers. *Agency Sales*, p. 30; and Dorn, E. M. (1999, March). Case method instruction in the business writing classroom. *Business Communication Quarterly, 62*(1), 51–52.

[12] Photo essay based on Kim, S. (2013, December 21). Underwear maker Hanes wages battle with Canadian hummus maker. ABC News. Retrieved from http://abcnews.go.com/Business/hanes-hummus-lawyer-pens-biting-rebuttal-response-hanes/story?id=21291945; CBC News. (December 18, 2013). Saskatoon hummus maker gets a wedgie from Hanes underwear. CBC News. Retrieved from http://www.cbc.ca/news/canada/saskatoon/saskatoon-hummus-maker-gets-a-wedgie-from-hanes-underwear-1.2469015

[13] Forbes, M. (1999). How to write a business letter. In K. Harty (Ed.), *Strategies for business and technical writing*. Boston: Allyn and Bacon, p. 108.

[14] Griffin Padgett, D. R., Cheng, S. S., & Parekh, V. (2013). The quest for transparency and accountability: Communicating responsibly to stakeholders in crises. *Asian Social Science, 9*(9). doi:10.5539/ass.v9n9p31; Browning, M. (2003, November 24). Work dilemma: Delivering bad news a good way. *Government Computer News*, p. 41; and Mowatt, J. (2002, February). Breaking bad news to customers. *Agency Sales*, p. 30.

[15] Engels, J. (2007, July). Delivering difficult messages. *Journal of Accountancy, 204*(1), 50–52. Retrieved from http://search.ebscohost.com; see also Lewis, B. (1999, September 13). To be an effective leader, you need to perfect the art of delivering bad news. *InfoWorld*, p. 124. Retrieved from http://books.google.com

[16] Bies, R. J. (2013, January). The delivery of bad news in organizations. *Journal of Management, 39*(1), 136–162. doi: 10.1177/0149206312461053

[17] Based on Lee, L. (2007, June 11). A smoothie you can chew on. *BusinessWeek*, p. 64.

# ACKNOWLEDGMENTS

**p. 193** Office Insider based on Engels, J. (2007, July). Delivering difficult messages. *Journal of Accountancy, 204*(1), 50. Retrieved from http://search.ebscohost.com

**p. 198** Office Insider based on Canavor, N. (2011, October 20). *Business writing in the digital age*. Thousand Oaks, CA: Sage, p. 63.

**p. 199** Office Insider based on Now go out and lead! (2007, January 8). *Bloomberg Businessweek*. Retrieved from http://www.businessweek.com/magazine/content/07_02/b4016083.htm

**p. 202** Office Insider based on Zimmerman, E. (2012, April 7). Accentuating the positive to angry customers. *The New York Times*. Retrieved from http://nytimes.com

**p. 204** Office Insider based on Mishory, J. (2004, June). Don't shoot the messenger: How to deliver bad news and still keep customers satisfied. *Sales & Marketing Management, 156*(6), 18. Retrieved from http://search.ebscohost.com

**p. 206** Office Insider based on Robertson, K. (2004, April). Saying no: How to deliver bad news to a customer. KR Consulting. Retrieved from http://www.krconsulting.com/saying-no-how-to-deliver-bad-news-to-a-customer

**p. 209** Office Insider based on Weeks, L. (2008, December 8). Read the blog: You're fired. National Public Radio. Retrieved from http://www.npr.org/templates/story/story.php?storyId=97945811

# CHAPTER 8

# Persuasive Messages

## OBJECTIVES
After studying this chapter, you should be able to

**8-1** Explain digital-age persuasion and identify time-proven persuasive techniques.

**8-2** Craft persuasive messages that request actions.

**8-3** Write compelling claims and deliver successful complaints.

**8-4** Understand interpersonal persuasion at work, and compose persuasive messages within organizations.

**8-5** Create effective and ethical direct-mail and e-mail sales messages employing the AIDA strategy: gaining attention, building interest, developing desire, and motivating action.

## 8-1 Understanding Persuasion in the Digital Age

In the digital age, businesses have moved toward leaner corporate hierarchies, simultaneously relying on teams, dismantling division walls, and blurring the lines of authority. Persuasive skills are becoming ever more important at work as teams and managers abandon the traditional command structure and focus instead on *influencing* others.[1] However, getting others to do what we want isn't easy. Persuasion is needed when we are making more than routine demands and facing skeptical audiences.

Experts say that the average American adult endures between 300 and 1,500 ads and other persuasive appeals a day.[2] As citizens and consumers, we need to be alert to persuasive practices and how they influence behavior. Being informed is our best defense. On the other hand, social media networks have put power into the hands of many. Persuasion guru B. J. Fogg points out that social media enable individuals or groups to reach virtually limitless audiences and practice "mass interpersonal persuasion."[3]

You have already studied techniques for writing routine request messages that require minimal persuasion. This chapter focuses on messages that require deliberate and skilled persuasion in the workplace. It also addresses selling, both offline and online.

### 8-1a How Has Persuasion Changed in the Digital Age?

The preoccupation with persuasion is not new. From the days of Aristotle in ancient Greece and Niccolò Machiavelli in Renaissance Italy, philosophers, politicians, and

226   Chapter 8: Persuasive Messages

businesspeople have longed to understand the art of influencing others. However, persuasion in the twenty-first century is different from persuasion in previous historic periods in distinct ways.[4] The most striking developments, summarized in this section, are less than three decades old.

**The Volume and Reach of Persuasive Messages Have Exploded.** TV, radio, the Internet, and mobile phones blast myriad messages to the far corners of the earth. A Pew Research study shows that American popular culture continues to soar abroad. Two thirds of people surveyed in 16 countries said they liked American music, films, and television—up 6 percent from five years earlier.[5]

**Persuasive Messages Spread at Warp Speed.** Popular TV shows such as *The X Factor* and their corporate sponsors use social media to engage the fans whose more than half a million social media comments instantly influence the contestants' dance routines, songs, and wardrobes. *American Idol* now clocks one million posts during a single show,[6] and citizen reporters deliver instant updates from disaster areas on Twitter and other social media networks.

**Organizations of All Stripes Are in the Persuasion Business.** Companies, ad agencies, PR firms, social activists, lobbyists, marketers, and more, spew persuasive messages. Although outspent by corporations that can sink millions into image campaigns, activists use social networks to rally their followers.

**Persuasive Techniques Are Subtler and More Misleading.** Instead of a blunt, pushy hard-sell approach, persuaders play on emotions by using flattery, empathy, nonverbal cues, and likability appeals. They are selling images and lifestyles, not products.[7] In this age of spin, the news media are increasingly infiltrated by partisan interests and spread messages masquerading as news.

**Persuasion Is More Complex and Impersonal.** American consumers are more diverse and don't necessarily think alike. To reach them, marketers carefully study various target groups and customize their appeals. Technology has increased the potential for distortion. People can "mash up" content, give it meanings the original source never intended, and blast it into the world in seconds.

## OFFICE INSIDER

*"Persuasion is your golden ticket to promotion. Master communicators feel in control of challenging situations because they understand the art of persuasion and they know how to recognize and use persuasive strategies."*

—Kurt Mortensen, author of *Maximum Influence* and an expert on persuasion

**LEARNING OBJECTIVE 1**
Explain digital-age persuasion and identify time-proven persuasive techniques.

## Workplace in Focus

At Our World Neighborhood Charter School in Queens, a third-grader who learned to write a persuasive letter in class decided to try his new skill to change the school's no-Pokémon policy. In a handwritten message to his teacher, the boy opened, "A lot of people in our class like Pokémon . . . I think we can use it educationally." Next, after explaining that the fantasy-card trading game teaches subtraction, addition, and multiplication, he made a request: "I was thinking we could have some friendly and educational competition as a center for math." The boy's letter closed, "If you can't, you are still a great teacher." The school lifted the ban and approved the game for math and recess. What made the student's message so persuasive?[8]

Chapter 8: Persuasive Messages

## Figure 8.1 Effective Persuasion Techniques

**Establish credibility**
- Show that you are truthful, experienced, and knowledgeable.
- Use others' expert opinions and research to support your position.

**Make a reasonable, specific request**
- Make your request realistic, doable, and attainable.
- Be clear about your objective. Vague requests are less effective.

**Tie facts to benefits**
- Line up plausible support such as statistics, reasons, and analogies.
- Convert the supporting facts into specific audience benefits.

**Recognize the power of loss**
- Show what others stand to lose if they don't agree.
- Know that people dread losing something they already possess.

**Expect and overcome resistance**
- Anticipate opposition from conflicting beliefs, values, and attitudes.
- Be prepared to counter with well-reasoned arguments and facts.

**Share solutions and compromise**
- Be flexible and aim for a solution that is acceptable to all parties.
- Listen to people and incorporate their input to create buy-in.

---

You probably recognize how important it is not only to become a skilled persuader, but also to identify devious messages and manipulation attempts directed at you. The delivery channels may have changed, but the principles of effective, time-tried persuasion outlined in Figure 8.1 still apply today.

When you want your ideas to prevail, start thinking about how to present them. Listeners and readers will be more inclined to accept what you are offering if you focus on important strategies, outlined in Figure 8.1 and further discussed throughout this chapter.

## 8-2 Planning and Writing Persuasive Requests

Direct claim messages, such as those you wrote in Chapter 6, are straightforward and direct. Persuasive requests, on the other hand, are generally more effective when they are indirect. Reasons and explanations should precede the main idea. To overcome possible resistance, the writer lays a logical foundation before delivering the request. A writing plan for persuasive requests requires deliberate development.

### WRITING PLAN FOR PERSUASIVE REQUESTS

- **Opening:** Capture the reader's attention and interest. Describe a problem, make an unexpected statement, suggest reader benefits, offer praise or compliments, or ask a stimulating question.
- **Body:** Build interest. Explain logically and concisely the purpose of the request. Prove its merit. Use facts, statistics, expert opinion, examples, and specific details. Focus on the reader's direct and indirect benefits. Reduce resistance. Elicit a desire to comply. Anticipate objections, offer counterarguments, establish credibility, demonstrate competence, and show the value of your proposal.
- **Closing:** Motivate action. Ask for a particular action. Make the action easy to take. Show courtesy, respect, and gratitude.

In this chapter you will learn to apply the preceding writing plan to messages that (a) request actions, (b) make claims and request adjustments that may meet with opposition, (c) persuade subordinates and supervisors, and (d) create effective direct-mail and e-mail sales messages.

**LEARNING OBJECTIVE 2**
Craft persuasive messages that request actions.

### 8-2a Crafting an Effective Persuasive Message

Convincing someone to change a belief or to perform an action when that person is reluctant requires planning and skill—and sometimes a little luck. A written request may require more preparation than a face-to-face request, but it can be more effective. For example, you may need to ask a businessperson to make a presentation to your club, or a company to encourage its employees to participate in a charity drive. Such messages require skill in persuasion.

Figure 8.2 shows a persuasive request from Sophia Tellez. Her research firm seeks to persuade other companies to complete a questionnaire revealing salary data. In most organizations, salary information is strictly confidential. What can Sophia do to convince strangers to part with such private information?

**Analyzing the First Draft.** The hurriedly written first version of the request in Figure 8.2 suffers from many faults. It fails to pique the interest of the reader in the opening. It also provides an easy excuse for Mr. Mosher to refuse (*filling out surveys can be tedious*). In the body, Mr. Mosher doesn't receive any incentive to accept the request. The writing is self-serving and offers few specifics. In addition, the draft does not anticipate objections and fails to suggest counterarguments. Last, the closing does not motivate action by providing a deadline or a final benefit.

**Revising the First Draft.** In the revised version shown in Figure 8.2, to gain attention, Sophia poses two short questions that spotlight the need for salary information. To build interest and establish trust, she states that Hunter Research has been collecting business data for a quarter century and has received awards. She ties her reasonable request to audience benefits.

## 8-3 Writing Effective Persuasive Claims and Complaints

As their name suggests, complaints deliver bad news. Some complaint messages just vent anger. However, if the goal is to change something (and why bother to write except to motivate change?), then persuasion is necessary. Persuasive claim and complaint messages may involve damaged products, mistaken billing, inaccurate shipments, warranty problems, limited return policies, insurance snafus, faulty merchandise, and so on.

An effective claim message makes a reasonable and valid request, presents a logical case with clear facts, and has a moderate tone. Anger and emotion are not effective persuaders.

### 8-3a Developing a Claim Message Logically

Strive for logical development in a claim message. You might open with sincere praise, an objective statement of the problem, a point of agreement, or a quick review of what you have done to resolve the problem. Then you can explain precisely what happened or why your claim is legitimate. Don't provide a blow-by-blow chronology of details; just hit the highlights. Be sure to enclose copies of relevant invoices, shipping orders, warranties, and payments. Close with a clear statement of what you want done: a refund, replacement, credit to your account, or other action. Be sure to think through the possibilities and make your request reasonable.

### 8-3b Adopting a Moderate Tone

The tone of your message is important. Don't suggest that the receiver intentionally deceived you or intentionally created the problem. Rather, appeal to the receiver's sense of responsibility and pride in the company's good name. Calmly express your disappointment in view of your high expectations of the product and of the company. Communicating your feelings without rancor is often the strongest appeal.

Charlotte Piroska's e-mail, shown in Figure 8.3, follows the persuasive strategy as she seeks credit for two VoIP (voice over Internet protocol) systems. Actually, she

---

**OFFICE INSIDER**

*"Complaining—when done well—can be a positive experience that benefits the company and person receiving the complaint, and which resolves a problem encountered by the person who is complaining."*

—David M. Rowell, publisher of *The Travel Insider*

**LEARNING OBJECTIVE 3**

Write compelling claims and deliver successful complaints.

Figure 8.2 Persuasive Request

**DRAFT**

Dear Mr. Mosher:

We need your help in collecting salary data for today's workers. Hunter Research has been collecting business data for 25 years, and we have received awards for accuracy. We know that filling out surveys can be tedious, but the results are very useful.
— Fails to pique interest; provides easy excuse

Companies trust the survey data we compile. We have been in this business long enough to know how important comparative salary data are to most organizations. Filling out our questionnaire will not take very long. If you wish, we could send you some of the results showing not only salaries, but also perks and other benefits.
— Does not promote direct and indirect benefits

Please fill out the enclosed questionnaire and call us if you have any questions. Thank you for your cooperation.
— Does not anticipate objections; fails to motivate action

**REVISION**

### HUNTER RESEARCH
599 Delaware Avenue, Buffalo, NY 14850  www.hunterresearch.com
PH 716.878.2300
FAX 716.878.4359

May 18, 2016

Mr. Brian H. Mosher
Walker Wealth Management
420 South Cayuga Street, Suite 250
Ithaca, NY 14850

Dear Mr. Mosher:

*Poses two short questions related to the reader* —
Have you ever added a unique job title but had no idea what compensation the position demanded? Has your company ever lost a valued employee to another organization that offered 20 percent more in salary for the same position?
— Gains attention

*Presents reader benefit tied to request explanation; establishes credibility* —
To remain competitive in hiring and to retain qualified workers, companies rely on survey data showing current salaries. Hunter Research has been collecting business data for a quarter century and has been honored by the American Management Association for its accurate data. We need your help in collecting salary data for today's workers. Information from the enclosed questionnaire will supply companies like yours with such data.
— Builds interest

*Anticipates and counters resistance to confidentiality and time/effort objections* —
Your information, of course, will be treated confidentially. The questionnaire takes but a few moments to complete, and it can provide substantial dividends for professional organizations just like yours that need comparative salary data.
— Elicits desire and reduces resistance

*Offers free salary data as a direct benefit* —
To show our gratitude for your participation, we will send you free comprehensive salary surveys for your industry and your metropolitan area. Not only will you find basic salaries, but you will also learn about bonus and incentive plans, special pay differentials, expense reimbursements, and perquisites such as a company car and credit card.

*Provides deadline and a final benefit to prompt action* —
Comparative salary data are impossible to provide without the support of professionals like you. Please complete the questionnaire and return it in the prepaid envelope before June 1, our spring deadline. Participating in this survey means that you will no longer be in the dark about how much your employees earn compared with others in your industry.
— Appeals to professionalism, an indirect benefit
— Motivates action

Sincerely yours,

HUNTER RESEARCH

*Sophia Tellez*

Sophia Tellez
Director, Survey Research

Enclosures

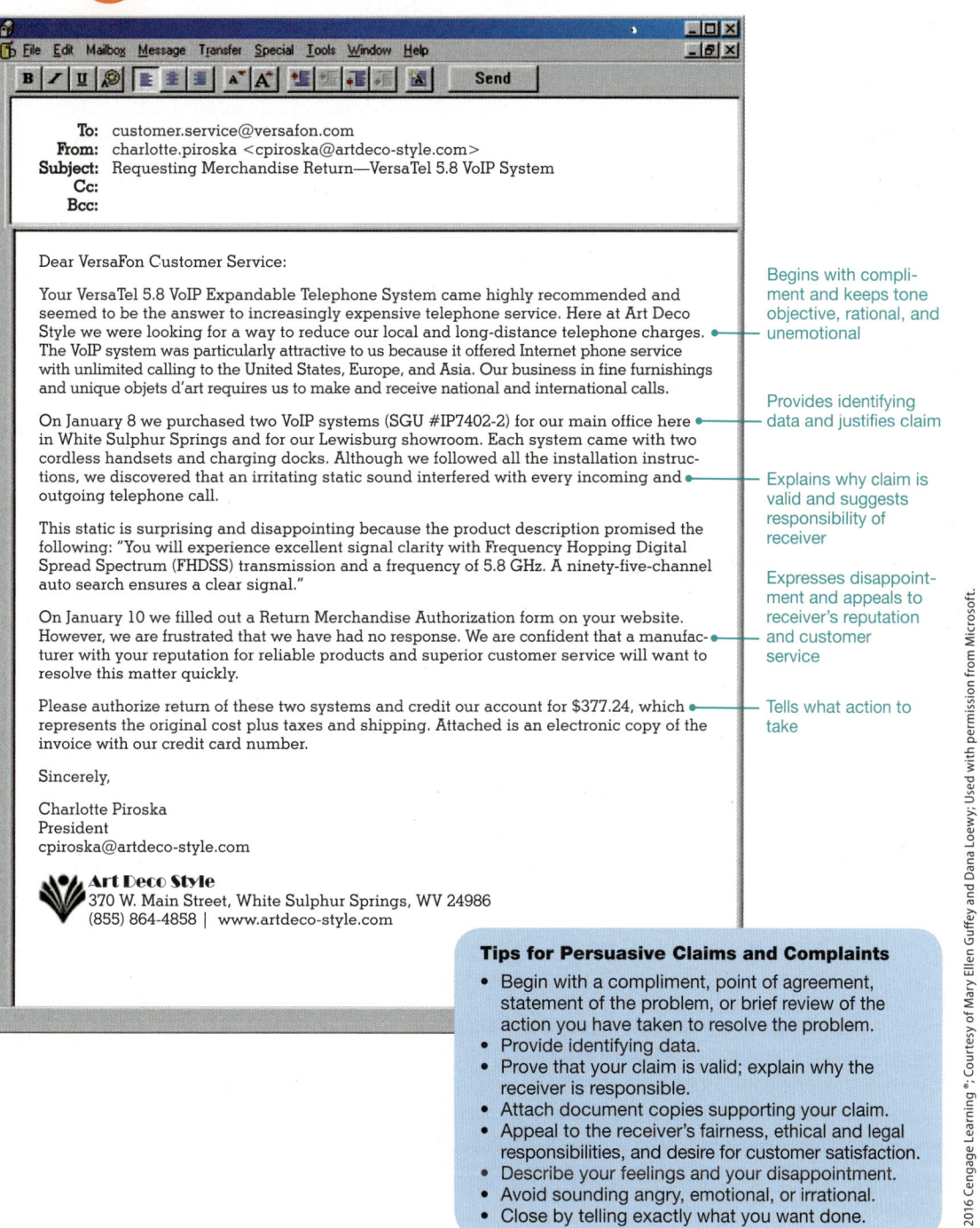

## Figure 8.3 Persuasive Claim (Complaint) E-Mail

**To:** customer.service@versafon.com
**From:** charlotte.piroska <cpiroska@artdeco-style.com>
**Subject:** Requesting Merchandise Return—VersaTel 5.8 VoIP System
**Cc:**
**Bcc:**

Dear VersaFon Customer Service:

Your VersaTel 5.8 VoIP Expandable Telephone System came highly recommended and seemed to be the answer to increasingly expensive telephone service. Here at Art Deco Style we were looking for a way to reduce our local and long-distance telephone charges. The VoIP system was particularly attractive to us because it offered Internet phone service with unlimited calling to the United States, Europe, and Asia. Our business in fine furnishings and unique objets d'art requires us to make and receive national and international calls. —— *Begins with compliment and keeps tone objective, rational, and unemotional*

On January 8 we purchased two VoIP systems (SGU #IP7402-2) for our main office here in White Sulphur Springs and for our Lewisburg showroom. Each system came with two cordless handsets and charging docks. Although we followed all the installation instructions, we discovered that an irritating static sound interfered with every incoming and outgoing telephone call. —— *Provides identifying data and justifies claim* / *Explains why claim is valid and suggests responsibility of receiver*

This static is surprising and disappointing because the product description promised the following: "You will experience excellent signal clarity with Frequency Hopping Digital Spread Spectrum (FHDSS) transmission and a frequency of 5.8 GHz. A ninety-five-channel auto search ensures a clear signal."

On January 10 we filled out a Return Merchandise Authorization form on your website. However, we are frustrated that we have had no response. We are confident that a manufacturer with your reputation for reliable products and superior customer service will want to resolve this matter quickly. —— *Expresses disappointment and appeals to receiver's reputation and customer service*

Please authorize return of these two systems and credit our account for $377.24, which represents the original cost plus taxes and shipping. Attached is an electronic copy of the invoice with our credit card number. —— *Tells what action to take*

Sincerely,

Charlotte Piroska
President
cpiroska@artdeco-style.com

**Art Deco Style**
370 W. Main Street, White Sulphur Springs, WV 24986
(855) 864-4858 | www.artdeco-style.com

---

**Tips for Persuasive Claims and Complaints**
- Begin with a compliment, point of agreement, statement of the problem, or brief review of the action you have taken to resolve the problem.
- Provide identifying data.
- Prove that your claim is valid; explain why the receiver is responsible.
- Attach document copies supporting your claim.
- Appeal to the receiver's fairness, ethical and legal responsibilities, and desire for customer satisfaction.
- Describe your feelings and your disappointment.
- Avoid sounding angry, emotional, or irrational.
- Close by telling exactly what you want done.

© 2016 Cengage Learning®; Courtesy of Mary Ellen Guffey and Dana Loewy; Used with permission from Microsoft.

---

was quite upset because her company was counting on these new Internet systems to reduce its phone bills. Instead, the handsets produced so much static that incoming and outgoing calls were all but impossible to hear.

However, Charlotte resolved to use a moderate tone in writing her claim/complaint e-mail because she knew that a calm, unemotional tone would be more effective than an angry one. She opted for a positive opening, a well-documented message, and a request for specific action in the closing.

## OFFICE INSIDER

*"In a networked organization, leaders have to use influence and powers of persuasion, which is much more complex and much more challenging than giving orders. Young leaders have the ability to operate in this new environment. They recognize that they're not working on the authoritarian model."*

—Phil Carroll, former chairman and chief executive officer at Fluor Corporation

**LEARNING OBJECTIVE 4**

Understand interpersonal persuasion at work, and compose persuasive messages within organizations.

## 8-4 Crafting Persuasive Messages in Digital-Age Organizations

The lines of authority are blurry in today's information-age workplaces, and the roles of executives are changing. Technology has empowered rank-and-file employees who can turn to their companies' intranets and don't need their managers to be information providers—formerly a crucial managerial role.

This huge shift in authority is affecting both the strategies for creating and the tone of workplace persuasive messages. You may still want to be indirect if you hope to persuade your boss to do something he or she will be reluctant to do; however, your boss, in turn, will be less likely to rely on the power of position and just issue commands. Rather, today's executives increasingly bank on persuasion to achieve buy-in from subordinates.[9]

This section focuses on messages flowing downward and upward within organizations. Horizontal messages exchanged among coworkers resemble the persuasive requests discussed earlier.

### 8-4a Persuading Employees: Messages Flowing Downward

Employees have traditionally expected to be directed in how to perform their jobs; therefore, instructions or directives moving downward from superiors to subordinates usually required little persuasion. Messages such as information about procedures, equipment, or customer service still use the direct strategy, with the purpose immediately stated.

However, employees are sometimes asked to volunteer for projects. For example, some organizations encourage employees to join programs to stop smoking, lose weight, or start exercising. Organizations may ask employees to participate in capacities outside their work roles—such as spending their free time volunteering for charity projects. In such cases, the writing plan for persuasive requests introduced earlier provides a helpful structure.

**Paying Attention to Tone.** Because many executives today rely on buy-in instead of exercising raw power,[10] messages flowing downward require attention to tone. Warm words and a conversational tone convey a caring attitude. Persuasive requests coming from a trusted superior are more likely to be accepted than requests from a dictatorial executive who relies on threats and punishments to secure compliance.

**Presenting Honest, Accurate Evidence.** The goal is not to manipulate employees or to seduce them with trickery. Rather, the goal is to present a strong but honest argument, emphasizing points that are important to the receiver or the organization. In business, honesty is not just the best policy—it's the only policy. People see right through puffery and misrepresentation. For this reason, the indirect strategy is effective only when supported by accurate, honest evidence.

### 8-4b Persuading the Boss: Messages Flowing Upward

Convincing management to adopt a procedure or invest in a product or new equipment requires skillful communication. Managers are just as resistant to change as others are. Providing facts, figures, and evidence is critical when submitting a recommendation to your boss. When selling an idea to management, strive to make a strong dollars-and-cents case.[11] A request that emphasizes how the proposal saves money or benefits the business is more persuasive than one that simply announces a good deal or tells how a plan works.

Persuasive messages traveling upward require a special sensitivity to tone. When asking supervisors to change views or take action, use words such as *suggest* and *recommend* rather than *you must* or *we should*. Avoid sounding pushy or argumentative. Strive for a conversational, yet professional, tone that conveys warmth, competence, and confidence.

When Marketing Manager Michael Cooper wanted his boss to authorize the purchase of a multifunction color laser copier, he knew he had to be persuasive. His memo, shown in Figure 8.4, illustrates an effective approach.

Notice that Michael's memo isn't short. A successful persuasive message typically takes more space than a direct message because proving a case requires evidence. In the end, Michael chose to send his memo as an e-mail attachment accompanied by a polite, short e-mail message because he wanted to keep the document format in Microsoft Word intact. He also felt that the message was too long to paste into his e-mail program. The subject line announces the purpose of the message without disclosing the actual request.

The strength of the persuasive document in Figure 8.4 is in the clear presentation of comparison figures showing how much money the company can save by purchasing a remanufactured copier.

## 8-5 Creating Effective Sales Messages in Print and Online

The best sales messages, whether delivered by postal mail or by e-mail, have much in common. Marketing professionals analyze and perfect every aspect of a sales message to encourage consumers to read and act on the message. This section presents techniques developed by experts for drafting effective sales messages, in print and online.

Sales letters are usually part of multichannel marketing campaigns. These letters are a powerful means to make sales, generate leads, boost retail traffic, solicit donations, and direct consumers to websites. Direct mail is a great channel for personalized, tangible, three-dimensional messages that are less invasive than telephone solicitations

### OFFICE INSIDER

"When you create the impression that you are a person of honesty and integrity, you will have a considerable advantage over someone who is perceived otherwise."

—Paul M. Sandler, litigation lawyer, writing on legal ethos

**LEARNING OBJECTIVE 5**
Create effective and ethical direct-mail and e-mail sales messages employing the AIDA strategy: gaining attention, building interest, developing desire, and motivating action.

## Workplace in Focus

As part of a recent marketing campaign, Taco Bell sent handwritten fan notes and jewelry to popular models in hopes of generating buzz. The highly personal letters, which marketers sent to Miss California Leah Cecil and swimsuit model Chrissy Teigen, among others, gushed statements like "You're cool, a great friend, and you like Taco Bell" and "Following you on Twitter was the best decision we ever made." To prove their affection, the marketers enclosed two rings that, worn together on the hand, spell Taco Bell. "We like you, so we wanted to give you this custom Taco Bell ring," explained one of the notes. The models were seen flashing their new friendship rings on Instagram and Twitter. How can communicators develop marketing messages that get attention?[12]

Chapter 8: Persuasive Messages

# Figure 8.4 Persuasive Message Flowing Upward

---

**To:** Gary Greer <gary.greer@smartmachinetools.com>
**From:** Michael Cooper <michael.cooper@smartmachinetools.com>
**Subject:** Saving Time and Money on Copying and Printing
**Cc:**
**Attached:** refurbished color copiers.docx (10 KB)

---

Gary,

Attached is a brief document that details our potential savings from purchasing a refurbished color laser copier. After doing some research, I discovered that these sophisticated machines aren't as expensive as one might think.

Please look at my calculations and let me know what you suggest that we to do improve our in-house production of print matter and reduce both time and cost for external copying.

Mike

**Michael Cooper**
*Marketing Assistant* * Smart Machine Tools, Inc.
800 S. Santa Fe Blvd. * City of Industry, CA 91715
213.680.3000 office / 213.680.3229 fax
michael.cooper@smartmachinetools.com

*Serves as cover e-mail to introduce attached memo in MS Word*
*Opens with catchy subject line*
*Does not reveal recommendation but leaves request for action to the attached memo*
*Provides an electronic signature with contact information*

---

## MEMORANDUM

**Date:** April 8, 2016
**To:** Gary Greer, Vice President
**From:** Michael Cooper, Marketing
**Subject:** Saving Time and Money on Copying

We are losing money on our current copy services and wasting the time of employees as well. Because our aging Canon copier is in use constantly and can't handle our growing printing volume, we find it increasingly necessary to send major jobs out to Copy Quick. Moreover, whenever we need color copies, we can't handle the work ourselves. Just take a look at how much we spend each month for outside copy service:

**Copy Costs: Outside Service**
| | |
|---|---:|
| 10,000 B&W copies/month made at Copy Quick | $ 700.00 |
| 1,000 color copies/month, $0.25 per copy (avg.) | 250.00 |
| Salary costs for assistants to make 32 trips | 480.00 |
| Total | $1,430.00 |

To save time and money, I have been considering alternatives. Large-capacity color laser copiers with multiple features (copy, e-mail, fax, LAN fax, print, scan) are expensive. However, reconditioned copiers with all the features we need are available at attractive prices. From Copy City we can get a fully remanufactured Xerox copier that is guaranteed and provides further savings because solid-color ink sticks cost a fraction of laser toner cartridges. We could copy and print in color for roughly the same as black and white. After we make an initial payment of $300, our monthly costs would look like this:

**Copy Costs: Remanufactured Copier:**
| | |
|---|---:|
| Paper supplies for 11,000 copies | $160.00 |
| Ink sticks and copy supplies | 100.00 |
| Labor of assistants to make copies | 150.00 |
| Monthly financing charge for copier (purchase price of $3,105 – $300 amortized at 10% with 36 payments) | 93.74 |
| Total | $503.74 |

As you can see, a remanufactured Xerox 8860MFP copier saves us more than $900 per month. For a limited time Copy City is offering a free 15-day trial offer, a free copier stand (a $250 value), free starter supplies, and free delivery and installation. We have office space available, and my staff is eager to add a second machine.

Please call me at Ext. 630 if you have questions. This copier is such a good opportunity that I have prepared a purchase requisition authorizing the agreement with Copy City. With your approval before May 1, we could have our machine by May 10 and start saving time and more than $900 every month. Fast action will also help us take advantage of Copy City's free start-up incentives.

*Summarizes problem*
*Uses headings and columns for easy comprehension*
*Provides more benefits*
*Makes it easy to grant approval*
*Describes topic without revealing request*
*Proves credibility of request with facts and figures*
*Highlights most important benefit*
*Counters possible resistance*
*Repeats main benefit with motivation to act quickly*

234 Chapter 8: Persuasive Messages

and less reviled than unsolicited e-mail. A recent study shows that tangible mail appears to have a greater emotional impact than virtual mail. MRI scans suggest that physical materials "leave a deeper footprint in the brain."[13] Figure 8.5 juxtaposes the most relevant features of traditional direct-mail and online sales messages.

### 8-5a Betting on Highly Targeted, Relevant Direct Mail

Although not as flashy as social media campaigns, direct mail still works as long as it is personalized and relevant.[14] Experts know that most recipients do look at their direct mail and respond to it; in fact, 79 percent of consumers act on direct mail immediately, whereas only 45 percent deal with e-mail right away.[15] Despite ever-increasing spending on digital and mobile advertising, more money still goes to traditional direct-mail marketing ($93.6 billion) than to online marketing ($62 billion).[16] The infographic in Figure 8.6 displays information about channel choice and consumer perceptions of the most common marketing media.

Professionals who specialize in traditional direct-mail services have made it a science. They analyze a market, develop an effective mailing list, study the product, prepare a sophisticated campaign aimed at a target audience, and motivate the reader to act. You have probably received many direct-mail packages, often called junk mail. Chances are they will keep coming, but they will be a lot more relevant to you and your spending habits.

### 8-5b Considering the Value of Sales Letters

We are most concerned here with the sales letter: its strategy, organization, and evidence. Because sales letters are usually written by specialists, you may never write one on the job. Why learn how to write a sales letter? Learning the techniques of sales writing will help you be more successful in any communication that requires persuasion and promotion. What's more, you will recognize sales strategies directed at you, which will make you a more perceptive consumer of ideas, products, and services.

> **OFFICE INSIDER**
>
> "Direct mail is perhaps one of the most powerful marketing media in use today. Few other marketing tools can deliver your message with exact precision at such a low cost. The amount of mail in your mailbox every day attests to the effectiveness of this medium (If it didn't work, your mailbox would be empty!)."
>
> —David Frey, president of Marketing Best Practices, Inc., Houston, Texas

Figure 8.5 Persuasive Sales Techniques in the Digital Age

## Characteristics of Traditional Versus Online Sales Messages

| Traditional Direct Mail (Sales Letter) | E-Commerce (E-Mail, Social Media Messages) |
|---|---|
| Creating static content (hard copy) | Creating dynamic digital content |
| Anticipating a single response (inquiry, sale) | Creating engagement instead of selling overtly |
| Resorting to "spray-and-pray" approach | Building one-to-one relationships and communities around brands |
| Single communication channel | Multiple communication channels |
| Limited response | Potentially unlimited responses |
| Monologue | Dialogue, potential for mass diffusion |
| Private response | Public, shared response |
| Asynchronous (delayed) response | Instant, real-time response possible |
| Passive | Interactive, participatory |
| Promoter-generated content | User-generated content |
| The needs of target groups must be anticipated and met in advance. | Consumers expect that brands understand their unique needs and deliver. |
| **Direct mail is preferred for information about insurance, financial services, and health care; excellent channel for offline customers.** | **Savvy brands respond nimbly to customer participation; today's sophisticated consumers dislike "hard sell."** |

Chapter 8: Persuasive Messages

## Figure 8.6 Channel Choice: Direct Mail and Social Media

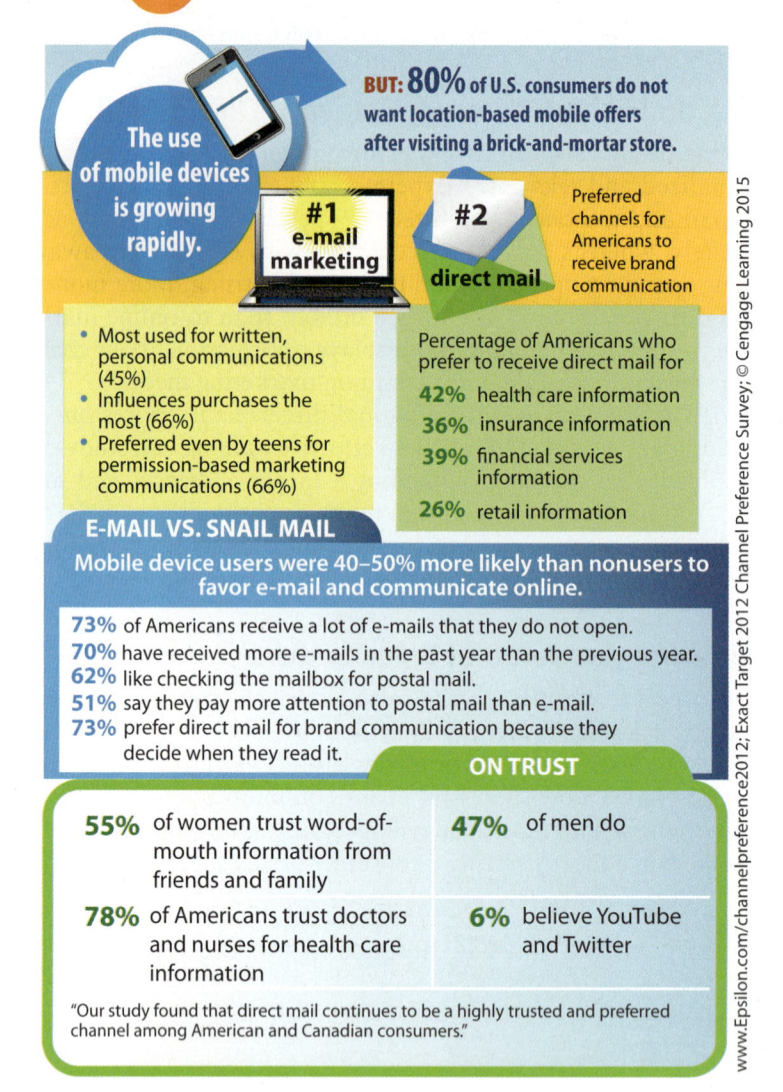

**The use of mobile devices is growing rapidly.**

**BUT:** 80% of U.S. consumers do not want location-based mobile offers after visiting a brick-and-mortar store.

**#1 e-mail marketing** and **#2 direct mail** — Preferred channels for Americans to receive brand communication

- Most used for written, personal communications (45%)
- Influences purchases the most (66%)
- Preferred even by teens for permission-based marketing communications (66%)

Percentage of Americans who prefer to receive direct mail for
- 42% health care information
- 36% insurance information
- 39% financial services information
- 26% retail information

### E-MAIL VS. SNAIL MAIL

Mobile device users were 40–50% more likely than nonusers to favor e-mail and communicate online.

- **73%** of Americans receive a lot of e-mails that they do not open.
- **70%** have received more e-mails in the past year than the previous year.
- **62%** like checking the mailbox for postal mail.
- **51%** say they pay more attention to postal mail than e-mail.
- **73%** prefer direct mail for brand communication because they decide when they read it.

### ON TRUST

- **55%** of women trust word-of-mouth information from friends and family
- **47%** of men do
- **78%** of Americans trust doctors and nurses for health care information
- **6%** believe YouTube and Twitter

"Our study found that direct mail continues to be a highly trusted and preferred channel among American and Canadian consumers."

www.Epsilon.com/channelpreference2012; ExactTarget 2012 Channel Preference Survey; © Cengage Learning 2015

---

Your primary goal in writing a sales message is to get someone to devote a few moments of attention to it. You may be promoting a product, a service, an idea, or yourself. In each case the most effective messages follow the AIDA strategy, illustrated in Figure 8.7: (a) gain attention, (b) build interest, (c) elicit desire and reduce resistance, and (d) motivate action. This is the same recipe we studied earlier in the writing plan for persuasive requests, but the ingredients are slightly different.

### WRITING PLAN FOR SALES MESSAGES: AIDA.

- **Opening:** Gain *attention*. Offer something valuable; promise a benefit to the reader; ask a question; or provide a quotation, fact, product feature, testimonial, startling statement, or personalized action setting.
- **Body:** Build *interest*. Describe central selling points and make rational and emotional appeals. Elicit *desire* in the reader and reduce resistance. Use testimonials, money-back guarantees, free samples, or performance tests.
- **Closing:** Motivate *action*. Offer a gift, promise an incentive, limit the offer, set a deadline, or guarantee satisfaction.

Figure 8.7 The AIDA Strategy for Sales Messages

| | STRATEGY | CONTENT | SECTION |
|---|---|---|---|
| **A** | Attention | Captures attention, creates awareness, makes a sales proposition, prompts audience to read on | Opening |
| **I** | Interest | Describes central selling points, focuses not on features of product/service but on benefits relevant to the reader's needs | Body |
| **D** | Desire | Reduces resistance, reassures the reader, elicits the desire for ownership, motivates action | Body |
| **A** | Action | Offers an incentive or gift, limits the offer, sets a deadline, makes it easy for the reader to respond, closes the sale | Closing |

From Guffey/Loewy, Essentials of Business Communication (with www.meguffey.com Printed Access Card), 9E. © 2013 Cengage Learning.

**Gaining Attention in Sales Messages.** One of the most critical elements of a sales message is its opening paragraph. This opener should be short (one to five lines), honest, relevant, and stimulating. Marketing pros have found that eye-catching typographical arrangements or provocative messages, such as the following, can hook a reader's attention:

- **Offer:** *Subscribe now and get a free iPad to enjoy your programming on the go!*
- **Promise:** *Now you can raise your sales income by 50 percent or even more with the proven techniques found in. . . .*
- **Question:** *Why wait in the Starbucks line for a pitiful paper cup when for $20 you can have the Chiseled Chrome Coffee Cup, a handsome stylish tumbler of your own to refill every morning?*
- **Quotation or proverb:** *Necessity is the mother of invention.*
- **Fact:** *The Greenland Eskimos ate more fat than anyone in the world. And yet . . . they had virtually no heart disease.*
- **Product feature and its benefit:** *The Atlas sock is made from cotton, polyester, and carbonized coffee. Yup! Coffee helps filter odor, but equally important, the sock uses pressure mapping and thermal imaging to create a ridiculously comfortable sock!*
- **Startling statement:** *Bigger houses cost less.*
- **Personalized action setting:** *It's 4:30 p.m. and you have to make a decision. You need everybody's opinion, no matter where they are. Before you pick up your phone and call them one at a time, pick up this card: WebEx Teleconference Services.*

Other openings calculated to capture attention include a solution to a problem, an anecdote, a personalized statement using the receiver's name, or a relevant current event.

**Building Interest With Rational and Emotional Appeals.** In this phase of your sales message, you should describe clearly the product or service. In simple language emphasize the central selling points that you identified during your prewriting analysis. Those selling points can be developed using rational or emotional appeals.

Chapter 8: Persuasive Messages

Rational appeals are associated with reason and intellect. They translate selling points into references to making or saving money, increasing efficiency, or making the best use of resources. In general, rational appeals are appropriate when a product is expensive, long-lasting, or important to health, security, or financial success.

Emotional appeals relate to status, ego, and sensual feelings. Appealing to the emotions is sometimes effective when a product is inexpensive, short-lived, or nonessential. Many clever sales messages, however, combine emotional and rational strategies for a dual appeal. Consider these examples:

### Rational Appeal
*You can buy the things you need and want, pay household bills, pay off higher-cost loans and credit cards—as soon as you are approved and your ChoiceCredit card account is opened.*

### Emotional Appeal
*Leave the urban bustle behind and escape to sun-soaked Tahiti! To recharge your batteries with an injection of sun and surf, all you need is your bathing suit, a little suntan lotion, and your ChoiceCredit card.*

### Dual Appeal
*New ChoiceCredit cardholders are immediately eligible for a $200 travel certificate and additional discounts at fun-filled resorts. Save up to 40 percent while lying on a beach in picturesque, sun-soaked Bora-Bora, the year-round luxury resort.*

A physical description of your product is not enough, however. Zig Ziglar, thought by some to be America's greatest salesperson, pointed out that no matter how well you know your product, no one is persuaded by cold, hard facts alone. In the end, people buy because of product benefits.[17] Your job is to translate those cold facts into warm feelings and reader benefits. Let's say a sales message promotes a hand cream made with aloe and cocoa butter extracts, along with vitamin A. Those facts become *Nature's hand helpers—including soothing aloe and cocoa extracts, along with firming vitamin A—form invisible gloves that protect your sensitive skin against the hardships of work, harsh detergents, and constant environmental assaults.*

**Reducing Resistance and Building Desire.** Marketing specialists use a number of techniques to overcome resistance and build desire. When price is an obstacle, consider these suggestions:

- Delay mentioning price until after you have created a desire for the product.
- Show the price in small units, such as the price per issue of a magazine.
- Demonstrate how the reader saves money—for instance, by subscribing for two or three years.
- Compare your prices with those of a competitor.

In addition, you need to anticipate objections and questions the receiver may have. When possible, translate these objections into selling points (*If you are worried about training your staff members on the new software, remember that our offer includes $1,000 worth of on-site one-on-one instruction*). Be sure, of course, that your claims are accurate and do not stretch the truth. Other techniques to overcome resistance and prove the credibility of the product include the following:

- **Testimonials:** "*I never stopped eating, yet I lost 107 pounds.*" —Tina Rivers, Greenwood, South Carolina

- **Names of satisfied users** (with permission, of course): *Enclosed is a partial list of private pilots who enthusiastically subscribe to our service.*
- **Money-back guarantee or warranty**: *We offer the longest warranties in the business—all parts and service on-site for five years!*
- **Free trial or sample**: *We are so confident that you will like our new accounting program that we want you to try it absolutely free.*
- **Performance tests, polls, or awards**: *Our TP-3000 was named Best Internet Phone, and Etown.com voted it Smartphone of the Year.*

**Motivating Action at the Conclusion of a Sales Message.** All the effort put into a sales message goes to waste if the reader fails to act. To make it easy for readers to act, you can provide a reply card, a stamped and preaddressed envelope, a toll-free telephone number, a smartphone-readable matrix barcode, a simple Web address, or a promise of a follow-up call. Because readers often need an extra push, consider including additional motivators, such as the following:

- **Offer a gift:** *You will receive a free iPad mini with the purchase of any new car.*
- **Promise an incentive:** *With every new, paid subscription, we will plant a tree in one of America's Heritage Forests.*
- **Limit the offer:** *Only the first 100 customers receive free travel mugs.*
- **Set a deadline:** *You must act before June 1 to take advantage of these low prices.*
- **Guarantee satisfaction:** *We will return your full payment if you are not entirely satisfied—no questions asked.*

The final paragraph of the sales message carries the punch line. This is where you tell readers what you want done and give them reasons for doing it. Most sales messages also include postscripts because they make irresistible reading. Even readers who might skim over or bypass paragraphs are drawn to a P.S. Therefore, use a postscript to reveal your strongest motivator, to add a special inducement for a quick response, or to reemphasize a central selling point.

## 8-5c Putting Together All the Parts of a Sales Message

A direct-mail sales letter is the number two preferred marketing medium right behind e-mail[18] because it can be personalized, directed to target audiences, and filled with a more complete message than other advertising media can. However, direct mail is expensive. That's why crafting and assembling all the parts of a sales message are so critical.

Figure 8.8 shows a sales letter addressed to individuals and families who may need health insurance. To prompt the reader to respond to the mailing, the letter incorporates the effective four-part AIDA strategy. The writer first establishes the need for health coverage. Then she develops a rational central selling point (a variety of affordable health plans for every budget offered without sales pressure and medical jargon) and repeats this selling point in all the components of the letter. This sales letter saves its strongest motivator—a free heart-rate monitor for the first 30 callers—for the high-impact P.S. line.

Although you want to be persuasive in sales letters, you must guard against overstepping legal and ethical boundaries. Be sure to check out the Communication Workshop at the end of this chapter to see specific examples of what is legal and what is not.

## 8-5d Writing Successful E-Mail Sales Messages

E-mail is the primary channel that consumers use to interact with brands today. It is the most used channel for written, personal communication (45 percent), and

> **OFFICE INSIDER**
>
> "The best form of marketing is the kind that does not feel like marketing. I'm going to buy from the brands that sell to me the least."
>
> —Giselle Abramovich, senior editor at the media company Digiday

### Figure 8.8 HealthSelect Sales Letter

**HealthSelect**
Insurance you can count on

Choose our health plans if you want VALUE!

Confused about health insurance? You're not alone.

📞 Call a licensed expert at **(877) 522-0417**.
💻 Visit us online at **choosehealth.com**.
📬 Return the completed reply card to us by mail.

June 17, 2016

Mr. Jared Klugman
350 South 2nd Street, Apt. B
Ashland, OR 97520

Dear Mr. Klugman:

*[Addresses common fear]* Do you think you can't afford quality health insurance? Let us try to change your mind. HealthSelect offers attractive health plans that fit a range of budgets, needs, and lifestyles. Whether you're a recent graduate, self-employed, retiring early, or working without health insurance, one of our plans could be right for you. *[Gains attention]*

*[Establishes need for health insurance]* Health care needs can rise at any time in life, even in healthy and fit individuals. Anyone can succumb to an infectious disease or become sidelined by an accident. Wouldn't you want to have peace of mind? Knowing that such an unfortunate event won't break the bank will give you peace of mind. *[Builds interest]*

*[Emphasizes central selling point and reader benefits]* **Choose from a variety of plans and benefits at affordable rates, starting at $110.***
Our individual and family plans feature important benefits to keep you healthy:
- Preventive care comes at no additional cost, so that you don't put off your annual exam!
- Generic and brand-name prescription drug coverage will save you money every time.
- Chiropractic care, acupuncture, and rehabilitation coverage will help keep you in shape.
- A range of deductible options that work for your budget will put coverage within reach.
- Optional dental, vision, and life insurance coverage will protect you from unexpected expense.

*[Elicits desire and reduces resistance]*

Visit our website **choosehealth.com** for lots of ideas on how you can achieve your wellness goals. Learn about discount programs that help you save money and achieve a healthier lifestyle—at no additional charge.

*[Repeats central sales pitch]* **Compare HealthSelect plans when you're ready. No obligation. No pressure. Simple!** Call us at **(877) 522-0417**, and we will answer your questions in clear, easy-to-understand language, no medical or bureaucratic jargon. We promise. No sales types will hound you, either. That's a promise too. *[Motivates action]*

Stay well,

*Danielle McCoy*
Danielle McCoy
Director of Individual and Family Care

*[Spotlights free offer in P.S. to prompt immediate reply]* P.S. Call **(877) 522-0417** today for your free quote or to apply for coverage. The first 30 callers will receive a free heart-rate monitor. We're here to help improve the health of the people we serve.

\* This rate may not apply to you. Rates vary based on age, location, and health history.

---

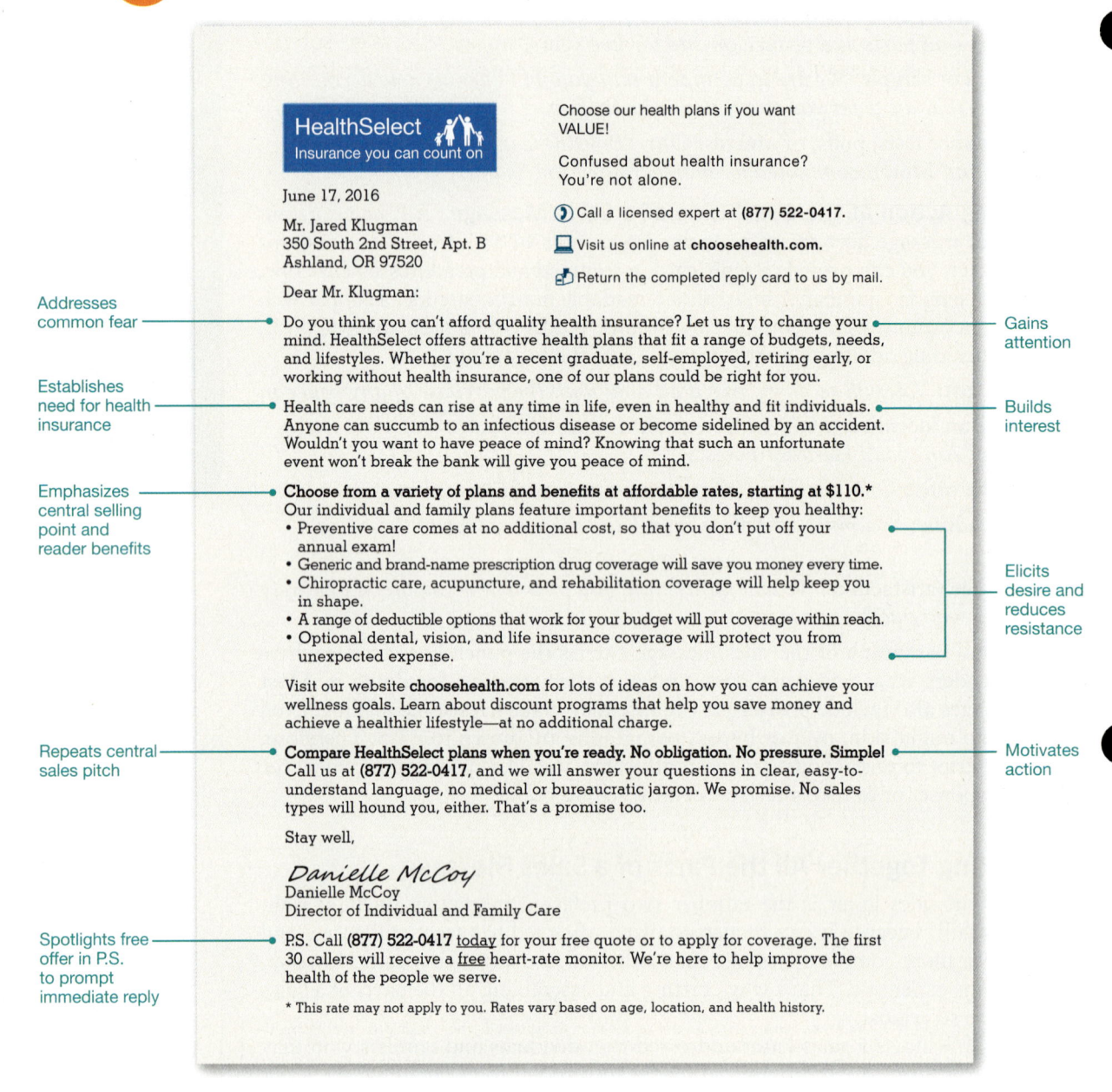

77 percent of consumers prefer permission-based marketing through e-mail.[19] E-mails cost about $7 per consumer response versus about $48 per response for traditional direct mail.[20]

Much like traditional direct mail, e-mail marketing can attract new customers, keep existing ones, encourage future sales, cross-sell, and cut costs. However, e-marketers can create and send a promotion in half the time it takes to print and distribute a traditional message. To reach today's consumer, marketers must target their e-mails well if they wish to even get their messages opened.

Meet Chef James Barry. The owner of Wholesome2Go, an organic food home-delivery service, knows that to achieve success today, he must cultivate relationships, not just push products.[21] A former personal chef for celebrities, James engages his clients by maintaining a website, tweeting updates, and posting on his Facebook and Pinterest pages. Wholesome2Go also has a YouTube channel. Frequently, Chef James sends persuasive e-mails in HTML format such as the one shown in Figure 8.9 that follows the four-part AIDA strategy.

On a practical level, you want to show how your persuasive message solves a problem, achieves a personal or work objective, or just makes life easier for your

Figure 8.9 Wholesome2Go Engages the Audience With Social Media

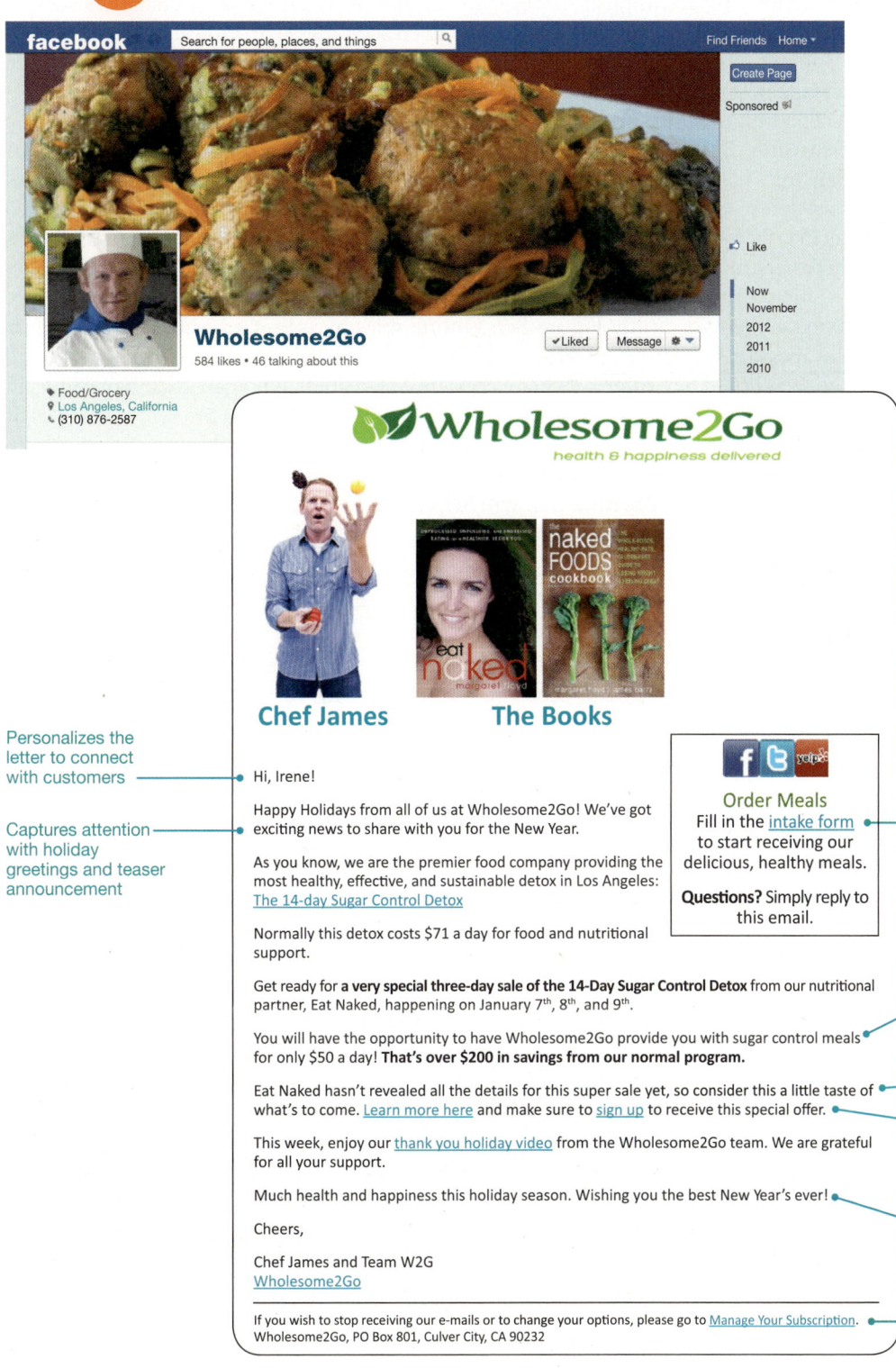

Chapter 8: Persuasive Messages

audience. Chef James understands that New Year's resolutions to eat healthy food and lose weight might reduce resistance to his offer.

When adapting persuasive requests to your audience, consider these questions that receivers will very likely be asking themselves: *Why should I? What's in it for me? What's in it for you? Who cares?*

### 8-5e Best Practices for Online Sales Messages

The goal of a persuasive message is to convert the receiver to your ideas and motivate action. To accomplish this feat in the age of social media, persuaders seek to build relationships with their audiences. Even so, a message without a clear purpose is doomed. Too often, inexperienced writers reach the end of the first draft of a message before discovering exactly what they want the receiver to think or do.

The first rule of e-marketing is to communicate only with those who have given permission. By sending messages only to "opt-in" folks, you greatly increase your open rate (i.e., the percentage of people who actually open the e-mail). E-mail users detest spam. However, receivers are surprisingly receptive to offers tailored specifically for them. Remember that today's customer is somebody—not anybody. Marketers must make it easy for the recipient to unsubscribe.

Some differences between traditional sales messages and e-marketing are obvious when you study Figure 8.9. Online sales messages are shorter than direct-mail messages, feature colorful graphics, and occasionally even come with sound or video clips. They offer a richer experience to readers who can click hyperlinks at will to access content that interests them. When such messages are sent out as ads or periodic e-newsletters coded in HTML, they may not have salutations or closings. Rather, they may resemble Web pages.

Here are a few guidelines that will help you create effective e-mail sales messages:

- **Craft a catchy subject line.** Include an audience-specific location (*Emporium in Vegas Opens Soon!*); ask a meaningful question (*What's Your Dream Vacation?*); and use no more than 50 characters. Promise realistic solutions. Offer discounts or premiums.
- **Keep the main information "above the fold."** E-mails should be top heavy. Primary points should appear early in the message to capture the reader's attention.
- **Make the message short, conversational, and focused.** Because on-screen text is taxing to read, be brief. Focus on one or two central selling points only.
- **Sprinkle testimonials throughout the copy.** Consumers' own words are the best sales copy. These comments can serve as callouts or be integrated into the text.
- **Provide a means for opting out.** It's polite and a good business tactic to include a statement that tells receivers how to be removed from the sender's mailing database.

### 8-5f Writing Short Persuasive Messages Online

Increasingly, writers are turning to social network posts to promote their businesses, further their causes, and build their online personas. As we have seen, social media are not primarily suited for overt selling; however, tweets and other online posts can be used to influence others and to project a professional, positive online presence.

Typically, organizations and individuals with followers post updates of their events, exploits, thoughts, and experiences. In persuasive tweets and posts, writers try to pitch offers, prompt specific responses, or draw the attention of their audiences to interesting events and media links. Figure 8.10 displays a sampling of persuasive tweets.

## Figure 8.10 Analyzing Persuasive Tweets

**Tweet promoting professional services by offering the reader a general benefit.**

> **Sandra Zimmer** @sandrazimmer
> Coaching for authentic presentations, public speaking & **persuasive messages** to help you shine. tinyurl.com/m5hrrx
> Expand ← Reply ⇄ Retweet ★ Favorite

**Tweet offering a freebie and testimonials to promote a book and urging action by restricting the availability of the freebie**

> **Jessica Brody** @JessicaBrody
> 5 autographed copies of UNREMEMBERED (UK edition) are up for grabs on Free Book Friday teens this week! Check it out! ow.ly/k5k6M

> **Delta** @Delta
> Be sure to enter our Kick It in NYC contest before the curtain closes. Enter now! oak.ctx.ly/r/1nwv pic.twitter.com/CRHxOwKe
> 📷 View photo ← Reply ⇄ Retweet ★ Favorite

**An airline creating urgency by suggesting that time to enter a contest is running out**

> **James Barry** @ChefJamesBarry
> The Sugar Control Detox is coming and at an insanely low price! This opportunity is available to everyone, no... fb.me/S2XDfTXB
> ▶ View media ← Reply ⇄ Retweet ★ Favorite

**Teaser tweet by a small business owner announcing an upcoming promotion**

> **richardbranson** @richardbranson
> Make this holiday story have a happy ending – sign the petition to put #educationfirst for children around the world virg.in/hap
> Expand

**A notable public figure advocating action for a cause, to sign a petition**

> **Army of Women** @ArmyofWomen
> Think #breastcancer should be a Nat. priority? Tell the president HERE:ow.ly/dnMd3
> Expand ← Reply ⇄ Retweet ★ Favorite

**A nonprofit organization requesting political action of advocacy for a popular cause**

> **Bill Gates** @BillGates
> Make your donations count. @CharityNav provides great information on the impact non-profits are actually having. b-gat.es/ThLBLJ
> Expand

**Notable philanthropist tweeting to motivate giving by reassuring followers of charities' merit**

> **Mike Bloomberg** @MikeBloomberg
> I've joined @Instagram. Follow me here: instagram.com/mikebloomberg
> Expand

**Tweet by a notable public figure announcing his new social network account and inviting followers along**

> **Guy Kawasaki** @GuyKawasaki
> Are you a writer? Here are some fantastic resources available free today as a download on the APE website.... fb.me/10bBh8apK
> Expand ← Reply ⇄ Retweet ★ Favorite

**Tweet by notable businessperson offering a free resource using an attention-getter**

© 2016 Cengage Learning®

Note that the compact format of a tweet requires extreme conciseness and efficiency. Don't expect the full four-part AIDA strategy to be represented in a 140-character Twitter message. Instead, you may see attention getters and calls for action, both of which must be catchy and intriguing. Regardless, many of the principles of persuasion discussed in this chapter apply even to micromessages.

## SUMMARY OF LEARNING OBJECTIVES

**8-1 Explain digital-age persuasion and identify time-proven persuasive techniques.**
- Business communicators need to use persuasion when making more than routine demands and facing a skeptical audience.
- Digital-age persuasion techniques are different from those used in earlier periods because the volume and reach of persuasive messages have exploded; messages now travel at warp speed; all kinds of organizations are persuaders; and persuasion is subtler and more misleading and has become more complex and impersonal.
- Effective persuasion involves establishing credibility; making specific, reasonable requests; linking facts to benefits; recognizing the power of loss; overcoming resistance; and sharing solutions and compromising.

Chapter 8: Persuasive Messages

**8-2 Craft persuasive messages that request actions.**
- Convincing a reluctant person requires planning and skill and sometimes a little luck.
- The writing plan for persuasive requests consists of an opening that captures the reader's attention; a body that establishes credibility, builds interest, and proves the merit of the request by using specific details; and a closing that motivates action while showing courtesy.

**8-3 Write compelling claims and deliver successful complaints.**
- Complaints and some persuasive claims deliver bad news; some vent anger, yet persuasion is necessary to effect change.
- Persuasive claims and complaints may involve damaged products, billing errors, wrong shipments, warranty problems, limited return policies, or insurance snafus.
- Employing a moderate tone, claim/complaint messages need to be logical and open with praise, a statement of fact or agreement, and a quick review of what was done to resolve the problem.
- In the body, writers highlight what happened and why the claim/complaint is legitimate; they enclose supporting documents such as invoices, shipping orders, warranties, and payments.
- The closing specifies what is to be done (e.g., a refund, replacement, or credit).

**8-4 Understand interpersonal persuasion at work, and compose persuasive messages within organizations.**
- Today's executives try to achieve buy-in from subordinates instead of forcing them to do things such as volunteer for projects or join programs that require lifestyle changes.
- Messages flowing downward require attention to tone and rely on honest, accurate evidence.
- Messages to management should provide facts, figures, and evidence and make strong dollars-and-cents cases for proposed ideas using a warm, professional tone.

**8-5 Create effective and ethical direct-mail and e-mail sales messages employing the AIDA strategy: gaining attention, building interest, developing desire, and motivating action.**
- Whether delivered by postal mail or by e-mail, marketers design sales messages to encourage consumers to read and act on the message.
- Sales letters are still an important part of multichannel marketing campaigns that can make sales, generate leads, boost retail traffic, solicit donations, and direct consumers to websites.
- The AIDA writing plan consists of an opening that gains attention, a body that builds interest and elicits desire, and a closing that motivates action by setting a deadline or presenting an incentive or a limited offer.
- Skilled e-marketers create catchy subject lines, start with the most important points, make the message conversational and focused, use testimonials, and allow readers to opt out.
- Short persuasive posts and tweets concisely pitch offers, prompt responses, and draw attention to events and media links. Principles of persuasion apply even to micromessages.

# CHAPTER REVIEW

1. List the characteristics of persuasion in the digital age. (Obj. 1)

2. List effective persuasion techniques. (Obj. 1)

3. What do claim/complaint messages typically involve, and how should they be crafted? (Obj. 3)

4. How can you ensure that your claim/complaint message is developed logically? (Obj. 3)

5. How have shifts in authority in digital-age organizations affected the strategies for creating goodwill and the tone of workplace persuasive messages? (Obj. 4)

6. When might persuasion be necessary in messages flowing upward? (Obj. 4)

7. What is the four-part AIDA writing plan for sales messages, and what does the acronym stand for? (Obj. 5)

8. What distinguishes rational, emotional, and dual appeals in persuasion? (Obj. 5)

9. Name the best practices for e-marketers hoping to write effective e-mail sales messages. (Obj. 5)

10. Describe the purpose and characteristics of persuasive tweets and other online posts. (Obj. 5)

# CRITICAL THINKING

11. *Recline in your first-class seat and sip a freshly stirred drink while listening to 12 channels of superb audio, or snooze* is an example of what type of persuasive appeal? How does it compare to the following: *Take one of four daily direct flights to Europe on our modern Airbus aircraft, and enjoy the most legroom of any airline. If we are ever late, you will receive coupons for free trips.* (Obj. 5)

12. The word *persuasion* turns some people off. What negative connotations can it have? (Objs. 1, 5)

13. What motivating impulse may prompt individuals to agree to requests that do not directly benefit themselves or their organizations? (Obj. 3)

14. How are direct-mail and e-mail sales messages similar, and how are they different? (Obj. 5)

15. Two students at Cambridge University in England raised more than $40,000 toward their university tuition by wearing business logos painted on their faces for a day.[22] Dunlop, however, went to the extreme by offering a set of free tires to those who would have the company's flying-D logo permanently tattooed somewhere on their bodies. Ninety-eight people complied.[23] Is it ethical for advertisers to resort to such promotions dubbed "skinvertising"? Do you think it's even effective? Would you participate? (Objs. 1, 5)

# WRITING IMPROVEMENT EXERCISES

## Direct and Indirect Strategies

**YOUR TASK.** For each of the following situations, check the appropriate writing strategy.

| Direct Strategy | Indirect Strategy | |
|---|---|---|
| _____ | _____ | 16. A request from the Society for the Prevention of Cruelty to Animals asking people to adopt animals and donate money |
| _____ | _____ | 17. An announcement that must convince employees to stop smoking, start exercising, and opt for a healthy diet to lower health care expenses and reduce absenteeism |
| _____ | _____ | 18. An e-mail message to employees asking them to come to the Operations Office to register and pick up new parking permits |
| _____ | _____ | 19. A message to your accountant asking her to reconsider her fee, which you think is exorbitant, considering that it was a bad year for your business |
| _____ | _____ | 20. A request for information about how to green up your office |
| _____ | _____ | 21. A letter to a grocery store requesting permission to display posters advertising a college fund-raising car wash |
| _____ | _____ | 22. A request for a refund by a buyer who purchased the wrong software but failed to uninstall it within the mandatory two-week return period. |
| _____ | _____ | 23. A request for correction of a routine billing error on your company credit card |
| _____ | _____ | 24. A letter to the local school board from a nearby convenience store owner expressing disapproval of a proposal allowing Coca-Cola to install vending machines on the school campus |
| _____ | _____ | 25. A memo to employees describing the schedule and menu selections of a new mobile catering service |

# RADICAL REWRITES

**Note:** Radical Rewrites are provided at www.cengagebrain.com for you to download and revise. Your instructor may show a suggested solution.

## 8.1 Radical Rewrite: Weak Persuasive Request Inviting Small Planet Speaker (Objs. 1, 2)

The following request from a program chair is intended to entice a prospective speaker, but it could be more much effective with a radical rewrite.

**YOUR TASK.** Analyze this poorly written request, and list at least five weaknesses. If your instructor directs, revise the letter implementing an effective persuasive strategy. Add appropriate information if needed.

---

Current date

Ms. Anna Lappé
418 North Jay Street
Brooklyn, NY 11212

Dear Ms. Lappé:

I am program chair for an upcoming member drive in Seattle. We would like very much to invite you to be our keynote speaker.

Our organization is called Sustainable Enterprises of Seattle, and we are a nonprofit dedicated to equipping the Northwest's citizens and decision makers with policy research and practical tools to advance long-term solutions to our region's most challenging challenges. We do many things including in-depth research. We offer commentary and analysis. All of these things we disseminate through e-mail, online, and in person.

We realize that you are extremely busy with your advocacy of the sustainability movement and as founding principal of the Small Planet Institute. But are you free on March 14? We are hoping you could address our group and talk about connecting the dots between the food on our plate and global warming—or do you call it global climate change? You have written that this country's food sector is both a central culprit in global warming and a key part of the solution. We would really like to learn how the world can be fed and the planet cooled through sustainable farming. We heard about you through your Facebook page and through your websites: Food MythBusters, Small Planet Fund, and Take a Bite Out of Climate Change.

We can offer only a small honorarium, although we could put you up at Seattle's eco-friendly Cedarbrook Lodge. Our mission is to make the Northwest a global model of sustainability. We envision sustainable communities, a green economy, and a healthy environment.

If you can speak to our group, we could, with your permission, possibly arrange to have copies of your latest book that you could sign.

Thank you and please let me know.

Sincerely,

---

List at least five weaknesses.

## 8.2 Radical Rewrite: Claim Letter From Seriously Displeased Customer (Objs. 1–3)

The following claim letter lodges a strong, almost insulting complaint, but the writer does little to persuade the receiver to meet his demands. Can you administer a radical rewrite that might make the request more successful?

**YOUR TASK.** Analyze this poorly written claim letter, and list at least five weaknesses. If your instructor directs, revise it.

Current date

Mr. Trenton Khalifa
VIP Copier Specialists
1532 Nashville Pike
Gallatin, TN 37012

Dear Ripoff Specialist:

Here are the dismal facts. My company recently purchased four of your *BizStar C500* photocopiers, which sounded great at the time. They promised 2-sided copies, fax, printer, and color scanning to my computer. This was perfect for my health care office. Your salesperson Carol Finley assured us that the BizStar C500 could handle our high volume of 3,000 copies a day. This sounded unlikely since the sales brochure suggested that the C500 was meant for 500 copies a day. Regardless, we listened to what Ms. Finley told us. And that was our big mistake! Our four C500 copiers are down every day, and my employees are screaming at me constantly. These machines are still under warranty, and I will admit that they do eventually get repaired. However, we can't get by with so much downtime.

Because I lost faith in your Ms. Finley, I telephoned the district manager, William Yamaguchi. I suggested that we trade in our four BizStar C500 copiers (which cost us $2,300 each) for two BizStar C1000 models (at $12,500 each). However, Mr. Yamaguchi said he would have to charge 50 percent depreciation on our C500 copiers. What a major rip-off! I think that 20 percent depreciation is more reasonable since we've had the machines only three months. Ms. Finley said she would get back to me, and I haven't heard from her since.

Now I'm forced to write to your headquarters because I have had no luck with either Ms. Finley or Mr. Yamaguchi, and I need to see some action on these machines. If you understood anything about business, you would see what a sweet deal I'm offering you. I'm willing to stick with your company and purchase your most expensive model—but I can't take such a steep loss on the C500 copiers. These copiers are relatively new; you should be able to sell them with no trouble. And think of all the money you will save by not having your repair technicians making constant trips to service our underpowered BizStar C500 copiers! Please let me hear from you immediately, or I may next turn to Yelp.

Sincerely yours,

List at least five weaknesses.

## 8.3 Radical Rewrite: Poor Persuasive E-Mail Flowing Upward—Miserable Meetings (Objs. 1, 2)

The following e-mail message suffers from many writing faults, including poor tone and poor persuasive strategy. It originated with a manager and is addressed to her boss.

**YOUR TASK.** List at least five writing weaknesses. Then revise the message implementing an effective persuasive strategy. See Chapter 11 for suggestions about improving meetings. Consider volunteering to help develop and carry out the policy being requested.

```
To:      Randolph Williams <rwilliams@fisherinc>
From:    Karissa Kuhn<kkuhn@fisherinc>
Subject: Miserable Staff Meetings
Cc:
```
Attached:

Good morning!

I wonder if you know how bad meetings are around here. We seem to have endless meetings that drag on and on forever. I myself attended five meetings within the building but also was forced to participate in three more conference call meetings. And that was just last week! Nearly every one of those meetings was poorly run. Some should never have been called because they merely announced information after a decision had already been made. Some could easily have been handled in an e-mail. Sometimes I think our meetings are really opportunities to socialize under the guise of "work." Our meetings are huge time suckers.

I'm going to level with you and tell it like it is. Something needs to be done about the lost productivity and sagging employee morale around here. No one likes to waste valuable time attending poorly run or unnecessary meetings. Apparently, our managers have not been trained in how to conduct meetings, although I realize that all of them are professional and have business training.

What we need is a meeting policy or something like that. We need some guidelines or training about how to conduct meetings. Has anyone thought of that? I can think of many ways to improve meetings. Could we please talk about this?

Karissa Kuhn

Project Manager

List at least five weaknesses.

## 8.4 Radical Rewrite: Favor Request—Facebook Flub? (Objs. 1, 2, and 5)

A student chose Facebook to request a recommendation from his professor. The following message suffers from many writing faults, including poor tone and flawed persuasive strategy.

**YOUR TASK.** Analyze the Facebook message and list at least five weaknesses. If your instructor directs, revise the message. Decide whether to use Facebook, of which the receiver is a member, or a conventional e-mail to make this request.

**New Message**

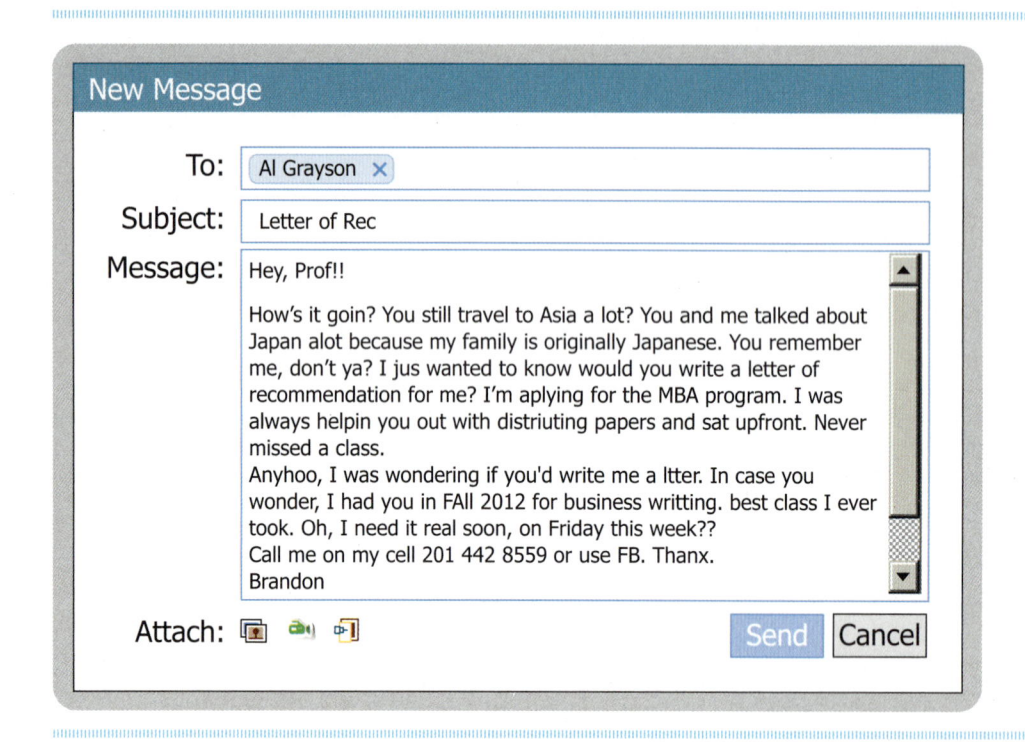

To: Al Grayson ×
Subject: Letter of Rec
Message:
Hey, Prof!!
How's it goin? You still travel to Asia a lot? You and me talked about Japan alot because my family is originally Japanese. You remember me, don't ya? I jus wanted to know would you write a letter of recommendation for me? I'm aplying for the MBA program. I was always helpin you out with distriuting papers and sat upfront. Never missed a class.
Anyhoo, I was wondering if you'd write me a ltter. In case you wonder, I had you in FAll 2012 for business writting. best class I ever took. Oh, I need it real soon, on Friday this week??
Call me on my cell 201 442 8559 or use FB. Thanx.
Brandon

Attach: [Send] [Cancel]

List at least five weaknesses.

## ACTIVITIES AND CASES

### 8.5 Analyzing Tweets: Identify Persuasive Techniques in Micromessages (Objs. 1, 5)
Communication Technology / Social Media / Web

As you have learned in this chapter, the time-tried AIDA sales technique is alive and well even in 140-character Twitter messages. Of course, we can't expect to find all four parts in a single tweet.

**YOUR TASK.** Study the following tweets and describe the persuasive techniques they employ. **Hint:** You may find that Twitter users rely on attention getters, calls for action, emotional appeals, incentives, and testimonials. They may also create urgency to stoke readers' interest. Chat about your findings in class or on your favorite course management platform. Your instructor may ask you to collect your own examples of persuasive tweets or other social media posts and discuss their frequency as well as effectiveness. After you have collected a sample large enough to allow you to generalize, compose an e-mail or post about your observations.

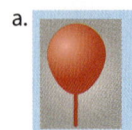

a. **lyft** @lyft 13 Nov
Get around your city with friendly, on-demand drivers for less than a cab. Use RIDE for $10 credit on your first Lyft http://lyft.com/app

© 2014 Lyft

250  Chapter 8: Persuasive Messages

b. **Delta** @Delta 25 Dec
Someone needs a vacay after the gift wrapping, elf wrangling & present delivering! #Santa #Christmas pic.twitter.com/nu8r4DmweL

c. **P&G Beauty** @PGBeauty 18 Dec
Got 5 minutes? Then you've got time to do this #gorgeous updo by @whoorl: http://spr.ly/6013dMRd

d. **John Deere** @JohnDeere 18 Dec
Hurry! 0% APR for 48 Months on wide range of new John Deere construction equipment. Offer ends Jan. 5 (Canada only) http://bit.ly/IV7Dnb

e. **Harley-Davidson** @harleydavidson 8 Nov
"When I ride there is only now, this moment. Clutch, throttle and brake. I am 100% focused." #harleywomen http://bit.ly/1d6pnW4

f. **Virgin Records** @virginrecords 4 Oct
Add your own Bastille-related photos to the @everlapse photo collage + stream "Bad Blood" at the same time.→ http://tmblr.co/Z8A2ZxwRp7tm

g. **taylor** @taylorcasey_ 29 Sep
An unbelievable day and concert!!! I like your shirt Dan #bastilleamerica http://instagram.com/p/e3zR-GqeiP/
Retweeted by Virgin Records

h. **Starbucks Coffee** @Starbucks 15 Oct
Signed petitions from across America are bound for D.C. tonight. Add your voice: http://sbux.co/H0qPPD #cometogether

i. **Southwest Airlines** @SouthwestAir 23 Dec
Two days left to enter for a chance to win a Wii U video game system from @NintendoAmerica and a pair of SWA tickets! http://www.southwest.com/Nintendo

## 8.6 Analyzing a Persuasive Appeal: From the Zappos Family to Yours (Objs. 1, 5)

**Communication Technology** | **Web**

Online shoe and apparel store Zappos seems to abide by a unique motto: "We are a service company that happens to sell." With a record-setting 10-hour customer service call,[24] Zappos bolstered its reputation for pleasing online shoppers. Therefore, it's perhaps not surprising that the online retailer sent this preholiday mailer with a coupon code to some of its less active customers:

*It just wouldn't be the holidays without you!*
*We'd love to see you again . . .*
*That's why we're giving you* **10% off** *your next Zappos.com order!*
*These coupons are very rare, but then again, you are very special.*
*Here's your handy-dandy coupon code to use during checkout:*
**ZMDR-500012**
*Can't wait to see you!*
*XOXO,*
*The Zappos Family*

Chapter 8: Persuasive Messages

**YOUR TASK.** Evaluate the persuasive appeal of this message. Which needs does this message address? How does it try to accomplish its goal, to sell merchandise? Do you think it's effective?

Can you point to similar examples of such an approach? Discuss in class or in writing. If your instructor directs, post your response and discuss it with peers on your course management system—Blackboard, Moodle, or a similar platform.

## 8.7 Persuasive Request: Please Write Me a Letter of Recommendation (Objs. 1, 2)
**E-mail**

As a student, you will need letters of recommendation to find a job, to apply for a scholarship or grant, or to enter graduate school. Naturally, you will consider asking one or several of your college instructors. You talk to a senior you know to find out how to get a busy professor to write you an effective letter. Your friend Mark has the following basic advice for you:

- Ask only instructors who have had the opportunity to observe your performance and may still remember you fondly. Two to five years after you attended a course of 20 to 40 students, your teachers many not recall you at all.
- Contact only instructors who can sing your praises. If your grades were poor, the endorsement won't be glowing. Some instructors refuse to write recommendations.

Make it easy for your instructors to agree to your request and to write a solid letter promptly by following these guidelines:

- Make the first request in person if possible; your former instructor will be more likely to remember you.
- Introduce yourself by name and try to point out something memorable you did to help your professor recall your performance.
- Have a copy of the job description, scholarship information, grant requirements, or graduate school application ready.
- Carry a copy of a recent polished résumé or promise to e-mail the requisite documents and any other information to help your recommender understand what you need.
- Confirm any agreement by e-mail promptly, and set a firm yet reasonable deadline by which the letter must be received. Don't expect to get a letter if you ask at the last minute.
- Gently nudge by e-mail to remind the recommender when the deadline is approaching.

**YOUR TASK.** Write a persuasive request by e-mail asking your instructor (or supervisor or manager) to write you a letter of recommendation for a job application, grant, scholarship, or graduate school application. Provide all relevant information to make it easy to write a terrific letter. Explain any attachments.

## 8.8 Persuasive Request: Seeking Dumps for TV Makeovers (Obj. 2)

As an intern at a major cable network, you have been given a task associated with a new show. The network plans to introduce a home makeover show called *Hideous Houses*. It will feature not only homes in desperate need of repair but also dwellings deluged with accumulated junk or those with haphazard additions. Producers say they are particularly interested in homes decked out in horrific colors, leopard prints, or disco, goth, or 1950s looks.

In preparation for the show, producers conducted multiple searches in three major cities and located hundreds of possible homes for the show. They did, however, want to avoid homes with structural damage suggesting that the home needed to be torn down. Instead, they focused on homes that were eyesores in the neighborhood and perhaps exhibited bad taste. In some cases, neighbors recommended "hideous houses" as possibilities for the upcoming show.

Homeowners could receive up to $20,000 worth of renovations as well as national exposure on a major cable network. Expert designers and contractors will be called in to renovate. To be eligible, participants must own the home, have a front yard, and provide two areas needing major help.

**YOUR TASK.** As part of your internship program, the producers of *Hideous Houses* ask you to prepare a persuasive message or a telephone script inviting a homeowner to participate in the show. The producer, who used to work with the Oprah show, cautions you to treat the owners with genuine respect. Given that the producers recognize that many people would be offended by being singled out for this program,[25] should you reveal the name of the program? Your goal is to obtain a callback so that you can discuss details.

## 8.9 Persuasive Request: Making a Case for Tuition Reimbursement (Obj. 2)
**Communication Technology**  **Team**

After working a few years, you would like to extend your college education on a part-time basis. You know that your education can benefit your employer, but you can't really afford the fees for tuition and books. You have heard that many companies offer reimbursement for tuition and books when employees complete approved courses with a grade of *C* or higher.

**YOUR TASK.** In teams discuss the best way to approach an employer whom you wish to persuade to start a tuition and books reimbursement program. How could such a program help the employer? Remember that the most successful requests help receivers see what's in it for them. What objections might your employer raise? How can you counter them? After discussing strategies in teams face-to-face or online, write a team memo or individual memos to your boss (at a company where you now work or one with which you are familiar). Persuade her or him to act on your persuasive request.

## 8.10 Persuasive Request: Junk Food Props Up School Budget (Obj. 2)

**Team** **Web**

"If I start to get huge, then, yeah, I'll cut out the chips and Coke," says 17-year-old Nicole O'Neill, as she munches sour cream-and-onion potato chips and downs a cold can of soda fresh from the snack machine. Most days her lunch comes from a vending machine. The trim high school junior, however, isn't too concerned about how junk food affects her weight or overall health. Although she admits she would prefer a granola bar or fruit, few healthy selections are available in school vending machines.

Vending machines loaded with soft drinks and snacks are increasingly under attack in schools and lunchrooms. Some school boards, however, see them as cash cows. In Gresham, Oregon, the school district is considering a lucrative soft drink contract. If it signs an exclusive 12-year agreement with Coca-Cola to allow vending machines at Gresham High School, the school district will receive $75,000 up front. Then it will receive an additional $75,000 three years later. Commission sales on the 75-cent drinks will bring in an additional $322,000 over the 12-year contract provided the school sells 67,000 cans and bottles every year. In the past the vending machine payments supported student body activities such as sending students to choir concerts and paying athletic participation fees. Vending machine funds also paid for an electronic reader board in front of the school and a sound system for the gym. The latest contract would bring in $150,000, which is already earmarked for new artificial turf on the school athletic field.

Coca-Cola's vending machines would dispense soft drinks, Fruitopia, Minute Maid juices, Powerade, and Dasani water. The hands-down student favorite, of course, is calorie-laden Coke. Because increasing childhood and adolescent obesity across the nation is a major health concern, the Gresham Parent Teacher Association (PTA) decided to oppose the contract. The PTA realizes that the school board is heavily influenced by the income generated from the Coca-Cola contract. It wonders what other school districts are doing about their vending machine contracts.

**YOUR TASK.** As part of a PTA committee, you have been given the task of researching and composing a persuasive but concise (no more than one page) letter addressed to the school board. Use the Web or databases to locate articles that might help you develop arguments, alternatives, and counterarguments. Meet with your team to discuss your findings. Then, individually or as a group, write a letter to the Board of Directors, Gresham-Barlow School District, P.O. Box 310, Gresham, OR 97033.

## 8.11 Persuasive Claim: Pricey Hotel Breakfast (Obj. 3)

As regional manager for an auto parts manufacturer, you and two other employees attended a conference in Lexington, Kentucky. You stayed at the Country Inn & Suites because your company recommends that employees use this hotel chain. Generally, your employees have liked their accommodations, and the rates have been within your company's budget.

Now, however, you are unhappy with the charges you see on your company's credit statement from Country Inn & Suites. When your department's administrative assistant made the reservations, she was assured that you would receive the weekend rates and that a hot breakfast—in the hotel restaurant, the Atrium—would be included in the rate. So you and the other two employees went to the restaurant and ordered a hot meal from the menu.

When you received the credit statement, though, you saw a charge for $132 for three champagne buffet breakfasts in the Atrium. You hit the ceiling! For one thing, you didn't have a buffet breakfast and certainly no champagne. The three of you got there so early that no buffet had been set up. You ordered pancakes and sausage, and for this you were billed $40 each. What's worse, your company may charge you personally for exceeding the maximum per diem rates.

In looking back at this event, you remember that other guests on your floor were having a continental breakfast in a lounge on your floor. Perhaps that's where the hotel expected all guests on the weekend rate to eat. However, your administrative assistant had specifically asked about this matter when she made the reservations, and she was told that you could order breakfast from the menu at the hotel's restaurant.

**YOUR TASK.** You want to straighten out this problem, and you can't do it by telephone because you suspect that you will need a written record of this entire mess. Online you have tried in vain to find an e-mail address for guest relations at the Lexington location. Write a persuasive claim to Customer Service, Country Inn & Suites, 1310 Darby Drive, Lexington, KY 40505. Should you include a copy of the credit card statement showing the charge?

## 8.12 Persuasive Claim: Nothing Magical About These Legal Fees (Obj. 3)

Originally a shipbuilding village, the town of Mystic, Connecticut, captures the spirit of the nineteenth-century seafaring era. However, it is best known for Mystic Pizza, a bustling local pizzeria featured in a movie that launched the film career of Julia Roberts. Today, customers line the sidewalk waiting to taste its pizza, called by some "a slice of heaven."

Chapter 8: Persuasive Messages

Assume that you are the business manager for Mystic Pizza's owners. They were approached by an independent vendor who wants to use the Mystic Pizza name and secret recipes to distribute frozen pizza through grocery and convenience stores. As business manager, you worked with a law firm, Giordano, Murphy, and Associates. This firm was to draw up contracts regarding the use of Mystic Pizza's name and quality standards for the product. When you received the bill from Henry Giordano, you were flabbergasted. It itemized 38 hours of attorney preparation, at $500 per hour, and 55 hours of paralegal assistance, at $150 per hour. The bill also showed $415 for telephone calls, which might be accurate because Mr. Giordano had to talk with the owners, who were vacationing in Italy at the time. You seriously doubt, however, that an experienced attorney would require 38 hours to draw up the contracts in question. When you began checking, you discovered that excellent legal advice can be obtained for $300 an hour.

**YOUR TASK.** Decide what you want to request, and then write a persuasive request to Henry Giordano, Attorney-at-Law, Giordano, Murphy, and Associates, 254 Sherborn Street, Boston, MA 02215. Include an end date and a reason for it.

## 8.13 Persuasive Claim: Toner Scam at Tony Florida Resort (Obj. 3)

Jeanine H. was new to her job as administrative assistant at the Aqualina Resort & Spa in Sunny Isles, Florida. Alone in the office one morning, she answered a phone call from Don, who said he was the resort's copier contractor. "Hey, look, Babydoll," Don purred, "the price on the toner you use is about to go way up. I can offer you a great price on this toner if you order right now." Jeanine knew that the copy machine regularly needed toner, and she thought she should probably go ahead and place the order to save the resort some money. Ten days later two bottles of toner arrived, and Jeanine was pleased at the perfect timing; the copy machine needed it right away. Three weeks later Helen, the bookkeeper, called to report a bill from Copyco Supplies for $960.43 for two bottles of toner. "What's going on here?" said Helen. "We don't purchase supplies from this company, and this price is totally off the charts!"[26]

Jeanine spoke to the manager, Javier Natali, who immediately knew what had happened. He blamed himself for not training Jeanine. "Never, never order anything from a telephone solicitor, no matter how fast-talking or smooth he sounds," warned Javier. He outlined an office policy for future supplies purchases. Only certain people can authorize or finalize a purchase, and purchases require a confirmed price including shipping costs settled in advance. However, what to do about this $960.43 bill? The resort had already begun to use the toner, although the current copies were looking faint and streaked.

**YOUR TASK.** As Javier Natali, decide how to respond to this obvious scam. Should you pay the bill? Should you return the unused bottle? Write a persuasive claim to Copyco Supplies, 8548 NW 88th Street, Miami, FL 33135. Supply any details necessary.

## 8.14 Persuasive Organizational Message Flowing Upward: Training Telecommuters (Obj. 4)

**E-mail** **Team** **Web**

Jared Johnson arose from bed in his New Hampshire home and looked outside to see a heavy snowstorm creating a fairyland of white. However, he felt none of the giddiness that usually accompanies a potential snow day. Such days were a gift from heaven when schools closed, businesses shut down, and the world ground to a halt. As an on-and-off telecommuter for many years, he knew that snow days were a thing of the past. These days, work for Jared Johnson and 20 percent of other workers around the globe is no farther than their home offices.[27]

More and more employees are becoming telecommuters, the well-publicized ban of telecommuting at Yahoo notwithstanding. They want to work at home, where they feel they can be more productive and avoid the hassle of driving to work. Some need to telecommute only temporarily while they take care of family obligations, births, illnesses, or personal problems. Others are highly skilled individuals who can do their work at home as easily as in the office. Businesses definitely see advantages to telecommuting. They don't have to supply office space for workers. What's more, as businesses continue to flatten management structures, bosses no longer have time to micromanage employees. Increasingly, they are leaving workers to their own devices.

However, the results have not been totally satisfactory. For one thing, in-house workers resent those who work at home. More important are problems of structure and feedback. Telecommuters don't always have the best work habits, and lack of communication is a major issue. Unless the telecommuter is expert at coordinating projects and leaving instructions, productivity can fizzle. Appreciating the freedom but recognizing that they need guidance, employees are saying, "Push me, but don't leave me out there all alone!"

As the human resources manager at your company, you already have 83 employees who are either full- or part-time telecommuters. With increasing numbers asking to work in remote locations, you decide that workers and their managers must receive training on how to do it effectively. You are considering hiring a consultant to train your prospective telecommuters and their managers. Another possibility is developing an in-house training program.

**YOUR TASK.** As human resources manager, you must convince Chris Crittenden, vice president, that your company needs a training program for all workers who are currently telecommuting or who plan to do so. Their managers should also receive training. You decide to ask your staff of four to help you gather information. Using the Web, you and your team read several articles on what such training should include. Now you must decide what action you want the vice president to take. Meet with you to discuss a training program? Commit to a budget item for future training? Hire a consultant or agency to come in and conduct training programs? Individually or as a team, write a convincing e-mail that describes the problem, suggests what the training should include, and asks for action by a specific date. Add any reasonable details necessary to build your case.

## 8.15 Persuasive Organizational Message Flowing Upward: Hey, Boss, I Have an Idea (Obj. 4)

**E-mail**

In your own work or organization experience, identify a problem for which you have a solution. Should a procedure be altered to improve performance? Would a new or different piece of equipment or software help you perform your work better? Could some tasks be scheduled more efficiently? Are employees being used most effectively? Could customers be better served by changing something? Do you want to work other hours or perform other tasks? Do you deserve a promotion? Do you have a suggestion to improve profitability?

**YOUR TASK.** Once you have identified a situation requiring persuasion, write a memo or an e-mail to your boss or organization head. Use actual names and facts. Employ the concepts and techniques in this chapter to help you convince your boss that your idea should prevail. Include concrete examples, anticipate objections, emphasize reader benefits, and end with a specific action to be taken.

## 8.16 Persuasive Organizational Message Flowing Downward: Saving Cash on Shipping (Obj. 4)

As office manager of a Seattle software company, write a memo persuading your technicians, engineers, programmers, and other employees to reduce the number of overnight or second-day mail shipments. Your FedEx and other shipping bills have been sky high, and you feel that staff members are overusing these services.

You think employees should send messages by e-mail. Sending a zipped file or PDF file as an e-mail attachment costs nothing. Compare this with $20 or $30 for FedEx service! Whenever possible, staff members should obtain the FedEx account number of the recipient and use it for charging the shipment. If staff members plan ahead and allow enough time, they can use UPS or FedEx ground service, which takes three to five days and is much cheaper. You wonder whether staff members consider whether the recipient is really going to use the message as soon as it arrives. Does it justify an overnight shipment? You would like to reduce overnight delivery services voluntarily by 50 percent over the next two months. Unless a sizable reduction occurs, the CEO threatens severe restrictions in the future.

**YOUR TASK.** Address your memo to all staff members. What other ways could employees reduce shipping costs?

## 8.17 Persuasive Organizational Message Flowing Downward: Become an Urban Farming Volunteer (Obj. 4)

**E-mail** **Web**

As employee relations manager of Paychex of San Francisco, one of your tasks is to promote Urban Farming, a global organization that has established almost 60,000 gardens in nearly 40 cities. Originating in the Detroit area, Urban Farming is a combined effort of major corporations. You must recruit 12 coworkers who will volunteer to plant gardens and teach community families about healthy eating.

Your task is to find volunteers in your company to start a community garden and in turn recruit other Paychex volunteers. San Francisco offers more than 5,000 vacant lots to choose from, and the city already manages 40 gardens. Paychex volunteers will be expected to attend training sessions and then to supervise and instruct participating members of the community. In return, employees will receive two hours of release time per week to work on their Urban Farming projects. The program has been very successful thus far, and the interest in community gardens is growing.

**YOUR TASK.** Learn more about Urban Farming by searching the Web. Then write a persuasive memo or e-mail with convincing appeals that will bring you 12 volunteers to work with Urban Farming.

## 8.18 Identifying the AIDA Strategy in Sales Messages (Obj. 5)

**E-mail**

**YOUR TASK.** Select a one- or two-page sales letter or promotional e-mail received by you or a friend. If you are unable to find a sales message, your instructor may have a collection. Study the sales message and then answer these questions:
a. What techniques capture the reader's attention?
b. Is the opening effective? Explain.
c. What is the central selling point?
d. Does the message use rational, emotional, or a combination of appeals? Explain.
e. What reader benefits are suggested?
f. How does the message build interest in the product or service?
g. How is price handled?
h. How does the message anticipate reader resistance and offer counterarguments?
i. What action is the reader to take? How is the action made easy?
j. What motivators spur the reader to act quickly?

Chapter 8: Persuasive Messages

## 8.19 Sales Letter: Pitaya—The Next "Superfruit"? (Obj. 5)

**E-mail**

Eric Helms is the founder and CEO of Juice Generation, a chain of juice and smoothie bars in New York City. He bought the exclusive rights to a year's supply of pitaya, a little-known softball-sized fruit of a cactus found in Nicaragua. The Vietnamese dragonfruit is the pitaya's Asian cousin. To prevent agricultural pests from entering the United States, the U.S Department of Agriculture (USDA) has mandated that only the fruit's frozen pulp may be shipped from Central America. The pitaya reportedly tastes like a cross between strawberries and wheatgrass and is said to contain an antioxidant believed to protect from cancer-causing free radicals. David Wolfe, author of *Superfoods*, is enthusiastic: "It's one of my favorite fruits of all time. It's superhigh in vitamin C and superhydrating." Yet even within health food circles, the fruit is still largely unknown.

The superpremium juice business that focuses on healthy exotic nectars (such as pomegranate and, most recently, the açaí berry) is a multibillion-dollar enterprise. The big players all have their brands—for example, Odwalla (Coca-Cola), Naked (PepsiCo), and Jamba Juice. Celebrities such as Russell Simmons and Gwyneth Paltrow have endorsed juicing. Selma Hayek, a longtime juicer, cofounded the Cooler Cleanse juice brand with Helms.

The term *superfruit* is a marketing term, referring to fruits heavy in antioxidants, but without any scientific or regulatory definition, says Jeffrey Blumberg, director of the USDA's antioxidants research laboratory. "As most natural fruits contain one or more positive nutrient attributes," Blumberg explains, "any one might be considered by someone 'super' in its own way." An industry primer is blunt: "Superfruits are the product of strategy, not something you find growing on a tree."[28] POM Wonderful lost a lawsuit to the Federal Trade Commission for deceptive advertising of its pomegranate juice.

Helms' Juice Generation partnered with a factory in Nicaragua that employs only single mothers to scoop and blend the fruit. The women pour the pulp into 3.5-ounce packets that are frozen for shipping. A packet of the Pink Pitaya Coco Blend, a mix of coconut, banana, and pitaya, costs $8.45. "You have to give people what they want, but also what they should be trying," Helms believes.[29]

**YOUR TASK.** Write a sales letter or a marketing e-mail promoting the Pink Pitaya Coco Blend. Your audience in this campaign will probably be gyms with in-house juice bars. Introduce the exotic pitaya fruit and explain its benefits. Cull information from the scenario to include a testimonial. Make sure your claims are ethical and legal.

## 8.20 E-Mail Marketing Message or Direct-Mail Sales Letter: Promoting Products and Services (Obj. 5)

**E-mail**

Identify a situation in your current job or a previous one in which a sales message is or was needed. Using suggestions from this chapter, write an appropriate sales message that promotes a product or service. Use actual names, information, and examples. If you have no work experience, imagine a business you would like to start, such as data processing, pet grooming, car detailing, tutoring, specialty knitting, balloon decorating, delivery service, child care, gardening, or lawn care.

**YOUR TASK.** Write a sales letter or an e-mail promoting your product or service to be distributed to your prospective customers. Be sure to tell them how to respond. You don't need to know HTML or have a Constant Contact account to craft a concise and eye-catching online sales message. Try designing it in Microsoft Word and saving it as a Web page (go to the **File** tab and select **Save as**; then in the **Save as type** line, select **Web page**). Consider adding graphics or photos—either your own or samples borrowed from the Internet. As long as you use them for this assignment and don't post (publish) them for all to see online, you are not violating copyright laws.

## 8.21 Micromessages: Analyzing Twitter Feeds for AIDA Components (Objs. 1, 2, and 5)

**Social Media** **Web**

People are increasingly sharing persuasive and promotional social media posts. Most of the persuasive micromessages incorporate some elements of sales techniques—individual AIDA components. Naturally, few of us would buy something solely on the basis of a tweet, but such micromessages are teasers or alerts, directing receivers to websites, video clips, and other media.

**Tip:** To find persuasive posts fast, view the ultra-brief LinkedIn member ads visible on the right side of most LinkedIn screens. Alternatively, visit the sponsored links at *Bloomberg Businessweek*. Determine whether tweets and posts ask questions, favor the "you" view, and use other features that are hallmarks of persuasion. Share your results in class. Analyze and critique each other's findings.

**Examples:**

Consider these LinkedIn posts with the commentary that follows:

> ***Senior Women Executives. Apply now to the Association of Women in Business. Register free.*** *Calls on a specific audience; uses the "you" view; free registration encourages compliance.*
>
> ***Spruce up Business Events. "Frank is fantastic." Skilled, fun, interactive musical entertainment.*** *Opts for vivid language and attracts attention with benefit in the opening; includes a claim resembling a testimonial.*
>
> ***Masters in Counseling. Earn a Chapman M.A. and jumpstart your career. Apply by Jan. 31.*** *Advertises graduate program as beneficial to career advancement; uses limited-time offer.*

Consider these tweets and the accompanying comments as models:

> ***With our updated Android app, share collections of photos with friends and family. Enjoy! http://wo.ly/gLknQ*** *Offers a benefit; conveys warmth (Enjoy!); provides a useful hyperlink.*
>
> ***Enjoy easier, smarter access to Delta with the new http://delta.com and Fly Delta apps for smartphones and iPad: http://oka.xtr.ly/m/1umh*** *Employs the "you" view; offers a benefit (easier, smarter access); prompts a response with convenient hyperlinks.*
>
> ***Please donate to @RedCrossAU Tasmanian Bushfires Appeal http://bit.ly/Xs4l7g All donations over $2 are tax deductible #redcross #tasfires*** *Starts with a direct call for action; points out the benefit that contributions are tax deductible.*

**YOUR TASK.** Examine a Twitter feed or other social media (e.g., LinkedIn) for persuasive micromessages that feature AIDA components such as attention getters, reader benefits, calls for action, limited-time offers, freebies, and so on. Arrange them in categories as shown in Figure 8.9.

## 8.22 Writing Persuasive Tweets and Posts (Objs. 1, 5)

`Social Media` `Web`

Being able to compose effective and concise micromessages and posts will positively contribute to your professional online persona.

**YOUR TASK.** Brainstorm to identify a special skill you have, an event you want others to attend, a charitable cause dear to your heart, or a product you like. Applying what you have learned about short persuasive messages online, write your own 140-character persuasive tweet or post. Use Figure 8.9 as a starting point and model.

## 8.23 Examining Puffery in Advertising (Objs. 1, 5)

`Communication Technology` `Social Media` `Web`

As discussed in the Communication Workshop at the end of this chapter, puffery in advertising may be tacky, but it is not illegal. Few of us take claims seriously that shout *the best pizza in town, the largest selection of electronics, the ultimate fresh breath, the world's juiciest hamburgers, the biggest pie money can buy,* or *the coldest beer.* After all, such exaggerated claims cannot be proven and do not fool anyone.

Serious, quantifiable claims, however, must be backed up with evidence or they could mean litigation: "Our chicken has less fat than a hamburger. It's better for you."[30] This bold claim was investigated, and the fried chicken restaurant had to stop using it in its advertising. Yes, the fried chicken had a little less total fat than a hamburger, but it contained more harmful transfat, sodium, and cholesterol, making it higher in calories—a decidedly unhealthy alternative. As the Federal Trade Commission points out, a restaurant can compare itself to others, but it must tell the truth.

**YOUR TASK.** Look for examples of puffery, and find ads that would need to prove their claims. How can you tell which is which? Discuss examples in class or in an online forum set up for your class.

Chapter 8: Persuasive Messages

# GRAMMAR/MECHANICS CHECKUP—8

## Commas 3

Review the Grammar/Mechanics Handbook Sections 2.10–2.15 for Questions 1–5. For Questions 6–15, also review Sections 2.01–2.09. Then study each of the following statements and insert necessary commas. In the space provided, write the number of commas you added; write *0* if no commas are needed. Also record the number of the G/M principle(s) illustrated. When you finish, compare your responses with those provided at the end of the book. If your answers differ, study carefully the principles shown in parentheses.

__2_____ (2.12)   **EXAMPLE**   The CEO named Betty Shiffman, not Martin Jiang, to the board of directors.

_____   1. "Perpetual optimism" said Colin Powell "is a force multiplier."

_____   2. The featured speakers are Laura Dendringer PhD and Pam Rankey MBA.

_____   3. We interviewed JoyLynn Reed on June 2 didn't we?

_____   4. Research shows that talking on a cell phone distracts drivers and quadruples their chances of getting into accidents such as rear-ending a car ahead of them.

_____   5. The bigger the monitor the clearer the picture.

## Review Commas 1, 2, 3

_____   6. As you may know information chips are already encoded in the visas of people who need them for work travel or study in this country.

_____   7. We think however that the new passports will be issued only to diplomats and other government employees beginning in August.

_____   8. To fill the vacant position we hope to hire Kimberly Creek-Lea who is currently working in Palm Beach Gardens.

_____   9. All things considered our conference will attract more participants if it is held in a resort setting such as Las Vegas Scottsdale or Orlando.

_____   10. If you examine the log closely you will see that we shipped 15 orders on Thursday; on Friday only 4.

_____   11. In the past ten years we have promoted over 30 well-qualified individuals many of whom started in accounting.

_____   12. Paul Miller who spoke to our class last week is the author of a book titled *The Digital Workplace*.

_____   13. A widely discussed study of productivity that was conducted by authoritative researchers revealed that workers in the United States are more productive than workers in Europe or Japan.

_____   14. America's secret productivity weapons according to the report were not bigger companies more robots or even brainier managers.

_____   15. As a matter of fact the report said that America's productivity resulted from a capitalistic system of unprotected hands-off competition.

## EDITING CHALLENGE—8

To fine-tune your grammar and mechanics skills, in every chapter you will be editing a message. The following message from server Joshua Rubin proposes a change in tipping policy to the general manager, Jeremy Roper. However, the message suffers from proofreading, spelling, grammar, punctuation, wordiness, and other writing faults that require correction. Study the guidelines in the Grammar/Mechanics Handbook as well as the lists of Confusing Words and Frequently Misspelled Words to sharpen your skills.

**YOUR TASK.** Edit the following message (a) by correcting errors in your textbook or on a photocopy using proofreading marks from Appendix A or (b) by downloading the message from the premium website at www.cengagebrain.com and correcting at your computer. Your instructor may show you a possible solution.

---

Current date

Mr. Jeremy Roper, General Manager
Monterey Plaza Hotel and Spa
440 Cannery Row
Monterey, CA 93940

Dear Mr. Roper:

I'm writing this letter to let you know that the wait staff at the Monterey Plazas popular Schooner Bistro restaurant would like to bring to your attention a serious problem. Even when us servers have gave good service some customer's leave no tip. Many of us have gotten together and decided to bring the problem and a possible solution to your attention per this letter.

Restaurants such as the famous French Laundry which is ranked as the countries finest restaurant, now add a 20 percent tip to the bill. All service charges go to the house and every one is paid a salary from that. Other restaurants are also printing gratuity guidelines on checks. In fact American Express now provides a calculation feature on it's terminals so that restaurants can chose the tip levels they want printed. In Europe a service charge of up to 20 percent is auto calculated, and added to a check.

Us servers are of the opinion that a suggested tip printed on checks would work good here at Schooner Bistro. We know that we give good service but some customers forget to tip. By printing a suggested tip on the check we remind them so that they won't forget. A printed suggested tip also does the math for them which is a advantage for customer's who are not to good with figures. In addition many of our customers are tourists from Europe. Who don't understand our tipping system.

Printing suggested tips on checks not only helps customers but also proves to the staff that you support them in there goal to recieve decent wages for the hard work they do. A few customers might resist, however these customers can always cross out the printed tip if they wish. If you have any doubts about the plan we could try it for a 6-month period, and monitor customers reactions.

We erge you to begin printing a suggested 20 percent tip on each customers bill. Our American express terminals are all ready equipt to do this. Please let us know your feelings about this proposal because its a serious concern to us.

Sincerely,

*Joshua Rubin*

Joshua Rubin
Server, Schooner Bistro

# COMMUNICATION WORKSHOP

## ETHICS

### What's Legal and What's Not in Sales Messages and Online Reviews

In promoting products and writing sales messages, be careful about the words you choose and the claims you make. How far can you go in praising and selling your product?

- **Puffery.** In a sales message, you can write, *Hey, we've got something fantastic! It's the very best product on the market!* Called "puffery," such promotional claims are not taken literally by reasonable consumers. However, consider the case of Dannon Yogurt, which settled a lawsuit for $45 million over allegedly deceptive claims that its products were "clinically proven" to relieve irregularity and helped people avoid catching colds or the flu.[31] The Federal Trade Commission charged that Dannon's claims were false and its advertising deceptive because it lacked proof.

- **Proving your claims.** If you write that three out of four dentists recommend your toothpaste, you had better have competent and reliable scientific evidence to support the claim. Such a claim goes beyond puffery and requires proof. According to a government report, as many as 20 percent of dietary supplements in the United States featured labels that made illegal claims to cure or treat diseases such as cancer and AIDS.[32] The $20 billion supplement industry is frequently in the sights of investigators and subject to litigation for misleading claims. Actress and *Dancing With the Stars* celebrity Kirstie Alley, whose struggle with weight loss is amply documented, was sued for allegedly making false statements over the Organic Liaison weight-loss program she touts.[33] In a litigious society, marketers who exaggerate are often taken to court.

- **Celebrities.** The unauthorized use of a celebrity's name, likeness, or nickname is not permitted in sales messages. Hollywood stars George Clooney and Julia Roberts joined forces to sue two audiovisual companies for misusing their names and images in selling projectors and entertainment systems. Hilary Swank filed a lawsuit claiming unauthorized use of her film *Million Dollar Baby* in ads.[34] Similarly, the White House does not approve the use of the president's name and likeness for commercial purposes. Weatherproof Garment Company was asked to remove a billboard in Times Square that showed Barack Obama wearing one of its coats above the caption "A Leader in Style."[35]

- **Misleading statements.** You cannot tell people that they are winners or finalists in a sweepstake unless they actually are. American Family Publishers was found guilty of sending letters tricking people into buying magazine subscription in the belief that they had won $1.1 million. Similarly, it is deceptive to invite unsuspecting consumers to cash a check that will then hook them into entering a legal contract or a subscription. Finally, companies may not misrepresent the nature, characteristics, qualities, or geographic origin of goods or services they are promoting.

- **Paying for favorable online reviews.** The Federal Trade Commission mandates full disclosure when a merchant and a promoter have a financial relationship. Legacy Learning Systems paid $250,000 to settle charges that it hired reviewers to recommend its videos on the Web.[36] Amazon and other online retailers have policies against buying positive reviews. Nonetheless, experts estimate that about one third of all Internet consumer reviews are fake.[37]

**CAREER APPLICATION.** Bring to class at least three promotional e-mails, sales letters, social media posts, or advertisements that may represent issues described here. What examples of puffery can you identify? Are claims substantiated by reliable evidence? What proof is offered? Do any of your examples include names, images, or nicknames of celebrities? How likely is it that the celebrity authorized this use? Have you ever received unwanted merchandise as part of a sales campaign? What were you expected to do with it?

# ENDNOTES

[1] White, E. (2008, May 19). Art of persuasion becomes key. *The Wall Street Journal*. Retrieved from http://online.wsj.com/article/SB121115784262002373.html; McIntosh, P., & Luecke, R. A. (2011). *Increase your influence at work*. New York: American Management Association, p. 4.

[2] Jones, J. P. (2004). *Fables, fashions, and facts about advertising: A study of 28 enduring myths*. Thousand Oaks, CA: Sage Publications (Kindle Edition), Chapter 2; Rosseli, F., Skelly, J. J., & Mackie, D. M. (1995). Processing rational and emotional messages: The cognitive and affective mediation of persuasion. *Journal of Experimental Social Psychology, 31*, 163.

[3] Fogg, B. J. (2008). Mass interpersonal persuasion: An early view of a new phenomenon. In: Proceedings. Third International Conference on Persuasive Technology 2008. Berlin, Germany: Springer.

[4] Discussion based on Perloff, R. M. (2010). *The dynamics of persuasion: Communication and attitudes in the twenty-first century* (4th ed.). New York: Routledge, pp. 4–5.

[5] Wike, R., & Krishnamurthy, V. (2012, June 13). Global opinion of Obama slips, international policies faulted. Pew Research Center. Retrieved from http://www.pewglobal.org/files/2012/06/Pew-Global-Attitudes-U.S.-Image-Report-FINAL-June-13-2012.pdf

[6] Halperin, S. (2012, December 19). "X Factor" sees significant social media strides. *The Hollywood Reporter*. Retrieved from http://www.hollywoodreporter.com/live-feed/x-factors-social-media-strategy-405485

[7] Perloff, R. M. (2010). *The dynamics of persuasion: Communication and attitudes in the twenty-first century* (4th ed.). New York: Routledge, p. 9.

[8] Boyle, C. (2011, June 16). Pokemon cards allowed in Queens school thanks to third-grader's persuasive letter to teacher. *New York Daily News*. Retrieved from http://www.nydailynews.com/new-york/education/pokemon-cards-allowed-queens-school-thanks-third-grader-persuasive-letter-teacher-article-1.130963

[9] McIntosh, P., & Luecke, R. A. (2011). *Increase your influence at work*. New York: AMACOM, p. 2.

[10] White, E. (2008, May 19). The art of persuasion becomes key. *The Wall Street Journal*. Retrieved from http://online.wsj.com/article/SB121115784262002373.html

[11] Pollock, T. (2003, June). How to sell an idea. *SuperVision*, p. 15. Retrieved from http://search.proquest.com

[12] Folan, K. (2013, May 20). Taco Bell targets b-list models with jewelry, weird love notes. Racked. Retrieved from http://racked.com/archives/2013/05/20/taco-bell-targets-blist-models-with-jewelry-weird-love-notes.php

[13] Millward Brown. (2009). Using neuroscience to understand the role of direct mail, p. 2. Retrieved from http://www.millwardbrown.com/Insights/CaseStudies/NeuroscienceDirectMail.aspx

[14] Direct mail statistics show B2B mailings are still effective. (2011, March 8). The Ballantine Corporation. Retrieved from http://www.ballantine.com/2011/03/08/direct-mail-statistics; Hartong, B. (2011, March). Revitalize your direct mail strategy. *Customer Interaction Solutions*, p. 10. Retrieved from http://proquest.umi.com

[15] Macleod, I. (2013, October). Infographic: Consumers more likely to deal with direct mail immediately compared to email. The Drum. Retrieved from http://www.thedrum.com/news/2013/10/23/infographic-consumers-more-likely-deal-direct-mail-immediately-compared-email DMA releases 2010 response rate trend report. (2010, June 15). Direct Marketing Association. Retrieved from http://www.the-dma.org/cgi/dispannouncements?article=1451; Hartong, B. (2011, March). Revitalize your direct mail strategy. *Customer Interaction Solutions*, p. 10. Retrieved from http://proquest.umi.com

[16] Jones, R. (2013, October 31). Data quality news: Direct mail is still a relevant marketing strategy in 2013. Experian. Retrieved from http://www.qas.com/data-quality-news/direct_mail_is_still_a_relevant_marketing_strategy_in_2013_9721.htm Statistical Fact Book. (2011). The Direct Marketing Association. Retrieved from http://www.the-dma.org/cgi/disppressrelease?article=1474+++++

[17] Ziglar, Z. (2004). The features, function and benefits technique. Retrieved from http://www.candogo.com/search/insight?i=3971; Lowenstein, M. (2007, September 24). Make both an emotional and rational appeal to your customers: Inside-out and outside-in commitment and advocacy. CustomerThink.net. Retrieved from http://www.customerthink.com/article/make_emotional_rational_appeal_customers

[18] ExactTarget. (2012). The 2012 channel preference survey. Retrieved from http://www.exacttarget.com/subscribers-fans-followers/sff14.aspx

[19] Ibid.

[20] Howard, T. (2008, November 28). E-mail grows as direct-marketing tool. *USA Today*, p. 5B.

[21] *Harvard Business Review on reinventing your marketing*. (2011, May 7). Boston: Harvard Business Press Books.

[22] Edwards, L. (2012, March 5). Are brands turning people into adverts with social media? Socialmedia Today. Retrieved from http://socialmediatoday.com/laurahelen/462175/are-brands-turning-people-adverts-social-media

[23] Tong, V. (2007, November 26). Tattoos: A new favorite of advertisers. Boston.com. Retrieved from http://www.boston.com/news/education/higher/articles/2007/11/26/tattoos_a_new_favorite_of_advertisers/?page=full

[24] Zappos' 10-hour long customer service call sets record. (2012, December 21). *The Huffington Post*. Retrieved from http://www.huffingtonpost.com/2012/12/21/zappos-10-hour-call_n_2345467.html?view=print

[25] Wadler, J. (2012, July 26). Home improvement, whether you asked for it or not. *The New York Times*, p. D2.

[26] Based on Fritscher-Porter, K. (2003, June/July). Don't be duped by office supply scam artists. *OfficePro*, pp. 9–10.

[27] Zbar, J. D. (2001, March). Training to telework. *Home Office Computing*, p. 72.

[28] Scenario based on Rubin, C. (2012, September 6). Pitaya: The selling of a superfruit. *Bloomberg Businessweek*. Retrieved from http://www.businessweek.com/articles/2012-09-06/pitaya-the-selling-of-a-superfruit

[29] Ibid.

[30] Scenario based on Federal Trade Commission. (n.d.). FTC fact sheet: It looks good … but is it true? Retrieved from http://www.consumer.ftc.gov/sites/default/files/games/off-site/youarehere/pages/pdf/FTC-Ad-Marketing_Looks-Good.pdf

[31] Federal Trade Commission. (2010, December 15). Dannon agrees to drop exaggerated health claims for Activia Yogurt and DanActive dairy drink. Retrieved from http://www.ftc.gov/news-events/press-releases/2010/12/dannon-agrees-drop-exaggerated-health-claims-activia-yogurt

[32] Burke, G. (2012, October 3). Dietary supplements illegally labeled: Dozens make false claims. Huffpost Healthy. Retrieved from http://www.huffingtonpost.com/2012/10/03/dietary-supplements-illegally-labeled-weight-loss-immune_n_1936670.html; U.S. Food and Drug Administration. (2012, September 4). Tips for older dietary supplement users. Retrieved from http://www.fda.gov/food/dietarysupplements/usingdietarysupplements/ucm110493.htm

[33] Saad, N. (2012, July 25). Kirstie Alley sued for false advertising over weight-loss program. *The Los Angeles Times*. Retrieved from http://articles.latimes.com/2012/jul/25/entertainment/la-et-mg-kirstie-alley-lawsuit-weight-loss-20120725

[34] Anand, S. (2012, June 19). George Clooney and Julia Roberts sue for unauthorized use of their names and images. Retrieved from http://www.lfirm.com/blog/2012/06/george-clooney-and-julia-roberts-sue-for-unauthorized-use-of-their-names-and-images.shtml

[35] Clifford, S. (2010, January 6). Coat maker transforms Obama photo into ad. *The New York Times*. Retrieved from http://www.nytimes.com/2010/01/07/business/media/07garment.html

[36] Streitfeld, D. (2012, January 26). For $2 a star, an online retailer gets 5-star reviews. *The New York Times*. Retrieved from http://www.nytimes.com/2012/01/27/technology/for-2-a-star-a-retailer-gets-5-star-reviews.html

[37] Streitfeld, D. (2012, August 25). The best book reviews money can buy. *The New York Times*. Retrieved from http://www.nytimes.com/2012/08/26/business/book-reviewers-for-hire-meet-a-demand-for-online-raves.html?pagewanted=all

# ACKNOWLEDGMENTS

**p. 227** Office Insider based on Mortensen, K. W. (2006, June 9). The ultra-prosperous study persuasion. EzineArticles. Retrieved from http://ezinearticles.com/?The-Ultra-Prosperous–Study–Persuasion&id=216435

**p. 229** Office Insider based on Rowell, D. M. (2008, January 4). How to create and structure a winning complaint: Being positive and fair gets you more. The Travel Insider. Retrieved from http://thetravelinsider.info/info/howtocomplain2.htm

**p. 232** Office Insider based on Lipnack, J. (2000-2004). Virtual teams: The future is now. Retrieved from http://www.linezine.com/7.2/articles/jlvtfin.htm

**p. 233** Office Insider based on Sandler, P. M. cited in Power of persuasion. (n.d.). SourceWatch. Retrieved from http://www.sourcewatch.org/index.php?title=Power_of_persuasion

**p. 235** Office Insider based on Frey, D. (2011, April 7). 8 reasons why direct mail is so powerful. Retrieved from http://www.facebook.com/note.php?note_id=10150167591671657&comments

**p. 239** Office Insider based on Abramovich, G. (2012, March 13). P&G's new approach to digital. Digiday. Retrieved from http://digiday.com/brands/pgs-new-approach-to-digital

# Business Reports

## UNIT 4

**CHAPTER 9**
Informal Reports

**CHAPTER 10**
Proposals and Formal Reports

# CHAPTER 9

# Informal Reports

## OBJECTIVES
After studying this chapter, you should be able to

**9-1** Explain informational and analytical report functions, organizational strategies, and writing styles.

**9-2** Describe typical report formats and understand the significance of effective headings.

**9-3** Determine the problem the report is addressing as well as the report's purpose, and gather significant secondary and primary information.

**9-4** Write short informational reports that describe routine tasks.

**9-5** Prepare short analytical reports that solve business problems.

## 9-1 Reporting in the Digital Age

Digital-age organizations are competing in a world of constant change due to innovative technology and the ability to generate and share data with vast audiences. Efficient reporting plays a critical role in helping organizations sift through data and make major decisions. Whether a company decides to launch a new product, expand into new markets, reduce expenses, improve customer service, or increase its social media presence, the decisions are usually based on information submitted in reports. Routine reports keep managers informed about work in progress. Focused reports help managers analyze the challenges they face before recommending solutions.

Business reports range widely in length, purpose, and delivery mode. Some are short, informal bulleted lists with status updates. Others are formal 100-page financial forecasts. Routine reports may be generated weekly or monthly, whereas focused reports appear irregularly and cover specific problems or situations. Report findings may be presented orally in a meeting or shared electronically on Web platforms. Many reports today are delivered digitally in e-mail messages, PDF (portable document format) files, or slide decks. These reports can then be shared on a company's intranet, posted on the Internet, or saved in cloud environments.

This chapter examines the functions, organizational strategies, writing styles, and formats of typical business reports. It discusses the importance of clearly identifying the problem to be solved and the specific purpose of the report. It also addresses the process of gathering accurate information from secondary and primary sources that can be used in short informational or analytical reports.

**LEARNING OBJECTIVE 1**
Explain informational and analytical report functions, organizational strategies, and writing styles.

## 9-1a Informational and Analytical Report Functions

Most reports fit into one of two broad categories: informational reports and analytical reports. Informational reports provide information and data only; analytical reports examine the data, draw conclusions, and sometimes make recommendations.

**Informational Reports.** Reports that present data without analysis or recommendations are primarily informational. For such reports, writers collect and organize facts, but they do not analyze the facts for readers. A trip report describing an employee's visit to a trade show, for example, is informational. Weekly status reports about an ongoing project are also informational. Other reports that present information without analysis include monthly sales reports, status updates, and government compliance reports.

**Analytical Reports.** Reports that provide data or findings, analyses, and conclusions are analytical. If requested, writers also supply recommendations. Analytical reports may intend to persuade readers to act or change their beliefs. For example, if you were writing a yardstick comparison report to evaluate several locations for a new automobile manufacturing plant, you would compare the locations using the same criteria and then provide a recommendation. Other reports that provide recommendations are feasibility studies (e.g., for expansion opportunities) and justification reports (e.g., for buying equipment or changing procedures).

## 9-1b Organizational Strategies

Like other business messages, reports may be organized directly or indirectly. The reader's anticipated reaction and the content of a report determine its organizational strategy, as illustrated in Figure 9.1. In long reports, such as corporate annual reports, some parts may be organized directly whereas other parts are arranged indirectly.

**Direct Strategy.** When you place the purpose for writing close to the beginning of a report, the organizational strategy is direct. Informational reports, such as the letter report shown in Figure 9.2, are usually arranged directly. In this letter the writer responds to a request for information about a legal services plan. Notice that the informational report opens with an introduction that provides details about the available plans. The facts about the plan's benefits, divided

### Workplace in Focus

In 2013, Coca-Cola's periodic sales reports showed four consecutive quarters of declining sales. Beverages leading the slump downward included the company's namesake Coke brand, as well as other carbonated drinks such as Sprite and Fanta. The drop was significant: according to the company's fourth quarter sales report, carbonated drink sales fell a full three percent. However, sales of the company's Powerade sports drink showed steady sales increases. What can Coca-Cola learn from this raw data, and what types of reports can turn this raw data into meaningful information to help managers fix sagging sales?[1]

Chapter 9: Informal Reports

## Figure 9.1 Audience Analysis and Report Organization

**Direct Strategy**
- If readers are informed
- If readers are eager to have results first
- If readers are supportive

**Informational Report**
- Introduction/Background
- Facts/Findings
- Summary

**Analytical Report**
- Introduction/Problem
- Conclusions/Recommendations
- Facts/Findings
- Discussion/Analysis

**Indirect Strategy**
- If readers need to be educated
- If readers need to be persuaded
- If readers may be disappointed or hostile

**Analytical Report**
- Introduction/Problem
- Facts/Findings
- Discussion/Analysis
- Conclusions/Recommendations

---

into three subtopics and identified by descriptive headings, follow. The report ends with a summary and a complimentary close.

Analytical reports may also be organized directly, especially when readers are supportive of or familiar with the topic. Many busy executives prefer this strategy because it gives them the results of the report immediately. They don't have to spend time wading through the facts, findings, discussion, and analyses to get to the two items they are most interested in—the conclusions and recommendations.

**Indirect Strategy.** The organizational strategy is indirect when the conclusions and recommendations, if requested, appear at the end of the report. Such reports usually begin with an introduction or description of the problem, followed by facts and explanations. They end with conclusions and recommendations. This strategy is helpful when readers are unfamiliar with the problem or when they must be persuaded. When readers may be disappointed in or hostile toward the report's findings, an indirect strategy works best. The writer is more likely to retain the reader's interest by first explaining, justifying, and analyzing the facts and then making recommendations. This strategy also seems most rational to readers because it follows the normal thought process: problem, alternatives (facts), solution.

### 9-1c Informal and Formal Writing Styles

Like other business messages, reports can range from informal to formal depending on their purpose, audience, and setting. Research reports from consultants to their clients tend to be more formal. Such reports must project objectivity, authority, and impartiality. However, depending on the industry, a report to a boss describing a trip to a conference is normally informal.

# Figure 9.2 Informational Report—Letter Format

**Apex Legal Services**
P.O. Box 465
Round Rock, TX 78664
(512) 248-8931
www.apexlegal.com

September 17, 2016

Ms. Ava Hammond, Office Manager
Lake Austin Homeowners
3902 Oak Hill Drive
Austin, TX 78134

Dear Ms. Hammond:

Subject: Request for Legal Services Plan for a Homeowners' Association

Thank you for your inquiry about a legal services plan for your homeowners' association. The following information describes our available plans and gives instructions for setting up a plan for your association.

**Introduction**

A legal services plan promotes preventive law by letting members talk to attorneys whenever problems arise. Prompt legal advice often prevents expensive litigation. Because groups can supply a flow of business to the plan's attorneys, groups can negotiate free consultations, follow-ups, and discounts.

Two types of plans are commonly available. The first, a free plan, offers free legal consultations and discounts for services when the participating groups are large enough to generate business for the plan's attorneys. The second type is the prepaid plan. Prepaid plans provide more benefits, but members must pay annual fees, usually $200 or more a year.

Because you inquired about a free plan for your homeowners' association, the following information describes how to set up such a program.

**Determine What Benefits Your Group Needs**

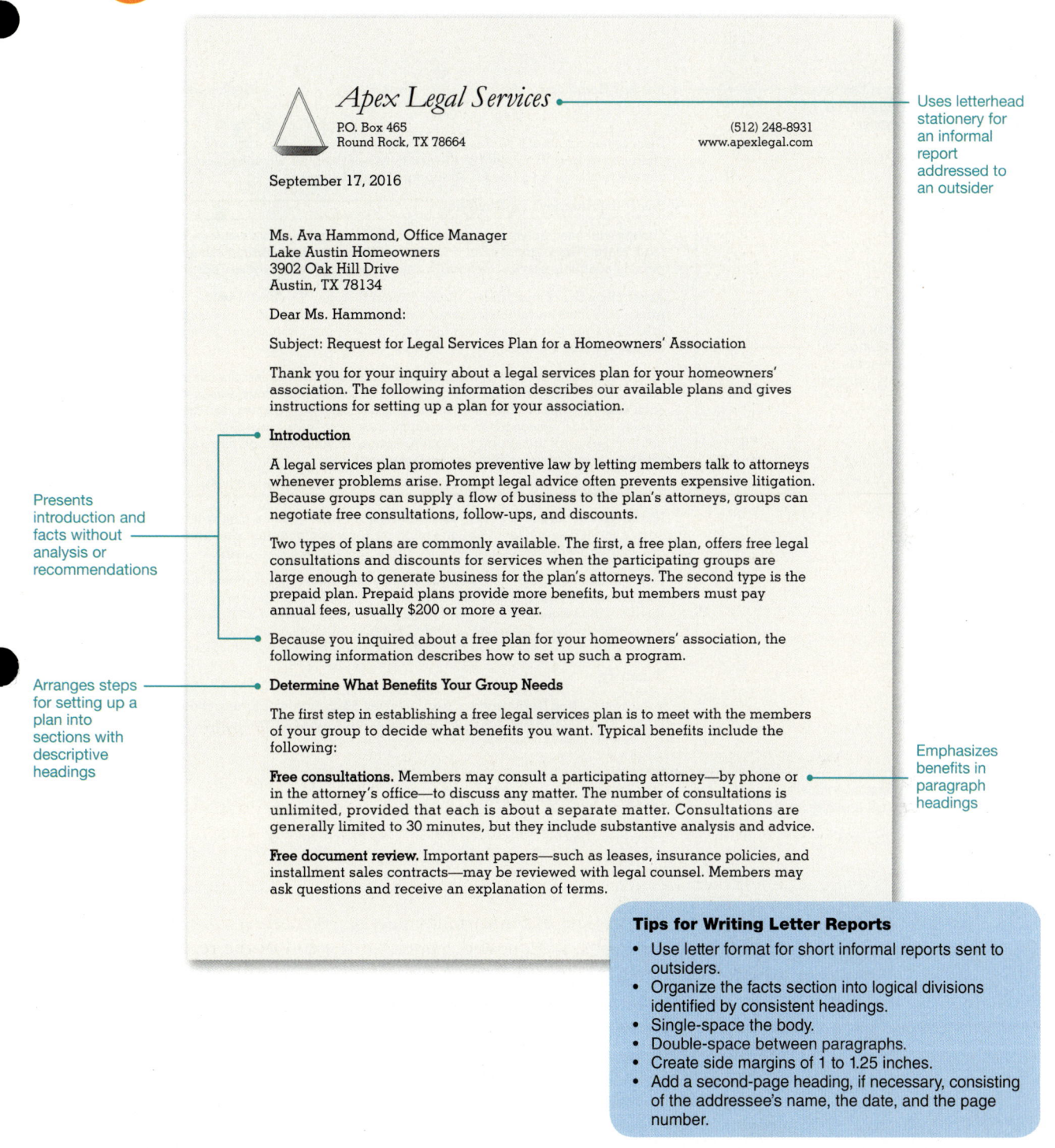

The first step in establishing a free legal services plan is to meet with the members of your group to decide what benefits you want. Typical benefits include the following:

**Free consultations.** Members may consult a participating attorney—by phone or in the attorney's office—to discuss any matter. The number of consultations is unlimited, provided that each is about a separate matter. Consultations are generally limited to 30 minutes, but they include substantive analysis and advice.

**Free document review.** Important papers—such as leases, insurance policies, and installment sales contracts—may be reviewed with legal counsel. Members may ask questions and receive an explanation of terms.

*Annotations:*
- Uses letterhead stationery for an informal report addressed to an outsider
- Presents introduction and facts without analysis or recommendations
- Arranges steps for setting up a plan into sections with descriptive headings
- Emphasizes benefits in paragraph headings

**Tips for Writing Letter Reports**
- Use letter format for short informal reports sent to outsiders.
- Organize the facts section into logical divisions identified by consistent headings.
- Single-space the body.
- Double-space between paragraphs.
- Create side margins of 1 to 1.25 inches.
- Add a second-page heading, if necessary, consisting of the addressee's name, the date, and the page number.

An office worker once called a grammar hotline service with this problem: "We've just sent a report to our headquarters, and it was returned with this comment, 'Put it in the third person.' What do they mean?" The hotline experts explained that management apparently wanted a more formal writing style, using third-person constructions (*the company* or *the researcher* instead of *we* and *I*). Figure 9.3, which compares the characteristics of formal and informal report-writing styles, can help you decide which style is appropriate for your reports. Note

Figure 9.2 (Continued)

---

Ms. Ava Hammond          Page 2          September 17, 2016

**Discount on additional services.** For more complex matters, participating attorneys charge members 75 percent of the attorney's normal fee. However, some attorneys choose to charge a flat fee for commonly needed services.

**Select the Attorneys for Your Plan**

Groups with geographically concentrated memberships have an advantage in forming legal plans. These groups can limit the number of participating attorneys and yet provide adequate service. Generally, smaller panels of attorneys are advantageous.

Assemble a list of candidates, inviting them to apply. The best way to compare prices is to have candidates submit their fees. Your group can then compare fee schedules and select the lowest bidder, if price is important. Arrange to interview attorneys in their offices.

After selecting an attorney or a panel, sign a contract. The contract should include the reason for the plan, what the attorney agrees to do, what the group agrees to do, how each side can end the contract, and the signature of both parties. You may also wish to include references to malpractice insurance, assurance that the group will not interfere with the attorney–client relationship, an evaluation form, a grievance procedure, and responsibility for government filings.

**Publicize the Plan to Your Members**

Members will not use a plan if they don't know about it, and a plan will not be successful if it is unused. Publicity must be vocal and ongoing. Announce it at the association's website, in newsletters, and at meetings.

Persistence is the key. All too frequently, leaders of an organization assume that a single announcement is all that's needed. They expect members to see the value of the plan and remember that it is available. Most organization members, though, are not as involved as the leadership. Therefore, it takes more publicity than the leadership usually expects to reach and maintain the desired level of awareness.

**Summary**

A successful free legal services plan involves designing a program, choosing the attorneys, and publicizing the plan. To learn more about these steps or to order a $45 how-to manual, call me at (512) 248-9282.

Sincerely,

*Gary T. Rodriguez, Esq.*
Gary T. Rodriguez, Esq.
Executive Director

---

*Annotations:*
- Identifies second page with a header
- Uses parallel headings for consistency and readability
- Includes complimentary close and signature

---

that, increasingly, formal reports writers use contractions and active-voice verbs. Today, report writers try to avoid awkward third-person references to themselves as *the researchers* or *the authors* because it sounds stilted and outdated.

**LEARNING OBJECTIVE 2**
Describe typical report formats and understand the significance of effective headings.

## 9-2 Report Formats and Heading Levels

The overall design of a formatted report should be visually appealing and professional looking. The report's design should include a hierarchy of meaningful headings that highlight major points, allowing readers to see the flow of ideas. Many corporations use templates or reporting software to standardize the look of their report in terms of formats and heading levels.

## 9-2a Typical Report Formats

The format of a report depends on its length, topic, audience, and purpose. After considering these elements, you will probably select one of the following formats or file types.

**Letter Format.** Use letter format for short informal reports (usually eight or fewer pages) addressed outside an organization. Prepared on office stationery, a letter report contains a date, inside address, salutation, and complimentary close, as shown in Figure 9.2. Although they may carry information similar to that found in correspondence, letter reports usually are longer and show more careful organization than typical letters. Meaningful headings guide the reader through the content.

**Memo and E-Mail Formats.** For short informal reports that stay within organizations, the memo format is appropriate. Memo reports begin with essential background information, using standard headings: *Date, To, From*, and *Subject*. Like letter reports, memo reports differ from regular memos in length, use of headings, and deliberate organization. Today, memo reports are rarely distributed in hard copy; rather, they are attached to e-mails or, if short, embedded in the body of e-mails.

**Manuscript Format.** For longer, more formal reports, use the manuscript format. These reports are usually printed on plain paper without letterhead. They begin with a title followed by systematically displayed headings and subheadings. You will see examples of proposals and formal reports using the manuscript format in Chapter 10.

**Forms and Templates.** Formerly, office workers used preprinted forms or templates for repetitive data, such as monthly sales reports, performance appraisals, merchandise inventories, and personnel and financial reports. Employees can now customize templates and forms and print them or distribute them electronically. Using standardized formats and headings saves a writer time and ensures that all required information is included.

### OFFICE INSIDER

"Third person makes ideas sound less subjective since it removes direct reference to the writer. . . . For example, 'Researchers first need to determine participants' (written in the third person) conveys a more formal, objective tone than 'You first need to determine participants' (second person) and 'I first needed to determine participants' (first person)."

—Kristie Sweet, content writer, Demand Media

### Figure 9.3 Report-Writing Styles

|  | Informal Writing Style | Formal Writing Style |
|---|---|---|
| **Appropriate Use** | • Short, routine reports<br>• Reports for familiar audiences<br>• Noncontroversial reports<br>• Internal use reports<br>• Internal announcements and invitations | • Lengthy, formal reports and proposals<br>• Research studies<br>• Controversial or complex reports<br>• External use reports<br>• Formal Invitations |
| **Overall Effect** | • Friendly tone<br>• Relationship building<br>• Casual | • Objectivity and accuracy<br>• Sense of professionalism and fairness<br>• Professional distance between writer and reader |
| **Writing Style Characteristics** | • Use of first-person pronouns (*I, we, me, my, us, our*)<br>• Use of contractions (*can't, don't*)<br>• Emphasis on active-voice verbs (*I conducted the study*)<br>• Shorter sentences<br>• Familiar words<br>• Conversational language | • Use of third person (*the researcher, the writer*) (depends on the circumstances)<br>• Absence of contractions (*cannot, do not*)<br>• Use of passive-voice verbs (*the study was conducted*)<br>• Professional, respectful language<br>• Absence of humor and figures of speech<br>• Elimination of "editorializing" (author's opinions and perceptions) |

Chapter 9: Informal Reports

**Digital Formats and PDF Files.** Writers often save and distribute reports as PDF files. This file type condenses documents while preserving the formatting and graphics. A report created with Microsoft Word, Excel, or PowerPoint can easily be saved as a PDF file. A PDF report might include links to external websites, a nice advantage over a printed report. Web-based reports may feature engaging multimedia effects, such as interactive charts and video.

**Infographics.** Infographics are visual representations of data or information. They can display complex information quickly and clearly, and they are easier to understand than written text. Infographics are also affordable and easily shared on social media platforms. In fact, good infographics can go viral when viewers embed and spread the word about it in their blogs and on their social media networks. Infographics can tell compelling stories that help all types of businesses attract and inform consumers.

**Digital Slide Decks.** Many business writers deliver their report information in digital slideshows, also called slide decks. These slides can be sent by e-mail, embedded on the Web, or posted on a company intranet. When used in reporting, slide decks may have more text than typical presentation slides. Photographs, tables, charts, and other visuals make slide decks more inviting to read than print pages of dense report text. Not surprisingly, communicators in the fields of marketing, technology, media, entertainment, and consulting are fond of using slide deck reports to summarize their statistics and other findings. Figure 9.4 shows several slides from global marketing company ExactTarget analyzing the Internet market in Germany.

Figure 9.4 Informal Reports Delivered as Slide Decks

Source: http://www.exacttarget.com/resource-center/digital-marketing/infographics/sff-german-digital-republic

Viewers may choose to download entire slide deck reports or even individual slides. One well-known free site for sharing slide decks is SlideShare. You can search SlideShare for presentations on various topics, download the presentation, and save it as a PDF or a PowerPoint file.

## 9-2b Effective Report Headings

Descriptive headings assist readers in comprehending the organization of a report. Viewers can see major ideas at a glance. Moreover, headings provide resting points for the mind and for the eye, breaking up large chunks of text into manageable and readable segments.

Report writers may use functional or talking headings, examples of which are shown in Figure 9.5. Functional headings are one- or two-word labels that show the sections of a report but provide little insight about the contents. Functional headings are sometimes useful for routine reports.

Talking headings provide more information and spark interest. Writers must make sure, however, that talking headings contribute to the overall organization and flow of ideas. With some planning, headings can combine the best attributes of both functional and talking, as the letter report in Figure 9.2 shows.

The best strategy for creating helpful talking headings is to write a few paragraphs first and then generate a talking heading that covers those paragraphs. To create effective report headings, follow these basic guidelines:

- **Construct a clear hierarchy of heading levels.** A hierarchy refers to the level of importance of the headings in a document. Some reports have one level of heading and others may have three. A heading's placement, size, and font should match those of the other headings in the same level. Writers may use varying font styles and sizes, but the hierarchy must be clear to the reader. Remember, too, that reports are easier to follow when they use not more than three heading levels. Figure 9.6 illustrates a document with a main heading (the title) and three heading levels.

- **Capitalize and emphasize carefully.** A writer might choose to use all capital letters for main titles, such as a report or chapter title. For first- and second-level headings, they follow the traditional rules for headings: capitalize the first letter of main words such as nouns, verbs, adjectives, adverbs, and so on. Do not capitalize articles (*a, an, the*), conjunctions (*and, but, or, nor*), and prepositions with three or fewer letters (*in, to, by, for*) unless they are the first or last words in the heading. Headings generally appear in bold font, as shown in Figure 9.6.

- **Create grammatically equal heading levels.** Try to create headings that are grammatically equal, or parallel, within the same level. For example, *Developing Product Teams* and *Presenting Plan to Management* are parallel headings; they both begin with an action word ending in *-ing*. *Development of Product Teams* and *Presenting Plan to Management* are not parallel headings.

Figure **9.5** Distinguishing Among Functional, Talking, and Combination Headings

**Functional Headings**
- Background
- Findings
- Personnel
- Production Costs

**Talking Headings**
- Lack of Space and Cost Compound Parking Program
- Survey Shows Support for Parking Fees

**Combination Headings**
- Introduction: Lack of Parking Reaches Crisis Proportions
- Parking Recommendations: Shuttle and New Structures

Figure 9.6 Varying Styles in Levels of Headings

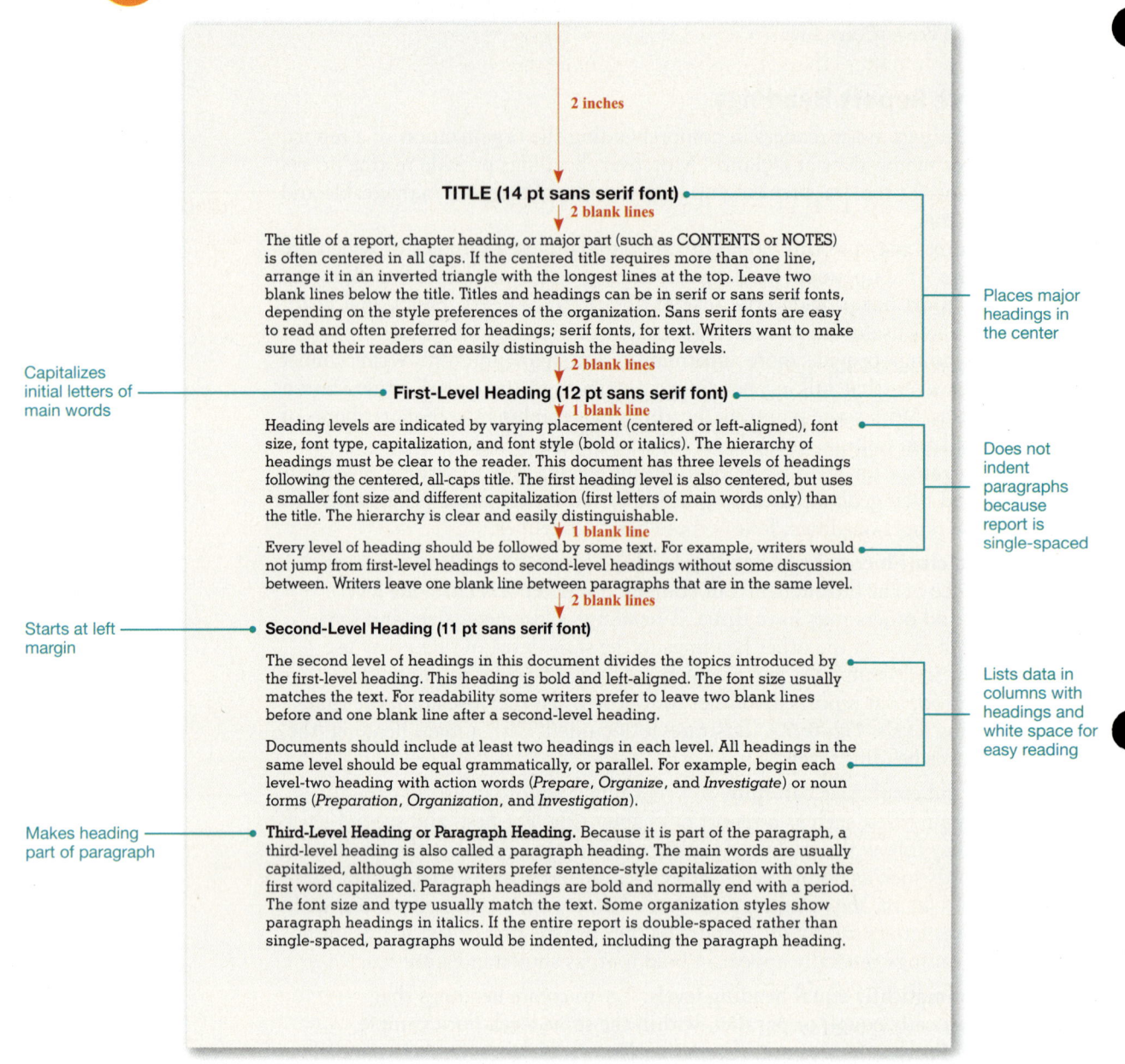

↓ 2 inches

**TITLE (14 pt sans serif font)**
↓ 2 blank lines

The title of a report, chapter heading, or major part (such as CONTENTS or NOTES) is often centered in all caps. If the centered title requires more than one line, arrange it in an inverted triangle with the longest lines at the top. Leave two blank lines below the title. Titles and headings can be in serif or sans serif fonts, depending on the style preferences of the organization. Sans serif fonts are easy to read and often preferred for headings; serif fonts, for text. Writers want to make sure that their readers can easily distinguish the heading levels.
↓ 2 blank lines

**First-Level Heading (12 pt sans serif font)**
↓ 1 blank line

Heading levels are indicated by varying placement (centered or left-aligned), font size, font type, capitalization, and font style (bold or italics). The hierarchy of headings must be clear to the reader. This document has three levels of headings following the centered, all-caps title. The first heading level is also centered, but uses a smaller font size and different capitalization (first letters of main words only) than the title. The hierarchy is clear and easily distinguishable.
↓ 1 blank line

Every level of heading should be followed by some text. For example, writers would not jump from first-level headings to second-level headings without some discussion between. Writers leave one blank line between paragraphs that are in the same level.
↓ 2 blank lines

**Second-Level Heading (11 pt sans serif font)**

The second level of headings in this document divides the topics introduced by the first-level heading. This heading is bold and left-aligned. The font size usually matches the text. For readability some writers prefer to leave two blank lines before and one blank line after a second-level heading.

Documents should include at least two headings in each level. All headings in the same level should be equal grammatically, or parallel. For example, begin each level-two heading with action words (*Prepare*, *Organize*, and *Investigate*) or noun forms (*Preparation*, *Organization*, and *Investigation*).

**Third-Level Heading or Paragraph Heading.** Because it is part of the paragraph, a third-level heading is also called a paragraph heading. The main words are usually capitalized, although some writers prefer sentence-style capitalization with only the first word capitalized. Paragraph headings are bold and normally end with a period. The font size and type usually match the text. Some organization styles show paragraph headings in italics. If the entire report is double-spaced rather than single-spaced, paragraphs would be indented, including the paragraph heading.

Callouts (left): Capitalizes initial letters of main words; Starts at left margin; Makes heading part of paragraph.

Callouts (right): Places major headings in the center; Does not indent paragraphs because report is single-spaced; Lists data in columns with headings and white space for easy reading.

- **For short reports use one or two heading levels.** In a short report, first-level headings might be bold and left-aligned; second-level headings might be bold paragraph headings.
- **Include at least one heading per report page, but don't end the page with a stand-alone heading.** Headings increase the readability and add visual appeal to report pages. Try to use at least one heading per page to break up blocks of text and reveal the content's topic. If a heading at the bottom of a page gets separated from the text that follows, move that heading to the top of the following page.
- **Apply punctuation correctly.** Stand-alone bold headings do not require end punctuation. Paragraph headings, on the other hand, are followed by a period, which separates them from the text that follows.

- **Keep headings short but clear.** One-word headings are emphatic but not always clear. For example, the heading *Project* does not adequately describe the expectations of a summer internship project for a Texas oil company. A better heading would be *(Company name)'s Internship Expectations*. Keep your headings brief (no more than eight words), but make them meaningful. Clarity is more important than brevity.

## 9-3 Defining the Purpose and Gathering Data

**LEARNING OBJECTIVE 3**
Determine the problem the report is addressing as well as the report's purpose, and gather significant secondary and primary information.

Because business reports are systematic attempts to compile data, answer questions, and solve problems, you'll want to be methodical and pay attention to their organization and structure. Make sure a report's purpose is clear. Also, think about your readers and how they will react to the conclusions or recommendations. This helps you know how much background material to gather, whether to organize the report directly or indirectly, and what level of formality to use.

Once the purpose is clear, you'll begin gathering needed data. Simple informal reports might not require much research or data analysis; however, complex reports might require extensive research and data analysis. Whatever the case, analyzing the problem the report will address and the purpose of the report will keep it on target and determine how much data and research is needed. The following guidelines will help you plan your report and gather relevant data.

### 9-3a Determine the Problem and Purpose

The first step in writing a report is analyzing or determining the problem the report will address. Preparing a written problem statement helps clarify the task. Suppose a pharmaceutical company wants to investigate the problem of high transportation costs for its sales representatives. Some sales reps visit clients using company-leased cars; others drive their own cars and are reimbursed for expenses. The leasing agreements for 12 cars expire in three months. The company wants to investigate the transportation choices and report the findings before the leases are renewed. The following problem statement helps clarify the reason for the report:

**Problem statement:** *The leases on all company cars will expire in three months. The company must decide whether to renew them or develop a new policy regarding transportation for sales reps. Expenses and reimbursement paperwork for employee-owned cars is excessive.*

A statement of purpose further defines the report's purpose and scope. To begin, develop questions that help clarify the purpose: Should the company compare the costs for buying and leasing cars? Should the company gather current data on reimbursement costs for those driving personal cars? Will the report writers evaluate the data and recommend a course of action? Should the sales reps' reactions be considered? Then write a statement of purpose that answers the questions.

**Statement of purpose:** *To recommend a plan that provides sales reps with cars to be used in their calls. The report will compare costs for three plans: outright ownership, leasing, and compensation for employee-owned cars. Data will include the sales reps' reactions to each plan.*

Preparing a written purpose statement is a good idea because it limits the scope and provides a standard that keeps the project on target. In writing useful purpose statements, choose action verbs telling what you intend to do: *analyze, choose, investigate, compare, justify, evaluate, explain, establish, determine*, and so on. Notice that the preceding purpose statement uses the action verbs *recommend* and *compare*.

Chapter 9: Informal Reports

## Workplace in Focus

Because of the Internet, gathering and analyzing survey data for business reports has never been easier. One Web-based company has turned the task of conducting surveys into a lot of monkey business—literally. Since launching in 1999, SurveyMonkey has become the world's largest survey company. The firm helps Fortune 500 companies conduct millions of surveys online daily. SurveyMonkey provides online templates and sound survey methodologies, and business managers simply plug-in the questions they need answered and hit Send. Surveys take place online, with results appearing in real time, ready for use in business reports. What are some of the most common uses of surveys in business?[2]

Some reports require only a simple statement of purpose (e.g., *to investigate expanded teller hours, to select a manager from among four candidates, to describe the position of accounts supervisor*). Many assignments, though, require expanded purpose statements.

### 9-3b Gather Information From Secondary and Primary Sources

One of the most important steps in writing a report is that of gathering information (research). A good report is based on solid, accurate, verifiable facts. This factual information falls into two broad categories: primary and secondary. Primary data result from firsthand experience and observation. Secondary data come from reading what others have experienced or observed and recorded. Typical sources of factual information for informal reports are (a) company records, (b) printed material, (c) electronic resources, (d) observation, (e) surveys and questionnaires, and (f) interviews.

**Company Records.** Many business reports begin with an analysis of company records and files. From these records you can observe past performance and methods used to solve previous problems. You can collect pertinent facts that will help determine a course of action.

**Printed Material.** Although some print resources are also available online, libraries should not be overlooked as an excellent source for many types of print resources. Some information in libraries is available only in print. Print sources include books, newspapers, and periodicals, such as magazines and journals.

**Electronic Resources.** An extensive source of current and historical information is available on the Web. From a computer or mobile device you can access storehouses of information provided by government sites, news media, periodicals, nonprofits, and businesses. Business researchers are also using Facebook comments, Twitter feeds, forum messages, and blog posts to gather information. For short informal reports, you will probably gather most of your data from online resources. Chapter 10 provides more detailed suggestions about online research and Web search tools.

**Observation.** In the absence of secondary sources, a primary source of data for many problems comes from personal observation and experience. For example, if you were writing a report on the need for a comprehensive policy on the use of social media, you might observe employees to see whether they are checking their social networks during the workday or sharing potentially damaging company information on their blogs, on Facebook, and on other social networks. Observation might yield incomplete results, but it is nonetheless a valid form of data collection.

**Surveys and Questionnaires.** When a report requires current user or customer feedback, you can collect the data efficiently and economically by using surveys and questionnaires. This is another primary source of information. For example, if you were part of a committee investigating the success of an employee carpooling program, you might gather data by distributing a questionnaire to the employees themselves. See Chapter 10 for more information about surveys.

**Interviews.** Talking with individuals directly concerned with the problem produces excellent firsthand information if published sources are not available. For example, if you would like to find ways to improve the hiring process of your company, you may want to interview your company's Human Resources director or several of the department hiring managers for the most accurate and relevant information. Interviews allow you to gather data from experts in their fields.

## 9-4 Writing Short Informational Reports

Now that you are familiar with the basics of gathering data, you are ready to enter that information into short informational or analytical reports. Informational reports often describe periodic, recurring activities (such as monthly sales or weekly customer calls) as well as situational, nonrecurring events (such as trips, conferences, and special projects). Short informational reports may also include summaries of longer publications. Most informational reports have one thing in common: a neutral or receptive audience. The readers of informational reports do not need to be persuaded; they simply need to be informed.

You can expect to write many informational reports as an entry-level or middle-management employee. These reports generally deliver nonsensitive data and are therefore written directly. Although the writing style is usually conversational and informal, the report contents must be clear to all readers. All headings, lists, and graphics should help a reader grasp major ideas immediately.

The principles of conciseness, clarity, courtesy, and correctness discussed in earlier chapters apply to report writing as well. Your ability to write effective reports can boost your visibility in a company and promote your advancement. Be familiar with the descriptions, guidelines, and examples of several types of informational reports.

### 9-4a Trip, Convention, and Conference Reports

Employees sent on business trips to conventions and conferences typically submit reports to document the events they attended and what they learned. Organizations may require documentation to show that their money was well spent in funding the travel. These reports often inform management about business trends, procedures, legal requirements, or other information that would affect their operations and products.

When writing a trip or conference report, you must select the most relevant material and organize it coherently. Generally, it is best not to use chronological sequencing (*in the morning we did X, at lunch we heard Y, and in the afternoon we did Z*). Instead, you should focus on three to five topics in which your reader will be interested. These items become the body of the report. Then simply add an introduction and a closing, and your report is organized. Here is a general outline for trip, conference, and convention reports:

- Begin by identifying the event (name, date, and location) and previewing the topics that were discussed.
- In the body, summarize the main topics that might benefit others in the organization. Use headings and bullets to add readability.
- Close by expressing appreciation, mentioning the value of the trip or event, and offering to share the information.
- Itemize your expenses, if requested, on a separate sheet.

### OFFICE INSIDER

*"A report is not the place to impress your audience with all the facts you can cram in—pare down to what is most important for your readers. Separate 'need to know' from 'nice to know.'"*

—Colorado State University, business writing teaching tips

**LEARNING OBJECTIVE 4**
Write short informational reports that describe routine tasks.

Chapter 9: Informal Reports

Madison Gardner was recently hired as a marketing specialist in the Marketing Department of a wireless devices and consumer electronics store in Seattle, Washington. Recognizing her lack of experience in online customer service, the marketing manager gave her permission to attend a two-day training conference titled Social Customer Service. Her boss, Bryce Corliss, encouraged Madison to attend, saying, "We are serious about increasing our social media involvement, and we want to build solid relationships with our customers while promoting our products. Come back and tell us what you learned from the experts." When she returned, Madison wrote the conference report shown in Figure 9.7. She included two topics that would most benefit the employees in her company.

### Figure 9.7 Conference Report

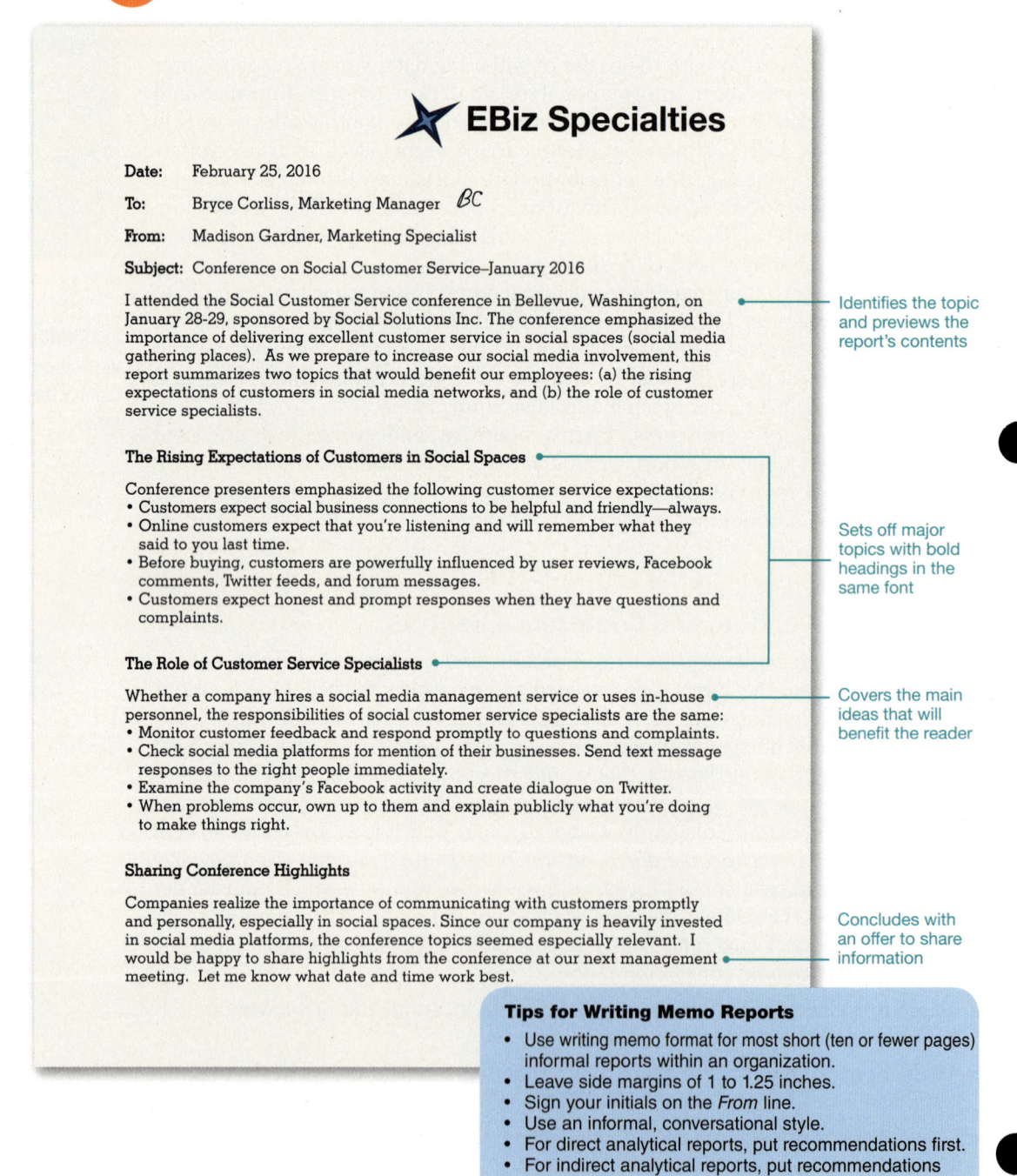

**EBiz Specialties**

**Date:** February 25, 2016
**To:** Bryce Corliss, Marketing Manager *BC*
**From:** Madison Gardner, Marketing Specialist
**Subject:** Conference on Social Customer Service–January 2016

I attended the Social Customer Service conference in Bellevue, Washington, on January 28-29, sponsored by Social Solutions Inc. The conference emphasized the importance of delivering excellent customer service in social spaces (social media gathering places). As we prepare to increase our social media involvement, this report summarizes two topics that would benefit our employees: (a) the rising expectations of customers in social media networks, and (b) the role of customer service specialists.

*— Identifies the topic and previews the report's contents*

**The Rising Expectations of Customers in Social Spaces**

Conference presenters emphasized the following customer service expectations:
- Customers expect social business connections to be helpful and friendly—always.
- Online customers expect that you're listening and will remember what they said to you last time.
- Before buying, customers are powerfully influenced by user reviews, Facebook comments, Twitter feeds, and forum messages.
- Customers expect honest and prompt responses when they have questions and complaints.

*— Sets off major topics with bold headings in the same font*

**The Role of Customer Service Specialists**

Whether a company hires a social media management service or uses in-house personnel, the responsibilities of social customer service specialists are the same:
- Monitor customer feedback and respond promptly to questions and complaints.
- Check social media platforms for mention of their businesses. Send text message responses to the right people immediately.
- Examine the company's Facebook activity and create dialogue on Twitter.
- When problems occur, own up to them and explain publicly what you're doing to make things right.

*— Covers the main ideas that will benefit the reader*

**Sharing Conference Highlights**

Companies realize the importance of communicating with customers promptly and personally, especially in social spaces. Since our company is heavily invested in social media platforms, the conference topics seemed especially relevant. I would be happy to share highlights from the conference at our next management meeting. Let me know what date and time work best.

*— Concludes with an offer to share information*

---

**Tips for Writing Memo Reports**
- Use writing memo format for most short (ten or fewer pages) informal reports within an organization.
- Leave side margins of 1 to 1.25 inches.
- Sign your initials on the *From* line.
- Use an informal, conversational style.
- For direct analytical reports, put recommendations first.
- For indirect analytical reports, put recommendations last.

## 9-4b Progress, or Interim, Reports

Continuing projects often require progress, or interim, reports to give status updates on the project. These reports may be external (advising customers regarding the headway of their projects) or internal (informing management of the status of activities). Follow this pattern when writing a progress report:

- Specify the purpose and nature of the project in the opening.
- Provide background information if it gives the reader a better perspective.
- Describe the work completed so far.
- Explain the work currently in progress, including names, activities, methods used, and locations.
- Describe current and anticipated problems. If possible, include possible remedies.
- Discuss future plans and completion dates in the closing.

As a location manager for Eagle Video Productions, Olivia Nevaeh frequently writes progress reports, such as the one shown in Figure 9.8. Producers want to

### Figure 9.8 Progress Report

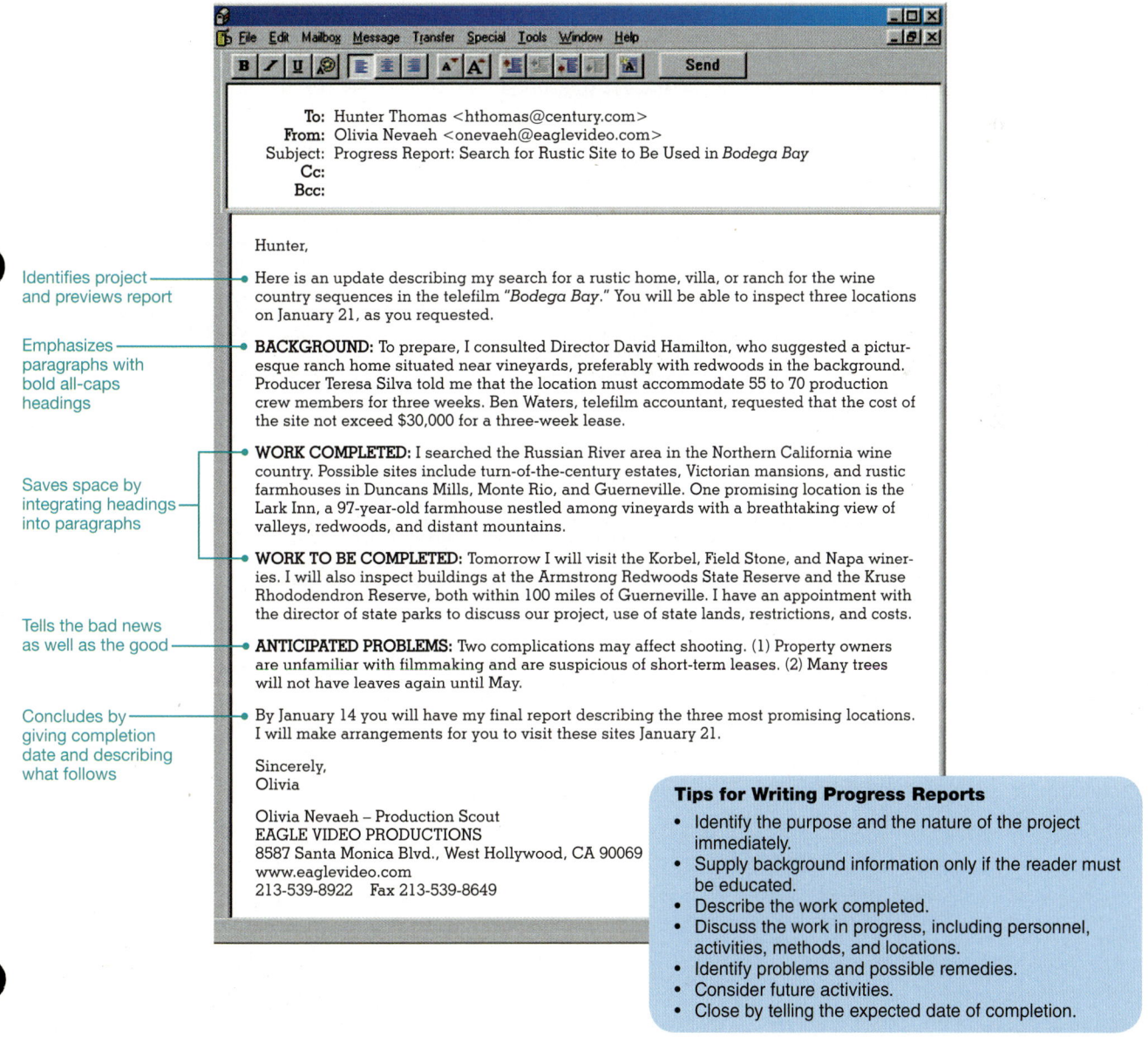

**To:** Hunter Thomas <hthomas@century.com>
**From:** Olivia Nevaeh <onevaeh@eaglevideo.com>
**Subject:** Progress Report: Search for Rustic Site to Be Used in *Bodega Bay*
**Cc:**
**Bcc:**

Hunter,

*Identifies project and previews report*

Here is an update describing my search for a rustic home, villa, or ranch for the wine country sequences in the telefilm "*Bodega Bay*." You will be able to inspect three locations on January 21, as you requested.

*Emphasizes paragraphs with bold all-caps headings*

**BACKGROUND:** To prepare, I consulted Director David Hamilton, who suggested a picturesque ranch home situated near vineyards, preferably with redwoods in the background. Producer Teresa Silva told me that the location must accommodate 55 to 70 production crew members for three weeks. Ben Waters, telefilm accountant, requested that the cost of the site not exceed $30,000 for a three-week lease.

*Saves space by integrating headings into paragraphs*

**WORK COMPLETED:** I searched the Russian River area in the Northern California wine country. Possible sites include turn-of-the-century estates, Victorian mansions, and rustic farmhouses in Duncans Mills, Monte Rio, and Guerneville. One promising location is the Lark Inn, a 97-year-old farmhouse nestled among vineyards with a breathtaking view of valleys, redwoods, and distant mountains.

**WORK TO BE COMPLETED:** Tomorrow I will visit the Korbel, Field Stone, and Napa wineries. I will also inspect buildings at the Armstrong Redwoods State Reserve and the Kruse Rhododendron Reserve, both within 100 miles of Guerneville. I have an appointment with the director of state parks to discuss our project, use of state lands, restrictions, and costs.

*Tells the bad news as well as the good*

**ANTICIPATED PROBLEMS:** Two complications may affect shooting. (1) Property owners are unfamiliar with filmmaking and are suspicious of short-term leases. (2) Many trees will not have leaves again until May.

*Concludes by giving completion date and describing what follows*

By January 14 you will have my final report describing the three most promising locations. I will make arrangements for you to visit these sites January 21.

Sincerely,
Olivia

Olivia Nevaeh – Production Scout
EAGLE VIDEO PRODUCTIONS
8587 Santa Monica Blvd., West Hollywood, CA 90069
www.eaglevideo.com
213-539-8922   Fax 213-539-8649

---

**Tips for Writing Progress Reports**

- Identify the purpose and the nature of the project immediately.
- Supply background information only if the reader must be educated.
- Describe the work completed.
- Discuss the work in progress, including personnel, activities, methods, and locations.
- Identify problems and possible remedies.
- Consider future activities.
- Close by telling the expected date of completion.

know what she is doing, and a phone call does not provide a permanent record. She provides background information to inform the director about her location specifications. She then includes information about what she is currently doing and what she plans to do next. She is up front about possible complications and concludes by giving a completion date. Olivia chose to use all-caps bold paragraph headings to make the report's sequence easy to follow. She also chose to follow the headings with a colon rather than a period.

### 9-4c Minutes of Meetings

Minutes summarize the proceedings of meetings. Most businesses post team meeting minutes to intranet sites soon after the meeting ends. The notes are then accessible to everyone who attended or who missed the meeting. Companies often use in-house templates for recording meeting minutes. Formal, traditional minutes, illustrated in Figure 9.9, are written for more formal meetings and

Figure 9.9 Formal Meeting Minutes

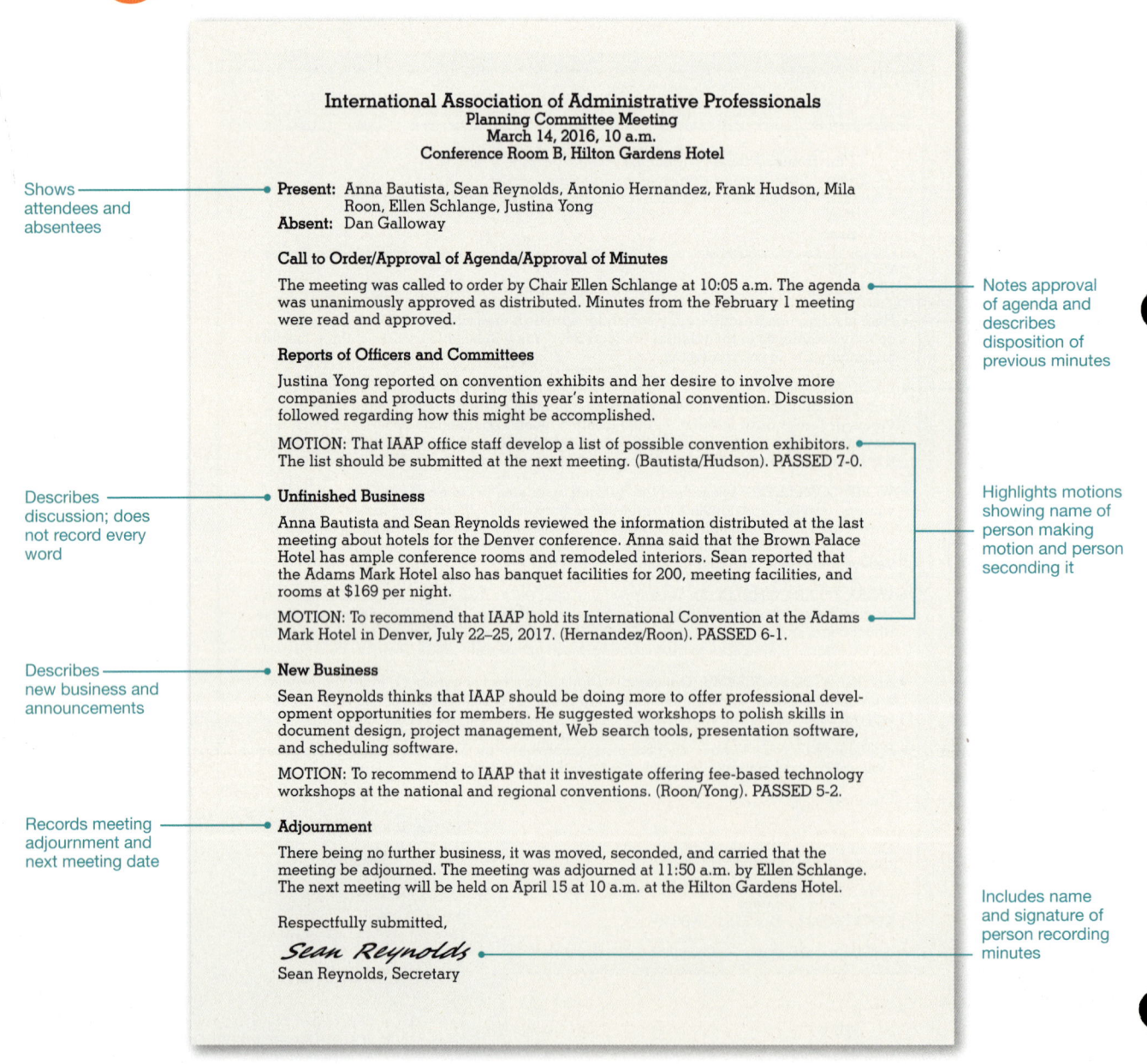

---

**International Association of Administrative Professionals**
**Planning Committee Meeting**
March 14, 2016, 10 a.m.
Conference Room B, Hilton Gardens Hotel

**Present:** Anna Bautista, Sean Reynolds, Antonio Hernandez, Frank Hudson, Mila Roon, Ellen Schlange, Justina Yong
**Absent:** Dan Galloway

**Call to Order/Approval of Agenda/Approval of Minutes**
The meeting was called to order by Chair Ellen Schlange at 10:05 a.m. The agenda was unanimously approved as distributed. Minutes from the February 1 meeting were read and approved.

**Reports of Officers and Committees**
Justina Yong reported on convention exhibits and her desire to involve more companies and products during this year's international convention. Discussion followed regarding how this might be accomplished.

MOTION: That IAAP office staff develop a list of possible convention exhibitors. The list should be submitted at the next meeting. (Bautista/Hudson). PASSED 7-0.

**Unfinished Business**
Anna Bautista and Sean Reynolds reviewed the information distributed at the last meeting about hotels for the Denver conference. Anna said that the Brown Palace Hotel has ample conference rooms and remodeled interiors. Sean reported that the Adams Mark Hotel also has banquet facilities for 200, meeting facilities, and rooms at $169 per night.

MOTION: To recommend that IAAP hold its International Convention at the Adams Mark Hotel in Denver, July 22–25, 2017. (Hernandez/Roon). PASSED 6-1.

**New Business**
Sean Reynolds thinks that IAAP should be doing more to offer professional development opportunities for members. He suggested workshops to polish skills in document design, project management, Web search tools, presentation software, and scheduling software.

MOTION: To recommend to IAAP that it investigate offering fee-based technology workshops at the national and regional conventions. (Roon/Yong). PASSED 5-2.

**Adjournment**
There being no further business, it was moved, seconded, and carried that the meeting be adjourned. The meeting was adjourned at 11:50 a.m. by Ellen Schlange. The next meeting will be held on April 15 at 10 a.m. at the Hilton Gardens Hotel.

Respectfully submitted,

*Sean Reynolds*
Sean Reynolds, Secretary

---

- Shows attendees and absentees
- Notes approval of agenda and describes disposition of previous minutes
- Describes discussion; does not record every word
- Highlights motions showing name of person making motion and person seconding it
- Describes new business and announcements
- Records meeting adjournment and next meeting date
- Includes name and signature of person recording minutes

legislative bodies. If you are assigned to take minutes, you will want to follow this general pattern:

- Begin with the name of the group, as well as the date, time, and place of the meeting.
- Identify the names of attendees and absentees.
- State whether the previous minutes were approved or revised.
- Record briefly the discussions of old business, new business, announcements, and committee reports.
- Include the precise wording of motions; record the votes and actions taken.
- Conclude with the name of the person recording the minutes. Formal minutes may require a signature.

### 9-4d Summaries

A summary compresses the main points from a book, report, article, website, meeting, or convention. A summary saves time by reducing a report or article by 85 to 95 percent. Employees are sometimes asked to write summaries that condense technical reports, periodical articles, or books so that a reader can skim the main ideas quickly. Students may be asked to write summaries of articles or chapters to sharpen their writing skills and confirm their knowledge of reading assignments.

Andrew Baxter, president of Health4Life, a chain of fitness centers, asked his administrative assistant Anne Randolph to search for current information on CEO involvement in social networks. Anne found an article on the social media habits of Fortune 500 CEOs and summarized them in a memo report shown in Figure 9.10. She used headings to highlight the article's main ideas and concluded with her overall reaction to the article. Summary reports of all types follow these general guidelines:

- State the main idea or purpose as well as the source of the document being summarized. Why was it written?
- If summarizing a report, highlight the research methods, findings, conclusions, and recommendations.
- Omit illustrations, examples, and references.
- Organize for readability by including headings and bulleted or enumerated lists.
- If requested to do so, include your reaction or overall evaluation of the document.

An *executive summary* summarizes a long report, proposal, or business plan. It covers what management needs to know about the full report, using headings and brief paragraphs. An example of an executive summary of a formal report is found in Chapter 10.

## 9-5 Preparing Short Analytical Reports

**LEARNING OBJECTIVE 5**
Prepare short analytical reports that solve business problems

You may recall that informational reports generally provide data only. This section describes three common types of analytical business reports: (a) justification/recommendation reports, (b) feasibility reports, and (c) yardstick reports. These reports involve collecting and analyzing data, evaluating the results, drawing conclusions, and making recommendations.

Analytical reports differ significantly from informational reports. Although both seek to collect and present data clearly, analytical reports also evaluate the data and typically try to persuade the reader to accept the conclusions and act on the recommendations. Informational reports emphasize facts; analytical reports emphasize reasoning and conclusions.

Figure 9.10   Article Summary

**Date:** March 3, 2016
**To:** Andrew Baxter, President
**From:** Anne Randolph, Administrative Assistant
**Subject:** Article Summary, "Are America's Top CEOs Getting More Social?"

*Introduces topic and publication information*

In response to your request for information about CEO involvement in social networks, I discovered an article from CEO.com that reported on social media habits of Fortune 500 CEOs. The company issued its yearly Social CEO Report titled "Are America's Top CEOs Getting More Social?" This article summary shows the social engagement of Fortune 500 CEOs in four major social networks.

*Provides headings to improve readability*

**Report Purpose and Research Methods**

CEO.com's report showed the levels of CEO involvement in four major social networks. Gathering the information for this article required searching for every CEO on the Fortune 500 list on Twitter, LinkedIn, Facebook, and Google+. Researchers verified the legitimacy of the CEOs' social profiles, made sure the content of the posts was relevant and believable, looked at the number and quality of followers, and checked to see that the account was maintained by or written by someone on behalf of the actual CEO.

*Highlights research methods*

**Social CEO Report Findings**

*Summarizes data from the article*

The report findings showed that 68 percent of Fortune 500 CEOs have no presence on the four major social networks (Twitter, Facebook, LinkedIn, or Google+). Of the 32 percent who are involved, LinkedIn and Twitter had the most CEO users, as shown in the following statistics:

**Twitter.** A total of 28 Fortune 500 CEOs are on Twitter, an improvement from the previous year's 18 CEOs. Of the 28 CEOs, 19 are considered active users, tweeting at least once every 100 days.

*Uses paragraph headings to increase readability*

**LinkedIn.** Currently, 140 Fortune 500 CEOs are on LinkedIn, which is a 25.9 percent increase from the previous year. LinkedIn appears to be the most popular network for CEOs.

**Facebook.** Currently, 35 Fortune 500 CEOs are on Facebook, compared to 38 the previous year. User growth is rather stagnant, although many CEOs have massive Facebook followings.

**Google+.** Only 5 Fortune 500 CEOs were found on Google+, compared to 4 last year. Google+ is obviously not popular with CEOs.

**Reaction to Article**

Not surprisingly, LinkedIn and Twitter are the most popular social networks for CEOs. For whatever reason, only a small percentage of Fortune 500 CEOs are engaged in social media currently. Their involvement, however, seems to be increasing. CEOs will continue to embrace social media to heighten the exposure of their companies. I agree with the article's assertion that CEOs who are involved in social media will see the rewards of increased customer loyalty and engagement.

*Includes overall evaluation of the article*

---

For some situations you may organize analytical reports directly with the conclusions and recommendations near the beginning. Directness is appropriate when the reader has confidence in the writer, based on either experience or credentials. Frontloading the recommendations also works when the topic is routine or familiar and the reader is supportive.

Directness can backfire, though. If you announce the recommendations too quickly, the reader may immediately object to a single idea. You may not have expected that this idea would trigger a negative reaction. Once the reader has an unfavorable mind-set, changing it may be difficult or impossible. A reader may also believe that you have oversimplified or overlooked something significant if you lay out all the recommendations before explaining how you arrived at them. When you must lead the reader through the process of discovering the solution or recommendation, use the indirect strategy: present conclusions and recommendations last.

Most analytical reports answer questions about specific problems and aid in decision making (e.g., *How can we use social media most effectively? Should we close the El Paso plant? Should we buy or lease company cars? How can we improve customer service?*). Analytical reports provide conclusions that help management answer these questions.

## 9-5a Justification/Recommendation Reports

Both managers and employees must occasionally write reports that justify or recommend actions, such as buying equipment, changing a procedure, hiring an employee, consolidating departments, or investing funds. These reports may also be called *internal proposals* because their persuasive nature is similar to that of external proposals (presented in Chapter 10). Large organizations sometimes prescribe how these reports should be organized and formatted; they often use forms with conventional headings. When you are free to select an organizational plan yourself, however, let your audience and topic determine your choice of the direct or indirect strategy.

**Direct Strategy.** For nonsensitive topics and recommendations that will be agreeable to readers, you can organize directly according to the following sequence:

- Identify the problem or need briefly.
- Announce the recommendation, solution, or action concisely and with action verbs.
- Explain more fully the benefits of the recommendation or steps necessary to solve the problem.
- Include a discussion of pros, cons, and costs.
- Conclude with a summary specifying the recommendation and necessary action.

**Indirect Strategy.** When a reader may oppose a recommendation or when circumstances suggest caution, do not rush to reveal your recommendation. Consider using the following sequence for an indirect approach to your recommendations:

- Refer to the problem in general terms, not to your recommendation, in the subject line.
- Describe the problem or need your recommendation addresses. Use specific examples, supporting statistics, and authoritative quotes to lend credibility to the seriousness of the problem.
- Discuss alternative solutions, beginning with the least likely to succeed.
- Present the most promising alternative (your recommendation) last.
- Show how the advantages of your recommendation outweigh its disadvantages.
- Summarize your recommendation. If appropriate, specify the action it requires.
- Ask for authorization to proceed if necessary.

Alexis D'Amico, an executive assistant at a large petroleum and mining company in Grand Prairie, Texas, received a challenging research assignment. Her boss, the director of Human Resources, asked her to investigate ways to persuade employees to quit smoking. Here is how she described her task: "We banned smoking many years ago inside our buildings and on the premises, but we never tried very hard to get smokers to actually kick their habits. My job was to gather information about the problem and learn how other companies have helped workers stop smoking. The report would go to my boss, but I knew he would pass it along to the management council for approval.

If the report were just for my boss, I would put my recommendation up front, because I'm sure he would support it. However, the management council may need to be persuaded because of the costs involved—and because some of them are smokers. Therefore, I put the alternative I favored last. To gain credibility, I footnoted my sources. I had enough material for a ten-page report, but I kept it to two pages in keeping with our company report policy." Alexis chose APA style to document her sources.

Alexis single-spaced her report, shown in Figure 9.11, because her company prefers this style. Some companies prefer the readability of double-spacing. Be sure to check with your organization for its preference before printing your reports.

### 9-5b Feasibility Reports

Feasibility reports examine the practicality and advisability of following a course of action. They answer this question: Will this plan or proposal work? Feasibility reports typically are internal reports written to advise on matters such

**Figure 9.11** Justification/Recommendation Report, APA Style

---

**Date:** October 11, 2016
**To:** Jackson Gill, Director, Human Resources
**From:** Alexis D'Amico, Executive Assistant *ADA*
**Subject:** Smoking Cessation Programs for Employees

At your request, I have examined measures that encourage employees to quit smoking. As company records show, approximately 23 percent of our employees still smoke, despite the antismoking and clean-air policies we adopted in 2015. To collect data for this report, I studied professional and government publications; I also inquired at companies and clinics about stop-smoking programs.

This report presents data describing the significance of the problem, three alternative solutions, and a recommendation based on my investigation.

**Significance of Problem: Health Care and Productivity Losses**

Employees who smoke are costly to any organization. The following statistics show the effects of smoking for workers and for organizations:

- Absenteeism is 40 to 50 percent greater among smoking employees.
- Accidents are two to three times greater among smokers.
- Bronchitis, lung and heart disease, cancer, and early death are more frequent among smokers (Arhelger, 2015, p. 4).

Although our clean-air policy prohibits smoking in the building, shop, and office, we have done little to encourage employees to stop smoking. Many workers still go outside to smoke at lunch and breaks. Other companies have been far more proactive in their attempts to stop employee smoking. Many companies have found that persuading employees to stop smoking was a decisive factor in reducing their health insurance premiums. Following is a discussion of three common stop-smoking measures tried by other companies, along with a projected cost factor for each (Rindfleisch, 2015, p. 4).

**Alternative 1: Literature and Events**

The least expensive and easiest stop-smoking measure involves the distribution of literature, such as "The Ten-Step Plan" from Smokefree Enterprises and government pamphlets citing smoking dangers. Some companies have also sponsored events such as the Great American Smoke-Out, a one-day occasion intended to develop group spirit in spurring smokers to quit. "Studies show, however," says one expert, "that literature and company-sponsored events have little permanent effect in helping smokers quit" (Mendel, 2014, p. 108).

   Cost: Negligible

---

*Avoids revealing recommendation immediately*

*Uses headings that combine function and description*

*Introduces purpose of report, tells method of data collection, and previews organization*

*Documents data sources for credibility, uses APA style citing author and year in the text*

as consolidating departments, offering a wellness program to employees, or hiring an outside firm to handle a company's accounting or social media presence. These reports may also be written by consultants called in to investigate a problem. The focus of these reports is on the decision: rejecting or proceeding with the proposed option. Because your role is not to persuade the reader to accept the decision,

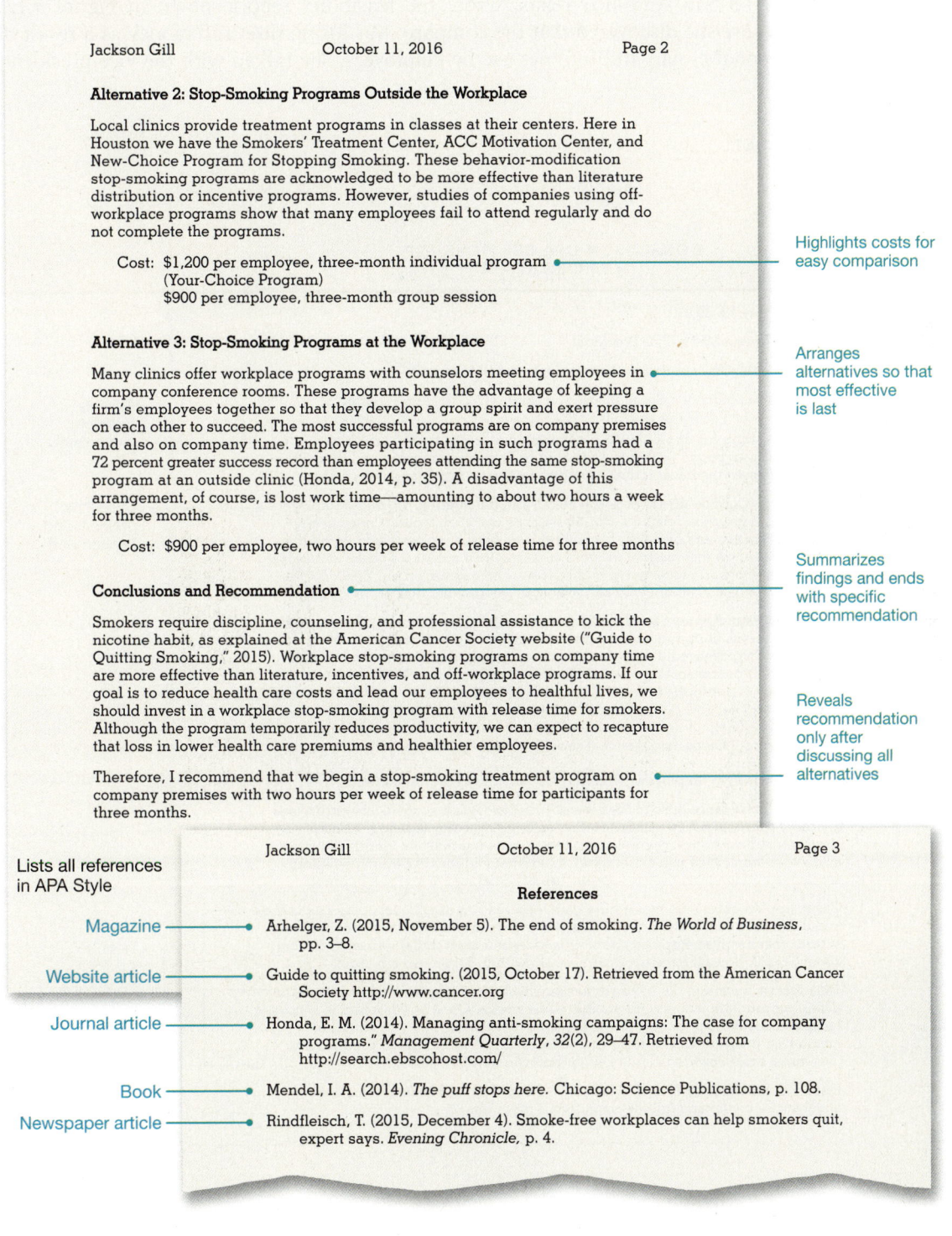

Figure 9.11 (Continued)

Jackson Gill     October 11, 2016     Page 2

**Alternative 2: Stop-Smoking Programs Outside the Workplace**

Local clinics provide treatment programs in classes at their centers. Here in Houston we have the Smokers' Treatment Center, ACC Motivation Center, and New-Choice Program for Stopping Smoking. These behavior-modification stop-smoking programs are acknowledged to be more effective than literature distribution or incentive programs. However, studies of companies using off-workplace programs show that many employees fail to attend regularly and do not complete the programs.

    Cost:  $1,200 per employee, three-month individual program — *Highlights costs for easy comparison*
           (Your-Choice Program)
           $900 per employee, three-month group session

**Alternative 3: Stop-Smoking Programs at the Workplace**

Many clinics offer workplace programs with counselors meeting employees in company conference rooms. These programs have the advantage of keeping a firm's employees together so that they develop a group spirit and exert pressure on each other to succeed. The most successful programs are on company premises and also on company time. Employees participating in such programs had a 72 percent greater success record than employees attending the same stop-smoking program at an outside clinic (Honda, 2014, p. 35). A disadvantage of this arrangement, of course, is lost work time—amounting to about two hours a week for three months.

— *Arranges alternatives so that most effective is last*

    Cost:  $900 per employee, two hours per week of release time for three months

**Conclusions and Recommendation**

Smokers require discipline, counseling, and professional assistance to kick the nicotine habit, as explained at the American Cancer Society website ("Guide to Quitting Smoking," 2015). Workplace stop-smoking programs on company time are more effective than literature, incentives, and off-workplace programs. If our goal is to reduce health care costs and lead our employees to healthful lives, we should invest in a workplace stop-smoking program with release time for smokers. Although the program temporarily reduces productivity, we can expect to recapture that loss in lower health care premiums and healthier employees.

— *Summarizes findings and ends with specific recommendation*

— *Reveals recommendation only after discussing all alternatives*

Therefore, I recommend that we begin a stop-smoking treatment program on company premises with two hours per week of release time for participants for three months.

Jackson Gill     October 11, 2016     Page 3

*Lists all references in APA Style*

**References**

*Magazine* — Arhelger, Z. (2015, November 5). The end of smoking. *The World of Business*, pp. 3–8.

*Website article* — Guide to quitting smoking. (2015, October 17). Retrieved from the American Cancer Society http://www.cancer.org

*Journal article* — Honda, E. M. (2014). Managing anti-smoking campaigns: The case for company programs." *Management Quarterly, 32*(2), 29–47. Retrieved from http://search.ebscohost.com/

*Book* — Mendel, I. A. (2014). *The puff stops here*. Chicago: Science Publications, p. 108.

*Newspaper article* — Rindfleisch, T. (2015, December 4). Smoke-free workplaces can help smokers quit, expert says. *Evening Chronicle*, p. 4.

you will want to present the decision immediately. In writing feasibility reports, consider these suggestions:

- Announce your decision immediately.
- Provide a description of the background and problem necessitating the proposal.
- Discuss the benefits of the proposal.
- Describe the problems that may result.
- Calculate the costs associated with the proposal, if appropriate.
- Show the time frame necessary for implementing the proposal.

Daisy Manaia-Payton, human resources manager for a large public accounting firm in San Antonio, Texas, wrote the feasibility report shown in Figure 9.12. Because she discovered that the company was losing time and money as a result of personal e-mail and Internet use by employees, she talked with the vice president,

## Figure 9.12 Feasibility Report

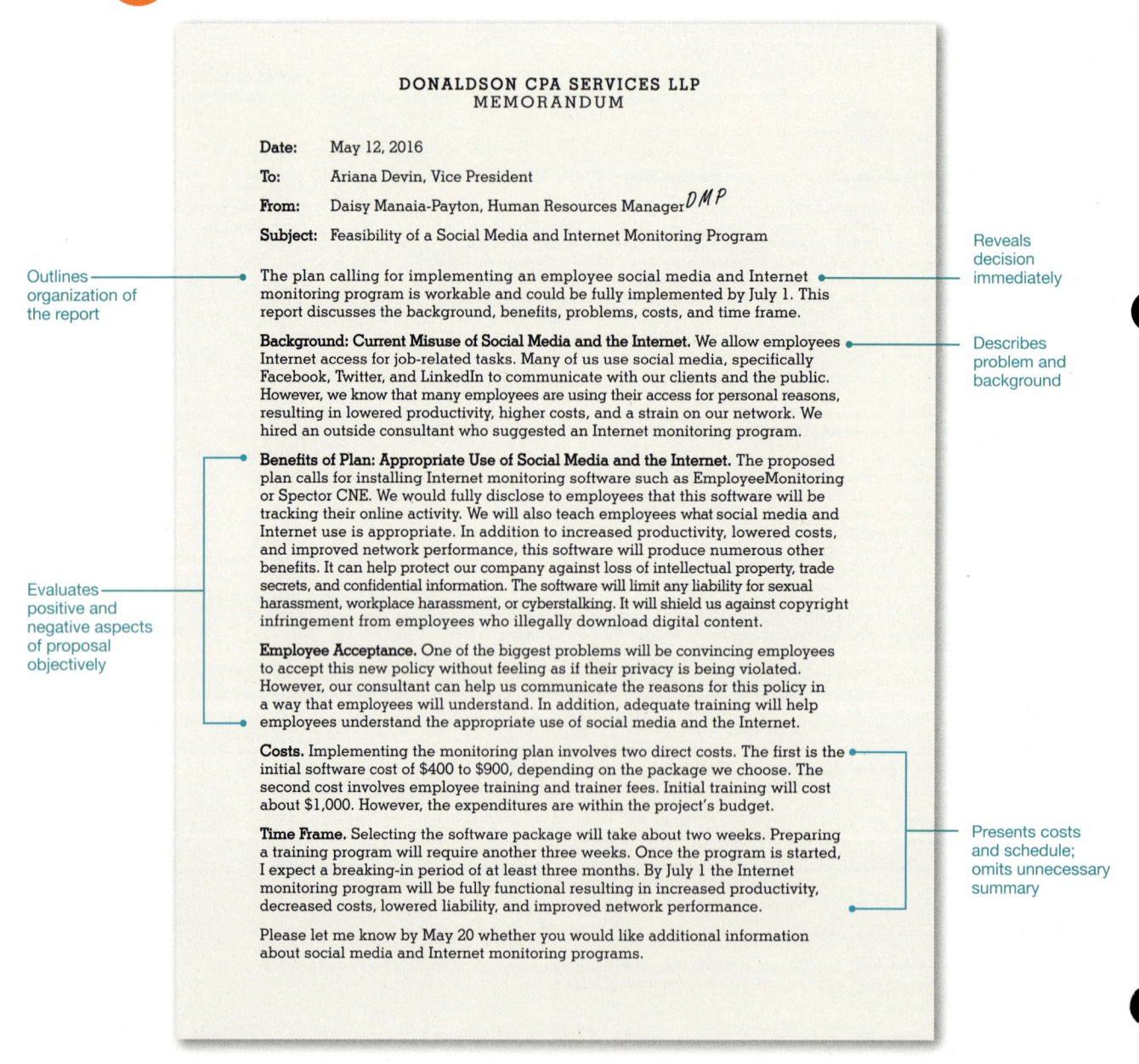

**DONALDSON CPA SERVICES LLP**
**MEMORANDUM**

**Date:** May 12, 2016
**To:** Ariana Devin, Vice President
**From:** Daisy Manaia-Payton, Human Resources Manager *DMP*
**Subject:** Feasibility of a Social Media and Internet Monitoring Program

The plan calling for implementing an employee social media and Internet monitoring program is workable and could be fully implemented by July 1. This report discusses the background, benefits, problems, costs, and time frame.

**Background: Current Misuse of Social Media and the Internet.** We allow employees Internet access for job-related tasks. Many of us use social media, specifically Facebook, Twitter, and LinkedIn to communicate with our clients and the public. However, we know that many employees are using their access for personal reasons, resulting in lowered productivity, higher costs, and a strain on our network. We hired an outside consultant who suggested an Internet monitoring program.

**Benefits of Plan: Appropriate Use of Social Media and the Internet.** The proposed plan calls for installing Internet monitoring software such as EmployeeMonitoring or Spector CNE. We would fully disclose to employees that this software will be tracking their online activity. We will also teach employees what social media and Internet use is appropriate. In addition to increased productivity, lowered costs, and improved network performance, this software will produce numerous other benefits. It can help protect our company against loss of intellectual property, trade secrets, and confidential information. The software will limit any liability for sexual harassment, workplace harassment, or cyberstalking. It will shield us against copyright infringement from employees who illegally download digital content.

**Employee Acceptance.** One of the biggest problems will be convincing employees to accept this new policy without feeling as if their privacy is being violated. However, our consultant can help us communicate the reasons for this policy in a way that employees will understand. In addition, adequate training will help employees understand the appropriate use of social media and the Internet.

**Costs.** Implementing the monitoring plan involves two direct costs. The first is the initial software cost of $400 to $900, depending on the package we choose. The second cost involves employee training and trainer fees. Initial training will cost about $1,000. However, the expenditures are within the project's budget.

**Time Frame.** Selecting the software package will take about two weeks. Preparing a training program will require another three weeks. Once the program is started, I expect a breaking-in period of at least three months. By July 1 the Internet monitoring program will be fully functional resulting in increased productivity, decreased costs, lowered liability, and improved network performance.

Please let me know by May 20 whether you would like additional information about social media and Internet monitoring programs.

*Annotations:*
- Outlines organization of the report
- Reveals decision immediately
- Describes problem and background
- Evaluates positive and negative aspects of proposal objectively
- Presents costs and schedule; omits unnecessary summary

Ariana Devin, about the problem. Ariana didn't want Daisy to take time away from her job to investigate what other companies were doing to prevent this type of problem. Instead, she suggested that they hire a consultant to investigate what other companies were doing to prevent or limit personal e-mail and Internet use. The vice president then wanted to know whether the consultant's plan was feasible. Although Daisy's report is only one page long, it provides all the necessary information: background, benefits, employee acceptance, costs, and time frame.

## 9-5c Yardstick Reports

Yardstick reports examine problems with two or more solutions. To determine the best solution, the writer establishes criteria by which to compare the alternatives. The criteria then act as a yardstick against which all the alternatives are measured, as shown in Figure 9.13. The yardstick approach is effective for companies that must

**Figure 9.13** Yardstick Report

Date: April 28, 2016
To: Tony Marshall, Vice President
From: Maria Rios, Benefits Administrator *M.R.*
Subject: Selecting Outplacement Services

Here is the report you requested April 1 investigating the possibility of CompuTech's use of outplacement services. It discusses the problem of counseling services for discharged staff and establishes criteria for selecting an outplacement agency. It then evaluates three prospective agencies and presents a recommendation based on that evaluation.

**Problem: Counseling Discharged Staff**

In an effort to reduce costs and increase competitiveness, CompuTech will begin a program of staff reduction that will involve releasing up to 20 percent of our workforce over the next 12 to 24 months. Many of these employees have been with us for ten or more years, and they are not being released for performance faults. These employees deserve a severance package that includes counseling and assistance in finding new careers.

**Solution and Alternatives: Outplacement Agencies**

Numerous outplacement agencies offer discharged employees counseling and assistance in locating new careers. This assistance minimizes not only the negative feelings related to job loss but also the very real possibility of litigation. Potentially expensive lawsuits have been lodged against some companies by unhappy employees who felt they were unfairly released.

In seeking an outplacement agency, we should find one that offers advice to the sponsoring company as well as to dischargees. The law now requires certain procedures, especially in releasing employees over forty. CompuTech could unwittingly become liable to lawsuits because our managers are uninformed of these procedures. I have located three potential outplacement agencies appropriate to serve our needs: Gray & Associates, Right Access, and Careers Plus.

**Establishing Criteria for Selecting Agency**

In order to choose among the three agencies, I established criteria based on professional articles, discussions with officials at other companies using outplacement agencies, and interviews with agencies. Here are the four groups of criteria I used in evaluating the three agencies:

1. <u>Counseling services</u>—including job search advice, résumé help, crisis management, corporate counseling, and availability of full-time counselors
2. <u>Administrative and research assistance</u>—including availability of administrative staff, librarian, and personal computers
3. <u>Reputation</u>—based on a telephone survey of former clients and listing with a professional association
4. <u>Costs</u>—for both group programs and executive services

Chapter 9: Informal Reports   285

Figure 9.13 (Continued)

---

Vice President Marshall     Page 2     April 28, 2016

**Discussion: Evaluating Agencies by Criteria**

Each agency was evaluated using the four criteria just described. Data comparing the first three criteria are summarized in Table 1.

Table 1

A COMPARISON OF SERVICES AND REPUTATIONS
FOR THREE LOCAL OUTPLACEMENT AGENCIES

|  | Gray & Associates | Right Access | Careers Plus |
|---|---|---|---|
| **Counseling services** | | | |
| Résumé advice | Yes | Yes | Yes |
| Crisis management | Yes | No | Yes |
| Corporate counseling | Yes | No | No |
| Full-time counselors | Yes | No | Yes |
| **Administrative, research assistance** | | | |
| Administrative staff | Yes | Yes | Yes |
| Librarian, research library | Yes | No | Yes |
| Personal computers | Yes | No | Yes |
| Listed by National Association of Career Consultants | Yes | No | Yes |
| Reputation (telephone survey of former clients) | Excellent | Good | Excellent |

**Counseling Services**

All three agencies offered similar basic counseling services with job-search and résumé advice. They differed, however, in three significant areas.

Right Access does not offer crisis management, a service that puts the discharged employee in contact with a counselor the same day the employee is released. Experts in the field consider this service especially important to help the dischargee begin "bonding" with the counselor immediately. Immediate counseling also helps the dischargee learn how to break the news to family members. Crisis management can be instrumental in reducing lawsuits because dischargees immediately begin to focus on career planning instead of concentrating on their pain and need for revenge. Moreover, Right Access does not employ full-time counselors; it hires part-timers according to demand. Industry authorities advise against using agencies whose staff members are inexperienced and employed on an "as-needed" basis.

In addition, neither Right Access nor Careers Plus offers regular corporate counseling, which I feel is critical in training our managers to conduct terminal interviews. Careers Plus, however, suggested that it could schedule special workshops if desired.

**Administrative and Research Assistance**

Both Gray & Associates and Careers Plus offer complete administrative services and personal computers. Dischargees have access to staff and equipment to assist them in their job searches. These agencies also provide research libraries, librarians, and databases of company information to help in securing interviews.

---

*Annotations:*
- Places table close to spot where it is first mentioned
- Summarizes complex data in table for easy reading and reference
- Highlights the similarities and differences among the alternatives
- Does not repeat obvious data from table

---

establish specifications for equipment purchases and then compare each manufacturer's product with the established specs. The yardstick approach is also effective when exact specifications cannot be established.

For example, a yardstick report might help a company decide on an inexpensive job perk. Perks are nontraditional benefits that appeal to current and future employees. Popular job perks include free food and beverages, flexible scheduling and telecommuting options, and on-site gyms and fitness classes. A yardstick report may help a company decide what job perks make the most sense. If the company wants to encourage long-term wellness, it might consider offering employees discounted fitness club memberships, on-site yoga classes, or ergonomic workstations. The yardstick report would describe and compare the three alternatives in terms of (a) costs, (b) long-term benefits, and (c) expected participation level.

Figure 9.13 (Continued)

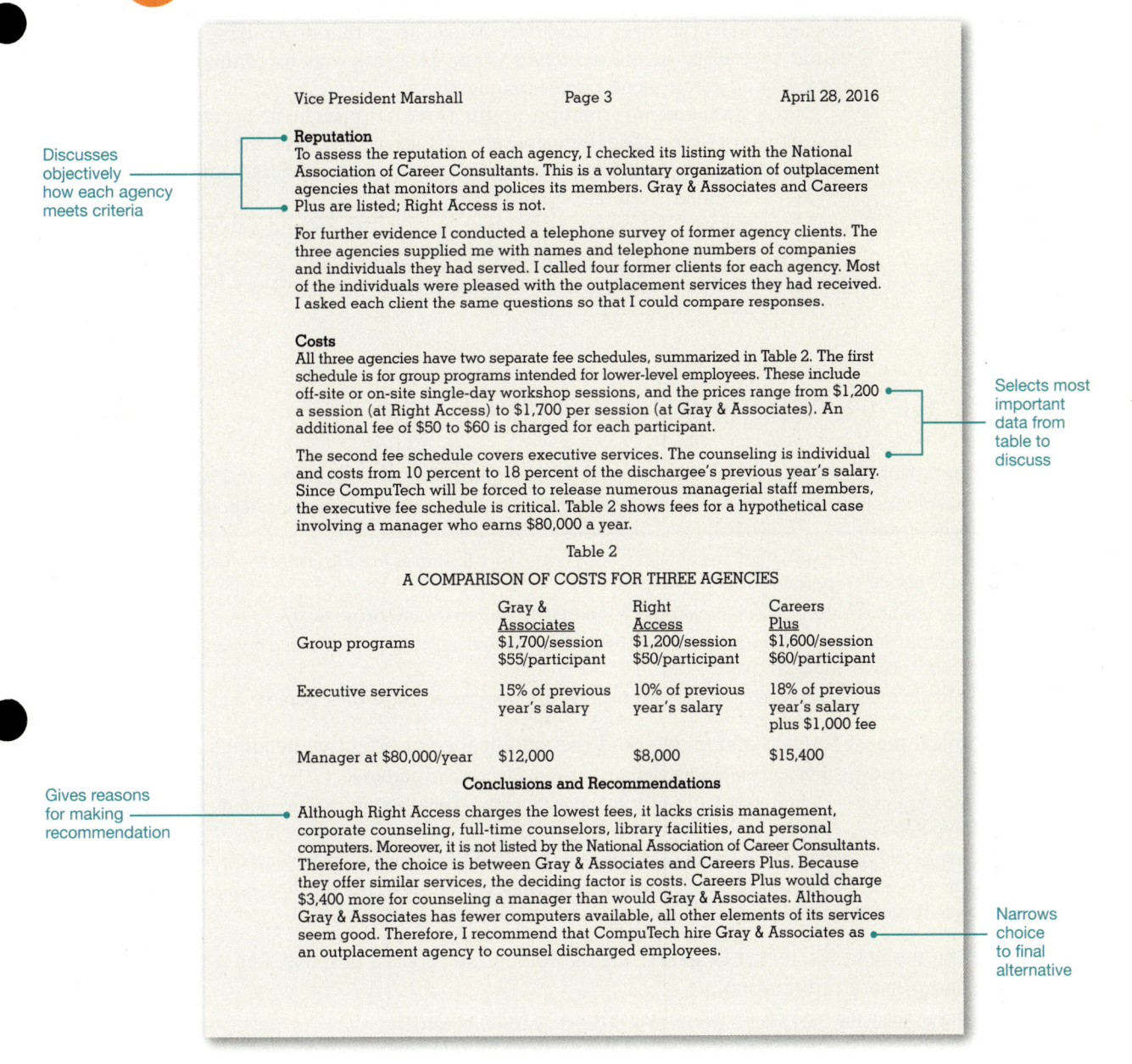

---

Vice President Marshall　　　　　Page 3　　　　　April 28, 2016

**Reputation**

To assess the reputation of each agency, I checked its listing with the National Association of Career Consultants. This is a voluntary organization of outplacement agencies that monitors and polices its members. Gray & Associates and Careers Plus are listed; Right Access is not.

For further evidence I conducted a telephone survey of former agency clients. The three agencies supplied me with names and telephone numbers of companies and individuals they had served. I called four former clients for each agency. Most of the individuals were pleased with the outplacement services they had received. I asked each client the same questions so that I could compare responses.

**Costs**

All three agencies have two separate fee schedules, summarized in Table 2. The first schedule is for group programs intended for lower-level employees. These include off-site or on-site single-day workshop sessions, and the prices range from $1,200 a session (at Right Access) to $1,700 per session (at Gray & Associates). An additional fee of $50 to $60 is charged for each participant.

The second fee schedule covers executive services. The counseling is individual and costs from 10 percent to 18 percent of the dischargee's previous year's salary. Since CompuTech will be forced to release numerous managerial staff members, the executive fee schedule is critical. Table 2 shows fees for a hypothetical case involving a manager who earns $80,000 a year.

Table 2
A COMPARISON OF COSTS FOR THREE AGENCIES

|  | Gray & Associates | Right Access | Careers Plus |
|---|---|---|---|
| Group programs | $1,700/session $55/participant | $1,200/session $50/participant | $1,600/session $60/participant |
| Executive services | 15% of previous year's salary | 10% of previous year's salary | 18% of previous year's salary plus $1,000 fee |
| Manager at $80,000/year | $12,000 | $8,000 | $15,400 |

**Conclusions and Recommendations**

Although Right Access charges the lowest fees, it lacks crisis management, corporate counseling, full-time counselors, library facilities, and personal computers. Moreover, it is not listed by the National Association of Career Consultants. Therefore, the choice is between Gray & Associates and Careers Plus. Because they offer similar services, the deciding factor is costs. Careers Plus would charge $3,400 more for counseling a manager than would Gray & Associates. Although Gray & Associates has fewer computers available, all other elements of its services seem good. Therefore, I recommend that CompuTech hire Gray & Associates as an outplacement agency to counsel discharged employees.

---

After interviewing employees and talking to people whose companies offer similar benefits, report writers would compare the alternatives and recommend the most workable job perk.

The real advantage to yardstick reports is that alternatives can be measured consistently using the same criteria. Writers using a yardstick approach typically do the following:

- Begin by describing the problem or need.
- Explain possible solutions and alternatives.
- Establish criteria for comparing the alternatives; tell how the criteria were selected or developed.
- Discuss and evaluate each alternative in terms of the criteria.
- Draw conclusions and make recommendations.

Maria Rios, benefits administrator for computer manufacturer CompuTech, was called on to write the report in Figure 9.13 comparing outplacement agencies. These agencies counsel discharged employees and help them find new positions; fees are paid by the former employer. Maria knew that downsizing and outsourcing would take place in the next two years. Her task was to compare outplacement agencies and recommend one to management.

Maria gathered information about three outplacement agencies and wanted to organize it systematically using a yardstick report. She chose to evaluate each agency using the following categories: counseling services, administrative and research assistance, reputation, and costs.

Maria showed the results of her research on Table 1 and Table 2 in Figure 9.13. She used the criteria as headings and discussed how each agency met, or failed to meet, each criterion. Making a recommendation was easy once Maria had created the tables and compared the agencies.

# SUMMARY OF LEARNING OBJECTIVES

**9-1 Explain informational and analytical report functions, organizational strategies, and writing styles.**
- Informational reports present data without analysis or recommendations, such as monthly sales reports, status updates, and compliance reports.
- Analytical reports provide data or findings, analyses, and conclusions. Examples include justification, recommendation, feasibility, and yardstick reports.
- Audience reaction and content determine whether a report is organized directly or indirectly.
- Reports organized directly reveal the purpose and conclusions immediately; reports organized indirectly place the conclusions and recommendations last.
- Like other business messages, reports can range from informal to formal, depending on their purpose, audience, and situation.

**9-2 Describe typical report formats and understand the significance of effective headings.**
- Report formats vary, depending on the report's length, topic, audience, and purpose.
- Common report formats include e-mail, letter, memo, and manuscript; digital reports can be created and shared as slide decks and infographics.
- Report headings add visual appeal and readability; they reveal the report's organization and flow of ideas.
- The hierarchy of heading levels should be clear to a reader; headings in the same level should use the same font size and style, placement, and capitalization.

**9-3 Determine the problem the report is addressing as well as the report's purpose, and gather significant secondary and primary information.**
- Clarifying the problem the report will address is the first step in writing a report.
- A purpose statement states the reasons for the report and answers the questions that prompted the report.
- Typical sources of secondary information used in reports are company records, books, journals, magazines, newspapers, and Web resources.
- Typical sources of primary, or firsthand, information used in reports are personal observations, surveys, questionnaires, and interviews with topic experts.

**9-4 Write short informational reports that describe routine tasks.**
- Informational reports provide information about recurring activities (e.g., monthly sales or project updates) as well as one-time events (e.g., trips, conferences, and special projects).
- Trip, convention, and conference reports include a preview of the topics covered, a summary of topics that will benefit the organization, and concluding thoughts about the overall value of the event.
- Progress, or interim, reports include a project description, background information, work completed, work in progress, problems encountered, and future plans.
- Meeting minutes include the names of attendees and absentees, a discussion of old and new business, committee reports, and decisions made.

**9-5** Prepare short analytical reports that solve business problems.
- Analytical reports, such as justification/recommendation, feasibility, and yardstick reports, evaluate information, draw conclusions, and make recommendations.
- Justification/recommendation reports are organized directly when the reader is supportive and indirectly when the reader needs persuasion to accept the recommendations.
- Feasibility reports are written directly and examine the practicality and advisability of following a course of action.
- Yardstick reports examine problems by using a standard set of criteria to compare several alternatives before recommending a solution.

# CHAPTER REVIEW

1. What is the difference between informational and analytical reports? Give an example of each. (Objs. 1, 4, and 5)

2. What factors determine whether a report should be written directly or indirectly? (Obj. 1)

3. What are the main report formats and when are they used? (Obj. 2)

4. What are the advantages of using forms and templates for recurring business reports? (Obj. 2)

5. Describe functional and talking headings and give an example of each. (Obj. 2)

6. Define primary research and give three examples. (Obj. 3)

7. What topics or sections should be included in a progress report? (Obj. 4)

8. What is a feasibility report? Are such reports generally intended for internal or external audiences? Explain your reasoning. (Obj. 5)

9. Describe a situation in which a yardstick report would be appropriate. (Obj. 5)

10. What is the advantage of using a slide deck to report information and statistics? (Obj. 5)

## CRITICAL THINKING

11. Under what circumstances would a recommendation report be written directly? Give an example. (Obj. 1)
12. Do you think informational reports should be written directly or indirectly? For what reasons would an analytical report be written with a direct or an indirect approach? State your reasoning. (Obj. 1)
13. What heading guidelines should you follow when writing a report? (Obj. 2)
14. What technology trends do you think will affect business reporting and delivery in the future? (Obj. 5)
15. How can report writers ensure that they present their information objectively and credibly? (Obj. 3)

## ACTIVITIES AND CASES

### 9.1 Informational Report: Added Value From Work or Volunteer Experience (Obj. 4)

Your instructor wants to learn about your current or former employment. Select a position you now hold or one that you have held in the past. If you have not been employed, choose a campus, professional, or community organization to which you belong. You may also select an internship or a volunteer experience.

**YOUR TASK.** Write an informational memo report to your instructor describing your current or former employment, an internship or volunteer experience, or your involvement in a professional or community group. Introduce the report by describing the company and its products or services, the organization's history and leadership, and its primary location. In the body of the report, add your title and job responsibilities, including the skills you need or needed to perform the job. Then describe the value and skills you gained from this experience. Your memo report should be single-spaced and 1 1/2 to 2 pages long. Add a meaningful subject line and descriptive headings for each section of the report.

## 9.2 Informational Report: Investigating a Career Path (Obj. 4)

**Web**

You are interested in exploring your career options to make sure you have the right skill set for your chosen field and that the future in that field looks promising. One of the best places to search is the latest *Occupational Outlook Handbook* compiled by the U.S. Bureau of Labor Statistics. Search the *Handbook* for your desired occupation using the **Search** box or find a career using the **A-Z Index**. This is a valid resource whether you are choosing a career or changing careers.

**YOUR TASK.** Write an informational memo report to your instructor that describes your desired career. In the report, summarize the information found in the *Handbook* about the nature of the work, working conditions, necessary qualifications, and the outlook for this career. Also summarize relevant information about typical salary ranges for this occupation. Add an appropriate introductory paragraph that describes the purpose of the report, and conclude with a brief paragraph summarizing what you learned from this investigation. For instance, after this investigation, do you still feel this career is a good fit for you? State your reasoning.

## 9.3 Informational Report: Fortune's 100 Best Companies to Work For (Obj. 4)

**Web**

You are intrigued by *Fortune's* annual list of the 100 best companies to work for. You want to work for one of them. You read the good news that many of them are hiring, so you begin searching for a company that has possibilities for you. After narrowing the list, you hone in on one that seems like the best fit.

**YOUR TASK.** Select a company from *Fortune's* list of 100 best companies to work for. Note the reasons *Fortune* added this company to the list, and note the company's ranking out of 100. Then review the company's website and gather information about the company's mission and goals, history, products and services, and current news releases. Find out where the home office is located, who leads the company, and how many employees work there. After researching the company, list your reasons for wanting to work there. In a memo report to your instructor, summarize your research findings. State the purpose, add appropriate section headings, and conclude with your thoughts on why you think this company is a good employment choice.

## 9.4 Informational or Feasibility Report: Cultural Competence Training (Objs. 4, 5)

**Web** **Intercultural**

Businesses see value in increasing the cultural competence of their employees. The makeup of the American population has changed, and diverse populations exist within organizations. Increasing intercultural awareness also helps employees understand those who have different perspectives and ways of doing things. It also lessens misunderstandings in terms of business etiquette, values, and behaviors when traveling to other countries.

Your company's HR director wants to build a curriculum for an in-house intercultural training class. You have been asked to search for websites that offer excellent information on intercultural business etiquette and communication. In your search you may discover the informative etiquette guides for specific countries by Kwintessential Ltd. (http://www.kwintessential.co.uk) and Executive Planet (www.executiveplanet.com).

**YOUR TASK.** Write a short memo report to Jeff Abrams, Director of Human Resources, listing at least five resources that offer excellent information on intercultural business etiquette and communication. List each site and the information it provides. You may also recommend the sites you found most helpful. If your instructor suggests, write this report as a feasibility study in memo format, describing the need for such a class, the benefits to employees, the costs associated with offering the class (workbooks, handouts), any anticipated problems, and a possible time frame for implementation. You may need to address hiring a knowledgeable presenter or an intercultural panel, scheduling a training room, and selecting suitable times—perhaps two-hour sessions during working hours. Other considerations: Will the training be mandatory or optional? How many sessions will be offered to accommodate most employees? What times of day work best for most employees? What credentials should the presenter have?

## 9.5 Progress Report: A Work in Progress (Obj. 4)

Think about someone who supports your decision to pursue your education and earn a degree. You want to let that person know how you are doing on your journey to complete your education. You decide to write a report describing your progress.

**YOUR TASK.** Prepare a progress report in letter format to a relative or friend who is supportive of your educational pursuits. You may organize the report as follows: (a) Describe your progress toward your educational goal; (b) summarize the work you have completed thus far; (c) discuss the work currently in progress, including your successes and challenges; and (d) outline your plans to accomplish your goal.

## 9.6 Progress Report: Checking In With Your Instructor (Obj. 4)
`E-mail`

If you are working on a lengthy formal or informal report for either this chapter or in the upcoming Chapter 10, you may want to keep your instructor informed of your progress and record any setbacks.

**YOUR TASK.** Send your instructor an e-mail report detailing the progress you are making on your long report assignment. Discuss (a) the purpose of the report, (b) the work already completed, (c) the work currently in progress, (d) problems encountered, (e) future activities, and (f) your schedule for completing the report.

## 9.7 Recommendation Report: Philanthropic Popularity (Obj. 5)
`Web`

Great news! MegaTech, the start-up company where you work, has become enormously successful. Now the owner wants to support a philanthropic program. He wants you to conduct research on philanthropic opportunities and recommend one. The owner is highly interested in projects that ease poverty and increase education in high-poverty regions. He is also interested in knowing what projects other companies are supporting. Based on this information, what projects can you recommend to the owner?

**YOUR TASK.** The owner wants you to investigate the philanthropic projects at 20 high-profile companies of your choice. Visit their websites and study programs such as volunteerism, matching funds, and charitable donations. In a recommendation report, discuss five of the best programs and recommend one that could serve as a philanthropic project for your company.

## 9.8 Justification/Recommendation Report: Developing a Social Media Use Policy (Obj. 5)
`Team` `Social Media` `Web`

A social media usage policy is a set of rules developed by organizations to regulate the use of social media by employees. As a manager in a midsized engineering firm, you see the need to draft such a policy. You have received reports that employees are using the Internet and social media sites during work hours to check Facebook and Twitter, look for jobs on LinkedIn, shop on eBay, and even play games online. You have also received reports that some employees have posted inappropriate comments about the company on Facebook. You have reason to worry about appropriate behavior, declining productivity, security problems, and liability issues. The executive council now wants to establish a social media policy, in addition to the already existing Internet policy, to clarify their policies on social media use and acceptable behavior. You are aware that the executive council needs to know that acceptable use of social media pertains to employees at work and at home. You decide to talk with other managers about the problem and to look at other companies' social media policies. You'll report your findings in a justification/recommendation report.

**YOUR TASK.** As a team, discuss the need for comprehensive social media use policies in general. Search for information about other firms' social media policies. Read about companies that are currently facing lawsuits over employees' inappropriate messages on social media networks. Find out what areas your policy should cover. Should the policy include guidelines for behavior on Facebook, Twitter, blogs, and wikis? Each member of the team should present and support his or her ideas regarding what should be included in the policy. Individually or as a team, write a convincing justification/recommendation report in memo format to the executive council based on the conclusions you draw from your research and discussion. Because you are recommending action, decide whether your approach should be direct or indirect.

## 9.9 Feasibility Report: Health and Wellness Perks (Obj. 5)
`Web`

Your company is considering adding some health and wellness perks that will interest current and future employees. Perks are benefits that are added above and beyond the normal medical coverage and sick pay. These wellness perks help in recruiting and retaining talented employees. You work for a smaller company that cannot compete with the great perks offered by giant companies such as Google and Amazon. However, small- and medium-sized companies are now adding health and wellness perks at little or no expense. You've been assigned to research and select three health and wellness perks that could be incorporated into your company's culture immediately. The company has a training room on-site for classes and a large lunchroom for lunchtime activities. You might consider the following options: a company-sponsored softball league, lunchtime walking groups, weekend hikes and bike trips, lunchtime classes on health and nutrition, or weekly yoga and cross-training classes. Search online for other possibilities, and be ready to suggest three company perks to your supervisor. Estimate the approximate costs associated with these perks, including administration costs. Then suggest an appropriate time frame for implementation.

**YOUR TASK.** Select three health and wellness perks that can be offered to employees at little or no cost. Write a memo report investigating the feasibility of adding the three perks. Begin by stating the decision to add the three perks. Then discuss the background leading up to the decision and the benefits of such programs. Estimate the approximate costs associated with each option, including administration costs, if any. Then suggest an appropriate time frame for implementation.

## 9.10 Minutes: Covering a Meeting for Someone Else (Obj. 4)

Attend an organized meeting at your school, in your community, in city government, or for a professional organization. Take notes and record the proceedings as if you were covering the meeting for a non-attender.

**YOUR TASK.** Write the meeting minutes using either a formal or informal format. Include all the data necessary, following the textbook instructions. Focus on committee reports, old and new business, motions and votes, decisions made, and action items for future meetings. Include the organization's name and the date, time, and location of the meeting in the heading.

## 9.11 Meeting Minutes: Team Meeting Notes (Obj. 4)
`Team`

When working on a formal report with a team, volunteer to take notes at a team meeting and be prepared to share the meeting minutes with your instructor, if requested. Follow the textbook instructions for meeting minutes.

**YOUR TASK.** Record the proceedings of a team meeting for a group project. Record the date and time of the meeting, the attendees' names, discussion items, decisions made, and the date of the next meeting.

## 9.12 Yardstick Report: Choosing a Live Chat Solution (Obj. 5)
`Web`

As an intern for a midsized online marketing company that sells outdoor and recreational clothing and equipment, you are anxious to comply with a request from the vice president of marketing. He wants to add a live chat feature on the company website to improve customer service with online shoppers. He is aware that online shoppers frequently accept invitations to chat live when they need help or have questions. What's more, they often turn into buyers. He asks you to research the most popular live chat software options, compare the features and monthly costs, and recommend one that the company could implement quickly.

**YOUR TASK.** Write a memo yardstick report to Vice President of Marketing Jon Stokes that compares the options. Search online for live chat support software, and look at several sources that list the most popular options for small and midsized companies. Choose five of the most frequently mentioned options, and compare them in terms of (a) monthly or yearly costs, (b) main features, and (c) ratings or reviews. Follow the instructions in the textbook for writing yardstick reports. Briefly discuss the background for the report, list the live chat alternatives, and compare them using the established criteria. Your comparison data may work best in a table. Draw conclusions and recommend a live chat solution that you believe will best meet the needs of the company.

## 9.13 Article or Infographic Summary: Current Social Media Marketing Trends (Objs. 2, 4)
`Social Media`  `Web`

With the rise of social media in business, your supervisor wants to stay abreast of the latest social media marketing trends. He asks you to research this topic and list the current trends with a brief explanation of each. You will format this document as an article summary.

**YOUR TASK.** Search for an article or infographic that addresses current or future social media marketing trends. In a memo report addressed to your boss, Jin Le, summarize the main ideas presented in the article or infographic. Be sure to identify the author, article title, publication name, and date of the article. If your source is an infographic, follow a similar procedure and identify the title, sponsoring website, source, and date, if available. Conclude with your overall opinion of the article or infographic.

## 9.14 Article Summary: Future Business Technology Trends (Obj. 4)
`Web`

Like many executives, your boss is too busy to sift through all the articles describing current technology trends and predictions for the future. She has assigned the task to you. She asks you to search for articles about future technology trends and write a summary of two of the best articles you found.

**YOUR TASK.** Write an article summary in memo format to Sandra Ellington that addresses two articles on future technology trends. Include an introduction, such as *As you requested, I am submitting two article summaries. . . .* Identify the author, article title, journal or website name, and date of publication for each article. Explain the purpose of each article and summarize three or four of its most important findings. Include an appropriate subject line and add meaningful headings. Your boss would also like a concluding statement indicating your overall reaction to the articles.

Chapter 9: Informal Reports

## 9.15 Seeking Infographic Reports (Obj. 2)
**Web**

With the explosive popularity of data visualization, visual media such as infographics will be around for a long time. Infographics share complex information quickly and clearly: they are readable, visually appealing, and content rich. As you examine excellent examples of infographics, you'll see how engaging they can be for presenting business-related information.

**YOUR TASK.** Find an infographic that visualizes intriguing business-relevant data. Look for the sources of the information (usually near the bottom in small print), and check to see that they are reliable. Answer the following questions, and prepare a short presentation on your findings: How much statistical information is provided in the infographic? Is the purpose of the infographic clear? Is the information clearly presented, easy to read, visually appealing, and insightful? Show your infographic and share your findings orally or in writing.

## 9.16 Report Topics for Informal Reports (Objs. 4, 5)
**Web** **Team**

A list of over 90 report topics is available at **www.cengagebrain.com**. The topics are divided into the following categories: accounting, finance, human resources, marketing, information systems, management, and general business/education/campus issues. You can collect information for many of these reports by using electronic databases and the Web. Your instructor may assign them as individual or team writing projects. All require critical thinking in collecting and organizing information into logical reports.

**YOUR TASK.** As directed by your instructor, select a topic from the report list at **www.cengagebrain.com**.

# GRAMMAR/MECHANICS CHECKUP—9

## Semicolons and Colons

Review Sections 2.16–2.19 in the Grammar/Mechanics Handbook. Then study each of the following statements. Insert any necessary punctuation. Use the delete sign to omit unnecessary punctuation. In the space provided, indicate the number of changes you made and record the number of the G/M principle(s) illustrated. (When you replace one punctuation mark with another, count it as one change.) If you make no changes, write *0*. This exercise concentrates on semicolon and colon use, but you will also be responsible for correct comma use. When you finish, compare your responses with those shown at the end of the book. If your responses differ, study carefully the principles shown in parentheses.

1 _____ (2.16b) **EXAMPLE** Sales meetings during prosperous times were lavish productions focused on entertainment; meetings today focus on training and motivation.

_____ 1. "Green" technologies are gaining a strong following consequently many industries are beginning to produce green products and recycling programs.

_____ 2. Cash resulting from holiday product sales does not arrive until January therefore our cash flow becomes critical in November and December.

_____ 3. We must negotiate short-term financing during the following months October November and December.

_____ 4. The largest American corporations offering financial services are: Bank of America and JPMorgan Chase.

_____ 5. Although some firms rarely need to borrow short-term money many businesses find that they require significant credit to pay for current production and sales costs.

_____ 6. A supermarket probably requires no short-term credit a seasonal company such as a ski resort however typically would need considerable short-term credit.

_____ 7. We offer three basic types of short-term lines of credit commercial paper and single-payer credit.

_____ 8. Speakers at the conference on credit include the following businesspeople Teresa Moore financial manager American International Investments Patrick Coughlin comptroller NationsBank and Margie Mullis legal counsel Fidelity National Financial.

_____  9.  The prime interest rate is set by one or more of the nation's largest banks and this rate is offered to a bank's best customers

_____  10. Many methods are used to calculate finance charges for example average daily balance adjusted balance two-cycle average daily balance and previous balance.

_____  11. Hot Topic which is a small clothing retailer with a solid credit rating recently applied for a loan however Union Bank refused the loan application because the bank was short on cash.

_____  12. When Hot Topic was refused by Union Bank its financial managers submitted applications to: Chemical Bank, Washington Mutual, and Wells Fargo.

_____  13. The cost of financing capital investments at the present time is very high therefore Hot Topic's managers elected to postpone certain expansion projects.

_____  14. Apple earns most of its income from the following: Macs, iPads, and iPhones.

_____  15. Several investors decided to pool their resources then they could find attractive investments for large-scale projects.

# EDITING CHALLENGE—9

To fine-tune your grammar and mechanics skills, in every chapter you will be editing a message. This progress report has problems with number usage, capitalization, punctuation, spelling, and other writing techniques you have studied. Study the guidelines in the Grammar/Mechanics Handbook as well as the lists of Confusing Words and Frequently Misspelled Words to sharpen your skills.

**YOUR TASK.** Edit the following message (a) by correcting errors in your textbook or on a photocopy using proofreading marks from Appendix A or (b) by downloading the message from the premium website at **www.cengagebrain.com** and correcting at your computer. Your instructor may show you a possible solution.

---

**To:** Kendra Montgomery <kmontgomery@scantastic.com>
**From:** Tim Shimoyama<tshimoyama@scantastic.com>
**Subject:** Committee Progress Report
**Cc:**
**Bcc:**

---

Kendra,

As per your request my committee and myself has been working for the past 3 months to find or the creation of a new name for our company. This message is describing our progress.

**Background:** Because of the fact that many potential customers did not recognize our document-scanning service from our current name you and other members of management created a committee to investigate changing our name to one that is more better and meaningful. People are intrigued by the name Scantastic, however they don't relate it to our service. Our committee was charged with the task of develloping a process for finding a new name, and avoiding hiring a professional naming firm which could cost as much as 35 thousand dollars.

**Work Completed:** The first thing our committee did was get together and set goals for our new name. We wanted a name that (a) is easy to spell, (b) has between 10 and 12 letters (c) is easy to type on a keyboard and (4) reflects what we do. We then engaged in the activity of brainstorming internally. We created a list of 90 names, and checked it against available domain name's in WHOIS the Web domain directory. After we finished we were left with about 30 name's. We created three groups of ten and asked employees to force rank them. Next we selected a group of customers who we trusted; and conducted interviews that were in depth. We asked which names they liked, and why. From this set of interviews we were able to make a reduction of the list to 4 possible names.

**Work to be Completed:** Our next step will be to send a e-mail survey to our list of several thousand customers, and get there feed back. When we receive the results of that survey we should be able to group the responses in to positive and negative groups. We will then present our findings, and our name recomendation to you and the management council.

By April 1 you will have our final report with the committees recommended name. We are happy to be part of the search for a new company name; as we move forward to increase brand recognition of our document-scanning service. Please do not hesitate to let me know if you need more information.

Tim Shimoyama, Chair
Renaming Committee
tshimoyama@scantastic.com

# COMMUNICATION WORKSHOP

## COLLABORATION

### Pulling Together a Successful Team Writing Project

Participating in group presentations and collaborating on written reports are good ways to develop teamwork skills. However, working with other people on team projects is often challenging and frustrating, particularly when team members don't carry their weight or when conflict occurs. Team projects can be productive and rewarding when members establish ground rules at the outset and adhere to guidelines such as those presented here.

## Preparing to Work Together

Smaller teams with two to five members tend to be more successful and have fewer challenges than larger teams. Before beginning the project, meet as a team and establish roles and ground rules.

- Select a team leader to coordinate and manage the project and a recorder to write and distribute the ground rules and take notes on each meeting's accomplishments.
- Decide how to distribute the workload. Perhaps certain team members have areas of expertise on the topic. Try to divide the workload equally.
- Decide whether your team will be governed by consensus (everyone must agree) or by majority rule.
- Compare team members' schedules, gather contact information, and agree on meeting times. Regularly held face-to-face team meetings are more beneficial than virtual meetings when collaborating on group projects. The group can decide how to involve those who miss a meeting.
- Discuss the value of sharing diverging opinions. When multiple viewpoints are shared, a better product results. Talk openly about conflict and how it should be focused on the issues, not on the people.
- Discuss how you will deal with members who are not meeting deadlines or doing their part.

## Planning the Document

Once you have established ground rules, you are ready to discuss the project and resulting document.

- Establish the document's specific purpose and identify the main issues involved.
- Discuss the audience(s) for the document and what appeal would help it achieve its purpose.
- Write a detailed outline of the report. What parts will be assigned to each team member? What graphics and visuals will be included in each part?
- Develop a work plan. Set deadlines for submitting the first drafts, for integrating the parts into one document, and for proofreading the final draft.
- Decide how the final document will look. What fonts and format will be used? What software will be used to create the report? Will the report need a cover sheet, a table of contents, or a list of citations?

## Collecting Information

The following suggestions will help teams gather accurate information:

- As a group, brainstorm ideas for gathering relevant information.
- Establish deadlines for collecting information from primary and secondary sources.
- Discuss ways to ensure the accuracy and currency of the information collected.

## Organizing, Writing, and Revising

As the project progresses, your team may wish to modify some of its earlier decisions.

- Review the proposed outline of your final document, and adjust it if necessary.
- Share the first drafts and have all members review them. Make sure all writers are using the same format, heading styles, and font sizes.
- Appoint the strongest writer to integrate all the parts, striving for a consistent voice. The report should read as if it were written by one person.

## Editing and Evaluating

Before submitting the document, meet and review the final copy.

- Review the document's overall design, format, and heading levels. Is the report's organization easy to follow?
- Although all members should review and suggest edits to the final document, assign a strong writer to copyedit the report for grammar and punctuation errors.
- Evaluate the final document. Discuss whether it fulfills its purpose and meets the needs of the audience.

## Using Online Collaboration Tools

Hosting companies such as PBWorks (**http://pbworks.com/content/edu+overview**) offer easy-to-use, free wiki accounts to educators to run in their classes without involving the IT department. Other writers prefer using Google Docs, a free document management solution that is popular in the workplace. Some writers prefer to create drafts in Microsoft Word and use the **Track Changes** feature to gather comments from multiple readers. Search online or ask educators and project managers what document-sharing platforms they prefer.

**CAREER APPLICATION.** Select a report topic from this chapter or Chapter 10. Assume that you are preparing the report as a team project. If you are working on a long report, your instructor may ask you to prepare individual progress reports as you develop your topic.

**YOUR TASK**

- Form a team of two to five members.
- Prepare to work together by following the suggestions in this workshop.
- Plan your report by establishing its purpose, analyzing the audience, writing a detailed outline, developing a work plan, and deciding how you want the final document to look.
- Collect information, organize it, and write the first draft.
- Use the same formatting, heading styles, and font sizes as other team members.
- Offer to proofread and make suggestions to the drafts of team members.

Your instructor may assign grades not only for the final report but also for team effectiveness and your individual contribution, as evaluated by fellow team members.

# ENDNOTES

[1] Photo essay based on Coyle, E. (2014, February 19). Sorry, Buffett: Coke's sales fizzle, shareholders' anger sizzles. Wall St. Cheat Sheet. Retrieved from http://wallstcheatsheet.com/technology/apple/sorry-buffett-cokes-sales-fizzle-shareholders-anger-sizzles.html

[2] Photo essay based on Eksteen, L. (2013, September 12). Six reasons why Survey Monkey is the bomb. The Media Online. Retrieved from http://themediaonline.co.za/2013/09/six-reasons-why-survey-monkey-is-the-bomb; Helft, M. (2011, September 15). SurveyMonkey turns online surveys into a hot business. Fortune Online. Retrieved from http://tech.fortune.cnn.com/2011/09/15/surveymonkey-online-surveys-hot-business

# ACKNOWLEDGMENTS

**p. 269** Office Insider based on Sweet, K. (n.d.). Writing in third person in APA style. Retrieved from http://classroom.synonym.com/writing-third-person-apa-style-2056.html

**p. 275** Office Insider based on Colorado State University. (n.d.). Writing business reports. Retrieved from http://wac.colostate.edu/teaching/tipsheets/writing_business_reports.pdf

# Proposals and Formal Reports

**CHAPTER 10**

## 10-1 Preparing Business Proposals

A *proposal* is a written offer to solve problems, provide services, or sell products. Proposals can mean life or death for a business. Why are they so important? Multimillion-dollar aerospace and engineering firms depend on proposals to compete for business. People running smaller businesses—such as electricians, contractors, plumbers, and interior designers—also depend on proposals to sell their services and products.

### 10-1a Types of Business Proposals

Writers prepare proposals for various reasons, such as asking for funds or promoting products and services to customers. Some proposals are brief; some are lengthy and complex. A proposal recipient could be a manager inside your company or a potential client outside your company. All types of proposals share two significant characteristics: (a) they use easy-to-understand language, and (b) they show the value and benefits of the product or services being recommended. Proposals may be classified as (a) informal or formal, (b) internal or external, and (c) solicited or unsolicited.

**Informal or Formal.** Informal proposals are short reports, often formatted as memos or letters. Proposal sections can vary, but an informal proposal might include the following parts: (a) an introduction or description of the problem, (b)

### OBJECTIVES
After studying this chapter, you should be able to

**10-1**
Understand the importance, purpose, and components of informal and formal proposals.

**10-2**
Describe the steps in writing and editing formal business reports.

**10-3**
Conduct research using primary and secondary sources, and understand how to assess the credibility of resources.

**10-4**
Identify the purposes and techniques of documenting and citing sources in business reports.

**10-5**
Convert report data into meaningful visual aids and graphics.

**10-6**
Describe the components of typical formal reports.

Chapter 10: Proposals and Formal Reports

299

**LEARNING OBJECTIVE 1**
Understand the importance, purpose, and components of informal and formal proposals.

pertinent background information or a statement of need, (c) the proposal benefits and schedule for completion, (d) the staffing requirements, (e) a budget analysis, and (f) a conclusion that may include an authorization request. Figure 10.2 shows an informal letter proposal to a Florida dentist who sought to improve patient satisfaction. The research company submitting the proposal describes the benefits of a patient survey to gather data about the level of patient satisfaction. As you can see, the proposal contains the basic components of an informal proposal.

Formal proposals are more complex and may range from 5 to 200 or more pages. In addition to the six basic parts of informal proposals, formal proposals may contain some or all of these additional parts: (a) a copy of a request for proposal (RFP), (b) a letter of transmittal, (c) an abstract or executive summary, (d) a title page, (e) a table of contents, (f) a list of figures, and (g) an appendix. Figure 10.1 shows the typical sections included in informal and formal proposals.

**Internal or External.** Proposal writers may submit internal proposals to management when they see benefits in changing a company policy, purchasing equipment, or adding new products and services. A company decision maker will review the proposal and accept or reject the idea. Internal proposals may resemble justification and recommendation reports, as discussed in Chapter 9. Most proposals, however, are external and addressed to clients and customers outside the company. An external sales proposal to a client would show how the company's goods or services would solve a problem or benefit the client.

Another type of external proposal is a grant request, written to obtain funding from agencies that support worthwhile causes. For example, Project C.U.R.E. submitted a successful grant request to Ronald McDonald House Charities to help reduce infant mortality in remote locations around the world.

Figure **10.1** Components of Informal and Formal Proposals

| Informal Proposals | Formal Proposals |
|---|---|
| Introduction | Copy of RFP (optional) |
| Background, problem, purpose | Letter of transmittal |
| Proposal, plan, schedule | Abstract or executive summary |
| Staffing | Title page |
| Budget | Table of contents |
| Conclusion and authorization | List of figures |
|  | Introduction |
|  | Background, problem, purpose |
|  | Proposal, plan, schedule |
|  | Staffing |
|  | Budget |
|  | Authorization |
|  | Appendix |

## Workplace in Focus

Following the glitch-ridden launch of Healthcare.gov in 2013, the U.S. government fired the site's chief programmer and awarded the $91 million e-commerce contract to Accenture, a Chicago-based technology company familiar with the government services sector. While the change was welcome news for millions of Americans needing health care, doubts arose after the public learned that Accenture won the contract through a noncompetitive "no bid" process. Confidence eroded even further when watchdog groups discovered a Justice Department investigation in which Accenture was accused of rigging bids and receiving financial "kickbacks." The U.S. Postal Service Inspector General's Office even urged terminating Accenture's government contracts due to ethics questions. What bidding process helps organizations award contracts fairly and judiciously?[1]

**Solicited (RFP) or Unsolicited.** When government organizations or businesses have a specific need, they prepare a *request for proposal (RFP)*, a document that specifies their requirements. Government agencies as well as private businesses use RFPs to solicit competitive bids from vendors. RFPs ensure that bids are comparable and that funds are awarded fairly. For example, the city of Las Vegas, Nevada, prepared a 30-page RFP seeking bids for a parking initiative from public and private funding sources.[2] Companies responding to these solicited proposals are careful to follow the RFP instructions explicitly, which might include following a specific proposal format.

Enterprising companies looking for work or special projects might submit unsolicited proposals. For example, the world-renowned architect who designed the Louvre Museum pyramid in Paris, I. M. Pei, was so intrigued by the mission of the Buck Institute for Age Research that he submitted an unsolicited proposal to design the biomedical research facility in Novato, California.[3] Pei's proposal must have impressed the decision makers, because the research facility now features his geometric elements and floating staircases.

Both large and small companies are likely to use RFPs to solicit bids on their projects. This enables them to compare prices from various companies on their projects. Not only do they want a good price from their project bidders, but they also want the legal protection offered by proposals, which are considered legal contracts.

When writing proposals, remember that they must be persuasive, not merely mechanical descriptions of what you can do. Like the persuasive sales messages discussed in Chapter 8, effective proposals must (a) get the reader's attention, (b) emphasize how your methods and products will benefit the reader, (c) showcase your expertise and build credibility, and (d) present ideas clearly and logically, making it easy for the reader to understand.

### 10-1b Components of Informal Proposals

The titles, or headings, of the components of informal proposals may vary, but the goals of the components are standard. Each of the following components of a typical informal proposal serves a purpose and contributes to its overall success.

Chapter 10: Proposals and Formal Reports

# Figure 10.2 Informal Letter Proposal

## 1 Prewriting

**Analyze:** The purpose of this letter proposal is to persuade the reader to accept this proposal.

**Anticipate:** The reader expects this proposal but must be convinced that this survey project is worth its hefty price.

**Adapt:** Because the reader will be resistant at first, use a persuasive approach that emphasizes benefits.

## 2 Drafting

**Research:** Collect data about the reader's practice and other surveys of patient satisfaction.

**Organize:** Identify four specific purposes (benefits) of this proposal. Specify the survey plan. Promote the staff, itemize the budget, and ask for approval.

**Draft:** Prepare a first draft, expecting to improve it later.

## 3 Revising

**Edit:** Revise to emphasize benefits. Improve readability with functional headings and lists. Remove jargon and wordiness.

**Proofread:** Check spelling of client's name. Verify dates and calculation of budget figures. Recheck all punctuation.

**Evaluate:** Is this proposal convincing enough to sell the client?

---

**Momentum RESEARCH**
3250 West Bay Street | phone 904.457.7332
Jacksonville, FL 32202 | fax 904.457.8614
email: info@momentum.com

May 30, 2016

Valerie Stevens, D.D.S.
490 Houston Street, Suite 301
Green Cove Springs, FL 32043

Dear Dr. Stevens:

Understanding the views of your patients is the key to meeting their needs. Momentum Research is pleased to propose a plan to help you become even more successful by learning what patients expect of your practice, so that you can improve your services.

**Background and Goals**

We know that you have been incorporating a total quality management approach in your practice. Although you have every reason to believe that your patients are pleased with your services, you may want to give them an opportunity to share what they like and suggest areas of improvement. Specifically, your goals are to survey your patients to (a) determine the level of their satisfaction with you and your staff, (b) collect and analyze their suggestions for improvement, (c) learn more about how they discovered you, and (d) compare the responses of your "preferred" and "standard" patients.

**Proposed Plan**

On the basis of our experience in conducting many local and national customer satisfaction surveys, Momentum proposes the following plan:

**Survey.** We will develop a short but thorough questionnaire that will collect the data you desire. Although the survey instrument will include both open-ended and closed questions, it will concentrate on the latter. Closed questions enable respondents to answer easily; they also facilitate systematic data analysis. The questionnaire will gauge patients' views of staff courtesy, professionalism, accuracy of billing, office atmosphere, and waiting time. After you approve it, the questionnaire will be sent to a carefully selected sample of 300 patients whom you have designated as "preferred" and "standard."

**Analysis.** Survey data will be analyzed by demographic segments, such as patient type, age, and gender. Using state-of-the-art statistical tools, our team of seasoned experts will study (a) satisfaction levels, (b) the reasons for satisfaction or dissatisfaction, and (c) the responses of your "preferred" compared to "standard" patients. Moreover, our team will give you specific suggestions for making patient visits more pleasant.

**Report.** You will receive a final report with the key findings clearly spelled out, Dr. Stevens. Our expert staff will draw conclusions based on the results. The report will include tables summarizing all responses, divided into preferred and standard patients.

---

*Annotations:*
- Grabs attention with "hook" that focuses on key benefit
- Uses opening paragraph to focus on key benefits
- Identifies four purposes of survey
- Announces heart of proposal
- Describes procedure for solving problem and achieving goals
- Divides proposed plan into logical, readable segments

Figure 10.2 (Continued)

*Annotations (left side):*
- Includes second-page heading
- Promotes credentials and expertise of key people
- Itemizes costs carefully because a proposal is a contract offer
- Makes response easy

*Annotations (right side):*
- Uses past-tense verbs to show that work has already started on the project
- Builds credibility by describing outstanding staff and facilities
- Closes by repeating key qualifications and main benefits
- Provides deadline

---

Dr. Valerie Stevens      Page 2      May 30, 2016

**Schedule.** With your approval, the following schedule has been arranged for your patient satisfaction survey:

| | |
|---|---|
| Questionnaire development and mailing | August 1–6 |
| Deadline for returning questionnaire | August 24 |
| Data tabulation and processing | August 24–26 |
| Completion of final report | September 1 |

**Staffing**

Momentum is a nationally recognized, experienced research consulting firm specializing in survey investigation. I have assigned your customer satisfaction survey to Dr. Joseph Hales, PhD, our director of research. Dr. Hales was trained at Emory University and has successfully supervised our research program for the past nine years. Before joining Momentum, he was a marketing analyst with T-Mobile.

Assisting Dr. Hales will be a team headed by Lesha Barber, our vice president for operations. Ms. Barber earned a BS degree in computer science and an MA degree in marketing from the University of Florida. She supervises our computer-aided telephone interviewing system and manages our 30-person professional staff.

**Budget**

| | Estimated Hours | Rate | Total |
|---|---|---|---|
| Professional and administrative time | | | |
| Questionnaire development | 3 | $175/hr. | $ 525 |
| Questionnaire mailing | 4 | 50/hr. | 200 |
| Data processing and tabulation | 12 | 50/hr. | 600 |
| Analysis of findings | 15 | 175/hr. | 2,625 |
| Preparation of final report | 5 | 175/hr. | 875 |
| Mailing costs | | | |
| 300 copies of questionnaire | | | 150 |
| Postage and envelopes | | | 300 |
| Total costs | | | $5,275 |

**Conclusion and Authorization**

We are convinced, Dr. Stevens, that our professionally designed and administered patient satisfaction survey will provide beneficial data for improving your practice. Momentum Research can have specific results for you by September 1 if you sign the enclosed duplicate copy of this letter and return it to us with a retainer of $2,500 so that we may begin developing your survey immediately. The rates in this offer are in effect only until October 1.

Sincerely,

*Vincent Diaz*
Vincent Diaz, President

VD:mem
Enclosure

---

**Introduction.** The proposal's introduction states the reasons for the proposal and highlights the writer's qualifications. To grab attention and be more persuasive, the introduction should strive to provide a "hook," such as the following:

- Hint at extraordinary results with details to be revealed shortly.
- Promise low costs or speedy results.
- Mention a remarkable resource (well-known authority, new computer program, and well-trained staff) available exclusively to you.
- Identify a serious problem (worry item) and promise a solution, to be explained later.
- Specify a key issue or benefit that you feel is the heart of the proposal.

Chapter 10: Proposals and Formal Reports

## Office Insider

"To conquer writer's block, begin with a bulleted list of what the customer is looking for. This list is like a road map; it gets you started and keeps you headed in the right direction."

—Mary Piecewicz, former Hewlett-Packard proposal manager

Before writing the proposal shown in Figure 10.2 on page 302, Vincent Diaz analyzed the request of Florida dentist, Valerie Stevens, and decided that she was most interested in improving service to her patients. Vincent focused on this issue in the opening sentence and offered his company's assistance in meeting Dr. Stevens' needs. The writer confidently proposes a plan to promote success in this strong introductory paragraph. In longer proposals the introduction may also describe the scope and limitations of the project.

**Background, Problem, and Purpose.** The background section identifies the problem and discusses the goals or purposes of the project. In an unsolicited proposal, your goal is to convince the reader that a problem exists. Therefore, you must present the problem in detail, discussing such factors as revenue losses, failure to comply with government regulations, or decreased customer satisfaction.

In a solicited proposal, your aim is to persuade the reader that you understand the reader's issues and that you have a realistic solution. If an RFP is involved, follow its requirements precisely and use the company's language in your description of the problem. For example, if the RFP asks for *the design of a maintenance program for wireless communication equipment*, do not call it a *customer service program for wireless products*. The background section might include segments titled *Statement of Need, Basic Requirements, Most Critical Tasks*, or *Important Secondary Problems*.

**Proposal, Plan, and Schedule.** In the proposal section itself, you would explain your plan for solving the problem. In some proposals this is tricky because you want to disclose enough of your plan to secure the contract, while being cautious about providing so much information that your services will not be needed. Without specifics, though, your proposal has little chance, so you must decide how much to reveal.

The proposal section often includes an implementation plan. If research is involved, state what methods you will use to gather the data. Remember to be persuasive by showing how your methods and products will benefit the reader. For example, show how the initial investment will pay off later. The proposal might even promise specific *deliverables*—tangible things your project will produce for the customer. A proposal deliverable might be a new website design or an online marketing plan. To add credibility, also specify how the project will be managed and audited. Most writers also include a schedule or timetable of activities showing the proposal's benchmarks for completion.

**Staffing.** The staffing section of a proposal describes the staff qualifications for implementation of the proposal as well as the credentials and expertise of the project leaders. In other words, this section may include the size and qualifications of the support staff. This section is a good place to endorse and promote your staff. The client sees that qualified people will be on board to implement the project. Even résumés may be included in this section. Experts, however, advise proposal writers against including generic résumés that have not been revised to mirror the RFP's requirements. Only well-tailored résumés will inspire the kind of trust in a team's qualifications that is necessary if a proposal is to be accepted.[4]

**Budget.** A central item in most proposals is the budget, a list of proposed project costs. Some proposal writers title this section *Statement of Costs*. You need to prepare this section carefully because it represents a contract; you cannot raise the project costs later—even if your costs increase.

In the proposal shown in Figure 10.2, Vincent Diaz decided to justify the budget for his firm's patient satisfaction survey by itemizing the costs. Whether the costs in a proposal are itemized or treated as a lump sum depends on the reader's needs and the proposal's goals.

304  Chapter 10: Proposals and Formal Reports

**Conclusion and Authorization.** The closing section should remind the reader of the proposal's key benefits and make it easy for the reader to respond. It might also include a project completion date as well as a deadline date beyond which the proposal offer will no longer be in effect. Writers of informal proposals often refer to this as a request for approval or authorization. The conclusion of the proposal in Figure 10.2 mentions a key benefit as well as a deadline for approval.

## 10-2 Writing and Editing Formal Business Reports

**LEARNING OBJECTIVE 2**
Describe the steps in writing and editing formal business reports.

A formal report may be defined as a document in which a writer analyzes findings, draws conclusions, and makes recommendations intended to solve a problem. Formal business reports are similar to formal proposals in length, organization, and tone. However, instead of solving problems, proposing changes, or responding to an RFP, formal reports present findings and recommendations based on research and data analysis. Report writers then present the recommendations to decision makers in the fields of business, industry, government, and education.

### 10-2a Steps for Writing Formal Business Reports

Writing a formal report is a difficult task. It requires planning, researching, and organizing. Because this is a complex process, writers are most successful when they follow specific steps, as outlined in the following sections.

**Determine the Purpose and Scope of the Report.** Like proposals and informal reports, formal reports begin with a purpose statement. Preparing a written purpose statement is helpful because it defines the focus of the report and provides a standard that keeps the project on target. Study the following purpose statement and notice the use of action words (*adding, writing,* and *establishing*):

> **Simple purpose statement:** *To recommend adding three positions to our sales team, writing a job description for the sales team leader, and establishing recruitment guidelines for sales team hiring.*

You can determine the scope of the report by defining the problem or problems that will be researched and analyzed. Then examine your limitations by considering these questions: How much time do you have to complete the report? How accessible is the data you need? How thorough should your research be, and what boundaries will help you limit the scope of this report? If interviews or surveys are appropriate, how many people should you contact, and what questions should you ask?

**Anticipate the Needs of the Audience.** Report writers know the information their readers want and need. Keep in mind that the audience may or may not be familiar with the topic. Your goal is to present key findings that are relevant to your audience. If you were reporting to a targeted audience of human resources managers, the following facts gathered from an employee survey would be considered relevant: *According to the company survey completed by 425 of our 515 employees, 72 percent of employees are currently happy with their health benefits package.* A good report writer considers the needs of the audience every step of the way.

**Decide on a Work Plan and Appropriate Research Methods.** A work plan is a tentative plan that guides the investigation. This plan includes a clear problem statement, a purpose statement, and a description of the research methods to be used. A good work plan also involves a tentative outline of the report's major sections and a logical work schedule for completion of major tasks, as illustrated in Figure 10.3.

## Figure 10.3 Work Plan for a Formal Report

**Statement of Problem**

Many women between the ages of 18 and 34 have trouble finding jeans that fit. Lee Jeans hopes to remedy that situation with its One True Fit line. We want to demonstrate to Lee that we can create a word-of-mouth campaign that will help it reach its target audience.

**Statement of Purpose**

*Defines purpose, scope, limits, and significance of report*

The purpose of this report is to secure an advertising contract from Lee Jeans. We will examine published accounts about the jeans industry and Lee Jeans in particular. In addition, we will examine published results of Lee's current marketing strategy. We will conduct focus groups of women in our company to generate campaign strategies for our pilot study of 100 BzzAgents. The report will persuade Lee Jeans that word-of-mouth advertising is an effective strategy to reach women in this demographic group and that BzzAgent is the right company to hire. The report is significant because an advertising contract with Lee Jeans would help our company grow significantly in size and stature.

**Research Strategy (Sources and Methods of Data Collection)**

*Describes primary and secondary data*

We will gather information about Lee Jeans and the product line by examining published marketing data and conducting focus group surveys of our employees. In addition, we will gather data about the added value of word-of-mouth advertising by examining published accounts and interpreting data from previous marketing campaigns, particularly those targeted toward similar age groups. Finally, we will conduct a pilot study of 100 BzzAgents in the target demographic.

**Tentative Outline**

*Factors problem into manageable chunks*

I. How effectively has Lee Jeans marketed to the target population?
   A. Historically, who has typically bought Lee Jeans products? How often? Where?
   B. How effective are the current marketing strategies for the One True Fit line?
II. Is this product a good fit for our marketing strategy and our company?
   A. What do our staff members and our sample survey of BzzAgents say about this product?
   B. How well does our pool of BzzAgents correspond to the target demographic in terms of age and geographic distribution?
III. Why should Lee Jeans engage BzzAgent to advertise its One True Fit line?
   A. What are the benefits of word of mouth in general and for this demographic in particular?
   B. What previous campaigns have we engaged in that demonstrate our company's credibility?

**Work Schedule**

*Estimates time needed to complete report tasks*

| | |
|---|---|
| Investigate Lee Jeans and One True Fit line's current marketing strategy | July 15–25 |
| Test product using focus groups | July 15–22 |
| Create campaign materials for BzzAgents | July 18–31 |
| Run a pilot test with a selected pool of 100 BzzAgents | August 1–21 |
| Evaluate and interpret findings | August 22–25 |
| Compose draft of report | August 26–28 |
| Revise draft | August 28–30 |
| Submit final report | September 1 |

**Conduct Research Using Primary and Secondary Sources.** Formal report writers conduct most of their research using *secondary sources*—that is, information that has been previously analyzed and compiled. Books, articles, Web documents, podcasts, correspondence, and annual reports are examples of secondary sources. In contrast, writers may conduct some of their research using primary sources—information and data gathered from firsthand experience. Interviews, observations, surveys, questionnaires, and meetings are examples of primary research. Research methods are discussed in the section "Conducting Primary and Secondary Research" later in this chapter.

**Organize, Analyze, and Draw Conclusions.** Formal report writers should organize their information logically and base their recommendations on solid facts to impress decision makers. They should analyze the findings and make sure they are relevant to the report's purpose.

When organizing your ideas, place your main topics and subtopics into an outline format as shown in Figure 10.4.

As you sort through your information, decide what information is substantiated and credible. Give readers only the information they need. Then arrange that information using one of the strategies shown in Figure 10.5. For example, if a company wants to design its own online surveys, management may request a report that compares the best survey software solutions. In this case, the compare/contrast strategy helps the report writer organize the data and compare the features and costs of each survey tool.

Conclude the report by summarizing your findings, drawing conclusions, and making recommendations. The way you conclude depends on the purpose of your report and what the reader needs. A well-organized report with conclusions based on solid data will impress management and other decision makers.

**Design Graphics to Clarify the Report's Message.** Presenting numerical or quantitative data visually helps your reader understand information readily. Trends, comparisons, and cycles are easier to comprehend when they are expressed graphically. These visual elements in reports draw attention, add interest, and

Figure 10.4 Outline Format

FORMS OF BUSINESS OWNERSHIP
I. **Sole proprietorship**
   A. Advantages of sole proprietorship
      1. Minimal capital requirements
      2. Control by owner
   B. Disadvantages of sole proprietorship
      1. Unlimited liability
      2. Limited management talent
II. **Partnership**
   A. Advantages of partnership
      1. Access to capital
      2. Management talent
      3. Ease of formation
   B. Disadvantages of partnership
      1. Unlimited liability
      2. Personality conflicts

Figure 10.5 Strategies for Organizing Report Findings

| Strategy Type | Data Arrangement | Useful Application |
| --- | --- | --- |
| Chronological | Arrange information in a time sequence to show history or development of topic. | Useful in showing time relationships, such as five-year profit figures or a series of events leading to a problem |
| Geographical | Organize information by geographic regions or locations. | Appropriate for topics that are easily divided into locations, such as East Coast, Northwest, etc. |
| Topic/Function | Arrange by topics or functions. May use a prescribed, conventional format. | Works well for topics with established categories or for recurring reports |
| Compare/Contrast | Present problem and show alternative solutions. Use consistent criteria. Show how the solutions are similar and different. | Best used for "before and after" scenarios or when comparing alternatives |
| Importance | Arrange from least to most important, lowest to highest priority, or lowest to highest value, etc. | Appropriate when persuading the audience to take a specific action or change a belief |
| Simple/Complex | Proceed from simple to more complex concepts or topics. | Useful for technical or abstract topics |
| Best Case/Worst Case | Describe the best and the worst possible scenarios. | Useful when dramatic effect is needed to achieve results; helpful when audience is uninterested or uninformed |

Chapter 10: Proposals and Formal Reports

often help readers gain information quickly. Visuals include drawings, graphs, maps, charts, photographs, tables, and infographics. This topic is covered in more depth in the section "Incorporating Meaningful Visual Aids and Graphics" later in this chapter.

### 10-2b What to Review When Editing Formal Business Reports

The final step in preparing a formal business report involves editing and proofreading. Because the reader is the one who determines the report's success, review the report as if you were the intended audience. Pay particular attention to the following elements:

- **Format.** Look at the report's format and assess the report's visual appeal.
- **Consistency.** Review the report for consistency in margins, page numbers, indents, line spacing, and font style.
- **Graphics.** Make sure all graphics have meaningful titles, are clear, and are placed in the report near the words that describe them.
- **Heading levels.** Check the heading levels for consistency in font style and placement. Headings and subheadings should be meaningful and help the reader follow the report's logic.
- **Accuracy.** Review the content for accuracy and clarity. Make sure all facts are documented.
- **Mechanics.** Correct all grammar, punctuation, capitalization, and usage errors. These errors will damage your credibility and might cause the reader to mistrust the report's content.

**LEARNING OBJECTIVE 3**
Conduct research using primary and secondary sources, and understand how to assess the credibility of resources.

## 10-3 Conducting Primary and Secondary Research

Research, or the gathering of information, is one of the most important steps in writing a report. Because a report is only as good as its data, you will want to spend considerable time collecting data before you begin writing.

As you analyze a report's purpose and audience, think about your research strategy and what data you will need to support your argument or explain your topic. Will the audience need a lot of background or contextual information? Will your readers appreciate statistics, case studies, or expert opinions? Will your data collection involve interviews or surveys?

Data sources fall into two broad categories, primary and secondary. Primary data result from gathering original data from firsthand experience, from interviews and surveys, or from direct observation. Secondary data result from reading what others have published, experienced, or observed. The makers of the energy drink Red Bull, for example, produce primary data when they give away samples, conduct interviews in the streets, and record the reactions of consumers. These same sets of data become secondary after they have been published in a newspaper article about the growing popularity of caffeinated energy drinks.

Secondary data sources are easier and cheaper to gather than primary data sources, which might involve interviewing large groups or sending out questionnaires. When considering primary and secondary sources, report writers usually focus first on secondary sources because most of their information will come from those sources.

### 10-3a Secondary Research Sources

Reviewing secondary sources can save time and effort. Find out first what has already been written about your topic. Most secondary material is available either in print or online. Common secondary research sources are journals, magazines, newspapers, and Web documents. You can find print resources such as books and periodicals in libraries. You can also find relevant information by searching online databases and reliable Web sources.

**Print Resources.** Although most report writers first look online for resource material, they should not underestimate libraries. In fact, libraries feature print resources that might not be available online.

If you are an infrequent library user, talk with a reference librarian about your writing project. Librarians will steer you in the right direction and help you understand their computer cataloging and retrieval systems.

**Books.** Although quickly outdated, books provide excellent historical, in-depth data. Like most contemporary sources, books can be located using the library's automated online catalog system.

**Periodicals.** Magazines, pamphlets, and journals are called *periodicals* because of their recurrent, or periodic, publication. Journals are compilations of scholarly articles. Articles in journals and other periodicals are extremely useful because they are concise, limited in scope, and current. Current publications are also digitized and available in full text online, often as PDF documents.

**Indexes.** University libraries offer online access to *The Readers' Guide to Periodical Literature*, a comprehensive index of popular, important periodicals. This index is now offered by EBSCO, a multidisciplinary resource composed of research databases, e-books, and e-journals. Contemporary business writers rely mostly on electronic indexes and research databases such as EBSCO to locate references, abstracts, and full-text articles from magazines, journals, and newspapers, such as *The New York Times*. When using Web-based online indexes, follow the on-screen instructions or ask a librarian for assistance.

**Online Databases.** As a writer of business reports, you will probably begin your secondary research with electronic resources. Online databases have become the staple of secondary research as they are fast and easy to use.

A *database* is a collection of information stored digitally so that it is accessible by computers or mobile electronic devices. Databases provide bibliographic information (titles of documents and brief abstracts) and full-text documents. Various databases contain a rich array of magazine, newspaper, and journal articles, as well as newsletters, business reports, company profiles, government data, reviews, and directories. The five databases most useful to business writers are ABI/INFORM (ProQuest), Business Source Premier (powered by EBSCOhost), JSTOR Business, Factiva (Dow Jones), and LexisNexis Academic. Figure 10.6 shows the ABI/INFORM Trade & Industry results page for a search on sustainable development and energy efficiency.

Efficient search strategies take time to master. Therefore, get advice from a librarian. Remember that college and public libraries as well as some employers offer free access to several commercial databases, sparing you the high cost of individual subscriptions.

**The Web.** Like most adults, you probably use the Web for entertainment, news, shopping, making travel arrangements, getting help with work projects, playing online games, or finding answers to questions. You may actively participate on Facebook, LinkedIn, Twitter, Instagram, or Pinterest. You have probably looked up directions on Google Maps and may have bid on or sold items on eBay. In short, you rely on the Internet daily for information and entertainment. The Web is also an effective research tool when you need valid information quickly.

**Web Search Tools.** Finding what you are looking for on the Web is less frustrating when you know about specialized search tools. Search engines, such as Google, Bing, and Yahoo Search, are popular tools that look for Web pages that match the keywords you enter. Another search tool is a Web directory, such as the Open Directory Project and WWW Virtual Library. Directories have human editors

## Figure 10.6 ABI/INFORM (ProQuest) Search Result Page

ABI/INFORM (ProQuest) is a comprehensive business research database that delivers more than 6,800 publications, nearly 80 percent of which are in full text. Users can access diverse publication types, including annual reports, newspapers, magazines, dissertations, scholarly journals, and business cases. Figure 10.6 shows that the search terms *sustainable development* and *energy efficiency* brought up 912 full-text search results.

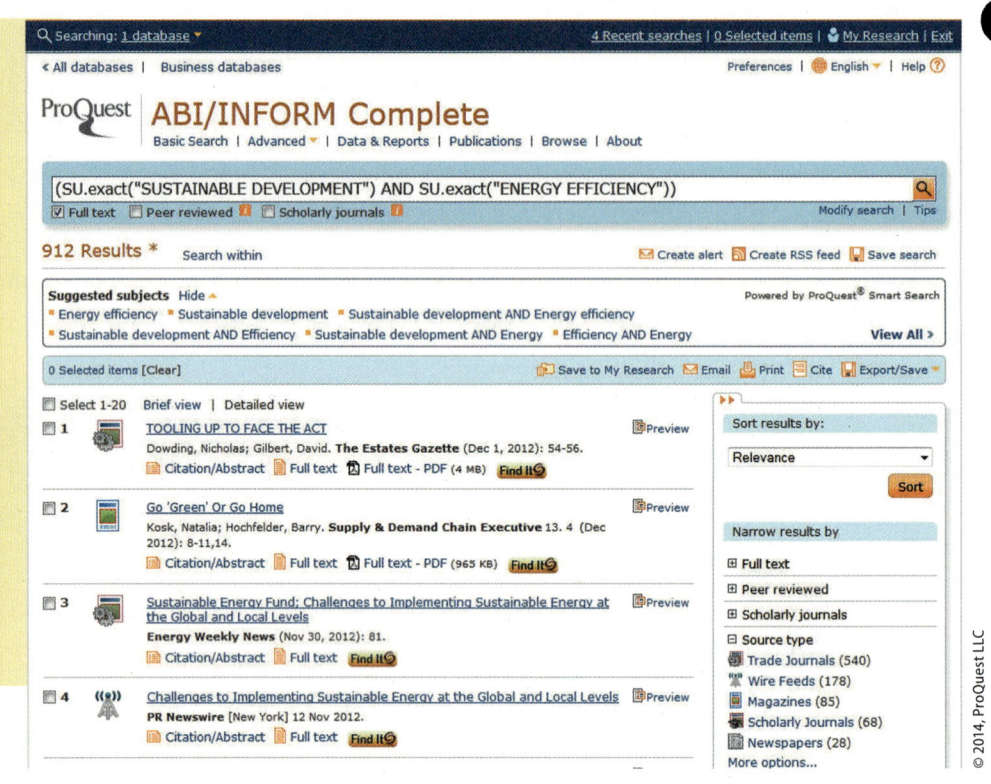

Source: http://search.proquest.com

that select and organize Web pages into subject categories. Metasearch engines, such as InfoSpace and WebCrawler, search through multiple search engines and summarize the results.

Both search engines and subject directories will help you find specific information. Figure 10.7 shows Business.com, a business search engine and subject directory in one. For best results, researchers should use various search tools and compare the quality of the search results.

**Web Search Operators.** When searching the Web, researchers might use a string of keywords with search operators to filter the results. Others may prefer using a search engine's Advance Search filters. Search operators help you narrow your search and find what you need. People who search regularly are familiar with the Boolean search operators, AND, OR, and NOT. You can narrow or broaden your search when you place these operators between words or groups of words. Check the Help section found on a search engine's website to see which search operators they recommend.

Google, undeniably one of the most popular search engines in the world, helps users search effectively on its pages titled Basic Search Tips and How to Search on Google. Google's Search Operators page gives tips for limiting results, and the Advanced Search page allows you to choose one or more filters to find the most relevant information. Google's search operators, some of which are shown in Figure 10.8, will help you search like an expert.

**Web Encyclopedias.** Encyclopedias are considered good sources of baseline information on most topics. The well-known general Web encyclopedia, Wikipedia, may provide helpful background information on topics that require more in-depth research. Because Wikipedia is written by amateurs, however, some schools and universities do not consider it a reliable source of information for research papers. Because anyone can contribute to or alter an article in Wikipedia,

Figure 10.7 Business.com

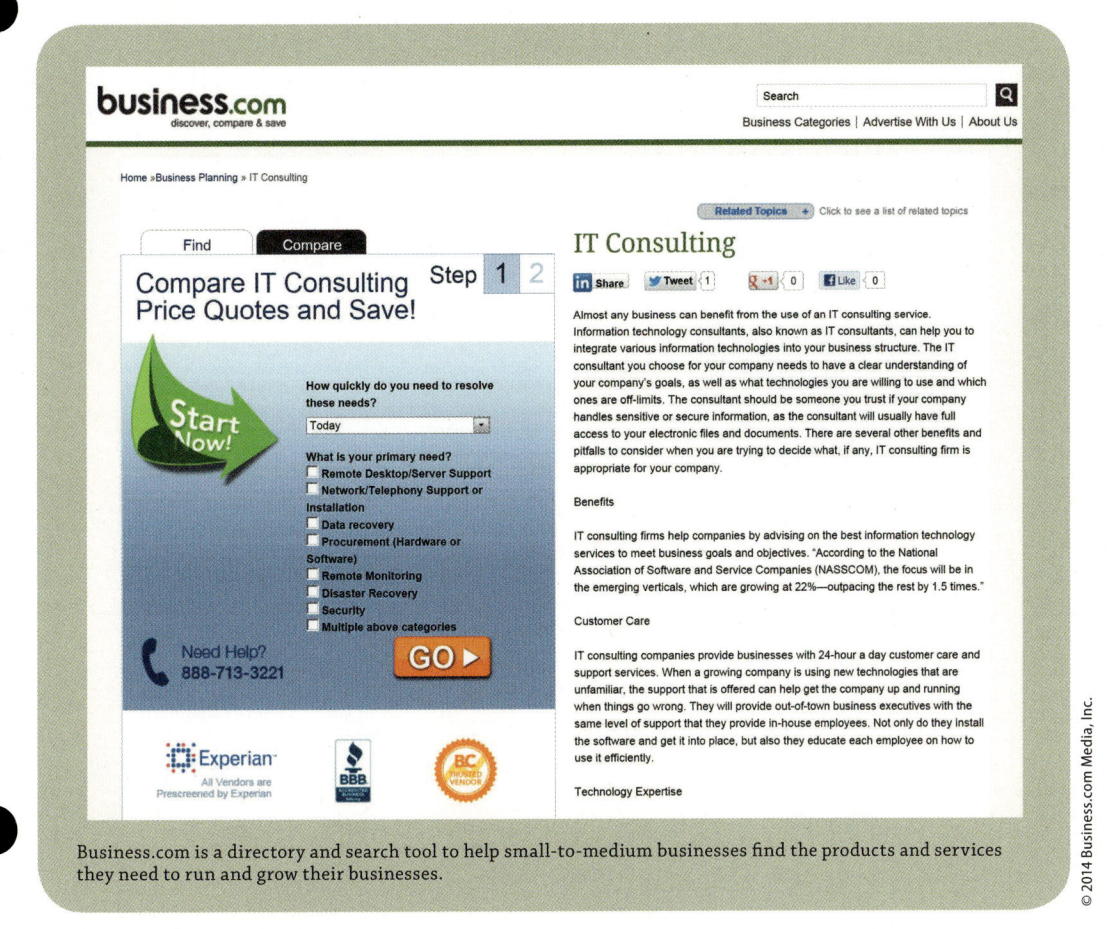

Business.com is a directory and search tool to help small-to-medium businesses find the products and services they need to run and grow their businesses.

the information might not be accurate or verifiable. In fact, Wikipedia's own disclaimer reminds readers that it cannot guarantee the validity of its information. However, this information-packed wiki site often provides its own references (bibliographies) so that you can locate the original sources of information and use them in your research.

**Web Resources and Their Credibility.** When searching the Web, you need to check the credibility and accuracy of the information you find. Anyone can publish on the Web, and credibility is sometimes difficult to determine. Wikis and unmoderated discussion forums are a case in point. The authorship may be unverifiable, and the credibility of the information may be questionable.

To assess the credibility of a Web page, you must scrutinize what you find and consider the following criteria:

- **Currency.** What is the date of the Web page? If the information is time sensitive and the site has not been updated recently, the site is probably not reliable.
- **Authority.** Who publishes or sponsors this Web page? Is information about the author or sponsoring organization available on the About Us page? Can the author be contacted? Be skeptical about data and assertions from individuals and organizations whose credentials are not verifiable.
- **Content.** Is the purpose of the page to entertain, inform, convince, or sell? Is the purpose readily apparent? Who is the intended audience, based on content, tone, and style? Evaluate the overall value of the content and see how it compares with other resources on this topic.

Chapter 10: Proposals and Formal Reports

311

### Figure 10.8 Google Search Operators

**SEARCH OPERATORS** — symbols or words that give you control over the results you see

**Search Smart with Google Operators**

**How Google Looks at Keyword Searches**

Google returns the most common spelling of a word, even if you have spelled it incorrectly.

Google ignores capitalization and most punctuation of keywords.

Google assumes the AND operator between all keywords, so no need to use AND or +.

| What do you want to do? | Try this. |
|---|---|
| Looking for an exact word, phrase, or song lyric? | Use **quotes** "top-level domains" "over the rainbow" |
| Want to exclude a word or a website from your results? | Add a space-[hyphen] **(-)** to exclude that word. Jaguar speed -car Pandas -site:Wikipedia.org |
| Looking for a definition? | Put **define** in front of any word. define loquacious |
| Want to search within a specific website or domain? | Include **site:** in your query (no spaces). Olympics site:nytimes.com Olympics site:.gov |
| Looking for sites that are similar to a well-known URL? (example: related news sites) | Use **related:** in front of the known URL. related:nytimes.com |
| Looking for an unknown word or term? (wildcard) | Use an asterisk **(*)**. "A * saved is a * earned" |
| Want results with one of several choices? | Include **OR** (in CAPS) between words. world cup winner 2013 OR 2014 |
| Want to see schedules and game scores of your favorite team? | Enter your team's name. Real Madrid |

- **Accuracy.** Do the facts that are presented seem reliable? Do you find errors in spelling, grammar, or usage? Do you see any evidence of bias? Are references provided? Do the external links work? Errors and missing references should alert you that the data may be questionable.

### 10-3b Primary Research Sources

Although you will start nearly every business report assignment by sifting through secondary sources, you will probably need primary data to add credibility and show the bigger picture. Business reports that solve specific current problems typically rely on primary, firsthand data. If, for example, management wants to discover the cause of increased employee turnover in its Seattle office, it might investigate employment trends in Seattle, prepare an employee survey about job satisfaction, and interview management for another perspective. Providing answers to business problems often means generating primary data through surveys, interviews, observation, or experimentation.

**Surveys.** Surveys collect data from groups of people. Before developing new products, for example, companies often survey consumers to learn about their preferences. Surveys gather data economically and efficiently from large groups of recipients. Moreover, people responding to surveys have time to consider their answers, which may improve the accuracy of the data.

Mailed or e-mailed surveys, of course, have disadvantages. Response rates may be low, and the returns may not represent an accurate sampling. Another disadvantage has to do with truthfulness. Some respondents may simply not respond accurately. In preparing print or electronic surveys, consider these suggestions:

- **Select the survey population carefully.** Many surveys question a small group of people (a *sampling*) and project the findings to a larger population. Let's say that a survey of your class reveals that the majority prefer *phở*, the Vietnamese meat and rice noodle soup. Can you then say that all students on other campuses prefer pho? For important surveys you will want to learn sampling techniques. As for pho, in a Sodexo survey the soup ranked among the top three comfort foods favored by American college students.[5] This comment implies that the researchers had a large sampling response from many college campuses.

- **Explain why the survey is necessary.** In a brief message, describe the need for the survey. Suggest how the responses will benefit a cause. If appropriate, offer to send recipients a copy of the findings.

- **Consider incentives.** If the survey is long and time-consuming, consider offering money (such as a $1 bill), coupons, gift certificates, or other incentives to encourage a response.

- **Limit the number of questions.** Resist the temptation to ask for too much. Request only information you will use. Don't, for example, include demographic questions (income, gender, age, and so forth) unless that information serves a purpose.

- **Use questions that produce quantifiable answers.** Check-off, multiple-choice, yes/no, and scale (or rank-order) questions, illustrated in Figure 10.9, provide quantifiable results that are easily tabulated. These *close-ended questions* require participants to choose from a limited number of responses determined by the researcher. Responses to *open-ended questions* (*What should the bookstore do about plastic bags?*) reveal interesting, but difficult-to-quantify, perceptions.[6] To obtain workable data, give survey participants a list of possible responses, as shown in items 1 through 4 of Figure 10.9, a college bookstore student survey. For scale and multiple-choice questions, try to present all the possible answer choices. Add an *Other* or *Don't know* category in case the choices seem insufficient to the respondent. Many surveys use scale questions because they capture degrees of feelings. Typical scale headings are *Strongly agree, Somewhat agree, Neutral* (or *No opinion*), *Somewhat disagree*, and *Strongly disagree*.

- **Avoid leading or ambiguous questions.** The wording of a question can dramatically affect responses to it.[7] When respondents were asked, "Are we spending too much, too little, or about the right amount on *assistance to the poor?*" 13 percent responded *Too much*. When the same respondents were asked, "Are we spending too much, too little, or about the right amount on *welfare?*" 44 percent responded *Too much*. Because words have different meanings for different people, you must strive to use objective language and pilot test your questions with typical respondents. Ask neutral questions (*Do CEOs earn too much, too little, or about the right amount?*). Also, avoid queries that ask two or more things (*Should the salaries of CEOs be reduced or regulated by government legislation?*). Instead, break them into separate questions (*Should the salaries of CEOs be reduced by government legislation? Should the salaries of CEOs be regulated by government legislation?*).

### Figure 10.9 College Bookstore Student Survey

**Shoreline College Bookstore**
STUDENT SURVEY

The Shoreline College Bookstore wants to do its part in protecting the environment. Each year we give away 45,000 plastic bags for students to carry off their purchases. We are considering changing from plastic to cloth bags or some other alternative, but we need your views.

Please place checks below to indicate your responses.

1. How many units are you presently carrying?      ___ Male
   ___ 15 or more units                                              ___ Female
   ___ 9 to 14 units
   ___ 8 or fewer units

2. How many times have you visited the bookstore this semester?
   ___ 0 times    ___ 1 time    ___ 2 times    ___ 3 times    ___ 4 or more times

3. Indicate your concern for the environment.
   ___ Very concerned    ___ Concerned    ___ Unconcerned

4. To protect the environment, would you be willing to change to another type of bag when buying books?
   ___ Yes
   ___ No

Indicate your feeling about the following alternatives.

|  | Agree | Undecided | Disagree |
|---|---|---|---|
| For major purchases the bookstore should | | | |
| 5. Continue to provide plastic bags. | ___ | ___ | ___ |
| 6. Provide no bags; encourage students to bring their own bags. | ___ | ___ | ___ |
| 7. Provide no bags; offer cloth bags at reduced price (about $3). | ___ | ___ | ___ |
| 8. Give a cloth bag with each major purchase, the cost to be included in registration fees. | ___ | ___ | ___ |
| 9. Consider another alternative, such as _____ | | | |

Please return the completed survey form to your instructor or to the survey box at the Shoreline College Bookstore exit. Your opinion counts.

*Thanks for your help!*

**Annotations:**
- Explains need for survey (use cover letter for longer surveys)
- Uses groupings that do not overlap (not *9 to 15* and *15 or more*)
- Uses scale questions to channel responses into quantifiable alternatives, as opposed to open-ended questions
- Allows respondent to add an answer in case choices provided seem insufficient
- Tells how to return survey form

---

- **Make it easy for respondents to return the survey.** If surveys are mailed, researchers often provide prepaid self-addressed envelopes to encourage a higher response rate. Since most people now have Internet access, Web surveys have grown in popularity because of their low cost, convenience, and quick response rate. Web-based survey companies such as SurveyMonkey and Zoomerang help users develop simple, template-driven surveys with a feature that allows them to collect the data and see real-time results.

- **Conduct a pilot study.** When considering a pilot study, try the questionnaire with a small group so that you can make needed adjustments. For example, the survey shown in Figure 10.9 revealed that female students generally favored cloth shopping bags and were willing to pay for them. Male students opposed purchasing cloth bags. By adding a gender category, researchers could verify this finding. The pilot study also revealed the need to ensure an appropriate representation of male and female students in the survey.

**Personal Interviews.** Excellent report information can come from personal interviews, particularly on topics about which little has been written. Interview those both inside and outside your company when gathering information for business reports. Scheduling and conducting personal interviews requires preparation and professionalism. See Figure 10.10 for a brief review of how to schedule and conduct an interview.

**Observation and Experimentation.** Some data can be obtained only through firsthand observation and investigation. If your study requires observation, the data you collect must be reliable. For example, a manager may want to learn how to improve customer service by sitting on the sales floor, observing interactions, and taking notes. The data-gathering observations must occur at regular intervals over a period of time in order for the data to be considered valid and reliable. Perhaps a customer service survey and personal interviews would also be part of this data collection.

If firsthand observation involves recording the session, secure permissions beforehand. Arrive early enough to introduce yourself and set up any equipment. Sometimes drop-in visits by company leaders result in firsthand information. Starbucks chief Howard Schultz frowns on research, advertising, and customer surveys. Instead of relying on sophisticated marketing research, Schultz visits 25 Starbucks locations a week to learn about his customers.[8]

Experimentation produces data suggesting causes and effects. Informal experimentation might be as simple as providing an optional customer service training course for employees and then observing whether the newly trained employees had fewer customer complaints than the untrained employees. Scientists would call the untrained employees the control group and the trained employees the experimental group. Informal experimentation has some merit if what you are trying to prove is relevant and valid.

Figure **10.10** Gathering Information Through Personal Interviews

### How to Schedule and Conduct an Interview

- **Locate an expert.** Interview knowledgeable individuals who are experts in their field.
- **Prepare for the interview.** Read all you can about the topic you will discuss so you can converse intelligently. Learn the name and background of the individual you are interviewing. Be familiar with the terminology of the topic. Let's say you are interviewing a corporate communication expert about the advantages of creating a corporate blog. You ought to be familiar with terms such as *brand management, RSS feeds, traffic,* and *damage control.*
- **Maintain a professional attitude.** Call before the interview to confirm the appointment, and arrive on time. You'll also want to be professional in your dress, language, and behavior.
- **Ask objective and open-ended questions.** Adopt a courteous, respectful attitude when asking questions. Open-ended questions encourage a variety of responses. Do not debate any issues and do not interrupt. You are there to listen, not to talk.
- **Watch the time.** Tell interviewees in advance how much time you'll need. Watch the clock and keep the interview discussion on track.
- **End graciously.** Conclude graciously with a general question, such as *Is there anything you would like to add?* Express your appreciation, and ask permission to contact the interviewee later if necessary.

**LEARNING OBJECTIVE 4**

Identify the purposes and techniques of documenting and citing sources in business reports.

## 10-4 Documenting and Citing Sources in Business Reports

In writing business reports, you will often build on the ideas and words of others. In Western culture, whenever you "borrow" the ideas or words of others, you must give credit to your information sources. This is called *documentation*. You can learn more about common documentation (or citation) styles in Appendix C.

### 10-4a Documentation Guidelines

Whether you quote or paraphrase another's words, you must document the source. To use the ideas of others skillfully and ethically, you need to know why, what, and how to document.

**Why Document.** As a careful writer, you should take pains to document report data properly for the following reasons:

- **To strengthen your argument and add credibility.** Including good data from reputable sources will convince readers of your credibility and the logic of your reasoning.
- **To protect yourself against charges of plagiarism.** Acknowledging your sources keeps you honest. *Plagiarism*, which is not only unethical but in some cases illegal, is the act of using others' ideas without proper documentation.
- **To help the reader learn more about the topic.** Citing references enables readers to pursue a topic further and make use of the information themselves.
- **To provide proper credit in an ever-changing world.** The world of business moves so quickly that words and ideas are often borrowed—which is acceptable when you give credit to your sources.

**What to Document.** When you write reports, you are continually dealing with other people's ideas. You are expected to conduct research, synthesize ideas, and build on the work of others. However, you must give proper credit for borrowed material. To avoid plagiarism, give credit whenever you use the following:[9]

- Another person's ideas, opinions, examples, or theory
- Any facts, statistics, graphs, and drawings that are not common knowledge
- Quotations of another person's actual spoken or written words
- Paraphrases of another person's spoken or written words
- Visuals, images, and any kind of electronic media

Information that is common knowledge requires no documentation. For example, the statement *The Wall Street Journal is a popular business newspaper* would require no citation. Statements that are not common knowledge, however, must be documented. For example, *Texas is home to two of the nation's top ten fastest-growing cities (100,000 or more population): Austin and San Antonio.* This statement requires a citation.

**How to Paraphrase.** In writing reports and using the ideas of others, you will probably rely heavily on *paraphrasing*, which means restating an original passage in your own words and in your own style. To do a good job of paraphrasing, follow these steps:

1. Read the original material intently to comprehend its full meaning.
2. Write your own version without looking at the original.

3. Avoid repeating the grammatical structure of the original and merely replacing words with synonyms.

4. Reread the original to be sure you covered the main points but did not borrow specific language.

To better understand the difference between plagiarizing and paraphrasing, study the following passages. Notice that the writer of the plagiarized version uses the same grammatical construction as the source and often merely replaces words with synonyms. Even the acceptable version, however, requires a reference to the source author.

### Source
We have seen, in a short amount of time, the disappearance of a large number of household brands that failed to take sufficient and early heed of the software revolution that is upending traditional brick-and-mortar businesses and creating a globally pervasive digital economy.[10]

### Plagiarized version
Many trusted household name brands disappeared very swiftly because they did not sufficiently and early pay attention to the software revolution that is toppling traditional physical businesses and creating a global digital economy. (Saylor, 2012)

### Acceptable paraphrase
Digital technology has allowed a whole new virtual global economy to blossom and very swiftly wiped out some formerly powerful companies that responded too late or inadequately to the disruptive force that has swept the globe. (Saylor, 2012)

**When and How to Quote.** On occasion, you will want to use the exact words of a source, but beware of overusing quotations. Documents that contain pages of spliced-together quotations suggest that writers have few ideas of their own. Wise writers and speakers use direct quotations for three purposes only:

- To provide objective background data and establish the severity of a problem as seen by experts
- To repeat identical phrasing because of its precision, clarity, or aptness
- To duplicate exact wording before making critical statements

When you must use a long quotation, try to summarize and introduce it in your own words. Readers want to know the gist of a quotation before they tackle it. For example, to introduce a quotation discussing the shrinking staffs of large companies, you could precede it with your words: *In predicting employment trends, Charles Waller believes the corporation of the future will depend on a small core of full-time employees.* To introduce quotations or paraphrases, use wording such as the following:

*According to Waller. . . .*

*Waller argues that. . . .*

*In his recent study, Waller reported. . . .*

Use quotation marks to enclose exact quotations, as shown in the following: "The current image," says Charles Waller, "of a big glass-and-steel corporate headquarters on landscaped grounds directing a worldwide army of tens of thousands of employees may soon be a thing of the past" (2013, p. 51).

## 10-4b Copyright and Fair Use

The Copyright Act of 1976 protects authors—literary, dramatic, and artistic—of published and unpublished works. The word *copyright* refers to "the right to copy," and a key provision is fair use. Under *fair use*, individuals have limited use of copyrighted material without requiring permission. These uses are for criticism, comment, news reporting, teaching, scholarship, and research. Unfortunately, the distinctions between fair use and infringement are not clearly defined.

**Four-Factor Test to Assess Fair Use.** What is fair use? Actually, it is a shadowy territory with vague and often disputed boundaries—now even more so with the addition of cyberspace. Courts use four factors as a test in deciding disputes over fair use:

- **Purpose and character of the use, particularly whether for profit.** Courts are more likely to allow fair use for nonprofit educational purposes than for commercial ventures.
- **Nature of the copyrighted work.** When information is necessary for the public good—such as medical news—courts are more likely to support fair use.
- **Amount and substantiality of the portion used.** Copying a 200-word passage from a 200,000-word book might be allowed but not 200 words from a 1,000-word article or a substantial part of a shorter work. A total of 300 words is mistakenly thought by many to be an acceptable limit for fair use, but courts have not upheld this figure.
- **Effect of the use on the potential market.** If use of the work may interfere with the author's potential profit from the original, fair use copying would not be allowed.

**How to Avoid Copyright Infringement.** Whenever you borrow words, charts, graphs, photos, music, and other media—in short, any *intellectual property*—be sure you know what is legal and acceptable. The following guidelines will help:

- **Assume that all intellectual property is copyrighted.** Nearly everything created privately and originally after 1989 is copyrighted and protected whether or not it has a copyright notice.
- **Realize that Internet items and resources are NOT in the public domain.** No contemporary intellectual or artistic creation is in the public domain (free to be used by anyone) unless the owner explicitly says so.
- **Observe fair-use restrictions.** Be aware of the four-factor test. Avoid appropriating large amounts of outside material.
- **Ask for permission.** You are always safe if you obtain permission. Write to the source, identify the material you wish to include, and explain where it will be used. Expect to pay for permission.
- **Don't assume that a footnote is all that is needed.** Including a footnote to a source prevents plagiarism but not copyright infringement. Anything copied beyond the boundaries of fair use requires permission.

### 10-4c Common Citation Formats

You can direct readers to your sources with parenthetical notes inserted into the text and with bibliographies. Figure 10.11 shows the most common citation formats presented by the Modern Language Association (MLA), the American Psychological Association (APA), and the Chicago Manual of Style (CMS). Learn more about using MLA and APA formats in Appendix C.

**LEARNING OBJECTIVE 5**
Convert report data into meaningful visual aids and graphics.

## 10-5 Incorporating Meaningful Visual Aids and Graphics

After collecting and interpreting information, you need to consider how best to present it. If your report contains complex data, you will want to display the information graphically in tables, charts, graphs, or even infographics. Graphics clarify

Figure 10.11 Comparing Bibliographic Citation Formats: MLA, APA, CMS

**Modern Language Association (MLA) Works Cited**

Saylor, M. The Mobile Wave: How Mobile Intelligence Will Change Everything. New York: Vanguard Press, 2012. Print.

Pazos, Pilar, Jennifer M. Chung, and Marina Micari. "Instant Messaging as a Task-Support Tool in Information Technology Organizations." *Journal of Business Communication* 50.1 (2013): 68–86. Print. doi:10.1177/0021943612465181

**American Psychological Association (APA) References**

Saylor, M. (2012). *The mobile wave: How mobile intelligence will change everything*. New York: Vanguard Press, p. ix.

Pazos, P., Chung J. M., & Micari, M. (2013, January). Instant messaging as a task-support tool in information technology organizations. *Journal of Business Communication, 50*(1), 68–86. doi:10.1177/0021943612465181

**Chicago Manual of Style (CMS) Bibliography**

Saylor, M. *The Mobile Wave: How Mobile Intelligence Will Change Everything*. New York: Vanguard Press, 2012.

Pazos, Pilar, Jennifer M. Chung, and Marina Micari. 2013. Instant Messaging as a Task-Support Tool in Information Technology Organizations. *Journal of Business Communication* 50:68–86. doi:10.1177/0021943612465181

data, add visual interest, and make complex data easy to understand. When incorporating graphics into your report, think about what type of graphic will display the information most effectively.

## 10-5a Matching Graphics and Objectives

When selecting a graphic, consider your objective. If your objective is to show changes over time, you may choose a line chart to display your data. Report writers select graphics (e.g., tables, bar charts, pie charts, or pictures) that will convey their information most effectively. Figure 10.12 summarizes appropriate uses for each type of graphic.

## 10-5b Using Tables, Charts, and Infographics

Why are graphics important? Report writers know that readers grasp meaning from visuals more quickly than they do from text. Therefore, they prefer to use tables and various types of charts and infographics to show data, relationships,

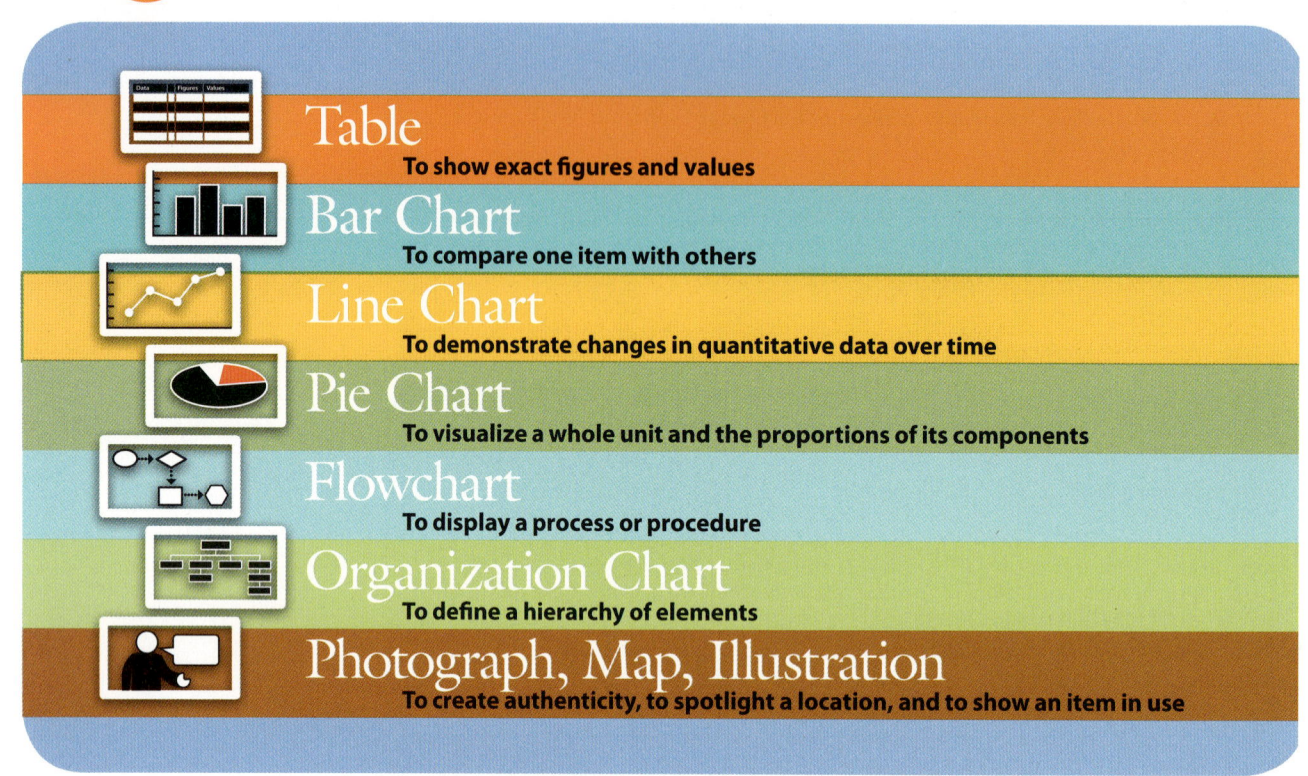

Figure **10.12** Matching Graphics to Objectives

**Table** — To show exact figures and values

**Bar Chart** — To compare one item with others

**Line Chart** — To demonstrate changes in quantitative data over time

**Pie Chart** — To visualize a whole unit and the proportions of its components

**Flowchart** — To display a process or procedure

**Organization Chart** — To define a hierarchy of elements

**Photograph, Map, Illustration** — To create authenticity, to spotlight a location, and to show an item in use

trends, and comparisons. Adding photographs, maps, illustrations, and diagrams also heightens visual interest and adds clarity to report information.

**Tables.** One of the most frequently used report graphics is the table. Because a *table* presents quantitative or verbal information in systematic columns and rows, it can clarify large quantities of data in small spaces. Here are tips for creating good tables, an example of which is shown in Figure 10.13.

- Add a meaningful title at the top of the table.
- Arrange items in a logical order (alphabetical, chronological, highest to lowest), depending on what you need to emphasize.
- Provide bold headings for rows and columns.
- Identify the units in which figures are given (percentages, dollars, hours) in the table title, in the column or row heading, in the first item of a column, or in a note at the bottom.
- Use *N/A* (*not available*) for missing data rather than leaving a cell empty.
- Make long tables easier to read by shading alternate lines or by leaving a blank line between groups of five.
- Place tables as close as possible to the place where they are mentioned in the text.

The table in Figure 10.13 presents data about the MPM Entertainment Company over several years, making it easy to compare several divisions over time. Notice that the year 2015 shows a projected income based on revenue growth during the years 2011 through 2014.

**Bar Charts.** *Bar charts* make visual comparisons by using horizontal or vertical bars of varying lengths. Bar charts are useful for comparing related items, illustrating

Figure **10.13** Table Summarizing Precise Data

| | Figure 1 | | | |
|---|---|---|---|---|
| | **MPM ENTERTAINMENT COMPANY** | | | |
| | Income by Division (in millions of dollars) | | | |
| | **Theme Parks** | **Motion Pictures** | **DVDs & Blu-ray Discs** | **Total** |
| 2012 | $15.8 | $39.3 | $11.2 | $66.3 |
| 2013 | 18.1 | 17.5 | 15.3 | 50.9 |
| 2014 | 23.8 | 21.1 | 22.7 | 67.6 |
| 2015 | 32.2 | 22.0 | 24.3 | 78.5 |
| 2016 (projected) | 35.1 | 21.0 | 26.1 | 82.2 |

Source: *Industry Profiles* (New York: DataPro, 2015) 225

changes in data over time, and showing segments as a part of a whole. Figures 10.16 and 10.17 need legends to explain the colors used in the chart. Note how the bar charts in Figures 10.14 to 10.17 display information in different ways.

Many techniques for constructing tables also hold true for bar charts. Here are a few additional tips:

- Keep the length and width of each bar and segment proportional.
- Include a total figure on the bar if it adds clarity for the reader and does not clutter the chart.
- Always start dollar or percentage amounts at zero.

**Line Charts.** Line charts show changes over time, thus indicating trends. The vertical axis is typically the dependent variable; the horizontal axis is the independent variable. Simple line charts (Figure 10.18) show just one variable. Multiple line charts (Figure 10.19) compare two or more data sets and require a legend to explain them. Here are some reminders when preparing line charts:

- Begin with a rectangular grid showing a vertical and horizontal axis.
- Place the time component (usually years) horizontally across the bottom.
- Label the vertical and horizontal axes (if needed) for clarification.

**Segmented Area (Surface) Charts.** Segmented area, or surface, charts (Figure 10.20) illustrate how the components of a whole change over time. If you want to stack the revenue increments for each division as shown in Figure 10.20, the top line indicates the total of the three division revenues. Area charts require a legend for clarity.

**Pie Charts.** Pie charts, or circle graphs, enable readers to see how the components, or wedges, relate to the whole. Pie charts are useful for showing percentages, as Figure 10.21 illustrates. For the most effective pie charts, follow these suggestions:

- Place the largest wedge near the top of the circle and arrange the others in descending order.
- Include the actual percentage for each wedge.
- Use four to six segments for best results; smaller wedges can be grouped in a segment labeled *Other*.

**Flowcharts.** Procedures are simplified and clarified in a flowchart, as shown in Figure 10.22. Whether you need to describe the procedure for handling a customer's purchase, highlight steps in solving a problem, or display a problem with a process,

**Figure 10.14** Vertical Bar Chart

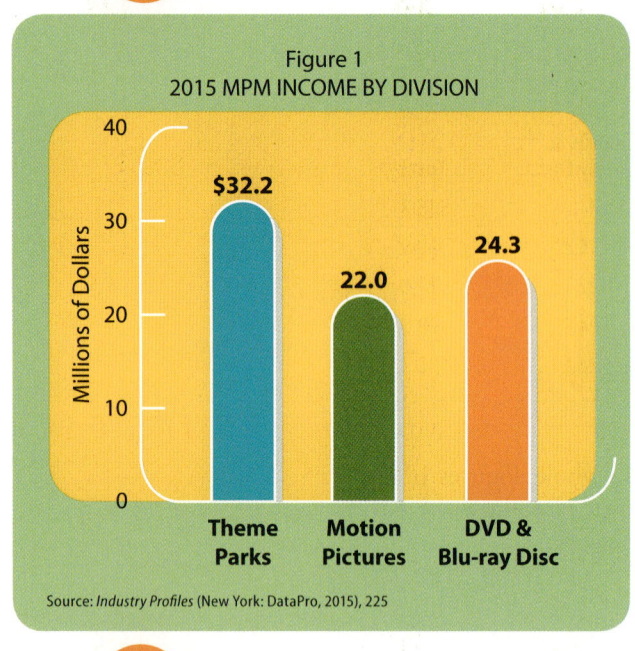

Figure 1
2015 MPM INCOME BY DIVISION

- Theme Parks: $32.2
- Motion Pictures: 22.0
- DVD & Blu-ray Disc: 24.3

(Millions of Dollars)

Source: *Industry Profiles* (New York: DataPro, 2015), 225

**Figure 10.15** Horizontal Bar Chart

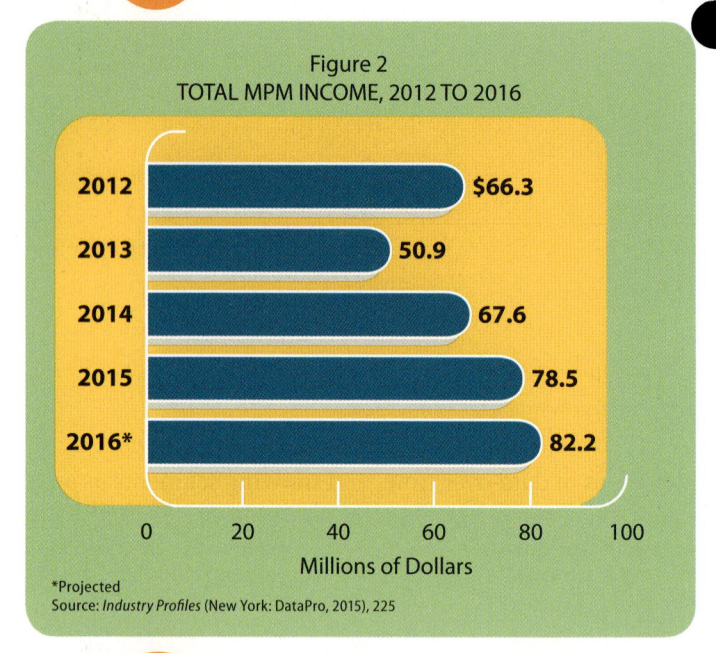

Figure 2
TOTAL MPM INCOME, 2012 TO 2016

- 2012: $66.3
- 2013: 50.9
- 2014: 67.6
- 2015: 78.5
- 2016*: 82.2

(Millions of Dollars)

*Projected
Source: *Industry Profiles* (New York: DataPro, 2015), 225

**Figure 10.16** Grouped Bar Chart

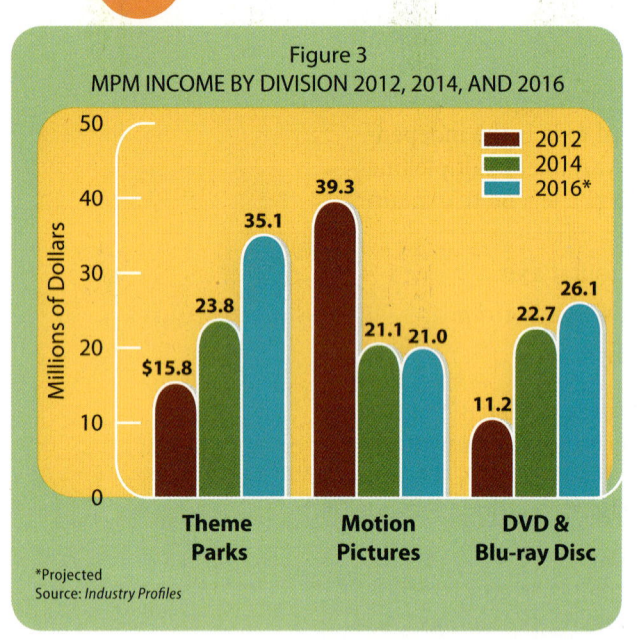

Figure 3
MPM INCOME BY DIVISION 2012, 2014, AND 2016

Legend: 2012, 2014, 2016*

- Theme Parks: $15.8, 23.8, 35.1
- Motion Pictures: 39.3, 21.1, 21.0
- DVD & Blu-ray Disc: 11.2, 22.7, 26.1

(Millions of Dollars)

*Projected
Source: *Industry Profiles*

**Figure 10.17** Segmented 100 Percent Bar Chart

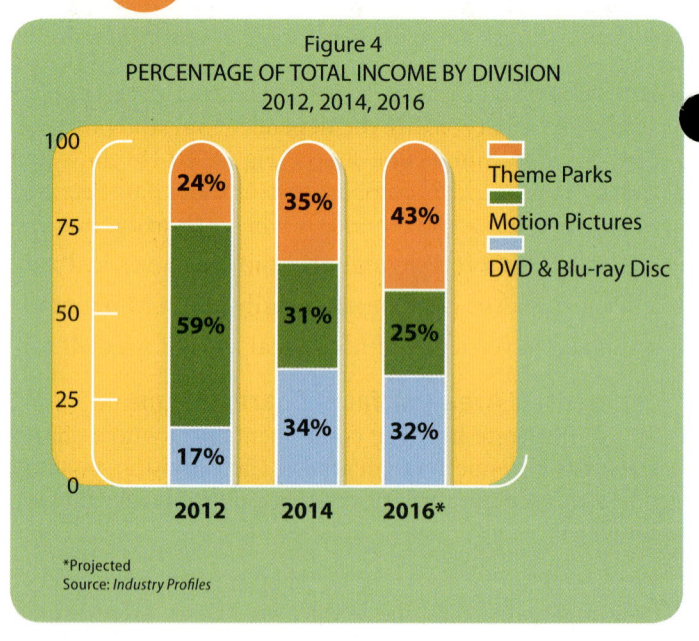

Figure 4
PERCENTAGE OF TOTAL INCOME BY DIVISION
2012, 2014, 2016

Legend: Theme Parks, Motion Pictures, DVD & Blu-ray Disc

- 2012: 24% / 59% / 17%
- 2014: 35% / 31% / 34%
- 2016*: 43% / 25% / 32%

*Projected
Source: *Industry Profiles*

flowcharts help the reader visualize the process. Traditional flowcharts use the following symbols:

- Ovals to designate the beginning and end of a process
- Diamonds to designate decision points
- Rectangles to represent major activities or steps

**Infographics.** An *infographic* is a visual representation of complex information in a format that is easy to understand. Compelling infographics tell a story by combining images and graphic elements, such as charts and diagrams. Because these data visualizations tend to be long, they are commonly shared in online environments.

Chapter 10: Proposals and Formal Reports

Figure **10.18** Simple Line Chart

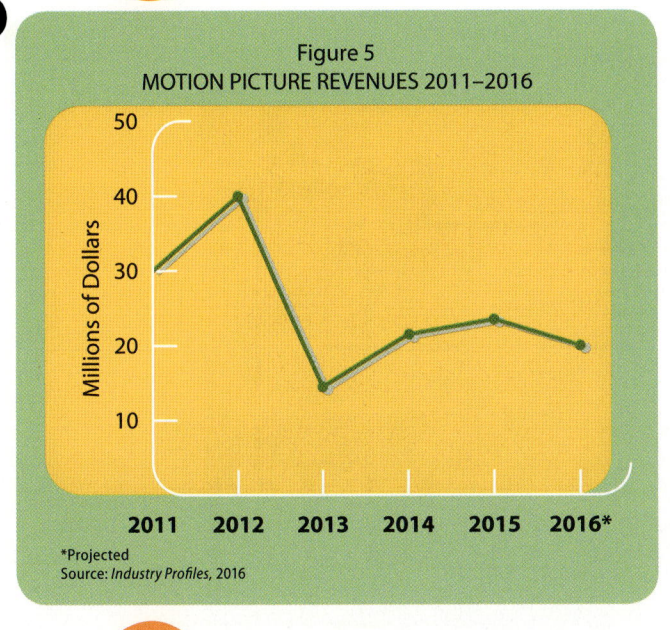

Figure 5
MOTION PICTURE REVENUES 2011–2016

*Projected
Source: *Industry Profiles*, 2016

Figure **10.19** Multiple Line Chart

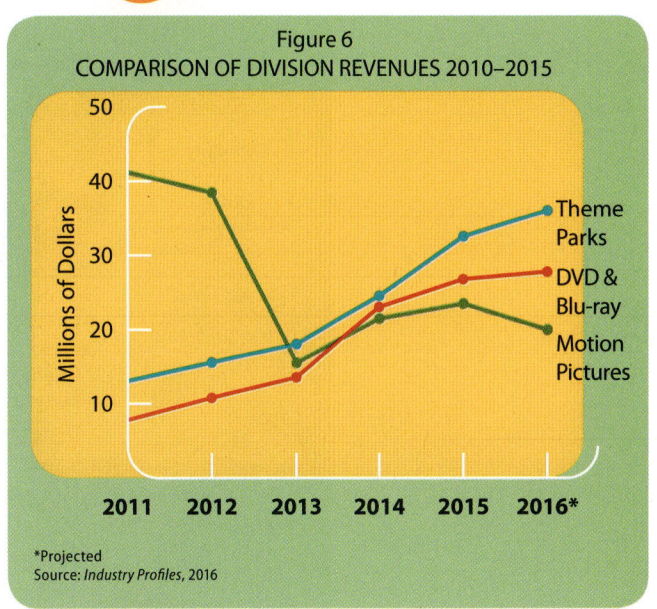

Figure 6
COMPARISON OF DIVISION REVENUES 2010–2015

*Projected
Source: *Industry Profiles*, 2016

Figure **10.20** Segmented Area (Surface) Chart

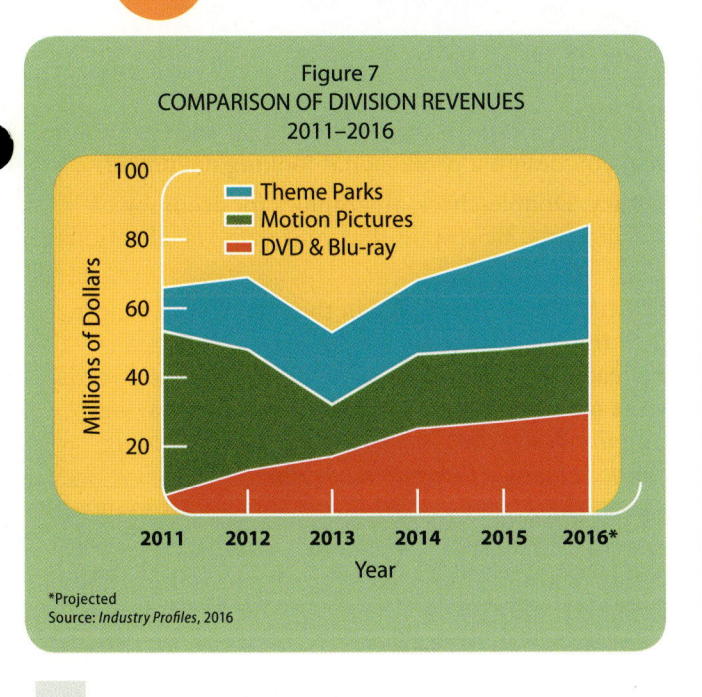

Figure 7
COMPARISON OF DIVISION REVENUES
2011–2016

*Projected
Source: *Industry Profiles*, 2016

Figure **10.21** Pie Chart

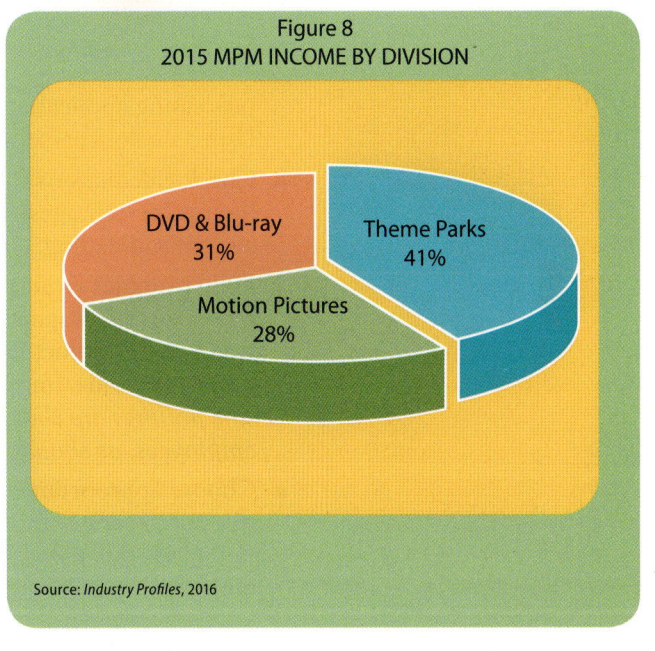

Figure 8
2015 MPM INCOME BY DIVISION

Source: *Industry Profiles*, 2016

## 10-5c Incorporating Graphics in Reports

Used appropriately, graphics make reports more interesting and easier to understand. When inserting graphics into your reports, follow these suggestions:

- **Consider the audience.** Will your graphics help the reader understand and retain the information? How many graphics are necessary? Longer technical reports may use more graphics than shorter informal reports do.
- **Use color wisely.** Colors used in graphics add visual appeal to a report. Warm colors such as yellow, orange, and red tend to advance on the page. In contrast, cool colors such as green, blue, and purple tend to recede. Most word

Chapter 10: Proposals and Formal Reports

**Figure 10.22** Flowchart

**FLOW OF CUSTOMER ORDER THROUGH XYZ COMPANY**

[Flowchart showing: Company receives order → Prepaid? → (No) Credit Department evaluates → Credit granted? → (Yes) Customer Service checks inventory; (No) Sales Manager responds → Customer. From Prepaid? (Yes) → Customer Service checks inventory → Goods available? → (No) Goods restocked; (Yes) Accounting prepares invoice → Shipping sends order → Customer.]

**Legend**
Operation
Decision
End

---

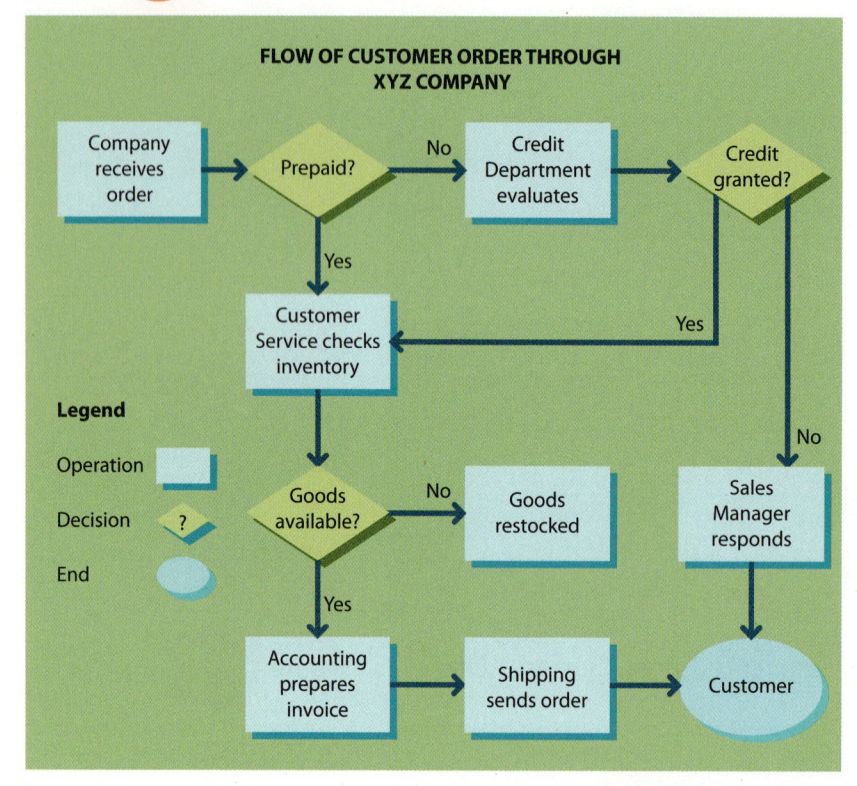

processing applications offer color palettes with a mix of warm and cool colors. Using a color theme will help you design a professional-looking document.

- **Check calculations for accuracy.** Double-check all graphics for accuracy of figures, percentages, and calculations. Be certain that your data visualizations are not misleading.
- **Place graphics strategically.** Mention every graphic in the text of your report, and place the graphic close to the point where it is mentioned. When referring to the graphic, help the reader understand its significance. In other words, be specific and summarize the main point of the graphic. Instead of saying, *The findings are shown in Figure 3*, say this: *Two thirds of the responding employees, as shown in Figure 3, favor a flextime schedule.*
- **Choose appropriate captions or titles.** Like reports, graphics may use "talking" titles or generic, functional titles. Talking titles are more persuasive; they tell the reader what to think. Functional titles make general references using nouns without interpreting the data.

| Talking Title | Functional Title |
|---|---|
| Rising Workplace Drug Testing Unfair and Inaccurate | Workplace Drug Testing |
| College Students' Diets Clogged With Fat | College Students and Nutrition |

Amateur designers can create captivating infographics using free online tools at sites such as Infogr.am, Piktochart, and Visual.ly. A few innovative companies have even turned reports and executive summaries into infographics. Another popular application of infographics is designing visual résumés, as shown in Figure 10.23.

Figure 10.23 Infographic Résumé

**Michael Anderson**
RÉSUMÉ / INFOGRAPHICS

theportfolio.ofmichaelanderson.com
lunyboy@yahoo.com | 304-382-5145
HC 63 BOX 2340 | ROMNEY, WV 26757

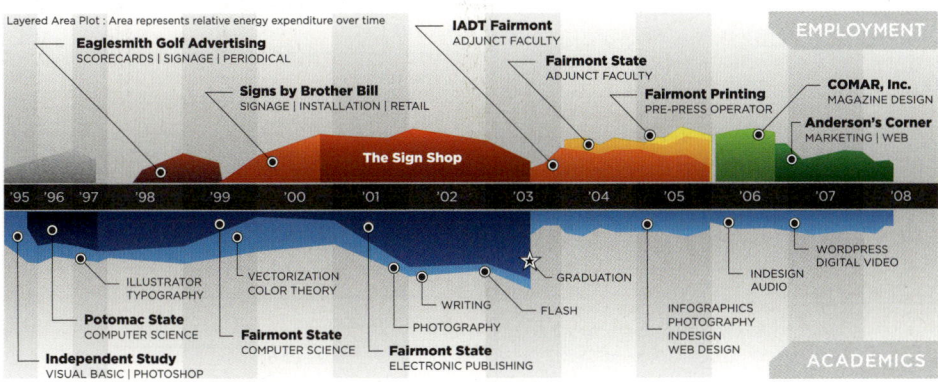

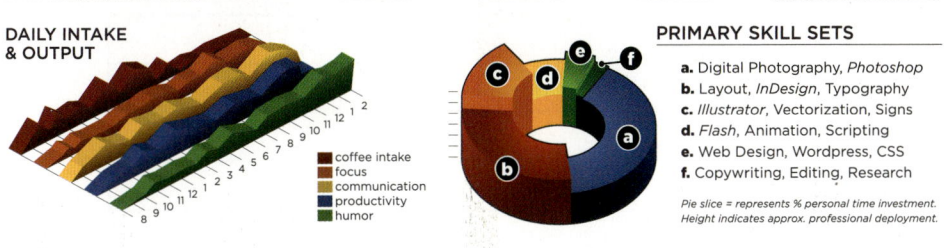

*Courtesy of Michael Anderson*

## 10-6 Understanding Report Components

**LEARNING OBJECTIVE 6**
Describe the components of typical formal reports.

Because formal business reports can be long and complex, they usually include more sections than routine informal business reports do. Figure 10.24 shows the components of informal and formal business reports. These components are standard and conventional; that is, the audience expects to see them in a professional report. You will find most of the components addressed here in Figure 10.25, a formal analytical report studying the economic impact of an industrial park on Flagstaff, Arizona.

### 10-6a Front Matter Components

The front matter of a formal report refers to the preliminary sections before the body section. Some front matter components are optional, but they typically appear in the following order: (a) report cover (optional), (b) title page, (c) letter or memo of transmittal (optional), (d) table of contents, (e) list of figures or tables (optional), and (f) executive summary. Writers often number these sections with lowercase Roman numerals; the title page, however, is normally not numbered. These components make it easy for the reader to find specific information quickly.

**Title Page.** The format of title pages may vary, but title pages often include the same elements. The report title page shown in Figure 10.25 follows MLA style and includes the following elements:

- Name of the report, often in uppercase letters (no underscore and no quotation marks)
- *Prepared for* (or *Submitted to*) followed by the name, title, and organization of the individual receiving the report

Chapter 10: Proposals and Formal Reports

Figure 10.24 Components of Informal and Formal Reports

**Informal Business Reports**

| Introduction |
| Body |
| Conclusions |
| Recommendations (if requested) |

**Formal Business Reports**

| Cover |
| Title page |
| Letter of transmittal |
| Table of contents |
| List of figures |
| Executive summary |
| Introduction |
| Body |
| Conclusions |
| Recommendations (if requested) |
| Appendix |
| References |

- *Prepared by* (or *Submitted by*) followed by the author's name and title
- Date of submission

**Letter or Memo of Transmittal.** Generally written on organization stationery, a letter or memorandum of transmittal may introduce a formal report. A transmittal letter or memo uses the direct strategy and is usually less formal than the report itself. The transmittal document typically (a) announces the topic of the report and tells how it was authorized; (b) briefly describes the project; (c) highlights the report's findings, conclusions, and recommendations; and (d) closes with appreciation for the assignment or instruction for follow-up actions. If a report is going to various readers, you would prepare a special transmittal letter or memo for each reader.

**Table of Contents.** The table of contents shows the main sections in the report and their page numbers. The proper title is *Contents* or *Table of Contents*. The table of contents includes front matter items, the body section's main headings and subheadings, and back matter sections, such as the appendix. Major headings are left-aligned, and leaders (spaced dots) help guide the eye to the page numbers.

**List of Figures.** For reports with many figures or tables, you may wish to list the figures to help readers locate them easily. This list may appear on the same page as the table of contents, space permitting. For each figure or table, include a title and page number. Some writers prepare separate lists for tables and figures. Because the model report in Figure 10.25 has few illustrations, the writer labeled them all *figures*.

**Executive Summary.** The purpose of an executive summary is to present an overview of the longer report for people who may not have time to read the entire document. Generally, an executive summary is prepared by the author of the report. However, you might be asked to write an executive summary of a published report or article written by someone else. In either case, the writer's goal is to summarize the report's major sections, such as the purpose, background, conclusions, and recommendations. Readers often go straight to the executive summary and look for the recommendations before glancing at the full report.

The one-page executive summary in Figure 10.25 includes headings that help direct the reader to the main sections. The format and headings of an executive summary may vary according to the organization's preferences.

## 10-6b Body Components

Body components of formal reports typically include the introduction and body sections. In the introduction, the writer briefly describes the report's contents. In the body, the longest and most substantive section, the writer discusses the problem and findings, before presenting conclusions and recommendations. Extensive and bulky materials that don't fit in the body belong in the appendix.

**Introduction.** Formal reports begin with an introduction to announce the topic and to set the stage for the reader. A good report introduction typically covers the following elements, although not necessarily in this order:

- **Background:** Events leading up to the problem or need
- **Problem or purpose:** Explanation of the problem or need that motivated the report
- **Significance:** Account of the importance of the report topic, which may include quotes from experts, journals, or Web resources
- **Scope:** Boundaries of the report, defining what will be included or excluded
- **Organization:** A road map or structure of the report

## Workplace in Focus

While casino gaming is harmless fun for most people, a 95-page report published by British Columbia's public health chief found that gaming is a serious problem for an increasing number of Canadians. According to the report, the number of British Columbians with a severe gambling habit rose from 13,000 to 31,000 over a five-year period, presenting a grave public health risk. To help regulators address the crisis, the report offered 17 recommendations, such as raising the gambling age, eliminating high-risk electronic gaming machines, and reducing the number of ATMs in casinos. Where can readers expect to find such important recommendations in lengthy formal reports?[10]

Jack Sullivan/Alamy

Chapter 10: Proposals and Formal Reports

Beyond these minimal introductory elements, consider adding any of the following information that may be relevant to your readers:

- **Authorization:** The name of whoever commissioned the report and its intended audience
- **Literature review:** A summary of other publications on this topic
- **Sources and methods:** A description of secondary sources (periodicals, books, databases) and methods of collecting primary data
- **Key terms:** Definitions of important and unfamiliar terms used in the report

**Report Body.** The body is the principal section in a formal report. It discusses, analyzes, interprets, and evaluates the research findings or solution to the initial problem. This is where you show the evidence that justifies your conclusions. Organize the body into main categories following your original outline.

The body section contains clear headings that explain each major section. Headings may be functional or talking. Functional heads (such as *Results of the Survey, Analysis of Findings*, or *Discussion*) help readers identify the general purpose of the section. Such headings are useful for routine reports or for sensitive topics that may upset readers. Talking heads (for example, *Findings Reveal Revenue and Employment Benefits*) are more descriptive and informative.

**Conclusions and Recommendations.** Writers know that the conclusions and recommendations section is most important to a reader. This section tells what the findings mean, particularly in terms of solving the original problem. Some writers prefer to intermix their conclusions with the analysis of the findings. Other writers place the conclusions before the body so that busy readers can examine them immediately. Still other writers combine the conclusions and recommendations. Most writers, though, present the conclusions after the body because readers expect this sequence. To improve readability, you may present the conclusions in a numbered or bulleted list.

### 10-6c Back Matter Components

The back matter of most reports includes a reference section and one or more appendixes. The reference section includes a bibliography of sources, and the appendix contains supplemental information or source documents. In organizing the back matter sections, use standard Arabic numerals to number the pages.

**Works Cited, References, or Bibliography.** If you use the MLA (Modern Language Association) referencing format, list all sources of information alphabetically in a section titled *Works Cited*. If you use the APA (American Psychological Association) format, list your sources in a section called *References*. Your listed sources must correspond to in-text citations in the report whenever you are borrowing words or ideas from published and unpublished resources.

### 10-6d Model Formal Report With MLA Format Plus Alternate APA Reference List

Formal reports in business generally aim to study problems and recommend solutions. In the formal report shown in Figure 10.25, Martha Montoya, senior research consultant with Sedona Development Company, examined the economic impact of a local industrial park on the city of Flagstaff, Arizona, resulting in this formal report.

Martha's report illustrates many of the points discussed in this chapter. Although it is a good example of the typical report format and style, it should not be viewed as the only way to present a report. This model report illustrates MLA in-text citations and references ("Works Cited"). The model also shows the report references in APA format ("References") so that you can compare the citation styles.

# Figure 10.25 Model Formal Report With MLA Citation Format and Alternate APA Reference List

*Includes report title in all caps with longer line above shorter line*

**ECONOMIC IMPACT OF COCONINO INDUSTRIAL PARK
ON THE CITY OF FLAGSTAFF**

*Highlights name of report recipient*

Prepared for
The Flagstaff City Council
Flagstaff, Arizona

*Identifies report writer*

Prepared by
Martha E. Montoya
Senior Research Consultant
Sedona Development Company

January 12, 2016

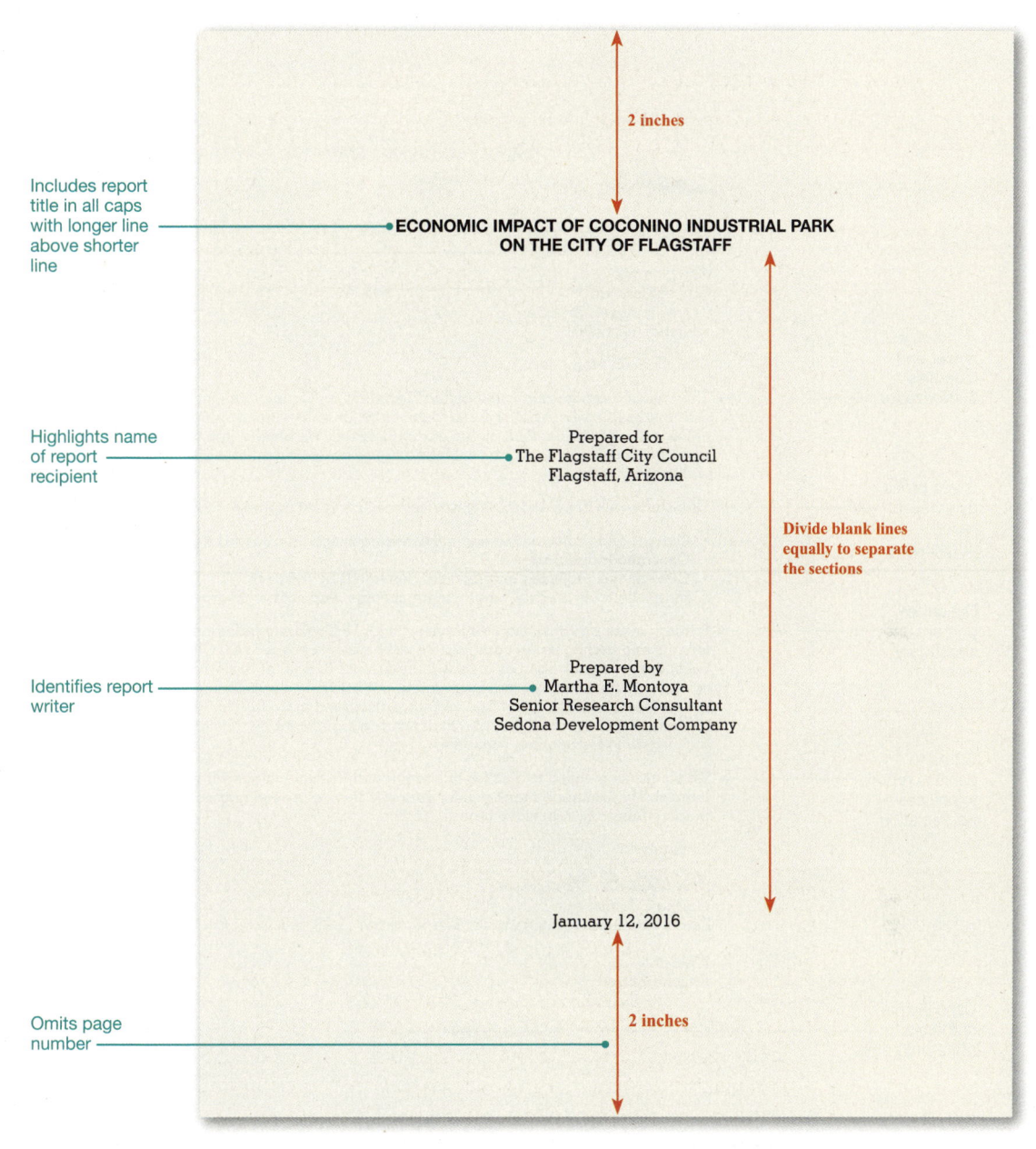

*Omits page number*

2 inches (top and bottom margins)

**Divide blank lines equally to separate the sections**

The title page is usually arranged in four evenly balanced areas. If the report is to be bound on the left, move the left margin and center point 0.25 inch to the right. Notice that no page number appears on the title page, although it is counted as page i. In designing the title page, be careful to avoid anything unprofessional—such as too many type fonts, italics, oversized print, and inappropriate graphics. Keep the title page simple and professional. This model report uses MLA documentation style. However, it does not illustrate double-spacing, the recommended format for research papers using MLA style. Instead, this model uses single-spacing, which saves space and is more appropriate for business reports.

Chapter 10: Proposals and Formal Reports

Figure 10.25 (Continued) Letter of Transmittal

## SEDONA DEVELOPMENT COMPANY
426 Saddle Rock Circle  www.sedonadevco.com
Sedona, Arizona 86340  928.450.3348

January 12, 2016

City Council
City of Flagstaff
211 West Aspen Avenue
Flagstaff, AZ 86001

Dear Council Members:

**Announces report and identifies authorization** → The attached report, requested by the Flagstaff City Council in a letter to Goldman-Lyon & Associates dated October 20, describes the economic impact of Coconino Industrial Park on the city of Flagstaff. We believe you will find the results of this study useful in evaluating future development of industrial parks within the city limits.

**Gives broad overview of report purposes** → This study was designed to examine economic impact in three areas:

- Current and projected tax and other revenues accruing to the city from Coconino Industrial Park
- Current and projected employment generated by the park
- Indirect effects on local employment, income, and economic growth

**Describes primary and secondary research** → Primary research consisted of interviews with 15 Coconino Industrial Park (CIP) tenants and managers, in addition to a 2014 survey of over 5,000 CIP employees. Secondary research sources included the Annual Budget of the City of Flagstaff, county and state tax records, government publications, periodicals, books, and online resources. Results of this research, discussed more fully in this report, indicate that Coconino Industrial Park exerts a significant beneficial influence on the Flagstaff metropolitan economy.

**Offers to discuss report; expresses appreciation** → We would be pleased to discuss this report and its conclusions with you at your request. My firm and I thank you for your confidence in selecting our company to prepare this comprehensive report.

Sincerely,

*Martha E. Montoya*

Martha E. Montoya
Senior Research Consultant

MEM:coe
Attachment

**Uses Roman numerals for prefatory pages** → ii

---

A letter or memo of transmittal announces the report topic and explains who authorized it. It briefly describes the project and previews the conclusions, if the reader is supportive. Such messages generally close by expressing appreciation for the assignment, suggesting follow-up actions, acknowledging the help of others, or offering to answer questions. The margins for the transmittal should be the same as for the report, about 1 to 1.25 inches for side margins. The dateline is placed 2 inches from the top, and the margins should be left-justified. A page number is optional.

Figure 10.25 (Continued) Table of Contents and List of Figures

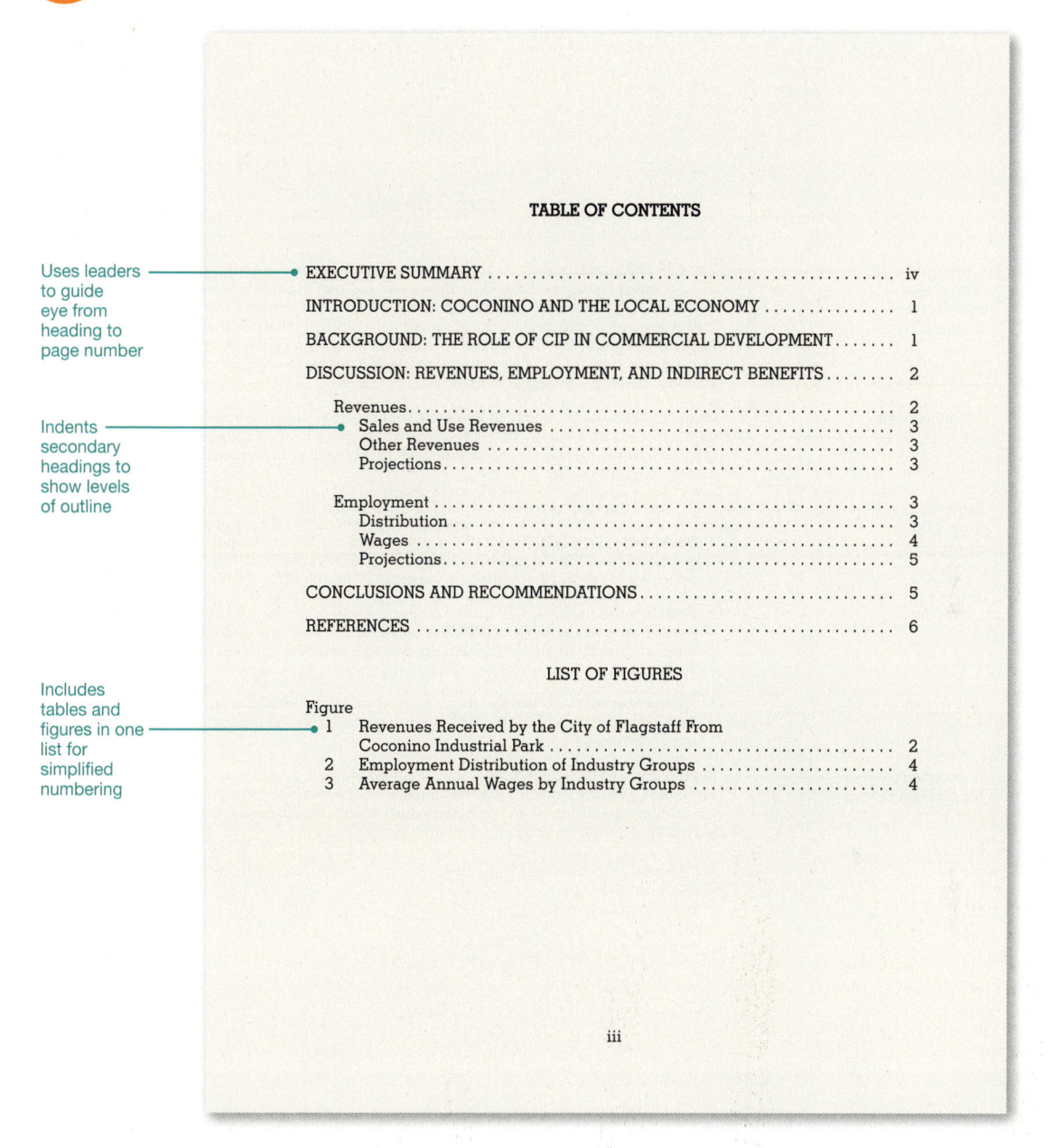

**TABLE OF CONTENTS**

Uses leaders to guide eye from heading to page number

| | |
|---|---|
| EXECUTIVE SUMMARY | iv |
| INTRODUCTION: COCONINO AND THE LOCAL ECONOMY | 1 |
| BACKGROUND: THE ROLE OF CIP IN COMMERCIAL DEVELOPMENT | 1 |
| DISCUSSION: REVENUES, EMPLOYMENT, AND INDIRECT BENEFITS | 2 |
|     Revenues | 2 |
|         Sales and Use Revenues | 3 |
|         Other Revenues | 3 |
|         Projections | 3 |
|     Employment | 3 |
|         Distribution | 3 |
|         Wages | 4 |
|         Projections | 5 |
| CONCLUSIONS AND RECOMMENDATIONS | 5 |
| REFERENCES | 6 |

Indents secondary headings to show levels of outline

**LIST OF FIGURES**

Includes tables and figures in one list for simplified numbering

| Figure | | |
|---|---|---|
| 1 | Revenues Received by the City of Flagstaff From Coconino Industrial Park | 2 |
| 2 | Employment Distribution of Industry Groups | 4 |
| 3 | Average Annual Wages by Industry Groups | 4 |

iii

Because the table of contents and the list of figures for this report are small, they are combined on one page. Notice that the titles of major report parts are in all caps, while other headings are a combination of upper- and lowercase letters. This duplicates the style within the report. Advanced word processing capabilities enable you to generate a contents page automatically, including leaders and accurate page numbering—no matter how many times you revise. Notice that the page numbers are right-justified.

Figure 10.25 (Continued) Executive Summary

## EXECUTIVE SUMMARY

*Opens directly with major research findings*

The city of Flagstaff can benefit from the development of industrial parks like the Coconino Industrial Park. Both direct and indirect economic benefits result, as shown by this in-depth study conducted by Sedona Development Company. The study was authorized by the Flagstaff City Council when Goldman-Lyon & Associates sought the City Council's approval for the proposed construction of a G-L industrial park. The City Council requested evidence demonstrating that an existing development could actually benefit the city.

*Identifies data sources*

Our conclusion that the city of Flagstaff benefits from industrial parks is based on data supplied by a survey of 5,000 Coconino Industrial Park employees, personal interviews with managers and tenants of CIP, city and state documents, and professional literature.

*Summarizes organization of report*

Analysis of the data revealed benefits in three areas:

- **Revenues.** The city of Flagstaff earned over $3 million in tax and other revenues from the Coconino Industrial Park in 2014. By 2020 this income is expected to reach $5.4 million (in constant 2014 dollars).

- **Employment.** In 2014, CIP businesses employed a total of 7,035 workers, who earned an average wage of $56,579. By 2020, CIP businesses are expected to employ directly nearly 15,000 employees who will earn salaries totaling over $998 million.

- **Indirect benefits.** Because of the multiplier effect, by 2020 Coconino Industrial Park will directly and indirectly generate a total of 38,362 jobs in the Flagstaff metropolitan area.

*Condenses recommendations*

On the basis of these findings, it is recommended that development of additional industrial parks be encouraged to stimulate local economic growth. The city would increase its tax revenues significantly, create much-needed jobs, and thus help stimulate the local economy in and around Flagstaff.

iv

For readers who want a quick overview of the report, the executive summary presents its most important elements. Executive summaries focus on the information the reader requires for making a decision related to the issues discussed in the report. The summary may include some or all of the following elements: purpose, scope, research methods, findings, conclusions, and recommendations. Its length depends on the report it summarizes. A 100-page report might require a 10-page summary. Shorter reports may contain 1-page summaries, as shown here. Unlike letters of transmittal (which may contain personal pronouns and references to the writer), the executive summary of a long report is formal and impersonal. It uses the same margins as the body of the report. See Chapter 9 for additional discussion of executive summaries.

Figure 10.25 (Continued) Page 1

**INTRODUCTION: COCONINO AND THE LOCAL ECONOMY**

This study was designed to analyze the direct and indirect economic impact of Coconino Industrial Park on the city of Flagstaff. Specifically, the study seeks answers to these questions:

- What current tax and other revenues result directly from this park? What tax and other revenues may be expected in the future?
- How many and what kinds of jobs are directly attributable to the park? What is the employment picture for the future?
- What indirect effects has Coconino Industrial Park had on local employment, incomes, and economic growth?

**BACKGROUND: THE ROLE OF CIP IN COMMERCIAL DEVELOPMENT**

The development firm of Goldman-Lyon & Associates commissioned this study of Coconino Industrial Park at the request of the Flagstaff City Council. Before authorizing the development of a proposed Goldman-Lyon industrial park, the city council requested a study examining the economic effects of an existing park. Members of the city council wanted to determine to what extent industrial parks benefit the local community, and they chose Coconino Industrial Park as an example.

For those who are unfamiliar with it, Coconino Industrial Park is a 400-acre industrial park located in the city of Flagstaff about 4 miles from the center of the city. Most of the land lies within a specially designated area known as Redevelopment Project No. 2, which is under the jurisdiction of the Flagstaff Redevelopment Agency. Planning for the park began in 1999; construction started in 2001.

The original goal for Coconino Industrial Park was development for light industrial users. Land in this area was zoned for uses such as warehousing, research and development, and distribution. Like other communities, Flagstaff was eager to attract light industrial users because such businesses tend to employ a highly educated workforce, are relatively quiet, and do not pollute the environment (Cohen C1). The city of Flagstaff recognized the need for light industrial users and widened an adjacent highway to accommodate trucks and facilitate travel by workers and customers coming from Flagstaff.

1

*Annotations:*
- Uses a bulleted list for clarity and ease of reading
- Lists three problem questions
- Describes authorization for report and background of study
- Includes APA citation with author name and date

The first page of a formal report generally contains the title printed 2 inches from the top edge. Headings for major parts of a report are centered in all caps. In this model document we show functional heads, such as *PROBLEM, BACKGROUND, FINDINGS,* and *CONCLUSIONS*. However, most business reports would use talking heads or a combination such as *FINDINGS REVEAL REVENUE AND EMPLOYMENT BENEFITS*. First-level headings (such as *Revenues* on page 2) are printed with bold upper- and lowercase letters. Second-level headings (such as *Distribution* on page 3) begin at the side, are bolded, and are written in upper- and lowercase letters. See Figure 9.6 for an illustration of heading formats. This business report is shown with single-spacing, although some research reports might be double-spaced. Always check with your organization to learn its preferred style.

**Figure 10.25 (Continued) Page 2**

The park now contains 14 building complexes with over 1.25 million square feet of completed building space. The majority of the buildings are used for office, research and development, marketing and distribution, or manufacturing uses. Approximately 50 acres of the original area are yet to be developed.

*Provides specifics for data sources* → Data for this report came from a 2014 survey of over 5,000 Coconino Industrial Park employees; interviews with 15 CIP tenants and managers; the annual budget of the city of Flagstaff; county and state tax records; and current books, articles, journals, and online resources. Projections for future revenues resulted from analysis of past trends and "Estimates of Revenues for Debt Service Coverage, Redevelopment Project Area 2" (Miller 79).

*Uses combination heads* → **DISCUSSION: REVENUES, EMPLOYMENT, AND INDIRECT BENEFITS**

*Previews organization of report* → The results of this research indicate that major direct and indirect benefits have accrued to the city of Flagstaff and surrounding metropolitan areas as a result of the development of Coconino Industrial Park. The research findings presented here fall into three categories: (a) revenues, (b) employment, and (c) indirect benefits.

**Revenues**

Coconino Industrial Park contributes a variety of tax and other revenues to the city of Flagstaff, as summarized in Figure 1. Current revenues are shown, along with projections to the year 2020. At a time when the economy is unstable, revenues from an industrial park such as Coconino can become a reliable income stream for the city of Flagstaff.

*Places figure close to textual reference* → Figure 1

**REVENUES RECEIVED BY THE CITY OF FLAGSTAFF FROM COCONINO INDUSTRIAL PARK**

Current Revenues and Projections to 2020

|  | 2014 | 2020 |
|---|---|---|
| Sales and use taxes | $1,966,021 | $3,604,500 |
| Revenues from licenses | 532,802 | 962,410 |
| Franchise taxes | 195,682 | 220,424 |
| State gas tax receipts | 159,420 | 211,134 |
| Licenses and permits | 86,213 | 201,413 |
| Other revenues | 75,180 | 206,020 |
| Total | $3,015,318 | $5,405,901 |

Source: Arizona State Board of Equalization Bulletin. Phoenix: State Printing Office, 2014, p. 28.

2

Notice that this formal report is single-spaced. Many businesses prefer this space-saving format. However, some organizations prefer double-spacing, especially for preliminary drafts. If you single-space, don't indent paragraphs. If you double-space, do indent the paragraphs. Page numbers may be centered 1 inch from the bottom of the page or placed 1 inch from the upper right corner at the margin. Your word processor can insert page numbers automatically. Strive to leave a minimum of 1 inch for top, bottom, and side margins. References follow the parenthetical citation style (or in-text citation style) of the Modern Language Association (MLA). Notice that the author's name and a page reference are shown in parentheses. The complete bibliographic entry for any in-text citation appears at the end of the report in the works-cited section.

### Sales and Use Revenues

As shown in Figure 1, the city's largest source of revenues from CIP is the sales and use tax. Revenues from this source totaled $1,966,021 in 2014, according to figures provided by the Arizona State Board of Equalization (28). Sales and use taxes accounted for more than half of the park's total contribution to the total income of $3,015,318.

### Other Revenues

Other major sources of city revenues from CIP in 2014 include alcohol licenses, motor vehicle in lieu fees, trailer coach licenses ($532,802), franchise taxes ($195,682), and state gas tax receipts ($159,420). Although not shown in Figure 1, other revenues may be expected from the development of recently acquired property. The U.S. Economic Development Administration has approved a grant worth $975,000 to assist in expanding the current park eastward on an undeveloped parcel purchased last year. Revenues from leasing this property may be sizable.

### Projections

Total city revenues from CIP will nearly double by 2020, producing an income of $5.4 million. This estimate is based on an annual growth rate of 0.65 percent, as projected by the Bureau of Labor Statistics.

## Employment

One of the most important factors to consider in the overall effect of an industrial park is employment. In Coconino Industrial Park the distribution, number, and wages of people employed will change considerably in the next six years.

### Distribution

A total of 7,035 employees currently work in various industry groups at Coconino Industrial Park. The distribution of employees is shown in Figure 2. The largest number of workers (58 percent) is employed in manufacturing and assembly operations. The next largest category, computer and electronics, employs 24 percent of the workers. Some overlap probably exists because electronics assembly could be included in either group. Employees also work in publishing (9 percent), warehousing and storage (5 percent), and other industries (4 percent).

Although the distribution of employees at Coconino Industrial Park shows a wide range of employment categories, it must be noted that other industrial parks would likely generate an entirely different range of job categories.

3

**Figure 10.25** (Continued) Page 4

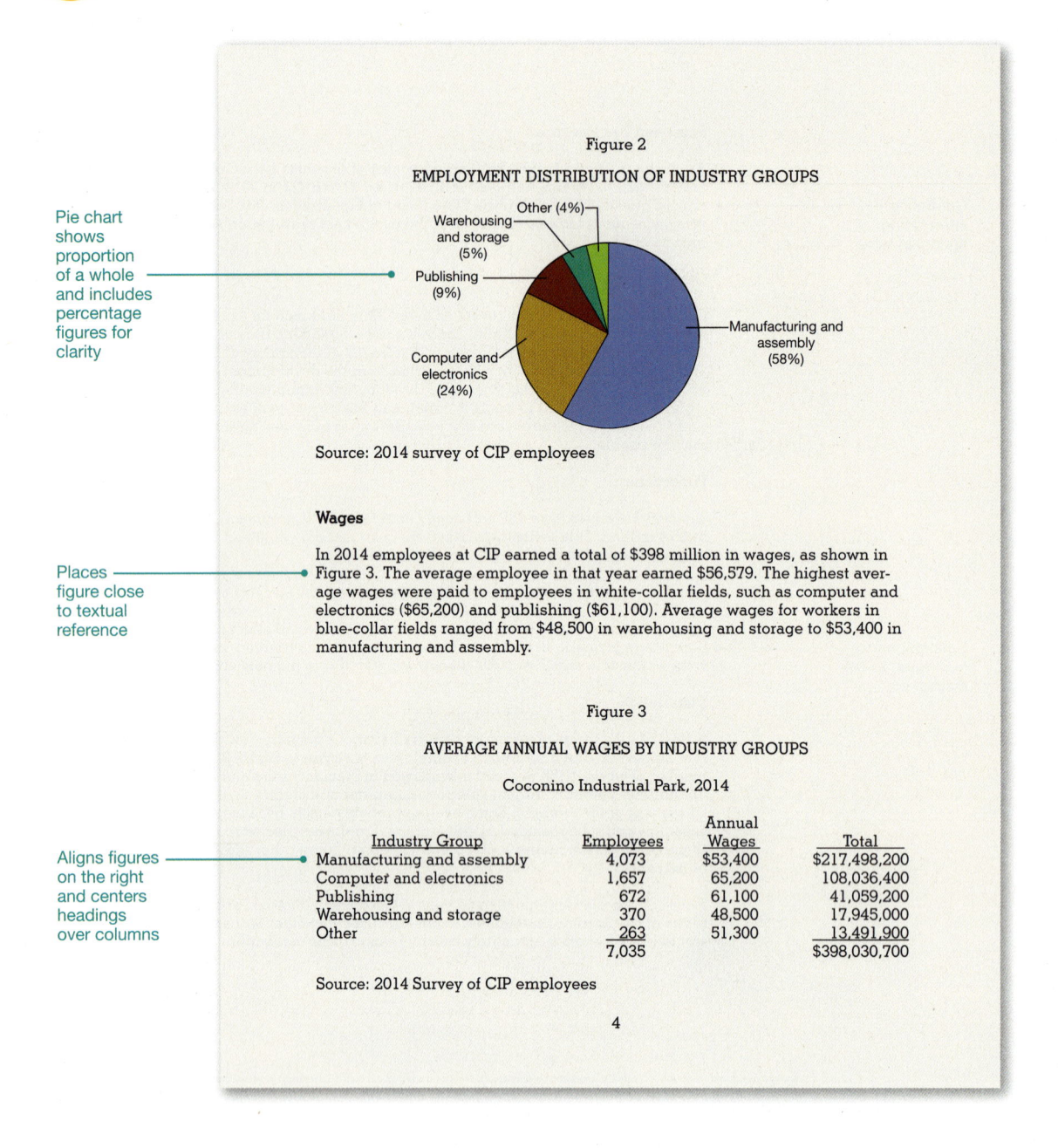

*Pie chart shows proportion of a whole and includes percentage figures for clarity*

Figure 2
EMPLOYMENT DISTRIBUTION OF INDUSTRY GROUPS

- Manufacturing and assembly (58%)
- Computer and electronics (24%)
- Publishing (9%)
- Warehousing and storage (5%)
- Other (4%)

Source: 2014 survey of CIP employees

**Wages**

*Places figure close to textual reference*

In 2014 employees at CIP earned a total of $398 million in wages, as shown in Figure 3. The average employee in that year earned $56,579. The highest average wages were paid to employees in white-collar fields, such as computer and electronics ($65,200) and publishing ($61,100). Average wages for workers in blue-collar fields ranged from $48,500 in warehousing and storage to $53,400 in manufacturing and assembly.

Figure 3

AVERAGE ANNUAL WAGES BY INDUSTRY GROUPS

Coconino Industrial Park, 2014

*Aligns figures on the right and centers headings over columns*

| Industry Group | Employees | Annual Wages | Total |
|---|---|---|---|
| Manufacturing and assembly | 4,073 | $53,400 | $217,498,200 |
| Computer and electronics | 1,657 | 65,200 | 108,036,400 |
| Publishing | 672 | 61,100 | 41,059,200 |
| Warehousing and storage | 370 | 48,500 | 17,945,000 |
| Other | 263 | 51,300 | 13,491,900 |
| | 7,035 | | $398,030,700 |

Source: 2014 Survey of CIP employees

4

If you use figures or tables, be sure to introduce them in the text (for example, *as shown in Figure 3*). Although it isn't always possible, try to place them close to the spot where they are first mentioned. To save space, you can print the title of a figure at its side. Because this report contains few tables and figures, the writer named them all "Figures" and numbered them consecutively.

Figure 10.25 (Continued) Page 5

### Projections

By 2020 Coconino Industrial Park is expected to more than double its number of employees, bringing the total to over 15,000 workers. The total payroll in 2020 will also more than double, producing over $998 million (using constant 2014 dollars) in salaries to CIP employees. These projections are based on a 9 percent growth rate (Miller 78), along with anticipated increased employment as the park reaches its capacity.

Future development in the park will influence employment and payrolls. One CIP project manager stated in an interview that much of the remaining 50 acres is planned for medium-rise office buildings, garden offices, and other structures for commercial, professional, and personal services (Novak interview). Average wages for employees are expected to increase because of an anticipated shift to higher-paying white-collar jobs. Industrial parks often follow a similar pattern of evolution (Badri, Rivera, and Kusak 41). Like many industrial parks, CIP evolved from a warehousing center into a manufacturing complex.

*Clarifies information and tells what it means in relation to original research questions*

### CONCLUSIONS AND RECOMMENDATIONS

Analysis of tax revenues, employment data, personal interviews, and professional literature leads to the following conclusions and recommendations about the economic impact of Coconino Industrial Park on the city of Flagstaff:

1. Sales tax and other revenues produced over $3 million in income to the city of Flagstaff in 2014. By 2020 sales tax and other revenues are expected to produce $5.4 million in city income.
2. CIP currently employs 7,035 employees, the majority of whom are working in manufacturing and assembly. The average employee in 2014 earned $56,579.
3. By 2020 CIP is expected to employ more than 15,000 workers producing a total payroll of over $998 million.
4. Employment trends indicate that by 2020 more CIP employees will be engaged in higher-paying white-collar positions.

On the basis of these findings, we recommend that the City Council of Flagstaff authorize the development of additional industrial parks to stimulate local economic growth. The direct and indirect benefits of Coconino Industrial Park strongly suggest that future commercial development would have a positive impact on the Flagstaff community and the surrounding region as population growth and resulting greater purchasing power would trigger higher demand.

As the Coconino example shows, gains in tax revenue, job creation, and other direct and indirect benefits would follow the creation of additional industrial parks in and around Flagstaff.

*Combines conclusions and recommendations*

*Uses a numbered list for clarity and ease of reading*

After discussing and interpreting the research findings, the writer articulates what she considers the most important conclusions and recommendations. Longer, more complex reports may have separate sections for conclusions and resulting recommendations. In this report they are combined. Notice that it is unnecessary to start a new page for the conclusions.

Figure 10.25 MLA Works Cited

**Works Cited**

*Arranges references in alphabetical order*

*Brochure* — Arizona State Board of Equalization. *Bulletin*. Phoenix State Printing Office, 2014, 26-29. Print.

*Journal with doi* — Badri, Joseph, H. Jose Rivera, and Michael E. Kusak. "A Comparison of Sustainability and Economic Development in Urban Industrial Parks." *Journal of Industrial Ecology*, 24.4 (2011): 233-268. Print. doi 10.1078/0366-6133.25.335

*Newspaper article* — Cohen, Andrew P. "Industrial Parks Invade Suburbia." *The New York Times* 14 Dec. 2014: C1. Print.

*Website without author or date* — Fighting Poverty and Protecting the Environment: Development of a Sustainable Technologies Industrial Park, (n.d.). Web. 7 June 2015.

*Book* — Miller, Aaron M. *Redevelopment Projects: Future Prospects*. New York: Rincon Press. Print.

*Online article* — Pearson, Sophie. "Travel to Work Characteristics for the 50 Largest Metropolitan Areas by Population in the United States." *The Wall Street Journal* 30 June 2013. Web. 3 July 2013.

*Government publication* — U.S. Department of Labor, Bureau of Labor Statistics. *Overview of the 2010-2020 Projections*. 2014: n pag. Web. 5 June 2015.

On this page the writer lists all references cited in the text as well as others that she examined during her research. The writer lists these citations following the MLA referencing style. Notice that all entries are arranged alphabetically. The *MLA Handbook for Writers of Research Papers,* Seventh Edition, 2009, requires italics for titles of books, magazines, newspapers, journals, and Web sites. For electronic sources, the following sequence is suggested: author or editor names; article name in quotation marks; title of website, project, or book in italics; any version numbers available; publisher information, including the publisher name and publishing date; page numbers, if available; medium of publication (such as *Web, Print,* or PDF); access date; and URL if necessary for retrieval or required by your instructor.

This works-cited page is shown with single-spacing, which is preferable for business reports. However, MLA style recommends double-spacing for research reports, including the works-cited page.

### Figure 10.25 Alternate References Shown in APA Style

**References**

*Arranges references in alphabetical order*

*Brochure* — Arizona State Board of Equalization Bulletin. (2014). Phoenix: State Printing Office, 26-29.

*Journal with doi* — Badri, J., Rivera, H., & Kusak, M. (2011) A comparison of sustainability and economic development in urban industrial parks. *Journal of Industrial Ecology, 24*(4), 233-268. doi: 10.1078/0366-6133.25.335

*Newspaper article* — Cohen, A. P. (2014, December 14). Industrial parks invade suburbia. *The New York Times*, p. C1.

*Website without author or date* — Fighting poverty and protecting the environment: Development of a sustainable technologies industrial park. Retrieved from http://www.smart-communities.ncat.org/success/northam.shtml

*Book* — Miller, A. M. (2013). *Redevelopment projects: Future prospects.* New York: Rincon Press.

*Online article* — Pearson, S. (2013, June 30). Travel to work characteristics for the 50 largest metropolitan areas by population in the United States. Retrieved from http://www.wsj.com/article 130630

*Government publication* — U.S. Department of Labor, Bureau of Labor Statistics. (2014). *Overview of the 2010-2020 Projections.* Retrieved from http://www.bls.gov/ooh/About/Projections-Overview.htm

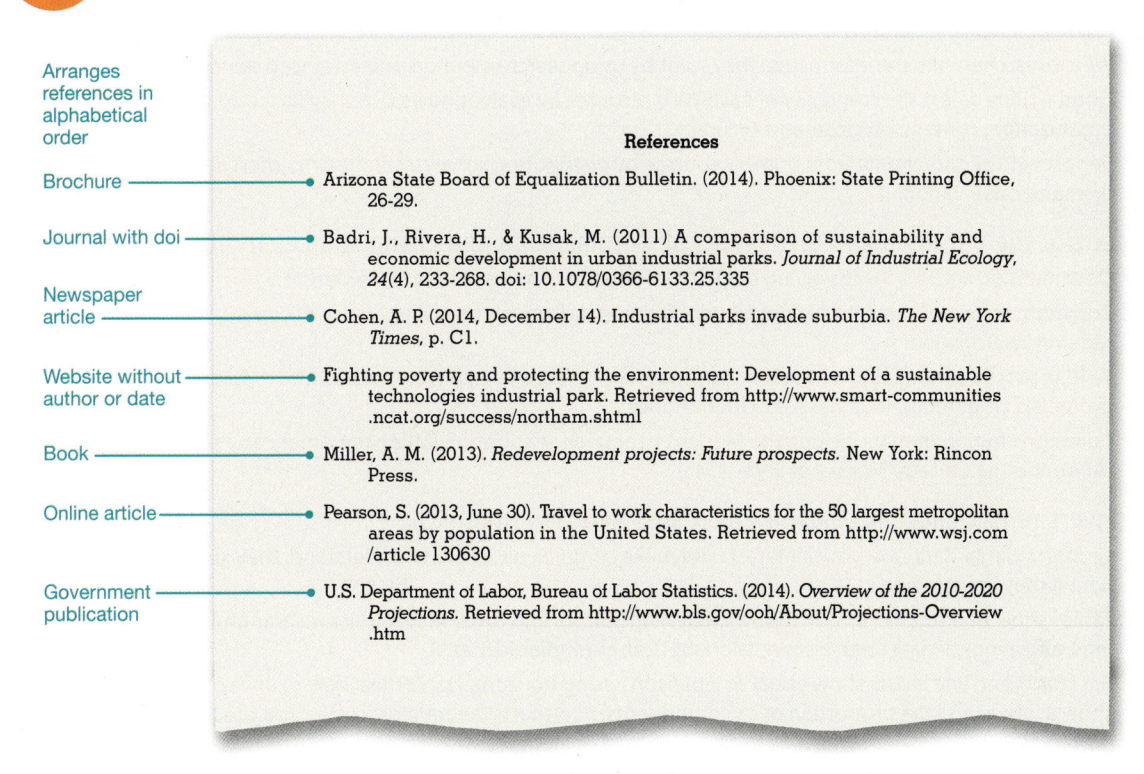

If this formal report had used APA referencing style, the references would appear as shown here. The writer lists all references cited in the text as well as the writer lists all references cited in the text as well as others that she examined during her research. The writer lists these citations following the APA referencing style. Notice that all entries are arranged alphabetically. Book and periodical titles are italicized, but they could be underlined. When referring to online items, she shows the full name of the citation and then identifies the URL as well as the date on which she accessed the electronic reference. This references page is shown with single-spacing, which is preferable for business reports. However, APA style recommends double-spacing for research reports, including the references page.

# SUMMARY OF LEARNING OBJECTIVES

**10-1 Understand the importance, purpose, and components of informal and formal proposals.**
- Proposals are written offers that solve problems, provide services, or sell products.
- Proposals may be solicited (requested by an organization) or unsolicited (written to offer a service, request funding, or solve a problem).
- Components of informal proposals often include an introduction; a background and purpose statement; a proposal, plan, and schedule; staffing requirements; a budget showing project costs; and a conclusion.
- Formal proposals often include additional components, such as a letter of transmittal, a title page, a table of contents, and an appendix.

**10-2 Describe the steps in writing and editing formal business reports.**
- Writers begin formal reports with a statement of purpose that defines the focus of the report.
- Report writers focus on their readers' needs and wants in order to present relevant findings.
- Researchers gather information from primary sources (firsthand observation, interviews, and surveys) and secondary sources (books, articles, journals, and the Web).
- Writers proofread and edit formal reports by reviewing the format, spacing and font consistency, graphics placement, heading levels, data accuracy, and mechanics.

Chapter 10: Proposals and Formal Reports

**10-3** Conduct research using primary and secondary sources, and understand how to assess the credibility of resources.
- Writers gather most of their research from secondary sources by reading what others have published in books, scholarly journals, magazines, and Web documents.
- Web researchers find the information they want by using search operators and advanced search features to filter the results.
- Good writers assess the credibility of each Web resource by evaluating its currency (last update), author or sponsoring organization, content, purpose, and accuracy.
- Report writers gather data from primary sources by distributing surveys, conducting interviews, and collecting data from firsthand observation.

**10-4** Identify the purposes and techniques of documenting and citing sources in business reports.
- Documenting sources means giving credit to information sources to avoid plagiarism.
- Copyright refers to "the right to copy"; under fair use, individuals have limited use of copyrighted material without requiring permission.
- Writers should assume that all intellectual property (words, charts, photos, music, and media) is copyrighted and protected whether or not it has a copyright notice.
- Common citation formats include the Modern Language Association (MLA), the American Psychological Association (APA), and the Chicago Manual of Style (CMS).

**10-5** Convert report data into meaningful visual aids and graphics.
- Graphics clarify data, add visual interest, and make complex data easy to understand; they should be placed close to where they are referenced.
- Tables show quantitative information in systematic tables and rows; they require meaningful titles, bold column headings, and a logical data arrangement (alphabetical, chronological, etc.)
- Bar charts and line charts show visual comparisons using horizontal or vertical bars or lines of varying lengths; pie charts show a whole and the proportion of its components; flowcharts diagram processes and procedures.
- Infographics, popular in online environments, combine images and graphic elements to illustrate information in an easy-to-understand format.

**10-6** Describe the components of typical formal reports.
- Front matter components of formal reports often include the following: title page, letter or memo of transmittal, table of contents, list of figures, and executive summary.
- Body components of formal reports include the introduction, the body, and the conclusions and recommendations.
- The body is the principal section of a formal report and discusses, analyzes, interprets, and evaluates the research findings before drawing conclusions.
- Back matter components of a formal report include a bibliography, which may be a works-cited or reference page, and any appendixes.

# CHAPTER REVIEW

1. For what reasons do writers prepare proposals? (Obj. 1)

2. For what reasons would government agencies and other firms use requests for proposals (RFPs)? Name an example of a project that might require an RFP. (Obj. 1)

3. What is the purpose of providing a "hook" in the introduction of a proposal? Give three examples. (Obj. 1)

4. What sources are considered secondary sources, and where can they be found? (Obj. 3)

5. What is the difference between an open-ended and close-ended survey question? Give an example of each. (Obj. 3)

6. Why should report writers document their sources? (Obj. 4)

7. Define the term *fair use*. When might using copyrighted material be considered fair use? (Obj. 4)

8. Why do report writers include visuals and graphics in reports? (Obj. 5)

9. What should the introduction to a formal business report include? (Obj. 6)

10. What information might be included in an appendix at the end of a formal report? (Obj. 6)

# CRITICAL THINKING

11. In what ways is a proposal similar to a persuasive sales message? (Obj. 1)

12. Some people say that business reports should not contain footnotes. If you were writing your first business report and did considerable research, what would you do about documenting your sources? (Objs. 3, 4, and 6)

13. Why do researchers often trust the reliability of information obtained from scholarly journals, major newspapers, and well-known magazines? Why should researchers use caution when accessing information from Wikipedia, online forums, and blogs? (Obj. 3)

14. Starbucks chief Howard Schultz frowns on research, advertising, and customer surveys. He conducts his own informal primary research by visiting 25 store locations a week and talking with his baristas, managers, and customers in person. This kind of observation, he insists, provides the information he needs most.[12] What are the pros and cons of such informal research to gather primary data? (Obj. 3)

15. Information graphics, also called *infographics*, are wildly popular, especially in online environments. Why do you think infographics continue to receive so much attention? How could infographics be useful in your field? (Obj. 5)

Chapter 10: Proposals and Formal Reports

# ACTIVITIES AND CASES

## 10.1 Proposal: Expanding the Use of Social Media (Objs. 1, 2)
**E-mail | Social Media | Web**

Businesses both large and small are flocking to social media platforms to engage consumers in conversations and also to drive sales through deals and coupons. Small businesses have found that social media and the Internet help them to level the playing field. They can foster closer relationships with clients and identify potential customers. Flirty Cupcakes owner Tiffany Kurtz says that Facebook and Twitter greatly helped her with product innovation, market expansion, and customer service.[13] Many other entrepreneurs are using social media to launch and expand their businesses. As an employee in a small business, you see opportunities to expand the use of social media. You want to first see how other companies are using social networks and then recommend the platforms you believe would be most useful to your business.

**YOUR TASK.** Search for small businesses that have used social media to expand their market share and promote their products and services. Select three businesses to study, and analyze their use of social media. What do they have in common? In what social media platforms are they engaged? What results have they seen? In an e-mail or memo to your instructor, describe briefly the three companies you selected. Explain how each company is using social media to promote and grow its business. Then write the introduction to a proposal that promotes expanding your company's use of social media. Include a brief description of the reasons for the proposal, specify the key benefits of using social networks, and state how the three companies you studied are using social media. Then recommend which social media platforms you believe would benefit your business.

## 10.2 Proposal: Workplace Problems Requiring Minor Expenditures (Obj. 1)

The ability to spot problems before they turn into serious risks is prized by most managers. Think about your current or past internship and work experiences. Do you see problems that could be solved with a small to moderate financial investment? Consider issues such as creating space for badly needed lunch and break rooms; offering stress-reducing health initiatives such as wellness programs and gym club memberships; replacing high-emission, gas-guzzling company vehicles; or increasing recycling efforts.

**YOUR TASK.** Discuss with your instructor the workplace problem that you have identified. Make sure you choose a relatively weighty problem that can be lessened or eliminated with a minor expenditure. Be sure to include a cost–benefit analysis. Address your unsolicited letter or memo proposal to your current or former boss and copy your instructor.

## 10.3 Proposal: Starting Your Own Business (Objs. 1, 3)
**Web**

Perhaps you have dreamed about one day owning your own company, or maybe you have already started a business. Proposals are offers to a very specific audience with whom you hope to do business. Think of a product or service that you like or know something about. On the Web or in electronic databases, research the market so that you understand going rates, prices, and costs. Search the Small Business Administration's website for valuable tips on how to launch and manage a business.

**YOUR TASK.** Choose a product or service you would like to offer to a particular audience, such as an upholstery business, a bakery featuring your favorite pastries or cakes, a photography business, a new Asian or European hair care line, massage therapy, or landscaping services. Discuss products and services as well as target audiences with your instructor. Write an informal letter addressed to a potential investor, Mr. Simon Lipton, 7430 Fondren Road, Houston, TX 77074. Keep the letter short and don't mention financing, as your goal is to first generate interest.

## 10.4 Proposal Writing Resources: Offering Assistance in Writing a Proposal (Objs. 1, 3)
**Web**

Many new companies with services or products to sell would like help writing unsolicited or solicited proposals. Your friend Teresa has started her own designer uniform company and has asked you for help. Her goal is to offer her colorful yet functional uniforms to hospitals and clinics. Before writing a proposal, however, she wants to learn more about the proposal-writing process.

**YOUR TASK.** Search the Web and find two sites that offer proposal writing advice. Avoid sites that want you to register or buy templates and books. Prepare a memo to Teresa in which you do the following:
a. Suggest two excellent sites where Teresa can learn the how-tos of creating an effective proposal.
b. Suggest headings for each section of Teresa's unsolicited proposal to promote her hospital/clinic uniforms.
c. Suggest two sites where Teresa can find free proposal templates.
d. Write a suggested introduction for Teresa's proposal.

## 10.5 Proposal: Informal Letter Proposing a Business Writing Workshop (Obj. 1)

**Team**

Business employees understand more than ever the importance of improving their writing skills. Whether e-mailing status updates to team members, writing a Web article, preparing meeting agendas, or corresponding with potential customers, employees must write concise, coherent, clear, error-free documents and messages. As the founder of Business Writing Solutions, you offer one- and two-day business writing workshops for businesses and organizations. Your website features writing tips, workshop descriptions, and your contact information. These workshops are presented on-site in corporate training rooms.

You received an e-mail inquiry from Human Resources Director Janet Somerfield, who is considering a one-day, on-site business writing workshop for employees in her midsized advertising agency. Janet is looking at several seminar companies who offer writing training. She asks about pricing, optimal class size, and course content. She also wants to know whether you can offer feedback on writing samples. Because Janet is considering other training options, you decide to respond with an informal proposal. Your goal is to meet her needs and win the contract.

Review the components of an informal proposal and include the appropriate components, which may include the following: an introduction, a statement of your goals and purpose, the proposed seminar details (time requirements, optimal class size, costs, location, schedule), and a conclusion. Organize the proposal, write meaningful headings, and choose a readable font. Decide where it is appropriate to mention the following advantages of improving writing skills in business environments:

- Excellent writing skills help build trusting relationships, improve one's professional image, and add to the credibility of an organization.
- Business associates appreciate clarity, conciseness, and results-focused messages.
- Better writing skills help employees advance their careers, which in turn improves retention.

The one-day workshop is offered in two 4-hour blocks in the client's training room. The course includes the following topics: (a) writing results-oriented e-mail messages; (b) structuring routine, persuasive, and negative news messages; (c) reviewing the most common grammar errors; and (d) designing documents for readability. You will also offer feedback on brief writing samples furnished by the participants. Employees who attend the workshop will earn a certificate of completion.

The cost of the writing workshop is $175 per person. If 15 employees participate, the cost would be $2,625. The cost includes workbooks and writing supplies for each participant.

**YOUR TASK.** Write an informal letter proposal promoting a one-day business writing workshop to Janet Somerfield, Director, Human Resources, Faulkner Advertising, 420 Fowler Avenue, Tampa, FL 33620.

## 10.6 Researching and Analyzing Findings: Service Learning Projects (Obj. 3)

**E-mail  Web**

Your school may be one that encourages service learning, a form of experiential learning. You could receive credit for a project that bridges academic and nonacademic communities. Because writing skills are in wide demand, you may have an opportunity to simultaneously apply your skills, contribute to the community, and expand your résumé. The National Service-Learning Clearinghouse describes service learning as "a teaching and learning strategy that integrates meaningful community service with instruction and reflection to enrich the learning experience, teach civic responsibility, and strengthen communities."[14] The Web offers many sites devoted to examples of students engaging in service learning projects.

**YOUR TASK.** Research possible service learning projects in this class or another. Your instructor may ask you to submit a memo or e-mail message analyzing your findings. Describe at least four completed service learning projects that you found on the Web. Draw conclusions about what made them successful or beneficial. What kinds of similar projects might be possible for you or for others in your class? Your instructor may use this as a research project or turn it into a hands-on project by having you find a service organization in your community in need of trained writers.

## 10.7 Executive Summary: Reviewing Articles and Summarizing Findings (Objs. 3, 5)

**Web**

Many managers and executives are too rushed to read long journal articles, but they are eager to stay current in their fields. Assume your boss has asked you to help him stay abreast of research in the field by submitting one executive summary every month on an article of interest.

**YOUR TASK.** In your field of study, select a professional journal, such as the *Journal of Management*. Using ProQuest, Factiva, EBSCO, or some other database, look for articles in your target journal. Select an article that is at least five pages long and is interesting to you. Write an executive summary in a memo format. Include an introduction that might begin with *The following executive summary of the* article titled "(title of article)" is from (source and date of publication). Then preview the main idea and summarize the most important findings of the study or article. Use descriptive, or "talking," headings rather than functional headings. Also summarize any recommendations made. Your boss would also like a concluding statement indicating your reaction to the journal article. Address your memo summary to Marcus E. Solomon.

## 10.8 Unsolicited Proposal: Requesting Funding for Your Campus Business Club (Obj. 1)

Professional associations often have student-organized chapters on college campuses. Let's say you are a member of a campus business club, such as the Society for the Advancement of Management (SAM), the American Marketing Association (AMA), the American Management Association (AMA), the Accounting Society (AS), the International Association of Administrative Professionals (IAAP), or the Association of Information Technology Professionals (AITP). Your club or association has managed its finances well, and therefore, it is able to fund monthly activities. However, membership dues are insufficient to cover any extras. You see the need for a special one-time seminar with a panel of experts or a keynote speaker that would benefit many business students. For example, you see value in inviting a panel of recruiters to come and discuss current job requirements and hiring processes. You must now request funding for this event.

**YOUR TASK.** Write an unsolicited letter or memo proposal to your program chair or business division dean to request one-time funding to cover the costs associated with this event. Identify your need or problem, provide the details of the event, mention the ways this event will benefit the attendees, support your claims with evidence, and provide a budget. Think ahead about costs associated with printing, appreciation gifts for the presenters, food and beverage needs, and other miscellaneous expenses.

## 10.9 Primary Research: Designing an Online Customer Service Survey (Obj. 3)
`Web`

Companies use surveys to continually improve their products and services. As a sales manager in a store selling wireless devices and electronics, you are interested in your customers' opinions about your sales associates and product quality, and in learning about their loyalty to your products. You plan to conduct a survey and use the results in an upcoming training workshop for your sales associates. You have obtained the e-mail addresses of customers who have opted in for product updates and reviews. You plan to design your own survey and want to get ideas by looking at examples of surveys and templates.

**YOUR TASK.** Search for free customer service survey templates, study the questions, and add the URL of the surveys you reviewed. Then design a customer service survey with a mix of seven or eight typical multiple-choice, scale, or open-ended questions.

## 10.10 Citations: Citing Secondary Resources Using MLA Format (Obj. 4)
`E-mail`

You will want to stay up-to-date on your career field by reading, saving current articles, and bookmarking valuable resources. Think about a current business topic related to your professional field that you would like to learn more about. This is your chance to learn more about, gather tips and strategies about, and follow current trends in your field of interest.

**YOUR TASK.** Look for three current (within the last two years) secondary research sources on a topic related to your field of study. In a memo or e-mail to your instructor, write a one-paragraph summary of each article or resource. Then list the citations for your three resources, using MLA standards. The citations should follow the format used on a works-cited page with citations in alphabetical order and using the hanging indent style.

## 10.11 Formal Business Report: Gathering Primary and Secondary Intercultural Data (Obj. 3)
`Intercultural` `Team` `Web`

U.S. businesses are expanding into foreign markets with manufacturing plants and branch offices. Many Americans, however, have little knowledge of or experience with people from other cultures. To prepare for participation in the global marketplace, you are to collect information for a report focused on an Asian, Latin American, European, or African country where English is not regularly spoken. Before selecting the country, though, consult your campus international student program for volunteers from other countries who are willing to be interviewed. Your instructor may make advance arrangements with international student volunteers.

**YOUR TASK.** In teams of three to five, collect information about your target country from electronic databases, the Web, and other sources. Then invite an international student from your target country to be interviewed by your group. As you conduct primary and secondary research, investigate the topics listed in Figure 10.26. Confirm what you learn in your secondary research by talking with your interviewee. When you complete your research, write a report for the CEO of your company (make up a name and company). Assume that your company plans to expand its operations abroad. Your report should advise the company's executives of the social customs, family life, societal attitudes, religious preferences and beliefs, education, and values of the target country. Remember that your company's interests are business oriented; do not dwell on tourist information. Compile your results and write the report.

Figure 10.26 Intercultural Interview Topics and Questions

**Social Customs**
- How do people react to strangers? Are they friendly? Reserved? Cautious? Suspicious?
- What is the typical greeting for friends? Family members and close friends? Business associates? Elderly people or relatives?
- What are appropriate topics of conversation in business settings? What topics should be avoided?
- What customs are associated with exchanging business cards?
- What are the hours of a typical work day?
- What are the attitudes toward personal space and touching?
- Is gift-giving appropriate when invited to someone's home? If so, what gifts are appropriate?
- What facial expressions or gestures are considered offensive? Is direct eye contact appropriate?
- What is the attitude toward punctuality in social situations? In business situations?
- What gestures indicate agreement? Disagreement? Frustration? Excitement?

**Family Life**
- What is a typical family unit? Do family units include extended family members?
- How do family life and family size differ in urban and rural settings?
- Do women and men have typical roles in families?
- Do women work outside of the home? In what occupations?
- Are children required by law to attend school? Do families value education?

**Housing, Clothing, and Food**
- How does housing differ in urban and rural areas? How does housing differ among various socioeconomic groups?
- What special occasions require traditional or ceremonial clothing?
- What types of clothing are considered inappropriate or in poor taste?
- What is appropriate business attire for men? For women?
- What are the typical eating times, and what foods are customary?
- What types of places, food, and drink are appropriate for business entertainment? Where is the seat of honor at a round table? At a rectangular table?

**Class Structure**
- Into what classes is society organized?
- Do racial, religious, or economic factors determine social status?
- Are there any minority groups? What is their social standing?

**Political Patterns**
- Are there any immediate threats or signs of political unrest in this country?
- How is political power manifested?
- What media channels are used for expressing political opinions?
- Is it appropriate to talk about politics in social situations?

**Religious Preferences and Beliefs**
- Are certain religious groups predominant?
- Do religious beliefs influence daily activities?
- Which places, objects, or animals are considered sacred?
- How do religious holidays affect business activities?

**Economic Norms**
- What are the country's principal exports and products?
- Are workers organized in unions?
- Are businesses owned by individuals, by large public corporations, or by the government?
- How is status shown in an organization? Private office? Floor level? Furnishings?
- Do business associates normally socialize before conducting business?

**Value Systems**
- Is competitiveness or cooperation more prized?
- Is politeness more important than honesty?
- To what extent is bribery accepted as a way of life?
- Do women own or manage businesses? If so, how are they treated?
- How do people perceive Americans? What behaviors exhibited by Americans are considered offensive?
- What was the hardest adjustment after coming to America?

## 10.12 Selecting Appropriate Graphics (Obj. 5)

> Team

In teams identify which type of graphic (table, bar chart, line chart, pie chart, flowchart, infographic, illustration, or map) would best illustrate the following data:
a. Figures comparing the sales of three brands of smartphones over the past 12 months
b. Statistics on the rise of six popular social media platforms (Facebook, Google+, Twitter, YouTube, Instagram, Pinterest) in five of the largest cities in the world
c. National unemployment rate figures for the last 12 months
d. Location of significant earthquakes in the world over the last 30 days
e. Date, time, and place of each game scheduled in the World Cup

f. Recruitment process from the time a job is advertised until the time an offer is made
g. Portion of national budget that goes to defense, social security, safety net programs, interest on debt, and Medicare/Medicaid

## 10.13 Evaluating Graphics (Obj. 5)
`Web`

**YOUR TASK.** Select four graphics from newspapers or magazines in hard copy or online. Look in *The Wall Street Journal*, *USA Today*, *Bloomberg Businessweek*, *U.S. News & World Report*, *Fortune*, *Forbes*, or other business news publications. Add the title and the source of each graphic. In an e-mail or memo to your instructor, critique each graphic based on what you have learned in this chapter. Do you think the graphic could have been expressed more effectively in text? How effective are the labels and headings used in this graphic? How was color used to add clarity? If a legend is used, describe its placement and effectiveness. Is the appropriate graphic form used? What is your overall impression of the effectiveness of the graphic?

## 10.14 Creating a Bar Chart and Writing a Title (Obj. 5)
`Web`

**YOUR TASK.** Create a bar chart comparing the current number of Internet users (by millions) in the following eight countries: United States, India, Japan, Brazil, Indonesia, China, United Kingdom, and Russia. Find statistics within the last year and name the source of your information. Arrange the bars according to the country with the highest number of users to the lowest. Add a chart title and appropriate labels.

## 10.15 Infographics: Telling a Story and Expressing Ideas (Obj. 5)
`Web`  `E-mail`

Information graphics, or infographics, are wildly popular, especially in online environments. Infographics can use color, text, images, data, diagrams, time lines, and charts to express ideas or tell a compelling story. You have heard that even nondesigners can create infographics, and you want to use this tool for presentations, reports, and employee training. By looking at examples of well-designed infographics and learning which websites offer free tools and templates, you will be well on your way to becoming an infographic designer.

**YOUR TASK.** Search for and examine excellent infographics featured online. Find three infographics on topics of interest to you. The topics may or may not be related. In an e-mail or memo to your instructor, promote the idea of using infographics and list the URLs for the infographic examples you found. Briefly describe the main ideas of each. Add a comment on what aspects make each infographic so compelling. Then search for one website that offers free infographic designs and templates. In your e-mail or memo, briefly describe what tools are available on this site and add the website name and URL. Conclude your message with a brief paragraph stating the reasons you believe infographics have become so popular and widely used.

## 10.16 Formal Report: Analyzing "Congressional Watchdog" Reports (Obj. 6)
`Web`

The U.S. Government Accountability Office (GAO) is a nonpartisan agency that works for Congress and investigates how the federal government spends taxpayer dollars. For this reason the agency is often called the congressional watchdog. These archived reports are available as portable document format (PDF) files. You'll be examining two reports from the GAO website.

**YOUR TASK.** Visit the U.S. GAO website at **http://www.gao.gov** and click the link for Reports and Testimonies at the top of the page. Narrow the date to find reports issued within the last six months. Then browse by topic and select two reports on the topics of Employment or Health Care. (You may choose one report from each topic or both reports from one topic.) For each report, click the link above the title to open the PDF version. Write a one-page analysis of the report. Include the title, date, and number of pages in the report. Read the summary and write a brief paragraph describing the purpose of the report. Describe what sections are included in the report. Also describe what types of graphics were included to display information.

## 10.17 Formal Report: Comparing Before Buying (Objs. 2–6)
`Web`  `Team`

Study a consumer product that you or a business might consider buying. This might be a notebook or laptop, a smartphone, a digital camera, a widescreen TV, an espresso machine, a car, a combination print/scan/fax machine, a powerful office printer, or some other product.

**YOUR TASK.** Use at least four primary and four secondary sources to research your product. Your primary research will be in the form of interviews with individuals (owners, users, salespeople, technicians) in a position to comment on attributes of your product. Secondary research will be in the form of print or electronic sources, such as magazine articles, marketing websites with user reviews, and company websites. Use electronic databases and the Web to find appropriate articles. Your report should analyze and discuss at least three comparable models or versions of the target product. Decide what criteria you will use to compare the models, such as price, features, warranty, and service. Create at least one original graphic to display report data. Include the following components in the report: table of contents, executive summary, introduction (including background, purpose, scope of the report, and research methods), findings (organized by comparison criteria), summary of findings, conclusions, recommendations, and bibliography. Address the report to your instructor. You may work individually, in pairs, or in teams.

## 10.18 Report Topics for Proposals and Formal Reports (Objs. 1–6)
*Team* *Web*

A list of nearly 100 Report Topics is available at the premium student site accessed at **www.cengagebrain.com**. Look under the tab Writing Resources. The topics are divided into the following categories: accounting, finance, personnel/human resources, marketing, information systems, management, and general business/education/campus issues. You can collect information for many of these reports by using electronic databases and the Web. Your instructor may assign them as individual or team projects. All involve critical thinking in organizing information, drawing conclusions, and making recommendations. The topics are appropriate for proposals and formal business reports.

**YOUR TASK.** As directed by your instructor, select a topic from the report list at **www.cengagebrain.com**.

# GRAMMAR/MECHANICS CHECKUP—10

## Apostrophes

Review Sections 2.20–2.22 in the Grammar/Mechanics Handbook. Then study each of the following statements. Underscore any inappropriate form. Write a correction in the space provided and record the number of the G/M principle(s) illustrated. If a sentence is correct, write C. When you finish, compare your responses with those at the back of the book. If your answers differ, study carefully the principles shown in parentheses.

years'        (2.20b)    **EXAMPLE**    In two <u>years</u> time, you could finish that degree.

_____    1. Did you know that Elizabeth Metz proposal was accepted?
_____    2. The company plans to double its earnings in three years time.
_____    3. All employees in the Human Resources Department must take their two weeks vacation before January 1.
_____    4. The attorneys agreed that Judge Millers comments were justified.
_____    5. Several employees records were accidentally removed from the files.
_____    6. The last witness testimony was the most convincing to the jury members.
_____    7. Lisas smoking led to health problems.
_____    8. I always get my moneys worth at my favorite restaurant.
_____    9. Three local companies went out of business last month.
_____    10. In one months time we hope to have our new website up and running.
_____    11. I need my boss signature on this expense claim.
_____    12. Only one legal secretaries document was error-free.
_____    13. Professor Sanchezes quizzes were always scheduled on Fridays.
_____    14. My companys stock price rose dramatically last month.
_____    15. In three months several businesses opening hours will change.

# EDITING CHALLENGE—10

To fine-tune your grammar and mechanics skills, in every chapter you will be editing a message. This executive summary suffers from wordiness, proofreading, spelling, grammar, punctuation, and other writing faults that require correction. Study the guidelines in the Grammar/Mechanics Handbook as well as the lists of Confusing Words and Frequently Misspelled Words to sharpen your skills.

**YOUR TASK.** Edit the following message (a) by correcting errors in your textbook or on a photocopy using proofreading marks from Appendix A or (b) by downloading the message from **www.cengagebrain.com** and correcting at your computer. Your instructor may show you a possible solution.

## EXECUTIVE SUMMARY

### Problem

To remain successful the U.S. tuna industry must grow it's markets abroad. Particularly in regard to japan. Which is one of the worlds largest consumers of tuna. Tuna consumption is on the decline in the United States, however it is increasing in japan. The problem that is occurring for the American tuna industry is developing appropriate marketing strategies to boost it's current sales in Japanese markets. The fact is that even though japan produces much of its tuna domestically they still must rely on imported tuna to meet its consumers demands.

### Summary of Findings

As shown herein, this report analyzes the Japanese market which at the current time consumes over eight hundred thousand tons of tuna per year. A single full grown bluefin tuna, the favorite species, can sell for $22,000. Much of the domestic consumption is supplied by imports which at this point in time total about 35% of sales. Our findings indicate that this trend will not only expand but also that Japans share of imports will continue to grow. The trend is alarming to Japans tuna industry leaders, because this important market, close to a $billion a year, is increasingly subject to the influence of foriegn imports. Declining catches by Japans own Tuna fleet as well as a sharp upward turn in food preference by affluent Japanese consumers, has contributed to this trend. In just two years time the demand for sashimi alone in Japan has increased in the amount of 15%.

The U.S. Tuna Industry are in the perfect position to meet this demand. Fishing techniques has been developed that maximize catch rates, while minimizing danger to the enviroment. Modern packaging procedures assure that tuna reaches Japan in the freshest possible condition. Let it be said that Japanese consumers have rated the quality of American tuna high. Which has only increased demand.

### Recommendations

Upon the completion of our analisys, we are prepared to reccommend the following 5 marketing strategys for the U.S. Tuna industry.
1. Farm greater suppys of tuna to export.
2. Establish new fisheries around the World.
3. We should market our own value-added products.
4. Fresh tuna should be sold direct to the Tokyo Central wholesale market.
5. Direct sales should be made to Japanese Supermarket chains.

# COMMUNICATION WORKSHOP

## TECHNOLOGY

### Evaluating the Credibility of Web Documents: Let the Reader Beware

Evaluating a website's credibility requires critical thinking and a good eye. Savvy Web users start the evaluation process by thinking about how they found the site in the first place. They may have accessed the site from the results page of a search engine or by following a link from a reputable site. Perhaps the site was recommended by a friend, which would add credibility. The processes for finding Web information may vary, but the reader alone is responsible for determining the validity, truthfulness, and integrity of that information. Because anyone with a computer and an Internet connection can publish on the Web, the reader must beware and wisely question all Web content.

Unlike the contents of journals, magazines, and newspapers found in research-oriented libraries, the content of most websites has not been reviewed by skilled editors. Some Web pages do not show authorship, credentials, or sponsoring organizations. The content cannot be verified. These sites have low credibility.

As a frequent Web user, you must learn to critically examine Web information for credibility. The following checklist of questions about authorship, publisher or sponsor, currency, content quality, and accuracy and organization will help you critically assess the validity of Web information.

## Authorship
- Who authored this page or article?
- Are the author's credentials easily found? If not, check the author's credentials online.
- Is the author affiliated with a reputable organization?
- Is the author's contact information, such as an e-mail address, easily found?
- Are the About page and the Contact page easy to spot?

## Publisher or Sponsor
- What organization publishes or sponsors this Web page? Is the publisher reputable?
- What domain is used in the URL? The domain name gives clues about who published the document (e.g., .com, .org, .edu, .gov, .net).
- Is the site published or sponsored in another country? Look for a two-letter code in the URL: .uk, .au, .br, .hu, .mx, .ca, .in.

## Currency
- When was the Web page published or last updated? Readers expect this information at the bottom of the page.
- Is this a website that requires current, updated information (e.g., science, medicine, current events)?
- Are all links on this Web page current and working? Broken links are red flags.

## Content Quality
- What is the purpose of the Web page? For example, does the page entertain, inform, persuade, sell, or express satire?
- Who is the intended audience of the page, based on its content, tone, and style?
- Do you see evidence of bias, and does the author acknowledge the bias?
- Does the site link to other reputable sites? Do those sites in turn link back to the site in question?
- Does the page contain distracting graphics or fill the screen with unwanted ads and pop-ups?

## Accuracy and Organization
- Does the information appear to be well researched?
- If the site contains statistics and facts, are sources, dates, and/or citations provided?
- Is the information well organized with main points clearly presented?
- Is the site well designed and easy to navigate? Good design adds credibility.
- Does the page have broken links or graphics that don't load?
- Are the graphics appropriately placed and clearly labeled?
- Does the site have spelling, grammar, or usage errors? Careless errors are red flags.

**CAREER APPLICATION.** As interns in a news-gathering service, you have been asked to assess the quality of the following websites. Think about whether you would recommend these sites as trustworthy sources of information.

- Beef Nutrition (**http://www.beefnutrition.org**)
- Edmunds (**http://www.edmunds.com**)
- EarthSave (**http://www.earthsave.org**)
- The White House (**http://www.whitehouse.net**)
- The White House (**http://www.whitehouse.gov**)
- GulfLINK (**http://www.gulflink.osd.mil**)
- The Anaheim White House Restaurant (**http://www.anaheimwhitehouse.com**)
- National Anti-Vivisection Society (**http://www.navs.org**)
- PETA (**http://www.peta.org**)
- WebMD (**http://www.webmd.com**)

- Petrol Direct (**http://www.petroldirect.com**)
- Buy Dehydrated Water (**http://www.buydehydratedwater.com/ci.htm**)
- Smithsonian (**http://www.si.edu**)
- Hootsuite (**https://hootsuite.com**)
- Bureau of Sasquatch Affairs (**http://zapatopi.net/bsa**)
- Mint (**https://www.mint.com**)
- DHMO.org (**http://www.dhmo.org**)
- Lonely Planet (**http://www.lonelyplanet.com**)
- Drudge Report (**http://www.drudgereport.com**)
- American Cancer Society (**http://www.cancer.org**)
- The Onion (**http://www.theonion.com**)
- Pacific Northwest Tree Octopus (**http://zapatopi.net/treeoctopus**)

**YOUR TASK.** If you decide to use teams, divide the preceding list among team members. If you are working individually, select four of the sites. Analyze each site using the checklist of questions in each category. Then summarize your evaluation of each site in a memo or e-mail report addressed to your boss (your instructor). Your report may also become part of a team presentation or a class discussion. Add a comment about whether you would recommend this site for researchers of news articles. Be careful—even a hoax site can seem reputable and trustworthy at first glance. Be careful not to label sites as good or bad. Even biased sites may have large audiences and some merit.

# ENDNOTES

[1] Photo essay based on Markon, J., and Crites, A. (2014, February 9). Accenture, hired to help fix HealthCare.gov, has had a series of stumbles. *The Washington Post.* Retrieved from http://www.washingtonpost.com/politics/accenture-hired-to-fix-healthcaregov-has-troubled-past/2014/02/09/3d1a2dc4-8934-11e3-833c-33098f9e5267_story.html

[2] City of Las Vegas. (2010, January 4). RFP for public private partnership parking initiative. Onvia DemandStar. Retrieved from http://www.lasvegasnevada.gov/Business/5990.htm?ID

[3] Buck Institute for Research on Aging. (n.d.). Architecture. Retrieved from http://www.buckinstitute.org/architecture

[4] Greenwood, G., & Greenwood, J. (2008). SBIR proposal writing basics: Resumes must be written well. Greenwood Consulting Group. Retrieved from http://www.g-jgreenwood.com/sbir_proposal_writing_basics91.htm

[5] Cohen, J. S. (2009, December 28). Top 10 favorite foods preferred by college students. *Chicago Tribune.* Retrieved from http://www.inyork.com/ci_14080691?source=most_viewed

[6] Giorgetti, D., & Sebastiani, F. (2003, December). Automating survey coding by multiclass text categories. *Journal of the American Society for Information Science and Technology, 54*(14), 1269. Retrieved from http://search.proquest.com

[7] Goldsmith, B. (2002, June). The awesome power of asking the right questions. *OfficeSolutions,* 52; and Bracey, G. W. (2001, November). Research-question authority. *Phi Delta Kappan,* 191.

[8] Berfield, S. (2009, August 17). Howard Schultz versus Howard Schultz. *BusinessWeek,* p. 31.

[9] Writing Tutorial Services, Indiana University. (n.d.). *Plagiarism: What it is and how to recognize and avoid it.* Retrieved from http://www.indiana.edu/~wts/pamphlets/plagiarism.shtml

[10] Photo essay based on Pemberton, K. (2013, October 22). Vancouver city staff to monitor how casinos adhere to health report recommendations. *The Vancouver Sun.* Retrieved from http://www.vancouversun.com/health/Vancouver+city+staff+monitor+casinos+adhere+health+report+recommendations/9069335/story.html

[11] Saylor, M. (2012). *The mobile wave: How mobile intelligence will change everything.* New York: Vanguard Press, p. ix.

[12] Berfield, S. (2009, August 17). Howard Schultz versus Howard Schultz. *BusinessWeek,* p. 31.

[13] Ratner, H. M. (2012, March 1). 9 businesses that social media built. *Today's Chicago Woman.* Retrieved from http://www.tcwmag.com/9-businesses-social-media-built

[14] Corporation for National and Community Service. (2013). What is service-learning? Retrieved from http://www.servicelearning.org/what-is-service-learning

# ACKNOWLEDGMENTS

**p. 304** Office Insider. Mary Piecewicz, Hewlett-Packard proposal manager, interview with Mary Ellen Guffey.

# Professionalism, Teamwork, Meetings, and Speaking Skills

## UNIT 5

**CHAPTER 11**
Professionalism at Work: Business Etiquette, Ethics, Teamwork, and Meetings

**CHAPTER 12**
Business Presentations

## CHAPTER 11

# Professionalism at Work: Business Etiquette, Ethics, Teamwork, and Meetings

**OBJECTIVES**
After studying this chapter, you should be able to

**11-1**
Understand professionalism, start developing business etiquette skills, and build an ethical mind-set—important qualities digital-age employers seek.

**11-2**
Use your voice as a communication tool, master face-to-face workplace interaction, foster positive relations on the job, and accept as well as provide constructive criticism gracefully.

**11-3**
Practice professional telephone skills and polish your voice mail etiquette.

**11-4**
Understand the importance of teamwork in today's digital-era workplace, and explain how you can contribute positively to team performance.

**11-5**
Discuss effective practices and technologies for planning and participating in productive face-to-face meetings and virtual meetings.

## 11-1 Developing Professionalism and Business Etiquette Skills at the Office and Online

Good manners and a businesslike, professional demeanor are among the top skills recruiters seek in applicants. Employers prefer courteous and professional job candidates over those who lack these skills and traits. With a potentially global audience watching, you can choose to project a positive, professional image, or you can embarrass yourself for years to come.[1] A journalist sums up the danger of overexposure: "Lives risk ruin from ill-considered pictures or utterances passed on and preserved for eternity."[2]

However, can you learn how to be courteous, civil, and professional? Of course! In this section you will study the professional characteristics most businesspeople value in workplace relationships. Next, you will be asked to consider the link between professional and ethical behavior on the job. Finally, by protecting your reputation offline and online, you can become the kind of professional that recruiters are looking to hire.

### 11-1a Understanding Professionalism and the Cost of Incivility

The term *professionalism* and its synonyms, such as *business etiquette* or *protocol*, *soft skills*, *social intelligence*, *polish*, and *civility*, all have one element in common. They describe *desirable workplace behavior*. Businesses have an interest in employees who get along and deliver positive results that enhance profits and boost the company's image. In the digital age, professionalism also means maintaining a *positive online presence*, a subject we discussed in Chapters 1 and 5 and will revisit in Unit 6, Employment Communication.

As workloads increase and face-to-face meetings decline, bad manners are becoming alarmingly common in the American workplace.[3] One survey showed that 71 percent of workers said they had been insulted, demeaned, ignored, or otherwise treated discourteously by their coworkers and supervisors.[4] Employers, of course, suffer from the resulting drop in productivity and exodus of talent. Employees, too, suffer. They worry about incidents, think about changing jobs, and cut back their efforts on the job. Another study showed that 12 percent of employees leave their jobs because of bullying and other uncivil acts they have experienced. The average cost of replacing each of these disgruntled employees is $50,000.[5]

Not surprisingly, businesses are responding to increasing incidents of "desk rage" and *cyberbullying* in American workplaces. Many organizations have established protocol procedures or policies to enforce civility. Following are a few traits and skills that define professional behavior to foster positive workplace relations.

**Civility.** Management consultant Patricia M. Buhler defines rising incivility at work as "behavior that is considered disrespectful and inconsiderate of others."[6] The editors of Wikipedia, the free online encyclopedia, clearly define undesirable behavior as follows: "Incivility consists of one or more of the following behaviours . . . personal attacks, rudeness, and disrespectful comments" that are disruptive, causing stress and conflict.[7] The largest wiki ever created wants to ensure that its more than 77,000 active contributors "treat each other with consideration and respect."[8]

**Polish.** You may hear businesspeople refer to someone as being *polished* or displaying *polish* when dealing with others. In her book with the telling title *Buff and Polish: A Practical Guide to Enhance Your Professional Image and Communication Style*, corporate trainer Kathryn J. Volin addresses making first impressions, shaking hands, improving one's voice quality, listening, presentation skills, and more. You will find pointers on developing many of these valuable traits of a polished business professional in this textbook and also in the Communication Workshop at that the end of this chapter.

**Business and Dining Etiquette.** Proper business attire, dining etiquette, and other aspects of your professional presentation can make or break your interview. Even a seemingly harmless act such as sharing a business meal can have a huge impact on your career. In the words of a Fortune 500 executive, "Eating is not an executive skill . . . but it is especially hard to imagine why anyone negotiating a rise to the top would consider it possible to skip mastering the very simple requirements . . . what else did they skip learning?"[9] This means that you will be judged on more than your college-bred expertise.

**Social Intelligence.** Occasionally you may encounter the expression *social intelligence*. In the words of one of its modern proponents, it is "The ability to get along well with others and to get them to cooperate with you."[10] Social intelligence points to a deep understanding of culture and life that helps us negotiate interpersonal and social situations. This type of intelligence can be much harder to acquire than simple etiquette. Social intelligence requires us to interact well, be perceptive, show sensitivity toward others, and grasp a situation quickly and accurately.

**Soft Skills.** Perhaps the most common definition of important interpersonal habits is *soft skills*, as opposed to *hard skills*, a term for the technical knowledge in your field. In a survey of managers, more than 60 percent cited soft skills as more important than hard skills (32 percent) and social media skills (7 percent) when evaluating on-the-job performance. The top three soft skills on the managers' wish list were the ability to prioritize work, a positive attitude, and teamwork skills.[11]

---

### OFFICE INSIDER

"Having excellent command of your online digital persona will enable you to quickly surpass those who present themselves weakly in the new competitive arena. Since you probably won't get a second chance, what kind of digital first impression will you choose to make?"

—Victor Urbach, management consultant

**LEARNING OBJECTIVE 1**

Understand professionalism, start developing business etiquette skills, and build an ethical mind-set—important qualities digital-age employers seek.

Chapter 11: Professionalism at Work: Business Etiquette, Ethics, Teamwork, and Meetings

## OFFICE INSIDER

"Civility on the job creates an atmosphere of respect and appreciation that ultimately translates to better reputation and, hence, to better business."

—Ronald M. Bosrock, founder and director of The Global Institute, a research center

Employers want managers and employees who are comfortable with diverse coworkers, who can listen actively to customers and colleagues, who can make eye contact, who display good workplace manners, and who possess a host of other interpersonal skills.

Simply put, all these attempts to explain proper behavior at work aim at identifying traits that make someone a good employee and a compatible coworker. You will want to achieve a positive image on the job and online to maintain a solid reputation. For the sake of simplicity, in the discussion that follows, the terms *professionalism*, *business etiquette*, and *soft skills* are used largely as synonyms.

### 11-1b Relating Professional Behavior to Ethics

A broad definition of professionalism also encompasses another crucial quality in a businessperson: *ethics*, or *integrity*. You may have a negative view of business after learning how reckless behavior by major banks contributed to the worst recession since the Great Depression. However, for every company that captures the limelight for misconduct, hundreds or even thousands of others operate honestly and serve their customers and the public well. The overwhelming majority of businesses wish to recruit ethical and polished graduates.

The difference between ethics and etiquette is minimal in the workplace. Ethics professor Douglas Chismar—and Harvard professor Stephen L. Carter before him—suggests that no sharp distinction between ethics and etiquette exists. How we approach the seemingly trivial events of work life reflects our character and attitudes when we handle larger issues. Our conduct should be consistently ethical and professional. Professor Chismar believes that "[w]e each have a moral obligation to treat each other with respect and sensitivity every day."[12] He calls on all of us to make a difference in the quality of life, morale, and productivity at work.

Figure 11.1 summarizes the many components of professional workplace behavior[13] and identifies six main dimensions that will ease your entry into the world of work.

## Workplace in Focus

From meetings and interviews to company parties and golf outings, nearly all workplace-related activities involve etiquette. Take Your Dog to Work Day, the ever-popular morale booster that keeps workers chained to their pets instead of the desk, has a unique set of guidelines to help maximize fun. For employees at the nearly one in five U.S. businesses that allow dogs at work, etiquette gurus say pets must be well behaved, housebroken, and free of fleas to participate in the four-legged festivity. Before bringing a dog to the office, check with immediate neighbors to see if any may be allergic to dogs. Remember, too, that dogs must not be allowed to wander around freely. At Amazon, dogs are required to be on-leash except when they're in an office with the door closed or behind a baby gate. Why is it important to follow proper business etiquette?

Figure 11.1 The Six Dimensions of Professional Behavior

*Wheel diagram with six sections around a central hub. Center segments: Courtesy/Respect, Appearance/Appeal, Tolerance/Tact, Honesty/Ethics, Reliability/Diligence, Collegiality/Sharing.*

- **Courtesy Respect**: Promptness; Giving and accepting criticism graciously; Apologizing for errors; Sincerity
- **Appearance Appeal**: Dining etiquette; Good hygiene and grooming; Attractive business attire
- **Tolerance Tact**: Ability to compromise; Fair treatment of others; Self-control
- **Honesty Ethics**: Truthfulness; Respecting others; Fair competition; Empathy
- **Reliability Diligence**: Dependability; Honoring commitments and keeping promises; Consistent performance
- **Collegiality Sharing**: Helpfulness; Showing up prepared; Delivering high-quality work

> ## OFFICE INSIDER
>
> "Unprofessional conduct around the office will eventually overflow into official duties. Few of us have mastered the rare art of maintaining multiple personalities."
>
> —Douglas Chismar, liberal arts program director at Ringling College of Art and Design

### 11-1c Gaining an Etiquette Edge in a Networked World

An awareness of courtesy and etiquette can give you a competitive edge in the job market. Etiquette, civility, and goodwill efforts may seem out of place in today's fast-paced, hyperconnected offices. However, when two candidates have equal qualifications, the one who appears to be more polished and professional is more likely to be hired and promoted. Moreover, most hiring managers are looking for new-hires who show enthusiasm, are eager to learn, volunteer to tackle even difficult tasks, and exhibit a positive attitude. You will not be hired to warm a seat.

In the networked professional environment of the digital era, you must manage and guard your reputation—at the office and online. How you present yourself in the virtual world, meaning how well you communicate and protect your "brand," may very well determine how successful your career will be. Thoughtful blog posts, astute comments on LinkedIn and Facebook, as well as competent e-mails will help you make a positive impression and show your professionalism.

This chapter focuses on developing interpersonal skills, telephone and voice mail etiquette, teamwork proficiency, and meeting management skills. These are some of the soft skills employers seek in the hyperconnected competitive work environments of the digital age.

## 11-2 Communicating Face-to-Face on the Job

You have learned that e-mail is the preferred communication channel at work because it is faster, cheaper, and easier than telephone, mail, or fax. You also know

**LEARNING OBJECTIVE 2**

Use your voice as a communication tool, master face-to-face workplace interaction, foster positive relations on the job, and accept as well as provide constructive criticism gracefully.

## OFFICE INSIDER

*"No question, technology is the Great Enabler. But, paradoxically, now the human bit is more, not less, important than ever before."*

—Tom Peters, business expert and author of *Re-Imagine!*

that businesspeople have embraced instant messaging, texting, and social media. However, despite its popularity and acceptance, communication technology can't replace the richness or effectiveness of face-to-face communication.[14] Imagine that you want to tell your boss how you solved a problem. Would you settle for a one-dimensional phone call, a text message, or an e-mail when you could step into her office and explain in person?

Face-to-face conversation has many advantages. It is the richest communication channel because you can use your voice and body language to make a point, convey warmth, and build rapport. You are less likely to be misunderstood because you can read feedback and make needed adjustments. In conflict resolution, you can reach a solution with fewer misunderstandings and cooperate to create greater levels of mutual benefit when communicating face-to-face.[15] Communicating in person remains the most effective of all communication channels, as you can see in Figure 11.2.

In this section you will explore professional interpersonal speaking techniques, starting with viewing your voice as a communication tool.

### 11-2a Using Your Voice as a Communication Tool

Studies suggest a strong correlation between voice and perceived authority and trust. Respondents typically favor lower-pitched voices in men and higher but not shrill female voices.[16] A voice carries so much nonverbal meaning that celebrities, actors, business executives, and everyday people consult coaches and speech therapists to help them shake bad habits or avoid sounding less intelligent than they are. You too can pick up valuable tips for using your voice most effectively

Figure 11.2 Media Richness and Communication Effectiveness

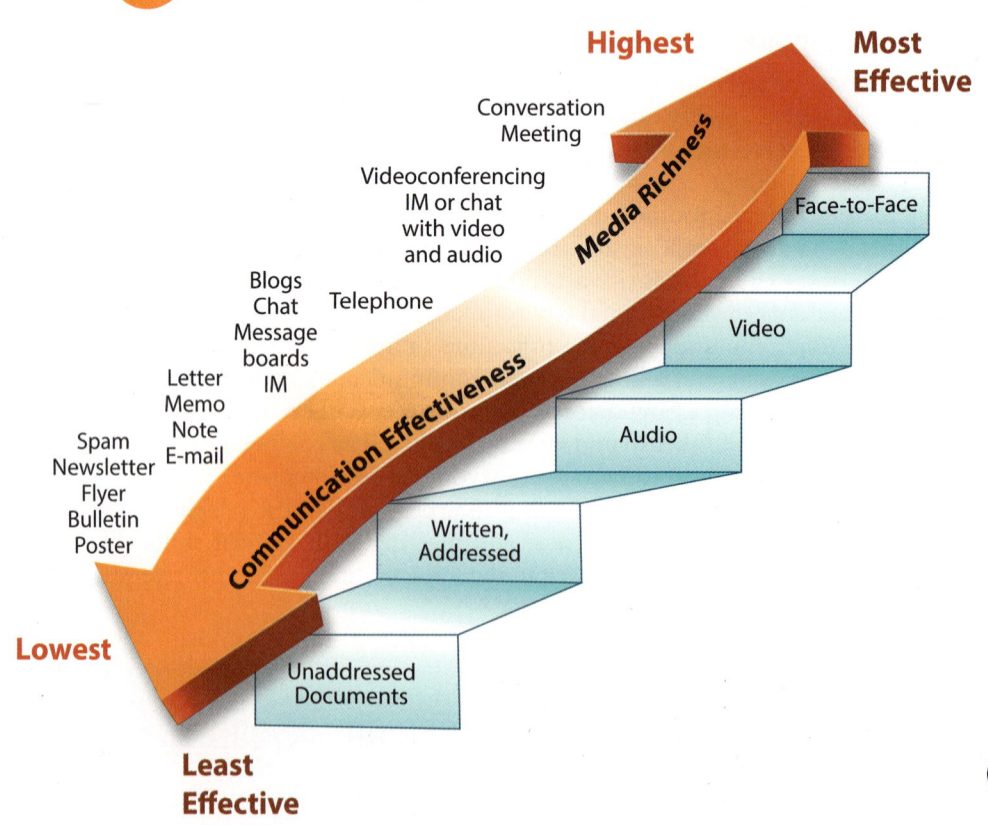

356  Chapter 11: Professionalism at Work: Business Etiquette, Ethics, Teamwork, and Meetings

by learning how to control your pronunciation, voice quality, pitch, volume, rate, and emphasis.

**Pronunciation.** Proper pronunciation involves saying words correctly and clearly with the accepted sounds and accented syllables. You will have a distinct advantage in your job if you pronounce words correctly. How can you improve your pronunciation? The best ways are to listen carefully to educated people, to look words up in the dictionary, and to practice. Many online dictionaries provide audio files so you can hear words pronounced correctly.

**Voice Quality.** The quality of your voice sends a nonverbal message to listeners. It identifies your personality and your mood. Some voices sound enthusiastic and friendly, conveying the impression of an upbeat person who is happy to be with the listener. However, voices can also sound controlling, patronizing, slow-witted, angry, bored, or childish. This does not mean that the speaker necessarily has that attribute. It may mean that the speaker is merely carrying on a family tradition or pattern learned in childhood. To check your voice quality, record your voice and listen to it critically. Is it projecting a positive quality about you? Do you sound professional?

**Pitch.** Effective speakers use a relaxed, controlled, well-pitched voice to attract listeners to their message. *Pitch* refers to sound vibration frequency; that is, the highness or lowness of a sound. Voices are most engaging when they rise and fall in conversational tones. Flat, monotone voices are considered boring and ineffectual.

**Volume and Rate.** The volume of your voice is the loudness or the intensity of sound. Just as you adjust the volume on your MP3 player or television set, you should adjust the volume of your speaking to the occasion and your listeners. *Rate* refers to the pace of your speech. If you speak too slowly, listeners can become bored and their attention can wander. If you speak too quickly, listeners may not be able to understand you. Most people normally talk at about 125 words a minute. Monitor the nonverbal signs of your listeners and adjust your volume and rate as needed.

**Emphasis.** By emphasizing or stressing certain words, you can change the meaning you are expressing. To make your message interesting and natural, use emphasis appropriately. Some speakers today are prone to *uptalk*. This is a habit of using a rising inflection at the end of a sentence resulting in a singsong pattern that makes statements sound like questions. Uptalk makes speakers seem weak and tentative. Their messages lack authority. On the job, managers wishing to sound confident and competent avoid uptalk.

**How well you handle workplace conversations helps determine your career success.**

## 11-2b Making Workplace Conversation Matter

Face-to-face conversation helps people work together harmoniously and feel that they are part of the larger organization. Workplace conversations may involve giving and taking instructions, providing feedback, exchanging ideas, brainstorming, participating in performance appraisals, or engaging in small talk about such things as families and sports. Following are several business etiquette guidelines that promote positive workplace conversations, both in the office and at work-related social functions.

## Office Insider

*"In today's fiercely competitive business arenas, etiquette and protocol intelligence will distinguish you from the crowd. While this unique intelligence alone may not get you anywhere, it will give you an edge that will make the difference between you and another person who is just as smart."*

—Dorothea Johnson, author and etiquette expert

**Use Correct Names and Titles.** Although the world seems increasingly informal, it is still wise to use titles and last names when addressing professional adults (*Ms. O'Malley, Mr. Santiago*). In some organizations senior staff members speak to junior employees on a first-name basis, but the reverse may not be encouraged. Probably the safest plan is to ask your supervisors how they want to be addressed. Customers and others outside the organization should always be addressed initially by title and last name. Wait for an invitation to use first names.

When you meet strangers, do you have trouble remembering their names? You can improve your memory considerably if you associate the person with an object, place, color, animal, job, adjective, or some other memory hook. For example, *technology pro Gina, L.A. Matt, silver-haired Mr. Elliott, baseball fan John, programmer Tanya, traveler Ms. Choi*. The person's name will also be more deeply imbedded in your memory if you use it immediately after being introduced, in subsequent conversation, and when you part.

**Choose Appropriate Topics.** In some workplace activities, such as social gatherings and interviews, you will be expected to engage in small talk. Stay away from controversial topics. Avoid politics, religion, and controversial current events that can trigger heated arguments. To initiate appropriate conversations, follow news sites such as CNN, Google News, and major newspapers online. Subscribe to e-newsletters and RSS feeds that deliver relevant news to you via e-mail. Listen to reputable radio and TV shows discussing current events. Try not to be defensive or annoyed if others present information that upsets you.

**Avoid Negative Remarks.** Workplace conversations are not the place to complain about your colleagues, your friends, the organization, or your job. No one enjoys listening to whiners. What's more, your criticism of others may come back to haunt you. A snipe at your boss or a complaint about a coworker may reach him or her, sometimes embellished or distorted with meanings you did not intend. Be circumspect in all negative judgments.

**Listen to Learn.** In conversations with managers, colleagues, subordinates, and customers, train yourself to expect to learn something. Being attentive is not only instructive but also courteous. Being receptive and listening with an open mind means not interrupting or prejudging. Let's say you wish to work at home for part of your workweek. You try to explain your ideas to your boss, but he cuts you off, saying, *It is out of the question; we need you here every day.* Suppose instead he had said, *I have strong reservations about your telecommuting, but maybe you will change my mind*, and then settles in to listen to your presentation. In this case, even if your boss refuses your request, you will feel that your ideas were heard.

**Give Sincere and Specific Praise.** The Greek philosopher Xenophon once said, "The sweetest of all sounds is praise." Probably nothing promotes positive workplace relationships better than sincere and specific praise. Whether the compliments and appreciation are traveling upward to management, downward to workers, or horizontally to colleagues, everyone responds well to recognition. Organizations run more smoothly and morale is higher when people feel appreciated. In your workplace conversations, look for ways to recognize good work

Active listening is an important, yet underused workplace skill.

and good people. Try to be specific. Instead of *You did a great job in leading that meeting*, say something more specific, such as *Your excellent leadership skills certainly kept that meeting short, focused, and productive.*

**Act Professionally in Social Situations.** You will likely attend many work-related social functions during your career, including dinners, picnics, holiday parties, and other events. It is important to remember that your actions at these events can help or harm your career. Dress appropriately, and avoid or limit alcohol consumption. Choose appropriate conversation topics, and make sure that your voice and mannerisms communicate that you are glad to be there.

## 11-2c Receiving Workplace Criticism Gracefully

Most of us hate giving criticism, but we dislike receiving it even more. However, giving and receiving criticism on the job is normal. The criticism may be given informally—for example, during a casual conversation with a supervisor or coworker. Sometimes the criticism is given formally—for example, during a performance evaluation. You need to accept and respond professionally when receiving criticism.

When being criticized, you may feel that you are being attacked. Your heart beats faster, your temperature shoots up, your face reddens, and you respond with the classic fight-or-flight reflex. You want to instantly retaliate or escape from the attacker. However, focusing on your feelings distracts you from hearing what is being said and prevents you from responding professionally. The following suggestions can help you respond positively to criticism so that you can benefit from it:

- **Listen without interrupting.** Even though you might want to protest, hear the speaker out.
- **Determine the speaker's intent.** Unskilled communicators may throw "verbal bricks" with unintended negative-sounding expressions. If you think the intent is positive, focus on what is being said rather than reacting to poorly chosen words.
- **Acknowledge what you are hearing.** Respond with a pause, a nod, or a neutral statement such as *I understand you have a concern.* This buys you time. Don't disagree, counterattack, or blame, which may escalate the situation and harden the speaker's position.
- **Paraphrase what was said.** In your own words, restate objectively what you are hearing.
- **Ask for more information if necessary.** Clarify what is being said. Stay focused on the main idea rather than interjecting side issues.
- **Agree—if the comments are accurate.** If an apology is in order, give it. Explain what you plan to do differently. If the criticism is on target, the sooner you agree, the more likely you will be to receive respect from the other person.
- **Disagree respectfully and constructively—if you feel the comments are unfair.** After hearing the criticism, you might say, *May I tell you my perspective?* Alternatively, you could say, *How can we improve this situation in a way you believe we can both accept?* If the other person continues to criticize, say, *I want to find a way to resolve your concern. When do you want to talk about it next?*
- **Look for a middle position.** Search for a middle position or a compromise. Be genial even if you don't like the person or the situation.
- **Learn from criticism.** Most work-related criticism is given with the best of intentions. You should welcome the opportunity to correct your mistakes and to learn from them. Responding positively to workplace criticism can help you improve your job performance. In the words of a career coach, if you make a mistake on the job, "own it and hone it."[17] Learn from it.

## Office Insider

"[T]here is no excuse for neglecting phone etiquette, even in a modern, technology-oriented office space with its inherent depersonalization. It is that very tendency to depersonalize that makes being personable on the phone more meaningful than in the past."

—Joshua Bjerke, writer, Recruiter.com

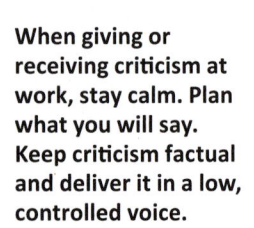

When giving or receiving criticism at work, stay calm. Plan what you will say. Keep criticism factual and deliver it in a low, controlled voice.

### 11-2d Providing Constructive Criticism on the Job

Today's workplace often involves team projects. As a team member, you will be called on to judge the work of others. In addition to working on teams, you can also expect to become a supervisor or manager one day. As such, you will need to evaluate subordinates. Good employees want and need timely, detailed observations about their work to reinforce what they do well and help them overcome weak spots. However, making that feedback constructive is not always easy. Depending on your situation, you may find the following suggestions helpful:

- **Mentally outline your conversation**. Think carefully about what you want to accomplish and what you will say. Find the right words and deliver them at the right time and in the right setting.

- **Generally, use face-to-face communication**. Most constructive criticism is best delivered in person. Personal feedback offers an opportunity for the listener to ask questions and give explanations. Occasionally, however, complex situations may require a different strategy. You might write out your opinions and deliver them by telephone or in writing. A written document enables you to organize your thoughts, include all the details, and be sure of keeping your cool. Remember, though, that written documents create permanent records—for better or worse.

- **Focus on improvement**. Instead of attacking, use language that offers alternative behavior. Use phrases such as *Next time, you could. . . .*"

- **Offer to help**. Criticism is accepted more readily if you volunteer to help eliminate or solve the problem.

- **Be specific**. Instead of a vague assertion such as *Your work is often late*, be more specific: *The specs on the Riverside job were due Thursday at 5 p.m., and you didn't hand them in until Friday.* Explain how the person's performance jeopardized the entire project.

    - **Avoid broad generalizations**. Don't use words such as *should, never, always* and other sweeping expressions because they may cause the listener to shut down and become defensive.

    - **Discuss the behavior, not the person**. Instead of *You seem to think you can come to work anytime you want*, focus on the behavior: *Coming to work late means that we have to fill in with someone else until you arrive.*

    - **Use the word *we* rather than *you***. Saying *We need to meet project deadlines* is better than saying *You need to meet project deadlines*. Emphasize organizational expectations rather than personal ones. Avoid sounding accusatory.

    - **Encourage two-way communication**. Even if well planned, criticism is hard to deliver. It may hurt the feelings of the employee. Consider ending your message like this: *It can be hard to hear this type of feedback. If you would like to share your thoughts, I'm listening.*

    - **Avoid anger, sarcasm, and a raised voice**. Criticism is rarely constructive when tempers flare. Plan in advance what you will say and deliver it in low, controlled, and sincere tones.

- **Keep it private**. Offer praise in public; offer criticism in private. "Setting an example" through public criticism is never a wise management policy, as AOL CEO Tim Armstrong learned after brutally firing a worker in front of more than 1,000 Patch news network employees.

## 11-3 Following Professional Telephone and Voice Mail Etiquette

**LEARNING OBJECTIVE 3**
Practice professional telephone skills and polish your voice mail etiquette.

Despite the heavy reliance on e-mail, the telephone is still an extremely important piece of equipment in offices. In a survey of business professionals, 83 percent said that e-mail is "critical/very important" to their productivity and success; 81 percent named the phone as "critical/very important." Both are the most indispensable communication tools today.[18] As a business communicator, you can be more productive, efficient, and professional by following some simple suggestions. This section focuses on telephone etiquette and voice mail techniques.

### 11-3a Making Telephone Calls Professionally

Before making a telephone call, decide whether the intended call is really necessary. Could you find the information yourself? If you wait a while, would the problem resolve itself? Perhaps your message could be delivered more efficiently by some other means—IMs or texts for a quick question, a telephone or videoconference to seek consensus or to brainstorm. Pick up the phone when something is urgent and can't wait. Consider using the following suggestions to make calls productive:

- **Plan a mini-agenda.** Have you ever had to make a second telephone call because you forgot an important item the first time? Before calling, jot down all the topics you need to discuss. Following an agenda guarantees not only a complete call but also a quick one.

- **Use a three-point introduction.** When placing a call, immediately (a) name the person you are calling, (b) identify yourself and your affiliation, and (c) give a brief explanation of your reason for calling. For example: *May I speak to Jeremy Johnson? This is Paula Soltani of Coughlin and Associates, and I'm seeking information about a software program called ZoneAlarm Internet Security.* This kind of introduction enables the receiving individual to respond immediately without asking further questions.

- **Be brisk if you are rushed.** For business calls when your time is limited, avoid questions such as *How are you?* Instead, say, *Lauren, I knew you'd be the only one who could answer these two questions for me.* Another efficient strategy is to set a "contract" with the caller: *Look, Lauren, I have only a few minutes, but I really wanted to get back to you.*

- **Be cheerful and accurate.** Let your voice show the same kind of animation that you radiate when you greet people in person. Try to envision the individual answering the telephone. A smile can affect the tone of your voice; therefore, even though the individual can't see you, smile at that person. Speak with an enthusiastic, attentive, and respectful tone. Moreover, be accurate about what you say. *Hang on a second; I will be right back* rarely is true. It is better to say, *It may take me two or three minutes to get that information.*

- **Be professional and courteous.** Remember that you are representing yourself and your company when you make phone calls. Use professional vocabulary and courteous language. Say *thank you* and *please* during your conversations. Don't eat, drink, or chew gum while talking on the phone. Articulate your words clearly. Avoid doing other work during the phone call so that you can focus entirely on the conversation.

- **Ending the call.** The responsibility for ending a call lies with the caller. This is sometimes difficult to do if the other person rambles on. You may need to use the following tactful cues: (a) *I have enjoyed talking with you*; (b) *I have*

*learned what I needed to know, and now I can proceed with my work*;
(c) *Thanks for your help*; (d) *I must go now, but may I call you again if I need . . . ?*;
or (e) *Should we talk again in a few weeks?*

- **Avoid telephone tag.** If you can't reach someone, ask when it would be best to call again. State that you will call at a specific time—and do it. If you ask a person to call you, give a time when you can be reached.
- **Leave complete voice mail messages.** Don't rush when leaving a voice mail message. Always enunciate clearly. Provide a complete message, including your name, telephone number, and the time and date of your call. Briefly explain your purpose so the receiver can be ready with the required information when returning your call.

### 11-3b Receiving Telephone Calls Professionally

Developing good telephone manners reflects well on you and on your organization. With a little forethought, you can project a professional image and make your telephone a productive tool in your communication tool belt.[19] You will be most successful on the job if you practice the following etiquette guidelines:

- **Answer promptly and courteously.** Try to answer the phone on the first or second ring if possible. Smile as you pick up the phone.
- **Identify yourself immediately.** In answering your telephone or someone else's, provide your name, title or affiliation, and a greeting. For example, *Juan Salinas, Digital Imaging Corporation. How may I help you?* Force yourself to speak clearly and slowly. The caller may be unfamiliar with what you are saying and fail to recognize slurred syllables.
- **Be responsive and helpful.** If you are in a support role, be sympathetic to callers' needs and show that you understand their situations. Instead of *I don't know*, try *That is a good question; let me investigate*. Instead of *We can't do that*, try *That is a tough one; let's see what we can do*. Avoid *No* at the beginning of a sentence. It sounds harsh because it suggests rejection.
- **Be cautious when answering calls for others.** Be courteous and helpful, but don't give out confidential information. It is better to say, *She is away from her desk* or *He is out of the office* than to report a colleague's exact whereabouts. Also be tight-lipped about sharing company information with strangers.
- **Take messages carefully.** Few things are as frustrating as receiving a potentially important phone message that is illegible. Repeat the spelling of names and verify telephone numbers. Write messages legibly and record their time and date.
- **Leave the line respectfully.** If you must put a call on hold, let the caller know and give an estimate of how long you expect the call to be on hold. Give the caller the option of holding. Say, *Would you prefer to hold, or would you like me to call you back?* If the caller is on hold for a long period of time, check back periodically.
- **Explain what you are doing when transferring calls.** Give a reason for transferring, and identify the extension to which you are directing the call in case the caller is disconnected.

### 11-3c Observing Smartphone Etiquette

The smartphone has become an essential part of communication in the workplace. No wonder: cellular phone ownership now stands at 91 percent of the U.S. population; 65 percent of Americans carry feature-rich smartphones.[20] Consumers own more electronic devices than ever, and the number of cell phone, netbook, PC, and tablet users keeps growing.[21] Some pundits are pronouncing the landline dead because 40 percent of Americans have cut the cord.[22]

Because so many people depend on their mobile devices, it is important to understand proper use and etiquette. When is it acceptable to take calls? Where should calls be made? Most of us have experienced thoughtless and rude cell phone behavior. Researchers say that the rampant use of mobile electronics has worsened workplace incivility. Rude users have generated a backlash. To avoid offending, smart business communicators practice cell phone etiquette, as outlined in Figure 11.3.

### 11-3d Making the Most of Voice Mail

Because telephone calls can be disruptive, most businesspeople are making extensive use of voice mail to intercept and screen incoming calls. Incoming information is delivered without interrupting potential receivers and without all the niceties that most two-way conversations require. Stripped of superfluous chitchat, voice mail messages allow communicators to focus on essentials. Voice mail also eliminates telephone tag, inaccurate message taking, and time zone barriers.

However, voice mail should not be overused. Individuals who screen all incoming calls cause irritation, resentment, and needless follow-up calls. Both receivers and callers can use etiquette guidelines to make voice mail work most effectively for them.

**On the Receiver's End.** Your voice mail should project professionalism and provide an easy way for your callers to leave messages for you. Here are some voice mail etiquette tips to follow:

- **Don't overuse voice mail.** Don't use voice mail to avoid taking phone calls. It is better to answer calls yourself than to let voice mail messages build up.

- **Prepare a professional, concise, friendly greeting.** Make your mechanical greeting sound warm and inviting, both in tone and content. Your greeting should be in your own voice, not a computer-generated voice. Identify yourself and your organization so that callers know they have reached the right number. Thank the caller and briefly explain that you are unavailable. Invite the caller to leave a message or, if appropriate, call back. Here's a typical voice mail greeting: *Hi! This is Larry Lopez of Proteus Software, and I appreciate your call. You have reached my voice mailbox because I'm either working with customers or talking on another line at the moment. Please leave your name, number, and reason for calling so that I can be prepared when I return your call.* Give callers an idea of when you will be available, such as *I'll be back at 2:30* or *I'll be out of my office until Wednesday, May 20*. If you screen your calls as a time management technique, try this message: *I'm not near my phone right now, but I should be able to return calls after 3:30.*

- **Test your message.** Call your number and assess your message. Does it sound inviting? Sincere? Professional? Understandable? Are you pleased with your tone? If not, record your message again until it conveys the professional image you want.

- **Change your message.** Update your message regularly, especially if you travel for your job.

Figure **11.3** Professional Cell Phone Use

**Show courtesy**
- Don't force others to hear your business.
- Don't make or receive calls in public places, such as post offices, banks, retail stores, trains, and buses.
- Don't allow your phone to ring in theaters, restaurants, museums, classrooms, and meetings.
- Apologize for occasional cell phone blunders.

**Keep it down**
- Speak in low, conversational tones. Cell phone microphones are sensitive, making it unnecessary to raise your voice.
- Choose a professional ringtone and set it on low or vibrate.

**Step outside**
- If a call is urgent, step outside to avoid being disruptive.
- Make full use of caller ID to screen incoming calls. Let voice mail take routine calls.

**Drive now, talk and text later**
- Talking while driving increases accidents almost fourfold, about the same as driving intoxicated.
- Texting while driving is even more dangerous. Don't do it!

Chapter 11: Professionalism at Work: Business Etiquette, Ethics, Teamwork, and Meetings

## OFFICE INSIDER

*"Teamwork is the ability to work together toward a common vision. The ability to direct individual accomplishments toward organizational objectives. It is the fuel that allows common people to attain uncommon results."*
—Andrew Carnegie

- **Respond to messages promptly.** Check your messages regularly, and try to return all voice mail messages within one business day.
- **Plan for vacations and other extended absences.** If you will not be picking up voice mail messages for an extended period, let callers know how they can reach someone else if needed.

**On the Caller's End.** When leaving a voice mail message, follow these tips:

- **Be prepared to leave a message.** Before calling someone, be prepared for voice mail. Decide what you are going to say and what information you are going to include in your message. If necessary, write your message down before calling.
- **Leave a concise, thorough message.** When leaving a message, always identify yourself using your complete name and affiliation. Mention the date and time you called and a brief explanation of your reason for calling. Always leave a complete phone number, including the area code, even if you think the receiver already has it. Tell the receiver the best time to return your call. Don't ramble.
- **Use a professional and courteous tone.** When leaving a message, make sure that your tone is professional, enthusiastic, and respectful. Smile when leaving a message to add warmth to your voice.
- **Speak slowly and articulate.** Make sure that your receiver will be able to understand your message. Speak slowly and pronounce your words carefully, especially when providing your phone number. If you suspect a poor connection, repeat the number before saying goodbye. The receiver should be able to write information down without having to replay your message.
- **Be careful with confidential information.** Don't leave confidential or private information in a voice mail message. Remember that anyone could gain access to this information.
- **Don't make assumptions.** If you don't receive a call back within a day or two after leaving a message, don't get angry or frustrated. Assume that the message wasn't delivered or that it couldn't be understood. Call back and leave another message, or send the person an e-mail.

## 11-4 Adding Value to Professional Teams

**LEARNING OBJECTIVE 4**
Understand the importance of teamwork in today's digital-era workplace, and explain how you can contribute positively to team performance.

As we discussed in Chapter 1, the workplace is changing. Collaboration is the rule today. As reported in a *BusinessWeek* study, a majority of white-collar professionals (82 percent) need to partner with others to complete their work.[23] Similarly, research by design company Gensler shows that the 2,000 knowledge workers surveyed nationally spent on average about 20 percent of their time collaborating.[24] Workers collaborate not only at their desks but also informally in hallways and unassigned work spaces or in rooms equipped with the latest teleconferencing tools. Many connect remotely with their smart electronic devices. Needless to say, solid soft skills rule in face-to-face as well as far-flung teams.

Teams can be effective in solving problems and in developing new products. Take, for example, the hugely successful collaboration between NASA and private aerospace company SpaceX in developing the PICA heat shield for SpaceX's Dragon spacecraft. The two organizations couldn't be more different, yet they capitalized on their respective strengths. NASA provided its expertise and testing facilities while SpaceX, with its characteristic speed and efficiency, completed the design and manufacture of the heat shield in less than four years.[25] Even critics of teamwork don't deny that organizations will most likely continue to rely on teams.[26]

Chapter 11: Professionalism at Work: Business Etiquette, Ethics, Teamwork, and Meetings

## 11-4a Understanding Teams and the Four Phases of Team Development

Today's workplace is teeming with teams. You might find yourself a part of a work team, project team, customer support team, supplier team, design team, planning team, functional team, cross-functional team, or some other group. All of these teams are formed to accomplish specific goals.

It's no secret that one of the most important objectives of businesses is finding ways to do jobs better at less cost. This objective helps explain the popularity of teams, which are formed for the following reasons:

- **Better decisions.** Decisions are generally more accurate and effective because group and team members contribute different expertise and perspectives.
- **Faster responses.** When action is necessary to respond to competition or to solve a problem, small groups and teams can act rapidly.
- **Increased productivity.** Because they are often closer to the action and to the customer, team members can see opportunities for improving efficiency.
- **Greater buy-in.** Decisions arrived at jointly are usually better received because members are committed to the solution and are more willing to support it.
- **Less resistance to change.** People who have input into decisions are less hostile, aggressive, and resistant to change.
- **Improved employee morale.** Personal satisfaction and job morale increase when teams are successful.
- **Reduced risks.** Responsibility for a decision is diffused, thus carrying less risk for any individual.

Regardless of their specific purpose, teams normally go through predictable phases as they develop. The psychologist B. A. Tuckman identified four phases: *forming*, *storming*, *norming*, and *performing*, as Figure 11.4 illustrates.[27] Some groups move quickly from *forming* to *performing*. Other teams may never reach the final stage of *performing*. However, most struggle through disruptive, although ultimately constructive, team-building stages.

## 11-4b Collaborating in Virtual Teams

Today you can expect to collaborate with coworkers in other cities and even in other countries. Such collaborations are referred to as *virtual teams*. This is a group of people who, aided by information technology, must accomplish shared tasks

Figure 11.4 Four Phases of Team Development in Decision Making

**Forming**
- Select members.
- Become acquainted.
- Build trust.
- Form collaborative culture.

**Storming**
- Identify problems.
- Collect and share information.
- Establish decision criteria.
- Prioritize goals.

**Norming**
- Discuss alternatives.
- Evaluate outcomes.
- Apply criteria.
- Prioritize alternatives.

**Performing**
- Select alternative.
- Analyze effects.
- Implement plan.
- Manage project.

## Office Insider

"People exposed to a diversity of information are at higher risk of seeing a new angle, a better way to frame ideas." Companies that harness such social capital "have better growth rates and better patent rates."

—Ronald S. Burt, sociologist, University of Chicago

largely without face-to-face contact across geographic boundaries, sometimes on different continents and across time zones.[28] Virtual teams have greater autonomy and require members who are more self-reliant than *co-located workers* are.[29]

Although Yahoo and Best Buy have recently reversed their acclaimed work-at-home policies, virtual teams are here to stay—for example, at SAP. Headquartered in Walldorf, Germany, software corporation SAP has established research and development centers in India, China, Israel, and the United States to save costs and to take advantage of global know-how. Each unit is highly specialized. Depending on the competence needed, virtual teams form and pool their expertise to complete particular assignments.[30] In the digital age, work is increasingly viewed as *what you do* rather than a place you go.

In some organizations, remote coworkers may be permanent employees from the same office or may be specialists called together for temporary projects. Regardless of the assignment, virtual teams can benefit from shared views, skills, and diversity.

### 11-4c Identifying Positive and Negative Team Behavior

How can you be a high-performing team member? Show your commitment to achieving the group's purpose by displaying positive behavior. For example, the most effective groups have members who are willing to establish rules and abide by them. They help to resolve differences and encourage a warm, supportive climate by praising and agreeing with others. When agreement is near, they move the group toward its goal by summarizing points of understanding. These and other positive traits are shown in Figure 11.5.

Not all groups, however, have members who contribute positively. Negative behavior is shown by those who constantly put down the ideas and suggestions of others. They may waste the group's time with unnecessary recounting of personal achievements or irrelevant topics. Also disturbing are team members who withdraw and refuse to be drawn out. To be a productive and welcome member of a work group, avoid the negative behaviors presented in Figure 11.5.

### 11-4d Defining Successful Teams

The use of teams has been called the solution to many ills in the current workplace.[31] Someone even observed that as an acronym TEAM means "Together, Everyone Achieves More."[32] However, teams that don't work well can actually increase frustration, lower productivity, and create employee dissatisfaction. Experts who have

Figure 11.5  Positive and Negative Group Behaviors

**Positive Group Behaviors**
- Setting rules and abiding by them
- Analyzing tasks and defining problems
- Contributing information and ideas
- Showing interest by listening actively
- Encouraging members to participate

**Negative Group Behaviors**
- Blocking the ideas of others
- Insulting and criticizing others
- Wasting the group's time
- Making improper jokes and comments
- Failing to stay on task
- Withdrawing, failing to participate

studied team dynamics and decisions have discovered that effective teams share some or all of the following characteristics.

**Stay Small and Embrace Diversity.** Teams may range from 2 to 25 members, although 4 or 5 is an optimal number for many projects. Larger groups have trouble interacting constructively, much less agreeing on actions.[33] Jeff Bezos, chairman and CEO of Amazon.com, reportedly said: "If you can't feed a team with two pizzas, the size of the team is too large."[34] Teams smaller than ten members tend to agree more easily on a common objective and form more cohesive units.[35] For the most creative decisions, teams generally have male and female members who differ in age, ethnicity, social background, training, and experience. The key business advantage of diversity is the ability to view a project from multiple perspectives. Many organizations are finding that diverse teams can produce innovative solutions with broader applications than homogeneous teams can.

**Agree on a Purpose.** An effective team begins with a purpose. Working from a general purpose to specific goals typically requires a huge investment of time and effort. Meaningful discussions, however, motivate team members to buy in to the project. When the Great Lakes Coast Guard faced the task of keeping commerce moving when the lakes and rivers froze, it brought all the stakeholders together to discuss the mission. The U.S. Coast Guard, the Canadian Coast Guard, and the maritime industry formed a partnership to clear and flush ice from the Great Lakes and connecting rivers during winter months. Agreeing on the purpose was the first step in developing a concerted team effort. Preseason planning and daily phone conferences cemented the mission and gained buy-in from all stakeholders.[36]

**Agree on Procedures.** The best teams develop procedures to guide them. They set up intermediate goals with deadlines. They assign roles and tasks, requiring all members to contribute equivalent amounts of real work. They decide how they will reach decisions, whether by majority vote, reaching consensus, or other methods. Procedures are continually evaluated to ensure movement toward the attainment of the team's goals.

**Confront Conflict.** Poorly functioning teams avoid conflict, preferring sulking, gossiping, or backstabbing. A better plan is to acknowledge conflict and address the root of the problem openly using the six-step plan outlined in Figure 11.6. Although it may feel emotionally risky, direct confrontation saves time and enhances team commitment in the long run. To be constructive, however, confrontation must be task oriented, not person oriented. An open airing of differences, in which all team members have a chance to speak their minds, should center on the

> **OFFICE INSIDER**
>
> "In order to foster more constructive conflict and feedback, remind your team and your colleagues about Don Corleone's [The Godfather] admonition that 'it's not personal, it's business.' Doing this will reinforce the notion that we can disagree about ideas and strategies, but still respect and like each other."
>
> —Ron Askenas, partner at Schaffer Consulting; Lisa Bodell, founder-CEO of FutureThink

Figure 11.6 Six Steps for Dealing With Conflict

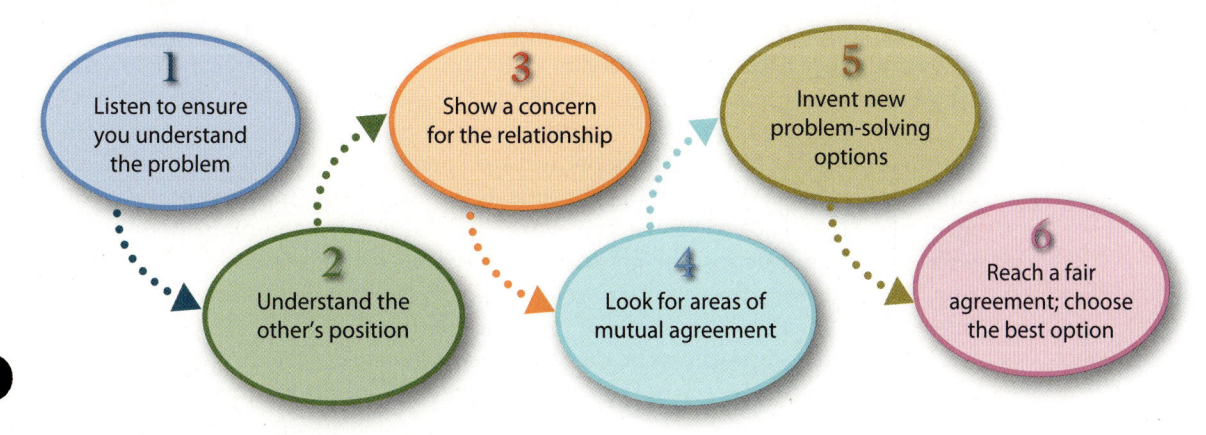

1. Listen to ensure you understand the problem
2. Understand the other's position
3. Show a concern for the relationship
4. Look for areas of mutual agreement
5. Invent new problem-solving options
6. Reach a fair agreement; choose the best option

Chapter 11: Professionalism at Work: Business Etiquette, Ethics, Teamwork, and Meetings

## OFFICE INSIDER

"'Mindful Meetings' are productive meetings with clear purpose and objectives, that involve the right people at the right time, and that use proven techniques to get the most out of the time invested. They don't happen by accident—key ingredients are preparation, good facilitation, balanced thinking, good recordkeeping, and appropriate follow-up."

—Janice Francisco, change facilitator and founder of BridgePoint Effect

strengths and weaknesses of the various positions and ideas—not on personalities. After hearing all sides, team members must negotiate a fair settlement, no matter how long it takes.

**Communicate Effectively.** The best teams exchange information and contribute ideas freely in an informal environment often facilitated by technology. Team members speak and write clearly and concisely, avoiding generalities. They encourage feedback. Listeners become actively involved, read body language, and ask clarifying questions before responding. Tactful, constructive disagreement is encouraged. Although a team's task is taken seriously, successful teams are able to inject humor into their interactions.

**Collaborate Rather Than Compete.** Effective team members are genuinely interested in achieving team goals instead of receiving individual recognition. They contribute ideas and feedback unselfishly. They monitor team progress, including what is going right, what is going wrong, and what to do about it. They celebrate individual and team accomplishments.

**Accept Ethical Responsibilities.** Teams as a whole have ethical responsibilities to their members, to their larger organizations, and to society. Members have a number of specific responsibilities to each other. As a whole, teams have a responsibility to represent the organization's view and respect its privileged information. They should not discuss with outsiders any sensitive issues without permission. In addition, teams have a broader obligation to avoid advocating actions that would endanger members of society at large.

**Share Leadership.** Effective teams often have no formal leader. Instead, leadership rotates to those with the appropriate expertise as the team evolves and moves from one phase to another. Many teams operate under a democratic approach. This approach can achieve buy-in to team decisions, boost morale, and create fewer hurt feelings and less resentment. In times of crisis, however, a strong team member may need to step up as a leader.

The skills that make you a valuable and ethical team player will serve you well when you run or participate in professional meetings.

**LEARNING OBJECTIVE 5**

Discuss effective practices and technologies for planning and participating in productive face-to-face meetings and virtual meetings.

## 11-5 Planning and Participating in Face-to-Face and Virtual Meetings

Business meetings consist of three or more people who assemble to pool information, solicit feedback, clarify policy, seek consensus, and solve problems. However, as growing numbers of employees work at distant locations, meetings have changed. Workers cannot always meet face-to-face. To be able to exchange information effectively and efficiently, you will need to know how to plan and participate in face-to-face as well as *virtual meetings*.

As you prepare to join the workforce, expect to attend meetings—lots of them! Estimates suggest that workers on average spend four hours a week in meetings and consider more than half of that time as wasted.[37] One business reporter called meetings "the black holes of the workday"[38]; another complained that "long-winded colleagues consume all available oxygen, killing good ideas by asphyxiation."[39] However, if meetings are well run, workers actually desire more, not fewer, of them.[40]

Moreover, meetings can be career-critical. Instead of treating them as thieves of your valuable time, try to see meetings as golden opportunities to demonstrate your leadership, communication, and problem-solving skills. To help you make the most of these opportunities, this section outlines best practices for running and contributing to successful meetings.

## 11-5a Preparing for the Meeting

A face-to-face meeting provides the most nonverbal cues and other signals that help us interpret the intended meaning of words. Thus, an in-person meeting is the richest of available media. Yet meetings are also costly, draining the productivity of all participants. If you are in charge of a meeting, determine your purpose, decide how and where to meet, choose the participants, invite them using a digital calendar, and organize an agenda.

**Determining the Purpose of the Meeting.** No meeting should be called unless it is important, can't wait, and requires an exchange of ideas. In a global poll, 77 percent of respondents stated that they preferred face-to-face meetings for deal-making and mission-critical decisions; however, more than two thirds liked to brainstorm and discuss complex technical concepts in person.[41]

If people are merely being informed, it's best to send an e-mail, text message, or memo. Pick up the phone or leave a voice mail message, but don't call a costly meeting. To decide whether the purpose of the meeting is valid, consult the key people who will be attending. Ask them what outcomes they desire and how to achieve those goals. This consultation also sets a collaborative tone and encourages full participation.

**Deciding How and Where to Meet.** Once you are sure that a meeting is necessary, you must decide whether to meet face-to-face or virtually. If you decide to meet in person, reserve a conference room. If you decide to meet virtually, select the appropriate media and make any necessary arrangements for your voice conference, videoconference, or Web conference. These communication technologies are discussed in Chapter 1.

**Selecting Meeting Participants.** The purpose of the meeting determines the number of participants, as shown in Figure 11.7. If the meeting purpose is motivational, such as an awards ceremony for sales reps of cosmetics giant Avon, then the number of participants is potentially unlimited. However, for high-stakes decisions, consultants recommend limiting the session to three to six key executives.[43] Other meetings may require a greater circle of stakeholders and those who will implement the decision. Let's consider Timberland's signature employee volunteer program. Company leaders might meet with managers, employee representatives, and community leaders to decide how best to "green" a community center, improve school grounds, or frame houses for families of tornado victims.[44]

## Workplace in Focus

While meetings rank high on employee lists of top time-killers at work, respected business leaders take action to never let a meeting go to waste. Amazon's Jeff Bezos places an empty chair at meetings to represent the customer's place in the room. Virgin Group founder Richard Branson stages meetings in nontraditional spaces—like poolside or at a park—to foster creativity. Stanford management professor Bob Sutton holds "stand up" meetings without chairs to keep gatherings brief and on-point. Former Apple chief Steve Jobs ejected individuals from meetings to weed out unnecessary participants. What other steps can managers take to make meetings more effective?[42]

Figure 11.7 Meeting Purpose and Number of Participants

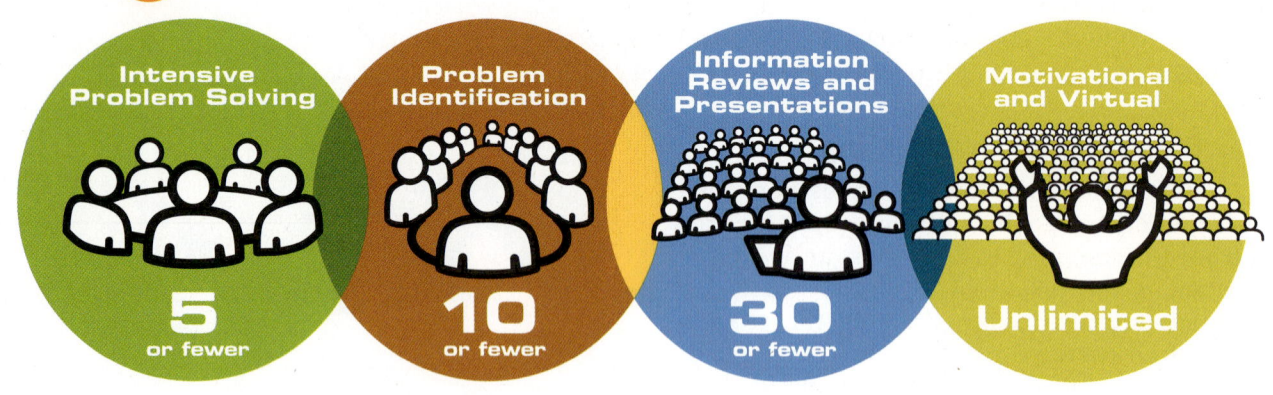

**Intensive Problem Solving** — 5 or fewer

**Problem Identification** — 10 or fewer

**Information Reviews and Presentations** — 30 or fewer

**Motivational and Virtual** — Unlimited

**Using Digital Calendars to Schedule Meetings.** Finding a time when everyone can meet is often difficult. Fortunately, digital calendars now make the task quicker and more efficient. Popular programs are Google Calendar, Apple Calendar, and the business favorite, Outlook Calendar, shown in Figure 11.8. Online calendars and mobile apps enable users to make appointments, schedule meetings, and keep track of daily activities. To schedule meetings, you enter a new meeting request and add the names of attendees. You select a date, enter a start and end time, and list the meeting subject and location. Then the meeting request goes to each attendee. Later you check the attendee availability tab to see a list of all meeting attendees. As the meeting time approaches, the program automatically sends reminders to attendees.

Figure 11.8 Using Calendar Programs

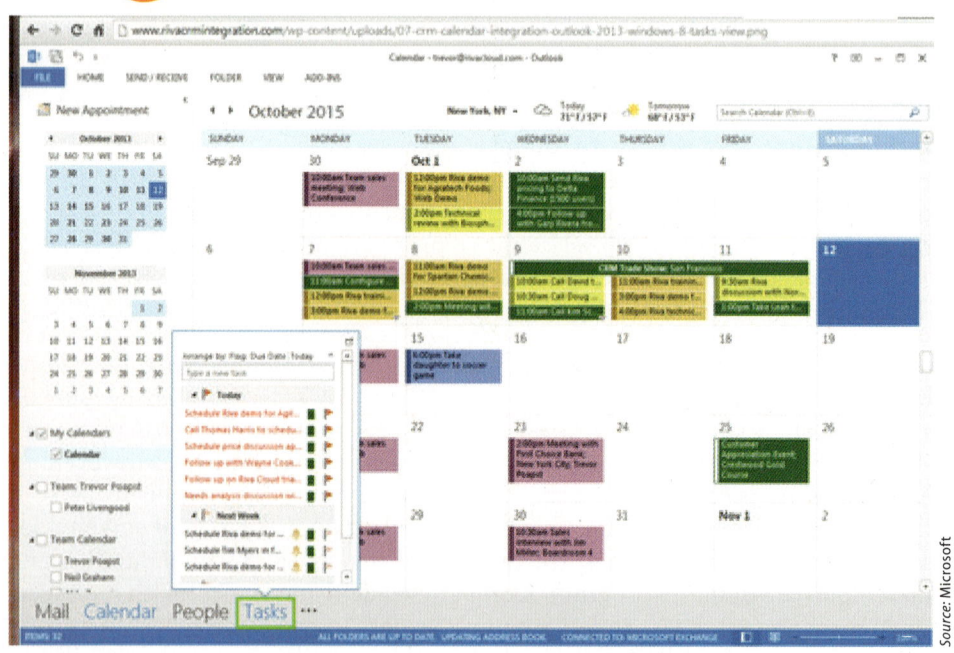

*Source: Microsoft*

370     Chapter 11: Professionalism at Work: Business Etiquette, Ethics, Teamwork, and Meetings

**Distributing an Agenda and Other Information.** At least two days before a meeting, distribute an agenda of topics to be discussed. Also include any reports or materials that participants should read in advance. For continuing groups, you might also include a copy of the minutes of the previous meeting. To keep meetings productive, limit the number of agenda items. Remember, the narrower the focus, the greater the chances for success. A good agenda, as illustrated in Figure 11.9, covers the following information:

- Date and place of meeting
- Start time and end time
- Brief description of each topic, in order of priority, including names of individuals who are responsible for performing some action
- Proposed allotment of time for each topic
- Any premeeting preparation expected of participants

### 11-5b Managing the Meeting

Whether you are the meeting leader or a participant, it is important to act professionally during the meeting. Meetings can be more efficient and productive if leaders and participants recognize how to get the meeting started, establish ground rules, move the meeting along, and handle conflict.

**Getting Started and Establishing Ground Rules.** Even if some participants are missing, start meetings promptly to avoid wasting time and irritating attendees. For

Figure 11.9 Typical Meeting Agenda

```
                        AGENDA
               Quantum Travel International
                      Staff Meeting
                    September 4, 2016
                       10 to 11 a.m.
                     Conference Room

   I.  Call to order; roll call

   II. Approval of agenda

   III. Approval of minutes from previous meeting

                                  Person        Proposed Time
   IV. Committee reports
       A. Website update          Jared         5 minutes
       B. Tour packages           Lakisha       10 minutes

   V.  Old business
       A. Equipment maintenance   John          5 minutes
       B. Client escrow accounts  Alicia        5 minutes
       C. Internal newsletter     Adrienne      5 minutes

   VI. New business
       A. New accounts            Garth         5 minutes
       B. Pricing policy for Asian tours  Minh  15 minutes

   VII. Announcements

   VIII. Chair's summary, adjournment
```

> **OFFICE INSIDER**
>
> "In many ways, leading a meeting is like juggling. A good leader keeps the balls in the air, stays focused, makes it a little entertaining, and ends with a big finish. Taking responsibility for this role is half the battle in leading good meetings. Remember, everyone wants somebody to lead."
>
> —Suzanne Bates, consultant and author of *Speak Like a CEO*

the same reasons, don't give quick recaps to latecomers. Open the meeting with a three- to five-minute introduction that includes the following:

- Goal and length of the meeting
- Background of topics or problems
- Possible solutions and constraints
- Tentative agenda
- Ground rules to be followed

Typical ground rules include communicating openly, being supportive, listening carefully, participating fully, confronting conflict frankly, silencing cell phones and other digital devices, and following the agenda. More formal groups follow parliamentary procedures based on Robert's Rules. The next step is to assign one participant to take minutes and one to act as a recorder. The recorder uses a computer and projector or stands at a flipchart or whiteboard to list the main ideas being discussed and agreements reached.

**Moving the Meeting Along.** An effective leader lets others talk and tries to involve all participants. Remember that the purpose of a meeting is to exchange views, not to hear one person, even the leader, do all the talking. If the group has one member who dominates, the leader might say, *Thanks, Gary, for that perspective, but please hold your next point while we hear how Rachel would respond to that*. To draw in reticent attendees, be positive, restate important points, and thank them for contributing. Ask people directly but kindly for input: *Do you have anything you wish to share?*[45]

To avoid allowing digressions to sidetrack the group, try generating a "parking lot" list. This is a list of important but divergent issues that should be discussed later. Another way to handle digressions is to say, *Folks, we are getting sidetracked here. Please forgive me for pressing on, but let's go back to the central issue of...* It is important to adhere to the agenda and the schedule. Equally important, when the group seems to have reached a consensus, is to summarize the group's position and see whether everyone agrees.

**Handling Conflict in Meetings.** As you learned earlier, conflict is natural and even desirable. However, it can also cause awkwardness and uneasiness. In meetings, conflict typically develops when people feel unheard or misunderstood. If two people clash, the best approach is to encourage each to make a complete case while group members give their full attention. Let each one question the other. Then, the leader should summarize what was said, and the participants should offer comments. The group may modify a recommendation or suggest alternatives before reaching consensus on a direction to follow.

### 11-5c Concluding the Meeting and Following Up

End the meeting at the agreed time or sooner. The leader should summarize all decisions, assigned tasks, and deadlines. It may be necessary to ask attendees to volunteer for completing action items. All participants should understand what was accomplished. One effective technique that encourages participation is "round-robin." Each person takes turns summarizing briefly his or her interpretation of what was decided and what happens next. Of course, this closure technique works best with smaller groups. The leader should conclude by asking the group to set a time for the next meeting. He or she should assure the group that a report will follow. Finally, the leader should thank participants for attending.

If minutes were taken, they should be distributed within a couple of days of the meeting. Meeting management programs and mobile apps enable you to follow a structured template such as that shown in Figure 11.10, which includes brief meeting minutes, key points and decisions, and action items. The leader needs to ensure that

Figure 11.10 E-Mail Meeting Minutes

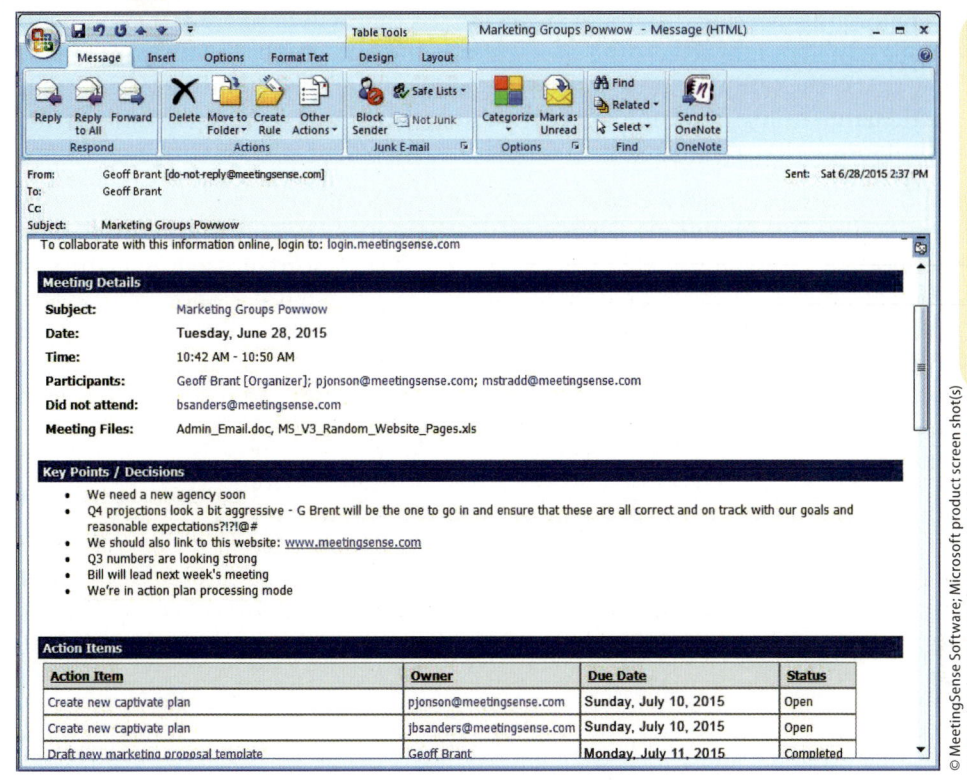

Meeting proceedings are efficiently recorded in a summary distribution template that provides subject, date, time, participant names, absentee names, meeting documents and files, key points, decisions, and action items.

decisions are executed. The leader may need to call participants to remind them of their assignments and also to solicit help if necessary.

### 11-5d Preparing for Virtual Meetings

Virtual meetings are real-time gatherings of dispersed participants who connect with communication technology. As travel costs rise and companies slash budgets, many organizations are cutting back on meetings that require travel.[46] Instead, they may meet in audioconferences using telephones or in videoconferences using the Internet. Steady improvements in telecommunications networks, software applications, and bandwidth continue to fuel the shift to virtual meetings. Like in-person meetings, virtual gatherings have many purposes, including training employees, making sales presentations, coordinating team activities, and talking to customers.

Saving travel costs and reducing employee fatigue are significant reasons for the digital displacement of business travel. Darryl Draper, a Subaru customer service training manager, estimates that when she traveled nine months out of the year, she reached about 100 people every six months at a cost of $300 a person. Thanks to virtual technology, she now reaches 2,500 people every six months at a cost of 75 cents a person.[47]

The following best practices recommended by experienced meeting facilitators will help you address premeeting issues such as technology glitches, scheduling across time zones, and language challenges.[48]

**Dealing With Technology.** To conduct successful virtual meetings or teleconferences, select the most appropriate technology. Be sure that everyone is able to participate fully using that technology. If someone can't see what is happening on screen, the entire meeting can be disrupted and delayed. Some participants may need coaching before the session begins. Figure 11.11 depicts a virtual design meeting and explains how Web conferencing works.

Before the meeting distribute any materials that will be shared. If documents will be edited or marked during the meeting, find out whether participants know how to use the online editing tools. To avoid panic at the last minute, encourage participants to log in 15 minutes early. Some programs require downloads and installations that can cause immense frustration and disruptions if not done early.

**Respecting the Needs of Dispersed Participants.** When setting the time of the meeting, use Coordinated Universal Time (UTC) so that group members in different time zones are not confused. Be particularly mindful of how the meeting schedule affects others. Avoid spanning a lunch hour, holding someone overtime, or making someone arrive extra early. However, virtual meetings across multiple time zones may inevitably disadvantage some participants. To be fair to all group members, rotate your meeting time so that everyone shares the burden of an inconvenient time.[49]

For global meetings decide what language you will use. If that language may be difficult for some participants, think about using simple expressions and repeating major ideas. Always follow up in writing.

### 11-5e Interacting Professionally in Virtual Meetings

Although the same good meeting management techniques discussed for face-to-face meetings prevail, additional skills and practices are important in virtual meetings. Creating ground rules, anticipating limited media richness, managing turn-taking, and humanizing the interaction with remote members all achieve the best results during virtual meetings.

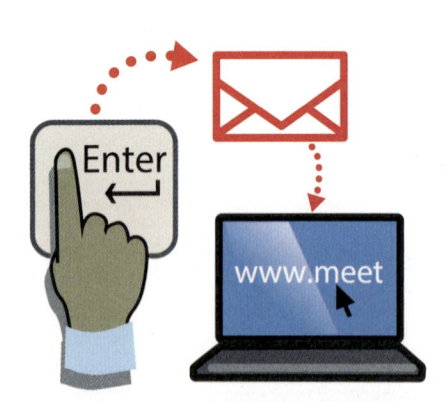

Figure 11.11 Understanding Web Conferencing

**1. E-Mail Contact:** Alan T., president of Sportster Marketing, an athletic gear company in Seattle, WA, sends an email to Meghan R., chief designer at NexxtDesign in Venice, CA, to discuss a new sports watch. The e-mail includes meeting date and time and a link to launch the session.

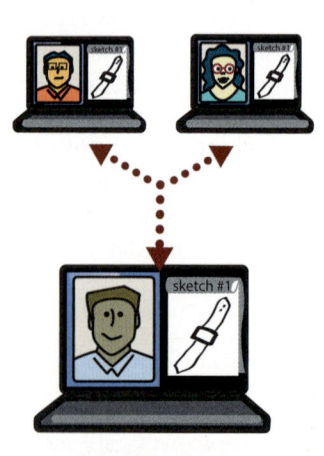

**2. Virtual Meeting:** When the Web conference begins, participants see live video of each other's faces on their screens. They look at photos of sports watches, share ideas, sketch designs on a shared "virtual whiteboard," and review contract terms.

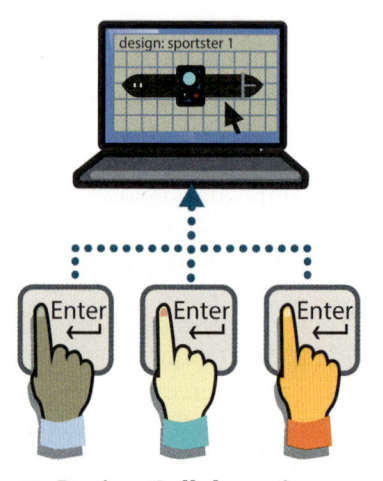

**3. Design Collaboration:** NexxtDesign artists and Sportster Marketing managers use peer-to-peer software that allows them to share spaces on each other's computers. The software enables them to take turns modifying the designs, and it also tracks all the changes.

**Establishing Ground Rules for Virtual Meetings.** Before beginning, explain how questions may be asked and answered. Many meeting programs allow participants to "raise their hands" with an icon on a side panel of the computer screen. Then they can type in their question for the leader and others to see. Unless the meeting involves people who know each other well, participants in audioconferences should always say their names before beginning to comment.

One of the biggest problems of virtual meetings is background noise from participants' offices or homes. You might hear dogs barking, telephones ringing, and toilets flushing. Meeting planners disagree on whether to require participants to put their phones on mute. Although the mute button reduces noise, it also prevents immediate participation and tends to deaden the conference. Remind the group to silence all electronic alerts and alarms.

As a personal ground rule, don't multitask—and that includes texting and checking e-mail—during virtual meetings. Giving your full attention is critical.

**Anticipating the Limitations of Virtual Technology.** Collaborating successfully in virtual meetings requires that you learn to manage limitations. Audioconferences in particular lack the richness that nonverbal cues provide during in-person meetings. Therefore, any small infraction or miscue can be blown out of proportion; words and tone can be easily misinterpreted. For example, when individuals meet face-to-face, they usually can recognize blank looks when people do not understand something being discussed. However, in virtual meetings participants and presenters cannot always see each other. "[Participants] will lose place, lose focus, and lose attention to the meeting," one meeting expert noted.[50] He also warned that participants won't tell you if they are lost.

As a result, when presenting ideas at a virtual meeting, you should be as precise as possible. Give examples and use simple language. Recap and summarize often. Confirm your understanding of what is being discussed. If you are a presenter, project an upbeat, enthusiastic, and strong voice. Without eye contact and nonverbal cues, the best way to keep the attention of the audience is through a powerful voice.

**Managing Turn-Taking and Other Meeting Procedures.** To encourage participation and avoid traffic jams with everyone talking at once, experts suggest a number of techniques. Participants soon lose interest if the leader is the only one talking. Therefore, encourage dialogue by asking questions of specific people. Often you will learn not only what the person is thinking but also what others feel but have not stated.

To elicit participation, go through the list of participants inviting each to speak for 30 seconds without interruption. If individuals have nothing to say, they may pass when their names are called. Leaders should avoid asking vague and leading questions such as *Does everyone agree?* Remote attendees cannot answer easily without drowning out each other's responses.

**Humanizing Virtual Meetings.** The technology we use to connect with far-flung coworkers can be impersonal and alienating. One final suggestion involves building camaraderie and trust. For teams with distant members, it helps to leave time before or after the scheduled meeting for small talk. A few moments of chat build personal bonds and establish a warm environment. Even with larger, unfamiliar groups, you can build trust and interest by dialing in early and greeting others as they join the group.

Virtual meetings are the wave of the future. Learning to plan and participate in them professionally will enhance your career as a business communicator.

# SUMMARY OF LEARNING OBJECTIVES

**11-1** Understand professionalism, start developing business etiquette skills, and build an ethical mindset—important qualities digital-age employers seek.

- Professionalism, good business etiquette, developed soft skills, social intelligence, polish, and civility are desirable workplace behaviors that are complemented by a positive online presence.
- Employers most want employees who can prioritize their work, work in teams, and exhibit a positive attitude in addition to displaying good workplace manners and other interpersonal skills.
- Professionalism means having integrity and being ethical; experts believe that no sharp distinction between ethics and etiquette exists. We should always treat others with respect.
- Practicing business etiquette on the job and online can put you ahead of others who lack polish.

**11-2** Use your voice as a communication tool, master face-to-face workplace interaction, foster positive relations on the job, and accept as well as provide constructive criticism gracefully.

- In-person communication is the richest communication channel; use your voice effectively by honing your pronunciation, voice quality, pitch, volume and rate, and emphasis.
- To excel in face-to-face conversations, use correct names and titles, choose appropriate topics, be positive, listen to learn, give sincere praise, and act professionally in social situations.
- When receiving criticism, avoid interrupting, paraphrase what you are hearing, agree if the criticism is accurate, disagree respectfully, look for compromise, and learn from criticism.
- When criticizing, plan your remarks, do it in person, focus on improvement, offer help, be specific, use the word *we*, encourage two-way communication, stay calm, and keep it private.

**11-3** Practice professional telephone skills and polish your voice mail etiquette.

- When calling, follow an agenda, use a three-point introduction, be brisk, try to sound cheerful, be professional and courteous, avoid phone tag, and leave complete voice mail messages.
- When answering, be courteous, identify yourself, be helpful, be cautious when answering calls for others, be respectful when putting people on hold, and explain why you are transferring calls.
- Practice smartphone etiquette by being considerate, observing quiet areas, using your indoor voice, taking only urgent calls, not calling or texting while driving, and choosing a professional ringtone.
- Prepare a friendly voice mail greeting and respond to messages promptly; as a caller, plan your message, be concise, watch your tone, speak slowly, and don't leave sensitive information.

**11-4** Understand the importance of teamwork in today's digital-era workplace, and explain how you can contribute positively to team performance.

- Teams are popular because they lead to better decisions, faster responses, increased productivity, greater buy-in, less resistance, improved morale, and reduced risks.
- The four phases of team development are forming, storming, norming, and performing.
- Virtual teams are collaborations among remote coworkers connecting with technology.
- Positive group behaviors include establishing and following rules, resolving differences, being supportive, praising others, and summarizing points of understanding.
- Negative behaviors include having contempt for others, wasting the team's time, and withdrawing.
- Successful teams are small and diverse, agree on a purpose and procedures, confront conflict, communicate well, don't compete but collaborate, are ethical, and share leadership.

**11-5** Discuss effective practices and technologies for planning and participating in productive face-to-face meetings and virtual meetings.

- Before a meeting businesspeople determine its purpose and location, choose participants, use a digital calendar, and distribute an agenda.
- Experienced meeting leaders move the meeting along and confront any conflict; they end the meeting on time, make sure everyone is heard, and distribute meeting minutes promptly.
- Virtual meetings save travel costs but require attention to communication technology and to the needs of dispersed participants regarding issues such as different time zones and language barriers.
- Virtual meetings demand specific procedures to handle questions, noise, lack of media richness, and turn-taking. Because they are impersonal, virtual meetings benefit from building camaraderie and trust.

## CHAPTER REVIEW

1. Is incivility common in the workplace? What might be its costs? (Obj. 1)

2. Define the five traits and skills listed in the chapter that demonstrate professionalism. (Obj. 1)

3. Explain the advantages of face-to-face conversation over other communication channels. (Obj. 2)

4. Why is voice an important communication tool, and how can businesspeople use it effectively? (Obj. 2)

5. How can you ensure that your telephone calls on the job are productive? Name at least six suggestions. (Obj. 3)

6. List at least five tips for receiving telephone calls professionally. (Obj. 3)

7. What are some of the reasons for the popularity of workplace teams? List at least five. (Obj. 4)

Chapter 11: Professionalism at Work: Business Etiquette, Ethics, Teamwork, and Meetings

8. Name the four phases of team development as identified by psychologist B. A. Tuckman, and explain what happens in each stage. (Obj. 4)

9. What is the best approach to address conflict in meetings? (Obj. 5)

10. What techniques can make virtual meetings as effective as face-to-face meetings? (Obj. 5)

# CRITICAL THINKING

11. Why is it particularly important to develop and maintain a professional, businesslike reputation in the knowledge-based economy of the digital era? (Obj. 1)
12. Think of typical workplace situations and how you might communicate in each. When would you seek an in-person conversation, pick up the phone, call a virtual meeting, or send an e-mail, IM, or text? (Objs. 1–5)
13. Try to recall situations in which you were criticized or dished out criticism yourself. Was the criticism constructive? Why or why not? How did you feel either as a giver or receiver of criticism? (Obj. 2)
14. Describe the advantages of face-to-face communication as opposed to interactions facilitated by technology such as telephones, e-mail, instant messaging, texting, the Web, social networking sites, and so on. When is face-to-face communication more effective? (Objs. 2, 3)
15. After much discussion and even conflict, your workplace team has finally agreed on Plan B, but you are firmly convinced that Plan A is a much better option. Your team is presenting Plan B to the whole department, and company executives are present. A vice president asks you for your opinion. Should you (a) keep your mouth shut, (b) try to persuade the team to adopt Plan A, (c) explain why you believe Plan A is a better plan, (d) tell the VP and all present that Plan B is not your idea, or (e) discuss one or two points you can agree on in Plan B? (Objs. 1, 4, and 5)

# ACTIVITIES AND CASES

## 11.1 Researching Professional Workplace Skills and Presenting Annotated Sources (Obj. 1)
**Team | Web**

You have seen that many definitions for *professionalism* exist. Recently, an opportunity to practice your research skills has arisen when your boss was invited to make a presentation to a group of human relations officers. He asked you and a small group of fellow interns to help him find articles about professionalism, soft skills, social intelligence, and other interpersonal qualities.

**YOUR TASK.** As a team, divide your research in such a way that each intern is responsible for one or two search terms, depending on the size of your group. Look for articles with definitions of *professionalism, business etiquette, civility, business ethics, social skills, soft skills,* and *social intelligence*. Find at least three useful articles for each search term. If you get bogged down in your research, consult with a business librarian on campus or report to your instructor. After compiling your findings, as a team, present your annotated works-cited list in an informational memo report to your boss, Ted Rollins.

## 11.2 Investigating Soft Skills: Employer Wish List (Obj. 1)
`Communication Technology` `Social Media` `Team` `Web`

What soft skills do employers request when they list job openings in your field?

**YOUR TASK.** Individually or in teams, check the listings at an online job board such as Monster, CollegeRecruiter, CareerBuilder, or CollegeGrad. Follow the instructions to search job categories and locations. Also check college resources and local newspaper listings of job openings. Find five or more listings in your field. Print or otherwise save the results of your search. Examine the skills requested. How often do the ads mention communication, teamwork, and computer skills? What tasks do the ads mention? Discuss your findings with your team members. Then prepare a list of the most frequently requested soft skills. Your instructor may ask you to submit your findings and/or report to the class. If you are not satisfied with the job selection at any job board, choose ads posted on websites of companies you admire or on LinkedIn.

## 11.3 Soft Skills: Personal Strengths Inventory (Obj. 1)

When hiring future workers, employers look for hard skills, which are those we learn, such as mastery of software applications or accountancy procedures, as well as soft skills. Soft skills are personal characteristics, strengths, and other assets a person possesses.

Studies have divided soft skills into four categories:

Thinking and problem solving

Oral and written communication

Personal qualities and work ethic

Interpersonal and teamwork

**YOUR TASK.** Using the preceding categories to guide you, identify your own soft skills, paying attention to attributes you think a potential employer would value. Prepare a list of at least four items for each of the four categories. For example, as evidence of problem solving, you might list a specific workplace or student problem you recognized and solved. You will want to weave these words and phrases into cover letters and résumés, which are covered in Chapter 13.

## 11.4 Making Concessions on the Job (Obj. 1)

Consider this statement from a young respondent in a recent survey of ethical decision making among young public relations professionals:

> At this point in my life, a job is a job, and in terms of ethics, I'll do what I have to do to keep my job; my personal feelings will take a back seat. With the economy so bad, it's just one of those things. I can't afford to let my personal feelings complicate my career.[51]

Do you agree that personal ethics must not get in the way of one's career? Under what circumstances would you hold your tongue and keep your head down at work?

**YOUR TASK.** Discuss this view with your classmates and instructor in light of what you have read in this chapter about ethics and etiquette.

## 11.5 Testing Your Voice Quality (Obj. 2)
`Team`

Recording your voice gives you a chance to learn how your voice sounds to others and provides an opportunity for you to improve its effectiveness. Don't be surprised if you fail to recognize your own voice or if it sounds strange to your ears.

**YOUR TASK.** Record yourself reading a newspaper or magazine article.
a. If you think your voice sounds a bit high, practice speaking slightly lower.
b. If your voice is low or expressionless, practice speaking slightly louder and with more inflection.
c. Ask a colleague, teacher, or friend to provide feedback on your pronunciation, pitch, volume, rate, and professional tone.

## 11.6 Choosing Communication Channels: How Rich Must the Media Be? (Obj. 2)

**Communication Technology** | **E-mail** | **Social Media**

**YOUR TASK.** First decide whether the following messages need to be communicated orally or in writing. After consulting the media richness diagram in Figure 11.2 on page 356, consider how rich the medium must be in each communication situation to convey the message most appropriately and reliably. Your choices can include e-mail, a letter, a report, texting, instant messaging, a telephone call, a live chat, teleconferencing, a face-to-face conversation, and a team meeting. Describe the advantages and disadvantages of each choice.

a. You are returning from a client visit to company headquarters, where you must attend an important department meeting. It looks as though you will be at least 15 minutes late. What are your options?
b. Working at 8 a.m. in your Boston office, you need to get in touch with your counterpart at your company's West Coast office and ask a few clarifying formatting questions about a report on which the two of you are collaborating.
c. John, the information technology vice president, must tell employees about a new company social media policy. He has two employees in mind who particularly need this information.
d. As soon as possible, you need to learn from Daryle in Document Imaging whether she can make copies of a set of engineering blueprints. If she cannot, you need her advice on where you can get it done.
e. As a manager in human resources, you must terminate three employees in a company-wide initiative to reduce costs.
f. It wasn't your fault, but an order for printed checks for a longtime customer was mishandled. The checks are not ready, and the customer is angry.
g. As chairman of the employee benefits committee, you have worked with your committee for two months evaluating several health plan options that meet new government standards. You are now ready to convey the recommendations of the committee to management.

## 11.7 Dishing Out and Taking It on the Chin: Constructive Criticism on the Job (Obj. 2)

No one likes to give it or receive it, but sometimes criticism is unavoidable, even desirable at times. Constructive criticism in the workplace is necessary when team members need feedback and managers must assess team effectiveness.

**YOUR TASK.** To remedy each of the following unprofessional actions, supply the appropriate solution following the guidelines provided in this chapter.

a. Manager Pete has a hot temper. He exploded when Jordan, one of his subordinates, came late to a staff meeting. Pete told Jordan that he hated his tardiness and that Jordan was always late.
b. Hot-headed manager Pete loudly confronted Bryana in her cubicle within earshot of staff. Bryana had requested time off as an important deadline was looming, and the project was already late.
c. Regional manager Karen delivered a stern lecture to an underperforming sales rep who was clearly stunned and hurt.
d. Barbara provided feedback to a dysfunctional team by spontaneously approaching team members in the hallway. Face-to-face with the argumentative team, she was at a loss for words and felt that she did not convey her points fully.
e. Supervisor Mark is tempted to deliver his negative feedback of a team member by e-mail.

## 11.8 Practicing Professional Telephone Skills (Obj. 3)

**Team**

Acting out the roles of telephone caller and receiver is an effective technique for improving skills. To give you such practice, your instructor will divide the class into pairs.

**YOUR TASK.** For each scenario take a moment to read and rehearse your role silently. Then play the role with your partner. If time permits, repeat the scenarios, changing roles.

**Partner 1**

a. You are the personnel manager of Sky Cellular, Inc. Call Gabriella Lawton, office manager at MagicTech Corporation. Inquire about a job applicant, Mabel Kung, who listed Ms. Lawton as a reference.
b. Call Ms. Lawton again the following day to inquire about the same job applicant, Mabel Kung. Ms. Lawton answers today, but she talks on and on, describing the applicant in great detail. Tactfully close the conversation.
c. You are now the receptionist for Markos Kallistos, of Kallistos Imports. Answer a call for Mr. Kallistos, who is

**Partner 2**

a. You are the receptionist for MagicTech Corporation. The caller asks for Gabriella Lawton, who is home sick today. You don't know when she will be able to return. Answer the call appropriately.
b. You are now Ms. Lawton, office manager. Describe Mabel Kung, an imaginary employee. Think of someone with whom you have worked. Include many details, such as her ability to work with others, her appearance, her skills at computing, her schooling, her ambition, and so forth.
c. You are now an administrative assistant for attorney Melanie Scheuble-Anderson. Call Markos Kallistos to verify a meeting

#### Partner 1 (Continued)

working in another office, at Ext. 2219, where he will accept calls.

d. You are now Markos Kallistos, owner of Kallistos Imports. Call your attorney, Melanie Scheuble-Anderson, about a legal problem. Leave a brief, incomplete message.

e. Call Ms. Scheuble-Anderson again. Leave a message that will prevent telephone tag.

#### Partner 2 (Continued)

date Ms. Scheuble-Anderson has with Mr. Kallistos. Use your own name in identifying yourself.

d. You are now the receptionist for attorney Melanie Scheuble-Anderson. Ms. Scheuble-Anderson is skiing in Aspen and will return in two days, but she does not want her clients to know where she is. Take a message.

e. Take a message again.

### 11.9 Recording a Professional Voice Mail Greeting (Obj. 3)
**Communication Technology | E-mail | Team | Web**

To present a professional image, smart businesspeople carefully prepare their outgoing voice mail greetings and announcements. After all, they represent their companies and want to be perceived as polished and efficient. Before recording a greeting, most workers plan and perhaps even jot down what they will say. To be concise, the greeting should not run longer than 25 seconds.

**YOUR TASK.** Use the guidelines in this chapter to plan your greeting. Invent a job title and the name of your company. Indicate when and how callers can reach you. Individually or as a team, record a professional voice mail greeting using a smartphone or another digital recording device. If the instructor directs, share your recording by sending it via e-mail to a designated address for evaluation. Alternatively, team members may be asked to exchange their recorded greetings for a peer critique. If you own an iPhone, a newer iPod Touch, or an iPad, download a free app such as Voice Memos that allows voice recordings. Android smartphone owners can likewise download a free voice recorder app. These mobile applications are easy to use, and when the recording is completed, you have the option of sharing it by e-mail, by Bluetooth, on Facebook, and so forth.

### 11.10 Leaving a Professional Voice Mail Message (Obj. 3)
**Communication Technology | Web**

Voice mail messages can be very effective communication tools as long as they are professional and make responding to them easy.

**YOUR TASK.** If your instructor allows, call his or her office number after hours or within a specified time frame. Plan what you will say; if needed, jot down a few notes. Leave a professional voice mail message as described in this chapter. Start by introducing yourself by name, then give your telephone number, and finally, leave a brief message about something you discussed in class, read in the chapter, or want the instructor to know about you. Speak slowly, loudly enough, and clearly, so your instructor won't need to replay your message.

### 11.11 Workplace Conflict: The Perils of Groupthink (Obj. 4)
**Team**

"Conflict can be good because you get the devil's advocate position," says Mary Osswald, senior manager at Kamehameha Schools, Honolulu, Hawaii. "Conflict usually comes because someone doesn't want change or doesn't agree with how you're making change. It certainly inspires better conversation and more thought about what's being done and why it's being done. It forces the project to evolve."[52] You learned about *groupthink* in Chapter 1. It describes a behavior characterized by a lack of critical thinking and extreme conformity to the values of a group.

The absence of conflict is not always a good sign, Ms. Osswald believes: "If you have a project with no conflict, you might have just as much of a leadership problem as if you were experiencing massive conflict. In such a case, Ms. Osswald suspects groupthink is at work: "It's very unlikely everybody always agrees with how the project activities are progressing. If you have zero conflict, my thought is you've got a bunch of 'yes men' who are keeping their mouths shut and simply doing what they think the leaders want."

**YOUR TASK.** Do you agree with Mary Osswald's views on workplace conflict and groupthink? Look back at your teamwork experience and consider tensions that arose. How were they addressed and settled? Have you worked on teams that were conflict free? Were you ever afraid to speak up? Could negative situations have been salvaged by using the tips suggested in this chapter? Discuss these and similar questions in small groups or in front of the class. If asked, provide a written assessment of your views on workplace conflict.

### 11.12 Resolving Workplace Conflict: Apply a Plan (Objs. 4, 5)
**Team**

Although conflict is a normal part of every workplace, if unresolved, it can create hard feelings and reduce productivity.

**YOUR TASK.** Analyze the following scenarios. In teams, discuss each scenario and apply the six-step procedure for dealing with conflict outlined in Figure 11.6. on page 367. Choose two of the scenarios to role-play, with two of your team members taking roles.

a. Meghan, an accountant, cannot complete her report until Matt, a salesman, provides her with all the necessary numbers and documentation. Meghan thinks that Matt is a procrastinator who forces her to deliver a rush job thus causing her great stress and increasing the likelihood of error. Matt believes that Meghan is exerting pressure on both of them and setting unrealistic deadlines. As the conflict is intensifying, productivity decreases.

b. A company policy manual is posted and updated at the company intranet, an internal website. Employees must sign that they have read and understand the manual. A conflict arises when team member Brian insists that employees should sign electronically. Fellow team member Erika thinks that a paper form should be signed by employees so that better records may be kept.

c. The author of a lengthy report refuses to collaborate with another colleague on future projects because she feels that the review of her document completed by the peer was superficial, short, and essentially useless. The report author is angry at the lack of attention her 25-page paper received.

d. Two management team members disagree on a new company social media policy. One wants to ban personal visits to Facebook and Twitter totally. The other thinks that an outright ban is impossible to implement and might raise the ire of employees. He is more concerned with limiting Internet misuse, including visits to online game, pornography, and shopping sites. The management team members agree that they need a social media policy, but they disagree on what to allow and what to prohibit.

## 11.13 Dealing With Dysfunction in Business Meetings (Obj. 5)

`E-mail` `Team`

As you have learned, facilitating a productive meeting requires skills that may be critical to your career success.

**YOUR TASK.** Individually or as a team, describe how you would deal with the following examples of unproductive or dysfunctional behavior and other challenges in a team meeting that you are running. Either report your recommendations verbally, or, if your instructor directs, summarize your suggestions in an e-mail or memo.

a. Ken likes to make long-winded statements and often digresses to unrelated subjects.
b. Esther keeps interrupting other speakers and dominates the discussion.
c. Pat and Rodrigo are hostile toward each other and clash over an agenda item.
d. Joanna arrives 15 minutes late and noisily unpacks her briefcase.
e. Sheri, Nora, and Jonathan are reading e-mails and texting under the table.
f. Kimberly is quiet, although she is taking notes and seems to be following the discussion attentively.
g. Jonathan, a well-known office clown, is telling off-color jokes while others are discussing the business at hand.
h. The meeting time is up, but the group has not met the objective of the meeting.

## 11.14 Meeting Malaise: Beyond Contempt (Obj. 5)

`Communication Technology` `Team` `Web`

"Meetings are indispensable when you don't want to do anything," observed the late economist John Kenneth Galbraith. This sentiment was echoed by Stanford professor Thomas Sowell who declared: "People who enjoy meetings should not be in charge of anything." Finally, management guru Peter Drucker claimed: "Meetings are a symptom of a bad organization. The fewer meetings, the better."

Much venomous ink has been spilled decrying meetings, but they won't go away because—despite their potential shortcomings—many workplace gatherings are necessary.

**YOUR TASK.** Examine the preceding quotations and perhaps other statements deriding meetings. Are they exaggerations or accurate assessments? If the assertions of wastefulness are true, what does that mean for the health of organizations conducting large numbers of meetings? Individually or as a team, search the Web for information in defense of meetings. Begin by discussing your own and classmates' experience with workplace meetings. Interview your parents, other relatives, and friends about meetings. Finding gripes is easy, but search the Web for advice on making meetings more effective. What information beyond the tips in this book can you find? In a class discussion or individually—perhaps in writing or in an electronic slide presentation if your instructor directs—introduce your findings.

## 11.15 Virtual Meetings: Improving Distance Meeting Buy-In (Obj. 5)

`Communication Technology` `Team` `Web`

Marina Elliot works at the headquarters for a large HMO that contracts with physician groups in various locations across the nation. Her position requires her to impose organizational objectives and systems on smaller groups that often resist such interference. Marina recently needed to inform regional groups that the home office was instituting a systemwide change to hiring practices. To save costs, she set up a Web conference between her office in Charlotte and others in Chicago, Denver, and Seattle. Marina set the meeting for 10 a.m. Eastern Standard Time. At the designated date and hour, she found that the Seattle team was not logged in and she had to delay the session. When the Seattle team finally did log in, Marina launched into her presentation. She explained the reasons behind the change in a PowerPoint presentation that contained complex data she had not distributed prior to the conference. Marina heard cell phone ringtones and typing in the background as she spoke. Still, she pushed through her one-hour presentation without eliciting any feedback.

**YOUR TASK.** In teams, discuss ways Marina might have improved the Web conference. Prepare a list of recommendations from your team.

## 11.16 Discussing a Group Project or Class Issue in a Virtual Meeting (Objs. 4, 5)
`Communication Technology` `E-mail` `Social Media` `Team`

Virtual meetings are extremely useful to dispersed workplace teams, and, yes, they may help harried college students. Some of them brave terrible traffic and commute vast distances to attend colleges and universities. When doing research for a group project, students often struggle to find a convenient time to meet because they may work on weekends or have family duties. Although wikis such as Google Docs can aid collaboration on shared files, a video chat conveys much more nuance than e-mail or IM can. Real-time video chatting allows for a fast exchange of information with almost the media richness of face-to-face conversations.

**YOUR TASK.** Settle on the type of communication software or app your team will use. Some popular group video chat applications are Skype, Google Hangouts, Fring, and WhatsApp. Following the guidelines in this chapter, prepare and conduct a virtual meeting with your collaborators. Ensure that everyone knows the technology; establish ground rules for the virtual meetings such as when to ask questions, letting everyone speak, and so forth. Your instructor may ask for deliverables by e-mail or in memo form such as an agenda and meeting minutes. You could also be required to write a short memo report on the experience, summarizing what you did before, during, and after the virtual meeting.

## 11.17 Visiting Virtual Office Hours (Objs. 2, 5)
`Communication Technology` `Social Media`

In distance courses in particular, some instructors hold virtual office hours. When using course management systems such as Blackboard and Moodle, your professors can create class chat rooms. At appointed times, you may join your instructor and your peers in the online chat room and ask questions, request clarification, or comment on the class and the teaching material. Some of your professors may offer video chat—for example, by Skype.

**YOUR TASK.** During virtual office hours, practice professional demeanor and courtesy. Your class is a workshop environment in which you are practicing appropriate workplace etiquette. Impress your instructor by following the guidelines in this chapter—for example, by offering a friendly, respectful greeting, introducing yourself, communicating clearly, writing correct prose, being an active participant in group meetings, providing and accepting constructive criticism, and exhibiting a positive can-do attitude. Plan your virtual visit as you would a professional phone conversation, also described in this chapter. Your instructor may give you informal feedback or decide to use a more formal assessment such as a performance appraisal.

# GRAMMAR/MECHANICS CHECKUP—11

## Other Punctuation

Although this checkup concentrates on Sections 2.23–2.29 in the Grammar/Mechanics Handbook, you may also refer to other punctuation principles. Insert any necessary and delete any unnecessary punctuation. In the space provided, indicate the number of changes you make and record the number of the G/M principle(s) illustrated. Count each mark separately; for example, a set of parentheses counts as 2. Replacing one punctuation mark with another counts as one change. If you make no changes, write 0. When you finish, compare your responses with those provided at the end of the book. If your responses differ, study carefully the specific principles shown in parentheses.

<u>   2   </u> (2.27) **EXAMPLE** (De-emphasize) Several cities chosen by *CNN/Money* as the best places to live in the United States (Alexandria, Chesapeake, Chantilly, and Reston) are in Virginia.

<u>          </u> 1. (Emphasize) The scholarship committee has invited three recipients Matt Martinez, Debbie Lee, and Traci Person to speak at the awards ceremony.

<u>          </u> 2. Could you please Dr. Kerlin check to be sure that my insurance information has been filed?

<u>          </u> 3. (De-emphasize) Our June financial figures see Appendix A show a sharp increase in operating expenses.

<u>          </u> 4. My friend and I wondered whether the application deadline was April 1 or April 15?

_____  5. Northwestern, Stanford, and Harvard these universities have three of the best MBA programs in the country.

_____  6. Warren Buffet said, Why not invest your assets in companies you really like

_____  7. Have you read The Wall Street Journal article titled Genetic Tests Create Pitfalls for Employers

_____  8. (Emphasize.) The biggest wine-producing states California, Washington, and Oregon are all located on the Pacific Coast.

_____  9. Have you received replies from Mr Francisco, M Arce, Ms Brenda Marini, and Dr Patricia Franzoia

_____  10. I enjoyed the chapter titled The Almost Perfect Meeting that appeared in Emily Post's book The Etiquette Advantage in Business.

_____  11. Donald Trump said, "Generally I like other people to fire, because it's always a lousy task" however, he has fired many people himself.

_____  12. Kevin asked whether sentences could end with two periods?

_____  13. Is today's meeting at 2 p m

_____  14. In business the term poison pill is defined as a defensive tactic used by a company to prevent a hostile takeover.

_____  15. Wow You've been working out haven't you

384  Chapter 11: Professionalism at Work: Business Etiquette, Ethics, Teamwork, and Meetings

ns and Meetings

Mountain View Parks and Recreation Board
Board Room, City Hall, 10 Main Street, Mountin View, Colorado
October 29, 2016

Present: Scott Almquist, Sue Hjortsberg, Bob Taft, Shirley Bailey, Michelle Esteban, Terri Rogers, David Kazanis
Absent: Kathie Muratore

The meeting was called to order at 7:03 pm in the evening by Vice Chair Michelle Esteban. Minutes from the September 28th meeting was read and approved.

**Old Business**

Manager Scott Almquist reported that a ten thousand dollar gift from the Partners of Parks & Recreation, Inc., had been recieved. The gift according to the donors request will be used for renovation of the Community Center. Bids were coming in considerable higher then anticipated, however, Mr. Almquist is confident that the project will move forewardd on schedule.

Sue Hjortsberg reported on her research into municipal park festivitys. She reccomended that Board members read an article titled Guide to Park Celebrations which appeared in the July issue of Park Management.

**New Business**

Discussion was held in a matter related to a donation request from Plains Real Estate Co., Inc. This donation involves three lots on Rancho Street, see pages 2-4 of your board packet. Because these lots is near Buffalo park Bob Taft stated that he couldn't hardly see any value in adding another "small lot" park to that area.

MOTION: To deny request from Plans Real Estate Co., Inc., to donate 3 lots on Rancho Street for Park purposes. (Taft/Bailey). Passed unanimously.

Discussion was held about proposed bonuses in view of the fact that the budget has been cut. Should the planned bonuses for three outstanding gardeners: Hector Valdez, Heather York, and Juan Rio, be postponed. The matter was tabled untill the next meeting.

Board members discussed the facility fee schedule for community use. David Kazanis suggested that fees should not be charged for Senior or Youth programs held in Mountain View facilitys but he thought that fees for adult sport's and fitness programs would need to be increase to cover added expenses.

MOTION: To increase fees for adult sport's and fitness programs held in Mountain View Park and Recreation District facilities. (Kazanis/Rogers). Failed 2-5.

**Adjournment**

The meeting was adjourned at 8:35 pm. The next meeting of the Mountain View Parks and Recreation Board will be held November 28th at the City Hall Board Room.

Respectfully submitted,

## COMMUNICATION WORKSHOP

### CAREER SKILLS

### Business Etiquette: Breaking the Smartphone Habit in Meetings

Not long ago it was almost a status symbol for professionals to "lay [their] BlackBerrys or iPhones on a conference table before a meeting—like gunfighters placing their Colt revolvers on the card tables in a saloon."[53] Businesspeople today often compulsively eyeball their smartphones and tablets to read e-mail, search Google, and check Facebook or Twitter during meetings. In fact, in a Robert Half survey of executives, 81 percent confessed to having committed more or less frequent smartphone etiquette violations during virtual meetings. At the same time, 76 percent stated that meeting participants who answered their e-mail or surfed the Internet would jeopardize their career prospects.[54] Workers tapping away at their smart devices may be a common sight, but the tide is turning. Increasingly, many professionals are tired of disruptions caused by electronic gadgets during meetings.

Etiquette consultants concur: "Electronic devices are like the smoking of the '90s," says Pamela Eyring, president of the Protocol School of Washington. "Companies are aggravated and losing productivity." Businesses hire her to enact formal policies and to teach workers "why it's not a good idea to be texting while your boss is speaking at the podium," Eyring says.[55] Nancy Flynn, executive director of the ePolicy Institute and author of *The Handbook of Social Media*, has this suggestion: "Require employees to turn off mobile devices during business-related meetings, seminars, conferences, luncheons and any other situation in which a ringing phone or tapping fingers are likely to disrupt proceedings or interrupt a speaker's or participant's train of thought."

Flynn notes that banning electronic devices in meetings is not just about interruptions: "You don't want employees shooting video via a smartphone during a meeting in which company secrets are discussed, then uploading the video to YouTube or sharing it with a competitor, reporter or other third party."[56] Organizations are only beginning to establish policies on smartphone use in meetings.

**CAREER APPLICATION.** Assume that you have been asked to develop a policy discussing the use of mobile electronic devices in meetings. Your boss can't decide whether to ask you to develop a short policy or a more rigorous one. Keep in mind that meeting participants could have legitimate reasons for using mobile electronic devices—for example, to take notes, look up calendar items, or fact-check a disputed point. How could this conflict between disruptive and valid uses of mobile devices in meetings be resolved?

**YOUR TASK.** As an individual or with a team, compose two documents: (a) a short statement that treats employees as grown-ups who can exercise intelligent judgment and (b) a more complete set of guidelines that spell out exactly what should and should not be done.

## ENDNOTES

[1] National Writing Project with DeVoss, D. N., Eidman-Aadahl, E., & Hicks, T. (2010). *Because digital writing matters*. San Francisco: Jossey-Bass, p. 150.
[2] Graff, J. (2013, December 27). Executive editor's note. *The Week*, p. 3.
[3] Chao, L. (2006, January 17). Not-so-nice costs. *The Wall Street Journal*, p. B1.
[4] Rubin, C. (2010, July 12). The high cost of rudeness in the workplace. *Inc.* Retrieved from http://www.inc.com/news/articles/2010/07/how-rudeness-affects-the-workplace.html; Yu, W. (2012, January 3). Workplace rudeness has a ripple effect. *Scientific American*. Retrieved from http://www.scientificamerican.com/article.cfm?id=ripples-of-rudeness; Jayson, S. (2011, August 9). Incivility a growing problem at work, psychologists say. *USA Today*. Retrieved from http://www.usatoday.com/news/health/wellness/story/2011/08/Incivility-a-growing-problem-at-work-psychologists-say/49854130/1
[5] Pearson, C., & Porath, C. (2009). *The cost of bad behavior: How incivility is damaging your business and what to do about it*. New York: Portfolio/Penguin.
[6] Buhler, P. M. (2003, April 1). Managing in the new millennium; workplace civility: Has it fallen by the wayside? *Supervision, 64*(4), pp. 20–22. Retrieved from http://search.proquest.com
[7] Wikipedia: Civility. (2013, November 27). Wikipedia. Retrieved from http://en.wikipedia.org/wiki/Wikipedia:Civility
[8] Ibid.
[9] Johnson, D. (1988–2006). Dine like a diplomat. Seminar Script. The Protocol School of Washington, Columbia, South Carolina.
[10] Albrecht, K. (2006). *Social intelligence: The new science of success*. San Francisco: Pfeiffer, p. 3.
[11] Schawbel, D. (2013, September 4). The soft skills managers want. *Bloomberg Businessweek*. Retrieved from http://www.businessweek.com/articles/2013-09-04/the-soft-skills-managers-want
[12] Chismar, D. (2001). Vice and virtue in everyday (business) life. *Journal of Business Ethics, 29*, 169–176. doi: 10.1023/A:1006467631038
[13] Hughes, T. (2008). Being a professional. Wordconstructions.com Retrieved from http://www.wordconstructions.com/articles/business/professional.html; Grove, C., & Hallowell, W. (2002). The seven balancing acts of professional behavior in the United States: A cultural values perspective. Grovewell.com. Retrieved from http://www.grovewell.com/pub-usa-professional.html
[14] Plantronics. (2010). How we work: Communication trends of business professionals. Retrieved from http://www.plantronics.com/media/howwework/brochure-role-of-voice.pdf; Martin, C. (2007, March 6). The importance of face-to-face communication at work. CIO.com. Retrieved from http://www.cio.com/article/29898/The_Importance_of_Face_to_Face_Communication_at_Work; Duke, S. (2001, Winter). E-mail: Essential in media relations, but no replacement for face-to-face communication. *Public Relations Quarterly*, p. 19.
[15] Lutz, K. (2013, April 3). Dispute resolution using online mediation. Harvard Law Program on Negotiation. Retrieved from http://www.pon.harvard.edu/daily/mediation/dispute-resolution-using-online-mediation;

Brenner, R. (2007, October 17). Virtual conflict. *Point Lookout*, Chaco Canyon Consulting. Retrieved from http://www.chacocanyon.com/pointlookout/071017.shtml; Drolet, A. L., & Morris, M. W. (2000, January). Rapport in conflict resolution: Accounting for how face-to-face contact fosters mutual cooperation in mixed-motive conflicts. *Journal of Experimental Social Psychology*, p. 26.

[16] Borkowska, B. (2011). Female voice frequency in the context of dominance and attractiveness perception. *Animal Behaviour, 82*(1), 55–59; Niculescu, A., van Dijk, B., Nijholt, A., Haizhou, L., & See, S. (2013, March 31). Making social robots more attractive: The effects of voice pitch, humor and empathy. *International Journal of Social Robotics, 5*(2), 171–191; Derrick, D. C., & Elkins, A. C. (2012, November 30). The sound of trust: Voice as a measurement of trust during interactions with embodied conversational agents. *Group Decision and Negotiation, 22*(5), 897–913.

[17] Tina Nicolai quoted in Smith, J. (2013, December 20). How to use your 2013 mistakes to build a better 2014 at work. *Forbes*. Retrieved from http://www.forbes.com/sites/jacquelynsmith/2013/12/20/how-to-use-your-2013-mistakes-to-build-a-better-2014

[18] Plantronics. (2010). How we work: Communication trends of business professionals. Retrieved from http://www.plantronics.com/media/howwework/brochure-role-of-voice.pdf

[19] Ibid.

[20] Smith, A. (2013, June 5). Smartphone ownership 2013. Pew Internet. Retrieved from http://pewinternet.org/Reports/2013/Smartphone-Ownership-2013/Findings.aspx; Nielsen. (2013, December 16). Consumer electronics ownership blasts off in 2013. Retrieved from http://www.nielsen.com/us/en/newswire/2013/consumer-electronics-ownership-blasts-off-in-2013.html

[21] Nielsen. (2013, December 16). Consumer electronics ownership blasts off in 2013. Retrieved from http://www.nielsen.com/us/en/newswire/2013/consumer-electronics-ownership-blasts-off-in-2013.html

[22] Love, D. (2013, December 27). The landline is dying and these numbers prove it. *Business Insider*. Retrieved from http://www.businessinsider.com/death-of-the-landline-2013-12; Blumberg, S. J., Luke, J. V. (2013, December). Wireless substitution: Early release of estimates from the National Health Interview Survey, January–June 2013. National Center for Health Statistics. Retrieved from www.cdc.gov/nchs/nhis.htm

[23] Vella, M. (2008, April 28). White-collar workers shoulder together—like it or not. *BusinessWeek*, p. 58.

[24] Gensler. (2013, June 26). Press release: Gensler releases 2013 U.S. workplace survey. Retrieved from www.gensler.com

[25] Chambers, A., & Rasky, D. (n.d.). NASA and SpaceX work together. *Ask Magazine*, p. 7. Retrieved from http://www.nasa.gov/pdf/489058main_ASK_40_space_x.pdf

[26] Coutu, D. (2009, May). Why teams don't work. *Harvard Business Review, 87*(5), 100. Retrieved from http://search.ebscohost.com; Cain, S. (2012, January 13). The rise of the new groupthink. *The New York Times*. Retrieved from http://www.nytimes.com/2012/01/15/opinion/sunday/the-rise-of-the-new-groupthink.html?pagewanted=all

[27] Discussion of Tuckman's model based on Robbins, H. A., & Finley, M. (2000). *The new why teams don't work*. San Francisco: Berrett-Koehler, Chapter 29.

[28] Zofi, Y. S. (2012). *A manager's guide to virtual teams*. New York: American Management Association, p. 1.

[29] Ferrazzi, K. (2013, December 18). To make virtual teams succeed, pick the right players. HBR Blog Network. Retrieved from http://blogs.hbr.org/2013/12/to-make-virtual-teams-succeed-pick-the-right-players

[30] Siebdrat, F., Hoegl, M., & Ernst, H. (2009, Summer). How to manage virtual teams. *MIT Sloan Management Review, 50*(4), 64. Retrieved from http://search.ebscohost.com

[31] Rey, J. (2010, June). Team building. *Inc., 32*(5), 68–71; Romando, R. (2006, November 9). Advantages of corporate team building. Ezine Articles. Retrieved from http://ezinearticles.com/?Advantages-of-Corporate-Team-Building&id=352961; Amason, A. C., Hochwarter, W. A., Thompson, K. R., & Harrison, A. W. (1995, Autumn). Conflict: An important dimension in successful management teams. *Organizational Dynamics, 24*(2), 1. Retrieved from http://search.ebscohost.com; Romando, R. (2006, November 9). Advantages of corporate team building. Ezine Articles. Retrieved from http://ezinearticles.com/?Advantages-of-Corporate-Team-Building&id=352961

[32] Ruffin, B. (2006, January). T.E.A.M. work: Technologists, educators, and media specialists collaborating. *Library Media Connection, 24*(4), 49. Retrieved from http://search.ebscohost.com

[33] Pratt, E. L. (2010). Virtual teams in very small classes. In R. Ubell (Ed.), *Virtual teamwork: Mastering the art and practice of online learning and corporate collaboration*. Hoboken, NJ: Wiley, pp. 93–94; Katzenbach, J. R., & Smith, K. (1994). *The wisdom of teams*. New York: HarperBusiness, p. 45.

[34] Ibid., p. 93.

[35] Ferrazzi, K. (2013, December 18). To make virtual teams succeed, pick the right players. HBR Blog Network. Retrieved from http://blogs.hbr.org/2013/12/to-make-virtual-teams-succeed-pick-the-right-players; Holtzman, Y., & Anderberg, J. (2011). Diversify your teams and collaborate: Because great minds don't think alike. *The Journal of Management Development, 30*(1), 79. doi: 10.1108/02621711111098389; Katzenbach, J., & Smith, D. (1994). *Wisdom of teams*. New York: HarperBusiness, p. 45.

[36] Callahan, D. (2009, April 21). Breaking the ice: Success through teamwork and partnerships. Retrieved from http://greatlakes.coastguard.dodlive.mil/2009/04/breaking-the-ice-success-through-teamwork-and-partnerships

[37] Phillips, A. (2012, May 9). Wasted time in meetings costs the UK economy £26 billion. Retrieved from http://www.businessrevieweurope.eu/business_leaders/wasted-time-in-meetings-costs-the-uk-economy-26-billion; Herring, H. B. (2006, June 18). Endless meetings: The black holes of the workday. *The New York Times*. Retrieved from http://www.nytimes.com

[38] Herring, H. B. (2006, June 18). Endless meetings: The black holes of the workday. *The New York Times*. Retrieved from http://www.nytimes.com

[39] Shellenbarger, S. (2012, May 16). Meet the meeting killers—In the office, they strangle ideas, poison progress; how to fight back. *The Wall Street Journal*. Retrieved from http://search.proquest.com

[40] Rogelberg, S. G., Shanock, L. R., & Scott, C. W. (2012). Wasted time and money in meetings: Increasing return on investment. *Small Group Research, 43*(2), 237. doi: 10.1177/1046496411429170

[41] Plantronics. (2010). How we work: Communication trends of business professionals. Retrieved from http://www.plantronics.com/media/howwework/brochure-role-of-voice.pdf

[42] Photo essay based on Codrea Rado, A. (2013, June 19). How Jeff Bezos, Richard Branson, and other business chiefs hold ruthlessly effective meetings. Quartz/Yahoo Finance. Retrieved from http://finance.yahoo.com/news/jeff-bezos-richard-branson-other-172057696.html

[43] Frisch, B., & Peck, J. (2010, May 14). Meetings: How many people should be in the room? *Bloomberg Businessweek*. Retrieved from http://www.businessweek.com/managing/content/may2010/ca2010054_344173.htm

[44] Timberland responsibility. (2012). Retrieved from http://responsibility.timberland.com/service/?story=3; Marquis, C. (2003, July). Doing well and doing good. *The New York Times*, p. BU 2.

[45] Tips on meetings: Three ways to encourage meeting participation. (2011, April 11). *Harvard Business Review*. Retrieved from http://hbr.org/web/management-tip/tips-on-meetings

[46] Lohr, S. (2008, July 22). As travel costs rise, more meetings go virtual. *The New York Times*. Retrieved from http://www.nytimes.com

[47] Ibid.

[48] Schlegel, J. (2012). Running effective meetings: Types of meetings. Salary.com. Retrieved from http://www.salary.com/running-effective-meetings-6; Cohen, M. A., Rogelberg, S. G., Allen, J. A., & Luong, A. (2011). Meeting design characteristics and attendee perceptions of staff/team meeting quality. *Group Dynamics: Theory, Research, and Practice, 15*(1), 100–101; Schindler, E. (2008, February 15). Running an effective teleconference or virtual meeting. *CIO*. Retrieved from www.cio.com. See also Brenowitz, R. S. (2004, May). Virtual meeting etiquette. Article 601, *Innovative Leader*. Retrieved from http://www.winstonbrill.com

[49] Tips on meetings: Two rules for making global meetings work. (2011, April 11). *Harvard Business Review*. Retrieved from http://hbr.org/web/management-tip/tips-on-meetings

[50] Schindler, E. (2008, February 15). Running an effective teleconference or virtual meeting. *CIO*. Retrieved from www.cio.com. See also Brenowitz, R. S. (2004, May). Virtual meeting etiquette. Article 601, *Innovative Leader*. Retrieved from http://www.winstonbrill.com

[51] Curtin, P. A., Gallicano, T., & Matthews, K. (2011, Spring). Millennials' approaches to ethical decision making: A survey of young public relations agency employees. *Public Relations Journal, 5*(2), 11.

[52] Scenario based on Hollingsworth, C. (2010, December). The peace process. *PM Network, 24*(12), 63. Retrieved from http://search.ebscohost.com

[53] Williams, A. (2008, June 24). At meetings, it's mind your BlackBerry or mind your manners. *The New York Times*, pp. A1, A3.

[54] Robert Half. (2011). Business etiquette: The new rules in a digital age, pp. 16, 23. Retrieved from http://www.roberthalf.com/business-etiquette

[55] O'Brien Coffey, J. (2011, September). How to manage smartphones at meetings. *Executive Travel Magazine*. Retrieved from http://www.executivetravelmagazine.com/articles/how-to-manage-smartphones-at-meetings

[56] Ibid.

# ACKNOWLEDGMENTS

**p. 353** Office Insider quoted in Canavor, N. (2012). *Business writing in the digital age*. Los Angeles: Sage, p. 4.

**p. 354** Office Insider based on Bosrock, R. M. (2005, October 5). Business forum: Good manners bring good results. *Star Tribune.com*. Retrieved from http://www.startribune.com/business/11050361.html?elr=KArksUUUoDEy3LGDiO7aiU

**p. 355** Office Insider based on Chismar, D. (2001). Vice and virtue in everyday (business) life. *Journal of Business Ethics*, 29, 169-176. doi: 10.1023/A: 1006467631038

**p. 356** Office Insider based on Begley, K. A. (2004). Face to face communication: Making human connections in a technology-driven world. NETg. Retrieved from http://www.axzopress.com/downloads/pdf/1560526998pv.pdf

**p. 358** Office Insider based on Johnson, D. (1988-2006). Dine like a diplomat. Seminar Script. The Protocol School of Washington, Columbia, South Carolina.

**p. 360** Office Insider based on Bjerke, J. (2013, November 12). The importance of your "phone voice" in business. Recruiter.com. Retrieved from http://www.recruiter.com/i/the-importance-of-your-phone-voice-in-business

**p. 364** Office Insider based on Lakey, D. M. (2007). *The board building cycle: Nine steps to finding, recruiting, and engaging nonprofit board members*. Washington, DC: BoardSource, p. 10.

**p. 366** Office Insider based on Edmondson, G. (2006, October 16). The secret of BMW's success. *Bloomberg Businessweek*. Retrieved from http://www.businessweek.com/magazine/content/06_42/b4005078.htm

**p. 367** Office Insider based on Askenas, R., & Bodell, L. (2013, October 16). Nice managers embrace conflict, too. HBR Blog Network. Retrieved from http://blogs.hbr.org/2013/10/nice-managers-embrace-conflict-too

**p. 368** Office Insider based on Francisco, J. (2007, November/December). How to create and facilitate meetings that matter. *The Information Management Journal*, p. 54. Retrieved from http://search.ebscohost.com

**p. 372** Office Insider based on Bates, S. (2011). Running a meeting: Ten rookie mistakes and how to avoid them. *Management Consulting News*. Retrieved from http://managementconsultingnews.com/article-suzanne-bates

# Business Presentations

## 12-1 Preparing Effective Business Presentations

Unlike motivational expert Anthony Robbins, activist Martin Luther King Jr., or the late Apple founder Steve Jobs, few of us will ever talk to an audience of millions—whether face-to-face or aided by technology. We won't be invited to give a TED Talk, motivate millions, or introduce a spectacular new product. At some point, however, all businesspeople have to inform others or sell an idea. Such informative and persuasive presentations are often conveyed in person and involve audiences of various sizes. If you are like most people, you have some apprehension when speaking in public. That's normal. Good speakers are made, not born. The good news is that you can conquer the fear of public speaking and hone your skills with instruction and practice.

### 12-1a Speaking Skills and Your Career

Many savvy future businesspeople fail to take advantage of opportunities in college to develop their speaking skills, even though such skills are often crucial for a successful career. As you have seen in Chapters 1 and 11, speaking skills rank very high on recruiters' wish lists. In a survey of employers, spoken communication took the top spot as the most desirable "soft skill" sought in job candidates. It even ranks above a strong work ethic, teamwork, analytical skills, and initiative.[1]

Speaking skills are useful at every career stage. You might, for example, have to make a sales pitch before customers, speak to a professional gathering, or describe

**OBJECTIVES**
After studying this chapter, you should be able to

**12-1**
Recognize various types of business presentations, and discuss two important first steps in preparing for any of these presentations.

**12-2**
Explain how to organize the introduction, body, and conclusion as well as how to build audience rapport in a presentation.

**12-3**
Understand visual aids and how to avoid ineffective PowerPoint practices.

**12-4**
Create an impressive, error-free multimedia presentation that shows a firm grasp of basic visual design principles.

**12-5**
Specify delivery techniques for use before, during, and after a presentation.

## OFFICE INSIDER

*"Presentation skills are a primary differentiator among you and your peers. Master your presentation skills, and become the master of your career options."*

—Andrew Dlugan, communication coach, public speaker

**LEARNING OBJECTIVE 1**

Recognize various types of business presentations, and discuss two important first steps in preparing for any of these presentations.

your company's expansion plans to your banker. This chapter prepares you to use speaking skills in making professional oral presentations, whether alone or as part of a team, whether face-to-face or virtually. Before we dive into the specifics of how to become an excellent presenter, the following section addresses the types of business presentations you may encounter in your career.

### 12-1b Understanding Presentation Types

A common part of a business professional's life is making presentations. Some presentations are informative, whereas others are persuasive. Some are face-to-face; others, virtual. Some are performed before big audiences, whereas others are given to smaller groups. Some presentations are elaborate; others are simple. Figure 12.1 shows a sampling of business presentations you may encounter in your career.

### 12-1c Knowing Your Purpose

Regardless of the type of presentation, you must prepare carefully to ensure that it is effective. The most important part of your preparation is deciding what you want to accomplish. Do you want to sell a health care program to a prospective client? Do you want to persuade management to increase the marketing budget? Whether your goal is to persuade or to inform, you must have a clear idea of where you are going. At the end of your presentation, what do you want your listeners to remember or do?

Sandra Castillo, a loan officer at First Fidelity Trust, faced such questions as she planned a talk for a class in small business management. (You can see the outline for her talk in Figure 12.4 on page 394.) Sandra's former business professor had asked her to return to campus and give his students advice about obtaining loans to start new businesses. Because Sandra knew so much about this topic, she found it difficult to extract a specific purpose statement for her presentation. After much thought she narrowed her purpose to this: *To inform potential entrepreneurs about three important factors that loan officers consider before granting start-up loans to launch small businesses.* Her entire presentation focused on ensuring that the students understood and remembered three principal ideas.

### Figure 12.1 Types of Business Presentations

**Briefing**
- Overview or summary of an issue, proposal, or problem
- Delivery of information, discussion of questions, collection of feedback

**Report**
- Oral equivalent of business reports and proposals
- Informational or persuasive oral account, simple or elaborate

**Podcast**
- Online, prerecorded audio clip delivered over the Web
- Opportunity to launch products, introduce and train employees, and sell products and services

**Virtual Presentation**
- Collaboration facilitated by technology (telepresence or Web)
- Real-time meeting online with remote colleagues

**Webinar**
- Web-based presentation, lecture, workshop, or seminar
- Digital transmission with or without video to train employees, interact with customers, and promote products

## 12-1d Knowing Your Audience

As in any type of communication, a second key element in preparation is analyzing your audience, anticipating its reactions, and adjusting to its needs if necessary. Audiences may fall into four categories, as summarized in Figure 12.2. By anticipating your audience, you have a better idea of how to organize your presentation. A friendly audience, for example, will respond to humor and personal experiences. A hostile audience demands a calm, controlled delivery style with objective data and expert opinion. Whatever type of audience you will face, remember to plan your presentation so that it focuses on audience benefits. People in your audience will want to know what's in it for them.

Other elements, such as the age, gender, education level, experience, and size of the audience, will affect your style and message. Analyze the following questions to determine your organizational pattern, delivery style, and supporting material:

- How will this topic appeal to this audience?
- How can I relate this information to my listeners' needs?
- How can I earn respect so that they accept my message?
- What would be most effective in making my point? Facts? Statistics? Personal experiences? Expert opinion? Humor? Cartoons? Graphic illustrations? Demonstrations? Case histories? Analogies?
- What measures must I take to ensure that this audience remembers my main points?

### Figure 12.2 Succeeding With Four Audience Types

| Audience Members | Organizational Pattern | Delivery Style | Supporting Material |
|---|---|---|---|
| **Friendly** | | | |
| They like you and your topic. | Use any pattern. Try something new. Involve the audience. | Be warm, pleasant, and open. Use lots of eye contact and smiles. | Include humor, personal examples, and experiences. |
| **Neutral** | | | |
| They are calm, rational; their minds are made up, but they think they are objective. | Present both sides of the issue. Use pro/con or problem/solution patterns. Save time for audience questions. | Be controlled. Do nothing showy. Use confident, small gestures. | Use facts, statistics, expert opinion, and comparison and contrast. Avoid humor, personal stories, and flashy visuals. |
| **Uninterested** | | | |
| They have short attention spans; they may be there against their will. | Be brief—no more than three points. Avoid topical and pro/con patterns that seem lengthy to the audience. | Be dynamic and entertaining. Move around. Use large gestures. | Use humor, cartoons, colorful visuals, powerful quotations, and startling statistics. |

> **Avoid** darkening the room, standing motionless, passing out handouts, using boring visuals, or expecting the audience to participate.

| | | | |
|---|---|---|---|
| **Hostile** | | | |
| They want to take charge or to ridicule the speaker; they may be defensive, emotional. | Organize using a noncontroversial pattern, such as a topical, chronological, or geographical strategy. | Be calm and controlled. Speak evenly and slowly. | Include objective data and expert opinion. Avoid anecdotes and humor. |

> **Avoid** a question-and-answer period, if possible; otherwise, use a moderator or accept only written questions.

Chapter 12: Business Presentations

## OFFICE INSIDER

*"Stories and punchlines pack power. Humor anchors key points. Humor makes your message memorable."*

—Dianna Booher, communication consultant and author

**LEARNING OBJECTIVE 2**

Explain how to organize the introduction, body, and conclusion as well as how to build audience rapport in a presentation.

## 12-2 Organizing Content for Impact and Audience Rapport

After determining your purpose and analyzing the audience, you are ready to collect information and organize it logically. Good organization and intentional repetition are the two most powerful keys to audience comprehension and retention. In fact, many speech experts recommend the following admittedly repetitious, but effective, plan:

**Step 1:** Tell them what you are going to tell them.
**Step 2:** Tell them.
**Step 3:** Tell them what you have told them.

Although it is redundant, this strategy works well because most people retain information best when they hear it repeatedly. Let's examine how to construct the three parts of an effective presentation: introduction, body, and conclusion.

### 12-2a Capturing Attention in the Introduction

How many times have you heard a speaker begin with, *It's a pleasure to be here.* Or, *Today I'm going to talk about....* Boring openings such as these get speakers off to a dull start. Avoid such banalities by striving to accomplish three goals in the introduction to your presentation:

- Capture listeners' attention and get them involved.
- Identify yourself and establish your credibility.
- Preview your main points.

If you are able to appeal to listeners and involve them in your presentation right from the start, you are more likely to hold their attention until the finish. Consider some of the techniques you used to open sales letters: a question, a startling fact, a joke, a story, or a quotation. Some speakers achieve involvement by opening with a question or command that requires audience members to raise their hands or stand up. Twelve techniques to gain and keep audience attention are presented in Figure 12.3.

To establish your credibility, you need to describe your position, knowledge, or experience—whatever qualifies you to speak. In addition, try to connect with your audience. Listeners respond particularly well to speakers who reveal something of themselves and identify with them. A consultant addressing office workers might reminisce about how she started as a temporary worker; a CEO might tell a funny story in which the joke is on him. Use humor if you can pull it off (not everyone can); self-effacing humor may work best for you.

After capturing attention and establishing your credibility, you will want to preview the main points of your topic, perhaps with a visual aid.

Take a look at Sandra Castillo's introduction, shown in Figure 12.4, to see how she integrated all the elements necessary for a good opening.

### 12-2b Organizing the Body of the Presentation

The most effective oral presentations focus on a few principal ideas. Therefore, the body of your short presentation (20 minutes or shorter) should include a limited number of main points—say, two to four. Develop each main point with adequate, but not excessive, explanation and details. Too many details can obscure the main

## Figure 12.3 Gaining and Keeping Audience Attention

Experienced speakers know how to capture the attention of an audience and how to maintain that attention throughout a presentation. You can spruce up your presentations by trying these twelve proven techniques.

- **A promise.** Begin with a realistic promise that keeps the audience expectant (for example, *By the end of this presentation, you will know how you can increase your sales by 50 percent!*).

- **Drama.** Open by telling an emotionally moving story or by describing a serious problem that involves the audience. Throughout your talk include other dramatic elements, such as a long pause after a key statement. Change your vocal tone or pitch. Professionals use high-intensity emotions such as anger, joy, sadness, and excitement.

- **Eye contact.** As you begin, command attention by surveying the entire audience to take in all listeners. Give yourself two to five seconds to linger on individuals to avoid fleeting, unconvincing eye contact. Don't just sweep the room and the crowd.

- **Movement.** Leave the lectern area whenever possible. Walk around the conference table or down the aisles of the presentation room. Try to move toward your audience, especially at the beginning and end of your talk.

- **Questions.** Keep listeners active and involved with rhetorical questions. Ask for a show of hands to get each listener thinking. The response will also give you a quick gauge of audience attention.

- **Demonstrations.** Include a member of the audience in a demonstration (for example, *I'm going to show you exactly how to implement our four-step customer courtesy process, but I need a volunteer from the audience to help me*).

- **Samples/props.** If you are promoting a product, consider using items to toss out to the audience or to award as prizes to volunteer participants. You can also pass around product samples or promotional literature. Be careful, though, to maintain control.

- **Visuals.** Give your audience something to look at besides yourself. Use a variety of visual aids in a single session. Also consider writing the concerns expressed by your audience on a flipchart, a whiteboard, or a smart board as you go along.

- **Attire.** Enhance your credibility with your audience by dressing professionally for your presentation. Professional attire will help you look competent and qualified, making your audience more likely to listen and take you seriously.

- **Current events/statistics.** Mention a current event or statistic (the more startling, the better) that is relevant to your topic and to which the audience can relate.

- **A quote.** Quotations, especially those made by well-known individuals, can be powerful attention-getting devices. The quotation should be pertinent to your topic, short, and interesting.

- **Self-interest.** Review your entire presentation to ensure that it meets the critical *What's-in-it-for-me* audience test. People are most interested in things that benefit them.

© iStockphoto.com/Izabela Habur

---

message, so keep your presentation simple and logical. Remember, listeners have no pages to refer to should they become confused.

When Sandra Castillo began planning her presentation, she understood that listeners are not good at separating major and minor points. Therefore, instead of drowning her listeners in information, she sorted out a few main ideas. In the banking industry, loan officers generally ask the following three questions of each budding entrepreneur: (a) Are you ready to "hit the ground running" in starting your business? (b) Have you done your homework? and (c) Have you made realistic projections of potential sales, cash flow, and equity investment? These questions would become her main points, but Sandra wanted to streamline them further so that her audience would be sure to remember them. She encapsulated the questions

**Figure 12.4** Outlining an Oral Presentation

### What Makes a Loan Officer Say Yes?

**I. INTRODUCTION**
- A. How many of you expect one day to start your own business? How many of you have all the cash available to capitalize that business when you start? *(Captures attention)*
- B. Like you, nearly every entrepreneur needs cash to open a business, and I promise you that by the end of this talk you will have inside information on how to make a loan application that will be successful. *(Involves audience)*
- C. As a loan officer at First Fidelity Trust, which specializes in small-business loans, I make decisions on requests from entrepreneurs like you applying for start-up money. *(Identifies speaker)*

  *Transition:* Your professor invited me here today to tell you how you can improve your chances of getting a loan from us or from any other lender. I have suggestions in three areas: experience, preparation, and projection. *(Previews three main points)*

**II. BODY** *(Establishes main points)*
- A. First, let's consider experience. You must show that you can hit the ground running.
  1. Demonstrate what experience you have in your proposed business.
  2. Include your résumé when you submit your business plan.
  3. If you have little experience, tell us whom you would hire to supply the skills that you lack.

     *Transition:* In addition to experience, loan officers will want to see that you have researched your venture thoroughly. *(Develops coherence with three planned transitions)*
- B. My second suggestion, then, involves preparation. Have you done your homework?
  1. Talk to local businesspeople, especially those in related fields.
  2. Conduct traffic counts or other studies to estimate potential sales.
  3. Analyze the strengths and weaknesses of the competition.

     *Transition:* Now that we've discussed preparation, we're ready for my final suggestion.
- C. My last tip is the most important one. It involves making a realistic projection of your potential sales, cash flow, and equity.
  1. Present detailed monthly cash-flow projections for the first year.
  2. Describe *What-if* scenarios indicating both good and bad possibilities.
  3. Indicate that you intend to supply at least 25 percent of the initial capital yourself.

     *Transition:* The three major points I've just outlined cover critical points in obtaining start-up loans. Let me review them for you.

**III. CONCLUSION**
- A. Loan officers are most likely to say yes to your loan application if you do three things: (1) prove that you can hit the ground running when your business opens; (2) demonstrate that you've researched your proposed business seriously; and (3) project a realistic picture of your sales, cash flow, and equity. *(Summarizes main points)*
- B. Experience, preparation, and projection, then, are the three keys to launching your business with the necessary start-up capital so that you can concentrate on where your customers, not your funds, are coming from. *(Provides final focus)*

---

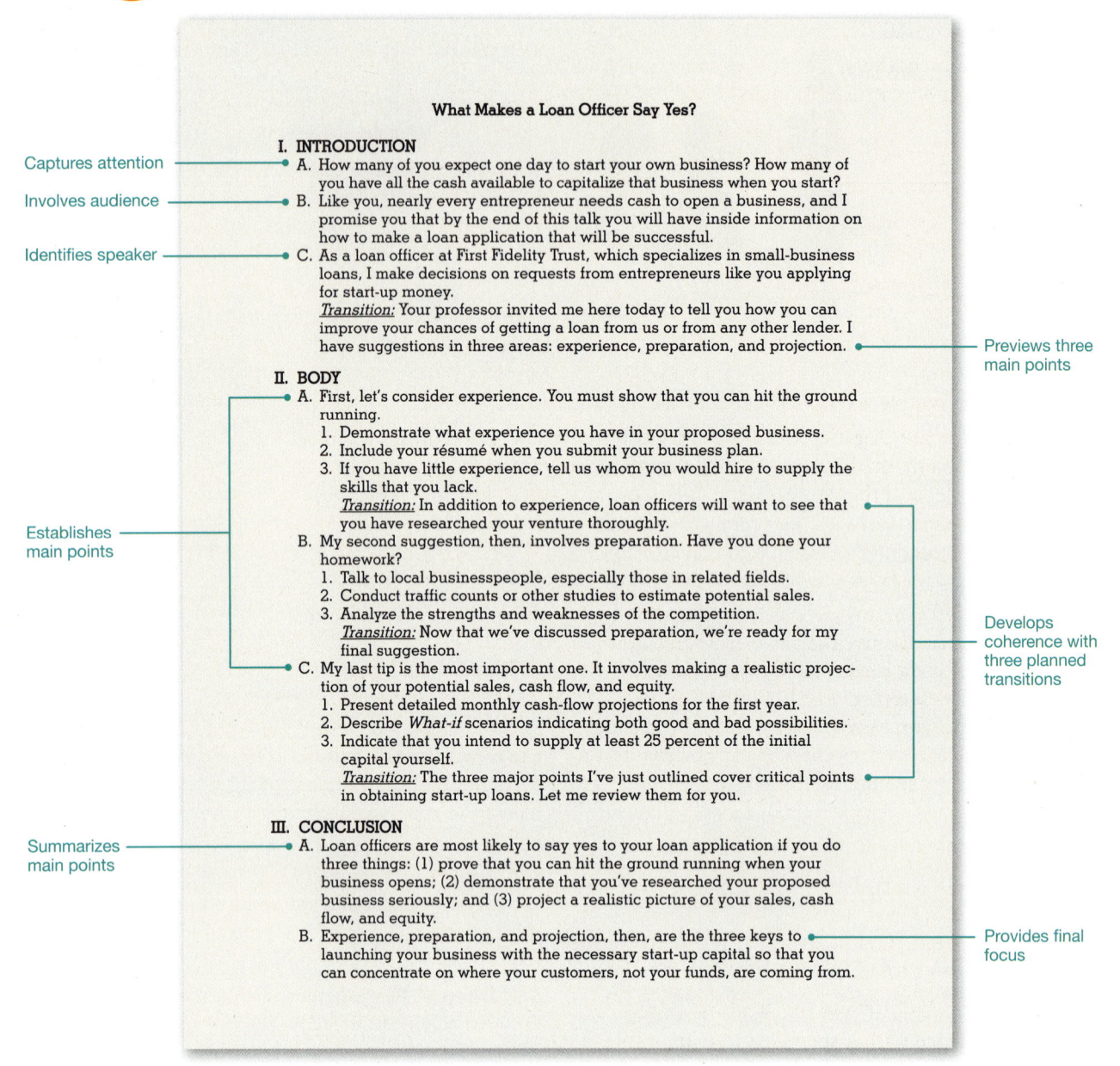

in three words: *experience, preparation*, and *projection*. As you can see in Figure 12.4, Sandra prepared a sentence outline showing these three main ideas. Each is supported by examples and explanations.

How to organize and sequence main ideas may not be immediately obvious when you begin working on a presentation. The following methods, which review and amplify those discussed in Chapter 10, provide many possible strategies and examples to help you organize a presentation:

- **Chronology:** A presentation describing the history of a problem, organized from the first sign of trouble to the present.
- **Geography/space:** A presentation about the changing diversity of the workforce, organized by regions in the country (East Coast, West Coast, and so forth).

- **Topic/function/conventional grouping:** A presentation discussing mishandled airline baggage, organized by names of airlines.
- **Comparison/contrast (pro/con):** A presentation comparing e-marketing with traditional direct mail.
- **Journalistic pattern (the six Ws):** A presentation describing how identity thieves can ruin your good name. Organized by *who, what, when, where, why,* and *how.*
- **Value/size:** A presentation describing fluctuations in housing costs, organized by prices of homes.
- **Importance:** A presentation describing five reasons a company should move its headquarters to a specific city, organized from the most important reason to the least important.
- **Problem/solution:** A presentation offering a solution to a problem of declining sales, such as reducing staff.
- **Simple/complex:** A presentation explaining the genetic modification of corn, organized from simple seed production to complex gene introduction.
- **Best case/worst case:** A presentation analyzing whether two companies should merge, organized by the best-case results (improved market share, profitability, employee morale) and the worst-case results (devalued stock, lost market share, employee malaise).

In the presentation outline shown in Figure 12.4, Sandra arranged the main points by importance, placing the most important point last, where it had maximum effect. When organizing any presentation, prepare a little more material than you think you will actually need. Savvy speakers always have something useful in reserve such as an extra handout, slide, or idea—just in case they finish early. At the same time, most speakers go about 25 percent over the time they spent practicing at home in front of the mirror. If your speaking time is limited, as it usually is in your classes, aim for less than the limit when rehearsing, so that you don't take time away from the next presenters.

## 12-2c Summarizing in the Conclusion

Nervous speakers often rush to wrap up their presentations because they can't wait to flee the stage. However, listeners will remember the conclusion more than any other part of a speech. That's why you should spend some time making it as effective as you can. Strive to achieve three goals:

- Summarize the main themes of the presentation.
- Leave the audience with a specific and memorable take-away.
- Include a statement that allows you to exit the podium gracefully.

A conclusion is like a punch line and must be memorable. Think of it as the high point of your presentation, a valuable kernel of information to take away. The valuable kernel of information, or take-away, should tie in with the opening or present a forward-looking idea. Avoid merely rehashing, in the same words, what you said before, but ensure that you will leave the audience with very specific information or benefits and a positive impression of you and your company. The take-away is the value of the presentation to the audience and the benefit audience members believe they have received. The tension that you built in the early parts of the talk now culminates in the close. Compare these poor and improved conclusions:

> **Poor conclusion:** *Well, I guess that's about all I have to say. Thanks for your time.*
> **Improved:** *In bringing my presentation to a close, I will restate my major purpose. . . .*
> **Improved:** *In summary, my major purpose has been to. . . .*
> **Improved:** *In conclusion, let me review my three major points. They are. . . .*

> **OFFICE INSIDER**
>
> "Rapport is what happens when you have everything in harmony. Your speech is right. The audience receives it well. They enjoy listening to it as much as you enjoy delivering it."
>
> —Susan Dugdale, writer, word lover, website creator, Toastmaster

Notice how Sandra Castillo, in the conclusion shown in Figure 12.4, summarized her three main points and provided a final focus to listeners.

If you are making a recommendation, you might end as follows: *In conclusion, I recommend that we retain Matrixx Marketing to conduct a telemarketing campaign beginning September 1 at a cost of X dollars. To do so, I suggest that we (a) finance this campaign from our operations budget, (b) develop a persuasive message describing our new product, and (c) name Lisa Beck to oversee the project.*

In your conclusion you could use an anecdote, an inspiring quotation, or a statement that ties in the opener and offers a new insight. Whatever you choose, be sure to include a closing thought that indicates you are finished.

### 12-2d Establishing Audience Rapport

Good speakers are adept at building audience rapport. They form a bond with the audience; they entertain as well as inform. How do they do it? From observations of successful and unsuccessful speakers, we have learned that the good ones use a number of verbal and nonverbal techniques to connect with their audiences. Their helpful techniques include providing effective imagery, supplying verbal signposts, and using body language strategically.

**Effective Imagery.** You will lose your audience quickly if you fill your talk with abstractions, generalities, and dry facts. To enliven your presentation and enhance comprehension, try using some of the techniques presented in Figure 12.5. However, beware of exaggeration or distortion. Keep your imagery realistic and credible.

**Verbal Signposts.** Speakers must remember that listeners, unlike readers of a report, cannot control the rate of presentation or read through pages to review main points. As a result, listeners get lost easily. Knowledgeable speakers help the audience recognize the organization and main points in an oral message with verbal signposts. They keep listeners on track by including helpful previews, summaries, and transitions, such as these:

- **Previewing**
  *The next segment of my talk presents three reasons for. . . .*
  *Let's now consider the causes of. . . .*

- **Summarizing**
  *Let me review with you the major problems I have just discussed.*
  *You see, then, that the most significant factors are. . . .*

- **Switching directions**
  *Thus far we have talked solely about . . . ; now let's move to. . . .*
  *I have argued that . . . and . . . , but an alternate view holds that. . . .*

You can further improve any oral presentation by including appropriate transitional expressions such as *first, second, next, then, therefore, moreover, on the other hand, on the contrary,* and *in conclusion.* These transitional expressions build coherence, lend emphasis, and tell listeners where you are headed. Notice in Sandra Castillo's outline in Figure 12.4 the specific transitional elements designed to help listeners recognize each new principal point.

**Nonverbal Messages.** Although what you say is most important, the nonverbal messages you send can also have a powerful effect on how well your audience receives your message. How you look, how you move, and how you speak can make or break your presentation. The following suggestions focus on nonverbal tips to ensure that your verbal message resonates with your audience.

- **Look terrific!** Like it or not, you will be judged by your appearance. For everything but small in-house presentations, be sure to dress professionally. The rule of thumb is that you should dress at least as well as the best-dressed person in the audience.

Figure 12.5 Engaging the Audience With Effective Imagery

**Metaphor** — Comparison between dissimilar things without the words *like* or *as*
- Our competitor's CEO is a snake when it comes to negotiating.
- My desk is a garbage dump.

**Analogy** — Comparison of similar traits between dissimilar things
- Product development is similar to conceiving, carrying, and delivering a baby.
- Downsizing is comparable to an overweight person's regimen of dieting and exercising.

**Personalized Statistics** — Statistics that affect the audience
- Look around you. Only three out of five graduates will find a job right after graduation.
- One typical meal at a fast food restaurant contains all the calories you need for an entire day.

**Worst- or Best-Case Scenario** — The worst or best that could happen
- If we don't back up now, a crash could wipe out all customer data.
- If we fix the system now, we can expand our customer files and also increase sales.

**Personal Anecdote** — A personal story
- Let me share a few personal blunders online and what I learned from my mistakes.
- I always worried about my pets while I was away. That's when I decided to start a pet hotel.

**Simile** — Comparison that includes the words *like* or *as*
- Our critics used our report like a drunk uses a lamppost—for support rather than illumination.
- She's as happy as someone who just won the lottery.

- **Animate your body.** Be enthusiastic and let your body show it. Stand with good posture to show confidence. Emphasize ideas to enhance points about size, number, and direction. Use a variety of gestures, but don't plan them in advance.
- **Punctuate your words.** You can keep your audience interested by varying your tone, volume, pitch, and pace. Use pauses before and after important points. Allow the audience to take in your ideas.
- **Get out from behind the podium.** Avoid standing rigidly behind the podium. Movement makes you look natural and comfortable. You might pick a few places in the room to walk to. Even if you must stay close to your visual aids, make a point of leaving them occasionally so that the audience can see your whole body.

Chapter 12: Business Presentations

## OFFICE INSIDER

"New, dynamic presentation tools like Prezi allow us to communicate design ideas with our clients in highly engaging and dynamic ways, liberating interesting conversations from the boredom of one-way presentations."

—Randy Howder, design strategist with Gensler

**LEARNING OBJECTIVE 3**

Understand visual aids and how to avoid ineffective PowerPoint practices.

- **Vary your facial expression**. Begin with a smile, but change your expressions to correspond with the thoughts you are voicing. You can shake your head to show disagreement, roll your eyes to show disdain, look heavenward for guidance, or wrinkle your brow to show concern or dismay.

Whenever possible, beginning presenters should have an experienced speaker watch them and give them tips as they rehearse. Your instructor is an important coach who can provide you with invaluable feedback. In the absence of helpers, record yourself and watch your nonverbal behavior on camera. Are you doing what it takes to build rapport?

## 12-3 Understanding Contemporary Visual Aids

Before you make a business presentation, consider this wise proverb: "Tell me, I forget. Show me, I remember. Involve me, I understand." Your goals as a speaker are to make listeners understand, remember, and act on your ideas. To get them interested and involved, include effective visual aids. Some experts say that we acquire as much as 85 percent of all our knowledge visually: "Professionals everywhere need to know about the incredible inefficiency of text-based information and the incredible effects of images," says developmental biologist John Medina.[2] Therefore, an oral presentation that incorporates visual aids is far more likely to be retained than one lacking visual enhancement.

Good visual aids serve many purposes. They emphasize and clarify main points, thus improving comprehension and retention. They increase audience interest, and they make the presenter appear more professional, better prepared, and more persuasive. Well-designed visual aids illustrate and emphasize your message more effectively than words alone; therefore, they may help shorten a meeting or achieve your goal faster. Good visuals also serve to jog the memory of a speaker, thus improving self-confidence, poise, and delivery.

### 12-3a Types of Visual Aids

Speakers have many forms of media at their fingertips to enhance their presentations. Figure 12.6 describes the pros and cons of several visual aids, both high-tech and low-tech, that can guide you in selecting the best one for any speaking occasion. Two of the most popular visuals for business presentations are multimedia slides and handouts. Zoom presentations, an alternative to multimedia slides, are growing in popularity.

**Multimedia Slides.** With today's excellent software programs—such as Microsoft PowerPoint, Apple Keynote, Apache OpenOffice Impress, Corel Presentations, and Adobe Presenter—you can create dynamic, colorful presentations with your desktop, laptop, tablet, or smartphone. The output from these programs is generally shown on a computer screen, a TV monitor, an LCD (liquid crystal display) panel, or a projection screen. With a little expertise and the right equipment, you can create multimedia presentations that include audio, videos, images, animation, and hyperlinks, as described in the next section on multimedia presentations. Digital slides can also be uploaded to a website or broadcast on the Web.

**Handouts.** You can enhance and complement your presentations by distributing pictures, outlines, brochures, articles, charts, summaries, or other supplements. Speakers who use multimedia presentation software often prepare a set of their slides along with notes to hand out to viewers. To avoid distractions and to keep control, you should announce and discuss handouts during the presentation but delay distributing them until after you finish.

Figure 12.6 Pros and Cons of Visual Aid Options

| | Pros | Cons |
|---|---|---|
| **High Tech** | | |
| **Multimedia Slides** | Create professional appearance with many color, art, graphic, and font options. Ability to incorporate video, audio, and hyperlinks. Easy to use and transport via removable storage media, Web download, or e-mail attachment. Inexpensive to update. | Present potential incompatibility issues. Require costly projection equipment and practice for smooth delivery. Tempt user to include razzle-dazzle features that may fail to add value. Too one-dimensional and linear. |
| **Zoom Presentations** | Nonlinear, 3D quality allows presenter to zoom in and out of content to show the "big picture" or specific details. Attractive templates. Ability to insert rich media. Presentations are interactive, cinematic, and dynamic. | Cloud-based, so Internet access is required. No way to edit images. Limited font choices. Because there are no separate slides, some users find it difficult to move around the canvas. Zooming can be distracting and even nauseating. |
| **Video** | Gives an accurate representation of the content; strong indication of forethought and preparation. | Creates potential for compatibility issues related to computer video formats. Expensive to create and update. |
| **Low Tech** | | |
| **Handouts** | Encourage audience participation. Easy to maintain and update. Enhance recall because audience keeps reference material. | Increase risk of unauthorized duplication of speaker's material. Can be difficult to transport. May cause speaker to lose audience's attention. |
| **Flipcharts or Whiteboards** | Provide inexpensive option available at most sites. Easy to (a) create, (b) modify or customize on the spot, (c) record comments from the audience, and (d) combine with more high-tech visuals in the same presentation. | Require graphics talent. Difficult for larger audiences to see. Prepared flipcharts are cumbersome to transport and easily worn with use. |
| **Props** | Offer a realistic reinforcement of message content. Increase audience participation with close observation. | Lead to extra work and expense in transporting and replacing worn objects. Limited use with larger audiences. |

**Zoom Presentations.** Many business presenters feel limited by multimedia slides, which tend to be linear. As a result, some communicators prefer more dynamic visual aids. Using software such as Prezi, which is a cloud-based presentation and storytelling tool, businesspeople can design 3D presentations. These 3D presentations allow the speaker to zoom out and in of images to help the audience better understand and remember content, details, and relationships.[3] Zoom presentations allow presenters to communicate their ideas in a more exciting, creative way. Audience members also seem to appreciate the cinematic, interactive quality of these presentations. Figure 12.7 shows what a typical Prezi canvas looks like during the design process.

Chapter 12: Business Presentations

Figure **12.7** Prezi Zoom Presentation

Prezi uses one canvas for a presentation rather than individual slides. Here is an example of the main canvas of a zoom presentation. Clicking on any section of this canvas will zoom in on detailed information. For example, if you click on the area around the tree roots, you will zoom in on a quote about thinking positively, as shown in the thumbnail images in the left pane.

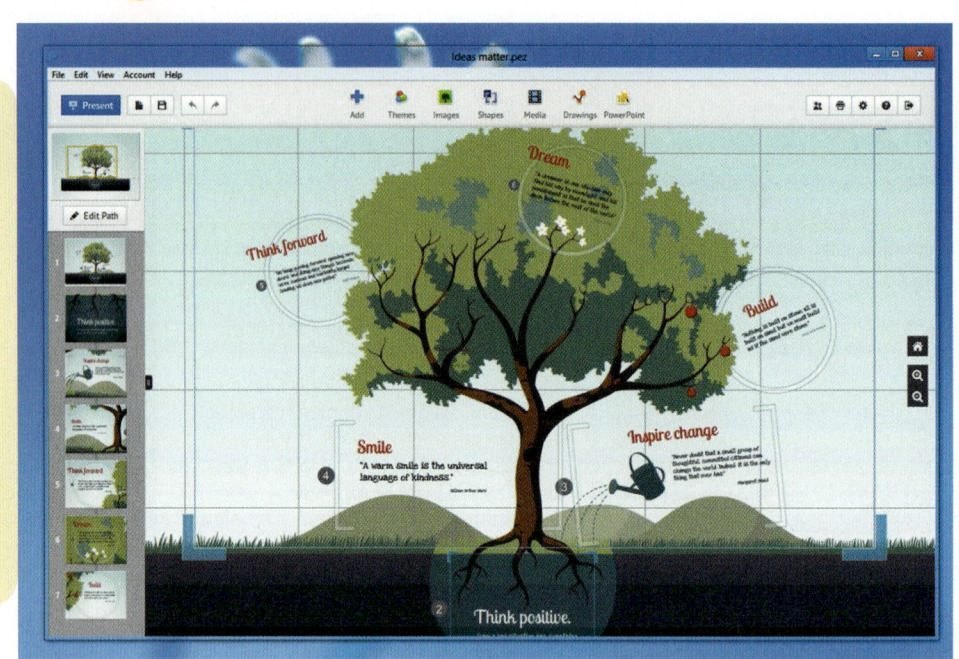

*Source:* http://prezi-a.akamaihd.net/presskit/Prezi%20Desktop/PreziDesktop_Windows.png

### 12-3b Moving Beyond PowerPoint Bullets

Few businesspeople would do without the razzle-dazzle of colorful images to make their points. Electronic slideshows, created using PowerPoint in particular, have become a staple of business presentations. However, overuse or misuse may be the downside of the ever-present PowerPoint slideshow. Over more than two decades of the software program's existence, millions of poorly created and badly delivered presentations have tarnished PowerPoint's reputation as an effective communication tool. Tools are helpful only when used properly.

In the last few years, several communication consultants have tried to show businesspeople how they can move "beyond bullet points." The experts recommend creating slideshows that tell a story and send a powerful message with much less text and more images.[4] Presentation guru Garr Reynolds urges readers to unleash their creativity: "Do not rely on Microsoft or Apple or anyone else to dictate your choices. Most of all, do not let mere habit—and the habits of others—dictate your decisions on how you prepare and design and deliver your presentations."[5] However, before breaking with established rules and expectations, we first need to understand design basics.

Even much-touted alternatives to PowerPoint, such as Prezi and SlideRocket, require some knowledge of the sound design principles covered in the next section. Figure 12.8 shows some of the tools that SlideRocket provides to create a visually rich presentation. The goal is to abandon boring bulleted lists.

**LEARNING OBJECTIVE 4**
Create an impressive, error-free multimedia presentation that shows a firm grasp of basic visual design principles.

## 12-4 Preparing Engaging Multimedia Presentations

Some presenters prefer to create their visuals first and then develop the narrative around their visuals. Others prepare their content first and then create the visual component. The risk associated with the first approach is that you may be tempted to spend too much time making your visuals look good and not enough time

Figure 12.8 SlideRocket Presentation

SlideRocket is a cloud-based presentation software. Like PowerPoint, it allows users to create slides, but it takes the emphasis off bullet points. Instead, SlideRocket offers numerous tools to help users create visually rich slides: stock photos, flash animation, 2D and 3D transitional effects, tables, and charts.

Source: http://www.sliderocket.com/product/

preparing your content. Remember that great-looking slides never compensate for thin content.

The following sections explain how to adjust your visuals to the situation and your audience. You will also receive how-to instructions for creating engaging and visually appealing PowerPoint, SlideRocket, and Prezi presentations.

## 12-4a Analyzing the Situation and Purpose

Making the best design choices for your presentation depends greatly on your analysis of the situation and the purpose of your slideshow. Will your slides be used during a live presentation? Will they be part of a self-running presentation such as in a store kiosk? Will they be saved on a server so that users can watch the presentation online at their convenience? Will they be sent as a PowerPoint show or a PDF slide deck to a client instead of a hard-copy report? Are you converting your presentation for viewing on smartphones or tablets?

If you are e-mailing the presentation or posting it online as a self-contained file, or slide deck, it should feature more text than one that you would deliver orally. If, on the other hand, you are creating slides for a live presentation, you will likely rely more on images than on text.

## 12-4b Adjusting Slide Design to Your Audience

Think about how you can design your presentation to get the most positive response from your audience. Audiences respond, for example, to the colors, images, and special effects you use. Primary ideas are generally best conveyed with bold colors such as blue, green, and purple. Because the messages that colors convey can vary from culture to culture, presenters must choose colors and other design elements carefully.

**The Meaning of Color.** In the United States, blue is the color of credibility, tranquility, conservatism, and trust. Therefore, it is the background color of choice for many business presentations and social media sites. Green relates to interaction, growth, money, and stability. It can work well as a background or an accent color. Purple can also work as a background or accent color. It conveys spirituality, royalty, dreams, and humor.[6] As for text, adjust the color in such a way that it provides high contrast so it is readable. White or yellow, for example, usually works well on dark backgrounds.

Adapt the slide colors based on where you will give the presentation. Use light text on a dark background for presentations in darkened rooms. Use dark text on

Chapter 12: Business Presentations

## OFFICE INSIDER

"Don't blame PowerPoint for the millions of poor presentations that are delivered every day. The hundreds of millions of dollars wasted every year in boring meetings with mind-numbing presentations [are] the fault of professionals and organizations not wanting to put in the hard work it takes to craft a clear, compelling message."

—Dave Paradi, presentation consultant

---

a light background for presentations in lighted rooms. Avoid using a dark font on a dark background, such as red text on a dark blue background. In the same way, avoid using a light font on a light background, such as white text on a pale blue background.

**The Power of Images.** Adapt the amount of text on your slide to how your audience will use the slides. As a general guideline, most graphic designers encourage the use of *the 6-x-6 rule*: "Six bullets per screen, max; six words per bullet, max."[7] You may find, however, that breaking this rule is sometimes necessary, particularly when your users will be viewing the presentation on their own with no speaker assistance. For most purposes, though, strive to break free from bulleted lists whenever possible and minimize the use of text.

When using presentation software such as PowerPoint, try to avoid long, boring bulleted lists. You can alter layouts by repositioning, resizing, or changing the fonts for the placeholders in which your title, bulleted list, organization chart, video clip, photograph, or other elements appear. Figure 12.9 shows how to make your slides visually more appealing and memorable even with relatively small changes.

Notice that the bulleted items on the Before Revision slide in Figure 12.9 are not parallel. The wording looks as if the author had been brainstorming or freewriting a first draft. The bullets on the After Revision slide are very short and well within the 6-x-6 rule, although they are complete sentences. The illustrations in the revised slide add interest and highlight the message. You may use stock photos that you can download from the Web for personal or school use without penalty, or consider taking your own digital pictures.

You can also use other PowerPoint features, such as SmartArt, to add variety and pizzazz to your slides. Converting pure text and bullet points to graphics, charts, and other images will keep your audiences interested and help them retain the information you are presenting.

**The Impact of Special Effects.** Just as you anticipate audience members' reactions to color and images, you can usually anticipate their reactions to special effects. Using animation and sound effects—flying objects, swirling text, clashing cymbals, and the like—only because they are available is not a good idea. Special effects distract your audience, drawing attention away from your main points. Add

---

**Figure 12.9** Revising and Enhancing Slides for Greater Impact

**Before Revision**

### Reasons for Selling Online

- Your online business can grow globally.
- Customer convenience.
- You can conduct your business 24/7.
- No need for renting a retail store or hiring employees.
- Reduce inquiries by providing policies and a privacy statement.
- Customers can buy quickly and easily.

**After Revision**

### Why You Should Sell Online

Grow business globally.　　Offer convenience to customers.　　Conduct business 24/7.

Save on rent and staff.　　Create policies to reduce inquiries.

The slide on the left contains bullet points that are not parallel and that overlap in meaning. The second and sixth bullet points say the same thing. Moreover, some bullet points are too long. After revision, the slide on the right has a more convincing title illustrating the "you" view. The bullet points are shorter, and each begins with a verb for parallelism and an emphasis on action. The illustrations add interest.

Chapter 12: Business Presentations

animation features only if doing so helps convey your message or adds interest to the content. When your audience members leave, they should be commenting on the ideas you conveyed—not on the wild swivels and sound effects. The zooming effect of Prezi presentations can add value to your presentation as long as it helps your audience understand connections and remember content. The motion should not make your listeners dizzy.

### 12-4c Building Your Business Presentation

After considering design principles and their effects, you are ready to start putting together your presentation. In this section you will learn how to organize and compose your presentation, which templates to choose, and how to edit, proofread, and evaluate your work.

**Organizing Your Presentation.** When you prepare your presentation, translate the major headings in your outline into titles for slides. Then build bullet points using short phrases. In Chapter 4 you learned to improve readability by using graphic highlighting techniques, including bullets, numbers, and headings. In preparing a PowerPoint, SlideRocket, or Prezi presentation, you will use those same techniques.

The slides (or canvas) you create to accompany your spoken ideas can be organized with visual elements that will help your audience understand and remember what you want to communicate. Let's say, for example, that you have three points in your presentation. You can create a blueprint slide that captures the three points in a visually appealing way, and then you can use that slide several times throughout your presentation. Near the beginning, the blueprint slide provides an overview of your points. Later, it provides transitions as you move from point to point. For transitions, you can direct your audience's attention by highlighting the next point you will be talking about. Finally, the blueprint slide can be used near the end to provide a review of your key points.

**Composing Your Presentation.** During the composition stage, many users fall into the trap of excessive formatting and programming. They fritter away precious time fine-tuning their slides or canvas and don't spend enough time on what they are going to say and how they will say it. To avoid this trap, set a limit for how much time you will spend making your slides or canvas visually appealing. Your time limit will be based on how many "bells and whistles" (a) your audience expects and (b) your content requires to make it understandable. Remember that not every point nor every thought requires a visual. In fact, it's smart to switch off the presentation occasionally and direct the focus to yourself. Darkening the screen while you discuss a point, tell a story, give an example, or involve the audience will add variety to your presentation.

Create a slide or canvas only if it accomplishes at least one of the following purposes:

- Generates interest in what you are saying and helps the audience follow your ideas
- Highlights points you want your audience to remember
- Introduces or reviews your key points
- Provides a transition from one major point to the next
- Illustrates and simplifies complex ideas

Consider perusing the Help articles built into your presentation software or purchasing one of many inexpensive guides to electronic slide presentations. Your presentations will be more appealing and you will save time if you know, for example, how to design with master slides and how to create your own templates.

**Working With Templates.** All presentation programs require you to (a) select or create a template that will serve as the background for your presentation and (b) make each slide by selecting a layout that best conveys your message. Novice and even advanced users often choose existing templates because they are designed by

---

### OFFICE INSIDER

*"Keep it simple. Limit the number of illustrations and reduce the number of words. One concept on a slide is sufficient. Remember: Less is better!"*

—Joyce Kupsh, PowerPoint expert and coauthor of *Presentation Design and Delivery*

professionals who know how to combine harmonious colors, borders, bullet styles, and fonts for pleasing visual effects. If you prefer, you can alter existing templates so they better suit your needs. Adding a corporate logo, adjusting the color scheme to better match the colors used on your organization's website, or selecting a different font are just some of the ways you can customize existing templates. One big advantage of templates is that they get you started quickly.

Be careful, though, of what one expert has labeled "visual clichés."[8] Overused templates and clip art that come preinstalled with PowerPoint, SlideRocket, and Prezi can weary viewers who have seen them repeatedly in presentations. Instead of using a standard template, search for *PowerPoint template*, *SlideRocket template*, or *Prezi template* in your favorite search tool. You will see hundreds of templates available as free downloads. Unless your employer requires that presentations all have the same look, your audience will appreciate fresh templates that complement the purpose of your presentation and provide visual variety.

**Revising and Proofreading.** Use the PowerPoint slide sorter view to rearrange, insert, and delete slides during the revision process. You can also use the Prezi editor to make any necessary changes to your canvas. This is the time to focus on making your presentation as clear and concise as possible. If you are listing items, be sure they all use parallel grammatical form. Figure 12.10 shows how to revise a PowerPoint slide to improve it for conciseness, parallelism, and other features. Study the design tips described in the first slide and determine which suggestions their author did not follow. Then compare it with the revised slide.

As you are revising, check carefully to find spelling, grammar, punctuation, and other errors. Use the PowerPoint, SlideRocket, or Prezi spell-check feature, but don't rely on it solely. Careful proofing, preferably from a printed copy of the slide-show, is a must. Nothing is as embarrassing as projecting errors on a huge screen in front of an audience. Also, check for consistency in how you capitalize and punctuate points throughout the presentation.

**Evaluating Your Presentation.** Finally, critically evaluate your slideshow. Is your message presented in a visually appealing way? Have you tested your slides on the equipment and in the room you will be using during your presentation? Do the

Figure **12.10** Designing More Effective Slides

**Before Revision**

DESIGN TIPS FOR SLIDE TEXT
1. STRIVE TO HAVE NO MORE THAN SIX BULLETS PER SLIDE AND NO MORE THAN SIX WORDS PER BULLET.
2. IF YOU USE UPPER- AND LOWERCASE TEXT, IT IS EASIER TO READ.
3. IT IS BETTER TO USE PHRASES RATHER THAN SENTENCES.
4. USING A SIMPLE HIGH-CONTRAST TYPE FACE IS EASIER TO READ AND DOES NOT DISTRACT FROM YOUR PRESENTATION.
5. BE CONSISTENT IN YOUR SPACING, CAPITALIZATION, AND PUNCTUATION.

**After Revision**

Design Tips for Slide Text
- Six or fewer bullets per slide
- Six or fewer words per bullet
- Concise phrases, not sentences
- Simple typeface
- Consistent spacing, capitalization, punctuation

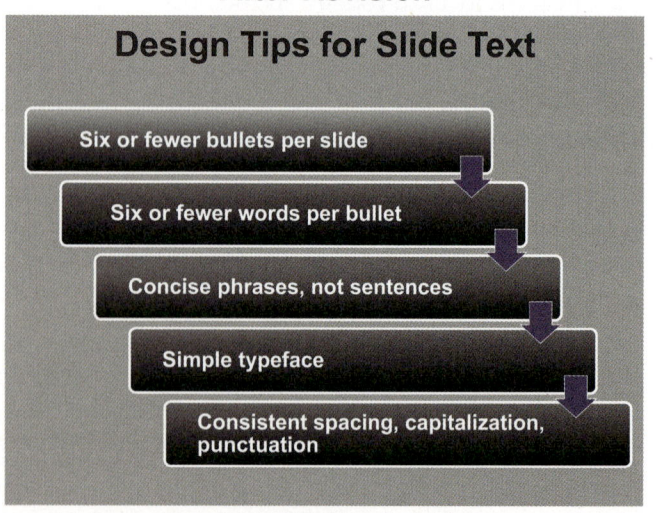

The slide on the left uses a difficult-to-read font style. In addition, the slide includes too many words per bullet and violates most of the slide-making rules it covers. After revision, the slide on the right provides a pleasing color combination, uses short bullet points in a readable font style, and creates an attractive list using PowerPoint SmartArt features.

Figure 12.11 PowerPoint Slides That Illustrate Multimedia Presentations

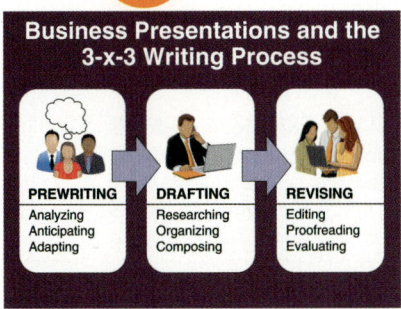

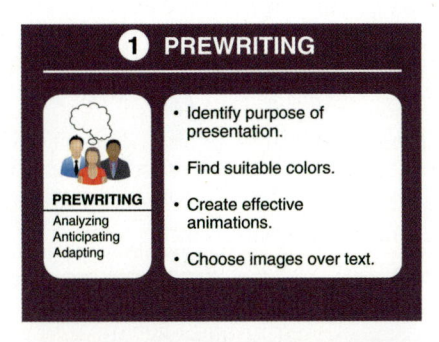

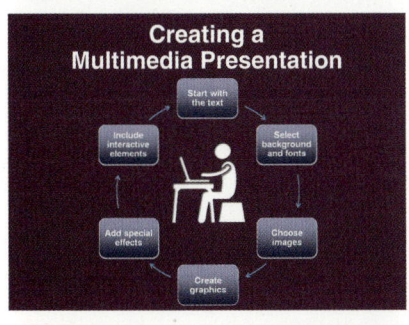

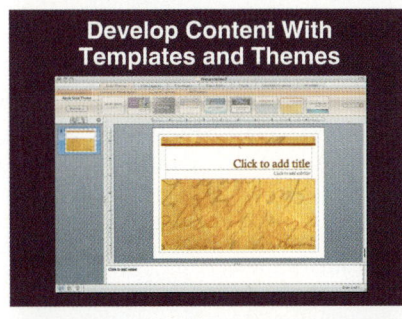

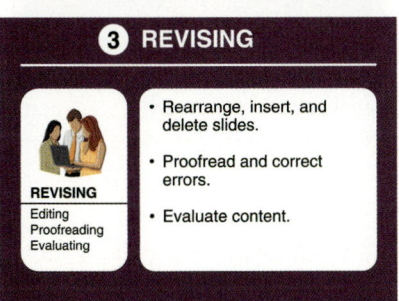

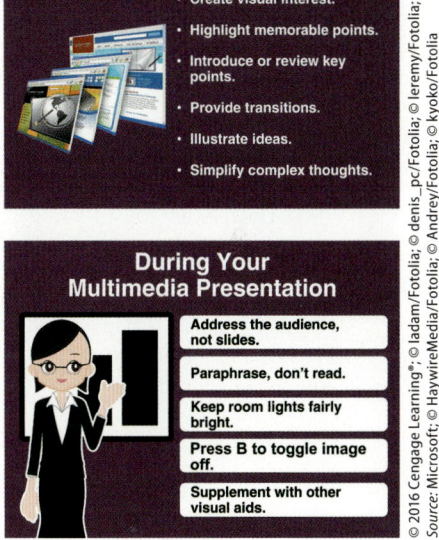

colors you selected work in this new setting? Are the font styles and sizes readable from the back of the room? Figure 12.11 shows examples of PowerPoint slides that incorporate what you have learned in this discussion.

The dark purple background and the matching hues in the slideshow shown in Figure 12.11 are standard choices for many business presentations. With an unobtrusive dark background, white fonts are a good option for maximum contrast and, hence, readability. The creator of the presentation varied the slide design to break the monotony of bulleted or numbered lists. Images and animated diagrams add interest and zing to the slides.

Some presenters allow their PowerPoint slides, SlideRocket slides, or Prezi canvases to steal their thunder. One expert urges speakers to "use their PowerPresence in preference to their PowerPoint."[9] Although multimedia presentations supply terrific sizzle, they cannot replace the steak. In developing a presentation, don't expect your slides to carry the show. You can avoid being upstaged by not relying totally on your slides or canvas. Remember that you are the main attraction!

## 12-4d Seven Steps to Making a Powerful Multimedia Presentation

We have now discussed many suggestions for making effective PowerPoint, SlideRocket, and Prezi presentations, but you may still be wondering how to put it all together. Figure 12.12 presents a step-by-step process for creating a powerful multimedia presentation.

Chapter 12: Business Presentations 405

Figure 12.12 Seven Steps to a Powerful Multimedia Presentation

**1. Start with the text.**
What do you want your audience to believe, do, or remember? Organize your ideas into an outline with major and minor points.

**2. Select background and fonts.**
Choose a template or create your own. Focus on consistent font styles, sizes, colors, and backgrounds. Try to use no more than two font styles in your presentation. The point size should be between 24 and 36, and title fonts should be larger than text font.

**3. Choose images that help communicate your message.**
Use relevant clip art, infographics, photographs, maps, or drawings to illustrate ideas. Microsoft Office Online is accessed in PowerPoint and contains thousands of clip art images and photographs, most of which are in the public domain and require no copyright permissions. Before using images from other sources, determine whether permission from the copyright holder is required.

**4. Create graphics.**
Use software tools to transform boring bulleted items into appealing graphics and charts. PowerPoint's SmartArt feature can be used to create organization charts, cycles and radials, time lines, pyramids, matrixes, and Venn diagrams. Use PowerPoint's Chart feature to develop various types of charts including line, pie, and bar charts. But don't overdo the graphics!

**5. Add special effects.**
To keep the audience focused, use animation and transition features to control when objects or text appear. With motion paths, 3D, and other animation options, you can move objects to various positions on the slide and zoom in and out of images and text on your canvas; or to minimize clutter, you can dim or remove them once they have served their purpose.

**6. Create hyperlinks.**
Make your presentation more interactive and intriguing by connecting to videos, spreadsheets, or websites.

**7. Move your presentation online.**
Make your presentation available by posting it to the Internet or an organization's intranet. Even if you are giving a face-to-face presentation, attendees appreciate these electronic handouts. The most complex option for moving your multimedia presentation to the Web involves a Web conference or broadcast. You can convert your presentations to PDF documents or send them via e-mail as files that open directly in PowerPoint or Prezi. SlideRocket presentations can be embedded in a website or blog to be viewed by anyone who visits the site.

**LEARNING OBJECTIVE 5**
Specify delivery techniques for use before, during, and after a presentation.

## 12-5 Polishing Your Delivery and Following Up

Once you have organized your presentation and prepared visuals, you are ready to practice delivering it. You will feel more confident and appear more professional if you know more about delivery methods and techniques to use before, during, and after your presentation.

406     Chapter 12: Business Presentations

## 12-5a Choosing a Delivery Method

Inexperienced speakers often hold on to myths about public speaking. They may believe that they must memorize an entire presentation or read from a manuscript to be successful. Let's debunk the myths and focus on effective delivery techniques.

**Avoid Memorizing Your Presentation.** Unless you are an experienced performer, you will sound robotic and unnatural if you try to recite your talk by heart. What's more, forgetting your place can be disastrous! That's why we don't recommend memorizing an entire oral presentation. However, memorizing significant parts—the introduction, the conclusion, and perhaps a meaningful quotation—can make your presentation dramatic and impressive.

**Don't Read From Your Notes.** Reading your business presentation to an audience from notes or a manuscript is boring, and listeners will quickly lose interest. Because reading suggests that you don't know your topic well, the audience loses confidence in your expertise. Reading also prevents you from maintaining eye contact. You can't see audience reactions; consequently, you can't benefit from feedback.

**Deliver Your Presentation Extemporaneously.** The best plan for delivering convincing business presentations, by far, is to speak extemporaneously, especially when you are displaying a multimedia presentation, such as a PowerPoint slideshow, SlideRocket slideshow, or Prezi canvas. Extemporaneous delivery means speaking freely, generally without notes, after preparing and rehearsing. This includes commenting on the multimedia visuals you have prepared. Reading notes or a manuscript in addition to a PowerPoint slideshow, SlideRocket slides, or a Prezi canvas will damage your credibility.

**Know When Notes Are Appropriate.** If you give a talk without multimedia technology, you may use note cards or an outline containing key sentences and major ideas, but beware of reading from a script. By preparing and then practicing with your notes, you can use them while also talking to your audience in a conversational manner. Your notes should be neither entire paragraphs nor single words. Instead, they should contain a complete sentence or two to introduce each major idea. Below the topic sentence(s), outline subpoints and illustrations. Note cards will keep you on track and prompt your memory, but only if you have rehearsed the presentation thoroughly.

## Workplace in Focus

Many people fear public speaking. And while tips for overcoming performance anxiety often suggest calming down before a presentation, one Harvard researcher says that the cure for stage fright is not relaxing oneself, but recasting anxiety as excitement—and embracing it. According to a recent study by Alison Wood Brooks of Harvard Business School, individuals who convinced themselves that their nervousness was "excitement" prior to giving a speech performed better than those who attempted to relax. Brooks argues that speakers can recast anxiety as excitement simply through active self-talk, such as saying aloud "I am excited" or "get excited." What other tips can speakers use to help overcome stage fright EN?[11]

Chapter 12: Business Presentations

### 12-5b Before Your Presentation

Speaking in front of a group will be less daunting if you prepare adequately and rehearse sufficiently. Being prepared and confident so you can interact with the audience, and being familiar with the equipment to limit surprises, will add to your peace of mind. Review the tips in the following sections for a smooth start.

**Prepare Thoroughly.** One of the most effective strategies for reducing stage fright is knowing your subject thoroughly. Research your topic diligently and prepare a careful sentence outline. One expert advises presenters to complete their PowerPoint slides, SlideRocket slides, or Prezi canvases a week before the actual talk and rehearse several times each day before the presentation.[10] Those who try to "wing it" usually suffer the worst butterflies—and give the worst presentations. Figure 12.13 offers tips for combating the fear of public speaking.

**Rehearse Repeatedly.** When you rehearse, practice your entire presentation. In PowerPoint you may print out speaker's notes, an outline, or a handout featuring miniature slides, which are excellent for practice. If you don't use an electronic slideshow, place your outline sentences on separate note cards. You may also wish to include transitional sentences to help you move to the next topic as you practice. Rehearse alone or before friends and family. Also consider making an audio or video recording of your rehearsals so you can evaluate your effectiveness.

### Figure 12.13 Conquering Stage Fright

Ever get nervous before making a presentation? Everyone does! And it's not all in your head, either. When you face something threatening or challenging, your body reacts in what psychologists call the fight-or-flight response. This physical reflex provides your body with increased energy to deal with threatening situations. It also creates those sensations—dry mouth, sweaty hands, increased heartbeat, and stomach butterflies—that we associate with stage fright. The fight-or-flight response arouses your body for action—in this case, making a presentation.

Because everyone feels some form of apprehension before speaking, it's impossible to eliminate the physiological symptoms altogether. However, you can reduce their effects with the following techniques:

- **Breathe deeply.** Use deep breathing to ease your fight-or-flight symptoms. Inhale to a count of ten, hold this breath to a count of ten, and exhale to a count of ten. Concentrate on your counting and your breathing; both activities reduce your stress.

- **Convert your fear.** Don't view your sweaty palms and dry mouth as evidence of fear. Interpret them as symptoms of exuberance, excitement, and enthusiasm to share your ideas.

- **Know your topic and come prepared.** Feel confident about your topic. Select a topic that you know well and that is relevant to your audience. Prepare thoroughly and practice extensively.

- **Use positive self-talk.** Remind yourself that you know your topic and are prepared. Tell yourself that the audience is on your side—because it is! Moreover, most speakers appear to be more confident than they feel. Make this apparent confidence work for you.

- **Take a sip of water.** Drink some water to alleviate your dry mouth and constricted voice box, especially if you're talking for more than 15 minutes.

- **Shift the spotlight to your visuals.** At least some of the time the audience will be focusing on your slides, transparencies, handouts, or whatever you have prepared—and not totally on you.

- **Ignore any stumbles.** If you make a mistake, ignore the stumble and keep going. Don't apologize or confess your nervousness. The audience will forget any mistakes quickly.

- **Feel proud when you finish.** You will be surprised at how good you feel when you finish. Take pride in what you have accomplished, and your audience will reward you with applause and congratulations. Your body, of course, will call off the fight-or-flight response and return to normal!

**Time Yourself.** Most audiences tend to get restless during longer talks. Therefore, try to complete your presentation in 20 minutes or less. If you have a time limit, don't go over it. Set a simple kitchen timer during your rehearsal to keep track of time. Better yet, use the PowerPoint function Rehearse Timings in the Slide Show tab to measure the length of your talk as you practice. Other presentation software packages offer similar features.

**Dress Professionally.** Dressing professionally for a presentation will make you look more credible to your audience. You will also feel more confident. If you are not used to professional attire, practice wearing it so you appear comfortable during your presentation.

**Request a Lectern.** Every beginning speaker needs the security of a high desk or lectern from which to deliver a presentation. It serves as a note holder and a convenient place to rest wandering hands and arms. Don't, however, lean on it. Eventually, you will want to interact with the audience without any physical barriers.

**Check the Room.** If you are using a computer, a projector, or sound equipment, be certain they are operational. Allow plenty of time to set up and test your equipment. Before you start, check the lighting, the electrical outlets, and the position of the viewing screen. Confirm that the places you plan to stand are not in the line of the projected image. Audience members don't appreciate having part of the slide displayed on your body. Ensure that the seating arrangement is appropriate to your needs. Make sure that all video or Web links are working and that you know how to operate all features the first time you try.

**Greet Members of the Audience.** Try to make contact with a few members of the audience when you enter the room, while you are waiting to be introduced, or when you walk to the podium. Your body language should convey friendliness, confidence, and enjoyment.

**Practice Stress Reduction.** If you feel tension and fear while you are waiting to speak, use stress-reduction techniques, such as deep breathing. Additional techniques to help you conquer stage fright are presented in Figure 12.13.

No matter how much time you put into preshow setup and testing, you still have no guarantee that all will go smoothly. Therefore, always bring backups of your presentation. Overhead transparencies and handouts of your presentation provide good substitutes. Transferring your presentation to a CD or a USB flash drive that could run from any available computer might prove useful as well. Likewise, copying your file to the cloud (e.g., Dropbox or Google Drive) or sending it to yourself as an e-mail attachment can be beneficial.

### 12-5c During Your Presentation

To stay in control during your talk, to build credibility, and to engage your audience, follow these time-tested guidelines for effective speaking:

**Start With a Pause and Present Your First Sentence From Memory.** When you first approach the audience, take a moment to make yourself comfortable. Establish your control of the situation. By memorizing your opening, you can immediately develop rapport with the audience through eye contact. You will also sound confident and knowledgeable.

**Maintain Eye Contact.** If the size of the audience overwhelms you, pick out two individuals on the right and two on the left. Talk directly to these people. Don't ignore listeners in the back of the room. Even when presenting to a large audience, try to make genuine, not fleeting eye contact with as many people as possible during your presentation.

## Office Insider

*"Don't be afraid to show enthusiasm for your subject. "I'm excited about being here today" says good things to an audience. It generally means that you are confident, you have something of value to say, and you are prepared to state your case clearly. Boredom is contagious."*

—Dianna Booher, communication consultant and author

**Control Your Voice and Vocabulary.** This means speaking in moderated tones but loudly enough to be heard. Eliminate verbal static, such as *ah, er, like, you know,* and *um.* Silence is preferable to meaningless fillers when you are thinking of your next idea.

**Show Enthusiasm.** If you are not excited about your topic, how can you expect your audience to be? Show passion for your topic through your tone, facial expressions, and gestures. Adding variety to your voice also helps to keep your audience alert and interested.

**Skip the Apologies.** Avoid weak openings, such as *I know you have heard this before, but we need to review it anyway.* Or: *I had trouble with my computer and the slides, so bear with me.* Unless the issue is blatant, such as not being able to load the presentation or make the projector work, apologies are counterproductive. Focus on your presentation.

**Slow Down and Know When to Pause.** Many novice speakers talk too rapidly, displaying their nervousness and making it very difficult for audience members to understand their ideas. Put the brakes on and listen to what you are saying. Pauses give the audience time to absorb an important point. Silence can be effective especially when you are transitioning from one point to another. Paraphrase and elaborate on what the listeners have seen. Don't read verbatim from the slides.

**Move Naturally.** If you have a lectern, don't hide behind it. Move about casually and naturally. Using a remote clicker to advance slides will give you the freedom to move about. Avoid fidgeting with your clothing, hair, or items in your pockets. Do not roll up your sleeves or put your hands in your pockets. Learn to use your body to express a point.

**Use Visual Aids Effectively.** You should discuss and interpret each visual aid for the audience. Move aside as you describe it so people can see it fully. Use a laser pointer if necessary, but steady your hand if it is shaking. Don't leave your slides on-screen when you finish discussing them; if you are not ready to continue, dim the slideshow. In Slide Show view in PowerPoint, press *B* on the keyboard to turn on or off the screen image by blackening it. Pressing *W* will turn the screen white. In Prezi, remember to zoom back out when necessary.

**Avoid Digressions.** Stick to your outline and notes. Don't suddenly include clever little anecdotes or digressions that occur to you on the spot. If it is not part of your rehearsed material, leave it out so you can finish on time.

**Summarize Your Main Points and Drive Home Your Message.** Conclude your presentation by reiterating your main points or by emphasizing what you want the audience to think or do. Once you have announced your conclusion, proceed to it directly.

### 12-5d After Your Presentation

As you are concluding you presentation, handle questions and answers competently and provide handouts, if appropriate. Try the following techniques:

**Distribute Handouts.** If you prepared handouts with data the audience will not need during the presentation, pass them out when you finish to prevent any distractions during your talk.

**Encourage Questions but Keep Control.** If the situation permits a question-and-answer period, announce it at the beginning of your presentation. Then, when you finish, ask for questions. Set a time limit for questions and answers. If you don't know the answer to a question, don't make one up or panic. Instead, offer to find the answer within a day or two. If you make such a promise to your audience, be sure to follow through. As you're answering questions, don't allow one individual to dominate the conversation. Keep the entire audience involved.

**Repeat Questions.** Although you may have heard the question, some audience members may not have. Begin each answer by repeating the question. This also gives you thinking time. Then, direct your answer to the entire audience.

**Reinforce Your Main Points.** You can use your answers to restate your primary ideas (*I'm glad you brought that up because it gives me a chance to elaborate on . . .*). In answering questions, avoid becoming defensive or debating the questioner.

**Avoid *Yes, but* Answers.** The word *but* immediately cancels any preceding message. Try replacing it with *and*. For example, *Yes, X has been tried. And Y works even better because. . . .*

**End With a Summary and Appreciation.** To signal the end of the session before you take the last question, say something like *We have time for just one more question.* As you answer the last question, try to work it into a summary of your main points. Then, express appreciation to the audience for the opportunity to present.

## SUMMARY OF LEARNING OBJECTIVES

**12-1** Recognize various types of business presentations, and discuss two important first steps in preparing for any of these presentations.
- Excellent presentation skills are sought by employers and will benefit you at any career stage.
- Presentation types include briefings, reports, podcasts, and webinars; they can be informative or persuasive, face-to-face or virtual, and complex or simple.
- Savvy speakers know what they want to accomplish and are able to adjust to friendly, neutral, uninterested, as well as hostile audiences.

**12-2** Explain how to organize the introduction, body, and conclusion as well as how to build audience rapport in a presentation.
- In the opening, capture the audience's attention, introduce yourself and establish your credibility, and preview your talk.
- Organize the body using chronology, space, function, comparison/contrast, a journalistic pattern, value/size, importance, problem/solution, simple/complex, or best case/worst case.
- In the conclusion, summarize the main topics of your talk, leave the audience with a memorable take-away, and end with a statement that provides a graceful exit.
- Build rapport by using effective imagery, verbal signposts, and positive nonverbal messages.

**12-3** Understand visual aids and how to avoid ineffective PowerPoint practices.
- Your audience is more likely to retain your talk if you use well-prepared visual aids.
- Good visuals emphasize and clarify main points, increase audience interest, prove you are professional, illustrate your message better than words alone, and serve to jog your memory.
- Common types of visual aids are multimedia slides, zoom presentations, videos, handouts, flipcharts and whiteboards, as well as props.
- In good hands PowerPoint is helpful, but you should focus on using more images and less text.

**12-4** Create an impressive, error-free multimedia presentation that shows a firm grasp of basic visual design principles.
- The purpose and the audience determine the slide design, which includes color, images, and special effects.
- Building a presentation involves organizing and composing slide content, avoiding overused templates, and revising, proofreading, and evaluating the final product.
- The seven steps to creating impressive multimedia slides are as follows: start with the text, select a template, choose images, create graphics, add special effects, create hyperlinks, and post online.

Chapter 12: Business Presentations

## 12-5 Specify delivery techniques for use before, during, and after a presentation.

- When delivering a business presentation, don't memorize your talk or read from notes; rather, speak extemporaneously and use notes only when you're not using presentation software.
- Before your presentation prepare and rehearse, time yourself, dress professionally, request a lectern, check the room, greet members of the audience, and practice stress reduction.
- During the presentation deliver your first sentence from memory, maintain eye contact, control your voice, show enthusiasm, slow down, move naturally, use visual aids skillfully, and stay on topic.
- After the presentation distribute handouts, encourage and repeat questions, reinforce your main points, avoid *Yes, but* answers, and end with a summary and appreciation.

# CHAPTER REVIEW

1. List and describe five types of presentations a business professional might make. (Obj. 1)

2. The age, gender, education level, experience, and size of the audience will affect your presentation style and message. List at least five questions you should answer to determine your organizational pattern, delivery style, and supporting material. (Obj. 1)

3. Which effective three-step organizational plan do many speech experts recommend, and why does it work well for oral presentations despite its redundancy? (Obj. 2)

4. What three goals should you accomplish in the introduction to your presentation? (Obj. 2)

5. Name at least eight techniques that can help you gain and keep audience attention. (Obj. 2)

6. List high-tech and low-tech visual aids that you can use when speaking to an audience. Which two are the most popular? (Obj. 3)

7. What is the 6-x-6 rule, and what might prompt a presentation slide creator to break it? (Obj. 4)

8. What questions might help you critically evaluate a slideshow? (Obj. 4)

9. Which delivery method is best for persuasive business presentations? Explain why. (Obj. 5)

10. How can speakers overcome stage fright? Name at least six helpful techniques. (Obj. 5)

## CRITICAL THINKING

11. Most people never address large audiences and live in fear of public speaking. Why then should you hone your presentation skills? (Obj. 1)
12. Communication expert Dianna Booher claims that enthusiasm is infectious and "boredom is contagious."[12] What does this mean for you as a presenter? How can you avoid being a boring speaker? (Objs. 2, 4, and 5)
13. Why do many communication consultants encourage businesspeople to move beyond bullet points? What do they recommend instead and why? (Obj. 3)
14. How can you prevent multimedia presentation software from stealing your thunder? (Obj. 4)
15. U.S. senator from New Jersey, Cory A. Booker, himself a popular and gifted orator, related his father's philosophy on public speaking as follows: "My dad worked for IBM. He said, 'Look, I can't sell products I don't believe in. People will see right through me. But if I'm passionate and have a deep conviction about what I'm doing, I'm the greatest salesman there is.'"[13] What qualities is Senator Booker describing, and why are they important in business? (Objs. 2, 5)

# ACTIVITIES AND CASES

## 12.1 Learning From the Best: Analyzing a Famous Speech (Objs. 1–5)

`Web`

**YOUR TASK.** Search online for a speech by a significant businessperson or well-known political figure. Consider watching the following iconic political speeches, thought to be among the best in the 20th century: Martin Luther King Jr.'s "I Have a Dream" speech, President Kennedy's inaugural address, and Franklin Delano Roosevelt's Pearl Harbor address.[14] If you prefer business tycoons dispensing advice, search for the best-known commencement speeches; for example, Steve Jobs' "Stay Hungry, Stay Foolish" Stanford address, Salman Khan's "Live Your Life Like It's Your Second Chance" speech, or Sheryl Sandberg's "Rocketship" commencement speech at Harvard. Transcripts of these and other well-known speeches are also available online.[15] Write a memo report or give a short presentation to your class critiquing the speech in terms of the following:

a. Effectiveness of the introduction, body, and conclusion
b. Evidence of effective overall organization
c. Use of verbal signposts to create coherence
d. Emphasis of two to four main points
e. Effectiveness of supporting facts (use of examples, statistics, quotations, and so forth)
f. Focus on audience benefits
g. Enthusiasm for the topic
h. Body language and personal mannerisms

## 12.2 Sizing Up Your Audience (Objs. 2, 4)

**YOUR TASK.** Select a recent issue of *Fortune, The Wall Street Journal, Fast Company, Bloomberg Businessweek, The Economist*, or another business periodical approved by your instructor. Based on an analysis of your classmates, select an article that will appeal to them and that you can relate to their needs. Submit to your instructor a one-page summary that includes the following: (a) the author, article title, source, issue date, and page reference; (b) a one-paragraph article summary; (c) a description of why you believe the article will appeal to your classmates; and (d) a summary of how you can relate the article to their needs.

## 12.3 Hiring a Famous Motivational Speaker (Objs. 1, 2, 4, and 5)

`Communication Technology` `Social Media` `Team` `Web`

Have you ever wondered why famous business types, politicians, athletes, and other celebrities can command high speaking fees? How much are they really making per appearance, and what factors may justify their sometimes exorbitant fees? You may also wonder how a motivational speaker or corporate trainer might benefit you and your class or your campus community. Searching for and selecting an expert is easy online with several commercial speaker bureaus vying for clients. All bureaus provide detailed speaker bios, areas of expertise, and fees. One even features video previews of its clients.

The three preeminent agencies for booking talent are Speakerpedia, BigSpeak Speakers Bureau, and Brooks International. Speakerpedia represents the likes of economist Nouriel Roubini, Donald Trump, Jack Welch, Richard Branson, and Suze Orman. BigSpeak standouts are Deepak Chopra, Dr. Susan Love, and distance swimmer Diana Nyad. Brooks International features financier and philanthropist Mike Milken and TV commentator and personal finance expert Terry Savage, among others. Imagine that you have a budget of up to $100,000 to hire a well-known public speaker.

**YOUR TASK.** In teams or individually, select a business-related category of speaker by visiting one of the speaker bureaus online. For example, choose several prominent personal finance gurus (Orman, Savage, and others) or successful entrepreneurs and venture capitalists (Branson, Trump, Jack Welch, and so forth). Other categories are motivational speakers, philanthropists, and famous economists. Study their bios for clues to their expertise and accomplishments. Comparing at least three, come up with a set of qualities that apparently make these people sought-after speakers. Consider how those qualities could enlighten you and your peers. To enrich your experience and enhance your knowledge, watch videos of your chosen speakers on YouTube or TED, if available. Check talent agencies, personal websites, and Facebook for further information. Write a memo report about your speaker group, or present your findings orally, with or without PowerPoint. If your instructor directs, recommend your favorite speaker and give reasons for your decision.

## 12.4 Follow Your Favorite Business Personality on Twitter (Objs. 1–5)

`Social Media` `Web` `Communication Technology`

**YOUR TASK.** On Twitter, in the Search window on top of the page, enter the name of the businessperson whose tweets you wish to follow. Donald Trump, Jack Welch, Richard Branson, Suze Orman, Guy Kawasaki, and other well-known businesspeople are avid Twitter users. Over the course of a few days, read the tweets of your favorite expert. After a while, you should be able to discern certain trends and areas of interest. Note whether and how your subject responds to queries from followers. What are his or her favorite topics? Report your findings to the class, verbally with notes or using PowerPoint. If you find particularly intriguing tweets and links, share them with the class.

## 12.5 Taming Stage Fright (Obj. 5)

**Team**

What scares you the most about making a presentation in front of your class? Being tongue-tied? Fearing all eyes on you? Messing up? Forgetting your ideas and looking silly?

**YOUR TASK.** Discuss the previous questions as a class. Then, in groups of three or four, talk about ways to overcome these fears. Your instructor may ask you to write a memo (individual or collective) summarizing your suggestions, or you may break out of your small groups and report your best ideas to the entire class.

## 12.6 How Much Speaking Can You Expect in Your Field? (Obj. 1)

**YOUR TASK.** Interview one or two individuals in your professional field. How is oral communication important in this profession? Does the need for oral skills change as one advances? What suggestions can these people make to newcomers to the field for developing proficient oral communication skills? Discuss your findings with your class.

## 12.7 Creating an Outline for an Oral Presentation (Obj. 2)

One of the hardest parts of preparing an oral presentation is developing the outline.

**YOUR TASK.** Select an oral presentation topic from the list in Activity 12.14, or suggest an original topic. Prepare an outline for your presentation using the following format:

**Title**
**Purpose**

|  | I. INTRODUCTION |
|---|---|
| **State your name** | A. |
| **Gain attention and involve the audience** | B. |
| **Establish credibility** | C. |
| **Preview main points** | D. |
| **Transition** | |
| | II. BODY |
| **Main point** | A. |
| **Illustrate, clarify, contrast** | 1. |
| | 2. |
| | 3. |
| **Transition** | |
| **Main point** | B. |
| **Illustrate, clarify, contrast** | 1. |
| | 2. |
| | 3. |
| **Transition** | |
| **Main point** | C. |
| **Illustrate, clarify, contrast** | 1. |
| | 2. |
| | 3. |
| **Transition** | |
| | III. CONCLUSION |
| **Summarize main points** | A. |
| **Provide final focus or take-away** | B. |
| **Encourage questions** | C. |

## 12.8 Learning From "Life After Death by PowerPoint" (Objs. 1–5)
**Social Media** | **Web**

**YOUR TASK.** Watch Don McMillan's now famous YouTube classic "Life After Death by PowerPoint 2012." Which specific PowerPoint ills is McMillan satirizing? Write a brief summary of the short clip for discussion in class. With your peers, discuss whether the bad habits the YouTube video parodies correspond with design principles introduced in this chapter.

## 12.9 Observing and Outlining a TED Talk (Objs. 1–5)
**E-mail** | **Social Media** | **Web**

To learn from the presentation skills of the best speakers today, visit the TED channel on YouTube or the TED website. Watch one or more of the 1,600 TED Talks (motto: *Ideas worth spreading*) available online. Standing at over one billion views worldwide, the presentations cover topics from the fields of technology, entertainment, and design (TED).

**YOUR TASK.** If your instructor directs, select and watch one of the TED Talks and outline it. You may also be asked to focus on the selected speaker's presentation techniques based on the guidelines you have studied in this chapter. Jot down your observations either as notes for a classroom discussion or to serve as a basis for an informative memo or e-mail. If directed by your instructor, compose a concise yet informative tweet directing Twitter users to your chosen TED Talk and commenting on it.

## 12.10 Talking About Your Job (Objs. 1–5)
**Communication Technology**

What if you had to create a presentation for your classmates and instructor, or perhaps a potential recruiter, that describes the multiple tasks you perform at work? Could you do it in a five-minute multimedia presentation?

Your instructors, for example, may wear many hats. Most academics (a) teach; (b) conduct research to publish; and (c) provide service to the department, college, university, and community. Can you see how those aspects of their profession lend themselves to an outline of primary slides (teaching, publishing, service) and second-level slides (instructing undergraduate and graduate classes, presenting workshops, and giving lectures under the *teaching* label)?

**YOUR TASK.** Now it's your turn to introduce the duties you perform (or performed) in a current or a past job, volunteer activity, or internship in a brief, simple, yet well-designed PowerPoint presentation. Your goal is to inform your audience of your job duties in a three- to five-minute talk. Use animation features and graphics where appropriate. Your instructor may show you a completed example of this project.

## 12.11 Calling All Angel Investors (Objs. 1–5)
**Communication Technology**

Venture capitalist and angel investor Guy Kawasaki believes that persuasive PowerPoint presentations should be no more than 10 slides long, last 20 minutes at most, and contain 30-point fonts or bigger (the 10/20/30 rule). Kawasaki is convinced that presentations deviating from this rule will fall short of their purpose, which is typically to reach some type of agreement.

Could you interest an investor such as Guy Kawasaki in your business idea? The venture capitalist believes that if you must use more than 10 slides to explain your business, you probably don't have one. Furthermore, Kawasaki claims that the 10 topics a venture capitalist cares about are the following:

1. Problem
2. Your solution
3. Business model
4. Underlying magic/technology
5. Marketing and sales
6. Competition
7. Team
8. Projections and milestones
9. Status and time line
10. Summary and call to action

**YOUR TASK.** Dust off that start-up fantasy you may have, and get to work. Prepare a slideshow that would satisfy Kawasaki's 10/20/30 rule: In 10 slides and a presentation of no more than 20 minutes, address the 10 topics that venture capitalists care about. Make sure that the fonts on your slides are at least 30 points in size.

## 12.12 Perfecting the Art of the Elevator Pitch (Objs 1, 2)

"Can you pass the elevator test?" asks presentation whiz Garr Reynolds in a new twist on the familiar scenario.[16] He suggests that this technique will help you sharpen your core message. In this exercise you need to pitch your idea in a few brief moments instead of the 20 minutes you had been granted with your vice president of product marketing. You arrive at her door for your appointment as she is leaving, coat and briefcase in hand. Something has come up. This meeting is a huge opportunity for you if you want to get the OK from the executive team. Could you sell your idea during the elevator ride and the walk to the parking lot? Reynolds asks. Although this scenario may never happen, you will possibly be asked to shorten a presentation, say, from an hour to 30 minutes or from 20 minutes to 5 minutes. Could you make your message tighter and clearer on the fly?

**YOUR TASK.** Take a business idea you may have, a familiar business topic you care about, or a promotion or raise you wish to request in a time of tight budgets. Create an impromptu two- to five-minute speech making a good case for your core message. Even though you won't have much time to think about the details of your speech, you should be sufficiently familiar with the topic to boil it down and yet be persuasive.

## 12.13 Understanding *Fortune* Lists (Objs. 1, 2)

`Web`

**YOUR TASK.** Using a research database, perform a search to learn how *Fortune* magazine determines which companies make its annual lists. Research the following lists. Then organize and present a five- to ten-minute informative talk to your class.
a. Fortune 500
b. Global 500
c. 100 Best Companies to Work For
d. America's Most Admired Companies

## 12.14 Something to Talk About: Topics for an Oral Presentation (Objs. 1–5)

`Communication Technology` `Web`

**YOUR TASK.** Select a report topic from the following suggestions or from the expanded list of Report Topics at **www.cengagebrain.com**. Prepare a five- to ten-minute oral presentation. Consider yourself an expert who has been called in to explain some aspect of the topic before a group of interested people. Because your time is limited, prepare a concise yet forceful presentation with effective visual aids.
a. What kind of incentives could your company offer to motivate employees to make healthier food choices and to exercise more?
b. How can businesses benefit from Facebook and Twitter? Cite specific examples in your chosen field.
c. Which is financially more beneficial to a business, leasing or buying copiers?
d. Tablet computers are eroding the market share previously held by laptops and netbooks. Which brands are businesses embracing and why? Which features are must-haves?
e. What kind of marketing works with students on college campuses? Word of mouth? Internet advertising? Free samples? How do students prefer to get information about goods and services?
f. How can consumers protect themselves from becoming victims of identity theft?
g. How can companies and nonprofits protect themselves from hackers?
h. How could an intercultural training program be initiated in your school?
i. Companies usually do not admit shortcomings. However, some admit previous failures and use them to strategic advantage. For example, Microsoft acknowledged the shortcomings of Windows 8, its redesigned operating system that users find confusing and annoying. Find three or more examples of companies admitting weaknesses, and draw conclusions from their strategies. Would you recommend this as a sound marketing ploy?
j. How can students and other citizens contribute to conserving gasoline and other fossil fuels to save money and help slow global climate change?
k. What is the career outlook in a field of your choice? Consider job growth, compensation, and benefits. What kind of academic or other experience is typically required in your field?
l. Find a recent "disruptive" (i.e., game-changing or groundbreaking) start-up and study its business model. What need does it fill? Is it about to change its industry significantly? What are its prospects? (For example, check out Uber, Airbnb, or Coursera.)
m. What is telecommuting, and for what kinds of workers is it an appropriate work alternative?
n. What options (think aid, grants, and scholarships) do students have to finance their college tuition and fees as costs continue to rise?
o. What is the economic outlook for a given product, such as hybrid cars, laptop computers, digital cameras, fitness equipment, or a product of your choice?
p. What is Bitcoin and why are banks and law enforcement authorities concerned?
q. What franchise would offer the best investment opportunity for an entrepreneur in your area?
r. How should a job candidate prepare for a video interview via Skype or FaceTime?
s. What should a guide to proper cell phone use include?
t. Are internships worth the effort?

u. Why should a company have a written e-mail and social media policy?
v. Where should your organization hold its next convention?
w. What is the outlook for real estate (commercial or residential) investment in your area?
x. What do personal assistants for celebrities do, and how does one become a personal assistant? (Investigate the Association of Celebrity Personal Assistants.)
y. What kinds of gifts are appropriate for businesses to give clients and customers during the holiday season?
z. What rip-offs are on the Federal Trade Commission's List of Top 10 Consumer Scams, and how can consumers avoid falling for them?

## 12.15 Impromptu or Extemporaneous Talk: Becoming a Professional Speaker (Objs. 1–5)

Communication Technology | Social Media | Web

Professional speakers come in two flavors. On the one hand, celebrities such as famous athletes, businesspeople, and politicians command astronomical fees. On the other hand, ordinary people who have built a following by marketing themselves well and providing useful content also ply the speaking circuit, but they do so at more moderate rates, ranging between $4,500 and $7,500 per speech. One expert estimates that 95 percent of professional speakers make less than $10,000 per speaking engagement, still a hefty sum.

Professional speaker Chris Widener[17] offers the following insights to aspiring speakers:

**Skip the speakers bureaus.** Before the Internet, speakers bureaus were helpful intermediaries with strong corporate ties. Today, newcomers can bypass them and go into business without them.

**Develop multiple sources of revenue.** Collecting speaking fees is one thing; selling one's CDs, DVDs, e-books, and print books is another. Widener sells up to $140,000 in products after a talk.

**Create free valuable content.** Widener wrote 450 articles on success and business that became his signature. After building a list of 100,000 people, he self-published his books.

**Develop a social media presence.** Between Facebook and Twitter, Widener has almost 900,000 followers. He self-markets his content but also pays for Facebook marketing and ads.

**Consider your fee your résumé.** The honorarium should match the speaker's accomplishments. Widener raises his fee as his reputation grows, after TV appearances, after publishing a new book, and after speaking at prestigious events.

**Think creatively to find the money.** Widener gets around associations' or companies' limited speakers budgets by, for example, targeting their "education budgets." Also, he encourages organizations to seek funding from several corporate sponsors to share the cost of paying him.

What other strategies might work to help you develop a following and be a sought-after speaker?

**YOUR TASK.** Use this activity to give a brief impromptu speech. Without much preparation, objectively paraphrase and summarize the information to convey to your listeners what it takes to become a successful professional speaker. Include all relevant details and organize your summary well. Alternatively, conduct additional research to learn how one might become a professional speaker. Use search terms such as *speakers bureau* and *Toastmasters*. Once you have assembled enough additional information, create a multimedia slideshow using presentation software or give a concise extemporaneous briefing. Be sure to outline your talk and to rehearse.

## 12.16 Reporting About a Relevant Business Topic in the Media (Objs. 1–3)

Social Media | Web

**YOUR TASK.** Find an intriguing business article, and verbally present it to the class with or without notes. Summarize the article and explain why you have chosen it and why you believe it's valuable. Another option is to select a short business-related video clip. First introduce the video and summarize it. Time permitting, show the video in class. Visit any business website—for example, *The Wall Street Journal*, *Forbes*, or *Bloomberg Businessweek*. If your instructor directs, compose a tweet recommending or commenting on your article or video clip. Of the available 140 characters, leave at least 10 for retweeting.

## 12.17 Persuasive Presentation: Become an Ambassador for a Cause Close to Your Heart (Objs. 1–5)

Communication Technology | Social Media | Web

Do you care deeply about a particular nonprofit organization or cause? Perhaps you have donated to a cancer charity or volunteered for a local faith-based nonprofit. The Red Cross, Greenpeace, and the World Wildlife Fund (WWF) may be household names, but thousands of lesser-known nonprofit organizations are also trying to make the world a better place.

Professional fund-raiser and nonprofit service expert Sarah W Mackey encourages volunteers-to-be to become ambassadors for their favorite organizations. Much like brand ambassadors, advocates for nonprofits should wear the nonprofit's logo, invite friends, tell their families, raise money, volunteer, and spread the word on social media, Mackey says.[18] Some nonprofits—for example, the California-based environmental group Heal the Bay—are proactive. They offer speaker training to volunteers eager to reach out to their communities and raise awareness.[19] Ambassadors do good, become professional speakers, and acquire valuable skills to put on their résumés, a win-win-win!

**YOUR TASK.** Select your favorite charity. If you need help, find your charity or cause by visiting GuideStar, a nongovernmental watchdog that monitors nonprofits, or simply google *list of nonprofits*. Learn as much as you can from your organization's website and from articles written about it. Also, vet your charity by checking it out on GuideStar. Then assemble your information into a logical outline, and create a persuasive oral presentation using presentation software. Your goal is not only to introduce the charity but also to inspire your peers to seek more information and to volunteer. Tip: Focus on the benefits, direct and indirect, of volunteering for this charity. Finally, if your instructor asks, practice writing tweets advocating for your organization and calling the public to action.

### 12.18 What Is My Credit Score and What Does It Mean? (Objs. 1–5)

**Web**

The program chair for the campus business club has asked you to present a talk to the group about consumer credit. He saw a newspaper article saying that only 10 percent of Americans know their credit scores. Many consumers, including students, have dangerous misconceptions about their scores. Not knowing your score could result in a denial of credit as well as difficulty obtaining needed services and even a job.

**YOUR TASK.** Using research databases and the Web, learn more about credit scores and typical misconceptions. For example, is a higher or lower credit score better? Can you improve your credit score by marrying well? If you earn more money, will you improve your score? If you have a low score, can you raise it? Can you raise your score by maxing out all of your credit cards? (One survey reported that 28 percent of consumers believed the latter statement was true!) Prepare an oral presentation with or without a multimedia slideshow appropriate for a student audience. Conclude with appropriate recommendations.

### 12.19 Creating a Multimedia Presentation (No additional research required) (Objs. 1–5)

You are a consultant and have been hired to improve the effectiveness of corporate trainers. These trainers frequently make presentations to employees on topics such as conflict management, teamwork, time management, problem solving, performance appraisals, and employment interviewing. Your goal is to teach these trainers how to make better presentations.

**YOUR TASK.** Create six visually appealing slides based on the following content, which will be spoken during your presentation titled Effective Employee Training. The comments shown here are only a portion of a longer presentation.

Trainers have two options when they make presentations. The first option is one-way communication in which the trainer basically dumps the information on the audience and leaves. The second option is a two-way approach that involves the audience. The benefits of the two-way approach are that it helps the trainer connect with the audience and reinforce key points, it increases audience retention rates, and it changes the pace and adds variety to the presentation. The two-way approach also encourages audience members to get to know each other. Because today's employees demand more than just a "talking head," trainers must engage their audiences by involving them in a dialogue.

If you decide to interact with your audience, you need to choose an approach that suits your delivery style. Also, think about which options your audience would be likely to respond to most positively. Let's consider some interactivity approaches now. Realize, though, that these ideas are presented to help you get your creative juices flowing. After reading the list, think about situations in which these options might be effective. You could also brainstorm to come up with creative ideas to add to this list.

- Ask employees to guess at statistics before revealing them.
- Ask an employee to share examples or experiences.
- Ask a volunteer to help you demonstrate something.
- Ask the audience to complete a questionnaire or worksheet.
- Ask the audience to brainstorm or list things as fast as possible.
- Ask a variety of question types to achieve different purposes.
- Invite the audience to work through a process or examine an object.
- Survey the audience.
- Pause to let the audience members read something to themselves.
- Divide the audience into small groups to discuss an issue.

# GRAMMAR/MECHANICS CHECKUP—12

## Capitalization

Review Sections 3.01–3.16 in the Grammar/Mechanics Handbook. Then study each of the following statements. Draw three underlines below any letter that should be capitalized. Draw a slash (/) through any capital letter that you wish to change to lowercase. Indicate in the space provided the number of changes you made in each sentence, and record the number of the G/M principle(s) illustrated. If you made no changes, write 0. When you finish, compare your responses with those provided at the back of the book. If your responses differ, study carefully the principles in parentheses.

__5__ (3.01, 3.06a) **EXAMPLE** Once the Management Team and the Union members finally agreed, mayor Johnson signed the Agreement.

1. All united passengers must exit the Plane at gate 16 when they reach the key west international airport.

2. Personal tax rates for japanese citizens are low by International standards; rates for japanese corporations are high, according to Iwao Nakatani, an Economics Professor at Osaka university.

3. Stephanie, an aspiring Entrepreneur, hopes to open her own Consulting Firm one day.

4. Randy plans to take courses in Psychology, Math, History, and english next semester.

5. Did you see *The new york times* article titled "Reebok to pay $25 million for toning shoe claims"?

6. I purchased the dell inspiron 2200, but you may purchase any Tablet Computer you choose.

7. According to a Federal Government report, any regulation of State and County banking must receive local approval.

8. The vice president of the united states said, "we continue to look for Foreign investment opportunities."

9. The Comptroller of Zarconi Industries reported to the President and the Board of Directors that the securities and exchange commission was beginning an investigation of their Company.

10. My Father, who lives near death valley, says that the Moon and Stars are especially brilliant on a cold, clear night.

11. Our Marketing Director met with Karin Bloedorn, Advertising Manager, to plan an Ad Campaign for our newly redesigned Smartphone.

12. In the Spring our Admissions Director plans to travel to venezuela, colombia, and ecuador to recruit new Students.

13. To reach Belle Isle park, which is located on an Island in the Detroit river, tourists pass over the Douglas MacArthur bridge.

14. On page 8 of the report, you'll find a list of all employees in our accounting department with Master's degrees.

15. Please consult figure 3.2 in chapter 5 for U.S. census bureau figures regarding non-english-speaking residents.

# EDITING CHALLENGE—12

To fine-tune your grammar and mechanics skills, in every chapter you will be editing a message. The following outline of a presentation written by your office manager has problems with capitalization, grammar, punctuation, spelling, proofreading, number expression, and other writing techniques you have studied. Study the guidelines in the Grammar/Mechanics Handbook as well as the lists of Confusing Words and Frequently Misspelled Words to sharpen your skills.

**YOUR TASK.** Edit the following message (a) by correcting errors in your textbook or on a photocopy using proofreading marks from Appendix A or (b) by downloading the message from **www.cengagebrain.com** and correcting at your computer. Your instructor may show you a possible solution.

### Developing an Office Recycling Plan

**I. Introduction**

Paper makes up about 40 percent of the solid waste stream in our City. By recycling our office paper we can help the Environment and save trees. Every ton of paper made from recycled fiber saves about 17 trees. It also saves about 25 gallons of Water, and reduces air pollution by an estimated 60 pounds. Here in our office we use a lot of white Paper. When Paper is recycled it goes into such products as tissue, paperboard, stationary, magazines, new office paper and other paper products. In interviewing 3 experts including Dr Walter Yang at the university of west virginia I learned how we can develop our own office recycling plan that could be implemented within 60 days.

**II. Body**

Companies can easily integrate Paper recycling into their normal business operations. One of the first steps is placing Recycling Bins next to employees desks. In addition the most successful programs conduct Seminars to educate employee. They also hire an Office Recycling Coordinator to facilitate the program. Some examples include the following:

- Bank of america initiated a program that grew from recycling 1,400 tons per year of computer and white paper to nearly fifteen thousand tons within 20 years. This Program saved nearly 500 thousand dollars in trash hauling fees.

- Hewlett Packard was able to divert 91 million pounds of Solid Waste, including 43 million pounds of Paper. H-P vice president william morris said that it saved more than 367,000 trees!

Our Vice President agrees with me that setting up a Office Recycling Program doesn't happen over night. It usually involves finding motivated employees, and educating the Office Staff. It may also require a Capitol investment in recycling bins.

A successful paper recycling plan will work best if we keep it very, very simple. First however we will need top Managements support. We must also provide sufficient instructions on what to put in, and what to keep out. We will need surveys, interviews and inspections to see how the Plan is working. Because the recycling bins and trash cans must be clean and items sorted properly we will need monitors checking to be sure every one is following instructions.

**III. Conclusion**

Paper recycling is relatively easy to do, we just need to make a committment. We could start with 5 of our 15 offices to work out the best procedures. If you all agree I will meet with the CEO within 1 week. If Management supports the idea our goal should be to start a Program within 2 months. Our Companies disposal costs can decrease dramatically and we can help the Environment as well. Let's do it!

## COMMUNICATION WORKSHOP

### WORKING WELL TOGETHER

### Effective and Professional Team Presentations

If you have been part of a team that created an oral presentation together, you know that the process can be frustrating. Sometimes team members don't carry their weight or produce poor-quality work. Very often members struggle to resolve conflict. On the other hand, team projects can be harmonious and productive when members establish ground rules and follow these steps:

- **Prepare to work together.** First, you should (a) compare schedules of team members in order to set up the best meetings times, (b) plan regular face-to-face and virtual meetings, and (c) discuss how you will deal with team members who are not contributing to the project or submitting shoddy work.

- **Plan the presentation.** Your team will need to agree on (a) the specific purpose of the presentation, (b) your audience, (c) the length of the presentation, (d) the types of visuals to include, and (e) the basic structure and content of the presentation.

- **Assign duties.** Once you decide what your presentation will cover, give each team member a written assignment that details his or her responsibilities, such as researching content, producing visuals, developing handouts, building transitions between segments, and showing up for team meetings and rehearsals.

- **Collect information.** To gather or generate information, teams can brainstorm together, conduct interviews, or search the Web. The team should set deadlines for collecting information and should discuss how to ensure the accuracy and currency of the information collected. Team members should exchange periodic progress reports on how their research is coming along.

- **Organize and develop the presentation.** Once your team has completed the research, start working on the presentation. Determine the organization of the presentation, compose a draft in writing, and prepare presentation slides and other visual aids. The team should meet often in person or online to discuss the presentation and to decide which members are responsible for delivering what parts of the presentation. Each member should build a transition to the next member's topic and strive for logical connections between segments.

- **Edit, rehearse, and evaluate.** Before you deliver the presentation, rehearse several times as a team. Make sure transitions from speaker to speaker are smooth. For example, a speaker might say, *Now that I have explained how to prepare for the meeting, Ashley is going to discuss how to get the meeting started.* Decide who will be responsible for advancing slides during the presentation (either on the computer or using a remote). Practice fielding questions if you plan to have a question-and-answer session. Decide how you are going to dress to look professional and competent. Run a spell-checker and proofread your presentation slides to ensure that the design, format, and vocabulary are consistent.

- **Deliver the presentation.** Show up on time for your presentation and wear appropriate attire. Deliver your part of the presentation professionally and enthusiastically. Remember that your audience is judging the team on its performance, not the individuals. Do what you can to make your team shine!

**CAREER APPLICATION.** Your boss named you to a team that is to produce an organizational social media communication strategy for your company. You know this assignment will end with an oral presentation to management. Your first reaction is dismay. You have been on teams before in the classroom, and you know how frustrating they can be. However, you want to give your best, and you resolve to contribute positively to this team effort.

**YOUR TASK.** In small groups or with the entire class, discuss effective collaboration. How can members contribute positively to teams? How should teams deal with members who aren't contributing or who have negative attitudes? What should team members do to ensure that the final presentation is professional and well coordinated? How can the team use technology to improve collaboration? If your instructor directs, summarize your findings in writing or in a brief presentation.

# ENDNOTES

[1] Korn, M. (2010, December 3). Wanted: Good speaking skills. *The Wall Street Journal*. Retrieved from Hire Education blog at http://blogs.wsj.com/hire-education/2010/12/03/wanted-good-speaking-skills

[2] Dr. John J. Medina quoted in Reynolds, G. (2010). *Presentation Zen design*. Berkeley, CA: New Riders, p. 97.

[3] The Basics. (2012). Retrieved from http://prezi.com/the-basics

[4] Atkinson, C. (2008). *Beyond bullet points* (2nd ed.). Redmond, WA: Microsoft Press.

[5] Reynolds, G. (2008). *Presentation Zen*. Berkeley, CA: New Riders, p. 220. See also Reynolds, G. (2010). *Presentation Zen design*. Berkeley, CA: New Riders.

[6] Booher, D. (2003). *Speak with confidence: Powerful presentations that inform, inspire, and persuade*. New York: McGraw-Hill Professional, p. 126. See also http://www.indezine.com/ideas/prescolors.html

[7] Bates, S. (2005). *Speak like a CEO: Secrets for commanding attention and getting results*. New York: McGraw-Hill Professional, p. 113.

[8] Sommerville, J. (n. d.). The seven deadly sins of PowerPoint Presentations. About.com: Entrepreneurs. Retrieved from http://entrepreneurs.about.com/cs/marketing/a/7sinsofppt.htm

[9] Ellwood, J. (2004, August 4). Less PowerPoint, more powerful points. *The Times* (London), p. 6.

[10] Graves, P. R., & Kupsh, J. (2011, January 21). Presentation design and delivery. Bloomington, IN: Xlibris, p. 10.

[11] Photo essay based on Berry, S. (2014, February 3). Suffer stage fright? Why you should get excited. *The Sydney Morning Herald*. Retrieved from http://www.smh.com.au/lifestyle/life/suffer-stage-fright-why-you-should-get-excited-20140203-31ww4.html

[12] Booher, D. (2011). Speak with confidence. AudioInk.

[13] Booker, C. (2013, April 11). How to get people to listen. *Bloomberg Businessweek*. Retrieved from http://www.businessweek.com/articles/2013-04-11/how-to-get-people-to-listen-by-newark-mayor-cory-booker

[14] Search YouTube or search the top 100 speeches at American Rhetoric: http://www.americanrhetoric.com/top100speechesall.html

[15] Nisen, M., & Guey, L. (2013, May 15). 23 of the best pieces of advice ever given to graduates. Business Insider. Retrieved from http://www.businessinsider.com/best-commencement-speeches-of-all-time-2013-5

[16] Reynolds, G. (2008). *Presentation Zen*. Berkeley, CA: New Riders, pp. 64ff.

[17] Clark, D. (2013, June 10). How to become a successful professional speaker. *Forbes*. Retrieved from http://www.forbes.com/sites/dorieclark/2013/06/10/how-to-become-a-successful-professional-speaker

[18] Mackey, S. W. (2012, November 4). Step up: Be an ambassador. Retrieved from http://sarahwmackey.com/2012/11/04/step-up-be-an-ambassador

[19] Volunteer. (n.d.). Heal the Bay. Retrieved from http://www.healthebay.org/volunteer

# ACKNOWLEDGMENTS

**p. 390** Office Insider based on Dlugan, A. (2008, April 10). 10 ways your presentation skills generate career promotions. Six Minutes. Retrieved from http://sixminutes.dlugan.com/2008/04/10/career-promotions-presentation-skills

**p. 392** Office Insider based on Booher, D. (2003). On speaking. Quotes by Dianna Booher. Booher Consultants. Retrieved from http://www.booher.com/quotes.html#speaking

**p. 396** Office Insider based on Dugdale, S. (n.d.). Building rapport—building harmony. Write-out-loud.com. Retrieved from http://www.write-out-loud.com/building-rapport.html

**p. 398** Office Insider based on Howder, R. (n.d.). About Prezi. Retrieved from http://prezi.com/about

**p. 402** Office Insider based on Paradi, D. (2004). PowerPoint sucks! No it doesn't!! Think Outside The Slide. Retrieved from http://www.bearriverbands.org/tech/paradi.pdf

**p. 403** Office Insider based on Kupsh, J. (2010, November 4). 15 guidelines to effective presentations. Training. Retrieved from http://www.trainingmag.com/article/15-guidelines-effective-presentations

**p. 410** Office Insider based on Booher, D. (2003). On speaking. Quotes by Dianna Booher. Booher Consultants. Retrieved from http://www.booher.com/quotes.html#speaking

# Employment Communication

## UNIT 6

**CHAPTER 13**
The Job Search and Résumés in the Digital Age

**CHAPTER 14**
Interviewing and Following Up

**CHAPTER 13**

# The Job Search and Résumés in the Digital Age

**OBJECTIVES**
After studying this chapter, you should be able to

**13-1**
Prepare to search for a job in the digital age by understanding the changing job market, identifying your interests, assessing your qualifications, and exploring career opportunities.

**13-2**
Develop savvy search strategies by recognizing job sources and using digital tools to explore the open job market.

**13-3**
Expand your job-search strategies by using both traditional and digital tools in pursuing the hidden job market.

**13-4**
Organize your qualifications and information into effective résumé segments to create a winning, customized résumé.

**13-5**
Optimize your job search and résumé by taking advantage of today's digital tools.

**13-6**
Draft and submit a customized cover message to accompany a print or digital résumé.

## 13-1 Job Searching in the Digital Age

There's no doubt about it. The job market has become increasingly complex and not just because of the economy, offshoring, outsourcing, and globalization. In this digital age, the Internet has fundamentally changed the way we search for jobs. Job boards, search engines, and social networks have all become indispensable tools in hunting for a job. Surprisingly, however, even in this digital age, personal networking and referrals continue to be the primary route to hiring.[1]

This chapter presents cutting-edge digital and personal networking strategies to help you land a job. You may be depressed about searching for a job because of the uncertain economy and highly competitive job market. However, you have a lot going for you. As a college student, think about your recent training, current skills, and enthusiasm. Remember, too, that you are less expensive to hire than older, experienced candidates. In addition, you have this book with the latest research, invaluable advice, and perfect model documents to guide you in your job search. Think positively! The more you understand the changing job market, the better equipped you will be to enter it wisely.

### 13-1a Understanding the Changing Job Market

Today, the major emphasis of the job search has changed. In years past the emphasis was on what the applicant wanted. Today it's on what the employer wants.[2] Employers are most interested in how a candidate will add value to their organizations. That's why today's most successful candidates customize their résumés to highlight their qualifications for each opening. In addition, career paths are no longer linear; most new-hires will not start in a job and steadily rise through the ranks. Jobs are more short-lived and people are constantly relearning and retraining.

The résumé is still important, but it may not be the document that introduces the job seeker these days. Instead, the résumé may come only after the candidate has established a real-world relationship. What's more, chances are that your résumé and cover message will be read digitally rather than in print. However, although some attention-grabbing publications scream that the "print résumé is dead," the truth is that every job hunter needs one. Whether offered online or in print, your résumé should be always available and current.

It's natural to think that the first step in finding a job is writing a résumé. However, that's a mistake. The job-search process actually begins long before you are ready to prepare your résumé. Regardless of the kind of employment you seek, you must invest time and effort in getting ready. Your best plan for landing the job of your dreams involves (a) analyzing yourself, (b) developing a job-search strategy, (c) preparing a résumé, and (d) knowing the hiring process, as illustrated in Figure 13.1.

**LEARNING OBJECTIVE 1**

Prepare to search for a job in the digital age by understanding the changing job market, identifying your interests, assessing your qualifications, and exploring career opportunities.

## 13-1b Beginning Your Job Search With Self-Analysis

The first step in a job search is analyzing your interests and goals and evaluating your qualifications. This means looking inside yourself to explore what you like and dislike so that you can make good employment choices. Career counselors charge large sums for helping individuals learn about themselves. You can do the same self-examination—without spending a dime. For guidance in choosing a career that eventually proves to be satisfying, consider the following questions:

- What are you passionate about? Can you turn this passion into a career?
- Do you enjoy working with people, data, or things?
- Would you like to work for someone else or be your own boss?
- How important are salary, benefits, technology support, and job stability?
- How important are working environment, colleagues, and job stimulation?
- Must you work in a specific city, geographical area, or climate?
- Are you looking for security, travel opportunities, money, power, or prestige?
- How would you describe the perfect job, boss, and coworkers?

Figure **13.1** Job Searching in the Digital Age

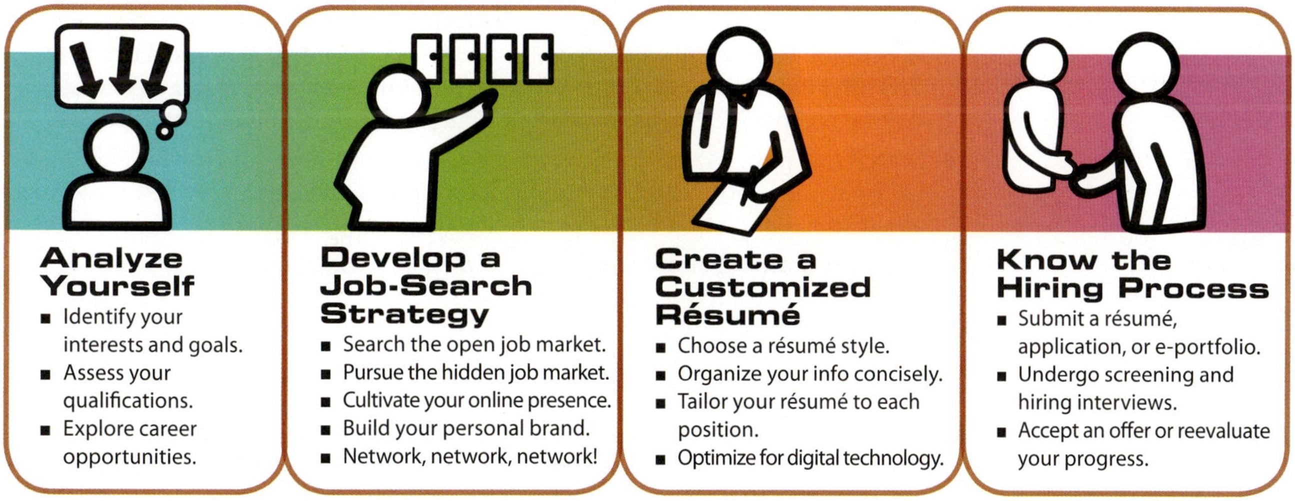

**Analyze Yourself**
- Identify your interests and goals.
- Assess your qualifications.
- Explore career opportunities.

**Develop a Job-Search Strategy**
- Search the open job market.
- Pursue the hidden job market.
- Cultivate your online presence.
- Build your personal brand.
- Network, network, network!

**Create a Customized Résumé**
- Choose a résumé style.
- Organize your info concisely.
- Tailor your résumé to each position.
- Optimize for digital technology.

**Know the Hiring Process**
- Submit a résumé, application, or e-portfolio.
- Undergo screening and hiring interviews.
- Accept an offer or reevaluate your progress.

Chapter 13: The Job Search and Résumés in the Digital Age

### 13-1c Assessing Your Qualifications

Beyond your interests and goals, take a good look at your qualifications. Remember that today's job market is not so much about what you want, but what the employer wants. What assets do you have to offer? Your responses to the following questions will target your thinking as well as prepare a foundation for your résumé. Always keep in mind, though, that employers seek more than empty assurances; they will want proof of your qualifications.

- What technology skills can you present? What specific software programs are you familiar with, what Web experience do you have, and what social media skills can you offer?
- Do you communicate well in speech and in writing? How can you verify these talents?
- What other skills have you acquired in school, on the job, or through activities? How can you demonstrate these skills?
- Do you work well with people? Do you enjoy teamwork? What proof can you offer? Consider extracurricular activities, clubs, class projects, and jobs.
- Are you a leader, self-starter, or manager? What evidence can you offer? What leadership roles have you held?
- Do you speak, write, or understand another language?
- Do you learn quickly? Are you creative? How can you demonstrate these characteristics?
- What unique qualifications can you offer that make you stand out among candidates?

### 13-1d Exploring Career Opportunities

The job picture in the United States is extraordinarily dynamic and flexible. On average, workers between ages eighteen and thirty-eight in the United States will have ten different employers over the course of their careers. The median job tenure of wage earners and salaried workers is 4.4 years with a single employer.[3] Although you may be frequently changing jobs in the future (especially before you reach age forty), you still need to train for a specific career now. In exploring job opportunities, you will make the best decisions when you can match your interests and qualifications with the requirements and rewards of specific careers. Where can you find the best career data? Here are some suggestions:

- **Visit your campus career center.** Most campus career centers have literature, inventories, career-related software programs, and employment or internship databases that allow you to explore such fields as accounting, finance, office technology, information systems, hotel management, and so forth. Some have well-trained job counselors who can tailor their resources to your needs. They may also offer career exploration workshops, job skills seminars, career days with visiting companies, assistance with résumé preparation, and mock interviews.
- **Search the Web.** Many job-search sites—such as Monster, CareerBuilder, and CollegeGrad—offer career-planning information and resources. You will learn about some of the best career sites in the next section.
- **Use your library.** Print and online resources in your library are especially helpful. Consult O*NET *Occupational Information Network*, *Dictionary of Occupational Titles*, *Occupational Outlook Handbook*, and *Jobs Rated Almanac* for information about job requirements, qualifications, salaries, and employment trends.
- **Take a summer job, internship, or part-time position in your field.** Nothing is better than trying out a career by actually working in it or in a related area. Many companies offer internships and temporary or part-time jobs

to begin training college students and to develop relationships with them. Unsurprisingly, lots of those internships turn into full-time positions. One recent study revealed that 60 percent of students who completed paid internships were offered full-time jobs.[4]

- **Interview someone in your chosen field.** People are usually flattered when asked to describe their careers. Inquire about needed skills, required courses, financial and other rewards, benefits, working conditions, future trends, and entry requirements.
- **Volunteer with a nonprofit organization.** Many colleges and universities encourage service learning. In volunteering their services, students gain valuable experience, and nonprofits appreciate the expertise and fresh ideas that students bring.
- **Monitor the classified ads.** Early in your college career, begin monitoring want ads and the websites of companies in your career area. Check job availability, qualifications sought, duties, and salary ranges. Don't wait until you are about to graduate to see how the job market looks.
- **Join professional organizations in your field.** Frequently, professional organizations offer student memberships at reduced rates. Such memberships can provide inside information on issues, career news, and jobs. Student business clubs and organization such as Phi Beta Lambda can also provide leadership development trainings, career tips, and networking opportunities.

## 13-2 Developing a Job-Search Strategy Focused on the Open Job Market

**LEARNING OBJECTIVE 2**
Develop savvy search strategies by recognizing job sources and using digital tools to explore the open job market.

Once you have analyzed what you want in a job and what you have to offer, you are ready to focus on a job-search strategy. You're probably most interested in the sources of today's jobs. Figure 13.2 shows the job source trends revealed by a Right Management survey of between 46,000 and 55,000 job seekers over a period of six years. Surprisingly, despite the explosion of digital job sources, person-to-person networking remains the No. 1 tool for finding a position. The job search, however, is changing, as the figure shows. The line between online and traditional networking blurs as technology plays an increasingly significant role. Carly McVey, Right Management executive, says, "Online social networking may not always be separate from traditional networking since one so often leads to the other. A job seeker uses the Internet to track down former associates or acquaintances and then reaches out to them in person."[5]

Both networking and online searching are essential tools in locating jobs, but where are those jobs? The *open job market* consists of jobs that are advertised or listed. The *hidden job market* consists of jobs that are never advertised or listed. Some analysts and authors claim that between 50 and 80 percent of all jobs are filled before they even make it to online job boards or advertisements.[6] Those openings are in the hidden job market, which we will explore shortly. First, let's start where most job seekers start—in the open job market.

### 13-2a Searching the Open Job Market

The open job market consists of positions that are advertised or listed publicly. Most job seekers start searching the open job market by using the Internet. Searching online is a common, but not always fruitful, approach. Both recruiters and job seekers complain about online job boards. Corporate recruiters say that the big job boards bring a flood of candidates, many of whom are not suited for the listed jobs. Job candidates grumble that listings are frequently outdated and fail to produce

## OFFICE INSIDER

*"I always tell my clients to apply online, but then find someone in the company you can fax, hand deliver or snail mail [your résumé] to. . . . If you are depending on electronic résumés alone, no one may ever see it."*

—Terry Pile, consultant, Career Advisors

### Figure 13.2 Trends in Sources of New Jobs

| | 2008 | 2010 | 2013 |
|---|---|---|---|
| **Networking** (person-to-person contacts) | 41% | 47% | **50%** |
| **Internet job boards** (such as Monster, CollegeGrad, and company websites) | 19% | 24% | **22%** |
| **Agencies** (search firms placing candidates for a fee) | 12% | 10% | **19%** |
| **Direct approach** (cold calling) | 9% | 8% | **8%** |
| **Newspapers/periodicals** (classified ads) | 7% | 2% | **1%** |
| **Other** (combination of above, direct referral, and luck) | 12% | 9% | **0%** |

Source: Based on a Right Management (ManpowerGroup) Survey of 46,000–55,000 job seekers

leads. Some career advisors call these sites black holes, into which résumés vanish without a trace. Almost as worrisome is the fear that an applicant's identity may be stolen through information posted at big boards.

Although the Internet may seem like a giant swamp where résumés disappear into oblivion, many job counselors encourage job seekers to spend a few minutes each day tracking online openings in their fields and locales. Moreover, job boards provide valuable job-search information such as résumé, interviewing, and salary tips. Job boards also serve as a jumping-off point in most searches. They inform candidates about the kinds of jobs that are available and the skill sets required.

However, job searching online can also be a huge time waster. Probably the most important tip you can apply is staying focused. In the hyperlinked utopia of endlessly fascinating sites, it's too easy to mindlessly follow link after link. Staying focused on a specific goal is critical. When you focus on the open job market, you will probably be checking advertised jobs on the big boards, company career sites, niche sites, LinkedIn, and other social networking sites.

**Exploring the Big Boards.** As Figure 13.2 indicates, the number of jobs found through all job boards is increasing; therefore, it makes sense to check them out. However, with tens of thousands of job boards and employment websites deluging the Internet, it's hard to know where to start. We suggest a few general sites as well as sites for college grads.

- **CareerBuilder** claims to be the largest online career site with more than 1 million jobs and 49 million résumés.

- **Monster** offers access to information on millions of jobs worldwide. It uses a search technology called 6Sense to match applicants with the best job opportunities. Many consider Monster to be the Web's premier job site.

- **CollegeGrad** describes itself as the "number one entry-level job site" for students and graduates. Applicants can search for entry-level jobs, internships, summer jobs, and jobs requiring one or more years of work experience.
- **Indeed** aggregates job listings from thousands of websites including company career pages, job boards, newspaper advertisements, associations, and blogs.

**Exploring Company Websites.** Probably the best way to find a job online is at a company's own website. Many companies now post job openings only at their own sites to avoid being inundated by the volume of applicants responding to postings at online job boards. A company's website is the first place to go if you have a specific employer in mind. You might find vision and mission statements, a history of the organization, and names of key hiring managers. Possibly you will see a listing for a position that doesn't fit your qualifications. Even though you're not right for this job, you have discovered that the company is hiring. Don't be afraid to send a résumé and cover message expressing your desire to be considered for future jobs. Rather than seeking individual company sites, you might prefer to visit aggregator LinkUp. It shows constantly updated job listings from small, midsized, and large companies.

**Checking Niche Sites.** If you seek a job in a specialized field, look for a niche site, such as Dice for technology jobs, Advance Healthcare Network for jobs in the medical field, and Accountemps for temporary accounting positions. Niche websites also exist for job seekers with special backgrounds or needs, such as GettingHired for disabled workers and Workforce50 for older workers. If you are looking for a short-term job, check out CoolWorks, which specializes in seasonal employment. Are you interested in living or working abroad? iHipo, the "high potential network," assists students and graduates in finding international internships, jobs, and graduate programs at businesses around the world. If you yearn for a government job, try USA Student Jobs, a website for students and recent graduates interested in federal service.

**Using LinkedIn and Social Networking Sites.** LinkedIn continues to dominate the world of job searching and recruiting. In a recent poll of 1,843 staffing professionals, 97 percent said they used LinkedIn as a recruiting tool.[7] At LinkedIn, job seekers can search for job openings directly, and they can also follow companies for the latest news and current job openings. (You will learn more about using LinkedIn when we discuss networking.) Beyond LinkedIn, other social networking sites such as Facebook and Twitter also advertise job openings and recruit potential employees. Because organizations may post open jobs to their Facebook or Twitter pages prior to advertising them elsewhere, you might gain a head start on submitting an application by following them on these sites.

When posting job-search information online, it's natural to want to put your best foot forward and openly share information that will get you a job. The challenge is striking a balance between supplying enough information and protecting your privacy. To avoid some of the risks involved, see Figure 13.3.

**Checking Newspapers.** Jobs in the open market may also be listed in local newspapers. Don't overlook this possibility, especially for local jobs. However, you don't have to buy a paper to see the listings. Most newspapers list their classified ads online.

## 13-3 Pursuing the Hidden Job Market With Networking

**LEARNING OBJECTIVE 3**
Expand your job-search strategies by using both traditional and digital tools in pursuing the hidden job market.

Not all available positions are announced or advertised in the open job market. As mentioned earlier, between 50 and 80 percent of jobs may be in the hidden job market.[8] Companies prefer not to openly advertise for a number of reasons. They don't welcome the deluge of unqualified candidates. What's more, companies

Figure **13.3** Protecting Yourself When Posting at Online Job Boards

- **Use reputable, well-known sites** and never pay to post your résumé.
- **Don't divulge personal data** such as your date of birth, social security number, or home address. Use your city and state or region in place of your home address.
- **Set up a separate e-mail account** with a professional-sounding e-mail address for your job search.
- **Post privately** if possible. Doing so means that you can control who has access to your e-mail address and other information.
- **Keep careful records** of every site on which you posted. At the end of your job search, remove all posted résumés.
- **Don't include your references** or reveal their contact information without permission.
- **Don't respond to "blind" job postings** (those without company names or addresses). Unfortunately, scammers use online job boards to post fake job ads to gather your personal information.

dislike hiring unknown quantities. Career coach Donald Asher, author of *Cracking the Hidden Job Market*, sets this scene: Imagine you are a hiring manager facing hundreds of résumés on your desk and a coworker walks in with the résumé of someone she vouches for. Which résumé do you think hits the top of the stack?[9] Companies prefer known quantities.

The most successful job candidates seek to transform themselves from unknown into known quantities through networking. More jobs today are found through referrals and person-to-person contacts than through any other method. That's because people trust what they know. Therefore, your goal is to become known to a large network of people, and this means going beyond close friends.

**Building a Personal Network.** Because most candidates find jobs today through networking, be prepared to work diligently to build your personal networks. This effort involves meeting people and talking to them about your field or industry so that you can gain information and locate possible job vacancies. Not only are many jobs never advertised, but some positions aren't even contemplated until the right person appears. One recent college grad underwent three interviews for a position, but the company hired someone else. After being turned down, the grad explained why he thought he was perfect for this company but perhaps in a different role. Apparently, the hiring manager agreed and decided to create a new job (in social media) because of the skills, personality, and perseverance of this determined young grad. Networking pays off, but it requires dedication. Here are three steps that will help you establish your own network:

Step 1. **Develop a contact list.** Make a list of anyone who would be willing to talk with you about finding a job. Figure 13.4 suggests possibilities. Even if you haven't talked with people in years, reach out to them in person or online. Consider asking your campus career center for alumni willing to talk with students. Also dig into your social networking circles, which we will discuss shortly.

Figure 13.4 Whom to Contact in Networking

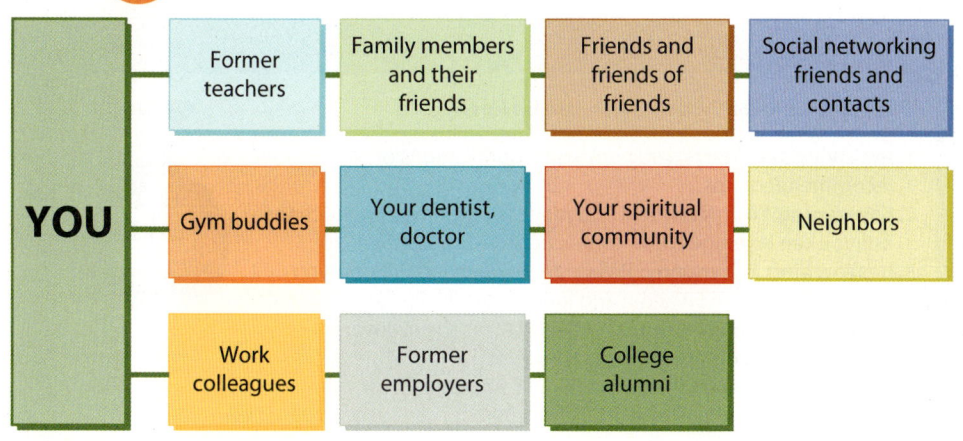

**YOU** — Former teachers | Family members and their friends | Friends and friends of friends | Social networking friends and contacts | Gym buddies | Your dentist, doctor | Your spiritual community | Neighbors | Work colleagues | Former employers | College alumni

**Step 2. Make contacts in person and online.** Call the people on your list or connect online. To set up a meeting in person, say, *Hi,_____. I'm looking for a job and I wonder if you could help me out. When could I come over to talk about it?* During your visit be friendly, well organized, polite, and interested in what your contact has to say. Provide a copy of your résumé, and try to keep the conversation centered on your job search. Your goal is to get two or more referrals. In pinpointing your request, ask, *Do you know of anyone who might have an opening for a person with my skills?* If the person does not, ask, *Do you know of anyone else who might know of someone who would?*

**Step 3. Follow up on your referrals.** Call or contact the people on your list. You might say something like, *Hello. I'm Stacy Rivera, a friend of Jason Tilden. He suggested that I ask you for help. I'm looking for a position as a marketing trainee, and he thought you might be willing to spare a few minutes and steer me in the right direction.* Don't ask for a job. During your referral interview, ask how the individual got started in this line of work, what he or she likes best (or least) about the work, what career paths exist in the field, and what problems must be overcome by a newcomer. Most important, ask how a person with your background and skills might get started in the field. Send an informal thank-you note to anyone who helps you in your job search, and stay in touch with the most promising people. Ask whether you could stay in contact every three weeks or so during your job search.

**Using Social Media to Network.** As digital technology continues to change our lives, job candidates have a powerful new tool at their disposal: social media networks. These networks not only keep you in touch with friends but also function beautifully in a job search. If you just send out your résumé blindly, chances are good that not much will happen. However, if you have a referral, your chances of getting a job multiply. Today's expansion of online networks results in an additional path to developing coveted referrals. Job seekers today are increasingly expanding their networking strategies to include social media sites such as LinkedIn, Facebook, and Twitter.

**Making the Most of LinkedIn to Search for a Job.** If you are looking for a job, LinkedIn is the No. 1 social media site for you to use. Although some young people have the impression that LinkedIn is for old fogies, that perception is changing as more and more college students and grads sign up. LinkedIn is where you can let recruiters know of your talents and where you begin your professional networking, as illustrated in Figure 13.5. For hiring managers to find your LinkedIn profile, however, you may need to customize your URL (uniform resource locator), which is the address of your page. To drive your name to the top of a Google search,

## Figure 13.5 Harnessing the Power of LinkedIn

**Five Ways College Students Can Use LinkedIn**

1. **Receiving Job Alerts.** LinkedIn sends notifications of recommended jobs.
2. **Leveraging Your Network.** You may start with two connections but you can leverage those connections to thousands.
3. **Researching a Company.** Before applying to a company, you can check it out on LinkedIn and locate valuable inside information.
4. **Getting Recommendations.** LinkedIn takes the awkwardness out of asking for recommendations. It's so easy!
5. **Helping Companies Find You.** Many companies are looking for skilled college grads, and a strong profile on LinkedIn can result in inquiries.

© iStockphoto.com/huronphoto

## Workplace in Focus

©Valua Vitaly/Shutterstock.com

Choosing the right words to describe yourself is important when setting up a career profile on social media. Each year LinkedIn publishes a list of the most popular self-descriptive words found in members' profiles. In 2013, the word that LinkedIn members used most frequently to represent themselves in the marketplace was "responsible." Other top keywords included "strategic," "creative," and "effective." Members use these buzzwords most frequently because they match the qualities that employers say they value in job candidates. What words would you use to describe yourself to a prospective employer?[12]

advises career coach Susan Adams, scroll down to the LinkedIn "public profile" on your profile page, and edit the URL. Try your first and last name and then your last name and first name, and then add a middle initial, if necessary. Test a variety of combinations with punctuation and spacing until the combination leads directly to your profile.[10]

In writing your LinkedIn career summary, use keywords and phrases that might appear in job descriptions. Include quantifiable achievements and specifics that reveal your skills. You can borrow most of this from your résumé. In the Work Experience and Education fields, include all of your experience, not just your current position. For the Recommendations section, encourage instructors and employers to recommend you. Having more recommendations in your profile makes you look more credible, trustworthy, and reliable. Career coach Adams even encourages job seekers to offer to write the draft for the recommender; in the world of LinkedIn, she says, this is acceptable.[11]

One of the best ways to use LinkedIn is to search for a company in which you are interested. Try to find company employees who are connected to other people you know. Then use that contact as a referral when you apply. You can also send an e-mail to everyone in your LinkedIn network asking for help or for people they could put you in touch with. Don't be afraid to ask an online contact for advice on getting started in a career and for suggestions to help a newcomer break into that career. Another excellent way to use a contact is to have that person look at your résumé and help you tweak it. Like Facebook, LinkedIn has status updates, and it's a good idea to update yours regularly so that your connections know what is happening in your career search.

Chapter 13: The Job Search and Résumés in the Digital Age

**Enlisting Other Social Networks in Job Hunting.** In addition to LinkedIn, job seekers can join Facebook, Twitter, and Google+ to find job opportunities, market themselves to companies, showcase their skills, highlight their experience, and possibly land that dream job. However, some career experts believe that social media sites such as Facebook do not mix well with business.[13] If you decide to use Facebook for professional networking, examine your profile and decide what you want prospective employers to see—or not see. Create a simple profile with minimal graphics, widgets, and photos. Post only content relevant to your job search or career, and choose your friends wisely.[14]

Employers often use these social media sites to check the online presence of a candidate. In fact, one report claimed that 91 percent of recruiters check Facebook, Twitter, and LinkedIn to filter out applicants.[15] Make sure your social networking accounts represent you professionally. You can make it easy for your potential employer to learn more about you by including an informative bio in your Twitter or Facebook profile that has a link to your LinkedIn profile. You can also make yourself more discoverable by posting thoughtful blog posts and tweets on topics related to your career goal.

### 13-3a Building Your Personal Brand

A large part of your job-search strategy involves building a brand for yourself. You may be thinking, *Who me? A brand?* Yes, absolutely! Even college grads should seriously consider branding because finding a job today is tough. Before you get into the thick of the job hunt, focus on developing your brand so that you know what you want to emphasize.

Personal branding involves deciding what makes you special and desirable in the job market. What is your unique selling point? What special skill set makes you stand out among all job applicants? What would your instructors or employers say is your greatest strength? Think about your intended audience. What are you promoting about yourself?

Try to come up with a tagline that describes what you do and who you are. Ask yourself questions such as these: Do you follow through with every promise? Are you a fast learner? Hardworking? What can you take credit for? It's OK to shed a little modesty and strut your stuff. However, do keep your tagline simple, short, and truthful so that it's easy to remember. See Figure 13.6 for some sample taglines appropriate for new grads.

Once you have a tagline, prepare a professional-looking business card with your name and tagline. Include an easy-to-remember e-mail address such as *firstname.lastname@domain.com*.

Now that you have your tagline and business card, work on an elevator speech. This is a pitch that you can give in 30 seconds or less describing who you are and what you can offer. Tweak your speech for your audience, and practice until you can say it naturally. Here's an example:[16]

Possible Elevator Speech for New Grad

*Hi, my name is _____. I will be graduating from _____ with a degree in _____. I'm looking to _____. I recently _____. May I take you out for coffee sometime to get your advice?*

## 13-4 Creating a Customized Résumé

In today's challenging and digital job market, the focus is not so much on what you want but on what the employer needs. That's why you will want to prepare a tailored résumé for every position you seek. The competition is so stiff today that

---

**OFFICE INSIDER**

*"I tell my clients, 'No résumé is ever one size fits all.' You shouldn't expect your résumé or your cover letter to be one size fits all. You have to expend the energy to customize the documents." Customization means tweaking the top half, including both the functional section and the job title, to match keywords found in the job listing itself.*

—Steve Burdan, certified professional résumé writer, TheLadders.com

**LEARNING OBJECTIVE 4**

Organize your qualifications and information into effective résumé segments to create a winning, customized résumé.

## Figure 13.6 Branding YOU

**4 Ways for Grads to Stand Out**
### Branding You

**Create your own tagline.**
Briefly describe what distinguishes you, such as *Talented at the Internet; Working harder, smarter; Super student, super worker; Love everything digital; Ready for a challenge; Enthusiasm plus fresh skills.*

**Distribute a business card.**
Include your name, tagline, and an easy-to-remember e-mail address. If you feel comfortable, include a professional headshot photo. Distribute it at all opportunities.

**Prepare an elevator speech.**
In 30 seconds, you need to be able to describe who you are and what problems your skills can solve. Tweak your speech for your audience, and practice until it feels natural.

**Build a powerful online presence.**
Prepare a strong LinkedIn profile dictating what comes up when people google your name. Consider adding Facebook and Twitter profile pages. Be sure all sites promote your brand positively.

© John Smith Design/Shutterstock.com

---

you cannot get by with a generic, all-purpose résumé. Although you can start with a basic résumé, you should customize it to fit each company and position if you want it to stand out from the crowd.

The Web has made it so easy to apply for jobs that recruiters are swamped with applications. As a job seeker, you have about five seconds to catch the recruiter's eye—if your résumé is even read by a person. It may very well first encounter an *applicant tracking system* (ATS). This software helps businesses automatically post openings, screen résumés, rank candidates, and generate interview requests. These automated systems make writing your résumé doubly challenging. Although your goal is to satisfy a recruiter or hiring manager, that person may never see your résumé unless it is selected by the ATS. You will learn more about applicant tracking systems shortly.

You may not be in the job market at this moment, but preparing a résumé now has advantages. Having a current résumé makes you look well organized and professional should an unexpected employment opportunity arise. Moreover, preparing a résumé early may reveal weaknesses and give you time to address them. If you have accepted a position, it's still a good idea to keep your résumé up-to-date. You never know when an opportunity might come along!

### 13-4a Choosing a Résumé Style

Résumés usually fall into two categories: chronological and functional. This section presents basic information as well as insider tips on how to choose an appropriate résumé style, determine its length, arrange its parts, and increase its chances of being selected by an applicant tracking system. You will also learn about adding a summary of qualifications, which busy recruiters welcome. Models of the résumé styles discussed in the following sections are shown in our comprehensive Résumé Gallery beginning on page 443.

**Chronological.** The most popular résumé format is the chronological format, shown in Figures 13.9 through 13.11 in our Résumé Gallery. The chronological résumé lists work history job by job but in reverse order, starting with the most recent position. Recruiters favor the chronological format because they are familiar with it and because it quickly reveals a candidate's education and experience. The chronological style works well for candidates who have experience in their field of employment and for those who show steady career growth, but it is less appropriate for people who have changed jobs frequently or who have gaps in their employment records. For college students and others who lack extensive experience, the functional résumé format may be preferable.

**Functional.** The functional résumé, shown in Figure 13.12 on page 446, focuses on a candidate's skills rather than on past employment. Like a chronological résumé, a functional résumé begins with the candidate's name, contact information, job objective, and education. Instead of listing jobs, though, the functional résumé groups skills and accomplishments in special categories, such as Supervisory and Management Skills or Retailing and Marketing Experience. This résumé style highlights accomplishments and can de-emphasize a negative employment history.

People who have changed jobs frequently, who have gaps in their employment records, or who are entering an entirely different field may prefer the functional résumé. Recent graduates with little or no related employment experience often find the functional résumé useful. Older job seekers who want to downplay a long job history and job hunters who are afraid of appearing overqualified may also prefer the functional format. Be aware, though, that online job boards may insist on the chronological format. In addition, some recruiters are suspicious of functional résumés, thinking the candidate is hiding something.

## 13-4b Deciding on Length

Experts disagree on how long a résumé should be. Conventional wisdom has always held that recruiters prefer one-page résumés. However, recruiters who are serious about candidates often prefer the kind of details that can be provided in a two-page or longer résumé. The best advice is to make your résumé as long as needed to present your skills to recruiters and hiring managers. Individuals with more experience will naturally have longer résumés. Those with fewer than ten years of experience, those making a major career change, and those who have had only one or two employers will likely have one-page résumés. Those with ten years or more of related experience may have two-page résumés. Finally, some senior-level managers and executives with a lengthy history of major accomplishments might have résumés that are three pages or longer.[17]

## 13-4c Organizing Your Information Into Effective Résumé Categories

Although résumés have standard categories, their arrangement and content should be strategically planned. A customized résumé emphasizes skills and achievements aimed at a particular job or company. It shows a candidate's most important qualifications first, and it de-emphasizes weaknesses. In organizing your qualifications and information, try to create as few headings as possible; more than six looks cluttered. No two résumés are ever exactly alike, but most writers consider including all or some of these categories: Main Heading, Career Objective, Summary of Qualifications, Education, Experience, Capabilities and Skills, Awards and Activities, Personal Information, and References.

**Main Heading.** Your résumé, whether chronological or functional, should start with an uncluttered and simple main heading. The first line should always be your name; add your middle initial for an even more professional look.

Format your name so that it stands out on the page. Following your name, list your contact information, including your address, phone number, and e-mail address. More recently, some candidates are omitting their street and city addresses as they consider such information unnecessary. Your telephone should be one where you can receive messages. The outgoing message at this number should be in your voice, it should state your full name, and it should be concise and professional. If you include your cell phone number and are expecting an important call from a recruiter, pick up only when you are in a quiet environment and can concentrate.

For your e-mail address, be sure it sounds professional instead of something like *toosexy4you@gmail.com* or *sixpackguy@yahoo.com*. Also be sure that you are using a personal e-mail address. Putting your work e-mail address on your résumé announces to prospective employers that you are using your current employer's resources to look for another job. If you have a website where an e-portfolio or samples of your work can be viewed, include the address in the main heading.

If you have an online presence, think about adding a *Quick Response* (QR) code to your résumé. This is a barcode that can be scanned by a smartphone, linking recruiters to your online portfolio or your LinkedIn profile page.

**Career Objective.** Opinion is divided about the effectiveness of including a career objective on a résumé. Recruiters think such statements indicate that a candidate has made a commitment to a career and is sure about what he or she wants to do. Yet, some career coaches today say objectives "feel outdated" and too often are all about what the candidate wants instead of what the employer wants.[18]

One job-trends researcher, Professor Charlyse Smith Diaz, contends that an objective should be included "only if it can be used persuasively to show how an applicant might fit with a company." She suggests three questions that might help a candidate decide whether to include an objective: "(1) Can you use a definitive, memorable descriptor? (2) Do you hold a required prerequisite or qualification for the position? (3) Are you seasoned in a specific profession?"[19] If you can answer yes to any of those questions, then include a career objective.

A well-written objective—customized for the job opening—makes sense, especially for new grads with fresh training and relevant skills. The objective can include strategic keywords for applicant tracking systems. If you decide to include an objective, focus on what you can contribute to the organization, not on what the organization can do for you.

**Poor:** To obtain a position with a well-established organization that will lead to a lasting relationship in the field of marketing. (Sounds vague and self-serving.)

**Improved:** To obtain a marketing position in which I use my recent training in writing and computer skills to increase customer contacts and expand brand penetration using social media. (Names specific skills and includes many nouns that might snag an applicant tracking system.)

Avoid the phrase *entry-level* in your objective, because it emphasizes lack of experience. If you omit a career objective, be sure to discuss your career goals in your cover message.

**Optional Summary of Qualifications.** "The biggest change in résumés over the last decade has been a switch from an objective to a summary at the top," says career expert Wendy Enelow.[20] Recruiters are busy, and smart job seekers add a summary of qualifications to their résumés to save the time of recruiters and hiring managers. Once a job is advertised, a hiring manager may get hundreds or even thousands of résumés in response. A summary at the top of your résumé makes it easier to read and ensures that your most impressive qualifications are not overlooked by a recruiter who is skimming résumés quickly. In addition, because résumés today may be viewed on tablets and smartphones, make sure that the first third spotlights your most compelling qualifications.

A summary of qualifications (also called a *career profile*, a *job summary*, or *professional highlights*) should include three to eight bulleted statements that prove that you are the ideal candidate for the position. When formulating these statements, consider your experience in the field, your education, your unique skills, awards you have won, certifications you hold, and any other accomplishments that you want to highlight. Strive to quantify your achievements wherever possible. Target the most important qualifications an employer will be looking for in the person hired for this position. Focus on nouns that might be selected as keywords by an applicant tracking system. Examples appear in Figures 13.9 and 13.11.

**Education.** The next component in a chronological résumé is your education—if it is more noteworthy than your work experience. In this section you should include the name and location of schools, dates of attendance, major fields of study, and degrees received. By the way, once you have attended college, you don't need to list high school information on your résumé.

Your grade point average and/or class ranking may be important to prospective employers. One way to enhance your GPA is to calculate it in your major courses only (for example, *3.6/4.0 in major*). It is not unethical so long as you clearly show that your GPA is in the major only. Looking to improve their hiring chances, some college grads are now offering an unusual credential: their scores on the Graduate Record Examination. Large companies and those specializing in computer software and financial services reportedly were most interested in applicants' GRE scores.[21]

Under Education you might be tempted to list all the courses you took, but such a list makes for dull reading and consumes valuable space. Refer to courses only if you can relate them to the position sought. When relevant, include certificates earned, seminars attended, workshops completed, scholarships awarded, and honors earned. If your education is incomplete, include such statements as *BS degree expected 6/18* or *80 units completed in 120-unit program*. Title this section Education, Academic Preparation, or Professional Training. If you are preparing a functional résumé, you will probably put the Education section below your skills summary, as Cooper Jackson has done in Figure 13.12.

**Work Experience or Employment History.** When your work experience is significant and relevant to the position sought, this information should appear before your education. List your most recent employment first and work backward, including only those jobs that you think will help you win the targeted position. A job application form may demand a full employment history, but your résumé may be selective. Be aware, though, that time gaps in your employment history will probably be questioned in the interview. For each position show the following:

- Employer's name, city, and state
- Dates of employment (month and year)
- Most important job title
- Significant duties, activities, accomplishments, and promotions

Your employment achievements and job duties will be easier to read if you place them in bulleted lists. Rather than list every single thing you have done, customize your information so that it relates to the target job. Your bullet points should be concise but not complete sentences, and they usually do not include personal pronouns (*I, me, my*). Strive to be specific:

| | |
|---|---|
| **Poor:** | Worked with customers |
| **Improved:** | Developed customer service skills by successfully interacting with 40+ customers daily |

---

## OFFICE INSIDER

*"Many résumé writers tend to aim for vague generalities and abstract attributes, focusing on their 'communication skills' and ability to work as a 'team player.' In a tough market, you need to move beyond these kinds of generic claims and focus on specifics. List each of your pertinent skills and responsibilities, and then back them up with fact-based bullets that explicitly prove your point."*

—Roberta Chinsky Matuson, president, Matuson Consulting

Whenever possible, quantify your achievements:

| | |
|---|---|
| Poor: | Did equipment study and report |
| Improved: | Conducted research and wrote final study analyzing equipment needs of 100 small businesses in Houston |
| Poor: | Was successful in sales |
| Improved: | Personally generated orders for sales of $90,000 annually |

In addition to technical skills, employers seek individuals with communication, management, and interpersonal capabilities. This means you will want to select work experiences and achievements that illustrate your initiative, dependability, responsibility, resourcefulness, flexibility, and leadership. Employers also want people who can work in teams.

| | |
|---|---|
| Poor: | Worked effectively in teams |
| Improved: | Collaborated with five-member interdepartmental team in developing ten-page handbook for temporary workers |
| Poor: | Joined in team effort on campus |
| Improved: | Headed 16-member student government team that conducted most successful voter registration in campus history |

Statements describing your work experience should include many nouns relevant to the job you seek. These nouns may match keywords sought by the applicant tracking system. To appeal to human readers, your statements should also include action verbs, such as those in Figure 13.7. Starting each of your bullet points with an action verb helps ensure that your bulleted lists are parallel.

**Capabilities and Skills.** Recruiters want to know specifically what you can do for their companies. Therefore, list your special skills. In this section be sure to include many nouns that relate to the targeted position. Include your ability to use

Figure 13.7 Action Verbs for a Powerful Résumé

| Communication Skills | Teamwork, Supervision Skills | Management, Leadership Skills | Research Skills | Clerical, Detail Skills | Creative Skills |
|---|---|---|---|---|---|
| clarified | advised | analyzed | assessed | activated | acted |
| collaborated | coordinated | authorized | collected | approved | conceptualized |
| explained | demonstrated | coordinated | critiqued | classified | designed |
| interpreted | developed | directed | diagnosed | edited | fashioned |
| integrated | evaluated | headed | formulated | generated | founded |
| persuaded | expedited | implemented | gathered | maintained | illustrated |
| promoted | facilitated | improved | interpreted | monitored | integrated |
| resolved | guided | increased | investigated | proofread | invented |
| summarized | motivated | organized | reviewed | recorded | originated |
| translated | set goals | scheduled | studied | streamlined | revitalized |
| wrote | trained | strengthened | systematized | updated | shaped |

the Web, software programs, social media, office equipment, and communication technology tools. Use expressions such as *proficient in, competent in, experienced in,* and *ability to* as illustrated in the following:

| | |
|---|---|
| **Poor:** | Have payroll experience |
| **Improved:** | Proficient in preparing federal, state, and local payroll tax returns as well as franchise and personal property tax returns |
| **Poor:** | Trained in computer graphics |
| **Improved:** | Certified in graphic design including infographics through an intensive 350-hour classroom program |
| **Poor:** | Have writing skills |
| **Improved:** | Competent in writing, editing, and proofreading reports, tables, letters, memos, e-mails, manuscripts, and business forms |

You will also want to highlight exceptional aptitudes, such as working well under stress, learning computer programs quickly, and interacting with customers. If possible, provide details and evidence that back up your assertions. Include examples of your writing, speaking, management, organizational, interpersonal, and presentation skills—particularly those talents that are relevant to your targeted job. For recent graduates, this section can be used to give recruiters evidence of your potential and to highlight successful college projects.

**Awards, Honors, and Activities.** If you have three or more awards or honors, highlight them by listing them under a separate heading. If not, put them in the Education or Work Experience section if appropriate. Include awards, scholarships (financial and other), fellowships, dean's list, honors, recognition, commendations, and certificates. Be sure to identify items clearly. Your reader may be unfamiliar, for example, with Greek organizations, honoraries, and awards; tell what they mean.

| | |
|---|---|
| **Poor:** | Recipient of Star award |
| **Improved:** | Recipient of Star award given by Pepperdine University to outstanding graduates who combine academic excellence and extracurricular activities |

It's also appropriate to include school, community, volunteer, and professional activities. Employers are interested in evidence that you are a well-rounded person. This section provides an opportunity to demonstrate leadership and interpersonal skills. Strive to use action statements.

| | |
|---|---|
| **Poor:** | Treasurer of business club |
| **Improved:** | Collected dues, kept financial records, and paid bills while serving as treasurer of 35-member business management club |

**Personal Data.** Résumés in the United States omit personal data, such as birth date, marital status, height, weight, national origin, health, disabilities, and religious affiliation. Such information doesn't relate to genuine occupational qualifications, and recruiters are legally barred from asking for such information. Some job seekers do, however, include hobbies or interests (such as skiing or photography) that might grab the recruiter's attention or serve as conversation starters. For example, let's say you learn that your hiring manager enjoys distance running. If you have run a marathon, you may want to mention it. Many executives practice tennis or golf, two sports highly suitable for networking. You could also indicate your willingness to travel or to relocate since many companies will be interested.

**References.** Listing references directly on a résumé takes up valuable space. Moreover, references are not normally instrumental in securing an interview—few companies check them before the interview. Instead, recruiters prefer that you bring to the interview a list of individuals willing to discuss your qualifications. Therefore, you should prepare a separate list, such as that in Figure 13.8, when you begin your job search. Consider three to five individuals, such as instructors, your current employer or previous employers, colleagues or subordinates, and other professional contacts. Ask whether they would be willing to answer inquiries regarding your qualifications for employment. Be sure, however, to provide them with an opportunity to refuse. No reference is better than a negative one. Better yet, to avoid rejection and embarrassment, ask only those contacts who you are confident will give you a glowing endorsement.

Do not include personal or character references, such as friends, family, or neighbors, because recruiters rarely consult them. Companies are more interested in the opinions of objective individuals who know how you perform professionally and academically. One final note: most recruiters see little reason for including the statement *References furnished upon request*. It is unnecessary and takes up precious space.

### 13-4d Online Résumé Reading Patterns

With increasing numbers of résumés being read online, it's wise for job applicants to know what researchers have found about how people read online text. Eye-tracking research revealed that people read text-based pages online in an F-shaped pattern.[22] That is, they read horizontally from the top of the page, concentrating on the top third and then focusing on the left side as they read downward. This roughly corresponds to the shape of a capital F. Smart applicants will arrange the most important information in the top section of the résumé. Additional significant information should appear at the beginning of each group down the left side.

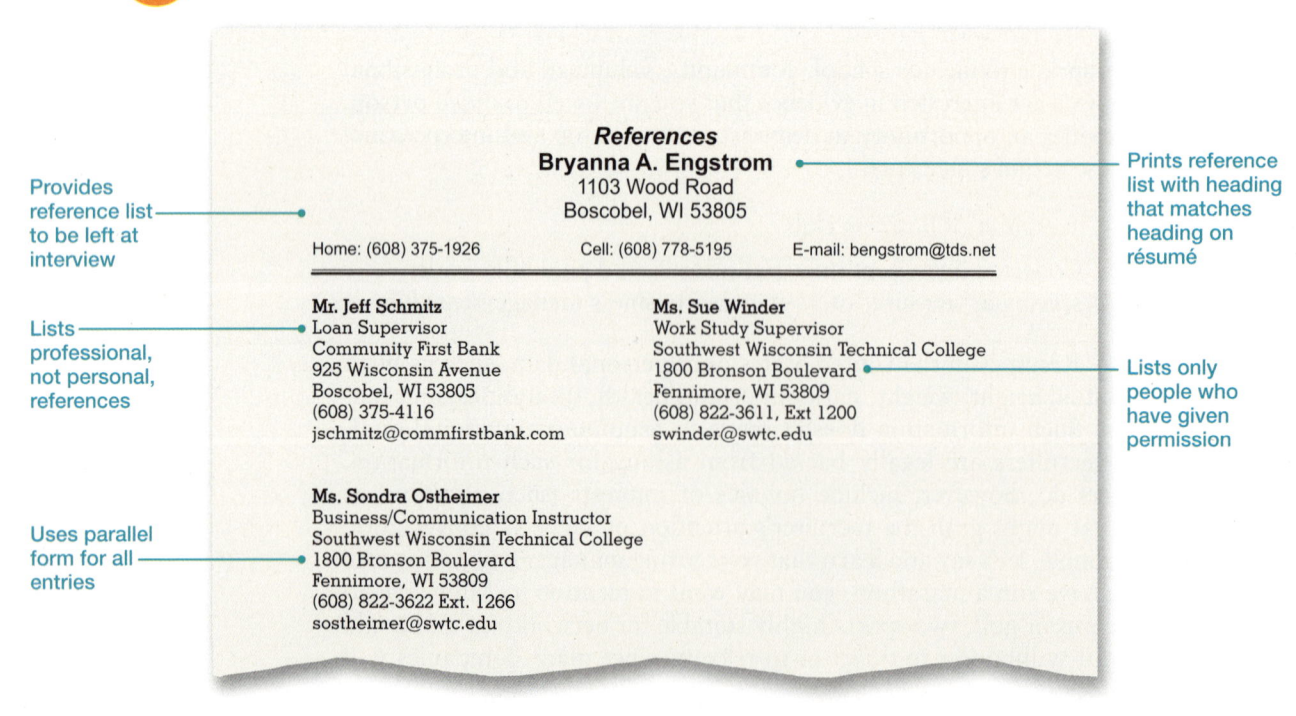

### Figure 13.8 Sample Reference List

**References**
**Bryanna A. Engstrom**
1103 Wood Road
Boscobel, WI 53805

Home: (608) 375-1926     Cell: (608) 778-5195     E-mail: bengstrom@tds.net

**Mr. Jeff Schmitz**
Loan Supervisor
Community First Bank
925 Wisconsin Avenue
Boscobel, WI 53805
(608) 375-4116
jschmitz@commfirstbank.com

**Ms. Sue Winder**
Work Study Supervisor
Southwest Wisconsin Technical College
1800 Bronson Boulevard
Fennimore, WI 53809
(608) 822-3611, Ext 1200
swinder@swtc.edu

**Ms. Sondra Ostheimer**
Business/Communication Instructor
Southwest Wisconsin Technical College
1800 Bronson Boulevard
Fennimore, WI 53809
(608) 822-3622 Ext. 1266
sostheimer@swtc.edu

Annotations:
- Provides reference list to be left at interview
- Lists professional, not personal, references
- Uses parallel form for all entries
- Prints reference list with heading that matches heading on résumé
- Lists only people who have given permission

## Résumé Gallery

### Figure 13.9 Chronological Résumé: Recent College Graduate With Related Experience

Bryanna Engstrom used a chronological résumé to highlight her work experience, most of which is related directly to the position she seeks. Although she is a recent graduate, she has accumulated experience in two part-time jobs and one full-time job. She included a summary of qualifications to highlight her skills, experience, and interpersonal traits aimed at a specific position.

Notice that Bryanna designed her résumé in two columns with the major categories listed in the left column. In the right column she included bulleted items for each of the four categories. Conciseness and parallelism are important in writing an effective résumé. In the *Experience* category, she started each item with an active verb, which improved readability and parallel form.

---

**Bryanna A. Engstrom**
1103 Wood Road
Boscobel, WI 53805

Home: (608) 375-1926   Cell: (608) 778-5195   E-mail: bengstrom@tds.net

**SUMMARY OF QUALIFICATIONS**

- Over three years' experience in administrative positions, working with business documents and interacting with customers
- Ability to keyboard (68 wpm) and use ten-key calculator (150 kpm)
- Proficient with Microsoft Word, Excel, Access, PowerPoint, SharePoint, and Publisher (passed MOS certification exam)
- Competent in Web research, written and oral communication, records management, desktop publishing, and proofreading and editing business documents
- Trained in QuickBooks, Flash, Photoshop, Dreamweaver

**EXPERIENCE**

**Administrative Assistant, Work Study**
Southwest Wisconsin Technical College, Fennimore, Wisconsin
August 2013–present
- Create letters, memos, reports, and forms in Microsoft Word
- Develop customized reports and labels using Microsoft Access
- Maintain departmental Microsoft Excel budget

**Loan Support Specialist**
Community First Bank, Boscobel, Wisconsin, May 2012– September 2013
- Prepared loan documents for consumer, residential, mortgage, agricultural, and commercial loans
- Ensured compliance with federal, state, and bank regulations
- Originated correspondence (oral and written) with customers and insurance agencies
- Ordered and interpreted appraisals, titles, and credit reports

**Customer Sales Representative**
Lands' End, Dodgeville, Wisconsin, Winter seasons 2012–2013
- Developed customer-service skills by serving 40+ online customers a day
- Resolved customer problems
- Entered catalog orders into computer system

**EDUCATION**

Southwest Wisconsin Technical College, Fennimore, Wisconsin
Major: Administrative Assistant with Help Desk certificate
AA degree expected May 2015. GPA in major: 3.8 (4.0 = A)

**ACTIVITIES AND AWARDS**

- Placed first in state BPA Administrative Assistant competition
- Served as SWTC Student Senate Representative
- Nominated for SWTC Ambassador Award (recognizes outstanding students for excellence in and out of classroom)

---

Annotations:
- Omits objective to keep all options open
- Focuses on skills and aptitudes that employers seek
- Uses present-tense verb for current job
- Arranges employment by job title for easy recognition
- Combines activities and awards to show extracurricular involvement

Chapter 13: The Job Search and Résumés in the Digital Age

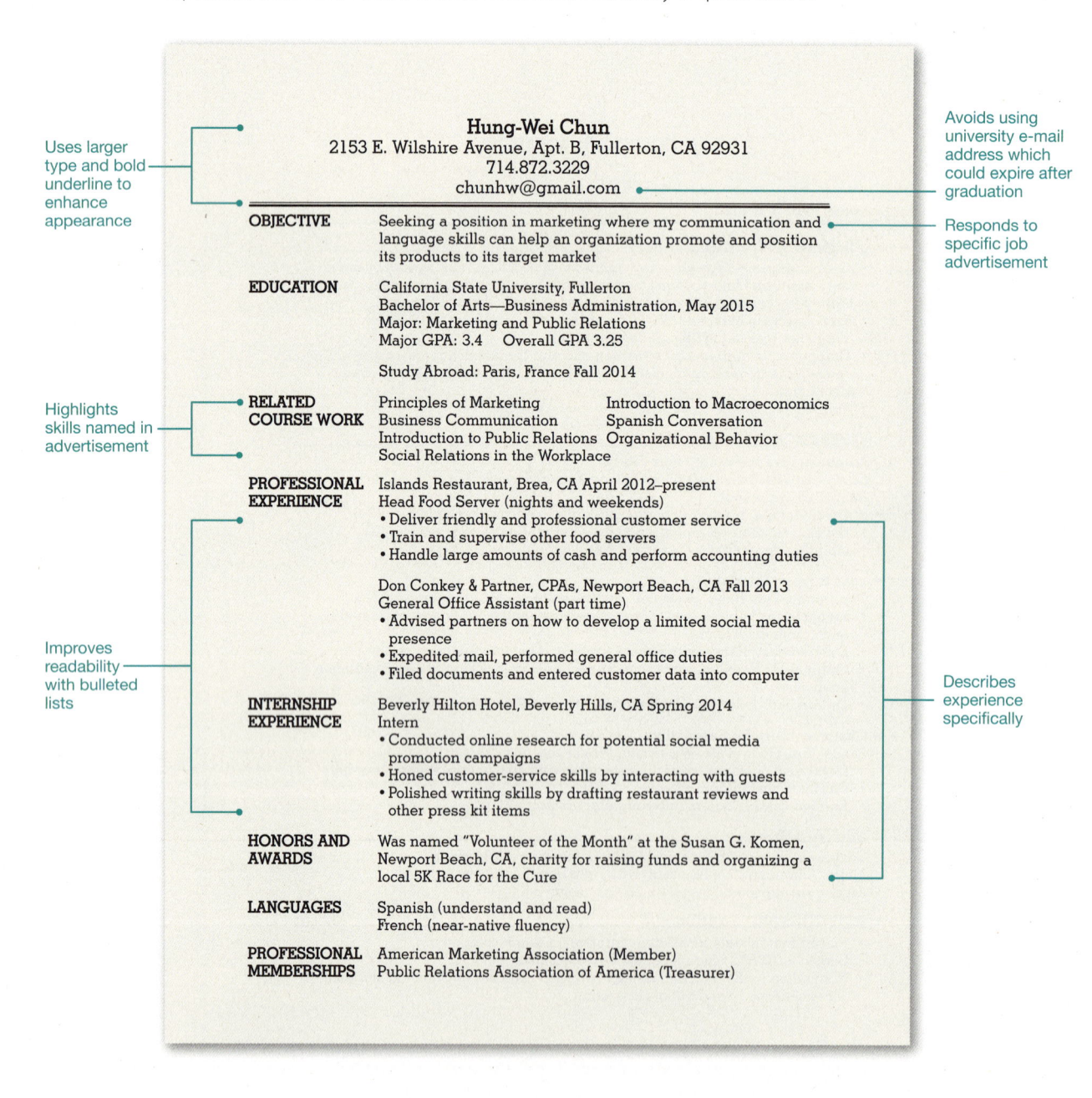

# Figure 13.10 Chronological Résumé: Current University Student With Limited Relevant Experience

Hung-Wei Chun used Microsoft Word to design a traditional chronological print-based résumé that he plans to give to recruiters at the campus job fair or during interviews. Notice that he formatted his résumé in two columns. An easy way to do this is to use the Word table feature and remove the borders so that no lines show.

Although Hung-Wei has work experience unrelated to his future employment, his résumé looks impressive because he has transferable skills. His internship is related to his future career, and his language skills and study abroad experience will help him score points in competition with other applicants. Hung-Wei's volunteer experience is also attractive because it shows him to be a well-rounded, compassionate individual. Because his experience in his future field is limited, he omitted a summary of qualifications.

---

**Hung-Wei Chun**
2153 E. Wilshire Avenue, Apt. B, Fullerton, CA 92931
714.872.3229
chunhw@gmail.com

**OBJECTIVE** — Seeking a position in marketing where my communication and language skills can help an organization promote and position its products to its target market

**EDUCATION** — California State University, Fullerton
Bachelor of Arts—Business Administration, May 2015
Major: Marketing and Public Relations
Major GPA: 3.4    Overall GPA 3.25

Study Abroad: Paris, France Fall 2014

**RELATED COURSE WORK**
- Principles of Marketing
- Business Communication
- Introduction to Public Relations
- Social Relations in the Workplace
- Introduction to Macroeconomics
- Spanish Conversation
- Organizational Behavior

**PROFESSIONAL EXPERIENCE**
Islands Restaurant, Brea, CA April 2012–present
Head Food Server (nights and weekends)
- Deliver friendly and professional customer service
- Train and supervise other food servers
- Handle large amounts of cash and perform accounting duties

Don Conkey & Partner, CPAs, Newport Beach, CA Fall 2013
General Office Assistant (part time)
- Advised partners on how to develop a limited social media presence
- Expedited mail, performed general office duties
- Filed documents and entered customer data into computer

**INTERNSHIP EXPERIENCE**
Beverly Hilton Hotel, Beverly Hills, CA Spring 2014
Intern
- Conducted online research for potential social media promotion campaigns
- Honed customer-service skills by interacting with guests
- Polished writing skills by drafting restaurant reviews and other press kit items

**HONORS AND AWARDS** — Was named "Volunteer of the Month" at the Susan G. Komen, Newport Beach, CA, charity for raising funds and organizing a local 5K Race for the Cure

**LANGUAGES**
Spanish (understand and read)
French (near-native fluency)

**PROFESSIONAL MEMBERSHIPS**
American Marketing Association (Member)
Public Relations Association of America (Treasurer)

---

Annotations:
- Uses larger type and bold underline to enhance appearance
- Highlights skills named in advertisement
- Improves readability with bulleted lists
- Avoids using university e-mail address which could expire after graduation
- Responds to specific job advertisement
- Describes experience specifically

## Figure 13.11 Chronological Résumé: University Graduate With Substantial Experience

Because Rachel has many years of experience and seeks executive-level employment, she highlighted her experience by placing it before her education. Her summary of qualifications highlighted her most impressive experience and skills. This chronological two-page résumé shows the steady progression of her career to executive positions, a movement that impresses and reassures recruiters.

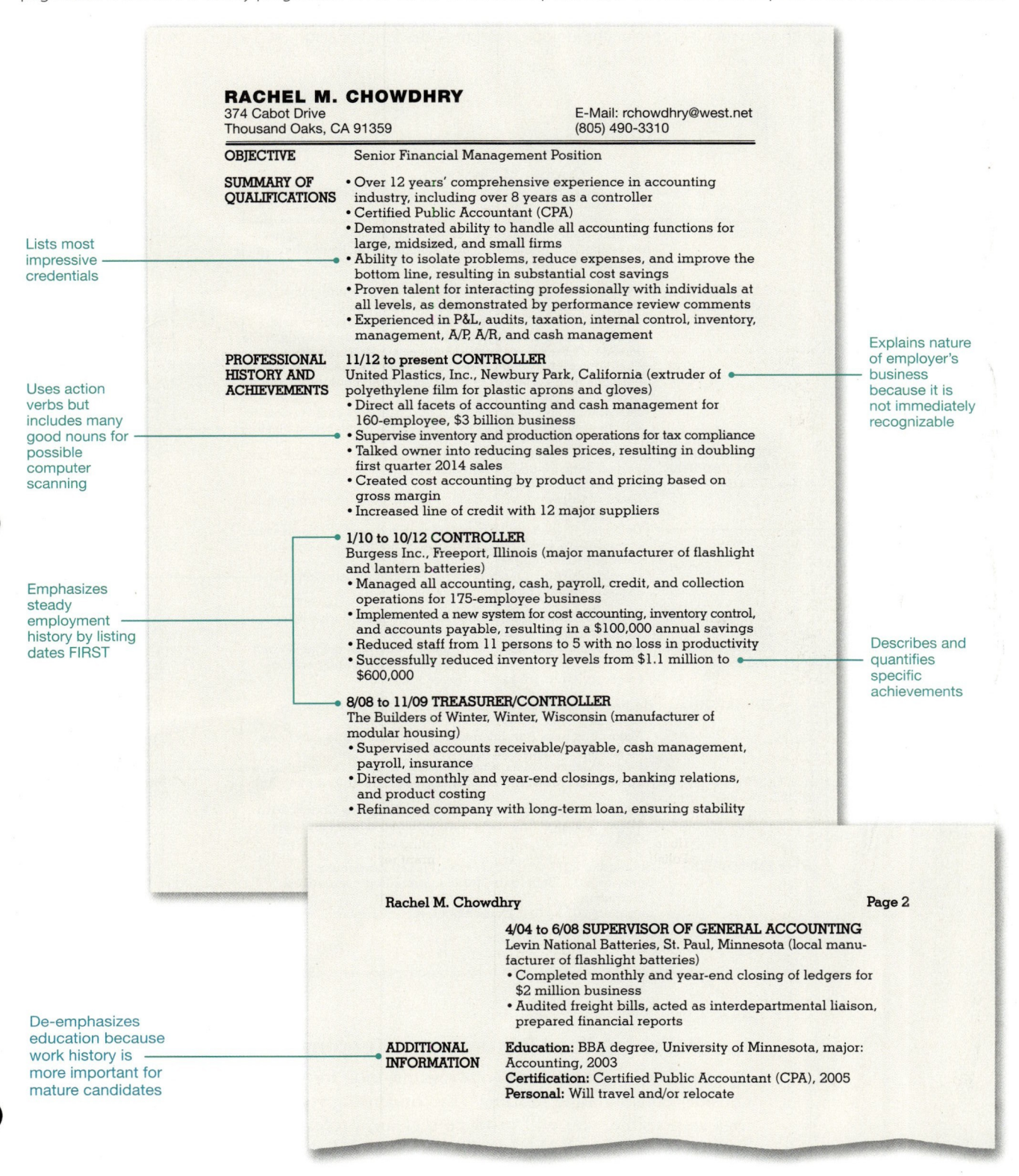

---

**RACHEL M. CHOWDHRY**
374 Cabot Drive
Thousand Oaks, CA 91359

E-Mail: rchowdhry@west.net
(805) 490-3310

---

**OBJECTIVE**  Senior Financial Management Position

**SUMMARY OF QUALIFICATIONS**
- Over 12 years' comprehensive experience in accounting industry, including over 8 years as a controller
- Certified Public Accountant (CPA)
- Demonstrated ability to handle all accounting functions for large, midsized, and small firms
- Ability to isolate problems, reduce expenses, and improve the bottom line, resulting in substantial cost savings
- Proven talent for interacting professionally with individuals at all levels, as demonstrated by performance review comments
- Experienced in P&L, audits, taxation, internal control, inventory, management, A/P, A/R, and cash management

*Lists most impressive credentials*

**PROFESSIONAL HISTORY AND ACHIEVEMENTS**

**11/12 to present CONTROLLER**
United Plastics, Inc., Newbury Park, California (extruder of polyethylene film for plastic aprons and gloves)
- Direct all facets of accounting and cash management for 160-employee, $3 billion business
- Supervise inventory and production operations for tax compliance
- Talked owner into reducing sales prices, resulting in doubling first quarter 2014 sales
- Created cost accounting by product and pricing based on gross margin
- Increased line of credit with 12 major suppliers

*Uses action verbs but includes many good nouns for possible computer scanning*

*Explains nature of employer's business because it is not immediately recognizable*

**1/10 to 10/12 CONTROLLER**
Burgess Inc., Freeport, Illinois (major manufacturer of flashlight and lantern batteries)
- Managed all accounting, cash, payroll, credit, and collection operations for 175-employee business
- Implemented a new system for cost accounting, inventory control, and accounts payable, resulting in a $100,000 annual savings
- Reduced staff from 11 persons to 5 with no loss in productivity
- Successfully reduced inventory levels from $1.1 million to $600,000

*Emphasizes steady employment history by listing dates FIRST*

*Describes and quantifies specific achievements*

**8/08 to 11/09 TREASURER/CONTROLLER**
The Builders of Winter, Winter, Wisconsin (manufacturer of modular housing)
- Supervised accounts receivable/payable, cash management, payroll, insurance
- Directed monthly and year-end closings, banking relations, and product costing
- Refinanced company with long-term loan, ensuring stability

---

Rachel M. Chowdhry                                                                 Page 2

**4/04 to 6/08 SUPERVISOR OF GENERAL ACCOUNTING**
Levin National Batteries, St. Paul, Minnesota (local manufacturer of flashlight batteries)
- Completed monthly and year-end closing of ledgers for $2 million business
- Audited freight bills, acted as interdepartmental liaison, prepared financial reports

**ADDITIONAL INFORMATION**
**Education:** BBA degree, University of Minnesota, major: Accounting, 2003
**Certification:** Certified Public Accountant (CPA), 2005
**Personal:** Will travel and/or relocate

*De-emphasizes education because work history is more important for mature candidates*

Chapter 13: The Job Search and Résumés in the Digital Age

# Figure 13.12 Functional Résumé: Recent College Graduate With Unrelated Part-Time Experience

Recent graduate Cooper Jackson chose this functional format to de-emphasize his meager work experience and emphasize his potential in sales and marketing. This version of his résumé is more generic than one targeted for a specific position. Nevertheless, it emphasizes his strong points with specific achievements and includes an employment section to satisfy recruiters. The functional format presents ability-focused topics. It illustrates what the job seeker can do for the employer instead of narrating a history of previous jobs. Although recruiters prefer chronological résumés, the functional format is a good choice for new graduates, career changers, and those with employment gaps.

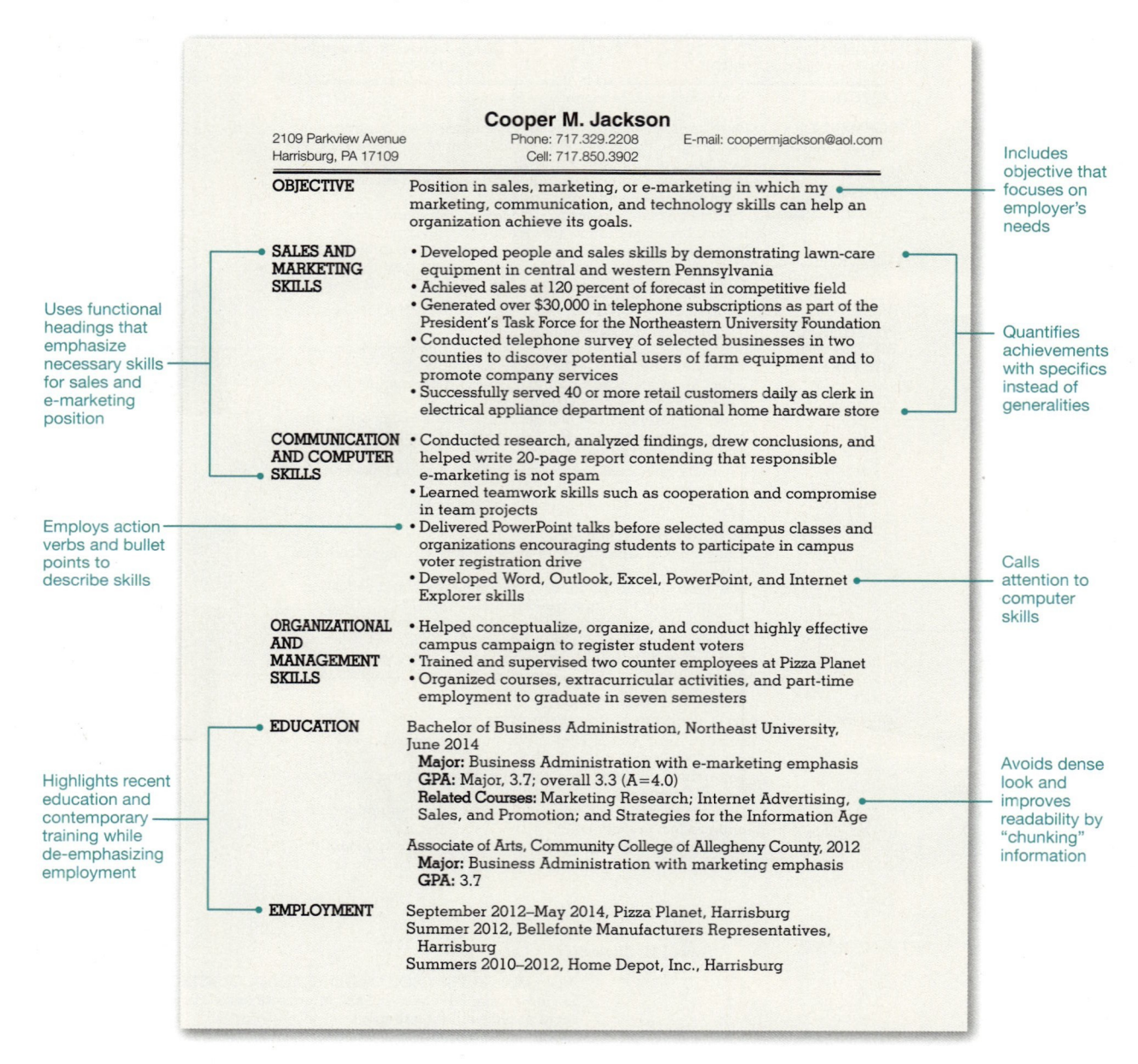

---

**Cooper M. Jackson**

2109 Parkview Avenue  Phone: 717.329.2208  E-mail: coopermjackson@aol.com
Harrisburg, PA 17109  Cell: 717.850.3902

**OBJECTIVE**
Position in sales, marketing, or e-marketing in which my marketing, communication, and technology skills can help an organization achieve its goals.

**SALES AND MARKETING SKILLS**
- Developed people and sales skills by demonstrating lawn-care equipment in central and western Pennsylvania
- Achieved sales at 120 percent of forecast in competitive field
- Generated over $30,000 in telephone subscriptions as part of the President's Task Force for the Northeastern University Foundation
- Conducted telephone survey of selected businesses in two counties to discover potential users of farm equipment and to promote company services
- Successfully served 40 or more retail customers daily as clerk in electrical appliance department of national home hardware store

**COMMUNICATION AND COMPUTER SKILLS**
- Conducted research, analyzed findings, drew conclusions, and helped write 20-page report contending that responsible e-marketing is not spam
- Learned teamwork skills such as cooperation and compromise in team projects
- Delivered PowerPoint talks before selected campus classes and organizations encouraging students to participate in campus voter registration drive
- Developed Word, Outlook, Excel, PowerPoint, and Internet Explorer skills

**ORGANIZATIONAL AND MANAGEMENT SKILLS**
- Helped conceptualize, organize, and conduct highly effective campus campaign to register student voters
- Trained and supervised two counter employees at Pizza Planet
- Organized courses, extracurricular activities, and part-time employment to graduate in seven semesters

**EDUCATION**
Bachelor of Business Administration, Northeast University, June 2014
   **Major:** Business Administration with e-marketing emphasis
   **GPA:** Major, 3.7; overall 3.3 (A=4.0)
   **Related Courses:** Marketing Research; Internet Advertising, Sales, and Promotion; and Strategies for the Information Age

Associate of Arts, Community College of Allegheny County, 2012
   **Major:** Business Administration with marketing emphasis
   **GPA:** 3.7

**EMPLOYMENT**
September 2012–May 2014, Pizza Planet, Harrisburg
Summer 2012, Bellefonte Manufacturers Representatives, Harrisburg
Summers 2010–2012, Home Depot, Inc., Harrisburg

---

Callouts (left): Uses functional headings that emphasize necessary skills for sales and e-marketing position; Employs action verbs and bullet points to describe skills; Highlights recent education and contemporary training while de-emphasizing employment.

Callouts (right): Includes objective that focuses on employer's needs; Quantifies achievements with specifics instead of generalities; Calls attention to computer skills; Avoids dense look and improves readability by "chunking" information.

### 13-4e Polishing Your Résumé and Keeping It Honest

As you continue to work on your résumé, look for ways to improve it. For example, consider consolidating headings. By condensing your information into as few headings as possible, you will produce a clean, professional-looking document. Study other résumés for valuable formatting ideas. Ask yourself what graphic highlighting

# Figure 13.13 Chronological Résumé: Student Seeking Internship

Although Haley has had one internship, she is seeking another as she is about to graduate. To aid her search, she prepared a chronological résumé that emphasizes her education and related coursework. She elected to omit her home address because she prefers that all communication take place digitally or by telephone. Her career objective states exactly the internship position she seeks.

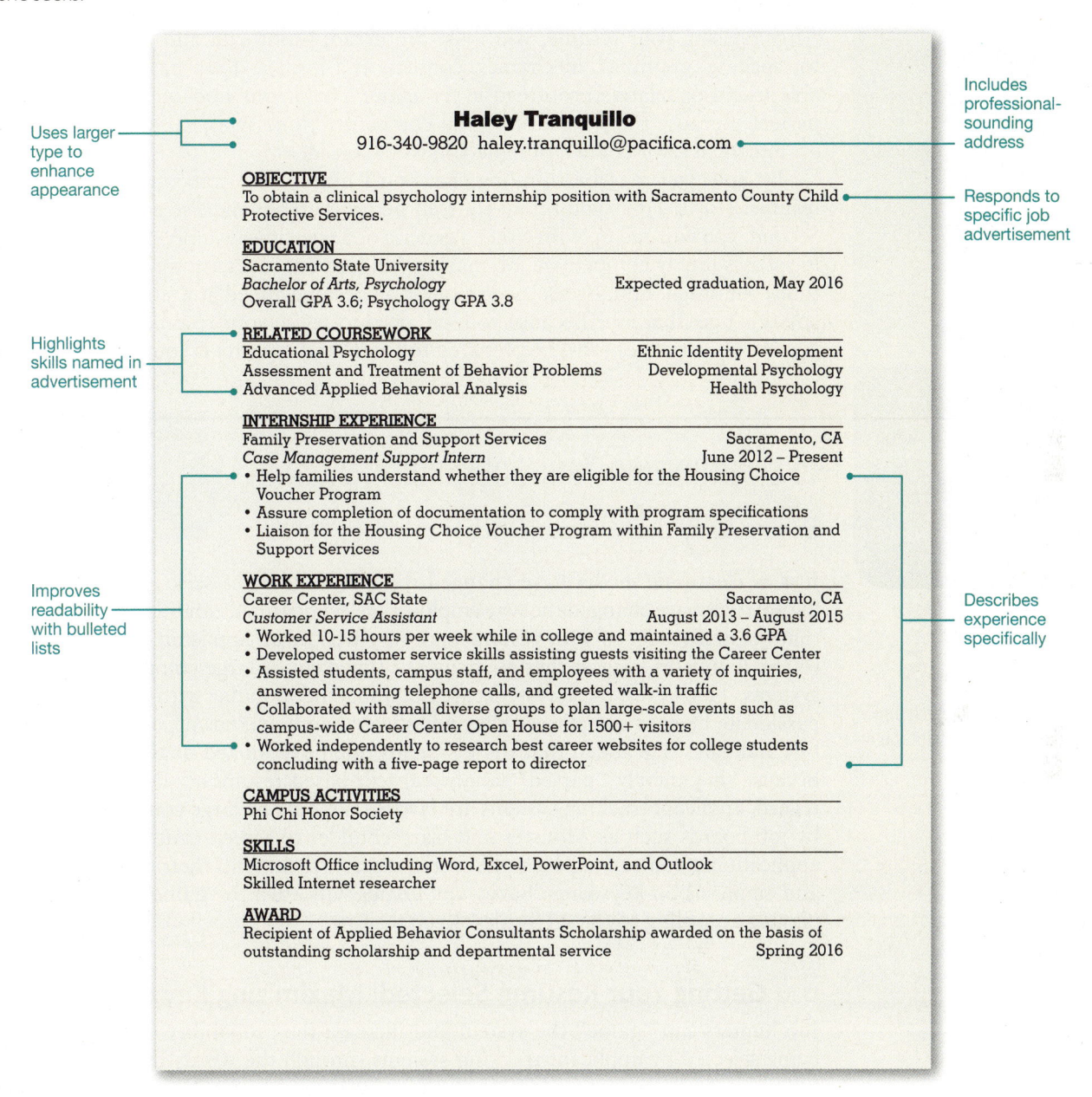

---

**Haley Tranquillo**
916-340-9820   haley.tranquillo@pacifica.com

**OBJECTIVE**
To obtain a clinical psychology internship position with Sacramento County Child Protective Services.

**EDUCATION**
Sacramento State University
*Bachelor of Arts, Psychology*                                Expected graduation, May 2016
Overall GPA 3.6; Psychology GPA 3.8

**RELATED COURSEWORK**
Educational Psychology                          Ethnic Identity Development
Assessment and Treatment of Behavior Problems    Developmental Psychology
Advanced Applied Behavioral Analysis             Health Psychology

**INTERNSHIP EXPERIENCE**
Family Preservation and Support Services                      Sacramento, CA
*Case Management Support Intern*                              June 2012 – Present
- Help families understand whether they are eligible for the Housing Choice Voucher Program
- Assure completion of documentation to comply with program specifications
- Liaison for the Housing Choice Voucher Program within Family Preservation and Support Services

**WORK EXPERIENCE**
Career Center, SAC State                                      Sacramento, CA
*Customer Service Assistant*                                  August 2013 – August 2015
- Worked 10-15 hours per week while in college and maintained a 3.6 GPA
- Developed customer service skills assisting guests visiting the Career Center
- Assisted students, campus staff, and employees with a variety of inquiries, answered incoming telephone calls, and greeted walk-in traffic
- Collaborated with small diverse groups to plan large-scale events such as campus-wide Career Center Open House for 1500+ visitors
- Worked independently to research best career websites for college students concluding with a five-page report to director

**CAMPUS ACTIVITIES**
Phi Chi Honor Society

**SKILLS**
Microsoft Office including Word, Excel, PowerPoint, and Outlook
Skilled Internet researcher

**AWARD**
Recipient of Applied Behavior Consultants Scholarship awarded on the basis of outstanding scholarship and departmental service                    Spring 2016

---

Annotations:
- Uses larger type to enhance appearance
- Includes professional-sounding address
- Responds to specific job advertisement
- Highlights skills named in advertisement
- Improves readability with bulleted lists
- Describes experience specifically

---

techniques you can use to improve readability: capitalization, underlining, indenting, and bulleting. Experiment with headings and styles to achieve a pleasing, easy-to-read message. Moreover, look for ways to eliminate wordiness. For example, instead of *Supervised two employees who worked at the counter*, try *Supervised two counter employees*. Review Chapter 4 for more tips on writing concisely.

A résumé is expected to showcase a candidate's strengths and minimize weaknesses. For this reason, recruiters expect a certain degree of self-promotion. Some

## OFFICE INSIDER

"Long-term damage can be done by lying on your résumé or 'spamming' (sending blanket copies everywhere). 'You're going to be remembered—and not in a positive way.' Also beware of submitting the same messages to multiple firms. ATS systems recognize duplicates, and the applicant immediately loses credibility."

—Colleen McCreary, chief people officer, Zynga, Inc.

**LEARNING OBJECTIVE 5**

Optimize your job search and résumé by taking advantage of today's digital tools.

---

résumé writers, however, step over the line that separates honest self-marketing from deceptive half-truths and flat-out lies. Distorting facts on a résumé is unethical; lying may be illegal. Most important, either practice can destroy a career. In the Communication Workshop at the end of this chapter, learn more about how to keep your résumé honest and the consequences of fudging the facts.

### 13-4f Proofreading Your Résumé

After revising your résumé, you must proofread, proofread, and proofread again for spelling, grammar, mechanics, content, and format. Then have a knowledgeable friend or relative proofread it yet again. This is one document that must be perfect. Because the job market is so competitive, one typo, misspelled word, or grammatical error could eliminate you from consideration.

By now you may be thinking that you'd like to hire someone to write your résumé. Don't! First, you know yourself better than anyone else could know you. Second, you will end up with either a generic or a one-time résumé. A generic résumé in today's highly competitive job market will lose out to a customized résumé nine times out of ten. Equally useless is a one-time résumé aimed at a single job. What if you don't get that job? Because you will need to revise your résumé many times as you seek a variety of jobs, be prepared to write (and rewrite) it yourself.

## 13-5 Optimizing Your Job Search With Today's Digital Tools

Just as electronic media have changed the way candidates seek jobs, these same digital tools have changed the way employers select qualified candidates. This means that the first reader of your résumé may very well be an applicant tracking system (ATS). Estimates suggest that as many as 90 percent of large companies use these systems.[23] However, these systems are not altogether popular with applicants. One passionate blogger complained that ATSs were highly inefficient, costly, and hated by candidates. He added that these systems often overlooked qualified candidates because they merely "parsed" (analyzed) text-based résumés.[24] Despite their low regard, applicant tracking systems are favored not only by large companies but also by job boards such as Monster and CareerBuilder to screen candidates and filter applications. You can expect to be seeing more of them with their restrictive forms and emphasis on keywords. Savvy candidates will learn to "game" the system by playing according to the ATS rules. Keep reading!

### 13-5a Getting Your Résumé Selected: Maximizing Keyword Hits

Job hunters can "game" the system and increase the probability of their résumés being selected by applicant tracking systems through the words they choose. The following techniques, in addition to those cited earlier, can boost the chance of having an ATS select your résumé:

- **Include specific keywords or keyword phrases.** Study carefully any advertisements and job descriptions for the position you want. Describe your experience, education, and qualifications in terms associated with the job advertisement or job description for this position.
- **Focus on nouns.** Although action verbs will make your résumé appeal to a recruiter, the applicant tracking system will often be looking for nouns in three categories: (a) a job title, position, or role (e.g., *accountant, Web developer, team leader*); (b) a technical skill or specialization (e.g., *Javascript, e-newsletter*

448   Chapter 13: The Job Search and Résumés in the Digital Age

*editor)*; and (c) a certification, a tool used, or specific experience (e.g., *Certified Financial Analyst, experience with WordPress*).[25]

- **Use variations of the job title.** Tracking systems may seek a slightly different job title from what you list. To be safe, include variations and abbreviations (e.g., *occupational therapist, certified occupational therapist*, or *COTA*). If you don't have experience in your targeted area, use the job title you seek in your objective.
- **Concentrate on the Skills section.** A majority of keywords sought by employees relate to specialized or technical skill requirements. Therefore, be sure the Skills section of your résumé is loaded with nouns that describe your skills and qualifications. See page 440 for more suggestions on skills categories.
- **Skip a keyword summary.** Avoid grouping nouns in a keyword summary because recruiters may perceive them to be manipulative.[26]

### 13-5b Showcasing Your Qualifications in a Career E-Portfolio

With the workplace becoming increasingly digital, you have yet another way to display your qualifications to prospective employers—the career e-portfolio. This is a collection of digital files that can be navigated with the help of menus and hyperlinks much like a personal website.

**What Goes in a Career E-Portfolio?** An e-portfolio provides viewers with a snapshot of your talents, accomplishments, and technical skills. It may include a copy of your résumé, reference letters, commendations for special achievements, awards, certificates, work samples, a complete list of your courses, thank-you letters, and other items that tout your accomplishments. An e-portfolio could also offer links to digital copies of your artwork, film projects, videos, blueprints, documents, photographs, multimedia files, and blog entries that might otherwise be difficult to share with potential employers.

Because e-portfolios offer a variety of resources in one place, they have many advantages, as seen in Figure 13.14. When they are posted on websites, they can be

> **OFFICE INSIDER**
>
> "Yes we all hate applicant tracking systems. When you have to fill in 20 fields in a form to apply for a job it makes your head spin. But these systems are badly needed and companies spend millions of dollars trying to make them easier to use and more valuable to candidates."
>
> —Josh Bersin, human resources and leadership consultant

Figure **13.14** Making a Career E-Portfolio

**Why create a career e-portfolio?**
- Demonstrate your technology skills.
- Support and extend your résumé.
- Present yourself in a lively format.
- Make data instantly accessible.
- Target a specific job.

**What goes in it?**
- Relevant course work
- Updated résumé, cover message
- Real work examples
- Recommendations
- Images, links, or whatever showcases your skills

**How to make and publish it?**
- Use a portfolio or blog template.
- Design your own website.
- Host at a university or private site.
- Publish its URL in your résumé and elsewhere.

Chapter 13: The Job Search and Résumés in the Digital Age

viewed at an employer's convenience. Let's say you are talking on the phone with an employer in another city who wants to see a copy of your résumé. You can simply refer the employer to the website where your résumé resides. E-portfolios can also be seen by many individuals in an organization without circulating a paper copy. However, the main reason for preparing an e-portfolio is that it shows off your talents and qualifications more thoroughly than a print résumé does.

Some recruiters may be skeptical about e-portfolios because they fear that such presentations will take more time to view than paper-based résumés do. As a result, nontraditional job applications may end up at the bottom of the pile or be ignored. That's why some applicants submit a print résumé in addition to an e-portfolio.

**How Are E-Portfolios Accessed?** E-portfolios are generally accessed at websites, where they are available around the clock to employers. If the websites are not password protected, however, you should remove personal information. Some colleges and universities make website space available for student e-portfolios. In addition, institutions may provide instruction and resources for scanning photos, digitizing images, and preparing graphics. E-portfolios may also be burned onto CDs and DVDs to be mailed to prospective employers.

To learn more about making a career e-portfolio, take a look at a tutorial written by a recent university graduate who tells exactly how he did it. This tutorial is available at the student website for this book: www.cengagebrain.com.

## 13-5c Expanding Your Employment Chances With a Video Résumé

Still another way to expand your employment possibilities is with a video résumé. Video résumés enable job candidates to present their experience, qualifications, and interests in video form. This format has many benefits. It allows candidates to demonstrate their public speaking, interpersonal, and technical skills more impressively than they can in traditional print résumés. Both employers and applicants can save recruitment and travel costs by using video résumés. Instead of flying distant candidates to interviews, organizations can see them digitally.

Video résumés are becoming more prevalent with the emergence of YouTube, inexpensive webcams, and widespread broadband. With simple edits on a computer, you can customize a video message to a specific employer and tailor your résumé for a particular job opening. In making a video résumé, dress professionally in business attire, just as you would for an in-person interview. Keep your video to three minutes or less. Explain why you would be a good employee and what you can do for the company that hires you.

Before committing time and energy to a video résumé, decide whether it is appropriate for your career field. Such presentations make sense for online, media, social, and creative professions. Traditional organizations, however, may be less impressed. Done well, a video résumé might give you an edge. Done poorly, however, it could bounce you from contention.

## 13-5d Wowing Them With an Infographic Résumé

A hot trend among creative types is the infographic résumé. It uses colorful charts, graphics, and time lines to illustrate a candidate's work history and experience. No one could deny that an infographic résumé really stands out. "Anyone looking at it," effuses blogger Randy Krum, "is 650% more likely to remember it days later."[27] Those preparing infographic résumés are often in the field of graphic design or journalism. James Coleman, a graduating senior from the University of Missouri, created an infographic résumé that secured a job. Shown in Figure 13.15, James's résumé uses a time line to track his experience and education. Colorful bubbles indicate his digital skills.

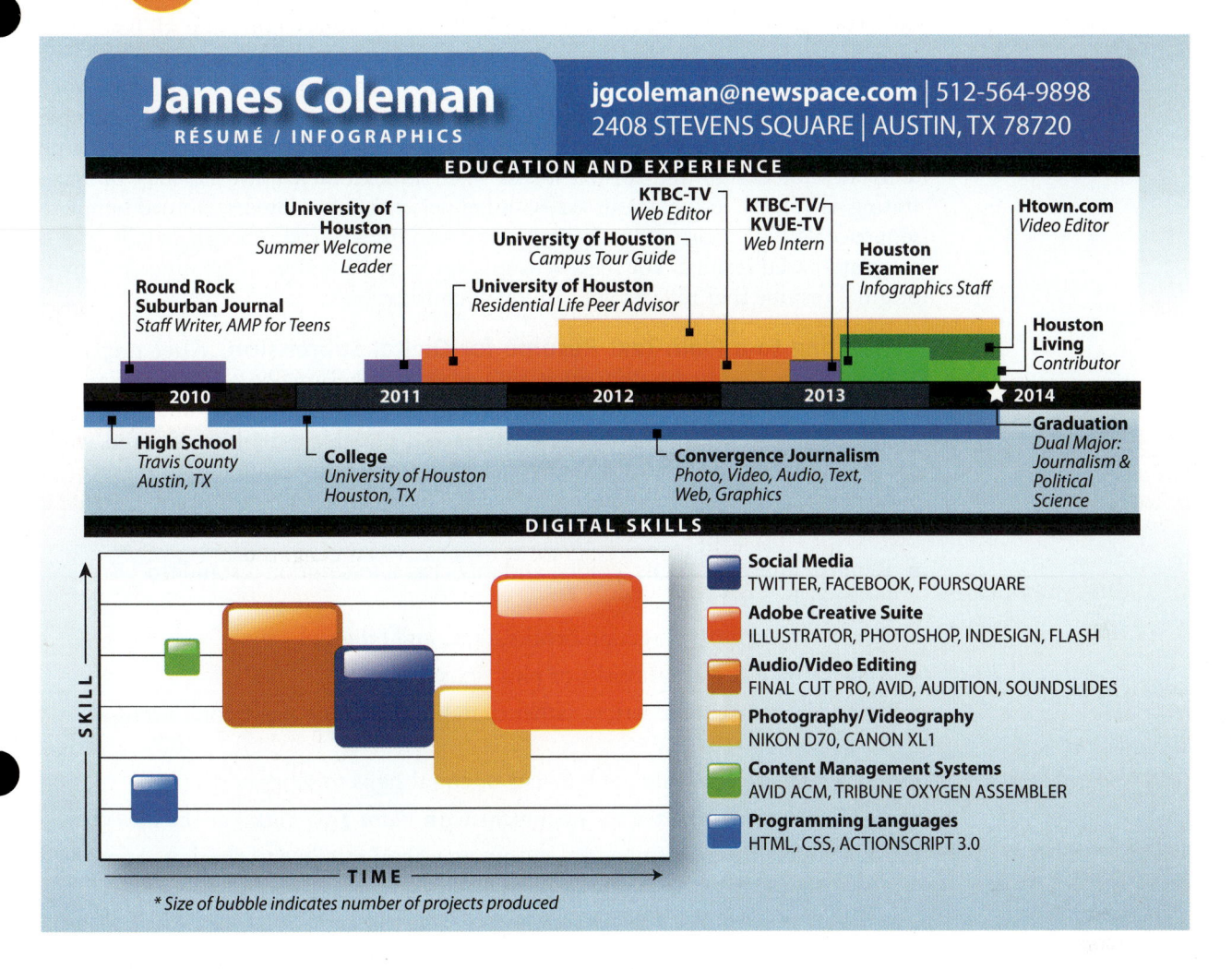

Figure **13.15** Infographics: A Novel Way to Show Education, Experience, and Skills

Most of us, however, are not talented enough to create professional-looking infographics. To the rescue are many companies that now offer infographic apps. Vizualize.me turns a user's LinkedIn profile information into a beautiful Web-based infographic. Re.vu also pulls in LinkedIn data to produce a stylish Web-based infographic. Brazen Careerist offers a Facebook application that generates an infographic résumé from a user's Facebook, Twitter, and LinkedIn information.

Will a dazzling infographic get you a job? Among hiring managers, the consensus is that infographic résumés help candidates set themselves apart, but such visual displays may not be appropriate for every kind of job.[28] In more traditional fields such as accounting and financial services, hiring managers want to see a standard print-based résumé. One hiring manager pointed out that traditional résumés evolved this way for a reason: they make comparison, evaluation, and selection easier for employers.[29]

### 13-5e How Many Résumés and What Format?

At this point you may be wondering how many résumés you should make, and what format they should follow. The good news is that you need only one basic résumé that you can customize for various job prospects and formats.

**Preparing a Basic Print-Based Résumé.** The one basic résumé you should prepare is a print-based traditional résumé. It should be attractively formatted to maximize readability. This résumé is useful (a) during job interviews, (b) for person-to-person networking situations, (c) for recruiters at career fairs, and (d) when you are competing for a job that does not require an electronic submission.

You can create a basic, yet professional-looking résumé by using your word processing program. The Résumé Gallery in this chapter provides ideas for simple layouts that are easily duplicated and adapted. You can also examine résumé templates for design and format ideas. Their inflexibility, however, may be frustrating as you try to force your skills and experience into a predetermined template sequence. What's more, recruiters who read hundreds of résumés can usually spot a template-based résumé. For these reasons, you may be better off creating your own original résumé that reflects your unique qualifications.

**Converting to a Plain-Text Résumé for Digital Submission.** After preparing a basic résumé, you can convert it to a plain-text résumé so that it is available for e-mailing or pasting into online résumé submission forms. Some employers prefer plain-text documents because they avoid possible e-mail viruses and word processing incompatibilities. Usually included in the body of an e-mail message, a plain-text résumé is immediately searchable. To make a plain-text résumé, create a new document, illustrated in Figure 13.16, in which you do the following:

- Remove images, designs, colors, and any characters not on a standard keyboard.
- Remove page breaks, section breaks, tabs, and tables.
- Replace bullets with asterisks or plus signs.
- Consider using capital letters rather than boldface type—but don't overdo the caps.
- Use white space or a line of hyphens or equal signs to separate sections.
- In Microsoft Word, save the document with *Plain Text* (*.txt) as the file type.
- Send yourself a copy embedded within an e-mail message to check its appearance. Also send it to a friend to try it out.

## 13-5f Submitting Your Résumé

The format you choose for submitting your résumé depends on what is required. If you are responding to a job advertisement, be certain to read the listing carefully to learn how the employer wants you to submit your résumé. Not following the prospective employer's instructions can eliminate you from consideration before your résumé is even reviewed. If you have any doubt about what format is desired, send an e-mail inquiry to a company representative, or call and ask. Most organizations request one of the following submission formats:

- **Word document.** Some organizations ask candidates to send their résumés and cover messages by surface mail. Others request that résumés be submitted as Word documents attached to e-mail messages, despite the fear of viruses.
- **Plain-text document.** As discussed earlier, many employers expect applicants to submit résumés and cover letters as plain-text documents. This format is also widely used for posting to an online job board or for sending by e-mail. Plain-text résumés may be embedded within or attached to e-mail messages.
- **PDF document.** For safety reasons some employers prefer PDF (portable document format) files. A PDF résumé looks exactly like the original and cannot be altered. Most computers have Adobe Acrobat Reader installed for easy reading of PDF files. Converting your résumé to a PDF file can be easily done by saving it as a PDF file, which preserves all formatting.

**Figure 13.16** Portion of Plain-Text Résumé

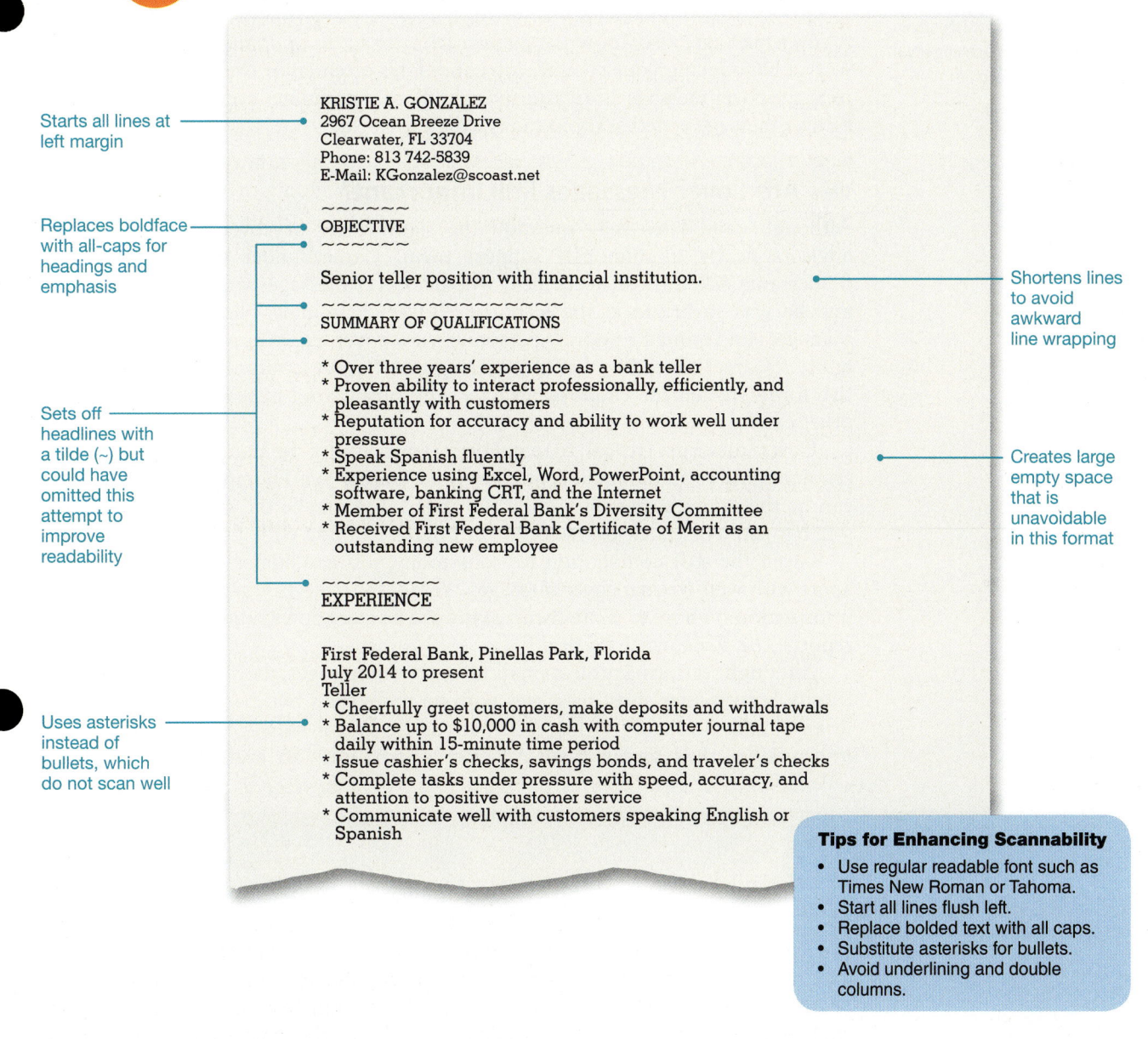

```
KRISTIE A. GONZALEZ
2967 Ocean Breeze Drive
Clearwater, FL 33704
Phone: 813 742-5839
E-Mail: KGonzalez@scoast.net

~~~~~~~
OBJECTIVE
~~~~~~~

Senior teller position with financial institution.

~~~~~~~~~~~~~~~~~~~~~~~
SUMMARY OF QUALIFICATIONS
~~~~~~~~~~~~~~~~~~~~~~~

* Over three years' experience as a bank teller
* Proven ability to interact professionally, efficiently, and
  pleasantly with customers
* Reputation for accuracy and ability to work well under
  pressure
* Speak Spanish fluently
* Experience using Excel, Word, PowerPoint, accounting
  software, banking CRT, and the Internet
* Member of First Federal Bank's Diversity Committee
* Received First Federal Bank Certificate of Merit as an
  outstanding new employee

~~~~~~~~~
EXPERIENCE
~~~~~~~~~

First Federal Bank, Pinellas Park, Florida
July 2014 to present
Teller
* Cheerfully greet customers, make deposits and withdrawals
* Balance up to $10,000 in cash with computer journal tape
  daily within 15-minute time period
* Issue cashier's checks, savings bonds, and traveler's checks
* Complete tasks under pressure with speed, accuracy, and
  attention to positive customer service
* Communicate well with customers speaking English or
  Spanish
```

Annotations:
- Starts all lines at left margin
- Replaces boldface with all-caps for headings and emphasis
- Sets off headlines with a tilde (~) but could have omitted this attempt to improve readability
- Uses asterisks instead of bullets, which do not scan well
- Shortens lines to avoid awkward line wrapping
- Creates large empty space that is unavoidable in this format

**Tips for Enhancing Scannability**
- Use regular readable font such as Times New Roman or Tahoma.
- Start all lines flush left.
- Replace bolded text with all caps.
- Substitute asterisks for bullets.
- Avoid underlining and double columns.

- **Company database.** Larger organizations may prefer that you complete an online form with your résumé information. This enables them to plug your data into their formats for rapid searching. You might be able to cut and paste the information from your résumé into the form.
- **Fax.** Although fading in office use, fax transmission might be requested. Sending your résumé via fax gets your information to an employer safely and quickly. However, because print quality is often poor, use the fax method only if requested or if a submission deadline is upon you. Then, follow up with your polished printed résumé.

Because your résumé is probably the most important message you will ever write, you will revise it many times. With so much information in concentrated form and with so much riding on its outcome, your résumé demands careful polishing, proofreading, and critiquing.

**LEARNING OBJECTIVE 6**
Draft and submit a customized cover message to accompany a print or digital résumé.

## 13-6 Creating Customized Cover Messages

A cover message, also known as a *cover letter* or *letter of application*, is a graceful way of introducing your résumé. Job candidates often labor over their résumés but treat the cover message as an afterthought. Some candidates even question whether a cover message is necessary in today's digital world.

### 13-6a Are Cover Messages Still Important?

Although candidates may question the significance of cover messages, career advisors nearly unanimously support them. CareerBuilder specialist Anthony Balderrama asked those in the field whether cover messages were a waste of time, and he was surprised at the response. "Overwhelmingly," he reported, "hiring managers and human resources personnel view cover letters as a necessity in the job hunt."[30] Career coach Heather Huhman agrees: "Cover letters allow you—in narrative form—to tell the employer exactly why hiring you, instead of the numerous other candidates, is a good decision."[31]

Cover messages reveal to employers your ability to put together complete sentences and to sound intelligent. Corporate trainer Sue Thompson declares, "You can be the smartest person within 100 miles, and maybe the right person for the job, but you will knock yourself right out of the running with a poor cover letter."[32]

Given the stiff competition for jobs today, job candidates can set themselves apart with well-written cover messages. Yet, despite the vast support for them and information on how to write them, many job hunters don't submit cover messages, reports *The Wall Street Journal*.[33]

Although recruiting professionals favor cover messages, they disagree about their length. Some prefer short messages with no more than two paragraphs embedded in an e-mail message.[34] Other recruiters desire longer messages that supply more information, thus giving them a better opportunity to evaluate a candidate's

## Workplace in Focus

Although many job seekers downplay cover letters, career advisors say that a cover message can be the difference between landing a job offer and losing one. Unlike résumés, which are factoid-driven, cover messages allow candidates to make a human connection and express creatively why they are right for the job. In one recent employment scenario, in which a Seattle woman earned a job with self-improvement firm Mindbloom, the applicant's letter opened, "Dear Mindbloomers: Please find my résumé for review in regards to no employment opportunities you have available at the moment." The woman proceeded to make a case for why the company should hire her as the "Director of Happiness," even though no such position existed. What tips can help job candidates write effective cover messages?[35]

*Courtesy of LinkedIn*

qualifications and writing skills. These recruiters argue that hiring and training new employees is expensive and time consuming; therefore, they welcome extra data to guide them in making the best choice the first time. Follow your judgment in writing a brief or a longer cover message. If you feel, for example, that you need space to explain in more detail what you can do for a prospective employer, do so.

Regardless of its length, a cover message should have three primary parts: (a) an opening that captures attention, introduces the message, and identifies the position; (b) a body that sells the candidate and focuses on the employer's needs; and (c) a closing that requests an interview and motivates action. When putting your cover message together, remember that the biggest mistake job seekers make when writing cover messages is being too generic. You should, therefore, write a personalized, customized cover message for every position that interests you.

## 13-6b Gaining Attention in the Opening

Your cover message will be more appealing—and more likely to be read—if it begins by addressing the reader by name. Rather than sending your letter to the *Hiring Manager* or *Human Resources Department*, try to identify the name of the appropriate individual. Kelly Renz, vice president for a recruiting outsourcing firm, says that savvy job seekers "take control of their application's destiny." She suggests looking on the company's website, doing an Internet search for a name, or calling the human resources department and asking the receptionist the name of the person in charge of hiring. Ms. Renz also suggests using LinkedIn to find someone working in the same department as the position in the posted job. This person may know the name of the hiring manager.[36] If you still cannot find the name of any person to address, you might replace the salutation of your letter with a descriptive subject line such as *Application for Marketing Specialist Position*.

How you open your cover message depends largely on whether the application is solicited or unsolicited. If an employment position has been announced and applicants are being solicited, you can use a direct approach. If you do not know whether a position is open and you are prospecting for a job, use an indirect approach. Whether direct or indirect, the opening should attract the attention of the reader. Strive for openings that are more imaginative than *Please consider this letter an application for the position of . . .* or *I would like to apply for. . . .*

**Openings for Solicited Jobs.** When applying for a job that has been announced, consider some of the following techniques to open your cover message:

- **Refer to the name of an employee in the company.** Remember that employers always hope to hire known quantities rather than complete strangers.

    *Brendan Borello, a member of your Customer Service Department, told me that Alliance Resources is seeking an experienced customer service representative. The enclosed summary of my qualifications demonstrates my preparation for this position.*

    *At the suggestion of Heather Bolger, in your Legal Services Department, I submit my qualifications for the position of staffing coordinator.*

    *Montana Morano, placement director at Southwest University, told me that Dynamic Industries has an opening for a technical writer with knowledge of Web design and graphics.*

- **Refer to the source of your information precisely.** If you are answering an advertisement, include the exact position advertised and the name and date of the publication. If you are responding to a position listed on an online job board, include the website name and the date the position was posted.

    *From your company's website, I learned about your need for a sales representative for the Ohio, Indiana, and Illinois regions. I am very interested*

> ## OFFICE INSIDER
>
> *"I see red flags when there is no cover letter along with a résumé. The absence of cover letters [suggests] to me that the candidate is lazy and is sending résumés in masses, rather than customizing or personalizing to each individual company of interest."*
>
> —Angela Ruggiero, senior account executive, Stanton Communications

Chapter 13: The Job Search and Résumés in the Digital Age

*in this position and am confident that my education and experience are appropriate for the opening.*

*My talent for interacting with people, coupled with more than five years of customer service experience, make me an ideal candidate for the director of customer relations position you advertised on the CareerJournal website on August 3.*

- **Refer to the job title, and describe how your qualifications fit the requirements.** Hiring managers are looking for a match between an applicant's credentials and the job needs.

*Ceradyne Company's marketing assistant opening is an excellent match with my qualifications. As a recent graduate of Western University with a major in marketing, I offer solid academic credentials as well as industry experience gained from an internship at Flotek Industries.*

*Will an honors graduate with a degree in recreation and two years of part-time experience organizing social activities for a convalescent hospital qualify for your position of activity director?*

*Because of my specialized training in finance and accounting at Michigan State University, I am confident that I have the qualifications you described in your advertisement for a staff accountant trainee.*

**Openings for Unsolicited Jobs.** If you are unsure whether a position actually exists, you might use a more persuasive opening. Because your goal is to convince this person to read on, try one of the following techniques:

- **Demonstrate an interest in and knowledge of the reader's business.** Show the hiring manager that you have done your research and that this organization is more than a mere name to you.

*Because Signa HealthNet, Inc., is organizing a new information management team for its recently established group insurance division, could you use the services of a well-trained information systems graduate who seeks to become a professional systems analyst?*

*I read with great interest the article in Forbes announcing the upcoming launch of US Bank. Congratulations on this new venture and its notable $50 million in loans precharter! The possibility of helping your bank grow is exciting, and I would like to explore a potential employment match that I am confident will be mutually beneficial.*

- **Show how your special talents and background will benefit the company.** Human resources managers need to be convinced that you can do something for them.

*Could your rapidly expanding publications division use the services of an editorial assistant who offers exceptional language skills, an honors degree from the University of Mississippi, and two years' experience in producing a campus literary publication?*

In applying for an advertised job, Shenice Williams wrote the solicited cover letter shown in Figure 13.17. Notice that her opening identifies the position advertised on the company's website so that the reader knows exactly what advertisement Shenice means. Using features on her word processing program, Shenice designed her own letterhead that uses her name and looks like professionally printed letterhead paper.

More challenging are unsolicited cover messages, such as the letter of Donald Vinton shown in Figure 13.18. Because he hopes to discover or create a job, his opening must grab the reader's attention immediately. To do that, he capitalizes

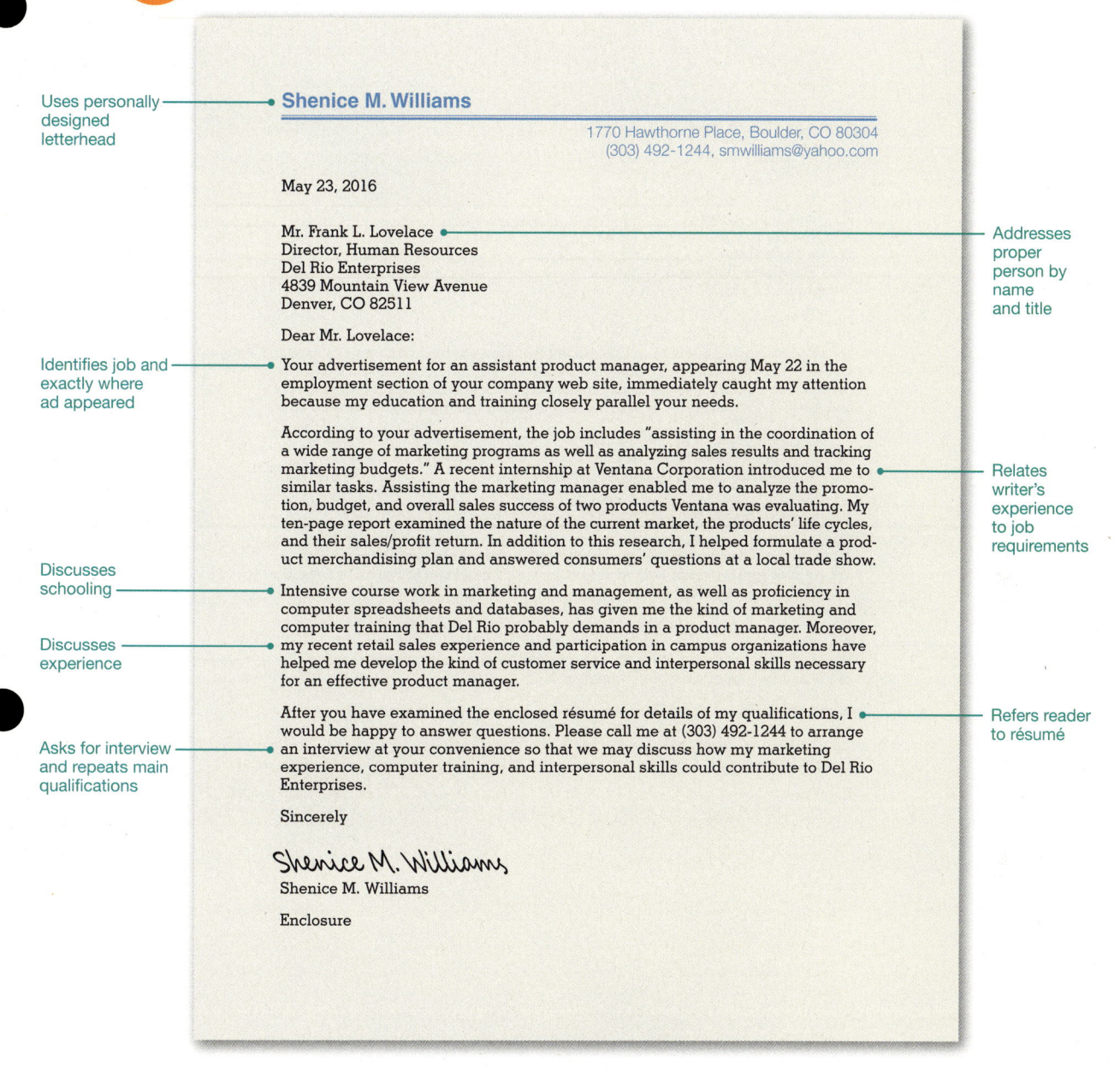

Figure 13.17 Solicited Cover Letter

*Uses personally designed letterhead*

**Shenice M. Williams**
1770 Hawthorne Place, Boulder, CO 80304
(303) 492-1244, smwilliams@yahoo.com

May 23, 2016

Mr. Frank L. Lovelace
Director, Human Resources
Del Rio Enterprises
4839 Mountain View Avenue
Denver, CO 82511

*Addresses proper person by name and title*

Dear Mr. Lovelace:

*Identifies job and exactly where ad appeared*

Your advertisement for an assistant product manager, appearing May 22 in the employment section of your company web site, immediately caught my attention because my education and training closely parallel your needs.

According to your advertisement, the job includes "assisting in the coordination of a wide range of marketing programs as well as analyzing sales results and tracking marketing budgets." A recent internship at Ventana Corporation introduced me to similar tasks. Assisting the marketing manager enabled me to analyze the promotion, budget, and overall sales success of two products Ventana was evaluating. My ten-page report examined the nature of the current market, the products' life cycles, and their sales/profit return. In addition to this research, I helped formulate a product merchandising plan and answered consumers' questions at a local trade show.

*Relates writer's experience to job requirements*

*Discusses schooling*

*Discusses experience*

Intensive course work in marketing and management, as well as proficiency in computer spreadsheets and databases, has given me the kind of marketing and computer training that Del Rio probably demands in a product manager. Moreover, my recent retail sales experience and participation in campus organizations have helped me develop the kind of customer service and interpersonal skills necessary for an effective product manager.

*Asks for interview and repeats main qualifications*

After you have examined the enclosed résumé for details of my qualifications, I would be happy to answer questions. Please call me at (303) 492-1244 to arrange an interview at your convenience so that we may discuss how my marketing experience, computer training, and interpersonal skills could contribute to Del Rio Enterprises.

*Refers reader to résumé*

Sincerely

*Shenice M. Williams*
Shenice M. Williams

Enclosure

on company information appearing in an online article. Donald purposely kept his cover letter short and to the point because he anticipated that a busy executive would be unwilling to read a long, detailed letter. Donald's unsolicited letter "prospects" for a job. Some job candidates feel that such letters may be even more productive than efforts to secure advertised jobs, because prospecting candidates face less competition and show initiative. Notice that Donald's letter uses a personal business letter format with his return address above the date.

### 13-6c Promoting Your Strengths in the Message Body

Once you have captured the attention of the reader and identified your purpose in the letter opening, you should use the body of the letter to plug your qualifications for this position. If you are responding to an advertisement, you will want to

## Figure 13.18 Unsolicited Cover Letter

2250 Turtle Creek Drive
Monroeville, PA 15146
May 29, 2016

Mr. Richard M. Jannis
Vice President, Operations
Sports World, Inc.
4907 Allegheny Boulevard
Pittsburgh, PA 16103

Dear Mr. Jannis:

Today's *Pittsburgh Examiner* online reports that your organization plans to expand its operations to include national distribution of sporting goods, and it occurs to me that you will be needing highly motivated, self-starting sales representatives and marketing managers. Here are three significant qualifications I have to offer:

- Four years of formal training in business administration, including specialized courses in sales management, retailing, marketing promotion, and consumer behavior
- Practical experience in demonstrating and selling consumer products, as well as successful experience in telemarketing
- Excellent communication skills and a strong interest in most areas of sports (which helped me become a sportscaster at Penn State radio station WGNF)

May we talk about how I can put these qualifications, and others summarized in the enclosed résumé, to work for Sports World as it develops its national sales force? I'll call during the week of June 5 to discuss your company's expansion plans and the opportunity for an interview.

Sincerely yours,

*Donald W. Vinton*

Donald W. Vinton

Enclosure

**Annotations:**
- Uses personal business style with return address above date
- Shows resourcefulness and knowledge of company
- Uses bulleted list to make letter easier to read
- Refers to enclosed résumé
- Keeps letter brief to retain reader's attention
- Takes initiative for follow-up

---

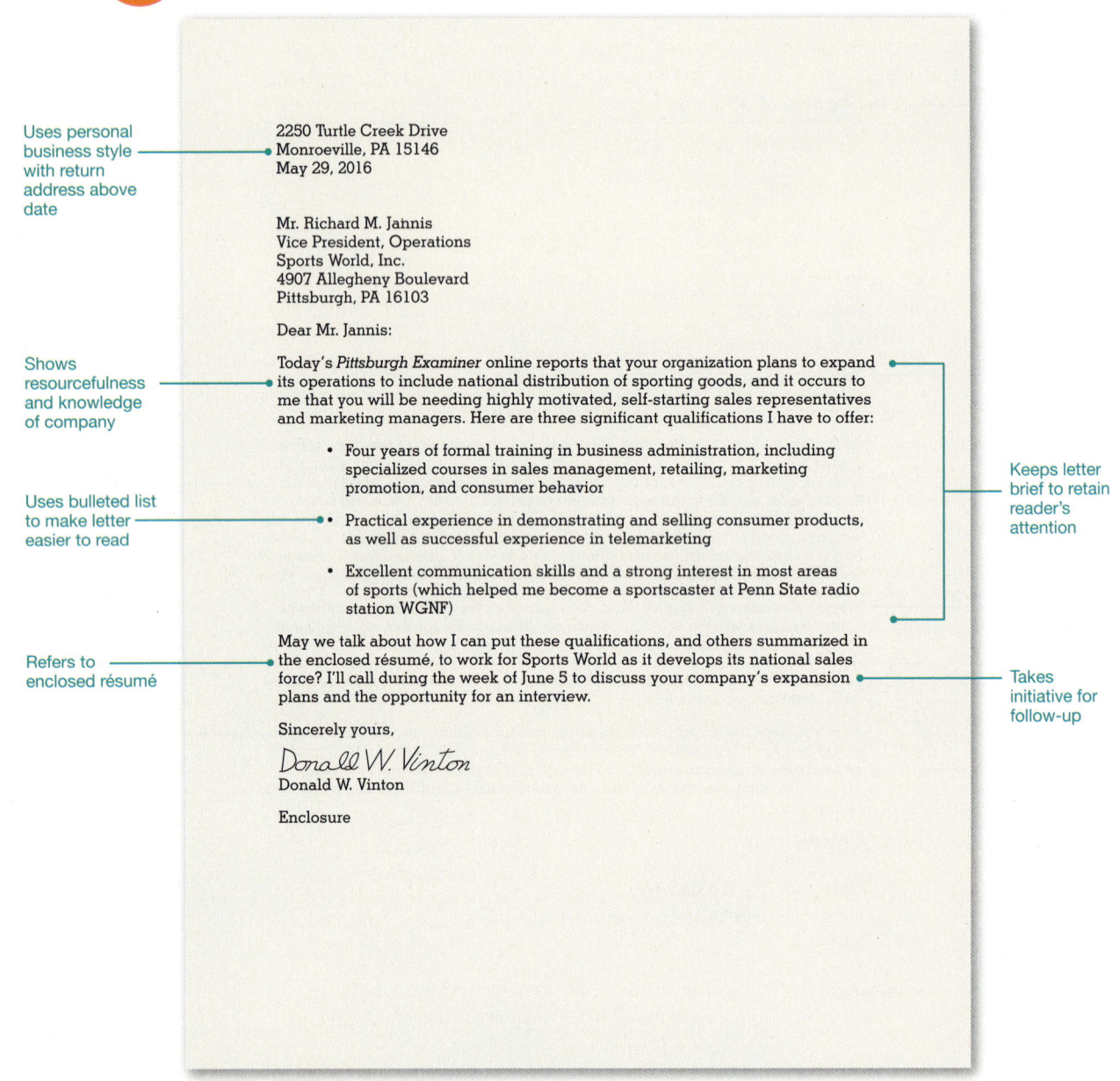

explain how your preparation and experience fulfill the stated requirements. If you are prospecting for a job, you may not know the exact requirements. Your employment research and knowledge of your field, however, should give you a reasonably good idea of what is expected for the position you seek.

It is also important to stress reader benefits. In other words, you should describe your strong points in relation to the needs of the employer. Hiring officers want you to tell them what you can do for their organizations. This is more important than telling what courses you took in college or what duties you performed in your previous jobs.

**Poor:** I have completed courses in business communication, report writing, and technical writing,

**Improved:** Courses in business communication, report writing, and technical writing have helped me develop the research and writing skills required of your technical writers.

Choose your strongest qualifications and show how they fit the targeted job. Remember that students with little experience are better off spotlighting their education and its practical applications:

**Poor:** I have taken classes that prepare me to be an administrative assistant.

**Improved:** Composing e-mail messages, business letters, memos, and reports in my business communication and office technology courses helped me develop the writing, language, proofreading, and computer skills mentioned in your ad for an administrative assistant.

In the body of your letter, you may choose to discuss relevant personal traits. Employers are looking for candidates who, among other things, are team players, take responsibility, show initiative, and learn easily. Don't just list several personal traits, though; instead, include documentation that proves you possess these traits. Notice how the following paragraph uses action verbs to paint a picture of a promising candidate:

*In addition to developing technical and academic skills at Florida Central University, I have gained interpersonal, leadership, and organizational skills. As vice president of the business students' organization, Gamma Alpha, I helped organize and supervise two successful fund-raising events. These activities involved conceptualizing the tasks, motivating others to help, scheduling work sessions, and coordinating the efforts of 35 diverse students. I enjoyed my success with these activities and look forward to applying my experience in your management trainee program.*

Finally, in this section or the next, refer the reader to your résumé. Do so directly or as part of another statement.

**Direct reference to résumé:** Please refer to the attached résumé for additional information regarding my education, experience, and skills.

**Part of another statement:** As you will notice from my enclosed résumé, I will graduate in June with a bachelor's degree in business administration.

## 13-6d Motivating Action in the Closing

After presenting your case, you should conclude by asking confidently for an interview. Don't ask for the job. To do so would be presumptuous and naïve. In requesting an interview, you might suggest reader benefits or review your strongest points. Sound sincere and appreciative. Remember to make it easy for the reader to agree by supplying your telephone number and the best times to call you. In addition, keep in mind that some hiring officers prefer that you take the initiative to call them. Avoid expressions such as *I hope*, which weaken your closing. Here are possible endings:

**Poor:** I hope to hear from you soon.

**Improved:** This brief description of my qualifications and the additional information on my résumé demonstrate my readiness to put my accounting skills to work for McLellan and Associates.

| | |
|---|---|
| | Please call me at (405) 488-2291 before 10 a.m. or after 3 p.m. to arrange an interview. |
| Poor: | I look forward to a call from you. |
| Improved: | To add to your staff an industrious, well-trained administrative assistant with proven Internet and communication skills, call me at (350) 492-1433 to arrange an interview. I look forward to meeting with you to discuss further my qualifications. |
| Poor: | Thanks for looking over my qualifications. |
| Improved: | I look forward to the opportunity to discuss my qualifications for the financial analyst position more fully in an interview. I can be reached at (213) 458-4030. |

## 13-6e Sending Your Résumé and Cover Message

Many applicants using technology make the mistake of not including cover messages with their résumés submitted by e-mail or fax. A résumé that arrives without a cover message makes the receiver wonder what it is and why it was sent. Some candidates either skip the cover message or think they can get by with a one-line cover such as this: *Please see attached résumé, and thanks for your consideration.*

How you submit your résumé depends on the employer's instructions, which usually involve one of the following methods:

- Submit both your cover message and résumé in an e-mail message. Convert both to plain text.
- Send your cover message in an e-mail and attach your résumé (plain text, Word document, or PDF).
- Send a short e-mail message with both your cover message and résumé attached.
- Send your cover message and résumé as printed Word documents by U.S. mail.

If you are serious about landing the job, take the time to prepare a professional cover message. What if you are e-mailing your résumé? Just use the same cover message you would send by surface mail, but shorten it a bit. As illustrated in Figure 13.19, an inside address is unnecessary for an e-mail recipient. Also, move your return address from the top of the letter to just below your name. Include your e-mail address and phone number. Remove tabs, bullets, underlining, and italics that might be problematic in e-mail messages. For résumés submitted by fax, send the same cover message you would send by surface mail. For résumés submitted as PDF files, send the cover message as a PDF also.

## 13-6f Final Tips for Successful Cover Messages

As you revise your cover message, notice how many sentences begin with *I*. Although it is impossible to talk about yourself without using *I*, you can reduce "I" domination with a number of thoughtful techniques. Make activities and outcomes, and not yourself, the subjects of sentences. Sometimes you can avoid "I" domination by focusing on the "you" view. Another way to avoid starting sentences with *I* is to move phrases from within the sentence to the beginning.

| | |
|---|---|
| Poor: | I took classes in business communication and computer applications. |
| Improved: | Classes in business communication and computer applications prepared me to. . . . (Make activities the subject.) |

Figure **13.19** E-Mail Cover Message

```
To:      Frank L. Lovelace <fllovelace@delrio.com>
From:    Shenice M. Williams <smwilliams@yahoo.com>
Subject: Application for Assistant Product Manager Position Advertised 5-22-16
Cc:
Bcc:
```
*Provides complete subject line identifying purpose*

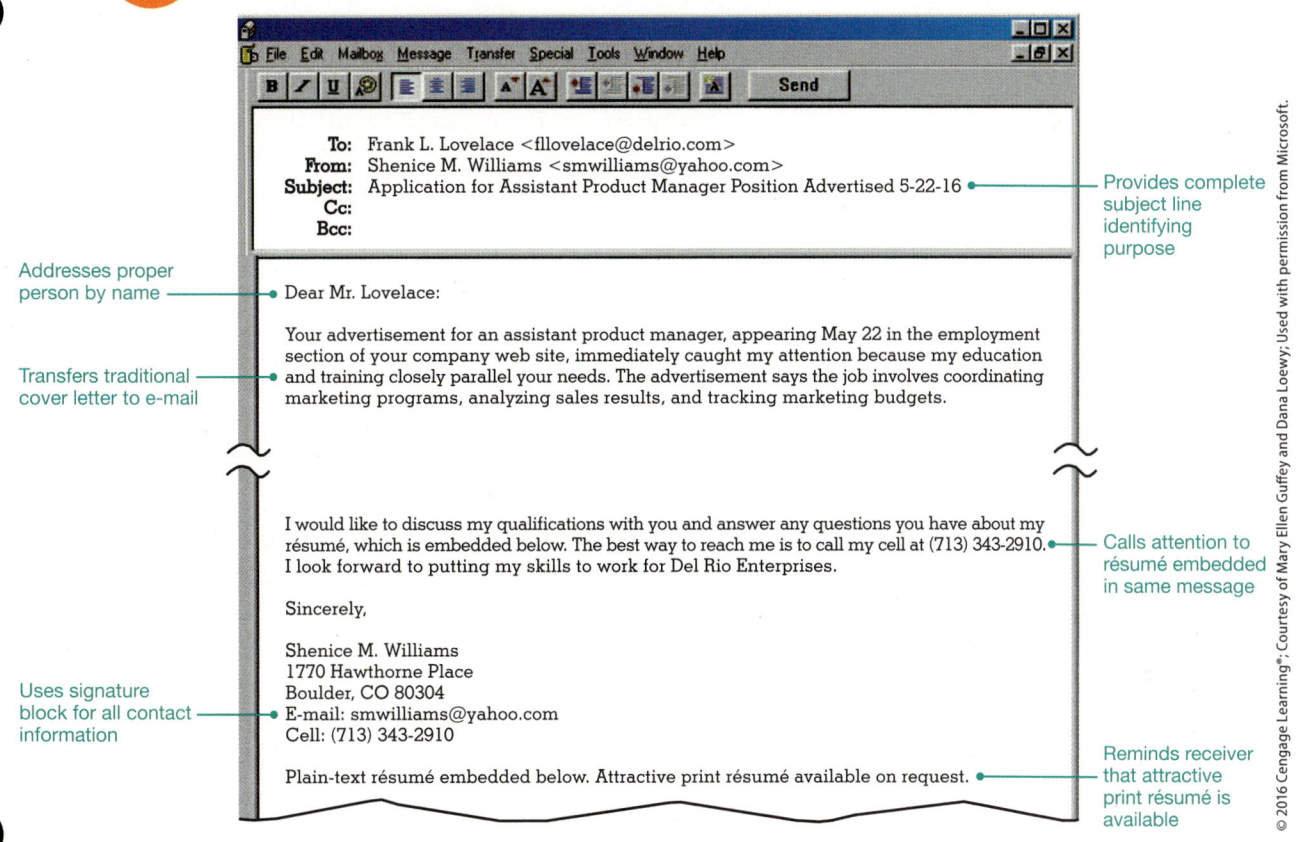

*Addresses proper person by name* — Dear Mr. Lovelace:

*Transfers traditional cover letter to e-mail* — Your advertisement for an assistant product manager, appearing May 22 in the employment section of your company web site, immediately caught my attention because my education and training closely parallel your needs. The advertisement says the job involves coordinating marketing programs, analyzing sales results, and tracking marketing budgets.

I would like to discuss my qualifications with you and answer any questions you have about my résumé, which is embedded below. The best way to reach me is to call my cell at (713) 343-2910. I look forward to putting my skills to work for Del Rio Enterprises.

*Calls attention to résumé embedded in same message*

Sincerely,

Shenice M. Williams
1770 Hawthorne Place
Boulder, CO 80304
*Uses signature block for all contact information* — E-mail: smwilliams@yahoo.com
Cell: (713) 343-2910

Plain-text résumé embedded below. Attractive print résumé available on request. — *Reminds receiver that attractive print résumé is available*

Other examples illustrate how to avoid starting too many sentences with *I*:

| | |
|---|---|
| **Poor:** | I enjoyed helping customers, which taught me to. . . . |
| **Improved:** | Helping customers was a real pleasure and taught me to. . . . (Make outcomes the subject.) |
| **Poor:** | I am a hardworking team player who. . . . |
| **Improved:** | You are looking for a hardworking team player who. . . . (Use the "you" view.) |
| **Poor:** | I worked to support myself all through college, thus building. . . . |
| **Improved:** | All through college, I worked to support myself, thus building. . . . (Move phrases to the beginning.) |

However, strive for a comfortable style. In your effort to avoid sounding self-centered, don't write unnaturally.

Like your résumé, your cover message must look professional and suggest quality. This means using a traditional letter style, such as block format. Also, be sure to print it on the same quality paper as your résumé. As with your résumé, proofread it several times yourself; then have a friend read it for content and mechanics. Don't rely on spell-check to find all the errors. Just like your résumé, your cover message must be perfect.

# SUMMARY OF LEARNING OBJECTIVES

**13-1** Prepare to search for a job in the digital age by understanding the changing job market, identifying your interests, assessing your qualifications, and exploring career opportunities.
- Searching for a job in this digital age has dramatically changed. Search engines, job boards, and social networks have all become indispensable tools in hunting for a job.
- Emphasis today is on what the employer wants, not what the candidate wants.
- Begin the job-search process by learning about yourself, your field of interest, and your qualifications. How do your skills match what employers seek?
- Search the Web, visit a campus career center, take a summer job, interview someone in your field, volunteer, or join professional organizations.
- Identify job availability, the skills and qualifications required, duties, and salaries.

**13-2** Develop savvy search strategies by recognizing job sources and using digital tools to explore the open job market.
- The primary sources of jobs today are networking (46 percent), Internet job boards and company websites (25 percent), and agencies (14 percent).
- In searching the open job market—that is, jobs that are listed and advertised—study the big job boards, such as CareerBuilder, Monster, and CollegeGrad.
- To find a job with a specific company, go directly to that company's website and check its openings and possibilities.
- Nearly all serious candidates today post profiles on LinkedIn.
- For jobs in specialized fields, search some of the many niche sites, such as Accountemps for temporary accounting positions or Dice for technology positions.

**13-3** Expand your job-search strategies by using both traditional and digital tools in pursuing the hidden job market.
- Estimates suggest that as many as 80 percent of jobs are in the hidden job market—that is, never advertised. Successful job candidates find jobs in the hidden job market through networking.
- An effective networking procedure involves (a) developing a contact list, (b) reaching out to these contacts in person and online in search of referrals, and (c) following up on referrals.
- Because electronic media and digital tools continue to change our lives, you should use social media networks—especially LinkedIn—to extend your networking efforts.
- Effective networking strategies include building a personal brand, preparing a professional business card with a tagline, composing a 30-second elevator speech that describes what you can offer, and developing a strong online presence.

**13-4** Organize your qualifications and information into effective résumé segments to create a winning, customized résumé.
- Because of intense competition, you must customize your résumés for every position you seek.
- Chronological résumés, which list work and education by dates, rank highest with recruiters. Functional résumés, which highlight skills instead of jobs, may be helpful for people with little experience, those changing careers, and those with negative employment histories.
- In preparing a résumé, organize your skills and achievements to aim at a particular job or company.
- Study models to effectively arrange the résumé main heading and the optional career objective, summary of qualifications, education, work experience, capabilities, awards, and activities sections.
- The most effective résumés include action verbs to appeal to human readers and job-specific nouns that become keywords selected by applicant tracking systems.
- As you complete your résumé, look for ways to strengthen it by polishing, proofreading, and checking for honesty and accuracy.

**13-5** Optimize your job search and résumé by taking advantage of today's digital tools.
- To increase the probability of having your résumé selected by an automated tracking system, include specific keywords, especially nouns that name job titles, technical skills, and tools used or specific experience.
- Consider preparing a career e-portfolio to showcase your qualifications. This collection of digital files can feature your talents, accomplishments, and technical skills. It may include examples of academic performance, photographs, multimedia files, and other items beyond what can be shown in a résumé.

- A video résumé enables you to present your experience, qualifications, and interests in video form.
- A hot trend among creative candidates is the infographic résumé, which provides charts, graphics, and time lines to illustrate a candidate's work history and experience.
- Most candidates, however, should start with a basic print-based résumé from which they can make a plain-text résumé stripped of formatting to be embedded within e-mail messages and submitted online.

**13-6** Draft and submit a customized cover message to accompany a print or digital résumé.
- Although cover messages are questioned by some in today's digital world, recruiters and hiring managers overwhelmingly favor them.
- Cover messages help recruiters make decisions, and they enable candidates to set themselves apart from others.
- In the opening of a cover message, gain attention by addressing the receiver by name and identifying the job. You might also identify the person who referred you.
- In the body of the message, build interest by stressing your strengths in relation to the stated requirements. Explain what you can do for the targeted company.
- In the body or closing, refer to your résumé, request an interview, and make it easy for the receiver to respond.
- If you are submitting your cover message by e-mail, shorten it a bit and include your complete contact information in the signature block.

# CHAPTER REVIEW

1. When preparing to search for a job, what should you do before writing a résumé? (Obj. 1)

2. What are the current trends in sources of new jobs? Which sources are trending upward and which are trending downward? (Obj. 2)

3. Although one may not actually find a job on the Internet, how can the big job boards be helpful to job hunters? (Obj. 2)

4. What is the hidden job market, and how can candidates find jobs in it? (Obj. 3)

5. In searching for a job, how can you build a personal brand, and why is it important to do so? (Obj. 3)

6. What is a customized résumé and why should you have one? (Obj. 4)

7. How do chronological and functional résumés differ, and what are the advantages and disadvantages of each? (Obj. 4)

8. What is an ATS, and how does it affect the way you prepare a résumé? (Obj. 5)

9. How can you maximize the keyword hits in your résumé? What three categories are most important? (Obj. 5)

10. What are the three parts of a cover message, and does each part contain? (Obj. 6)

# CRITICAL THINKING

11. How has job searching for candidates and job placement for hiring managers changed in the digital age? In your opinion, have the changes had a positive or a negative effect? Why? (Obj. 1)

12. The authors of *Guerrilla Marketing for Job Hunters*[37] claim that every year 50 million U.S. jobs are filled, almost all without a job posting. Why do you think businesses avoid advertising job openings? If jobs are unlisted, how can a candidate locate them? (Obj. 3)

13. Some employment authors claim that the paper résumé is dead or dying. What's behind this assertion, and how should current job candidates respond? (Obj. 4)

14. Why might it be more effective to apply for unsolicited jobs than for advertised jobs? Discuss the advantages and disadvantages of letters that "prospect" for jobs. (Obj. 6)

15. Some jobs are advertised even when a leading candidate has the position nailed down. The candidate could be an internal applicant or someone else with an inside track. Although not required by law, management policies and human resources departments at many companies demand that hiring managers list all openings on job boards or career sites. Often, hiring managers have already selected candidates for these "phantom" jobs. Do you believe it is ethical to advertise jobs that are not really available?[38]

# RADICAL REWRITES

**Note:** Radical Rewrites are provided at **www.cengagebrain.com** for you to download and revise. Your instructor may show a suggested solution.

## 13.1 Radical Rewrite: Rescuing a Slapdash Résumé (Obj. 4)

The following poorly organized and written résumé needs help to remedy its misspellings, typos, and inconsistent headings.

**YOUR TASK.** Analyze Isabella's sad résumé. List at least eight weaknesses. Your instructor may ask you to revise sections of this résumé before showing you an improved version.

### Résumé of Isabella R. Jimenez
1340 East Phillips Ave., Apt. D Littleton, CO 80126
Phone 455-5182 • E-Mail: Hotchilibabe@gmail.com

**OBJECTIVE**

I'm dying to land a first job in the "real world" with a big profitable company that will help me get ahead in the accounting field.

**SKILLS**

Word processing, Internet browsers (Explorer and Google), Powerpoint, Excel, type 40 wpm, databases, spreadsheets; great composure in stressful situations; 3 years as leader and supervisor and 4 years in customer service

**EDUCATION**

Arapahoe Community College, Littleton, Colorado. AA degree Fall 2013

Now I am pursuing a BA in Accounting at CSU-Pueblo, majoring in Accounting; my minor is Finance. My expected degree date is June 2015; I recieved a Certificate of Completion in Entry Level Accounting in December 2012.

I graduated East High School, Denver, CO in 2009.

**Highlights:**
- Named Line Manger of the Month at Target, 08/2009 and 09/2010
- Obtained a Certificate in Entry Level Accounting, June 2012
- Chair of Accounting Society, Spring and fall 2013
- Dean's Honor List, Fall 2014
- Financial advisor training completed through Primerica (May 2014)
- Webmaster for M.E.Ch.A, Spring 2015

**Part-Time Employment**

Financial Consultant, 2014 to present
I worked only part-time (January 2014-present) for Primerica Financial Services, Pueblo, CO to assist clients in refinancing a mortgage or consolidating a current mortgage loan and also to advice clients in assessing their need for life insurance.

Target, Littleton, CO. As line manager, from September 2008-March 2012, I supervised 22 cashiers and front-end associates. I helped to write schedules, disciplinary action notices, and performance appraisals. I also kept track of change drawer and money exchanges; occasionally was manager on duty for entire store.

Mr. K's Floral Design of Denver. I taught flower design from August, 2008 to September, 2009. I supervised 5 florists, made floral arrangements for big events like weddings, send them to customers, and restocked flowers.

List at least eight weaknesses.

## 13.2 Radical Rewrite: Inadequate Cover Letter (Obj. 6)

The following cover letter accompanies Isabella Jimenez's résumé (**Radical Rewrite 13.1**). Like her résumé, the cover letter needs major revision.

**YOUR TASK.** Analyze Isabella's cover letter and list at least eight weaknesses. Your instructor may ask you to revise this letter before showing you an improved version.

---

To Whom It May Concern:

I saw your internship position yesterday and would like to apply right away. It would be so exiting to work for your esteemed firm! An internship would really give me much needed real-world experience and help my career.

I have all the qualifications you require in your add and more. I am a junior at Colorado State University-Pueblo and an Accounting major (with a minor in Finance). Accounting and Finance are my passion and I want to become a CPA and a financial advisor. I have taken Intermediate I and II and now work as a financial advisor with Primerica Financial Services in Pueblo. I should also tell you that I was at Target for four years. I learned alot, but my heart is in accounting and finance.

I am a team player, a born leader, motivated, reliable, and I show excellent composure in stressful situation, for example, when customers complain. I put myself through school and always carry at least 15 units while working part time.

You will probably agree that I am a good candidate for your internship position, which should start July 1. I feel that my motivation, passion, and strong people skills will serve your company well.

Sincerely,

---

List at least eight weaknesses.

# ACTIVITIES AND CASES

## 13.3 Beginning Your Job Search With Self-Analysis (Obj. 1)
*E-mail*

**YOUR TASK.** In an e-mail or a memo addressed to your instructor, answer the questions in the section "Beginning Your Job Search With Self-Analysis" on page 427. Draw a conclusion from your answers. What kind of career, company, position, and location seem to fit your self-analysis?

## 13.4 Evaluating Your Qualifications (Obj. 1–3)

**YOUR TASK.** Prepare four worksheets that inventory your qualifications in these areas: employment; education; capabilities and skills; and awards, honors, and activities. Use active verbs when appropriate and specific nouns that describe job titles and skills.

a. **Employment.** Begin with your most recent job or internship. For each position list the following information: employer; job title; dates of employment; and three to five duties, activities, or accomplishments. Emphasize activities related to your job goal. Strive to quantify your achievements.

b. **Education.** List degrees, certificates, and training accomplishments. Include courses, seminars, and skills that are relevant to your job goal. Calculate your grade point average in your major.

c. **Capabilities and skills.** List all capabilities and skills that qualify you for the job you seek. Use words and phrases such as *skilled, competent, trained, experienced*, and *ability to*. Be sure to include **nouns** that describe keywords relevant to your career field. Also list five or more qualities or interpersonal skills necessary for success in your field. Write action statements demonstrating that you possess some of these qualities. Empty assurances aren't good enough; try to show evidence (*Developed teamwork skills by working with a committee of eight to produce a . . .*).

d. **Awards, honors, and activities.** Explain any awards that the reader might misunderstand. List campus, community, and professional activities that suggest you are a well-rounded individual or possess traits relevant to your target job.

## 13.5 Choosing a Career Path (Obj. 1)
*Web*

Many people know amazingly little about the work done in various occupations and the training requirements.

**YOUR TASK.** Use the online *Occupational Outlook Handbook* at **http://www.bls.gov/ooh**, prepared by the Bureau of Labor Statistics (BLS), to learn more about an occupation of your choice. This is the nation's premier source for career information. The career profiles featured here cover hundreds of occupations and describe what people in these occupations do, the work environment, how to get these jobs, salaries, and more. You can browse categories including highest paying, fastest growing, and most new jobs.

Find the description of a position for which you could apply in two to five years. Learn about what workers do on the job, working conditions, training and education needed, earnings, and expected job prospects. Print the pages from the *Occupational Outlook Handbook* that describe employment in the area in which you are interested. If your instructor directs, attach these copies to the cover letter you will write in **Activity 13.9**.

## 13.6 Searching the Job Market (Obj. 1)
*Web*

Where are the jobs? Even though you may not be in the market at the moment, become familiar with the kinds of available positions because job awareness should be an important part of your education.

**YOUR TASK.** Clip or print a job advertisement or announcement from (a) the classified section of a newspaper, (b) a job board on the Web, (c) a company website, or (d) a professional association listing. Select an advertisement or announcement describing the kind of employment you are seeking now or plan to seek when you graduate. Save this advertisement or announcement to attach to the résumé you will write in **Activity 13.8**.

## 13.7 Posting a Résumé on the Web (Obj. 2)
`E-mail` `Web`

Learn about the procedure for posting résumés at job boards on the Web.

**YOUR TASK.** Prepare a list of three websites where you could post your résumé. In a class discussion or in an e-mail to your instructor, describe the procedure involved in posting a résumé and the advantages for each site.

## 13.8 Writing Your Résumé (Obj. 4)

**YOUR TASK.** Using the data you developed in **Activity 13.4**, write your résumé. Aim it at the full-time job, part-time position, or internship that you located in **Activity 13.6**. Attach the job listing to your résumé. Also prepare a list of references. Revise your résumé until it is perfect.

## 13.9 Preparing Your Cover Message (Obj. 6)
`E-mail`

**YOUR TASK.** Using the job listing you found for **Activity 13.6**, write a cover message introducing your résumé. Decide whether it should be a letter or an e-mail. Again, revise until it is perfect.

## 13.10 Using LinkedIn to Assist You in Your Job Search (Obj. 2)
`Social Media`

LinkedIn is the acknowledged No. 1 site for job seekers and recruiters. It's free and easy to join. Even if you are not in the job market yet, becoming familiar with LinkedIn can open your eyes to the kinds of information that employers seek and also give you practice in filling in templates such as those that applicant tracking systems employ.

**YOUR TASK.** To become familiar with LinkedIn, set up an account and complete a profile. This consists of a template with categories to fill in. The easiest way to begin is to view a LinkedIn video taking you through the steps of creating a profile. Search for *LinkedIn Profile Checklist*. It discusses how to fill in information in categories such as the following:

- **Photo.** Your photo doesn't have to be fancy. Just take a cell phone shot in front of a plain background. Wear a nice shirt and smile.
- **Headline.** Use a tagline to summarize your professional goals.
- **Summary.** Explain what motivates you, what you are skilled at, and where you want to go in the future.
- **Experience.** List the jobs you have held and be sure to enter the information precisely in the template categories. You can even include photos and videos of your work.

You can fill in other categories such as Organizations, Honors, Publications, and so forth. After completing a profile, discuss your LinkedIn experience with classmates. If you already have an account set up, discuss how it operates and your opinion of its worth. How can LinkedIn help students now and in the future?

## 13.11 Tweeting to Find a Job (Obj. 5)
`Web` `Social Media` `Team`

Twitter résumés are a new twist on job hunting. While most job seekers struggle to contain their credentials on one page, others are tweeting their credentials in 140 characters or fewer! Here is an example from TheLadders.com:

> RT #Susan Moline seeks a LEAD/SR QA ENG JOB http://bit.ly/1ThaW @TalentEvolution - http://bit.ly/QB5DC @TweetMyJobs.com #résumé #QA-Jobs-CA

Are you scratching your head? Let's translate: (a) RT stands for retweet, allowing your Twitter followers to repeat this message to their followers. (b) The hashtag (#) always means *subject;* prefacing your name, it makes you easy to find. (c) The uppercase abbreviations indicate the job title, here *Lead Senior Quality Assurance Engineer*. (d) The first link is a "tiny URL," a short, memorable Web address or alias provided free by TinyURL.com and other URL-shrinking services. The first short link reveals the job seeker's Talent Evolution profile page; the second directs viewers to a job seeker profile created on TweetMyJobs.com. (e) The hashtags indicate the search terms used as seen here: name, quality assurance jobs in California, and the broad term *résumé*. When doing research from within Twitter, use the @ symbol with a specific Twitter user name or the # symbol for a subject search.

**YOUR TASK.** As a team or individually, search the Web for *tweet résumé*. Pick one of the sites offering to tweet your résumé for you—for example, TweetMyJobs.com or Tweet My Résumé. Describe to your peers the job-search process via Twitter presented on that website. Some services are free, whereas others come with charges. If you select a commercial service, critically evaluate its sales pitch and its claims. Is it worthwhile to spend money on this service? Do clients find jobs? How does the service try to demonstrate that? As a group or individually, share the results with the class.

## 13.12 Analyzing and Building Student E-Portfolios (Obj. 5)

**Communication Technology | Web | Team**

Take a minute to conduct a Google search on your name. What comes up? Are you proud of what you see? If you want to change that information—and especially if you are in the job market—think about creating a career e-portfolio. Building such a portfolio has many benefits. It can give you an important digital tool to connect with a large audience. It can also help you expand your technology skills, confirm your strengths, recognize areas in need of improvement, and establish goals for improvement. Many students are creating e-portfolios with the help of their schools.

**YOUR TASK NO. 1.** Before attempting to build your own career e-portfolio, take a look at those of other students. Use the Google search term *student career e-portfolio* to see lots of samples. Your instructor may assign you individually or as a team to visit specific digital portfolio sites and summarize your findings in a memo or a brief oral presentation. You could focus on the composition of the site, page layout, links provided, software tools used, colors selected, or types of documents included.

**YOUR TASK NO. 2.** Next, examine websites that provide tutorials and tips on how to build career e-portfolios. One of the best sites can be found by searching for *career e-portfolios San Jose State University*. Your instructor may have you individually or as team write a memo summarizing tips on how to create an e-portfolio and choose the types of documents to include. Alternatively, your instructor may ask you to actually create a career e-portfolio.

## 13.13 Exploring Infographic Résumés (Obj. 5)

**E-mail | Web**

The latest rage in résumés is infographics. However, are they appropriate for every field?

**YOUR TASK.** Using your favorite browser, locate 10 to 15 infographic résumés. Select your favorite top three. Analyze them for readability, formatting, and color. How many use time lines? What other similarities do you see? What career fields do they represent? Do you find any in your career field? In terms of your career field, what are the pros and cons of creating an infographic résumé? Do you think an infographic résumé would improve your chances of securing an interview? In an e-mail to your instructor, summarize your findings and answer these questions.

# GRAMMAR/MECHANICS CHECKUP—13

## Number Style

Review Sections 4.01–4.13 in the Grammar/Mechanics Handbook. Then study each of the following pairs. Assume that these expressions appear in the context of letters, reports, or memos. Write *a* or *b* in the space provided to indicate the preferred number style, and record the number of the G/M principle illustrated. When you finish, compare your response with those at the end of the book. If your responses differ, study carefully the principles in parentheses.

a_____ (4.01a) **EXAMPLE** (a) three cell phones (b) 3 cell phones

_____ 1. (a) fifteen employees (b) 15 employees

_____ 2. (a) Third Avenue (b) 3rd Avenue

_____ 3. (a) twenty-one new phone apps (b) 21 new phone apps

_____ 4. (a) September 1st (b) September 1

_____ 5. (a) thirty dollars (b) $30

_____ 6. (a) on the 15th of July (b) on the fifteenth of July

_____ 7. (a) at 4:00 p.m. (b) at 4 p.m.

_____ 8. (a) 3 200-page reports (b) three 200-page reports

| | | |
|---|---|---|
| _____ | 9. (a) over fifty years ago | (b) over 50 years ago |
| _____ | 10. (a) 2,000,000 people | (b) 2 million people |
| _____ | 11. (a) fifteen cents | (b) 15 cents |
| _____ | 12. (a) a thirty-day warranty | (b) a 30-day warranty |
| _____ | 13. (a) 2/3 of the e-mails | (b) two thirds of the e-mails |
| _____ | 14. (a) two printers for 15 employees | (b) 2 printers for 15 employees |
| _____ | 15. (a) 6 of the 130 messages | (b) six of the 130 messages |

# EDITING CHALLENGE—13

To fine-tune your grammar and mechanics skills, in every chapter you will be editing a message. This résumé has problems with number usage, capitalization, spelling, proofreading, and other writing techniques. Study the guidelines in the Grammar/Mechanics Handbook as well as the lists of Confusing Words and Frequently Misspelled Words to sharpen your skills.

**YOUR TASK.** Edit the following message (a) by correcting errors in your textbook or on a photocopy using proofreading marks from Appendix A or (b) by downloading the message from the premium website at **www.cengagebrain.com**.

## Amanda J. Copeland

3010 East 8th Avenue  acopeland@charter.com
Monroe, Mich. 48162

**SUMMARY OF QUALIFICATIONS**
- Over three years experience in working in customer relations
- Partnered with Assistant Manager to create mass mailing by merging three thousand customers names and addresses in ad campaign
- Hold AA Degree in Administrative Assisting
- Proficient with MS Word, excel, powerpoint, and the internet

**EXPERIENCE**

**Administrative Assistant,** Monroe Mold and Machine Company, Munroe, Michigan
June 2015 to present
- Answer phones, respond to e-mail and gather information for mold designers
- Key board and format proposals for various machine Platforms and Configurations
- Help company with correspondence to fulfill it's guarantee that a prototype mold can be produced in less than 1 week
- Worked with Assistant Manger to create large customer mailings
- Use the internet to Research prospective customers; enter data in Excel

**Shift Supervisor,** Monroe Coffee Shop, Monroe, Michigan
May 2014 to May 2015
- Trained 3 new employees, opened and closed shop handled total sales
- Managed shop in the owners absence
- Builded satisfied customer relationships

**Server, Hostess, Expeditor, Busser,** Roadside Girll, Toledo, Ohio
April 2012 to April 2014
- Created customer base and close relationships with patrons of resterant
- Helped Owner expand menu from twenty to thirty-five items
- Develop procedures that reduce average customer wait time from sixteen to eight minutes

**AWARDS AND ACHEIVEMENTS**
- Deans List, Spring, 2015, Fall, 2014
- Awarded 2nd prize in advertise essay contest, 2014

**EDUCATION**
- AA degree, Munroe Community College, 2015
- Major: Office Administation and Technology
    GPA in major: 3.8 (4.0 = A)

# COMMUNICATION WORKSHOP

### ETHICS

## Fudging the Facts on Résumés: Worth the Risk?

Given today's brutal job market, it might be tempting to puff up your résumé. You certainly wouldn't be alone in telling fibs or outright whoppers. A CareerBuilder survey of 8,700 workers found that 8 percent admitted to lying on their résumés; however, the same study found that of the 3,100 hiring managers surveyed, 49 percent caught a job applicant lying on some part of his or her résumé. Worse, 57 percent of employers will automatically dismiss applicants who misrepresent any part of their résumés.[39] It's a risky game, warns recruiter Dennis Nason. Background checks are much easier now, he says, with the Internet and professionals who specialize in sniffing out untruths.[40]

After they have been hired, candidates may think they are safe—but organizations often continue the checking process. If hiring officials find a discrepancy in a GPA or prior experience and the error is an honest mistake, they meet with the new-hire to hear an explanation. If the discrepancy wasn't a mistake, they will likely fire the person immediately.

No job seeker wants to be in the unhappy position of explaining résumé errors or defending misrepresentation. Avoiding the following actions can keep you off the hot seat:

- **Enhancing education, grades, or honors.** Some job candidates claim degrees from colleges or universities when in fact they merely attended classes. Others increase their grade point averages or claim fictitious honors. Any such dishonest reporting is grounds for dismissal when discovered.
- **Inflating job titles and salaries.** Wishing to elevate their status, some applicants misrepresent their titles or increase their past salaries. For example, one technician called himself a programmer when he had actually programmed only one project for his boss. A mail clerk who assumed added responsibilities conferred upon herself the title of supervisor.
- **Puffing up accomplishments.** Job seekers may inflate their employment experience or achievements. One clerk, eager to make her photocopying duties sound more important, said that she assisted the *vice president in communicating and distributing employee directives*. Similarly, guard against taking sole credit for achievements that required many people. When recruiters suspect dubious claims on résumés, they nail applicants with specific—and often embarrassing—questions during their interviews.
- **Altering employment dates.** Some candidates extend the dates of employment to hide unimpressive jobs or to cover up periods of unemployment and illness. Although their employment histories may have no gaps, their résumés are dishonest and represent potential booby traps.

**CAREER APPLICATION.** Cassidy M. finally got an interview for the perfect job. The big problem, however, is that she padded her résumé a little by making the gaps in her job history a bit smaller. Oh, yes, and she increased her last job title from administrative assistant to project manager. After all, she was really doing a lot of his work. Now she's worried about the upcoming interview. She's considering coming clean and telling the truth. On the other hand, she wonders whether it is too late to submit an updated résumé and tell the interviewer that she noticed some errors. Of course, she could do nothing. A final possibility is withdrawing her application. In groups, discuss Cassidy's options. What would you advise her to do? Why?

## ENDNOTES

[1] Adams, S. (2011, June 7). Networking is still the best way to find a job, survey says. Retrieved from http://www.forbes.com/sites/susanadams/2011/06/07/networking-is-still-the-best-way-to-find-a-job-survey-says; see also Stevens-Huffman, L. (2012, August 9). Networking is still the best way to find a job. Retrieved from http://news.dice.com/2012/08/09/networking-most-effective-way-find-job

[2] Waldman, J. (2012, February 26). 10 differences between the job search of today and of yesterday. Retrieved from http://www.careerrealism.com/job-search-differences

[3] Bureau of Labor Statistics. (2010, September 14). Economic news release: Employee tenure summary. Retrieved from http://www.bls.gov/news.release/tenure.nr0.htm. See also Kimmit, R. M. (2007, January 23). Why job churn is good. *The Washington Post*, p. A17. Retrieved from http://www.washingtonpost.com/wp-dyn/content/article/2007/01/22/AR2007012201089.html

[4] Adams, S. (2012, July 25). Odds are your internship will get you a job. Retrieved from http://www.forbes.com/sites/susanadams/2012/07/25/odds-are-your-internship-will-get-you-a-job

[5] Adams, S. (2011, June 7). Networking is still the best way to find a job, survey says. Retrieved from http://www.forbes.com/sites/susanadams/2011/06/07/networking-is-still-the-best-way-to-find-a-job-survey-says

[6] Mathison, D., & Finney, M. I. (2009). *Unlock the hidden job market: 6 steps to a successful job search when times are tough*. Upper Saddle River, NJ: Pearson Education, FI Press. See also Poplinger, H., as reported by Jessica Dickler (2009, June 10) in The hidden job market. Retrieved from CNNMoney.com at http://money.cnn.com/2009/06/09/news/economy/hidden_jobs

[7] Adams, S. (2013, February 5). New survey: LinkedIn more dominant than ever among job seekers and recruiters, but Facebook poised to gain. Retrieved from http://www.forbes.com/sites/susanadams/2013/02/05/new-survey-linked-in-more-dominant-than-ever-among-job-seekers-and-recruiters-but-facebook-poised-to-gain

[8] Mathison, D., & Finney, M. I. (2009). *Unlock the hidden job market: 6 steps to a successful job search when times are tough*. Upper Saddle River, NJ: Pearson Education, FI Press. See also Poplinger, H., as reported by Jessica Dickler (2009, June 10) in The hidden job market. Retrieved from CNNMoney.com at http://money.cnn.com/2009/06/09/news/economy/hidden_jobs

[9] Richardson, V. (2011, March 16). Five ways inside the 'hidden job market.' Retrieved from http://www.dailyfinance.com/2011/03/16/five-ways-inside-the-hidden-job-market

[10] Adams, S. (2012, March 27). Make LinkedIn help you find a job. Retrieved from http://www.forbes.com/sites/susanadams/2012/04/27/make-linkedin-help-you-find-a-job-2

[11] Ibid.
[12] Williams, N. (2013, December 12). How to strategically use buzzwords on LinkedIn. *U.S. News & World Report*. Retrieved from http://money.usnews.com/money/blogs/outside-voices-careers/2013/12/12/how-to-strategically-use-buzzwords-on-linkedin
[13] Doyle, A. (n.d.). Facebook and professional networking. Retrieved from http://jobsearch.about.com/od/networking/a/facebook.htm
[14] Ibid.
[15] Swallow, E. (2011, October 23). How recruiters use social networks to screen candidates. Retrieved from http://mashable.com/2011/10/23/how-recruiters-use-social-networks-to-screen-candidates-infographic
[16] Hansen, K. (n.d.). From *Tell me about yourself: Storytelling that propels careers* (Ten Speed Press). Excerpt appearing in Heather Huhman's blog at http://www.personalbrandingblog.com/how-to-write-your-60-second-elevator-pitch
[17] Isaacs, K. (2012). How to decide on résumé length. Retrieved from http://career-advice.monster.com/resumes-cover-letters/resume-writing-tips/how-to-decide-on-resume-length/article.aspx
[18] Green, A. (2012, June 20). 10 things to leave off your résumé. Retrieved from http://money.usnews.com/money/blogs/outside-voices-careers/2012/06/20/10-things-to-leave-off-your-resume
[19] Diaz, C. (2013, December). Updating best practices: Applying on-screen reading strategies to résumé writing. *Business Communication Quarterly*, 76(4), 427–445.
[20] Korkki, P. (2007, July 1). So easy to apply, so hard to be noticed. *The New York Times*. Retrieved from http://www.nytimes.com/2007/07/01/business/yourmoney/01career.html
[21] Berrett, D. (2013, January 25). My GRE score says I'm smart. Hire me. *The Chronicle of Higher Education*, A4.
[22] Diaz, C. (2013, December). Updating best practices: Applying on-screen reading strategies to résumé writing. *Business Communication Quarterly*, 76(4), 427–445. See also Nielsen, J. (2006, April 17). F-shaped pattern for reading web content. Retrieved from http://www.nngroup.com/articles/f-shaped-pattern-reading-web-content.
[23] Struzik, E., IBM expert quoted in Weber, L. (2012, January 24). Your résumé vs. oblivion. *The Wall Street Journal*, p. B6.
[24] Harris, C. (2012, February 15). Why applicant tracking systems are the weakest link. Retrieved from http://www.unrabble.com/blog/why-applicant-tracking-systems-are-the-weakest-link
[25] Optimalresume.com. (n.d.). Optimizing your résumé for scanning and tracking. Retrieved from http://www.montclair.edu/CareerServices/OptimalsScannedresumes.pdf
[26] Ibid.
[27] Krum, R. (2012, September 10). Is your résumé hopelessly out of date? Retrieved from http://infonewt.com/blog/2012/9/10/infographic-resumes-interview-by-the-art-of-doing.html
[28] Larsen, M. (2011, Nov. 8). Infographic résumés: Fad or trend? Retrieved from http://www.recruiter.com/i/infographic-resumes
[29] Ibid.
[30] Balderrama, S. (2009, February 26). Do you still need a cover letter? Retrieved from http://msn.careerbuilder.com/Article/MSN-1811-Cover-Letters-Resumes-Do-You-Still-Need-a-Cover-Letter
[31] Quoted in Doyle, A. (2012, July 14). Do you need a cover letter? Retrieved from http://jobsearch.about.com/b/2012/07/14/do-you-need-a-cover-letter.htm
[32] Quoted in Balderrama, S. (2009, February 26). Do you still need a cover letter? Retrieved from http://msn.careerbuilder.com/Article/MSN-1811-Cover-Letters-Resumes-Do-You-Still-Need-a-Cover-Letter
[33] Needleman, S. E. (2010, March 9). Standout letters to cover your bases. *The Wall Street Journal*, p. D4.
[34] Balderrama, S. (2009, February 26). Do you still need a cover letter? Retrieved from http://msn.careerbuilder.com/Article/MSN-1811-Cover-Letters-Resumes-Do-You-Still-Need-a-Cover-Letter
[35] Grant, A. (2011, March 1). Proactive Job-Search Strategy: Pitch Your Dream Company. *U.S. News & World Report*. Retrieved from http://money.usnews.com/money/careers/articles/2011/03/01/proactive-job-search-strategy-pitch-your-dream-company
[36] Korkki, P. (2009, July 18). Where, oh where, has my application gone? *The New York Times*. Retrieved from http://www.nytimes.com/2009/07/19/jobs/19career.html?_r=1&scp=1&sq=Where,%20oh%20where,%20has%20my%20application%20gone&st=cse
[37] Levinson, J. C., & Perry, D. (2011). *Guerrilla marketing for job hunters 3.0*. Hoboken, NJ: John Wiley & Sons.
[38] Weber, L., & Kwoh, L. (2013, January 9). Beware the phantom job listing. *The Wall Street Journal*, pp. B1 and B6.
[39] Zupek, R. (2008, March 27). Honesty is the best policy in résumés and interviews. Retrieved from Careerbuilder.com at http://msn.careerbuilder.com/Article/MSN-1854-Cover-Letters-Resumes-Honesty-is-the-Best-Policy-in-R%C3%A9sum%C3%A9s-and-Interviews
[40] Quoted in Purdy, C. (n.d.). The biggest lies job seekers tell on their résumés—and how they get caught. Retrieved from http://career-advice.monster.com/resumes-cover-letters/resume-writing-tips/the-truth-about-resume-lies-hot-jobs/article.aspx

# ACKNOWLEDGMENTS

**p. 430** Office Insider based on quotation in Giang, V. (2013, September 14). 3 reasons why the paper resume isn't dead. Retrieved from http://www.businessinsider.com/why-the-paper-resume-isnt-dying-any-2013-9#ixzz2sDbs8OYV
Figure 13.2 based on Right Management survey. Most Expect to Get New Job by Networking (2013). Retrieved from http://www.right.com/news-and-events/press-releases/2013-press-releases/item24727.aspx?x=24727

**p. 435** Office Insider based on quotation in Vaas, L. (n.d.). Customize your résumé for that plum job. Retrieved from http://www.theladders.com/career-advice/customize-resume-for-plum-job

**p. 439** Office Insider based on Matuson, R. C. (n.d.). Recession-proof your career. Retrieved from http://www.hcareers.com/us/resourcecenter/tabid/306/articleid/522/default.aspx

**p. 448** Office Insider based on quotation in Needleman, S. (2010, February 2). Job hunters, beware. *The Wall Street Journal*. Retrieved from http://online.wsj.com/news/articles/SB10001424052748704107204575039361105870740

**p. 449** Office Insider based on Bersin, J. (2013, July 4). The hottest trends in corporate recruiting. Retrieved from http://www.forbes.com/sites/joshbersin/2013/07/04/the-9-hottest-trends-in-corporate-recruiting/2

**p. 455** Office Insider based on quotation in Needleman, S. (2010, March 9). Standout letters to cover your bases. *The Wall Street Journal*, p. D4.

# CHAPTER 14
# Interviewing and Following Up

## OBJECTIVES
After studying this chapter, you should be able to

**14-1** Explain the purposes and types of job interviews, including screening, one-on-one, panel, group, sequential, stress, and online interviews.

**14-2** Describe what to do *before* an interview, including ensuring professional phone techniques, researching the target company, rehearsing success stories, cleaning up digital dirt, and fighting fear.

**14-3** Describe what to do *during* an interview, including controlling nonverbal messages and answering typical interview questions.

**14-4** Describe what to do *after* an interview, including thanking the interviewer, contacting references, and writing follow-up messages.

**14-5** Prepare additional employment documents such as applications, rejection follow-up messages, acceptance messages, and resignation letters.

## 14-1 Purposes and Types of Employment Interviews

Employment is a major part of everyone's life; therefore, the job interview takes on enormous importance. Most people consider job interviews extremely stressful. However, the more you learn about the process and the better prepared you are, the less stress you will feel. Moreover, a job interview is a two-way street. It is not just about being judged by the employer. You, the applicant, will be using the job interview to evaluate the employer. Do you really want to work for this organization?

This chapter will increase your interviewing effectiveness and confidence by explaining the purposes and kinds of interviews and how to prepare for them. You will learn how to project a professional image throughout the interview process. You will also pick up tips for responding to recruiters' favorite questions and learn how to cope with illegal questions and salary matters. Moreover, you will learn what you should do as a successful follow-up to an interview. First, though, you need to know the purposes of employment interviews and what types you might encounter in your job search.

### 14-1a Purposes of Job Interviews

You may know that from the employer's perspective, the interview is an opportunity to (a) assess your abilities in relation to the requirements of the position; (b) discuss your training, experience, knowledge, and abilities in more detail; (c) see what drives and motivates you; and (d) decide whether you would fit into the organization.

For you as a job candidate, though, an interview also has several purposes. It is an opportunity to (a) convince the employer of your potential, (b) learn more about the job and the company, and (c) expand on the information in your résumé. This is the time for you to gather information about whether you would fit into the company culture. You should also be thinking about whether this job suits your career goals.

## 14-1b Types of Job Interviews

Job applicants generally face two kinds of interviews: screening interviews and hiring/placement interviews. You must succeed in the first to proceed to the second. Once you make it to the hiring/placement interview, you will find a variety of interview styles, including one-on-one, panel, group, sequential, stress, and online interviews. You will be better prepared if you know what to expect in each type of interview.

**Screening Interviews.** Screening interviews serve to eliminate applicants who fail to meet minimum requirements. Companies use screening interviews to save time and money by weeding out lesser-qualified candidates before scheduling face-to-face interviews. Although some are conducted during job fairs or on college campuses, many screening interviews take place on the telephone. Online screening questionnaires in multiple-choice format are another popular screening method preferred, for example, by accounting firm KPMG.[1] Screening interviews can also take place online, via Skype, for instance. In a recent poll, 63 percent of HR managers stated that they often conducted video interviews, up from 14 percent a year earlier.[2]

During a screening interview, the interviewer will probably ask you to provide details about the education and experience listed on your résumé; therefore, you must be prepared to promote and illustrate your qualifications. Remember that the person conducting the screening interview is trying to determine whether you should move on to the next step in the interview process. Even though the screening interview may be short, don't treat it casually. If you don't perform well, it may be your last interview with that organization. You can use the tips that follow in this chapter to succeed during the screening process.

**Hiring/Placement Interviews.** The most promising candidates selected from screening interviews are invited to hiring/placement interviews. Hiring managers want to learn whether candidates are motivated, qualified, and a good fit for the position. Their goal is to learn how the candidate would fit into their organization. Conducted in depth, hiring/placement interviews may take many forms.

**One-on-One Interviews.** In one-on-one interviews, which are the most common type, you can expect to sit down with a company representative and talk about the job and your qualifications. If the representative is the hiring manager, questions will be specific and job related. If the representative is from human resources, the questions will probably be more general.

**Panel Interviews.** Panel interviews are typically conducted by people who will be your supervisors and colleagues. Usually seated around a table, interviewers take turns asking questions. Panel interviews are advantageous because they save the company time and money, and they show you how the staff works together. If possible before these interviews, try to gather basic biographical information about each panel member. When answering questions, maintain eye contact with the questioner as well as with the others.[3]

**Group Interviews.** Sometimes derisively called cattle-call interviews, group interviews occur when a company interviews several candidates for the same position at the same time. Some employers—for example, IBM, various airlines, and secondary school systems—use this technique to measure leadership skills and communication styles. During a group interview, stay focused on the interviewer,

## OFFICE INSIDER

*"The reason group interviews are so effective is you get to see the entire group at one time and are able to rank those candidates. If they're in the room, they've met minimum expectations for what we're looking for in the role . . . I'm really looking for cultural fit."*

—Jodie Shaw, CEO of the business coaching company ActionCOACH

**LEARNING OBJECTIVE 1**

Explain the purposes and types of job interviews, including screening, one-on-one, panel, group, sequential, stress, and online interviews.

**Group interviews can be stressful and frustrating for interviewees. However, employers who use this tool believe that "cattle-call" interviews allow them to rank candidates quickly in the categories of teamwork, leadership, and stress management.**

and treat the other candidates with respect.[4] Even if you are nervous, try to remain calm, take your time when responding, and express yourself clearly. The key during a group interview is to make yourself stand out from the other candidates in a positive way.[5]

**Sequential Interviews.** In a sequential interview, you meet individually with two or more interviewers one-on-one over the course of several hours or days. For example, you may meet with human resources representatives, your hiring manager, and potential future supervisors and colleagues in your division or department. You must listen carefully and respond positively to all interviewers. Promote your qualifications to each one; don't assume that any interviewer knows what was said in a previous interview. Keep your responses fresh, even when repeating yourself many times over.

Subsequent interviews also tend to be more in depth than first interviews, which means that you need to be even more prepared and know even more about the company. According to Chantal Verbeek-Vingerhoed, head of enterprise talent for ING, during subsequent interviews, "They dig deeper into your technical skills, and make connections about how you'd add value and solve issues in the department. If you know the exact job requirements and expectations, you can really shine."[6]

**Stress Interviews.** Stress interviews are meant to test your reactions during nerve-racking situations and are common for jobs in which you will face significant stress. You may be forced to wait a long time before being greeted by the interviewer. You may be given a test with an impossible time limit, or one or more of the interviewers may treat you rudely.

Another stress interview technique is to have interviewers ask questions at a rapid rate. If asked rapid-fire questions from many directions, take the time to slow things down. For example, you might say, *I would be happy to answer your question, Ms. X, but first I must finish responding to Mr. Z*. If greeted with silence (another stress technique), you might say, *Would you like me to begin the interview? Let me tell you about myself*. Or ask a question such as *Can you give me more information about the position?* One career expert says, "The key to surviving stress interviews is to remain calm, keep a sense of humor, and avoid getting angry or defensive."[7]

**Online, Video, and Virtual Interviews.** Don't be surprised if you are asked to participate in a virtual interview for one or more of the positions in which you are interested. Many companies today use technology to interview job candidates from a distance. For example, savvy companies such as Zappos use webcams and videoconferencing software to conduct long-distance interviews. Virtual interviews save job applicants and companies time and money, especially when applicants are not in the same geographic location as the company. The same rules apply whether you are face-to-face with your interviewers or looking into a camera.

No matter what interview type you encounter, you will feel more comfortable and be less stressed if you understand the anatomy of the interview process, as summarized in Figure 14.1. Following are specific tips on what to do before, during, and after the interview.

**LEARNING OBJECTIVE 2**

Describe what to do *before* an interview, including ensuring professional phone techniques, researching the target company, rehearsing success stories, cleaning up digital dirt, and fighting fear.

## 14-2 Before the Interview

If you do well in the screening interview, you may be invited to an in-person or online meeting. Consider yourself an active job seeker. Being active in the job market means that you should be prepared to be contacted by potential employers.

Figure 14.1 Anatomy of the Job Interview Process

**1. Know the interviewing sequence.**
- Expect a telephone screening interview.
- If you are successful, next comes the hiring interview.
- Be prepared to answer questions in a one-on-one, panel, group, or video interview.

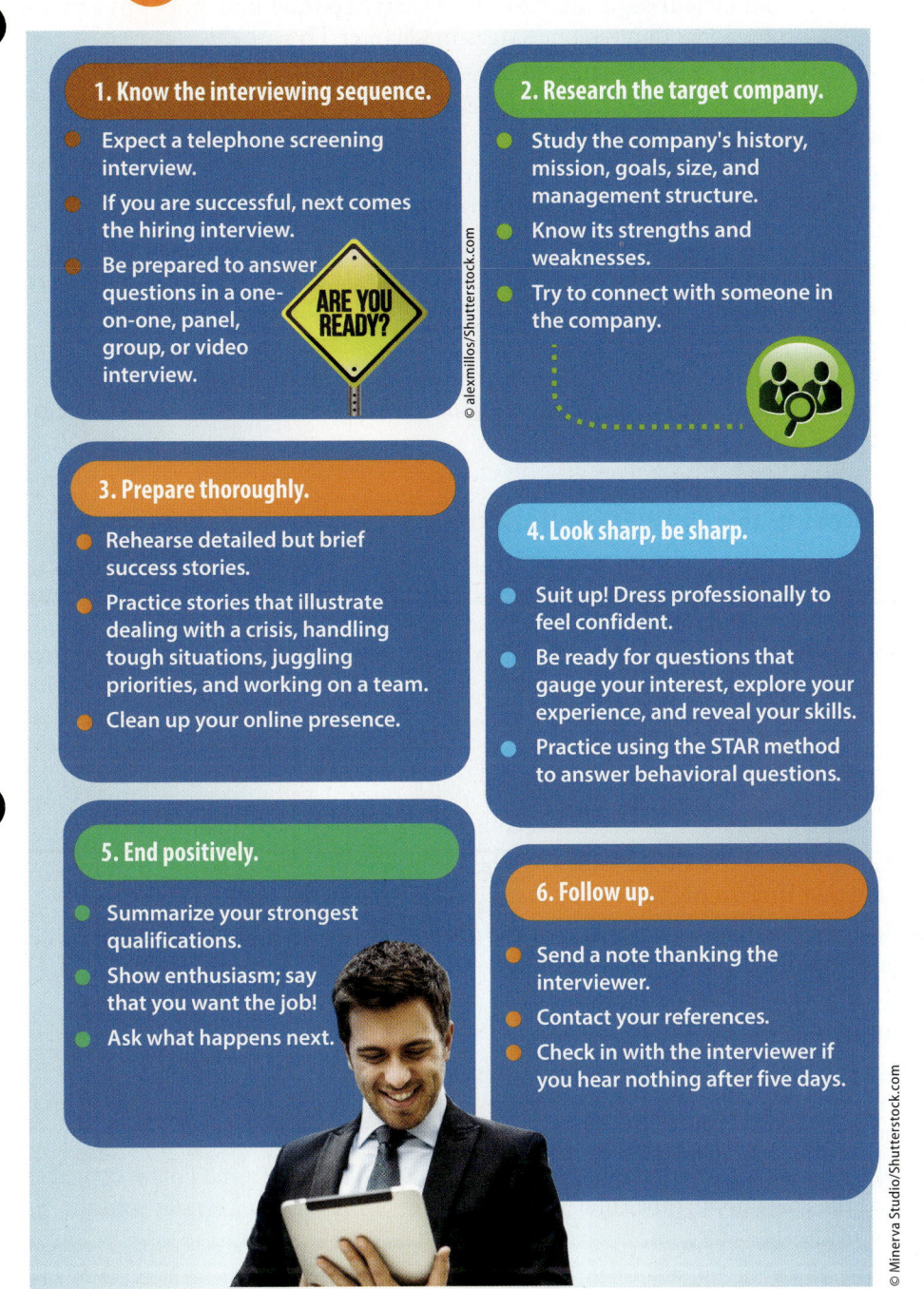

**2. Research the target company.**
- Study the company's history, mission, goals, size, and management structure.
- Know its strengths and weaknesses.
- Try to connect with someone in the company.

**3. Prepare thoroughly.**
- Rehearse detailed but brief success stories.
- Practice stories that illustrate dealing with a crisis, handling tough situations, juggling priorities, and working on a team.
- Clean up your online presence.

**4. Look sharp, be sharp.**
- Suit up! Dress professionally to feel confident.
- Be ready for questions that gauge your interest, explore your experience, and reveal your skills.
- Practice using the STAR method to answer behavioral questions.

**5. End positively.**
- Summarize your strongest qualifications.
- Show enthusiasm; say that you want the job!
- Ask what happens next.

**6. Follow up.**
- Send a note thanking the interviewer.
- Contact your references.
- Check in with the interviewer if you hear nothing after five days.

## 14-2a Ensuring Professional Phone Techniques

Once you are actively looking for a job, anytime the phone rings, it could be a potential employer. Most employers like to contact job applicants by phone to set up interviews because they can judge how well applicants communicate over the phone. Make sure your voice mail greeting sounds professional. If sharing a phone line, alert roommates or family members. To make the best impression, try these tips:

- When using voice mail, make sure that your greeting is concise and professional, with no distracting background sounds. The greeting should be in your own voice and include your full name for clarity. You can find more tips for creating professional outgoing messages in Chapter 11.
- Family members or roommates can affect the first impression an employer has of you. Explain to them the importance of acting professionally and taking complete messages.
- If you have children, prevent them from answering the phone during your job search. Children of all ages are not known for taking good messages!
- If you have put your cell phone number on your résumé, don't answer unless you are in a good location to carry on a conversation with an employer. It is hard to focus while driving, even with hands-free equipment, or while eating in a noisy restaurant!
- To be in total control when you expect a return call from a prospective employer, screen your calls. Organize your materials and ready yourself psychologically for the conversation.

### 14-2b Making the First Conversation Impressive

Whether you answer the phone directly or return an employer's call, make sure you are prepared for the conversation. Remember that this is the first time the employer has heard your voice. How you conduct yourself on the phone will create a lasting impression. To make that first impression a positive one, follow these tips:

- On your cell phone or near your landline, keep a list of positions for which you have applied.
- Treat any call from an employer just like an interview. Use a professional tone and businesslike language. Be polite and enthusiastic, and sell your qualifications.
- If caught off guard by the call, ask whether you can call back in a few minutes. Take that time to organize your materials and yourself.
- Have your résumé available so you can answer any questions that come up. Also, have your list of references, a calendar, and a virtual or paper notepad handy.
- Be prepared for a screening interview. As discussed earlier, this might occur during the first phone call.
- Take good notes during the phone conversation. Obtain accurate directions, and verify the spelling of your interviewer's name. If you will be interviewed by more than one person, get all of their names.
- If given a choice, ask for an interview on Tuesday at 10:30 a.m. This is considered the most opportune time. Avoid the start of the day on Monday and the end of the day on Friday.[8]
- Before you hang up, reconfirm the date and time of your interview. You could say something like *I look forward to meeting with you next Wednesday at 2 p.m.*

### 14-2c Researching the Target Company

Once you have scheduled an in-person or online interview, you need to start preparing for it. One of the most important steps in effective interviewing is gathering detailed information about a prospective employer. Never enter an interview cold. Recruiters are impressed by candidates who have done their homework.

**Scouring the Web for Important Company Data.** Search the potential employer's website, news sources, trade journals, and industry directories.

Unearth information about the job, the company, and the industry. Learn all you can about the company's history, mission and goals, size, geographic locations, and number of employees. Check out its customers, competitors, culture, management structure, reputation in the community, financial condition, strengths and weaknesses, and future plans, as well as the names of its leaders.

**Analyzing the Company's Advertising.** In addition to its online presence, examine the company's ads and promotional materials, including sales and marketing brochures. One candidate, a marketing major, spent a great deal of time poring over brochures from an aerospace contractor. During his initial interview, he shocked and impressed the recruiter with his knowledge of the company's guidance systems. The candidate had, in fact, relieved the interviewer of his least-favorite task—explaining the company's complicated technology.

**Locating Inside Information.** Use social media networks such as LinkedIn and Twitter. "Like" the company on Facebook and comment shrewdly on the organization's status updates and other posts. Beyond these sites, check out employee review websites such as Glassdoor and TheFIT to get the inside scoop on what it's like to work there. Online tools such as InTheDoor and LinkedIn's Job Insider toolbar can help you discover whether you know someone who already works at the company.

Try to connect with someone who is currently employed—but not working in the immediate area where you wish to be hired. Be sure to seek out someone who is discreet. Blogs are also excellent sources for insider information and company research. One marketing specialist calls them "job posting gold mines."[9] In addition, don't forget to google the interviewer.

As you learn about a company, you may uncover information that convinces you that this is not the company for you. It is always better to learn about negatives early in the process. More likely, though, the information you collect will help you tailor your interview responses to the organization's needs. You know how flattered you feel when an employer knows about you and your background. That feeling works both ways. Employers are pleased when job candidates take an interest in them.

> **OFFICE INSIDER**
>
> "Whoever said 80 percent of success is just showing up wasn't thinking about job interviews. Thoroughly preparing for an interview makes a huge difference in how well you do. And it can also make you a lot less nervous."
>
> —Alison Green, management consultant and blogger

## Workplace in Focus

Since career experts advise not to ask about salary or benefits during a first interview, job candidates often feel disadvantaged during the recruitment process. Many organizations conceal their job salaries out of fear that higher qualified employees won't apply, or that less-qualified employees will expect the high end of the salary range. Thankfully, job seekers aren't stuck in the dark. Web sites such as salary.com and payscale.com provide accurate salary information for most jobs by profession and region. By taking time to research salaries, candidates can empower themselves to make better career choices. What facts should candidates know about a company before interviewing?[10]

Chapter 14: Interviewing and Following Up

## OFFICE INSIDER

"One wonderful thing about stories is that often they reveal more skills in the candidate than the interviewer originally asks for. For example, the interviewer asks you a question based on leading global teams. You tell a story that reveals not only leadership skills, but also problem solving, time management, and communication skills . . . with positive quantified results. The story is told with such conviction and confidence that it covers potentially four questions."

—Katharine Hansen, career/job search author

Who hasn't had an "oops" moment after pressing *Send*? Similarly, some social media users are still oblivious to privacy settings and post inappropriate content that can sabotage their career plans. Before searching for a job, candidates should clean up their digital act.

### 14-2d Preparing and Practicing

The most successful job candidates never go into interviews unprepared. They rehearse success stories and practice answers to typical questions. They clean up digital dirt and plan their responses to any problem areas on their résumés. As part of their preparation before the interview, they decide what to wear, and they gather the items they plan to take with them.

**Rehearsing Success Stories.** To feel confident and be able to sell your qualifications, prepare and practice success stories. These stories are specific examples of your educational and work-related experience that demonstrate your qualifications and achievements. Look over the job description and your résumé to determine what skills, training, personal characteristics, and experience you want to emphasize during the interview. Then prepare a success story for each one. Incorporate numbers, such as dollars saved or percentage of sales increase, whenever possible. Your success stories should be detailed but brief. Think of them as 30-second sound bites.

Practice telling your success stories until they fluently roll off your tongue and sound natural. Then in the interview be certain to find places to insert them. Tell stories about (a) dealing with a crisis, (b) handling a tough interpersonal situation, (c) successfully juggling many priorities, (d) changing course to deal with changed circumstances, (e) learning from a mistake, (f) working on a team, and (g) going above and beyond expectations.[11] Of course, the claims you make on your résumé and during the interview must be consistent with your online presence.[12]

**Cleaning Up Digital Dirt.** Potential employers definitely screen a candidate's online presence using Google and social media sites such as Facebook, LinkedIn, and Twitter.[13] One study revealed that nearly 70 percent of recruiters found something online that caused them not to hire a candidate.[14] The top reasons cited for not considering an applicant after an online search were that the candidate (a) posted provocative or inappropriate photographs or information; (b) posted content about drinking or doing drugs; (c) talked negatively about current or previous employers, colleagues, or clients; (d) exhibited poor communication skills; (e) made discriminatory comments; (f) lied about qualifications; or (g) revealed a current or previous employer's confidential information.[15]

In Chicago the president of a small consulting company was about to hire a summer intern when he discovered the student's Facebook page. The candidate described his interests as "smokin' blunts [cigars hollowed out and stuffed with marijuana], shooting people and obsessive sex."[16] The executive quickly lost interest in this candidate. Even if the student was merely posturing, it showed poor judgment. Teasing photographs and provocative comments about drinking, drug use, and sexual exploits make students look immature and unprofessional. Think about cleaning up your online presence by following these steps:

- **Remove questionable content.** Remove any incriminating, provocative, or distasteful photos, content, and links that could make you look unprofessional to potential employers.

- **Stay positive.** Don't complain about things in your professional or personal life online. Even negative reviews you have written on sites such as Amazon can turn employers off.

- **Be selective about your list of friends.** You don't want to miss out on an opportunity because you seem to associate with negative, immature, or unprofessional people. Your best bet is to make your personal social networking pages private.

- **Avoid joining groups or fan pages that may be viewed negatively.** Remember that online searches can turn up your online activities, including group memberships, blog posts, replies to posts, and so on. If you think any activity you are involved in might show poor judgment, remove yourself immediately.
- **Don't discuss your job search if you are still employed.** Employees can find themselves in trouble with their current employers by writing status updates or sending tweets about their job searches.
- **Set up a professional social networking page or create your own personal website.** Use Facebook, LinkedIn, or other social networking sites to create a professional page. Many employers actually find information during their online searches that convinces them to hire candidates. Make sure your professional page demonstrates creativity, strong communication skills, and well-roundedness.[17]

### OFFICE INSIDER

*"Most employers nowadays hop on Google to search a name as a preliminary step, either before or right after the interview. A positive and strong online presence can play a tremendous part in the employer's first impression."*

—Monique Tatum, author of *Jumping Off the Curb and Into SEO Traffic*

## 14-2e Traveling To and Arriving At Your Interview

The big day has arrived! Ideally, you are fully prepared for your interview. Now you need to make sure everything goes smoothly. That means making sure the trip to the potential employer's office goes well and that you arrive on time.

**Avoiding Being Rushed.** On the morning of your interview, give yourself plenty of time to groom and dress. Then make sure you can arrive at the employer's office without being rushed. If something unexpected happens that will to cause you to be late, such as an accident or bridge closure, call the interviewer right away to explain what is happening. Most interviewers will be understanding, and your call will show that you are responsible. On the way to the interview, don't smoke, don't eat anything messy or smelly, and don't load up on perfume or cologne. Arrive at the interview five or ten minutes early, but not earlier. If you are very early, wait in the car or in a café nearby. If possible, check your appearance before going in.

**Being Polite and Pleasant.** When you enter the office, be courteous and congenial to everyone. Remember that you are being judged not only by the interviewer but also by the receptionist and anyone else who sees you before and after the interview. They will notice how you sit, what you read, and how you look. Introduce yourself to the receptionist, and wait to be invited to sit. You may be asked to fill out a job application while you are waiting. You will find tips for doing this effectively later in this chapter.

**Greeting the Interviewer and Making a Positive First Impression.** Greet the interviewer confidently, and don't be afraid to initiate a handshake. Doing so exhibits professionalism and confidence. Extend your hand, look the interviewer directly in the eye, smile pleasantly, and say, *I'm pleased to meet you, Mr. Thomas. I am Constance Ferraro*. In this culture a firm, not bone-crushing, handshake sends a nonverbal message of poise and assurance. After introductions, wait for the interviewer to offer you a chair. Make small talk with upbeat comments, such as *This is a beautiful headquarters* or *I'm very impressed with the facilities you have here*. Don't immediately begin rummaging in your briefcase for your résumé. Being at ease and unrushed suggest that you are self-confident.

## 14-2f Fighting Fear

Other than public speaking, employment interviews are the most dreaded events in people's lives. One survey revealed that job interviews are more stressful than going on a blind date, being pulled over by the police, or taking a final exam without studying.[18] One of the best ways to overcome fear is to know what happens in a typical interview. You can further reduce your fears by following these suggestions:

Chapter 14: Interviewing and Following Up

- **Practice interviewing.** Try to get as much interviewing practice as you can—especially with real companies. The more times you experience the interview situation, the less nervous you will be. If offered, campus mock interviews also provide excellent practice, and the interviewers will offer tips for improvement.
- **Prepare thoroughly.** Research the company. Know how you will answer the most frequently asked questions. Be ready with success stories. Rehearse your closing statement. Knowing that you have done all you can to be ready for the interview is a tremendous fear preventive.
- **Understand the process.** Find out ahead of time how the interview will be structured. Will you be meeting with an individual, or will you be interviewed by a panel? Is this the first of a series of interviews? Don't be afraid to ask about these details before the interview so an unfamiliar situation won't catch you off guard.
- **Dress professionally.** If you know you look sharp, you will feel more confident.
- **Breathe deeply.** Take deep breaths, particularly if you feel anxious while waiting for the interviewer. Deep breathing makes you concentrate on something other than the interview and also provides much-needed oxygen.
- **Know that you are not alone.** Everyone feels some anxiety during a job interview. Interviewers expect some nervousness, and a skilled interviewer will try to put you at ease.
- **Remember that an interview is a two-way street.** The interviewer isn't the only one who is gleaning information. You have come to learn about the job and the company. In fact, during some parts of the interview, you will be in charge. This should give you courage.

**LEARNING OBJECTIVE 3**

Describe what to do *during* an interview, including controlling nonverbal messages and answering typical interview questions.

## 14-3 During the Interview

Throughout the interview the interviewer will be trying to learn more about you, and you should be learning more about the job and the organization. You will be answering questions and asking your own questions. Your demeanor, body language, and other nonverbal cues will also be on display. Although you may be asked some unique questions, many interviewers ask standard, time-proven questions, which means that you can prepare your answers ahead of time.

### 14-3a Sending Positive, Professional Nonverbal Messages

What comes out of your mouth and what is written on your résumé are not the only messages an interviewer receives from you. Nonverbal messages also create powerful impressions on people. You have already sent nonverbal cues to your interviewer by arriving on time, being courteous, dressing professionally, and greeting the receptionist confidently. You can send positive nonverbal messages during face-to-face and online interviews by following these tips:

- **Control your body movements.** Keep your hands, arms, and elbows to yourself. Don't lean on a desk. Keep your feet on the floor. Don't cross your arms in front of you. Keep your hands out of your pockets.
- **Exhibit good posture.** Sit erect, leaning forward slightly. Don't slouch in your chair; at the same time, don't look too stiff and uncomfortable. Good posture demonstrates confidence and interest.
- **Practice appropriate eye contact.** A direct eye gaze, at least in North America, suggests interest and trustworthiness. If you are being interviewed by a panel, remember to maintain eye contact with all interviewers.

- **Use gestures effectively.** Nod to show agreement and interest. Gestures should be used as needed, but not overused.
- **Smile enough to convey a positive attitude.** Have a friend give you honest feedback on whether you generally smile too much or not enough.
- **Listen attentively.** Show the interviewer you are interested and attentive by listening carefully to the questions being asked. This will also help you answer questions appropriately. Do not interrupt any speaker.
- **Turn off your cell phone or other electronic devices.** Avoid the embarrassment of having your smartphone ring, ping, or even as much as buzz, during an interview. Turn off your electronic devices completely; don't just switch them to vibrate.
- **Don't chew gum.** Chewing gum during an interview is distracting and unprofessional.
- **Sound enthusiastic and interested—but sincere.** The tone of your voice has an enormous effect on the words you say. Avoid sounding bored, frustrated, or sarcastic during an interview. Employers want employees who are enthusiastic and interested.
- **Avoid empty words.** Filling your answers with verbal pauses such as *um*, *uh*, *like*, and *basically* communicates that you are unprepared and unprofessional. Also avoid annoying distractions such as clearing your throat repeatedly or sighing deeply.
- **Be confident, but not cocky.** Most recruiters want candidates who are self-assured but not too casual or even arrogant. Let your body language, posture, dress, and vocal tone prove your confidence. Speak at a normal volume and enunciate words clearly without mumbling.[19]

Naturally, hiring managers make subjective decisions based on intuition, but they need to ferret out pleasant people who fit in. To that end, some recruiters apply "the airport test" to candidates, asking themselves, "Would I want to be stuck in the airport for 12 hours with this person if my flight were delayed?"[20]

## 14-3b Preparing to Answer Interview Questions

Remember that the way you answer questions can be almost as important as what you say. Use the interviewer's name and title from time to time when you answer. *Yes, Ms. Lyon, I would be pleased to tell you about. . . .* People like to hear their own names. Be sure you are pronouncing the name correctly, and don't overuse this technique. Avoid answering questions with a simple *yes* or *no*; elaborate on your answers to better promote yourself and your assets.

During the interview don't be afraid to clarify vague questions. Some interviewers are inexperienced and ill at ease in the role. You may ask your own question to understand what was asked, such as *By ____, do you mean ____?* Consider closing out some of your responses with *Does that answer your question, Mr. Cruz?* or *Would you like me to elaborate on any particular experience?*

Always aim your answers at the key characteristics interviewers seek: expertise, competence, motivation, interpersonal skills, decision-making skills, enthusiasm for the company and the job, and a pleasing personality. Remember to stay focused on your strengths. Bring up a weakness only if asked directly, and in such a case explain how you are working to overcome it.

As you respond, be sure to use good English and enunciate clearly. Avoid slurred words such as *gonna* and *din't*, as well as slangy expressions such as *yeah*, *like*, and *ya know*. As you practice answering expected interview questions, it is always a good idea to make a recording. Is your speech filled with verbal static?

You can't expect to be perfect in an employment interview. No one is. However, you can avert sure disaster by avoiding certain topics and behaviors such as those described in Figure 14.2.

---

### OFFICE INSIDER

*"Most people, even after spending hours slaving over a perfect résumé, fail to put in the necessary preparation for the most important part of the process: the interview!"*

—Carole Martin, interview coach and author of *Interview Fitness Training*

Figure **14.2** Ten Interview Actions to Avoid

**1. Don't be late or too early.** Arrive five to ten minutes before your scheduled interview.

**2. Don't be rude or annoying.** Treat everyone you come into contact with warmly and respectfully. Avoid limp handshakes, poor eye contact or staring, and verbal ticks such as *like*, *you know*, and *umm*.

**3. Don't criticize anyone or anything.** Don't criticize your previous employer, supervisors, colleagues, or job. The tendency is for interviewers to wonder if you would speak about their companies similarly.

**4. Don't act unprofessionally.** Don't discuss controversial subjects, and don't use profanity. Don't answer your cell phone or fiddle with it. Silence all electronic devices so that they don't even buzz, or turn them off completely. Don't bring food or coffee.

**5. Don't emphasize salary or benefits.** Don't address salary, vacation, or benefits early in an interview. Let the interviewer set the pace; win him or her over first.

**6. Don't focus on your imperfections.** Never dwell on your liabilities or talk negatively about yourself.

**7. Don't interrupt.** Interrupting is not only impolite but also prevents you from hearing a complete question or remark. Don't talk too much or too little. Answer interview questions to the best of your ability, but avoid rambling as much as terseness.

**8. Don't bring someone along.** Don't bring a friend or relative with you to the interview. If someone must drive you, ask that person to drop you off and come back later.

**9. Don't appear impatient or bored.** Your entire focus should be on the interview. Don't glance at your watch, which can imply that you are late for another appointment. Be alert and show interest in the company and the position.

**10. Don't act desperate.** A sure way to turn off an interviewer is to appear desperate. Don't focus on why you need the job; focus on how you will add value to the organization.

### 14-3c Anticipating Typical Interview Questions

Employment interviews are all about questions, and many of the questions interviewers ask are not new. You can anticipate a large percentage of questions that will be asked before you ever walk into a conference room. Although you can't anticipate every question, you can prepare for various types.

This section presents questions that may be asked during employment interviews. To get you thinking about how to respond, we have provided an answer for, or a discussion of, one or more of the questions in each of the following groups. As you read the remaining questions in each group, think about how you could respond most effectively. For additional questions, contact your campus career center, or consult one of the career websites listed in Chapter 13. If you rehearse success stories and anticipate interview questions, you will steer clear of the most common interview pitfalls shown in Figure 14.3.

Figure 14.3 What Can Go Wrong in a Job Interview?

**Most Common Interview Mistakes**

- 71% Answering a cell phone or texting
- 69% Dressing inappropriately
- 69% Appearing uninterested
- 66% Appearing arrogant
- 63% Denigrating a former employer
- 59% Talking while chewing gum

**Most Outrageous Interview Behavior**

- **Providing a detailed listing** of how the previous employer angered the candidate
- **Hugging** the hiring manager at the end of the interview
- **Eating all the candy** from the candy bowl while trying to answer questions
- **Blowing her nose** and lining up the used tissues on the table in front of her
- **Throwing his beer can** in the outside trash bin before coming into the office
- **Having a friend come in and say,** "How much longer?"

Source: Based on CareerBuilder survey of more than 2,400 hiring managers. Retrieved from http://www.careerbuilder.com/share/aboutus/pressreleasesdetail.aspx?id=pr614&sd=1%2F12%2F2011&ed=12%2F31%2F2011

**Questions to Get Acquainted.** After opening introductions, recruiters generally try to start the interview with personal questions designed to put you at ease. They are also striving to gain an overview to see whether you will fit into the organization's culture. When answering these questions, keep the employer's needs in mind and try to incorporate your success stories.

1. Tell me about yourself.

   Experts agree that you must keep this answer short (one to two minutes tops) but on target. Use this chance to promote yourself. Stick to educational, professional, or business-related strengths; avoid personal or humorous references. Be ready with at least three success stories illustrating characteristics important to this job. Demonstrate responsibility you have been given; describe how you contributed as a team player. Try practicing this formula: *I have completed a _____ degree with a major in _____. Recently I worked for _____ as a _____. Before that I worked for _____ as a _____. My strengths are _____ (interpersonal) and _____ (technical).* Try rehearsing your response in 30-second segments devoted to your education, work experience, qualifications, and skills.

## Office Insider

*"Occasionally you bump into a talented and competent candidate . . . who's so lacking in the EQ components of humility and realness that you can't take a chance. This young man had a lot of the right stuff, but when he started telling us that he had never made a mistake in his life and didn't expect to, we knew we'd heard enough."*

—Jack and Suzy Welch, management consultants and authors

2. What are your greatest strengths?
   Stress your strengths that are related to the position, such as *I am well organized, thorough, and attentive to detail.* Tell success stories and give examples that illustrate these qualities: *My supervisor says that my research is exceptionally thorough. For example, I recently worked on a research project in which I. . . .*

3. Do you prefer to work by yourself or with others? Why?
   This question can be tricky. Provide a middle-of-the-road answer that not only suggests your interpersonal qualities but also reflects an ability to make independent decisions and work without supervision.

4. What was your major in college, and why did you choose it?

5. What are some things you do in your spare time?

**Questions to Gauge Your Interest.** Interviewers want to understand your motivation for applying for a position. Although they will realize that you are probably interviewing for other positions, they still want to know why you are interested in this particular position with their organization. These types of questions help them determine your level of interest.

1. Why do you want to work for [name of company]?
   Questions like this illustrate why you must research an organization thoroughly before the interview. The answer to this question must prove that you understand the company and its culture. This is the perfect place to bring up the company research you did before the interview. Show what you know about the company, and discuss why you want to become a part of this organization. Describe your desire to work for this organization not only from your perspective but also from its point of view. What do you have to offer that will benefit the organization?

2. Why are you interested in this position?

3. What do you know about our company?

4. Why do you want to work in the _____ industry?

5. What interests you about our products (or services)?

**Questions About Your Experience and Accomplishments.** After questions about your background and education and questions that measure your interest, the interview generally becomes more specific with questions about your experience and accomplishments. Remember to show confidence when you answer these questions. If you are not confident in your abilities, why should an employer be?

1. Why should we hire you when we have applicants with more experience or better credentials?
   In answering this question, remember that employers often hire people who present themselves well instead of others with better credentials. Emphasize your personal strengths that could be an advantage with this employer.
   Are you a hard worker? How can you demonstrate it? Have you had recent training? Some people have had more years of experience but actually have less knowledge because they have done the same thing over and over. Stress your experience using the latest methods and equipment. Be sure to mention your computer training and Internet savvy. Emphasize that you are open to new ideas and learn quickly. Tell success stories to support your claims. Above all, show that you are confident in your abilities.

2. Describe the most rewarding experience of your career so far.

3. How have your education and professional experiences prepared you for this position?

4. What were your major accomplishments in each of your past jobs?

5. What was a typical workday like?
6. What job functions did you enjoy most? Least? Why?
7. Tell me about your computer skills.
8. Who was the toughest boss you ever worked for and why?
9. What were your major achievements in college?
10. Why did you leave your last position? *OR:* Why are you leaving your current position?

**Questions About the Future.** Questions that look into the future tend to stump some candidates, especially those who have not prepared adequately. Employers ask these questions to see whether you are goal oriented and to determine whether your goals are realistic.

1. Where do you expect to be five (or ten) years from now?
   Formulate a realistic plan with respect to your present age and situation. The important thing is to be prepared for this question. It is a sure kiss of death to respond that you would like to have the interviewer's job! Instead, show an interest in the current job and in making a contribution to the organization. Talk about the levels of responsibility you would like to achieve. One employment counselor suggests showing ambition but not committing to a specific job title. Suggest that you hope to have learned enough to have progressed to a position in which you will continue to grow. Keep your answer focused on educational and professional goals, not personal goals.
2. If you got this position, what would you do to be sure you fit in?
3. This is a large (or small) organization. Do you think you would like that environment?
4. Do you plan to continue your education?
5. What do you predict for the future of the _____ industry?
6. How do you think you can contribute to this company?
7. What would you most like to accomplish if you get this position?
8. How do you keep current with what is happening in your profession?

**Challenging Questions.** The following questions may make you uncomfortable, but the important thing to remember is to answer truthfully without dwelling on your weaknesses. As quickly as possible, convert any negative response into a discussion of your strengths.

1. What is your greatest weakness?
   It is amazing how many candidates knock themselves out of the competition by answering this question poorly. Actually, you have many choices. You can present a strength as a weakness (*Some people complain that I'm a workaholic or too attentive to details*). You can mention a corrected weakness (*Because I needed to learn about designing websites, I took a course*). You could cite an unrelated skill (*I really need to brush up on my Spanish*). You can cite a learning objective (*One of my long-term goals is to learn more about international management. Does your company have any plans to expand overseas?*). Another possibility is to reaffirm your qualifications (*I have no weaknesses that affect my ability to do this job*). Be careful that your answer doesn't sound too cliché (*I tend to be a perfectionist*) and instead shows careful analysis of your abilities.
2. What type of people do you have no patience for?
   Avoid letting yourself fall into the trap of sounding overly critical. One possible response is, *I have always gotten along well with others. But I confess that I can be irritated by complainers who don't accept responsibility.*

3. If you could live your life over, what would you change and why?
4. How would your former (or current) supervisor describe you as an employee?
5. What do you want the most from your job?
6. What is your grade point average, and does it accurately reflect your abilities?
7. Have you ever used drugs?
8. Who in your life has influenced you the most and why?
9. What are you reading right now?
10. Describe your ideal work environment.
11. Is the customer always right?
12. How do you define success?

**Situational Questions.** Questions related to situations help employers test your thought processes and logical thinking. When using situational questions, interviewers describe a hypothetical situation and ask how you would handle it. Situational questions differ based on the type of position for which you are interviewing. Knowledge of the position and the company culture will help you respond favorably to these questions. Even if the situation sounds negative, keep your response positive. Here are just a few examples:

1. You receive a call from an irate customer who complains about the service she received last night at your restaurant. She is demanding her money back. How would you handle the situation?
2. If you were aware that a coworker was falsifying data, what would you do?
3. Your supervisor has just told you that she is dissatisfied with your work, but you think it is acceptable. How would you resolve the conflict?
4. Your supervisor has told you to do something a certain way, and you think that way is wrong and you know a far better way to complete the task. What would you do?
5. Assume that you are hired for this position. You soon learn that one of the staff is extremely resentful because she applied for your position and was turned down. As a result, she is being unhelpful and obstructive. How would you handle the situation?
6. A colleague has told you in confidence that she suspects another colleague of stealing. What would your actions be?
7. You have noticed that communication between upper management and first-level employees is eroding. How would you solve this problem?

**Behavioral Questions.** Instead of traditional interview questions, you may be asked to tell stories. The interviewer may say, *Describe a time when . . .* or *Tell me about a time when. . . .* To respond effectively, learn to use the storytelling, or STAR, technique, as illustrated in Figure 14.4. Ask yourself, what the Situation or Task was, what Action you took, and what the Results were.[21] Practice using this method to recall specific examples of your skills and accomplishments. To be fully prepared, develop a coherent and articulate STAR narrative for every bullet point on your résumé. When answering behavioral questions, describe only educational and work-related situations or tasks, and try to keep them as current as possible. Here are a few examples of behavioral questions:

1. Tell me about a time when you solved a difficult problem.
Tell a concise story explaining the situation or task, what you did, and the result. For example, *When I was at Ace Products, we continually had a problem of excessive back orders. After analyzing the situation, I discovered that orders went through many unnecessary steps. I suggested that we eliminate much paperwork. As a result, we reduced back orders by 30 percent.*

Figure 14.4 Using the STAR Technique to Answer Behavioral Interview Questions

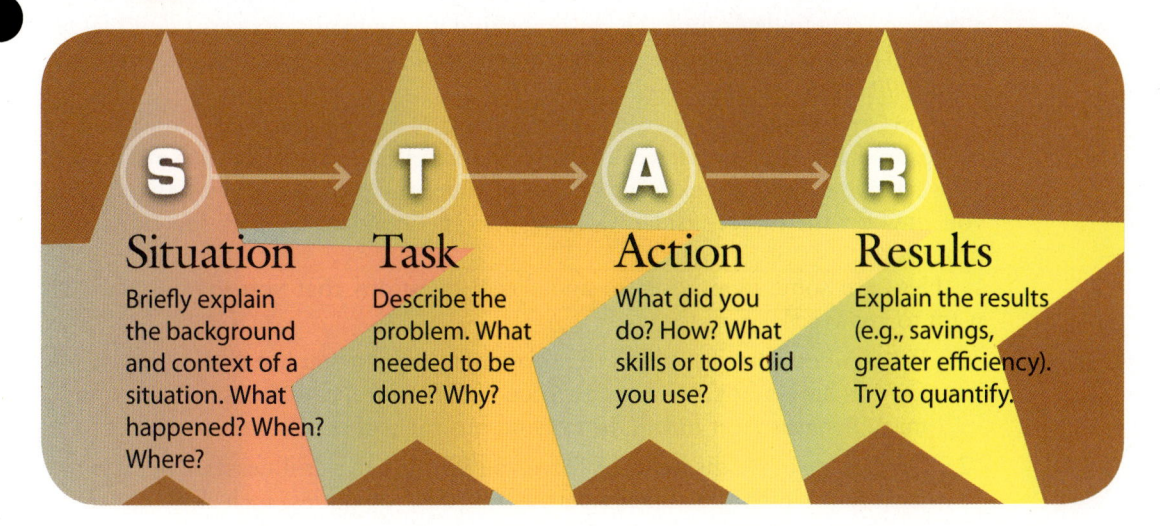

**S** → **T** → **A** → **R**

**Situation**
Briefly explain the background and context of a situation. What happened? When? Where?

**Task**
Describe the problem. What needed to be done? Why?

**Action**
What did you do? How? What skills or tools did you use?

**Results**
Explain the results (e.g., savings, greater efficiency). Try to quantify.

Go on to emphasize what you learned and how you can apply that learning to this job. Practice your success stories in advance so you will be ready.

2. Describe a situation in which you were able to use persuasion to convince someone to see things your way.
   The recruiter is interested in your leadership and teamwork skills. You might respond, I have learned to appreciate the fact that the way you present an idea is just as important as the idea itself. When trying to influence people, I put myself in their shoes and find some way to frame my idea from their perspective. I remember when I. . . .
3. Describe a time when you had to analyze information and make a recommendation.
4. Describe a time that you worked successfully as part of a team.
5. Tell me about a time that you dealt with confidential information.
6. Give me an example of a time when you were under stress to meet a deadline.
7. Tell me about a time when you had to go above and beyond the call of duty to get a job done.
8. Tell me about a time you were able to deal with another person successfully even though that person did not like you personally (or vice versa).
9. Give me an example of when you showed initiative and took the lead.
10. Tell me about a recent situation in which you had to deal with an upset customer or coworker.

**Illegal and Inappropriate Questions.** Federal laws prohibit employment discrimination based on gender, age, religion, color, race, national origin, and disability. In addition, federal civil service statutes and many state and city laws prohibit employment discrimination based on factors such as sexual orientation.[22] Therefore, it is inappropriate for interviewers to ask any question related to these areas. These questions become illegal, though, only when a court of law determines that the employer is asking them with the intent to discriminate.[23] Most illegal interview questions are asked innocently by inexperienced interviewers. Some are only trying to be friendly when they inquire about your personal life or family. Regardless of the intent, how should you react?

If you find the question harmless and if you want the job, go ahead and answer it. If you think that answering it would damage your chance to be hired, try to

Chapter 14: Interviewing and Following Up

deflect the question tactfully with a response such as *Could you tell me how my marital status relates to the responsibilities of this position?* or, *I prefer to keep my personal and professional lives separate.* If you are uncomfortable answering a question, try to determine the reason behind it; you might answer, *I don't let my personal life interfere with my ability to do my job*, or, *Are you concerned with my availability to work overtime?*

Another option, of course, is to respond to any inappropriate or illegal question by confronting the interviewer and threatening a lawsuit or refusing to answer. However, you could not expect to be hired under these circumstances. In any case, you might wish to reconsider working for an organization that sanctions such procedures.

Here are some inappropriate and illegal questions that you may or may not want to answer:[24]

1. What is your marital status? Are you married? Do you live with anyone? Do you have a boyfriend (or girlfriend)? (However, employers can ask your marital status after hiring for tax and insurance forms.)

2. Do you have any disabilities? Have you had any recent illnesses? (But it is legal to ask if the person can perform specific job duties, such as *Can you carry a 50-pound sack up a 10-foot ladder five times daily?*)

3. I notice you have an accent. Where are you from? What is the origin of your last name? What is your native language? (However, it is legal to ask what languages you speak fluently if language ability is related to the job.)

4. Have you ever filed a workers' compensation claim or been injured on the job?

5. Have you ever had a drinking problem or been addicted to drugs? (But it is legal to ask if a person uses illegal drugs.)

6. Have you ever been arrested? (But it is legal to ask, *Have you ever been convicted of____?* when the crime is related to the job.)

7. How old are you? What is your date of birth? When did you graduate from high school? (But it is legal to ask, *Are you 16 years [or 18 years or 21 years] old or older?* depending on the age requirements for the position.)

8. Of what country are you a citizen? Are you a U.S. citizen? Where were you born? (But it is legal to ask, *Are you authorized to work in the United States?*)

9. What is your maiden name? (But it is legal to ask, *What is your full name?* or, *Have you worked under another name?*)

10. Do you have any religious beliefs that would prevent you from working weekends or holidays? (An employer can, however, ask you if you are available to work weekends and holidays or otherwise within the company's required schedule.)

11. Do you have children? Do you plan to have children? Do you have adequate child-care arrangements? (However, employers can ask for dependent information for tax and insurance purposes after you are hired. Also, they can ask if you would be able to travel or work overtime on occasion.)

12. How much do you weigh? How tall are you? (However, employers can ask you about your height and weight if minimum standards are necessary to safely perform a job.)[25]

### 14-3d Asking Your Own Questions

Usually, near the end of the interview, you will be asked whether you have any questions. The worst thing you can do is say *no*, which suggests that you are not interested in the position. Instead, ask questions that will help you gain information and impress the interviewer with your thoughtfulness and interest in the position. Remember that this interview is a two-way street. You must be happy with the prospect of working for this organization. You want a position that matches your skills and personality. Use this opportunity to learn whether this job is right for you. Be aware that you don't have to wait for the interviewer to ask you for questions. You can ask your own questions throughout the interview to learn more about the company and position. Here are some questions you might ask:

1. What will my duties be (if not already discussed)?
2. Tell me what it is like working here in terms of the people, management practices, workloads, expected performance, and rewards.
3. What training programs are available from this organization? What specific training will be given for this position?
4. Who would be my immediate supervisor?
5. What is the organizational structure, and where does this position fit in?
6. Is travel required in this position?
7. How is job performance evaluated?
8. Assuming my work is excellent, where do you see me in five years?
9. How long do employees generally stay with this organization?
10. What are the major challenges for a person in this position?
11. What do you see in the future of this organization?
12. What do you like best about working for this organization?
13. May I have a tour of the facilities?
14. When do you expect to make a decision?

Do not ask about salary or benefits, especially during the first interview. It is best to let the interviewer bring those topics up first.

## 14-3e Ending Positively

After you have asked your questions, the interviewer will signal the end of the interview, usually by standing up or by expressing appreciation that you came. If not addressed earlier, you should at this time find out what action will follow. Demonstrate your interest in the position by asking when it will be filled or what the next step will be. Too many candidates leave the interview without knowing their status or when they will hear from the recruiter. Don't be afraid to say that you want the job!

Before you leave, summarize your strongest qualifications; show your enthusiasm for obtaining this position. Thank the interviewer for a constructive interview and for considering you for the position. Ask the interviewer for a business card, which will provide the information you need to write a thank-you note, which is discussed later. You might also ask whether you may stay in touch through LinkedIn.

Shake the interviewer's hand with confidence, and acknowledge anyone else you see on the way out. Be sure to thank the receptionist. Departing gracefully and enthusiastically will leave a lasting impression on those responsible for making the final hiring decision.

# 14-4 After the Interview

After leaving the interview, immediately make notes of what was said in case you are called back for a second interview. Write down key points that were discussed, the names of people you spoke with, and other details of the interview. Ask yourself what went really well and what you could improve. Note your strengths and

**LEARNING OBJECTIVE 4**

Describe what to do *after* an interview, including thanking the interviewer, contacting references, and writing follow-up messages.

## OFFICE INSIDER

"Thank-you notes matter: They give you a terrific opportunity to follow up with the decision-maker right away. I encourage job seekers to get thank-you notes out (to each individual they've met in the interview process) immediately after the interview. Same day. From your laptop in the parking lot, if you really want to wow them."

—Jenny Foss, job search strategist, career coach

weaknesses during the interview so you can work to improve in future interviews. Next, write down your follow-up plans. To whom should you send thank-you messages? Will you contact the employer by phone? By e-mail? If so, when? Then be sure to follow up on those plans, beginning with writing a thank-you e-mail or letter and contacting your references.

### 14-4a Thanking Your Interviewer

After a job interview, you should always send a thank-you note, e-mail, or letter. This courtesy sets you apart from other applicants, most of whom will not bother. Your message also reminds the interviewer of your visit and shows your good manners and genuine enthusiasm for the job.

Follow-up thank-you messages are most effective if sent immediately after the interview. Experts believe that a thoughtful follow-up note carries as much weight as the cover letter or e-mail does. Almost nine out of ten senior executives admit that in their evaluation of a job candidate they are swayed by a written thank-you.[26] In your thank-you message, refer to the date of the interview, the exact job title for which you were interviewed, and specific topics discussed. "An effective thank-you letter should hit every one of the employer's hot buttons," author and career consultant Wendy Enelow says.[27]

The majority of hiring managers (87 percent) find thank-you e-mails acceptable; recruiters in more formal companies may prefer handwritten notes or traditional letters.[28] However, precious few interviewers like to receive text messages: only 10 percent. The rest frown upon inappropriate messages such as *Thx for the intrvw!*[29] In any case, avoid worn-out phrases, such as *Thank you for taking the time to interview me*. Be careful, too, about overusing *I*, especially to begin sentences. Most important, show that you really want the job and that you are qualified for it. Notice how the letter in Figure 14.5 conveys enthusiasm and confidence.

If you have been interviewed by more than one person, send a separate thank-you message to each interviewer. It is also a good idea to send a thank-you message to the receptionist and to the person who set up the interview. Your preparation and knowledge of the company culture will help you determine whether a traditional thank-you letter sent by mail or an e-mail is more appropriate. Make sure that you write your e-mail using professional language, standard capitalization, and proper punctuation. One job candidate makes a follow-up e-mail her standard practice. She summarizes what was discussed during the face-to-face interview and adds information that she had not thought to mention during the interview.[30]

### 14-4b Contacting Your References

Once you have thanked your interviewer, it is time to alert your references that they may be contacted by the employer. You might also have to request a letter of recommendation to be sent to the employer by a certain date. As discussed in Chapter 13, you should have already asked permission to use these individuals as references, and you should have supplied them with a copy of your résumé and information about the types of positions you are seeking

To provide the best possible recommendation, your references need information. What position have you applied for with what company? What should they stress to the prospective employer? Let's say you are applying for a specific job that requires a letter of recommendation. Professor Sherman has already agreed to be a reference for you. To get the best letter of recommendation from Professor Sherman, help her out. Write an e-mail or letter telling her about the position, its requirements, and the recommendation deadline. Include copies of your résumé, college transcript, and, if applicable, the job posting or ad with detailed information about the opening. You might remind her of a positive experience with you that she could use in the recommendation. Remember that recommenders need evidence

Figure 14.5 Interview Follow-Up Message

**Eugene H. Vincente**

1308 Big Ridge Rd., Apt. 3, Biloxi, MS 39530
(228) 627-4362, evincente@gmail.com

May 28, 2016

Mr. André G. Mercier
3D Signs
5505 Industrial Parkway, Ste. 200
New Orleans, LA 70129

Dear Mr. Mercier:

Talking with you Friday, May 27, about the graphic designer position was both informative and interesting.

Thanks for describing the position in such detail and for introducing me to Ms. Sasaki, the senior designer. Her current project designing an annual report in four colors sounds fascinating as well as quite challenging.

Now that I've learned in greater detail the specific tasks of your graphic designers, I'm more than ever convinced that my computer and creative skills can make a genuine contribution to your graphic productions. My training in design and layout using PhotoShop and InDesign ensures that I could be immediately productive on your staff.

You will find me an enthusiastic and hardworking member of any team effort. As you requested, I'm enclosing additional samples of my work. I'm eager to join the graphics staff at your New Orleans headquarters, and I look forward to hearing from you soon.

Sincerely,

*Eugene H. Vincente*

Eugene H. Vincente

Enclosures

- Mentions the interview date and specific job title
- Highlights specific skills for the job
- Shows good manners, appreciation, and perseverance—traits that recruiters value
- Uses customized lettherhead but could have merely typed street and city address above dateline
- Personalizes the message by referring to topics discussed in the interview
- Reminds reader of interpersonal skills as well as enthusiam and eagerness for this job

---

to support generalizations. Give them appropriate ammunition, as the student has done in the following request:

*Dear Professor Sherman:*

*Recently, I interviewed for the position of administrative assistant in the Human Resources Department of Global Hospitality. Because you kindly agreed to help me, I am now asking you to write a letter of recommendation to Global.*

*The position calls for good organizational, interpersonal, and writing skills, as well as computer experience. To help you review my skills and training, I enclose my résumé. As you*

In a reference request letter, tell immediately why you are writing. Identify the target position and company.

Specify the job requirements to help the recommender know what to stress.

Chapter 14: Interviewing and Following Up

may recall, I earned an A in your business communication class last fall; and you commended my long report for its clarity and organization.

*Please send your letter to Mr. Connor Gordon at Global Hospitality before July 1 in the enclosed stamped, addressed envelope. I'm grateful for your support and promise to let you know the results of my job search.*

*Sincerely,*

### 14-4c Following Up

The standard advice to job candidates is to call to follow up a few days after the interview. However, some experts suggest that cold calling a hiring manager is risky. You may be putting a busy recruiter on the spot and force him or her to search for your application. In addition, don't assume you are the only candidate; multiply your phone call by the 200 applicants some hiring managers interview.[31] Therefore, you don't want to be a pest. An e-mail to find out how the decision process is going may be your best bet because such a message is much less intrusive. If you asked about it in the interview, you might follow up with the interviewer through a message on LinkedIn.

If you believe it is safe to follow up by phone, or if the recruiter suggested it, practice saying something like, *I'm wondering what else I can do to convince you that I'm the right person for this job*, or, *I'm calling to find out the status of your search for the ____ position*. When following up, it is important to sound professional and courteous. Sounding desperate, angry, or frustrated that you have not been contacted can ruin your chances. The following follow-up e-mail message would impress the interviewer:

*Dear Ms. Stein:*

*I enjoyed my interview with you last Thursday for the project manager position. You should know that I'm very interested in this opportunity with Enterprise Solutions. Because you mentioned that you might have an answer this week, I'm eager to know how your decision process is coming along. I look forward to hearing from you.*

*Sincerely,*

Depending on the response you get to your first follow-up request, you may have to follow up additional times.[32] Keep in mind, though, that some employers won't tell you about their hiring decision unless you are the one hired. Don't harass the interviewer, and don't force a decision. If you don't hear back from an employer within several weeks after following up, it is best to assume that you didn't get the job and to continue with your job search.

**LEARNING OBJECTIVE 5**
Prepare additional employment documents such as applications, rejection follow-up messages, acceptance messages, and resignation letters.

## 14-5 Preparing Additional Employment Documents

Although the résumé and cover letter are your major tasks, other important documents and messages are often required during the job-search process. You may need to complete an employment application form and write follow-up letters. You might also have to write a letter of resignation when leaving a job. Because each of these tasks reveals something about you and your communication skills, you will want to put your best foot forward. These documents often subtly influence company officials to offer a job.

Sidenotes: Provide a stamped, addressed envelope. Inquire courteously; beware of sounding angry or desperate.

## 14-5a Application Form

Some organizations require job candidates to fill out job application forms instead of, or in addition to, submitting résumés. This practice permits them to gather and store standardized data about each applicant. Whether the application is on paper or online, follow the directions carefully and provide accurate information. The following suggestions can help you be prepared:

- Carry a card or notes saved on your mobile device summarizing vital statistics not included on your résumé. If you are asked to fill out a paper application form in an employer's office, you will need a handy reference to the following data: graduation dates; beginning and ending dates of all employment; salary history; full names, titles, and present work addresses of former supervisors; full addresses and phone numbers of current and previous employers; and full names, occupational titles, occupational addresses, and telephone numbers of people who have agreed to serve as references.
- Look over all the questions before starting.
- Fill out the form neatly, using blue or black ink. Many career counselors recommend printing your responses; cursive handwriting can be difficult to read.
- Answer all questions honestly. Write *Not applicable* or *N/A* if appropriate. Don't leave any sections blank.
- Use accurate spelling, grammar, capitalization, and punctuation.
- If asked for the position desired, give a specific job title or type of position. Don't say, *Anything* or *Open*. These answers make you look unfocused; moreover, they make it difficult for employers to know what you are qualified for or interested in.
- Be prepared for a salary question. Unless you know what comparable employees are earning in the company, the best strategy is to suggest a salary range or to write *Negotiable* or *Open*. See the Communication Workshop at the end of this chapter for tips on dealing with money matters while interviewing.
- Be prepared to explain the reasons for leaving previous positions. Use positive or neutral statements such as *Relocation, Seasonal, To accept a position with more responsibility, Temporary position, To continue education,* or *Career change*. Avoid explanations such as *Fired, Quit, Didn't get along with supervisor,* or *Pregnant*.
- Check the application before submitting to make sure it is complete and that you have followed all instructions. Sign and date the application.

If asked to input data into fields on an electronic application, have a flash drive ready or access your cloud drive to retrieve digital records that you can carefully copy and paste into windows on electronic forms.

## 14-5b Application or Résumé Follow-Up Message

If your résumé or application generates no response within a reasonable time, you may decide to send a short follow-up e-mail or letter such as the following. Doing so (a) jogs the memory of the hiring manager, (b) demonstrates your serious interest, and (c) allows you to emphasize your qualifications or to add new information.

Dear Ms. Ma:

*Please know that I am still interested in becoming an administrative support specialist with Asawa Commercial, Inc.*

Open by reminding the reader of your interest.

---

**OFFICE INSIDER**

"People spend much more time trying to find a new job than they do planning a proper exit. You can never be sure how secure any job is. It's important that you leave positive professional impressions with every employer so you can receive a good reference and keep the door open to returning if ever appropriate."

—Patty Prosser, chair, OI Partners, a global coaching, leadership development, and consulting firm

*Since submitting an application [or résumé] in May, I have completed my degree and have been employed as a summer replacement for office workers in several downtown offices. This experience has honed my word processing and communication skills. It has also introduced me to a wide range of office procedures.*

*Please keep my application in your active file and let me know when my formal training, technical skills, and practical experience can go to work for you.*

*Sincerely,*

### 14-5c Rejection Follow-Up Message

If you didn't get the job and you think it was perfect for you, don't give up. Employment specialists encourage applicants to respond to a rejection. The candidate who was offered the position may decline, or other positions may open up. In a rejection follow-up e-mail or letter, it is OK to admit that you are disappointed. Be sure to add, however, that you are still interested and will contact the company again in a month in case a job opens up. Then follow through for a couple of months—but don't overdo it. You should be professional and persistent, not annoying. Here is an example of an effective rejection follow-up message:

*Dear Mr. Connolly:*

*Although disappointed that someone else was selected for your accounting position, I appreciate your promptness and courtesy in notifying me.*

*Because I am confident that you would benefit from my technical and interpersonal skills in your fast-paced environment, please consider keeping my résumé in your active file. My desire to become a productive member of Goldfine Manufacturers staff remains strong.*

*Our interview on _____ was very enjoyable, and I especially appreciate the time you and Ms. Katz spent describing your company's expansion into international markets. To enhance my qualifications, I have enrolled in a course in international accounting at CSU.*

*Should you have an opening for which I am qualified, you may reach me at (818) 719-3901. In the meantime, I will call you in a month to discuss employment possibilities.*

*Sincerely,*

### 14-5d Job Acceptance or Rejection Message

When all your hard work pays off, you will be offered the position you want. Although you will likely accept the position over the phone, it is a good idea to follow up with an acceptance e-mail or letter to confirm the details and to formalize the acceptance. Your acceptance message might look like this:

*Dear Ms. Reed:*

*It was a pleasure talking with you earlier today. As I mentioned, I am delighted to accept the position of social media manager with SkyVault Networks, in your Portland office. I look forward to becoming part of the SkyVault team and starting work on a variety of exciting and innovative projects.*

*As we agreed, my starting salary will be $46,000, with a full benefits package including health and life insurance, retirement plan, and two weeks of vacation per year.*

*I look forward to starting my position with SkyVault Networks on September 15, 2016. Before that date I will send you the completed tax and insurance forms you need. Thanks again for everything, Ms. Reed.*

*Sincerely,*

Include the specific starting date.

If you must turn down a job offer, show your professionalism by writing a sincere letter. This letter should thank the employer for the job offer and explain briefly that you are turning it down. Taking the time to extend this courtesy could help you in the future if this employer has a position you really want. Here's an example of a job rejection letter:

*Dear Mr. Levitt:*

*Thank you very much for offering me the position of sales representative with Trimble Pharmacology. It was a difficult decision to make, but I have accepted a position with another company.*

Thank the employer for the job offer and decline the offer without giving specifics.

*I appreciate your showing me your headquarters and introducing me to your staff, and I wish Trimble Pharmacology much success in the future.*

Express gratitude and best wishes for the future.

*Sincerely,*

## 14-5e Resignation Letter

After you have been in a position for a period of time, you may find it necessary to leave. Perhaps you have been offered a better position, or maybe you have decided to return to school full-time. Whatever the reason, you should leave your position gracefully and tactfully. Although you will likely discuss your resignation in person with your supervisor, it is a good idea to document your resignation by writing a formal letter. Some resignation letters are brief, whereas others contain great detail. Remember that many resignation letters are placed in personnel files; therefore, you should format and write yours using the professional business letter–writing techniques you learned earlier. Here is an example of a basic letter of resignation:

*Dear Ms. Washington:*

*This letter serves as formal notice of my resignation from Sienna Logistics, effective Friday, August 19. I have enjoyed serving as your staff accountant for the past two years, and I am grateful for everything I have learned during my employment with Sienna Logistics.*

Confirm the exact date of resignation. Remind the employer of your contributions.

*Please let me know what I can do over the next two weeks to help you prepare for my departure. I would be happy to help with finding and training my replacement.*

Offer assistance to prepare for your resignation.

*Thanks again for providing such a positive employment experience. I will long remember my time here.*

Offer thanks and end with a forward-looking statement.

*Sincerely,*

Although the employee who wrote the preceding resignation letter gave the standard two-week notice, you may find that a longer notice is necessary. The higher your position and the greater your responsibility, the longer the notice you give your employer should be. You should, however, always give some notice as a courtesy.

## Workplace in Focus

After a successful 12-year term at Goldman Sachs, derivatives director Greg Smith caused a stir when he resigned suddenly from the prestigious Wall Street institution. Instead of sending a polite resignation letter to bosses, Smith submitted a dramatic op-ed to the *New York Times* that criticized his employer. In the piece, Smith characterized the company's culture as "toxic and destructive," and he shamed managers who sought personal gain at clients' expense. "I hope this can be a wake-up call to the board of directors," Smith wrote. "People who care only about making money will not sustain this firm—or the trust of its clients—for very much longer." Are there ways for an employee to leave a firm on good terms?[33]

Writing job acceptance, job rejection, and resignation letters requires effort. That effort, however, is worth it because you are building bridges that may carry you to even better jobs in the future.

## SUMMARY OF LEARNING OBJECTIVES

**14-1** Explain the purposes and types of job interviews, including screening, one-on-one, panel, group, sequential, stress, and online interviews.
- An interviewer wants to (a) find out whether your skills are right for the job, (b) discuss your abilities in detail, (c) probe for motivation, and (d) see whether you would fit into the organization.
- An interviewee has a chance to (a) show potential, (b) learn about the job and company, and (c) elaborate on the information in the résumé.
- Screening interviews help companies weed out lesser-qualified candidates before scheduling face-to-face hiring/placement interviews with the most promising applicants.
- Hiring interviews include one-on-one, panel, group, sequential, stress, and online or virtual interviews.

**14-2** Describe what to do *before* an interview, including ensuring professional phone techniques, researching the target company, rehearsing success stories, cleaning up digital dirt, and fighting fear.
- Aim to make a good first impression on the phone by being polite and enthusiastic, recording a professional voice mail greeting, and alerting any housemates.
- Research the company on the Web, analyze its advertising and media presence, and try to locate insider information; then prepare by rehearsing success stories and cleaning up any digital dirt.
- Allow plenty of time for traveling to the interview; greet the interviewer politely and be pleasant.
- Fight fear by preparing thoroughly and dressing professionally; remember to breathe.

**14-3** Describe what to do *during* an interview, including controlling nonverbal messages and answering typical interview questions.
- Be aware of your body language, exhibit good posture, maintain eye contact, use gestures effectively, listen, smile, turn off your cell phone, don't chew gum, use proper speech, and be confident.
- Aim your answers at the key characteristics interviewers seek; focus on your strengths.
- Expect questions designed to get acquainted, gauge your interest, determine your accomplishments, probe for future plans, and challenge you; anticipate situational, behavioral, and inappropriate questions.
- Demonstrate interest by asking your own questions; end positively and say goodbye graciously.

**14-4** Describe what to do *after* an interview, including thanking the interviewer, contacting references, and writing follow-up messages.
- Send a thank-you note, e-mail, or letter immediately after the interview to each interviewer, but do not text message; reiterate your interest and qualifications, but avoid overused phrases.
- Alert your references to expect recruiter calls, and give them the appropriate information so they can support generalizations about you with specific evidence.
- A few days after the interview, follow up by e-mail or by calling the recruiter, if you believe it's safe, but don't be a pest. If you call, be professional and courteous.

**14-5** Prepare additional employment documents such as applications, rejection follow-up messages, acceptance messages, and resignation letters.
- Follow-up messages reveal a lot about you and your communication skills; prepare each with care.
- To fill out application forms neatly and accurately, carry records summarizing your vital statistics.
- In an application or résumé follow-up message, remind the recruiter of your application, demonstrate serious interest, and emphasize your qualifications.
- Even if you didn't get the job, write a follow-up e-mail or letter; be persistent yet not annoying.
- When accepting a job, follow up in writing to confirm what was discussed; when declining an offer, be professional and sincere. Thank the interviewer and courteously turn down the position.
- If you decide to resign, write a graceful and tactful formal letter to document your decision.

# CHAPTER REVIEW

1. During a job interview, do the interviewer and the interviewee want the same thing? How do their purposes differ? (Obj. 1)

2. Briefly describe the types of hiring/placement interviews you may encounter. (Obj. 1)

3. Career coaches warn candidates to never enter a job interview "cold." What does this mean, and how can a candidate heed the warning? (Obj. 2)

4. What are success stories, and how can you use them? (Obj. 2)

5. Should candidates be candid with interviewers when asked about their weaknesses? (Obj. 3)

6. What are situational and behavioral interview questions, and how can you craft responses that will make a favorable impression on the interviewer? (Obj. 3)

7. List the steps you should take immediately following your job interview. (Obj. 4)

8. How can you help your references provide the best possible recommendation? (Obj. 4)

9. If you receive a job offer, why is it important to write an acceptance message, and what should it include? (Obj. 5)

10. Is it a good idea to follow up after a job rejection? Why or why not? (Obj. 5)

# CRITICAL THINKING

11. Online multiple-choice questionnaires are a hot trend in recruiting, experts say.[34] Employers may ask not only how applicants would handle tricky situations, but also how happy they are or how much they have stolen from their previous employer. The multiple-choice format poses a dilemma for the applicant whether to be truthful or say what the employer might want to hear. Is this practice fair? What are some advantages and disadvantages of this practice? (Objs. 1, 2)

12. "Like criminal background checks and drug tests, the social media check is quickly becoming an automatic part of the hiring process," asserts Melissa Bell, editor of BlogPost for *The Washington Post*.[35] Do you believe employers are justified or ethical in making these kinds of searches before hiring? Does this assume that candidates may be criminals? Isn't this similar to snooping? (Objs. 1, 2)

13. What can you do to appear professional when a potential employer contacts you by phone for a screening interview or to schedule a job interview? (Obj. 2)

14. If you are asked an illegal interview question, why is it important to first assess the intentions of the interviewer? (Obj. 3)

15. A recruiter is checking the online presence of an outstanding candidate and discovers from her social media posts that she is 18 weeks pregnant—and happily so. The position involves a big project going live just as the candidate would take maternity leave. He decides to eliminate this candidate. Is his action legal? Ethical? What lesson could be learned about posting private information online? (Objs. 1, 2)

# ACTIVITIES AND CASES

## 14.1 Surviving Cattle-Call Interviews (Obj. 1)
*Social Media* *Web*

Group interviews are not for the fainthearted, and opinions on the practice are mixed. "Cattle-call" interviews can be stressful, shocking, even demeaning, some participants feel. One interviewee for an executive-level public relations position described being herded into a room with 200 other applicants where interviewers started bellowing questions at participants. Employers who like this tool say that cattle-call interviews are fair and efficient because they allow the quick ranking of candidates in categories such as teamwork, leadership, and stress management.

**YOUR TASK.** To deepen your understanding of group interviews, search the Web for articles and blogs using the keywords *group job interviews* or *cattle-call interviews*. Job-search advice sites offer tips on coping with the anxiety of group interviewing. Collect the advice and report your insights in class or in a written document as determined by your instructor.

## 14.2 The Kiss of Death to Job Prospects or a Job Offer? (Objs. 1, 2)
*E-mail* *Social Media* *Team* *Web*

What turns off hiring managers who browse candidates' social media sites? A Harris Interactive/CareerBuilder study[36] shows employers' pet peeves about applicants' social media presence. The research also reveals recruiters' favorite findings that may improve a candidate's job prospects. Here is an overview of how employers responded:

*Social Media Behavior Hurting Job Seekers*

| | |
|---|---|
| Candidates posted information about themselves drinking or using drugs. | 49 percent |
| Candidates posted provocative or inappropriate photos or information. | 45 percent |
| Candidates' screen names were unprofessional. | 29 percent |
| Candidates badmouthed previous employers. | 26 percent |
| Candidates made discriminatory comments related to race, gender, religion, etc. | 23 percent |
| Candidates lied about qualifications. | 21 percent |
| Candidates were linked to criminal behavior. | 21 percent |
| Candidates had poor communication skills. | 17 percent |

Conversely, social media behavior that impresses recruiters includes the following positive impressions: creative (48 percent), got a good feel for candidate's personality (43 percent), great communication skills (42 percent), well rounded/wide range of interests (41 percent), and conveyed a professional image (38 percent).

**YOUR TASK.** Conduct a social media audit in your course. Armed with the knowledge acquired in this chapter and the information in this activity, critically evaluate fellow students' social media sites, whether Facebook, Instagram, Google+, Twitter, LinkedIn, etc. In pairs or larger groups, look for positive attributes as well as negative criteria that may repel hiring managers. Report your findings orally or compile them in an e-mail or memo. If you identify negative behavior, discuss remedies—how to remove offensive material.

## 14.3 Learning What Jobs Are Really About Through Blogs, Facebook, and Twitter (Obj. 2)
`Social Media` `Web`

Blogs and social media sites such as Facebook and Twitter are becoming important tools in the job-search process. By accessing blogs, company Facebook pages, and Twitter feeds, job seekers can locate much insider information about a company's culture and day-to-day activities.

**YOUR TASK.** Using the Web, locate a blog that is maintained by an employee of a company where you would like to work. Monitor the blog for at least a week. Also, access the company's Facebook page and monitor Twitter feeds for at least a week. Prepare a short report summarizing what you learned about the company through reading the blog postings, status updates, and tweets. Include a statement of whether this information would be valuable during your job search.

## 14.4 Using Glassdoor to Prepare for Interviews and Find Salary Data (Objs. 1, 2)
`Social Media` `Web` `E-mail`

You may be familiar with LinkedIn, the social network devoted to all things career. Perhaps you have a profile on LinkedIn. However, did you know that Glassdoor is another superb source of job-search information, postings, and reviews? In anonymous posts, Glassdoor dishes on company reviews, salary comparisons, CEO approval ratings, interviews, and more. If you want authentic insider data about job interviews and other invaluable information, check out Glassdoor.

Let's say you wish to know what LinkedIn is like as an employer and how happy applicants are with LinkedIn's interview process. You would search by company and could refine your search by targeting a specific job title and location. You would see that at 4.6, the career network has a high rating overall and that its CEO Jeff Weiner has achieved a stellar 98 percent approval rating.

**YOUR TASK.** At the Glassdoor site, search for your dream employer. You can select from industries or search for companies by name. Examine the reviews and the interview modalities. How happy are interviewees and current workers with their employer? Share your results with the class and, if asked, report your findings in a document—a memo, e-mail, or informal report.

## 14.5 Warren Buffett's Career Advice to Millennials (Objs. 1–5)

Warren Buffett, the billionaire investor and Berkshire Hathaway CEO, is a welcome speaker about career success. In a live stream video chat with a career advice site,[37] Buffett gave advice often heard from successful businesspeople about finding one's passion and learning how to communicate effectively. He shared that, as a student, he had been terrified of public speaking, but that a Dale Carnegie class changed his life. Furthermore, Buffett recommended finding and associating with the right role models. He advised women to "stop holding yourself back" and to seek male mentors. Moreover, he recommended becoming involved with growing businesses because they offer more opportunities than established businesses do.

More remarkable perhaps is Buffett's advice not to work for someone who won't pay employees fairly and to "never give up searching for the job that you're passionate about." He added: "Forget about the pay. When you're associating with the people that you love, doing what you love, it doesn't get any better than that." Buffett says he reads six hours every day to grow intellectually.

**YOUR TASK.** Evaluate this advice critically. Consider questions such as the following: How much of Buffett's advice can you apply immediately? What can you do in the medium or long term? Discuss the issues of fair pay and being passionate about work. Do many people genuinely love the work they do? Is it necessary to love one's work to do it well? If your instructor directs, you could interview friends and family using Buffett's tips to gather more views about success and happiness.

## 14.6 Yes, You Can Interview People in Fewer Than 140 Characters! (Objs. 1, 3)
`Social Media` `Team` `Web`

Digital marketing strategist, angel investor, and best-selling author Jay Baer published an e-book, *The Best of Twitter 20* that presents 22 Twitter interviews (twitterviews) he conducted with social media luminaries. The experts, to whom Baer posed 20 questions in no more than 140 characters within approximately 90 minutes, include Joseph Jaffe, Gary Vaynerchuk, Spike Jones, and Amber Naslund.

**YOUR TASK.** Search for a phrase such as *Baer and The Twitter 20*. Visit Baer's blog Convince&Convert, download the free e-book, or read it online. You can also access the individual links on Baer's website, taking you directly to the social media expert of your choice. Study the twitterviews. Then, if your instructor directs, team up for a role-play, in which one student acts as the interviewer and the other plays the interviewee. The roles can be switched after a while. Prepare at least five concise career-related questions that you will convert into tweets. In turn, your counterpart will tweet back his or her answers. If you don't want to use a live Twitter feed, type up your tweets in a word processing program that will allow you to count characters. You can model your list of tweets on Baer's transcript format.

## 14.7 Telling Effective Success Stories (Obj. 2)

You can best showcase your talents if you are ready with your own success stories that illustrate how you have developed the skills or traits required for your targeted position.

**YOUR TASK.** Prepare success stories that highlight required skills or traits. Select three to five stories to develop into answers to potential interview questions. For example, here is a typical question: *How does your background relate to the position we have open?* A possible response: *As you know, I have just completed an intensive training program in _____. In addition, I have over three years of part-time work experience in a variety of business settings. In one position I was selected to manage a small business in the absence of the owner. I developed responsibility and customer service skills in filling orders efficiently, resolving shipping problems, and monitoring key accounts. I also inventoried and organized products worth over $200,000. When the owner returned from a vacation to Florida, I was commended for increasing sales and received a bonus in recognition of my efforts.* People relate to and remember stories. Try to shape your answers into memorable stories.

## 14.8 Cleaning up Digital Dirt (Obj. 2)

**Web**

Before embarking on your job hunt, you may want to know what employers might find if they searched your personal life in cyberspace, specifically on Facebook, Twitter, Instagram, and so forth. Running your name through Google and other search engines, particularly enclosed in quotation marks to lower the number of hits, is usually the first step. To learn even more, try some of the people-search sites such as 123people, Snitch.name, and PeekYou. They collect information from a number of search engines, websites, and social networks.

**YOUR TASK.** Use Google, 123people, and another search tool to explore the Web for your full name, enclosed in quotation marks. In Google, don't forget to run an Image search at **http://www.google.com/images** to find any photos of questionable taste. If the instructor requests, share your insights with the class—not the salacious details, but general observations—or write a short memo summarizing the results.

## 14.9 Talent Assessments: Evaluating Job Scenarios (Objs. 1, 2)

**Web**

What do Macy's, PetSmart, Radio Shack, Walmart, and Burger King have in common? They use preemployment testing to identify applicants who will fit into the organization. Unlike classical aptitude tests that began in the military, today's online multiple-choice tests assess integrity, collegiality, and soft skills in general.

To give you a flavor of these talent assessments,[38] here are three typical scenarios:

| 1. You have learned that eye contact is important in communication. How much eye contact should you have when conversing with someone in a professional environment? | 2. You are attending an important meeting with colleagues who are more senior than you are. How much should you speak at the meeting? | 3. You just found out that people at work are spreading a bad rumor about you that is untrue. How would you respond? |
|---|---|---|
| A At all times. You want to make sure the person knows you are paying attention. | A You should look very interested but not speak at all unless they request it. | A Tell everybody that it is not true. You need to clear your name. |
| B About 60-70 percent of the time | B You should speak only when the topic is of your expertise. | B Don't react to it at all. It'll blow over eventually. |
| C Every now and then. You don't want to make the other person uncomfortable. | C You should try to talk as much as possible to show your knowledge. | C Find out who started it so you talk to them to make sure that they will never do it again. |
| D About half the time | D You should speak in the beginning of the meeting and every now and then. | D Talk to others about another coworker's rumor so people will forget about yours. |

Chapter 14: Interviewing and Following Up

**YOUR TASK.** Answer the questions; then compare your answers with those of your classmates. Discuss the scenarios. What specific skills or attributes might each question be designed to measure? Do you think such questions are effective? What might be the best way to respond to the scenarios? Your instructor may share the correct answers with you. If your instructor directs, search the Web for more talent assessment questions. Alternatively, your instructor might ask you to create your own workplace (or college) scenarios to help you assess an applicant's soft skills. As a class you could compare questions/scenarios and quiz each other.

## 14.10 Getting Ready to Wear Interview Attire (Objs. 2, 3)

Web

As you prepare for your interview by learning about the company and the industry, don't forget a key component of interview success: creating a favorable first impression by wearing appropriate business attire. Job seekers often have nebulous ideas about proper interview wear. Some wardrobe mishaps include choosing a conservative "power suit" but accessorizing it with beat-up casual shoes or a shabby bag. Grooming glitches include dandruff on dark suit fabric, dirty fingernails, and mothball odor. Women sometimes wrongly assume that any black clothing items are acceptable, even if they are too tight, revealing, sheer, or made of low-end fabrics. Most image consultants agree that workplace wardrobe falls into three main categories: business formal, business casual, and casual. Only business formal is considered proper interview apparel.

**YOUR TASK.** To prepare for your big day, search the Web for descriptions and images of *business formal*. You may research *business casual* and *casual* styles, but for an interview, always dress on the side of caution—conservatively. Compare prices and look for suit sales to buy one or two attractive interview outfits. Share your findings (notes, images, and price range for suits, solid shoes, and accessories) with the class and your instructor.

## 14.11 Rehearsing Interview Questions (Obj. 3)

Team

Practice makes perfect in interviewing. The more often you rehearse responses to typical interview questions, the closer you are to getting the job.

**YOUR TASK.** Select three questions from each of these question categories discussed in this chapter: questions to get acquainted, questions to gauge your interest, questions about your experience and accomplishments, questions about the future, and challenging questions. Write your answers to each set of questions. Try to incorporate skills and traits required for the targeted position, and include success stories where appropriate. Polish these answers and your delivery technique by practicing in front of a mirror or by making an audio or video recording. Your instructor may make this assignment a group activity in class.

## 14.12 Anticipating Situational Interview Questions (Obj. 3)

Team  Web

Situational interview questions can vary widely from position to position. You should know enough about a position to understand some of the typical situations you would encounter regularly.

**YOUR TASK.** Use your favorite search tool to locate typical job descriptions of a position in which you are interested. Based on these descriptions, develop a list of six to eight typical situations someone in this position would face; then write situational interview questions for each of these scenarios. In pairs, role-play interviewer and interviewee, alternating with each question.

## 14.13 Examining Behavioral Interview Questions (Obj. 3)

Team  Web

Behavioral interview questions are increasingly popular, and you will need a little practice before you can answer them easily.

**YOUR TASK.** Use your favorite search tool to locate lists of behavioral questions on the Web. Select five skills areas such as communication, teamwork, and decision making. For each skill area, find three behavioral questions that you think would be effective in an interview. In pairs, role-play interviewer and interviewee, alternating with each question. You goal is to answer effectively in one or two minutes. Remember to use the STAR method when answering.

## 14.14 Compiling a Digital or Paper Interview Cheat Sheet (Objs. 2, 3)

Even the best-rehearsed applicants sometimes forget to ask the questions they prepared, or they fail to stress their major accomplishments in job interviews. Sometimes applicants are so rattled they even forget the interviewer's name. To help you keep your wits during an interview, make a cheat sheet—whether paper or digital—that summarizes key facts, answers, and questions. Review it before the interview and again as the interview is ending to be sure you have covered everything that is critical.

**YOUR TASK.** Prepare a cheat sheet with the following information:
Day and time of interview:
Meeting with (name[s] of interviewer[s], title, company, city, state, zip, telephone, cell, fax, e-mail):
Major accomplishments (four to six):
Management or work style (four to six):
Things you need to know about me (three or four items):
Reason I left my last job:
Answers to difficult questions (four or five answers):
Questions to ask interviewer:
Things I can do for you:

## 14.15 Responding to Inappropriate and Illegal Interview Questions (Obj. 3)

Although some questions are considered inappropriate and potentially illegal by the government, many interviewers ask them anyway—whether intentionally or unknowingly. Being prepared is important.

**YOUR TASK.** Assume you are being interviewed at one of the top companies on your list of potential employers. The interviewing committee consists of a human resources manager and the supervising manager of the department where you would work. At various times during the interview, the supervising manager asks questions that make you feel uncomfortable. For example, he asks whether you are married. You know this question is inappropriate, but you see no harm in answering it. Then, however, he asks how old you are. Because you started college early and graduated in three and a half years, you are worried that you may not be considered mature enough for this position. However, you have most of the other qualifications required, and you are convinced you could succeed on the job. How should you answer this question?

## 14.16 Asking Your Own Questions (Obj. 3)

When it is your turn to ask questions during the interview process, be ready.

**YOUR TASK.** Decide on three to five questions that you would like to ask during an interview. Write these questions out and practice asking them to help you sound confident and sincere.

## 14.17 Embracing Mock Interviews (Obj. 3)
**Team**

One of the best ways to understand interview dynamics and to develop confidence is to role-play the parts of interviewer and candidate in a mock interview.

**YOUR TASK.** Choose a partner for this activity. Each partner makes a list of two interview questions for each of the eight interview question categories presented in this chapter. In team sessions you and your partner role-play an actual interview. One acts as interviewer; the other is the candidate. Prior to the interview, the candidate tells the interviewer the job he or she is applying for and the name of the company. For the interview, the interviewer and candidate should dress appropriately and sit in chairs facing each other. The interviewer greets the candidate and makes the candidate comfortable. The candidate gives the interviewer a copy of his or her résumé. The interviewer asks three (or more depending on your instructor's time schedule) questions from the candidate's list. The interviewer may also ask follow-up questions, if appropriate. When finished, the interviewer ends the meeting graciously. After one interview, partners reverse roles and repeat.

## 14.18 YouTube: Critiquing Interview Skills (Obj. 3)
**Web**

The adage *Practice makes perfect* is especially true for interviewing. The more you confront your fears in mock or real interviews, the calmer and more confident you will be when your dream job is on the line. Short of undergoing your own interview, you can also learn from observation. YouTube and other video sites offer countless video clips showing examples of excellent, and poor, interviewing techniques.

**YOUR TASK.** Visit YouTube or search the Internet for interview videos. Select a clip that you find particularly entertaining or informative. Watch it multiple times and jot down your observations. Then summarize the scenario in a paragraph or two. Provide examples of interview strategies that worked and those that didn't, applying the information you learned in this chapter. If required, share your insights about the video with the class.

## 14.19 Minding Your Table Manners (Obj. 3)

**Web**

Although they are less likely for entry-level candidates, interviews over business meals are a popular means to size up the social skills of a job seeker, especially in second and subsequent interviews. Candidates coveting jobs with a lot of face-to-face contact with the public may be subjected to the ultimate test: table manners. Interviews are nerve-racking and intimidating enough, but imagine having to juggle silverware, wrangle potentially messy food, and keep your clothing stain free—all this while listening carefully to what is being said around the table and giving thoughtful, confident answers.

**YOUR TASK.** Researching tips can help you avoid the most common pitfalls associated with interviews over meals. Use your favorite search engine and try queries such as *interview dining tips, interviewing over meals*, and so forth. Consider the credibility of your sources. Are they authorities on the subject? Compile your list of tips and jot down your sources. Share the list with your peers. If you instructor directs, discuss the categories of advice provided. Then, as a class assemble a list of the most common interview tips.

## 14.20 Thanking the Interviewer (Obj. 4)

You have just completed an exciting employment interview, and you want the interviewer to remember you.

**YOUR TASK.** Write a follow-up thank-you letter to Ronald T. Ranson, Human Resources Development, Electronic Data Sources, 1328 Peachtree Plaza, Atlanta, GA 30314 (or a company of your choice). Make up any details needed.

## 14.21 Following Up After Submitting Your Résumé

**E-mail**

A month has passed since you sent your résumé and cover letter in response to a job advertisement. You are still interested in the position and would like to find out whether you still have a chance.

**YOUR TASK.** Write a follow-up e-mail or letter to an employer of your choice that does not offend the reader or damage your chances of employment.

## 14.22 Refusing to Take *No* for an Answer

After an excellent interview with Electronic Data Sources (or a company of your choice), you are disappointed to learn that someone else was hired. However, you really want to work for EDS.

**YOUR TASK.** Write a follow-up message to Ronald T. Ranson, Human Resources Development, Electronic Data Sources, 1328 Peachtree Plaza, Atlanta, GA 30314 (or a company of your choice). Indicate that you are disappointed but still interested.

## 14.23 Accepting a Job Offer

Your dream has come true: you have just been offered an excellent position. Although you accepted the position on the phone, you want to send a formal acceptance letter.

**YOUR TASK.** Write a job acceptance letter to an employer of your choice. Include the specific job title, your starting date, and details about your compensation package. Make up any necessary details.

## 14.24 Evaluating Your Course

Your boss has paid your tuition for this course. As you complete the course, he or she asks you for a letter about your experience in the course.

**YOUR TASK.** Write a letter to a boss in a real or imaginary organization explaining how this course made you more valuable to the organization.

# GRAMMAR/MECHANICS CHECKUP—14

## Total Review

This exercise reviews all of the guidelines in the Grammar/Mechanics Handbook as well as the lists of Confusing Words and Frequently Misspelled Words. Use proofreading marks to correct capitalization, number expression, grammar, punctuation, and spelling in the following sentences. When you finish, compare your responses with those at the end of the book.

**EXAMPLE** The board ~~have~~ *has* voted to give all employee*'s* retroactive pay ~~rises~~ *raises*.

1. In the Fall each of the companys plan to increase it's hiring.

2. Our accounting department processed expense claims for Ryan and I, but Ryans was lost.

3. The Marketing Manager assigned Jennifer and I the best 2 new sales territorys.

4. The telephone has rang at least 3 times with the same incredibal recorded message.

5. 3 types of similar storms' of the tropics are: cyclones, typhoons and hurricanes.

6. Its to early to determine whether we'll make a profit before September 15th.

7. If I was her I would pay off the principal of the loan immediatly.

8. German shoppers generally bring there own bags for grocerys, therefore they were unaccustomed to Walmarts bagging techniques.

9. Mary Beth Merrin, a Professor at the University, asked that research reports contain the following sections, Introduction, body, summary, and bibliography.

10. If we had saw the senders invoice we would have payed it quick.

11. When convenent will you please send me 4 copys of that vendors most recent contract?

12. Do you think Jacob and him placed they're report on the boss desk last night.

13. About 1/2 of Pizza Huts eight thousand outlets will make deliverys, the others focuses on walk in customers.

14. Every thing accept labor and parts is covered in you're five year warranty.

15. When Kerry completes her degree she plans to apply for employment in: Scottsdale, Dallas or Atlanta.

# EDITING CHALLENGE—14

To fine-tune your grammar and mechanics skills, in every chapter you have been editing a message. This interview follow-up letter has problems with wordiness, number usage, capitalization, spelling, proofreading, and other writing techniques. Study the guidelines in the Grammar/Mechanics Handbook as well as the lists of Confusing Words and Frequently Misspelled Words to sharpen your skills.

**YOUR TASK.** Edit the following message (a) by correcting errors in your textbook or on a photocopy using proofreading marks from Appendix A or (b) by downloading the message from **www.cengagebrain.com** and correcting at your computer. Your instructor may show you a possible solution.

291 Green Avenue
Columbus, OH 43207
June 17, 2016

Ms. Karen Dermott
Upper Arlington Agency
439 Marble Cliff Drive
Columbus, OH 43310

Dear Ms. Dermott:

It was extremely enjoyable to talk with you on thursday about the Assistant Account Manager position at the Upper Arlington Agency. The position as you presented it seems to be a excelent match for my training and skills. The creative approach to Account Management that you described, confirmed my desire to work in a imaginative firm such as the Upper Arlington Agency.

In addition to an enthusiastic attitude I would bring to the position strong communication skills, and the ability to encourage others to work cooperatively within the department. My Graphic Arts training and experience will help me work with staff artists, and provide me with a understanding of the visual aspects of you work.

I certainly understand your departments need for strong support in the administrative area. My attention to detail and my organizational skills will help to free you to deal with more pressing issues in the management area. Despite the fact that it was on my résumé I neglected to emphasize during our interview that I had worked for 2 summers as a temporary office worker. This experience helped me to develop administrative support and clerical skills as well as to understand the every day demands of a busy office.

Thanks for taking the time to interview me, and explain the goals of your agency along with the dutys of this position. As I mentioned during the interview I am very interested in working for the Upper Arlingtin agency, and look forward to hearing from you about this position. In the event that you might possibly need additional information from me or facts about me, all you need to do is shoot me an e-mail at ddenova@buckeye.com.

Sincerely,

*Darcy Denova*

Darcy Denova

## COMMUNICATION WORKSHOP

### CAREER SKILLS

## Let's Talk Money: Negotiating a Salary

Does the idea of negotiating a salary scare you? If yes, you are hardly alone. Recent graduates generally don't have much bargaining leverage when pursuing entry-level positions. However, it does not hurt to try if you bring some special expertise or experience to the table.[39] If you have proved your worth throughout the interview process, employers may want to negotiate with you. To discuss compensation effectively, though, you must be prepared for salary questions, and you should know what you are worth. You also need to know basic negotiation strategies. As negotiation expert Chester L. Karrass said, "In business, you don't get what you deserve, you get what you negotiate."[40] The following negotiating rules, recommended by career experts, can guide you to a better beginning salary.[41]

### Rule No. 1: Avoid discussing salary for as long as possible in the interview process.

The longer you delay salary discussion, the more time you will have to convince the employer that you are worth what you are asking for. Ideally, you should try to avoid discussing salary until you know for sure that the interviewing company is making a job offer. The best time for you to negotiate your salary is between the time you are offered the position and the time you accept it. Wait for the employer to bring salary up first. If salary comes up and you are not sure whether the job is being offered to you, it is time for you to be blunt. Here are some things you could say:

*Are you making me a job offer?*

*What is your salary range for positions with similar requirements?*

*I'm very interested in the position, and my salary would be negotiable.*

*Tell me what you have in mind for the salary range.*

### Rule No. 2: Know in advance the probable salary range for similar jobs in similar organizations.

Many job-search websites provide salary information. One of the best sources for salary and other candid insider information is Glassdoor. It allows you to search by region, so you know what similar jobs are paying in your area. The important thing here is to think in terms of a wide salary range. Let's say you are hoping to start at between $46,000 and $50,000. To an interviewer, you might say, *I was looking for a salary in the high forties to the low fifties*. This technique is called bracketing. In addition, stating your salary range in an annual dollar amount sounds more professional than asking for an hourly wage. Be sure to consider such things as geographic location, employer size, industry standards, the state of the economy, and other factors to make sure that the range you come up with is realistic.

### Rule No. 3: When negotiating, focus on what you are worth, not on what you need.

Throughout the interview and negotiation process, focus continually on your strengths. Make sure the employer knows everything of value that you will bring to the organization. You have to prove that you are worth what you are asking for. Employers pay salaries based on what you will accomplish on the job and contribute to the organization. When discussing your salary, focus on how the company will benefit from these contributions. Don't bring personal issues into the negotiation process. No employer will be willing to pay you more because you have bills to pay, mouths to feed, or debt to settle.

### Rule No. 4: Never say *no* to a job before it is offered.

Why would anyone refuse a job offer before it is made? It happens all the time. Let's say you were hoping for a salary of $45,000. The interviewer tells you that the salary scheduled for this job is $40,000. You respond, *Oh, that is out of the question!* Before you were offered the job, you have, in effect, refused it. Instead, wait for the job offer; then start negotiating your salary.

### Rule No. 5: Ask for a higher salary first, and consider benefits.

Within reason, always try to ask for a higher salary first. This will leave room for this amount to decrease during negotiations until it is closer to your original expectations. Remember to consider the entire compensation package when negotiating. You may be willing to accept a lower salary if benefits such as insurance, flexible hours, time off, and retirement are attractive.

### Rule No. 6: Be ready to bargain if offered a low starting salary.

Companies are often willing to pay more for someone who interviews well and fits their culture. If the company seems right to you and you are pleased with the sound of the open position but you have been offered a low salary, say, *That is somewhat lower than I had hoped, but this position does sound exciting. If I were to consider this, what sorts of things could I do to quickly become more valuable to this organization?* Also discuss such factors as bonuses based on performance or a shorter review period. You could say something like, *Thanks for the offer. The position is very much what I wanted in many ways, and I am delighted at your interest. If I start at this salary, may I be reviewed within six months with the goal of raising the salary to _____?*

Another possibility is to ask for more time to think about the low offer. Tell the interviewer that this is an important decision and you need some time to consider the offer. The next day you can call and say, *I am flattered by your offer, but I cannot accept because the salary is lower than I would like. Perhaps you could reconsider your offer or keep me in mind for future openings.*

## Rule No. 7: Be honest.

Be honest throughout the entire negotiation process. Don't inflate the salaries of your previous positions to try to get more money. Don't tell an employer that you have received other job offers unless it is true. These lies can be grounds for being fired later on.

## Rule No. 8: Get the final offer in writing.

Once you have agreed on a salary and compensation package, get the offer in writing. You should also follow up with a position acceptance message—letter or e-mail—as discussed earlier in the chapter.

**CAREER APPLICATION.** You have just passed the screening interview and have been asked to come in for a personal interview with the human resources representative and the hiring manager of a company where you are very eager to work. Although you are delighted with the company, you have promised yourself that you will not accept any position that pays less than $50,000 to start.

**YOUR TASK.** With a partner, role-play the positions of interviewer and interviewee. The interviewer sets the scene by discussing preliminaries and offers a salary of $46,500. The interviewee responds to preliminary questions and to the salary offer. Then, reverse roles and repeat the scenario.

# ENDNOTES

[1] Zacharias, Y. (2013 November 30). So, on a scale of one to 10 . . . ; Online multiple-choice questionnaire is the hot new tool for screening job applicants. *The Vancouver Sun*. Retrieved from http://global-factiva.com

[2] Pofeldt, E. (2013, September). Ace your next interview. *Money*, p. 1. Retrieved from http://search.ebscohost.com

[3] Ziebarth, B. (2009, December 10). Tips to ace your panel job interview. Associated Content, Inc. Retrieved from http://voices.yahoo.com/tips-ace-panel-job-interview-5036880.html

[4] Reynolds Lewis, K. (2011, July 6). Group interview or cattle call? *Fortune*/CNNMoney. Retrieved from http://management.fortune.cnn.com/2011/07/06/group-job-interview-or-cattle-call

[5] Crisante, D. (2009, June 15). How to succeed in a group interview. CareerFAQs. Retrieved from http://www.careerfaqs.com.au/job-interview-tips/1116/How-to-succeed-in-a-group-interview

[6] Weiss, T. (2009, May 12). Going on the second interview. *Forbes*. Retrieved from http://www.forbes.com/2009/05/12/second-interview-advice-leadership-careers-basics.html

[7] Hansen, R. (2010). Situational interviews and stress interviews: What to make of them and how to succeed in them. Quintessential Careers. Retrieved from http://www.quintcareers.com/situational_stress_interviews.html

[8] Breslin, S. (2011, November 25). 7 weird job tips. Retrieved from http://www.forbes.com/sites/susannahbreslin/2012/11/25/7-weird-job-interview-tips

[9] Gold, T. (2010, November 28). How social media can get you a job. Marketing Trenches. Retrieved from http://www.marketingtrenches.com/marketing-careers/how-social-media-can-get-you-a-job

[10] Photo essay based on Green, A. (2013, September 30). Why employers won't name a salary range first. U.S. News & World Report. Retrieved from http://money.usnews.com/money/blogs/outside-voices-careers/2013/09/30/why-employers-wont-name-a-salary-range-first

[11] Ryan, L. (2007, May 6). Job seekers: Prepare your stories. Ezine Articles. Retrieved from http://practicaljobsearchadvice.blogspot.com/2007/05/job-seekers-prepare-your-stories.html

[12] Carniol, A. (2013, January 6). How to tell your story in job interviews. Mashable. Retrieved from http://mashable.com/2013/01/06/tips-job-interviews

[13] Haefner, R. (2009, June 10). More employers screening candidates via social networking sites. CareerBuilder. Retrieved from http://www.careerbuilder.com/Article/CB-1337-Getting-Hired-More-Employers-Screening-Candidates-via-Social-Networking-Sites

[14] Lynch, B. (2010, January 28). Online reputation in a connected world. [Presentation]. Data Privacy Day. Retrieved from http://www.microsoft.com

[15] Haefner, R. (2009, June 10). More employers screening candidates via social networking sites. CareerBuilder. Retrieved from http://www.careerbuilder.com/Article/CB-1337-Getting-Hired-More-Employers-Screening-Candidates-via-Social-Networking-Sites

[16] Finder, A. (2006, June 11). For some, online persona undermines a résumé. *The New York Times*. Retrieved from http://www.nytimes.com/2006/06/11/us/11recruit.html?_r=1&scp=1&sq=For%20some,%20online%20persona%20undermines&st=cse&oref=slogin

[17] Haefner, R. (2009, June 10). More employers screening candidates via social networking sites. CareerBuilder. Retrieved from http://www.careerbuilder.com/Article/CB-1337-Getting-Hired-More-Employers-Screening-Candidates-via-Social-Networking-Sites/

[18] Active listening for interview success: How your ears can help you land the job. (n.d.). Hcareers.com. Retrieved from http://www.hcareers.com/us/resourcecenter/tabid/306/articleid/250/default.aspx

[19] Korkki, P. (2009, September 13). Subtle cues can tell an interviewer "pick me." *The New York Times*. Retrieved from http://www.nytimes.com

[20] Susan L. Hodas cited in Korkki, P. (2009, September 13). Subtle cues can tell an interviewer "pick me." *The New York Times*. Retrieved from http://www.nytimes.com

[21] Tyrell-Smith, T. (2011, January 25). Tell a story that will get you hired. *Money/U.S. News & World Report*. Retrieved from http://money.usnews.com/money/blogs/outside-voices-careers/2011/01/25/tell-a-story-that-will-get-you-hired

[22] The U.S. Equal Employment Opportunity Commission. (2009, November 21). Federal laws prohibiting job discrimination: Questions and Answers. Retrieved from http://www.eeoc.gov/facts/qanda.html

[23] Lucas, S. (2012, February 29). When illegal interview questions are legal. CBS Moneywatch. Retrieved from http://www.cbsnews.com/news/when-illegal-interview-questions-are-legal

[24] Ibid.; 30 interview questions you can't ask and 30 sneaky, legal alternatives to get the same info. (2007, November 15). *HR World*. Retrieved from http://www.hrworld.com/features/30-interview-questions-111507

[25] Ibid.

[26] Quast, L. (2013, August 26). Job seekers: No, the interview thank you note is not dead. *Forbes*. Retrieved from http://www.forbes.com/sites/lisaquast/2013/08/26/job-seekers-no-the-interview-thank-you-note-is-not-dead; Lublin, J. S. (2008, February 5). Notes to interviewers should go beyond a simple thank you. *The Wall Street Journal*, p. B1. Retrieved from http://proquest.umi.com

[27] Ibid.

[28] Korkki, P. (2009, September 13). Subtle cues can tell an interviewer "pick me." *The New York Times*. Retrieved from http://www.nytimes.com

[29] Quast, L. (2013, August 26). Job seekers: No, the interview thank you note is not dead. *Forbes*. Retrieved from http://www.forbes.com/sites/lisaquast/2013/08/26/job-seekers-no-the-interview-thank-you-note-is-not-dead

[30] Olson, L. (2010, September 16). Why you should never skip the interview thank-you note. *Money/U.S. News & World Report*. Retrieved from http://money.usnews.com/money/blogs/outside-voices-careers/2010/09/16/why-you-should-always-send-an-interview-thankyou-note; Needleman, S. E. (2006, February 7). Be prepared when opportunity calls. *The Wall Street Journal*, p. B4.

[31] Green, A. (2010, December 27). How to follow up after applying for a job. *Money/U.S. News & World Report*. Retrieved from http://money.usnews.com/money/blogs/outside-voices-careers/2010/12/27/how-to-follow-up-after-applying-for-a-job

[32] Korkki, P. (2009, August 23). No response after an interview? What to do. *The New York Times*. Retrieved from http://www.nytimes.com.

[33] Photo essay based on Smith, G. (2012, March 14). Why I am leaving Goldman Sachs. The New York Times. Retrieved from http://www.nytimes.com/2012/03/14/opinion/why-i-am-leaving-goldman-sachs.html

[34] Zacharias, Y. (2013, November 30). So, on a scale of one to 10 . . . ; Online multiple-choice questionnaire is the hot new tool for screening job applications. *The Vancouver Sun*, p. D3. Retrieved from http://www.vancouversun.com/business/scale/9232136/story.html

[35] Bell, M. (2011, July 15). More employers using firms that check applicants' social media history. *The Washington Post*. Retrieved from http://www.washingtonpost.com/lifestyle/style/more-employers-using-firms-that-check-applicants-social-media-history/2011/07/12/gIQAxnJYGI_story.html

[36] Fayerman, P. (2013, July 5). Social media sinks job prospects for many applicants: CareerBuilder study. *The Vancouver Sun*. Retrieved from http://blogs.vancouversun.com/2013/07/05/social-media-sinks-job-prospects-for-many-applicants-careerbuilder-study

[37] Giang, V., & Guey, L. (2013, May 8). Warren Buffett shared some great career advice for millennials. Business Insider. Retrieved from http://www.businessinsider.com/warren-buffett-becomes-a-mentor-to-young-women-2013-5#ixzz2XCWLDCaF

[38] Soft skills test. (n.d.). Retrieved from http://www.everythingsoftskills.com/resource/testsquizzes

[39] Vogt, P. (n. d.). Entry-level salary (probably) isn't as negotiable as you think. Monster.com. Retrieved from http://career-advice.monster.com/salary-benefits/negotiation-tips/entry-level-salary-negotiable/article.aspx

[40] About Karrass: The Karrass Story. (n.d.). Retrieved from https://www.karrass.com/why-karrass

[41] Malhotra, D. (2014, April). 15 rules for negotiating a job offer. *Harvard Business Review*. Retrieved from http://hbr.org/2014/04/15-rules-for-negotiating-a-job-offer/ar/3; Boardman, J. (n.d.). Know what you're worth BEFORE your salary negotiation. CBsalary.com. Retrieved from http://www.cbsalary.com; Dawson, R. (2006). *Secrets of power salary negotiating*. Franklin Lakes, NJ: Career Press, pp. 117–125; Hansen, R. S. (n.d.). Job offer too low? Use these key salary negotiation techniques to write a counter proposal letter. Quintessential Careers. Retrieved from http://www.quintcareers.com/salary_counter_proposal.html; Hansen, R. S. (n.d.). Salary negotiation do's and don'ts for job-seekers. Quintessential Careers. Retrieved from http://www.quintcareers.com/salary-dos-donts.html; Ireland, S. (n.d.). Salary negotiation skills. Retrieved from http://susanireland.com/salarywork.html; Powell, J. (n.d.). Salary negotiation: The art of the deal. Resume-Resource. Retrieved from http://www.resume-resource.com/article16.html

# ACKNOWLEDGMENTS

**p. 475** Office Insider based on Reynolds Lewis, K. (2011, July 6). Group interview or cattle call? *Fortune*/CNNMoney. Retrieved from http://management.fortune.cnn.com/2011/07/06/group-job-interview-or-cattle-call

**p. 479** Office Insider based on Green, A. (2011, February 7). How to prepare for a job interview. *Money/U.S. News & World Report*. Retrieved from http://money.usnews.com/money/blogs/outside-voices-careers/2011/02/07/how-to-prepare-for-a-job-interview

**p. 480** Office Insider based on McIntosh, B. (2013, April 30). How to ace an interview with job success stories. Retrieved from http://www.biospace.com/News/how-to-ace-an-interview-with-job-success-stories/294802

**p. 481** Office Insider based on Zupek, R. (2009, October 12). "Digital dirt" can haunt your job search. CNN.com. Retrieved from http://edition.cnn.com/2009/LIVING/worklife/10/24/cb.digital.trail.job.search/index.html

**p. 483** Office Insider based on Martin, C. (2001). *Interview fitness training*. San Ramon, CA: Interview Publishing.

**p. 486** Office Insider based on Welch, J., & Welch, S. (2008, July 7). Hiring is hard work. *Businessweek*, p. 80.

**p. 492** Office Insider based on Foss, J. (2012, May 12). 4 non-annoying ways to follow up after an interview. *Forbes*. Retrieved from http://www.forbes.com/sites/dailymuse/2012/05/30/4-non-annoying-ways-to-follow-up-after-an-interview/2

**p. 495** Office Insider based on Ford, S. (2012, March 7). The 10 biggest mistakes when leaving your job. Retrieved from http://www.oipartners.net/news-detail/12-03-07/The_10_Biggest_Mistakes_When_Leaving_Your_Job.aspx

# Appendix A: Correction Symbols and Proofreading Marks

In marking your papers, your instructor may use the following symbols or abbreviations to indicate writing weaknesses. Studying these symbols and suggestions will help you understand your instructor's remarks. Knowing this information can also help you evaluate and improve your own memos, e-mails, letters, reports, and other writing. These symbols are keyed to your Grammar/Mechanics Handbook and to the text.

| | |
|---|---|
| **Adj** | Hyphenate two or more adjectives that are joined to create a compound modifier before a noun. See G/M 1.17e. |
| **Adv** | Use adverbs, not adjectives, to describe or limit the action. See G/M 1.17d. |
| **Apos** | Use apostrophes to show possession. See G/M 2.20–2.22. |
| **Assgn** | Follow the assignment instructions. |
| **Awk** | Recast to avoid awkward expression. |
| **Bias** | Use inclusive, bias-free language. See Chapter 2, page 50. |
| **Cap** | Use capitalization appropriately. See G/M 3.01–3.16. |
| **CmConj** | Use a comma before the coordinating conjunction in a compound sentence. See G/M 2.05. |
| **CmDate** | Use commas appropriately in dates, addresses, geographical names, degrees, and long numbers. See G/M 2.04. |
| **CmIn** | Use commas to set off internal sentence interrupters. See G/M 2.06c. |
| **CmIntr** | Use commas to separate introductory clauses and certain phrases from independent clauses. See G/M 2.06. |
| **CmSer** | Use commas to separate three or more items (words, phrases, or short clauses) in a series. See G/M 2.01. |
| **Coh** | Improve coherence between ideas. Repeat key ideas, use pronouns, or use transitional expressions. See Chapter 3, pages 75–76. |
| **Cl** | Improve the clarity of ideas or expression so that the point is better understood. |
| **CS** | Avoid comma-splice sentences. Do not use a comma to splice (join) two independent clauses. See Chapter 3, page 70. |
| **CmUn** | Avoid unnecessary commas. See G/M 2.15. |
| **:** | Use a colon after a complete thought that introduces a list of items. Use a colon in business letter salutations and to introduce long quotations. See G/M 2.17–2.19. |
| **Direct** | Use the direct strategy by emphasizing the main idea. See Chapter 3, pages 66–68. |
| **Dash** | Use a dash to set off parenthetical elements, to emphasize sentence interruptions, or to separate an introductory list from a summarizing statement. See G/M 2.26. |
| **DM** | Avoid dangling modifiers by placing modifiers close to the words they describe or limit. See Chapter 3, page 74. |

| | |
|---|---|
| Filler | Avoid fillers such as *there are* or long lead-ins such as *this is to inform you that*. See Chapter 4, page 92. |
| Format | Choose an appropriate format for this document. |
| Frag | Avoid fragments by expressing ideas in complete sentences. A fragment is a broken-off part of a sentence. See Chapter 3, page 70. |
| GH | Use graphic highlighting (bullets, lists, indentions, or headings) to enhance readability. See Chapter 4, pages 100–101. |
| MM | Avoid misplaced modifiers by placing modifiers close to the words they describe or limit. See Chapter 3, page 74. |
| Num | Use number or word form appropriately. See G/M 4.01–4.13. |
| Ob | Avoid stating the obvious. |
| Org | Improve organization by grouping similar ideas. |
| Par | Express ideas in parallel form. See Chapter 3, pages 73–74. |
| Paren | Use parentheses to set off nonessential sentence elements such as explanations, directions, questions, or references. See G/M 2.27. |
| Period | Use one period to end a statement, command, indirect question, or polite request. See G/M 2.23. |
| Pos | Express an idea positively rather than negatively. See Chapter 2, page 47. |
| PosPro | Use possessive-case pronouns to show ownership. See G/M 1.07 and 1.08d. |
| Pro | Use nominative-case pronouns as subjects of verbs and as subject complements. Use objective-case pronouns as objects of prepositions and verbs. See G/M 1.07 and 1.08. |
| ProAgr | Make pronouns agree in number and gender with the words to which they refer (their antecedents). See G/M 1.09. |
| ProVag | Be sure that pronouns such as *it, which, this,* and *that* refer to clear antecedents. |
| ? | Use a question mark after a direct question and after statements with questions appended. See G/M 2.24. |
| Quo | Use quotation marks to enclose the exact words of a speaker or writer; to distinguish words used in a special sense; or to enclose titles of articles, chapters, or other short works. See G/M 2.28. |
| Redun | Avoid expressions that repeat meaning or include unnecessary words. See Chapter 4, page 93. |
| RunOn | Avoid run-on (fused) sentences. A sentence with two independent clauses must be joined by a coordinating conjunctions (*and, or, nor, but*) or by a semicolon (;). See Chapter 3, page 70. |
| Sp | Check misspelled words. |
| Self | Use *self*-ending pronouns only when they refer to previously mentioned nouns or pronouns. See G/M 1.08h. |
| ; | Use a semicolon to join closely related independent clauses. A semicolon is also an option to join separate items in a series when one or more of the items contain internal commas. See G/M 2.16. |
| Shift | Avoid a confusing shift in verb tense, mood, or voice. See G/M 1.15c. |
| Trans | Use an appropriate transition. See Chapter 3, page 76. |
| Tone | Use a conversational, positive, and courteous tone that promotes goodwill. See Chapter 2, page 47. |
| You | Focus on developing the "you" view. See Chapter 2, page 45. |

**VbAgr**     Make verbs agree with subjects. See G/M 1.10.
**VbMood**   Use the subjunctive mood to express hypothetical (untrue) ideas. See G/M 1.12.
**VbTnse**   Use present-tense, past-tense, and part-participle forms correctly. See G/M 1.13.
**VbVce**    Use active- and passive-voice verbs appropriately. See G/M 1.11.
**WC**       Focus on precise word choice. See Chapter 4, page 98.
**Wordy**    Avoid wordiness including flabby expressions, long lead-ins, unnecessary *there is/are* fillers, redundancies, and trite business phrases. See Chapter 4, pages 91–94.

## Proofreading Marks

| Proofreading Mark | Draft Copy | Final Copy |
|---|---|---|
| ⌒ Align horizontally | TO: Rick Munoz | TO: Rick Munoz |
| ‖ Align vertically | 166.32<br>132.45 | 166.32<br>132.45 |
| ≡ Capitalize | Coca-cola<br>sending a pdf file | Coca-Cola<br>sending a PDF file |
| ⌒ Close up space | meeting at 3 p. m. | meeting at 3 p.m. |
| ][ Center | ]Recommendations[ | Recommendations |
| ⌿ Delete | in my final judgement | in my judgment |
| ∨ Insert apostrophe | our companys product | our company's product |
| ∧ Insert comma | you will of course | you will, of course, |
| = / ∧ Insert hyphen | tax free income | tax-free income |
| ⊙ Insert period | Ms Holly Hines | Ms. Holly Hines |
| ⌄⌄ Insert quotation mark | shareholders receive a bonus. | shareholders receive a "bonus." |
| # Insert space | wordprocessing program | word processing program |
| / Lowercase (remove capitals) | the Vice President<br>HUMAN RESOURCES | the vice president<br>Human Resources |
| ⊏ Move to left | ⊏I. Labor costs | I. Labor costs |
| ⊐ Move to right | A. Findings of study ⊐ |    A. Findings of study |
| ◯ Spell out | aimed at 2 depts | aimed at two departments |
| ¶ Start new paragraph | ¶Keep the screen height of your computer at eye level. | Keep the screen height of your computer at eye level. |
| ..... Stet (don't delete) | officials talked openly | officials talked openly |
| ∼ Transpose | accounts recievable | accounts receivable |
| bf Use boldface | Conclusions bf | **Conclusions** |
| ital Use italics | The Perfect Résumé ital | *The Perfect Résumé* |

Appendix A: Correction Symbols and Proofreading Marks

# Appendix B: Document Format Guide

Business communicators produce numerous documents that have standardized formats. Becoming familiar with these formats is important because business documents actually carry two kinds of messages. Verbal messages are conveyed by the words chosen to express the writer's ideas. Nonverbal messages are conveyed largely by the appearance of a document and its adherence to recognized formats. To ensure that your documents carry favorable nonverbal messages about you and your organization, you will want to give special attention to the appearance and formatting of your e-mails, letters, envelopes, and fax cover sheets.

## E-Mail

E-mail continues to be a primary communication channel in the workplace. Chapter 5 presents guidelines for preparing e-mails. This section provides additional information on formats and usage. The following suggestions, illustrated in Figure B.1 and also in Figure 5.1 on page 124, may guide you in setting up the parts of any e-mail. Always check, however, with your organization to ensure that you follow its practices.

***To* Line.** Include the receiver's e-mail address after *To*. If the receiver's address is recorded in your address book, you just have to click it. Be sure to enter all addresses very carefully since one mistyped letter prevents delivery.

***From* Line.** Most mail programs automatically include your name and e-mail address after *From*.

**Figure B.1 Typical E-Mail**

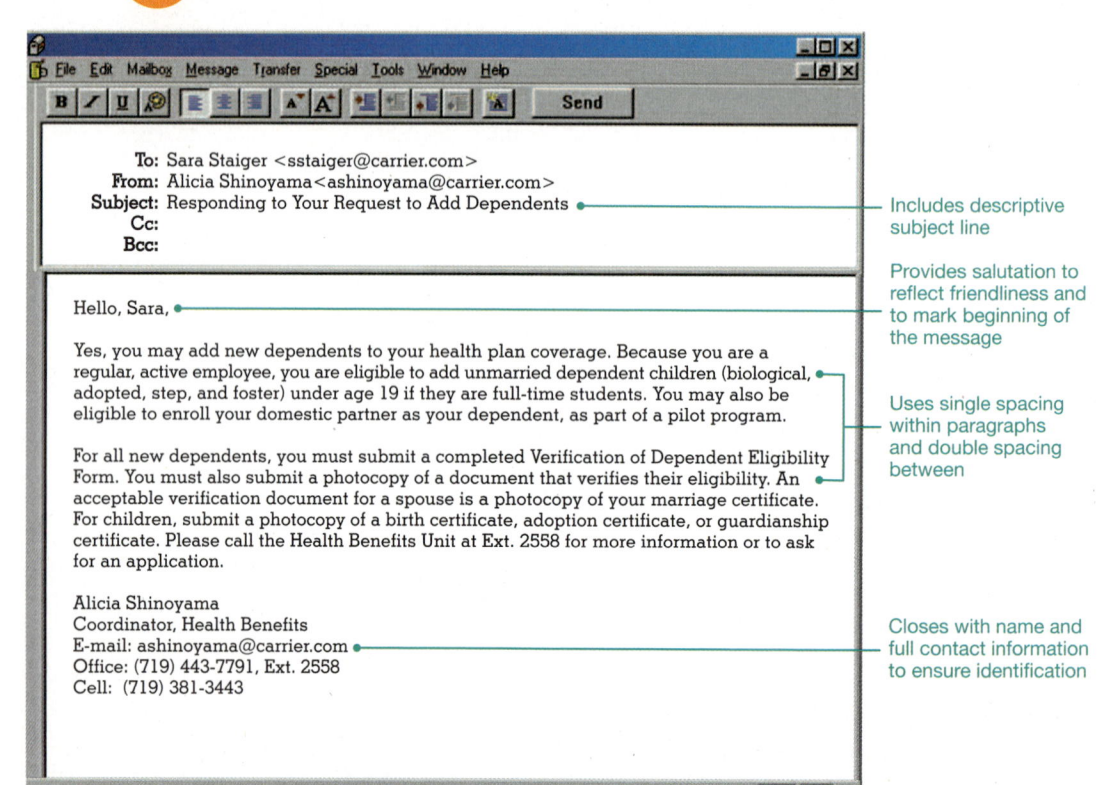

```
To:       Sara Staiger <sstaiger@carrier.com>
From:     Alicia Shinoyama <ashinoyama@carrier.com>
Subject:  Responding to Your Request to Add Dependents
Cc:
Bcc:

Hello, Sara,

Yes, you may add new dependents to your health plan coverage. Because you are a
regular, active employee, you are eligible to add unmarried dependent children (biological,
adopted, step, and foster) under age 19 if they are full-time students. You may also be
eligible to enroll your domestic partner as your dependent, as part of a pilot program.

For all new dependents, you must submit a completed Verification of Dependent Eligibility
Form. You must also submit a photocopy of a document that verifies their eligibility. An
acceptable verification document for a spouse is a photocopy of your marriage certificate.
For children, submit a photocopy of a birth certificate, adoption certificate, or guardianship
certificate. Please call the Health Benefits Unit at Ext. 2558 for more information or to ask
for an application.

Alicia Shinoyama
Coordinator, Health Benefits
E-mail: ashinoyama@carrier.com
Office: (719) 443-7791, Ext. 2558
Cell:   (719) 381-3443
```

- Includes descriptive subject line
- Provides salutation to reflect friendliness and to mark beginning of the message
- Uses single spacing within paragraphs and double spacing between
- Closes with name and full contact information to ensure identification

***Cc* and *Bcc*.** Insert the e-mail address of anyone who is to receive a copy of the message. *Cc* stands for "carbon copy" or "courtesy copy." Don't be tempted, though, to send needless copies just because it is easy. *Bcc* stands for "blind carbon copy." Some writers use *bcc* to send a copy of the message without the addressee's knowledge. Writers also use the *bcc* line for mailing lists. When a message is sent to a number of people and their e-mail addresses should not be revealed, the *bcc* line works well to conceal the names and addresses of all receivers.

**Subject.** Identify the subject of the e-mail with a brief but descriptive summary of the topic. Be sure to include enough information to be clear and compelling. Capitalize the initial letters of main words. Main words are all words except (a) the articles *a*, *an*, and *the*; (b) prepositions containing two or three letters (such as *at*, *to*, *on*, *by*, *for*); (c) the word *to* in an infinitive (*to work*, *to write*); and (d) the word *as*—unless any of these words are the first or last word in the subject line.

**Salutation.** Include a brief greeting, if you like. Some writers use a salutation such as *Dear Sara* followed by a comma or a colon. Others are more informal with *Hi, Sara; Hello, Sara; Good morning*; or *Greetings*.

**Message.** Ideally, cover just one topic in your message, and try to keep your total message under three screens in length. Single-space and be sure to use both upper- and lowercase letters. Double-space between paragraphs.

**Closing.** Conclude an e-mail, if you like, with *Cheers, Best wishes*, or *Warm regards*, followed by your name and complete contact information. Some people omit their e-mail address because they think it is provided automatically. However, programs and routers do not always transmit the address. Therefore, always include it along with other identifying information in the closing.

**Attachment.** Use the attachment window or button to select the path and file name of any file you wish to send with your e-mail. You can also attach a Web page to your message.

## Business Letters

Business communicators write business letters primarily to correspond with people outside the organization. Letters may go to customers, vendors, other businesses, and the government, as discussed in Chapters 6, 7, and 8. The following information will help you format your letters following conventional guidelines.

### Conventional Letter Placement, Margins, and Line Spacing

To set up business letters using conventional guidelines, follow these guidelines:

- For a clean look, choose a sans serif font such as Arial, Calibri, Tahoma, or Verdana. For a more traditional look, choose a serif font such as Times New Roman. Use a 10-point, 11-point, or 12-point size.
- Use a 2-inch top margin for the first page of a letter printed on letterhead stationery. This places the date on line 12 or 13. Use a 1-inch top margin for second and succeeding pages.
- Justify only the left margin. Set the line spacing to single.
- Choose side margins according to the length of your letter. Set 1.5-inch margins for short letters (under 200 words) and 1-inch margins for longer letters (200 or more words).
- Leave from two to ten blank lines following the date to balance the message on the page. You can make this adjustment after keying your message.

## Formatting Letters With Microsoft Word 2007, 2010, and 2013

If you are working with Microsoft Word 2007, 2010, or 2013, the default margins are set at 1 inch and the default font is 11-point Calibri. The default setting for line spacing is 1.15, and the paragraph default is 10 points of blank space following each paragraph or each tap of the Enter key. Many letter writers find this extra space excessive, especially after parts of the letter that are normally single-spaced. The model documents in this book show conventional single-spacing with one blank line between paragraphs.

To format your documents with conventional spacing and yet retain a clean look, change the Microsoft defaults to the following: Arial font set for 11 points, line spacing at 1.0, and spacing before and after paragraphs at 0.

## Spacing and Punctuation

For some time typists left two spaces after end punctuation (periods, question marks, and so forth). This practice was necessary, it was thought, because typewriters did not have proportional spacing and sentences were easier to read when two spaces separated them. Professional typesetters, however, never followed this practice because they used proportional spacing, and readability was not a problem. Influenced by the look of typeset publications, many writers now leave only one space after end punctuation. As a practical matter, however, it is not wrong to use two spaces.

## Business Letter Parts

Professional-looking business letters are arranged in a conventional sequence with standard parts. Following is a discussion of how to use these letter parts properly. Figure B.2 illustrates the parts of a block style letter. See Chapter 6 for additional discussion of letters and their parts.

**Letterhead.** Most business organizations use 8½ × 11-inch paper printed with a letterhead displaying their official name, street address, Web address, e-mail address, and telephone and fax numbers. The letterhead may also include a logo and an advertising message.

**Dateline.** On letterhead paper you should place the date one blank line below the last line of the letterhead or 2 inches from the top edge of the paper (line 12 or 13). On plain paper place the date immediately below your return address. Because the date goes on line 12 or 13, start the return address an appropriate number of lines above it. The most common dateline format is as follows: *June 9, 2016*. Don't use *th* (or *rd, nd* or *st*) when the date is written this way. For European or military correspondence, use the following dateline format: *9 June 2016*. Notice that no commas are used.

**Addressee and Delivery Notations.** Delivery notations such as *E-MAIL TRANS-MISSION, FEDEX, MESSENGER DELIVERY, CONFIDENTIAL,* or *CERTIFIED MAIL* are typed in all capital letters two blank lines above the inside address.

**Inside Address.** Type the inside address—that is, the address of the organization or person receiving the letter—single-spaced, starting at the left margin. The number of lines between the dateline and the inside address depends on the size of the letter body, the type size (point or pitch size), and the length of the typing lines. Generally, one to nine blank lines are appropriate.

Be careful to duplicate the exact wording and spelling of the recipient's name and address on your documents. Usually, you can copy this information from the letterhead of the correspondence you are answering. If, for example, you are responding to *Jackson & Perkins Company*, do not address your letter to *Jackson and Perkins Corp.*

Always be sure to include a courtesy title such as *Mr., Ms., Mrs., Dr.,* or *Professor* before a person's name in the inside address—for both the letter and the envelope. Although many women in business today favor *Ms.*, you should use whatever title the addressee prefers.

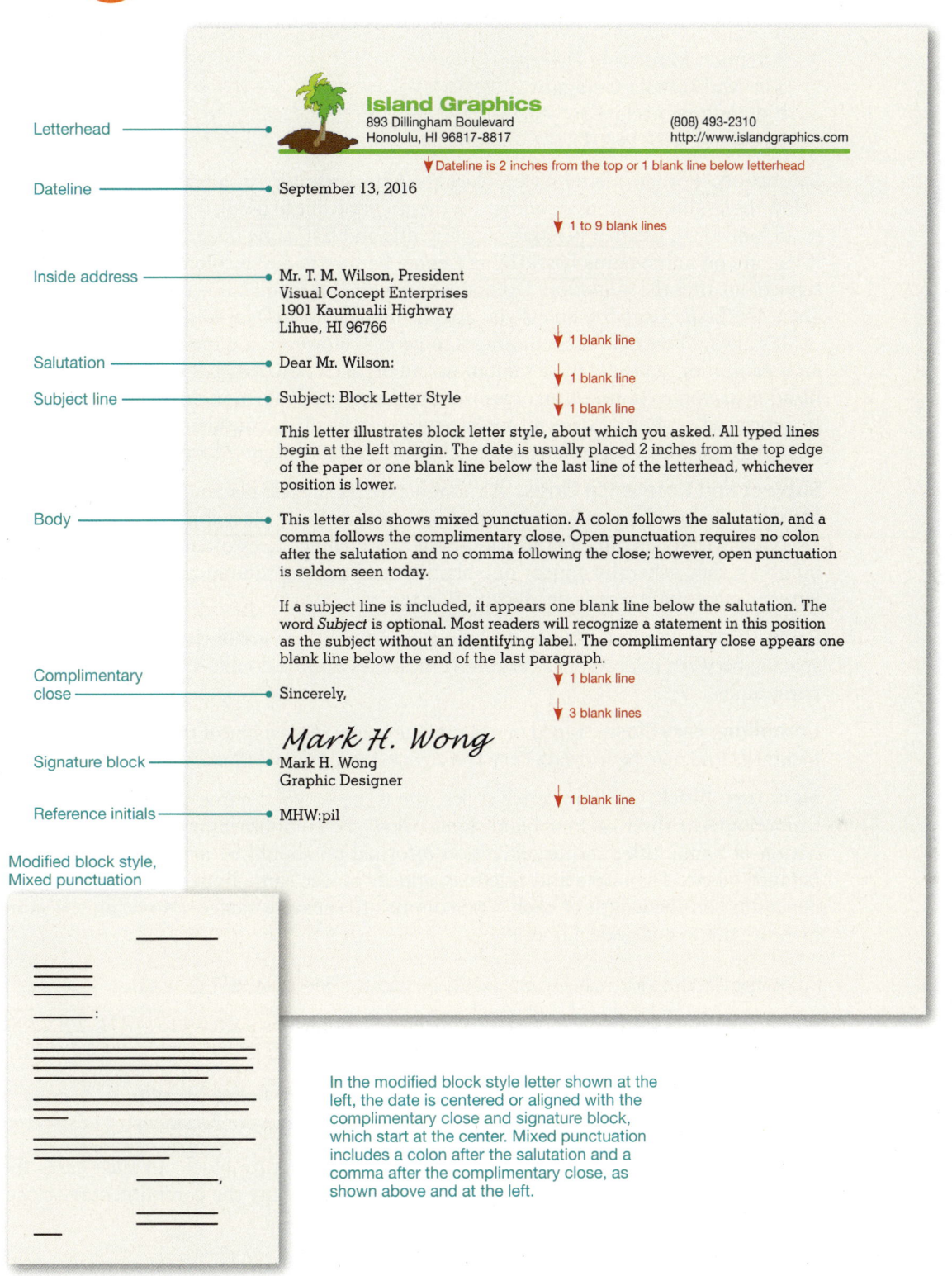

Figure B.2 Block and Modified Block Letter Styles

**Letterhead**

**Island Graphics**
893 Dillingham Boulevard
Honolulu, HI 96817-8817
(808) 493-2310
http://www.islandgraphics.com

▼ Dateline is 2 inches from the top or 1 blank line below letterhead

**Dateline** — September 13, 2016

▼ 1 to 9 blank lines

**Inside address** —
Mr. T. M. Wilson, President
Visual Concept Enterprises
1901 Kaumualii Highway
Lihue, HI 96766

▼ 1 blank line

**Salutation** — Dear Mr. Wilson:

▼ 1 blank line

**Subject line** — Subject: Block Letter Style

▼ 1 blank line

This letter illustrates block letter style, about which you asked. All typed lines begin at the left margin. The date is usually placed 2 inches from the top edge of the paper or one blank line below the last line of the letterhead, whichever position is lower.

**Body** — This letter also shows mixed punctuation. A colon follows the salutation, and a comma follows the complimentary close. Open punctuation requires no colon after the salutation and no comma following the close; however, open punctuation is seldom seen today.

If a subject line is included, it appears one blank line below the salutation. The word *Subject* is optional. Most readers will recognize a statement in this position as the subject without an identifying label. The complimentary close appears one blank line below the end of the last paragraph.

▼ 1 blank line

**Complimentary close** — Sincerely,

▼ 3 blank lines

*Mark H. Wong*

**Signature block** — Mark H. Wong
Graphic Designer

▼ 1 blank line

**Reference initials** — MHW:pil

**Modified block style, Mixed punctuation**

In the modified block style letter shown at the left, the date is centered or aligned with the complimentary close and signature block, which start at the center. Mixed punctuation includes a colon after the salutation and a comma after the complimentary close, as shown above and at the left.

In general, avoid abbreviations such as *Ave.* or *Co.* unless they appear in the printed letterhead of the document being answered.

**Attention Line.** An attention line allows you to send your message officially to an organization but to direct it to a specific individual, officer, or department.

However, if you know an individual's complete name, it is always better to use it as the first line of the inside address and avoid an attention line. Placing an attention line first in the address block enables you to paste it directly onto the envelope:

Attention Marketing Director
The MultiMedia Company
931 Calkins Avenue
Rochester, NY 14301

**Salutation.** For most letter styles, place the letter greeting, or salutation, one blank line below the last line of the inside address or the attention line (if used). If the letter is addressed to an individual, use that person's courtesy title and last name (*Dear Mr. Lanham*). Even if you are on a first-name basis (*Dear Leslie*), be sure to add a colon (not a comma or a semicolon) after the salutation. Do not use an individual's full name in the salutation (not *Dear Mr. Leslie Lanham*) unless you are unsure of gender (*Dear Leslie Lanham*).

It's always best to address messages to people. However, if a message is addressed to an organization, consider these salutations: an organization of men (*Gentlemen*), an organization of women (*Ladies*), an organization of men and women (*Ladies and Gentlemen*). If a message is addressed to an undetermined individual, consider these salutations: a woman (*Dear Madam*), a man (*Dear Sir*), a title (*Dear Customer Service Representative*).

**Subject and Reference Lines.** Although experts suggest placing the subject line one blank line below the salutation, many businesses actually place it above the salutation. Use whatever style your organization prefers. Reference lines often show policy or file numbers; they generally appear one blank line above the salutation. Use initial capital letters for the main words or all capital letters.

**Body.** Most business letters and memorandums are single-spaced, with double-spacing between paragraphs. Very short messages may be double-spaced with indented paragraphs.

**Complimentary Close.** Typed one blank line below the last line of the letter, the complimentary close may be formal (*Very truly yours*) or informal (*Sincerely* or *Cordially*).

**Signature Block.** In most letter styles, the writer's typed name and optional identification appear three or four blank lines below the complimentary close. The combination of name, title, and organization information should be arranged to achieve a balanced look. The name and title may appear on the same line or on separate lines, depending on the length of each. Use commas to separate categories within the same line, but not to conclude a line.

Sincerely yours,

Jeremy M. Wood, Manager
Technical Sales and Services

Cordially yours,

Casandra Baker-Murillo
Executive Vice President

Some organizations include their names in the signature block. In such cases the organization name appears in all caps one blank line below the complimentary close, as shown here:

Cordially,

LIPTON COMPUTER SERVICES

Shelina A. Simpson
Executive Assistant

**Reference Initials.** If used, the initials of the typist and writer are typed one blank line below the writer's name and title. Generally, the writer's initials are capitalized and the typist's are lowercased, but this format varies.

**Enclosure Notation.** When an enclosure or attachment accompanies a document, a notation to that effect appears one blank line below the reference initials. This notation reminds the typist to insert the enclosure in the envelope, and it reminds the recipient to look for the enclosure or attachment. The notation may be spelled out (*Enclosure, Attachment*), or it may be abbreviated (*Enc., Att.*). It may indicate the number of enclosures or attachments, and it may also identify a specific enclosure (*Enclosure: Form 1099*).

**Copy Notation.** If you make copies of correspondence for other individuals, you may use *cc* to indicate courtesy copy, *pc* to indicate photocopy, or merely *c* for any kind of copy. A colon following the initial(s) is optional.

**Second-Page Heading.** When a letter extends beyond one page, use plain paper of the same quality and color as the first page. Identify the second and succeeding pages with a heading consisting of the name of the addressee, the page number, and the date. Use the following format or the one shown in Figure B.3:

Ms. Sara Hendricks                    2                    May 3, 2016

Both headings appear six blank lines (1 inch) from the top edge of the paper followed by two blank lines to separate them from the continuing text. Avoid using a second page if you have only one line or the complimentary close and signature block to fill that page.

**Plain-Paper Return Address.** If you prepare a personal or business letter on plain paper, place your address immediately above the date. Do not include your name; you will type (and sign) your name at the end of your letter. If your return address

Figure B.3  Second-Page Heading

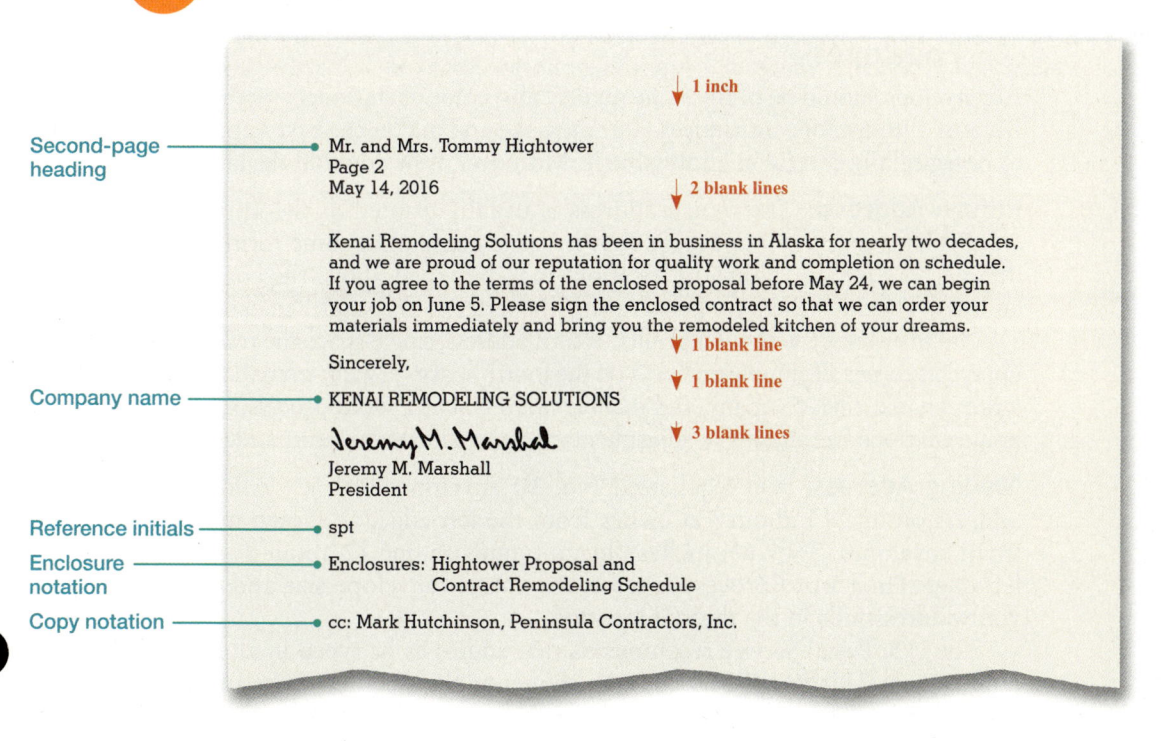

Second-page heading:
Mr. and Mrs. Tommy Hightower
Page 2
May 14, 2016

Kenai Remodeling Solutions has been in business in Alaska for nearly two decades, and we are proud of our reputation for quality work and completion on schedule. If you agree to the terms of the enclosed proposal before May 24, we can begin your job on June 5. Please sign the enclosed contract so that we can order your materials immediately and bring you the remodeled kitchen of your dreams.

Sincerely,

Company name: KENAI REMODELING SOLUTIONS

*Jeremy M. Marshall*
Jeremy M. Marshall
President

Reference initials: spt

Enclosure notation: Enclosures: Hightower Proposal and Contract Remodeling Schedule

Copy notation: cc: Mark Hutchinson, Peninsula Contractors, Inc.

contains two lines, begin typing so that the date appears 2 inches from the top. Avoid abbreviations except for a two-letter state abbreviation.

580 East Leffels Street<br>
Springfield, OH 45501<br>
December 14, 2016

Ms. Ellen Siemens
Escrow Department
TransOhio First Federal
1220 Wooster Boulevard
Columbus, OH 43218-2900

Dear Ms. Siemens:

For letters in the block style, type the return address at the left margin. For modified block style letters, start the return address at the center to align with the complimentary close.

## Letter and Punctuation Styles

Most business letters today are prepared in either block or modified block style, and they generally use mixed punctuation.

**Block Style.** In the block style, shown in Figure B.2, all lines begin at the left margin. This style is a favorite because it is easy to format.

**Modified Block Style.** The modified block style differs from block style in that the date and closing lines appear in the center, as shown at the bottom of Figure B.2. The date may be (a) centered, (b) begun at the center of the page (to align with the closing lines), or (c) backspaced from the right margin. The signature block—including the complimentary close, writer's name and title, or organization identification—begins at the center. The first line of each paragraph may begin at the left margin or may be indented five or ten spaces. All other lines begin at the left margin.

**Mixed Punctuation Style.** Most businesses today use mixed punctuation, shown in Figure B.2. This style requires a colon after the salutation and a comma after the complimentary close. Even when the salutation is a first name, a colon is appropriate.

## Envelopes

An envelope should be of the same quality and color of stationery as the letter it carries. Because the envelope introduces your message and makes the first impression, you need to be especially careful in addressing it. Moreover, how you fold the letter is important.

**Return Address.** The return address is usually printed in the upper left corner of an envelope, as shown in Figure B.4. In large companies some form of identification (the writer's initials, name, or location) may be typed above the company name and address. This identification helps return the letter to the sender in case of nondelivery.

On an envelope without a printed return address, single-space the return address in the upper left corner. Beginning on line 3 on the fourth space (½ inch) from the left edge, type the writer's name, title, company, and mailing address. On a word processor, select the appropriate envelope size and make adjustments to approximate this return address location.

**Mailing Address.** On legal-sized No. 10 envelopes (4⅛ × 9½ inches), begin the address on line 13 about 4¼ inches from the left edge, as shown in Figure B.4. For small envelopes (3⅝ × 6½ inches), begin typing on line 12 about 2½ inches from the left edge. On a word processor, select the correct envelope size and check to be sure your address falls in the desired location.

The U.S. Postal Service recommends that addresses be typed in all caps without any punctuation. This Postal Service style, shown in the small envelope in Figure B.4, was originally developed to facilitate scanning by optical character readers. Today's OCRs,

Figure B.4  Envelope Formats

Rick Lopez
Oak Park Financial Services
4910 Lake Street
Oak Park, IL 60719-4910

↓ 1½ inches
CERTIFIED MAIL – RETURN RECEIPT REQUESTED

2 inches

4¼ inches →

Shield Security Systems
Attention Accounting Department
2108 Geneva Road, Suite 210
Elmhurst, IL 60219-2108

No. 10 envelope,
upper- and lowercase format

↓ line 3
TINISHA JAMES
1390 DANDINI BLVD
→ RENO NV 89512
½ inch

2 inches
→ MR WILLIAM R EVERSON
3210 W ROOSEVELT RD
LITTLE ROCK AR 72203-2280

2½ inches

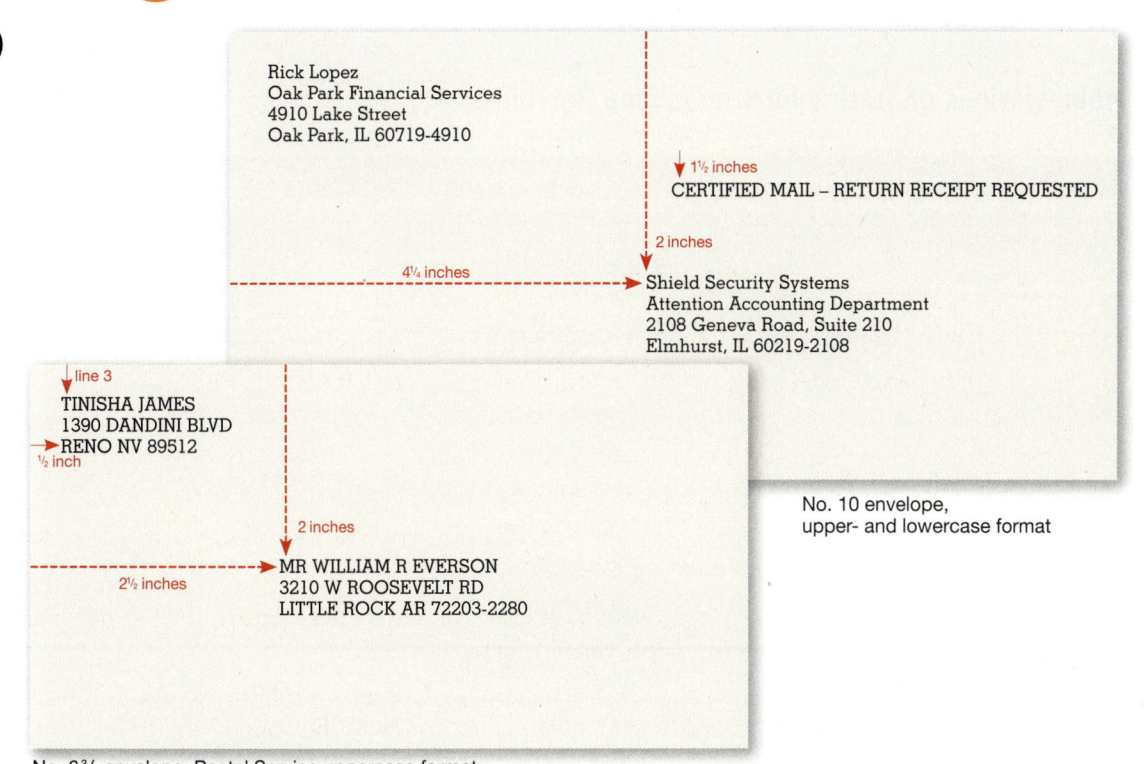

No. 6¾ envelope, Postal Service uppercase format

however, are so sophisticated that they scan upper- and lowercase letters easily. Many companies today do not follow the Postal Service format because they prefer to use the same format for the envelope as for the inside address. If the same format is used, writers can take advantage of word processing programs to copy the inside address to the envelope, thus saving keystrokes and reducing errors. Having the same format on both the inside address and the envelope also looks more professional and consistent. For those reasons you may choose to use the familiar upper- and lowercase combination format. However, you should check with your organization to learn its preference.

In addressing your envelopes for delivery in this country or in Canada, use the two-letter state and province abbreviations shown in Figure B.5. Notice that these abbreviations are in capital letters without periods.

**Folding.** The way a letter is folded and inserted into an envelope sends additional nonverbal messages about a writer's professionalism and carefulness. Most businesspeople follow the procedures shown here, which produce the least number of creases to distract readers.

For large No. 10 envelopes, begin with the letter face up. Fold slightly less than one third of the sheet toward the top, as shown in the following diagram. Then fold down the top third to within ⅓ inch of the bottom fold. Insert the letter into the envelope with the last fold toward the bottom of the envelope.

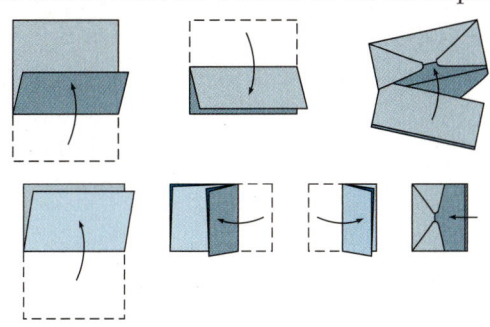

Appendix B: Document Format Guide

A-11

For small No. 6¾ envelopes, begin by folding the bottom up to within ⅓ inch of the top edge. Then fold the right third over to the left. Fold the left third to within ⅓ inch of the last fold. Insert the last fold into the envelope first.

## Figure B.5 Abbreviations of States, Territories, and Provinces

| State or Territory | Two-Letter Abbreviation | State or Territory | Two-Letter Abbreviation |
|---|---|---|---|
| Alabama | AL | North Carolina | NC |
| Alaska | AK | North Dakota | ND |
| Arizona | AZ | Ohio | OH |
| Arkansas | AR | Oklahoma | OK |
| California | CA | Oregon | OR |
| Canal Zone | CZ | Pennsylvania | PA |
| Colorado | CO | Puerto Rico | PR |
| Connecticut | CT | Rhode Island | RI |
| Delaware | DE | South Carolina | SC |
| District of Columbia | DC | South Dakota | SD |
| Florida | FL | Tennessee | TN |
| Georgia | GA | Texas | TX |
| Guam | GU | Utah | UT |
| Hawaii | HI | Vermont | VT |
| Idaho | ID | Virgin Islands | VI |
| Illinois | IL | Virginia | VA |
| Indiana | IN | Washington | WA |
| Iowa | IA | West Virginia | WV |
| Kansas | KS | Wisconsin | WI |
| Kentucky | KY | Wyoming | WY |
| Louisiana | LA | **Canadian Province** | |
| Maine | ME | Alberta | AB |
| Maryland | MD | British Columbia | BC |
| Massachusetts | MA | Labrador | LB |
| Michigan | MI | Manitoba | MB |
| Minnesota | MN | New Brunswick | NB |
| Mississippi | MS | Newfoundland | NF |
| Missouri | MO | Northwest Territories | NT |
| Montana | MT | Nova Scotia | NS |
| Nebraska | NE | Ontario | ON |
| Nevada | NV | Prince Edward Island | PE |
| New Hampshire | NH | Quebec | PQ |
| New Jersey | NJ | Saskatchewan | SK |
| New Mexico | NM | Yukon Territory | YT |
| New York | NY | | |

# Appendix C: Documentation Formats

For many reasons business writers are careful to properly document report data. Citing sources strengthens a writer's argument, as you learned in Chapter 10 on page 316, while also shielding the writer from charges of plagiarism. Moreover, good references help readers pursue further research. As a business writer, you can expect to routinely borrow ideas and words to show that your ideas are in sync with the rest of the business world, to gain support from business leaders, or simply to save time in developing your ideas. To be ethical, however, you must show clearly what you borrowed and from whom.

Source notes tell where you found your information. For quotations, paraphrases, graphs, drawings, or online images you have borrowed, you need to cite the original authors' names, full publication titles, and the dates and facts of publication. The purpose of source notes, which appear at the end of your report, is to direct your readers to the complete references. Many systems of documentation are used by businesses, but they all have one goal: to provide clear, consistent documentation.

Rarely, business writers use content notes, which are identified with a raised number at the end of the quotation. At the bottom of the page, the number is repeated with a remark, clarification, or background information.

During your business career, you may use a variety of documentation systems. The two most common systems in the academic world are those of the American Psychological Association (APA) and the Modern Language Association (MLA). Each organization has its own style for text references and bibliographic lists. This book uses a modified MLA style. However, business organizations may use their own documentation systems.

Before starting any research project, whether for a class or in a business, inquire about the preferred documentation style. For school assignments ask about specifics. For example, should you include URLs and dates of retrieval for Web sources? For workplace assignments ask to see a previous report either in hard-copy version or as an e-mail attachment.

In your business and class writing, you will usually provide a brief citation in parentheses that refers readers to the complete reference that appears in a references or works-cited section at the end of your document. Following is a summary of APA and MLA formats with examples.

## American Psychological Association Format

First used primarily in the social and physical sciences, the American Psychological Association (APA) documentation format uses the author-date method of citation. This method, with its emphasis on current information, is especially appropriate for business. Within the text, the date of publication of the referenced work appears immediately after the author's name (Rivera, 2014), as illustrated in the brief APA example in Figure C.1. At the end of the report, all references appear alphabetically on a page labeled "References." The APA format does not require a date of retrieval for online sources, but you should check with your instructor or supervisor about the preferred format for your class or organization. For more information about the APA format, see the *Publication Manual of the American Psychological Association*, Sixth Edition (Washington, DC: American Psychological Association, 2009).

**APA In-Text Format.** Within your text, document each text, figure, or personal source with a short description in parentheses. Following are selected guidelines summarizing the important elements of APA style.

## Figure C.1 Portions of APA Text Page and References

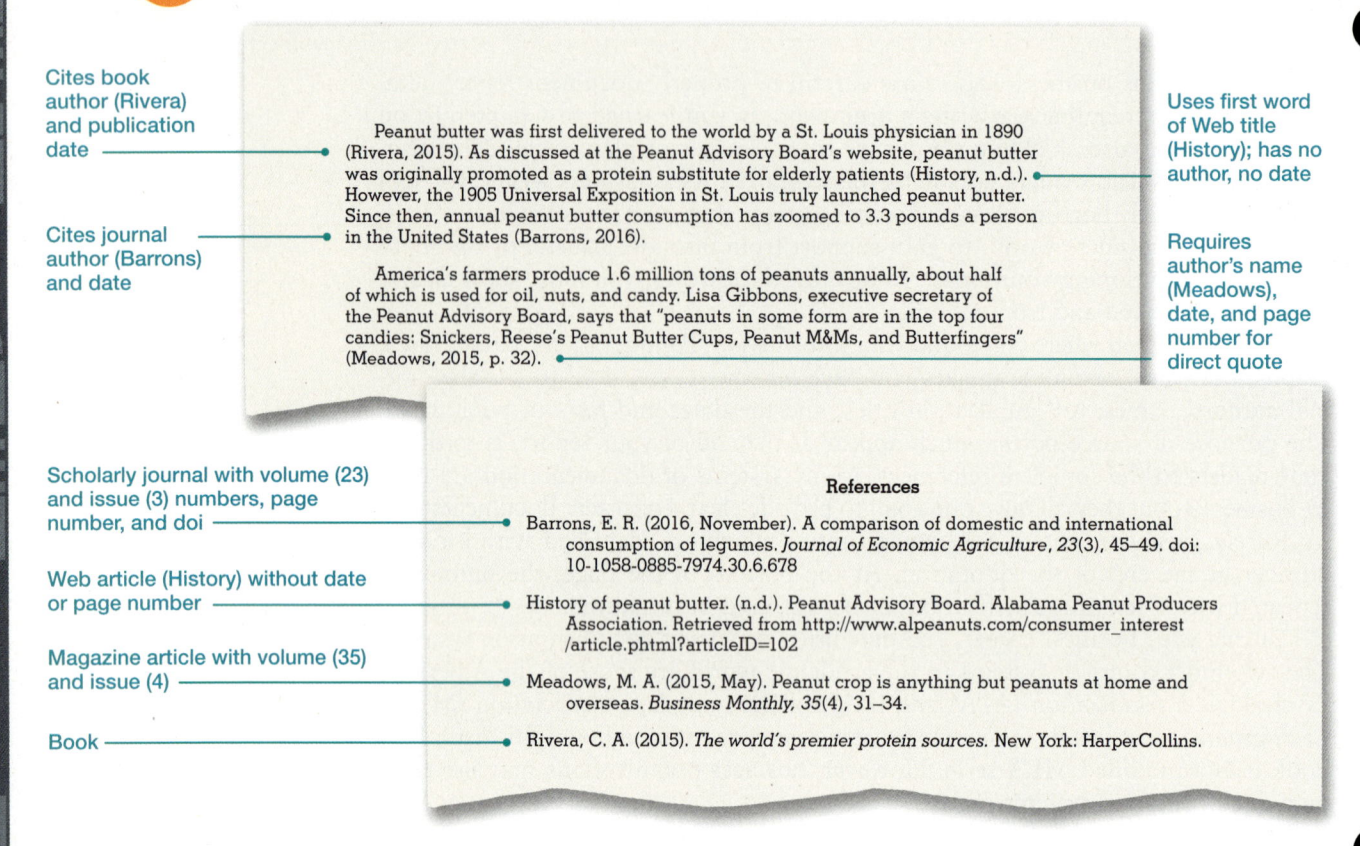

**Cites book author (Rivera) and publication date**

Peanut butter was first delivered to the world by a St. Louis physician in 1890 (Rivera, 2015). As discussed at the Peanut Advisory Board's website, peanut butter was originally promoted as a protein substitute for elderly patients (History, n.d.). However, the 1905 Universal Exposition in St. Louis truly launched peanut butter. Since then, annual peanut butter consumption has zoomed to 3.3 pounds a person in the United States (Barrons, 2016).

**Cites journal author (Barrons) and date**

America's farmers produce 1.6 million tons of peanuts annually, about half of which is used for oil, nuts, and candy. Lisa Gibbons, executive secretary of the Peanut Advisory Board, says that "peanuts in some form are in the top four candies: Snickers, Reese's Peanut Butter Cups, Peanut M&Ms, and Butterfingers" (Meadows, 2015, p. 32).

**Uses first word of Web title (History); has no author, no date**

**Requires author's name (Meadows), date, and page number for direct quote**

### References

**Scholarly journal with volume (23) and issue (3) numbers, page number, and doi**

Barrons, E. R. (2016, November). A comparison of domestic and international consumption of legumes. *Journal of Economic Agriculture*, *23*(3), 45–49. doi: 10-1058-0885-7974.30.6.678

**Web article (History) without date or page number**

History of peanut butter. (n.d.). Peanut Advisory Board. Alabama Peanut Producers Association. Retrieved from http://www.alpeanuts.com/consumer_interest/article.phtml?articleID=102

**Magazine article with volume (35) and issue (4)**

Meadows, M. A. (2015, May). Peanut crop is anything but peanuts at home and overseas. *Business Monthly*, *35*(4), 31–34.

**Book**

Rivera, C. A. (2015). *The world's premier protein sources*. New York: HarperCollins.

---

- For a direct quotation, include the last name of the author(s), if available, and the year of publication; for example, *(Meadows, 2015, p. 32)*. If no author is shown in the text or on a website, use a shortened title or a heading that can be easily located on the References page; for example, *(History, n.d.)*.
- If you mention the author in the text, do not use the name again in the parenthetical reference. Just cite the date; for example, *According to Meadows (2015)*.
- Search for website dates on the home page or at the bottom of Web pages. If no date is available for a source, use *n.d.*

**APA References Format.** At the end of your report, in a section called "References," list all references alphabetically by author, or by title if no author is available. To better understand the anatomy of an APA scholarly journal article reference, see Figure C.2.

## Figure C.2 Anatomy of an APA Journal Article Reference

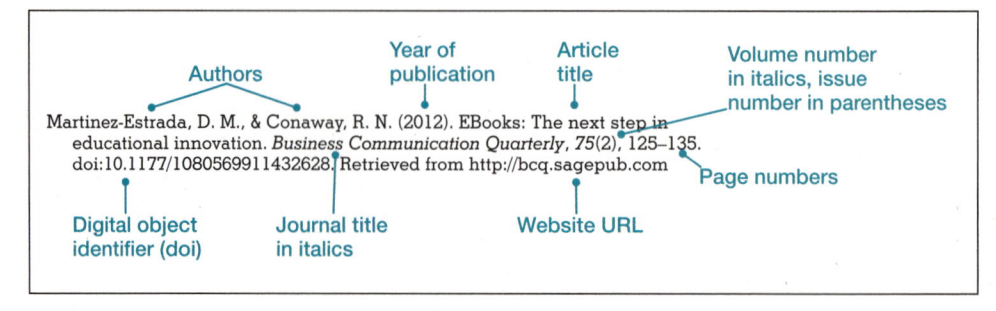

Martinez-Estrada, D. M., & Conaway, R. N. (2012). EBooks: The next step in educational innovation. *Business Communication Quarterly*, *75*(2), 125–135. doi:10.1177/1080569911432628. Retrieved from http://bcq.sagepub.com

- **Authors**
- **Year of publication**
- **Article title**
- **Volume number in italics, issue number in parentheses**
- **Page numbers**
- **Digital object identifier (doi)**
- **Journal title in italics**
- **Website URL**

As with all documentation methods, APA has specific capitalization, punctuation, and sequencing rules, some of which are summarized here:

- Include the last name of the author(s) followed by initials. APA is gender neutral, so first and middle names are not spelled out; for example, *(Martinez-Estrada, D. M.)*.
- Show the date of publication in parentheses immediately after the author's name. A magazine citation will also include the month and day in the parentheses.
- Use sentence-style capitalization for all titles except journal article titles. Do not use quotation marks.
- Italicize titles of magazines, newspapers, books, and journals.

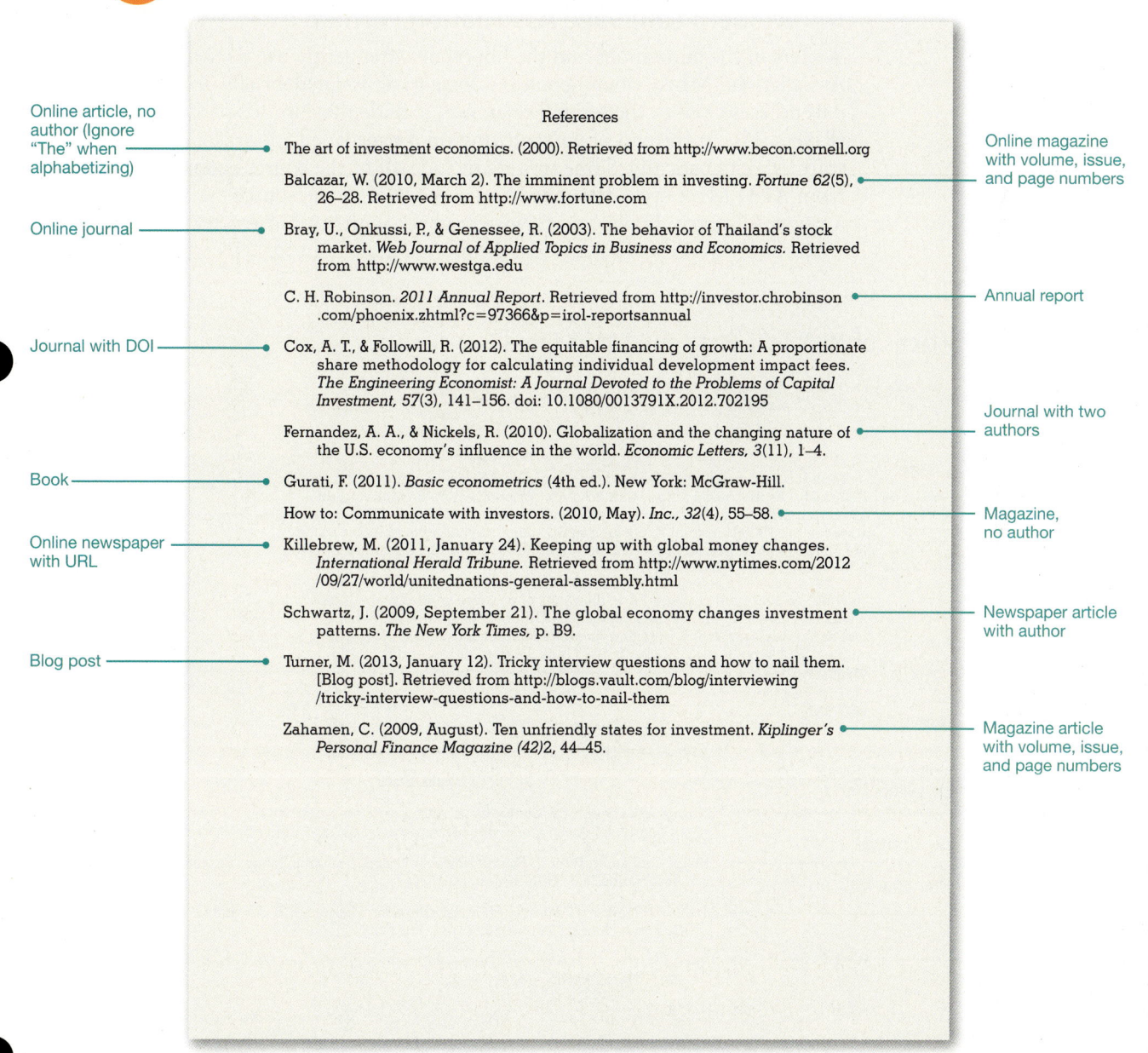

### Figure C.3 APA Sample References

**References**

**Online article, no author (Ignore "The" when alphabetizing)**
The art of investment economics. (2000). Retrieved from http://www.becon.cornell.org

**Online magazine with volume, issue, and page numbers**
Balcazar, W. (2010, March 2). The imminent problem in investing. *Fortune 62*(5), 26–28. Retrieved from http://www.fortune.com

**Online journal**
Bray, U., Onkussi, P., & Genessee, R. (2003). The behavior of Thailand's stock market. *Web Journal of Applied Topics in Business and Economics.* Retrieved from http://www.westga.edu

**Annual report**
C. H. Robinson. *2011 Annual Report*. Retrieved from http://investor.chrobinson.com/phoenix.zhtml?c=97366&p=irol-reportsannual

**Journal with DOI**
Cox, A. T., & Followill, R. (2012). The equitable financing of growth: A proportionate share methodology for calculating individual development impact fees. *The Engineering Economist: A Journal Devoted to the Problems of Capital Investment, 57*(3), 141–156. doi: 10.1080/0013791X.2012.702195

**Journal with two authors**
Fernandez, A. A., & Nickels, R. (2010). Globalization and the changing nature of the U.S. economy's influence in the world. *Economic Letters, 3*(11), 1–4.

**Book**
Gurati, F. (2011). *Basic econometrics* (4th ed.). New York: McGraw-Hill.

**Magazine, no author**
How to: Communicate with investors. (2010, May). *Inc., 32*(4), 55–58.

**Online newspaper with URL**
Killebrew, M. (2011, January 24). Keeping up with global money changes. *International Herald Tribune.* Retrieved from http://www.nytimes.com/2012/09/27/world/unitednations-general-assembly.html

**Newspaper article with author**
Schwartz, J. (2009, September 21). The global economy changes investment patterns. *The New York Times,* p. B9.

**Blog post**
Turner, M. (2013, January 12). Tricky interview questions and how to nail them. [Blog post]. Retrieved from http://blogs.vault.com/blog/interviewing/tricky-interview-questions-and-how-to-nail-them

**Magazine article with volume, issue, and page numbers**
Zahamen, C. (2009, August). Ten unfriendly states for investment. *Kiplinger's Personal Finance Magazine (42)*2, 44–45.

Note: Although APA style prescribes double spacing for the references page, we show single spacing to conserve space and to represent preferred business usage.

- Include the digital object identifier (DOI) when available for online periodicals. If no DOI is available, include the home page URL unless the source is difficult to retrieve without the entire URL.
- Break a URL or DOI only before a mark of punctuation such as a period or slash.
- If the website content may change, as in a wiki, include a retrieval date; for example, *Retrieved 7 July 2016 from http://www.encyclopediaofmath.org/index.php/MainPage*.
- Please note, however, that many instructors require that all Web references be identified by their URLs.
- For articles easily obtained from an online college database, provide the print information only. Do not include the database name or an accession number unless the article is discontinued or was never published.

For a comprehensive list of APA documentation format examples, see Figure C.3.

## Modern Language Association Format

Writers in the humanities and the liberal arts frequently use the Modern Language Association (MLA) documentation format, illustrated briefly in Figure C.4. In parentheses close to the textual reference, include the author's name and page cited (Rivera 25). At the end of your writing on a page titled "Works Cited," list all the sources alphabetically. Some writers include all of the sources consulted. Differing from APA, MLA style does not require the URL if the source can be located with a keyword search. However, it's wise to check with your instructor or organization

### Figure C.4 Portions of MLA Text Page and Works Cited

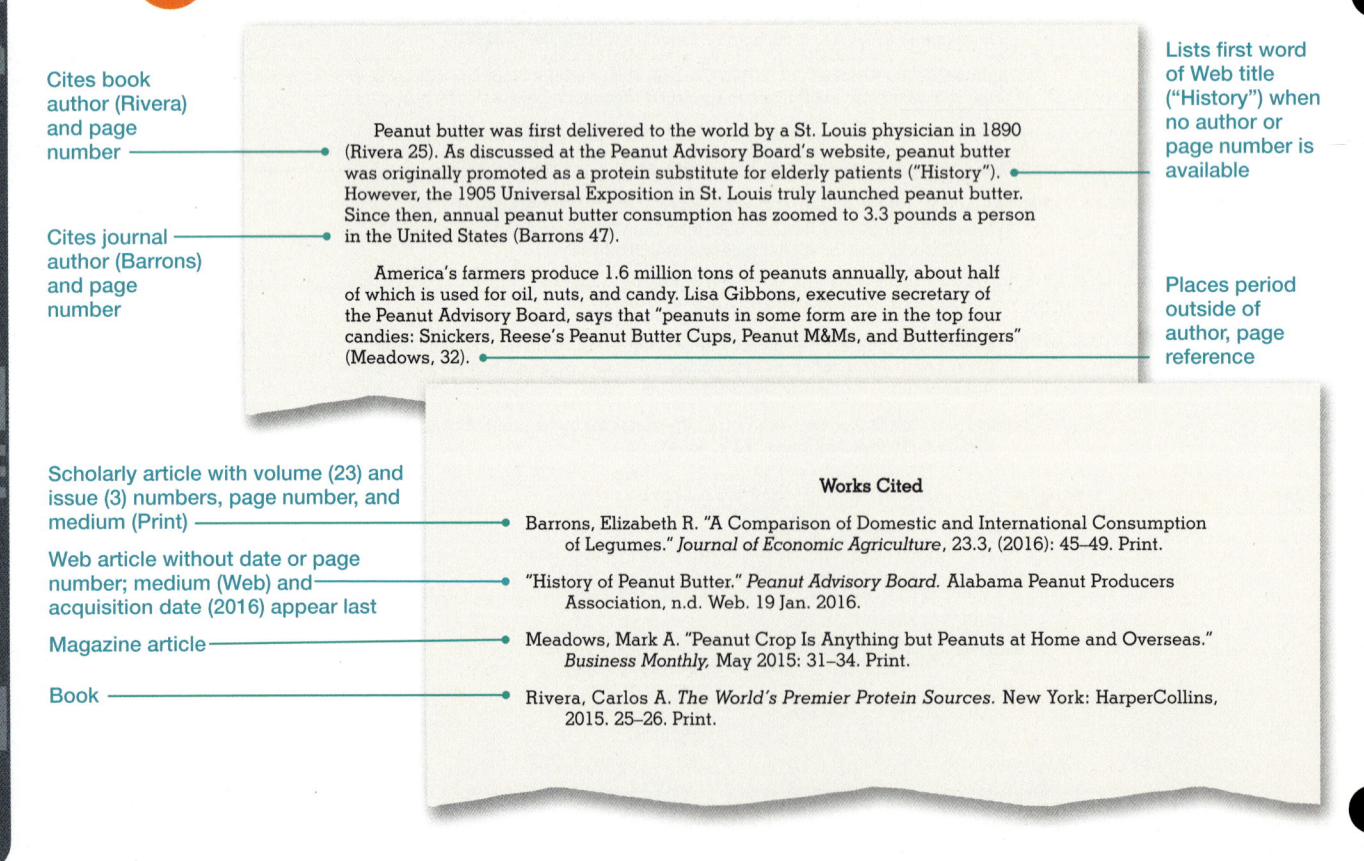

Cites book author (Rivera) and page number

Peanut butter was first delivered to the world by a St. Louis physician in 1890 (Rivera 25). As discussed at the Peanut Advisory Board's website, peanut butter was originally promoted as a protein substitute for elderly patients ("History"). However, the 1905 Universal Exposition in St. Louis truly launched peanut butter. Since then, annual peanut butter consumption has zoomed to 3.3 pounds a person in the United States (Barrons 47).

Lists first word of Web title ("History") when no author or page number is available

Cites journal author (Barrons) and page number

America's farmers produce 1.6 million tons of peanuts annually, about half of which is used for oil, nuts, and candy. Lisa Gibbons, executive secretary of the Peanut Advisory Board, says that "peanuts in some form are in the top four candies: Snickers, Reese's Peanut Butter Cups, Peanut M&Ms, and Butterfingers" (Meadows, 32).

Places period outside of author, page reference

**Works Cited**

Scholarly article with volume (23) and issue (3) numbers, page number, and medium (Print)

Barrons, Elizabeth R. "A Comparison of Domestic and International Consumption of Legumes." *Journal of Economic Agriculture*, 23.3, (2016): 45–49. Print.

Web article without date or page number; medium (Web) and acquisition date (2016) appear last

"History of Peanut Butter." *Peanut Advisory Board.* Alabama Peanut Producers Association, n.d. Web. 19 Jan. 2016.

Magazine article

Meadows, Mark A. "Peanut Crop Is Anything but Peanuts at Home and Overseas." *Business Monthly,* May 2015: 31–34. Print.

Book

Rivera, Carlos A. *The World's Premier Protein Sources.* New York: HarperCollins, 2015. 25–26. Print.

to see what is required. Another notable way MLA differs from APA is in the identification of the publication medium such as *Print* or *Web*. For more information, consult the *MLA Handbook for Writers of Research Papers*, Seventh Edition (New York: The Modern Language Association of America, 2009).

**MLA In-Text Format.** Following any borrowed material in your text, provide a short parenthetical description. Here are selected guidelines summarizing important elements of MLA style:

- For a direct quotation, enclose in parentheses the last name of the author(s), if available, and the page number without a comma; for example, *(Rivera 25)*. If a website has no author, use a shortened title of the page or a heading that is easily found on the works-cited page; for example, *("History")*.
- If you mention the author in the text, do not use the name again in parentheses; for example, *According to Rivera (27) . . . .*
- Search for website dates on the home page or on each Web page for use in the in-text citation. If no page number is available, use a paragraph number; for example, *(Killebrew par. 4)*. If neither a page number nor a paragraph number is available, cite the website in your text; for example, *The Inc. website about how to communicate with investors says that. . . .*

**MLA Works-Cited Format.** In a section called "Works Cited," list all references alphabetically by author or, if no author is available, by title. As with all documentation methods, MLA has specific capitalization and sequencing rules. Some of the most significant are summarized here:

- Include the author's last name first, followed by the first name and initial; for example, *(Rivera, Charles A.)*.
- Enclose in quotation marks the titles of articles, essays, stories, chapters of books, pages in websites, individual episodes of television and radio broadcasts, and short musical compositions.
- Italicize the titles of books, magazines, newspapers, and journals.
- Include the medium of the publication, such as *Web, Print, Radio, Television, Film*.
- Include the URL only if the online site cannot be located by a keyword search. However, for class assignments, check to learn whether your instructor requires URLs, database names, and retrieval dates.

To better understand the anatomy of the format of an MLA scholarly journal article reference, see Figure C.5. For a comprehensive list of MLA documentation format examples, see Figure C.6.

**Figure C.5** Anatomy of an MLA Journal Article Reference

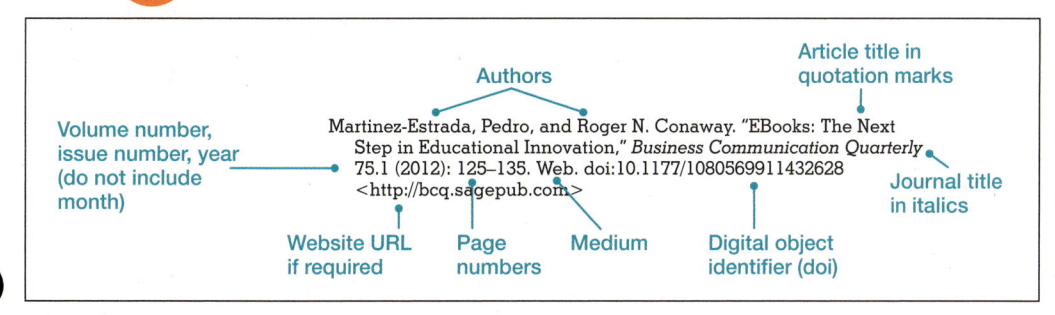

Martinez-Estrada, Pedro, and Roger N. Conaway. "EBooks: The Next Step in Educational Innovation," *Business Communication Quarterly* 75.1 (2012): 125–135. Web. doi:10.1177/1080569911432628 <http://bcq.sagepub.com>

- Authors
- Article title in quotation marks
- Journal title in italics
- Volume number, issue number, year (do not include month)
- Website URL if required
- Page numbers
- Medium
- Digital object identifier (doi)

Figure C.6 MLA Sample References

## Works Cited

Balcazar, William. "The Imminent Problem in Investing." *Fortune* 2 March 2010: 26–28. Web. 5 Jan. 2013.

Bray, Unoki, Peter Ohkussi, and Ronni Genessee. "The Behavior of Thailand's Stock Market." *Web Journal of Applied Topics in Business and Economics* (2003): n. pag. Web. 22 Dec. 2012.

C. H. Robinson. *2011 Annual Report*. Web. 22 Dec. 2012.

Cox, Arthur T., and Robert Followill. "The Equitable Financing of Growth: A Proportionate Share Methodology for Calculating Individual Development Impact Fees." *The Engineering Economist: A Journal Devoted to the Problems of Capital Investment* 57.3 (2012): 141–156. Web. 6 Jan. 2013.

Fernandez, Anthony A., and Roberto Nickels. "Globalization and the Changing Nature of the U.S. Economy's Influence in the World." *Economic Letters* 3.11 (2010): 1–4. Print.

Gurati, Fredrik. *Basic Econometrics*. 4th ed. New York: McGraw-Hill, 2011. Print.

"How to: Communicate with Investors." *Inc.* May 2010: 55–58. Print.

Killebrew, Matthew. "Keeping Up with Global Money Changes." *International Herald Tribune* 24 Jan. 2011: 22+. Web. 24 Dec. 2012.

Schwartz, John. "The Global Economy Changes Investment Patterns." *The New York Times* 21 Sept. 2009, late ed.: B9. Print.

"The Art of Investment Economics." (2000): 1. Web. 24 Dec. 2012. <www.becon.cornell.org>.

Turner, Michelle. "Tricky Interview Questions and How to Nail Them." *Vault Blogs*. Vault Career Intelligence. Blog post. 12 Jan. 2013.

Zahamen, Cecil. "Ten Unfriendly States for Investment." *Kiplinger's Personal Finance Magazine* Aug. 2009: 44–45. Print.

**Annotations (left side):**
- Online magazine article. *Note:* Include date and page numbers but not volume or issue, even if available
- Annual report from website
- Journal article with two authors
- Magazine article without author. No period after magazine title unless part of title
- Newspaper article with author and edition
- Blog post

**Annotations (right side):**
- Online journal without page, volume, or issue numbers
- Online journal with volume (57) and issue (3) numbers
- Book
- Online newspaper
- Unsigned online article with URL if required
- Magazine article. Include date but not volume or issue numbers

Note: Check with your instructor about whether to cite URLs. Although MLA suggests using them only if necessary, many schools require students to include all URLs in their research papers.

# Grammar/Mechanics Handbook

## Introduction

Because many students need a quick review of basic grammar and mechanics, we provide a number of resources in condensed form. The Grammar/Mechanics Handbook, which offers you a rapid systematic review, consists of four parts:

- **Grammar/Mechanics Diagnostic Pretest.** This 65-point pretest helps you assess your strengths and weaknesses in eight areas of grammar and mechanics. Your instructor may later give you a posttest to assess your improvement.
- **Grammar/Mechanics Profile.** The G/M Profile enables you to pinpoint specific areas in which you need remedial instruction or review.
- **Grammar/Mechanics Review.** Provided here is a concise review of basic principles of grammar, punctuation, capitalization, and number style. The review also provides reinforcement and quiz exercises that help you interact with the principles of grammar and test your comprehension. The guidelines not only provide a study guide for review but will also serve as a reference manual throughout the writing course. The grammar review can be used for classroom-centered instruction or for self-guided learning.
- **Confusing Words and Frequently Misspelled Words.** A list of selected confusing words, along with a list of 160 frequently misspelled words, completes the Grammar/Mechanics Handbook.

## More Help to Improve Your Grammar Skills

Some of you want all the help you can get in improving your language skills. For additional assistance with grammar and language fundamentals, *Essentials of Business Communication*, 10e, offers you unparalleled interactive and print resources at **www.cengagebrain.com**.

- **Your Personal Language Trainer.** In this self-paced learning tool, Dr. Guffey acts as your personal trainer in helping you pump up your language muscles. *Your Personal Language Trainer* provides the rules plus hundreds of sentence applications so that you can try out your knowledge and build your skills with immediate feedback and explanations.
- **Sentence Competency Skill Builders** offer interactive exercises similar to the grammar/mechanics checkups in this book. These drills focus on common writing weaknesses so that you can learn to avoid them.
- **Spell Right!** presents frequently misspelled words along with exercises to help you improve your skills.
- **Advanced Grammar/Mechanics Checkups** take you to the next level in language confidence. These self-teaching exercises provide challenging sentences that test your combined grammar, punctuation, spelling, and usage skills.

A more comprehensive treatment of grammar, punctuation, and usage can be found in Clark and Clark's *A Handbook for Office Professionals* or Guffey's *Business English*. The first step in your systematic review of grammar and mechanics involves completing a diagnostic pretest found on the next page.

# Grammar/Mechanics Diagnostic Pretest

Name _____

This diagnostic pretest is intended to reveal your strengths and weaknesses in using the following:

| | | |
|---|---|---|
| plural nouns | adjectives | punctuation |
| possessive nouns | adverbs | capitalization style |
| pronouns | prepositions | number style |
| verbs | conjunctions | |

The pretest is organized into sections corresponding to the preceding categories. In Sections A through H, each sentence is either correct or has one error related to the category under which it is listed. If a sentence is correct, write C. If it has an error, underline the error and write the correct form in the space provided. When you finish, check your answers with your instructor and fill out the Grammar/Mechanics Profile at the end of the test.

## A. Plural Nouns

**EXAMPLE:** Large companys hire numerous CPAs and accountants. — companies

1. All job candidates are asked whether they can work on Saturday's.
2. All company e-mails arrive in batch's at regular intervals during the day.
3. Both of Jeff's sister-in-laws worked as administrative assistants at different facilities.
4. Neither the Sanchezes nor the Harris's knew about the changes in beneficiaries.
5. Since the early 2000s, most judicial systems and attornies have invested in packages that detect computer viruses.

## B. Possessive Nouns

6. We sincerely hope that the jurys judgment reflects the stories of all the witnesses.
7. In a little over two months time, the analysts finished their reports.
8. Ms. Porters staff is responsible for all accounts receivable for customers purchasing electronics parts.
9. At the next stockholders meeting, we will discuss benefits for employees and dividends for shareholders.
10. For the past 90 days, employees in the sales department have complained about Mr. Navetta smoking.

## C. Pronouns

**EXAMPLE:** Whom did you ask to replace Francisco and I? — me

11. The chief and myself were quite willing to send copies to whoever requested them.
12. Much of the project assigned to Samantha and I had to be reassigned to Matt and them.
13. Although it's CPU was noisy, the computer worked for Jeremy and me.
14. Just between you and me, only you and I know that she will be transferred.
15. My friend and I applied at GE because of their excellent benefits.

GM-2

Grammar/Mechanics Handbook

## D. Verb Agreement

**EXAMPLE:** The list of payments have to be approved by the boss. — has

16. This cell phone and its calling plan costs much less than I expected.
17. A description of the property, together with several other legal documents, were submitted by my attorney.
18. There are a wide range of proposals for reducing e-mail overload.
19. Neither the manager nor the employees in the office think the solution is fair.
20. Because of the holiday, our committee were unable to meet.

## E. Verb Mood, Voice, and Tense

21. If I was in charge, I would certainly change things.
22. To make a copy, first open the disk drive door and then you insert the disk.
23. If I could chose any city, I would select Hong Kong.
24. Those contracts have laid on his desk for more than two weeks.
25. The auditors have went over these accounts carefully, and they have found no discrepancies.

## F. Adjectives and Adverbs

26. Until we have a more clearer picture of what is legal, we will proceed cautiously.
27. Britney thought she had done good in her job interview.
28. A recently appointed official was in charge of monitoring peer to peer file-sharing systems.
29. Robert only has two days before he must submit his end-of-the-year report.
30. The architects submitted there drawings in a last-minute attempt to beat the deadline.

## G. Prepositions and Conjunctions

31. Can you tell me where the meeting is scheduled at?
32. It seems like we have been taking this pretest forever.
33. Our investigation shows that cell phones may be cheaper then landlines.
34. My courses this semester are totally different than last semester's.
35. Do you know where this shipment is going to?

## H. Commas

For each of the following sentences, insert any necessary commas. Count the number of commas that you added. Write that number in the space provided. All punctuation must be correct to receive credit for the sentence. If a sentence requires no punctuation, write C.

**EXAMPLE:** Because of developments in theory and computer applications, management is becoming more of a science. — 1

36. For example management determines how orders assignments and responsibilities are delegated to employees.
37. Your order Ms. Lee will be sent from Memphis Tennessee on July 1.

Grammar/Mechanics Handbook

GM-3

38. When you need service on any of your equipment we will be happy to help you Mr. Lopez.

39. Michelle Wong who is the project manager at TeleCom suggested that I call you.

40. You have purchased from us often and your payments in the past have always been prompt.

## I. Commas and Semicolons 1

Add commas and semicolons to the following sentences. In the space provided, write the number of punctuation marks that you added.

41. The salesperson turned in his report however he did not indicate the time period it covered.

42. Interest payments on bonds are tax deductible dividend payments are not.

43. We are opening a branch office in Scottsdale and hope to be able to serve all your needs from that office by the middle of January.

44. As suggested by the committee we must first secure adequate funding then we may consider expansion.

45. When you begin to research a report consider many sources of information namely think about using the Internet, books, periodicals, government publications, and databases.

## J. Commas and Semicolons 2

46. After our chief had the printer repaired it jammed again within the first week although we treated it carefully.

47. Our experienced courteous staff has been trained to anticipate your every need.

48. In view of the new law that went into effect on April l our current liability insurance must be increased therefore we need to adjust our budget.

49. As stipulated in our contract your agency will develop a social media program and supervise our media budget.

50. As you know Ms. Okui we aim for long-term business relationships not quick profits.

## K. Other Punctuation

Each of the following sentences may require colons, question marks, quotation marks, periods, parentheses, and underscores, as well as commas and semicolons. Add the appropriate punctuation to each sentence. Then in the space provided, write the total number of marks that you added or changed.

**EXAMPLE:** Fully recharging your digital camera's battery see page 6 of the instruction manual takes only 90 minutes.

51. The following members of the department volunteered to help on Saturday Kim Carlos Dan and Sylvia.

52. Mr Phillips, Miss Reed and Mrs Garcia usually arrived at the office by 8 30 a m.

53. We recommend that you use hearing protectors see the warning on page 8 when using this electric drill.

54. Did the president really say "All employees may take Friday off

55. We are trying to locate an edition of BusinessWeek that carried an article titled Who Is Reading Your E-Mail

## L. Capitalization

For each of the following sentences, underline any letter that should be capitalized. In the space provided, write the number of words you marked.

**EXAMPLE:** vice president rivera devised a procedure for expediting purchase orders from area 4 warehouses.    4

56. although english was his native language, he also spoke spanish and could read french.
57. on a trip to the east coast, uncle henry visited the empire state building.
58. karen enrolled in classes in history, german, and sociology.
59. the business manager and the vice president each received a new dell computer.
60. james lee, the president of kendrick, inc., will speak to our conference in the spring.

## M. Number Style

Decide whether the numbers in the following sentences should be written as words or as figures. Each sentence either is correct or has one error. If it is correct, write *C*. If it has an error, underline it and write the correct form in the space provided.

**EXAMPLE:** The bank had 5 branches in three suburbs.    five

61. More than 3,000,000 people have visited the White House in the past five years.
62. Of the 28 viewer comments we received regarding our online commercial, only three were negative.
63. We set aside forty dollars for petty cash, but by December 1 our fund was depleted.
64. The meeting is scheduled for May fifth at 3 p.m.
65. In the past five years, nearly fifteen percent of the population changed residences at least once.

## Grammar/Mechanics Profile

In the spaces at the right, place a check mark to indicate the number of correct answers you had in each category of the Grammar/Mechanics Diagnostic Pretest.

|  |  | Number Correct ||||| 
|---|---|---|---|---|---|---|
|  |  | 5 | 4 | 3 | 2 | 1 |
| 1–5 | Plural Nouns | ___ | ___ | ___ | ___ | ___ |
| 6–10 | Possessive Nouns | ___ | ___ | ___ | ___ | ___ |
| 11–15 | Pronouns | ___ | ___ | ___ | ___ | ___ |
| 16–20 | Verb Agreement | ___ | ___ | ___ | ___ | ___ |
| 21–25 | Verb Mood, Voice, and Tense | ___ | ___ | ___ | ___ | ___ |
| 26–30 | Adjectives and Adverbs | ___ | ___ | ___ | ___ | ___ |
| 31–35 | Prepositions and Conjunctions | ___ | ___ | ___ | ___ | ___ |
| 36–40 | Commas | ___ | ___ | ___ | ___ | ___ |
| 41–45 | Commas and Semicolons 1 | ___ | ___ | ___ | ___ | ___ |
| 46–50 | Commas and Semicolons 2 | ___ | ___ | ___ | ___ | ___ |
| 51–55 | Other Punctuation | ___ | ___ | ___ | ___ | ___ |
| 56–60 | Capitalization | ___ | ___ | ___ | ___ | ___ |
| 61–65 | Number Style | ___ | ___ | ___ | ___ | ___ |

Note: 5 = have excellent skills; 4 = need light review; 3 = need careful review; 2 = need to study rules; 1 = need serious study and follow-up reinforcement.

# Grammar/Mechanics Review

## Parts of Speech (1.01)

**1.01 Functions.** English has eight parts of speech. Knowing the functions of the parts of speech helps writers better understand how words are used and how sentences are formed.

a. **Nouns:** name persons, places, things, qualities, concepts, and activities (for example, *Kevin, Phoenix, computer, joy, work, banking*).
b. **Pronouns:** substitute for nouns (for example, *he, she, it, they*).
c. **Verbs:** show the action of a subject or join the subject to words that describe it (for example, *walk, heard, is, was jumping*).
d. **Adjectives:** describe or limit nouns and pronouns and often answer the questions *what kind? how many?* and *which one?* (for example, *red* car, *ten* items, *good* manager).
e. **Adverbs:** describe or limit verbs, adjectives, or other adverbs and frequently answer the questions *when? how? where?* or *to what extent?* (for example, *tomorrow, rapidly, here, very*).
f. **Prepositions:** join nouns or pronouns to other words in sentences (for example, desk *in* the office, ticket *for* me, letter *to* you).
g. **Conjunctions:** connect words or groups of words (for example, you *and* I, Mark *or* Jill).
h. **Interjections:** express strong feelings (for example, *Wow! Oh!*).

## Nouns (1.02–1.06)

Nouns name persons, places, things, qualities, concepts, and activities. Nouns may be classified into a number of categories.

**1.02 Concrete and Abstract.** Concrete nouns name specific objects that can be seen, heard, felt, tasted, or smelled. Examples of concrete nouns are *telephone, dollar, Cadillac,* and *tangerine*. Abstract nouns name generalized ideas such as qualities or concepts that are not easily pictured. *Emotion, power,* and *tension* are typical examples of abstract nouns.

Business writing is most effective when concrete words predominate. It is clearer to write *We need 16-pound copy paper* than to write *We need office supplies*. Chapter 4 provides practice in developing skill in the use of concrete words.

**1.03 Proper and Common.** Proper nouns name specific persons, places, or things and are always capitalized *(General Electric, Baltimore, Jennifer)*. All other nouns are common nouns and begin with lowercase letters *(company, city, student)*. Rules for capitalization are presented in Sections 3.01–3.16.

**1.04 Singular and Plural.** Singular nouns name one item; plural nouns name more than one. From a practical view, writers seldom have difficulty with singular nouns. They may need help, however, with the formation and spelling of plural nouns.

### 1.05 Guidelines for Forming Noun Plurals

a. Add *s* to most nouns *(chair, chairs; mortgage, mortgages; Monday, Mondays)*.
b. Add *es* to nouns ending in *s, x, z, ch,* or *sh (bench, benches; boss, bosses; box, boxes; Lopez, Lopezes)*.
c. Change the spelling in irregular noun plurals *(man, men; foot, feet; mouse, mice; child, children)*.
d. Add *s* to nouns that end in *y* when *y* is preceded by a vowel *(attorney, attorneys; valley, valleys; journey, journeys)*.
e. Drop the *y* and add *ies* to nouns ending in *y* when *y* is preceded by a consonant *(company, companies; city, cities; secretary, secretaries)*.
f. Add *s* to the principal word in most compound expressions *(editors in chief, fathers-in-law, bills of lading, runners-up)*.
g. Add *s* to most numerals, letters of the alphabet, words referred to as words, degrees, and abbreviations *(5s, 2000s, Bs, ands, CPAs, qts.)*.
h. Add *'s* only to clarify letters of the alphabet that might be misread, such as *A's, I's, M's,* and *U's* and *i's, p's,* and *q's*. An expression like *c.o.d.s* requires no apostrophe because it would not easily be misread.

**1.06 Collective Nouns.** Nouns such as *staff, faculty, committee, group,* and *herd* refer to a collection of people, animals, or objects. Collective nouns may be considered singular or plural depending on their action. See Section 1.10i for a discussion of collective nouns and their agreement with verbs.

## Review Exercise A—Nouns

In the space provided for each item, write *a* or *b* to complete the following statements accurately. When you finish, compare your responses with those provided. Answers are provided for odd-numbered items. Your instructor has the remaining answers. For each item on which you need review, consult the numbered principle shown in parentheses.

1. Two of the contest (a) *runner-ups*, (b) *runners-up* protested the judges' choice. _____
2. Several (a) *attorneys*, (b) *attornies* worked on the case together. _____
3. Please write to the (a) *Davis's*, (b) *Davises* about the missing contract. _____
4. The industrial complex has space for nine additional (a) *companys*, (b) *companies*. _____
5. That accounting firm employs two (a) *secretaries*, (b) *secretarys* for five CPAs. _____
6. Four of the wooden (a) *benches*, (b) *benchs* must be repaired. _____
7. The home was constructed with numerous (a) *chimneys*, (b) *chimnies*. _____
8. Tours of the production facility are made only on (a) *Tuesdays*, (b) *Tuesday's*. _____
9. We asked the (a) *Lopez's*, (b) *Lopezes* to contribute to the fund-raising drive. _____
10. Both my (a) *sister-in-laws*, (b) *sisters-in-law* agreed to the settlement. _____
11. The stock market is experiencing abnormal (a) *ups and downs*, (b) *up's and down's*. _____
12. Three (a) *mouses*, (b) *mice* were seen near the trash cans. _____
13. This office is unusually quiet on (a) *Sundays*, (b) *Sunday's*. _____
14. Several news (a) *dispatchs*, (b) *dispatches* were released during the strike. _____
15. Two major (a) *countries*, (b) *countrys* will participate in arms negotiations. _____
16. Some young children have difficulty writing their (a) *bs* and *ds*, (b) *b's* and *d's*. _____
17. The (a) *board of directors*, (b) *boards of directors* of all the major companies participated in the surveys. _____
18. In their letter the (a) *Metzes*, (b) *Metzs* said they intended to purchase the property. _____
19. In shipping we are careful to include all (a) *bill of sales*, (b) *bills of sale*. _____
20. Over the holidays many (a) *turkies*, (b) *turkeys* were consumed. _____

---

1. b (1.05f)  3. b (1.05b)  5. a (1.05e)  7. a (1.05d)  9. b (1.05b)  11. a (1.05g)  13. a (1.05a)  15. a (1.05e)  17. b (1.05f)  19. b (1.05f) (Only odd-numbered answers are provided. Consult your instructor for the others.)

Grammar/Mechanics Handbook

GM-7

## Pronouns (1.07–1.09)

Pronouns substitute for nouns. They are classified by case.

**1.07 Case.** Pronouns function in three cases, as shown in the following chart.

| **Nominative Case** *(Used for subjects of verbs and subject complements)* | **Objective Case** *(Used for objects of prepositions and objects of verbs)* | **Possessive Case** *(Used to show possession)* |
| --- | --- | --- |
| I | me | my, mine |
| we | us | our, ours |
| you | you | your, yours |
| he | him | his |
| she | her | her, hers |
| it | it | its |
| they | them | their, theirs |
| who, whoever | whom, whomever | whose |

### 1.08 Guidelines for Selecting Pronoun Case

a. Pronouns that serve as subjects of verbs must be in the nominative case:

*He* and *I* (not *Him* and *me*) decided to apply for the jobs.

b. Pronouns that follow linking verbs (such as *am, is, are, was, were, be, being, been*) and rename the words to which they refer must be in the nominative case:

It must have been *she* (not *her*) who placed the order. (The nominative-case pronoun *she* follows the linking verb *been* and renames *it*.)

If it was *he* (not *him*) who called, I have his number. (The nominative-case pronoun *he* follows the linking verb *was* and renames *it*.)

c. Pronouns that serve as objects of verbs or objects of prepositions must be in the objective case:

Mr. Andrews asked *them* to complete the proposal. (The pronoun *them* is the object of the verb *asked*.)

All computer printouts are sent to *him*. (The pronoun *him* is the object of the preposition *to*.)

Just between you and *me*, profits are falling. (The pronoun *me* is one of the objects of the preposition *between*.)

d. Pronouns that show ownership must be in the possessive case. Possessive pronouns (such as *hers, yours, ours, theirs,* and *its*) require no apostrophes:

I bought a cheap cell phone, but *yours* (not *your's*) is expensive.

All parts of the machine, including *its* (not *it's*) motor, were examined.

The house and *its* (not *it's*) contents will be auctioned.

Don't confuse possessive pronouns and contractions. Contractions are shortened forms of subject–verb phrases (such as *it's* for *it is*, *there's* for *there is*, and *they're* for *they are*).

e. When a pronoun appears in combination with a noun or another pronoun, ignore the extra noun or pronoun and its conjunction. In this way pronoun case becomes more obvious:

The manager promoted Jeff and *me* (not *I*). (Ignore *Jeff and*.)

f.  In statements of comparison, mentally finish the comparative by adding the implied missing words:

   Next year I hope to earn as much as *she*. (The verb *earns* is implied here: … *as much as she earns*.)

g.  Pronouns must be in the same case as the words they replace or rename. When pronouns are used with appositives, ignore the appositive:

   A new contract was signed by *us* (not *we*) employees. (Temporarily ignore the appositive *employees* in selecting the pronoun.)

   *We* (not *us*) citizens have formed our own organization. (Temporarily ignore the appositive *citizens* in selecting the pronoun.)

h.  Pronouns ending in *self* should be used only when they refer to previously mentioned nouns or pronouns:

   The CEO *himself* answered the telephone.

   Robert and *I* (not *myself*) are in charge of the campaign.

i.  Use objective-case pronouns as objects of the prepositions *between, but, like* and *except*:

   Everyone but John and *him* (not *he*) qualified for the bonus.

   Employees like Miss Gillis and *her* (not *she*) are hard to replace.

j.  Use *who* or *whoever* for nominative-case constructions and *whom* or *whomever* for objective-case constructions. In making the correct choice, it's sometimes helpful to substitute *he* for *who* or *whoever* and *him* for *whom* or *whomever*:

   For *whom* was this book ordered? *(This book was ordered for him/whom?)*

   *Who* did you say would drop by? *(Who/He … would drop by?)*

   Deliver the package to *whoever* opens the door. (In this sentence the clause *whoever opens the door* functions as the object of the preposition *to*. Within the clause itself, *whoever* is the subject of the verb *opens*. Again, substitution of *he* might be helpful: *He/Whoever opens the door.*)

## 1.09 Guidelines for Making Pronouns Agree With Their Antecedents.

Pronouns must agree with the words to which they refer (their antecedents) in gender and in number.

a.  Use masculine pronouns to refer to masculine antecedents, feminine pronouns to refer to feminine antecedents, and neuter pronouns to refer to antecedents without gender:

   The man opened *his* office door. (Masculine gender applies.)

   A woman sat at *her* desk. (Feminine gender applies.)

   This computer and *its* programs fit our needs. (Neuter gender applies.)

b.  Use singular pronouns to refer to singular antecedents:

   Common-gender pronouns (such as *him* or *his*) traditionally have been used when the gender of the antecedent is unknown. Sensitive writers today, however, prefer to recast such constructions to avoid gender-biased pronouns. Study these examples for bias-free pronouns. See Chapter 2 for additional discussion of bias-free language.

   Each student must submit *a* report on Monday.

   All students must submit *their* reports on Monday.

   Each student must submit *his or her* report on Monday. (This alternative is least acceptable since it is wordy and calls attention to itself.)

c. Use singular pronouns to refer to singular indefinite subjects and plural pronouns for plural indefinite subjects. Words such as *anyone, something*, and *anybody* are considered indefinite because they refer to no specific person or object. Some indefinite pronouns are always singular; others are always plural.

| Always Singular | | | Always Plural |
|---|---|---|---|
| anybody | either | nobody | both |
| anyone | everyone | no one | few |
| anything | everything | somebody | many |
| each | neither | someone | several |

Somebody in the group of touring women left *her* (not *their*) purse in the museum.

Either of the companies has the right to exercise *its* (not *their*) option to sell stock.

d. Use singular pronouns to refer to collective nouns and organization names:

The engineering staff is moving *its* (not *their*) facilities on Friday. (The singular pronoun *its* agrees with the collective noun *staff* because the members of *staff* function as a single unit.)

Jones, Cohen, & Chavez, Inc., *has* (not *have*) canceled *its* (not *their*) contract with us. (The singular pronoun *its* agrees with *Jones, Cohen, & Chavez, Inc.*, because the members of the organization are operating as a single unit.)

e. Use a plural pronoun to refer to two antecedents joined by *and*, whether the antecedents are singular or plural:

Our company president and our vice president will be submitting *their* expenses shortly.

f. Ignore intervening phrases—introduced by expressions such as *together with, as well as*, and *in addition to*—that separate a pronoun from its antecedent:

One of our managers, along with several salespeople, is planning *his* retirement. (If you wish to emphasize both subjects equally, join them with *and*: One of our managers *and* several salespeople are planning *their* retirements.)

g. When antecedents are joined by *or* or *nor*, make the pronoun agree with the antecedent closest to it:

Neither Jackie nor Kim wanted *her* (not *their*) desk moved.

## Review Exercise B—Pronouns

In the space provided for each item, write *a, b*, or *c* to complete the statement accurately. When you finish, compare your responses with those provided. For each item on which you need review, consult the numbered principle shown in parentheses.

1. Send e-mail copies of the policy to the manager or (a) *me*, (b) *myself*.
2. James promised that he would call; was it (a) *him*, (b) *he* who left the message?
3. Much preparation for the seminar was made by Mrs. Washington and (a) *I*, (b) *me* before the brochures were sent out.
4. The Employee Benefits Committee can be justly proud of (a) *its*, (b) *their* achievements.
5. A number of inquiries were addressed to Jeff and (a) *I*, (b) *me*, (c) *myself*.
6. (a) *Who*, (b) *Whom* did you say the letter was addressed to?
7. When you visit Franklin Savings Bank, inquire about (a) *its*, (b) *their* certificates.
8. All e-mail messages for Taylor and (a) *I*, (b) *me*, (c) *myself* will become part of the lawsuit.
9. Apparently one of the female applicants forgot to sign (a) *her*, (b) *their* application.

10. Both the printer and (a) *it's*, (b) *its* cover are missing.

11. I've never known any man who could work as fast as (a) *him*, (b) *he*.

12. Just between you and (a) *I*, (b) *me*, the stock price will fall by afternoon.

13. Give the supplies to (a) *whoever*, (b) *whomever* ordered them.

14. (a) *Us*, (b) *We* employees have been given an unusual voice in choosing benefits.

15. When he finally found a job, Dante, along with many other recent graduates, described (a) *his*, (b) *their* experience in an employment blog.

16. Either James or Robert must submit (a) *his*, (b) *their* report next week.

17. Any woman who becomes a charter member of this organization will be able to have (a) *her*, (b) *their* name inscribed on a commemorative plaque.

18. We are certain that (a) *our's*, (b) *ours* is the smallest camera phone available.

19. Everyone has completed the reports except Debbie and (a) *he*, (b) *him*.

20. Lack of work disturbs Mr. Thomas as much as (a) *I*, (b) *me*.

1. a (1.08h) 3. b (1.08c) 5. b (1.08c, 1.08e) 7. a (1.09d) 9. a (1.09b) 11. b (1.08f) 13. a (1.08j) 15. a (1.09f) 17. a (1.09b) 19. b (1.08i)

## Cumulative Editing Quiz 1

Use proofreading marks (see Appendix A) to correct errors in the following sentences. All errors must be corrected to receive credit for the sentence. Check with your instructor for the answers.

**EXAMPLE:** Max and ~~her~~ *she* started ~~there~~ *their* own company in early 2000~~s~~'s.

1. Neither the citys nor the countys would take responsibility for there budget overruns.
2. Can we keep this matter just between you and I?
3. Only a few attornies still have private secretarys.
4. Our staff committee gave their recommendation to the president and I as soon as they finished deliberating.
5. Theres really no excuse for we citizens to have no voice in the matter.
6. The manager and myself will deliver supplies to whomever ordered them.
7. Many basketball and football star's earn huge salaries.
8. Are you sure that this apartment is their's?
9. Each student must submit their report on Monday.
10. Both the network administrator and myself are concerned about the increase in personal Web use and it's tendency to slow productivity.

## Verbs (1.10–1.15)

Verbs show the action of a subject or join the subject to words that describe it.

### 1.10 Guidelines for Agreement With Subjects.
One of the most troublesome areas in English is subject–verb agreement. Consider the following guidelines for making verbs agree with subjects.

Grammar/Mechanics Handbook

GM-11

a. A singular subject requires a singular verb:

   The stock market *opens* at 10 a.m. (The singular verb *opens* agrees with the singular subject *market*.)

   He *doesn't* (not *don't*) work on Saturday.

b. A plural subject requires a plural verb:

   On the packing slip several items *seem* (not *seems*) to be missing.

c. A verb agrees with its subject regardless of prepositional phrases that may intervene:

   This list of management objectives *is* extensive. (The singular verb *is* agrees with the singular subject *list*.)

   Every one of the letters *shows* (not *show*) proper form.

d. A verb agrees with its subject regardless of intervening phrases introduced by *as well as, in addition to, such as, including, together with*, and similar expressions:

   An important memo, together with several contracts, *is* missing. (The singular verb *is* agrees with the singular subject *memo*.)

   The president, as well as several other top-level executives, *approves* of our proposal. (The singular verb *approves* agrees with the subject *president*.)

e. A verb agrees with its subject regardless of the location of the subject:

   Here *is* one of the contracts about which you asked. (The verb *is* agrees with its subject *one*, even though it precedes *one*. The adverb *here* cannot function as a subject.)

   There *are* many problems yet to be resolved. (The verb *are* agrees with the subject *problems*. The word *there* does not function as a subject.)

   In the next office *are* several printers. (In this inverted sentence, the verb *are* must agree with the subject *printers*.)

f. Subjects joined by *and* require a plural verb:

   Analyzing the reader and organizing a strategy *are* the first steps in message writing. (The plural verb *are* agrees with the two subjects, *analyzing* and *organizing*.)

   The tone and the wording of the message *were* persuasive. (The plural verb *were* agrees with the two subjects, *tone* and *wording*.)

g. Subjects joined by *or* or *nor* may require singular or plural verbs. Make the verb agree with the closer subject:

   Neither the memo nor the report *is* ready. (The singular verb *is* agrees with *report*, the closer of the two subjects.)

h. The following indefinite pronouns are singular and require singular verbs: *anyone, anybody, anything, each, either, every, everyone, everybody, everything, many a, neither, nobody, nothing, someone, somebody*, and *something*:

   Either of the alternatives that you present *is* acceptable. (The verb *is* agrees with the singular subject *either*.)

i. Collective nouns may take singular or plural verbs, depending on whether the members of the group are operating as a unit or individually:

   Our management team *is* united in its goal.

   The faculty *are* sharply divided on the tuition issue. (Although acceptable, this sentence sounds better recast: The faculty *members* are sharply divided on the tuition issue.)

j. Organization names and titles of publications, although they may appear to be plural, are singular and require singular verbs.

   Clark, Anderson, and Horne, Inc., *has* (not *have*) hired a marketing consultant.

   *Thousands of Investment Tips is* (not *are*) again on the best-seller list.

**1.11 Voice.** Voice is that property of verbs that shows whether the subject of the verb acts or is acted upon. Active-voice verbs direct action from the subject toward the object of the verb. Passive-voice verbs direct action toward the subject.

| | |
|---|---|
| **Active voice:** | Our employees *send* many e-mail messages. |
| **Passive voice:** | Many e-mail messages *are sent* by our employees. |

Business writers generally prefer active-voice verbs because they are specific and forceful. However, passive-voice constructions can help a writer be tactful. Chapter 3 presents strategies for effective use of active- and passive-voice verbs.

**1.12 Mood.** Three verb moods express the attitude or thought of the speaker or writer toward a subject: (a) the indicative mood expresses a fact; (b) the imperative mood expresses a command; and (c) the subjunctive mood expresses a doubt, a conjecture, or a suggestion.

| | |
|---|---|
| **Indicative:** | I *am looking* for a job. |
| **Imperative:** | *Begin* your job search with the want ads. |
| **Subjunctive:** | I wish I *were* working. |

Only the subjunctive mood creates problems for most speakers and writers. The most common use of subjunctive mood occurs in clauses including *if* or *wish*. In such clauses substitute the subjunctive verb *were* for the indicative verb *was*:

  If he *were* (not *was*) in my position, he would understand.

  Mr. Simon acts as if he *were* (not *was*) the boss.

  We wish we *were* (not *was*) able to ship your order.

The subjunctive mood can maintain goodwill while conveying negative information. The sentence *We wish we were able to ship your order* sounds more pleasing to a customer than *We cannot ship your order*. However, for all practical purposes, both sentences convey the same negative message.

**1.13 Tense.** Verbs show the time of an action by their tense. Speakers and writers can use six tenses to show the time of sentence action; for example:

| | |
|---|---|
| **Present tense:** | I *work*; he *works*. |
| **Past tense:** | I *worked*; she *worked*. |
| **Future tense:** | I *will work*; he *will work*. |
| **Present perfect tense:** | I *have worked*; he *has worked*. |
| **Past perfect tense:** | I *had worked*; she *had worked*. |
| **Future perfect tense:** | I *will have worked*; he *will have worked*. |

### 1.14 Guidelines for Verb Tense

a. Use present tense for statements that, although introduced by past-tense verbs, continue to be true:

  What did you say his name *is*? (Use the present tense *is* if his name has not changed.)

b. Avoid unnecessary shifts in verb tenses:

  The manager *saw* (not *sees*) a great deal of work yet to be completed and *remained* to do it herself.

Although unnecessary shifts in verb tense are to be avoided, not all the verbs within one sentence have to be in the same tense; for example:

  She *said* (past tense) that she *likes* (present tense) to work late.

**1.15 Irregular Verbs.** Irregular verbs cause difficulty for some writers and speakers. Unlike regular verbs, irregular verbs do not form the past tense and past participle by adding -ed to the present form. Here is a partial list of selected troublesome irregular verbs. Consult a dictionary if you are in doubt about a verb form.

### Troublesome Irregular Verbs

| Present | Past | Past Participle *(always use helping verbs)* |
|---|---|---|
| begin | began | begun |
| break | broke | broken |
| choose | chose | chosen |
| come | came | come |
| drink | drank | drunk |
| go | went | gone |
| lay (to place) | laid | laid |
| lie (to rest) | lay | lain |
| ring | rang | rung |
| see | saw | seen |
| write | wrote | written |

a. Use only past-tense verbs to express past tense. Notice that no helping verbs are used to indicate simple past tense:

   The auditors *went* (not *have went*) over our books carefully.

   He *came* (not *come*) to see us yesterday.

b. Use past-participle forms for actions completed before the present time. Notice that past-participle forms require helping verbs:

   Steve *had gone* (not *had went*) before we called. (The past-participle *gone* is used with the helping verb *had*.)

c. Avoid inconsistent shifts in subject, voice, and mood. Pay particular attention to this problem area because undesirable shifts are often characteristic of student writing.

   **Inconsistent:** When Mrs. Taswell read the report, the error was found. (The first clause is in the active voice; the second, passive.)

   **Improved:** When Mrs. Taswell read the report, she found the error. (Both clauses are in the active voice.)

   **Inconsistent:** The clerk should first conduct an inventory. Then supplies should be requisitioned. (The first sentence is in the active voice; the second, passive.)

   **Improved:** The clerk should first conduct an inventory. Then he or she should requisition supplies. (Both sentences are in the active voice.)

   **Inconsistent:** All workers must wear security badges, and you must also sign a daily time card. (This sentence contains an inconsistent shift in subject from *all workers* in the first clause to *you* in the second clause.)

   **Improved:** All workers must wear security badges, and they must also sign a daily time card.

   **Inconsistent:** Begin the transaction by opening an account; then you enter the customer's name. (This sentence contains an inconsistent shift from the imperative mood in the first clause to the indicative mood in the second clause.)

   **Improved:** Begin the transaction by opening an account; then enter the customer's name. (Both clauses are now in the imperative mood.)

## Review Exercise C—Verbs

In the space provided for each item, write *a* or *b* to complete the statement accurately. When you finish, compare your responses with those provided. For each item on which you need review, consult the numbered principle shown in parentheses.

1. Our directory of customer names and addresses (a) *was* (b) *were* out-of-date.
2. There (a) *is*, (b) *are* a customer-service engineer and two salespeople waiting to see you.
3. Improved communication technologies and increased global competition (a) *is*, (b) *are* changing the world of business.
4. Crews, Meliotes, and Bove, Inc., (a) *has*, (b) *have* opened an office in Boston.
5. Yesterday Mrs. Phillips (a) *choose*, (b) *chose* a new office on the second floor.
6. The man who called said that his name (a) *is*, (b) *was* Hernandez.
7. Our management team and our attorney (a) *is*, (b) *are* researching the privacy issue.
8. Either of the flight times (a) *appears*, (b) *appear* to fit my proposed itinerary.
9. If you had (a) *saw*, (b) *seen* the rough draft, you would better appreciate the final copy.
10. Across from our office (a) *is*, (b) *are* the parking structure and the information office.
11. Although we have (a) *began*, (b) *begun* to replace outmoded equipment, the pace is slow.
12. Specific training as well as ample experience (a) *is*, (b) *are* important for that position.
13. Changing attitudes and increased job opportunities (a) *is*, (b) *are* resulting in increased numbers of working women.
14. Neither the organizing nor the staffing of the program (a) *has been*, (b) *have been* completed.
15. If I (a) *was*, (b) *were* you, I would ask for a raise.
16. If you had (a) *wrote*, (b) *written* last week, we could have sent a brochure.
17. The hydraulic equipment that you ordered (a) *is*, (b) *are* packed and will be shipped Friday.
18. One of the reasons that sales have declined in recent years (a) *is*, (b) *are* lack of effective online advertising.
19. Either of the proposed laws (a) *is*, (b) *are* going to affect our business negatively.
20. Merger statutes (a) *requires*, (b) *require* that a failing company accept bids from several companies before merging with one.

1. a (1.10c)   3. b (1.10f)   5. b (1.15a)   7. b (1.10f)   9. b (1.15b)   11. b (1.15b)   13. b (1.10f)   15. b (1.12)
17. a (1.10a)   19. a (1.10h)

## Review Exercise D—Verbs

In the following sentence pairs, choose the one that illustrates consistency in use of subject, voice, and mood. Write *a* or *b* in the space provided. When you finish, compare your responses with those provided. For each item on which you need review, consult the numbered principle shown in parentheses.

Grammar/Mechanics Handbook

1. (a) You need more than a knowledge of technology; one also must be able to interact well with people.
   (b) You need more than a knowledge of technology; you also must be able to interact well with people.

2. (a) Tim and Jon were eager to continue, but Bob wanted to quit.
   (b) Tim and Jon were eager to continue, but Bob wants to quit.

3. (a) The salesperson should consult the price list; then you can give an accurate quote to a customer.
   (b) The salesperson should consult the price list; then he or she can give an accurate quote to a customer.

4. (a) Read all the instructions first; then you install the printer program.
   (b) Read all the instructions first, and then install the printer program.

5. (a) She was an enthusiastic manager who always had a smile for everyone.
   (b) She was an enthusiastic manager who always has a smile for everyone.

1. b (1.15c)   3. b (1.15c)   5. a (1.14b)

## Cumulative Editing Quiz 2

Use proofreading marks (see Appendix A) to correct errors in the following sentences. All errors must be corrected to receive credit for the sentence. Check with your instructor for the answers.

1. The production cost and the markup of each item is important in calculating the sale price.
2. Sheila acts as if she was the manager, but we know she is not.
3. The committee are reconsidering their decision in view of recent health care legislation.
4. My all-in-one computer and it's lightweight keyboard is attractive but difficult to use.
5. Waiting in the outer office is a job applicant and a sales representative who you told to stop by.
6. Each applicant could have submitted his application online if he had went to our website.
7. One of the reasons she applied are that she seen the salarys posted at our website.
8. Either of the options that you may chose are acceptable to Jake and myself.
9. Although there anger and frustration is understandable, both editor in chiefs decided to apologize and reprint the article.
10. The Lopez'es, about who the article was written, accepted the apology graciously.

### Adjectives and Adverbs (1.16–1.17)

Adjectives describe or limit nouns and pronouns. They often answer the questions *what kind? how many?* or *which one?* Adverbs describe or limit verbs, adjectives, or other adverbs. They often answer the questions *when? how? where?* or *to what extent?*

**1.16 Forms.** Most adjectives and adverbs have three forms, or degrees: positive, comparative, and superlative.

|  | Positive | Comparative | Superlative |
|---|---|---|---|
| **Adjective:** | clear | clearer | clearest |
| **Adverb:** | clearly | more clearly | most clearly |

Some adjectives and adverbs have irregular forms.

|  | Positive | Comparative | Superlative |
|---|---|---|---|
| **Adjective:** | good | better | best |
|  | bad | worse | worst |
| **Adverb:** | well | better | best |

Adjectives and adverbs composed of two or more syllables are usually compared by the use of *more* and *most;* for example:

> The Payroll Department is *more efficient* than the Shipping Department.
> Payroll is the *most efficient* department in our organization.

## 1.17 Guidelines for Use

a. Use the comparative degree of the adjective or adverb to compare two persons or things; use the superlative degree to compare three or more:

> Of the two plans, which is *better* (not *best*)?
>
> Of all the plans, we like this one *best* (not *better*).

b. Do not create a double comparative or superlative by using *-er* with *more* or *-est* with *most*:

> His explanation couldn't have been *clearer* (not *more clearer*).

c. A linking verb (*is, are, look, seem, feel, sound, appear,* and so forth) may introduce a word that describes the verb's subject. In this case be certain to use an adjective, not an adverb:

> The characters on the monitor look *bright* (not *brightly*). (Use the adjective *bright* because it follows the linking verb *look* and modifies the noun *characters*.)
>
> The company's letter made the customer feel *bad* (not *badly*). (The adjective *bad* follows the linking verb *feel* and describes the noun *customer*.)

d. Use adverbs, not adjectives, to describe or limit the action of verbs:

> The business is running *smoothly* (not *smooth*). (Use the adverb *smoothly* to describe the action of the verb *is running. Smoothly* tells how the business is running.)
>
> Don't take his remark *personally* (not *personal*). (The adverb *personally* describes the action of the verb *take*.)
>
> Serena said she did *well* (not *good*) on the test. (Use the adverb *well* to tell how she did.)

e. Two or more adjectives that are joined to create a compound modifier before a noun should be hyphenated:

> The *four-year-old* child was tired.
>
> Our agency is planning a *coast-to-coast* campaign.

Hyphenate a compound modifier following a noun only if your dictionary shows the hyphen(s):

> Our speaker is very *well-known*. (Include the hyphen because most dictionaries do.)
>
> The tired child was four years old. (Omit the hyphens because the expression follows the word it describes, *child*, and because dictionaries do not indicate hyphens.)

f. Keep adjectives and adverbs close to the words they modify:

> She asked for *a cup of hot coffee* (not *a hot cup of coffee*).
>
> Patty *had only two days* of vacation left (not *only had two days*).
>
> Students may sit in the *first five rows* (not *in five first rows*).
>
> He *has saved almost* enough money for the trip (not *has almost saved*).

Grammar/Mechanics Handbook

g. Don't confuse *there* with the possessive pronoun *their* or the contraction *they're*:

   Put the documents *there*. (The adverb *there* means "at that place or at that point.")

   *There* are two reasons for the change. (The pronoun *there* is used as function word to introduce a sentence or a clause.)

   We already have *their* specifications. (The possessive pronoun *their* shows ownership.)

   *They're* coming to inspect today. (The contraction *they're* is a shortened form of *they are*.)

### Review Exercise E—Adjectives and Adverbs

In the space provided for each item, write *a*, *b*, or *c* to complete the statement accurately. If two sentences are shown, select *a* or *b* to indicate the one expressed more effectively. When you finish, compare your responses with those provided. For each item on which you need review, consult the numbered principle shown in parentheses.

1. After the interview, Tim looked (a) *calm*, (b) *calmly*.

2. If you had been more (a) *careful*, (b) *carefuler*, the box might not have broken.

3. Because we appointed a new manager, the advertising campaign is running (a) *smooth*, (b) *smoothly*.

4. To avoid a (a) *face to face*, (b) *face-to-face* confrontation, she sent an e-mail.

5. Darren completed the employment test (a) *satisfactorily*, (b) *satisfactory*.

6. I felt (a) *bad*, (b) *badly* that he was not promoted.

7. Which is the (a) *more*, (b) *most* dependable of the two cars?

8. Can you determine exactly what (a) *there*, (b) *their*, (c) *they're* company wants us to do?

9. Of all the copiers we tested, this one is the (a) *easier*, (b) *easiest* to operate.

10. (a) Mr. Aldron almost was ready to accept the offer.
    (b) Mr. Aldron was almost ready to accept the offer.

11. (a) We only thought that it would take two hours for the test.
    (b) We thought that it would take only two hours for the test.

12. (a) Please bring me a glass of cold water.
    (b) Please bring me a cold glass of water.

13. (a) The committee decided to retain the last ten tickets.
    (b) The committee decided to retain the ten last tickets.

14. New owners will receive a (a) *60-day*, (b) *60 day* trial period.

15. The time passed (a) *quicker*, (b) *more quickly* than we expected.

16. We offer a (a) *money back*, (b) *money-back* guarantee.

17. Today the financial news is (a) *worse*, (b) *worst* than yesterday.

18. Please don't take his comments (a) *personal*, (b) *personally*.

19. You must check the document (a) *page by page*, (b) *page-by-page*.

20. (a) We try to file only necessary paperwork.
    (b) We only try to file necessary paperwork.

1. a (1.17c)  3. b (1.17d)  5. a (1.17d)  7. a (1.17a)  9. b (1.17a)  11. b (1.17f)  13. a (1.17f)  15. b (1.17d)
17. a (1.17a)  19. a (1.17e)

# Prepositions (1.18)

Prepositions are connecting words that join nouns or pronouns to other words in a sentence. The words *about, at, from, in,* and *to* are examples of prepositions.

## 1.18 Guidelines for Use

a. Include necessary prepositions:

   What type *of* software do you need (not *what type software*)?

   I graduated *from* high school two years ago (not *I graduated high school*).

b. Omit unnecessary prepositions:

   Where is the meeting? (Not *Where is the meeting at?*)

   Both printers work well. (Not *Both of the printers*.)

   Where are you going? (Not *Where are you going to?*)

c. Avoid the overuse of prepositional phrases.

   | **Weak:** | We have received your application for credit at our branch in the Fresno area. |
   |---|---|
   | **Improved:** | We have received your Fresno credit application. |

d. Repeat the preposition before the second of two related elements especially when the second element is distant from the first:

   Applicants use the résumé effectively by summarizing their most important experiences and *by* relating their education to the jobs sought.

e. Include the second preposition when two different prepositions modify a single object:

   George's appreciation *of* and aptitude *for* computers led to a promising career.

# Conjunctions (1.19)

Conjunctions connect words, phrases, and clauses. They act as signals, indicating when a thought is being added, contrasted, or altered. Coordinate conjunctions (such as *and, or, but*) and other words that act as connectors (such as *however, therefore, when, as*) tell the reader or listener in what direction a thought is heading. They are like road signs signaling what's ahead.

## 1.19 Guidelines for Use

a. Use coordinating conjunctions to connect only sentence elements that are parallel or balanced.

   | **Weak:** | His report was correct and written in a concise manner. |
   |---|---|
   | **Improved:** | His report was correct and concise. |
   | **Weak:** | Management has the capacity to increase fraud, or reduction can be achieved through the policies it adopts. |
   | **Improved:** | Management has the capacity to increase or reduce fraud through the policies it adopts. |

b. Do not use the word *like* as a conjunction:

   It seems *as if* (not *like*) this day will never end.

c. Avoid using *when* or *where* inappropriately. A common writing fault occurs in sentences with clauses introduced by *is when* and *is where*. Written English ordinarily requires a noun (or a group of words functioning as a noun) following the linking verb *is*. Instead of acting as conjunctions in these constructions, the words *where* and *when* function as adverbs, creating faulty grammatical equations (adverbs cannot complete equations set up by linking verbs). To avoid the problem, revise the sentence, eliminating *is when* or *is where*.

Grammar/Mechanics Handbook

| | |
|---|---|
| **Weak:** | A bullish market is when prices are rising in the stock market. |
| **Improved:** | A bullish market is created when prices are rising in the stock market. |
| **Weak:** | A flowchart is when you make a diagram showing the step-by-step progression of a procedure. |
| **Improved:** | A flowchart is a diagram showing the step-by-step progression of a procedure. |
| **Weak:** | A podcast is where a prerecorded audio program is posted to a website. |
| **Improved:** | A podcast is a prerecorded audio program posted to a website. |

A similar faulty construction occurs in the expression *I hate when*. English requires nouns, noun clauses, or pronouns to act as objects of verbs, not adverbs.

| | |
|---|---|
| **Weak:** | I hate when we're asked to work overtime. |
| **Improved:** | I hate it when we're asked to work overtime. |
| **Improved:** | I hate being asked to work overtime. |

d. Don't confuse the adverb *then* with the conjunction *than*. *Then* means "at that time"; *than* indicates the second element in a comparison:

> We would rather remodel *than* (not *then*) move.

> First, the equipment is turned on; *then* (not *than*) the program is loaded.

## Review Exercise F—Prepositions and Conjunctions

In the space provided for each item, write *a* or *b* to indicate the sentence that is expressed more effectively. When you finish, compare your responses with those provided. For each item on which you need review, consult the numbered principle shown in parentheses.

1. (a) The chief forgot to tell everyone where today's meeting is.
   (b) The chief forgot to tell everyone where today's meeting is at.

2. (a) She was neither aware of nor interested in the company insurance plan.
   (b) She was neither aware nor interested in the company insurance plan.

3. (a) Mr. Samuels graduated college last June.
   (b) Mr. Samuels graduated from college last June.

4. (a) "Flextime" is when employees arrive and depart at varying times.
   (b) "Flextime" is a method of scheduling worktime in which employees arrive and depart at varying times.

5. (a) Both employees enjoyed setting their own hours.
   (b) Both of the employees enjoyed setting their own hours.

6. (a) I hate when my cell loses its charge.
   (b) I hate it when my cell loses its charge.

7. (a) What style of typeface should we use?
   (b) What style typeface should we use?

8. (a) Business letters should be concise, correct, and written clearly.
   (b) Business letters should be concise, correct, and clear.

9. (a) Mediation in a labor dispute occurs when a neutral person helps union and management reach an agreement.
   (b) Mediation in a labor dispute is where a neutral person helps union and management reach an agreement.

10. (a) It looks as if the plant will open in early January.
    (b) It looks like the plant will open in early January.

11. (a) We expect to finish up the work soon.
    (b) We expect to finish the work soon.

12. (a) At the beginning of the program in the fall of the year at the central office, we experienced staffing difficulties.
    (b) When the program began last fall, the central office experienced staffing difficulties.

13. (a) Your client may respond by e-mail or a telephone call may be made.
    (b) Your client may respond by e-mail or by telephone.

14. (a) A résumé is when you make a written presentation of your education and experience for a prospective employer.
    (b) A résumé is a written presentation of your education and experience for a prospective employer.

15. (a) Stacy exhibited both an awareness of and talent for developing innovations.
    (b) Stacy exhibited both an awareness and talent for developing innovations.

16. (a) This course is harder then I expected.
    (b) This course is harder than I expected.

17. (a) An ombudsman is an individual hired by management to investigate and resolve employee complaints.
    (b) An ombudsman is when management hires an individual to investigate and resolve employee complaints.

18. (a) I'm uncertain where to take this document to.
    (b) I'm uncertain where to take this document.

19. (a) By including accurate data and by writing clearly, you will produce effective messages.
    (b) By including accurate data and writing clearly, you will produce effective messages.

20. (a) We need computer operators who can load software, monitor networks, and files must be duplicated.
    (b) We need computer operators who can load software, monitor networks, and duplicate files.

1. a (1.18b)   3. b (1.18a)   5. a (1.18b)   7. a (1.18a)   9. a (1.19c)   11. b (1.18b)   13. b (1.19a)   15. a (1.18e)
17. a (1.19c)   19. a (1.18d)

# Cumulative Editing Quiz 3

Use proofreading marks (see Appendix A) to correct errors in the following sentences. All errors must be corrected to receive credit for the sentence. Check with your instructor for the answers.

1. Her new computer is definitely more faster then her previous computer.

2. Max said that he felt badly that he missed his appointment with you and myself.

3. Neither the managers nor the union are happy at how slow the talks are progressing.

4. Just between you and I, we have learned not to take the boss's criticism personal.

5. After completing a case by case search, the consultant promised to send his report to Carlos and I.

6. If you was me, which of the two job offers do you think is best?

7. Did your team members tell you where there meeting is at?

Grammar/Mechanics Handbook

8. Jason felt that he had done good on the three hour certification exam.

9. It seems like our step by step instructions could have been more clearer.

10. I hate when I'm expected to finish up by myself.

# Punctuation Review

## Commas 1 (2.01–2.04)

**2.01 Series.** Commas are used to separate three or more equal elements (words, phrases, or short clauses) in a series. To ensure separation of the last two elements, careful writers always use a comma before the conjunction in a series:

> Business letters usually contain a dateline, address, salutation, body, and closing. (This series contains words.)

> The job of an ombudsman is to examine employee complaints, resolve disagreements between management and employees, and ensure fair treatment. (This series contains phrases.)

> Trainees complete basic keyboarding tasks, technicians revise complex documents, and editors proofread completed projects. (This series contains short clauses.)

**2.02 Direct Address.** Commas are used to set off the names of individuals being addressed:

> Your inquiry, *Mrs. Johnson*, has been referred to me.

> We genuinely hope that we may serve you, *Mr. Lee*.

**2.03 Parenthetical Expressions.** Skilled writers use parenthetical words, phrases, and clauses to guide the reader from one thought to the next. When these expressions interrupt the flow of a sentence and are unnecessary for its grammatical completeness, they should be set off with commas. Examples of commonly used parenthetical expressions follow:

| | | |
|---|---|---|
| all things considered | however | needless to say |
| as a matter of fact | in addition | nevertheless |
| as a result | incidentally | no doubt |
| as a rule | in fact | of course |
| at the same time | in my opinion | on the contrary |
| consequently | in the first place | on the other hand |
| for example | in the meantime | therefore |
| furthermore | moreover | under the circumstances |

> *As a matter of fact*, I wrote to you just yesterday. (Phrase used at the beginning of a sentence.)

> We will, *in the meantime*, send you a replacement order. (Phrase used in the middle of a sentence.)

> Your satisfaction is our first concern, *needless to say*. (Phrase used at the end of a sentence.)

Do not use commas if the expression is necessary for the completeness of the sentence:

> Kimberly had *no doubt* that she would finish the report. (Omit commas because the expression is necessary for the completeness of the sentence.)

**2.04 Dates, Addresses, and Geographical Items.** When dates, addresses, and geographical items contain more than one element, the second and succeeding elements are normally set off by commas.

a. Dates:

   The conference was held February 2 at our home office. (No comma is needed for one element.)

   The conference was held February 2, 2015, at our home office. (Two commas set off the second element.)

   The conference was held Tuesday, February 2, 2015, at our home office. (Commas set off the second and third elements.)

   In February 2015 the conference was held. (This alternate style omitting commas is acceptable if only the month and year are written.)

b. Addresses:

   The letter addressed to Mr. Jim W. Ellman, 600 Via Novella, Agoura, CA 91306, should be sent today. (Commas are used between all elements except the state and zip code, which in this special instance act as a single unit.)

c. Geographical items:

   She moved from Toledo, Ohio, to Champaign, Illinois. (Commas set off the state unless it appears at the end of the sentence, in which case only one comma is used.)

In separating cities from states and days from years, many writers remember the initial comma but forget the final one, as in the examples that follow:

   The package from Austin, Texas{,} was lost.

   We opened June 1, 2010{,} and have grown steadily since.

## Review Exercise G—Commas 1

Insert necessary commas in the following sentences. In the space provided, write the number of commas that you added. Write *C* if no commas are needed. When you finish, compare your responses with those provided. For each item on which you need review, consult the numbered principle shown in parentheses.

1. As a rule we do not provide complimentary tickets.

2. You may be certain Mr. Martinez that your policy will be issued immediately.

3. I have no doubt that your calculations are correct.

4. The safety hazard on the contrary can be greatly reduced if workers wear rubber gloves.

5. Every accredited TV newscaster radio broadcaster and blogger had access to the media room.

6. Deltech's main offices are located in Boulder Colorado and Seattle Washington.

7. The employees who are eligible for promotions are Terry Evelyn Vicki Rosanna and Steve.

8. During the warranty period of course you are protected from any parts or service charges.

9. Many of our customers include architects engineers attorneys and others who are interested in database management programs.

10. I wonder Mrs. Stevens if you would send my letter of recommendation as soon as possible.

11. The new book explains how to choose appropriate legal protection for ideas trade secrets copyrights patents and restrictive covenants.

12. The factory is scheduled to be moved to 2250 North Main Street Ann Arbor Michigan 48107 within two years.

Grammar/Mechanics Handbook

13. You may however prefer to correspond directly with the manufacturer in Hong Kong.

14. Are there any alternatives in addition to those that we have already considered?

15. The rally has been scheduled for Monday January 12 in the football stadium.

16. A check for the full amount will be sent directly to your home Mr. Jefferson.

17. Goodstone Tire & Rubber for example recalled 400,000 steelbelted radial tires because some tires failed their rigorous tests.

18. Kevin agreed to unlock the office open the mail and check all the equipment in my absence.

19. In the meantime thank you for whatever assistance you are able to furnish.

20. Research facilities were moved from Austin Texas to Santa Cruz California.

---

1. rule, (2.03)   3. C (2.03)   5. newscaster, radio broadcaster, (2.01)   7. Terry, Evelyn, Vicki, Rosanna, (2.01)   9. architects, engineers, attorneys, (2.01)   11. ideas, trade secrets, copyrights, patents, (2.01)   13. may, however, (2.03)   15. Monday, January 12, (2.04a)   17. Rubber, for example, (2.03)   19. meantime, (2.03)

## Commas 2 (2.05–2.09)

**2.05 Independent Clauses.** An independent clause is a group of words that has a subject and a verb and that could stand as a complete sentence. When two such clauses are joined by *and, or, nor,* or *but,* use a comma before the conjunction:

> We can ship your merchandise July 12, but we must have your payment first.
>
> Net income before taxes is calculated, and this total is then combined with income from operations.

Notice that each independent clause in the preceding two examples could stand alone as a complete sentence. Do not use a comma unless each group of words is a complete thought (that is, has its own subject and verb).

> Our CPA calculates net income before taxes *and* then combines that figure with income from operations. (No comma is needed because no subject follows *and*.)

**2.06 Dependent Clauses.** Dependent clauses do not make sense by themselves; for their meaning they depend on independent clauses.

a. **Introductory clauses.** When a dependent clause precedes an independent clause, it is followed by a comma. Such clauses are often introduced by *when, if,* and *as*:

> *When your request came*, we responded immediately.
>
> *As I mentioned earlier*, Mrs. James is the manager.

b. **Terminal clauses.** If a dependent clause falls at the end of a sentence, use a comma only if the dependent clause is an afterthought:

> We have rescheduled the meeting for October 23, *if this date meets with your approval*. (Comma used because dependent clause is an afterthought.)
>
> We responded immediately *when we received your request*. (No comma is needed.)

c. **Essential versus nonessential clauses.** If a dependent clause provides information that is unneeded for the grammatical completeness of a sentence, use commas to set it off. In determining whether such a clause is essential or nonessential, ask yourself whether the reader needs the information contained in the clause to identify the word it explains:

> Our district sales manager, *who just returned from a trip to the Southwest District*, prepared this report. (This construction assumes that there is only one district sales manager. Because the sales manager is clearly identified, the dependent clause is not essential and requires commas.)

The salesperson *who just returned from a trip to the Southwest District* prepared this report. (The dependent clause in this sentence is necessary to identify which salesperson prepared the report. Therefore, use no commas.)

The position of assistant sales manager, *which we discussed with you last week*, is still open. (Careful writers use *which* to introduce nonessential clauses. Commas are also necessary.)

The position *that we discussed with you last week* is still open. (Careful writers use *that* to introduce essential clauses. No commas are used.)

**2.07 Phrases.** A phrase is a group of related words that lacks both a subject and a verb. A phrase that precedes a main clause is followed by a comma if the phrase contains a verb form or has four or more words:

*Beginning November 1*, Worldwide Savings will offer two new combination checking/savings plans. (A comma follows this introductory phrase because the phrase contains the verb form *beginning*.)

*To promote our plan*, we will conduct an extensive social media advertising campaign. (A comma follows this introductory phrase because the phrase contains the verb form *to promote*.)

*In a period of only one year*, we were able to improve our market share by 30 percent. (A comma follows the introductory phrase—actually two prepositional phrases—because its total length exceeds four words.)

*In 2015* our organization installed a multiuser system that could transfer programs easily. (No comma needed after the short introductory phrase.)

**2.08 Two or More Adjectives.** Use a comma to separate two or more adjectives that equally describe a noun. A good way to test the need for a comma is this: Mentally insert the word *and* between the adjectives. If the resulting phrase sounds natural, a comma is used to show the omission of *and*:

We're looking for a *versatile, error-free* operating system. (Use a comma to separate *versatile* and *error-free* because they independently describe *operating system*. *And* has been omitted.)

Our *experienced, courteous* staff is ready to serve you. (Use a comma to separate *experienced* and *courteous* because they independently describe *staff*. *And* has been omitted.)

It was difficult to refuse the *sincere young* telephone caller. (No commas are needed between *sincere* and *young* because *and* has not been omitted.)

**2.09 Appositives.** Words that rename or explain preceding nouns or pronouns are called *appositives*. An appositive that provides information not essential to the identification of the word it describes should be set off by commas:

James Wilson, *the project director for Sperling's*, worked with our architect. (The appositive, *the project director for Sperling's*, adds nonessential information. Commas set it off.)

## Review Exercise H—Commas 2

Insert only necessary commas in the following sentences. In the space provided, indicate the number of commas that you added for each sentence. If a sentence requires no commas, write *C*. When you finish, compare your responses with those provided. For each item on which you need review, consult the numbered principle shown in parentheses.

1. A corporation must register in the state in which it does business and it must operate within the laws of that state.

2. The manager made a point-by-point explanation of the distribution dilemma and then presented his plan to solve the problem.

3. If you will study the cost analysis you will see that our company offers the best system at the lowest price.

Grammar/Mechanics Handbook

4. Molly Epperson who amassed the greatest number of sales points won a bonus trip to Hawaii.

5. The salesperson who amasses the greatest number of sales points will win a bonus trip to Hawaii.

6. To promote goodwill and to generate international trade we are opening offices in South Asia and in Europe.

7. On the basis of these findings I recommend that we retain Jane Rada as our counsel.

8. Scott Cook is a dedicated hardworking employee for our company.

9. The bright young student who worked for us last summer will be able to return this summer.

10. When you return the completed form we will be able to process your application.

11. We will be able to process your application when you return the completed form.

12. The employees who have been with us over ten years automatically receive additional insurance benefits.

13. Knowing that you wanted this merchandise immediately I took the liberty of sending it by FedEx.

14. The central processing unit requires no scheduled maintenance and has a self-test function for reliable performance.

15. A tax credit for energy-saving homes will expire at the end of the year but Congress might extend it if pressure groups prevail.

16. Stacy Wilson our newly promoted office manager has made a number of worthwhile suggestions.

17. For the benefit of employees recently hired we are offering a two-hour seminar regarding employee benefit programs.

18. Please bring your suggestions and those of Mr. Mason when you attend our meeting next month.

19. The meeting has been rescheduled for September 30 if this date meets with your approval.

20. Some of the problems that you outline in your recent memo could be rectified through more stringent purchasing procedures.

---

1. business, (2.05)  3. analysis, (2.06a)  5. C (2.06c)  7. findings, (2.07)  9. C (2.08)  11. C (2.06b)
13. immediately, (2.07)  15. year, (2.05)  17. hired, (2.07)  19. September 30, (2.06b)

## Commas 3 (2.10–2.15)

**2.10 Degrees and Abbreviations.** Degrees following individuals' names are set off by commas. Abbreviations such as *Jr.* and *Sr.* are also set off by commas unless the individual referred to prefers to omit the commas:

> Anne G. Turner, *MBA*, joined the firm.
>
> Michael Migliano, *Jr.*, and Michael Migliano, *Sr.*, work as a team.
>
> Anthony A. Gensler *Jr.* wrote the report. (The individual referred to prefers to omit commas.)

The abbreviations *Inc.* and *Ltd.* are set off by commas only if a company's legal name has a comma just before this kind of abbreviation. To determine a company's practice, consult its stationery or a directory listing:

> Firestone and Blythe, *Inc.*, is based in Canada. (Notice that two commas are used.)

> Computers *Inc.* is extending its franchise system. (The company's legal name does not include a comma before *Inc.*)

**2.11 Omitted Words.** A comma is used to show the omission of words that are understood:

> On Monday we received 15 applications; on Friday, only 3. (Comma shows the omission of *we received*.)

**2.12 Contrasting Statements.** Commas are used to set off contrasting or opposing expressions. These expressions are often introduced by such words as *not, never, but,* and *yet*:

> The president suggested cutbacks, *not* layoffs, to ease the crisis.

> Our budget for the year is reduced, *yet* adequate.

> The greater the effort, the greater the reward.

If increased emphasis is desired, use dashes instead of commas, as in *Only the sum of $100—not $1,000—was paid on this account.*

**2.13 Clarity.** Commas are used to separate words repeated for emphasis. Commas are also used to separate words that may be misread if not separated:

> The building is a long, long way from completion.

> Whatever is, is right.

> No matter what, you know we support you.

**2.14 Quotations and Appended Questions**

a. A comma is used to separate a short quotation from the rest of a sentence. If the quotation is divided into two parts, two commas are used:

> The manager asked, "Shouldn't the managers control the specialists?"

> "Perhaps the specialists," replied Tim, "have unique information."

b. A comma is used to separate a question appended (added) to a statement:

> You will confirm the shipment, won't you?

**2.15 Comma Overuse.** Do not use commas needlessly. For example, commas should not be inserted merely because you might drop your voice if you were speaking the sentence:

> One of the reasons for expanding our East Coast operations is{,} that we anticipate increased sales in that area. (Do not insert a needless comma before a clause.)

> I am looking for an article titled{,} "State-of-the-Art Communications." (Do not insert a needless comma after the word *titled*.)

> Customers may purchase many food and nonfood items in convenience stores *such as*{,} 7-Eleven and Stop-N-Go. (Do not insert a needless comma after *such as*.)

> We have{,} at this time{,} an adequate supply of parts. (Do not insert needless commas around prepositional phrases.)

## Review Exercise I—Commas 3

Insert only necessary commas in the following sentences. Remove unnecessary commas with the delete sign ( ). In the space provided, indicate the number of commas inserted or deleted in each sentence. If a sentence requires no changes, write *C*. When you finish, compare your responses with those provided. For each item on which you need review, consult the numbered principle shown in parentheses.

Grammar/Mechanics Handbook

1. We expected Anna Cortez not Tyler Rosen to conduct the audit.
2. Brian said "We simply must have a bigger budget to start this project."
3. "We simply must have" said Brian "a bigger budget to start this project."
4. In August customers opened at least 50 new accounts; in September only about 20.
5. You returned the merchandise last month didn't you?
6. In short employees will now be expected to contribute more to their own retirement funds.
7. The better our advertising and recruiting the stronger our personnel pool will be.
8. Mrs. Delgado investigated selling her stocks not her real estate to raise the necessary cash.
9. "On the contrary" said Mr. Stevens "we will continue our present marketing strategies."
10. Our company will expand into surprising new areas such as, women's apparel and fast foods.
11. What we need is more not fewer suggestions for improvement.
12. Randall Clark Esq. and Jonathon Georges MBA joined the firm.
13. "America is now entering" said President Saunders "the Age of Information."
14. One of the reasons that we are inquiring about the publisher of the software is, that we are concerned about whether that publisher will be in the market five years from now.
15. The talk by D. A. Spindler PhD was particularly difficult to follow because of his technical and abstract vocabulary.
16. The month before a similar disruption occurred in distribution.
17. We are very fortunate to have, at our disposal, the services of excellent professionals.
18. No matter what you can count on us for support.
19. Mrs. Sandoval was named legislative counsel; Mr. Freeman executive advisor.
20. The data you are seeking can be found in an article titled, "The 100 Fastest Growing Games for Smartphones."

1. Cortez, Rosen, (2.12)   3. have," said Brian, (2.14a)   5. month, (2.14b)   7. recruiting, (2.12)   9. contrary," Stevens, (2.14a)   11. more, not fewer, (2.12)   13. entering," Saunders, (2.14a)   15. Spindler, PhD, (2.10)   17. have at our disposal (2.15)   19. Freeman, (2.11)

## Cumulative Editing Quiz 4

Use proofreading marks (see Appendix A) to correct errors and omissions in the following sentences. All errors must be corrected to receive credit for the sentence. Check with your instructor for the answers.

1. E-mails must be written clear and concise, to ensure that receivers comprehend the message quick.
2. Our next sales campaign of course must target key decision makers.
3. In the meantime our online sales messages must include more then facts testimonials and guarantees.

4. The Small Business Administration which provide disaster loans are establishing additional offices in Miami New Orleans and Biloxi.

5. Because we rely on e-mail we have reduced our use of faxes, and voice messages.

6. In business time is money.

7. "The first product to use a bar code" said Alice Beasley "was Wrigley's gum."

8. In 1908, the Model T went into production in Henry Ford's plant in Detroit Michigan.

9. As Professor Perez predicted the resourceful well trained graduate was hired quick.

10. The company's liability insurance in view of the laws that went into effect January 1 need to be increased.

# Semicolons (2.16)

## 2.16 Independent Clauses, Series, Introductory Expressions

a. **Independent clauses with conjunctive adverbs.** Use a semicolon before a conjunctive adverb that separates two independent clauses. Some of the most common conjunctive adverbs are *therefore, consequently, however,* and *moreover*:

> Business messages should sound conversational; *therefore*, writers often use familiar words and contractions.
>
> The bank closes its doors at 5 p.m.; *however*, the ATM is open 24 hours a day.

Notice that the word following a semicolon is *not* capitalized (unless, of course, that word is a proper noun).

b. **Independent clauses without conjunctive adverbs.** Use a semicolon to separate closely related independent clauses when no conjunctive adverb is used:

> Bond interest payments are tax deductible; dividend payments are not.
>
> Ambient lighting fills the room; task lighting illuminates each workstation.

Use a semicolon in *compound* sentences, not in *complex* sentences:

> After one week the paper feeder jammed; we tried different kinds of paper. (Use a semicolon in a compound sentence.)
>
> After one week the paper feeder jammed, although we tried different kinds of paper. (Use a comma in a complex sentence. Do not use a semicolon after *jammed*.)

The semicolon is very effective for joining two closely related thoughts. Don't use it, however, unless the ideas are truly related.

c. **Series with internal commas.** Use semicolons to separate items in a series when one or more of the items contains internal commas:

> Delegates from Miami, Florida; Freeport, Mississippi; and Chatsworth, California, attended the conference.
>
> The speakers were Kevin Lang, manager, Riko Enterprises; Henry Holtz, vice president, Trendex, Inc.; and Margaret Woo, personnel director, West Coast Productions.

d. **Introductory expressions.** Use a semicolon when an introductory expression such as *namely, for instance, that is,* or *for example* introduces a list following an independent clause:

> Switching to computerized billing are several local companies; namely, Ryson Electronics, Miller Vending Services, and Black Home Heating.
>
> The author of a report should consider many sources; for example, books, periodicals, databases, and newspapers.

## Colons (2.17–2.19)

### 2.17 Listed Items

a. **With colon.** Use a colon after a complete thought that introduces a formal list of items. A formal list is often preceded by such words and phrases as *these, thus, the following*, and *as follows*. A colon is also used when words and phrases like these are implied but not stated:

> Additional costs in selling a house involve *the following:* title examination fee, title insurance costs, and closing fee. (Use a colon when a complete thought introduces a formal list.)

> Collective bargaining focuses on several key issues: cost-of-living adjustments, fringe benefits, job security, and work hours. (The introduction of the list is implied in the preceding clause.)

b. **Without colon.** Do not use a colon when the list immediately follows a *to be* verb or a preposition:

> The employees who should receive the preliminary plan are James Sears, Monica Spears, and Rose Lopez. (No colon is used after the verb *are*.)

> We expect to consider equipment for Accounting, Legal Services, and Payroll. (No colon is used after the preposition *for*.)

### 2.18 Quotations.
Use a colon to introduce long one-sentence quotations and quotations of two or more sentences:

> Our consultant said: "This system can support up to 32 users. It can be used for decision support, computer-aided design, and software development operations at the same time."

### 2.19 Salutations.
Use a colon after the salutation of a business letter:

Gentlemen:     Dear Mrs. Seaman:     Dear Jamie:

## Review Exercise J—Semicolons, Colons

In the following sentences, add semicolons, colons, and necessary commas. For each sentence indicate the number of punctuation marks that you added. If a sentence requires no punctuation, write *C*. When you finish, compare your responses with those provided. For each item on which you need review, consult the numbered principle shown in parentheses.

1. Technological advances make full-motion video viewable on small screens consequently mobile phone makers and carriers are rolling out new services and phones.

2. Our branch in Sherman Oaks specializes in industrial real estate our branch in Canoga Park concentrates on residential real estate.

3. The sedan version of the automobile is available in these colors Olympic red metallic silver and Aztec gold.

4. If I can assist the new manager please call me however I will be gone from June 10 through June 15.

5. The individuals who should receive copies of this announcement are Jeff Doogan Alicia Green and Kim Wong.

6. We would hope of course to send personal letters to all prospective buyers however we have not yet decided just how to do this.

7. Many of our potential customers are in Southern California therefore our promotional effort will be strongest in that area.

8. Since the first of the year we have received inquiries from one attorney two accountants and one information systems analyst.

9. Three dates have been reserved for initial interviews January 15 February 1 and February 12.

10. Several staff members are near the top of their salary ranges and we must reclassify their jobs.
11. Several staff members are near the top of their salary ranges we must reclassify their jobs.
12. Several staff members are near the top of their salary ranges therefore we must reclassify their jobs.
13. If you apply for an Advantage Express card today we will waive the annual fee moreover you will earn 10,000 bonus miles and reward points for every $1 you spend on purchases.
14. Monthly reports from the following departments are missing Legal Department Human Resources Department and Engineering Department.
15. Monthly reports are missing from the Legal Department Human Resources Department and Engineering Department.
16. Since you became director of that division sales have tripled therefore I am recommending you for a bonus.
17. The convention committee is considering Portland Oregon New Orleans Louisiana and Phoenix Arizona.
18. Several large companies allow employees access to their personnel files namely General Electric Eastman Enterprises and Infodata.
19. Sherry first asked about salary next she inquired about benefits.
20. Sherry first asked about the salary and she next inquired about benefits.

---

1. screens; consequently, (2.16a)   3. colors: Olympic red, metallic silver, (2.01, 2.17a)   5. Doogan, Alicia Green, (2.01, 2.17b)   7. California; therefore, (2.16a)   9. interviews: January 15, February 1, (2.01, 2.17a)   11. ranges; (2.16b)   13. today, fee; moreover, (2.06a, 2.16a)   15. Department, Human Resources Department, (2.01, 2.17b)   17. Portland, Oregon; New Orleans, Louisiana; Phoenix, (2.16c)   19. salary; (2.16b)

## Apostrophes (2.20–2.22)

**2.20 Basic Rule.** The apostrophe is used to show ownership, origin, authorship, or measurement.

**Ownership:** We are looking for *Brian's keys*.
**Origin:** At the *president's suggestion*, we doubled the order.
**Authorship:** The *accountant's annual report* was questioned.
**Measurement:** In *two years' time* we expect to reach our goal.

a. **Ownership words not ending in *s*.** To place the apostrophe correctly, you must first determine whether the ownership word ends in an *s* sound. If it does not, add an apostrophe and an *s* to the ownership word. The following examples show ownership words that do not end in an *s* sound:

   the employee's file          (the file of a single employee)
   a member's address           (the address of a single member)
   a year's time                (the time of a single year)
   a month's notice             (notice of a single month)
   the company's building       (the building of a single company)

Grammar/Mechanics Handbook

b. **Ownership words ending in s**. If the ownership word does end in an s sound, usually add only an apostrophe:

| | |
|---|---|
| several employees' files | (files of several employees) |
| ten members' addresses | (addresses of ten members) |
| five years' time | (time of five years) |
| several months' notice | (notice of several months) |
| many companies' buildings | (buildings of many companies) |

A few singular nouns that end in *s* are pronounced with an extra syllable when they become possessive. To these words, add 's.

    my boss's desk    the waitress's table    the actress's costume

Use no apostrophe if a noun is merely plural, not possessive:

    All the sales representatives, as well as the assistants and managers, had their names and telephone numbers listed in the directory.

**2.21 Names Ending in *s* or an *s* sound.** The possessive form of names ending in *s* or an *s* sound follows the same guidelines as for common nouns. If an extra syllable can be pronounced without difficulty, add 's. If the extra syllable is hard to pronounce, end with an apostrophe only.

| **Add apostrophe and s** | **Add apostrophe only** |
|---|---|
| Russ's computer | New Orleans' cuisine |
| Bill Gates's business | Los Angeles' freeways |
| Mrs. Jones's home | the Morrises' family |
| Mr. Lopez's desk | the Lopezes' pool |

Individual preferences in pronunciation may cause variation in a few cases. For example, some people may prefer not to pronounce an extra *s* in examples such as *Bill Gates' business*. However, the possessive form of plural names is consistent: *the Joneses' home, the Burgesses' children, the Bushes' car*. Notice that the article *the* is a clue in determining whether a name is singular or plural.

**2.22 Gerunds.** Use 's to make a noun possessive when it precedes a gerund, a verb form used as a noun:

    Mr. Smith's smoking prompted a new office policy. (*Mr. Smith* is possessive because it modifies the gerund *smoking*.)

    It was Betsy's careful proofreading that revealed the discrepancy.

## Review Exercise K—Apostrophes

Insert necessary apostrophes and corrections in the following sentences. In the space provided for each sentence, write the corrected word. If none were corrected, write *C*. When you finish, compare your responses with those provided. For each item on which you need review, consult the numbered principle shown in parentheses.

1. In five years time, Lisa hopes to repay all of her student loans.
2. If you go to the third floor, you will find Mr. Londons office.
3. All the employees personnel folders must be updated.
4. In a little over a years time, that firm was able to double its sales.
5. The Harrises daughter lived in Florida for two years.
6. A patent protects an inventors invention for 17 years.
7. Both companies headquarters will be moved within the next six months.
8. That position requires at least two years experience.

9. Some of their assets could be liquidated; therefore, a few of the creditors received funds.
10. All assistants workstations were equipped with Internet access.
11. The package of electronics parts arrived safely despite two weeks delay.
12. Many nurses believe that nurses notes are not admissable evidence.
13. According to Mr. Cortez latest proposal, all employees would receive an additional holiday.
14. Many of our members names and addresses must be checked.
15. His supervisor frequently had to correct Jacks financial reports.
16. We believe that this firms service is much better than that firms.
17. Mr. Jackson estimated that he spent a years profits in reorganizing his staff.
18. After paying six months rent, we were given a receipt.
19. The contract is not valid without Mrs. Harris signature.
20. It was Mr. Smiths signing of the contract that made us happy.

1. years' (2.20b)   3. employees' (2.20b)   5. Harrises' (2.21)   7. companies' (2.20b)   9. C (2.20b)
11. weeks' (2.20b)   13. Cortez's (2.21)   15. Jack's (2.20)   17. year's (2.20a)   19. Harris's (2.21)

## Cumulative Editing Quiz 5

Use proofreading marks (see Appendix A) to correct errors and omissions in the following sentences. All errors must be corrected to receive credit for the sentence. Check with your instructor for the answers.

1. Mark Zuckerberg worked for years to build Facebook however it was years' before the company made a profit.
2. E-businesses has always been risky, online companys seem to disappear as quick as they appear.
3. According to a leading data source three of the top European entertainment companys are the following Double Fusion, Jerusalem, Israel, Echovoc, Geneva, Switzerland, and IceMobile, Amsterdam, The Netherlands.
4. By the way Tess e-mail was forwarded to Mr. Lopezes incoming box in error and she was quite embarrassed.
5. The SECs findings and ruling in the securitys fraud case is expected to be released in one hours time.
6. Only one HMOs doctors complained that they were restricted in the time they could spend listening to patients comments.
7. Any one of the auditors are authorized to conduct an independent action however only the CEO can change the councils directives.
8. Charles and Les mountain bicycles were stole from there garage last night.
9. Five of the worst computer passwords are the following your first name, your last name, the Enter key, *Password*, and the name of a sports' team.
10. On January 15 2015 we opened an innovative full equipped fitness center.

Grammar/Mechanics Handbook

GM-33

# Other Punctuation (2.23–2.29)

## 2.23 Periods

a. **Ends of sentences.** Use a period at the end of a statement, command, indirect question, or polite request. Although a polite request may have the same structure as a question, it ends with a period:

> Corporate legal departments demand precise skills from staff members. (End a statement with a period.)

> Get the latest data by reading current periodicals. (End a command with a period.)

> Mr. Rand wondered whether we had sent any follow-up literature. (End an indirect question with a period.)

> Would you please reexamine my account and determine the current balance. (A polite request suggests an action rather than a verbal response.)

b. **Abbreviations and initials.** Use periods after initials and after many abbreviations.

| | | |
|---|---|---|
| R. M. Johnson | c.o.d. | Ms. |
| p.m. | a.m. | Mr. |
| Inc. | i.e. | Mrs. |

The latest trend is to omit periods in degrees and professional designations: BA, PhD, MD, RN, DDS. Use just one period when an abbreviation falls at the end of a sentence:

> Guests began arriving at 5:30 p.m.

## 2.24 Question Marks.
Direct questions are followed by question marks:

> Did you send your proposal to Datatronix, Inc.?

Statements with questions added are punctuated with question marks:

> We have completed the proposal, haven't we?

## 2.25 Exclamation Points.
Use an exclamation point after a word, phrase, or clause expressing strong emotion. In business writing, however, exclamation points should be used sparingly:

> Incredible! Every terminal is down.

## 2.26 Dashes.
The dash (constructed at a keyboard by striking the hyphen key twice in succession) is a legitimate and effective mark of punctuation when used according to accepted conventions. As a connecting punctuation mark, however, the dash loses effectiveness when overused.

a. **Parenthetical elements.** Within a sentence a parenthetical element is usually set off by commas. If, however, the parenthetical element itself contains internal commas, use dashes (or parentheses) to set it off:

> Three top salespeople—Tom Judkins, Tim Templeton, and Mary Yashimoto—received bonuses.

b. **Sentence interruptions.** Use a dash to show an interruption or abrupt change of thought:

> News of the dramatic merger—no one believed it at first—shook the financial world.

> Ship the materials Monday—no, we must have them sooner.

Sentences with abrupt changes of thought or with appended afterthoughts can usually be improved through rewriting.

c. **Summarizing statements.** Use a dash (not a colon) to separate an introductory list from a summarizing statement:

> Sorting, merging, and computing—these are tasks that our data processing programs must perform.

**2.27 Parentheses.** One means of setting off nonessential sentence elements involves the use of parentheses. Nonessential sentence elements may be punctuated in one of three ways: (a) with commas, to make the lightest possible break in the normal flow of a sentence; (b) with dashes, to emphasize the enclosed material; and (c) with parentheses, to de-emphasize the enclosed material. Parentheses are frequently used to punctuate sentences with interpolated directions, explanations, questions, and references:

> The cost analysis (which appears on page 8 of the report) indicates that the copy machine should be leased.

> Units are lightweight (approximately 13 oz.) and come with a leather case and operating instructions.

> The latest laser printer (have you heard about it?) will be demonstrated for us next week.

A parenthetical sentence that is not embedded within another sentence should be capitalized and punctuated with end punctuation:

> The Model 20 has stronger construction. (You may order a Model 20 brochure by circling 304 on the reader service card.)

### 2.28 Quotation Marks

a. **Direct quotations.** Use double quotation marks to enclose the exact words of a speaker or writer:

> "Keep in mind," Mrs. Frank said, "that you'll have to justify the cost of networking our office."

> The boss said that automation was inevitable. (No quotation marks are needed because the exact words are not quoted.)

b. **Quotations within quotations.** Use single quotation marks (apostrophes on the keyboard) to enclose quoted passages within quoted passages:

> In her speech, Mrs. Deckman remarked, "I believe it was the poet Robert Frost who said, 'All the fun's in how you say a thing.'"

c. **Short expressions.** Slang, words used in a special sense, and words following *stamped* or *marked* are often enclosed within quotation marks:

> Jeffrey described the damaged shipment as "gross." (Quotation marks enclose slang.)

> Students often have trouble spelling the word "separate." (Quotation marks enclose words used in a special sense.)

> Jobs were divided into two categories: most stressful and least stressful. The jobs in the "most stressful" list involved high risk or responsibility. (Quotation marks enclose words used in a special sense.)

> The envelope marked "Confidential" was put aside. (Quotation marks enclose words following *marked*.)

In the four preceding sentences, the words enclosed within quotation marks can be set in italics, if italics are available.

d. **Definitions.** Double quotation marks are used to enclose definitions. The word or expression being defined should be underscored or set in italics:

> The term *penetration pricing* is defined as "the practice of introducing a product to the market at a low price."

e. **Titles.** Use double quotation marks to enclose titles of literary and artistic works, such as magazine and newspaper articles, chapters of books, movies, television shows, poems, lectures, and songs. Names of major publications—such as books, magazines, pamphlets, and newspapers—are set in italics (underscored).

> Particularly helpful was the chapter in Smith's *Effective Writing Techniques* titled "Right Brain, Write On!"

In the *Los Angeles Times* appeared John's article, "E-Mail Blunders"; however, we could not locate it online.

 f. **Additional considerations.** In this country periods and commas are always placed inside closing quotation marks. Semicolons and colons, on the other hand, are always placed outside quotation marks:

Mrs. James said, "I could not find the article titled 'Cell Phone Etiquette.'"

The president asked for "absolute security": All written messages were to be destroyed.

Question marks and exclamation points may go inside or outside closing quotation marks, as determined by the form of the quotation:

Sales Manager Martin said, "Who placed the order?" (The quotation is a question.)

When did the sales manager say, "Who placed the order?" (Both the incorporating sentence and the quotation are questions.)

Did the sales manager say, "Ryan placed the order"? (The incorporating sentence asks a question; the quotation does not.)

"In the future," shouted Bob, "ask me first!" (The quotation is an exclamation.)

**2.29 Brackets.** Within quotations, brackets are used by the quoting writer to enclose his or her own inserted remarks. Such remarks may be corrective, illustrative, or explanatory:

Mrs. Cardillo said, "OSHA [Occupational Safety and Health Administration] has been one of the most widely criticized agencies of the federal government."

## Review Exercise L—Other Punctuation

Insert necessary punctuation in the following sentences. In the space provided for each item, indicate the number of punctuation marks that you added. Count sets of parentheses, dashes, and quotation marks as two marks. Emphasis or de-emphasis will be indicated for some parenthetical elements. When you finish, compare your responses with those provided. For each item on which you need review, consult the numbered principle shown in parentheses.

1. Will you please send me your latest catalog

2. (Emphasize) Three of my friends Carmen Lopez, Stan Meyers, and Ivan Sergo were promoted.

3. Mr Lee, Miss Evans, and Mrs Rivera have not responded.

4. We have scheduled your interview for 4 45 p m

5. (De-emphasize) The appliance comes in limited colors black, ivory, and beige, but we accept special orders.

6. The expression de facto means exercising power as if legally constituted.

7. Was it the president who said "This, too, will pass

8. Should this package be marked Fragile

9. Did you see the Newsweek article titled How Far Can Wireless Go

10. Amazing All sales reps made their targets

---

1. catalog. (2.23a) 3. Mr. Mrs. (2.23b) 5. colors (black, ivory, and beige) (2.26a) 7. said, pass"? (2.28f)
9. *Newsweek* "How Go?" (2.28e)

## Cumulative Editing Quiz 6

Use proofreading marks (see Appendix A) to correct errors and omissions in the following sentences. All errors must be corrected to receive credit for the sentence. Check with your instructor for the answers.

1. We wondered whether Ellen Hildago PhD would be the speaker at the Cairo Illinois event?

2. Our operating revenue for 2015 see Appendix A exceeded all the consultants expectations.

3. Four features, camera, text messaging, Web access, and voice mail—are what Americans want most on there cell phones.

4. Louis Camilleri CEO of Philip Morris said "We're being socially responsible in a rather controversial industry.

5. Kym Andersons chapter titled Subsidies and Trade Barriers appears in the book How to Spend $50 Billion to Make the World a Better Place.

6. Wasnt it Zack Woo not Ellen Trask who requested a 14 day leave.

7. Was it Oprah Winfrey who said that the best jobs are those we'd do even if we didn't get paid.

8. The word mashup is a technology term that is defined as a website that uses content from more then one source to create a completely new service.

9. Miss. Rhonda Evers is the person who the employees council elected as there representative.

10. Would you please send a current catalog to Globex, Inc?

## Style and Usage

### Capitalization (3.01–3.16)

Capitalization is used to distinguish important words. However, writers are not free to capitalize all words they consider important. Rules or guidelines governing capitalization style have been established through custom and use. Mastering these guidelines will make your writing more readable and more comprehensible.

**3.01 Proper Nouns.** Capitalize proper nouns, including the *specific* names of persons, places, schools, streets, parks, buildings, holidays, months, agreements, websites, software programs, apps, games, historical periods, and so forth. Do not capitalize common nouns that make only *general* references.

| Proper nouns | Common nouns |
| --- | --- |
| Instagram, Flixster, WorldMate | popular mobile apps |
| Mexico, Canada | U.S. trading partners |
| El Camino College | a community college |
| Sam Houston Park | a park in the city |
| Phoenix Room, Statler Inn | a meeting room in the hotel |
| Memorial Day, New Year's Day | two holidays |

Grammar/Mechanics Handbook

| | |
|---|---|
| Google, Facebook, Wikipedia | popular websites |
| George Washington Bridge | a bridge |
| Consumer Product Safety Act | a law to protect consumers |
| PowerPoint, Photoshop, Excel | software programs |
| Will Rogers World Airport | a municipal airport |
| January, February, March | months of the year |

**3.02 Proper Adjectives.** Capitalize most adjectives that are derived from proper nouns:

| | |
|---|---|
| Greek symbol | British thermal unit |
| Roman numeral | Freudian slip |
| Xerox copy | Hispanic markets |

Do not capitalize the few adjectives that, although originally derived from proper nouns, have become common adjectives through usage. Consult your dictionary when in doubt:

| | |
|---|---|
| manila folder | diesel engine |
| venetian blinds | china dishes |

**3.03 Geographic Locations.** Capitalize the names of *specific* places such as continents, countries, states, mountains, valleys, lakes, rivers, oceans, and geographic regions:

| | |
|---|---|
| New York City | Great Salt Lake |
| Allegheny Mountains | Pacific Ocean |
| San Fernando Valley | Delaware Bay |
| the East Coast | the Pacific Northwest |

**3.04 Organization Names.** Capitalize the principal words in the names of all business, civic, educational, governmental, labor, military, philanthropic, political, professional, religious, and social organizations:

| | |
|---|---|
| Genentech | Board of Directors, Midwest Bank |
| *The Wall Street Journal*\* | San Antonio Museum of Art |
| New York Stock Exchange | Securities and Exchange Commission |
| United Way | National Association of Letter Carriers |
| Commission to Restore the Statue of Liberty | Association of Information Systems Professionals |

**3.05 Academic Courses and Degrees.** Capitalize particular academic degrees and course titles. Do not capitalize general academic degrees and subject areas:

Professor Bernadette Ordian, *PhD*, will teach *Accounting* 221 next fall.

Mrs. Snyder, who holds *bachelor's* and *master's degrees*, teaches *marketing* classes.

Jim enrolled in classes in *history, business English*, and *management*.

**3.06 Personal and Business Titles**

a. Capitalize personal and business titles when they precede names:

| | |
|---|---|
| Vice President Ames | Uncle Edward |
| Board Chairman Frazier | Councilman Herbert |
| Governor G. W. Thurmond | Sales Manager Klein |
| Professor McLean | Dr. Samuel Washington |

---

\**Note:* Capitalize *the* only when it is part of the official name of an organization, as printed on the organization's stationery.

b. Capitalize titles in addresses, salutations, and closing lines:

| | |
|---|---|
| Mr. Juan deSanto | Very truly yours, |
| Director of Purchasing | |
| Space Systems, Inc. | Clara J. Smith |
| Boxborough, MA 01719 | Supervisor, Marketing |

c. Generally, do not capitalize titles of high government rank or religious office when they stand alone or follow a person's name in running text:

The president conferred with the joint chiefs of staff and many senators.

Meeting with the chief justice of the Supreme Court were the senator from Ohio and the mayor of Cleveland.

Only the cardinal from Chicago had an audience with the pope.

d. Do not capitalize most common titles following names:

The speech was delivered by Robert Lynch, *president*, Academic Publishing. Lois Herndon, *chief executive officer*, signed the order.

e. Do not capitalize common titles appearing alone:

Please speak to the *supervisor* or to the *office manager*.

Neither the *president* nor the *vice president* could attend.

However, when the title of an official appears in that organization's minutes, bylaws, or other official document, it may be capitalized.

f. Do not capitalize titles when they are followed by appositives naming specific individuals:

We must consult our *director of research*, Ronald E. West, before responding.

g. Do not capitalize family titles used with possessive pronouns:

| | |
|---|---|
| my mother | your father |
| our aunt | his cousin |

h. Capitalize titles of close relatives used without pronouns:

Both *Mother* and *Father* must sign the contract.

## 3.07 Numbered and Lettered Items.
Capitalize nouns followed by numbers or letters (except in page, paragraph, line, and verse references):

| | |
|---|---|
| Flight 34, Gate 12 | Plan No. 2 |
| Volume I, Part 3 | Warehouse 33-A |
| Invoice No. 55489 | Figure 8.3 |
| Model A5673 | Serial No. C22865404-2 |
| State Highway 10 | page 6, line 5 |

## 3.08 Points of the Compass.
Capitalize *north, south, east, west*, and their derivatives when they represent *specific* geographical regions. Do not capitalize the points of the compass when they are used in directions or in general references:

| **Specific regions** | **General references** |
|---|---|
| from the South | heading north on the highway |
| living in the Midwest | west of the city |
| Easterners, Southerners | western Nevada, southern Indiana |
| going to the Middle East | the northern part of the United States |
| from the East Coast | the east side of the street |

Grammar/Mechanics Handbook

**3.09 Departments, Divisions, and Committees.** Capitalize the names of departments, divisions, or committees within your own organization. Outside your organization capitalize only *specific* department, division, or committee names:

> The inquiry was addressed to the *Legal Department* in our *Consumer Products Division*.
>
> John was appointed to the *Employee Benefits Committee*.
>
> Send your résumé to their *human resources division*.
>
> A *planning committee* will be named shortly.

**3.10 Governmental Terms.** Do not capitalize the words *federal, government, nation,* or *state* unless they are part of a specific title:

> Unless *federal* support can be secured, the *state* project will be abandoned.
>
> The *Federal Deposit Insurance Corporation* protects depositors from bank failure.

**3.11 Product Names.** Capitalize product names only when they refer to trademarked items. Except in advertising, common names following manufacturers' names are not capitalized:

| | |
|---|---|
| Magic Marker | Dell computer |
| Kleenex tissues | Swingline stapler |
| Q-tip swab | ChapStick lip balm |
| Levi 501 jeans | Excel spreadsheet |
| DuPont Teflon | Canon camera |

**3.12 Literary Titles.** Capitalize the principal words in the titles of books, magazines, newspapers, articles, movies, plays, songs, poems, and reports. Do *not* capitalize articles (*a, an, the*), short conjunctions *(and, but, or, nor)*, and prepositions of fewer than four letters (*in, to, by, for*) unless they begin or end the title:

> Jackson's *What Job Is for You?* (Capitalize book titles.)
>
> Gant's "*Software for the Executive Suite*" (Capitalize principal words in article titles.)
>
> "*Performance Standards to Go By*" (Capitalize article titles.)
>
> "*The Improvement of Fuel Economy With Alternative Fuels*" (Capitalize report titles.)

**3.13 Beginning Words.** In addition to capitalizing the first word of a complete sentence, capitalize the first word in a quoted sentence, independent phrase, item in an enumerated list, and formal rule or principle following a colon:

> The business manager said, "*All* purchases must have requisitions." (Capitalize first word in a quoted sentence.)
>
> Yes, if you agree. (Capitalize an independent phrase.)
>
> Some of the duties of the position are as follows:
>
> 1. *Editing* and formatting Word files
> 2. *Arranging* video and teleconferences
> 3. *Verifying* records, reports, and applications (Capitalize items in a vertical enumerated list.)
>
> One rule has been established through the company: *No* smoking is allowed in open offices. (Capitalize a rule following a colon.)

**3.14 Celestial Bodies.** Capitalize the names of celestial bodies such as *Mars, Saturn,* and *Neptune*. Do not capitalize the terms *earth, sun,* or *moon* unless they appear in a context with other celestial bodies:

> Where on *earth* did you find that manual typewriter?
>
> *Venus* and *Mars* are the closest planets to *Earth*.

**3.15 Ethnic References.** Capitalize terms that refer to a particular culture, language, or race:

| | |
|---|---|
| Asian | Hebrew |
| Caucasian | Indian |
| Latino | Japanese |
| Persian | Judeo-Christian |

**3.16 Seasons.** Do not capitalize seasons:

In the *fall* it appeared that *winter* and *spring* sales would increase.

## Review Exercise M—Capitalization

In the following sentences, correct any errors that you find in capitalization. Underscore any lowercase letter that should be changed to a capital letter. Draw a slash (/) through a capital letter that you wish to change to a lowercase letter. In the space provided, indicate the total number of changes you have made in each sentence. If you make no changes, write *0*. When you finish, compare your responses with those provided.

**EXAMPLE:** Bill McAdams, currently Assistant Manager in our Personnel department, will be promoted to Manager of the Employee Services division.     5

1. My Uncle and I used powerpoint to make a simple marketing video featured on youtube.
2. Our company will soon be moving its operations to the west coast.
3. Marilyn Hunter, mba, received her bachelor's degree from Ohio university in athens.
4. The President of Datatronics, Inc., delivered a speech titled "Taking off into the future."
5. Please ask your Aunt and your Uncle if they will come to the Attorney's office at 5 p.m.
6. Your reservations are for flight 32 on american airlines leaving from gate 14 at 2:35 p.m.
7. Once we establish an organizing committee, arrangements can be made to rent holmby hall.
8. Dylan was enrolled in history, spanish, business communications, and physical education courses.
9. Either the President or the Vice President of the company will make the decision about purchasing xerox copiers.
10. Rules for hiring and firing Employees are given on page 7, line 24, of the Contract.
11. Some individuals feel that american companies do not have the sense of loyalty to their employees that japanese companies do.
12. Where on Earth can we find better workers than Robots?
13. The secretary of state said, "we must protect our domestic economy from foreign competition."
14. After crossing the sunshine skyway bridge, we drove to Southern Florida for our vacation.
15. All marketing representatives of our company will meet in the empire room of the red lion motor inn.
16. Richard Elkins, phd, has been named director of research for spaceage strategies, inc.
17. The special keyboard for the Dell Computer must contain greek symbols for Engineering equations.

Grammar/Mechanics Handbook

18. After she received a master's degree in electrical engineering, Joanne Dudley was hired to work in our product development department.

19. In the Fall our organization will move its corporate headquarters to the franklin building in downtown los angeles.

20. Dean Amador has one cardinal rule: always be punctual.

---

1. uncle PowerPoint YouTube (3.06g, 3.01)   3. MBA University Athens (3.01, 3.05)   5. aunt uncle attorney's (3.06e, 3.06g)   7. Holmby Hall (3.01)   9. president vice president Xerox (3.06e, 3.11)   11. American Japanese (3.02)   13. We (3.13)   15. Empire Room Red Lion Motor Inn (3.01)   17. computer Greek engineering (3.01, 3.02, 3.11)   19. fall Franklin Building Los Angeles (3.01, 3.03, 3.16)

## Cumulative Editing Quiz 7

Use proofreading marks (see Appendix A) to correct errors and omissions in the following sentences. All errors must be corrected to receive credit for the sentence. Check with your instructor for the answers.

1. I wonder whether president Jackson invited our Marketing Vice President to join the upcoming three hour training session?

2. Our Sales Manager said that you attending the two day seminar is fine however we must find a replacement.

3. The boston marathon is an annual Sporting Event hosted by the City of Boston, Massachusetts on patriot's day the third monday of April.

4. Steve Chen one of the founders of YouTube hurried to gate 44 to catch flight 246 to north carolina.

5. Jake noticed that the english spoken by asians in hong kong sounded more british than american.

6. Memorial day is a Federal holiday therefore banks will be closed.

7. Because the package was marked fragile the mail carrier handled it careful.

8. Money traders watched the relation of the american dollar to the chinese yuan, the european euro and the japanese yen.

9. My Aunt and me travel South each Winter to vacation in Southern Georgia with our friends the Gonzalez's.

10. Mary Minnick former Executive Vice President of the Coca-cola company now serves as president of the companys marketing, strategy, and innovation department.

### Number Style (4.01–4.13)

Usage and custom determine whether numbers are expressed in the form of figures (for example, *5, 9*) or in the form of words (for example, *five, nine*). Numbers expressed as figures are shorter and more easily understood, yet numbers expressed as words are necessary in certain instances. The following guidelines are observed in expressing numbers in written sentences. Numbers that appear on business forms—such as invoices, monthly statements, and purchase orders—are always expressed as figures.

### 4.01 General Rules

a. The numbers *one* through *ten* are generally written as words. Numbers above *ten* are written as figures:

> The bank had a total of *nine* branch offices in *three* suburbs.
>
> All *58* employees received benefits in the *three* categories shown.
>
> A shipment of *45,000* lightbulbs was sent from *two* warehouses.

b. Numbers that begin sentences are written as words. If a number beginning a sentence involves more than two words, however, the sentence should be revised so that the number does not fall at the beginning.

> *Fifteen* color options are available in our latest smartphone lineup.
>
> A total of 156 companies participated in the promotion (not *One hundred fifty-six companies participated in the promotion*).

### 4.02 Money.
Sums of money $1 or greater are expressed as figures. If a sum is a whole dollar amount, omit the decimal and zeros (whether or not the amount appears in a sentence with additional fractional dollar amounts):

> We budgeted *$300* for a digital camera, but the actual cost was *$370.96*.
>
> On the invoice were items for *$6.10*, *$8*, *$33.95*, and *$75*.

Sums less than $1 are written as figures that are followed by the word *cents*:

> By shopping carefully, we can save *15 cents* per unit.

### 4.03 Dates.
In dates, numbers that appear after the name of the month are written as cardinal figures (*1, 2, 3*, etc.). Those that stand alone or appear before the name of a month are written as ordinal figures *(1st, 2nd, 3rd*, etc.):

> The Personnel Practices Committee will meet *May 7*.
>
> On the *5th* day of February and again on the *25th*, we placed orders.

In domestic business documents, dates generally take the following form: *January 4, 2015*. An alternative form, used primarily in military and foreign correspondence, begins with the day of the month and omits the comma: *4 January 2015*.

### 4.04 Clock Time.
Figures are used when clock time is expressed with *a.m.* or *p.m.* Omit the colon and zeros in referring to whole hours. When exact clock time is expressed with the contraction *o'clock*, either figures or words may be used:

> Mail deliveries are made at *11 a.m.* and *3:30 p.m.*
>
> At *four* (or *4*) *o'clock* employees begin to leave.

### 4.05 Addresses and Telephone Numbers

a. Except for the number *one*, house numbers are expressed in figures:

> 540 Elm Street                17802 Washington Avenue
> One Colorado Boulevard        2 Highland Street

b. Street names containing numbers *ten* or lower are written entirely as words. For street names involving numbers greater than *ten*, figures are used:

> 330 Third Street              3440 Seventh Avenue
> 6945 East 32nd Avenue         4903 West 23rd Street

c. Telephone numbers are expressed with figures. When used, the area code is placed in parentheses preceding the telephone number:

>Please call us at *(818) 347-0551* to place an order.

>Mr. Sims asked you to call *(619) 554-8923*, Ext. 245, after 10 a.m.

**4.06 Related Numbers.** Numbers are related when they refer to similar items in a category within the same reference. All related numbers should be expressed as the largest number is expressed. Thus if the largest number is greater than *ten*, all the numbers should be expressed in figures:

>Only *5* of the original *25* applicants completed the processing. (Related numbers require figures.)

>The *two* plans affected *34* employees working in *three* sites. (Unrelated numbers use figures and words.)

>Exxon Oil operated *86* rigs, of which *6* were rented. (Related numbers require figures.)

>The company hired *three* accountants, *one* customer-service representative, and *nine* sales representatives. (Related numbers under ten use words.)

**4.07 Consecutive Numbers.** When two numbers appear consecutively and both modify a following noun, generally express the first number in words and the second in figures. If, however, the first number cannot be expressed in one or two words, place it in figures also (*120 70-cent* stamps). Do not use commas to separate the figures.

>Historians divided the era into *four 25-year* periods. (Use word form for the first number and figure form for the second.)

>We ordered *ten 30-page* color brochures. (Use word form for the first number and figure form for the second.)

>Did the manager request *150 100-watt* bulbs? (Use figure form for the first number since it would require more than two words.)

**4.08 Periods of Time.** Seconds, minutes, days, weeks, months, and years are treated as any other general number. Numbers above *ten* are written in figure form. Numbers below *ten* are written in word form unless they represent a business concept such as a discount rate, interest rate, or warranty period:

>This business was incorporated over *50* years ago. (Use figures for a number above *ten*.)

>It took *three* hours to write this short report. (Use words for a number under *ten*.)

>The warranty period is limited to *2* years. (Use figures for a business term.)

**4.09 Ages.** Ages are generally expressed in word form unless the age appears immediately after a name or is expressed in exact years and months:

>At the age of *twenty-one*, Elizabeth inherited the business.

>Wanda Tharp, *37*, was named acting president.

>At the age of *4 years and 7 months*, the child was adopted.

**4.10 Round Numbers.** Round numbers are approximations. They may be expressed in word or figure form, although figure form is shorter and easier to comprehend:

>About *600* (or *six hundred*) stock options were sold.

>It is estimated that *1,000* (or *one thousand*) people will attend.

For ease of reading, round numbers in the millions or billions should be expressed with a combination of figures and words:

>Facebook estimates that it has *1.11 billion* users.

>More than *163 million* viewers watched last year's Super Bowl game.

**4.11 Weights and Measurements.** Weights and measurements are expressed with figures:

> The new deposit slip measures *2* by *6 inches*.
>
> Her new suitcase weighed only *2 pounds 4 ounces*.
>
> Toledo is *60 miles* from Detroit.

**4.12 Fractions.** Simple fractions are expressed as words. Complex fractions may be written either as figures or as a combination of figures and words:

> Over *two thirds* of the stockholders have already voted.
>
> This microcomputer will execute the command in *1 millionth* of a second. (A combination of words and numbers is easier to comprehend.)
>
> She purchased a *one-fifth* share in the business.*

**4.13 Percentages and Decimals.** Percentages are expressed with figures that are followed by the word *percent*. The percent sign (%) is used only on business forms or in statistical presentations:

> We had hoped for a *7 percent* interest rate, but we received a loan at *8 percent*.
>
> Over *50 percent* of the residents supported the plan.

Decimals are expressed with figures. If a decimal expression does not contain a whole number (an integer) and does not begin with a zero, a zero should be placed before the decimal point:

> The actuarial charts show that *1.74* out of *1,000* people will die in any given year.
>
> Inspector Norris found the setting to be *.005* inch off. (Decimal begins with a zero and does not require a zero before the decimal point.)
>
> Considerable savings will accrue if the unit production cost is reduced *0.1* percent. (A zero is placed before a decimal that neither contains a whole number nor begins with a zero.)

**Quick Chart—Expression of Numbers**

| Use Words | Use Figures |
|---|---|
| Numbers *ten* and under | Numbers *11* and over |
| Numbers at beginning of sentence | Money |
| Ages | Dates |
| Fractions | Addresses and telephone numbers |
| | Weights and measurements |
| | Percentages and decimals |

## Review Exercise N—Number Style

Write the preferred number style on the lines provided. Assume that these numbers appear in business correspondence. When you finish, compare your responses with those provided. For each item on which you need review, consult the numbered principle shown in parentheses.

1. (a) 2 laptops                (b) two laptops
2. (a) Seventh Avenue           (b) 7th Avenue
3. (a) sixty sales reps         (b) 60 sales reps
4. (a) November ninth           (b) November 9
5. (a) forty dollars            (b) $40

---

*Notes:* Fractions used as adjectives require hyphens.

6. (a) on the 23rd of May    (b) on the twenty-third of May
7. (a) at 2:00 p.m.    (b) at 2 p.m.
8. (a) 4 two-hundred-page books    (b) four 200-page books
9. (a) at least 15 years ago    (b) at least fifteen years ago
10. (a) 1,000,000 viewers    (b) 1 million viewers
11. (a) twelve cents    (b) 12 cents
12. (a) a sixty-day warranty    (b) a 60-day warranty
13. (a) ten percent interest rate    (b) 10 percent interest rate
14. (a) 4/5 of the voters    (b) four fifths of the voters
15. (a) the rug measures four by six feet    (b) the rug measures 4 by 6 feet
16. (a) about five hundred people attended    (b) about 500 people attended
17. (a) at eight o'clock    (b) at 8 o'clock
18. (a) located at 1 Wilshire Boulevard    (b) located at One Wilshire Boulevard
19. (a) three computers for twelve people    (b) three computers for 12 people
20. (a) 4 out of every 100 licenses    (b) four out of every 100 licenses

---

1. b (4.01a)   3. b (4.01a)   5. b (4.02)   7. b (4.04)   9. a (4.08)   11. b (4.02)   13. b (4.13)   15. b (4.11)
17. a or b (4.04)   19. b (4.06)

## Cumulative Editing Quiz 8

Use proofreading marks (see Appendix A) to correct errors and omissions in the following sentences. All errors must be corrected to receive credit for the sentence. Check with your instructor for the answers.

1. My partner and myself will meet at our attorneys office at three p.m. on June ninth to sign our papers of incorporation.

2. Emily prepared 2 forty page business proposals to submit to the Senior Account Manager.

3. Of the 235 e-mail messages sent yesterday only seven bounced back.

4. Your short term loan for twenty-five thousand dollars covers a period of sixty days.

5. Each new employee must pick up their permanent parking permit for lot 3-A before the end of the 14 day probationary period.

6. 259 identity theft complaints were filed with the Federal trade commission on November second alone.

7. Robertas 11 page report was more easier to read then Davids because her's was better organized and had good headings.

8. Every morning on the way to the office Tatiana picked up 2 lattes that cost a total of eight dollars.

9. Taking 7 years to construct the forty thousand square foot home of Bill Gates reportedly cost more then fifty million dollars.

10. Many companys can increase profits nearly ninety percent by retaining only 5% more of there current customers.

# Confusing Words

| | |
|---|---|
| accede: | to agree or consent |
| accept: | to receive |
| adverse: | opposing; antagonistic |
| advice: | suggestion, opinion |
| advise: | to counsel or recommend |
| affect: | to influence |
| all ready: | prepared |
| all right: | satisfactory |
| already: | by this time |
| alright: | unacceptable variant spelling |
| altar: | structure for worship |
| alter: | to change |
| appraise: | to estimate |
| apprise: | to inform |
| ascent: | (n) rising or going up |
| assent: | (v) to agree or consent |
| assure: | to promise |
| averse: | unwilling; reluctant |
| capital: | (n) city that is seat of government; wealth of an individual; (adj) chief |
| capitol: | building that houses state or national lawmakers |
| cereal: | breakfast food |
| cite: | to quote; to summon |
| coarse: | rough texture |
| complement: | that which completes |
| compliment: | (n) praise, flattery; (v) to praise or flatter |
| conscience: | regard for fairness |
| conscious: | aware |
| council: | governing body |
| counsel: | (n) advice, attorney; (v) to give advice |
| course: | a route; part of a meal; a unit of learning |
| credible: | believable |
| creditable: | good enough for praise or esteem; reliable |
| desert: | arid land; to abandon |
| dessert: | sweet food |
| device: | invention or mechanism |
| devise: | to design or arrange |
| disburse: | to pay out |
| disperse: | to scatter widely |
| effect: | (n) outcome, result; (v) to bring about, to create |
| elicit: | to draw out |
| ensure: | to make certain |
| envelop: | (v) to wrap, surround, or conceal |
| envelope: | (n) a container for a written message |
| every day: | each single day |
| everyday: | ordinary |
| exceed: | over a limit |
| except: | to exclude; (prep) but |
| farther: | a greater distance |
| formally: | in a formal manner |
| formerly: | in the past |
| further: | additional |
| grate: | (n) a frame of crossed bars blocking a passage; (v) to reduce to small particles; to cause irritation |
| great: | (adj) large in size; numerous; eminent or distinguished |
| hole: | an opening |
| illicit: | unlawful |
| imply: | to suggest indirectly |
| infer: | to reach a conclusion |
| insure: | to protect from loss |
| lean: | (v) to rest against; (adj) not fat |
| liable: | legally responsible |
| libel: | damaging written statement |
| lien: | (n) a legal right or claim to property |
| loose: | not fastened |
| lose: | to misplace |
| miner: | person working in a mine |
| minor: | a lesser item; person under age |
| patience: | calm perseverance |
| patients: | people receiving medical treatment |
| personal: | private, individual |
| personnel: | employees |
| plaintiff: | (n) one who initiates a lawsuit |
| plaintive: | (adj) expressive of suffering or woe |
| populace: | (n) the masses; population of a place |
| populous: | (adj) densely populated |
| precede: | to go before |
| precedence: | priority |
| precedents: | events used as an example |
| principal: | (n) capital sum; school official; (adj) chief |
| principle: | rule of action |
| proceed: | to continue |
| serial: | arranged in sequence |
| sight: | a view; to see |
| site: | location |

Grammar/Mechanics Handbook

| | | | |
|---|---|---|---|
| *stationary:* | immovable | *to:* | a preposition; the sign of the infinitive |
| *stationery:* | writing material | | |
| *than:* | conjunction showing comparison | *too:* | an adverb meaning "also" or "to an excessive extent" |
| *their:* | possessive form of *they* | *two:* | a number |
| *then:* | adverb meaning "at that time" | *waiver:* | abandonment of a claim |
| *there:* | at that place or point | *waver:* | to shake or fluctuate |
| *they're:* | contraction of *they are* | *whole:* | complete |

## 160 Frequently Misspelled Words

| | | | |
|---|---|---|---|
| absence | desirable | independent | prominent |
| accommodate | destroy | indispensable | qualify |
| achieve | development | interrupt | quantity |
| acknowledgment | disappoint | irrelevant | questionnaire |
| across | dissatisfied | itinerary | receipt |
| adequate | division | judgment | receive |
| advisable | efficient | knowledge | recognize |
| analyze | embarrass | legitimate | recommendation |
| annually | emphasis | library | referred |
| appointment | emphasize | license | regarding |
| argument | employee | maintenance | remittance |
| automatically | envelope | manageable | representative |
| bankruptcy | equipped | manufacturer | restaurant |
| becoming | especially | mileage | schedule |
| beneficial | evidently | miscellaneous | secretary |
| budget | exaggerate | mortgage | separate |
| business | excellent | necessary | similar |
| calendar | exempt | nevertheless | sincerely |
| canceled | existence | ninety | software |
| catalog | extraordinary | ninth | succeed |
| changeable | familiar | noticeable | sufficient |
| column | fascinate | occasionally | supervisor |
| committee | feasible | occurred | surprise |
| congratulate | February | offered | tenant |
| conscience | fiscal | omission | therefore |
| conscious | foreign | omitted | thorough |
| consecutive | forty | opportunity | though |
| consensus | fourth | opposite | through |
| consistent | friend | ordinarily | truly |
| control | genuine | paid | undoubtedly |
| convenient | government | pamphlet | unnecessarily |
| correspondence | grammar | permanent | usable |
| courteous | grateful | permitted | usage |
| criticize | guarantee | pleasant | using |
| decision | harass | practical | usually |
| deductible | height | prevalent | valuable |
| defendant | hoping | privilege | volume |
| definitely | immediate | probably | weekday |
| dependent | incidentally | procedure | writing |
| describe | incredible | profited | yield |

GM-48

Grammar/Mechanics Handbook

# Key to Grammar/Mechanics Checkups

## Chapter 1
**1.** countries (1.05e) **2.** CEOs (1.05g) **3.** attorneys (1.05d) **4.** Sundays, Mondays (1.05a) **5.** turkeys (1.05d) **6.** Alvarezes (1.05b) **7.** 1950s (1.05g) **8.** brothers-in-law (1.05f) **9.** klutzes (1.05b) **10.** inquiries (1.05e) **11.** Anthonys (1.05a) **12.** C (1.05d) **13.** liabilities (1.05e) **14.** C (1.05h) **15.** women (1.05c)

## Chapter 2
**1.** she (1.08b) **2.** his (1.09b) **3.** him (1.08c) **4.** Whom (1.08j) **5.** yours (1.08d) **6.** me (1.08c) **7.** I (1.08a) **8.** its (1.08d) **9.** whoever (1.08j) **10.** me (1.08i) **11.** he (1.08f) **12.** us (1.08g) **13.** her (1.09c) **14.** its (1.09g) **15.** he and I (1.08a)

## Chapter 3
**1.** is (1.10c) **2.** has (1.10i) **3.** offers (1.10d) **4.** are (1.10e) **5.** has (1.10i) **6.** were (1.12) **7.** C (1.10h) **8.** gone (1.15) **9.** lain (1.15) **10.** is (1.10h) **11.** believe (1.10b) **12.** b (1.15c) **13.** b (1.15c) **14.** a (1.15c) **15.** a (1.14b)

## Chapter 4
**1.** tried-and-true (1.17e) **2.** ten-year-old (1.17e) **3.** bright (1.17c) **4.** quickly (1.17d) **5.** delete *more* (1.17b) **6.** work-related (1.17e) **7.** their (1.17g) **8.** spur-of-the-moment (1.17e) **9.** C (1.17e) **10.** well-thought-out (1.17e) **11.** change-of-address (1.17e) **12.** case-by-case (1.17e) **13.** delete *more* (1.17b) **14.** bad (1.17c) **15.** smoothly (1.17d)

## Chapter 5
**1.** a (1.19d) **2.** b (1.19c) **3.** b (1.19d) **4.** b (1.19c) **5.** b (1.19a) **6.** a (1.18a) **7.** b (1.18b) **8.** b (1.18c) **9.** b (1.18a) **10.** b (1.18e) **11.** b (1.19a) **12.** a (1.19b) **13.** b (1.19c) **14.** a (1.18b) **15.** b (1.19c)

## Chapter 6
**1.** 2 (2.03) **2.** 2 (2.02) **3.** 2 (2.01) **4.** 0 **5.** 1 (2.03) **6.** 4 (2.04c) **7.** 1 (2.03) **8.** 2 (2.04a) **9.** 2 (2.01) **10.** 4 (2.04b) **11.** 2 (2.03) **12.** 2 (2.01) **13.** 1 (2.02) **14.** 2 (2.03) **15.** 4 (2.04c)

## Chapter 7
**1.** 1 (2.06a) **2.** 1 (2.05) **3.** 0 (2.05) **4.** 2 (2.06c) **5.** 1 (2.08) **6.** 0 (2.06c) **7.** 2 (2.09) **8.** 1 (2.07) **9.** 1 (2.06a) **10.** 1 (2.07) **11.** 2 (2.01) **12.** 3 (2.06a, 2.04a) **13.** 1 (2.06c) **14.** 3 (2.06a, 2.04a) **15.** 1 (2.05)

## Chapter 8
**1.** 2 (2.14a) **2.** 3 (2.10) **3.** 1 (2.14b) **4.** 0 (2.15) **5.** 1 (2.12) **6.** 3 (2.06a, 2.01) **7.** 2 (2.03) **8.** 2 (2.07, 2.06c) **9.** 3 (2.03, 2.01) **10.** 2 (2.06a, 2.11) **11.** 2 (2.07, 2.09) **12.** 2 (2.06c, 2.15) **13.** 0 (2.06c) **14.** 4 (2.06c, 2.01) **15.** 2 (2.03, 2.08)

## Chapter 9
**1.** 2 (2.16a) **2.** 2. (2.16a) **3.** 3 (2.17a, 2.01) **4.** 1 (2.17b) **5.** 1 (2.06a) **6.** 3 (2.03, 2.16b) **7.** 3 (2.17a, 2.01) **8.** 9 (2.16c, 2.17a) **9.** 1 (2.05) **10.** 5 (2.16d, 2.01) **11.** 4 (2.06c, 2.16a) **12.** 2 (2.06a, 2.17b) **13.** 2 (2.16a) **14.** 0 (2.17a) **15.** 1 (2.16b)

## Chapter 10
**1.** Metz's (2.21) **2.** years' (2.20b) **3.** weeks' (2.20b) **4.** Miller's (2.20a) **5.** employees' (2.20b) **6.** witness's (2.20b) **7.** Lisa's (2.22) **8.** money's (2.20a) **9.** C (2.20b) **10.** month's (2.20a) **11.** boss's (2.20b) **12.** secretary's (2.20a) **13.** Sanchez's (2.21) **14.** company's (2.20a) **15.** businesses' (2.20b)

## Chapter 11
**1.** 2 (2.26a) **2.** 3 (2.02, 2.23a) **3.** 2 (2.27) **4.** 1 (2.23a) **5.** 1 (2.26c) **6.** 2 (2.28f) **7.** 4 (2.28e, 2.28f) **8.** 2 (2.26a) **9.** 5 (2.23b, 2.24) **10.** 3. (2.28e) **11.** 1 (2.28f) **12.** 1 (2.23a) **13.** 3 (2.23b, 2.24) **14.** 3 (2.28d) **15.** 3 (2.24, 2.25, 2.14)

## Chapter 12
**1.** 7 (3.01, 3.07) **2.** 6 (3.15, 3.01, 3.04, 3.06d) **3.** 3 (3.01) **4.** 4 (3.05) **5.** 8 (3.04, 3.12) **6.** 4 (3.11) **7.** 4 (3.10) **8.** 4 (3.06c, 3.01, 3.13) **9.** 8 (3.06e, 3.09) **10.** 5 (3.06g, 3.03, 3.14) **11.** 7 (3.06e, 3.11) **12.** 7 (3.16, 3.06e, 3.03) **13.** 4 (3.01, 3.03) **14.** 3 (3.09, 3.05) **15.** 5 (3.07, 3.04, 3.15)

## Chapter 13
**1.** b (4.01a) **2.** a (4.05b) **3.** a (4.01a) **4.** b (4.03) **5.** b (4.02) **6.** a (4.03) **7.** b (4.04) **8.** b (4.07) **9.** b (4.08) **10.** b (4.10) **11.** b. (4.02) **12.** b (4.08) **13.** b (4.12) **14.** a (4.06) **15.** a (4.06)

## Chapter 14
1. In the **fall** each of the **companies plans** to increase **its** hiring.
2. Our **Accounting Department** processed expense claims for Ryan and **me**, but **Ryan's** was lost.
3. The **marketing manager** assigned Jennifer and **me** the best **two** new sales **territories**.
4. The telephone has **rung** at least **three** times with the same **incredible** recorded message.
5. **Three** types of similar **storms** of the tropics **are [delete colon]** cyclones, **typhoons,** and hurricanes.
6. **It's too** early to determine whether we'll make a profit before **September 15**.
7. If I **were she,** I would pay off the **principle** of the loan **immediately**.
8. German shoppers generally bring **their** own bags for **groceries; therefore,** they were unaccustomed to **Walmart's** bagging techniques.
9. Mary Beth Merrin, a **professor** at the **university**, asked that research reports contain the following **sections: introduction**, body, summary, and bibliography.

10. If we had **seen** the **sender's invoice,** we would have **paid** it **quickly.**
11. When **convenient**, will you please send me **four copies** of that **vendor's** most recent **contract.**
12. Do you think Jacob and **he** placed **their** report on the **boss's** desk last **night?**
13. About **one half** of Pizza **Hut's 8,000** outlets will make **deliveries;** the others **focus** on **walk-in** customers.
14. **Everything except** labor and parts is covered in **your five**-year warranty.
15. When Kerry completes her **degree,** she plans to apply for employment **in [delete colon]** Scottsdale, **Dallas,** or Atlanta.

# Index

*Italic page numbers indicate illustrative information in figures.*

## A

Abbreviations
　avoid, 20
　commas with, GM-26–GM-27
　of states, territories, and provinces, A-12
　texting style, 46
ABI/INFORM (ProQuest), 309
　search result page, *310*
Abstract nouns, GM-6
Abstract or executive summary, formal proposals, 300, *300*
Academic courses and degrees, capitalization of, GM-38
Acceptance message, job, 496–497
Accuracy, editing formal business reports, 308
Acronyms, avoid, 20
Action
　motivating at conclusion of sales message, 239
　rejecting requests for, 202–203
　verbs for powerful résumés, 440
Action request, concluding claim with, 165
Action-specific verbs, 20
Active voice, 73, GM-13
Activities, résumé information, 441
Adaptation, 44
Adapting the message, 3-x-3 writing process, 39
Adapting to audience
　bias-free language, 50–51
　developing you view, 45–46
　preferring plain language and familiar words, 51
　sounding conversational but professional, 46–47
　spotlighting audience benefits, 44–45
Address
　commas with, GM-22–GM-23
　number style of, GM-43–GM-44
Addressee notations, business letters, A-6
Adjectives, GM-16–GM-18
　capitalization of proper, GM-38
　commas with two or more, GM-25
　forms, GM-16–GM-17
　function of, GM-6
　guidelines for use, GM-17–GM-18
Adjustment, 168
Adjustment messages, 168–171
Adobe Presenter, 398
Advance Search filters, 310
Adverbs, GM-16–GM-18
　forms, GM-16–GM-17
　function of, GM-6
　guidelines for use, GM-17–GM-18
Age
　biased language, 50
　number style of, GM-44
　workforce diversity, 20
　Workforce50, 431
Agencies, *430*

Agenda of meeting, distributing, 371, *371*
Agreement, buffer to open indirect negative messages, 198
Agreement guidelines
　for pronoun antecedent, GM-9–GM-10
　for verb-subject, GM-11–GM-12
AIDA (attention, interest, desire, action), 236
　strategy for sales messages, 237
All caps, 71
Alternate references shown in APA style, *339*
Ambiguous wording, avoid, 20
American Psychological Association (APA), 318, A-13
　format, 328, A-13–A-16
　in-text format, A-13–A-14
　journal article reference, anatomy of, *A-14*
　reference format, 3, A-14–A-16
　references, 319
　sample references, *A-15*
　style, justification/recommendation report, *282–283*
　text page and references, portions of, *A-14*
Analogy, 397
Analysis
　audience, 266
　begin job search with self-analysis, 427
　budget, 300, *300*
Analytical reports, 265
　feasibility reports, 282–285
　justification/recommendation reports, 281–282
　preparing short, 279–288
　yardstick reports, 285–288
Analytical-reasoning, 3
Analyze, formal business reports, 307
Analyzing
　negative news strategies, 194–197
　persuasive tweets, *243*
　the audience, 41–44
　the situation and purpose, multimedia presentations, 401
　3-x-3 writing process, 39
Answers, avoid *yes, but*, 411
Anticipating
　the audience, 41–44
　3-x-3 writing process, 39
　typical interview questions, 484–490
Anytime, anywhere and nonterritorial offices, 6–7
APA. *See* American Psychological Association
Apache OpenOffice Impress, 398
Apology
　composing effective negative messages, 198–202

　defined, 198
　law, 170
　skip during presentation, 410
Apostrophes, GM-31–GM-32
Appearance, 13–14
　business documents, 13
　personal, 13–14
Appended questions, commas with, GM-27
Appendix, formal proposals, 300, *300*
Apple Calendar, 370
Apple Keynote, 398
Applicant tracking system (ATS), 436, 448
Application follow-up message, 495–496
Application form, 495
Appositives, commas with, GM-25
Appreciation, buffer to open indirect negative messages, 198
Article summary, *280*
ATS. *See* applicant racking system, 436
Attachment, e-mail, A-5
Attention
　capturing in introduction, 392
　faking, 10
　gaining in sales messages, 237
　gaining in the opening of cover message, 455–457
Attention line, business letters, A-7–A-8
Audience
　adapting message to, 39, 44–47
　analysis and report organizations, 266
　analyzing, 39, 41–44
　anticipating, 39, 41–44, 305
　attention, *393*
　benefits, 44–45
　communicating with diverse workplace, 21–22
　engaging with effective imagery, *397*
　greet members before presentation, 409
　knowing your, 391
　multimedia presentations adjusting slide design to, 401–403
　of short information reports, 275
　primary, *42*
　profiling, 42, *43*
　receptive, direct strategy for, 66–67, *68*
　secondary, *42*
　types of, *391*
　unreceptive, indirect strategy for, 67–68, *68*
Audience rapport
　establishing, 396–398
　organizing content for, 392–398
Audience-focused message, 45
Authority, lines of, 232

Authorization request, informal proposals, 300, *300*
Awards, résumé information, 441

## B

Back matter components, body components of formal business reports, 328
Background
　informal proposals, 299, *300*, 304
　multimedia presentation, *406*
Bad news
　announcing directly, *195*
　announcing to employees and public, 209–210
　best communication channel, 209
　cushioning of, 200–201
　delivering in person within organizations, 207–208
　delivering sensitively, *197*
　direct strategy, 194–195
　follow-up message, *205*
　indirect strategy, 196, *196*
　intranet post, 209–210
　managing within organizations, 206–210
　refusing workplace requests, 208–209
　strategically positioning of, 200
　*See also* Negative news; Negative messages
Bar charts, 320–321, *320*, *322*
Barriers to effective listening, overcoming, 10
*Bcc*, e-mail, A-5
Beginning words, capitalization of, GM-40
Behavior
　dimensions of, *355*
　identifying positive and negative team, 366
　relating to ethics, 354–355
　workplace, 352
　positive and negative group, 366
Behavioral questions, interview questions, 488–489
　using STAR technique to answer, *489*
Best case/worst case strategy for organizing the body of oral presentation, 395
　organizing report findings, *307*
Best practices for
　better e-mail, *125*
　instant messaging and texting on the job, 129
　online sales messages, 242
Bias-free language, 50–51
Bibliographic citation formats, comparing, *319*
Bibliography, 328
Bing, 309
Block letter style, *A-7*, A-10

Index　　　　I-1

## B

Blogging
  crisis communication, 133–134
  customer relations, 133–134
  for business, 132–136
  internal communication, 135
  market research, 134
  online communities, 134–135
  public relations, 133–134
  recruiting, 135
  viral marketing, 134
Blogs, 6, *43*, 66, 479
  best practices, 135–136
  podcasts, and wikis, collaboration with, *9*
Body
  adjustment message, 170
  blog best practices, 135
  business letters, A-8
  cover message, 457–459
  formal business reports, 327–328
Boldface, 71
Booher, Dianna, 66
Books, secondary source, 309
Boolean search operators, 310
Boss, messages to persuade, 232–233
Brackets, GM-36
Brand, building personal, 435, *436*
Briefings, types of business presentations, *390*
*Brilliant Email*, 121
Budget analysis, informal proposals, 300, *300*
Budget, component of informal proposal, 304
Buffer to open indirect negative messages, 197–198
Buffett, Warren, 13
Bulleted lists, 100–101
Bullying, 129
Business
  blogging for, 132–136
  how companies blog, 133–135
  making podcasts and wikis work for, 130–132, *132*
  webcasts, 131
  writing goals, 38
  writing techniques, developing, 71–75
Business communicators in low-and high-context cultures, 16
Business documents, eye appeal of, 13
Business etiquette, 130, 352–355
Business letters, A-5–A-12
  confidentiality, 157
  formality and sensitivity, 157
  formatting, 157–158
  parts of, A-6-A-10
  permanent record, 157
  persuasive, 157
  understanding, 156–157
Business messages
  applying phase 3 of writing process, 90–95
  being positive rather than negative, 47–49
  employing bias-free language, 50–51
  evaluating effectiveness of, 105
  expressing courtesy, 49
  making it clear, 95–98
  preferring plain language and familiar words, 51

primary purpose to inform and persuade, 41–42
  proofreading, 103–105
  revising for conciseness, 91–94
  secondary purpose to promote goodwill, 42
  sounding conversational but professional, 46–47
  using precise, vigorous words, 51
Business podcasts
  delivering and accessing, 131
  how organizations use, 131
  or webcasts, 131
Business presentations
  after, 410–411
  before, 408–409
  combating stage fright, *408*
  delivery method, 407
  during, 409–410
  organizing content for impact and audience rapport, 392–398
  polishing your deliver and following up, 406–411
  preparing, 389–391
  speaking skills and your career, 389–390
  types of, 390, *390*
  understanding contemporary visual aids, 398–400
  *See also* Multimedia presentations; Oral presentations
Business proposals
  informal or formal, 299–300
  internal or external, 300
  preparing, 299–305
  solicited (RFP) or unsolicited, 301
  types of, 299–301
Business reports, 264
  defining purpose and gathering data for, 273–275
  documenting and citing sources in, 316–318
  writing and editing formal, 305–308
Business Source Premier (EBSCO), 309
Business titles, capitalization of, GM-38–GM39
Business.com, 310, *311*
Businesses generate wide range of messages, 3–4
Businesses use social networks, 136–137
  potential risks of, 138–139
Businesslike, professional e-mail message, *4*
Buzzwords, 96–97

## C

Calendar programs, *370*
Campus career center, 428
Capabilities, résumé information, 440–441
Caperton, Gaston, 3
Capitalization, 101, 271, GM-37–GM-41
Career e-portfolio, making, 449
Career objective, résumé information, 438
Career opportunities, exploring, 428–429
Career profile, 439

Career sifter, 2
CareerBuilder, 428, 430, 448, 454
Carlson, Chris, 121
Carter, Stephen L., 354
Case
  guidelines for selecting pronoun, GM-8–GM-9
  of pronouns, GM-8
Category headings, 101
Cattle-call interviews, 475
*Cc*, e-mail, A-5
Celestial bodies, capitalization of, GM-40
Cell phones
  or other electronic devices, turn off during the interview, 483
  projecting professionalism, *6*
Channel, 37
  choice, direct mail and social media, *236*
  selecting best, 43–44
Charts
  bar, 320–321
  line, 321
  pie, 321, *323*
  segmented area (surface), 321, *323*
Chat, 46
Chicago Manual of Style (CMS), 318
  bibliography, *319*
Chismar, Douglas, 354, 355
Chitchat, 46
Chronological résumé
  graduate with related experience, *443*
  graduate with substantial experience, *445*
  student seeking internship, *447*
  student with limited relevant experience, *444*
  style, 437
Chronological sequencing, 275
Chronological strategy for organizing report findings, *307*
Chronology, organizing the body of oral presentation, 394
Citation formats, 318
Civility, 352, 353
Claim message
  adopting a moderate tone, 229–231
  developing logically, 229
Claims, 164
  denying, 206
  direct, 164–167
  refusing typical, 202–206
  writing plan for refusing typical, 202
Clarify the report's message, formal business reports, 307–308
Clarity
  commas with, GM-27
  communicating negative news, 193
  instruction messages, 164
  revising for, 95–98
  short information reports, 275
Classified ads, 429
Clichés, 96
Clock time, number style of, GM-43
Close-ended questions, surveys, 313
Closing
  adjustment message, 171
  cover message, 459–460
  e-mail, A-5

negative messages, 201–202
  request messages, 159
Cloud, 120
  computing, *8*
Cloud-based presentation, 399
Collaboration, 364
  in teams, 368
  software, 4
Collaborative technologies, communication and, *8–9*
Collective nouns, GM-7
Collectivist, 16
CollegeGrad, 428, 431
Colons, GM-30
Color, meaning of in multimedia presentations, 401–402
Commas, GM-22–GM-27
  overuse of, GM-27
Comma-splice sentences, 70
Committee names, capitalization of, GM-40
Common nouns, GM-6
Communicating face-to-face on the job, 355–360
Communication
  collaborative technologies and, *8–9*
  defined, 36
  in teams, 368
  recognizing how culture affects, 14–18
  style, 17
  with diverse workplace audiences, 21–22
Communication channels, comparing rich and lean, *43*
Communication process, understanding, 36–38, *37*
Communication skills
  learning nonverbal, 11–14
  your pass to success, 2–3
Communication technology, 2, 17–18, 356
  rapidly changing, 5–6
Company blogs, 4
Company database, submitting your résumé, 453
Company records, gather information from, 274
Company websites, exploring, 431
Comparative form of adjectives and adverbs, GM-16–GM-17
Compare/contrast strategy for organizing
  body of oral presentation, 395
  report findings, *307*
Complaints
  and reviews, posting online, 167, *167*
  direct, 164–167
Complex documents, proofreading, 104–105
Complex sentence, 69
Compliance, risk of IM and texting, 129
Complimentary close, business letters, A-8
Composing
  first draft, 69–71
  negative messages, 197–202
  multimedia presentations, 403
Compound sentence, 69
Compound-complex sentence, 69
Comprehension, numbering and bulleting lists for, 100–101

I-2                                                                                                                                                                                                                                           Index

Conciseness
  aids clarity in understanding drug facts, 95
  principles of apply to writing short information reports, 275
  revising for, 91–94
Conclusion
  and authorization, informal proposal, 300, 300, 305
  formal business reports, 307, 328
  oral presentations summarizing in, 395–396
Concrete nouns, GM-6
Condolences, sending, 174
Conference report, 275–276, 276
Confidentiality, business letters safeguard, 157
Conflict
  dealing with, 367
  handling in meetings, 372
  teams confront, 367–368
Confusing words, GM-47–GM-48
Conjunctions, GM-19–GM-20
  functions of, GM-6
  guidelines for use, GM-19–GM-20
Consecutive numbers, number style of, GM-44
Consistency, editing formal business reports, 308
Constructive criticism, providing on the job, 360
Contact list, building personal network, 432–433
Content
  notes, A-13
  organizing for impact and audience rapport, 392–398
Context, 15–16
Contractions, 20
Contrasting statements, commas with, GM-27
Contributions, recognizing employees for, 173–174
Control voice and vocabulary during presentation, 410
Convention report, 275–276
Conversation
  face-to-face, 43, 122, 356
  interview, 478
  workplace, 357–359
Conversational and informal writing style for short information reports, 275
Conversational but professional, business messages, 46–47
Coordinated Universal Time (UTC), 374
Copy notation, business letters, A-9
Copyright and fair use, 317–318
Corel Presentations, 398
Correction symbols, A-1–A-3
Correctness, principles of apply to writing short information reports, 275
Cost, benefit of IM and texting, 128
Courtesy
  expressing, 49
  principles of apply to writing short information reports, 275
Cover letter or message, 454
  body, 457–459
  closing, 459–460
  customized, 454–461

final tips, 460–461
importance of, 454–455
opening, 455–457
sending, 460
solicited jobs, 455–456, 457
unsolicited jobs, 456–457, 458
Crisis communication, companies blog, 133–134
Critical-thinking, 3
Criticism in workplace, 359
Crowdsourcing, 132, 134
Cultural differences and social networking, 18
Cultural divides, bridging, 17–18
Culture
  comparing low- and high-context, 15
  defined, 15
  group-centered, 16
  recognizing how it affects communication, 14–18
Culture dimension
  communication style, 17
  context, 15
  individualism, 16
  power distance, 17
  time orientation, 16–17
Customer
  adjustment letter, 169
  comments, 161
  dealing with disappointed, 203–204
  relations, 133–134
  response e-mail, 160
  reviews online, 161
Cyberbullying, 353

D
Dangling modifiers, 74–75
Dashes, 71, GM-34
Data sources, 308
Database, 309
Dateline, business letters, A-6
Dates
  commas with, GM-22–GM-23
  number style of, GM-43
Decimals, number style of, GM-45
Decision making, four phases of team development in, 365
Decisions, better with teams, 365
Decoding, 38
  skills, 14
Deference, 17
Degrees, commas with, GM-26–GM-27
Deliverables, 304
Delivery method of presentation, 407
Delivery notations, business letters, A-6
Denying claims, 206
Department names, capitalization of, GM-40
Dependent clauses, commas with, GM-24–GM-25
Desire, building in sales messages, 238–239
Desk rage, 353
Diction, levels of, 47
Dictionary of Occupational Titles, 428
Digital age
  e-mail messages and memos, preparing, 120–127
  job searching in, 426–429, 427

organizations, crafting persuasive messages in, 232–233
reporting in, 264–268
understanding changing job market, 426–427
understanding persuasion in, 226–229
Digital convergence, 9
Digital dirt, 480–481
Digital documents, revising, 92
Digital format, 270
Digital media, 3, 17–18
Digital message, 38
Digital revolution, writing skills matter, 3–4
Digital slide decks, 270
Digital tools, optimizing job search with today's, 448–453
Digressions, avoid during presentation, 410
Direct address, commas with, GM-22
Direct approach (cold calling), 430
Direct claim e-mail, 166
Direct claims and complaints, 164–167
Direct mail, 233
Direct referral and luck, 430
Direct request letter, block style, 158
Direct request messages, writing plan for, 159
Direct strategy
  and indirect strategies for negative messages, comparing, 194
  for delivering negative news, 194–196
  for receptive audiences, 66–67
  justification/recommendation reports, 281
  organizational strategies for reports, 265–266
Direct-mail
  marketing, 235
  sales letter, 239
  sales messages, 235
Directness, 280
  equated with honesty, 196
Directories, 309–310
Disability biased language, 51
Disabled workers, GettingHired, 431
Disappointed customers, dealing in print with, 203–204
Diversity
  in workforce, 20
  teams embrace, 367
Division names, capitalization of, GM-40
Documentation, 316
  common citation formats, 318
  copyright and fair use, 317–318
  formats, A-13–A-18
  guidelines, 316–317
  paraphrase, 316–317
  quote, 317
Documents
  design improves readability, 102
  enhancing readability through design, 98–103
  format guide, A-4–A-12
  proofreading complex, 104–105
  proofreading routine, 103–104
  revising digital and print, 92
Donation request, refusing, 203
Down-editing, 125

Drafting
  second phase of 3-x-3 writing process, 39–40
  well-organized, paragraphs, 75–76
Dropbox, 409

E
EBSCO, 309
Editing, 90
  3-x-3 writing process, 40
Education
  bonus, 7
  drives your income, 5
  résumé information, 439
Efficiency, benefit of IM and texting, 129
Electronic presentations, 9
Electronic resources, gather information from, 274
E-mail(s), 3, 5, 36, 43, 46, 121, A-4–A-5
  best practices for, 125
  close effectively, 123
  comparing memos and, 126–127
  controlling your inbox, 123–124
  cover message, 461
  denying a claim, 207
  drafting professional, 122–123
  everlasting evidence, 121
  format, 269
  goodwill messages, 174–175
  include greeting, 122–123
  knowing when it is appropriate, 122
  meeting minutes, 373
  organize body for readability and tone, 123
  overload, 121
  projecting professionalism, 6
  replying efficiently with down-editing, 125
  routine messages, 156–158
  subject line, 122
  typical, A-4
  why people complain, 121
E-mail message
  businesslike and professional, 4
  preparing in digital-age, 120–127
  reports delivered as, 264
  request, formatting, 124
  writing techniques to improve, 48
E-mail replies, writing plan for, 160
E-mail sales messages, 239
  guidelines for, 242
  writing successful, 239–242
E-marketing, 242
Emotional appeal, building interest with, 237–238
Empathy, 19, 45
  composing effective negative messages, 199
  conveying in negative news, 193
Emphasis
  developing, 71–73
  using your voice as a communication tool, 357
Employability skills, 5
Employee morale, improved with teams, 365

Index I-3

Employees
  announcing bad news to, 209–210, *210*
  downward flowing messages to persuade, 232
  recognizing for their contributions, 173–174
  writing plan for announcing negative news to, 209
Employment
  documents, 494–498
  history, résumé information, 439–440
  interviews, purposes and types of, 474–476
Empty words
  avoiding during the interview, 483
  purging, 93–94
Enclosure notations, business letters, A-9
Encoding, 37
Engagement, 133
Enthusiasm, show during presentation, 410
Envelope, business letters, A-10–A-12
  formats, *A-11*
E-portfolio, 449–450
Ethical communication, key to, 197
Ethical responsibilities, teams accept, 368
Ethics, 354
  information age workplace, 5
  relating professional behavior to, 354–355
  renewed emphasis on, 7
Ethnic references, capitalization of, GM-41
Ethnically biased language, 50
Ethnicity, workforce diversity, 20
Ethnocentrism, 18–19
Etiquette
  business, 130, 353
  online and office skills, 352–355
  smartphone, 362–363
  telephone and voice mail, 361–364
  texting, 130, *130*
Evaluating, 90
  effectiveness of message, 105
  slide presentations, 404–405
  3-x-3 writing process, 40
Exclamation points, GM-34
Executive summary, 279, 300, *300*, 326–327, *332*
Experience, organizing body in oral presentations, 394
Experimentation, primary research source, 315
External proposals, 300
Exuberance, 97
Eye contact
  during the interview, 482
  maintain during presentation, 409
  nonverbal skills, 14
  silent messages sent by body, 12

# F

Facebook, 4, 6, 36, 42, 66, 94, 120, 121, 136, 137, 161, 205, 240–241, 309, 431, 433, 435, 451, 479, 480–481
  big companies rule on, *137*
  Messenger, 127, 128
  model, adopting, 137
Face-to-face
  communication on the job, 355–360
  conversation, *43*, 122, 356
  meetings, planning and participating in, 368–375
Facial expression, silent messages sent by body, 12
Factiva (Dow Jones), 309
Fair use and copyright, 317–318
Fairness, communicating negative news, 193
Familiar words, 51
Favors
  rejecting requests for, 202–203
  sending thanks for, 172–173
Fax, 6
  submitting your résumé, 453
Feasibility reports, 282–285, *284*
Feedback, 11, 38
Fillers, 92–93
First draft, 69–71
Flabby expressions, 91
Flattened management hierarchies, 7
  information age workplace, 5
Fletcher, Theo, 21
Flexible working arrangements, 6
Flipcharts, *399*
Flowchart, 321–322, *324*
  matching graphics to objectives, *320*
Focused reports, 264
Fogg, B. J., 226
Folding, business letters, A-11–A-12
Follow-up message
  acceptance and rejection, 496–497
  application, 495–496
  résumé, 495–496
Fonts
  changes in, 71
  multimedia presentation, *406*
  types and sizes of, 100
Footnote, 318
Forbes, Malcolm, 206
Formal business reports, 325–339, *326*
  writing and editing, 305–308
Formal meeting minutes, *278*
Formal proposals, 299–300, *300*
Formal research methods, 65–66
Formal writing style, 266–268, *269*
Formality and sensitivity, business letters convey, 157
Format, 103
  APA, 328
  APA in-text, A-13–A-14
  APA reference, 3, A-14–A-16
  business letters, 157–158
  citation, 318, *319*
  digital, 270
  document guide, A-4–A-12
  documentation, A-13–A-18
  editing formal business reports, 308
  e-mail, *124*, 269
  envelope, *A-11*
  letter, 267–268, 269, A-6
  manuscript, 269
  memo, 125, *126*, 269
  MLA in-text, A-17
  MLA, A-16–A-18

MLA referencing, 328
MLA works-cited, A-17
outline, *67*, 307
report, 269–271
résumé, 451–452
Forming, team development, 365
Forms and templates, 269
Forums, 6
Fractions, number style of, GM-45
Fragments, 70
Franklin, Ben, 44
Freebies, 201
Freewriting, 69
*From* line, e-mail, A-4
Front matter components, 325–327
Frontloading, 67
  message, 159
  recommendations, 280
FTC template, negative news, 196
Functional heads, 271, 328
Functional résumé, 437, *446*
Future perfect tense, GM-13
Future tense, GM-13

# G

Gender biased language, 50
Gender, workforce diversity, 20
Generation Y, 136
Geographic locations, capitalization of, GM-38
Geographical items, commas with, GM-22–GM-23
Geographical strategy for organizing report findings, *307*
Geography/space, organizing body of oral presentation, 394
Gerunds, apostrophes with, GM-33
Gestures, 12
  during the interview, 483
Gift, express thanks for, 172
Global competition, 5
  heightened, 7
Global knowledge workers, 121
Globalization and workplace diversity, 20
Goodwill messages, 171–175
  expressing sympathy, 174
  e-mail, 174–175
  replying to, 174
  saying thank you, 172–174
Google, 46, 65, 136, 309, 310, 433, 480
  Calendar, 370
  Docs, 132
  Drive, 409
  Google+, 435
  Maps, 309
  News, 358
  Search Operators, *309*, *310*
  Sites, 132
Government job, USA Student Jobs, 431
Governmental terms, capitalization of, GM-40
Grammar, 103
Grammatically equal levels, report headings, 271
Grandstanding, 10
Grant proposals, 300
Graphics
  editing formal business reports, 308
  incorporating into reports, 323–325

  matching graphics and objectives, 319, *320*
  multimedia presentation, *406*
Greeting, e-mail, 122–123
Group interviews, 475–476
Group-centered cultures, 16
Grouped bar chart, *322*
Grouping, 66
Groupthink, 21

# H

Hall, Edward T., 13, 15
Handouts, 398, *399*
  distribute after presentation, 410
Harmony and acceptance, 21
Headings, 328
  adding for visual impact, 101–103
  distinguishing among functional, talking, and combination, *271*
  formal business reports, 308
  include at least one per report page, 272
  report headings, 273
  varying styles in levels, *272*
Hedging, equated with deceit, 196
Hidden job market, 429
  pursuing with networking, 431–435
Hierarchy of levels, effective report headings, 271
High potential network, iHipo, 431
High-context cultures
  communicators in, 16
  more collectivist, 16
Hiring/placement interviews, 475
Horizontal bar chart, *322*
Hospitality, extending thanks for, 173
Hyperlinks, multimedia presentation, *406*

# I

Idioms, avoid, 20
Illegal and inappropriate interview questions, 489–490
Illustration, matching graphics to objectives, *320*
IM. *See* Instant messaging
Image
  power of in multimedia presentations, 402, *406*
  projecting and maintaining professional, 5
Imagery, establishing audience rapport, 396
Immediacy, benefit of IM and texting, 129
Impact, organizing content for, 392–398
Imperative mood, 162, GM-13
Importance
  organizing the body of oral presentation, 395
  strategy for organizing report findings, *307*
Incivility, understanding cost of, 352–354
Income, education drivers, 5
Indeed, 431
Independent clauses
  commas with, GM-24
  semicolons with, GM-29

Indexes, secondary source, 309
Indicative mood, 162, GM-13
Indirect strategy
    and direct strategies for negative messages, comparing, *194*
    delivering negative news, 196, *196*
    justification/recommendation reports, 281–282
    organizational strategies for reports, 266
    unreceptive audiences, 67–68
Individualism, 16
Influence, 226
Influencers, 130, 134
Infogr.am, 324
Infographic résumé, *325*, 450–451, *451*
Infographics, 270, 322
Informal experimentation, 315
Informal letter proposal, *302*–303
Informal proposals, 299–300, *300*
    components of, *300*, 301–305
Informal reports
    components of, *326*
    delivered as slide decks, *270*
Informal research methods, 64–65
Informal writing style, 266–268, *269*
Information
    gathering through personal interviews, *315*
    organizing, 66–68
    rejecting requests for, 202–203
    researching background, 64
Information age workplace
    anytime, anywhere and nonterritorial offices, 6–7
    flattened management hierarchies, 7
    heightened global competition, 7
    meeting challenges of, 5–9
    rapidly changing communication technologies, 5–6
    renewed emphasis on ethics, 7
    self-directed work groups and virtual teams, 7
Information report, letter format, *267–268*
Informational e-mails, writing plan for, 122
Informational reports, 265, 275–279
Inside address, business letters, A-6–A-7
Instagram, 4, 233, 309
Instant access, twenty-first-century workplace, 2
Instant messaging (IM), 3, 5–6, 36, *43*, 46, 127, *127*
    benefits of, 128, 129
    best practices for, 129
    how to use on the job, 129
    impact of, 128–129
    risks of, 129
Instruction messages, 158–164
    dividing into steps, 162
    learning more about, 164
    provide clear explanations, 164
    revising, 163–164
    watch your tone, 164
    writing plan for, 162
Integrity, 354
Intellectual property, 318
Intercultural audiences
    oral communication with, 19–20
    written communication with, 20

Intercultural communication, 17–18
Intercultural workplace skills, building, 18–22
Interest, building in sales messages, 237–238
Interim reports, 277–278
Interjections, function of, GM-6
Internal communication, companies blog, 135
Internal proposals, 281, 300
Internal request, refusing, *208*
International graduate programs, internships, and jobs, iHipo, 431
Internet, 429
    job boards (Monster, CollegeGrad, and company websites), *430*
    projecting professionalism, 6
Internship, summer job, or part-time position, 428–429
Interoffice memos, writing, 125–127
Interview, 429
    actions to avoid, *484*
    after, 491–494
    anticipating questions during, 484–490
    answer questions during, 483
    asking your own questions during, 490–491
    before, 476–482
    clean up digital dirt before, 480–481
    contacting references, 492–494
    during, 482–491
    ending positively, 491
    fighting fear, 481–482
    following up after, 492, *493*, 494
    gather information from, 275
    greet interviewer and make positive first impression, 481
    preparing and practicing before, 480–481
    primary research source, 315
    sending positive, nonverbal messages during, 482–483
    travelling to and arriving at, 481
Interview questions
    about the future, 487
    about your experience and accomplishments, 486–487
    behavioral questions, 488–489
    challenging, 487–488
    illegal and inappropriate questions, 489–490
    situational questions, 488
    to gauge your interest, 486
    to get acquainted, 485–486
Intranet post, announcing bad news to employees and public, 209–210
Introduction
    capturing attention in, 392
    formal business reports, 327–328
    informal proposals, 299, *300*, 303–304
Introductory expressions, semicolons with, GM-29
Irregular verbs, GM-14
Italics, 71

## J

Jargon, 51
    avoid, 20
Job acceptance and rejection message, 496–497

Job boards, 426, 429–431
Job hunting, enlisting other social networks in, 435
Job interview, 474–475, 475–476, *477*, 485
    See also Employment interviews; Interview
Job market, understanding changing, 426–427
Job search
    assessing your qualifications, 428
    beginning with self-analysis, 427
    building personal brand, 435
    career opportunities, 428–429
    digital tools, 448–453
    hidden job market, 431–435
    in digital age, 426–429, *427*
    online, 429–431
    open job market, 429–431
Job summary, 439
Jobs
    solicited, 455–456
    trends in sources of, *430*
    unsolicited, 456–457
*Jobs Rated Almanac*, 428
Justification/recommendation reports, 281–282
    APA style, *282–283*

## K

KakaoTalk, 128
Keep it short and simple. *See* KISS formula
Key competencies, 5
Keywords, 448–449
KISS formula (keep it short and simple), 95

## L

Language
    bias-free, 50–51
    choices based on audience profile, 43
    plain, 51
    positive and negative, 49
    problems, 10
    specialized, 51
Laptop computers, 6
Lead-ins, limiting long, 91–92
Letter, 43
Letter format, 269
    informational report, *267–268*
Letter of application, 454
Letter of transmittal, *330*
    formal proposals, 300, *300*
    front matter components of formal business report, 326
Letter placement, business letters, A-5
Letter replies, writing plan for, 160
Letter styles
    block and modified block, *A-7*
    business letters, A-10
Lettered items, capitalization of, GM-39
Letterhead, business letters, A-6
Letters
    business, A-5–A-12
    resignation, 497–498
    routine messages, 156–158
Liability burden, risk of IM and texting, 129

Library, 428
Line charts, *320*, 321, *323*
Line spacing, business letters, A-5
LinkedIn, 136, 309, 430, 451, 454, 479, 480–481, 494
    making most of, *433–434*, *434*
    using, 431
List of figures, *331*
    formal business report, 326
    formal proposals, 300, *300*
Listed items, colons with, GM-30
Listening
    barriers to effective, 10
    during the interview, 483
    skills, 10–11
Literary titles, capitalization of, GM-40
Low-text cultures
    communicators in, 16
    tend to value individualism, 16

## M

Mailing address, business letters, A-10–A-11
Main idea, label, 72
Malware (malicious software programs), 129
Manuscript format, 269
Map, matching graphics to objectives, *320*
Margins, 99
    business letters, A-5
Market research, companies blog, 134
Mashable, 98
Meaning, crucial element in definition of communication, 36
Measurements, number style of, GM-45
Mechanics
    achieving emphasis through, 71–72
    editing formal business reports, 308
Media richness and communication effectiveness, *356*
Media, using professionally (dos and don'ts), *138*
Medical fields, Advance Healthcare Network, 431
Meeting management programs, 372
Meetings
    concluding and following up, 372–373
    distributing an agenda and other information, 371, *371*
    face-to-face and virtual, 368–375
    handling conflict in, 372
    managing, 371–372
    preparing for, 369–371
    purpose and number of participants, 369, *370*
    using digital calendars to schedule, 369–370
Memo of transmittal, formal business report, 326
Memos, *43*
    and e-mails, comparing, 126–127
    delivering instructions, *163*
    format, 125, *126*, 269
    preparing in digital-age, 120–127
    routine messages, 156–158
    writing interoffice, 125–127
    writing plan for replies, 160

Messages
    adjustment, 168–171
    application or résumé follow-up, 495–496
    audience focus, 45
    businesses generate wide range of, 3–4
    e-mail, A-5
    evaluating effectiveness of, 105
    flowing downward, persuading employees, 232
    flowing upward, persuading the boss, 232–233
    goodwill, 171–175
    instruction, 158–164
    job acceptance and rejection, 496–497
    nonverbal, 396–398
    request, 158–164
    response, 158–164
    sender focus, 45
Metaphor, *397*
Metasearch engines, 310
Microblogging, writing concisely for, 94–95
Microsoft PowerPoint, 398
Microsoft Word 2007, 2010, and 2013, formatting letters with, A-6
Minorities, workforce diversity, 20
Minutes of meetings, 278
Mishra, Gaurav, 18
Misplaced modifiers, 74–75
Misspelled words, GM-48
Mobile apps, 372
Mobility, twenty-first-century workplace, 2
Model formal report with MLA
    citation format and alternate APA reference list, *329–339*
    format plus alternate APA reference list, *328–339*
Modern Language Association (MLA), 318, A-13
    format, A-16–A-18
    in-text format, A-17
    journal article reference, anatomy of, *A-17*
    referencing format, 328
    sample references, *A-18*
    text page and works cited, portions of, *A-16*
    works cited, *319, 338,* A-17
Modified block letter style, *A-7, A-10*
Money
    number style of, GM-43
    rejecting requests for, 202–203
Monster, 428, 430, 448
MLA. *See* Modern Language Association
Multimedia presentations
    adjusting slide design to audience, 401–403
    analyzing situation and purpose, 401
    building business presentation, 403
    preparing, 400–406
    seven steps to, 405–406, *406*
    slides that illustrate, *405*
    *See also* Business presentations; Oral presentations
Multimedia slides, 398, *399*
Multiple line chart, *323*

# N

N/A (not available), 320
Names, 103
    apostrophes with, GM-32
National origin, workforce diversity, 20
Neeleman, 199
Negative language, 49
Negative messages
    apologizing, 198–202
    closing pleasantly, 201–202
    comparing direct and indirect strategies for, *194*
    composing, 197–202
    cushioning the bad news, 200–201
    opening indirect messages with a buffer, 197–198
    presenting the reasons, 199–200
    showing empathy, 199
    *See also* Bad news; Negative news
Negative news
    achieving goals in communicating, 193
    communicating effectively, 192–193
    strategies, analyzing, 194–197
    to employees, writing plan for announcing, 209
    *See also* Bad news; Negative messages
Negative posts and reviews online, responding to, 204–206
Networked world, gaining an etiquette edge in, 355
Networking (person-to-person contacts), *430*
    pursuing hidden job market with, 431–435
    whom to contact, *443*
Newspapers, checking open job market, 431
Newspapers/periodicals (classified ads), *430*
Niche sites, checking, 431
Noise, 38
Nominative case, GM-8
Nonterritorial workspaces, 7
Nonverbal communication
    defined, 11–12
    skills, 11–14
Nonverbal distractions, 10
Nonverbal messages, A-4
    establishing audience rapport, 396–398
Nonverbal skills, building strong, 14
Norming, team development, 365
Noun plurals, guidelines for forming, GM-6
Nouns, GM-6–GM-7
    abstract, GM-6
    collective, GM-7
    common, GM-6
    concrete, GM-6
    function of, GM-6
    plural, GM-6
    proper, GM-6
    singular, GM-6
Number style, GM-42–GM-45
    general rules, GM-43
Numbered items, capitalization of, GM-39
Numbered lists, 100–101
Numbers, 103

# O

*O*NET Occupational Information Network*, 428
Objective case, GM-8
Observation
    gather information from, 274
    primary research source, 315
Observe yourself on video, 14
*Occupational Outlook Handbook*, 428
Omitted words, commas with, GM-27
One-on-one interviews, 475
Online
    environment, 18
    interviews, 476
    multimedia presentation, 406
    responding to customer, 161
    résumé reading patterns, 442–446
    social networking, 429
    vs. traditional sales messages, *235*
    writing short persuasive messages, 242–243
Online communities, companies blog, 134–135
Online databases, secondary source, 309
Online job boards, 429, *432*
Online post, guidelines for responding to, 162
Online reviews and complaints, *167*
Open Directory Project, 309
Open job market, searching, 429–431
Open offices, *8*
Open-ended questions, surveys, 313
Opening
    cover messages, 455–457
    direct claim with clear statement, 165
    for solicited jobs, 455–456
    for unsolicited jobs, 456–457
    indirect negative messages with a buffer, 197–198
    paragraph, blog best practices, 135
Oral communication, 3
    with intercultural audiences, 19–20
Oral presentations
    capturing attention in introduction, 392
    establishing audience rapport, 396–398
    knowing your audience, 391
    knowing your purpose, 390
    organizing the body of, 392–395
    outline, *394*
    polishing your deliver and following up, 406–411
    speaking skills and your career, 389–390
    summarizing in conclusion, 395–396
    understanding contemporary visual aids, 398–400
    understanding types of, 390
    *See also* Business presentations; Multimedia presentations
Organization chart, matching graphics to objectives, *320*
Organization names, capitalization of, GM-38

Organizational strategies for reports, 265–266
Organizations
    in persuasion business, 227
    managing bad news within, 206–210
Organizing
    content, business presentations, 392–398
    body, business presentations, 392–395
    formal business reports, 307
    3-x-3 writing process, 40
    your presentations, 403
Outline, 66
    format, *307*
    oral presentation, *394*

# P

Panel interviews, 475
Paper trail, 121
Paragraphs
    building coherence, 75–76
    controlling length, 76
    drafting well-organized, 75–76
Parallelism, 73–74, 101
Paraphrasing, 316–317
Parentheses, GM-35
Parenthetical expressions, commas with, GM-22
Participants
    in virtual meetings, respecting needs of dispersed, 374
    purpose and number of participants, *370*
    selecting, 369
Parts of speech, GM-6
Passive voice, 73, GM-13
    to cushion bad news, 200–201
Past perfect tense, GM-13
Past tense, GM-13
PDF document, submitting résumé as, 452
PDF (portable document format) files, 270
    reports delivered as, 264
Peer-to-peer tools, 6
Percentages, number style of, GM-45
Performing, team development, 365
Periodicals, secondary source, 309
Periods, GM-34
Periods of time, number style of, GM-44
Perks, 286
Permanent record, business letters provide, 157
Personal anecdote, *397*
Personal appearance, 13–14
Personal brand, building, 435
Personal data, résumé information, 441
Personal interviews, primary research source, 315, *315*
Personal networking, 426
    hidden job market, 432–433
Personal titles, capitalization of, GM-38–GM39
Personalized statistics, *397*
Person-to-person contacts, 432
Person-to-person networking, 429
Persuasion
    effective techniques, *228*
    understanding in digital age, 226–229

I-6   Index

Persuasive claims and complaints
　e-mail, 231
　writing effective, 229–231
Persuasive messages
　business letters deliver, 157
　crafting, 228–229
　first draft, analyzing and revising, 229
　flowing downward to employees, 232
　flowing upward to the boss, 232–233, 234
　in digital-age organizations, 232–233
　online, 242–243
　volume and reach of, 227
Persuasive request, 230
　planning and writing for, 228–229
Persuasive sales techniques in digital age, 235
Peters, Tom, 356
Phishing (fraudulent schemes), 129
Photograph, matching graphics to objectives, 320
Phrases, commas with, GM-25
Physical barriers, listening, 10
Pie charts, 321, 323
　matching graphics to objectives, 320
Piktochart, 324
Pilot study, surveys, 314–315
Pinterest, 4, 6, 120, 241, 309
Pitch, 357
Plagiarism, 316
Plain language, 51
Plain-paper return address, business letters, A-9–A-10
Plain-text résumé for digital submission, 452, 453
Plural nouns, GM-6
Podcasting, 131
Podcasts
　blogs, and wikis, collaboration with, 9
　business, 130–132
　types of business presentations, 390
Points of the compass, capitalization of, GM-39
Polish, 352, 353
Positive and negative group behaviors, 366
Positive form of adjectives and adverbs, GM-16–GM-17
Positive language, 49
Positive messages, routine messages, 156–158
Positive online presence, 353
Possessive case, GM-8
Post, Emily, 198
Post, Peter, 198
Posts, respectfully respond to, blog best practices, 136
Posture
　during the interview, 482
　silent messages sent by body, 12
Power Distance Index, 17
PowerPoint, 400
　bullets, moving beyond, 400
　presentations, 401–406
　slides that illustrate multimedia presentations, 405
Precise words, 51
Preparation, organizing the body in oral presentations, 394

Prepositions, GM-19
　function of, GM-6
　guidelines for use, GM-19
Presence functionality, 129
Presence technology, 9
Present perfect tense, GM-13
Present tense, GM-13
Presentations. See Business presentations; Multimedia presentations; Oral presentations
Prewriting, first phase of 3-x-3 writing process, 39
Prezi, 399, 400
　presentations, 401–406
　zoom presentation, 400
Primary audience, 42
Primary research sources, 312–315
　formal business reports, 306
　observation and experimentation, 315
　personal interviews, 315
　surveys, 313–315
Primary sources
　formal research methods, 65–66
　gather information from, 274–275
Print documents, revising, 92
Print resources, secondary source, 309
Print-based résumé, 452
Printed material, gather information from, 274
Problem statement, preparing written, 273
Procedures, teams agree on, 367
Product names, capitalization of, GM-40
Productivity, increased with teams, 365
Professional behavior, 355
　relating to ethics, 354–355
Professional cell phone use, 363
Professional highlights, 439
Professional organizations, joining, 429
Professional teams
　adding value to, 364–368
　collaborating in virtual teams, 365–366
　defining successful teams, 366–368
　identifying positive and negative team behavior, 366
　understanding teams and the four phases of team development, 365
Professional telephone and voice mail etiquette, 361–364
Professionalism, 5
　developing at office and online, 352–355
　projecting when you communicate, 6
　understanding, 352–354
Profiling the audience, 42, 42
Progress report, 277, 277–278
Pronouns, GM-8–GM-10
　case of, GM-8
　function of, GM-6
　guidelines for making pronouns-antecedents agreement, GM-9–GM-10
　guidelines for selecting case, GM-8–GM-9
Pronunciation, 357

Proofreading, 90, 103–105
　accuracy matters in business, 103
　blog best practices, 135
　complex documents, 104–105
　marks, 104, A-3
　résumé, 448
　routine documents, 103–104
　slide presentations, 404
　3-x-3 writing process, 40
Proper adjectives, capitalization of, GM-38
Proper nouns, GM-6
　capitalization of, GM-37–GM-38
Proposals, 299
　benefits and schedule for completion, 300, 300
　components of informal, 304
　external, 300
　formal, 299–300, 300
　grant, 300
　informal, 299–300, 300
　internal, 281, 300
Props, 399
Protocol, 352
Psychological barriers, effective listening, 10
Psychological compensation, 170
Public, announcing bad news to, 209–210
Public profile, 434
Public relations, companies blog, 133–134
Publication Manual of the American Psychological Association, A-13
Punctuation, 101, 103
　apply correctly for effective report headings, 272
　business letters, A-6
　other, GM-34–GM-36
　styles, A-10
Purpose
　and number of participants of meeting, 370
　and scope, formal business reports, 305
　and situation, multimedia presentations, 401
　determining, 41–42
　knowing your, 390
　preparing written statement of, 273–274
　teams agree on, 367

# Q

Qualifications
　showcasing in career e-portfolio, 449–450
　summary of, résumé information, 438–439
Question marks, GM-34
Questionnaires, gather information from, 274–275
Questions
　encourage but keep control, 410–411
　preparing to answer during interview, 483
　repeat after presentation, 411
Quick Response (QR) code, 438
Quotation marks, GM-35–GM-36
Quotations
　colons with, GM-30
　commas with, GM-27
Quotes, 317

# R

Race, workforce diversity, 20
Racially biased language, 50
Rapport
　oral presentations establishing audience, 396–398
　organizing content of business presentations for audience, 392–398
Rational appeal, building interest with, 237–238
Readability
　enhancing through document design, 98–103, 102
　professional e-mail, 123
Readers' Guide to Periodical Literature, The, 309
Reasons, presenting in negative messages, 199–200
Reasons-before-refusal plan, 206
Receiver, 38
Recommendations, body components of formal business reports, 328
Recruiting, companies blog, 135
Redundancies, 93
Reference format, APA, 3, A-14–A-16
Reference initials, business letters, A-9
Reference line, business letters, A-8
Reference list, 442
References, 328
　back matter components, 328
　contacting after interview, 492–494
　résumé information, 442
Referrals, 426, 432
　building personal network, 432–433
Refusing donation request, 203
Refusing internal request, 208
Refusing typical requests and claims, 202–206
　dealing with disappointed customers in print, 203–204
　denying claims, 206
　responding to negative posts and reviews online, 204–206
Refusing workplace requests, 208–209
Rejection message, 496–497
　follow-up, 496
Related numbers, number style of, GM-44
Relative pronouns, 20
Religion, workforce diversity, 20
Report components, understanding, 325–339
Report findings, strategies for organizing, 307
Report formats, 269–271
　and heading levels, 268–273
　effective report headings, 271–273
Report headings, 271–273
Reporting in digital-age, 264–268
　informal and formal writing styles, 266–268
　organizational strategies, 265–266

Index　　I-7

Reports, *43*
　analytical, 265
　components of informal and formal, *326*
　feasibility, 282–285
　formal business, 305–308
　incorporating graphics in, 323–325
　informational, 265
　justification/recommendation, 281–282
　organizational strategies for, 265–266
　progress or interim, 277–278
　research, 266
　short analytical, 279–288
　trip, convention, and conference, 275–276
　types of business presentations, *390*
　varying styles in levels of headings, *272*
　writing style, *269*
　yardstick, 285–288
Request a lectern before presentation, 409
Request for proposal (RFP), 301
　copy of, formal proposals, 300, 300
Request messages, 158–164
　big idea first, 159
　closing with appreciation and action request, 159
　creating, 159
　providing details, 159
Requests
　refusing internal, *208*
　refusing typical, 202–206
　refusing workplace, 208–209
　rejecting, for favors, money, information, and action, 202–203
　responding to, 160–161
　writing plan for persuasive, 228
Research, 64, 274–275
　conducting primary and secondary, 308–315
　electronic access to, 65
　formal business reports, 305, 306
　formal methods, 65–66
　informal methods, 64–65
　manual, 65
　reports, 266
　3-x-3 writing process, 39
Resignation letter, 497–498
Respect, 17
Response, faster with teams, 365
Response messages, 158–164
　to customer comments online, *161*, 161–162
　to requests, 160–161
　writing plan for, 159
Résumé, 427
　action verbs for powerful, *440*
　customized, 435–448
　faxing, 453
　follow-up message, 495–496
　gallery, *443*–447
　how many and what format, 451–452
　keyword "hits", 448–449
　length of, 437
　online at company database, 453
　organizing information into categories, 437–442

PDF document, 452
plain-text document, 452
polishing, 446–448
print-based, 452
proofreading, 448
sending, 460
style, 436–437
submitting, 452–453
word document, 452
Return address, business letters, A-10
Reviews and complaints, writing online, *167*
Revising
　and enhancing slides for greater impact, *402*
　digital and print documents, *92*
　for clarity, 95–98
　for conciseness, 91–94
　multimedia presentations, 404
　third phase of 3-x-3 writing process, 40, 90–95
RFP. *See* Request for proposal
Riccardi, Toni, 21
Richness of channel, 44
Risks, reduced with teams, 365
Robert's Rules, 372
Round numbers, number style of, GM-44
Round-robin, 372
Routine documents, proofreading, 103–104
Routine reports, 264
Run-on (fused) sentences, 70

## S

Sales letters, 233, *240*
　considering value of, 235–239
Sales messages
　AIDA strategy, *237*
　best practices for online, 242
　building interest with rational and emotional appeals, 237–238
　direct mail, 235
　gaining attention in, 237
　in print and online, 233–243, *235*
　motivating action at conclusion of, 239
　putting together all parts of, 239
　reducing resistance and building desire, 238–239
　writing plan for, 236
Salutation
　business letters, A-8
　colons with, GM-30
　e-mail, A-5
Sampling, survey population, 313
Sans serif typefaces, 99–100
Scientific experiments, formal research methods, 66
Scratch list, 66
Screening interviews, 475
Search engines, 309, 310, 426
Seasonal employment, CoolWorks, 431
Seasons, capitalization of, GM-41
Secondary audience, *42*, 43
Secondary research sources, 308–312
　formal business reports, 306
　online databases, 309
　print resources, 309
　the Web, 309

Secondary sources, gather information from, 274–275
Second-page heading, business letters, A-9, A-9
Security breach message, direct strategy for negative news, 195, *195*
Security, risk of IM and texting, 129
Seeley, Dr. Monica, 121
Segmented 100 percent bar chart, *322*
Segmented area (surface) charts, 321, *323*
Self-analysis, beginning job search with, 427
Self-directed work groups, 7
Semicolons, GM-29
Sender
　encodes idea, 37
　has idea, 36–37
　selects channel and transmits message, 37–38
Sender-focused message, 45
Sensitivity
　and formality, business letters convey, 157
　conveying in negative news, 193
Sentence fragments, 46
Sentences
　achieving variety with, 69
　avoiding common faults, 70
　composing first draft, 69–71
　favoring short, 71
　place important idea first or last in, 72
　support, 75
　topic, 75
Sequential interviews, 476
Series
　commas in, GM-22
　semicolons with, GM-29
Serif typefaces, 99–100
Sexting, 129
Sexual orientation, workforce diversity, 20
Shirky, Clay, 18
Short message service (SMS), 128
Short messaging channels, 46
Short reports, report headings use one or two levels in, *272*
Short sentences, 71
Short-term jobs, CoolWorks, 431
Signature block, business letters, A-8
Silent messages, 12–13
Simile, *397*
Simple line chart, *323*
Simple sentence, 69
Simple/complex
　strategy for organizing report findings, *307*
　organizing the body of oral presentation, 395
Singular nouns, GM-6
Situational questions, interview questions, 488
6-x-6 rule, 402
6Sense, 430
Skills, résumé information, 440–441
Skype, 127, 128, 475
Slang, 46, 96–97
　avoid, 20
Slide decks, 270
　reports delivered as, 264
SlideRocket, 400
　presentation, *401*, 401–406

Slides
　designing more effective, *404*
　revising and enhancing for great impact, *402*
　that illustrate multimedia presentations, *405*
SlideShare, 271
Smart mobile devices, *9*
SmartArt, 402
Smartphones, 6, 362–363
Social intelligence, 352, 353
Social interaction, four space zones for, *13*
Social media, *9*, 17–18
　networks, posting on, 94–95
　presence, 3
　sites, 4
　using to network, 433–435
　Wholesome2Go engages audience with, *241*
Social networking, 136–139
　bridging cultural divides and, 17–18
　sites, 139, 431
Social networks, 426
　businesses potential risk of, 138–139
　how businesses use, 136–137
　tapping into, 136
Society for Information Management survey, 3
Soft skills, 5, 352, 353–354, 389
Solicited cover letter, *457*
Solicited jobs, 455–456
Source notes, A-13
Space, silent messages sent by, 12–13
Spacing, business letters, A-6
Speaking skills and your career, 389–390
Special effects, multimedia presentations impact of, 402–403, *406*
Specialized language, 51
Speech habits, projecting professionalism, *6*
Speed, benefit of IM and texting, 128
Spelling, 103
Spim (IM spam), 129
Sports references, avoid, 20
Staffing requirements, 300, *300*, 304
Stage fright, combating, *408*
STAR (storytelling) technique, 488
Stereotypes, 19
Storming, team development, 365
Strategizing, 66
Stress interviews, 476
Style, achieving emphasis through, 72–73
Subject directories, 310
Subject, e-mail, A-5
Subject line
　business letters, A-8
　professional e-mail drafting of, 122
Subjunctive mood, GM-13
Summaries, 279
Summary and appreciation, end with, 411
Summary of qualifications, résumé information, 438–439
Superlative form of adjectives and adverbs, GM-16–GM-17
Support sentences, 75
SurveyMonkey, 274

I-8　　　　Index

Surveys
    gather information from, 274–275
    primary research source, 313–315
Sympathy, expressing, 174

# T

Table of contents, *331*
    formal proposals, 300, *300*
    formal business report, 326
Table summarizing precise data, *321*
Tables, 319–323, *320*
Tablets, projecting professionalism, *6*
Tabulation, 71
Talking heads, 271, 328
Target company, 478–479
Team behavior, identifying positive and negative, 366
Team development, four phases of, 365, *365*
Teams
    adding value to professional, 364–368
    collaborating in virtual, 365–366
    confront conflict, 367–368
    defining successful, 366–368
    stay small and embrace diversity, 367
Teamwork, 3, 7
Technical fields need strong communication skills, 3
Technology
    dealing with in virtual meetings, 373–374
    jobs, Dice, 431
TED Talks, 131, *131*
Telephone, *43*, 122
    numbers, number style of, GM-43–GM-44
    projecting professionalism, *6*, 361–362
    VoIP, *8*
Teleworkers, 7
Templates, multimedia presentations, 403–404
Territory, silent messages sent by, 12–13
Text alerts, Centers for Disease Control, *128*
Text alignment, 99
Text messaging, 6, 127
    business etiquette and, 130
Text, multimedia presentation, *406*
Texting, 4, 121
    benefits of, 128, 129
    best practices for, 129
    how to use on the job, 129
    impact of, 128–129
    projecting professionalism, *6*
    risks of, 129
Thanks, 172–174
    expressing for a gift, 172
    extending for hospitality, 173
    sending for a favor, 172–173, *173*
Think Wikipedia, 132
Thought speed, listening, 10
3-x-3 writing process. *See* Writing process (3-x-3)
3D presentations, 399
Time
    orientation, 16–17
    silent messages sent by, 12–13
    yourself before presentation, 409
Title page
    formal proposals, 300, *300*
    front matter components of formal business report, 325–326
*To* line, e-mail, A-4
Tolerance, 19
Tone
    choices based on audience profile, 43
    courteous, 49
    in persuasive claims, 229–231
    informal conversational instead of formal pretentious, 46
    instruction messages, 164
    of message, 47–49
    professional e-mail, 123
Topic sentences, 75
Topic/function strategy for organizing report findings, *307*
Topic/function/conventional grouping, organizing the body of oral presentation, 395
Track changes, 119
Traditional vs. online sales messages, characteristics of, *235*
Transitional expressions to build coherence, *76*
Trip report, 275–276
Trite business phrases, 96
Tumblr, 42, 94
Twenty-first-century workplace, mastering tools for success in, 2–9
Twitter, 4, 6, 18, 36, 42, 46, 66, 94, 120, 136, 205, 227, 233, 309, 431, 433, 435, 451, 479, 480
Type fonts and sizes, capitalizing on, 100
Typefaces, 99–100
    with different personalities for different purposes, *99*
Typical requests and claims, refusing, 202–206

# U

Underlining, 71
Unethical communicators, 197
Unobtrusiveness, benefit of IM and texting, 128
Unsolicited cover letter, *458*
Unsolicited jobs, 456–457
Uptalk, 357
URL (uniform resource locator), 433

# V

Vcasting, 131
Verb tense, guidelines for, GM-13
Verbal messages, A-4
Verbal signposts, establishing audience rapport, 396
Verbs, GM-11–GM-14
    action, *440*
    action-specific, 20
    buried, 97
    function of, GM-6
    guidelines for agreement with subjects, GM-11–GM-12
    irregular, GM-14
    mood, GM-13
    tense, GM-13
    voice, GM-13
Version confusion, 132
Vertical bar chart, *322*
Video, *399*
    chat, *43*
    interviews, 476
    résumé, expanding employment chances with, 450
Videoconferencing, 6, *9*
Vigorous words, 51
Viral marketing, 134
Virtual interviews, 476
Virtual meetings
    anticipating limitations of, 375
    dealing with technology, 373–374
    ground rules for, 375
    humanizing of, 375
    interacting professionally in, 374–375
    managing turn-taking and other meeting procedures, 375
    planning and participating in, 368–375
    preparing for, 373
    respecting needs of dispersed participants, 374
Virtual presentations, types of business presentations, 390
Virtual teams, 7
    collaborating in, 365–366
Viruses, 129
Visual aids
    incorporating graphics and, 318–325
    options, pros and cons of, *399*
    types of, 398–400
    understanding contemporary, 398–400
    use effectively during presentation, 410
Visual résumés, 324
Visual.ly, 324
Visualize.me, 451
Vivid words, 72
Voice
    as a communication tool, 356–357
    quality, 357
    recognition, *8*
    using active and passive, 73
Voice Conferencing, *8*
Voice mail, 6
    caller's end, 364
    making the most of, 363–364
    projecting professionalism, *6*
    receiver's end, 363–364
VoIP (voice over internet protocol systems), 128, 229
Volume and rate, 357
Volunteering, 429

# W

Watzlawick, Paul, 12
Web, 309–312
    encyclopedias, 310
    professionals survey, 3
    search operators, 310
    search tools, 309–310
    searching, 428
Web 2.0, *8*, 130
    social networking, 136–139
Web conferencing, *9*
    understanding, 374
Web sources, credibility of, 311–312
Webcasting, 131
Webcasts, business, 131
WebCrawler, 310
Webinars, types of business presentations, 390
WebSphere, 132
WeChat, 128
Weights, number style of, GM-45
WhatsApp, 127, 128
White space, 99
Whiteboards, *399*
WIIFM (what's in it for me?), 42, 44
Wiki farms, 132
Wikia, 132
Wikipedia, 310, 353
Wikis, 4, 6, *43*, 66
    advantages of, 132
    blogs, and podcasts, collaboration with, *9*
    collaborating with, 132
    creating with Google sites and Google docs, *133*
    making work for business, 130–132
Wikispaces, 132
Women, workforce diversity, 20
Word document, submitting résumé as, 452
Words
    capitalization of beginning, GM-40
    choosing positive in negative message, 200
    confusing, GM-47–GM-48
    empty, 93–94, 483
    familiar, 51
    low-and high-context cultures communicate differently with, 17
    misspelled, GM-48
    nonagreement of nonverbal cues and, 12
    precise, 51, 98
    vigorous, 51
    vivid, 72
Work experience, résumé information, 439–440
Work plan, formal business reports, 305–306, *306*
Work shifter, 6
Workforce diversity
    benefits of, 21
    communicating with diverse workplace audiences on the job, 21–22
Workforce50 for older workers, 431
Workplace
    conversation, making it matter, 357–359
    criticism, receiving gracefully, 359
    diversity, globalization and, 20
    messages, drafting, 63–66
    requests, refusing, 208–209
    texting and messaging, 127–130
    tools for success in twenty-first-century, 20–9
Works cited, 328
    back matter components, 328
Worst- and best-case scenario, *397*

Index I-9

Writing
- and editing formal business reports, 305–308
- for microblogging and posting on social media networks, 94–95
- persuasive claims and complaints, 229–231
- short informational reports, 275–279
- short persuasive messages online, 242–243
- successful e-mail sales messages, 239–242

Writing instructions, instruction messages, 164

Writing plan for
- adjustment messages, 168
- announcing negative news to employees, 209
- direct claim, 164
- direct request and response messages, 159
- e-mail, memo, and letter replies, 160
- informational e-mails, 122
- instruction messages, 162
- persuasive requests, 228
- refusing typical requests and claims, 202
- sales messages, AIDA, 236

Writing process (3-x-3), *40*, *64*
- applying phase 3, 90–95
- defining your goals, 38
- drafting, 39–40
- editing, 40
- evaluating, 40
- introducing, 39–40
- organizing, 40
- pacing of, 40–41
- prewriting, 39
- proofreading, 40
- researching, 39
- revising, 40
- scheduling, *41*
- using as a guide, 38–41

Writing techniques
- additional expert, 47–51
- being positive rather than negative, 47–49
- business, 71–75
- developing emphasis, 71–73
- developing parallelism, 73–74
- employing bias-free language, 50–51
- escaping dangling and misplaces modifiers, 74–75
- expressing courtesy, 49
- preferring plain language and familiar words, 51
- to improve e-mail message, applying expert, *48*
- using active and passive voice effectively, 73
- using precise, vigorous words, 51

Written communication with intercultural audiences, 20

WWW Virtual Library, 309

# Y

Yahoo Search, 309
Yammer, 137
Yardstick reports, 285–288, *285–287*
You view, developing, 45–46
YouTube, 4, 6, 131, 241, 450

# Z

Ziglar, Zig, 238
Zombie nouns, 97
Zoom presentations, 398, 399, *399*